A 2015 edition full of promise

We taste over 20,000 wines a year and this year is no exception. Our 2015 selection features 3,000 wines, most of which come from French and European wine regions. Increasingly though, we are bringing other countries into the fold and 2015 sees the inclusion of wines from Argentina, South Africa and as far away as China, with many newcomers from Chile and even Mexico waiting in the wings for 2016.

For free access to all of our tasting results, visit our website: www.gilbertgaillard.com. With nine online guides in as many languages, you can browse through our commentaries using a wide range of search criteria, from scores to prices and appellations. If you already know the name of a wine or a property you're looking for, it's even quicker!

We wish you many new finds and look forward to your next visit.

Gilbert & Gaillard

CONTENTS

Register at the international Gilbert & Gaillard contest

- Free access in 9 languages
- 50.000 wines online

GILBERT & GAILLARD

Stay connected...   www.gilbertgaillard.com

HOW TO USE THIS GUIDE

THE ORDER OF THE WINES :

We have chosen to present wines by region (Alsace, Beaujolais…), then by appellation with each company or château listed in alphabetical order, and finally by tasting scores in descending order.

INDEX: There are two indexes at the back of the book: one for wines and producers (page 526) and one for appellations (page 568)

WINE SCORES :

Our tasting notes are scored on a 100 point scale, which gives enough range to evaluate every characteristic that we taste in a wine. Below are the different levels that make up this scoring:

95-100/100 : an outstanding wine, when a great "terroir" meets exceptional winemaking expertise.

90-94/100 : a superlative wine combining finesse, complexity and remarkable winemaking.

85-89/100 : a wine of extremely high standard, which we enjoyed for its typicity and character.

80-84/100 : a quality wine combining balance, structure and neatness for a pleasurable wine drinking experience.

75-79/100 : a wine deemed acceptable.

70-74/100 : a wine with defects, unacceptable.

65-69/100 : a wine with major defects, inadmissible.

50-64/100 : unacceptable wine, not worthy for sale.

Note : wines scoring less than 75/100 are not included in our publications.

THE COLOUR OF THE WINES :

▼ Red wine

▼ Dry white wine

▼ Rose wine

▼ Sweet white wine

▼ sparkling brut or extra-brut

▼ sparkling brut rose

▼ Liqueur wine

▼ Brandy

▼ Appetiser

SPECIFIC CONDITIONS

Bordeaux - P. 66-111

1er Cru Classé du Médoc 1855 or 1er Cru Classé de Sauternes 1855:
First Classed Growth 1855

2e Cru Classé du Médoc 1855 or 2e Cru Classé de Sauternes1855:
Second Classed Growth 1855

3e Cru Classé du Médoc 1855: Third Classed Growth 1855

4e Cru Classé du Médoc 1855: Fourth Classed Growth 1855

5e Cru Classé du Médoc 1855: Fifth Classed Growth 1855

1er Grand Cru Classé de Saint-Émilion A: First Classed Growth A category

1er Grand Cru Classé de Saint-Émilion B: First Classed Growth B category

Cru Classé: Classed Growth

OTHER FEATURES

ORG: Organic wine

CONV: in the process of converting to organic production

ECO: this abbreviation is found in the section on Italian wines (pages 451-498) and indicates wines produced in keeping with sustainable development

CV ECO: in the process of converting to wines produced in keeping with sustainable development

Prices mentioned in this book are guideline and can vary depending on point of sale.The shops, wineries or publisher can in no way be held responsible for this.

PRESENTATION

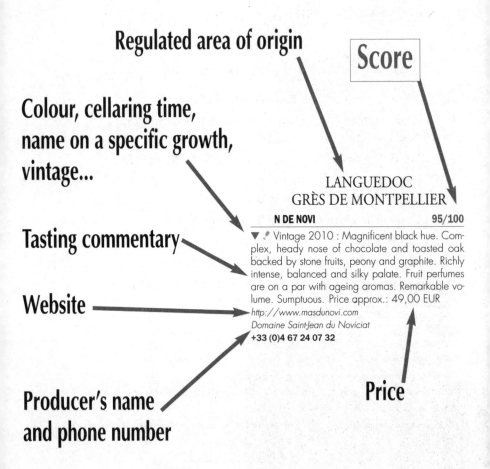

Regulated area of origin

Score

Colour, cellaring time, name on a specific growth, vintage...

LANGUEDOC
GRÈS DE MONTPELLIER

N DE NOVI   95/100

Tasting commentary ▼ ♪ Vintage 2010 : Magnificent black hue. Complex, heady nose of chocolate and toasted oak backed by stone fruits, peony and graphite. Richly intense, balanced and silky palate. Fruit perfumes are on a par with ageing aromas. Remarkable volume. Sumptuous. Price approx.: 49,00 EUR

Website http://www.masdunovi.com
Domaine Saint-Jean du Noviciat
+33 (0)4 67 24 07 32

Producer's name and phone number

Price

GILBERT & GAILLARD
AWARDS

Only for the best

Gilbert & Gaillard

ALSACE

ONE OF FRANCE'S BEST KEPT SECRETS

Alsace has long been famous as one of the most food and wine-loving regions in the whole of France. Its wines are capable of creating unsuspected harmonies and providing flavours that complement each other. What for example is the secret alchemy that brings pikeperch (zander) together with Riesling, foie gras with Tokay-Pinot Gris, Munster cheese with Gewurztraminer and kugelhopf with Crémant? An extraordinary diversity to discover.

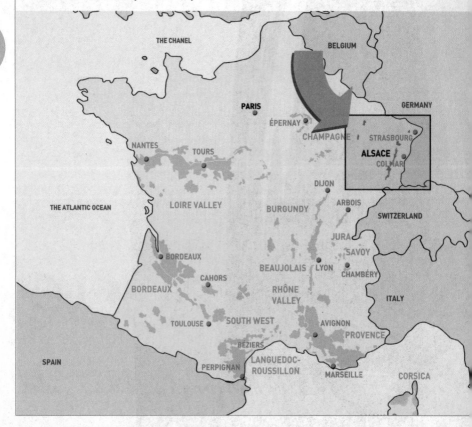

THE CHANEL

BELGIUM

PARIS

GERMANY

ÉPERNAY

CHAMPAGNE   STRASBOURG

NANTES

ALSACE

TOURS

COLMAR

DIJON

THE ATLANTIC OCEAN

LOIRE VALLEY

BURGUNDY

ARBOIS

SWITZERLAND

JURA

BORDEAUX

SAVOY

BEAUJOLAIS   LYON

CHAMBÉRY

BORDEAUX

CAHORS

RHÔNE
VALLEY

ITALY

TOULOUSE   SOUTH WEST

AVIGNON

PROVENCE

BÉZIERS

SPAIN

LANGUEDOC-
ROUSSILLON

PERPIGNAN

MARSEILLE

CORSICA

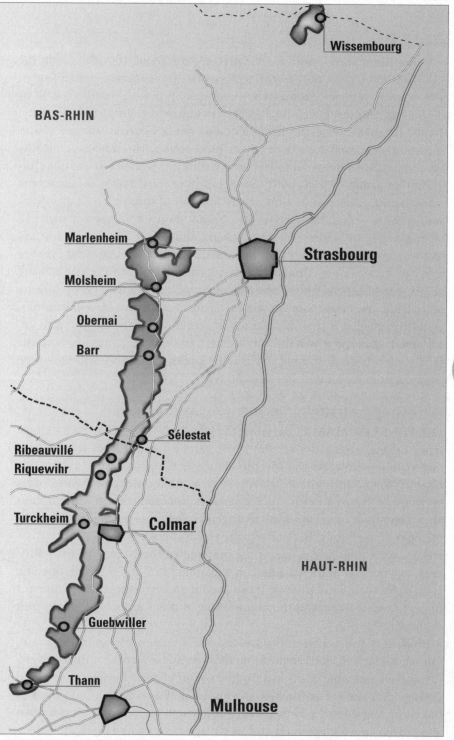

The Alsace wine-growing area stretches for about 100 kms along the western section of the Vosges mountains from Marlenheim to Thann, with a small northern enclave at Wissembourg. It is at the northern limit of the vine-growing area and white grape varieties are therefore in the majority. 14,000 hectares of vines are laid out at altitudes of between 200 and 400 m and yield an annual average of 150 million bottles. The wine-growing area has a generally south or south-east aspect. This is the perfect location for following the famous Alsace Wine Route. But most importantly, it enables the vines to take advantage of a maximum amount of sunshine in the growing and ripening period. In addition, its position means it enjoys a remarkable microclimate: «A warm temperature band showed up on the slopes and half-way up the hills, where the temperature is 1 to 1.5° higher than on the lower or upper slopes. This band is not located exactly on the south-facing slopes, but in general on the steepest slope» (Claude Sittler, 1990). On the other hand, the Alsace wine-growing soils are characterised by a great geological diversity that is probably unique in French vine growing. The vine has colonised chalk, marly-chalk, sandy-clay, clayey-loam, gypseous, volcanic sandstone, schistous, granitic and granitic gneiss soils. As we will see, some grape varieties are happier in particular types of soil.

THE GRAPE VARIETIES OF ALSACE- A DISTINCTIVE FAMILY

THE WINES OF ALSACE: including the grand crus - are made from a single type of grape, except for Crémant which can be blended from several separate varieties. However the specific nature of the Alsace varieties remains essential for producing very distinctive wines. All knowledgeable wine lovers know that there are 7 original grape varieties and can list them without thinking. Here they are in more detail, together with another, less well-known member of the family, but one equally worth considering.

• **Sylvaner** • this variety, one of the best-known in Alsace, was discredited years ago because of high yields. If it is handled well and if its late ripening is carefully taken into account, it can produce a wine that is remarkable for its lightness, is lively and thirst-quenching and has aromas of young fruit or flowers.

• **Riesling** • this is one of the greatest white grape varieties in the world. On sandy-clay soils the «gentle aromatic» - as it is sometimes called - gives a dry and elegant wine of distinction, the colour of crystal, with delicate fruit (orange peel and exotic fruits) and with floral and mineral (flinty) hints. It has surprising finesse, power, balance and length on the palate. It can ripen at relatively low temperatures and its vintage years mature perfectly.

- **Gewürztraminer** • the most aromatic grape variety grown in the area, it is used to make the most famous of the Alsace wines on marly-chalk soils. It comes from a selection of the most aromatic Savagnin Rose or Traminer varieties. The wine, full of vigour, well-rounded, with a powerful structure, offers great complexity. In it are found scents of acacia, lily, rose, carnation, honey, cardamom, spices (gewürz = spicy), cinnamon, clove, pepper, lychee, grapefruit and quince. This superb and generous wine is capable of maturing marvellously. The finest vintages bestow upon the wine a touch of sweetness.
- **Muscat** • this gives an aromatic wine that is heady yet dry and which is nothing like the Muscats from the south. It has inimitable fruit and flower aromas with a veritable explosion of acacia, box, rosewood and geranium.
- **Pinot Blanc** • this variety, which gives of its best on a loamy soil, gives a soft, supple wine full of freshness and with subtle aromatic hints. It has become one of the basic varieties of Crémant d'Alsace.
- **Pinot Gris** • this is the proper name of the Alsace Tokay (Grauer Tokayer). It is happy in deep soils and clayey-loam conglomerates. Its powerful, well-structured, even opulent wine is very long on the palate and releases aromas of dried fruit, fruit tree wood, undergrowth and game, where a hint of smoked meat can be detected. It is most certainly one of Alsace's greatest wines.
- **Pinot Noir** • this is Alsace's only red wine grape variety. Perfect when it has found a sandy or chalky soil, it is made into rosé or red wine. The latter, which has the characteristic colour of claret, develops flavours of small red fruits where the cherry dominates.
- **Klevener** • this variety of the former Traminer or Savagnin Rose gives a full-bodied and well-balanced wine. Under the decree of 4th February 1997, only the communes of Bougheim, Getwiller, Heiligenstein and Obernai can use the name «Klevener de Heiligenstein».

WHAT ARE THE PRODUCTION CONDITIONS?

Alsace wines normally show the grape variety on the label and are made 100% from that grape. A blend of two or more varieties is called Edelzwicker. The appellation wines have a yield per hectare of 8,000 litres with a minimum alcohol level of 8.5°. The production conditions for the 50 Grands Crus reduce the yield to 6,000 litres/hectare with 10° minimum for Riesling and Muscat, and 12° for Gewürztraminer or Pinot Gris. Their areas have been set out by the I.N.A.O. (the National Institute for Appellations d'Origine) on the basis of very strict geological and climatic criteria. The «Vendange tardive» (late harvest) and the «Sélection de grains nobles» (selection of superior over-

13

ripe grapes), which have been official Alsace specialities since 1984, have won a place in the hearts of all wine lovers.

«Vendange tardive» is only practised on the Gewürztraminer, Pinot Gris, Riesling and Muscat grapes, both for Vin d'Alsace A.C. and for the Grands Crus. Harvesting when they are overripe increases the available sugar within the berry, especially if it has begun to be covered with the noble rot. The wines then reach the pinnacle of their development and are real masterpieces. The «Sélections de grains nobles» are harvested by hand, with successive pickings of grapes affected by botrytis cinerea. The resulting concentration gives a powerful wine with complex aromas that is exceptionally long on the palate and has an unparalleled long life.

The Crémant d'Alsace sparkling wines, the vast majority of which are white, are produced by the traditional method of a second fermentation in the bottle. They are made from one or more grape varieties (Pinot Blanc, Riesling, Pinot Gris and occasionally Chardonnay). Crémant Rosé is made from the Pinot Noir. Strict production conditions that are very close to those for the Vin d'Alsace appellation and an irreproachable quality have been the basis of the success of the Crémants. Wonderful grands crus The fame of Alsace wine was initially built upon the sure foundation of its grape varieties. But connoisseurs, and even more so the winemakers themselves, have long recognised that such and such a wine from such and such a place was better than a commune's general production. In a deliberate move, the producers therefore decided to put those parcels of land that for centuries had been the glory of Alsace wine back onto their pedestal. If we leaf through the fact sheets of the terroirs where the 50 current Grands Crus are produced, we immediately see that these thousand-year old vineyards cover all the steepest slopes of the hills sheltering them from cold winds that these are very often in the shape of a bowl, a crescent or an arc that encourages exposure to the sun; that there is little topsoil; that the wine-growing parcels are located on gravel that both warms the soil and gives good drainage; and that thanks to a specific micro-climate, rainfall is low. This is effectively the jewel in the crown of Alsace wine. By taking this step, Alsace has not only gone back to its roots, but rediscovered its best wines.

REVIEW OF RECENT VINTAGES

• **2010** • 20 percent volume decrease on 2009 yet abundant fruit and freshness. A vintage for pleasure.

• **2011** • Drought in the spring and rainfall at the start of the summer yielded a fruity, ripe vintage with low acidity. The wines will be early-drinking, except for the superlative sites which always produce wines with ageability.

• **2012** • Despite a somewhat disrupted growth cycle, this vintage is well balanced. The Crémant wines are remarkable, and the Pinots (whether Pinot Blanc, Pinot Gris or Pinot Noir) are excellent. The other grape varieties do not stand out to the same degree, but are very respectable all the same.

• **2013** • A vintage that ripened well and offers up some fairly high levels of acidity, guaranteeing a very bright future. The Gewurztraminers are very promising, the Rieslings are classic with abundant minerality, the Pinots blancs et Pinots gris show great maturity and the Pinots noirs are well-crafted.

THREE APPELLATIONS FOR ONE REGION

A.C. VIN D'ALSACE

These wines must be bottled in the area of production and in the slender bottle characteristic of Alsace wine. They are available in all the authorised grape varieties. This is unique in France and ratified by the I.N.A.O., taking account of both the actual history of the rebuilding of the Alsace vine-growing area post phylloxera and of a Rhine tradition. They have been part of the great A.C. family since 1962.

A.C. ALSACE GRAND CRU

Only four grape varieties are permitted for the A.C. Alsace Grand Cru: Gewürztraminer, Riesling, Muscat and Pinot Gris. The label must include A.C. Alsace Grand Cru and show the locality, the grape variety and the year. Twenty-five localities were selected in 1983. Then in 1992, the National Institute for Appellations d'Origine ratified the definition of 25 new parcels. From that time, Alsace has prided itself on a new appellation made up of 51 Grands Crus. The wines produced in these areas have rare elegance and great finesse, and also power, quality and distinction. The best years give wines that can be laid down for a long time.

A.C. CRÉMANT D'ALSACE

Created in 1976, this has been given an unprecedented welcome by wine-lovers, as Crémant d'Alsace is the top appellation sparkling wine drunk in France, ahead of Clairette de Die. It is made by 500 producers who put nearly 20 million bottles on the market. It has the particular feature of being able to blend the various recommended grape varieties which must all come from the regional appellation area.

• • •

15

2015
ALSACE WINES

ALSACE GEWURZTRAMINER

P. HUMBRECHT   92/100

Org▼✎ Steiner-t 2010 : Bright, pale hue, green tints. Refined nose of ripe tropical and white fruits with lychee. Suave attack, a delightful medium dry with beautiful concentrated, fresh presence and precise, ethereal aromas. Fine mineral and spice notes. Very persistent. Wonderful.
Price approx.: 25,00 EUR
http://www.vins-humbrecht.fr
Maison Humbrecht
+33 (0)3 89 49 62 97

PAUL SCHNEIDER   91/100

▼✎ Vendanges Tardives 2011 : Light yellow with green tints. Complex nose showing smoke, toast and mineral notes, white peach and a faint tropical touch. Mellow, velvety, concentrated and lively palate of candied citrus, raisin and a range of spices. Marvellous.
Price approx.: 22,00 EUR
http://www.vins-paul-schneider.fr
Paul Schneider
+33 (0)3 89 41 50 07

P. HUMBRECHT   91/100

Org▼✎ Jean 2010 : Brilliant pale hue with green tints. Racy, tropical nose (lychee) with yellow peach. Beautifully round, full mouthfeel with enjoyably precise, delicate aromas. A light, lively and expressive medium dry wine, highly drinkable at any time of day.
Price approx.: 21,00 EUR
http://www.vins-humbrecht.fr
Maison Humbrecht
+33 (0)3 89 49 62 97

DOMAINES SCHLUMBERGER   90/100

▼✎ Les Princes Abbés 2012 : Limpid, light gold. Expressive nose showing huge typicity with lychee and rose petal scents. Abundant freshness immediately at point of entry and extremely pure expression. The finish stays focused and persistent. A wine for pleasure.
Price approx.: 14,00 EUR
www.domaines-schlumberger.com
Domaines Schlumberger
+33 (0)3 89 74 27 00

DOMINIQUE ET JULIEN FREY   89/100

Org▼✎ Clos St Sébastien 2012 : Light gold. Distinctive, elegant nose showing great restraint with predominant floral and peppery notes. Substantial richness on the palate balanced by freshness. The aromas take on a pronounced tropical dimension. Highly successful and very well-crafted.
Price approx.: 15,00 EUR
http://www.vinsfreybio.com
Domaine Charles Frey
+33 (0)3 88 92 41 04

CHRISTOPHE RIEFLÉ   89/100

▼✎ Vintage 2011 : Yellow-gold. Expressive, endearing nose showing huge typicity, halfway between floral notes, exotic fruits and rose petal. The palate displays the same emblematic varietal character augmented by freshness and persistency. A top-flight offering.
Price approx.: 6,20 EUR
http://www.vins-christophe-riefle.com
Christophe Riefle
+33 (0)3 89 49 77 85

WOLFBERGER   88/100

▼✎ Vendanges Tardives 2012 : Crystalline yellow with green tints. Expressive nose of lychee, yellow peach, mango and fine spice. Mild attack, impression of harmony, lush, velvety, pure and lively palate. Persistent finish that stays precise and pure. A wonderful wine for hedonists.
Price approx.: 22,95 EUR
http://www.wolfberger.com
Cave Vinicole d'Eguisheim - Wolfberger
+33 (0)3 89 22 20 20

ROBERT KLINGENFUS   88/100

▼✎ Clos des Chartreux 2012 : Attractive yellow-gold. Distinctive nose blending floral, peppery and tropical fruit notes. More of the same on the palate which shows seductive freshness and intensity. Compelling tropical finish with accents of lychee and ginger.
Price approx.: 12,00 EUR
Domaine Robert Klingenfus
+33 (0)3 88 38 07 06

DOMAINE ANDRÉ BLANCK ET SES FILS 88/100

▼✎ Altenburg 2013 : Vibrant light yellow with green tints. Racy, fruity nose offering up peach and lychee. Soft, fleshy and suave palate. Absolutely delicious, concentrated yet lively. Spice comes to the fore with a smoke touch on the finish. Invigorating and generous.
Price approx.: 8,60 EUR
http://www.andreblanck.com
Domaine André Blanck et ses Fils
+33 (0)3 89 78 24 72

MEYBLUM & FILS 87/100

▼♪ Prestige : Light yellow with green tints. Expressive floral nose with a trace of lychee. Ethereal, soft and lively palate with perfumes of rose petal and fine spice. A delicious style wine that would go down well at family reunions.
Price approx.: 13,00 EUR
http://www.meyblum-et-fils.com
MVP Wines

DOMAINE SCHAEFFER-WOERLY 87/100

Conv▼♪ Vieilles Vignes 2012 : Light gold. Subdued nose showing signature aromas of rose petal, mild spice and lychee. A supple, well-balanced wine with a lovely interaction between mildness, perfume and freshness. Exotic fruit-driven finish. Should work perfectly with Asian foods.
Price approx.: 9,00 EUR
www.schaeffer-woerly.com
Schaeffer-Woerly
+33 (0)3 88 92 40 81

WOLFBERGER 85/100

▼♪ Vintage 2013 : Brilliant light gold with green tints. Refined nose of rose petal, fine spice, mango and lychee. Full, silky substance invigorated by a robust freshness. Lovely tropical spicy aromas are exuded in the foreground. Sheer pleasure.
Price approx.: 7,10 EUR
http://www.wolfberger.com
Cave Vinicole d'Eguisheim - Wolfberger
+33 (0)3 89 22 20 20

HORCHER 85/100

▼♪ Sélection 2012 : Brilliant light yellow with green tints. Distinctive nose of lychee, ripe peach and fine spice. Soft, focused and easy-drinking palate that is honest and spice-infused. A wine for pleasure that works well at family reunions.
Price approx.: 8,70 EUR
www.vin-horcher.com
Domaine Horcher
+33 (0)3 89 47 93 26

BESTHEIM 83/100

▼♪ Classic 2013 : Light gold. Distinctive nose driven by rose and lychee. Lovely sweet entry. Focused perfume and freshness. A Gewurztraminer showing at its best when young, equally suitable as an aperitif or with dessert.
Price approx.: 7,25 EUR
http://www.bestheim.com
Bestheim
+33 (0)3 89 49 09 29

ALSACE GRAND CRU (CÉPAGES DIVERS)

DOMAINE CHARLES SPARR 89/100

▼♪ Brand 2011 : Yellow-gold. Delicate nose exuding mild spice tones, white flowers and toast notes. Soft attack on the palate with a refined mouthfeel and clear-cut aromas with oak imparting beautiful complexity. Highly unusual.
Price approx.: 20,00 EUR
http://www.domaine-vin-alsace.com
Domaine Charles Sparr
+33 (0)3 89 47 92 14

ALSACE GRAND CRU GEWURZTRAMINER

DOMAINE PIERRE FRICK 92/100

Org▼♪ Steinert - Vendanges Tardives 2010 : Light golden hue. Focused, expressive, creamy nose with yellow peach and a spice dimension. Fleshy attack, soft, delightful palate with ethereal opulence reinforced by elegant freshness. Precise and natural. Spicy and vibrant with a honeyed touch. Real allure.
Price approx.: 26,00 EUR
http://www.pierrefrick.com
Domaine Pierre Frick
+33 (0)3 89 49 62 99

HORCHER 92/100

▼♪ Mandelberg 2012 : Brilliant pale yellow with green tints. Racy nose of graphite, smoke, lychee and fine spices. Harmonious, silky, rich and highly drinkable palate with mellowness nicely balanced by exuberance. A real treat. Perfect for foie gras.
Price approx.: 12,40 EUR
www.vin-horcher.com
Domaine Horcher
+33 (0)3 89 47 93 26

DOMAINE ANDRÉ BLANCK ET SES FILS 91/100

▼♪ Schlossberg 2013 : Brilliant gold, green tints. Fairly reticent nose showing ripe yellow peach, mango and fine spices. Soft, nervy, rich palate revealing lovely easy-drinking generosity, splendid aromatic purity and refreshing drive. Elegant austerity on the finish. Beautiful.
Price approx.: 11,40 EUR
http://www.andreblanck.com
Domaine André Blanck et ses Fils
+33 (0)3 89 78 24 72

DOMAINES SCHLUMBERGER   91/100

▼🍷 Kessler 2008 : Glistening golden hue. Expressive, endearing nose intermixing candied fruit notes, fresh mushroom and fruit butter. Savoury freshness, expression and balance on the palate. A stylistic exercise nicely controlled by the right amount of acidity.

Price approx.: 21,50 EUR

www.domaines-schlumberger.com

Domaines Schlumberger

+33 (0)3 89 74 27 00

EDMOND RENTZ   89/100

▼🍷 Froehn 2012 : Crystalline pale yellow with green tints. Racy nose of lychee and yellow peach with fine spices. Soft, full and velvety presence on the palate, extremely vigorous and expressing refined mineral and spice notes with precision and moderation.

www.edmondrentz.com

Edmond Rentz

+33 (0)3 89 47 90 17

PAUL SCHNEIDER   89/100

▼🍷 Grand cru Eichberg 2011 : Light gold with green tints. Elegant nose of rose petal, fine spice and white-fleshed fruits. Velvety, medium-dry attack, beautiful aromatic exuberance clearly flowing into spice. Its liveliness makes it a suitable partner for cream-based sauces.

Price approx.: 12,00 EUR

http://www.vins-paul-schneider.fr

Paul Schneider

+33 (0)3 89 41 50 07

FALLER   89/100

▼🍷 Kirchberg 2012 : Attractive, limpid light gold. Suggestions of white flowers, tropical fruits and a honeyed touch on the nose. A pleasant, mellow wine on the palate with tropical aromas of lychee and ginger supported by freshness.

Price approx.: 24,00 EUR

Robert Faller et Fils

+33 (0)3 89 73 60 47

BESTHEIM   89/100

▼🍷 Mambourg 2011 : Yellow-gold. Predominant spice on the nose primarily recalling pepper. The palate is rich and well-balanced with the nose aromatics carrying through coupled with candied fruits. A classic wine already showing accessibility.

Price approx.: 11,50 EUR

http://www.bestheim.com

Bestheim

+33 (0)3 89 49 09 29

JEAN-LOUIS SCHOEPFER   88/100

▼🍷 Hengst 2011 : Yellow-gold. Distinctive nose with accents of tropical fruits and rose petal. The same pleasurable archetypal aromas recur on the palate, supported by lovely freshness. The fruit and floral aromas flow into persistent peppery notes on the finish.

Price approx.: 10,50 EUR

Jean-Louis Schoepfer

+33 (0)3 89 80 71 29

DOMAINE CHARLES SPARR   88/100

▼🍷 Sporen 2011 : Limpid pale yellow. Delicate, distinctive nose showing peppery notes, tropical fruits and lovely finesse. The palate is equally very distinctive even though youthfulness prevents it from fully revealing itself. A rich, heady style that needs time.

Price approx.: 18,00 EUR

http://www.domaine-vin-alsace.com

Domaine Charles Sparr

+33 (0)3 89 47 92 14

HORCHER   86/100

▼🍷 Sporen 2012 : Attractive light gold. Fairly distinctive, pure nose with a pronounced floral streak. Fruit and spice enter after swirling. The palate is well-balanced, fresh, aromatic and distinctive. Fairly seductive finish with notes of pepper, ginger and spice.

Price approx.: 14,70 EUR

www.vin-horcher.com

Domaine Horcher

+33 (0)3 89 47 93 26

ALSACE GRAND CRU PINOT GRIS

DOMAINES SCHLUMBERGER   91/100

▼🍷 Kessler 2010 : Limpid, light gold. Inviting, distinctive nose recalling ripe plum and apricot with a touch of crispness. The palate marries hallmark varietal richness with intense aromas and impeccable freshness. A fairly persistent, pleasant style marked by purity.

Price approx.: 17,00 EUR

www.domaines-schlumberger.com

Domaines Schlumberger

+33 (0)3 89 74 27 00

CHÂTEAU OLLWILLER   90/100

▼🍷 Ollwiller 2009 : Light yellow-gold. Generous nose of smoke, yellow peach, dried fruits, refined spice and a patisserie touch. Mellow, fleshy and concentrated palate with a substantial freshness

preventing heaviness. Superb spice and honeyed aromas. Beautiful persistency.
Price approx.: 10,44 EUR
http://www.cavevieilarmand.com
Cave Vinicole du Vieil Armand
+33 (0)3 89 76 73 75

EDMOND RENTZ 90/100

▼♪ Froehn 2011 : Intense yellow-gold. Pleasurable nose of ripe yellow peach, refined spice, liquorice and a tropical note. Silky attack, a fleshy, generous medium-dry. Very refined and elegant with a delicate, invigorating exuberance and long spicy finish. Real pleasure.
www.edmondrentz.com
Edmond Rentz
+33 (0)3 89 47 90 17

PAUL SCHNEIDER 89/100

▼♪ Grand cru Steinert 2010 : Brilliant pale gold with green tints. Racy nose showing great precision with white peach, a pineapple dimension and liquorice. A delicious, fleshy, spice-driven wine with exuberant expression supported by refined acidity. Faint mineral austerity.
Price approx.: 12,00 EUR
http://www.vins-paul-schneider.fr
Paul Schneider
+33 (0)3 89 41 50 07

BESTHEIM 88/100

▼♪ Zinnkoepflé 2011 : Yellow-gold. Classic nose suggestive of ripe plum. Beautiful acidity on the palate. Clean, crisp attack showing fruity aromas with lots of drive. The finish is richer and more candied. A potential partner for foie gras.
Price approx.: 11,50 EUR
http://www.bestheim.com
Bestheim
+33 (0)3 89 49 09 29

ALSACE
GRAND CRU RIESLING

DOMAINES SCHLUMBERGER 95/100

▼♪ Kitterlé 2008 : Limpid, pale yellow. Expressive nose showing predominant mineral perfumes of gunflint and limestone. Clean, full attack with extremely precise mineral and fruit aromas coupled with impressive length. Textbook style.
Price approx.: 20,50 EUR
www.domaines-schlumberger.com
Domaines Schlumberger
+33 (0)3 89 74 27 00

ROBERT KLINGENFUS 93/100

▼♪ Bruderthal 2008 : Pale gold. Refined, mature nose opening up to fresh mushroom and dried fruits then revealing a mineral character of hydrocarbon. Ample palate with a full, mellow attack. Bone dry, fruity and mineral in the middle palate. A superlative Riesling.
Price approx.: 15,00 EUR
Domaine Robert Klingenfus
+33 (0)3 88 38 07 06

DOMAINES SCHLUMBERGER 92/100

▼♪ Kessler 2009 : Appealing limpid, light gold. Elegant nose gradually revealing perfumes of ripe white fruits and candied lemon. A rich, full-bodied and generous wine on the palate showing aromatic precision, freshness and persistency.
Price approx.: 17,50 EUR
www.domaines-schlumberger.com
Domaines Schlumberger
+33 (0)3 89 74 27 00

BESTHEIM 92/100

▼♪ Mambourg 2010 : Alluring pale limpid gold. Delicate, distinctive nose marrying mineral and lemony notes. Excellent expression. The palate also displays great purity in the same very classic vein. Extremely pure sense of place.
Price approx.: 10,00 EUR
http://www.bestheim.com
Bestheim
+33 (0)3 89 49 09 29

DOMAINE DES MARRONNIERS 91/100

▼♪ Kastelberg 2012 : Beautiful light gold. The nose exudes candied citrus aromas with fairly reticent mineral undertones. Silky texture, fat and refined sweetness showcase the fruit. Mineral infused finish. An all-round, signature Grand Cru with a great future ahead.
Price approx.: 19,60 EUR
www.guy-wach.fr
Domaine des Marronniers
+33 (0)3 88 08 93 20

CHÂTEAU OLLWILLER 90/100

▼♪ Ollwiller 2010 : Brilliant yellow with green tints. Racy nose of lime, citrus and a mineral dimension. Full attack leading into a soft, rich palate bursting with energy. Beautiful, full-on mineral scents (hydrocarbon, chalk). Deserves flavoursome fish.
Price approx.: 11,14 EUR
http://www.cavevieilarmand.com
Cave Vinicole du Vieil Armand
+33 (0)3 89 76 73 75

EDMOND RENTZ   90/100

▼✦ Schoenenbourg 2011 : Brilliant light yellow, green tints. Racy nose of liquorice, hydrocarbon and lemon. Full attack, delightful, mouth-coating substance, beautiful clearly-delineated, striking perfumes. A soft wine showing a proud sense of place. Set aside for sophisticated foods.
www.edmondrentz.com
Edmond Rentz
+33 (0)3 89 47 90 17

DOMAINE DES MARRONNIERS   90/100

▼✦ Moenchberg 2012 : Limpid gold. Complex nose showing a touch of exotic fruits with mineral and wild flower undertones. Delicate palate with a lush texture and substantial aromatic presence with a lovely soft finish. A savoury great growth that has yet to fully reveal itself.
Price approx.: 17,05 EUR
www.guy-wach.fr
Domaine des Marronniers
+33 (0)3 88 08 93 20

DOMAINE ANDRÉ BLANCK ET SES FILS 89/100

▼✦ Schlossberg 2013 : Brilliant yellow with green tints. Racy nose with fruit suggestions of lime and grapefruit and a mineral note. The palate is fleshy and concentrated and driven by substantial exuberance. It flows into a beautiful austere mineral and lemony finish.
Price approx.: 9,90 EUR
http://www.andreblanck.com
Domaine André Blanck et ses Fils
+33 (0)3 89 78 24 72

ROBERT KLINGENFUS   89/100

▼✦ Bruderthal 2011 : Alluring yellow-gold. Delightfully intense nose marrying candied lemon notes, ripe white fruit and a patisserie touch flowing into mineral aromas. Very full, fresh and perfumed palate showing medium body and length.
Price approx.: 14,00 EUR
Domaine Robert Klingenfus
+33 (0)3 88 38 07 06

FALLER   88/100

▼✦ Geisberg 2012 : Limpid, light gold. The nose recalls white fruits with a floral touch on first pour. Easy-drinking style on the palate with a fresh attack dominated by the same delightful aromas. An accessible great growth drinking well now.
Price approx.: 25,00 EUR
Robert Faller et Fils
+33 (0)3 89 73 60 47

DOMAINE AIMÉSTENTZ   88/100

Org▼✦ Sommerberg 2012 : Beautiful light gold. Rich nose recalling stewed white fruit, mineral and dried fruit aromas. Lovely softness at point of entry supported by focused perfume. Balance and freshness. A great growth that is very full yet also accessible.
Price approx.: 12,30 EUR
http://www.vins-stentz.fr
Domaine Aiméstentz
+33 (0)3 89 80 63 77

DOMAINE DES MARRONNIERS   88/100

▼✦ Wiebelsberg 2012 : Light gold. Young, subdued nose showing accents of ripe citrus fruits and flowers. Mineral tones after swirling. Soft, mellow palate showing seductive youthful aromatics that make it accessible already. A crowd-pleasing great growth.
Price approx.: 17,40 EUR
www.guy-wach.fr
Domaine des Marronniers
+33 (0)3 88 08 93 20

DOMAINE DES MARRONNIERS   88/100

▼✦ Kastelberg - Vendanges Tardives 2011 : Light gold. Complex nose of honey, almond, quince and rose with a mineral touch. A supple, young, sweet wine still a little backward in terms of aroma. Boasts the prerequisites of a great wine. Just needs to develop more aroma, substance and sweetness.
Price approx.: 29,50 EUR
www.guy-wach.fr
Domaine des Marronniers
+33 (0)3 88 08 93 20

DOMAINE CHARLES SPARR   88/100

▼✦ Brand 2011 : Yellow hue bordering on pale with green tints. Subtle fruit on the nose opening up to fleeting mineral tones. More expressive fruity aromas on the palate with a crisp touch and subtle mineral note. The finish is slightly mellow.
Price approx.: 13,00 EUR
http://www.domaine-vin-alsace.com
Domaine Charles Sparr
+33 (0)3 89 47 92 14

Prices mentioned in this book are guideline and can vary depending on point of sale. The shops, wineries or publisher can in no way be held responsible for this.

DOMAINE CHARLES SPARR

90/100

▼ **Schoenenbourg 2011**

Light yellow. Refined nose marrying floral, fruity and mineral notes. On the palate, a pronounced mineral dimension imparts a degree of austerity yet great structure characterises the whole. Abundant freshness on the finish imparted by a lemony note.

Price approx.: 14 EUR
Serving temperature: 8-10°
Ready to drink: 2015-2017

The estate's vineyards stretch over 20 hectares located primarily on hillside sites. They encompass four great growths, each with its own distinct personality: Brand in Turckheim; Mambourg in Sigolsheim; and Sporen and Schoenenbourg in Riquewihr.
Winegrowers for 12 generations, three of which still manage the property, the family's successive heirs have all shared the same passion. Charles, who represents the youngest generation, has broken the mould by converting the estate to organic wine growing, thereby strengthening the wines' authenticity and subtlety. Guided tours of the winery can be organised by arrangement.

Domaine Charles Sparr
8 avenue Mequillet - 68340 Riquewihr
Tel: (+33) 3 89 47 92 14 - Fax: (+33) 3 89 47 99 31
E-mail: pierre.sparr@wanadoo.fr
Website: http://www.domaine-vin-alsace.com

SCHAEFFER-WOERLY — 87/100

Conv ▼🔊 Frankstein 2012 : Light gold. Refined, subdued nose with smoke, mineral and dried fruit accents. Delicate palate boasting lovely mellowness. Fruit expression is pleasantly crisp. A harmonious, supple great growth, pleasurable from its early years on.
Price approx.: 11,50 EUR
www.schaeffer-woerly.com
Schaeffer-Woerly
+33 (0)3 88 92 40 81

ALSACE MUSCAT

ROBERT KLINGENFUS — 85/100

▼🔊 Clos des Chartreux 2012 : Pale yellow. Subdued nose showing accents of fresh grape with a faint vegetal touch. The palate clearly focuses on lightness, freshness and fruity perfumes, particularly grape. A distinctive, refreshing style, ideal for the aperitif.
Price approx.: 12,00 EUR
Domaine Robert Klingenfus
+33 (0)3 88 38 07 06

ALSACE PINOT BLANC

DOMAINE ANDRÉ BLANCK ET SES FILS — 86/100

▼🔊 Rosenburg 2013 : Brilliant pale yellow with green tints. Pleasurable nose of white-fleshed fruits. Round attack leading into a full, fairly fleshy palate showing lovely clean, precise, exuberant aromas. A wine that would sit very well alongside a mild curry.
Price approx.: 6,80 EUR
http://www.andreblanck.com
Domaine André Blanck et ses Fils
+33 (0)3 89 78 24 72

MEYBLUM & FILS — 85/100

▼🔊 Prestige 2012 : Brilliant pale gold. Compelling nose suggestive of golden delicious apple with a floral tone. Supple attack leading into a round, likeable palate bolstered by an effective liveliness that marks the finish. A flavoursome partner for vegetable terrine.
Price approx.: 11,00 EUR
http://www.meyblum-et-fils.com
MVP Wines

JEAN-LOUIS SCHOEPFER — 84/100

▼🔊 Vintage 2012 : Limpid, light yellow in colour. Pleasant nose marrying floral and white fruit notes. Fresh, fruity and well-balanced at point of entry. A no-frills wine that pairs with terrines or fish.

Price approx.: 5,50 EUR
Jean-Louis Schoepfer
+33 (0)3 89 80 71 29

HORCHER — 83/100

▼🔊 Vintage 2012 : Brilliant pale hue with green tints. Fairly shy nose of white fruits with a floral note. Supple attack, soft, easy-drinking and likeable palate. A well-balanced, accessible Pinot pairing with vegetable terrine.
Price approx.: 6,20 EUR
www.vin-horcher.com
Domaine Horcher
+33 (0)3 89 47 93 26

ALSACE PINOT GRIS

DOMINIQUE ET JULIEN FREY — 90/100

Org ▼🔊 Quintessence 2011 : Golden hue. Expressive, refined nose with dried fruit, Seville orange, quince and rhubarb tones. Extremely crunchy style. Rich attack on the palate flowing into a mid-palate balanced by evident acidity. Long finish revealing more of the nose complexity.
Price approx.: 15,00 EUR
http://www.vinsfreybio.com
Domaine Charles Frey
+33 (0)3 88 92 41 04

CHRISTOPHE RIEFLÉ — 89/100

▼🔊 Côte de Rouffach 2011 : Beautiful golden hue. The nose marries notes of ripe, almost jammy fruits with a smoky mineral background. Abundant freshness, richness and velvety smoothness on the palate. A highly distinctive style exuding rich, focused and long-lasting fruit.
Price approx.: 6,35 EUR
http://www.vins-christophe-riefle.com
Christophe Riefle
+33 (0)3 89 49 77 85

DOMAINE ANDRÉ BLANCK & SES FILS — 87/100

▼🔊 Clos Schwendi 2013 : Brilliant yellow. Expressive nose showing a core of fruits with a whiff of smoke and yellow peach. Soft, fleshy and rich palate with refined spice, savoury exuberance increasing in intensity and precise aromas. An assertive, precise Pinot gris.
Price approx.: 8,60 EUR
http://www.andreblanck.com
Domaine André Blanck et ses Fils
+33 (0)3 89 78 24 72

WOLFBERGER — 87/100

▼🔊 Vendanges Tardives 2012 : Brilliant yellow with faint green tints. Complex smoky nose showing refined spice, peach stone and patisserie touches.

Mild attack leading into a silky, concentrated palate revealing more of the nose aromatics and an impression of vanilla. A real treat.
Price approx.: 19,95 EUR
http://www.wolfberger.com
Cave Vinicole d'Eguisheim - Wolfberger
+33 (0)3 89 22 20 20

MEYBLUM & FILS   87/100

▼.♪ Prestige 2012 : Brilliant pale gold. Pleasant nose of white peach, pear and refined patisserie touches. On the palate, a soft, svelte wine showing exuberant, clear-cut expression with a marked spice accent mid-palate. Fresh, expressive and long-lasting finish.
Price approx.: 13,00 EUR
http://www.meyblum-et-fils.com
MVP Wines

PAUL SCHNEIDER   87/100

▼♪ Cuvée Saint Urbain 2012 : Light yellow, green tints. Promising nose of white peach with smoke, mineral and tropical tones. Supple palate, a soft, velvety and full wine that is very welcoming with refined acidity and an array of spice driving the mid-palate. A good, distinctive Pinot gris.
Price approx.: 8,50 EUR
http://www.vins-paul-schneider.fr
Paul Schneider
+33 (0)3 89 41 50 07

DOMAINES SCHLUMBERGER   87/100

▼♪ Les Princes Abbés 2012 : Beautiful limpid pale yellow. Fairly subdued nose of ripe fruits with crisp accents. Wonderful balance, fullness and fairly intense perfume on the palate. A full-bodied style pairing with white meats or stews.
Price approx.: 10,00 EUR
www.domaines-schlumberger.com
Domaines Schlumberger
+33 (0)3 89 74 27 00

DOMAINE AIMÉSTENTZ   86/100

Org▼♪ Rosenberg 2013 : Light yellow with green tints. Endearing nose of yellow peach with spice and smoke notes. On the palate, a fairly svelte, rich and lively wine with lovely intense aromas and a crunchy, dynamic and fruity finish. A successful offering.
Price approx.: 9,10 EUR
http://www.vins-stentz.fr
Domaine Aiméstentz
+33 (0)3 89 80 63 77

Detailed instructions are featured at

the start of the book.

WOLFBERGER   86/100

▼♪ Hospices de Strasbourg 2012 : Brilliant pale yellow. Subdued, creamy nose showing an impression of white fruits. Soft attack leading into a fleshy, silky palate with some spicy and honeyed touches. A delicious wine pairing with Asian foods.
Price approx.: 9,30 EUR
http://www.wolfberger.com
Cave Vinicole d'Eguisheim - Wolfberger
+33 (0)3 89 22 20 20

WOLFBERGER   86/100

▼♪ Vintage 2013 : Light yellow with green tints. Shy nose of white peach with a tropical touch. Round attack, fleshy, silky substance supported by delicate freshness. Lovely expressive, generous mouthfeel showing refined spice. Uncork for a mild
Price approx.: 7,60 EUR
http://www.wolfberger.com
Cave Vinicole d'Eguisheim - Wolfberger
+33 (0)3 89 22 20 20

DOMINIQUE ET JULIEN FREY   86/100

Org▼♪ Cuvée de l'Ours 2012 : Limpid, light yellow. Subdued nose of jammy fruits and citrus. Tell-tale varietal style on the palate which is ripe, fruity and spicy. Clean finish recalling stone fruits. A distinctive, well-balanced Pinot gris pairing with white meats.
Price approx.: 8,90 EUR
http://www.vinsfreybio.com
Domaine Charles Frey
+33 (0)3 88 92 41 04

JEAN-LOUIS SCHOEPFER   85/100

▼♪ Vintage 2012 : Light yellow. Suggestions of stone fruits with a pronounced almond note on the nose. Freshness, expression and intensity are key themes on the palate. An easy-drinking, well-balanced style for the aperitif or a cold starter.
Price approx.: 5,90 EUR
Jean-Louis Schoepfer
+33 (0)3 89 80 71 29

HORCHER   85/100

▼♪ Grains de Terroir 2009 : Pale gold. Distinctive nose reminiscent of ripe fruits, plum, apricot and a touch of dried fruit. On the palate, a very rich style yet nonetheless revealing the varietal's tell-tale acidity. More of the typical nose aromas with a crisp, stewed finish.
Price approx.: 11,40 EUR
www.vin-horcher.com
Domaine Horcher
+33 (0)3 89 47 93 26

HORCHER — 84/100

▼✔ Sélection 2011 : Light yellow with faint green tints. Pleasant nose intermixing yellow and white peaches with a dash of spice. Supple attack, soft, fresh and very drinkable palate with some patisserie notes. An enjoyable Pinot gris that works with a wide array of foods.
Price approx.: 8,70 EUR
www.vin-horcher.com
Domaine Horcher
+33 (0)3 89 47 93 26

WOLFBERGER — 83/100

▼✔ Vintage 2013 : Deep ruby with dark purple tints. Pleasant nose suggestive of morello cherry coupled with a floral dimension. Fresh palate dominated by robust, crunchy fruit showing full-on expression and subtle, underlying vegetal ageing notes. An enjoyable wine.
Price approx.: 6,95 EUR
http://www.wolfberger.com
Cave Vinicole d'Eguisheim - Wolfberger
+33 (0)3 89 22 20 20

ALSACE PINOT NOIR

CHÂTEAU OLLWILLER — 87/100

▼✔ Vintage 2009 : Limpid hue starting to evolve. Seductive nose of ripe black cherry, kirsch and a touch of undergrowth. Supple, rich palate showing refined spices and a firm finish. Still fairly shy but a beautiful promising wine all the same.
Price approx.: 9,23 EUR
http://www.cavevieilarmand.com
Cave Vinicole du Vieil Armand
+33 (0)3 89 76 73 75

ROBERT KLINGENFUS — 85/100

▼✔ Signature 2011 : Slightly mature light red. Suggestions of ripe cherry with a trace of spice on the nose. Clean, fruit-forward attack on the palate. Lightweight structure. More of the same pleasant ripe cherry tone on the mid-palate and finish.
Price approx.: 9,00 EUR
Domaine Robert Klingenfus
+33 (0)3 88 38 07 06

JEAN-LOUIS SCHOEPFER — 85/100

▼✔ Prestige 2011 : Light red. Suggestions of ripe cherry with Morello cherry on the nose. Fruit leads the way on the palate. Lightweight structure yet nevertheless good aromatic focus. Uncork for cold cuts and barbecued foods.
Price approx.: 6,90 EUR
Jean-Louis Schoepfer
+33 (0)3 89 80 71 29

DOMINIQUE ET JULIEN FREY — 85/100

Org▼✔ Quintessence 2011 : Light red. Nose of red fruits and spices with a touch of morello cherry. On the palate, a fresh wine with melted tannins displaying focused fruity notes. The finish is delightful and driven by ripe cherry and redcurrant tones. A wine for sharing.
Price approx.: 12,50 EUR
http://www.vinsfreybio.com
Domaine Charles Frey
+33 (0)3 88 92 41 04

ALSACE RIESLING

DOMAINE PIERRE FRICK — 91/100

Org▼✔ Rot - Murlé 2009 : Brilliant, vibrant pale yellow. Racy lemony nose with a balsamic dimension. Honest, round and lively palate showing exuberant lemon aromas flowing into suggestions of plum and fine spice mid-palate. Focused, aromatic finish. Absolutely beautiful.
Price approx.: 12,80 EUR
http://www.pierrefrick.com
Domaine Pierre Frick
+33 (0)3 89 49 62 99

DOMAINES SCHLUMBERGER — 90/100

▼✔ Vendanges Tardives 2009 : Attractive limpid golden hue. Fruity nose of citrus fruit butter with a lemony mineral touch. Beautiful well-balanced, aromatic attack on the palate. The mid-palate is fairly powerful with persistent lemony and spice notes. Lots of character.
Price approx.: 35,00 EUR
www.domaines-schlumberger.com
Domaines Schlumberger
+33 (0)3 89 74 27 00

DOMINIQUE ET JULIEN FREY — 89/100

Org▼✔ Quintessence 2012 : Limpid, pale gold. Expressive nose marrying fresh grape notes with a subtle smoky mineral tone. The palate is velvety yet rich with predominant mineral perfumes. A fairly elegant, authentic Riesling.
Price approx.: 15,00 EUR
http://www.vinsfreybio.com
Domaine Charles Frey
+33 (0)3 88 92 41 04

BRAND & FILS — 88/100

Org▼✔ Kefferberg 2011 : Bright golden yellow. Racy nose intermixing mineral and floral notes backed by citrus. Silky, round and generous palate. A bone dry Riesling that is fairly reticent at the

moment. Fresh lemon on the mid-palate. Real sense of place. Keep for a while.
Price approx.: 7,90 EUR
Domaine Lucien Brand & fils
+33 (0)3 88 38 17 71

DOMAINE DES MARRONNIERS   88/100

▼♪ Andlau 2012 : Beautiful light gold. Ripe nose with accents of citrus and white fruits over mineral and smoke undertones. A generous, full Riesling marked by freshness with nicely showcased perfume. A distinctive wine pairing perfectly with freshwater fish in a sauce.
Price approx.: 9,80 EUR
www.guy-wach.fr
Domaine des Marronniers
+33 (0)3 88 08 93 20

ROBERT KLINGENFUS   88/100

▼♪ Signature 2012 : Pale gold. Refined, expressive nose marrying fruit and mineral notes. On the palate, a lovely compromise between fruit, freshness and fullness. Persistent mineral perfumes recur on the finish. A delightful, distinctive Riesling for premium fish.
Price approx.: 7,50 EUR
Domaine Robert Klingenfus
+33 (0)3 88 38 07 06

DOMAINES SCHLUMBERGER   87/100

▼♪ Les Princes Abbés 2012 : Light yellow, green tints. Pleasant, expressive nose with accents of white flowers and a floral and mineral touch. Fresh attack on the palate with more of the same delightful, focused aromas. Beautiful balance. An accessible Riesling for starters.
Price approx.: 9,70 EUR
www.domaines-schlumberger.com
Domaines Schlumberger
+33 (0)3 89 74 27 00

DOMAINE CHARLES SPARR   87/100

▼♪ Altenbourg 2011 : Light yellow with green tints. Archetypal nose marrying white fruits and minerality. Fairly dense, fresh attack revealing more of the same pleasant features. Persistent, fruity and quite easy-drinking finish with a stone fruit tone.
Price approx.: 12,00 EUR
http://www.domaine-vin-alsace.com
Domaine Charles Sparr
+33 (0)3 89 47 92 14

WILLM   85/100

▼♪ Réserve 2013 : Brilliant light hue with green tints. Pleasant nose with floral notes entwined with

citrus fruits. Fairly round mouthfeel driven by good liveliness and lovely exuberant, precise lemony aromas that linger. A good, distinctive Riesling.
Price approx.: 5,95 EUR
http://www.wolfberger.com
Cave Vinicole d'Eguisheim - Wolfberger
+33 (0)3 89 22 20 20

MEYBLUM & FILS   85/100

▼♪ Prestige 2012 : Brilliant light yellow with green tints. Subdued nose of lime, lemon and tangerine. Forthright, lively and closely-integrated palate with floral perfumes coupled with fruit followed by a faint mineral streak. A well-made Riesling.
Price approx.: 11,00 EUR
http://www.meyblum-et-fils.com
MVP Wines

PAUL SCHNEIDER   85/100

▼♪ Vieilles Vignes 2012 : Pale, crystalline hue with green tints. Expressive nose intermixing citrus, a refined mineral tone and a patisserie touch. Supple attack, a likeable palate with lemon and grapefruit overtones. Pleasurable and supported by effective freshness.
Price approx.: 8,30 EUR
http://www.vins-paul-schneider.fr
Paul Schneider
+33 (0)3 89 41 50 07

JEAN-LOUIS SCHOEPFER   85/100

▼♪ Vintage 2012 : Pale yellow with green tints. Pleasant, focused nose recalling white flowers with a mineral touch. Lightweight framework on the palate with focus on freshness. The finish is denser. A likeable Riesling pairing with seafoods.
Price approx.: 5,50 EUR
Jean-Louis Schoepfer
+33 (0)3 89 80 71 29

DOMAINE AIMÉSTENTZ   84/100

Org▼♪ Vintage 2013 : Brilliant light hue with green tints. Expressive nose of fresh and candied citrus with pine. Light, lively palate revealing more of the citrus fruits. Upright and showing honest expression with a lovely lemony finish. An enjoyable wine.
Price approx.: 6,90 EUR
http://www.vins-stentz.fr
Domaine Aiméstentz
+33 (0)3 89 80 63 77

WOLFBERGER 84/100

▼🍷 Vintage 2013 : Brilliant pale hue with green tints. Compelling nose of white flowers and citrus fruits. Ethereal and lively palate with a lemony character, striking aromas and a degree of austerity. A little bottle age will enhance its charm. Set aside for shellfish.
Price approx.: 5,95 EUR
http://www.wolfberger.com
Cave Vinicole d'Eguisheim - Wolfberger
+33 (0)3 89 22 20 20

HORCHER 83/100

▼🍷 Sélection 2012 : Pale gold. Fairly subdued nose with accents of white flowers and fresh fruits. On the palate, quite a distinctive, light, fruit-driven style with a slightly bitter finish faintly reminiscent of almond. An accessible Riesling for grilled fish.
Price approx.: 9,70 EUR
www.vin-horcher.com
Domaine Horcher
+33 (0)3 89 47 93 26

BESTHEIM 82/100

▼🍷 Lieu dit Rebgarten 2013 : Light gold. The nose is driven by citrus and dried fruits. Supple, soft palate showing a low level of concentration. Pleasant, focused fruit. A very accessible Riesling that works well from the aperitif onwards.
Price approx.: 7,75 EUR
http://www.bestheim.com
Bestheim
+33 (0)3 89 49 09 29

ALSACE SYLVANER

DOMINIQUE ET JULIEN FREY 89/100

Org▼🍷 Fraîcheur Gourmande 2012 : Clean yellow with a light gold streak. Focused, heady nose marrying white fruit and almond notes. A fresh, full-bodied wine on the palate revealing more of the same aromatic traits. An expressive, persistent style for gourmet foods.
Price approx.: 7,00 EUR
http://www.vinsfreybio.com
Domaine Charles Frey
+33 (0)3 88 92 41 04

DOMAINE PIERRE FRICK 88/100

Org▼🍷 Bergweingarten 2009 : Brilliant light yellow, green tints. Pleasant nose recalling ripe white fruits and mirabelle plum. Ethereal, focused and vibrant palate. Lovely natural impression. A sweet wine with floral and honeyed notes and an aromatic

finish. Delightfully successful.
Price approx.: 12,60 EUR
http://www.pierrefrick.com
Domaine Pierre Frick
+33 (0)3 89 49 62 99

DOMAINE SCHAEFFER-WOERLY 85/100

Conv▼🍷 Vintage 2012 : Pale gold. Subtle citrus fruit on the nose. Expressive palate boasting fat. Lovely freshness showcasing the fruit. A lively, generous Sylvaner that makes the perfect partner for pies, quiches and fish terrines.
Price approx.: 5,80 EUR
www.schaeffer-woerly.com
Schaeffer-Woerly
+33 (0)3 88 92 40 81

CRÉMANT DALSACE

DOMAINE CHARLES SPARR 89/100

▼🍷 Chardonnay Hallelujah : Light gold. Refined nose driven by almond, hazelnut and a touch of pastry. Vinous, ample and full-bodied palate dominated by more of the nose aromatics. Beautiful length and freshness. A superlative Crémant.
Price approx.: 13,00 EUR
http://www.domaine-vin-alsace.com
Domaine Charles Sparr
+33 (0)3 89 47 92 14

DOMINIQUE ET JULIEN FREY 88/100

Org▼🍷 Extra brut Plaisir perlant 2010 : Light yellow. Mature nose of ripe white fruits, stone fruits and a touch of toast, pastries and mocha. A full wine on the palate with delicious mature perfumes dominated by toasted notes and mild spices. A compelling effort.
Price approx.: 8,90 EUR
http://www.vinsfreybio.com
Domaine Charles Frey
+33 (0)3 88 92 41 04

BESTHEIM 87/100

▼🍷 Brut Prestige : Light yellow. Elegant nose intermixing white fruits and biscuit tones. The palate is full, fruity, focused and delightful. More of the same persistency driven by crisp, fruity notes. An extremely refined Crémant for gourmet foods.
Price approx.: 10,95 EUR
http://www.bestheim.com
Bestheim
+33 (0)3 89 49 09 29

DOMAINE AIMÉSTENTZ   86/100

Org▼🍷 Brut Chardonnay 2012 : Light yellow with a beautiful, fine effervescence. Expressive nose recalling white flowers. Ethereal palate revealing more of the floral aromas, with lovely aromatic intensity. A nicely-crafted, refined Crémant, very enjoyable as an aperitif.
Price approx.: 9,50 EUR
http://www.vins-stentz.fr
Domaine Aiméstentz
+33 (0)3 89 80 63 77

PAUL SCHNEIDER   86/100

▼🍷 Brut : Light yellow with good effervescence. Extremely fresh nose showing delicate floral aromatics and white fruits. On the palate, an ethereal Crémant revolving around freshness and focused, crunchy aromas bolstered by beautiful, substantial foam.
Price approx.: 8,30 EUR
http://www.vins-paul-schneider.fr
Paul Schneider
+33 (0)3 89 41 50 07

DOMAINE AIMÉSTENTZ   86/100

Org▼🍷 Brut Cuvée Prestige : Light gold. Refined mineral and fruity nose of apple and pear. A soft, light Crémant displaying crisp, crunchy fruit aromatics. Freshness frames the whole. Very refined and delicate.
Price approx.: 8,05 EUR
http://www.vins-stentz.fr
Domaine Aiméstentz
+33 (0)3 89 80 63 77

CHRISTOPHE RIEFLÉ   85/100

▼🍷 Brut : Light yellow. Focused nose marrying white fruits and biscuit notes. Wonderful balance on the palate with suppleness the primary feature. Creamy effervescence showing off the same delightful aromas. A pretty wine.
Price approx.: 5,70 EUR
http://www.vins-christophe-riefle.com
Christophe Riefle
+33 (0)3 89 49 77 85

DOMINIQUE ET JULIEN FREY   84/100

Org▼🍷 Extra Brut Plaisir Perlant 2009 : Pale gold. Nose of dried fruits, apricot and white fruits. Nervy, generous mouthfeel where exuberance highlights perfume. A Crémant that wakens the palate.
Price approx.: 8,90 EUR

http://www.vinsfreybio.com
Domaine Charles Frey
+33 (0)3 88 92 41 04

BESTHEIM   82/100

▼🍷 Brut rosé : Beautiful clean pink. Extremely focused nose of red fruits. The palate is quite lively and fruit-driven with crisp strawberry notes on the finish. Set aside for a red-fruit based dessert.
Price approx.: 8,50 EUR
http://www.bestheim.com
Bestheim
+33 (0)3 89 49 09 29

BESTHEIM   82/100

▼🍷 Brut : Light yellow. The nose is a halfway house between vegetal and fruit notes. Clean attack leading into a fairly lively mid-palate. A well-balanced, simple and accessible dry sparkling wine across the palate.
Price approx.: 7,50 EUR
http://www.bestheim.com
Bestheim
+33 (0)3 89 49 09 29

OTHER ALSACE A.O.C.

WOLFBERGER   85/100

▼🍷 Black Papillon 2013 : Pale crystalline hue with green tints. Appealing nose of lycee, refined spice and a floral touch. On the palate, a very likeable, round, rich and easy-drinking wine showcasing spice aromatics. Fairly dry and nervy, pairing with creamy sauces.
Price approx.: 7,30 EUR
http://www.wolfberger.com
Cave Vinicole d'Eguisheim - Wolfberger
+33 (0)3 89 22 20 20

BEAUJOLAIS

A WINE REGION WITH A STORY TELL

The Beaujolais wine region lies to the east of central France. It takes its name from the small town of Beaujeu. It starts off below Macon, in Burgundy, and stretches south, virtually down to the northern gateway to Lyon. The vast majority of its wines are red with a few rosés, though a small proportion of white wines are also produced in the north. Beaujolais wines boast a distinctive aromatic personality derived from a unique combination of the three fundamental elements of winegrowing: grape varietals, terroir and climate.

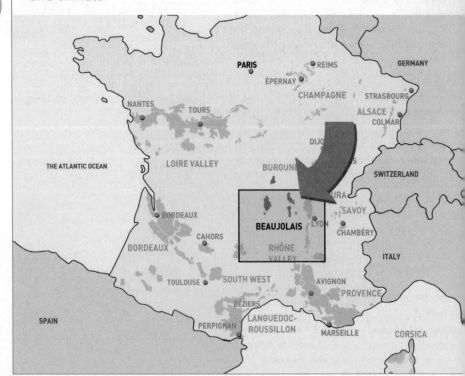

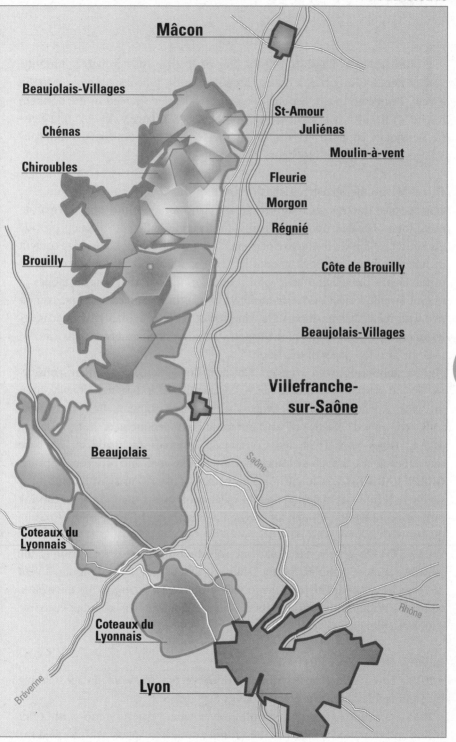

Mâcon

Beaujolais-Villages

St-Amour

Chénas

Juliénas

Moulin-à-vent

Chiroubles

Fleurie

Morgon

Régnié

Brouilly

Côte de Brouilly

Beaujolais-Villages

Villefranche-
sur-Saône

Beaujolais

Coteaux du
Lyonnais

Coteaux du
Lyonnais

Saône

Rhône

Brévenne

Lyon

The region's flagship wines are of course its growths: Brouilly, Chénas, Chiroubles, Côte de Brouilly, Fleurie, Juliénas, Morgon, Moulin à Vent, Regnié and Saint-Amour (see map), which are situated in the northern reaches of the area. The southern part of the region is largely devoted to a generic Beaujolais appellation, further sub-divided into two more tiers, Beaujolais-Villages and Beaujolais Supérieur.

This is where the archetypal characteristics of the Gamay varietal bloom. The granite soils, intermingled with shale and sandstone, form a perfect environment for it. Isolated pockets of soil with a slightly different make-up provide the substance for the distinctive personalities of the growths: higher clay content in Juliénas; manganese-rich granite in Chénas; silica and granite intermingled in the Fleurie appellation area; granite and 'green horn' shale on the slopes of Mount Brouilly... (A.C. Côte de Brouilly). When these characteristics are combined with the craftsmanship of the winegrower, each Beaujolais growth achieves its fullest expression. Some of the region's proudest standard bearers are featured over the next few pages of this book.

The neighbouring wine region, Coteaux du Lyonnais, is often considered to be part of Beaujolais: since Roman times, it has traditionally been the vine growing garden of Lyon. Gamay reigns supreme here on granite soils, comprised chiefly of metamorphic and sedimentary rock. Classed as A.C. wines since 1984, red Coteaux du Lyonnais are made in the same way as Beaujolais, though a balance of wines are also rosé, and occasionally white.

GRAPE VARIETALS: «Gamay noir à jus blanc», or black Gamay with white juice, for the reds (the vast majority) and the balance of rosés. Chardonnay for the tiny proportion of whites, though also some Pinot blanc and Aligoté in the Coteaux du Lyonnais area.

WINE STYLES: generic Beaujolais are soft, fruit-driven reds for quaffing; the growths are more complex and the better vintages of Morgon and Moulin à Vent can even be cellared. The rosés are in their prime when young, as are the whites, which are acidulous, vigorous wines. Both are delicious served as appetisers or with soft, fresh goat's cheese.

REVIEW OF RECENT VINTAGES

• **2010** • Low quantity caused by millerandage yet nevertheless a vintage boasting fruit and faultless structure after a hot, dry September.

• **2011** • A strange growing season like everywhere else in France with a hot spring and unsettled weather in the summer until late August which saved the day. The berries were small and often very healthy with normal cluster weight. The wines should be destined for an honourable future.

• **2012** • Yields were low due to climatic disturbances, but the general quality is good thanks to a dry spell at the beginning of September that encouraged ripening. A fruity vintage that is not likely to go down in history, but is nonetheless very well made.

• **2013** • A fairly late vintage, reminding wine growers of 1983 which enjoyed a remarkable life. Let's hope the 2013s follow the same route. The grapes had to be sorted but produced wonderful levels of acidity and overall, beautifully crafted wines.

THE BEAUJOLAIS APPELLATIONS

A.C. BEAUJOLAIS AND BEAUJOLAIS SUPÉRIEUR

OVERVIEW: the vineyard runs north to south over a stretch of land 90 kilometres long and 15 kilometres wide. Covering three cantons and 55 towns and villages, it starts off in Leynes, below Macon, and extends southwards to the canton of Abresle. The boundaries of this entire region are etched by the river Arlais in the north, the Monts du Lyonnais range in the west, the Saône in the east and by another river, the Turdine, in the south.

Virtually all of the wines classed as AC Beaujolais and Beaujolais Supérieur are made south of Villefranche-sur-Saône.

The vast majority of the wines are red, drawn from the Gamay varietal. The whites, drawn from Chardonnay, account for just 2% of overall production. The minimum alcohol requirement for Beaujolais is 10%, which is raised to 11% for Beaujolais Supérieur.

Most of the wines are sold as 'nouveau' and three-quarters of these are sold via shipping companies.

CLIMATE AND SOILS: there are two types of soils. In the north, they are crystalline, granite with traces of manganese. In the southern section, they are comprised of sedimentary rocks and are predominantly calcareous clay. The vineyards are planted on hillside sites along the myriad rivers which provide drainage for the region. In the northern reaches, home to the growths, the ground is shallow and permeable. Most wines classed as AC Beaujolais are grown in the southern part of the region. The temperate climate has a pronounced continental influence, with potentially harsh winters and hot summers. The Beaujolais hills shield the vineyard from westerly winds and with their east and south facings, the vines clock up a good deal of sunlight hours.

WINE STYLES: Beaujolais wines are neither crushed nor destemmed prior to vinting. Whole clusters enter the vats and ferment inside the skins producing fresh, fruit-forward, lively wines for quaffing. Their ruby-red hue with purple-blue tints and fragrance of small red fruit (red currant, blackcurrant, raspberry...) reward early drinking. Everyday home cooking and cooked cold pork meats are perfect drinking partners.

A.C. BEAUJOLAIS-VILLAGES

OVERVIEW: the appellation area covers 39 towns and villages in the Rhône departments and a further eight in Saône-et-Loire. The appellation runs from Leynes in the north to Denicé. Village names to look for are Odenas, Montmelas, Vauxrenard, Rivolet, Saint-Lager... This particular wine region also embraces nine of the ten Beaujolais growths. The soils here are crystalline and are predominantly formed of shale and granite which is where Gamay flourishes. The alcohol requirement for Beaujolais-Villages is 10.5%. They account for a quarter of the entire region's output. Fact: although winegrowers are entitled to state the name of their village on the label, very few actually do.

WINE STYLES: they display a cherry-red hue and fragrances of red fruit, predominantly strawberry and blackcurrant. Occasionally they exude notes of leather, spices or game. They are also more robust than AC Beaujolais wines. These fruit-driven, lively, well-balanced, round wines are smooth and harmonious and can be drunk young or laid down. Saveloy cooked in brioche, grilled chitterlings sausage, coq au vin, red meat, Lyon cheeses, suckling pig, stew, grilled chicken... are all dishes that enhance these qualities.

A.C. BROUILLY

OVERVIEW: the most southerly and extensive of the Beaujolais growths. The vineyard encircles Brouilly hill, through Saint-Lager, Cercié, Quincié, Odenas, Saint-Etienne-la-Varende and Charentay. There were vines growing on the southern slopes of the hill as far back as the 4th century and up until the 17th century the wines were drunk locally. It is sometimes dubbed 'the wine of love'. Several different soil profiles can be found here. In Saint-Etienne-la-Varende, Quincié and Odenas, sandy clay soils rest on granite. On limestone marl bedrock, the soil is formed of limestone, silica and sandstone stones. On one hillside facing due south in Cercié, 22 hectares of vines are entitled to carry the 'pisse vieille' label which is the only climatically distinct site recognised in Brouilly.

WINE STYLES: Brouilly are well-structured wines. They are soft, delicate, lively wines which are firm, robust, powerful and fruity. They are also harmonious, round and have relatively good vinosity with pleasant tannins. They display an intense ruby-style hue and fragrances of blueberry, blackberry, fresh grapes, kirsch, cherry and mineral notes. Brouilly partners well with red meats, barbecues, cooked cold pork meats and goat's cheeses.

A.C. CHÉNAS

OVERVIEW: this growth takes its name from the oak trees that were the area's original inhabitants. The appellation extends over Chénas and La-Chapelle-de-Guinchay in the Rhône and Saône-et-Loire departments. Situated between Juliénas and Saint-Amour in the north and Moulin-à-Vent in the south, it is one of Beaujolais' smallest growths. The greater part of the appellation overlooks the Mauvaise valley. Due to the area's microclimate, the grapes are harvested earlier than in other parts of the region. In the upper reaches of the appellation, the soils are granite and as they descend towards the valley floor the ground turns into clay silica. The surface soil is littered with stones and as a whole the soils are meagre and light. Fact: the local co-operative winery produces roughly half of total output.

WINE STYLES: Chenas has a deep hue and floral fragrances, predominantly peony, rose and violet. As it ages, it sometimes develops spicy, woody notes. The wines have bouquet, they are soft, fleshy, voluptuous and warm. They have elegant, long-lasting tannins which mellow with age. They exude a more marked bouquet than Juliénas and tend to be more similar in style to Moulin-à-Vent. Their average cellar life is 5 to 8 years. La-Chapelle-de-Guinchay tends to produce softer wines. An expression often used to describe them is of 'bunches of flowers resting on a basket of velvet'. They deserve to be paired with roasted red meats, meat served with a sauce, quail, pigeons with peas, cheeses, veal cutlets with chestnuts…

A.C. CHIROUBLES

OVERVIEW: 50 kilometres north of Lyon, the Chiroubles appellation is situated west of Fleurie and north of Morgon. Planted on terraces creating a bowl formation, this growth boasts the highest elevation in Beaujolais (between 250 to 400 m). The hillsides planted to vines act as a natural barrier. Consequently, the temperature range is greater than in the other growths. The soils are meagre, permeable and homogeneous, comprising shallow granite sand.

WINE STYLES: Chiroubles are ethereal, brilliant, light, soft wines which have a pleasant bouquet, are lively and easy drinking. They are also elegant, delicate, well-balanced with very discrete tannins, which earns them a reputation as 'feminine' wines. They could be described as archetypal Beaujolais with their light vermilion hue, fragrances of violet, peony, lily-of-the-valley, iris, raspberry and woodland fruits. They are also some of the quickest-maturing wines in Beaujolais and should be drunk young. An expression often used to describe them is that they 'caress you inside'. Serve with rabbit terrine in aspic, grilled meats, cooked cold pork meats, grilled or chitterlings sausages, poultry, white meats, lamb shoulder, Charolais cheeses…

A.C. CÔTE DE BROUILLY

OVERVIEW: the wine growing area climbs the steep slopes of the Brouilly hills, around Saint-Lager, Quincié, Cercié and Odenas. Vines can be traced back here to the 4th and 5th centuries which means that this AC lays a claim to being Beaujolais' oldest appellation; it also claims to be protected by the Virgin. Located in its midst is the chapel of Nôtre-Dame-du-Raisin, which was inaugurated in 1857 and since then has hosted an annual pilgrimage. The soils in Côte de Brouilly have truly definable characteristics: crystalline and volcanic rocks known as Brouilly 'blue stone'. Shale and diorite also known as 'green horn'.

WINE STYLES: Côte-de-Brouilly display a deep ruby-red hue and fragrances of fresh grapes, red fruit (raspberry, blueberry), kirsch, iris and notes of vanilla. They are flavoursome, have well-balanced mellowness and vinosity. They are robust, ample, fleshy and have good structure. They are long on the palate and well-balanced with elegant tannins. Their ageing capacity is greater than for Brouilly and they can even be firm when young. Because of their structure, they can be paired with red meats, either roasted or served with a sauce, rib steak with marrow, poultry (goose, duck, Bresse chicken), grilled chitterlings sausage, rabbit stew, cheese tart…

A.C. FLEURIE

OVERVIEW: the Fleurie appellation covers just one village of the same name, which is adjacent to Chiroubles, Morgon and Moulin-à-Vent. The vineyard has a south-east and north-west aspect, and whilst some vines are located on steep inclines, others occupy more gentle slopes. The soils are meagre and are formed of crystal granite with a smattering of clay in the eastern portion of the appellation. Around the chapel of the Black Virgin, on the steepest summits of the appellation, they become skeletal whereas those below the village have a higher clay content. INAO has identified thirteen different climate types within the appellation area: Les Côtes, Le Bon Cru, La Roilette, Les Moriers, Les Roches, Les Garants, Poncié, Montgenas, La Chapelle des Bois, La Madone, Grille Midi, Champagne and La Joie du Palais. Fact: a large share of the wines are made by the local co-operative winery.

WINE STYLES: Fleurie displays a deep cherry-red hue and fragrances of peach, red fruit like blackcurrant, floral notes with iris, violet and rose. Occasionally they are slightly spicy. The wines are fleshy, elegant, velvety, fruit-driven and feminine. Wines grown in the upper reaches of the appellation are more delicate and aromatic whilst those drawn from the lower slopes have more structure. If Moulin-à-Vent is considered to be the 'king' of Beaujolais then, by the same measure, Fleurie is the 'queen' of the growths. The wines can be laid down. Serve with chitterlings sausage, duck with cherries, leg of lamb, white meats and poultry.

A.C. JULIÉNAS

OVERVIEW: this growth is situated in the far northern part of the region and embraces Juliénas, Juillé and Emeringes in the Rhône and Pruzilly in Saône-et-Loire. It is located between Chénas in the south and Saint-Amour in the northwest. Juliénas grows at the crux of two contrasting worlds: Chardonnay territory in the Mâcon region, and Gamay in Beaujolais. The vines have south-west and north-west exposure and are sheltered from the northerly and easterly winds.
They are planted on soils made up of shale and granite with pockets of clay. The western portion of the appellation is granite with some manganese, whilst in the east, the soils are deeper and have greater clay content.

WINE STYLES: Juliénas displays a deep hue and its fragrances are predominantly peony, violet, red fruit (red currant, wild strawberry, raspberry), cinnamon, blackcurrant and vine peach. Occasionally spicy notes can be detected. The wines are generous, well-structured, powerful, rich and virile and, apart from the odd exception, they should be drunk when aged between two to five years. However, wines grown in Juillé and Emeringes mature earlier, whilst those drawn from more clayey soils need longer to reveal their full potential. Enjoy with red meats, either roasted or served with a sauce, barbecues, poultry or coq au vin.

A.C. MORGON

OVERVIEW: this Beaujolais growth encircles Villié-Morgon, 25 km from Mâcon and from Villefranche-sur-Saône. Its boundaries are formed by Chiroubles and Fleurie in the north and Régnié in the south-west. The appellation area is crisscrossed with streams travelling west to east. It is the most extensive Beaujolais growth, along with Brouilly. The appellation has even lent its name to a verb: a young Beaujolais with similar characteristics to a Burgundy is said 'to morgon'. The soils are formed of altered, friable crystalline rocks, dubbed 'rotten earth'. The granite in this particular area is intermingled with clay and sand. The ground is manganoan and pyritic which is said to enhance a wine's ageing capacity.
WINE STYLES: Morgon has a distinctive garnet-red hue and fragrances of stone fruits (apricot, peach, cherry, plum), kirsch, pear drops, strawberry, red currant,

blackcurrant and raspberry. In hot years, aromas of very ripe fruit develop. The wines are hearty, full-bodied, fleshy and robust, particularly those from the Côte de Py, which tend to display the hallmark depth of a Morgon. These are some of the region's best laying-down wines and they need time to express their full potential. Some growers, however, have opted for early-drinking alternatives.

Since 1985, Morgon has been divided into six climatically distinct sites: Les Charmes (well-structured wines), Corcelettes, Côte du Py (extremely robust, laying down wines), Douby (softer on the palate), Les Grands Crus (round, pleasant, aromatic) and Les Micouds (middle of the road). Morgon pairs well with sirloin steak, meat served with a sauce (pheasant), game, coq au vin, mutton stew, duck with onions, or a leg of lamb.

A.C. MOULIN À VENT

OVERVIEW: this growth takes its name from an old 15th century windmill. It embraces Chénas (Rhône) and Romanèche-Thorins (Saône-et-Loire) and is adjacent to Juliénas, Fleurie and Chénas. Moulin à Vent boasts five site-specific vineyards: Grand Carquelin, Champ de la Cour, Les Thorins, La Roche and Rochegrès. The first four are located in the vicinity of the windmill, whilst the latter one is situated in the upper portion of the appellation, on the border with Fleurie. The vines are planted on rolling hills facing east. The soils are formed of friable pink granite (known locally as 'gore'), rich in manganese oxide, which is said to impart Moulin à Vent wines their hallmark characteristics.

Wine styles: they display a ruby-red hue and fragrances of red fruit (cherries) and floral notes, predominantly iris, violet and rose. As they age, they develop aromas of ripe red fruits, spices, truffle, musk, sometimes even game. Moulin à Vent wines are concentrated, full-bodied, powerful, robust and rich in tannins. They are considered to be the most suitable laying-down wines. They have garnered a reputation as being as graceful as Beaujolais and as prestigious as Burgundy. Enjoy with beef casserole, roasted red meats, game or cheeses.

A.C. RÉGNIÉ

OVERVIEW: Beaujolais' most westerly growth. It embraces Régnié-Durette and Latignié, 25 km north-west of Villefranche-sur-Saône, and was the last Beaulolais growth to be officially recognised. Prior to that, the local wines were ranked top amongst Beaujolais-Villages. The vineyard unfolds gently down towards the floor of the Ardières valley. To the north-west, mount Avenas acts a natural barrier for the vines. The soils, which are light and poor, are made up of pink granite, relatively rich in minerals and containing clay in parts.

WINE STYLES: Régnié wines are fruity, quaffing wines. They are well-balanced, pleasant and mature well, with delicate tannins. Their cherry-red hue, fragrances of red (raspberry, red currant, blackcurrant) and black fruits (blueberries, blackberries), occasionally ripe peach, floral (honeysuckle) and spicy notes, reward early drinking. Serve with grilled red meats, chitterlings sausage, ham in parsley aspic, knuckle of ham, hot dried sausage, potato tart or cheeses.

A.C. SAINT-AMOUR

OVERVIEW: Beaujolais' most northerly growth, located in Amour-Bellevue. The village is said to derive its name from Amor (subsequently Saint-Amateur), a Roman soldier who survived a massacre and then sought refuge in Gaul where he later became a missionary. The village was thus named after him.

The appellation area, which is situated on the border with Mâcon, is also home to white Beaujolais and Saint-Véran (from Chardonnay). Set against the backdrop of mount Bessay, the terroir here is formed of limestone though also granite with patches of shale and sandstone. The terrain is clay-silica scattered with stones and rocky debris.

WINE STYLES: the area produces two styles of wines: powerful, voluptuous wines with good structure, fat and harmony, for cellaring. These are relatively tannic with an intense hue ranging from crimson to garnet-red, exuding fragrances of apricot, peach, apple, crushed strawberries, raspberry and peony. Alternatively, it produces wines destined for early drinking, fleshy, soft, light and elegant which conjure up aromas of kirsch, spices and floral notes (mignonette). Each style suits different foods, ranging from red to white meat, cooked cold pork meats and cheeses.

A.C. COTEAUX DU LYONNAIS

OVERVIEW: covering an extensive 48 towns and villages, this appellation stretches westwards along the right banks of the Rhone. It occupies a strip of land 40 km long by 30 km wide and is sandwiched between Beaujolais in the north and the Côtes-du-Rhône in the south. The vines are planted on hillside and plateaux sites facing east or south-east. The lion's share of the wines are red, with a balance of whites making up the remaining 5%.

WINE STYLES: red Coteaux du Lyonnais boast a cherry-red hue and fragrances of raspberry and cherry. They are light, fruity wines for quaffing, best enjoyed when served with cooked cold pork meats (chitterlings sausages, paté, hot dried sausage), poultry, roasted or braised red meats, stew, roast poultry and cheeses. The whites have a yellow hue with hints of green and develop aromas of citrus fruit, grapefruit and exotic fruits. They are the perfect match for pike quenelles. The rosés are fresh, intense, fruity and elegant wines, which are great as thirst-quenchers.

• • •

2015
BEAUJOLAIS WINES

BEAUJOLAIS SUPÉRIEUR

LE PUITS DE BESSON   81/100

▼♪ Vintage 2013 : Deeply-coloured purple-blue. Pleasurable nose blending cherry and violet. The palate is lively and full with predominant red fruit. A Beaujolais that is still young and poised to open up. Firm finish. Uncork for cold cuts.
Price approx.: 4,50 EUR
http://www.lepuitsdubesson.com
Domaine Le Puits du Besson
+33 (0)4 74 68 66 64

BEAUJOLAIS VILLAGES

CHÂTEAU DE L'HESTRANGE   87/100

▼♪ Vintage 2013 : Light salmon-pink. Pleasurable nose driven by red fruit sweets backed by spice. Supple, robust and generous palate that nonetheless leaves a sensation of freshness. Peppery character on the finish. A nicely crafted, powerful rosé.
Price approx.: 6,00 EUR
http://www.lhestrange.com
Domaine Metge-Toppin
+33 (0)9 63 63 84 86

DOMAINE DES GRANDES BRUYÈRES   87/100

Org▼♪ Vintage 2013 : Limpid crimson with dark purple tints. Pleasurable nose intermixing red and black fruits. On the palate, an ethereal, crunchy, likeable wine with clearly-delineated fruit expression, assertiveness and honesty. Very convincing. A nicely crafted, natural wine.
Price approx.: 7,00 EUR
www.vins-teissedre.com
Les Vins Jean-Pierre Teissèdre
+33 (0)4 74 03 48 02

CHÂTEAU DE L'HESTRANGE   84/100

▼♪ Vintage 2013 : Attractive crimson with dark purple. Intense nose of red fruit sweets. Light, soft palate emphasising crunchy, simple and delicious fruit. Joyful Gamay expression, drinking best chilled with a group of family or friends.
Price approx.: 6,00 EUR

http://www.lhestrange.com
Domaine Metge-Toppin
+33 (0)9 63 63 84 86

DOMAINE DES GRANDES BRUYÈRES   81/100

▼♪ Vintage 2011 : Light gold. Intense nose driven by dried fruits and white flowers. Slightly austere, firm palate with power prevailing over the fruit. A well-structured Beaujolais pairing with fish in a cream sauce.
Price approx.: 8,00 EUR
www.vins-teissedre.com
Les Vins Jean-Pierre Teissèdre
+33 (0)4 74 03 48 02

BEAUJOLAIS

LE PUITS DE BESSON   84/100

▼♪ Vintage 2011 : Bright, pale yellow. Pleasant focused nose of pip fruit (apple, pear) with floral notes. Lively attack leading into a full palate with beautiful concentration. Fat is very perceptible as are the fruity nose aromatics. A nicely crafted white Beaujolais.
Price approx.: 5,50 EUR
http://www.lepuitsdubesson.com
Domaine Le Puits du Besson
+33 (0)4 74 68 66 64

DOMAINE DE CHAMP FLEURY   83/100

▼♪ Vintage 2013 : Brilliant pale salmon-pink. The nose is a tad blurred with red fruits and a tangy touch. Clean palate with red fruits supported by effective freshness, augmented by a spice note. An unpretentious wine for country-style foods.
Price approx.: 5,00 EUR
http://www.domaine-du-champ-fleury.com
Domaine de Champ Fleury
+33 (0)4 74 67 08 20

BROUILLY

DOMAINE COMTE DE MONSPEY   90/100

▼♪ Cuvée du Commandeur 2013 : Deep colour, crimson tints. Profound nose opening up to ripe red fruits with a mineral dimension and hint of spice. Beautiful presence on the palate. Full, well-structured and fat yet also remarkably fresh. A lovely wine that does real justice to its appellation.
Price approx.: 14,00 EUR
Domaine Comte de Monspey
+33 (0) 26 47 02 62

CHÂTEAU DE LA CHAIZE — 90/100

▼♪ Cuvée Vieilles Vignes 2011 : Deep red. Profound, open nose with ripe red fruit aromas augmented by animal and earthy notes. Lush palate that is mild yet fresh and displays ultra ripe fruit. Full, harmonious and pleasurable across the palate.
Price approx.: 15,00 EUR
http://www.chateaudelachaize.com
Château de la Chaize
+33 (0)4 74 03 41 05

DOMAINE COMTE DE MONSPEY — 88/100

▼♪ Vieilles Vignes 2013 : Attractive dark purple. Delightful, focused, expressive nose with a floral and fruit character augmented by a pleasant mineral dimension of earth. Supple, fleshy palate enhanced by savoury freshness. A Brouilly that is fresh, closely-integrated and persistent.
Price approx.: 9,00 EUR
Domaine Comte de Monspey
+33 (0) 26 47 02 62

DOMAINE BERTRAND — 88/100

▼♪ Vintage 2011 : Deep crimson, dark purple tints. Pleasant nose marrying floral notes of violet, fruit (cassis, raspberry, blackberry) and spice undertones. Supple, full and fruity palate with silky tannins. Excellent balance. Persistent spicy finish. A Brouilly for pleasure.
Price approx.: 8,00 EUR
http://www.domainebertrand.fr
Domaine Bertrand
+33 (0)4 74 66 85 96

CHÂTEAU DE LA CHAIZE — 88/100

▼♪ Vintage 2012 : Attractive colour tinged with dark purple. Focused, precise nose revolving around red fruits with subtle mineral and peppery touches. Delightful, easy-drinking palate. A sensation of freshness underscores the fruit. A soft, crunchy Brouilly.
Price approx.: 10,50 EUR
http://www.chateaudelachaize.com
Château de la Chaize
+33 (0)4 74 03 41 05

HENRY FESSY — 87/100

▼♪ Les Brûlées 2012 : Ruby-red. Nose of jammy red fruits with subtle spice in the background. On the palate, beautiful quality fresh fruit. A delightful, crunchy style showing fruit overtones. Fresh and crisp. A very enjoyable Brouilly.
Price approx.: 13,80 EUR
www.henryfessy.com
Vins Henry Fessy

HENRY FESSY — 86/100

▼♪ Plateau de Bel Air 2012 : Young-looking garnet. Delightful nose recalling redcurrant, raspberry and strawberry sweets. Crunchy, easy-drinking palate showing charmingly fresh fruit. All the pleasure of simplicity that works well with grilled poultry.
Price approx.: 10,30 EUR
www.henryfessy.com
Vins Henry Fessy

DOMAINE DE TANTE ALICE — 86/100

▼♪ Pisse-Vieille 2012 : Deep crimson tinged with ruby. Subdued nose driven by violet, red fruits and mineral undertones. Focused, full, rich and delightful palate revealing spice. Vibrant and robust. Long-lasting spicy finish. A Brouilly that will appeal to lovers of the style.
Price approx.: 7,00 EUR
www.tante-alice.com
Domaine de Tante Alice
+33 (0)4 74 66 89 33

CHIROUBLES

STEEVE CHARVET — 89/100

▼♪ Vieilles Vignes 2011 : Robe grenat assez soutenu. Nez racé évoquant la griotte, les épices douces, fond boisé élégant. Attaque suave, bouche ample, fondue, nerveuse, finement épicée, élevage bien présent mais harmonieusement intégré. Cru ambitieux bien réussi.
Price approx.: 10,00 EUR
http://www.chauvet-gites-vins.fr
Steeve Charvet
+33 (0)4 74 69 13 08

CÔTE DE BROUILLY

CHÂTEAU DES RAVATYS — 89/100

▼♪ Mathilde Courbe 2011 : Deep ruby with crimson highlights. Pleasant nose intermixing floral, fruity and toast notes. Generous, full-on expression on the palate. A delightful fresh, full wine revealing a spice streak on the finish. Gets our vote of approval.
Price approx.: 9,40 EUR
http://www.chateaudesravatys.com
Château des Ravatys
+33 (0)4 74 66 80 35

HENRY FESSY · 85/100

▼♪ Vintage 2012 : Young garnet. Focused nose of red berry fruits and woodland aromatics. A soft, supple wine boasting savoury exuberance. The fruit is crunchy and persistent. Distinctive. An inspiration for a Sunday lunch of roast chicken.
Price approx.: 9,20 EUR
www.henryfessy.com
Vins Henry Fessy

LE PUITS DE BESSON · 83/100

▼♪ Vintage 2011 : Slightly evolved dark purple. Endearing nose driven by red fruits with a vegetal touch in the background. Supple, full attack. The palate shows seductive ripe red fruits. Firmer, spicy finish. A Côte de Brouilly drinking well from now on.
Price approx.: 7,20 EUR
http://www.lepuitsdubesson.com
Domaine Le Puits du Besson
+33 (0)4 74 68 66 64

FLEURIE

ANNE SOPHIE DUBOIS · 89/100

▼♪ Clepsydre 2011 : Fairly deep ruby. Expressive nose intermixing smoky, floral and fruity touches. On the palate, a light, invigorating wine with focused, exuberant aromas. Subtle proportions and lots of craftmanship. A delicious, old-fashioned wine. Extremely delightful.
Price approx.: 15,00 EUR
http://anne-sophiedubois.blogspot.fr
Anne-Sophie Dubois
+33 (0)4 74 69 84 45

DOMAINE GAGET · 88/100

▼♪ La Madone 2012 : Slightly evolved cherry-red. Endearing nose driven by red fruits with earthy undertones. Elegant, fleshy and closely-integrated palate revealing more of the nose aromatics. Beautifully balanced. The finish is slightly firmer. A seductive Fleurie.
Price approx.: 9,00 EUR
Domaine Gaget
+33 (0)4 74 04 20 75

DOMAINE PARDON · 88/100

▼♪ Vintage 2012 : Deep, young colour. Endearing nose exuding jammy aromatics of strawberry, raspberry and cherry. A delightful Fleurie showing seductively fresh perfume. Very supple with beautiful substance. Deliciously drinkable from now on.
Price approx.: 8,00 EUR
http://www.vinspardon.fr
Domaine Pardon
+33 (0)4 74 04 86 97

DOMAINE BERTRAND · 88/100

▼♪ Les Déduits 2011 : Dark purple with crimson tints. Pleasant nose opening up after swirling to red fruits and undergrowth. Full, velvety palate showing good concentration and nicely showcased red fruit. Beautiful structure. Persistent pepper-infused finish. Very successful.
Price approx.: 8,50 EUR
http://www.domainebertrand.fr
Domaine Bertrand
+33 (0)4 74 66 85 96

CHÂTEAU DE RAOUSSET · 88/100

▼♪ Grille Midi 2011 : Appealing deep crimson. Crisp nose intermixing red fruits, flowers and spice with a touch of toast at the end. Powerful, hot, full and fruity palate showing balance and mellow tannins. Spice-infused mid-palate. An elegant Fleuri appealing to lovers of the style.
Price approx.: 8,50 EUR
http://www.chateauderaousset.com
Château de Raousset
+33 (0)4 74 69 17 28

ANNE SOPHIE DUBOIS · 87/100

▼♪ L'Alchimiste 2011 : Limpid ruby. Appealing nose of redcurrant, red fruits, morello cherry and a touch of oak. Easy-drinking, ethereal and fresh palate with clearly-delineated aromas and a welcome, overall impression of natural character. A real pleasure and perfect as a quaffer.
Price approx.: 12,00 EUR
http://anne-sophiedubois.blogspot.fr
Anne-Sophie Dubois
+33 (0)4 74 69 84 45

CHÂTEAU DES LABOURONS · 86/100

▼♪ Vintage 2012 : Young colour. Nose of ripe raspberry and wild strawberry. Very supple palate with easy-drinking fruit. Lovely freshness and lightness enhancing the fruit. A distinctive Fleurie, ready to drink now and perfect with leg of lamb.
Price approx.: 12,00 EUR
www.henryfessy.com
Vins Henry Fessy

COMTE DE MONSPEY · 86/100

▼♪ Le Debuché 2013 : Ruby with dark purple. Focused nose showing pronounced floral accents

backed by red berry fruits. Fine-grained mouthfeel supported by a lively, tense structure. A vibrant Fleurie showing instant accessibility.
Price approx.: 9,50 EUR
Domaine Comte de Monspey
+33 (0) 26 47 02 62

MORGON

JOËL LACOQUE 95/100

▼♪ Côte du Py Cuvée Marie Jeanne 2011 : Beautiful deep ruby. Magnificent nose offering wonderful mineral, smoke and floral expression layered over ripe red fruits. Silky attack, full-bodied, generous, tense and iron-like palate. Refined, precise, natural. Delicious. A superlative Côte du Py.
Price approx.: 11,50 EUR
Joël Lacoque
+33 (0)4 74 69 16 52

DOMAINE DES SOUCHONS 91/100

▼♪ Cuvée Claude Pillet 2011 : Deep garnet with evolved highlights. Mature nose of mild spices, smoke, mocha, subtle oak and red fruits. Silky, full and delicious palate showing wonderful salinity and judicious use of oak. Persistent, spicy finish. A sterling quality Morgon.
Price approx.: 16,00 EUR
http://www.1752.fr
Les vins 1752
+33 (0)4 74 69 14 45

CHÂTEAU DE PIZAY 89/100

▼♪ Grand Cras 2013 : Attractive purple-blue with crimson tints. Honest nose suggestive of ripe red and black berry fruits. Very supple attack leading into a delightful velvety, silky palate. Focused, precise fruit. Balance, finesse and elegance. A promising wine.
Price approx.: 8,95 EUR
http://www.vins-chateaupizay.com
Vins de Pizay
+33 (0)4 74 66 26 10

DOMAINE GAGET 89/100

▼♪ Côte du Py 2012 : Lightly-coloured cherry-red. Pleasant nose intermixing red fruits, spices and mineral notes with animal undertones. Supple attack, concentrated, fleshy, full palate showing fruit and spice. Well-balanced substance. Fresh, spice-driven finish. Very compelling.
Price approx.: 7,80 EUR

Domaine Gaget
+33 (0)4 74 04 20 75

JOËL LACOQUE 89/100

▼♪ Côte du Py 2012 : Fairly deep ruby with purple highlights. Subdued nose of red fruits with a mineral note. Seductive attack, full, round, ripe and tense palate with vigour and clear expression. The mid-palate shows more of a spice streak with some tannins on the finish.
Price approx.: 6,80 EUR
Joël Lacoque
+33 (0)4 74 69 16 52

DOMAINE DUFOUR 88/100

▼♪ Les Champs Brûlés 2012 : Limpid ruby. Pleasant nose suggestive of red fruits with a hint of spice. On the palate, a round, full and expressive wine supported by effective freshness. Consistent palate with a touch of firmness allowing for a measure of ageability.
Price approx.: 6,70 EUR
Dufour Père et Fils
+33 (0)4 74 04 35 46

ARMAND CHARVET 86/100

▼♪ Côte du Py 2011 : Limpid garnet with crimson tints. Attractive nose showing spice, flowers and red fruit with subtle oak in the background. Delightful, ethereal palate with a faint crispness and clearly-delineated aromas. Hint of firmness on the finish. An enjoyable wine.
Price approx.: 8,30 EUR
http://www.charvet-gites-vins.fr
Domaine Armand Charvet
+33 (0)4 74 69 13 08

ALAIN FOREST 83/100

▼♪ Vintage 2011 : Fairly light colour with evolved highlights. Mature nose of jammy fruits revealing vegetal and mineral notes after swirling. The attack is supple without lacking fullness, leading into a more rectilinear, firmer mid-palate. Serve with poultry in a sauce.
Price approx.: 7,00 EUR
Alain Forest
+33 (0)4 74 69 25 69

Prices mentioned in this book are guideline and can vary depending on point of sale. The shops, wineries or publisher can in no way be held responsible for this.

MOULIN À VENT

DOMAINE DUFOUR   91/100

▼♪ Vintage 2012 : Young, limpid ruby. Subdued, racy and smoke-infused nose with red fruits and a mineral tone. Aromatic attack, good presence on the palate, rich, virile and spicy revealing beautiful, closely-integrated tannins. Keep before serving with red meats.

Price approx.: 9,60 EUR

Dufour Père et Fils

+33 (0)4 74 04 35 46

DOMAINE FOND MOIROUX   89/100

CONV▼♪ Vintage 2011 : Intense red with young highlights. Elegant vanilla oak on the nose dominating the fruit. Seductive, silky, ethereal and lively palate where precise, intense fruit aromas are a good match for the ageing notes. Hint of firmness. Elegant and expressive.

Price approx.: 15,00 EUR

http://www.fondmoiroux.com

Domaine de la Fond Moiroux

+33 (0)4 74 67 47 48

DOMAINE BERTRAND   88/100

▼♪ Vintage 2011 : Deep purple-blue. Delightful nose driven by red fruits and violet with earthy undertones. Elegant, light and supple palate with fruit supported by freshness. A delicate Moulin à Vent pairing well with a platter of fine cheeses.

Price approx.: 9,50 EUR

http://www.domainebertrand.fr

Domaine Bertrand

+33 (0)4 74 66 85 96

DOMAINE MORTET   88/100

▼♪ Vintage 2012 : Young, limpid ruby. Subdued yet promising nose of red fruits, violet and iris. The fruit really comes into its own on the palate which is round, concentrated and generous, suffused with spice and supported by silky tannins. Expertly crafted.

Price approx.: 8,00 EUR

www.domaine-mortet.fr

Domaine Mortet

+33 (0)3 85 35 55 51

COMTE DE MONSPEY   87/100

▼♪ Les Honneurs 2013 : Dark purple. Endearing nose with upfront red fruit, plum flesh and a floral dimension. Full attack leading into a livelier, more structured mid-palate. The fruit is augmented by a lingering peppery note. Serve with red meats.

Price approx.: 9,00 EUR

Domaine Comte de Monspey

+33 (0) 26 47 02 62

DOMAINE MORTET   87/100

▼♪ Les Rouchaux 2011 : Fairly deep ruby. Appealing nose of jammy red fruits. The palate is sappy and boasts lovely youthful acidity and generous, focused fruit. A distinctive Moulin à Vent that would sit well alongside grilled poultry. A successful wine.

Price approx.: 9,00 EUR

www.domaine-mortet.fr

Domaine Mortet

+33 (0)3 85 35 55 51

DOMAINE FOND MOIROUX   87/100

▼♪ Vintage 2010 : Ruby-hued. The nose is still young and dominated by oak (vanilla) backed by red berry fruits. Youthful palate marked by savoury acidity, balance of oak and fruit and aromatic persistency. A racy Moulin à Vent that needs decanting.

Price approx.: 15,00 EUR

http://www.fondmoiroux.com

Domaine de la Fond Moiroux

+33 (0)4 74 67 47 48

RÉGNIÉ

CLOS DE PONCHON   89/100

▼♪ Cuvée Tradition - élevé en fût de chêne 2011 : Limpid ruby. Delightful nose showing a cornucopia of red and black berry fruits with oak presence in the background. Silky attack, rich, mellow and delicious palate. Hint of firmness on the finish. Traditional yet compelling in style. Keep for a while.

Price approx.: 7,80 EUR

Dufour Père et Fils

+33 (0)4 74 04 35 46

BORDEAUX

A LAND OF SUPERLATIVE QUALITY AND DIVERSITY

No other wine region in the world sparks as much passion as Bordeaux. Ask around and you won't find a single wine lover who does not have well-formed opinions about Bordeaux wines, how they taste, their varieties, their unrivalled terroirs and even their prices.

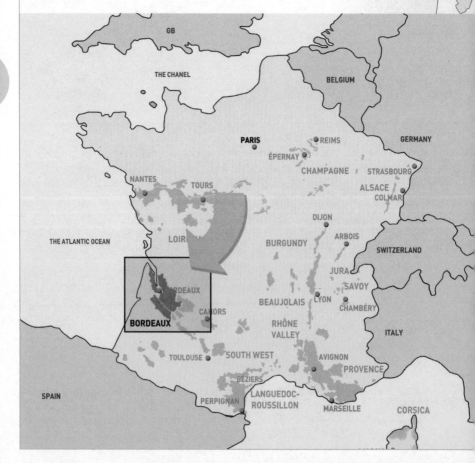

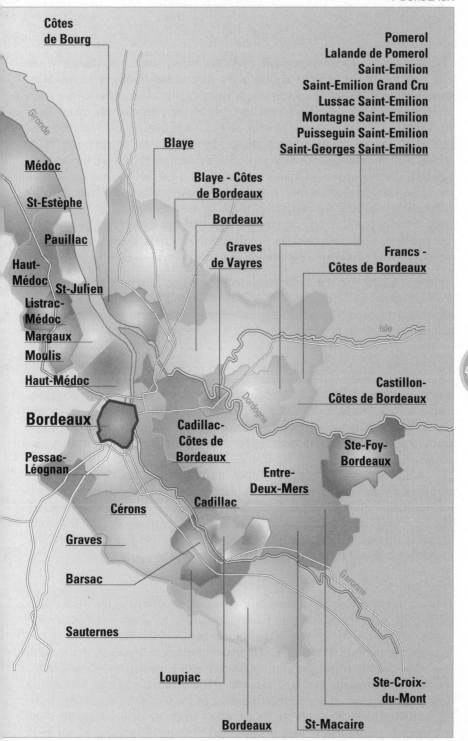

Côtes
de Bourg

Pomerol
Lalande de Pomerol
Saint-Emilion
Saint-Emilion Grand Cru
Lussac Saint-Emilion
Montagne Saint-Emilion
Puisseguin Saint-Emilion
Saint-Georges Saint-Emilion

Blaye

Médoc

Blaye - Côtes
de Bordeaux

St-Estèphe

Bordeaux

Pauillac

Graves
de Vayres

Haut-
Médoc St-Julien

Francs -
Côtes de Bordeaux

Listrac-
Médoc

Margaux

Moulis

Haut-Médoc

Castillon-
Côtes de Bordeaux

Bordeaux

Cadillac-
Côtes de
Bordeaux

Ste-Foy-
Bordeaux

Pessac-
Léognan

Entre-
Deux-Mers

Cérons Cadillac

Graves

Barsac

Sauternes

Loupiac

Ste-Croix-
du-Mont

Bordeaux St-Macaire

Gironde

Isle

Dordogne

Garonne

45

With its 120,000 hectares (300,000 acres) under AC-classed vines, the Bordeaux wine region is the revered behemoth of French wine growing, though its boundaries fit snugly within a single department. Four components factor into the quality of this unparalleled wine region. Firstly, a favoured vineyard site along the Gironde plateau, on gently undulating land. A climate particularly conducive to wine growing, marked by maritime influences rising off the Atlantic which combine with a matrix of distinct local traits (incline, topography, aspect) to form a myriad of microclimates. Once these then partner up with all the various soil types, they form the third component which will determine the 'terroirs' most suitable for producing quality wines. Last comes a range of noble grape varieties painstakingly selected through trial and error by the people who care (grape growers, wine makers…), whose labour can in many ways be considered the fifth component of Bordeaux's success.

So here you have the tremendous alchemy of the Bordeaux wine region. And as these components do not work in unison, the result is a cornucopia of styles, sufficiently numerous to form territorial entities with their own distinct personalities.

LE MÉDOC

Situated between the Gironde estuary and the Atlantic Ocean, the Médoc peninsula, meaning 'middle land' in local patois, is Bordeaux's prodigy with prestigious names such as Margaux or Pauillac… Here, a combination of sandy, stony and clay soils - the famous 'graves' or gravel - deposited by the Garonne over thousands of years, retain heat during the day before gradually releasing it. They also regulate drainage.

The Médoc is primarily home to Cabernet-Sauvignon, a late-ripening varietal renowned for its tannins and powerful blackcurrant aromas, dominating its fellow varietals, Merlot, Cabernet Franc and Petit-Verdot (not extensively planted). The area covers eight appellations: six 'communal' appellations, Listrac, Moulis, Margaux, Pauillac, Saint-Estèphe and Saint-Julien, and two 'sub-regions', Médoc to the far north and Haut-Médoc at the southern end.

LES GRAVES

This area is situated south of Bordeaux, extending south-east of the Médoc with similar soil types, in addition to which are sand, clay, shelly sand (limestone with shells), and sometimes even quartz and quartzite. The land is home to two red wine appellations, Pessac-Léognan on the outskirts of Bordeaux, to the north (an AC since 1987 embracing all the Graves classed growths), and Graves, in the south. Wines from the northern part are well-structured, powerful reds with a deep hue and good cellaring capacity, whilst in the south the wines tend to be lighter and more delicate on the palate. All of them are drawn from the same red varietals grown in the Médoc. However, both the northern and southern parts also have the capacity to produce powerful, mouth-filling whites, with a delicate bouquet and extensive ageing potential. They are drawn from Semillon, a productive, hardy varietal well-suited to oak ageing, and Sauvignon, a lively, aromatic varietal.

THE REALMS OF THE SWEET WINES

South of the Graves, this area straddling the Garonne river is home to the sweet wines: Loupiac and Sainte-Croix-du-Mont along the right bank, Sauternes, Barsac and Cérons along the left bank…. These prestigious appellations are fortunate to have a climate conducive to producing a microscopic fungus - botrytis cinerea - which develops by sucking water out from inside the grapes, hence concentrating sugars in the wines. Vintages where the wines fully express all the rich, subtle aromas imparted by the fungus are occasionally referred to as 'botrytised' years. These outstanding wines can only be drawn from three varietals - Semillon (70%), Sauvignon (25%) and Muscadelle (5%) - in that order, though the latter varietal, whilst highly aromatic on gravely and calcareous clay soils, is not widely planted because it does not always ripen easily.

THE LIBOURNE AREA

Fanning out from the northern banks of the Dordogne, with the town of Libourne as its focal point, this area is primarily a red wine region where Bordeaux's most ubiquitous grape variety (Merlot with 53.5%) is by far the most predominant. Here it produces a clutch of world-famous wines like Canon-Fronsac, Fronsac, Pomerol, Lalande de Pomerol and the highly celebrated Saint-Emilion Grand Cru… Though slightly less renowned, Montagne-Saint-Emilion, Lussac and Puisseguin offer enticing alternatives. These particular vineyard sites provide this varietal with extremely varied soil types based on a backbone of clay (calcareous clay, clay-gravel, clay-sand…) where it forms a perfect partnership with Cabernet Franc (or Bouchet), yielding generous, racy, powerful wines with subtle aromas.

CÔTES-DE-BORDEAUX WINES

Although this region is geographically extensive, the wines it produces are not as heterogeneous as one might imagine. They share a similar landscape, consisting of hilly slopes of clay-limestone soils along the banks of the Dordogne and the Garonne, as well as a south to southeast orientation -another feature they have in common is they are excellent value for money.

Côtes-de-Bordeaux is made up of seven appellations. In the north, on the right bank of the Gironde, across from Médoc, lie the vineyards of Blaye, Côtes-de-Bourg and Blaye Côtes-de-Bordeaux, which produce red wines that are rustic yet agreeable. Further south are two appellations around the town of Libourne: Francs Côtes-de-Bordeaux and Castillon Côtes-de-Bordeaux to the east, entirely dev oted to reds, and Graves-de-Vayres to the west, which produces interesting reds and whites. South of this lies Cadillac Côtes-de-Bordeaux, which stretches along the Garonne River from Bordeaux to Langon. Benefiting from very good conditions, today these vineyards produce quality wines that are highly appreciated by demanding consumers. The unique Carménère grape is still grown here, a variety that produces excellent wines with a rich taste and deep colour, with a structure that is rather similar to Cabernet Franc.

ENTRE-DEUX-MERS

Set between the Garonne and the Dordogne, this is Bordeaux's most extensive wine growing region, stretching almost 30 kilometres wide and a good 60 km long. Home of the dry whites (primarily Entre-Deux-Mers), this area is now governed by strict regulations. To be entitled to appellation status, the wines must be drawn from 70% Semillon, Sauvignon and Musca-delle and no more than 30% Merlot Blanc or 10% Ugni blanc, Mauzac and Colombard.

WINE STYLES

The red wines are evidently blends (chiefly Cabernets and Merlot). They are well-structured and tannic, with intense aromas of blackcurrant and are often able to withstand the test of time. The most prestigious appellations are all of the above and much more, displaying incomparable finesse and exceptional complexity.
The dry whites, which more often than not are also blends (Semillon-Sauvignon), cover a range of styles. White Bordeaux and Entre-Deux-Mers are lively, floral, fruity wines, in their prime when young. Graves and Pessac-Léognan have a longer life span due to a more ample structure, often enhanced by oak-ageing. Lastly come the sweet whites, legally required to come from the Semillon, Sauvignon and Muscadelle trio, which no longer need an introduction: Sauternes, Barsac, Cérons, Loupiac and Sainte-Croix-du-Mont acquired star status aeons ago. In good years, their structure keeps them fresh and young after decades in the bottle.

REVIEW OF RECENT VINTAGES

• **2006** • Both a classic and uneven vintage, lacking the concentration of the 2005s yet still promising in terms of balance and elegance.
• **2007** • Although the summer was mediocre, the autumn was magnificent. The red wines are soft, moderately concentrated and have a bouquet of ripe fruit. They can be drunk when young. The dry white wines are excellent, and the dessert wines amazing.
• **2008** • With a relatively cool August and a sunny end of September, 2008 was a rather mixed year, producing red wines that are fruity, lively and elegant, not without a certain power. The whites are very fresh, and the dessert wines moderately rich.
• **2009** • An exceptional, monumental vintage, particularly for the red wines. Bordeaux reds have never before reached such concentration. They are powerful, complete and deep. The Grands Crus will age well, while the humbler wines can be enjoyed already. The dry whites and dessert wines are full-bodied, sometimes perhaps a bit overly so, but there are also some excellent examples that are balanced with freshness.

• **2010** • Record concentrations due to the drought that prevailed throughout the summer. The 2010 vintage broke all previous records for phenolic concentration and alcoholic strength. However, unlike 2009, August stayed relatively cool thus ensuring slightly higher acidity levels, particularly in the Cabernets. Vintage 2010 saw successful wines when power and concentration took a back seat to freshness and the purity of the fruit.

• **2011** • After a warm, dry spring, July and August were unsettled leading to an inconsistent vintage. Some successful dry and sweet whites. The reds are a more mixed bunch with two main taste profiles: enjoyable, fruity and fairly full-bodied wines and another group showing more pronounced tannins and a measure of dryness on the finish.

• **2012** • In contrast to 2011, the spring was disrupted by precipitation and slow flowering, with the weather improving only in mid-July. The dry white wines are well made, while the dessert wines are decent without being excellent, and the reds are variable (particularly in Médoc). However, the wines are generally pleasant, with mature tannins and well-defined fruit.

• **2013** • Even before the grapes entered the wineries, the vintage received bad press, but in actual fact, the outcome is not bad at all. The wines are fruit-driven and harmonious with some wonderfully successful offerings, particularly in Pomerol and the Médoc. The dry whites are decent and the noble-rot wines atypical, with a lot less concentration than usual.

49

LES APPELLATIONS BORDELAISES

A.C. BARSAC

OVERVIEW: AC Barsac is grown in and around the town of Barsac on the left bank of the Garonne. All wines produced within AC Barsac can be labelled as Sauternes, however this only works one way.

WINE STYLES: Traditionally, Barsacs are considered to be moderately lighter than Sauternes, perhaps because the soil has greater sand and clay content and the terrain is marginally flatter. As a rule of thumb, Barsacs display a characteristically beautiful golden colour, running the gamut from pale gold for the youngest to deep amber for the most mature. They exude a full, deep nose. On the palate, they develop flavours of acacia honey, the flesh of white peach, almond, toast and above all botrytised grapes which, over time, mellow and become more complex and harmonious. Enjoy with baked sole fillets in a creamy hollandaise sauce, smoked salmon, or chocolate cake.

BLAYE AOC

OVERVIEW: The vineyards of Blaye are located on the right bank of the Gironde, around 50 kilometres northwest of Bordeaux. The vineyards stretch over a large area of 6,000 hectares (of which 90% are planted with red varieties) and are cultivated by 700 winegrowers. The Blaye AOC produces still red wines.

WINE STYLES: These red wines are quite smooth, with a bouquet of spices, prune and ripe fruit that can develop over time to give musky hints. They develop an attractive brick-red colour during ageing.

BLAYE CÔTES-DE-BORDEAUX AOC

OVERVIEW: This winegrowing area shares the same territory as Blaye AOC, separated from the Médoc by the Gironde estuary. The Blaye Côtes-de-Bordeaux reds are mainly produced from Merlot and have a deep colour and fruity notes. They are pleasant, easy-drinking wines that go well with meat and cheese. The Blaye Côtes-de- Bordeaux whites are principally made from Sauvignon, giving them their pale yellow colour, nose of citrus and broom, as well as a nice bite and long finish, making them intensely subtle wines. These whites are ideal for an apéritif or with seafood.

WINE STYLES: Blaye Côtes-de-Bordeaux AOC wines are typically more delicate that those of Blaye AOC, as the grapes can be markedly different. The dominant aromas are white flowers, yellow fruits and broom. They can be served with seafood.

AC BORDEAUX

OVERVIEW: AC Bordeaux covers the entire Gironde department, with the exception of wetlands, valley floors and the sandy soils of the Landes woodlands. It applies only to red wines (dry whites are governed by a specific dry Bordeaux appellation). Legally, they can only be made from Cabernet-Sauvignon, Cabernet Franc, Merlot, Malbec, Petit Verdot and Carmenere. Four different soil types form the Bordeaux appellation area: marshlands (recent alluvial soils edging the Garonne and the Dordogne), gravely soils made up of gravel and quartz, calcareous clay earth, extremely widespread on hillside sites, and 'boulbenes' (loamy soils characteristic of the Entre-Deux-Mers plateaux). The wines are made traditionally in temperature-controlled stainless steel or lined concrete tanks. They can be aged in oak but this is optional.

WINE STYLES: As a rule of thumb, red AC Bordeaux wines boast a fine cherry-red colour, they are well-balanced, harmonious and fruity, not overly robust and reward early drinking.

AC BORDEAUX SEC

OVERVIEW: Grown in the same area as red Bordeaux, dry Bordeaux are made from Semillon, Sauvignon and Muscadelle.

WINE STYLES: They offer floral, fruity fragrances, are relatively fat and rarely woody. At their best when served young, with seafood, fish and poultry.

AC BORDEAUX SUPÉRIEUR

OVERVIEW: The AC Bordeaux Supérieur fits within the Bordeaux appellation area and can be used for reds and whites, both dry and sweet. There are two major differences between the two: Bordeaux Supérieur has lower yields and a higher minimum alcohol content than Bordeaux. However the varietal range for the reds is identical: Cabernet-Sauvignon, Cabernet Franc, Merlot, Malbec, Petit Verdot, Carmenere; and for the whites: Semillon, Sauvignon and Muscadelle.

WINE STYLES: They are more robust and fuller wines than 'basic' Bordeaux. Bordeaux Supérieur wines have red fruit (raspberry) and black fruit (blackcurrant) aromas, with a dash of vanilla for the oak-aged wines. They pair well with sirloin steak cooked over a fire of vine twigs, pan-fried Bayonne ham and roast beef with shallot chutney.

The sweet white wines are rich in alcohol and sugar with scents of honey, acacia, plum and tobacco. They make perfect appetisers or accompaniments to white meat and foie gras.

AC BORDEAUX HAUT-BENAUGE

OVERVIEW: The Haut-Benauge region is set like a lone island amidst the sea of Entre-Deux-Mers vines. Its soils are calcareous clay and clay-silica. The Bordeaux-Haut-Benauge appellation applies only to sweet white wines which account for one third of the area's output: Semillon, Sauvignon and Muscadelle.

WINE STYLES: The dry white wines display a pale yellow hue with hints of green. They are soft, supple, fruity, easy-drinking wines. Predominant aromas are flinty and floral notes.

51

AC BORDEAUX ROSÉ

OVERVIEW: Bordeaux's rosé wines are labelled under the regional appellations Bordeaux Rosé and Bordeaux Clairet. They can produced anywhere in the Gironde department, providing the land is suitable for wine growing. They are drawn from the same varietals as red wines. Bordeaux rosés are briefly macerated (for 10-18 hours) to impart some colour and are then run off and bottled shortly after.

WINE STYLES: Fresh, fruity wines rewarding early drinking, the rosés are lighter than the Clairets. Fragrances of blackcurrant, redcurrant, raspberry and strawberry intermingle with caramel, orange peel and grapefruit... Try as an appetiser or with fish or cooked cold pork meats.

AC BORDEAUX CLAIRET

OVERVIEW: Bordeaux Clairets, blended from Cabernet-Sauvignon, Cabernet Franc, Merlot, Malbec, Petit Verdot and Carmenere, are vinted in the same way as the rosés. However, because they macerate for longer (24 to 36 hours), their colour is deeper and tannin content higher. Some of them spend a short period in oak.

WINE STYLES: The Clairets display fruit (peach, raspberry, redcurrant, straw-berry, lychee) and floral aromas (seringa, rose, orange blossom) with a hint of primary bud aromas. They are more appropriate for a meal time, served with cooked cold pork meats, kebabs, grilled fish...

AC CADILLAC CÔTES-DE-BORDEAUX

OVERVIEW: Cadillac AOC, located to the north of Loupiac on the right bank of the Garonne, produces white dessert wines. Until 1973, Cadillac was part of the Premières Côtes-de-Bordeaux appellation. Today, 22 districts have the right to claim this AOC, but many winegrowers continue to use Premières Côtes-de-Bordeaux AOC. The wines are produced from Sémillon, Sauvignon and Muscadelle.

WINE STYLES: These wines are elegant, aromatic, fruity and full. They are good apéritif wines, but also go well with foie gras and sweet-and-sour dishes such as caramelised pork.

AC CANON-FRONSAC

OVERVIEW: In the Libourne area only two villages are entitled to carry the Canon-Fronsac appellation - Fronsac and Saint-Michel-de-Fronsac - and even then, the grapes can only come from specific vineyard sites. The vines (Cabernet-Sauvignon, Cabernet Franc, Merlot and Malbec) are planted on hillside sites where the soils are calcareous clay or clay-sand on a limestone bedrock.

WINE STYLES: Canon-Fronsac wines (exclusively reds) are on the whole deeply-coloured, fat, fleshy wines whilst at the same time revealing suppleness and elegance with a delicate, slightly spicy flavour and a distinctive bouquet. With good cellaring potential, they develop aromas of red fruits, pepper, spices and truffle. They pair well with marinated or roast meats, preserved duck or goose, poultry and pears cooked in wine.

AC CASTILLON CÔTES-DE-BORDEAUX

OVERVIEW: Some 40 kilometres east of Bordeaux, on the northeast border of the Gironde region, Castillon is known for the battle in 1453 that brought an end to the Hundred Years' War. There are nine districts that have the right to claim the appellation. The area benefits from a favourable climate for growing grapes. The soils are rich in iron and limestone and lie on clay-limestone or limestone slopes. The grape varieties used are Merlot, Cabernet Sauvignon, Cabernet Franc and Malbec.

WINE STYLES: The wines resemble those around Saint-Émilion, although they are less tannic and need to age for several years in order to soften. They have an intense colour and are structured, powerful, balanced and fleshy. They develop aromas of prune, spices and animal notes. They pair well with red meat, either barbecued or prepared with a sauce, game and strong cheeses.

AC CÉRONS

OVERVIEW: this appellation covers around 120 hectares in Cérons, Illats and Podensac on the left bank of the Garonne, thirty or so kilometres south-east of Bordeaux. Set within the Graves appellation area, it only produces sweet wines from Semillon, Sauvignon and Muscadelle grapes harvested when overripe and picked in batches as they ripen.

WINE STYLES: Cérons is an elegant sweet wine, perhaps slightly lighter and vigorous than Sauternes. It is a good match for foie gras, white meat served in a sauce or blue cheeses (Roquefort).

AC CÔTES DE BLAYE

OVERVIEW: This area fits within the AC Blaye region, looking out over the Gironde to the Médoc. It only produces white wines and these must legally be blended from at least two varietals, usually Colombard, with a balance of Semillon, Sauvignon or Muscadelle.

WINE STYLES: As a rule, wines entitled to use the Côtes de Blaye appellation tend to be more refined than those labelled AC Blaye, mainly because the varietal range can be noticeably different. Predominant aromas are white blossom, yellow fruit and broom. Food pairings include fish or seafood.

AC CÔTES DE BORDEAUX SAINT-MACAIRE

OVERVIEW: This appellation lies to the extreme southeast of Cadillac Côtes-de-Bordeaux AOC over some ten districts (including Saint-Macaire) on the right bank of the Garonne. Only whites (dessert and dry wines) made from Sémillon, Sauvignon, Sauvignon Gris and Muscadelle can be labelled with this AOC. Both the dry and moelleux dessert wines are produced from grapes harvested at a late stage of ripening. The liquoreux dessert wines are produced from overripe grapes affected by noble rot.

WINE STYLES: These sweet wines, more or less botrytised depending on the year, are subtle, quite full-bodied yet soft, and best drunk when young. They have a bouquet with notes of honey, acacia and tobacco. They can be drunk as an apéritif and also pair well with white meat and foie gras.

AC CÔTES-DE-BOURG

OVERVIEW: This appellation sits on the right bank of the Dordogne, near the confluence with the Garonne, some 30 kilometres northeast of Bordeaux. It spreads over the district of Bourg-sur-Gironde. The hillsides generally have clay-limestone or clay-gravel soils. The vineyards along the banks of the Gironde estuary are particularly well protected from freezing due to the influence of the Atlantic Ocean. This area is often called 'Gironde's Little Switzerland' for its green, hilly landscapes. Its red wines are made from Cabernet Sauvignon, Cabernet Franc, Merlot and Malbec. Its whites are made from Sémillon, Sauvignon, Muscadelle, Merlot Blanc and Colombard.

WINE STYLES: Côtes-de-Bourg wines are mainly red. The whites were once used as the base wine for making Cognac. Today some of them are distilled into Fine de Bordeaux, a brandy that received recognition in 1974. The red wines are robust, well-structured and highly aromatic, with a deep, brilliant purple colour. They have surprising roundness and velvety tannins. They pair wonderfully with poultry, roast beef with boletus mushrooms or leg of lamb.

AC CÔTES DE CASTILLON

OVERVIEW: Located 40 kilometres east of Bordeaux, along the north-east border

53

of Gironde, Castillon is famous for the 1453 battle which ended the 100 Years' War. Nine towns and villages are entitled to use the appellation. The area is blessed with a climate conducive to wine growing. The soils are rich in iron and limestone on hillside sites of calcareous clay or just clay. The wines are blended from the varietals Merlot, Cabernet-Sauvignon, Cabernet Franc and Malbec.

WINE STYLES: The wines are similar in style to the Saint-Emilion satellite appellations although they tend to be less tannic and take a few years to mellow. Their hue is intense and they are well-constituted, powerful, well-balanced and fleshy. They develop aromas of prunes, spices and animal notes. They are suitable partners for red meats either grilled or served with a sauce, game or mature cheeses.

AC CRÉMANT DE BORDEAUX

OVERVIEW: Crémants are sparkling wines which can be made anywhere within the Bordeaux appellation area from both the red and white varietals used in Gironde. They are made using the traditional method with secondary fermentation in the bottle after a blend of sugar and yeasts has been added.

WINE STYLES: Crémants can generally divided into three different styles: 'blancs de blancs' made from Semillon, Sauvignon and Muscadelle, Crémant Rosé made from red Bordeaux varietals and blended white Crémant, a combination of red and white varietals. With their pale yellow colour, Crémants are usually fresh and lively. They can be served as appetisers, or with fish, shellfish, white meats, cheeses or desserts.

AC ENTRE-DEUX-MERS

OVERVIEW: this extensive appellation should actually be called 'Entre-Deux-Rivières' (or between two rivers) as it sits between the Dordogne and the Garonne. It produces white wines only, from Sauvignon, Semillon and Muscadelle, with just over 2,000 hectares on-stream. Red wines grown here are labelled as Bordeaux or Bordeaux Supérieur.

WINE STYLES: these are dry, fresh, fruity wines which have become rounder over the past few years. Characteristic aromas of citrus fruit (lemon, grapefruit), peach and occasionally exotic fruit (lychee) are present. Try with seafood or fish.

AC ENTRE-DEUX-MERS HAUT-BENAUGE

OVERVIEW: The Entre-Deux-Mers Haut-Benauge region is set like a lone island amidst the sea of Entre-Deux-Mers vines; only a clutch of villages producing dry white wines are entitled to use it. The appellation applies only to white wines which account for one third of the area's output. Varietals used are Sauvignon, Semillon and Muscadelle.

WINE STYLES: These dry white wines display a pale yellow hue with hints of green. They are soft, supple, fruity, easy-drinking wines. They develop aromas of flint and floral notes. They can be served either as an appetiser or with seafood or grilled fish.

AC FRANCS-CÔTES DE BORDEAUX

OVERVIEW: This appellation extends east from Puisseguin-Saint-Émilion and Lussac-Saint-Émilion. It covers the districts of Francs, Saint-Cibard and Tayac. In the valleys, the soils are clay, and the hillsides have clay-limestone soil over marly or limestone subsoils. The red grape varieties are Cabernet Sauvignon, Cabernet Franc, Merlot, Malbec, Petit Verdot and Carménère. The white varieties are Sémillon, Sauvignon and Muscadelle.

WINE STYLES: The red wines have a rich colour and are opulent and full-bodied, characterised by harmonious tannins. They have notes of red fruits (red currant) and spices, with woody notes when young that evolve over time to aromas of game and leather. The dry white wines are fat and complex with floral, woody fragrances. The dessert wines, which are produced only when the harvest and weather allow, are powerful, fat, well balanced and endowed with an attractive wealth of aromas.

AC FRONSAC

OVERVIEW: Set within the Libourne region, this appellation embraces Fronsac, La Rivière, Saint-Germain-la-Rivière, Saint-Michel-de-Fronsac, Saint-Aignan, Saillans and Galgon. Soil types range from modern alluvium along the marshland bordering the Dordogne and the Isle to calcareous clay and clay-sand. Only wines blended from Cabernet-Sauvignon, Cabernet Franc, Merlot and Malbec are made here.

WINE STYLES: As a general rule, Fronsac wines are deeply-coloured (vermilion red or deep ruby hue, occasionally turning a topaz shade with age), fat, fleshy and well-balanced, though at the same time supple and delicate with a distinctive flavour and bouquet. They are laying-down wines which develop aromas of pepper, spices and truffle.

AC GRAVES

OVERVIEW: The extensive region of Graves, which runs parallel with the banks of the Garonne, is Bordeaux's oldest wine growing area. AC Graves wines hail primarily from the stretch of land between La Brède and Langon, encircling the Barsac and Sauternes appellations. In 1987, it parted company with AC Pessac-Léognan in the north which embraces all the classed growths. The gravel-strewn outcrops near Bordeaux and sandy gravel soils further south are home to vineyards blessed with a particularly mild climate. The red wines are blended from Merlot; Cabernet-Sauvignon, Cabernet Franc, Petit Verdot and Malbec. The whites from Semillon, Sauvignon and Muscadelle.

WINE STYLES: The red wines are supple, elegant, well-structured, delicate and well-balanced with an enticing bouquet (red berries, violet, liquorice, peach). They generally mature harmoniously and pair well with roast white meats (veal, lamb) and cheeses (brie, coulommiers). The white wines, which bear the tell-tale characteristics of Bordeaux wines and are amongst the best the region has to offer, are dry, elegant, fleshy, lively wines that linger on the palate and boast a layered aromatic profile: honey, wax, muscat and acacia blossom when they are made from Semillon; more predominant citrus and exotic fruits when Sauvignon is the backbone varietal. Enjoy with shellfish, fish and white meats served with a sauce.

AC GRAVES DE VAYRES

OVERVIEW: This diminutive appellation situated near Libourne, along the left bank of the Dordogne, embraces just two villages: Vayres and Arveyres. It is entirely surrounded by the northern section of the Entre-Deux-Mers appellation.

WINE STYLES: The wines display a ruby-red hue and are delicate and elegant with a supple, well-balanced tannic structure. They are equally suited to early drinking and laying down. They boast fragrances of cherry, redcurrant, blackcurrant, strawberry and notes of liquorice, leather and vanilla. Whites made predominantly from Sauvignon are dry with a pleasant bouquet, brimming with freshness on the palate. The sweet whites, drawn from over-ripe Semillon grapes, display an attractive straw-yellow hue. On the palate, they are generous and overwhelmingly supple. The scale of production remains, however, boutique.

AC GRAVES SUPÉRIEURES

OVERVIEW: This AC produces sweet white wines from Semillon, Sauvignon and Muscadelle. Minimum natural sugar content in the must is 221g/l and alcoholic strength must be in excess of 13.5%. Wine making practices are identical to those in Sauternes.

WINE STYLES: Graves Supérieures are sweet white wines with a distinctive bouquet and great length on the palate. Golden yellow in colour, they display a characteristic balance between acidity and sweetness with toasted, honey notes and occasionally dried fruit. They partner well with fresh or pan-fried foie gras and desserts.

AC HAUT-MÉDOC

OVERVIEW: The regional Haut-Médoc appellation forms the southern part of the Medoc peninsula. It covers 29 towns and villages from Blanquefort in the south as far as Saint-Seurin-de-Cadourne in the north, including the communal appellations Saint-Estèphe, Pauillac, Saint-Julien, Moulis, Listrac-Médoc and Margaux. Dotted throughout the region are the star-studded châteaux producing some of the world's greatest wines.

The region is home to five classed growths, hundreds of Bourgeois growths producing some of Bordeaux's finest wines and five co-operative wineries. The soil make-up comprises gravel from the Quaternary era, deposited by the Garonne and shaped into outcrops. The temperate climate is strongly defined by the Atlantic and the nearby estuary. The wines are made traditionally at controlled temperatures and subsequently aged in oak for 12 to 18 months.

WINE STYLES: Blended from Cabernet-Sauvignon, Cabernet Franc, Merlot, Malbec, Petit Verdot and Carmenere, the wines are elegant, with great finesse and a layered bouquet. They are reasonably robust and perfectly suited to laying down. They conjure up aromas of ripe red fruit, notes of roasted coffee, mild spices (liquorice, vanilla…) and sweet pepper, sometimes prune. They pair well with Normandy-style veal cutlets, roast meats or game.

CLASSED GROWTHS:
Château La Lagune (3rd growth),
Château La Tour Carnet (4th growth),
Château Camensac, Château Cantemerle and
Château Belgrave (all three 5th growths).

AC LALANDE-DE-POMEROL

OVERVIEW: The Lalande-de-Pomerol appellation area embraces just two villages, Lalande-de-Pomerol itself and Néac, situated north of Saint-Emilion and Pomerol. In fact, only a tiny river, the Barbanne, separates them from Pomerol. Soil types range from clay and clay-gravel in the east to gravel in the north and north-east, and sand in the western reaches. Vines thrive here in hot sunny climes, blessed with sufficient rainfall. Red varietals: Merlot, Cabernet-Sauvignon, Cabernet Franc and Malbec.

WINE STYLES: Deeply coloured red wines, powerful and velvety with a pleasant mouthfeel. Predominant aromas are truffle, violet and undergrowth. They are a good match for roast beef, duck and unfermented cheeses.

AC LISTRAC-MÉDOC

OVERVIEW: Officially recognised in 1957, Listrac is the youngest of the six communal appellation areas in Haut-Médoc.It is also the furthest away from the Gironde estuary, set on the border between the wine growing areas of Medoc and its woodlands. The soils are either gravely or calcareous clay. The nearby ocean and the estuary provide a temperate climate.

WINE STYLES: The wines are all of a consistent standard. Deeply coloured, tannic and well-structured, they display a virile, fleshy personality. Predominant aromas are ripe red and black fruit, vanilla or caramel, roasted coffee, dark chocolate and spices. They can be served with beef casserole or preserved duck. There are no classed growths within this communal appellation.

AC LOUPIAC

OVERVIEW: This appellation is situated 40 km from Bordeaux along the right bank of the Garonne, near Sainte-Croix-du-Mont. The vines are planted on hillside sites where the soils are either calcareous clay or clay-sand. This south-facing area is blessed with a microclimate conducive to the onset of noble rot. Varietals for blending are Semillon, Sauvignon and Muscadelle.

WINE STYLES: Loupiac are fruity wines with a well-balanced mellowness. They are delicate, elegant, firm and generous, developing aromas of crystallised fruit (apricot), honey and gingerbread. They pair well with roast duck or duck breasts.

AC LUSSAC-SAINT-EMILION

OVERVIEW: Lussac-Saint-Emilion is one of Saint-Emilion's four satellite appellations. Set in the village of Lussac, it is a red-wine only appellation. The wines are grown on average 10-hectare plots by around a hundred growers. The vineyards are planted on plateaux and hillside sites where soil types are calcareous clay in the south eastern portion and gravely in the west, though there are pockets of sand and clay. The wines are blended from Merlot, Cabernet Franc, Cabernet-Sauvignon, Malbec and Carmenère.

WINE STYLES: Lussac's hallmark character traits are sourced in its 'terroir'. The wines display a distinctively intense colour, finesse and generosity. They are well-balanced, full and suitable for laying down. They can be paired with grilled or roast meats and game.

AC MARGAUX

OVERVIEW: Situated on a plateau 6 km long by 2 km wide, the appellation encompasses five villages (Margaux, Cantenac, Soussans, Arsac and Labarde). It is not only the most extensive appellation in the Haut-Médoc, it is also the most southerly.

The core of the appellation is in Cantenac and Margaux along a string of prime hillock sites. The vineyards are planted on a plateau of gravel flanked by gravely outcrops. They in fact boast the deepest layer of gravel throughout the whole of the Médoc and have the stoniest soils.

WINE STYLES: These delicate, refined wines are rich, subtle and elegant. They are reputedly the Medoc's most 'feminine' wines. Their aromas cover a broad spectrum, predominantly violet, rose and raspberry. Recommended pairings include venison fillet, rack of lamb, hare or roast partridge, morels in puff pastry, sweetbreads and veal cutlets with chanterelles. In fact, they enhance all red meats and mild flavoured game.

CLASSED GROWTHS:
First growth: *Château Margaux.*
Second growths: *Château Brane-Cantenac, Château Dufort-Viviens, Château Lascombes, Château Rauzan-Gassies, Château Rauzan-Ségla.*
Third growths: *Château Boyd-Cantenac, Château Kirwan, Château d'Issan, Château Giscours, Château Malescot Saint-Exupéry, Château Cantenac-Brown, Château Palmer, Château Ferrière, Château Desmirail, Château Marquis d'Alesme Becker.*
Fourth growths: *Château Prieuré-Lichine, Château Pouget, Château Marquis de Terme.*
Fifth growths: *Château Dauzac, Château du Tertre.*

AC MÉDOC

OVERVIEW: AC Médoc is situated in the northern part of Médoc, around the towns and villages north of Saint-Seurin-de-Cadourne. Interspersed amongst the calcareous clay soils are less frequent occurrences of gravel. The temperate climate is strongly defined by the Atlantic ocean and the nearby estuary. The wines are made traditionally at controlled temperatures. They are matured for varying periods of time either under oak or in tanks.

WINE STYLES: AC Médoc is a red-wine only appellation. The wines display a brilliant cherry-red hue. On both the nose and the palate they have distinctive fruit aromas (blackcurrant, red fruit). These superbly round, delicate, supple wines tend to mature well. They can be enjoyed from an early age and served with grilled sirloin steak, cooked cold meats and cheeses.

AC MONTAGNE SAINT-EMILION

OVERVIEW: Of the four Saint-Emilion satellite appellations, this AC has the greatest acreage. Its soil type is quite similar to that of nearby Saint-Emilion: calcareous clay hillside sites on a subsoil of limestone, clay-silica or loam. The wines are blended from Merlot, Cabernet Franc, Cabernet-Sauvignon, Malbec and Carmenere.

WINE STYLES: With a hue of varying intensity, these wines are fresh, powerful, rich and mild. Tannins are quite present but the wines remain supple and display extremely pleasant characteristic floral, fruity notes. They partner with game and poultry served in a sauce.

AC MOULIS

OVERVIEW: Situated on the left bank of the Gironde, in Haut-Médoc, the Moulis appellation area embraces seven villages (Moulis, Listrac-Médoc, Lamarque, Arcins, Avensan, Castelnau-de-Médoc, Cussac-Fort-Médoc). Forty or so wine growers share the appellation and 14 of those boast Bourgeois growth status. The vines grow on outcrops studded with gravel of Pyrenean origin or deposited by the Garonne.

WINE STYLES: The wine boasts great finesse and an elegant bouquet supported by a strong framework and good length. An intense ruby-red colour, it is both seductive yet virile. For some, it is the epitome of a Médoc, with the potential finesse of Margaux, the complexity of a Saint-Julien and the strength of a Pauillac. Their tannin content makes Moulis capable of considerable longevity. They exude aromas of prunes and leather as well as spicy and vanilla notes. They can be served with stew, casseroles, sirloin steak with a shallot sauce, leg of mutton…

AC PAUILLAC

OVERVIEW: Pauillac is a Médoc communal appellation. It boasts an impressive concentration of top-flight wines with three of the five First Growths within its boundaries (Lafite, Latour and Mouton-Rothschild). The vines are planted on a virtually unbroken ridge stretching from Saint-Julien in the south to Saint-Estèphe in the north. Only a few hundred metres of m arshland separate them from the

waters of the Gironde estuary. The soils are gravely with sandy deposits, providing superb drainage. The nearby ocean and estuary define a warm temperate climate.
WINE STYLES: Pauillac's red wines, whose principal varietal is Cabernet-Sauvignon, are some of the Médoc's most concentrated wines. Rich and complex, they have a well-structured, harmonious body bolstered by a fine tannic structure. They are robust, elegant, distinguished wines with a great ability to age. They develop fragrances of raspberry, blackcurrant, rose, violet, iris, cedar and cigar box. Enjoy with Pauillac lamb, roast wood pigeon, rack of veal with chanterelles.
CLASSED GROWTHS:
First Growths: *Château Lafite Rothschild, Château Latour, Château Mouton Rothschild.*
Second Growths: *Château Pichon-Longueville (Baron), Château Pichon-Longueville (Comtesse de Lalande).*
Fourth Growth: Château Duhart-Milon-Rothschild.
Fifth Growths: *Château Batailley, Château Haut-Batailley, Château Clerc Milon, Château Croizet-Bages, Château Grand-Puy Ducasse, Château Grand-Puy Lacoste, Château Haut-Bages Libéral, Château Lynch-Bages, Château Lynch-Moussas, Château Pédesclaux, Château Pontet-Canet, Château d'Armailhac.*

AC PESSAC-LÉOGNAN

OVERVIEW: Pessac-Léognan, which was given its own appellation in 1987, is set in the heart of Graves country. It embraces ten towns and villages south of Bordeaux (Pessac, Talence, Villemanve d'Ornon, Léognan, Martillac, Mérignac, Gradignan, Cadaujac, Canéjan, Saint-Médard d'Eyrans). The terrain forms gravel outcrops and has good drainage. Bordered by pine forests then the ocean to the west and the Garonne to the east, the Graves region enjoys an extremely mild climate.
The wines are made traditionally at controlled temperatures. The reds are aged in oak as are the whites which are both fermented and matured under oak, almost invariably on the lees.
WINE STYLES: Pessac-Léognan scales the quality heights with elegant, complex wines. Displaying a highly attractive garnet-red hue, they show concentration and structure and are blessed with a finely woven texture, spanning a broad range of aromas. Ripe fruit, spices (pepper, liquorice) and humus aromas intermingle with smoky, chocolaty notes. The white wines are dry, vigorous, elegant, fleshy wines, velvety on the palate exuding an extremely refined bouquet (honey, acacia flowers, butter, dried fruit (peach, apricot), crystallised citrus fruit). The reds pair with roast poultry and meat served in a sauce; the whites with shellfish, pike served with a butter sauce… Both red and white Pessac-Léognan are wines for laying down and will keep for between 5 to 20 years.
CLASSED GROWTHS:
First growth (Official 1855 Classification): *Château Haut-Brion.*
Classed growths: *Château Bouscaut, Château Carbonnieux, Domaine de Chevalier, Château Couhins, Château Couhins-Lurton, Château de Fieuzal, Château Haut-Bailly, Château La Mission Haut-Brion, Château La Tour Haut-Brion, Château Latour*

Martillac, Château Laville Haut-Brion, Château Malartic-Lagravière, Château Olivier, Château Pape-Clément, Château Smith Haut-Lafitte.

AC POMEROL

OVERVIEW: Pomerol is a village situated near Libourne. The hillsides of Saint-Emilion roll down to Pomerol ending in a plateau carved into terraces which gently descend towards the valley floor. The soils are predominantly gravel interspersed with layers of clay. The subsoil however is shot through with a kind of iron-rich sandstone called 'iron dross' which in some cases imparts very distinctive characteristics to the wines.

Despite the fact that Pomerol is one of the most renowned and popular wines in the world, it has no official classification.

WINE STYLES: Pomerol wines are rich in colour, powerful and brimming with body, roundness and generosity, though they also boast finesse and an overwhelmingly rich bouquet. Red fruit, truffle and violet form the backbone of its aromatic range. Pomerol is an all-rounder which can be paired with all sorts of food, including foie gras. It sits nicely alongside dishes such as roast beef en croûte, jugged hare, lamprey in a red wine sauce, mushrooms and most cheeses.

AC PUISSEGUIN-SAINT-EMILION

OVERVIEW: This is one of Saint-Emilion's four satellite appellations, with a total 120 growers, one third of whom belong to the local co-operative. The soil is primarily calcareous clay with a rocky, stony subsoil. A large proportion of the vineyards enjoy a south, south-east aspect and a dry microclimate. The wines grown here are red, drawn from Merlot, Cabernet Franc (or Bouchet) Cabernet-Sauvignon and very occasionally Malbec.

WINE STYLES: Puisseguin-Saint-Emilion wines have good depth of colour. They are powerful, well-constituted, delicate, harmonious wines. The more mature wines pair well with white meat whilst the younger versions are better suited to red meat and game.

AC SAINTE-CROIX-DU-MONT

OVERVIEW: Situated 45 km south-south-east of Bordeaux, this appellation sits on the opposite bank of the Garonne to Sauternes. The soils are calcareous clay in type with fossils set on a subsoil of limestone or gravel. The vines are planted on plateaux or hillside sites. The wines are blended from Semillon, Sauvignon and Muscadelle.

WINE STYLES: These sweet wines are fruity, rich and elegant with a well-balanced mellowness. They have a high sugar and alcohol content. They pair with melon, roast chicken or quenelles.

AC SAINTE-FOY-BORDEAUX

OVERVIEW: Set in the north-eastern corner of Gironde, this appellation embraces 19 towns and villages. Sainte-Foy-Bordeaux produces dry and sweet white wines and reds. Red wines are blended from Cabernet-Sauvignon, Cabernet Franc, Merlot, Malbec and Petit Verdot and white wines primarily from Semillon, Sauvignon and Muscadelle.

WINE STYLES: The red wines have good depth of colour and can be supple or robust. Depending on how they are made, they are either suitable for early drinking or should be kept. They display aromas of red fruit, undergrowth, leather and notes of vanilla. The dry whites are round with a touch of acidity, exuding discrete, appealing fragrances. The sweet whites show a pale yellow hue, finesse and mellowness, with scents of honey, linden and muscat.

AC SAINT-EMILION

OVERVIEW: Saint-Émilion is near the town of Libourne to the east of the Gironde. It dates back to the end of the 13th century, when Emilianus, a monk from Brittany, settled there. Saint-Émilion was a winegrowing region well before Médoc. Although Médoc is made up of very large estates, several hundred small winegrowers cultivate the vineyards of Saint-Émilion. The appellation consists of eight districts: Saint-Émilion, Saint-Christophe-des-Bardes, Saint-Étienne-de-Lisse, Saint-Hippolyte, Saint-Laurent-des-Combes, Saint-Pey-d'Armens, Saint-Sulpice-de-Faleyrens and Vignonet, as well as part of Libourne. As the topography of the area is varied, the grapes produce very different wines depending on the orientation and location of the vines. Saint-Émilion has four main types of terroir: a limestone plateau near the town, a large terrace of siliceous-clay gravel stretching in the direction of Libourne, clay-limestone hillsides and valleys, and the sand and gravel plain of the Dordogne valley, which produces lighter wines.

WINE STYLES: Saint-Émilion produces only reds, which are plum-coloured and reputed for their generous, warm, powerful character and opulent bouquet. Saint-Émilion AOC wines are nonetheless less full-bodied than Saint-Émilion grands crus. The main aromas are red fruit jam, spices and coffee. It pairs well with lamprey à la bordelaise, duck casserole or goose confit.

AC SAINT-ÉMILION GRAND CRU

OVERVIEW: Produced in the same winegrowing area as Saint-Émilion AOC, the grand crus are found on the best terrains: the clay-limestone hillsides, the plateau or the gravel terrace. Its wines are produced according to strict rules: a maximum yield of 46 hectolitres per hectare (in contrast with 53 for other Saint-Émilion wines), a minimum natural level of alcohol (11.5° in contrast with 11°) and final tasting before authorization. The crus classés concern only Saint-Émilion Grand Cru AOC.

CRUS CLASSÉS: Saint-Émilion is ranked to distinguish premiers grands crus classés and grands crus classés. This ranking is reviewed every ten years. All these wines belong to the Saint-Émilion Grand Cru appellation, however not all the wines of this AOC are grands crus classés. Within the premiers grands crus classés, there are two categories, A and B.

GRANDS CRUS CLASSES :

Château l'Arrosée, Château Fleur Cardinale, Château Monbousquet, Château Balestard la Tonnelle, Château La Fleur Morange, Château Moulin du Cadet, Château Barde-Haut, Château Fombrauge*, Clos de l'Oratoire, Château Bellefont-Belcier, Château Fonplégade, Château Pavie Decesse, Château Bellevue, Château Fonroque, Château Peby Faugères*, Château Berliquet, Château Franc Mayne, Château Petit Faurie de Soutard, Château Cadet-Bon, Château Grand Corbin, Château de Pressac*, Château Capdemourlin, Château Grand Corbin-Despagne, Château le Prieuré, Château le Chatelet, Château Grand Mayne, Château Quinault l'Enclos*, Château Chauvin, Château les Grandes Murailles, Château Ripeau, Château Clos de Sarpe, Château Grand-Pontet, Château Rochebelle, Château la Clotte, Château Guadet, Château Saint-Georges-Cote-Pavie, Château la Commanderie, Château Haut-Sarpe, Clos Saint-Martin, Château Corbin, Clos des Jacobins, Château Sansonnet, Château Côte de Baleau, Couvent des Jacobins, Château la Serre, Château la Couspaude, Château Jean Faure, Château Soutard, Château Dassault, Château Laniote, Château Tertre Daugay, Château Destieux, Château Larmande Château la Tour Figeac, Château la Dominique, Château Laroque, Château Villemaurine, Château Faugères*, Château Laroze, Château Yon-Figeac, Château Faurie de Souchard, Clos la Madeleine, Château de Ferrand*, Château la Marzelle.

* Châteaux promoted in 2012

AC SAINT-ESTÈPHE

63

OVERVIEW: This is the most northerly of the six Haut-Médoc communal appellations. Set on gravely outcrops with a stony limestone, and occasionally clayey subsoil, it is a red-wine only appellation. The five 1855 classed growths account for just 20% of overall production, underscoring the crucial role of the Bourgeois growths and the lesser wine growers, at the root of the area's diverse wine styles.

WINE STYLES: As a rule, Saint-Estèphe wines tend to have great depth of colour and a robust structure which does not compromise their finesse. They have a full tannic structure and cover a broad aromatic spectrum. They are robust, though not unpleasantly so, and are extremely well-suited to cellaring. Ripe red fruit and spices are the predominant aromas. Serve with large game, roast meat or meat served in a sauce, and a choice of cheeses.

CLASSED GROWTHS:

Second growths: *Château Cos d'Estournel, Château Montrose.* Third growth: *Château Calon-Ségur.*

Fourth growth: *Château Lafon-Rochet.*

Fifth growth: *Château Cos Labory.*

AC SAINT-GEORGES SAINT-EMILION

OVERVIEW: This is the smallest of the Saint-Emilion satellite appellations and in fact most growers sell their wines as Montagne-Saint-Emilion. The vineyards are located exclusively along rolling hillsides and face south or south-west. The range of varietals is traditional with Merlot, Cabernet Franc, Cabernet-Sauvignon, Malbec and Carmenere.

WINE STYLES: The consistency of the terrain is mirrored in the quality of the wines. They display an intense crimson hue, are fruity and gain complexity as they mature. They are well-constituted, mild, fat and boast velvety tannins. They enhance red meat and game.

AC SAINT-JULIEN

OVERVIEW: Saint-Julien sits within a rectangle, 5 km long by 3.5 km wide, south of Pauillac. Roughly three-quarters of Saint-Julien wines are made by its 11 classed growths. Outcrops of gravel from the Quaternary era deposited by the Garonne are home to its vineyards, as are silica-type soils to the west. The nearby ocean and the estuary provide a mild temperate climate.

WINE STYLES: Saint-Julien wines display an intense colour. They are subtle, well-balanced, elegant and show great length on the palate with a delicate, tell-tale bouquet. With their aromas of red fruit, mild spices, leather, vanilla… they boast a considerable ability to age. Enjoy with red meat, game, duck…

CLASSED GROWTHS:
Second growths: *Château Léoville Las Cases, Château Léoville-Poyferré, Château Léoville-Barton, Château Gruaud-Larose, Château Ducru-Beaucaillou.*
Third growths: *Château Lagrange, Château Langoa-Barton.* Fourth growths: *Château Talbot, Château Saint-Pierre, Château Beychevelle, Château Branaire-Ducru.*

AC SAINTE-FOY-BORDEAUX

OVERVIEW: Located in the east of the Gironde region and covering 19 districts, the appellation of Sainte-Foy-Bordeaux produces dry and sweet white wines as well as reds. The red varieties used are Cabernet Sauvignon, Cabernet Franc, Merlot, Malbec and Petit Verdot. The main white varieties are Sémillon, Sauvignon and Muscadelle.

WINE STYLES: The red wines are rich in colour, smooth and full-bodied. Depending on the vinification method, they can be drunk when young or can be kept. They have a bouquet of red fruits, undergrowth, leather and notes of vanilla. The dry whites are round and slightly acidic and have subtle, flattering aromas. The dessert wines are pale yellow in colour, with a delicate and mild palate with scents of honey, lime flower and Muscat.

AC SAUTERNES

OVERVIEW: Sauternes, considered to be one of the greatest sweet white wines in the world, comes from an area located in the southern part of the Graves. This regional appellation embraces 5 villages: Sauternes, Fargues, Bommes, Preignac and Barsac. The cold waters of the river Ciron, which cuts through Sauternes, flow into the warmer Garonne, producing the autumn mists which envelop the vineyard in the evening and linger until the following morning. These climatic conditions are conducive to the formation of noble rot. Soil make-up is extremely varied, covering the gamut from gravel, to clay, silica and limestone or all four simultaneously. Subsoil is primarily clay though patches of limestone or gravel are also present. The wines are made from white varietals prone to 'Botrytis cinerea' (noble rot) such as Semillon (80% of the blend), Sauvignon and Muscadelle. Climate permitting, noble rot forms and the grapes are late harvested by painstakingly combing through the vineyard time after time. The grapes become shrivelled with extremely high sugar concentration. To comply with legislation, natural alcohol content in the finished wine must be between 15% and 12% actual alcohol. The difference between the two comes from the unfermented sugar. Residual sugar content must be at least 45g per litre.

Once the grapes have been harvested, they have to be handled with great care and must be pressed as gently as possible. The wines are fermented either in tanks or barrels and are usually matured under oak for anything between 18 to 36 months.

WINE STYLES: AC Sauternes yields sweet white wines displaying an old gold hue. They are rich, unctuous wines bolstered by a touch of acidity which allows them to age well. They exhibit fragrances of citrus fruit, acacia honey, apricot and hazelnut. Serve chilled as an appetiser, with foie gras, dishes cooked in a butter sauce, elaborate white meat dishes or desserts.

65

CLASSED GROWTHS:

Wines from Sauternes are classed either as AC Sauternes or AC Barsac, or occasionally both.

Superior First growth: *Château d'Yquem (Sauternes).*

First growths: *Château la Tour Blanche (Sauternes), Château Lafaurie-Peraguey (Sauternes), Château Rayne Vigneau (Sauternes), Château Suduiraut (Sauternes), Château Coutet (Sauternes and Barsac), Château Climens (Sauternes and Barsac), Château Guiraud (Sauternes), Château Rieussec (Sauternes), Château Rabaud-Promis (Sauternes), Château Sigalas Rabaud, Château Clos Haut-Peraguey (Sauternes).*

Second growths: *Château Doisy-Daëne (Sauternes and Barsac), Château Doisy Védrines (Sauternes and Barsac), Château d'Arche (Sauternes), Château Filhot (Sauternes), Château Broustet (Sauternes and Barsac), Château Nairac (Sauternes and Barsac), Château Caillou (Sauternes and Barsac), Château Suau (Sauternes and Barsac), Château de Malle (Sauternes), Château Romer du Hayot (Sauternes), Château Doisy Dubroca (Sauternes and Barsac), Château Lamothe Despujols (Sauternes), Château Lamothe (Sauternes), Château de Myrat (Sauternes and Barsac).*

● ● ●

2015
BORDEAUX WINES

BLAYE CÔTES DE BORDEAUX

CHÂTEAU CANTINOT   91/100

▼ Orbite 2010 : Beautiful garnet. Expressive nose driven by black fruits, prune, vanilla and liquorice. Explosive, round, concentrated and fruity palate with polished tannins. Lovely freshness, balance and power. A very successful wine pairing with ribsteak.
Price approx.: 50,00 EUR
www.chateau-cantinot.com
Château Cantinot
+33 (0)5 57 64 31 70

LES TOURS DE CANTINOT   89/100

▼ Vintage 2009 : Slightly evolved garnet. Mature nose driven by ripe black fruits and spice with a menthol touch. Fruity, full palate that is powerful yet supple. Impeccable balance. Lingering, spice-infused finish. A consummate wine pairing with roast meats.
Price approx.: 30,00 EUR
www.chateau-cantinot.com
Château Cantinot
+33 (0)5 57 64 31 70

CHÂTEAU GIGAULT   88/100

▼ Cuvée Viva 2010 : Beautiful deep red, still in its y outh. Ripe, profound nose with accents of cassis and redcurrant. Wonderfully sappy palate with fine-grained tanniins yet a substantial framework. The finish is heady, persistent and fruit-forward. A racy wine.
Price approx.: 15,50 EUR
http://www.chateau-gigault.fr
Château Gigault
+33 (0) 57 32 62 59

CHÂTEAU CANTINOT   88/100

▼ Orbite 2011 : Deep garnet. Mature, complex nose driven by black fruits, spice and a hint of smoke in the background. Supple, full and fruity palate with tightly-wound tannins. Beautiful balance and freshness. Lingering vegetal finish. Enjoyable with red meats.
Price approx.: 50,00 EUR
www.chateau-cantinot.com
Château Cantinot
+33 (0)5 57 64 31 70

CHÂTEAU HAUT-COLOMBIER   87/100

CONV ▼ Vintage 2013 : Brilliant light yellow. Pleasant nose driven by citrus and gunflint. Fairly lively attack leading into a rich, round and supple palate. Well-balanced with focused aromas. Persistent, spice-infused finish. A successful wine pairing with oily fish.
Price approx.: 8,00 EUR
www.chateauhautcolombier.com
Vignobles Jean Chéty et Fils
+33 (0)5 57 42 10 28

CHÂTEAU LES AUBIERS   87/100

▼ Vintage 2012 : Attractive garnet hue. The nose is driven by ripe cassis, redcurrant and raspberry. Beautifully dense palate with restrained tannin presence and upfront fruit. Silky mouthfeel. A refined, full Blaye pairing with tournedos in a peppercorn sauce.
Price approx.: 5,00 EUR
http://www.grandmoulin.com
Robin
+33 (0)5 57 32 62 06

CHÂTEAU CANTINOT   87/100

▼ Vintage 2010 : Slightly evolved garnet. Mature nose driven by blackberry and cassis with spice and animal undertones. The palate is concentrated and full with tight-knit tannins. Fresh, well-balanced structure. Long-lasting spicy finish. Real allure, drink with cheese.
Price approx.: 18,00 EUR
www.chateau-cantinot.com
Château Cantinot
+33 (0)5 57 64 31 70

CHÂTEAU LES MARÉCHAUX   86/100

▼ Vintage 2010 : Deeply-coloured garnet. Distinctive nose varying between vegetal and ripe red and black fruit perfumes. A well-balanced, tannic Blaye revealing fruity aromas. Assertive power. A focused, classic style calling for grilled or roast red meats.
Price approx.: 10,00 EUR
http://www.vignobles-rs.com
Château Les Maréchaux

CHÂTEAU BELLE COLINE   86/100

▼ Vintage 2011 : Deeply-coloured, young red. The nose is ripe and profound and the fruit flows into mineral and oak tones. Full attack leading into a mid-palate revealing fresh aromatics. Lingering spice touch on the finish.
Price approx.: 15,00 EUR
http://www.chateau-belle-coline.com
Château Gigault
+33 (0) 57 32 62 59

CHÂTEAU LE VIROU 86/100

▼ Les Vieilles Vignes 2012 : Concentrated garnet. Predominant vanilla oak on the nose with plum, blackberry and redcurrant undertones. The oak has mellowed nicely already and allows the fruit to shine through. Trace of tannins on the finish. A good Blaye that needs decanting.
Price approx.: 5,60 EUR
www.chateaux-en-bordeaux.com
Châteaux en Bordeaux

CHÂTEAU HAUT-COLOMBIER 86/100

▼ Vintage 2012 : Deep, young colour. Smoky nose backed by ripe black fruits. The palate still shows tannin influence with bolder fruit expression on the finish. Quality aromatics combined with a quality mouthfeel. A Blaye with a good future ahead.
Price approx.: 8,00 EUR
www.chateauhautcolombier.com
Vignobles Jean Chéty et Fils
+33 (0)5 57 42 10 28

CHÂTEAU LA TONNELLE DE GRILLET 86/100

▼ Vintage 2013 : Beautiful young, deep colour. Nose of fresh blackberry, cassis and cherry backed by peony and violet. The palate is still a little muted but beautiful quality fruit supported by proud tannins can be sensed. A little patience is needed for full enjoyment.
Price approx.: 5,00 EUR
http://www.grandmoulin.com
Robin
+33 (0)5 57 32 62 06

CHÂTEAU LE GRAND MOULIN 86/100

▼ Vintage 2012 : Young garnet. Heady, fruit-driven nose showing blackcurrant, blackberry and raspberry with a vegetal touch in the background. Very supple, mouth-coating palate with polished tannins and beautiful fruit presence. Finesse is the name of the game here.
Price approx.: 5,00 EUR
http://www.grandmoulin.com
Robin
+33 (0)5 57 32 62 06

CHÂTEAU LES AUBIERS 86/100

▼ Vintage 2013 : Beautiful deep, young colour. Distinctive nose of fresh fruit coupled with earth notes. Well-balanced, chewy palate showing fine-grained tannins and beautiful aromatic presence with fruit stealing the show on the finish. A good wine for red meats.
Price approx.: 5,00 EUR
http://www.grandmoulin.com
Robin
+33 (0)5 57 32 62 06

CHÂTEAU LA HAIE 85/100

Org▼ Vintage 2011 : Crimson with garnet. Nose of jammy plum, black cherry and raspberry with vegetal undercurrents. Full palate still showing exuberance. The tannins are upfront and refined with fruit playing a supporting role. A distinctive Blaye, all-set for a good future.
Price approx.: 0,08 EUR
http://www.chateau-la-haie.com
Château La Haie
+33 (0)6 72 94 53 37

CHÂTEAU LES GRAVES DU CHAMP DES CHAILS 85/100

▼ Vintage 2013 : Beautifully youthful colour. Alluring nose of fresh red fruits. A supple, soft wine with tannins that have already mellowed. Lovely, easy-drinking youthful fruit perfumes. A seductively drinkable Blaye from now on.
Price approx.: 5,00 EUR
http://www.grandmoulin.com
Robin
+33 (0)5 57 32 62 06

CHÂTEAU CAILLETEAU BERGERON 84/100

▼ Tradition 2012 : Beautiful vibrant red with purple-blue tints. Pleasant nose intermixing black fruits with a roasted coffee and oak tone. Supple attack on the palate with mellow tannins. The mid-palate and finish are firmer but stay well-balanced.
Price approx.: 6,00 EUR
http://www.cailleteau-bergeron.com
Château Cailleteau Bergeron
+33 (0)5 57 42 11 10

EXCELLENCE IX 84/100

▼ Vintage 2012 : Beautiful, young vibrant red. Fruity and spicy nose showing lovely intensity. Wonderful sappy attack flowing into a more oak-driven mid-palate and finish yet the palate stays fresh and aromatic. Set aside for red meats and barbecues.
Price approx.: 5,00 EUR
www.chateau-segonzac.com
Château Segonzac
+33 (0)5 57 42 18 16

CHÂTEAU LE GRAND MOULIN 84/100

▼ Vintage 2013 : Pale gold. Floral nose of meadow and boxwood with a touch of nettle and citrus. A crisp Blaye with a thirst-quenching exuberance that imparts a good measure of acidity allowing the palate to cope with the rest of the meal and wines. A good palate starter.
Price approx.: 4,50 EUR
http://www.grandmoulin.com
Robin
+33 (0)5 57 32 62 06

CHÂTEAU LE GRAND MOULIN 84/100

▼♪ Vintage 2013 : Deeply-coloured with dark purple tints. Refined nose of ripe red and black fruits. Supple palate with polished tannins. Freshness nicely supports perfume. A crowd-pleasing Blaye.
Price approx.: 5,00 EUR
http://www.grandmoulin.com
Robin
+33 (0)5 57 32 62 06

CHÂTEAU CROIX PICARD 84/100

▼♪ Vintage 2013 : Young, dark purple. Alluring nose of fresh red and black fruits. A soft, supple Blaye showing beautiful freshness. Wonderful substance nicely highlights the fruit. A very approachable wine.
Price approx.: 5,00 EUR
http://www.grandmoulin.com
Robin
+33 (0)5 57 32 62 06

CHÂTEAU HAUT LANDON 84/100

▼♪ Vintage 2013 : Deeply-coloured dark purple. Inviting nose of forest fruits. A classic, well-made Blaye offering up savoury fresh fruit. Perceptible, fine-grained tannins. The ideal companion for grilled red meats.
Price approx.: 5,00 EUR
http://www.grandmoulin.com
Robin
+33 (0)5 57 32 62 06

CHÂTEAU CHEVALIERS DES BRARDS 84/100

▼♪ Cuvée Prestige 2013 : Young dark purple. The nose boasts beautifully ripe cassis, cherry and redcurrant. A supple Blaye offering up savoury fruity freshness. Mellow tannins. Balance and generous aromatics. The perfect partner for grilled meats.
Price approx.: 5,00 EUR
http://www.grandmoulin.com
Robin
+33 (0)5 57 32 62 06

CHÂTEAU PEYREBRUNE LE VIGNEAU 84/100

▼♪ Vintage 2012 : Deep, young colour. Crisp nose of blackcurrant, cherry and raspberry. Supple, light and fruity palate with polished tannins and abundant freshness highlighting the fruit. A charming Blaye drinking well even in its youth.
Price approx.: 5,00 EUR
http://www.grandmoulin.com
Robin
+33 (0)5 57 32 62 06

CHÂTEAU LA GRANGE D'ORLÉAN 83/100

▼♪ Vintage 2012 : Deep, young colour. Nose of overripe fruits with spicy undercurrents. Warm palate with melted tannins. The nose aromatics carry through. Assertive power. Uncork for lamb chops served with a wine-based sauce.
Price approx.: 5,00 EUR
http://www.grandmoulin.com
Robin
+33 (0)5 57 32 62 06

CHÂTEAU CAPVILLE 83/100

▼♪ Cuvée Prestige 2013 : Deep, young colour. Nose of ripe red and black fruits. Full mouthfeel setting the stage for fruit expression, freshness and suppleness. A crowd-pleasing Blaye ready to drink now.
http://www.grandmoulin.com
Robin
+33 (0)5 57 32 62 06

CHATEAU FONTARABIE 83/100

▼♪ Vintage 2013 : Clear, limpid and vibrant red. Dashing nose marrying red fruits and a vanilla oak tone. Same aromatic profile on the palate which reveals savoury freshness and balance. A pleasant style that is already accessible.
Price approx.: 6,00 EUR
http://www.vignoblesfaure.fr
Vignobles A. Faure
+33 (0)5 57 42 68 80

MEYBLUM & FILS 82/100

▼♪ Vintage 2012 : Deeply-coloured garnet. Fine nose of vanilla oak backed by ripe red and black fruits. A young Blaye, still slightly tannic. Fruit presence framed by a fairly lightweight mouthfeel. Ready to drink now.
Price approx.: 10,00 EUR
http://www.meyblum-et-fils.com
MVP Wines

CHÂTEAU HAUT SOCIONDO 81/100

▼♪ Vintage 2013 : Deep, young colour. Heady nose suggestive of peony and fresh strawberry, raspberry and redcurrant. Lightweight palate with supple tannins and fresh, vibrant perfume. An instantly accessible Blaye.
Price approx.: 5,00 EUR
http://www.grandmoulin.com
Robin
+33 (0)5 57 32 62 06

CHÂTEAU LA GRAVETTE 79/100

▼♪ Millésime 2013 : Belle robe rouge, jeune d'aspect. Nez expressif où le fruit se mêle de notes végétales- terreuses. Bouche légère, relativement équilibrée mais toujours avec cette tonalité végétale

persistante. On l'appréciera légèrement frais et sans tarder.
Price approx.: 2,20 EUR
http://www.vignobles-roux.com
Vignobles Roux
+33 (0)5 56 61 98 93

BORDEAUX CLAIRET

CHÂTEAU THIEULEY 88/100

▼♪Vintage 2013 : Brilliant deep pink. Focused nose driven by redcurrant, cherry and strawberry. Supple, full and generous palate with full-on fruit expression. Persistent, spice-infused finish. A deliciously seductive wine that works best as an aperitif.
Price approx.: 6,10 EUR
www.thieuley.com
Vignobles Francis Courselle
+33 (0)5 56 23 00 01

BORDEAUX ROSÉ

CHÂTEAU THIEULEY 87/100

▼♪Vintage 2013 : Brilliant light salmon-pink. Pleasant nose of red fruits and boiled sweets. Round, full and delicious palate with full-on, focused fruit expression. Intense finish driven by mild spices. A crunchy wine that works well as an aperitif or with summer starter.
Price approx.: 6,10 EUR
www.thieuley.com
Vignobles Francis Courselle
+33 (0)5 56 23 00 01

CHÂTEAU HAUT- COLOMBIER 86/100

CONV▼♪Vintage 2013 : Very deeply-coloured vibrant pink. The nose is driven by cherry and redcurrant. Supple, rich palate revealing focused aromas. Well-balanced and pleasurable. Crisp finish. A salad enjoyable wine that works well with a summer starter.
Price approx.: 6,00 EUR
www.chateauhautcolombier.com
Vignobles Jean Chéty et Fils
+33 (0)5 57 42 10 28

CHÂTEAU CASTENET 86/100

▼♪Vintage 2013 : Brilliant cherry-red. Fairly subdued nose driven by focused redcurrant and cherry. Lively attack leading into an ethereal, well-balanced palate with predominant red fruit. Savoury freshness drives the finish. A successful rosé for pleasure.

Price approx.: 5,80 EUR
Castenet
+33 (0)5 56 61 40 67

CHÂTEAU LAMOUROUX 86/100

▼♪ Vintage 2013 : Light orange hue. Inviting nose driven by citrus and red berry fruits with floral undertones. Very supple, round and fat palate revealing focused, crunchy aromas. A good rosé for pleasure, drinking well at any time of the day.
Price approx.: 9,00 EUR
www.le-grand-enclos.com
Grand Enclos du Château de Cérons
+33 (0)5 56 27 01 53

BORDEAUX SEC

CHÂTEAU THIEULEY 87/100

▼♪Cuvée Francis Courselle 2011 : Fairly deep, brilliant light gold. Subdued nose opening up to notes of almond and hazelnut backed by a hint of spice. Mild attack leading into a delicate, velvety and round mid-palate exuding more of the nose aromas. Crisp finish. Serve with fish.
Price approx.: 8,60 EUR
www.thieuley.com
Vignobles Francis Courselle
+33 (0)5 56 23 00 01

CHÂTEAU THIEULEY 87/100

▼♪Vintage 2013 : Brilliant light yellow with green tints. Delightful nose driven by green grass and white fruits. Well-balanced, supple, full and delicious palate with focused, clear-cut aromas. Intense finish driven by mild spices. A sterling wine.
Price approx.: 6,10 EUR
www.thieuley.com
Vignobles Francis Courselle
+33 (0)5 56 23 00 01

BORDEAUX SUPÉRIEUR

GRAND VIN DE REIGNAC 90/100

▼♪Vintage 2010 : Extremely concentrated black hue. Complex nose of smoky oak with chocolate backed by jammy black fruits. Remarkably intense, silky and supple palate with an aromatic elegance supported by fine-grained tannins. A Bordeaux Supérieur competing with the best.
Price approx.: 22,00 EUR
www.reignac.com
Château de Reignac
+33 (0)5 56 20 41 05

CHÂTEAU FRACHET — 87/100

▼✎ Prestige 2012 : Beautiful deep colour with a youthful sparkle. Refined nose of toasted oak backed by flowers and wild berries. Balanced palate that is not excessively robust due to quality tannins. Expressive fruity and floral perfumes enhanced by oak. A reliable choice.

Price approx.: 8,50 EUR

www.chateaux-en-bordeaux.com

Châteaux en Bordeaux

CHÂTEAU AUX GRAVES DE LA LAURENCE — 87/100

▼✎ Réserve Traditionnelle - élevée en fûts de chêne 2010 : Deep garnet. On the nose, elegant dark fruits, fine spice and subtle oak. Suave attack leading into a very enjoyable full, sappy palate with drive. Silky tannins stay in the wings. Already delicious.

Price approx.: 8,80 EUR

Château Aux Graves de la Laurence

+33 (0)6 82 05 21 94

CHÂTEAU FILLON — 87/100

▼✎ L'Apogée 2010 : Crimson. Concentrated nose displaying focused fruit delicately framed by notes of fresh oak. The palate shows seductive volume and refined, closely-integrated substance. Mouth-filling freshness frames the whole and imparts length. A successful wine.

Price approx.: 7,50 EUR

http://www.bestheim.com

Bestheim

+33 (0)3 89 49 09 29

CHÂTEAU VERMONT — 86/100

▼✎ Prestige 2012 : Deep garnet. Predominant vanilla oak on the nose backed by ripe fruits. Supple palate with fine-grained tannins, beautiful balance, substance and aromas, with fruit still taking a backseat to oak. Racy, needs time for greater enjoyment. Patience!

Price approx.: 6,50 EUR

http://www.chateau-vermont.fr/

Château Vermont

+33 (0)5 56 23 90 16

CHÂTEAU PASCAUD — 86/100

▼✎ Réserve 2010 : Beautiful deep colour, still in its youth. Nose of ripe red fruits coupled with a faint undergrowth tone. Mellow attack on the palate with ripe tannins. Lovely freshness and aromatic intensity with fruit still to the fore.

Price approx.: 6,30 EUR

Château Jalousie Beaulieu

+33 (0)5 57 74 30 13

CHÂTEAU DE L'HERMITAGE — 86/100

▼✎ Vieilli en fût de chêne 2010 : Deep garnet. Racy nose showing refined spice and toast, backed by black fruits. Fullness on the palate, svelte, rich and spicy presence with closely-integrated fine tannins. A convincing generic with a beautiful structure, deserves 3-5 years cellaring.

Price approx.: 7,00 EUR

http://www.chateau-hermitage.com

Vignobles Lopez

+33 (0)5 56 71 57 58

CHÂTEAU LA PEYRÈRE DU TERTRE — 86/100

▼✎ Cuvée Jean 2012 : Deep garnet with purple-blue tints. Racy nose of ripe black fruits with fine spices and beautiful toasted oak in the background. Elegant, harmonious framework on the palate with concentration and refined tannins boding well for the future. Very compelling.

Price approx.: 10,00 EUR

http://www.chateaulapeyrere.com

Château La Peyrère du Tertre

+33 (0)5 56 65 41 86

CHÂTEAU BRAN DE COMPOSTELLE — 86/100

CONV▼✎ Cuvée Louisa 2012 : Fairly deep garnet. Intense, pleasant nose of black fruits (cassis, blackberry) and prunes backed by oak. Supple, velvety and mouth-coating palate with silky tannins balancing the whole. Upfront fruit. Beautiful length. A successful wine.

Price approx.: 5,55 EUR

Vignobles Gagne

+33 (0)5 56 23 98 50

MUSE DE LA FAVIÈRE — 86/100

▼✎ Vintage 2011 : Beautiful young, vibrant red. Nose of red fruits enhanced by more tropical spice and tobacco tones. The same aromatic influence carries through to the palate, generating a faint bitterness. Quite pronounced ageing aromas. Pair with strongly-flavoured food.

Price approx.: 6,00 EUR

http://www.lafaviere.fr

Château La Favière

+33 (0)5 57 49 72 08

CHÂTEAU LA FAVIÈRE — 86/100

▼✎ Intégrale 2011 : Young, vibrant red. The nose is dominated by oak and toast notes with tropical-like scents. The palate displays lovely fullness on the attack. The mid-palate is firmer with more of the pronounced oak influence. An acquired taste.

Price approx.: 35,00 EUR

http://www.lafaviere.fr

Château La Favière

+33 (0)5 57 49 72 08

CHÂTEAU LAMOTHE-VINCENT 86/100

▼.✦ Héritage 2012 : Deep garnet, dark purple tints. Pleasurable nose of morello cherry and blackcurrant backed by toasted oak. Harmonious framework on the palate that is fairly full, suave and framed by some tannins. Vegetal presence on the finish. Needs a little more time.

Price approx.: 7,80 EUR

http://www.lamothe-vincent.com

Château Lamothe-Vincent

+33 (0)5 56 23 96 55

CHÂTEAU LAMOTHE-VINCENT 86/100

▼.✦ Le Grand Rossignol - Les Crus 2011 : Purple-blue hue. Expressive nose of ripe fruits adorned with empyreumatic tones. Compelling. Focused attack on the palate leading into a slightly more oaked mid-palate. Oak is more upfront on the finish although aromas display a degree of purity.

Price approx.: 18,00 EUR

http://www.lamothe-vincent.com

Château Lamothe-Vincent

+33 (0)5 56 23 96 55

CHÂTEAU LAJARRE 86/100

▼.✦ Eléonore 2012 : Deep garnet with dark purple tints. On the nose, morello cherry, redcurrant and toasted oak. Exuberant attack with no sign of shyness. Fresh, full and spicy palate with some supporting tannins. A promising wine that needs a little more bottle time.

Château Lajarre

+33 (0)5 57 40 50 59

CHÂTEAU AUX GRAVES DE LA LAURENCE 86/100

▼.✦ Vintage 2012 : Deep garnet. Pleasant nose of stone fruits and cassis with a toast dimension. Suave attack, seductive, velvety and rich palate showing a lovely harmonious impression. Very elegant tannins frame the whole. An expertly crafted generic, already enjoyable now.

Price approx.: 5,40 EUR

Château Aux Graves de la Laurence

+33 (0)6 82 05 21 94

CHÂTEAU AUX GRAVES DE LA LAURENCE 86/100

▼.✦ Réserve Traditionnelle - élevée en fûts de chêne 2011 : Beautiful deep garnet. Alluring nose blending red and black fruits (cassis, blackberry) with oak, liquorice and spice notes. Generous, velvety attack with upfront tannins, a touch of freshness and a slightly lean finish. Drink with barbecued foods.

Price approx.: 8,60 EUR

Château Aux Graves de la Laurence

+33 (0)6 82 05 21 94

CHÂTEAU PRIEURÉ MARQUET 86/100

▼.✦ Vintage 2012 : Dark garnet with youthful highlights. Cherry, refined spices and a floral note on the nose. Supple attack, lovely full, nervy, fresh substance with a welcome likeability. Vegetal component on the finish. Nicely crafted across the palate.

Price approx.: 6,50 EUR

Château Prieuré Marquet

+33 (0)6 07 88 05 81

CHÂTEAU SERCILLAN 86/100

▼.✦ Vintage 2010 : Deep crimson with a beautiful sparkle. Focused, profound nose with precise aromas of ripe black fruits and subtle liquorice notes. Remarkably melted, full palate with polished, closely-integrated tannins and evident fruit. A nicely-crafted Bordeaux supéri.

Price approx.: 5,50 EUR

Château Majureau

+33 (0)5 57 43 00 25

CHÂTEAU FILLON 86/100

▼.✦ Cuvée Première 2010 : Attractive deep garnet. Focused nose revealing a harmonious blend of black fruit and oak. Generous attack, tightly-wound, polished and well-integrated texture. Long-lasting fruit supported by freshness. A handsome wine.

Price approx.: 5,95 EUR

http://www.bestheim.com

Bestheim

+33 (0)3 89 49 09 29

CHÂTEAU CASTENET 86/100

▼.✦ Vintage 2010 : Beautiful garnet red. Distinctive nose halfway between vegetal aromas and ripe red and black fruits. Refined tannins imparting a very supple mouthfeel coupled with focused fruit and freshness. A good Bordeaux in a good vintage.

Price approx.: 7,60 EUR

Castenet

+33 (0)5 56 61 40 67

CHÂTEAU CAP DE FER 85/100

▼.✦ Vintage 2010 : Attractive garnet with faint bricking. Profound nose opening up gradually to notes of red and black fruits with delicate spice touches. Pleasant attack on the palate, fairly refined tannins and a freshness that enhances focused fruit.

Price approx.: 6,50 EUR

Domaines Jean Guillot

+33 (0)6 07 31 79 22

> Detailed instructions are featured at
>
> the start of the book.

CHÂTEAU PASCAUD 85/100

▼♪ Vintage 2010 : Deeply-coloured with pronounced mature highlights. Mature nose of jammy fruits backed by undergrowth. A nicely open wine offering up fruit and freshness thanks to welcome supple tannins. Drink now with roast beef.
Price approx.: 4,50 EUR
Château Jalousie Beaulieu
+33 (0)5 57 74 30 13

CHÂTEAU DE L'HERMITAGE 85/100

▼♪ Vintage 2011 : Fairly deep garnet. Expressive nose of black cherry, fine spices and a touch of truffle. Harmonious, full, suave and spicy palate supported by a robust structure which dominates on the finish. Everything is in place, patience is required.
Price approx.: 5,00 EUR
http://www.chateau-hermitage.com
Vignobles Lopez
+33 (0)5 56 71 57 58

CHÂTEAU LA FAVIÈRE 85/100

▼♪ Vintage 2011 : Beautiful red tinged with purple-blue. Nose of black fruits coupled with tones of cocoa and toast. Same personality on the palate which offers up quite a lot of substance. A balanced wine with a very unusual range of aromatics.
Price approx.: 11,00 EUR
http://www.lafaviere.fr
Château La Favière
+33 (0)5 57 49 72 08

CHÂTEAU LA TUILERIE DU PUY 85/100

▼♪ Cuvée Grand Chêne 2012 : Concentrated hue with dark purple tints. Nose of refined toasted oak backed by red and black fruits. Supple palate with tannins and oak that are already mellow with focused fruit presence. A racy Bordeaux calling for barbecued foods.
Price approx.: 7,90 EUR
Château la Tuilerie du Puy
+33 (0)5 56 61 61 92

CHÂTEAU D'ABZAC 85/100

▼♪ Elevé en fût de chêne 2011 : Intense garnet showing faint bricking. Promising nose of coffee, mild spices and toast notes. Elegant, lively palate with exuberant aromas mirroring the nose and supported by fine, closely-integrated tannins. An ambitious generic that is already delicious
Price approx.: 7,00 EUR
http://www.chateau-abzac.com
Château d'Abzac
+33 (0)5 57 49 32 82

CHÂTEAU MAISON NOBLE ST-MARTIN 85/100

▼♪ Vintage 2012 : Beautiful dark, young garnet. Compelling nose with toast and roasted coffee backed by dark fruits. A charming wine on the palate boasting a full, ripe and succulent mouthfeel with spice. A robust structure directs the finish. Patience!
Price approx.: 8,00 EUR
http://www.chateaumaisonnoble.com
Château Maison Noble Saint Martin
+33 (0)5 56 71 86 53

CHÂTEAU LESTRILLE CAPMARTIN 85/100

▼♪ Vintage 2010 : Beautiful dark garnet. Expressive nose of overripe black fruits with some mild spices. Velvety, full and invigorating palate showing spice. Exuberance marks the finish. A good traditional wine that will become more harmonious with bottle age.
Price approx.: 7,70 EUR
http://www.lestrille.com
Jean-Louis Roumage
+33 (0)5 57 24 51 02

CHÂTEAU GARON LA TUILIÈRE 84/100

▼♪ Vintage 2013 : Deeply-coloured garnet. Intense nose driven by cassis, blackberry and redcurrant with a dash of spice. Well-balanced palate with ripe tannins. Lovely focused fruit, freshness and length. Drinking well now or suitable for cellaring. Pair with lamb chops.
Price approx.: 6,50 EUR
http://www.chateau-darzac.Com
Vignobles Claude Barthe
+33 (0)5 57 84 55 04

CHÂTEAU DARZAC 84/100

▼♪ Vintage 2013 : Young-looking dark purple. Classic nose of red and black berry fruits. The nose aromatics carry through to the palate and are supple, long and fresh. Youthful firmness on the finish. Would work with all types of red meat.
Price approx.: 6,50 EUR
http://www.chateau-darzac.Com
Vignobles Claude Barthe
+33 (0)5 57 84 55 04

CHÂTEAU LESPARRE 84/100

▼♪ Vintage 2012 : Medium intense garnet. Mature nose revealing aromas of undergrowth (damp earth) with a whiff of smoke. A supple, mellow wine on the palate with light tannins. Harmonious, perfumed and persistent. Drink with red meats.
Price approx.: 7,00 EUR
http://www.chateaulesparre.com
Michel Gonet et Fils
+33 (0)5 57 24 51 23

CHÂTEAU LAFITE MONTEIL 84/100

▼.'Vintage 2010 : Beautiful ruby-red. Fairly subdued nose opening up after swirling to a compromise between ripe fruit and oak. On the palate, a reserved, mellow style on the attack, then becoming firmer though with increasingly intense fruit expression. Still some potenti

Price approx.: 8,00 EUR

http://www.chateau-lafite-monteil.com

Château Lafite Monteil

+33 (0)5 40 12 93 95

CHÂTEAU HAUT LANDON 84/100

▼.'Vintage 2012 : Deeply-coloured garnet. Focused nose of ripe red and black fruits with spicy undercurrents. Balance, refined, polished tannins and fruit presence. A Bordeaux showing good suppleness. Grilled lamb chops would seem to be the perfect partner.

Price approx.: 5,00 EUR

http://www.grandmoulin.com

Robin

+33 (0)5 57 32 62 06

CHÂTEAU DE RIBEBON 84/100

▼.'Vintage 2011 : Garnet, ruby tints. Endearing nose of ripe red fruits, vegetal aromas and earthy undertones. Fruit-driven attack, supple, full and concentrated palate. Beautiful freshness, tightly-wound tannins. Fairly clean, tannic finish. A Bordeaux supérieur drinking

Price approx.: 10,00 EUR

Vignobles Aubert

+33 (0)5 57 40 04 30

CHÂTEAU LES GRAVIÈRES DE LA BRANDILLE
84/100

▼.' Cuvée Prestige 2011 : Deeply-coloured young red. The nose is fairly dashing, marrying red fruits and oak notes. Round and fresh at point of entry showing fruit expression. The mid-palate and finish are firmer with a more pronounced oak presence.

Price approx.: 10,00 EUR

Vignobles Borderie

+33 (0)5 57 69 83 01

CHÂTEAU HAUT POUGNAN 84/100

▼.' Cuvée Prestige - élevée en fûts de chêne 2012 : Clean, fairly deeply-coloured red. Subdued nose opening up to mineral and smoke notes. The palate is robust and fairly powerful yet shows focused aromatic expression displaying both red fruit and liquorice.

Price approx.: 5,50 EUR

http://www.haut-pougnan.fr

Château Haut Pougnan

+33 (0)5 56 23 06 00

CHÂTEAU LES MOUTINS 84/100

▼.' Vintage 2012 : Beautiful vibrant red. Very enticing, expressive nose driven by ripe red fruit. The palate is supple and melted with polished tannins. Freshness and fruit are also present. A seductive wine ready to drink now.

Price approx.: 5,50 EUR

http://www.haut-pougnan.fr

Château Haut Pougnan

+33 (0)5 56 23 06 00

CHÂTEAU L'ESCART 84/100

Org▼.' Cuvée Eden 2012 : Beautiful deeply-coloured, young red. The nose displays red fruit and mild spice tones. The same aromas recur on the palate where oak plays a substantial part. Well-balanced throughout but in an international style.

Price approx.: 9,00 EUR

Château l'Escart

+33 (0)5 56 77 53 19

CHÂTEAU BOIS DE FAVEREAU 83/100

▼.' Cuvée Jean-Jules 2012 : Deeply-coloured garnet. Smoky oak on the nose with ripe red and black fruits. The palate is supple at point of entry despite upfront tannins. The finish shows more of the fruit. Would work well with rib-eye steak. Has the potential to soften more.

Price approx.: 5,50 EUR

http://www.mortier.com

J.J Mortier et Cie

CHÂTEAU LAFITE MONTEIL 83/100

▼.' Vintage 2011 : Fairly deep garnet. Subdued nose showing spice notes, black fruits and oak presence. The palate is clearly-defined, fresh and nervy with honest aromatic expression. The vegetal component makes the finish a tad bitter but that will change with time.

Price approx.: 8,00 EUR

Château Lafite Monteil

+33 (0)5 40 12 93 95

CHÂTEAU HAUT LANDON 83/100

▼.'Vintage 2013 : Dark purple. Nose of black fruits and stone fruits. Supple attack marked by a youthful exuberance leading into a mid-palate driven by freshness and fruit. A classic wine that needs a few more months in bottle for full enjoyment. A Bordeaux for barbecues.

Price approx.: 5,00 EUR

http://www.grandmoulin.com

Robin

+33 (0)5 57 32 62 06

ARNOZAN 83/100

▼.✦Réserve des Chartrons Elevé en Fûts de chêne 2012 : Deeply-coloured ruby. Expressive nose of stewed red berry fruits. Supple, seductive palate dominated by fruit. Evident, tightly-wound tannins. Firm, vegetal finish. Classic in style. A Bordeaux supérieur pairing with red meats.
Price approx.: 4,90 EUR
http://www.producta.com
Producta Vignobles
+33 (0)5 57 81 18 18

CHÂTEAU DE RIBEBON 83/100

▼.✦Vintage 2012 : Deep garnet with ruby highlights. Aromatic nose driven by red berry fruits, animal notes (leather) and undergrowth. The palate shows seductive fruit, polished tannins, beautiful concentration and balance. Forthright, spicy finish. Drink with red meats.
Price approx.: 10,00 EUR
Vignobles Aubert
+33 (0)5 57 40 04 30

CHÂTEAU L'ESCART 83/100

Org▼.✦ O. Khayam 2012 : Dark hued with purple-blue highlights. Extremely heady nose of cherries in brandy. Powerful at point of entry with prominent tannins. The generous nose aromas follow through. A Bordeaux with a real sense of place that works best with food.
Price approx.: 15,00 EUR
Château l'Escart
+33 (0)5 56 77 53 19

CHATEAU HAUT CRUZEAU 83/100

▼.✦ Vintage 2011 : Clean red. Nose of ripe red fruits with a touch of fruits in brandy. On the palate, a clean, fruity wine with an assertive character. Suppleness and aromatic honesty are key themes on the palate.
Price approx.: 9,00 EUR
http://www.regis-chevalier.com
Château Haut Cruzeau
+33 (0)5 56 21 11 11

CHÂTEAU CAP DE FER 83/100

▼.✦ Vintage 2009 : Beautiful clean, slightly mature red. Evolved nose of ripe red fruits with a faint jammy touch. A degree of power and evident tannins on the palate with ultra ripe fruit aromatics. A wine at maturity pairing with red meats.
Price approx.: 6,20 EUR
Domaines Jean Guillot
+33 (0)6 07 31 79 22

LESTONNAT 82/100

▼.✦ Merlot Cabernet Sauvignon 2012 : Intense garnet with purple-blue tints. Expressive nose dominated by finely toasted oak. Oak influence stays to the fore on the palate. Fresh, svelte and spicy with a fine-grained tannin framework. Keep for a few years.
Price approx.: 6,00 EUR
http://lestonnat.com
Lestonnat
+33 (0)7 86 72 60 40

CHÂTEAU SERCILLAN 82/100

▼.✦ Vintage 2013 : Beautiful vibrant red. Honest nose showing suggestions of cherries in brandy. Supple structure on the palate with ripe, mellow tannins. More of the cherries in brandy aromas on the finish. A simple, honest and accessible wine.
Price approx.: 6,00 EUR
Château Majureau
+33 (0)5 57 43 00 25

CHÂTEAU CASTENET 82/100

▼.✦ Vintage 2012 : Deeply-coloured young garnet. Vanilla oak dominates on the nose backed by ripe red and black fruits. Very supple palate showing a low level of concentration. Oak combines with the fruit. A classic Bordeaux Supérieur, ready to drink now.
Price approx.: 7,70 EUR
Castenet
+33 (0)5 56 61 40 67

CHÂTEAU VRAI CAILLOU 82/100

▼.✦Vintage 2011 : Deeply-coloured garnet. Pleasurable, open nose driven by black fruits and spice. Supple, harmonious and mellow attack, again driven by fruit leading into a forthright, spicy mid-palate capped off with a hint of bitterness. Pair with grilled meats.
Price approx.: 5,50 EUR
GFA des Pommier
+33 (0)5 56 61 31 56

CHÂTEAU DE RIBEBON 82/100

▼.✦Vintage 2013 : Fairly deep garnet with youthful tints. Expressive nose of ripe, dark fruits backed by undergrowth. Supple, fruit-driven palate with tightly-wound tannins. Smooth, well-balanced mouthfeel. Fairly forthright finish with fruit petering out slightly. Keep.
Price approx.: 10,00 EUR
Vignobles Aubert
+33 (0)5 57 40 04 30

CHÂTEAU LES GRAVIÈRES DE LA BRANDILLE
79/100

▼♪ Vintage 2011 : Deeply-coloured young red. Ripe nose marrying red fruit notes and a vegetal touch. The palate is supple, melted and shows more of the same, fairly rustic aromatic range.
Price approx.: 6,00 EUR
Vignobles Borderie
+33 (0)5 57 69 83 01

CHÂTEAU CASTENET
78/100

▼♪ Vintage 2011 : Deeply-coloured garnet. Mellow oak on the nose yet the fruit is quite reticent. Lightweight concentration on the palate, fairly fluid mouthfeel and fruit that lacks vibrancy. Drink now.
Price approx.: 7,70 EUR
Castenet
+33 (0)5 56 61 40 67

BORDEAUX

CHÂTEAU LAMOTHE-VINCENT
88/100

▼♪ Intense 2013 : Light gold with green tints. Distinctive, intense nose driven by citrus, peach and tropical fruits. Mellow attack leading into a rich, velvety palate with clear-cut aromas. Elegant and well-balanced. Enjoyable with a seafood platter.
Price approx.: 6,50 EUR
http://www.lamothe-vincent.com
Château Lamothe-Vincent
+33 (0)5 56 23 96 55

CHATEAU MARJOSSE
88/100

▼♪ Vintage 2012 : Deep garnet. Expressive nose with aromas of cassis, blackberry and fine oak undertones. Beautiful clean, enjoyable, harmonious and easy-drinking attack revealing seductive freshness and silky tannins. Firm trace on the finish. Successful, promising, will.
Price approx.: 9,60 EUR
Château Marjosse
+33 (0)5 57 55 57 80

CHÂTEAU BELLE-GARDE
88/100

▼♪ Cuvée élevée en fûts de chêne 2012 : Deep, young colour. Complex floral nose with black fruits backed by toasted, spicy oak. Full, elegant, powerful wine. Impeccable balance between fruit and oak, both of which fit nicely into the palate. A successful offering.
Price approx.: 6,50 EUR
www.vignobles-ericduffau.com
Vignobles Eric Duffau
+33 (0)5 57 24 49 12

CHÂTEAU HAUT VIEUX CHÊNE
87/100

▼♪ Vintage 2013 : Deep garnet with dark purple tints. Intense fruity nose of cassis, blackberry and raspberry with spice notes in the background. A powerful, warm style on the palate with evident, tightly-wound tannins. Balance, freshness and lovey aroma. A successful wine
Price approx.: 5,00 EUR
http://www.grandmoulin.com
Robin
+33 (0)5 57 32 62 06

CHÂTEAU LAMOTHE-VINCENT
87/100

▼♪ Vintage 2013 : Brilliant light gold. Heady nose of citrus, white flowers and tropical fruits. Round, supple, fleshy and mouth-coating palate with the same aromas carrying through. Lovely fat and persistent finish driven by toast notes. Serve with fine fish.
Price approx.: 5,00 EUR
http://www.lamothe-vincent.com
Château Lamothe-Vincent
+33 (0)5 56 23 96 55

CHÂTEAU LAMOTHE-VINCENT
87/100

▼♪ Héritage 2013 : Brilliant light yellow. Pleasant nose driven by grapefruit and blackcurrant bud. Lively attack, supple, round, full and powerful palate with aroma to the fore. Persistent fresh finish. Harmonious. Drink with fish in a sauce.
Price approx.: 7,50 EUR
http://www.lamothe-vincent.com
Château Lamothe-Vincent
+33 (0)5 56 23 96 55

CHÂTEAU DE PERRE
86/100

▼♪ Vintage 2013 : Limpid, pale gold. Expressive nose halfway between pear and citrus notes and floral perfumes (boxwood, blackcurrant bud). Beautiful freshness at point of entry. Perfume has already been released and coats the palate. An instantly enjoyable Sauvignon.
Price approx.: 4,00 EUR
www.vignobles-mayle.com
Château de Perre
+33 (0)5 56 62 83 31

CHÂTEAU ROQUE-PEYRE
86/100

▼♪ Vintage 2011 : Beautifully youthful colour. Nose of crunchy cassis, blackberry and raspberry. A supple Bordeaux with fine-grained tannins underscoring a very drinkable array of fruit aromatics. Its generous aromas make it a good partner for lamb chops. A good Bordeaux.
Price approx.: 5,50 EUR
Vignobles Vallette
+33 (0)5 53 24 77 98

MENUTS 86/100

▼✔ Vintage 2011 : Beautiful deeply-coloured red. Profound nose of ripe cherry with morello cherry. Pleasant, fleshy attack on the palate with a delightful array of ripe fruit aromatics. Mellow mid-palate and very harmonious finish.
Price approx.: 8,00 EUR
http://www.maisonriviere.fr
Maison Rivière
+33 (0)5 57 55 59 59

CHÂTEAU SAINTE BARBE 86/100

▼✔ Merlot 2011 : Beautiful vibrant red. Pleasant nose marrying fruit and spice with a mineral touch in the background. Supple tannins on the palate with savoury freshness and ripe, persistent fruit. A lovely, very distinctive wine.
Price approx.: 5,50 EUR
http://www.chateausaintebarbe.com
Château Sainte Barbe
+33 (0)5 56 77 49 57

CHÂTEAU VERMONT 85/100

▼✔ Vintage 2013 : Deeply-coloured dark purple. Fruit-driven nose showing cassis, raspberry and redcurrant. Well-balanced palate with tannin presence not obscuring fruit expression. A classic, well-made Bordeaux that needs a little more bottle time. Recommended for ribsteak
Price approx.: 5,50 EUR
Château Vermont
+33 (0)5 56 23 90 16

CHÂTEAU JULIAN 85/100

▼✔ Vintage 2013 : Brilliant pale gold. Lovely tropical nose coupled with floral notes. Impeccable acidity coats the palate along with crunchy tropical flavours. Gets the taste buds racing. A very good introductory wine.
Price approx.: 5,50 EUR
www.vignobles-dulon.com
Dulon
+33 (0)5 56 23 69 16

CHÂTEAU LAGRUGÈRE 85/100

Org▼✔ l'Essentiel 2013 : Vibrant red with cherry-red tints. Seductive nose reminiscent of cherry and peony. Supple attack, lovely succulence on the palate, impression of lightness, emergence of a nicely proportioned structure though a tad angular. Cellaring should sort it out.
Price approx.: 5,00 EUR
http://www.chateau-hermitage.com
Vignobles Lopez
+33 (0)5 56 71 57 58

LA CHAPELLE DE BORDEAUX 85/100

▼✔ Vintage 2012 : Intense, young-looking garnet. Medium focus on the nose with aromas of redcurrant, cassis and fine spices after swirling. Very light, tense palate showing a natural impression. Finesse is the key theme. A real treat that we recommend.
Price approx.: 6,50 EUR
Direct Wines Le Chai au Quai
+33 (0)5 57 40 13 31

LA CROIX DE BORDEAUX 85/100

▼✔ Vintage 2012 : Deep garnet with dark purple tints. Promising nose of cherry, redcurrant and spice touches. Suave attack leading into an easy-drinking, full and nervy palate perfumed with lovely clean, honest aromas. Hint of firmness on the finish. A convincing generic.
Price approx.: 6,50 EUR
Direct Wines Le Chai au Quai
+33 (0)5 57 40 13 31

CHÂTEAU FAYAU 85/100

▼✔ Vintage 2013 : Pale gold. Highly perfumed nose of pineapple and pink grapefruit with a lovely floral presence. An easy-drinking Bordeaux for quaffing showing seductive honesty and fresh aromas. Ideal for the aperitif and nibbles.
Price approx.: 4,50 EUR
http://www.medeville.com
Jean Médeville et Fils
+33 (0)5 57 98 08 08

CHÂTEAU GABELOT 85/100

▼✔ Elevé en fûts de chêne 2012 : Deep colour, dark purple tints. Nose of refined toasted oak backed by black fruits. Silky texture on the palate with oak that doesn't obscure the fruit and polished tannins. Generous aromatics that will become more extensive over time. A good Bordeaux.
Price approx.: 4,50 EUR
http://www.medeville.com
Jean Médeville et Fils
+33 (0)5 57 98 08 08

CHÂTEAU SAINT-GENÈS 85/100

▼✔ Vintage 2011 : Crimson with garnet. Endearing nose of heady oak backed by ripe red and black fruits. The palate is chewy and boasts upfront spicy oak tannins. Fruit contemplates the whole. A good Bordeaux that should preferably be given a little more bottle time.
Price approx.: 5,50 EUR
www.thieuley.com
Vignobles Francis Courselle
+33 (0)5 56 23 00 01

CHÂTEAU BELLE-GARDE 85/100

▼♪ Vintage 2012 : Young ruby. Enticing nose of peony and violet with raspberry and blackberry undercurrents. The palate is nicely balanced by ripe, fine-grained tannins. Beautiful fruit presence, length and personality. A very dashing, enjoyable Bordeaux for red meats.
Price approx.: 5,00 EUR
www.vignobles-ericduffau.com
Vignobles Eric Duffau
+33 (0)5 57 24 49 12

LA PERLE DU VALLIER 85/100

▼♪ Vintage 2012 : Limpid pale gold. Delicate nose blending white fruit notes and toasted tones. Fresh at point of entry leading into a powerful, rich mid-palate revealing more of the same aromatic spectrum. A heady, food-friendly style for fish.
Price approx.: 7,10 EUR
www.vignobles-dulon.com
Dulon
+33 (0)5 56 23 69 16

CHÂTEAU PENIN 85/100

▼♪ Grande Sélection 2011 : Garnet. Nose of slightly jammy ripe red fruits with a hint of spice. Fairly fresh, aromatic attack flowing into a firmer mid-palate. Fruit and spice expression on the finish. A generous, food-friendly style.
Price approx.: 9,50 EUR
http://www.chateaupenin.com
Vignobles Carteyron
+33 (0)5 57 24 46 98

CHÂTEAU DE HARTES 85/100

▼♪ Vintage 2013 : Deeply-coloured with purple-blue tints. Fairly muted nose of black fruits. Wonderful ample, fruity attack. Highly perfumed middle palate with accents of black fruits and liquorice candy. Fresh, easy-drinking finish revealing more of the same aromatics.
Price approx.: 5,00 EUR
http://www.toutigeac.com
Château Toutigeac
+33 (0)5 56 23 90 10

CHÂTEAU FONTBONNE 84/100

▼♪ Vintage 2012 : Attractive colour with garnet tints. Endearing nose with red fruit aromas enhanced by a pleasant vegetal and spice dimension. Suppleness and roundness are key qualities on the palate. A generous, perfumed Bordeaux showing more of the spice dimension.
Price approx.: 5,10 EUR
Château Fontbonne
+33 (0)5 56 23 49 36

CHÂTEAU HAUT BARAILLOT 84/100

▼♪ Vintage 2013 : Deeply-coloured garnet. Vanilla-infused nose with fresh red and black fruits. Well-balanced palate with fine-grained tannins, unobtrusive oak presence and strong fruit development. A structured Bordeaux with the potential for greater fruit expression.
Price approx.: 5,50 EUR
Château Vermont
+33 (0)5 56 23 90 16

CHÂTEAU GRAND JEAN 84/100

▼♪ Vintage 2013 : Pale gold. Distinctive nose suggestive of boxwood, blackcurrant bud and pink grapefruit. Fresh, crisp attack leading into a more supple mid-palate with focused, crunchy fruit. A good white for shellfish, drinking best whilst still young.
Price approx.: 5,50 EUR
www.vignobles-dulon.com
Dulon
+33 (0)5 56 23 69 16

CUVÉE LUMINE 84/100

CONV▼♪ Vintage 2013 : Limpid garnet. Pleasurable nose of red and black cherries with lovely floral scents. Supple attack, clean, light and fairly round palate with refined spice, enhanced by subtle oak. Hint of firmness, spice-infused finish. A successful generic.
Price approx.: 4,00 EUR
http://www.chateau-hermitage.com
Vignobles Lopez
+33 (0)5 56 71 57 58

CATHERINE LUCAS 84/100

▼♪ Vintage 2013 : Brilliant light yellow with green tints. Expressive nose of tropical and white-fleshed fruits with a vanilla note. Round attack leading into a fresh, velvety and mellow palate showing medium concentration, balance and oak enhancing the fruit.
Price approx.: 8,00 EUR
http://www.chateaulapeyrere.com
Château La Peyrère du Tertre
+33 (0)5 56 65 41 86

CHÂTEAU BRAN DE COMPOSTELLE 84/100

CONV▼♪ Vintage 2012 : Crimson with garnet. Ripe nose showing a predominant ripe red and black fruit streak with a floral and spice presence. Well-balanced palate with ripe, mellow tannins and a lovely show of fruit. A classic, well-made Bordeaux, perfect for red meat.
Price approx.: 4,30 EUR
Vignobles Gagne
+33 (0)5 56 23 98 50

BARTON & GUESTIER — 84/100

▼♪ Passeport 2012 : Fairly young, vibrant red. Generous nose of stone fruits. More of the same aromatics on the palate which shows lovely fine-grained tannins and balance. Fruit undertones flow into a delicate oak and mineral tone.
Price approx.: 10,00 EUR
http://www.barton-guestier.com
Barton & Guestier
+33 (0)5 56 95 48 00

DOMAINE DU BALLAT — 84/100

▼♪ Vintage 2011 : Slightly mature, intense garnet. Pleasant nose of plum, cassis, some spice and a toast note. Lovely mellow, suave presence, light on the palate. An invigorating, easy-drinking wine with lovely honest aromas and a hint of firmness on the finish. Good.
Price approx.: 3,90 EUR
Domaine du Ballat
+33 (0)5 56 76 41 33

CHÂTEAU DE BON AMI — 84/100

▼♪ Cuvée Tradition 2012 : Quite deep, young colour. Fruit-driven nose of cassis, raspberry and blackberry. Fairly fleshy, well-balanced palate with fruit overtones. A nicely crafted Bordeaux, ready to drink now with grilled meats.
Price approx.: 5,95 EUR
Château la Tuilerie du Puy
+33 (0)5 56 61 61 92

CHÂTEAU LE GRAND MOULIN — 84/100

▼♪ Vintage 2013 : Pale orange. Endearing nose driven by sugar-coated almonds and red berry fruits. Quite a delightful, round and supple palate with a welcome freshness. Focused fruit. Would work equally well as an appetiser or with barbecued foods.
Price approx.: 4,50 EUR
http://www.grandmoulin.com
Robin
+33 (0)5 57 32 62 06

CHÂTEAU MOULIN DE VIGNOLLE — 84/100

▼♪ Vintage 2013 : Light yellow. The nose is predominantly floral with aromas of boxwood and blackcurrant bud backed by grapefruit and pineapple. Beautiful exuberance from point of entry, focused Sauvignon aromas, substance and freshness. A good white to kick off a meal.
Price approx.: 4,50 EUR
http://www.grandmoulin.com
Robin
+33 (0)5 57 32 62 06

CHÂTEAU JEAN DE BEL AIR — 84/100

▼♪ Vintage 2012 : Appealing deep garnet. Endearing nose of stone fruits, mild spices and lovely toasted oak. Supple attack, velvety, full and fresh palate that leaves a good impression. Spicy, firm and vegetal finish that needs time to achieve greater harmony.
Price approx.: 7,60 EUR
http://www.chateaumaisonnoble.com
Château Maison Noble Saint Martin
+33 (0)5 56 71 86 53

CHÂTEAU PENIN — 84/100

▼♪ Natur 2012 : Young garnet with purple-blue. Focused fruity nose faintly reminiscent of ripe redcurrant. Fresh, fruity attack on the palate leading into a more tannic mid-palate. The fruit is tinged with notes of liquorice. A fairly traditional style.
Price approx.: 8,10 EUR
http://www.chateaupenin.com
Vignobles Carteyron
+33 (0)5 57 24 46 98

CHÂTEAU FONDARZAC — 83/100

▼♪ Vintage 2013 : Young dark purple. Appealing fruit-driven nose of redcurrant, raspberry and blackberry backed by spice and smoke. More of the predominant fruit aromas on the palate. Very supple and crunchy. An enjoyable Bordeaux, drinking well whilst young and fruit forw.
Price approx.: 4,90 EUR
http://www.chateau-darzac.Com
Vignobles Claude Barthe
+33 (0)5 57 84 55 04

CHÂTEAU PRADEAU - MAZEAU — 83/100

▼♪ Vintage 2013 : Pretty garnet and dark purple. Endearing, fruit-driven nose with a slightly spicy floral dimension. Supple, perfumed and well-balanced palate. A classic, likeable Bordeaux pairing with red meats.
Price approx.: 5,00 EUR
http://www.toutigeac.com
Château Toutigeac
+33 (0)5 56 23 90 10

CHÂTEAU TOUTIGEAC — 83/100

▼♪ Vintage 2013 : Attractive dark purple. Delightful young nose showing floral and fruity perfumes. Lovely supple, mellow palate. A Bordeaux that is polished yet fresh. Enjoy with white meats.
Price approx.: 5,00 EUR
http://www.toutigeac.com
Château Toutigeac
+33 (0)5 56 23 90 10

CLOSERIE SAINT - VINCENT 83/100

▼ Grand Pavillon 2013 : Pale yellow with green tints. Distinctive nose marrying grapefruit with some floral notes. Lively attack leading into a supple, full palate showing beautiful freshness. Somewhat hot on the finish. Drink with oily fish.
Price approx.: 5,00 EUR
http://www.grandmoulin.com
Robin
+33 (0)5 57 32 62 06

FRENCH CELLARS 83/100

▼ Merlot - Cabernet sauvignon 2012 : Deeply-coloured garnet. Nose of red and black fruits with vegetal undertones. The palate offers up lovely uplifting fruit, mellow tannins and freshness. A well-made Bordeaux that is already accessible. Perfect for a kebab party.
Price approx.: 3,25 EUR
http://www.winesoverland.com
Wines Overland

MEYBLUM & FILS 83/100

▼ Vintage 2012 : Young, dark purple. Fruit-driven nose showing raspberry, strawberry and blackcurrant. A soft Bordeaux with lightweight concentration, offering up a lovely fruity freshness. Perfect from now on.
Price approx.: 7,50 EUR
http://www.meyblum-et-fils.com
MVP Wines

CHÂTEAU LE TRÉBUCHET 83/100

▼ Vintage 2011 : Faintly mature red. Nose of ripe red fruits coupled with a slightly smoky tone. A full, fleshy wine with crunchy fruit aromas. The finish is a little firmer but stays balanced. Drink from now on.
Price approx.: 6,00 EUR
Vignobles Berger
+33 (0)5 56 71 42 28

DOMAINE DU BALLAT 83/100

▼ Vintage 2012 : Deep garnet. Expressive nose intermixing redcurrant and cassis. On the palate, a supple, likeable, light and fruity wine showing a skilful blend of fruits and spices with vegetal undertones. A simple Bordeaux for enjoying with the family.
Price approx.: 3,90 EUR
Domaine du Ballat
+33 (0)5 56 76 41 33

CHÂTEAU LA GRAVE PEYNET 83/100

▼ Vintage 2011 : Intense garnet. Fairly subdued nose of stone fruits with a toast note. Quite full, well-

balanced and nervy palate perfumed with delightful focused, honest aromas. What more could you ask for? Needs to gain a little more harmony.
Price approx.: 3,90 EUR
Domaine du Ballat
+33 (0)5 56 76 41 33

CHÂTEAU LES FERMENTEAUX 83/100

▼ Vintage 2013 : Beautifully young colour. Subtly fruity and floral nose. Very supple palate showing a seductive youthfulness, freshness and fruit. A classic, well-made Bordeaux.
Price approx.: 5,00 EUR
http://www.grandmoulin.com
Robin
+33 (0)5 57 32 62 06

CHÂTEAU LA GRAVE PEYNET 83/100

▼ Vintage 2013 : Deep, young-looking garnet. Expressive nose of stone fruits and black berries with a spice note. A wine with real drive on the palate displaying a degree of density and lovely aromatic honesty. Firm finish. A well-made generic. Keep for a while.
Price approx.: 3,90 EUR
Domaine du Ballat
+33 (0)5 56 76 41 33

CHATEAU DU CROS 83/100

▼ Vintage 2013 : Pale gold. Expressive nose reminiscent of boxwood, nettle and citrus flowing into a tropical touch of pineapple after swirling. Very fresh, fragrant attack leading into a more forthright mid-palate. A simple, pleasant Sauvignon drinking best in its youth.
Price approx.: 6,70 EUR
http://www.chateauducros.com
Vignobles Boyer
+33 (0)5 56 62 99 31

CHÂTEAU LES MOUTINS 83/100

▼ Vintage 2013 : Pale yellow with green tints. Distinctive nose showing accents of white flowers and meadow. A very pleasant, vibrant and crisp style on the palate. Its freshness makes it a good companion for a seafood platter.
Price approx.: 5,00 EUR
http://www.haut-pougnan.fr
Château Haut Pougnan
+33 (0)5 56 23 06 00

Prices mentioned in this book are guideline and can vary depending on point of sale. The shops, wineries or publisher can in no way be held responsible for this.

CHÂTEAU SAINTE BARBE 83/100

▼♪ Vintage 2011 : Beautiful, fairly deep, vibrant red. The nose shows pronounced, yet beautiful quality oak. More of the same on the palate where fruit is still slightly backward and oak takes up the vacant space. An oaked style showing no sense of place.
Price approx.: 9,60 EUR
http://www.chateausaintebarbe.com
Château Sainte Barbe
+33 (0)5 56 77 49 57

CHÂTEAU PRADEAU-MAZEAU 83/100

▼♪ Vintage 2012 : Dark hue with purple-blue tints. Concentrated nose of black fruits. On the palate, supple attack with polished tannins. Upfront fruit with delicate spice in the background. A well-balanced, accessible style that would work well with barbecues.
Price approx.: 4,50 EUR
http://www.toutigeac.com
Château Toutigeac
+33 (0)5 56 23 90 10

CHÂTEAU DE PERRE 82/100

▼♪ Vintage 2013 : Young garnet. Compelling, fruit-driven nose with reducurrant, blackberry and raspberry. A Bordeaux showing lovely suppleness, mellow tannins and focused fruit, pairing well with flank steak.
Price approx.: 4,00 EUR
www.vignobles-mayle.com
Château de Perre
+33 (0)5 56 62 83 31

CHÂTEAU FAYAU 82/100

▼♪ Vintage 2013 : Deep garnet with dark purple tints. Pleasant nose intermixing refined spice, flowers and ripe cassis and black cherry. Supple attack, lovely, closely-integrated, round presence. Harmonious framework, hint of firmness on the finish. An enjoyable wine.
Price approx.: 4,50 EUR
http://www.medeville.com
Jean Médeville et Fils
+33 (0)5 57 98 08 08

CHÂTEAU HAUT CORMIER 82/100

▼♪ Vintage 2013 : Deeply-coloured with dark purple tints. Subtle fruit on the nose (blackcurrant, raspberry). A supple, soft, fresh and well-balanced Bordeaux. Lovely fruit presence. Already enjoyable with grilled steak.
Price approx.: 5,00 EUR
http://www.grandmoulin.com
Robin
+33 (0)5 57 32 62 06

CHÂTEAU LE ROUDIER 82/100

▼♪ Vintage 2013 : Young, dark purple. The nose is driven by fresh red and black fruits. The palate shows pronounced exuberance and youthful fruit. A little fiery, its lightweight substance should rapidly help it achieve balance.
Price approx.: 5,00 EUR
http://www.grandmoulin.com
Robin
+33 (0)5 57 32 62 06

CHÂTEAU LUSSAN 82/100

▼♪ Vintage 2013 : Medium deep, young colour. Fruit-driven nose of redcurrant, raspberry and strawberry. Lightweight concentration on the palate that shows seductive fruity freshness. Drinking well from now on with grilled meats. Classic simplicity.
Price approx.: 5,00 EUR
http://www.grandmoulin.com
Robin
+33 (0)5 57 32 62 06

CHÂTEAU MOULIN DE VIGNOLLE 82/100

▼♪ Vintage 2013 : Very young, deep colour. Fresh blackcurrant, blackberry and raspberry drive the nose. Supple palate showing lightweight concentration and more of the same fruit. A Bordeaux that shows at its best whilst young and still fresh.
Price approx.: 5,00 EUR
http://www.grandmoulin.com
Robin
+33 (0)5 57 32 62 06

MISSION SAINT VINCENT 82/100

▼♪ Réserve 2012 : Deep ruby. Crunchy red berry fruits on the nose backed by toast. Lively attack leading into a full, fruity, concentrated and rich palate. Undergrowth to the fore. Forthright, firm finish. An aromatic Bordeaux that would work well with barbecued foods.
Price approx.: 4,35 EUR
http://www.producta.com
Producta Vignobles
+33 (0)5 57 81 18 18

CHÂTEAU LES ANCRES 82/100

▼♪ Vintage 2012 : Deep garnet, still in its youth. Seductive nose recalling black cherry and peony. On the palate, a likeable, full and fleshy wine revealing tannins that are a tad severe and a vegetal finish. Well-balanced. Needs cellaring for a few years.
Price approx.: 5,00 EUR
http://www.vignoblespelle.com
Vignobles Pellé
+33 (0)5 56 63 60 90

CHÂTEAU MAISON NOBLE ST-MARTIN 82/100

▼🌙 Vintage 2013 : Brilliant orange-pink. Heady nose of ripe red fruits. The palate is focused and fruit-forward with a lingering ripe, crisp tone. An honest wine that would pair well with grilled fish.
Price approx.: 7,40 EUR
http://www.chateaumaisonnoble.com
Château Maison Noble Saint Martin
+33 (0)5 56 71 86 53

DOMAINE DE VALMENGAUX 82/100

Org▼🌙 Vintage 2011 : Beautiful purple-blue colour. Powerful, heady nose of red and black fruits. Substantial tannin framework on the palate even though it is coupled with fruit. A fairly virile yet well-balanced style. Serve with red meats.
Price approx.: 16,00 EUR
Domaine de Valmengaux
+33 (0)5 57 74 48 92

CHÂTEAU PUY DE GUIRANDE 81/100

▼🌙 Vintage 2013 : Young, dark purple. The nose is midway between fresh fruits and vegetal notes. A classic, lightweight Bordeaux with supple tannins. Pleasant freshness creating a drink-now style.
Price approx.: 5,00 EUR
http://www.grandmoulin.com
Robin
+33 (0)5 57 32 62 06

CHÂTEAU CHAMPS DE LUCAS 81/100

▼🌙 Vintage 2012 : Deep garnet with dark purple tints. Shy nose of black cherry and black berry fruits. Suave attack, full, rich and invigorating palate flowing into a robust structure and vegetal dimension. An honest Bordeaux calling for patience.
Price approx.: 5,00 EUR
http://www.vignoblespelle.com
Vignobles Pellé
+33 (0)5 56 63 60 90

CHÂTEAU LARTIGUE-CÈDRES 81/100

▼🌙 Vintage 2012 : Garnet with young highlights. Pleasurable nose recalling blackberry and raspberry. Supple attack, closely-integrated, suave and accessible palate that shows charm. Then comes the finish with pronounced vegetal accents that proves to be fairly bitter.
Price approx.: 5,00 EUR
www.chateaulartigue-cedres.fr
Château Lartigue Les Cèdres
+33 (0)5 56 30 10 28

CHÂTEAU JULIAN 81/100

▼🌙 Vintage 2012 : Beautiful vibrant red. Fairly subdued nose marrying fruity notes and mineral tones. On the palate, tannin presence, stuffing and a degree of firmness. Fruit is present on the finish clad with notes of spice.
Price approx.: 6,80 EUR
www.vignobles-dulon.com
Dulon
+33 (0)5 56 23 69 16

CLOSERIE SAINT VINCENT 80/100

▼🌙 Vintage 2013 : Young, deep colour. Nose of overripe red fruits. A light Bordeaux with a fruit-driven attack leading into a more linear mid-palate. Drinking well from now on.
Price approx.: 5,00 EUR
http://www.grandmoulin.com
Robin
+33 (0)5 57 32 62 06

CHÂTEAU HAUT POUGNAN 80/100

▼🌙 Sauvignon 2013 : Pale yellow. The nose marries white flower notes with a mineral touch of gunflint. On the palate, a vibrant, crisp style that is simple and accessible. A potential partner for whitebait.
Price approx.: 5,00 EUR
http://www.haut-pougnan.fr
Château Haut Pougnan
+33 (0)5 56 23 06 00

CHÂTEAU HAUT VIEUX CHÊNE 79/100

▼🌙 Vintage 2013 : Youthful appearance. Subdued fruit on the nose. More of the same subtle aromas on the palate coupled with a vegetal-driven finish. A Bordeaux pairing with food off the specials board.
Price approx.: 5,00 EUR
http://www.grandmoulin.com
Robin
+33 (0)5 57 32 62 06

CHÂTEAU FONTBONNE 79/100

▼🌙 Vintage 2011 : Ruby-hued. Open nose with fruity aromas under oak influence. Warm palate with a supple attack contrasting with the firmer, tannin-driven mid-palate. Fruit plays second fiddle to oak. Firm finish. Serve with meats in a sauce.
Price approx.: 5,00 EUR
Château Fontbonne
+33 (0)5 56 23 49 36

CHÂTEAU CALEBRET 76/100

▼♪ Cuvée Premium 2013 : Crimson with dark purple. Fairly subdued nose driven by ripe red and black fruits. On the palate, quite a fluid mouthfeel. Light-bodied with simple fruit. A Bordeaux suitable for the dish of the day.

Price approx.: 4,00 EUR

www.vignobles-mayle.com

Château de Perre

+33 (0)5 56 62 83 31

CADILLAC CÔTES DE BORDEAUX

CHÂTEAU FAYAU 87/100

▼♪Vintage 2010 : Deeply coloured with mature highlights. Nose of ripe, jammy fruits with forest and earth undertones. Supple palate, soft mouthfeel and polished tannins showcasing focused, dense fruit. The pleasure continues over nice length. A very compelling wine.

Price approx.: 5,60 EUR

http://www.medeville.com

Jean Médeville et Fils

+33 (0)5 57 98 08 08

CHÂTEAU COURTADE-DUBUC 86/100

▼♪ Cuvée Rubis 2009 : Deeply-coloured, young garnet. Heady nose of ripe red fruits bordering on jammy. Lovely sappy palate with ripe tannins and a persistent finish where fruit and spice are entwined. A beautifully crafted, fully mature wine.

Price approx.: 8,50 EUR

www.courtade-dubuc.com

Château Courtade-Dubuc

+33 (0)5 56 20 77 07

CHATEAU CLOS CHAUMONT 86/100

▼♪Vintage 2011 : Deeply-coloured, vibrant red. Ripe nose with accents of morello cherry and oak undertones tinged with cocoa accents. Polished attack with mellow tannins. The aromas are impeccably showcased and the same aromatic touch imparted by the oak recurs.

Price approx.: 20,50 EUR

http://www.closchaumont.com

Château Clos Chaumont

+33 (0)5 56 23 37 23

CHÂTEAU CLOS BOURBON 86/100

▼♪Cuvée La Rose Bourbon 2011 : Slightly evolved colour. The nose is driven by dark fruit backed by vanilla and liquorice. Supple attack, round palate brimming with lovely polished tannins. Savoury freshness, balance, fruit aromas and finish. A stellar wine pairing with cheese or meat.

Price approx.: 6,40 EUR

Clos Bourbon

+33 (0) 56 762 99 31

CHÂTEAU LE THYS 84/100

▼♪ Vintage 2012 : Beautiful deep colour, youthful tints. Fairly muted on the nose with black fruits, oak tones and a whiff of roasted coffee. Relatively mellow on the palate with more of the same pleasant aromatics. An idiosyncratic style drinking well now or in a year or

Price approx.: 5,50 EUR

www.chateau-birot.com

Fournier Casteja

+33 (0)5 56 62 68 16

CHÂTEAU DE BIROT 84/100

▼♪ Vintage 2012 : Deep garnet with dark purple tints. Expressive nose of refined spices, ripe plum and a floral tone. Fresh, full and succulent palate which is charming with a vegetal presence coupled with fruit. Hint of firmness on the finish. A good traditional Côtes.

Price approx.: 8,50 EUR

www.chateau-birot.com

Fournier Casteja

+33 (0)5 56 62 68 16

DOMAINE DE BAVOLIER 82/100

▼♪ Vintage 2011 : Beautiful clean red. Focused fruity nose with crisp red berry notes. The palate is crunchy, fresh and fleshy. The aromatic personality of the nose recurs with pleasant balance. A delightful style for barbecued foods.

Price approx.: 4,40 EUR

Domaine de Bavolier

+33 (0)5 56 20 76 72

CADILLAC

CHÂTEAU FAYAU 86/100

▼♪ Vintage 2011 : Yellow-gold. Subdued nose with accents of white fruits and a touch of toast. A degree of concentration and shy aromatic expression on the palate. A fresh, young wine, still backward in coming forward.

Price approx.: 8,10 EUR

http://www.medeville.com

Jean Médeville et Fils

+33 (0)5 57 98 08 08

CASTILLON CÔTES DE BORDEAUX

CLOS PUY ARNAUD   87/100
▼.✒Vintage 2011 : Beautiful radiant dark red. Endearing, precise nose blending red and black fruits, liquorice and graphite notes. Fleshy, crunchy attack framed by freshness. Lively, mineral and persistent mid-palate. A pleasant, robust personality.
Price approx.: 30,00 EUR
http://www.clospuyarnaud.com
Thierry Valette
+33 (0)5 57 47 90 33

CHÂTEAU CASTEGENS   86/100
▼.✒Vintage 2010 : Deeply-coloured with garnet tints. Appealing nose of jammy redcurrant, blackberry and cassis. Soft palate with a silky, heady mouthfeel. Delicious fruit expression. A generous Castillon, nearing its ultimate goal.
Price approx.: 8,00 EUR
http://chateau-pitray.com
Château Pitray
+33 (0)5 57 40 63 35

CHÂTEAU CANON MONTSÉGUR   86/100
▼.✒ Gaspard 2011 : Deep, young-looking garnet. Elegant nose intermixing blackberry, black berry fruits, a floral element and fine spice. Deliciously fresh, crunchy and fruity palate leading into a more vegetal mid-palate with a hint of firmness. Balanced. Keep for a few yea.
Price approx.: 6,90 EUR
Château Lajarre
+33 (0)5 57 40 50 59

CHÂTEAU BREHAT   86/100
▼.✒Vintage 2011 : Beautiful young, vibrant red. Subtle fruit on the nose, opening up to subtle earthy mineral notes after swirling. Wonderful clean attack on the palate with supple tannins and ripe, focused fruit. A coherent, well-balanced and aromatic offering.
Price approx.: 9,00 EUR
http://www.vins-jean-de-monteil.com
Château Haut Rocher
+33 (0)5 57 40 18 09

Prices mentioned in this book are guideline and can vary depending on point of sale. The shops, wineries or publisher can in no way be held responsible for this.

CHÂTEAU HYOT   85/100
▼.✒ Vintage 2013 : Limpid garnet with purple-blue highlights. Pleasurable nose suggestive of plum, morello cherry and fine spices. Clean, round and likeable palate with a faint floral streak and firm, vegetal finish. Well-balanced. Needs a few more years bottle age.
Price approx.: 10,00 EUR
Vignobles Aubert
+33 (0)5 57 40 04 30

CHÂTEAU HYOT   85/100
▼.✒Vintage 2012 : Light garnet with crimson tints. Pleasant nose suggestive of prune, red fruits and mild spices. Supple attack leading into a pleasurable round, smooth and fruity palate. Well-balanced. Firmer, vegetal finish. A promising wine. Keep.
Price approx.: 10,00 EUR
Vignobles Aubert
+33 (0)5 57 40 04 30

CHÂTEAU HYOT   85/100
▼.✒Vintage 2011 : Deep garnet, crimson tints. Delightful nose driven by red berry fruits, undergrowth and vanilla undertones. Deliciously supple, full and fruity palate with skilfully crafted tannins. Beautiful harmony. Firmer finish. A compelling wine pairing with red mea.
Price approx.: 10,00 EUR
Vignobles Aubert
+33 (0)5 57 40 04 30

CHÂTEAU GERMAN   85/100
▼.✒Vintage 2012 : Deeply-coloured ruby. Pleasant nose driven by red fruits, toast notes and oak undertones. Supple, tannic and concentrated palate with free-flowing fruit expression. Hint of spice and tannin on the finish. A successful Bordeaux that needs a little more bot.
Price approx.: 10,00 EUR
Vignobles Aubert
+33 (0)5 57 40 04 30

CHÂTEAU GERMAN   84/100
▼.✒Vintage 2011 : Deep crimson, ruby tints. Delightful, honest nose marrying currants and oak undertones. Supple attack, fine, round, full and very fruity palate with mellow tannins. Wonderful balance. More forthright mid-palate. Vegetal finish. An enjoyable wine.
Price approx.: 10,00 EUR
Vignobles Aubert
+33 (0)5 57 40 04 30

CHÂTEAU GERMAN — 83/100

▼✦ Vintage 2013 : Brilliant, deep ruby. After swirling, the nose opens up to red fruits with a touch of toast and smoke. Fairly lively attack, supple, round palate where tannins prevail over fruit. Oak note on the palate. Well-balanced. Bitterness on the finish. Keep.

Price approx.: 10,00 EUR

Vignobles Aubert

+33 (0)5 57 40 04 30

CHÂTEAU LAVERGNOTTE — 76/100

Org▼✦ Millésime 2013 : Robe rubis, reflets violines. Nez généreux de fruits rouges très mûrs. La bouche s'articule autour d'une charpente vive, mince.Un bordeaux qu'il conviendra d'appre'cier le'ge`rement frais.

Price approx.: 2,90 EUR

http://www.vignobles-roux.com

Vignobles Roux

+33 (0)5 56 61 98 93

CÔTES DE BORDEAUX

CLOS SAINT-ANNE — 88/100

▼✦ Vintage 2012 : Deep garnet with dark purple tints. Pleasant nose suggestive of black cherry, refined spice and subtle fine oak. Very seductive palate with a full, mellow and lively mouthfeel. Harmonious framework supported by silky tannins. Sheer pleasure.

Price approx.: 8,60 EUR

www.thieuley.com

Vignobles Francis Courselle

+33 (0)5 56 23 00 01

CHÂTEAU DE POTIRON — 87/100

▼✦ Cuvée Exceptionnelle 2010 : Young, deeply-coloured vibrant red. Profound nose showing accents of red fruits and liquorice with a whiff of smoke in the background. Lovely sappy palate with velvety tannins and a polished mouthfeel. The finish is firmer yet stays full and well-balanced

Price approx.: 28,00 EUR

http://www.chateaudepotiron.com

Château de Potiron

+33 (0)5 56 72 19 76

CHÂTEAU BOUTEILLEY — 85/100

▼✦ Vintage 2011 : Beautiful clean red. Super ripe nose with notes of jammy red fruits, a touch of roasted coffee and liquorice. Refined mouthfeel, polished tannins and freshness enhancing focused fruit. The finish is evolved yet pleasant.

Price approx.: 6,83 EUR

Domaines Jean Guillot

+33 (0)6 07 31 79 22

CHÂTEAU DE POTIRON — 85/100

▼✦ Cuvée Privilège 2011 : Clean, medium dense red. Pleasant nose recalling ripe red fruits, primarily strawberry. On the palate, a round, supple and melted wine showcasing more of the same delightful aromas. An open, accessible style, already drinking well.

Price approx.: 9,00 EUR

http://www.chateaudepotiron.com

Château de Potiron

+33 (0)5 56 72 19 76

CHÂTEAU DE POTIRON — 84/100

▼✦ Cuvée Exceptionnelle 2011 : Fairly deep, young red. The nose marries accents of ripe fruits with tones of oak and mild spices. On the palate, a powerful, sappy wine with ripe tannins and quite a pleasant aromatic tone of jammy fruits.

Price approx.: 22,00 EUR

http://www.chateaudepotiron.com

Château de Potiron

+33 (0)5 56 72 19 76

DOMAINE DE MARTET — 82/100

▼✦ Vintage 2012 : Beautiful deep red with purple-blue. Muted nose of black fruits with a hint of spice. On the palate, a dense wine showing fruit tinged with a touch of bitterness. Balanced throughout and drinking well soon with grilled foods.

Price approx.: 7,00 EUR

www.chateau-birot.com

Fournier Casteja

+33 (0)5 56 62 68 16

CHÂTEAU PENEAU — 80/100

▼✦ Elevé en foudre de chêne 2011 : Fairly deeply-coloured garnet. Mature nose with accents of ripe fruits, undergrowth, vegetal undertones and mild spice notes. Supple attack flowing into a more linear mid-palate. A wine showing instant accessibility pairing well with roast meats.

Price approx.: 4,95 EUR

www.chateaupeneau.free.fr

Château Peneau

+33 (0)5 56 23 05 10

CÔTES DE BOURG

CHÂTEAU HAUT-MACÔ — 89/100

▼✦ Cuvée Jean Bernard 2010 : Deeply-coloured young red. Pleasant nose blending floral and fruity notes with delicate spicy nuance. Beautiful robust yet mellow attack on the palate. Very fine-grained tannins imparting lots of elegance. Fresh, fruity finish.

Price approx.: 7,70 EUR
www.hautmaco.com
Château Haut-Macô
+33 (0)5 57 68 81 26

CHÂTEAU MOULIN DE BEL AIR   88/100

▼.♪ Vintage 2012 : Beautiful young red with purple-blue. Very honest, fruit-driven nose showing suggestions of cassis and ripe redcurrant in the main. Free-rein expression on the palate which offers up very fresh fruit framed by polished tannins. A delightful wine for shari.
Price approx.: 6,00 EUR
Château Moulin de Bel Air
+33 (0)5 57 64 21 91

CHÂTEAU GRAND-MAISON   88/100

▼.♪ Grand Vin 2010 : Concentrated garnet. Intense nose of empyreumatic oak coupled with nicely ripe red and black fruit. Sappy mouthfeel, impeccable balance of oak and fruit and beautiful length. Tannic force shows restraint. An extremely generous Bourg.
Price approx.: 14,50 EUR
http://www.grandmaison-bourg.com
Château Grand-Maison
+33 (0)6 08 88 10 69

CHÂTEAU HAUT-MACÔ   87/100

▼.♪ Vintage 2011 : Beautiful deep vibrant red. Profound, focused and alluring nose of black fruits. Clean attack on the palate, ripe and nicely mellowed tannins. Freshness and fruit are predominant with savoury stone fruit aromatics.
Price approx.: 5,21 EUR
www.hautmaco.com
Château Haut-Macô
+33 (0)5 57 68 81 26

CHÂTEAU HAUT-GUIRAUD   87/100

▼.♪ Vintage 2012 : Deeply-coloured purple-blue. Subdued nose gradually opening up to oak and peppery notes. The palate is dense yet mellow. The same, fairly elegant spice and oak aromatics follow through with a very fresh fruity tone on the finish.
Price approx.: 6,70 EUR
http://www.chateauhautguiraud.com
Bonnet et Fils
+33 (0)5 57 64 91 39

CHÂTEAU PUY D'AMOUR   86/100

▼.♪ Cuvée Grain de Folie n°5 2011 : Young, deep garnet. Relatively mature yet focused and endearing nose of jammy red fruits. Lovely volume

on the palate showing a delightful robust yet mellow framework. A well-balanced wine at its peak with a beautiful lengthy finish.
Price approx.: 5,00 EUR
http://www.grandmoulin.com
Robin
+33 (0)5 57 32 62 06

CHÂTEAU VIEUX LIGAT   86/100

▼.♪ Vintage 2010 : Limpid garnet. Pleasant nose of black cherry and mild spices with a whiff of truffle. Harmonious palate centring on a full, succulent and fresh mouthfeel supported by fine tannins. Vegetal and spicy finish. A successful wine.
Price approx.: 5,00 EUR
http://www.grandmoulin.com
Robin
+33 (0)5 57 32 62 06

CHÂTEAU GROS MOULIN   86/100

▼.♪ Vintage 2010 : Dark garnet. Appealing nose of stone fruits, cassis, some spice and subtle oak. Suave attack leading into a fairly virile palate framed by a robust structure revealing a generous mix of spice and fruit aromas. A good, characterful wine.
Price approx.: 6,70 EUR
Château Gros Moulin
+33 (0)5 57 68 41 56

CHÂTEAU GRAND-MAISON   86/100

▼.♪ Cuvée Spéciale 2010 : Deeply-coloured with garnet highlights. Rich nose of empyreumatic oak backed by jammy fruits. Fairly warm palate with tannins. Aromatic balance. An honest, focused Bourg displaying a perfect blend of fruit and oak perfumes. Calls for red meats.
Price approx.: 8,50 EUR
http://www.grandmaison-bourg.com
Château Grand-Maison
+33 (0)6 08 88 10 69

CHATEAU HAUT-GUIRAUD   85/100

▼.♪ Péché du Roy 2012 : Deep garnet with dark purple highlights. Compelling nose of black berries, mild spices and elegant toasted oak. The palate shows seductive harmony, purity, tension and a silky structure guaranteeing its future. Vegetal and spice-driven finish. Promising.
Price approx.: 13,70 EUR
http://www.chateauhautguiraud.com
Bonnet et Fils
+33 (0)5 57 64 91 39

CHÂTEAU VIEUX PLANTIER 84/100

▼♪ Vintage 2012 : Deep garnet. Refined nose marrying red fruits and vegetal notes backed by vanilla. The palate shows seductive fruity aromas, suppleness and beautiful concentration. Youthfulness is revealed in a fairly firm finish. Keep for 2 to 3 years.

Price approx.: 5,00 EUR

www.chateau-vieux-plantier.com

Château Vieux Plantier

+33 (0)5 57 64 34 60

CHÂTEAU MOULIN DES RICHARDS 83/100

▼♪ Vintage 2013 : Young, medium-deep colour. Endearing nose driven by fresh fruit and peony. The tannins are still fairly tightly-wound on the palate. Lovely fruit-driven finish. A traditional Bourg that needs decanting for full enjoyment.

Price approx.: 5,00 EUR

http://www.grandmoulin.com

Robin

+33 (0)5 57 32 62 06

CHÂTEAU PONT DE LA TONNELLE 83/100

▼♪ Vintage 2009 : Evolved garnet. Mature nose intermixing black fruits and spice with game undertones. Supple palate showing medium concentration. Fruit is supported by freshness. Fairly firm finish. Drink now with roast meats.

Price approx.: 6,30 EUR

www.chateau-vieux-plantier.com

Château Vieux Plantier

+33 (0)5 57 64 34 60

CHÂTEAU PLAISANCE 83/100

▼♪ Vintage 2012 : Fairly deep, clear garnet-red. Pleasant fruity notes on the nose with candied undertones and cocoa notes. Extremely delightful range of aromatics on the palate. Focused finish driven by quite distinctive liquorice tones.

Price approx.: 8,00 EUR

http://www.vignoblesplaisance.com

Vignobles Plaisance

+33 (0)5 57 42 68 80

CHÂTEAU CROIX PICARD 82/100

▼♪ Vintage 2013 : Young, dark purple. Nose of fresh fruits and flowers. Very supple palate with a fruity freshness to the fore. A Bourg for sharing, drinking well from now on with steak in a peppercorn sauce.

Price approx.: 5,00 EUR

http://www.grandmoulin.com

Robin

+33 (0)5 57 32 62 06

CHÂTEAU BELAIR-COUBET 82/100

▼♪ Cuvée Tradition 2012 : Beautiful young, vibrant red. Nose of red fruits underscored by subtle spicy oak. Robust, fleshy attack on the palate with fairly pronounced bitterness revealing assertive oak influence. Fruit presence on the finish. Keep.

Price approx.: 8,00 EUR

http://www.vignoblesfaure.fr

Vignobles A. Faure

+33 (0)5 57 42 68 80

CHÂTEAU HAUT MOUSSEAU 80/100

▼♪ Vintage 2011 : Beautiful dark, young hue with purple-blue tints. The nose is strangely mature and driven by salt and dried meat tones. The palate offers up a fairly austere character although fruit is present on the finish. Light-bodied and quite mature.

Price approx.: 6,70 EUR

www.vignobles-briolais.com

Vignobles Briolais

+33 (0)5 57 64 34 38

CHÂTEAU VIEUX GOMBEAUDS 78/100

▼♪ Millésime 2011 : Belle robe rouge vif. Nez où le fruit est relativement absent, légère touche végétale. En bouche une attaque neutre, équilibrée, une évolution plus puissante où s'expriment le fruit et le végétal.

Price approx.: 2,25 EUR

http://www.vignobles-roux.com

Vignobles Roux

+33 (0)5 56 61 98 93

ENTRE-DEUX-MERS

CHÂTEAU MARJOSSE 88/100

▼♪ Vintage 2012 : Light gold. Distinctive nose halfway between wild flowers, white and tropical fruits. A powerful, full-bodied wine. Full mouthfeel with nicely showcased perfume and beautiful freshness. A top-flight Entre-Deux-Mers pairing with poached crayfish.

Price approx.: 8,00 EUR

Château Marjosse

+33 (0)5 57 55 57 80

CHÂTEAU DARZAC 87/100

▼♪ Vintage 2013 : Light gold. Extremely delightful nose showing accents of white fruits, peach and wild flowers. Restrained acidity on the palate with delicious tropical flavours coupled with a freshness bordering on menthol. Set aside for mild spice-flavoured pike.

Price approx.: 5,70 EUR

http://www.chateau-darzac.Com
Vignobles Claude Barthe
+33 (0)5 57 84 55 04

CHÂTEAU CASTENET 86/100

▼♪ Vintage 2013 : Brilliant light yellow with young highlights. Pleasant nose marrying citrus fruits, coconut and pip fruits. Lively attack, soft, crisp palate with fruit supported by savoury freshness. Well-balanced with a lingering spicy finish. A successful wine.
Price approx.: 5,80 EUR
Castenet
+33 (0)5 56 61 40 67

CHÂTEAU LA TUILERIE DU PUY 86/100

▼♪ Cuvée Tradition 2013 : Pale gold. Tropical-style nose of peach and pineapple with floral undercurrents. Lovely crisp palate boasting fieriness and exuberance coupled with crunchy young aromatics. A white wine for sharing with friends over a lengthy aperitif.
Price approx.: 5,45 EUR
Château la Tuilerie du Puy
+33 (0)5 56 61 61 92

CHÂTEAU HAUT POUGNAN 86/100

▼♪ Vintage 2013 : Pale yellow. Subdued nose showing predominant accents of white flowers with faint vegetal touches. Lovely texture and a beautiful marriage of richness and exuberance on the palate. Elegant, well-balanced and persistent. Serve with seafood and shellfish.
Price approx.: 5,00 EUR
http://www.haut-pougnan.fr
Château Haut Pougnan
+33 (0)5 56 23 06 00

CHÂTEAU GRAND JEAN 84/100

▼♪ Vintage 2013 : Brilliant pale gold. Refined nose showing subtle citrus fruit and flowers. A very thirst-quenching, distinctive wine with lovely suppleness, freshness and crisp aromatics. The palate stays very fresh. A perfect wine for the aperitif.
Price approx.: 5,50 EUR
www.vignobles-dulon.com
Dulon
+33 (0)5 56 23 69 16

CHÂTEAU VRAI CAILLOU 83/100

▼♪ Vintage 2013 : Pale gold. Nose of white fruits and wild flowers. A light Entre-Deux-Mers with simple, pleasant fruit. Beautiful overall freshness. The perfect wine for prawns and cockles.

Price approx.: 5,50 EUR
GFA des Pommier
+33 (0)5 56 61 31 56

CHÂTEAU MAISON NOBLE ST-MARTIN 83/100

▼♪ Vintage 2013 : Light yellow. Subdued nose with floral and tangy notes. Ultra ripe palate delivering persistent, crisp perfumes. The finish is framed by a pleasant floral touch. Try with spicy foods.
Price approx.: 7,10 EUR
http://www.chateaumaisonnoble.com
Château Maison Noble Saint Martin
+33 (0)5 56 71 86 53

FRANCS CÔTES DE BORDEAUX

CHÂTEAU PUY-GALLAND 84/100

▼♪ Vintage 2013 : Garnet with dark purple tints. Suggestions of blackberry and morello cherry on the nose with a jammy note. Supple attack, clean, full and reticent palate supported by robust freshness and closely-integrated tannins. A Francs respectful of traditions. Keep.
Price approx.: 5,00 EUR
http://www.grandmoulin.com
Robin
+33 (0)5 57 32 62 06

CHÂTEAU PUY-GALLAND 83/100

▼♪ Vintage 2012 : Deeply-coloured purple-blue. Heady nose of ripe fruits and floral notes. More of the same aromatic intensity on the palate within a noticeable framework. Harmonious and fruity. Drinking well now.
Price approx.: 5,70 EUR
Vignobles Labatut
+33 (0)5 57 40 63 50

FRONSAC

CHÂTEAU DALEM 89/100

▼♪ Vintage 2011 : Concentrated colour, still in its youth. Refined nose of vanilla oak backed by wild fruits. Full, rich palate with a generous range of aromatics. Lovely balance and fusion of fruit and oak. A modern wine that will become more assertive over time.
Price approx.: 21,50 EUR
http://www.chateau-dalem.com
Vignobles Brigitte Rullier
+33 (0)5 57 84 34 18

CHÂTEAU VRAY HOUCHAT　　　　88/100

▼.✔Vintage 2011 : Slightly mature, deep colour. Pleasant nose marrying fruity and fresh notes with elegant touches of oak and roasted coffee. Beautiful aromatic presence on the palate with polished tannins and lengthy aromatic expression showing savoury spice and fruit.
Price approx.: 6,00 EUR
Château Les Roches de Ferrand
+33 (0)5 57 24 95 16

CHÂTEAU DE LA HUSTE　　　　87/100

▼.✔Vintage 2011 : Deeply-coloured garnet. Nose of smoky oak backed by ripe fruits. Ageing scents are present on the attack before leading into a lovely fruity texture. A balanced, silky and self-assured Fronsac. Very compelling.
Price approx.: 13,50 EUR
http://www.chateau-dalem.com
Vignobles Brigitte Rullier
+33 (0)5 57 84 34 18

CHÂTEAU LES ROCHES DE FERRAND　85/100

▼.✔ Vintage 2011 : Fairly mature, deep colour. Fruity nose coupled with elegant oak tones. Quite mellow, ripe tannins on the palate and relatively opulent aromatic expression. A lush style that is already ready to drink.
Price approx.: 7,90 EUR
Château Les Roches de Ferrand
+33 (0)5 57 24 95 16

GRAVES DE VAYRES

CHÂTEAU LESPARRE　　　　　87/100

▼.✔ Vintage 2012 : Deep garnet. Pleasurable nose intermixing fine spice notes, roasted coffee and beautiful fruit undertones. Velvety palate displaying an impression of harmony. Seductive with beautiful burgeoning complexity. A top-flight Graves de Vayres that needs to matu.
Price approx.: 9,90 EUR
http://www.chateaulesparre.com
Michel Gonet et Fils
+33 (0)5 57 24 51 23

CHÂTEAU DU PETIT PUCH　　　87/100

▼.✔Vintage 2010 : Deeply-coloured with slightly evolved highlights. Nose of ripe red fruits with faint toast and smoke tones. Lovely volume and polished tannins on the palate. Fruit is nicely showcased with a very fresh spice tone on the finish.
Price approx.: 14,00 EUR

www.chateaupetitpuch.com
Château du Petit Puch
+33 (0)5 57 24 52 36

CHÂTEAU DU PETIT PUCH　　　86/100

▼.✔ Vintage 2009 : Fairly dense, slightly evolved colour. Beautiful fusion of fruit and oak on the nose. On the palate, a medium-bodied yet very harmonious wine with lovely intense fruit aromas. The finish introduces pleasant liquorice and mild spice tones.
www.chateaupetitpuch.com
Château du Petit Puch
+33 (0)5 57 24 52 36

CHÂTEAU DU PETIT PUCH　　　86/100

▼.✔Vintage 2011 : Slightly mature, clean red. Ripe nose marrying red berry fruits and a subtle spice tone. Fruit, freshness and velvety tannins on the palate. Charming, light and fruity across the palate with plenty of ageability left.
Price approx.: 13,00 EUR
www.chateaupetitpuch.com
Château du Petit Puch
+33 (0)5 57 24 52 36

CHÂTEAU TOULOUZE　　　　　86/100

▼.✔Grande Cuvée 2011 : Deep garnet. Compelling nose showing roasted coffee, spice and toast notes. A traditional style on the palate, not lacking in intensity and exuberance. Still a little firmness and a vegetal trace on the finish. A successful wine. Patience!
Price approx.: 11,45 EUR
http://www.chateauxcailley.com
Châteaux Cailley
+33 (0)5 56 30 85 47

CHÂTEAU LATHIBAUDE　　　　79/100

▼.✔ Vintage 2012 : Medium intense garnet. After swirling, the nose opens up to notes of ripe red fruits and menthol. Supple, warm attack, in contrast to the upright, slightly lean mid-palate. An immediately accessible wine pairing with white meats.
Price approx.: 7,90 EUR
http://www.chateaulesparre.com
Michel Gonet et Fils
+33 (0)5 57 24 51 23

CHÂTEAU LA PONTÊTE　　　　79/100

▼.✔ Vintage 2010 : Red with evolved highlights. Super ripe nose marrying jammy fruit notes with a touch of earth. Lightweight attack on the palate with more of the same open aromas yet also quite crisp, upfront perfumes. Drink fairly well-chilled now.
Price approx.: 6,00 EUR
Château La Pontête
+33 (0)5 57 74 76 99

CHÂTEAU LA PONTÊTE — 78/100

▼🍷 Fût de Chêne 2010 : Slightly evolved red. Notes of ripe fruits, spice and liquorice stick on the nose. On the palate, the range of aromatics is marked by bitterness even though fruit and spice are present. Oak obscures the grape aromas.
Price approx.: 8,00 EUR
Château La Pontête
+33 (0)5 57 74 76 99

GRAVES SUPÉRIEURES

CHÂTEAU DE MONBAZAN — 88/100

Org▼🍷 Vintage 2011 : Golden hue. Seemingly concentrated, focused nose revealing candied citrus, dried fruits, apricot and citrus notes. Extremely concentrated palate with the fruity nose aromatics augmented by tones of fruit paste and calisson sweets. Set aside for poultry.
Price approx.: 18,00 EUR
Château de Monbazan
+33 (0)5 56 62 42 82

GRAVES

THOMAS BARTON — 90/100

▼🍷 Réserve 2012 : Brilliant pale gold. Complex nose of yellow fruits, citrus and floral notes backed by gunflint and mellow oak. Very supple attack leading into a velvety, mouth-coating palate showing impeccable balance and focused fruit. Elegant and very flavoursome!
Price approx.: 12,00 EUR
http://www.barton-guestier.com
Barton & Guestier
+33 (0)5 56 95 48 00

CHÂTEAU DE CHANTEGRIVE — 90/100

▼🍷 Caroline 2012 : Brilliant light yellow. Delightful nose showing lovely aromas of citrus, exotic fruits and delicate oak undercurrents. Fleshy, silky and closely-integrated attack leading into a fresh mid-palate with persistent aromas centering on fruit. A compelling wine.
Price approx.: 15,00 EUR
www.chantegrive.com
Château de Chantegrive
+33 (0)5 56 27 17 38

CHÂTEAU DE CHANTEGRIVE — 89/100

▼🍷 Vintage 2010 : Dark hued. Full nose with accents of ripe red and black fruits with a light toasted mineral touch. On the palate, a dense, tightly-wound wine with refined, polished tannins. Fullness and freshness enhance persistent fruit.
Price approx.: 14,00 EUR
www.chantegrive.com
Château de Chantegrive
+33 (0)5 56 27 17 38

DE SERREY — 88/100

▼🍷 Vintage 2011 : Beautiful dark colour still in its youth. Wonderful quality fruit on the nose with an oak dimension recalling graphite. On the palate, dense attack, evident yet velvety tannins with the same, quite noble oak presence. A nicely crafted wine.
Price approx.: 28,00 EUR
http://www.deserrey.com
De Serrey
+33 (0)6 67 79 00 87

CHÂTEAU PRIEURÉ-LES-TOURS — 87/100

▼🍷 Vintage 2012 : Deep garnet. Focused, profound nose centring on nicely ripe fruit. Full, generous palate with closely-integrated ripe tannins. Well-balanced, fairly well-structured and pairing with roast beef.
Price approx.: 6,40 EUR
Les Domaines de la Mette
+33 (0)556671818

CHÂTEAU PRIEURÉ-LES-TOURS — 87/100

▼🍷 Cuvée Clara 2013 : Light gold. Menthol and vanilla oak on the nose backed by citrus, peach and white fruits. Refined oak at point of entry supported by savoury fruity acidity on the finish. Balance and freshness. A distinctive Graves, inviting from now on.
Price approx.: 5,80 EUR
Les Domaines de la Mette
+33 (0)556671818

CHÂTEAU MARGÈS — 87/100

▼🍷 Vintage 2012 : Red with purple-blue tints. Fairly subdued nose of red fruits. Lovely substance on the palate, a mellow wine showing more of the fruit enhanced by spice and oak notes. A coherent style that is already poised for enjoyment.
Price approx.: 6,90 EUR
http://www.chateau-pouyanne.com
Château Pouyanne
+33 (0)5 56 62 51 73

GRAND ENCLOS DU CHÂTEAU DE CÉRONS — 87/100

▼🍷 Vintage 2011 : Beautiful deep red. Fairly elegant nose opening up to a fruity tone and subtle oak after swirling. Wonderful attack on the palate, dense mouthfeel and polished tannins. A young wine with aromatic expression still backward in coming forward.
Price approx.: 23,00 EUR
www.le-grand-enclos.com
Grand Enclos du Château de Cérons
+33 (0)5 56 27 01 53

CHÂTEAU MAGENCE — 86/100

▼🌡Elevé en fûts de chêne 2011 : Deeply-coloured garnet. Refined nose of toasted oak backed by ripe black fruits. Supple, well-balanced palate. Mellow tannins, nicely restrained oak presence supported by fruit. An elegant Graves yet to fully reveal itself. Enjoy with a fine cut of beef.

http://www.magence.com
Château Magence
+33 (0)5 56 63 07 05

CHÂTEAU MILLET — 86/100

▼🌡 Cuvée Henri 2013 : Light gold. Appealing nose of lime, white fruits, almond and vanilla. Soft palate showing seductively elegant body and crunchy vanilla-infused fruit perfumes. A classic, well-made Graves, drinking well already. Fish in a cream sauce is the obvious partner.

Price approx.: 5,80 EUR
Les Domaines de la Mette
+33 (0)556671818

CHÂTEAU DE MONBAZAN — 86/100

Org▼🌡 Vintage 2011 : Slightly mature red. Ripe nose recalling cherry flesh. Savoury fruit on the palate with abundant freshness and beautiful persistence on the finish. A delightful, distinctive Graves drinking well now.

Price approx.: 9,00 EUR
Château de Monbazan
+33 (0)5 56 62 42 82

CHÂTEAU CAILLIVET — 86/100

▼🌡 Vintage 2011 : Dark hued with youthful tints. Generous nose with accents of fruits in brandy. The palate displays beautiful quality fruit and a fairly rectilinear structure. Its relative firmness is counterbalanced by delightful aromatics. A beautiful ripe, balanced win.

Price approx.: 12,00 EUR
www.chateaucaillivet.com
Château Caillivet
+33 (0)5 56 76 23 19

CHÂTEAU DE RESPIDE — 86/100

▼🌡Callipyge 2011 : Deep garnet. Predominant burnt oak and mocha on the nose backed by ripe red and black fruits. The palate offers up balanced fruit and oak with mellow tannins. A robust structure supports the whole. A Graves that has benefited from oak ageing.

Price approx.: 12,00 EUR
www.chateau-de-respide.com
Vignobles Bonnet
+33 (0)5 56 63 24 24

CHÂTEAU DE RESPIDE — 86/100

▼🌡 Callipyge 2012 : Light gold. Attractive toasted oak on the nose with boxwood, citrus

and a tropical touch. A Graves boasting a full mouthfeel, well-balanced blend of oak and fruit and abundant freshness. Would benefit from more bottle age or decanting.

Price approx.: 11,00 EUR
www.chateau-de-respide.com
Vignobles Bonnet
+33 (0)5 56 63 24 24

CHÂTEAU POUYANNE — 86/100

▼🌡 Tradition 2012 : Red with purple-blue highlights. Ripe fruity nose suggestive of garden berry fruits. The palate offers up lovely crunchy fruit framed by evident substance and ripe tannins. A balanced wine drinking well now.

Price approx.: 6,90 EUR
http://www.chateau-pouyanne.com
Château Pouyanne
+33 (0)5 56 62 51 73

CHÂTEAU LAMOUROUX — 86/100

▼🌡 Vintage 2013 : Pale gold. Delightful nose with a strong floral theme backed by white fruits, citrus and tropical fruits. A very supple, very soft and very refreshing Graves. Expressive perfume with abundant freshness. A sun-filled wine pairing with an entire meal.

Price approx.: 11,00 EUR
www.le-grand-enclos.com
Grand Enclos du Château de Cérons
+33 (0)5 56 27 01 53

CHÂTEAU LAMOUROUX — 86/100

▼🌡Cuvée Saint Martin 2011 : Beautiful, fairly deep red. Focused nose showing accents of red fruits and a hint of spice. The palate is delightfully supple and marries distinctive fruit (cherries) with a delectable liquorice and spice tone. Lovely typicity.

Price approx.: 12,90 EUR
www.le-grand-enclos.com
Grand Enclos du Château de Cérons
+33 (0)5 56 27 01 53

CHÂTEAU MAGENCE — 85/100

▼🌡 Elevé en fûts de chêne 2013 : Light gold. The needs to be aerated well to develop perfumes of vanilla with lemony undertones. Nice crisp attack opening up the palate. Oak then becomes more upfront yet stays balanced and harmonious. Boasts potential.

http://www.magence.com
Château Magence
+33 (0)5 56 63 07 05

CHÂTEAU MARTIN — 85/100

▼🌡Vintage 2012 : Deeply-coloured. Classic nose revealing aromas of nicely ripe red fruits with a subtle touch of smoke. Fullness and fat on the palate, an honest, harmonious and fairly persistent style. Subtle touch of bitterness on the finish. Serve with red meats.

Price approx.: 6,40 EUR
Les Domaines de la Mette
+33 (0)556671818

CHÂTEAU MILLET   85/100

▼♪Vintage 2012 : Deep garnet. Nose of ripe red fruits enhanced by a subtle undergrowth note. Fairly concentrated palate with tightly-wound tannins. Closely-integrated, mellow and warm attack. Well-balanced and pairing with roast meats.

Price approx.: 6,40 EUR
Les Domaines de la Mette
+33 (0)556671818

CHÂTEAU BOYREIN   85/100

▼♪ Vintage 2013 : Light yellow. Harmonious nose halfway between grapefruit, pineapple and tropical fruits and boxwood and broom perfumes. A supple Graves showing a lovely thirst-quenching freshness, an acidity that lifts the palate and fruit supporting the whole.

Price approx.: 6,70 EUR
http://www.medeville.com
Jean Médeville et Fils
+33 (0)5 57 98 08 08

CHÂTEAU D'ARCHAMBEAU   85/100

▼♪ Vintage 2011 : Beautiful young, concentrated red. Ripe nose recalling cherry flesh. On the palate, a degree of firmness although the tannins are well-integrated. Fruit takes on heady cherry in brandy tones. A generous style wine.

Price approx.: 9,50 EUR
Vignobles Dubourdieu
+33 (0)5 56 62 51 46

CHÂTEAU HAUT-MAYNE   85/100

▼♪ Vintage 2013 : Pale gold. Crisp nose blending wild flowers, citrus and tropical fruits. A supple, light style showing seductive freshness and fruit. A delightful, simple Graves pairing with goat's cheese canapés.

Price approx.: 7,50 EUR
http://www.chateauducros.com
Vignobles Boyer
+33 (0)5 56 62 99 31

CHÂTEAU HAUT-MAYNE   85/100

▼♪ Vintage 2012 : Vibrant garnet with crimson tints. Pleasant nose of cherry, strawberry, peony

and subtle oak. The palate focuses on fruit and is easy-drinking, invigorating and svelte with fine supporting tannins. A fairly angular finish calls for patience.

Price approx.: 7,50 EUR
http://www.chateauducros.com
Vignobles Boyer
+33 (0)5 56 62 99 31

CHÂTEAU BOYREIN   84/100

▼♪Vintage 2012 : Intense garnet, still in its youth. Pleasant nose showing a basket of red and black fruits with a floral touch. Round attack, delightful palate with focused, exuberant aromas. Likeable, easy-drinking fruit to the fore. A Graves drinking well from now on.

Price approx.: 5,70 EUR
http://www.medeville.com
Jean Médeville et Fils
+33 (0)5 57 98 08 08

CHÂTEAU MAGENCE   83/100

▼♪ Vintage 2013 : Pale gold. The nose is still slightly muted, revealing accents of citrus and tropical fruits. The palate shows more of the subtle aromatics probably due to the young age of the wine. An elegant mouthfeel should help release the aromas.

http://www.magence.com
Château Magence
+33 (0)5 56 63 07 05

CHÂTEAU CHANTELOISEAU   82/100

▼♪ Cuvée Jean Jules 2012 : Deeply-coloured with mature highlights. Nose of jammy fruits backed by vegetal oak. A light Graves, slightly linear in terms of aromatics. Mellow tannins and oak. Uncork from now on for barbecues.

Price approx.: 5,90 EUR
http://www.mortier.com
J.J Mortier et Cie

CHÂTEAU D'ARCHAMBEAU   81/100

▼♪ Vintage 2013 : Light gold. Very young, slightly awkward nose with floral and citrus undercurrents and an earthy note. Reserved palate. Substance forms a backdrop and fruit is poised to follow through. Warm finish. A Graves that needs to be tasted again in better conditi.

Price approx.: 10,00 EUR
Vignobles Dubourdieu
+33 (0)5 56 62 51 46

CHÂTEAU CAILLIVET 79/100

▼♪ In 2012 : Deep garnet with dark purple tints. The nose lacks focus and shows red fruits with a floral trace after swirling. Suave attack with lovely intensity. A svelte, tense and spicy wine. The mid-palate is vegetal and a tad bitter. Firm finish. Keep.
Price approx.: 7,90 EUR
www.chateaucaillivet.com
Château Caillivet
+33 (0)5 56 76 23 19

HAUT-MÉDOC

CHÂTEAU CISSAC 89/100

▼♪ Vintage 2011 : Beautiful, fairly deep red. Profound nose of red and black fruits with subtle oak in the background. Tannins of impeccable quality on the palate, honest attack leading into a very fresh, full and fruity mid-palate. Quite a successful wine.
Price approx.: 12,50 EUR
http://www.chateau-cissac.com
Château Cissac
+33 (0)5 56 59 58 13

CHÂTEAU CAMBON LA PELOUSE 89/100

▼♪ Vintage 2009 : Beautiful dark red, still in its youth. Profound, expressive and elegant nose marrying fruit and mineral aromas. Wonderful dense, expressive attack on the palate marrying the same racy tones augmented by seductive fullness.
Price approx.: 15,80 EUR
www.cambon-la pelouse.com
Cambon La Pelouse
+33 (0)5 57 88 40 32

CHÂTEAU DE MALLERET 89/100

▼♪ Vintage 2011 : Deep young red. Profound nose of black fruits coupled with mint and mild spice tones. On the palate, a dense, tightly-wound, full wine, still very much in its infancy. Aromatic expression is still reticent despite evident fruit on the finish.
Price approx.: 18,50 EUR
http://www.chateau-malleret.fr
Château de Malleret
+33 (0)5 56 35 05 36

LE BARON DE MALLERET 89/100

▼♪ Vintage 2010 : Dark red. Pleasant nose with black fruit, dark chocolate and toffee aromas entwined. Powerful soft, silky attack on the palate. Full mid-palate leading into a perfumed finish of fruit, liquorice and menthol notes.
Price approx.: 9,80 EUR

http://www.chateau-malleret.fr
Château de Malleret
+33 (0)5 56 35 05 36

CHÂTEAU BRAUDE FELLONNEAU 89/100

▼♪ Vintage 2010 : Beautiful deep, young red. The nose opens up gradually to black fruit tones, mineral and spice notes. Wonderfully sappy palate. A wine that is full-bodied yet melted. Youthfulness imparts a touch of bitterness.
Price approx.: 20,00 EUR
www.chateau-mongravey.fr
Mongravey
+33 (0)5 56 58 84 51

CHÂTEAU CITRAN 89/100

▼♪ Vintage 2011 : Beautiful clean, slightly mature red. Relatively muted on the nose opening up to oak and spice tones. Pleasurable framework on the palate, supple tannins and evident fruit. The finish displays a hint of firmness. Keep.
Price approx.: 11,50 EUR
http://www.citran.com
Château Citran
+33 (0)5 56 58 21 01

CHÂTEAU HAUT-BELLEVUE 89/100

▼♪ Vintage 2011 : Beautiful young, deep red. Nose of black fruits underscored by delicately roasted coffee and oak. Lovely framework on the palate revealing more of the same components. Oak is still present but should rapidly take a back seat to fruit.
Price approx.: 11,00 EUR
http://www.chateauhautbellevue.fr
Haut-Bellevue
+33 (0)5 56 58 91 64

FRENCH CELLARS 88/100

▼♪ Vintage 2011 : Deep colour, garnet tints. Refined nose of empyreumatic oak coupled with blackberry, cherry and cassis. Soft, polished palate with silky substance and aromatic typicity. Oak presence does not obscure the fruit. A beautiful, delicate, refined Haut-Médoc.
Price approx.: 9,00 EUR
http://www.winesoverland.com
Wines Overland

CHÂTEAU DU MOULIN ROUGE 88/100

▼♪ Vintage 2011 : Young-looking vibrant red. Delicate nose marrying notes of black fruits, oak and roasted coffee. Lovely sappy palate with ripe tannins and racy oak. An all-round Haut-Médoc, at its peak, with wonderful potential.
Château du Moulin Rouge
+33 (0)5 56 58 91 13

CHÂTEAU PEYRABON 88/100

▼🍷 Vintage 2011 : Young-looking garnet. Subdued fruit on the nose entwined with vegetal and mineral tones. Supple attack flowing into a palate that focuses on elegance. A tense, svelte, racy and spicy wine supported by fine tannins. A pleasure to drink in 4-6 years' time.
Price approx.: 11,67 EUR
www.chateau-peyrabon.com
Château Peyrabon
+33 (0)5 56 59 57 10

CHÂTEAU CAMBON LA PELOUSE 88/100

▼🍷 Vintage 2011 : Deep young red. Pleasant, racy nose showing fruit entwined with a subtle toasted oak tone. Beautiful attack on the palate with dense substance and fairly polished, ripe tannins. Young and still a little fiery yet promising.
Price approx.: 13,50 EUR
www.cambon-la pelouse.com
Cambon La Pelouse
+33 (0)5 57 88 40 32

CHÂTEAU DE BRAUDE 88/100

▼🍷 Vintage 2011 : Beautiful vibrant young red. Fairly racy nose of ripe black fruits with mineral undertones of graphite. The palate shows a seductive refined texture, polished tannins and focused fruit that lingers. A wine without artifice showing impeccable balance.
Price approx.: 13,00 EUR
www.chateau-mongravey.fr
Mongravey
+33 (0)5 56 58 84 51

CHÂTEAU ANEY 88/100

▼🍷 Vintage 2011 : Garnet hue with ruby highlights. Focused nose showing a delightful mix of quality red fruit and refined, subtle oak. Good staying power on the palate. Full, warm and melted attack. More of the fruit supported by good exuberance imparting freshness.
Price approx.: 13,00 EUR
Château Aney
+33 (0)5 56 58 94 89

CHÂTEAU PUY CASTÉRA 86/100

▼🍷 Vintage 2011 : Limpid garnet. Pleasant nose intermixing red and black fruits with a floral note and elegant oak. Supple attack, a wine displaying lovely vibrant succulence on the palate with accessible aromas and fine tannins framing the whole.
Price approx.: 11,50 EUR
www.puycastera.fr
Château Puy Castéra
+33 (0)5 56 59 58 80

CHÂTEAU DU BREUIL 86/100

▼🍷 Vintage 2011 : Fairly deep, young garnet. On the nose, ripe tones marry the fruit with a more animal, smoky dimension. Beautiful attack on the palate, very full and melted with a clear focus on freshness and fruit. A charming wine.
Price approx.: 7,50 EUR
http://www.chateau-cissac.com
Château Cissac
+33 (0)5 56 59 58 13

CHÂTEAU TROIS MOULINS 86/100

▼🍷 Vintage 2012 : Vibrant red. Dashing nose of ripe garden berry fruits with a faint mineral oak touch. Fairly lightweight on the palate but skilful ageing imparts substance, freshness and aroma. An authentic, well-balanced style.
Price approx.: 8,00 EUR
www.cambon-la pelouse.com
Cambon La Pelouse
+33 (0)5 57 88 40 32

CHÂTEAU TROIS MOULINS 86/100

▼🍷 Vintage 2011 : Beautiful young, vibrant red. Nose of ripe red and black fruits with earthy mineral aromas in the background. Robust attack on the palate and evident, well-integrated tannins. Freshness enhances focused fruit and imparts great harmony to the whole.
Price approx.: 7,50 EUR
www.cambon-la pelouse.com
Cambon La Pelouse
+33 (0)5 57 88 40 32

LE BARON DE MALLERET 86/100

▼🍷 Vintage 2011 : Clean red. Fairly compelling nose of red fruits with a whiff of spice. On the palate, a melted, pleasant wine revealing more of the fruit and spice duo. The finish is still under oak influence. Drink as a food wine for barbecues.
Price approx.: 9,80 EUR
http://www.chateau-malleret.fr
Château de Malleret
+33 (0)5 56 35 05 36

CHÂTEAU TOUR MARCILLANET 86/100

▼🍷 Vintage 2010 : Fairly lightly-coloured yet young red. Mature nose of slightly jammy red fruits. Suppleness, fruit and aromatic expression are central themes on the palate. A very pleasant wine, ready to drink now with red meats.
Price approx.: 17,00 EUR
http://www.chateau-tour-marcillanet.fr
Château Tour Marcillanet
+33 (0)5 56 59 92 94

CHÂTEAU HOURTIN-DUCASSE   86/100

▼🍷 Vintage 2011 : Beautiful clean red with youthful tints. Dusty nose lacking in fruit and showing sawdust. More obscured aromas on the palate with accents of fresh nuts bordering on garlicky. Same after a second tasting.

Price approx.: 12,00 EUR

Vignobles Marengo Père et Fils

+33 (0)5 56 59 56 92

CHÂTEAU LE MEYNIEU   84/100

▼🍷 Vintage 2011 : Beautiful clean red. Enticing, expressive nose marrying ripe fruits and fairly unconventional oak. More of the same slightly atypical aromas on the palate with a strong exotic slant on the oak. A potential partner for Antipodean foods.

Price approx.: 10,50 EUR

http://www.domaines-pedro.com

Domaines Pedro

+33 (0)5 56 73 32 10

LALANDE DE POMEROL

CHÂTEAU LES HAUTS-CONSEILLANTS 88/100

▼🍷 Vintage 2010 : Young red. Ripe nose with red and black fruits taking on earthy and smoky tones. Lovely melted character on the palate showing fruit expression even though oak notes recur on the finish. Still young, will keep.

Price approx.: 19,95 EUR

http://www.chateauleshautsconseillants.com

Pierre Bourotte SAS

CHÂTEAU LE GRAVILLOT   87/100

▼🍷 Vintage 2011 : Young red. Extremely endearing nose of red berry fruits. Beautiful mouthfeel with silky tannins. Although the finish is slightly firmer, fruit remains present. Would work with a prime cut of beef.

Price approx.: 14,90 EUR

www.vignobles-brunot.fr

Vignobles JB Brunot & Fils

+33 (0)5 57 55 09 99

CHÂTEAU VIEILLE DYNASTIE   87/100

▼🍷 Eléonore 2011 : Deeply-coloured young red. The nose marries vegetal and fruity notes with a whiff of smoke. Full palate, polished mouthfeel and very silky tannins. Fruit expression enjoys substantial exposure. Perfect for red meats.

Price approx.: 20,00 EUR

Vignobles Borderie

+33 (0)5 57 69 83 01

CHÂTEAU AU PONT DE GUITRES   86/100

▼🍷 Vintage 2011 : Clean red. Focused, ripe fruity nose with subtle mineral oak undertones. Beautiful attack on the palate with very mellow tannins and quite a velvety mouthfeel. The mid-palate and finish are slightly firmer but very aromatic. A pleasurable wine.

Price approx.: 10,50 EUR

Château Les Roches de Ferrand

+33 (0)5 57 24 95 16

CHÂTEAU VOSELLE   86/100

▼🍷 Vintage 2011 : Dark, young red. Mature nose showing a combination of black fruits and earthy, mineral notes. A dense, tightwound style on the palate which is sappy with expressive perfume. A pleasant wine, already showing well.

Price approx.: 9,10 EUR

Château Voselle

+33 (0)5 57 51 61 77

CHÂTEAU LA CROIX SAINT-ANDRÉ   86/100

▼🍷 Vintage 2011 : Deep red. Ultra ripe nose of jammy-like cherry. Lightweight stuffing on the palate with upfront tannins combining to produce a slightly rustic style. Drink now or, say, white meats.

Price approx.: 18,00 EUR

Château La Croix Saint André

+33 (0)5 57 84 36 67

VIEUX CHATEAU GACHET   83/100

▼🍷 Vintage 2011 : Young, deep red. Predominant oak notes on the nose with vanilla and mild spice aromas. More of the same on the palate where fruit clearly plays a supporting role. Oak ageing and tannins are central themes. An acquired taste.

Price approx.: 12,00 EUR

www.vignobles-g-arpin.com

Vignobles G. Arpin

+33 (0)9 71 58 23 49

LISTRAC-MÉDOC

CHÂTEAU MAINE LALANDE   88/100

▼🍷 Vintage 2011 : Beautiful deep young red. A mix of red fruits and fairly upfront oak on the nose. Lovely sappy palate, melted tannins and intense fruit and liquorice aromas. A compelling full and persistent wine.

Price approx.: 18,00 EUR

http://www.chateau-mayne-lalande.com

Vignobles Lartigue

+33 (0)5 56 58 27 63

CHATEAU CAP LÉON VEYRIN — 87/100

▼.✔ Vintage 2011 : Beautiful deep purple-blue. Ripe nose with red fruit rapidly joined by oak tones. Beautiful dense, full-bodied attack. Upfront yet well-integrated tannins. Lovely fruit-driven finish. A distinctive, promising wine.

Price approx.: 16,00 EUR
www.vignobles-meyre.com
Vignobles Meyre
+33 (0)5 56 58 07 28

CHÂTEAU LIOUNER — 87/100

▼.✔ Vintage 2011 : Dark young red. Extremely compelling nose showing delicate toast and roasted coffee accents with slightly backward fruit. A very honest, forthright and tightly-wound wine on the palate where oak prevails a little over the fruit. Great potential. Keep.

Price approx.: 14,50 EUR
Bosq et fils
+33 (0)5 56 58 05 62

LE LISTRAC DE LA MOULINE — 87/100

▼.✔ Vintage 2011 : Beautiful appearance of deep garnet. Fairly intense fruity nose with accents of ripe cherry and redcurrant. On the palate, a full, tightly-wound wine. Present yet well-integrated tannins. The finish is still powerful. Keep.

Price approx.: 12,00 EUR
http://www.chateaulamouline.com
Coubris JLC
+33 (0)5 56 17 13 17

LOUPIAC

CHÂTEAU DU CROS — 89/100

▼.✔ Vintage 2011 : Brilliant yellow-gold. Delightful nose driven by quince and candied citrus, brimming with freshness. Beautiful concentration on the palate with showcased aromas of quince, honey and rhubarb. Well-balanced. A successful Loupiac pairing with foie gras.

Price approx.: 15,10 EUR
http://www.chateauducros.com
Vignobles Boyer
+33 (0)5 56 62 99 31

CHÂTEAU SÉGUR DU CROS — 82/100

▼.✔ Vintage 2011 : Light gold. Alluring honeyed nose with tropical fruits and citrus. Fairly supple palate showing medium concentration and a welcome freshness. A very accessible Loupiac.

Price approx.: 9,20 EUR
http://www.chateauducros.com
Vignobles Boyer
+33 (0)5 56 62 99 31

LUSSAC-SAINT-EMILION

CHÂTEAU LA CLAYMORE — 89/100

▼.✔ Vintage 2011 : Vibrant red. Highly endearing nose where red fruits are entwined with roasted coffee and toast notes. Excellent quality texture, silky tannins and fruit expression on the finish, again underscored by the same elegant oak tones.

Price approx.: 10,70 EUR
http://www.chateaulaclaymore.com
Château La Claymore
+33 (0)5 57 74 67 48

CHÂTEAU LES COMBES — 88/100

▼.✔ Louis Gabriel 2011 : Dark hued with vibrant red highlights. Profound, concentrated nose of black fruits with a touch of graphite. Full attack on the palate showing stuffing, melted tannins and a well-balanced mid-palate still under oak influence. A successful wine.

Price approx.: 16,00 EUR
Vignobles Borderie
+33 (0)5 57 69 83 01

CHÂTEAU BEL-AIR — 87/100

▼.✔ Vintage 2011 : Deep, young garnet. Profound, subtle and evolving nose. Black fruits are entwined with a pleasant mineral tone. Pleasant attack on the palate, full of freshness with fairly fine-grained tannins and focused aromatic expression. An elegant style wine.

Price approx.: 12,00 EUR
http://www.chateaubelair.fr
Château Bel-Air
+33 (0)5 57 74 60 40

CHÂTEAU TOUR DE GRENET — 86/100

▼.✔ Vintage 2011 : Deeply-coloured garnet. Delightful nose of morello cherry, cherry flesh and oak undertones with mineral accents. Robust attack on the palate, focused aromatic expression with fruit and quality oak entwined. Good craftmanship.

Price approx.: 9,70 EUR
www.vignobles-brunot.fr
Vignobles JB Brunot & Fils
+33 (0)5 57 55 09 99

CHÂTEAU DE TABUTEAU — 84/100

▼.✔ Vintage 2011 : Slightly mature, light red. Quite delightful, endearing fruity nose. More of the same aromatics on the palate which is more supple than powerful and concentrated. Compelling and focused across the palate. Serve with grilled foods.

Price approx.: 8,00 EUR
http://www.durand-laplagne.com
Vignobles Sylvie et Bertrand Bessou
+33 (0)5 57 74 63 07

CHÂTEAU PUY-GALLAND 84/100
▼.✔Vintage 2012 : Deeply-coloured purple-blue. Nose of ripe forest fruits. The palate is robust yet mellow and exudes pleasant aromas intermixing mineral and fruity notes. An authentic, enjoyable style.
Price approx.: 9,10 EUR
Vignobles Labatut
+33 (0)5 57 40 63 50

CHÂTEAU LES VIEILLES PIERRES 83/100
▼.✔Vintage 2011 : Deeply-coloured garnet. Nose of ripe fruits backed by smoky vanilla oak. Chewy palate with noticeable, fine-grained tannins, assertive aromatic maturity and a warm finish. A distinctive Lussac that still needs decanting.
Price approx.: 7,80 EUR
http://www.mortier.com
JJ Mortier et Cie

ROC DE LUSSAC 82/100
▼.✔ Vintage 2012 : Beautiful young, vibrant red. The nose marries fruit and oak notes. On the palate, fruit is nicely showcased, freshness is a feature and the tannins are polished. A very harmonious, accessible style for barbecues or grilled foods.
Price approx.: 6,90 EUR
http://www.producta.com
Producta Vignobles
+33 (0)5 57 81 18 18

MARGAUX

CHÂTEAU DESMIRAIL 93/100
▼.✔ Vintage 2010 : Beautiful dark red, still in its youth. Profound nose recalling bigarreau cherry and ripe morello cherry with delicate oak undertones. On the palate, a very full, powerful wine. Ripe tannins impart elegance and length. A delightful wine needing more bottl.
Price approx.: 35,00 EUR
www.desmirail.com
Château Desmirail
+33 (0)5 57 88 34 33

CHEVALIER DE LASCOMBES 92/100
▼.✔Vintage 2009 : Beautiful, slightly mature red. Pleasant, expressive nose with delicate aromas of red berry fruits. Fruit is entwined with a generous, fleshy attack on the palate. The mid-palate and finish are augmented by delightful spice tones. A lovely wine.
Price approx.: 28,00 EUR
http://www.chateau-lascombes.com
Château Lascombes
+33 (0)5 57 88 70 66

CHÂTEAU MARQUIS DE TERME 92/100
▼.✔ Vintage 2011 : Beautiful young, vibrant red. Delicate nose opening up to oak and empyreumatic notes with fruit developing after swirling. On the palate, lovely volume, polished tannins and more expressive fruit. A fairly promising, robust wine.
Price approx.: 33,00 EUR
http://www.chateau-marquis-de-terme.com
Château Marquis de Terme
+33 (0)5 57 88 30 01

CHÂTEAU SIRAN 90/100
▼.✔Vintage 2011 : Vibrant red. Delightful, expressive nose marrying notes of black fruits, spice, toast and cocoa bean. Generous attack on the palate leading into a powerful mid-palate. Heady, expressive aromas that linger. A wine providing instant enjoyment.
Price approx.: 22,75 EUR
http://www.chateausiran.com
Vignobles Miailhe
+33 (0)5 57 88 34 04

M DE MALLERET 89/100
▼.✔Vintage 2011 : Deep young red. Delicate nose opening up to black fruit notes, subtle oak with roasted coffee and touches of ripe currants. Extremely mature palate showing a distinctive oak structure and heady fruit notes.
Price approx.: 25,00 EUR
http://www.chateau-malleret.fr
Château de Malleret
+33 (0)5 56 35 05 36

CHÂTEAU MONGRAVEY 89/100
▼.✔Vintage 2011 : Beautiful young red. Racy nose opening up after swirling to refined spice notes, black fruit and subtle roasted coffee and oak. Full, silky attack on the palate with fruit and freshness. Lovely sappy, crunchy and well-balanced palate.
Price approx.: 22,00 EUR
www.chateau-mongravey.fr
Mongravey
+33 (0)5 56 58 84 51

CHÂTEAU GRAND TAYAC 88/100
▼.✔ Vintage 2011 : Ruby-hued. The nose opens up to red fruit notes and subtle, menthol-infused oak with an animal touch in the background. The palate is still young, tightly-wound and displays tightly-knit tannins and a degree of firmness. Should melt.
Price approx.: 20,00 EUR
http://www.chateauhautbellevue.fr
Haut-Bellevue
+33 (0)5 56 58 91 64

CHÂTEAU LASCOMBES

97/100

▼ **Vintage 2009**

Beautiful dense red, still in its youth. Expressive nose still marked by oak presence coupled with lovely intense ripe red fruit. On the palate, a rich, silky and full wine starting to fully deliver its power. Poised for a great future.

Price approx.: 100 EUR
Serving temperature: 16-18°
Ready to drink: 2018-2020

This estate is one of the oldest in Médoc. Its first wines made by the Chevalier de Lascombes – who gave his name to the second of the estate's wines – as early as the first half of the 18th century. The estate covers 112 hectares in the Margaux appellation. Its new owners, the Health Professionals Mutual Fund (MACSF), have entrusted the existing team to continue producing a wine that is fully in keeping with its rank of second cru classé, as they have been over the last decade, most notably with the more recent vintages: 2006, 2008, 2009 and 2010 achieve a rare level of fullness. Seminars can be organised at the estate, benefiting from a superb setting and an outstanding welcome.

Château Lascombes
1 cours de Verdun - 33460 Margaux
Tel: (+33) 5 57 88 70 66 - Fax: (+33) 5 57 88 72 17
E-mail: contact@chateau-lascombes.fr
Website: http://www.chateau-lascombes.com

CHÂTEAU TAYAC   88/100

▼♪Vintage 2010 : Beautiful young red. Striking nose with accents of ripe currants with subtle oak in the background. Wonderful structure on the palate with melted tannins although the oak imparts a degree of power on the finish. A successful wine with a bright future.

Price approx.: 20,00 EUR

www.chateautayac-margaux.com

Chateau Tayac

+33 (0)5 57 88 33 06

CHÂTEAU CONFIDENCE DE MARGAUX 87/100

▼♪Vintage 2011 : Concentrated colour, young tints. Complex nose of empyreumatic oak with mocha coupled with notes of ripe red and black fruits. Supple palate with a full mouthfeel and oak that is already very mellow allowing fruit to gradually unfurl.

Price approx.: 25,00 EUR

Château Confidence

+33 (0)6 07 03 19 60

MONGRAVEY   87/100

▼♪Vintage 2010 : Young deep red. Fairly profound fruity nose with black fruits augmented by oak and mineral notes. Quite a full mouthfeel with ripe yet evident tannins. Fruit expression is shortened by medium body.

Price approx.: 45,00 EUR

www.chateau-mongravey.fr

Mongravey

+33 (0)5 56 58 84 51

MÉDOC

CHÂTEAU DAVID   89/100

▼♪Vintage 2012 : Young, vibrant red. Pleasant nose of red and black berry fruits. After swirling, a subtle roasted coffee and oak tone is revealed. Velvety attack with mellow tannins and impeccably showcased fruit over substantial length. A wonderfully successful wine.

Price approx.: 8,50 EUR

Château David

+33 (0)5 56 09 44 62

CHÂTEAU LES ORMES SORBET   89/100

▼♪ Vintage 2011 : Deeply-coloured with purple-blue. Elegant nose showing expressive, complex oak, notes of cocoa, roasted coffee and graphite. Dense attack on the palate, refined tannins and beautiful fullness. The finish showcases the complex nose aromas. Leave to mature.

Price approx.: 16,75 EUR

www.ormes-sorbet.com

Jean Boivert et Fils

+33 (0)5 56 73 30 30

CHÂTEAU VERNOUS   88/100

▼♪ Vintage 2012 : Beautiful deep red with purple-blue. The nose seems concentrated and delivers fruit and oak notes. On the palate, a young, tightly-wound wine with ripe tannins and delicate oak. A traditional yet elegant style that needs more bottle time.

Price approx.: 8,90 EUR

www.chateaux-en-bordeaux.com

Châteaux en Bordeaux

CHÂTEAU DAVID   88/100

▼♪Vintage 2011 : Beautiful clean red. Aromatic nose with fruit enhanced by delicate spice tones. On the palate, a mellow wine with lovely density. Pleasant fruit and spice aromatics are revealed with a liquoricy touch on the finish.

Price approx.: 8,50 EUR

Château David

+33 (0)5 56 09 44 62

CHÂTEAU CARMENÈRE   88/100

▼♪Vintage 2011 : Beautiful deep red. Profound, focused nose of red and black fruits with liquorice and roasted coffee tones. Full attack on the palate with refined tannins and elegant, complex aromatic expression. Beautiful long-lasting finish suffused with aroma.

Price approx.: 15,00 EUR

Château Carmenère

+33 (0)6 52 70 63 28

CHÂTEAU DE CONQUES   88/100

▼♪Vintage 2011 : Beautiful deep, young red. The nose is fairly refined and displays oak and roasted coffee scents. Delicate framework on the palate, melted tannins and the same idiosyncratic aromas. Quite an elegant, distinctive style.

Price approx.: 10,00 EUR

www.ormes-sorbet.com

Jean Boivert et Fils

+33 (0)5 56 73 30 30

L'ELITE DU CHATEAU HAUT BARRAIL   88/100

▼♪ Vintage 2011 : Deep, young red. Heady, powerful nose marrying black fruits and an oaked mineral tone. A fairly robust wine with evident yet quite well melted tannins. Oak influence is still pronounced on the finish.

Price approx.: 20,00 EUR

www.vieux-chateau-landon.com

Gillet Cyril

+33 (0)5 56 41 50 42

CHÂTEAU L'ESTRAN   88/100

▼♪Vintage 2011 : Beautiful, fairly deep garnet. Focused nose showing very honest ripe strawberry and cherry. Wonderful mouthfeel with supple

tannins and more of the same expressive fruit. A lovely liquoricy tone shines through on the finish.
Price approx.: 10,00 EUR
http://www.listran.com
SC Crété
+33 (0)5 56 09 48 59

CHÂTEAU CASTERA   88/100
▼.✔ Vintage 2011 : Clean red. Ripe, delicate nose delivering clear-cut fruit. Melted mouthfeel with focused aromas on the palate. Full-bodied with a finish that stays firm. A well-built wine capable of withstanding the test of time.
Price approx.: 14,50 EUR
http://www.chateau-castera.com
Prestom
+33 (0)5 56 73 20 60

CHÂTEAU DE PANIGON   87/100
▼.✔ Vintage 2012 : Beautiful clean red. Pleasant nose of red and black fruits underscored by a subtle mineral touch. Wonderful mouthfeel, quality fruit and pleasurable tannins. A characterful wine with a very enjoyable aromatic finish.
Price approx.: 8,50 EUR
DWL France
+33 (0)5 56 41 37 00

CHÂTEAU LE BOURDIEU   87/100
▼.✔ Vintage 2011 : Slightly evolved red. Delightful nose of ripe red fruits like strawberry and raspberry. Beautiful harmony on the palate, mellow tannins and expressive fruit with crisp red berries recurring, coupled with a faint spice touch on the finish.
Price approx.: 11,00 EUR
www.lebourdieu.fr
Château Le Bourdieu
+33 (0)5 56 41 58 52

CHÂTEAU SIGOGNAC   87/100
▼.✔ Vintage 2011 : Deep garnet with youthful highlights. Pure nose of black cherry with some fine spice and a floral component. The palate is fairly reticent yet displays an impression of harmony and delicious fleshy, fresh substance supported by a robust structure. Keep.
Price approx.: 11,90 EUR
http://www.chateau-sigognac.fr
Château Sigognac
+33 (0)5 56 09 05 04

Prices mentioned in this book are guideline and can vary depending on point of sale. The shops, wineries or publisher can in no way be held responsible for this.

CHATEAU FONTIS   87/100
▼.✔ Vintage 2011 : Dark, vibrant red. Compelling, intense fruity nose with spice in the background. A degree of stuffing and power on the palate with upfront yet quality oak. A traditional style wine that will keep.
Price approx.: 13,00 EUR
http://www.ormes-sorbet.com
Chateau Fontis
+33 (0)5 56 73 30 30

CHÂTEAU HOURBANON   87/100
▼.✔ Vintage 2011 : Beautiful young deep red. Sterling quality fruit on the nose (currants) underscored by spice notes. On the palate, a robust yet melted wine with the quality nose aromatics carrying through. A traditional Médoc.
Price approx.: 9,00 EUR
Château Hourbanon
+33 (0)5 56 41 02 88

CHÂTEAU VIEUX ROBIN   87/100
▼.✔ Vintage 2009 : Clean, slightly evolved red. Evolving nose intermixing notes of ripe morello cherry, liquorice and a subtle touch of oak. Fruity, velvety attack leading into a more powerful mid-palate and a finish structured by oak. A traditional Médoc.
Price approx.: 16,00 EUR
http://www.chateau-vieux-robin.com
Château Vieux Robin
+33 (0)5 56 41 50 64

CHÂTEAU FLEUR LA MOTHE   87/100
▼.✔ Vintage 2011 : Fairly deep, young colour. Intense nose with roasted coffee and spiced oak aromas. Full, harmonious attack on the palate where the fruit and oak work well together. Firmer mid-palate and finish. Drink with rib-eye steak grilled over vine twigs.
Price approx.: 13,00 EUR
http://www.chateaufleurlamothe.fr
Château Fleur La Mothe
+33 (0)5 56 59 67 06

CHÂTEAU PONTAC GADET   86/100
▼.✔ Optimus 2010 : Concentrated young garnet. Refined nose showing an empyreumatic touch with a floral and ripe fruit presence. The palate is immediately seductive with polished tannins, freshness, ripe fruit presence and integrated oak. Roast red meats would do the trick.
Price approx.: 15,00 EUR
www.vignobles-briolais.com
Vignobles Briolais
+33 (0)5 57 64 34 38

CHÂTEAU LAULAN DUCOS 86/100

▼✦Vintage 2011 : Deep, young colour. Pleasant nose marrying fruity and oaked notes. The palate is harmonious despite oak presence. Fruit recurs on the finish with delicious tones of ripe cherry. Beautifully honest and expressive.
Price approx.: 15,00 EUR
http://www.laulanducos.com
Château Laulan Ducos
+33 (0)5 56 09 42 37

CHÂTEAU CHANTEMERLE 86/100

▼✦ Vintage 2011 : Deeply-coloured young red. Pleasant nose opening up to notes of ripe fruits, spice and oak. A degree of power, forthrightness and evident tannins on the palate. A powerful, uncompromising style. Keep.
Price approx.: 10,90 EUR
http://www.chateauchantemerle.com
Château Chantemerle
+33 (0)5 56 41 69 71

CHÂTEAU L'ESTRAN 86/100

▼✦Cuvée Prestige 2010 : Medium deep, clean red. Nose of red fruits intermixed with notes of vanilla and mild spice. Power forms the backbone on the palate with evident tannins punctuated by a hint of bitterness and fruit that remains in a supporting role.
Price approx.: 10,00 EUR
http://www.listran.com
SC Crété
+33 (0)5 56 09 48 59

CHÂTEAU BOURBON LA CHAPELLE 86/100

▼✦Vintage 2011 : Beautiful clean red. Delightful nose blending red fruits and a vanilla tone. On the palate, a supple, fruit-driven wine revealing more of the refined spice touch that lingers on the finish.
Price approx.: 7,00 EUR
http://www.chateau-castera.com
Prestom
+33 (0)5 56 73 20 60

CHÂTEAU PONTAC GADET 85/100

▼✦Vintage 2011 : Deep colour, still in its youth. Inviting fruity presence on the nose with empyreumatic undertones. The palate displays suppleness. Very fresh attack bringing out the fruit. Polished tannins. A distinctive Médoc that doesn't beat about the bush.
Price approx.: 9,50 EUR
www.vignobles-briolais.com
Vignobles Briolais
+33 (0)5 57 64 34 38

CHÂTEAU AMOUR 85/100

▼✦ Vintage 2012 : Attractive clean red. Forward nose of ripe cassis and prune with touches of spice and cocoa. Beautiful attack on the palate and ripe, mellow tannins. A balanced wine even if the finish is slightly more generous. Drinking well from now on.
Price approx.: 6,50 EUR
DWL France
+33 (0)5 56 41 37 00

CHÂTEAU ESCOT 85/100

▼✦ Vintage 2012 : Intense garnet, crimson tints. Pleasurable nose of ripe stone fruits, black berries and toast notes. Supple attack leading into a full, round and nervy palate with some well-integrated tannins, fine spices and a slightly bitter vegetal presence on the fin.
Price approx.: 13,90 EUR
www.chateau-d-escot.com
Château d'Escot
+33 (0)5 56 41 06 92

CHÂTEAU LES TROIS MANOIRS 85/100

▼✦ Vintage 2011 : Beautiful vibrant red. Nose of cherries in brandy with faint oak and smoke touches in the backdrop. A full, powerful yet melted wine on the attack. The finish is a lot firmer and needs foods in a sauce for full enjoyment.
Price approx.: 8,90 EUR
http://www.chateauchantemerle.com
Château Chantemerle
+33 (0)5 56 41 69 71

CHÂTEAU DES CABANS 85/100

▼✦Vintage 2011 : Deeply-coloured young red. Pleasant nose halfway between ripe fruit and oak. A powerful, rustic style on the palate with robust tannins. A characterful wine that pairs well with meats in a sauce.
Price approx.: 12,00 EUR
http://www.vignobles-philippeberard.com
Philippe Bérard
+33 (0)5 56 41 50 67

CHÂTEAU CARMENÈRE 84/100

▼✦Petite Réserve 2012 : Beautiful vibrant red. The nose marries fruit and oak notes. Very honest, harmonious and supple palate. A Médoc with a fruit-driven framework boasting lovely persistency and a fairly distinctive style.
Price approx.: 8,00 EUR
Château Carmenère
+33 (0)6 52 70 63 28

LES HAUTS DE TOUSQUIRON 84/100

▼✦ Cuvée Lucie 2010 : Fairly deep, slightly evolved colour. Very open nose showing jammy fruits and a touch of undergrowth. Clean, fruit-driven attack. A rectilinear wine showing open aromatic expression. Ready to drink now.

Price approx.: 13,00 EUR

Vignobles Beuvin

+33 (0)6 66 77 66 36

MONTAGNE-SAINT-EMILION

CHÂTEAU GACHON   84/100

▼.❦ Cuvée Les Petits Rangas 2011 : Concentrated garnet. The nose focuses on oak on first pour with ripe red and black fruit presence after swirling. The palate shows velvety tannins and predominant oak that does not obscure fruit expression. A modern Montagne that just needs a little more.

Price approx.: 8,70 EUR

http://www.mortier.com

J.J Mortier et Cie

CHÂTEAU MONTAIGUILLON   84/100

▼.❦ Vintage 2011 : Beautiful young, vibrant red. The nose is midway between fruit and oak notes. Tightwound, dense attack on the palate. The tannins are ripe, albeit a little prominent still but fruit is present and persistent. A rustic, yet effective style.

Price approx.: 12,00 EUR

http://www.montaiguillon.com

Château Montaiguillon

+33 (0)5 57 74 62 34

CHÂTEAU ROUDIER   84/100

▼.❦ Vintage 2010 : Appealing garnet. Endearing nose of ripe fruits with delicate vanilla undercurrents. On the palate, a dense, compact and rustic style marked by tannins that are ripe yet impinge slightly on the fruit. Drink as a food wine with red meats.

Price approx.: 14,40 EUR

www.vignoblescapdemoulin.com

Vignobles Capdemourlin

+33 (0)5 57 74 62 06

CHÂTEAU PIRON   84/100

▼.❦ Vintage 2011 : Clean, medium deep red. Nose of ripe red fruits with subtle mineral oak undercurrents. On the palate, beautiful tannin framework and velvety tannins although the finish is slightly firmer. A wine with a real sense of place.

Price approx.: 5,80 EUR

www.domaine-fressineau-chateau-piron.com

Château Piron

+33 (0)5 57 74 61 57

CHATEAU GACHON   82/100

▼.❦ Vintage 2011 : Attractive deep, young red. Delightful nose marrying red fruits, mild spice notes and lots of freshness. The tannins are fairly upfront

on the palate and tinged with a touch of bitterness. Balanced yet firm across the palate.

Price approx.: 8,00 EUR

www.vignobles-g-arpin.com

Vignobles G. Arpin

+33 (0)9 71 58 23 49

MOULIS

CHÂTEAU BISTON-BRILLETTE   89/100

▼.❦ Vintage 2011 : Beautiful vibrant red. Focused fruity nose with subtle mineral oak undercurrents. The palate displays wonderful density and evident, ripe tannins framed by fairly elegant oak. A wine still in the initial phases of ageing where fruit needs to come forward.

Price approx.: 15,50 EUR

www.chateaubistonbrillette.com

Château Biston-Brillette

+33 (0)5 56 58 22 86

CHÂTEAU LA MOULINE   89/100

▼.❦ Vintage 2011 : Deep red. Pleasantly intense nose with delicate accents of ripe red fruits. The palate shows seductive velvety tannins and polished texture. More of the freshness and fruit intensity over good length. Already drinking well now.

Price approx.: 15,00 EUR

http://www.chateaulamouline.com

Coubris JLC

+33 (0)5 56 17 13 17

CHÂTEAU HAUT-BELLEVUE   88/100

▼.❦ Vintage 2011 : Beautiful young vibrant red. Expressive, youthful nose with perfumes of violet and blackcurrant bud. Lovely sappy palate, melted tannins and fruit impeccably enhanced by freshness. A distinctive, delightful style, already enjoyable to drink.

Price approx.: 15,00 EUR

http://www.chateauhautbellevue.fr

Haut-Bellevue

+33 (0)5 56 58 91 64

CHÂTEAU LAGORCE BERNADAS   87/100

▼.❦ Vintage 2011 : Garnet-hued with young highlights. Fairly shy nose blending black cherry, mild spices and a floral note. Supple attack, rich palate with lovely fleshy proportions. Well-balanced, coherent and very likeable with a fine tannin framework. A successful wine.

Price approx.: 13,10 EUR

Château Lagorce Bernadas

+33 (0)5 53 24 77 98

CHÂTEAU MYON DE L'ENCLOS 87/100

▼♪Vintage 2011 : Dark hued with young highlights. Heady nose blending ripe cassis notes, oak and mild spices. Beautiful tannin backbone on the palate with substance and polished tannins. Youthfulness imparts a hint of firmness that should fade.
Price approx.: 14,00 EUR
http://www.chateau-mayne-lalande.com
Vignobles Lartigue
+33 (0)5 56 58 27 63

CHÂTEAU BISTON 87/100

▼♪Vintage 2011 : Appealing vibrant red. Intense, focused nose of red fruits suggestive of cherry flesh and ripe redcurrant. Lovely sappy palate, ripe, melted tannins and a pleasurable aromatic personality. Savoury long-lasting fruit. A first-rate wine.
Price approx.: 10,00 EUR
www.chateaubistonbrillette.com
Château Biston-Brillette
+33 (0)5 56 58 22 86

DOMAINE DE LAGORCE DE LA MOULINE 87/100

▼♪Vintage 2011 : Beautiful, fairly deep, youthful garnet. Quite subtle nose of red fruits becoming more expressive after swirling. Supple at point of entry, crunchy fruit and melted tannins. Aromatic, harmonious and extremely enjoyable across the palate.
Price approx.: 8,50 EUR
http://www.chateaulamouline.com
Coubris JLC
+33 (0)5 56 17 13 17

PAUILLAC

CHÂTEAU LA FLEUR PEYRABON 89/100

▼♪ Vintage 2011 : Deep garnet with purple-blue highlights. Subdued, racy nose of toast with fine spice. The palate shows drive with spice, blackcurrant, black fruits and beautiful, closely-integrated silky tannins. A good Pauillac focusing on elegance. Keep for a few years.
Price approx.: 19,17 EUR
www.chateau-peyrabon.com
Château Peyrabon
+33 (0)5 56 59 57 10

CHÂTEAU BELLEGRAVE 88/100

▼♪ Vintage 2011 : Deeply-coloured garnet. Young nose that needs aerating, revealing perfumes halfway between ripe vegetal, toasted oak and jammy fruits. Fairly supple palate framed

by generous substance. Balanced perfumes and substantial tannin presence. A distinctive Paui.
Price approx.: 23,00 EUR
www.chateau-bellegrave.com
Château Bellegrave
+33 (0)5 56 59 05 53

PESSAC-LÉOGNAN

GRANDE CUVÉE DE CHÂTEAU D'ECK 92/100

▼♪Vintage 2012 : Intense hue with crimson tints. Refined nose with fruit augmented by a delicate oak note infused with a hint of spice (black pepper). The palate is full yet fresh with a lovely fine texture, persistency and fruit married with oak. A successful wine.
Price approx.: 29,00 EUR
http://www.chateaulesparre.com
Michel Gonet et Fils
+33 (0)5 57 24 51 23

CHÂTEAU LE SARTRE 91/100

▼♪Vintage 2012 : Light yellow with green tints. Elegant nose marrying floral notes, citrus fruits and mild spices. Beautiful attack on the palate with delightful, intense aromas of exotic fruits and mild spices. A racy wine for noble fish or shellfish.
Price approx.: 19,50 EUR
http://www.lesartre.com
Château Le Sartre
+33 (0)5 56 64 08 78

CHÂTEAU DU SARTRE 90/100

▼♪Vintage 2011 : Attractive young vibrant red. Profound nose showing red and black fruits coupled with a subtle oak touch. Powerful attack with beautiful substance. A wine structured by oak ageing. Full, fairly classic in style and nicely crafted.
Price approx.: 19,50 EUR
http://www.lesartre.com
Château Le Sartre
+33 (0)5 56 64 08 78

CHÂTEAU FERRAN 90/100

▼♪Vintage 2012 : Limpid, light yellow colour. Expressive nose showing lovely focus, blending white flowers, tropical fruits, citrus. The same highly invigorating personality recurs on the palate with predominant crisp perfumes tinged with exotic wood.
Price approx.: 14,00 EUR
www.chateauferran.com
Château Ferran
+33 (0)9 77 64 23 11

CHÂTEAU LÉOGNAN — 90/100

▼.✔Vintage 2010 : Concentrated colour with garnet glints. Rich nose of toasted oak backed by ripe fruits. Delicate mouthfeel with melted oak, evident and refined tannins and persistent fruit. A superlative wine that is now fully up to speed. A successful effort.
Price approx.: 34,50 EUR
Château de Léognan

CHÂTEAU HAUT NOUCHET — 89/100

▼.✔Vintage 2009 : Vibrant garnet with bricking. Racy nose of pure black fruits, mild spices, roasted coffee and a touch of truffle. Seductive fleshy palate with toast, supported by invigorating freshness and well-integrated silky tannins. Very successful.
Price approx.: 23,50 EUR
http://www.hautnouchet.com
Château Haut-Nouchet

CHÂTEAU FERRAN — 89/100

▼.✔Vintage 2011 : Clean red. The nose is muted on first pour then opens up to complex mineral and mild spice tones. Beautiful mouthfeel, freshness and fullness with supple tannins. Extremely classic in style. Would benefit from a few more years' bottle age.
Price approx.: 13,50 EUR
www.chateauferran.com
Château Ferran
+33 (0)9 77 64 23 11

CHÂTEAU HAUT NOUCHET — 88/100

▼.✔ Vintage 2010 : Dark garnet. Savoury nose of fine spices, a touch of smoke and ripe black fruits. Velvety attack leading into a full, rich and nervy palate. A generous wine framed by a robust structure.ˮ Beautiful long life ahead, but requires patience!
Price approx.: 23,50 EUR
http://www.hautnouchet.com
Château Haut-Nouchet

CHÂTEAU HAUT NOUCHET — 88/100

▼.✔Vintage 2010 : Brilliant pale hue. Racy nose of white fruits with a trace of toast and mineral impression. Full palate, generous aromatic expression and oak notes blending harmoniously with the fruit and spice mix. Consistent and persistent. Successful and distinctive.
Price approx.: 23,50 EUR
http://www.hautnouchet.com
Château Haut-Nouchet

CHÂTEAU SAINT EUGÉNE — 87/100

▼.✔Martillac 2012 : Young, vibrant red. Ripe nose marrying red fruits and a delicate touch of jam and spice. Silky attack leading into a relatively full mid-palate. Fruit is nicely enhanced by freshness. Fleshy and quite persistent finish. Beautiful.
Price approx.: 11,90 EUR
http://www.chateaulesparre.com
Michel Gonet et Fils
+33 (0)5 57 24 51 23

CHÂTEAU HAUT NOUCHET — 87/100

▼.✔Vintage 2011 : Brilliant pale yellow. Compelling nose of ripe white fruits with vanilla oak. Round attack, easy-drinking palate with lightness and freshness the key themes. Refined oak influence and lovely spicy fruit persistency. Successful. Serve with fish gratin.
Price approx.: 23,50 EUR
http://www.hautnouchet.com
Château Haut-Nouchet

LE S DU SARTRE — 87/100

▼.✔ Vintage 2012 : Pale yellow with green tints. Hallmark nose showing accents of white flowers, meadow and honeysuckle. Beautiful freshness on the palate and predominant floral tones. A delightful perfumed style that would pair well with shellfish.
Price approx.: 12,50 EUR
http://www.lesartre.com
Château Le Sartre
+33 (0)5 56 64 08 78

LE S DU SARTRE — 86/100

▼.✔Vintage 2011 : Beautiful deep garnet. Focused nose showing suggestions of garden berry fruits, becoming headier after swirling. A robust wine with a clean attack on the palate. The nose aromatics recur and are quite persistent on the finish.
Price approx.: 12,50 EUR
http://www.lesartre.com
Château Le Sartre
+33 (0)5 56 64 08 78

CHÂTEAU HAUT LAGRANGE — 85/100

▼.✔Vintage 2008 : Deep garnet with bricking. Mature nose of peony and black cherries with a trace of roasted coffee and an impression of elegance, confirmed on the palate. A velvety, mellow and nervy wine still under oak influence. A classic, successful Léognan.
Price approx.: 12,50 EUR
http://www.hautlagrange.com
Château Haut-Lagrange
+33 (0)5 56 64 09 93

CHÂTEAU HAUT LAGRANGE 83/100

▼♪ Vintage 2011 : Intense garnet. Shy floral nose. Suave attack leading into a lightweight palate that is not lacking in elegance although expression is still backward. The right amount of toasted oak influence and silky supporting tannins. Keep for a few years.
Price approx.: 12,00 EUR
http://www.hautlagrange.com
Château Haut-Lagrange
+33 (0)5 56 64 09 93

CHÂTEAU D'ECK 81/100

▼♪ Vintage 2012 : Deep garnet. Pleasurable nose of stone fruits, fine spices and elegant toasted oak. Suave attack leading into a consistent palate centring on elegance. The mid-palate flows into a finish emphasising vegetal aromas. Leave to mature.
Price approx.: 15,00 EUR
http://www.chateaulesparre.com
Michel Gonet et Fils
+33 (0)5 57 24 51 23

POMEROL

CHÂTEAU ENCLOS HAUT-MAZEYRES 92/100

▼♪Vintage 2010 : Young red. Plesant nose revealing red and black fruits, liquorice sweet tones and elegant, toasted oak. Real fruit quality on the palate, texture and racy expression confirming the successful marriage of fruit and oak.
Price approx.: 28,00 EUR
Château Enclos Haut-Mazeyres
+33 (0)5 57 51 16 69

CHATEAU FRANC MAILLET 92/100

▼♪Vintage 2011 : Beautiful deep, vibrant red. Pleasant, delicate nose of ripe red and black berry fruits. Dense, sappy attack on the palate with melted tannins and a degree of fullness. Lovely persistent fruit, hallmark features and velvety texture.
Price approx.: 22,00 EUR
www.vignobles-g-arpin.com
Vignobles G. Arpin
+33 (0)9 71 58 23 49

CHÂTEAU LA GANNE 90/100

▼♪Vintage 2011 : Deep red. Appealing profound, delicate nose intermixing ripe red fruit, oak and a mineral touch. A highly distinctive wine on the palate with a full, silky entry and velvety tannins. Nicely showcased fruit and a young finish that stays slightly firm.
Price approx.: 23,00 EUR

http://www.chateau-laganne.com
Château La Ganne
+33 (0)5 57 51 18 24

PUISSEGUIN-SAINT-EMILION

CHÂTEAU DURAND-LAPLAGNE 85/100

▼♪ Grande Sélection 2010 : Slightly mature red. Nose of ripe red fruits bordering on jammy. Clean, balanced and robust attack. The mid-palate and finish are firmer yet stay balanced. Drink now.
Price approx.: 9,50 EUR
http://www.durand-laplagne.com
Vignobles Sylvie et Bertrand Bessou
+33 (0)5 57 74 63 07

CHÂTEAU DURAND-LAPLAGNE 85/100

▼♪Les Terres Rouges 2011 : Beautiful vibrant red. Nose of red and black fruits coupled with a liquorice touch. On the palate, a mellow, savoury style showing a harmonious blend of fruit and oak. Savoury finish showing liquoricy accents.
Price approx.: 7,50 EUR
http://www.durand-laplagne.com
Vignobles Sylvie et Bertrand Bessou
+33 (0)5 57 74 63 07

CHATEAU LANBERSAC 85/100

▼♪ Vintage 2011 : Deep garnet, young tints. Beautiful nose of morello cherry, toast and refined spices. On the palate, a silky, light and delightful wine focusing on elegance. The mid-palate reveals ageing aromas that are a tad strict but everything will fall into place so.
Price approx.: 9,50 EUR
www.vignobles-lannoye.com
Françoise et Philippe Lannoye
+33 (0)5 57 55 23 28

SAINTE-CROIX-DU-MONT

CHÂTEAU LA CAUSSADE 89/100

▼♪ Le Portail 2013 : Brilliant golden yellow. Intense nose showing splendid jammy, tropical and spice notes. Silky, concentrated yet lively palate still under oak influence. Impeccable proportions. A superb botrytised wine, exceptional for the AOC. Great future ahead. Bravo!
Château La Rame
+33 (0)5 56 62 01 50

SAINT-EMILION GRAND CRU

CHÂTEAU FIGEAC   95/100

▼♪ Vintage 2011 : Deep purple-blue. Delicate nose showing a subtle marriage of black fruits and oak, mild spice and toast tones. Remarkable quality texture on the palate. Fine-grained tannins and focused, persistent fruit. Complexity is the only component still to come.

Price approx.: 90,00 EUR

http://www.chateau-figeac.com

Famille Manoncourt

+33 (0)5 57 24 72 26

CHÂTEAU LAROQUE   91/100

▼♪ Vintage 2011 : Deep, clean red. Fruity nose showing great honesty and marrying notes of redcurrant and morello cherry. On the palate, a young, harmonious wine showing seductive honesty and classicism. Should gain in complexity with more bottle time.

Price approx.: 26,00 EUR

http://www.chateau-laroque.com

Château Laroque

+33 (0)5 57 24 77 28

CHÂTEAU FRANC PATARABET   90/100

▼♪ Cuvée Les Menuts Vieilles Vignes 2010 : Clean red showing faint signs of evolution. A mix of ripe red fruits and a floral tone on the nose with slightly more mature notes after swirling. Impeccable harmony on the palate with abundant freshness and mellow character. Promising dense finish.

Price approx.: 17,50 EUR

http://www.franc-patarabet.com

Faure Barraud

+33 (0)5 57 24 65 93

CHÂTEAU GRAND CORBIN MANUEL   90/100

▼♪ Vintage 2011 : Beautiful deep colour. Focused, expressive nose with sterling quality fruit to the fore and melted oak. Well-structured, full and restrained palate showing a lovely touch of freshness and fruit expression. An expertly crafted Saint-Emilion.

Price approx.: 20,00 EUR

www.grandcorbinmanuel.fr

Château Grand Corbin Manuel

+33 (0)5 57 25 09 68

CHÂTEAU BALESTARD LA TONNELLE   90/100

▼♪ Vintage 2011 : Deep garnet. Concentrated, expressive nose blending black fruits, cocoa, graphite notes and a whiff of smoke. Powerful palate with evident substance. Robust and firm across the palate, capped off with liquoricy notes.

Needs more bottle time.

Price approx.: 35,50 EUR

www.vignoblescapdemoulin.com

Vignobles Capdemourlin

+33 (0)5 57 74 62 06

CHÂTEAU CAP DE MOURLIN   90/100

▼♪ Vintage 2011 : Beautiful young vibrant red. Distinctive fruity nose of ripe redcurrant with oak and vanilla undertones. Very full palate with lots of substance and evident oak showing a bitter tone. A robust, dense style that needs more bottle time.

Price approx.: 32,00 EUR

www.vignoblescapdemoulin.com

Vignobles Capdemourlin

+33 (0)5 57 74 62 06

PETIT FIGEAC   89/100

▼♪ Vintage 2011 : Beautiful deeply-coloured purple-blue. Fairly profound black fruit on the nose which becomes more expressive after swirling. The palate offers up a silky attack and polished mid-palate with extremely honest fruit. Very pure expression.

Price approx.: 35,00 EUR

http://www.chateau-figeac.com

Famille Manoncourt

+33 (0)5 57 24 72 26

FRENCH CELLARS   89/100

▼♪ Vintage 2011 : Deep colour, garnet tints. Refined nose of smoky oak backed by morello cherry, cassis, raspberry. Soft, supple palate, elegant substance, refined oak influence, focused fruit expression, polished tannins. A full, distinctive and rich St Emilion. Wonderful.

Price approx.: 11,00 EUR

http://www.winesoverland.com

Wines Overland

CHÂTEAU CANTENAC   89/100

▼♪ Sélection Madame 2011 : Beautiful vibrant red. Profound nose of black fruits with delicate mineral and oak notes. On the palate, a delicate tannin framework showcasing clear-cut fruit aromas. Lovely finish that stays fruit-driven. A very successful, delicate wine.

Price approx.: 15,00 EUR

http://www.chateau-cantenac.fr

Château Cantenac

+33 (0)5 57 51 35 22

Detailed instructions are featured at the start of the book.

CHÂTEAU FRANC PATARABET 89/100

▼ ♪ Vintage 2011 : Beautiful vibrant red, still in its youth. Pleasant nose marrying red fruit notes and heady floral perfumes. A likeable, fruity wine on the palate displaying savoury freshness. The finish is slightly firmer but stays harmonious.

Price approx.: 10,00 EUR

http://www.franc-patarabet.com

Faure Barraud

+33 (0)5 57 24 65 93

CHÂTEAU CADET-BON 89/100

▼ ♪ Vintage 2011 : Dark-hued with youthful highlights. Nose of ripe black berry fruits with mineral oak in the background. Great ripeness on the palate with savoury quality oak. Aromatic, still firm throughout and punctuated by a hint of bitterness yet showing promise.

Price approx.: 30,00 EUR

http://www.cadet-bon.com

Château Cadet-Bon

+33 (0)5 57 74 43 20

CHÂTEAU LA ROSE CÔTES ROL 89/100

▼ ♪ Vintage 2010 : Beautiful young, clean red. Ripe nose where fruit is entwined with quite an elegant earthy tone. Lovely chewy palate, ripe tannins showing no bitterness and highly expressive fruit conducive to lengthy exposure. A pretty wine with a real sense of place.

Price approx.: 15,00 EUR

www.larosecotesrol.com

Vignobles Mirande

+33 (0)5 57 24 71 28

CHÂTEAU DE PRESSAC 89/100

▼ ♪ Vintage 2011 : Beautiful deep, vibrant red. Delightful nose marrying ripe fruit and an elegant oak tone. On the palate, a savoury, compelling wine impeccably showcasing focused fruit. The finish is ripe and slightly jammy yet stays delicious.

Price approx.: 23,50 EUR

http://www.chateau-de-pressac.com

Vignobles Quenin

+33 (0)5 57 40 18 02

CHÂTEAU GRAND-PONTET 89/100

▼ ♪ Vintage 2013 : Fairly deep purple-blue. Reticent nose with accents of black fruits and cherry jam. Powerful attack on the palate with noticeable tannins. Very fiery aromatic expression hovering between black fruits and oak. A generous wine that needs more bottle age.

http://www.chateaugrandpontet.com

Château Grand-Pontet

+33 (0)5 57 74 46 88

CHÂTEAU HAUT-PEZAT 89/100

▼ ♪ Vintage 2010 : Young, vibrant red. Ripe, profound nose marrying notes of redcurrant and blackcurrant with chocolatey undertones. Beautiful fullness on entry with extremely melted tannins. Long-lasting finish showing liquoricy accents. A wine for pleasure.

Price approx.: 9,50 EUR

www.vignobles-dulon.com

Dulon

+33 (0)5 56 23 69 16

CHÂTEAU BÉARD LA CHAPELLE 89/100

▼ ♪ Vintage 2012 : Beautiful dark red. Profound nose of red and black berry fruits with subtle spicy oak undercurrents. Dense at point of entry with a full mouthfeel and degree of firmness yet also lots of balance and freshness. Persistent finish suffused with ripe fruit.

Price approx.: 16,00 EUR

http://www.beardlachapelle.com

Château Béard la Chapelle

+33 (0)6 21 89 18 28

CHÂTEAU PIGANEAU 88/100

▼ ♪ Vintage 2011 : Beautiful young, fairly deep red. Compelling nose with elegant accents of black fruits coupled with very noble oak aromas of roasted coffee. Lovely mouthfeel with polished tannins, freshness and focused aromas. A deftly-crafted wine.

Price approx.: 14,00 EUR

www.vignobles-brunot.fr

Vignobles JB Brunot & Fils

+33 (0)5 57 55 09 99

CHÂTEAU CANTENAC 88/100

▼ ♪ Passion et Tradition 2011 : Deep garnet with youthful tints. Racy nose of toast with a touch of roast coffee, elegant black fruits and a floral note. Lovely impression of harmony on the palate, delightful, lively mouthfeel with real drive, framed by silky tannins. A promising wine.

Price approx.: 18,00 EUR

http://www.chateau-cantenac.fr

Château Cantenac

+33 (0)5 57 51 35 22

CHÂTEAU HAUT ROCHER 88/100

▼ ♪ Vintage 2011 : Young, deep red. Profound nose with fruit and spice accents. On the palate, clean attack, supple, velvety tannins and ripe fruit supported by freshness. Savoury, crunchy finish heralding good ageability.

Price approx.: 17,50 EUR

http://www.vins-jean-de-monteil.com

Château Haut Rocher

+33 (0)5 57 40 18 09

CHÂTEAU BÉARD LA CHAPELLE 88/100

▼♪ Vintage 2011 : Beautiful vibrant red. Subdued nose of black fruits with faint spice touches. Pleasant fullness on the palate, lots of balance and mellowness even though the finish is slightly firmer. A pleasant wine that needs a little more bottle time.

Price approx.: 15,00 EUR

http://www.beardlachapelle.com

Château Béard la Chapelle

+33 (0)6 21 89 18 28

CHÂTEAU PETIT FAURIE DE SOUTARD 88/100

▼♪ Vintage 2011 : Deeply-coloured with ruby tints. Honest nose showing nicely crafted upfront red fruit enhanced by fine oak that is subtly infused with spice. Warm, still fiery palate displaying aromas of fruits in brandy and chocolate. Touch of firmness on the finish.

Price approx.: 28,50 EUR

www.vignoblescapdemoulin.com

Vignobles Capdemourlin

+33 (0)5 57 74 62 06

CHÂTEAU HAUT-PEZAT 88/100

▼♪ Vintage 2011 : Beautiful clean red. Endearing nose boasting focused fruit with a distinctive crisp red fruit streak. Beautiful stuffing, fullness and melted tannins on the palate. Freshness highlights clear-cut fruit. Lovely persistency on the finish. Complex and promis.

Price approx.: 9,50 EUR

www.vignobles-dulon.com

Dulon

+33 (0)5 56 23 69 16

CHÂTEAU FRANC PIPEAU 87/100

▼♪ Descombes 2011 : Beautiful, quite deeply-coloured young red. Nose of ripe red fruits recalling cherry with a fairly pronounced floral touch. Supple, mellow attack on the palate with subtle tannins. A delightful, fruit-driven style with a firmer finish revealing ageability.

Price approx.: 15,00 EUR

www.chateaucarteau.com

Vignobles Jacques Bertrand

+33 (0)5 57 24 73 94

CHÂTEAU LANIOTE 87/100

▼♪ Grand Cru Classé de Saint-Emilion 2011 : Dense colour with vibrant red highlights. Nose of jammy red and black fruits. Ultra ripe palate showing more of the same exuberant perfumes with oak undertones structuring the whole. Slightly extreme in style at the moment.

Price approx.: 31,00 EUR

http://www.laniote.com

Château Laniote

+33 (0)5 57 24 70 80

CHÂTEAU MONDORION 87/100

▼♪ Cuvée Etoiles 2008 : Fairly deep, clean red. Mature nose of ripe red berry fruits with a whiff of smoke. The palate is quite shy on the attack then flows into a more expressive mid-palate driven by ripe red fruit with a heady fruity finish imparting a degree of harmony.

Price approx.: 15,50 EUR

http://funique.grandenclos@orange.fr

Château Mondorion

+33 (0)5 56 27 01 53

CHÂTEAU HAUT VEYRAC 87/100

▼♪ Vintage 2010 : Beautiful vibrant red. Ultra ripe fruit marries with tropical tones supported by oak on the nose. Fairly full at point of entry with upfront fruit leading into an oaked mid-palate that stays harmonious. Interesting style across the palate.

Price approx.: 19,00 EUR

http://www.chateau-haut-veyrac.com

Château Haut Veyrac

+33 (0)5 57 40 02 26

CHÂTEAU PINDEFLEURS 87/100

▼♪ Vintage 2011 : Beautiful deep garnet. The nose shows pronounced oak influence with fruit expression after swirling. On the palate, a medium-bodied wine in a clean, fruity style. The finish is dominated by an evident tannin structure. Drink as a food wine with red meats.

Price approx.: 17,50 EUR

www.pindefleurs.fr

Vignobles Dominique Lauret

+33 (0)5 57 24 72 95

CHÂTEAU CARTEAU 86/100

▼♪ Côtes Daugay 2011 : Deep, young garnet. Compelling nose of black fruits with elegant toasted oak and a faint mineral note. Invigorating palate with a lovely velvety mouthfeel. A fairly full wine with a firm, vegetal and spicy finish. Everything is in place, leave to mature.

Price approx.: 16,00 EUR

www.chateaucarteau.com

Vignobles Jacques Bertrand

+33 (0)5 57 24 73 94

CHÂTEAU DE LA COUR 86/100

▼♪ Vintage 2011 : Fairly deep, vibrant red. Nose of relatively ripe red fruits with clear suggestions of cherry. Lightweight mouthfeel with polished tannins, fruit and freshness. Ultra ripe finish intimating that it should be enjoyed now.

Price approx.: 18,00 EUR

http://chateaudelacour.com

Château de la Cour

+33 (0)5 57 84 64 95

CHÂTEAU DU ROCHER 86/100

▼♪ Vintage 2011 : Deep garnet with dark purple highlights. Elegant nose of black berries, cassis and spice notes. On the palate, a supple, likeable and harmonious wine with little depth and a robust framework. Vegetal, spicy finish. Uncork in 4-5 years' time.

Price approx.: 15,00 EUR

www.baron-de-montfort.com

Baron de Montfort - Château du Rocher

+33 (0)5 57 40 18 20

CHÂTEAU AMBE TOUR POURRET 86/100

▼♪ Vintage 2011 : Beautiful dark garnet, dark purple tints. Shy nose of black berries, morello cherry, a floral touch and subtle toasted oak. Full, nervy palate with lovely seductive roundness and upfront elegance. A fairly robust structure dominates on the finish.

Price approx.: 20,00 EUR

http://www.vignobles-lannoye.com

Château Tour Pourret

+33 (0)5 57 55 23 28

CHÂTEAU HAUT GRAVET 86/100

▼♪ Vintage 2011 : Dark garnet with youthful tints. Pleasant nose of plum, refined spice and subtle oak. Aromatic attack, suave, nervy presence, fairly rich on the palate with quite a robust structure characterising the mid-palate and a vegetal finish.

Price approx.: 20,00 EUR

Vignobles Aubert

+33 (0)5 57 40 04 30

CHÂTEAU TOUR GRAND FAURIE 86/100

▼♪ Vintage 2007 : Limpid garnet. Pleasurable nose of mild spices, toast, mushroom and liquorice. Supple attack, fairly free-flowing palate revolving around a lovely structure that still needs to mellow. Its lightness makes it suitable for drinking early.

Price approx.: 16,00 EUR

www.tourgrandfaurie.com

Château Tour Grand Faurie

+33 (0)5 57 74 49 03

CHÂTEAU MONDORION 86/100

▼♪ Vintage 2011 : Beautiful deep, vibrant red. Subdued nose with reticent fruit. A well-balanced wine on the palate with polished tannins and fruit slightly tinged with bitterness. A classic style that works.

Price approx.: 25,00 EUR

http://funique.grandenclos@orange.fr

Château Mondorion

+33 (0)5 56 27 01 53

CHÂTEAU HAUTE NAUVE 85/100

▼♪ Millésime 2011 : Robe grenat limpide. Nez savoureux, finement épicé, grillé, réglissé, prune, griotte. Au palais un vin aérien à la matière aimable, soyeuse, fraîche, nette, encadrée par une structure bien dosée. Finale végétale. Un bon millésime classique, à attendre.

Price approx.: 13,00 EUR

http://www.chateauhaute-nauve.fr

Château Haute Nauve

+33 (0)5 57 24 73 21

CHÂTEAU HAUTE NAUVE 85/100

▼♪ Son Altesse de Haute-Nauve 2011 : Robe grenat limpide. Nez prometteur, châtaigne grillée, épices douces, réglisse, prune. Bouche franche, souple, légère, où on retrouve les arômes du nez. Structure solide sous-jacente. Finale fraîche, épicée, végétale. Bon vin de style traditionnel.

Price approx.: 17,50 EUR

http://www.chateauhaute-nauve.fr

Château Haute Nauve

+33 (0)5 57 24 73 21

CHÂTEAU JEAN VOISIN FAGOUET 85/100

▼♪ Millésime 2010 : Robe grenat marqué. Nez de fruits mûrs, arrière-plan sur le végétal, la terre. Bouche étoffée, d'une agréable souplesse qui met en avant un fruit mûr de qualité. Une cuvée qui a su tirer profit du millésime 2010.

Price approx.: 6,80 EUR

http://www.vignobles-roux.com

Vignobles Roux

+33 (0)5 56 61 98 93

CHÂTEAU TOUR GRAND FAURIE 85/100

▼♪ Vintage 2011 : Deep garnet. Racy nose of mild spices, plum and morello cherry with subtle toasted oak. On the palate, a full, velvety, fresh and savoury wine supported by tannins that are a tad severe, introducing a measure of bitterness on the finish. Keep.

Price approx.: 17,00 EUR

www.tourgrandfaurie.com

Château Tour Grand Faurie

+33 (0)5 57 74 49 03

CHÂTEAU HAUT VEYRAC 85/100

▼♪ Vintage 2011 : Young, vibrant red. Pronounced oak on the nose with tropical accents slightly obscuring the fruit. The palate displays a substantial structure with lots of extraction. Fruit is present but vies for a place alongside bitter, spicy oak tones.

Price approx.: 18,00 EUR

http://www.chateau-haut-veyrac.com

Château Haut Veyrac

+33 (0)5 57 40 02 26

CHÂTEAU JEAN VOISIN FAGOUET   82/100

▼♪ Millésime 2011 : Robe grenat. Nez sur le fruit (cassis, mûre, groseille). Un saint-émilion souple, de concentration légère. On apprécie le fruit. Facile d'accès et à boire.

Price approx.: 6,80 EUR

http://www.vignobles-roux.com

Vignobles Roux

+33 (0)5 56 61 98 93

SAINT-EMILION

CHÂTEAU BEAURANG   87/100

▼♪ Vintage 2011 : Slightly mature garnet. Pleasant, focused fruit on the nose. The palate offers up lovely fruit with subtle oak undercurrents infused with liquorice and roasted coffee accents. A very enjoyable, authentic style.

Price approx.: 10,50 EUR

www.chateau-beaurang.com

Vignobles Puyol

+33 (0)5 57 24 73 31

THOMAS BARTON   86/100

▼♪ Réserve 2011 : Slightly mature, deep colour. Pleasant nose of ripe fruits coupled with a delicate spice note bordering on cocoa. Lovely fresh, mellow palate showing a degree of aromatic intensity. A wine ready to drink now with meats in a sauce.

Price approx.: 15,00 EUR

http://www.barton-guestier.com

Barton & Guestier

+33 (0)5 56 95 48 00

JOSEPH D'ARAGON   86/100

▼♪ Vintage 2012 : Fairly deep, vibrant red. Nose of ripe fruits recalling strawberry coulis-like notes. The palate displays a strong fruit theme and is pleasantly fresh and crunchy. Polished tannins and pleasant harmony with lingering fruit on the finish.

Price approx.: 8,50 EUR

www.chateau-beaurang.com

Vignobles Puyol

+33 (0)5 57 24 73 31

CHÂTEAU ROCHER-FIGEAC   85/100

▼♪ Vintage 2012 : Deeply-coloured garnet. Vanilla oak on the nose backed by fresh red and black fruits. Supple, well-balanced palate showing

---

a pleasant blend of oak and fruit perfumes. A consistent, modern wine, still tannic and needing a little bottle age for full enjoyme.

Price approx.: 9,95 EUR

http://www.mortier.com

JJ Mortier et Cie

SAINT-ESTÈPHE

CHÂTEAU TRONQUOY-LALANDE   89/100

▼♪ Vintage 2010 : Dark hue with highlights still in their youth. Fairly elegant, expressive nose marrying black fruits with racy oak. Beautiful attack on the palate with ripe, polished tannins. Sappy with fruit and freshness. A full wine, armed to last.

Price approx.: 32,00 EUR

http://www.tronquoy-lalande.com

Château Tronquoy-Lalande

+33 (0)5 56 59 30 12

CHÂTEAU LA PEYRE   88/100

▼♪ Vintage 2011 : Garnet. Refined nose of toasted oak with vegetal and ripe fruit undertones. Supple palate with refined tannins and evident oak that does not obscure the fruit. Firmer finish. A distinctive wine that needs more time to provide full enjoyment.

Price approx.: 18,00 EUR

http://www.chateaulapeyre.fr

Château La Peyre

+33 (0)5 56 59 32 51

CHÂTEAU POMYS   87/100

▼♪ Vintage 2011 : Limpid garnet. Pleasurable nose of red and black fruit basket aromas with fine spices and lovely toasted oak. Aromatic attack with a measure of vigour. Rich, nervy and well-balanced with silky tannins. A good, traditional and enjoyable Saint-Estèphe.

Price approx.: 18,00 EUR

www.chateaupomys.com

Arnaud SA

+33 (0)5 56 59 32 26

CHÂTEAU SAINT ESTÈPHE   86/100

▼♪ Vintage 2011 : Beautiful vibrant red. Fruit-driven nose with suggestions of cherries in brandy in the background. On the palate, a balanced, medium-bodied wine with harmonious fruit and tannins. An accessible style, drinking well from now on.

Price approx.: 17,00 EUR

www.chateaupomys.com

Arnaud SA

+33 (0)5 56 59 32 26

Detailed instructions are featured at

the start of the book.

CHÂTEAU CLAUZET   84/100

▼♪ Vintage 2011 : Beautiful deep red. On the nose, a generous wine with accents of cherries in brandy. On the palate, real power at point of entry with more of the same generosity which slightly overshadows the fruit. A slight lack of coordination, more harmony is needed.
Price approx.: 22,50 EUR
http://www.chateauclauzet.com
Baron Velge
+33 (0)5 56 59 34 16

CHÂTEAU DE CÔME   84/100

▼♪ Vintage 2011 : Vibrant red. Generous nose marrying black fruits with a mineral and earthy tone. On the palate, a wine framed by very upfront oak tannins placing the fruit slightly in the background. Needs to unfold and become more harmonious.
Price approx.: 18,50 EUR
http://www.chateauclauzet.com
Baron Velge
+33 (0)5 56 59 34 16

CHÂTEAU LAVILLOTTE   83/100

▼♪ Vintage 2011 : Limpid garnet. Expressive nose dominated by lightly toasted oak. Oak ageing still influences the palate at the moment. Lightweight, fresh substance and balance across the palate. Let's wait until room is made for the fruit.
Price approx.: 14,00 EUR
http://www.domaines-pedro.com
Domaines Pedro
+33 (0)5 56 73 32 10

SAINT-GEORGES
SAINT-EMILION

CHÂTEAU FEYTIT DIVON   87/100

▼♪ Vintage 2010 : Deep garnet. Pleasant nose suggestive of stone fruits, mild spices and a floral dimension. Beautiful silky, full and harmonious presence that is still backward and supported by a robust, closely-integrated structure. Harmonious mid-palate. Shows potential.
Price approx.: 13,00 EUR
www.tourgrandfaurie.com
Château Tour Grand Faurie
+33 (0)5 57 74 49 03

CHÂTEAU FEYTIT DIVON   84/100

▼♪ Vintage 2011 : Deep garnet. Seductive nose of morello cherry, plum, fine spice and subtle toasted oak in the background. Round attack, full, succulent palate set in a vigorous, spicy framework. Slightly free-flowing, vegetal finish with tannins that are a tad austere.
Price approx.: 11,00 EUR
www.tourgrandfaurie.com
Château Tour Grand Faurie
+33 (0)5 57 74 49 03

SAINT-JULIEN

CHÂTEAU LÉOVILLE BARTON   97/100

▼♪ Vintage 2008 : Deeply-coloured, still young. Focused, profound nose recalling cassis, black fruits, coffee, graphite and a hint of spice. Lovely presence, dense, fine texture, lingering freshness, elegant oak and silky tannins. A superlative wine still full of promise.
www.leoville-barton.com
Château Léoville Barton
+33 (0)5 56 59 06 05

CHÂTEAU LANGOA BARTON   91/100

▼♪ Vintage 2007 : Deeply-coloured with evolved highlights. Mature nose with jammy aromas opening up to notes of autumnal undergrowth. More of the same aromatic presence on the palate which is full, melted, lingering and fresh, punctuated by a mineral note of graphite.
www.leoville-barton.com
Château Léoville Barton
+33 (0)5 56 59 06 05

CHÂTEAU DU GLANA   90/100

▼♪ Vintage 2011 : Deeply-coloured with youthful tints. Profound, concentrated nose opening up after swirling to beautiful red fruit and a subtle earthy note. Ample, full and well-structured palate, still a little fiery. Savoury freshness. Needs more bottle age.
Price approx.: 21,00 EUR
www.chateau-du-glana.com
Château du Glana
+33 (0)5 56 59 06 47

CHÂTEAU DE LA BRIDANE   89/100

▼♪ Vintage 2011 : Beautiful young red. Profound nose opening up to black fruit tones and balsamic and mineral notes. Evident yet melted structure on the palate with ripe, well-integrated tannins. Firmer finish reverting to mineral and graphite aromas.
Price approx.: 19,00 EUR
http://www.vignobles-saintout.com
Vignobles Bruno Saintout
+33 (0)5 56 59 91 70

SAUTERNES

CHÂTEAU LAMOTHE   91/100

▼♪ Vintage 2011 : Attractive yellow-gold. Highly restrained, delicate nose with accents of mild spices, white fruits and herbs. Lovely velvety attack and concentration on the palate coupled with abundant freshness. Overall impression of great nobility.

Price approx.: 27,00 EUR

http://www.lamothe-despujols.com

Château Lamothe Despujols

+33 (0)5 56 76 67 89

CHÂTEAU DE VEYRES   89/100

▼♪ Vintage 2011 : Attractive old gold. Fairly intense nose showing accents of beeswax, honey and a touch of exotic fruits. The palate is extremely concentrated and delivers the same delicious aromas. The finish is augmented by a welcome touch of citrus. Very compelling.

Price approx.: 22,00 EUR

Clos de la Vicairie

+33 (0)5 56 76 85 69

CHÂTEAU DES ROCHERS   86/100

▼♪ Vintage 2012 : Deep gold. Fairly subdued nose with accents of jammy fruits, a touch of oak and varnish. A measure of freshness on the palate with more upfront aromas of spice and candied citrus. Concentrated, harmonious structure. Lingering spicy finish.

Price approx.: 14,00 EUR

http://www.chateauvoigny.com

Vignobles Bon

+33 (0)5 56 63 28 29

BURGUNDY

A MULTI-FACETED WINE REGION

The wine region of Burgundy is a jigsaw puzzle with myriad pieces; understanding its intricacies requires both time and patience. The aim of this wine guide is to provide the ways and means of finding one's way around the appellations, climate-specific sites, first growths and great growths; a map of the region also locates all the appellations... In this multi-faceted wine region, there are only a few large, clear-cut geographical entities. Before detailing them, here is an overall picture of the area.

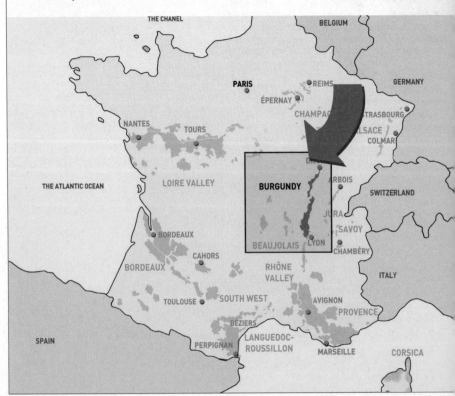

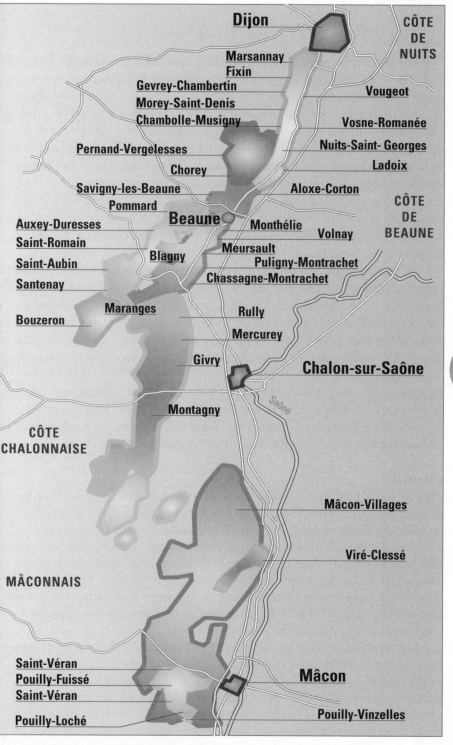

Dijon

CÔTE
DE
NUITS

Marsannay
Fixin
Gevrey-Chambertin
Vougeot
Morey-Saint-Denis
Chambolle-Musigny
Vosne-Romanée
Pernand-Vergelesses
Nuits-Saint- Georges
Chorey
Ladoix
Savigny-les-Beaune
Aloxe-Corton
Pommard
CÔTE
DE
BEAUNE
Beaune
Monthélie
Auxey-Duresses
Volnay
Saint-Romain
Meursault
Saint-Aubin
Blagny
Puligny-Montrachet
Santenay
Chassagne-Montrachet
Maranges
Rully
Bouzeron
Mercurey
Givry
Chalon-sur-Saône

Montagny
Saône

CÔTE
CHALONNAISE

Mâcon-Villages

Viré-Clessé

MÂCONNAIS

Saint-Véran
Pouilly-Fuissé
Mâcon
Saint-Véran

Pouilly-Loché
Pouilly-Vinzelles

The diversity of Burgundy is so great that it is impossible to generalise, either about its geography, the appellations, the different climates, aspects, soil permeability or structure...

The character of the wines covers such a broad spectrum that it would be a challenge to do so. There are two generalisations, however, that can be made, on the climatic influences and area under vine. Burgundy's climate is defined both by westerly maritime winds, which shed most of their rainfall over the Morvan mountain range, and continental influences which bring the predominantly cold, dry northerly winds that vines need to ward off disease. On-stream area under vine covers around 26,000 hectares, equivalent to roughly 6% of French vineyard acreage, spread over 3 departments: Yonne, 6,200 hectares, Côte-d'Or, 9,550 and Saône-et-Loire, 10,950 ha.

On the varietal front, three leading actors take centre stage, with a clutch of supporting roles. The vast majority of red wines are drawn from Pinot noir, Burgundy's quintessential noble varietal, and the whites from Chardonnay, though Bourgogne Aligoté is also made from the grape of the same name.

Although they are made on a more boutique scale, in Yonne, red wines around Auxerre are made entirely or partly from the Cesar grape variety, or occasionally from Tressot (virtually obsolete). In the northern part of Côte-d'Or and Yonne, Sacy, Pinot blanc and Melon are blended into Crémant de Bourgogne. Sauvignon, far from its favoured sites here, is used in Saint-Bris-le Vineux (Yonne). The stage is now set, enter Burgundy's large geographical entities, from the northernmost reaches down to the northern boundaries of Beaujolais in Rhône-Alpes.

CHABLIS

Chablis wines belong to the elite circle of legendary French wines. They are often copied but remain peerless. Running the gamut from the Grands Crus (7 in number), the Premiers Crus (around 40), down through to the 'generic' or Petit Chablis, they all have one point in common: they are all drawn from the Chardonnay varietal, which thrives here on Kimmeridgian calcareous clay marl. The only cloud on this otherwise unspoilt horizon, is the harsh weather conditions which bring frequent bouts of frost in the winter and spring. Yet, this is precisely what gives Chablis its highly distinctive character. The same goes for its neighbours around Auxerre and Tonnerre.

The northern part of Burgundy is anything but uniform. The first area, around Auxerre, boasts Irancy (south of Auxerre), a red wine from Pinot noir and the native varietal Cesar, and Saint-Bris, a young AC (January 2003) drawn from Sauvignon and yielding fresh, fruity wines, as its flag bearers. In the second area, around Tonnerre, east of Chablis, this role is played by Epineuil, a fruity red wine made from Pinot noir. North and south of this area, Côte Saint-Jacques near

Joigny (north of Auxerre) and Vézelay (south of Auxerre) also produce noteworthy wines.

CÔTE DE NUITS

Wines from the Côte de Nuits boast two great qualities: they are delicate and complex. From the gateway of Dijon in the north down to Corgoloin, the most southerly outpost, the Côtes de Nuits is a string of jewels, threading together twenty or more of France's greatest growths and its finest flagships: Chambertin, Clos-Saint-Denis, Bonnes Mares, Clos de Tart, Musigny, Grands-Echezeaux, Clos de Vougeot, Richebourg, Romanée-Conti…are just some of the more famous names. Pinot noir is by far the most ubiquitous grape variety here, covering at least 99% of the area under vine, on a mixture of soil types formed of encrinal limestone and Bajocian marl, strewn, sometimes profusely, with stony scree. The soil type is so unusual that no great white wine has ever been grown here.

CÔTE DE BEAUNE

This is where the white wines are avenged: Corton-Charlemagne, Chevalier-Montrachet, Bâtard-Montrachet, Montrachet… Seven of Côte de Beaune's eight great growths are white from Chardonnay, with just one embracing both red and white wines, the famous Corton. From Ladoix, the name of both an appellation and a hamlet in the parish of Ladoix-Serrigny north of Beaune, to Maranges, the northern gateway to Saône-et-Loire, Côte de Beaune unravels a string of great growths on marl or Middle or Upper Oxfordian limestone soils. These enable it to produce, particularly around Chassagne-Montrachet and Puligny-Montrachet, some of the greatest white wines in the world.

CÔTE CHALONNAISE

Once it passes Chagny, the Côte widens, branches out, grows in size… Basically, it breathes. Four main ACs share an area no less than 25 kilometres by seven : Rully, Mercurey, Givry and Montagny (the last one is whites only) which, along with Bourgogne Aligoté and Bouzeron (a village appellation also made from Aligoté), form the backbone of the Côte Chalonnaise range.

The soil type here is predominantly Jurassic: calcareous clay along the Dheune valley, which provides some unexpected ground for Chardonnay to thrive on; or brown limestone for Pinot noir.

Interestingly, the Crémant de Bourgogne appellation, which is used widely throughout Burgundy, actually originated in Rully (in Saône-et-Loire).

MÂCONNAIS

Stretching from Saint-Gengoux-le-National down to the northern frontiers of Beaujolais, the Mâconnais can be divided into two distinct areas: in the north, the 'sub-regional' appellations of white (from Chardonnay) and red wines (from Gamay) : Mâcon, Mâcon Supérieur, Mâcon-Villages, intermingled with a clutch of village ACs like Mâcon-Loché, Mâcon-Prissé, Mâcon-Fuissé, Mâcon-Cruzille and Viré-Clessé. Moving south lies the second portion of the appellation, home to the other village appellations which yield some great white wines such as Saint-Véran, Pouilly-Fuissé, Pouilly-Loché and Pouilly-Vinzelles.

The Mâconnais is a frontier land, where the climate alternates between continental influences, and the occasional bout of frost they bring with them, and Mediterranean influences, and their characteristic sunshine and moderate rainfall. This creates just the right balance for the primarily calcareous-clay-type soils to yield their finest qualities before they metamorphose into granite in northern Beaujolais.

WINE STYLES

Summing up the multifarious flavours encountered in Burgundy, home to both the greatest growths and basic wines, is a tall order. In a nutshell, though, Pinot noir delivers sterling quality red fruit aromas and boasts remarkably elegant expression. The whites alternate between great suppleness and a commensurate amount of complexity in the great growths (Chablis, Meursault…), and pleasantly graceful, simple freshness (Aligoté, Mâcon-villages, Bourgogne Chardonnay…). Chardonnay expresses varietal aromas of hazelnut and wild flowers. Crémants can prove remarkable, provided the vines grow on limestone soils.

REVIEW OF RECENT VINTAGES

• **2008** • The red wines are very successful, with a lovely aroma of fruit, good concentration, and rounded and silky tannins. They can be drunk when young, but the best show a promising potential for aging. The whites are powerful with a ripe nose and above all an acidity that guarantees freshness. A great year.

• **2009** • It seems that years ending in nine are lucky in Burgundy: think of 1959, 1989 and, more recently, 1999. The 2009 reds are full-bodied and very ripe, sometimes with a jammy nose. They can easily be enjoyed when young. The whites are also full-bodied and some give off exotic aromas.

• **2010** • Well-balanced, fresh, pure whites. The minerality evident on the palate is archetypal of Burgundy sites. The reds show fresh red fruit aromatics, great perfume and unfurl silky tannins and wonderful harmony between acidity and roundness.

• **2011** • Very unusual weather patterns leading to one of the sixth-earliest vintages in 300 years! A vintage where the winegrower came into his own, as is often the case in Burgundy. Good reds with consistency between villages and growths. The whites can tend to suffer from a lack of acidity but will be perfect when young.

• **2012** • This region experienced every type of weather in 2012: a mild winter, a cool spring that brought frost, a hot May, a cool, rainy June, and an unstable summer that included a heat wave, hail and thunderstorms. The yield was rather low, but the wines have turned out quite well. The whites are expressive, with a very well-balanced palate. The reds are dense, with mature, silky tannins. This vintage is likely to be ready to drink soon.

• **2013** • A low-yielding vintage with virtually no fruit at all around Pommard and Volnay after the passage of hailstorms. However, the wines are extremely pure, brimming with fruit and showing good balance, both for the reds and the whites.

THE BURGUNDY APPELLATIONS

AC ALOXE-CORTON

OVERVIEW: a village appellation in the Côte de Beaune, set in the village of the same name and the neighbouring village of Ladoix-Serrigny. The wines are virtually all reds from Pinot noir with a minute proportion of whites grown on 1.7 ha. The soils are formed of whitish marl and brown or yellowish Callovian or Upper Bathonian limestone.

Climate sites classed as first growths: Several climate-specific sites are classed as first growths (37.5 ha in total). In Aloxe-Corton: Les Valozières, Les Paulands, Les Maréchaudes, Clos des Maréchaudes, Les Chaillots, Les Fournières, Clos du Chapitre, Les Guérets, Les Vercots. In Ladoix-Serrigny : Clos des Maréchaudes, La Maréchaude, Les Petites Folières, Les Moutottes, La Coutière, La Toppe au Vert.

WINE STYLES: the red wines display a crimson hue. They conjure up aromas of red or black fruit (cherry), spices, toast; over time, they take on tones of truffles and leather. In the early years, the reds reveal a strong tannic character, they are firm, generous and elegant. They can be enjoyed with game, guinea fowl, cheeses…

AC AUXEY-DURESSES

OVERVIEW: a village appellation in the Côte de Beaune, set halfway between Meursault and Saint-Romain. In the past, the majority of the wines were sold under the Côte de Beaune-Villages label. The appellation area is surrounded by hills and there are two distinct soil types: those that are conducive to red wines (calcareous clay) and those more suitable for whites (limestone marl).

Climate sites classed as first growths: approximately 30 ha are classed as first growths: Climat du Val, Clos du Val, Les Bréterins, La Chapelle, Reugne, Les Duresses, Bas des Duresses, Les Grands Champs, Les Ecusseaux.

WINE STYLES: three-quarters of the wines are red from Pinot noir. They display a reasonably pale hue, aromas of blackcurrant, raspberry, blackberry, animal, musk and smoky notes. They are harmonious, lively, supple, slightly tannic wines which pair well with braised ham, grilled or roast meats. They are also well-balanced and deep. The whites, with their translucid hue, develop aromas of hazelnut, russet apple, fresh almonds. They combine creaminess with good   acidity and can be served with oven-cooked fish or even poultry served in a cream sauce.

AC BÂTARD-MONTRACHET GRAND CRU

OVERVIEW: A great growth appellation in the Côte de Beaune, located in the villages of Puligny-Montrachet (6.02 ha) and Chassagne-Montrachet (5.85 ha), with a combined total of 11.24 ha. Chardonnay grows here on calcareous clay type soils with high stone and clay content. Bâtard-Montrachet wines are rich, heady, firm white wines with fragrances of almonds, hawthorn and honey. They can be paired with fish served in a sauce or shellfish.

AC BEAUNE

OVERVIEW: Beaune is Côte d'Or's most extensive village appellation. It is famed for its Hospices wine auction which is held at the end of November and is used as a gauge for the region's wine economy. The proceeds provide funding for the local hospital. The vines grow primarily on hillside sites where the soil is brown limestone interspersed with clay or sand.

Climate sites classed as first growths: the appellation boasts 42 first growths with a total 317.55 ha under vine (equating to ¾ of the area): Les Boucherottes, Les Vignes Franches, Clos des Ursules, Les Chouacheux, Les Epenotes, Le Clos des Mouches, Les Montrevenots, Les Aigrots, Les Sizies, Pertuisots, Clos Saint-Landry, Les Avaux, Les Tuvilains, Belissand, Les Seurey, Clos e la Mousse, Les Reversées, Les Sceaux, Les Teurons, Clos du Roi, Blanches Fleurs, A l'Ecu, Clos de l'Ecu, Les Fèves, Les Cent Vignes, Les Marconnets, En Genêt, En l'Orme, Les Perrières, Les Bressandes, Les Toussaints, Les Grèves, Sur les Grèves, Sur les Grèves-Clos-Sainte-Anne, Aux Cras, Le Bas des Teurons, Aux Coucheria, Clos de la Feguine, Montée Rouge, La Mignotte, Clos des Avaux, Champs Pimont.

WINE STYLES: 90% of output is red, made from Pinot noir. The wines boast a deep hue and fruity aromas (cherry, strawberry) with animal undertones developing down the years. Although they are invariably elegant, they vary in structure. The wines from the centre and south of the appellation tend to be powerful and tannic, whilst those from the north are more supple and delicate. The whites (10% of output), with their pale yellow colour, are fat, rich and unctuous. Their acidity enhances their structure and releases aromas of hazelnuts and occasionally tropical fruits (pineapple). The reds sit well alongside marinated meats, poultry and cheeses.

AC BIENVENUES-BÂTARD-MONTRACHET

OVERVIEW: A great growth in the Côte de Beaune located in the village of Puligny-Montrachet, yielding white wines only, from Chardonnay. The appellation covers just 3.53 ha. Its quality and characteristics make it highly reminiscent of Bâtard-Montrachet, which is quite logical since this area extends out eastwards from Bâtard-Montrachet. Bâtard-Montrachet, Bienvenues-Bâtard-Montrachet and Criots-Bâtard-Montrachet have only been classed as individual appellations since the 1937.

AC BLAGNY

OVERVIEW: the only village appellation in Burgundy which does not carry a village name. Blagny is in fact a hamlet which straddles both Meursault and Puligny-Montrachet. The appellation covers only red wines since the whites are labelled Meursault or Puligny-Montrachet.

Climate sites classed as first growths: Blagny boasts 4.08 ha of first growths. In Meursault: La Jeunelotte, La Pièce sous le Bois, Sous le Dos d'Ane, Sous Blagny. In Puligny-Montrachet: Sous le Puits, La Garenne or Sur La Garenne, Hameau de Blagny.

WINE STYLES: Blagny are firm, robust and reasonably well-constituted red wines. Difficult to approach when young, they cellar well. They display pleasant aromas of blackcurrant and strawberry and match well with Epoisses cheese.

AC BONNES-MARES GRAND CRU

OVERVIEW: Most of this 16.24-hectare vineyard is located in the village of Chambolle-Musigny in the Côte de Nuits though the most northerly plots are in Morey-Saint-Denis. The area is divided between more than forty wine growers. The soil comprises a thin layer of limestone on a bedrock of Jurassic limestone, lightened by stones and gravel. These red wines are robust, powerful, dense and elegant and are famed for their lengthy lifespan. With a crimson hue, they display aromas of spices, animal notes and a hint of undergrowth. Enjoy with fillet steak in sauce chasseur, duck with truffles, wild game.

AC BOURGOGNE

OVERVIEW: AC Bourgogne is the umbrella name given to appellation wines throughout Burgundy. Pinot noir is the only permitted varietal for the regional appellation though in Yonne, two old traditional varieties - Cesar and Tressot - which have become virtually obsolete, can also be used.

WINE STYLES: the range of wine styles is extremely diversified due to the possibilities afforded by blending wines from very different growing environments or 'terroirs'. As a rule, the red wines display a moderately intense hue with crimson tints. Down the years, the colour turns ruby then orangy-red. Predominant aromas are cherry, raspberry and occasionally floral notes. As the wines age, humus, venison, truffle, stewed fruit and mild spices enter the scene.

The wine structure is supple, with moderate tannins and occasionally quite distinct acidity. Early-drinking is rewarded and pairings include white meat, vol-au-vents, ham, kidneys, lamb...The whites display the tell-tale aromas of Chardonnay : white flowers, almonds and fresh hazelnuts, lemon, occasionally augmented by woody notes. The balance between fat and freshness is one of their strong points. Try with chicken, oven-cooked fish, scallops...

Some villages in Yonne are entitled to add their name to the Bourgogne appellation. Although this relatively new classification rewards growers geared to making quality wines, actual output remains quite low.

• **Bourgogne Chitry** • Located south-east of Auxerre, on the border with Chablis, in the village of Chitry. The soil is formed of Kimmeridgian limestone marl. The elegant, fruity wines pair with grilled or roast red meat, duck, sauteed veal or beef bourguignon. The generous, round whites are a perfect match for poultry or fish.

• **Bourgogne Côte d'Auxerre** • The area is set south-east of Auxerre in the villages of Augy, Quenne, Saint Bris le Vineux, Vincelottes, Champs-sur-Yonne, Vaux and Auxerre.

The reds are full with delicate tannins and fragrances of raspberry and morello cherry. The whites are fat and delicate with aromas of hazelnut and flowers.

• **Bourgogne Côte Saint-Jacques** • This area located north-west of Auxerre on south, south-east facing hillsides overlooking the Yonne, covers the village of Joigny in the Yonne department. This is Burgundy's most northerly wine region and fewer than 13 hectares are labelled under the appellation annually.

• **Bourgogne Coulanges-la-Vineuse** • The aptly named village of Coulanges, south of Auxerre, has lent its name to this area covering Charentenay, Coulanges La Vineuse, Escolives-Sainte Camille, Jussy, Migé, Mouffy and Val de Mercy in the Yonne department.

• **Bourgogne Epineuil** • The growing area is located north-east of Chablis, near Tonnerre in the village of Epineuil. Grown on calcareous clay soils, the reds are tannic, elegant wines suitable for laying down. Try with red meat, roast poultry or veal stew. The fruity, soft whites are well-suited to fish.

• **Bourgogne Tonnerre** • An area located north-east of Chablis, on plots set in the villages of Epineuil, Dannemoine, Junay, Molosmes, Tonnerre and Vézinnes in the Yonne department.

Bourgogne Vezelay: centring on the famous basilica where tourists flock, providing a ready-made clientele, this appellation covers around 50 hectares in the villages of Asquins, Saint Père, Tharoiseau and Vézelay in the Yonne department.

AC BOURGOGNE ALIGOTÉ

OVERVIEW: a regional appellation grown throughout Burgundy which takes its name from the eponymous varietal. Most Aligotés are made in the Côte Chalonnaise.

WINE STYLES: Bourgogne Aligoté are light, lively, vigorous wines that are supple, delicate, fresh and moderately well-constituted with acidulous overtones. They exhibit a white gold colour with greenish tints, and exude fragrances of grape, green apple, vanilla and lemon. Try with cooked cold pork meats, fried or grilled fish, snails, oven-baked pike-perch, goats cheeses.

AC BOURGOGNE CLAIRET

These rosé wines can be grown throughout Burgundy. They are fruity and supple and must comply with the same regulations as for AC Burgundy. Pinot noir is the sole grape variety, except in Yonne, where it can be augmented with Cesar and Trousseau. They pair well with barbecues or cooked cold pork meats.

AC BOURGOGNE CÔTE CHALONNAISE

OVERVIEW: 44 towns and villages in Saône-et-Loire are entitled to this appellation: canton of Buxy (18 villages), Chagny (11 villages), Givry (12 villages) and Mont Saint Vincent (3 villages). The area was awarded AC status in 1990 so that growers outside the boundaries of the other local appellations (Mercurey, Givry, Rully and Montagny) could enjoy their own appellation. Production conditions are identical to those for AC Bourgogne.

WINE STYLES: the red wines are light, supple, delicate and round with fragrances of red fruits (cherry, raspberry, strawberry), bay, and pleasant tannins and acidity. Try with veal stew. The whites are rich, with a pleasant bouquet, developing aromas of flowers and dried fruit.

AC BOURGOGNE HAUTES CÔTES DE BEAUNE

OVERVIEW: the steep gradient separating Burgundy's 'mountain' from the valley floor of the Saône, is not only the prerogative of the Côte de Beaune and its northerly neighbour, the Côte de Nuits. Tucked away at higher elevations are the Hautes Côtes, an extremely fragmented area where vines have been growing at altitudes of between 300 and 450 metres since time immemorial. 22 villages in the Côte d'Or department and 7 in Saône-et-Loire are entitled to use this appellation.

WINE STYLES: drawn from Pinot noir and Chardonnay, these wines are lighter than those of the Côte, their acidity greater. They reward earlier drinking too and are approachable, pleasant wines from an aromatic perspective. Enjoyable with barbecues (reds), fish or shellfish (whites).

AC BOURGOGNE HAUTES CÔTES DE NUITS

OVERVIEW: the Hautes Côtes de Nuits borders on the Hautes Côtes de Beaune in the north and covers 16 villages in Côte d'Or, dotted between Dijon and Maranges, as well as the upper reaches of 4 localities in the Côtes de Nuits area. The vineyards are home to Pinot noir and Chardonnay vines and, despite their high elevation, they enjoy excellent aspect and suitable soils.

WINE STYLES: the reds exhibit a relatively deep hue and sterling quality fruit. On the palate, they display a pleasant mellowness, fat and freshness. Although they are quite robust, they are still soft and fruity, thereby pairing well with poultry for example. The whites are of a good standard, quite generous and highly aromatic. Try with langoustine and other shellfish.

AC BOURGOGNE ORDINAIRE AND BOURGOGNE GRAND ORDINAIRE (COTEAUX BOURGUIGNONS)

These appellations are on the wane. The area shares the same boundaries as AC Bourgogne, stretching over Côte d'Or, the Rhone, Yonne and Saône-et-Loire and covering 385 towns and villages. Gamay is allowed to be blended into the reds, alongside Pinot noir. The red wines have lower alcohol content than AC Bourgogne. Try with ham, duck with green pepper... The whites come primarily from Chardonnay and Aligoté and partner with snails, and the rosés go with cooked cold pork meats, barbecues and crudités.

AC BOURGOGNE PASSE-TOUT-GRAINS

OVERVIEW: the name of this appellation is a give-away as to the type of wine made here, because contrary to the other Burgundy ACs, this appellation is a blend of several varietals: at least 1/3 Gamay and at most 2/3 Pinot noir. Bourgogne Passe-Tout-Grains is made throughout the region, thereby covering 91 towns and villages in Côte d'Or, 85 in the Rhone, 154 in Saône-et-Loire and 54 in Yonne. The best wines come from sites in Côte d'Or on the valley floor.

WINE STYLES: with a deep colour and aromas of violet, fruit and animal notes in the early years, this is a quaffing wine, fruity and rustic with a certain amount of acidity.

AC BOUZERON

OVERVIEW: this particular site embraces two villages, Bouzeron and Chassey Le Camp, in the Saône-et-Loire department. The reputation of its Aligoté wines is long-established, entitling it to add its name to the Bourgogne Aligoté appellation initially, then subsequently warranting it an outright village appellation in 1998. The best Bourgogne Aligoté hail from this site and from Chitry.

WINE STYLES: Bouzeron wines display a pale yellow hue with greenish tints. They exhibit aromas of vanilla, are soft and silky on the palate and are enjoyable with cooked cold pork meats, fried or grilled fish and snails.

AC CHABLIS

OVERVIEW: Chablis is located not far from Auxerre, midway between Dijon and Paris. It grows along the hills flanking the river Serein and boasts a south/south-east aspect. It is Burgundy's most northerly appellation and embraces more than 18 towns and villages. Soil types ranging from marl to Jurassic limestone (Kimmeridgian) littered with marine fossils provide a foothold for the vines. The climate in Chablis is continental, with harsh winters, potentially disastrous spring frosts and scorching summers. Booming sales have led to the constant expansion of the region since the 1960s.

WINE STYLES: Chablis are white wines drawn from Chardonnay. They display recognisable aromas of acacia, honeysuckle, fern, honey, toast, hazelnut and mushroom. They boast elegant, complex fruitiness, and characteristic liveliness and fat. Whilst basic Chablis, usually vinted in vats, rewards early drinking, the more structured first growths have a cellaring capacity ranging from 5 to 10 years. Try with seafood, fish and snails.

123

CHABLIS PREMIER CRU

OVERVIEW: Here the vineyard classification system really comes into its own. The core of the wine region is formed of seven climate-specific sites comprising the Grand Cru appellation (see specific heading) and forty or so climate-specific sites classed as Chablis Premiers Crus, labelled under 17 denominations: Les Beauregards, Beauroy, Berdiot, Chaume de Talma, Côte de Jouan, Côte de Léchet, Côte de Vaubarousse, Fourchaume, Les Fourneaux, Monts de Milieu, Montée de Tonnerre, Montmains, Vaillons, Vau Ligneau, Vau de Vey, Vaucoupin, Vosgros. The rest of the appellation is entitled to use the basic AC Chablis appellation. The outlying area, with its Portlandian limestone soils, is home to the Petit Chablis appellation.

WINE STYLES: Chablis 1er Cru wines are more robust though also more delicate than basic Chablis. Their lifespan ranges from 5 to 10 years and many of them spend some time under oak. They are the perfect match for grilled crayfish, lobster, fish in a white sauce, snails, seafood, oysters, goats cheese and veal stew.

AC CHABLIS GRAND CRU

OVERVIEW: in the heart of the Chablis area, seven great growth climate-specific sites occupy a hillside overlooking the right bank of the Serein. These are Blanchot

(12.2 ha), Bougros (14.35 ha), Les Clos (25.87 ha), Grenouilles (9.38 ha), Les Preuses (10.81 ha), Valmur (10.55 ha) and Vaudésir (15.43 ha). The climate-specific site of La Moutonne, belonging to the Long Depaquit estate, is not officially classed as such by AC law. However 95 % of La Moutonne's vineyards are located in the Vaudésir appellation and 5% in Les Preuses, hence the owner sells La Moutonne under the Chablis Grand Cru appellation. This particular hillside, with the characteristic calcareous marl of Chablis, provides remarkable drainage and aspect for Chardonnay (known locally as Beaunois), which explains the outstanding potential of the wines.

WINE STYLES: Chablis Grand Cru exhibit a greenish-yellow hue and exude fragrances of honey, hazelnut and mineral notes. They are concentrated wines, often firm when young, which develop fat and mellowness over time. Good vintages will age for between 10 to 15 years, developing intense aromas of dried fruit, toast, gingerbread, slightly oxidised notes and occasionally gun flint. Serving them with oysters in a cream sauce, fish in a sauce, poultry, veal stew… enhances their flavour.

AC CHAMBERTIN GRAND CRU

A 13-hectare great growth in the Côte de Nuits, in the village of Gevrey-Chambertin. The vines grow halfway up a gently sloping hill, to the south of the village of Chambertin on marl or calcareous marl soils scattered with tiny stones. Woodland to the west shelters the vines from the wind. The red wines exhibit a liquorice hue, they are full-bodied, vigorous, robust, racy, generous and full, with good cellaring capacity. Try with game, coq au Chambertin, flavoursome cheeses…

AC CHAMBERTIN CLOS DE BÈZE GRAND CRU

These wines can be sold as Chambertin   Clos de Bèze or AC Chambertin. Conversely, Chambertin cannot be sold as Chambertin Clos de Bèze. Located between Chambertin and Mazis-Chambertin, this site of just under 15 hectares is set at a higher elevation than Chambertin and its soils are shallower. The wines are sensual, opulent, delicate, with a powerful structure. They pair with game.

AC CHAMBOLLE-MUSIGNY

OVERVIEW: Chambolle-Musigny grows in the heart of the Côte de Nuits. Half of the village boasts either first or great growth status. The soils are limestone with stones or gravel, imparting greater finesse to the wines.

WINE STYLES: this appellation has a reputation for producing the most delicate and most feminine of all the wines in Côte d'Or. With an intense hue displaying purple then garnet-red tints as it ages, this is a racy wine boasting elegant tannins and very little acidity. The first growths are firm, with greater concentration. Deep aromas of raspberry, stewed strawberry, violet, undergrowth, spices, morello cherry, liquorice… Try with young pigeon, veal Orloff, fatted chicken, young wild boar, duck with girolle mushrooms.

CLIMATE SITES CLASSED AS FIRST GROWTHS:
(just over 50 hectares): *Les Véroilles, Les Sentiers, Les Baudes, Les Noirots, Les Lavrottes, Les Fuées, Aux Beaux Bruns, Aux Echanges, Les Charmes, Les Plantes, Aux Combottes, Derrière la Grange, Les Gruenchers, Les Groseilles, Aux Combottes, Les Feusselottes, Les Chatelots, Les Cras, Les Carrières, Les Chabiots, Les Amoureuses, Les Borniques, Les Hauts Doix, La Combe d'Orveau.*

AC CHAPELLE-CHAMBERTIN GRAND CRU

This 5.5-hectare appellation is located in the northern part of the Côte de Nuits, in the village of Gevrey-Chambertin. The soils are slightly richer than in Griotte-Chambertin and the wines are some of the fruitiest of the Chambertin great growths. They are robust and virile like Gevrey, yet more delicate. Their aromas are comparable to those of Clos de Bèze although they lack their grand finish. They sit nicely alongside fish in a sauce, though also shellfish and roast white meats.

125

AC CHARMES CHAMBERTIN GRAND CRU

A 28.97-hectare site adjacent to Mazoyères-Chambertin, in fact the production areas for Charmes-Chambertin and Mazoyères-Chambertin are identical. The soils are calcareous marl in type with an extremely high proportion of limestone. Charmes are less tannic, rounder and lighter than the other Chambertin great growths. They develop aromas of violet, liquorice and vanilla and woody undertones. They pair with wild boar, venison or pheasant.

AC CHASSAGNE-MONTRACHET

OVERVIEW: located in the far south of the Côte de Beaune, in the villages of Chassagne-Montrachet (Côte d'Or) and Remigny (Saône-et-Loire), this appellation area covers just over 300 hectares, half of which is divided between 55 first growths and 3 great growths. Chardonnay grows on clayey white limestone in the north-east, Pinot noir on the limestone marl in the north-west and south-west.

WINE STYLES: the white wines are fat, opulent, robust and golden in colour. They are dry, firm and long on the palate. Aromas reminiscent of almonds, ripe apple, white flowers, honey, fern and hawthorn are present, along with mineral notes and a hint of hazelnut, though also tropical fruit such as pineapple and grapefruit. The red wines conjure up aromas of blackcurrant, raspberry and a comprehensive range of ripe fruit, and venison. The wines are clean and round, fleshy, well-constituted, supply and velvety with delicate tannins.

CLIMATE SITES CLASSED AS FIRST GROWTHS:
Clos Saint-Jean, Cailleret, Les Chaumées, Les Vergers, Les Chenevottes, Les Macherelles, En Remilly, Dent de Chien, Vide Bourse, Blanchot-Dessus, La Maltroie, Les Brussonnes, Morgeot, Abbaye de Morgeot, Bois de Chassagne, La Grande Montagne, La Boudriotte, Les Champs Gains, Tonton Marcel, Champs Jendreau, Chassagne, Chassagne du Clos Saint-Jean, Clos Chareau, Clos Pitois, En Cailleret, En Virondot, Ez Crets, Ez Crottes, Francemont, Guerchère, La Cardeuse, La Chapelle, La Grande Borne, La Romanée, La Roquemaure, Les Baudines, Les Boirettes, Les Bondues, Les Chaumes, Les Combards, Les Commes, Les Embazées, Les Fairendes, Les Grandes Ruchottes, Les Grands Clos, Les Murées, Les Pasquelles, Les Petites Fairendes, Les Petits Clos, Les Places, Les Rebichets, Petingeret, Tête du Clos, Vigne Blanche and Vigne Derrière.

AC CHEVALIER-MONTRACHET GRAND CRU

This 7.47-hectare site is set above Puligny-Montrachet in a horizontal strip. The vines are planted on thin, stony soil of clayey white limestone and face east and south-east. With their body, firmness, mellowness and intensity they make pleasant wines to drink, though their most recognisable characteristics are their great finesse and delicacy. Sporting a bright golden hue, aromas of hazelnut, honey, almond, amber and exotic fruits, they pair with turbot and fish in a sauce, lobster, white meats.

AC CHOREY-LÈS-BEAUNE

OVERVIEW: the village is located in the vicinity of Beaune, in the plain, level with Savigny on an imaginary line from Dijon to Beaune. The appellation boasts no first growths.

WINE STYLES: predominantly red wines with fragrances of raspberry, morello cherry and blackcurrant, leading into crystallised fruit. They are light, supple, fruity, with low acidity and tannins. Their elegance outweighs their tannin content. They are delicate and feminine and are usually at their peak within their first decade. Pair with poultry fricassee, barbecued meats, mildly flavoured game birds or roast guinea fowl...

AC CLOS DES LAMBRAYS GRAND CRU

Located in the village of Morey-Saint-Denis between Clos-Saint-Denis and Clos de Tart, this 7.04 ha growth is, like Clos de Tart, a monopoly (owned by a German industrialist). In actual fact, it is a virtual monopoly as a few ares belong to neighbouring growers. The growth is set in the heart of the village and occupies a marl hillside which turns into calcareous clay at the foot of the hill. The wines combine power with finesse. They display fragrances of truffle and humus though rarely fruit. A perfect match for game, red meat and vacherin cheese.

AC CLOS DE LA ROCHE GRAND CRU

Covering almost 13.41 hectares, this Morey-Saint-Denis great growth occupies a hillside site with a due east aspect overlooking the road from Gevrey to Morey. The marl-rich, limestone soils impart structure and depth to these red wines, which are duly deep, well-constituted wines exhibiting great structure and body, whilst at the same time remaining delicate and graceful with bundles of fruit. The cellaring capacity of the wines is one of the longest in Burgundy, reaching and indeed extending beyond 20 years. Try with game or roast meat.

AC CLOS DE TART GRAND CRU

This 7.5-hectare Clos, established in 1141, is today a monopoly, owned entirely by a single owner (Maison J. Mommessin). It sits north of Morey-Saint-Denis, between Bonnes Mares and Clos des Lambrays. The soils are formed of shallow scree, covering a limestone bedrock. These red wines exude fragrances of strawberry, violet, and subsequently spices and undergrowth as they mature. With an extensive cellaring capacity, they are powerful, robust, elegant, silky and down the years become graceful. Their strong tannic framework mellows with age. Try with venison, leg of lamb…

127

AC CLOS DE VOUGEOT GRAND CRU

With its 50 hectares under vine, this great growth is the largest in the Côte d'Or and is located in the village of Vougeot, north of Nuits-Saint-Georges. Created between the 11th and 14th centuries by the monks of Cîteaux who built a wall around it, the growth is currently divided between almost 80 different owners ! The soil types are extremely varied. The higher elevations adjacent to Bonnes-Mares and Grands-Echezeaux, are home to light, gravely chalk resting on a bedrock of oolitic limestone. Further down the slopes, the soil is softer limestone containing clay and gravel and at the very bottom, it is rich in alluvial clay.

Classic Clos de Vougeot displays a deep red colour and aromas of red and black fruit (cherries, blackcurrant, blackberries), undergrowth and violet. As it matures, it develops aromas of fur, truffle and musk. A robust, firm, lively wine in its youth, it exhibits delicate tannins and a discrete touch of acidity. As a rule, the better wines come from the plots in the upper reaches of the Clos, though with such a great vineyard and range of growers, the wines cover a broad spectrum. Try with pheasant with apples.

AC CLOS SAINT-DENIS GRAND CRU

Located in the village of Morey-Saint-Denis, between Clos de la Roche and Clos des Lambrays. The original area under vine was a diminutive 2 hectares but this has been extended to a current area of 5.99 ha. Clos Saint-Denis red wines are moderately full but their aromatic range covers a broad spectrum: red and black fruit, spices, tobacco, musk… Try with poultry and game, or why not Peking duck as some people suggest !

AC CORTON GRAND CRU

The Corton great growth occupies the southern slopes of the Corton hillside overlooking the village of Aloxe-Corton. The only red great growth in the Côte de Beaune, it extends over 160 ha with barely a hundred of those on-stream. Voltaire used to say that he would rather drink this wine in private than serve it to his guests. White wines are also grown on 4.53 hectares. Corton wines display a deep-coloured hue and fragrances of red fruit (blackcurrant, cherry), truffle, leather, a touch of humus and spices. They are powerful wines, blessed with good acidity. Laying-down wines, they can be slightly firm over the first few years. Try with small or large game.

SOME CLIMATE SITE NAMES CAN BE ADDED TO THAT OF THE APPELLATION:

In Aloxe-Corton: *Les Pougets, Les Languettes, Le Corton, Les Renardes, Les Grèves, Le Clos du Roi, Les Chaumes, Les Perrières, Les Bressandes, Les Paulands, Les Maréchaudes, Les Fiètres, Le Meix Lallemand, Clos des Meix, Les Combes, La Vigne au Saint.*

In Ladoix-Serrigny: *Le Rognet et Corton, Clos des Cortons, Les Moutottes, Les Carrières, Basses Mourottes, Hautes Mourottes, Les Vergennes, Les Grandes Lolières, La Toppe au vert.*

AC CORTON CHARLEMAGNE (AND CHARLEMAGNE) GRAND CRU

This fifty or so hectare great growth extends westwards from Corton on the hill of the same name. Its climate sites straddle the villages of Aloxe-Corton, Ladoix and Pernand-Vergelesses. Corton-Charlemagne is the only wine area bearing the name of two emperors: Curtis d'Othon, hence the name Corton, and of course Charlemagne, who donated his vines to Saint-Andoche abbey in Saulieu in 775. Chardonnay thrives here on the limestone-rich soils, steep inclines facing south-west and north-east and a microclimate which ensures cooler temperatures. The appellation also embraces that of Charlemagne, which is no longer used.

These white wines with their golden hue display complex fragrances of citrus peel, fresh almonds, cinnamon, walnut, exotic fruits, honey, dried fruit, spices (pepper). Corton-Charlemagne are lively, fresh, full, rich, unctuous wines with great length, intensity, body, complexity and elegance. They are slightly firm when young and require a few years to fully express their qualities. Try with lobster Americaine, fish in a cream sauce, some white meats and certain types of cheese (Munster and blue).

AC CÔTE-DE-BEAUNE-VILLAGES

OVERVIEW: with the exception of Aloxe-Corton, Beaune, Pommard and Volnay, all of the village ACs in the Côte de Beaune are entitled to use this appellation and can choose between their own appellation or Côte-de-Beaune-Villages. Growers can also state the name of their village after 'Côte de Beaune' on labels.

WINE STYLES: depending on whether they are harvested in the northern portion of the appellation or in the south, wine styles can vary immensely. Those from the north display a light hue with elegant, supple, delicate, round aromas and pleasant tannins. Those from the south boast a deeper hue and a more marked tannic structure, they are well-rounded with good acidity.

AC CÔTE DE BEAUNE

OVERVIEW: stretching over the outlying hills around the town of Beaune, this appellation covers around 25 ha. It should not be confused with 'Côte de Beaune', the geographical term used to described the southern half of Côte d'Or (as opposed to Côte de Nuits in the north).

WINE STYLES: the wines are highly reminiscent of those from Beaune, with a relatively dark hue and typical red fruit fragrances such as strawberry, blackcurrant and cherry. Try with marinated meats such as beef, poultry, game birds or cooked cold pork meats.

129

AC CÔTE DE NUITS-VILLAGES

OVERVIEW: the villages entitled to use this appellation are Fixin, Brochon, Premeaux-Prissey, south-west of Dijon and Comblanchien and Corgoloin south of Nuits-Saint-Georges. Soil types vary greatly, ranging from predominantly limestone with patches of marl in the north, to stonier soils with a touch of clay in the south.

WINE STYLES: the wines are aromatic (blackberry, cherry, raspberry, blackcurrant, leading into liquorice and venison as they age) and mature rapidly. Wines from the south are supple, fruity and more delicate, whilst those from the north display a good tannic framework and fat. Such diversity is not only down to the varying soil make-up, but also the aspect of the vineyards and the climate. Try with poached eggs in a red wine sauce, beef bourguignon, mildly-flavoured cheeses...

AC CRÉMANT DE BOURGOGNE

OVERVIEW: Crémant is made throughout virtually the whole of Burgundy, but primarily in Yonne and the Côte Chalonnaise. Permitted varietals are divided into two groups: Pinot noir, Pinot gris and Chardonnay(first group); Gamay, Aligoté, Melon and Sacy (second group). In the final blend, varietals in the first group must account for at least 30%, whilst Gamay is restricted to a maximum 20%.

Rules governing production: a basic yield of 7,500 kg/ha, i.e. 50 hl/ha, hand harvesting, an extraction rate restricted to 100 litres of juice per 150 kg of grapes, horizontal storage for at least nine months… After disgorging, CO2 in Crémant de Bourgogne must be under at least 3.5 atmospheres of pressure.

WINE STYLES: Crémant has a brilliant hue, it is ethereal, light, fresh, vigorous, fruity and round with good liveliness imparted by Pinot noir. The best Crémants hail from the Rully area (Saône-et-Loire) and from Saint-Bris in Yonne. They are equally delicious as an appetiser with cheese puffs ('gougères') or with a main course of seafood.

AC CRIOTS BÂTARD-MONTRACHET GRAND CRU

This 1.57 ha great growth is entirely located in the village of Chassagne-Montrachet, in a place called Les Criots, south-west of Beaune. These great (and rare) white wines bear the tell-tale characteristics of the Montrachet great growths. They are dry yet not harsh and reveal remarkable fruit. Try with lobster or crayfish.

AC ECHEZEAUX GRAND CRU

This 34.79 ha great growth is located in the village of Flagey-Echézeaux in the Côte de Nuits. It yields elegant, velvety, fleshy wines with power and concentration. They boast delicate tannins and a long-lasting finish. With a deep red hue, they display fragrances of red and black fruit, cocoa bean, exotic wood and musk. They pair well with game birds (woodcock, partridge), lamb and soft, creamy cheeses.

AC FIXIN

OVERVIEW: with around a hundred hectares under vine located a few kilometres south of Dijon, this is one of the more northerly Côte de Nuits village appellations. It is geared virtually entirely to producing red wines and a large proportion of them are actually labelled under the Côte de Nuits-Villages appellation.

Climate sites classed as first growths: in Fixin: Arvelets, Clos du Chapitre, Clos Napoléon, Le Meix Bas, Clos de la Perrière, Hervelets. In Brochon: Clos de la Perrière.

WINE STYLES: grown on Bajocian limestone type soils with patches of marl, the reds are well-constituted, generous, robust, relatively tannic and rich in alcohol. Firm and blessed with good acidity, they exhibit animal or even wild notes (fur, musk), as well as red and black fruit (blackcurrant, cherry, blackberry). Try with a leg of lamb, game, red meat in a sauce, mature cheeses.

AC GEVREY-CHAMBERTIN

OVERVIEW: the vineyards in this Côte de Nuits wine area embrace two villages: Gevrey-Chambertin and Brochon, about 10 km from Dijon. They cover almost

410 ha and are divided into two parts by 'Lavaux Coomb'. The soil is formed of Bajocian encrinal limestone and upper Lias clay marl.

WINE STYLES: their deep hue covers a broad spectrum ranging from cherry-red to garnet. They display distinctive fragrances of red or black fruit (blackcurrant), animal notes, musk, fur, liquorice, bilberry, prune, nutmeg, pepper, leather. Wines from the steeper slopes are solid, powerful and generous, whilst those from the flatter soils tend to be more elegant. In the early years, they are often tannic, and the first growths remain firm throughout. Try with poultry, beef tenderloin, small or large game.

THE AREA IS HOME TO 26 FIRST GROWTHS:
La Bossière, La Romanée, Poissenot, Estournelles-Saint-Jacques, Clos des Varoilles, Lavaut Saint-Jacques, Champeaux, Petits Cazetiers, Combe au Moine, Les Goulots, Aux Combottes, Bel Air, Cherbaudes, Petite Chapelle, En Ergot, Clos Prieur, La Perrière, Au Closeau, Issarts, Les Corbeaux, Craipillot, Fonteny, Clos du Chapitre, Clos Saint-Jacques, Les Cazetiers, Champonet.

AC GIVRY

OVERVIEW: this appellation sits west of Chalon-sur-Saône, and occupies a strip 6km long by 3km wide. Reputedly Henry IV's favourite wines, they are grown in the village of Givry and the immediate vicinity, forming a barrier against urban sprawl.

WINE STYLES: the reds display a deep ruby-red hue with aromas of wild fruit, redcurrant, a touch of spices and animal tones, liquorice, raspberry and under-growth. They are round, warm, delicate, lively, moderately robust wines. Try with white meat in a sauce. The whites display a golden colour with floral aromas such as thyme, wild rose, mineral and citrus notes (lemon). Smooth on the palate, they are rich, subtle and delicate with good length and fresh flavours. Enjoy with fish or tarts.

CLIMATE SITES CLASSED AS FIRST GROWTHS:
Clos du Cras Long, Clos des Vernoy, Les Grandes Vignes, Clos Marceaux, Les Garnds Prétans, Clos de la Barraude, Petit Marole, Clos du Celiiers aux Moines, Clos Charlé, Servoisine, Les Bois Chevaux, Clos Saint-Pierre, Clos Saint-Paul, Clos Salomon, A Vigne Rouge, Clos Jus, Crausot, Crémillons, En Choué, La Grande Berge, La Plante, Le Paradis, Le Petit Prétan, Le Vigron, les Bois Gautiers, Champ Nalot, En Veau, La Brûlée, La Matrosse, La Grande Berge, La Petite Berge, Le Champ Lalot, Le Médenchot, Le Pied du Clou, Le Vernoy, Les Combes, Les Galaffres, Pied de Chaume and Clos Marole.

AC GRANDS ECHEZEAUX GRAND CRU

Located in the village of Flagey-Echezeaux, this growth has a misleading name: it is in fact four times smaller than neighbouring Echezeaux (7.53 ha) with just one plot (as opposed to 11 for Echezeaux). It has a due east aspect, gentle inclines,

131

and the soil is calcareous clay. Good drainage is provided by the myriad stones here. These combine to produce silky, full, deep red wines, which are more powerful and generous than the Echezeaux. Similarly, they are also longer on the palate. They display aromas of cherry, strawberry, blackcurrant and raspberry, leading into a bouquet of musk, leather and undergrowth as they mature. They pair well with roast meals, meat served with a sauce, game (venison, wild boar) and mildly-flavoured cheeses.

AC GRIOTTE-CHAMBERTIN GRAND CRU
This 2.7 ha growth is located in the village of Gevrey-Chambertin. The soil is strewn with small stones over a Bajocian bedrock. The wines are red, fleshy, delicate and soft. Their framework is bolstered more by their tannins than their acidity and they develop aromas of jammy cherries as they age. A suitable partner for white meat and poultry.

AC IRANCY
OVERVIEW: the appellation is located 15 km south of Auxerre, in and around Irancy, Vincelottes and Cravant in the Yonne department. Site-specific names (Palotte, Les Cailles, Les Mazelots…) can be appended to that of Irancy though in actual fact few growers do.
WINE STYLES: Irancy display a deep hue and fragrances of cherry, blackcurrant, spices, violet and 'terroir'. They are solid, robust, tannic wines which are lively and long-lasting on the palate. Although they can be slightly bitter in the early years, they have a prolonged cellaring capacity. The hallmark characteristics of these wines are partly derived from frequent use of the Cesar varietal, which is blended with Pinot. Try with coq au vin, kidneys in a Madeira sauce, beef bourguignon and cheeses.

AC LADOIX
OVERVIEW: Ladoix is in fact not a village but a hamlet within the parish of Ladoix-Serrigny. With around 140.95 ha under vine, it is nevertheless considered as a village appellation and embraces 11 climate sites classed as first growths.
WINE STYLES: with their fragrances of raspberry, cherry and undergrowth, the red wines are relatively robust and fleshy, with body and character. The first growths display great structure and more predominant tannins. Try with veal liver, roasted red meats, game. With their aromas of ripe apple, fresh fig and walnut, the whites are firm when young, gradually mellowing as they age.
CLIMATE SITES CLASSED AS FIRST GROWTHS:
La Micaude, La Corvée, Le Clou d'Orge, Les Joyeuses, Bois Roussot, Basses Mourottes, En Naget, Le Rognet et Corton, les Buis,
Les Grêchons et Foutrières and Hautes Mourottes.

AC LA GRANDE RUE GRAND CRU

This 1.65-ha growth is set within the boundaries of Vosne-Romanée, between Romanée-Conti and La Tâche. It is under the sole ownership of Domaine Lamarche and was classed as recently as 1992. The soil is limestone in type, rich in iron with a stony, rocky or clay-marl subsoil. The wines are subtle and delicate whilst at the same time robust, well-constituted and powerful, combining to produce harmony and distinction. They are chewy and boast similarities with the neighbouring growths. Their musky fragrances and violet and raspberry tones are a joy to the senses.

AC LA TÂCHE GRAND CRU

A 6 ha great growth located in the village of Vosne Romanée. The limestone soils are shallow and particularly poor here. The growth is a monopoly of Domaine de la Romanée-Conti. Red La Tâche wines are concentrated and powerful on the nose. Although they can be very discrete when young, they gradually acquire complexity and finesse as they mature. Try with poultry-based dishes.

AC LATRICIÈRES CHAMBERTIN GRAND CRU

This 7.35 ha growth is located in the village of Gevrey-Chambertin, on the other side of the road from Chambertin. A thin layer of silica modifies the soil type, making it harder. Pinot noir is the sole grape variety and the wines are vigorous, virile and racy with a pleasant bouquet. Their finesse sets them apart from the other growths. Less powerful than the Chambertins, they boast fragrances of moss, undergrowth and game.

AC MÂCON AND MÂCON SUPÉRIEUR

(followed by the name of a locality)

OVERVIEW: barely 100 towns and villages with a combined are under vine of 2,391 ha are entitled to this appellation, which more or less fits within the same area as the district of Mâcon.

WINE STYLES: their hue covers a broad spectrum ranging from cherry-red to deep ruby-red with purplish tints. These are quaffing wines, light, pleasant and round on the palate, with well-balanced tannins. The whites display a limpid hue with green gold tints. They are supple wines with fragrances of citronella, fern and musk, which reward early drinking.

AC MÂCON-VILLAGES

OVERVIEW: this white wine appellation embraces 26 groups of towns and villages in the Mâcon area, including Azé, Chaintré, Chasselas, Chardonnay, Cruzille, Davayé, Fuissé, Igé, Lugny, Milly-Lamartine, Péronne, Pierreclos,

Solutré-Pouilly, La Roche-Vineuse, Vergisson and Verzé. Overall area under vine is slightly in excess of 1,300 ha. The Burgundy climate draws out good varietal expression from Chardonnay. Wood is a less prominent flavour component than in Côte de Beaune and the prices are a lot more affordable too.

WINE STYLES: with a brilliant hue sporting greenish tints, the wines display aromas of hazelnut, almond, white peach, fern, butter and white flowers (hawthorn, acacia and wild rose), with lemony undertones. They boast a clean, silky attack, are fat, noticeably rich in alcohol with well-balanced acidity. Try with monkfish steak in a green pepper sauce, trout, chitterlings sausage, seafood, fish served with a sauce, white meats.

AC MARANGES

OVERVIEW: this 163 ha appellation is divided between three villages located in the far southern tip of the Côte de Beaune in Saône-et-Loire : Dezize, Sampigny and Cheilly, each of which is entitled to add its name to that of the appellation. Seven climate sites are classed as first growths within the appellation.

WINE STYLES: Maranges wines have a deep colour and aromas of red fruit and undergrowth. When fully mature, they develop aromas of fur and game. They are solid, robust, rich, tannic, fleshy wines which are full and firm. Try with a leg of venison, ribsteak, rabbit with a mushroom sauce, jugged hare.

CLIMATE SITES CLASSED AS FIRST GROWTHS:
In Cheilly-les-Maranges: *Les clos Roussots, la Fussière, Clos de la Boutière.*
In Dezize: *La Fussière, Clos de la Fussière, La Croix aux Moines.*
In Sampigny: *Les Clos Roussots, Le Clos des Rois, Le Clos des Loyères.*

AC MARSANNAY

OVERVIEW: this is the most northerly appellation in the Côte de Nuits, embracing three villages: Marsannay-la-Côte, Couchey and Chenôve. It is unusual in that it produces all three colours of wine: red, white and rosé. The rosé wines are made from Pinot noir and the appellation has built up its entire reputation as a producer of rosé. Out of an overall area under vine of 210 ha, 35 ha are dedicated to its rosé wine which is considered to be the best in Burgundy.

WINE STYLES: the reds, with their fragrances of blackcurrant, dried prunes and wild blackberry are clean, light, supple and scented. Try with cooked cold pork meats, or grilled meats. The rosés with their aromas of peach, strawberry and raspberry, display a hue ranging from salmon-pink to pale ruby-red. They are powerful, soft and fruity with good acidity. The fleshy, fat, full, supple whites have a long-lasting flavour and pair well with grilled fish.

AC MAZIS-CHAMBERTIN GRAND CRU

This 8.79-ha growth is adjacent to Clos de Bèze, south of Gevrey-Chambertin.

The soils are extremely shallow, particularly in the upper reaches of the Clos The vineyards are planted to Pinot noir, which yields lighter, less austere wines than Chambertin. They are delicate, smooth, opulent, powerful wines bolstered by a good tannic framework, hence their need to mature. They display fragrances of red fruit leading into leather. They pair well with large game.

AC MAZOYÈRES-CHAMBERTIN GRAND CRU

This is a 1.72-ha growth (area on-stream) in the village of Gevrey-Chambertin. The soil is strewn with stones and has a strong limestone bias. The red wines offer crystallised aromas of stone fruits and leathery notes. Production areas for Charmes-Chambertin and Mazoyères-Chambertin are identical but most of the wines are usually labelled as Charmes-Chambertin.

AC MERCUREY

OVERVIEW: set midway between Rully and Givry, the boundaries of this appellation are etched by Mount Morin and the Orbiset river. With 646 ha under vine, including 32 classed as first growths, the Mercurey appellation produces almost as much wine as the other ACs in the Côte Chalonnaise (Givry, Rully, Montagny). The wines are grown in the village of Mercurey and in the immediate vicinity.

WINE STYLES: the reds exhibit aromas of small red fruit (blackcurrant, raspberry, morello cherry, strawberry) with undertones of leather and undergrowth. They have body, are chewy, rich, robust and well-balanced. They pair nicely with pheasant and tenderloin steak with ceps. The whites, with their golden colour and aromas of cinnamon, exotic fruit, amber and walnut, are fat and elegant. They are the perfect partner for fish served with a sauce.

CLIMATE SITES CLASSED AS FIRST GROWTHS:
Clos Marcilly, Les Croichots, La Cailloute, Les Combins, Les Champs Martin, Clos des Barraults, Clos des Myglands, Le Clos l'Evêque, Clos Voyens, Grand Clos Fortoul, Clos des Grands Voyens, Les Naugues, Les Crêts, Clos Tonnerre, Les Vasées, Les Byots, Sazenay, La Bondue, La Levrière, La Mission, Le Clos du Roy, Griffères, Les Velley, Clos du Château de Montaigu, Les Montaigus, Clos des Montaigus, Les Fourneaux, La Chassière, Les Ruelles, Les Naugues, Les Puillets, Les Saumonts and Clos de Paradis.

AC MEURSAULT

OVERVIEW: the village of Meursault is situated 8 km south-west of Beaune in Côte d'Or. The southern part of the village boasts the greatest concentration of first growths, which number 20 or so in total, including the flagship Les Perrières and Clos des Perrières. Of the appellation's 394 ha expanse, 105 ha are classed as first growths. The soil is formed of white marl on a Jurassic limestone bedrock. The proportion of clay here is higher than in the other appellations.

WINE STYLES: 95% of the wines are white. They display a golden hue and develop aromas of russet apple, crusty bread, hazelnut, bitter or dried almonds, foliage. Rich in alcohol, they exhibit fat and opulence. Try with foie gras, fish in a sauce, fatted chicken in a cream sauce or shellfish. Very occasionally red wines are made. They boast aromas of raspberry and are delicate with good structure, requiring a few years' ageing before they fully reveal their character.

CLIMATE SITES CLASSED AS FIRST GROWTHS:
Les Cras, Les Caillerets, Les Santenots Blancs, Les Plures, Les Santenots du Milieu, Charmes, La Jeunellotte, La Jeune-Lotte, La Pièce sous le Bois, Sous le Dos d'Ane, Sous Blagny, Perrières, Clos des Perrières, Genevrières, Le Porusot, Les Bouchères, Les Gouttes d'Or, Blagny, Les Ravelles, Porusot.

AC MONTAGNY

OVERVIEW: this is the Côte Chalonnaise's most southerly appellation, embracing four villages and an area under vine slightly in excess of 310 ha. The vines grow on hillside sites facing east-south-east and enjoy good sunshine exposure. The appellation is for white wines only and the AC boasts 49 climate sites classed as first growths. The vast majority of the wines are produced by the co-operative winery in Buxy.

WINE STYLES: with their golden colour, they offer aromas of lemon and grapefruit with tones of hazelnut, almond, fern and mineral notes. These white wines are racy and attractive with a delicate bouquet. They are soft, well-balanced, fresh, refined and elegant, with good length. Try with seafood, langoustine, fish served with a sauce or goats cheese.

CLIMATE SITES CLASSED AS FIRST GROWTHS:
In Montagny: *Vignes Saint-Pierre, les Combes, Saint-Ytage,*
Les Chaumelottes, Champ Toizeau, Vignes sur le Cloux, Les Garchères,
Vignes Couland, Les Bouchots, Les Burnins, Les Perrières, Les Treuffères, Montcuchot,
Vigne du Soleil, Les Maroques, Les Beaux Champs, les Macles, Creux de Beaux
Champs, L'Epaule, Les Platières, Les Jardins, les Coères, Saint-Morille,
Les Vignes Derrière, Les Bordes, Les Las, Les Gouresses, Les Paquiers, Montorge,
Les Resses, Le Cloux, Sous les Feilles.
In Buxy: *La Grande Pièce, Le Cos Chaudron, Les Vignes des près, Le Vieux Château,*
La Condemine du Vieux Château, Le Clouzot,
Les Pidances, Les Coudrettes, Les Vignes Longues, Cornevent, Mont Laurent,
Les Bonneveaux, Les Bassets.
In Saint-Vallerin: *Les Paquiers, Les Cradoulettes, Les Coères, La Moullière, Les Resses.*
In Jully-lès-Buxy: *Les Coères, Les Chaniots, Chazelle.*

AC MONTHÉLIE

OVERVIEW: the village of Monthélie is located south of Volnay, more or less in the heart of the Côte de Beaune. Formerly owned by the Dukes of Burgundy and Cluny abbey, the appellation actually fits within quite a snug area. It sits on both sides of a coomb which is narrow to the north then opens up in the south. The appellation's 110 ha are devoted primarily to red wines. Life focuses so intensely on wine growing here that according to a local saying, a chicken could die of starvation during the grape harvest.

WINE STYLES: the reds exhibit an intense hue with purplish tints. They display aromas of red or black berries (cherry, bilberry, blackcurrant, redcurrant), prune, undergrowth, fern, mushrooms, violet, with a liquorice finish. They are robust, elegant, fresh wines in the early years with the potential to mature well. The first growths display more up-front tannins, imparting greater structure. Try with roast lamb, poultry served with a sauce, game birds, cheeses. A tiny proportion of the wines are white, which are relatively mellow with good acidity. Try them with quenelles or poached fish with melted butter.

CLIMATE SITES CLASSED AS FIRST GROWTHS:
Les Riottes, Sur la Velle, Le Meix Bataille, Le Clos Gauthey, Les Vignes Rondes,
Le Cas Rougeot, La Taupine, Les Champs Fulliot, Le Village, Le Château Gaillard,
Clos des Toisières, Le Clou des Chênes, Les Barbières, Les Clous and Les Duresses.

137

AC MONTRACHET GRAND CRU

This Côte de Beaune growth straddles Chassagne and Puligny-Montrachet. The soil is limestone and the vines face south-east, which is conducive to good sunshine exposure. The highest elevations are home to soils of steep Rauracien limestone, followed by Callovian limestone further down and ultimately Bathonian limestone at the foot of the hill. They are shallow and poor. The 8 or so hectares of this great growth are divided amongst 20 or so different owners, who grow a single variety: Chardonnay. The white wines are racy, elegant, opulent, deep and intense with lashings of body. With their bright golden hue, they display fragrances of hazelnut, dried fruit, fern, butter and honey, unfolding into more mineral notes as they age. They pair with shellfish, sole in a white butter sauce and poultry in a cream sauce.

AC MOREY-SAINT-DENIS

OVERVIEW: set in the heart of the Côte de Nuits, this appellation boasts five great growths (Clos de la Roche, Clos Saint-Denis, Clos de Tart, Clos des Lambrays and part of Bonnes-Mares) and 20 first growths. The D122 road acts as boundary between the great growths in the west and the first growths. The combined area of the growths accounts for two-thirds of the appellation.

WINE STYLES: the reds boast good structure, body, vigour, elegance and delicacy. Their well-balanced structure makes them suitable for laying down. They combine the mellowness and finesse of Chambolle with the power and structure of Gevrey Chambertin. With their relatively deep-coloured hue, their aromas of red fruits (cherry morello cherry, blackcurrant), and their woody, spicy or animal nuances, they pair well with game, red meat and very mature cheeses.

CLIMATE SITES CLASSED AS FIRST GROWTHS:
Les Genavrières, Monts Luisants, Les Chaffots, Clos Baulet, Les Blanchards, Les Gruenchers, La Riotte, Les Milandes, Les Faconnières, Les Charrières, Clos des Ormes, Aux Charmes, Aux Cheseaux, Les Chenevery, Le Village, Les Sorbès, Clos Sorbè, La Bussière, Les Ruchots, Côte Rôtie.

AC MUSIGNY GRAND CRU

Musigny sits on a relatively steep incline, overlooking Clos de Vougeot. One property, Domaine de Vogüé, owns 7 of the growth's total 9.32 ha., which cover a limestone rock terrace. Patches of red clay are dotted here though there is less limestone than in other parts. In fact, the soils veer more towards clay than chalk and are covered with a shallow layer of loam. The red wines are made from Pinot noir and the whites from Chardonnay. Musigny are well-balanced, supple wines with body. They are refined with delicate tannins and great length on the palate. Their aromatic spectrum embraces fragrances of strawberry, raspberry, violet and undergrowth. They pair with duck, poached chicken with bite-sized vegetables, capon and lamb.

AC NUITS-SAINT-GEORGES

OVERVIEW: this appellation covers both Nuits-Saint-Georges and Premeaux-Prissey. Stretching over a 4 km strip, the area is split into two parts, one located north of the town, the other in the far south of Nuits-Saint-Georges. Middle Jurassic limestone and marl soils are home to the vines here. The red wines are made from Pinot noir whilst a clutch of whites are produced from Chardonnay.

WINE STYLES: Nuits-Saint-Georges is a generous, well-constituted, robust wine with a strong framework and a powerful, complex bouquet. On the nose, it is fruity with notes of blackcurrant, cherry, prune stones, truffle and leather with nuances of undergrowth. It conjures up earthy, even gamey notes. Nuits-Saint-Georges can be served with roast red meat, mutton, Brie or Pont l'Evêque cheese.

CLIMATE SITES CLASSED AS FIRST GROWTHS:
In Nuits-Saint-Georges: *Aux Champs Perdrix, En la Perrière Noblot, Les Damodes, Aux Boudots, Aux Cras, La Richemone, Aux Murgers, Aux Vignerondes, Aux Chaignots, Aux Thorey, Aux Argillas, Aux Bousselots, Les Perrières, Les Hauts Pruliers, Château gris, Les Crots, Rue de Chaux, Les Procès, Les Pruliers, Roncière, Les Saints-Georges, Les Cailles, Les Porrets Saint-Georges, Clos des Porrets Saint-Georges,*

Les Vallerots, Les Poulettes, Les Chabœufs, Les Vaucrains, Chaînes Carteaux.
In Premeaux : *Clos des Grandes Vignes, Clos de la Maréchale, Clos Arlot, Les Terres Blanches, Les Didiers, Clos des Forêts Saint-Georges, Aux Perdrix, Clos des Corvées, Clos des Corvées Pagets, Clos Saint-Marc, Les Argilières, Clos des Argilières.*

AC PERNAND-VERGELESSES

OVERVIEW: the appellation is located 8 km north of Beaune. Clayey, iron-rich, limestone and marl soils (Bathonian and Oxfordian) provide a foothold for the vines on sloping terrain, predominantly facing west or even north-west. 65 percent of the village's wines are red (Pinot noir). The whites (Chardonnay) come from the mountain at Corton.

WINE STYLES: the reds are firm in their early years, aromatic, elegant, ample and tannic. They display aromas of small red fruit (blackcurrant, redcurrant), liquorice, undergrowth, musk and floral notes. Try with stuffed fatted chicken, lamb, cheeses. The whites are solid wines with body, character and good acidity. They display a brilliant hue, aromas of vanilla, strawberry, citrus fruit (lemon, apple), honey, amber and are slightly spicy. Enjoyable with fish, either grilled or served with a cream sauce.

CLIMATE SITES CLASSED AS FIRST GROWTHS:
Clos Berthet, Sous Frétille, Village de Pernand, Creux de la Net, En Caradeux, Ile des Vergelesses, Les Fichots, Vergelesses.

AC PETIT CHABLIS

OVERVIEW: Petit Chablis grow on the rim of the Chablis wine region on Portlandian limestone soils (secondary era) which form the foundations of the plateaux.

WINE STYLES: considered as early wines, Petit Chablis are lively, fresh, clean, soft, pleasant and light. They have less staying power than Chablis and are usually at their peak within their first year. They display mineral, fruity and floral (acacia) type fragrances, a style particularly well-suited to cooked cold pork meats, seafood, grilled fish, jellied ham with parsley, snails…

AC POMMARD

OVERVIEW: situated 3 km west of Beaune, the area faces east and south-east. Although the appellation does not boast any great growths, it is home to 28 first growths which cover 37% of the appellation area. The soils are formed of soft, reasonably clayey limestone and Pinot noir is the sole grape variety.

WINE STYLES: Pommard have an intense colour (red-black) and are robust, warm and full-bodied, with great cellaring capacity. The wines from the northern part of the appellation tend to be softer than those from the south. Acidity is in the foreground, coupled with a certain amount of astringency. Pommard are firm and feature among the most tannic wines Burgundy has to offer. They have an intense bouquet with blackcurrant, musk, game, raspberry, bilberry and gingerbread. On the palate, notes of vanilla and liquorice are present. They can be served with game and mature, distinctive cheeses.

CLIMATE SITES CLASSED AS FIRST GROWTHS:
La Chanière, Les Charmots, La Platière, Les Arvelets, Les Saussiles, Les Pezerolles, En Largillière, Les Grands Epenots, Clos des Epeneaux, Les Petits Epenots, Les Boucherottes, Le Clos Micot, Les Combes-Dessus, Clos de Verger, Clos de la Commaraine, La Refène, Clos Blanc, Le Village, Derrière Saint-Jean, Les Rugiens-Bas, Les Chaponnières, Les Croix Noires, Les Poutures, Les Bertins, Les Fremiers, Les Jarolières, Les Rugiens-Hauts, Les Chanlins-Bas.

AC POUILLY-FUISSÉ

OVERVIEW: the production area embraces four villages situated in the southern part of the Mâconnais. The vines grow over a series of natural amphitheatres facing east and south-east, forming sites where winds to the west are deflected by the rocky ridges of Solutré and Vergisson. Although the appellation area does not boast any first growths, it is home to fifty or so climate-specific sites which can be stated on the label provided the wine has an ABV of 12% instead of 11% and has been aged at least until the 1st April following the harvest. The limestone-marl soils reveal various stages of the Jurassic era (Bathonian, Bajocian, Oxfordian, Kimmeridgian), promoting a varied range of 'terroirs'.

WINE STYLES: these white wines are well-balanced, rich, harmonious, lively and fleshy with powerful aromas and a long-lasting finish. Wines drawn from soils referred to as deep (clay marl) are powerful, fat and full. Those which come from stonier soils with only a thin layer of vegetation, are more mineral and delicate. Solutré wines are rich whilst those of Vergisson are more elegant though also lighter. With a greenish-yellow hue, they display aromas of dried fruit such as grilled almonds, hazelnut, floral notes including honeysuckle, hawthorn, lily, honey and linden, though also gun-flint, warm brioche, gingerbread and a taste reflecting its 'terroir'. They pair with sweetbread, veal steak in a cream sauce, scallops and fish served with a sauce.

CLIMATE-SPECIFIC SITES:
In Fuissé: *Vignes des Champs, Les Prâles, Les Brûlés, En Chatenet, Les Perrières, Les Vignes Blanches, Le Clos, Les Ménétrières, Au Bourg, Les Travers, Les Murgers, Les Châtaigniers, Bois Seguin, Plan de Bourdon, Aux Prats, Clos Gaillard, Sur les Moulins.*
In Solutré-Pouilly: *Lamure, Les Quarts, La Frairie, Aux Champ Roux, Le Clos, En Servy, Aux Gerbaux, Vigne du Riat, Aux Chailloux, Aux Bouthières, Aux Peloux, En Courtesse, En Bertilonne.*

In Vergisson: *Aux Vignes Dessus, Aux Charmes, Ronchevrat, Martelet, En France, Sur la Roche, La Côte, Les Croux, Les Crays, En Caramentrant, La Maréchaude.*
In Chaintré: *Maison du Villard, Aux Murs, Les Chevrières, En Vallée, Le Clos de M. Noly, En Cenan, La Bergerie, Aux Quarts, Les Plessys, Les Châtaigneries, La Grande Chattière, Les Hauts de Savy, Les Plantes Vieilles, Le Clos Ressier, Les Fourneaux, Les Verchères.*

AC POUILLY-VINZELLES

OVERVIEW: Pouilly-Vinzelles and neighbouring Pouilly-Loché belong to the most southerly group of Burgundy appellations. The two appellations in fact dovetail. The wines are grown and vinted in exactly the same way as in Pouilly-Fuissé; what differentiates them is the local soil type (predominantly Jurassic calcareous clay with patches of clay).

WINE STYLES: these white wines are highly reminiscent of Pouilly-Fuissé wines, with less body. Pouilly-Vinzelles are dry, lively, vigorous and warm with well-balanced mellowness. Sporting a greenish-yellow hue, they display aromas of honey, peony, acacia, pear, hazelnut and occasionally game. Try with fresh-water fish such as pike perch and pike, shellfish, white meats such as veal or goats cheeses.

141

AC POUILLY-LOCHÉ

Pouilly-Loché display a straw-yellow hue with aromas of wild rose, honeysuckle, apricot jam, quince, grilled almond, vanilla notes rounded off with mineral tones. Try them with a seafood platter, oven-baked sea bream, fish terrine. Fact: Pouilly-Loché can revert to the lesser Pouilly-Vinzelles appellation, whereas Pouilly-Vinzelles cannot upgrade to Pouilly-Loché.

AC PULIGNY-MONTRACHET

OVERVIEW: the village of Puligny is situated roughly a dozen kilometres from Beaune. The vines grow over the rolling, east facing hills which unfold behind the village as far as Blagny hamlet. The soil is calcareous clay, strewn with stones and is home to a predominant proportion of white wines. The red wines grown within the appellation area are also entitled to use AC Blagny or Côte de Beaune Village. The village's reputation centres on its four world-famous great growths (Montrachet, Bâtard-Montrachet, Chevalier-Montrachet and Bienvenues-Bâtard-Montrachet).

WINE STYLES: the whites are a pale yellow colour. They are rich, with great length on the palate and subtle acidity. Their texture and body are firm, with aromas of freshly-cut grass, butter, fern, hazelnut, marzipan, white flowers, acacia honey, exotic fruits and occasionally amber and quince. These sterling wines are the perfect partners for shellfish, fish served in a sauce, turbot, fatted chicken, strong-smelling cheeses. The less common reds pair with roast red meat, game birds and mild cheeses.

CLIMATE SITES CLASSED AS FIRST GROWTHS:
Sous le Puits, La Garenne, Hameau de Blagny, La Truffière, Champ Gain, Les Chalumeaux, Champ Canet, Clos de la Garenne, Les Folatières, Le Cailleret, Les Demoiselles, Les Pucelles, Clavaillon, Les Perrières, Clos de la Mouchère, Les Combettes, Les Referts.

AC RICHEBOURG GRAND CRU

Vines here grow on the higher part of the slope north of Romanée and Romanée-Conti. 10 growers share the growth's 7.4 ha. The soils are limestone with high clay content and the wines are drawn from Pinot noir. With their ruby-red hue, the wines are robust, intense, warm and highly expressive. They develop fragrances of ripe fruit, musk and leather.

AC ROMANÉE GRAND CRU

Burgundy's most minute growth (0.84 ha) overlooks Romanée-Conti. The texture of the soil is less clayey than in Romanée-Conti and the gradient steeper. The shallow soil combination lays on a limestone foundation and is littered with stones. Only Pinot noir grapes are grown here. The wines are hard when young and are racy, powerful, velvety and mellow. They boast body, flesh and fat with fragrances of black fruit, cherry and undergrowth, and require a few years' patience before they reach their fullest expression. They pair with thrush, partridge, veal and cheeses.

AC ROMANÉE-CONTI GRAND CRU

This 1.63 ha great growth is a monopoly of Domaine de la Romanée-Conti. It is set within the Vosne-Romanée appellation area to the west of the village. This red wine is extremely rich, powerful, full, well-constituted, sturdy and suave, with great aromatic length. It boasts a rich, sometimes opulent texture. With its crimson hue, it displays fragrances of ripe or crystallised red and black fruit (black cherry, bilberry), violet, resin, humus, musk, leather and animal notes. They are the ideal partner for any sophisticated dish.

AC ROMANÉE-SAINT-VIVANT GRAND CRU

From a size perspective, this is Vosne-Romanée's leading growth (9.4 ha), taking its name from Saint-Vivant monastery which was founded in 900. It is currently divided between 6 growers. The soils are deeper than in the other growths, combining limestone and clay. The wines are velvety, graceful, well-constituted, feminine and delicate, they are intense though less powerful than the neighbouring growths. They display fragrances of ripe red (cherry) and black fruit or crystallised fruit though also spices and rose. Recommended with pheasant, venison and hare.

AC RUCHOTTES-CHAMBERTIN GRAND CRU

This 3.3 ha site is adjacent to Clos de Bèze and Mazis-Chambertin in the village of Gevrey-Chambertin. It is a hillside site, yielding magnificently well-balanced red wines which pair well with red meat, roast or sautéed poultry, large game and strong, refined cheeses.

AC RULLY

OVERVIEW: Rully sits south of Chagny, in the northern reaches of the Côte Chalonnaise. The appellation embraces Rully and Chagny, boasting 23 first growths in the foothills of Mount Folie, Mount Varot and Mount Montpalais. The soils are clayey with a predominant proportion of limestone and marl. The red wines are made from Pinot noir, the whites from Chardonnay. Interestingly, Rully specialises in sparkling wines which are now used to make Crémant de Bourgogne.

WINE STYLES: the whites are robust, lively, well-balanced, delicate and subtle. They display a pale golden hue, with aromas of apple, hazelnut, spices and occasionally violet. The reds are elegant, delicate, fleshy and lively and their staying power makes them reminiscent of Mercurey wines. They display a glistening ruby-red hue and aromas of lilac, freshly-cut grass, violet, raspberry, cherry and crushed strawberries. The reds make a suitable partner for free-range poultry and white meats, the whites for pike quenelles, snails, veal escalope with a cream sauce and all white meats in a sauce.

CLIMATE SITES CLASSED AS FIRST GROWTHS:
In Rully: *Le Meix Caillet, Marissou, La Fosse, Les Pierres, Pillot, Raclot, Cloux, Rabourcé, Chapitre, Préaux, Molesme, Agneux, La Bressande, Champs Cloux, Le Meix Cadot, Montpalais, Grésigny, Margotés, Le Rearde, Vauvry, la Pucelle.*
In Chagny: *Clos du Chaigne, Clos Saint-Jacques.*

AC SAINT-AUBIN

OVERVIEW: Saint-Aubin is a village appellation in Côte d'Or located between Chassagne and Puligny-Montrachet. The appellation produces red wine from Pinot noir and white from Chardonnay. Two-thirds of the vineyards boast first growth status and although the area is primarily geared to producing red wines, its reputation is based on its whites. The vines enjoy a south-west or south-south-east aspect.

WINE STYLES: the whites display a pale golden hue and fragrances of green almonds, beeswax, hazelnut, cinnamon, amber and a touch of pepper. They are rich, harmonious, delicate and elegant wines. The reds display a deep colour with fragrances of blackcurrant, black cherry and a touch of leather. The reds pair with game patés, stuffed duck and lamb with girolle mushrooms and the whites with trout in a cream sauce or salmon with basil.

143

CLIMATE SITES CLASSED AS FIRST GROWTHS:
*Derrière la Tour, En Créot, Bas de Vermarain in the east, Les Champlots, In Gamay,
La Chatenière, En Remilly, Les Murgers des Dents de Chien, Les Combes,
Le Charmoix, Village, Les Castets, Derrière chez Edouard, Le Puits, Sur le Sentier du
Clou, Echaille, En la Ranché, En Montceau, En Vollon à l'Est, Es Champs, Le Bas de
Gamay à l'Est, Les Combes au Sud, Les Cortons, Les Perrières, Les Travers de Marinot,
Marinot, Pitangeret, Sous Roche Dumay, Vignes Moingeon and Les Frionnes.*

AC SAINT-BRIS

OVERVIEW: Saint-Bris is grown in 7 villages in Yonne, a dozen kilometres south-east of Auxerre. The vineyards extend over a plateau of stony, limestone soils and are entirely planted to Sauvignon, making them unique in Burgundy.
WINE STYLES: these are fresh, pleasant, delicate, long-lasting, generous wines which are lively when young. They display fragrances of blackcurrant leaves, exotic fruits, acidulous fruits, gun-flint... They are equally delicious as appetisers or with fish, shellfish, grilled chitterlings sausage and cheese.

AC SAINT-ROMAIN

OVERVIEW: this area is located not far from Auxey-Duresses, at high elevations, on extremely stony limestone hills. Two varietals are grown here: Pinot noir for the reds and Chardonnay for the whites. There are no first growths within the appellation area.
WINE STYLES: the reds are lively and slightly austere in their early years. As they mature, they acquire elegance from their mellow tannins. They display fragrances of cherry, redcurrant and blackcurrant bud leading into smoky tones and macerated fruits as they age. The whites are vigorous, clean and fresh, acquiring mellowness with age. They display vegetal scents, linden and honeysuckle, white flowers, toast, ripe yellow fruit such as mirabelle plums and honey.

AC SAINT-VÉRAN

OVERVIEW: the appellation area is located between the Mâconnais and Beaujolais, with eight villages entitled to use the name. The vineyards enjoy a south-south-east aspect and grow on Jurassic calcareous clay and limestone soils. The terrain is rugged in places and Chardonnay is the sole varietal used here.
WINE STYLES: the wines are dry, round and soft. They display a pale greenish-gold hue and aromas of hazelnut, grilled almonds, honey, gun-flint, white flesh fruit such as pear and peach, though also acacia and honeysuckle. They can be served with oysters, chitterlings sausages, eel with parsley, grilled salmon in a hollandaise sauce, white meats…

AC SANTENAY

OVERVIEW: vineyards in Santenay stretch from east to west, running alongside the Dheune river, fifteen or so kilometres from Beaune. The soils are formed of hard limestone interspersed with marl. One of the oddities here is the way in which the vines are pruned: Guyot pruning is most commonly used in Burgundy, but in Santenay it is supplanted by Royat cordon pruning because of the depth and richness of the soils; this slows down the ageing process of the vines.

WINE STYLES: although they are only moderately concentrated, they can be firm when young, maturing towards greater depth… They display aromas of almond, strawberry, chestnut and prunes for the mature wines. They pair with grilled ribsteak, coq au vin, beef bourguignon…The whites, which are few and far between, are dry, robust and vigorous with an extremely well-developed fragrance.

CLIMATE SITES CLASSED AS FIRST GROWTHS:
La Comme, Les Gravières, Clos de Tavannes, Les Gravières-Clos de Tavannes, Beauregard, Clos Faubard, Clos des Mouches, Beaurepaire, Passetemps, La Maladière, Grand Clos Rousseau, Clos Rousseau.

AC SAVIGNY LES BEAUNE

OVERVIEW: situated north of Beaune, this area is encircled by Beaune mountain in the south and Noël and Chenôve forests in the north. The vineyards are divided into two parts: one west of the village, the other further south-east. One of Savigny's claims to fame is as the home of Dr Guyot who lent his name to a system of pruning. The first growths are planted on two different types of soil: the ones in the south occupy sandy, gravely soil whilst those in the north grow on richer soils formed of limestone and iron-rich clay. The varietals used for the appellation are Chardonnay and Pinot blanc for the whites and Pinot noir for the reds.

WINE STYLES: with their brilliant colour, the reds are pleasant wines with low tannin content and acidity. They are supple, light and graceful. The first growths hailing from the south are light and soft and reward early drinking. Wines from the north are more robust and reward patience. Predominant aromas in the red wines are morello cherry, blackcurrant, strawberry and undergrowth. The whites are lively in the early years then mellow with age. They are harmonious, delicate and sturdy with fragrances of hawthorn, hazelnut, apple and occasionally exotic fruits. They pair with white meat, poultry, scallops, fish…

CLIMATE SITES CLASSED AS FIRST GROWTHS:
Les Charnières, Les Talmettes, Les Vergelesses, Bataillière, Basses Vergelesses, Aux Fourneaux, Champ Chevrey, Les Lavières, Aux Gravains, Petits Godeaux, Aux Serpentières, Aux Clous, Aux Guettes, Les Rouvrettes, Les Narbantons,

145

Les Peuillets, Les Marconnets, La Dominode, Les Jarrons, Les Hauts Jarrons, Redrescul, Les Hauts Marconnets.

AC VIRÉ-CLESSÉ

OVERVIEW: Viré-Clessé embraces four villages in the Mâconnais. It is farmed by 70 growers over a combined area under vine of 390 hectares. The only permitted grape variety is Chardonnay. The vines grow either halfway up hillsides or at the summit on calcareous clay soils. In Clessé, the limestone dates back to the Oxfordian period whilst in Viré, Bajocian bedrock prevails. The entire area enjoys an east/south-east aspect.

WINE STYLES: wines bearing the Viré-Clessé appellation display characteristic aromas of hawthorn, exotic fruit and rose. They are lively, fruity, supple, harmonious wines with great length on the palate. They are the perfect partner for fish, either grilled or served with a sauce, frogs legs or oysters.

AC VOLNAY

OVERVIEW: a Côte de Beaune appellation where over half of the vineyards are classed as first growths. The village of Volnay sits between Meursault, in the south, and Pommard, in the north. Interestingly, 29 hectares of vines within Meursault are entitled to the Volnay first growth appellation, in which case they become Volnay-Santenots. Whites are also grown here and, depending on the specific plots, they are entitled to use the Meursault, Meursault first growth or Meursault-Santenots appellations.

WINE STYLES: they are round, velvety, silky, soft and full. They are prime examples of the Côte de Beaune's most 'feminine' wines. They mature more rapidly than Pommard. Their hue runs the gamut from vermilion to deep ruby-red. They display aromas of raspberry, strawberry, cherry, blackberry, mushroom, violet, spices and vanilla. They pair with veal kidneys, partridges, thrushes, marinated meats and soft cheeses such as reblochon or brie.

CLIMATE SITES CLASSED AS FIRST GROWTHS:
In Volnay: *Chanlin, Pitures-Dessus, Lassolle, Clos des Ducs, Le Village, Clos de la Cave des Ducs, Clos de l'Audignac, Clos de la Chapelle, Clos du château des Ducs, Clos de la Rougeotte, Frémiets-Clos de la Rougeotte, Clos de la Barre, Clos de la Bousse d'Or, Les Brouillards, Les Mitans, En l'Ormeau, Les Angles, Pointes d'Angle, Frémiets, La Gigotte, Les Grands Champs, Les Lurets, Robardelle, Carelle sous la Chapelle, Carelles, Le Ronceret, Les Aussy, Champans, Les Caillerets, Les Caillerets-Clos des 60 Ouvrés, En Chevret, Taille Pieds, Clos du Verseuil, Clos des Chênes.*
In Meursault: *Santenots Blancs, Les Santenots du Milieu, Les Santenots- Dessous, Clos des Santenots, Les Plures, Les Vignes Blanches.*

AC VOSNE-ROMANÉE

OVERVIEW: the appellation embraces the villages of Vosne-Romanée and Flagey-Echezeaux. The soils are limestone with varying amounts of clay on reasonably steep inclines which provide for efficient drainage. Pinot noir is the only permitted varietal. Vosne-Romanée is the privileged home of some of the most prestigious wines in the world, boasting eight great growths: Romanée-Conti, Romanée-Saint-Vivant, Echezeaux, Grands Echezeaux, La Romanée, La Grande-Rue, La Tâche and Richebourg.

WINE STYLES: the most predominant character trait here is the silkiness of the wines with subtle tannins and acidity. The wines are fleshy with excellent length. On the palate, they are powerful yet epitomise delicacy, lacking any form of aggressiveness. They display fragrances of cherry, strawberry, undergrowth, blackcurrant, boxwood and spices with notes of mint and bitter almond. They pair with pheasant paté, roast hare, venison steak and roast beef.

CLIMATE SITES CLASSED AS FIRST GROWTHS:
Les Beaux Mont, Les Suchots, Aux Brûlées, La Croix Rameau, Clos des Réas, Les Gaudichots, Les Chaumes, Aux Malconsorts, Au-Dessus des Malconsorts, Cros Parentoux, Aux Reignots, En Orveaux, Les Rouges, Les Petits Monts.

147

AC VOUGEOT

OVERVIEW: 73% of the hamlet of Vougeot is given over to vineyards. Although it is renowned world-wide for Clos de Vougeot château (a great growth), it also produces wines under a village appellation and as first growths, to the southeast, on the border with Chambolle-Musigny. The soil types are varied: they are limestone combined with varying amounts of clay. The two permitted varietals are Pinot noir (reds) and Chardonnay (whites).

WINE STYLES: the reds are harmonious, elegant, racy and pleasantly round. With their sparkling crimson, dark ruby-red colour, they are powerful and complex with truffle, violet, animal nuances, blackcurrant, raspberry, blackberry and bilberry. As they age, they develop aromas of venison and havana cigars. Try with partridge or a leg of venison. The whites are fruity, supple, dry and relatively robust first growths. On the palate, they are round, fleshy and long-lasting with excellent balance. They partner well with foie gras or salmon in a sorrel sauce.

CLIMATE SITES CLASSED AS FIRST GROWTHS:
Les Cras, Le Clos Blanc, Les Petits Vougeots, Clos de la Perrière.

• • •

2015
BURGUNDY WINES

ALOXE CORTON

Domaine Poulleau Père & Fils 89/100

▼⋅ Vintage 2012 : Medium intense, limpid hue. Racy nose of morello cherry, refined spice and quality oak. Suave attack, ripe, tense palate focusing on elegance. Fine-grained tannins ensure a degree of ageability. A pretty and accessible wine.
www.poulleau.com
Domaine Poulleau
+33 (0)3 80 21 26 52

AUXEY-DURESSES

GUY BOCARD 85/100

▼⋅ 1er Cru En Reugnes 2011 : Beautiful lightly-coloured, vibrant red. Ripe perfumes realling cherries in brandy adorn the nose. Fleshy attack on the palate leading into a full mid-palate with focused aromas revealing fairly good quality fruit. Would work with white meats.
Price approx.: 20,00 EUR
Domaine Guy Bocard
+33 (0)3 80 21 26 06

BONNES MARES GRAND CRU

(See page 149)

BOURGOGNE CÔTE CHALONNAISE

DOMAINE DE L'EVÊCHÉ 86/100

▼⋅ Clos de l'Evêché 2012 : Brilliant garnet. Endearing nose blending ripe red berry fruits and fine oak. Full attack, fine-grained texture framed by fat and a fresh middle palate. A closely-integrated, persistent and likeable style.
Price approx.: 7,90 EUR
http://www.domainedeleveche.com
Vincent Joussier
+33 (0)3 85 44 30 43

DOMAINE DE L'EVÊCHÉ 86/100

▼⋅ Reviller 2012 : Limpid, pale yellow with green tints. Pleasurable nose blending ripe white fruits and a delicate

floral note. Light, elegant and well-balanced palate showing more of the nose aromatics. Charming. Quite a crunchy wine. A successful effort.
Price approx.: 7,60 EUR
http://www.domainedeleveche.com
Vincent Joussier
+33 (0)3 85 44 30 43

BOURGOGNE EPINEUIL

DOMAINE DE L'ABBAYE 86/100

CONV▼⋅ Cuvée Juliette 2012 : Deep, young garnet. Nose of garden fruits suggestive of cassis and blueberry with subtle oak undertones. A fresh, crunchy and fruity wine. Lovely sappy, balanced palate with a subtle mineral and oak-infused finish.
Price approx.: 18,00 EUR
http://www.bourgognevin.com
Dominique Gruhier Vigneron
+33 (0)3 86 55 32 51

BOURGOGNE GRAND ORDINAIRE

CHÂTEAU DE L'HESTRANGE 85/100

▼⋅ Vintage 2013 : Ruby with dark purple tints. Nose of crunchy ripe red berry fruits with spice in the background. Ethereal, fresh and supple palate with mellow tannins. Upfront aromas that linger. A summery wine that works well with cold cuts.
Price approx.: 7,50 EUR
http://www.lhestrange.com
Domaine Metge-Toppin
+33 (0)9 63 63 84 86

BOURGOGNE HAUTES CÔTES DE BEAUNE

MANOIR DE MERCEY 88/100

▼⋅ Au Paradis 2012 : Appealing ruby-red. Focused, precise nose of fresh red fruits and subtle oak. Seductively refined, closely-integrated texture bordering on silky at point of entry. Well-integrated and flowing into fine tannins. A trace of firmness is perceptible on the finish.
www.berger-rive.fr
Domaine Gérard Berger-Rive & Fils
+33 (0)3 85 91 13 81

MANOIR DE MERCEY 85/100

▼⋅ Clos des Dames 2012 : Light yellow with green tints. Refined, floral and vegetal-dominant nose enhanced by subtle oak. Supple, silky and perfumed attack leading

DOMAINE FOUGERAY DE BEAUCLAIR

Bonnes-Mares Grand Cru 2012

▼ Vibrant red. Delightful ripe nose with accents of cherry and redcurrant, heady yet not overbearingly so. Powerful, generous attack with full-on fruit expression. Fine-grained tannins and persistent, delicious fruit aromas. Beautiful!

+33 3 80 52 21 12

95/100

---

into a fresher mid-palate capped off with a subtle trace of sourness. Serve preferably well-chilled.
www.berger-rive.fr
Domaine Gérard Berger-Rive & Fils
+33 (0)3 85 91 13 81

DOMAINE CLAUDE NOUVEAU · 81/100

▼ ✦ Vieilles Vignes 2011 : Cherry-red. The nose opens up to ripe red fruits coupled with a fairly upfront oak dimension. Quite a powerful, full palate bordering on warm. The attack is mellow though the finish is firmer and marked by oak tannins.
Price approx.: 10,40 EUR
http://www.claudenouveau.com
Domaine Claude Nouveau
+33 (0)3 85 91 13 34

BOURGOGNE HAUTES CÔTES DE NUITS

DOMAINE MICHEL GROS · 87/100

▼ ✦ Vintage 2010 : Limpid ruby. Subdued yet promising nose of morello cherry, red fruits and elegant oak undercurrents. Supple attack, consistent, tense palate with lovely aromatic drive enhanced by a clutch of spices. Hint of firmness. Nicely crafted across the palate.
Price approx.: 11,30 EUR
http://www.domaine-michel-gros.com
Domaine Michel Gros
+33 (0)3 80 61 04 69

BOURGOGNE TONNERRE

DOMINIQUE GRUHIER · 85/100

CONV ▼ ✦ Vintage 2012 : Brilliant pale yellow with green tints. Expressive nose of white flowers with a mineral dimension. Displays charm on the palate, offering up refined, focused scents and lovely fleshy roundness.

Aromatic finish. A successful Tonnerre.
Price approx.: 8,90 EUR
http://www.bourgognevin.com
Dominique Gruhier Vigneron
+33 (0)3 86 55 32 51

BOURGOGNE

DOMAINE POULLEAU PÈRE & FILS · 87/100

▼ ✦ Vintage 2012 : Fairly light, limpid colour. Delightful nose of red fruits with a floral note and subtle oak. Suave attack, delicious, ethereal palate showing lovely fleshy roundness and well-integrated, refined freshness. A pleasurable Burgundy for everyday drinking.
Price approx.: 9,00 EUR
www.poulleau.com
Domaine Poulleau
+33 (0)3 80 21 26 52

GUY BOCARD · 86/100

▼ ✦ Chardonnay 2011 : Pale crystalline hue. Beautiful nose of ripe white fruits, a whiff of flowers and supporting vanilla oak. Promising albeit slightly disjointed palate at the moment. Fairly ethereal and fresh with more oak influence than fruit. A little bottle time will do the trick.
Price approx.: 12,00 EUR
Domaine Guy Bocard
+33 (0)3 80 21 26 06

DOMAINE DE CHAMP FLEURY · 86/100

▼ ✦ Vintage 2013 : Light yellow with green tints. Suggestions of white-fleshed fruits with a floral touch on the nose. Supple attack, full, concentrated mouthfeel with a beautiful silky texture and impression of harmony. Enjoyable with pike.
Price approx.: 6,40 EUR
http://www.domaine-du-champ-fleury.com
Domaine de Champ Fleury
+33 (0)4 74 67 08 20

MEYBLUM & FILS   85/100

▼🔸 Pinot Noir 2011 : Garnet. Nose of ultra ripe red fruits recalling cherry and redcurrant. The palate is mellow, silky and fruity. Lovely quality tannins and aromatic focus. A well-made Pinot noir for sharing, with fruit to the fore.
Price approx.: 18,00 EUR
http://www.meyblum-et-fils.com
MVP Wines

DOMAINE DE CHAMP FLEURY   84/100

▼🔸 Vintage 2013 : Limpid, ruby-hued with young tints. Redcurrant, morello cherry and floral touches on the nose. Honest, forthright, full and fruit-driven palate with a lovely trace of crispness. A hint of spice and firmness on the finish. A pleasant generic for cold cuts.
Price approx.: 7,00 EUR
http://www.domaine-du-champ-fleury.com
Domaine de Champ Fleury
+33 (0)4 74 67 08 20

GUY BOCARD   83/100

▼🔸 Pinot Noir 2011 : Attractive clean red. Nose of ripe red fruits. On the palate, a light wine with fleshy and crisp aromas. A delightful, easy-drinking style pairing with a platter of cold meats.
Domaine Guy Bocard
+33 (0)3 80 21 26 06

CHÂTEAU DE L'HESTRANGE   81/100

▼🔸 Chardonnay 2013 : Beautiful gold. The nose is still subdued and reveals notes of white flowers and citrus fruits. The palate also shows restrained aromatics and freshness. The finish is firm and mineral-dominated. Should round out over time.
Price approx.: 7,50 EUR
http://www.lhestrange.com
Domaine Metge-Toppin
+33 (0)9 63 63 84 86

CHABLIS GRAND CRU

DOMAINE JEAN COLLET & FILS   92/100

CONV▼🔸 Valmur 2012 : Brilliant pale yellow with yellow tints. Racy, mineral and smoky nose with fruit undertones. On the palate, a profound wine with powerful aromatics that make it austere at the moment. An intense finish reveals its underlying quality though. Very promising.
Price approx.: 33,00 EUR
http://www.domaine-collet.fr
Domaine Jean Collet & fils
+33 (0)3 86 42 11 93

CHABLIS PREMIER CRU

CHÂTEAU DE FLEYS   91/100

▼🔸 Mont de Milieu - Vieilles Vignes 2011 : Light gold. Slightly reticent nose gradually opening up to white flowers, dried fruits, smoke... Rich, full-bodied palate. Silky mouthfeel asserting its Chardonnay varietal personality. Fruit is released. A racy first growth. Decant or keep.
Price approx.: 14,80 EUR
http://www.chablis-philippon.com
Domaine du Château de Fleys
+33 (0)3 86 42 47 70

DOMAINE JEAN COLLET & FILS   90/100

▼🔸 Montée de Tonnerre - Elevé en fûts de chêne 2012 : Brilliant light yellow, green tints. Beautiful silica aromas on the nose backed by ripe white fruits. Fresh, slender palate where spice touches combine with lemony fruit. Beautiful aromatic intensity. Austere finish. A wonderful wine all set for the future.
Price approx.: 16,00 EUR
http://www.domaine-collet.fr
Domaine Jean Collet & fils
+33 (0)3 86 42 11 93

DOMAINE DE LA MANDELIÈRE   90/100

▼🔸 Les Fourneaux 2012 : Beautiful light yellow with green tints. Racy nose opening up after swirling to mineral, vegetal and floral notes with fruit and a touch of lemon in the background. Wonderful presence, fullness and silky texture on the palate with beautiful balance of fat and nervousness. A nice wine.
Domaine de la Mandelière
+33 (0)3 86 42 19 30

DOMAINE JOLLY ET FILS   89/100

▼🔸 Fourchaume L'Homme Mort 2012 : Light gold. Complex mineral and smoke infused nose with white fruits, almond, honeysuckle and acacia. A 1st growth that is young yet already boasts lots of elegance, volume, fullness and substance. More reserved fruit, all-set for the future. Very promising.
Domaine Jolly et Fils
+33 (0)3 86 47 42 31

DOMAINE JEAN COLLET & FILS   89/100

▼🔸 Vaillons 2012 : Brilliant light yellow with green tints. Subdued nose of white flowers with a mineral dimension. Round attack, fairly fleshy, lively palate with generous perfume. Already accessible and loaded with charm. Uncork for Chablis-style ham.
Price approx.: 14,00 EUR
http://www.domaine-collet.fr
Domaine Jean Collet & fils
+33 (0)3 86 42 11 93

DOMAINE JEAN COLLET & FILS — 88/100

🍷 Montmains 2012 : Brilliant light yellow with green tints. Shy nose showing mineral presence backed by fruit. Delicious, full, silky and concentrated mouthfeel driven by effective freshness yet still not very exuberant. Will blossom with time.
Price approx.: 14,00 EUR
http://www.domaine-collet.fr
Domaine Jean Collet & fils
+33 (0)3 86 42 11 93

DOMAINE CHARLY NICOLLE — 88/100

🍷 Mont de Milieu 2012 : Light gold. Delicate nose with a distinct linden and hawthorn streak backed by almonds, pear, citrus fruits. Same elegance on the palate with a supple mouthfeel and beautiful freshness enhancing perfume. A distinctive 1st growth with the best yet to come.
http://www.chablis-charlynicolle.com
Domaine Charly Nicolle
+33 (0)3 86 42 80 08

DOMAINE DE LA MANDELIÈRE — 88/100

🍷 Mont de Milieu 2012 : Deeply-coloured light yellow. Ripe nose suggestive of lemon zest with lovely floral undercurrents. Full, fat and lush on the palate, leaving a sensation of suppleness. A generous, rich wine, pairing with fish in a sauce.
Domaine de la Mandelière
+33 (0)3 86 42 19 30

DOMAINE CHANTEMERLE — 87/100

🍷 Fourchaume 2012 : Brilliant hue tinged with green. Subdued nose intermixing lemon and white-fleshed fruits. Full, generous, expressive and taut palate showing only fruit aromatics for the moment. Slightly fleeting finish. More cellar time should bring out more personality.
Price approx.: 10,50 EUR
http://www.chablis-boudin.com
Domaine Chantemerle
+33 (0)3 86 42 18 95

DOMAINE CHARLY NICOLLE — 87/100

🍷 Les Fourneaux 2012 : Pale gold. Appealing nose of dried fruits coupled with notes of butter and white flowers with a mineral touch. Slightly muted in terms of aromatics yet showing a seductively full mouthfeel, freshness and crispness. Keep.
http://www.chablis-charlynicolle.com
Domaine Charly Nicolle
+33 (0)3 86 42 80 08

CHÂTEAU DE FLEYS — 86/100

🍷 Mont de Milieu 2011 : Pale gold. A mix of floral and ripe fruit notes on the nose with tones bordering on tropical. This carries through to the palate which is generous, supple and enhanced by a honey-like tone. A warm, perfumed wine pairing with cooked fish dishes.
Price approx.: 12,50 EUR
http://www.chablis-philippon.com
Domaine du Château de Fleys
+33 (0)3 86 42 47 70

CHABLIS

CHÂTEAU DE FLEYS — 89/100

🍷 Vieilles Vignes 2011 : Beautiful light gold. Intense nose with accents of butter, almond, hazelnut, honeysuckle… Lush, mouth-filling palate. Very persistent, distinctive perfumes. Powerful and fresh. A successful wine.
Price approx.: 9,50 EUR
http://www.chablis-philippon.com
Domaine du Château de Fleys
+33 (0)3 86 42 47 70

DOMAINE LE VERGER — 88/100

🍷 Vintage 2012 : Brilliant light gold. Distinctive nose recalling fresh butter, hawthorn and sweet almond. Fruit is present at point of entry and extends the finish. Generous, mouth-coating and concentrated substance. A young Chablis, soon punching above its weight.
Price approx.: 12,00 EUR
http://www.chablis-geoffroy.com
Domaine Alain Geoffroy
+33 (0)3 86 42 43 76

DOMAINE JOLLY ET FILS — 87/100

🍷 Vintage 2012 : Pale hue, brilliant tints. Expressive, distinctive nose driven by almond, honey and white flowers. Fat palate showing volume and a focused array of aromatics supported by savoury acidity. Youthful firmness on the finish. A beautiful Chablis with good potential.
Domaine Jolly et Fils
+33 (0)3 86 47 42 31

DOMAINE JEAN COLLET & FILS — 87/100

🍷 Chablis 2012 : Brilliant light gold with green tints. Distinctive nose of citrus coupled with a refined mineral tone. Lightweight palate, beautiful tension and a generous array of focused lemony aromas that are fairly austere, as they should be. Highly successful.
Price approx.: 9,10 EUR
http://www.domaine-collet.fr
Domaine Jean Collet & fils
+33 (0)3 86 42 11 93

Prices mentioned in this book are guideline and can vary depending on point of sale. The shops, wineries or publisher can in no way be held responsible for this.

DOMAINE CHANTEMERLE 86/100

▼ 🖊 Vintage 2012 : Brilliant pale gold, green tints. Subdued nose of white flowers with a silica touch. Clean palate displaying a fairly full, focused and consistent mouthfeel marrying flowers, white fruits and a lemony dimension. Fairly exuberant. A Chablis for pleasure.

Price approx.: 7,50 EUR

http://www.chablis-boudin.com

Domaine Chantemerle

+33 (0)3 86 42 18 95

DOMAINE CHARLY NICOLLE 86/100

▼ 🖊 Ancestrum 2012 : Pale gold. Refined nose with accents of almonds, white fruits and linden. Supple palate boasting savoury acidity. Soft perfumes and a silky mouthfeel. A refreshing yet elegant Chablis. Drinking well from the start of the meal onwards.

http://www.chablis-charlynicolle.com

Domaine Charly Nicolle

+33 (0)3 86 42 80 08

CHÂTEAU DE FLEYS 86/100

▼ 🖊 Vintage 2012 : Light yellow. Refined nose of white-fleshed fruits and floral notes unfurling a slightly tropical character after swirling. Rich, fleshy and closely-integrated palate revealing more of the tropical fruit notes. A delightful wine, enjoy whilst young.

Price approx.: 7,80 EUR

http://www.chablis-philippon.com

Domaine du Château de Fleys

+33 (0)3 86 42 47 70

DOMAINE DE LA MANDELIÈRE 85/100

▼ 🖊 2012 : Limpid, light gold. Focused nose blending notes of fresh grass and white-fleshed fruits. Fairly generous, fleshy attack. A rich, perfumed style, nicely balanced by good exuberance that lingers. A successful 2012.

Domaine de la Mandelière

+33 (0)3 86 42 19 30

CHARMES-CHAMBERTIN GRAND CRU

DOMAINE HENRI REBOURSEAU 92/100

▼ 🖊 Vintage 2001 : Orange-brown colour. Complex nose suggestive of damp earth, autumnal undergrowth and stone fruits. Ethereal structure with lace-like tannins. Exuberance prevails mid-palate, imparting a more nervy profile. Superb persistency.

Price approx.: 99,00 EUR

http://www.domaine-rebourseau.fr

Domaine Henri Rebourseau

+33 (0)3 80 51 88 94

CHOREY-LÈS-BEAUNE

DOMAINE POULLEAU PÈRE & FILS 89/100

▼ 🖊 Vintage 2012 : Medium intense, limpid hue. Lovely nose of morello cherry and plum with a touch of spice. Supple attack, round, easy-drinking and enjoyable palate. Fresh, spice-infused finish with a hint of firmness. Perfect for pork pie.

www.poulleau.com

Domaine Poulleau

+33 (0)3 80 21 26 52

CLOS DE VOUGEOT GRAND CRU

(See page 153)

CÔTE DE NUITS-VILLAGES

DOMAINE FOUGERAY DE BEAUCLAIR 88/100

▼ 🖊 Vintage 2012 : Beautiful intense ruby. Pleasurable nose of red fruits, liquorice and subtle spice. Velvety, rich palate showing a lovely impression of harmony supported by a robust structure. Tense and generous. A convincing effort.

Price approx.: 20,10 EUR

http://www.fougeraydebeauclair.fr

Domaine Fougeray de Beauclair

+33 (0)3 80 52 21 12

CRÉMANT DE BOURGOGNE

CLAUDE GHEERAERT 86/100

▼ 🖊 Brut Tradition : Light gold. Refined nose driven by hazelnut, white fruits and a touch of red berry fruits. A full, generous Crémant showing seductive vinosity, exuberance and freshness. A food-friendly fizz.

Price approx.: 7,20 EUR

http://www.cremant-gheeraert.fr

Ghéeraert Claude

+33 (0)3 80 93 71 67

FIXIN

DOMAINE FOUGERAY DE BEAUCLAIR 89/100

▼ 🖊 Clos Marion 2012 : Limpid ruby. Shy nose of cherry and refined spice. Velvety, rich and harmonious mouthfeel enveloping exuberance and extremely refined tannins. Still reticent but everything is in place. Poised for greatness. Patience!

Price approx.: 31,50 EUR

http://www.fougeraydebeauclair.fr

Domaine Fougeray de Beauclair

+33 (0)3 80 52 21 12

DOMAINE HENRI REBOURSEAU

95/100

▼ Clos de Vougeot 2002

Deep colour with magnificent orange-brown tints. Profound nose revealing jammy red fruits, undergrowth and leather notes.
Beautiful presence on the palate with a subtle balance between nicely retained power and wonderful exuberance. Great length, great wine.

Price approx.: 143 EUR
Serving temperature: 15-17°
Ready to drink: From now on

In 1919, General Henri Rebourseau turned his father's vines around their 18th-century home into a vineyard. His son Pierre later took over, helping the estate to prosper into the 1980s. Today, one of the general's great grandchildren, Jean de Surrel, manages the estate. It stretches over 13 hectares, forming a patchwork of extremely well-situated terroirs: from Gevrey-Chambertin to Premier Cru Le Fonteny, passing through Charmes-Chambertin, Mazis-Chambertin, Chambertin and Chambertin-Clos-De-Bèze. All the wealth and diversity of the terroirs of Gevrey-Chambertin are found here, not to mention the emblematic Clos de Vougeot, of which the estate owns 2.20 hectares located at the heart of the walled vineyard.

Domaine Henri Rebourseau
10 place du Monument - 21220 Gevrey Chambertin
Tel: (+33) 3 80 51 88 94 - Fax: (+33) 3 80 34 12 82
E-mail: domaine@rebourseau.com
Website: http://www.domaine-rebourseau.fr

GEVREY-CHAMBERTIN

CHÂTEAU DE BEAUFORT   93/100

▼♪ 1er Cru Les Champeaux 2006 : Faint bricking. Nose of jammy fruits flowing into dried fig with a touch of undergrowth after swirling. Beautiful full, ethereal palate. Lightweight mouthfeel showing lovely fat and remarkable freshness. A consummate Gevrey, almost feminine in style.
www.david-de-beaufort.com
Château de Beaufort
+33 (0)6 28 27 10 38

DOMAINE PHILIPPE LECLERC   91/100

▼♪ 1er Cru La Combe aux Moines 2010 : Intense garnet, young tints. Generous, mineral nose showing morello cherry, spice and subtle oak. On the palate, a virile, svelte and very vigorous wine with racy, intense aromas that have yet to evolve. Persistent finish. A fine wine, respectful of tradition.
Price approx.: 49,00 EUR
http://www.philippe-leclerc.com
Domaine Philippe Leclerc
+33 (0)3 80 34 30 72

DOMAINE PHILIPPE LECLERC   90/100

▼♪ Gevrey Chambertin en Champs 2010 : Deep garnet. Racy, expressive nose of red fruits, morello cherry, a touch of toast and smoke and a mineral impression. Tense palate displaying beautiful unfurling complexity, menthol, spice and vegetal touches and coffee. The tannins have virtually mellowed. Superb.
Price approx.: 28,00 EUR
http://www.philippe-leclerc.com
Domaine Philippe Leclerc
+33 (0)3 80 34 30 72

DOMAINE HENRI REBOURSEAU   90/100

▼♪ Vintage 2000 : Attractive hue with bricking. Mature nose combining dried fruits, undergrowth and animal notes. Fat, mellow and supple at point of entry, more vibrant mid-palate. Beautiful staying power and lovely length. A marvellous partner for small game.
Price approx.: 39,00 EUR
http://www.domaine-rebourseau.fr
Domaine Henri Rebourseau
+33 (0)3 80 51 88 94

IRANCY

ERIC DARLES   87/100

▼♪ Vintage 2009 : Medium intense hue with initial signs of ageing. Pleasurable, distinctive nose of morello cherry and vegetal notes. A robust, full, mellow and generous wine with exhilarating freshness. Still a tad angular. Vegetal, spicy finish. Needs 3-5 years more.

Price approx.: 9,40 EUR
Domaine Eric Darles
+33 (0)3 86 42 57 31

ERIC DARLES   85/100

▼♪ Boudardes 2008 : Limpid hue. Characterful, savoury nose showing fine spice and stone fruits. Supple attack leading into a suave, juicy palate revealing an impression of harmony yet quite indefinable. The mid-palate flows into a fairly dry vegetal finish. Watch this space.
Price approx.: 10,70 EUR
Domaine Eric Darles
+33 (0)3 86 42 57 31

MÂCON-CHARDONNAY

CHÂTEAU DE MESSEY   87/100

▼♪ Les Crêts 2012 : Light yellow showing a beautiful sparkle. Profound nose with aromas of ripe fruits (plum flesh). Wonderful presence on the palate, fat and fullness. A fresh, melted style revealing lovely focus. Perfect for fish or white meats.
Price approx.: 11,00 EUR
www.demessey.com
Château de Messey
+33 (0)3 85 51 33 83

MÂCON-CRUZILLE

CHÂTEAU DE MESSEY   87/100

▼♪ Clos des Avoueries 2012 : Light yellow-gold. Profound, focused nose developing perfumes of tropical fruits (pineapple). Lush, rich and full palate revealing more of the tropical-like character. May take aback but certainly very compelling with sweet and sour foods.
Price approx.: 11,50 EUR
www.demessey.com
Château de Messey
+33 (0)3 85 51 33 83

MÂCON-MILLY-LAMARTINE

CAVE DU PÈRE TIENNE   85/100

▼♪ Vintage 2009 : Limpid, deeply-coloured, first signs of ageing. Interesting nose of vegetal and animal notes with a whiff of toast backed by red fruit. Supple attack, seductive, fleshy and full palate supported by fine tannins. Characterful. Needs a little more time.
Price approx.: 6,90 EUR
http://perso.wanadoo.fr/caveduperetienne
Cave Du Père Tienne
+33 (0)3 85 37 78 05

DOMAINE PHILIPPE LECLERC

93/100

▼ 1er Cru Les Cazetiers 2009

Limpid garnet, starting to mature. Distinguished nose of coffee and mild spices with a mineral impression. Velvety, mellow yet nervy palate. A heady, warm and virile wine, already quite mature. Obvious vintage effect. Perfect for roast boar.

Price approx.: 46 EUR
Serving temperature: 15-17°
Ready to drink: 2015-2018

Philippe Leclerc has a clearly defined set of principles which allows him to produce flavoursome and charming wines. Vines are selected for their quality rather than their yields. Philippe prefers to keep old vines and occasionally replace the odd plant rather than uproot entire plots; he believes that vines show at their best from the age of 30, when the roots delve deep into the soil and impart a truly complex sense of place and typicality to the grapes, and therefore the wines. During the harvest, the grapes are treated with care so that their skins remain intact and the juice does not undergo oxidation before it enters the tanks. These guiding principles ensure consistent quality in the wines. Philippe's bottlings are not only archetypally Burgundian in style, they also have excellent ageing capacity.

Domaine Philippe Leclerc
9 rue des Halles - 21220 Gevrey Chambertin
Tel: (+33) 3 80 34 30 72 - Fax: (+33) 3 80 34 17 39
E-mail: philippe.leclerc60@wanadoo.fr
Website: http://www.philippe-leclerc.com

MÂCON-VILLAGES

CLOS DE CONDEMINE 87/100

▼🍷 Monopole Luquet 2013 : Light yellow with green tints. Powerful, mineral nose of gunflint backed by fruit notes. The palate displays a fleshy, full and concentrated mouthfeel, effectively invigorated by refined freshness. Would work with a crab salad.

Price approx.: 6,95 EUR

http://www.domaine-luquet.com

Domaine Roger Luquet

+33 (0)3 85 35 60 91

MARANGES

DOMAINE CLAUDE NOUVEAU 88/100

▼🍷 1er Cru La Fussière 2011 : Beautiful ruby. Inviting nose of raspberry and redcurrant enhanced by refined oak. Fleshy, closely-integrated attack leading into a full mid-palate showing tannin expression. Still young yet balanced and persistent. A compelling wine.

Price approx.: 15,00 EUR

http://www.claudenouveau.com

Domaine Claude Nouveau

+33 (0)3 85 91 13 34

MARSANNAY

DOMAINE FOUGERAY DE BEAUCLAIR 91/100

▼🍷 Saints-Jacques 2012 : Deeply-coloured ruby. Perfumed nose of cherry, redcurrant and a floral dimension. Silky attack, full, invigorating palate showing marvellous, archetypal Pinot aromas, and focusing successfully on finesse. The same is true for the structure. Superb.

Price approx.: 23,70 EUR

http://www.fougeraydebeauclair.fr

Domaine Fougeray de Beauclair

+33 (0)3 80 52 21 12

DOMAINE FOUGERAY DE BEAUCLAIR 87/100

▼🍷 Les Aiges Pruniers 2012 : Brilliant golden yellow. Fairly subtle, creamy nose showing ripe white fruits and vanilla oak in the background. Svelte, invigorating palate where fruit is augmented by a fine mineral presence and becomes more expressive. Spicy mid-palate. Keep for a while.

Price approx.: 16,70 EUR

http://www.fougeraydebeauclair.fr

Domaine Fougeray de Beauclair

+33 (0)3 80 52 21 12

DOMAINE FOUGERAY DE BEAUCLAIR 87/100

▼🍷 Les Favières 2012 : Deeply-coloured ruby with young tints. Shy yet elegant nose of stone fruits with a touch of spice. Velvety, tense and fairly full palate. Quite robust and framed by fine tannins. A nicely crafted Marsannay. Cellar for 3-5 years.

Price approx.: 19,90 EUR

http://www.fougeraydebeauclair.fr

Domaine Fougeray de Beauclair

+33 (0)3 80 52 21 12

MERCUREY

DOMAINE JEAN MARÉCHAL 91/100

▼🍷 Clos L'Evêque 2012 : Appealing, deep colour. Refined nose focusing on red berry fruits with well-integrated oak. The palate shows seductive fullness, fleshy character, fine, closely-integrated oak as well as clearly-delineated fruit. A nicely crafted wine.

Price approx.: 15,00 EUR

Domaine Jean Marechal

+33 (0)3 85 45 11 29

DOMAINE MICHEL JUILLOT 90/100

▼🍷 Les Vignes de Maillonge 2012 : Brilliant light yellow with green tints. Racy nose intermixing white fruits and refined mineral and liquoricy dimensions. Lively, generous palate with lovely silky body and exuberant, racy and precise aromas. Very compelling.

Price approx.: 16,00 EUR

www.domaine-michel-juillot.fr

Domaine Michel Juillot

+33 (0)3 85 98 99 89

DOMAINE MICHEL JUILLOT 89/100

▼🍷 Les Vignes de Maillonge 2012 : Brilliant ruby. Compelling nose of redcurrant and black cherry with a floral dimension. Fresh attack leading into an exuberant, fruity palate with refined spice and lots of vigour. Focused with some elegant, well-integrated tannins. Subtle oak. Beautiful.

Price approx.: 15,50 EUR

www.domaine-michel-juillot.fr

Domaine Michel Juillot

+33 (0)3 85 98 99 89

DOMAINE MICHEL JUILLOT 89/100

▼🍷 1er Cru Clos des Barraults 2011 : Limpid ruby. Pleasurable nose of ripe cherry with fine vegetal notes. The fruit aromatics carry through to the palate in a crunchy, dynamic style then flow into a degree of vegetal sourness mid-palate. Should sort itself out with time.

Price approx.: 24,00 EUR

www.domaine-michel-juillot.fr

Domaine Michel Juillot

+33 (0)3 85 98 99 89

MANOIR DE MERCEY — 89/100

▼🖋 Chateaubeau 2012 : Beautiful ruby. Delightful, focused nose with red fruit aromas augmented by a delicate animal and spice touch. Full mouthfeel framed by lovely fat. Clear fruit expression supported by a forthright structure. A wine for pleasure.

www.berger-rive.fr
Domaine Gérard Berger-Rive & Fils
+33 (0)3 85 91 13 81

DOMAINE JEAN MARÉCHAL — 87/100

▼🖋 Clos Barraults 2012 : Ruby showing youthful tints. Endearing nose marrying ripe red fruits and pronounced oak. Fullness, fat and exuberance on the palate. A fruit-driven attack leads into prevailing oak on the finish. Wait for it to mellow.

Price approx.: 15,00 EUR
Domaine Jean Marechal
+33 (0)3 85 45 11 29

MEURSAULT

GUY BOCARD — 96/100

▼🖋 1er Cru Charmes 2011 : Brilliant hue with green tints. Magnificent blend of silica, ripe white fruits, a floral touch and well concealed toasted oak on the nose. Tension is the key theme on the palate which is ethereal, silky and pure with precise, racy aromas. Marvellous.

Price approx.: 39,00 EUR
Domaine Guy Bocard
+33 (0)3 80 21 26 06

GUY BOCARD — 92/100

▼🖋 Limozin 2011 : Brilliant hue with green tints. A harmonious blend of fruit and flowers on the nose. Supple attack, beautiful full, silky and rich substance with lots of charm. Profound and tense with a finish that is still slightly rigid but very promising. A real treat.

Price approx.: 29,00 EUR
Domaine Guy Bocard
+33 (0)3 80 21 26 06

DOMAINE ALAIN PATRIARCHE — 91/100

▼🖋 Les Tillets 2012 : Light yellow with green tints. Delectable, profound nose intermixing a lemony, menthol character and excellent, subtly toasted oak. Although the palate is still young it shows seductively balanced fat and freshness, a melted attack and persistency. Keep.

http://www.alainpatriarche.com
Domaine Alain Patriarche
+33 (0)3 80 21 24 48

GUY BOCARD — 90/100

▼🖋 Les Narvaux 2011 : Light yellow with green tints. Beautiful racy nose with flowers, vanilla and ripe

white fruits. Very supple, fresh palate showing medium concentration, exemplary purity, some spice and ageing tones on the finish. A stellar wine that will be ready quite soon.

Price approx.: 29,00 EUR
Domaine Guy Bocard
+33 (0)3 80 21 26 06

GUY BOCARD — 88/100

▼🖋 Vieilles Vignes 2011 : Brilliant hue with green tints. Subdued nose with delicate fruity scents and a refined mineral dimension. Lightness and freshness are primary features on the palate which shows lovely round succulence and charm. Nicely present ageing aromas and spice.

Price approx.: 22,00 EUR
Domaine Guy Bocard
+33 (0)3 80 21 26 06

MEURSAUT-BLAGNY

DOMAINE ALAIN PATRIARCHE — 96/100

▼🖋 1er Cru La Pièce sous Bois 2012 : Light yellow-gold with green tints. Refined, profound nose with aromas of ripe lemon, fennel and subtle oak. Very harmonious palate showing lovely fullness, fat, mellowness and freshness. A full, elegant and persistent style. Very compelling.

http://www.alainpatriarche.com
Domaine Alain Patriarche
+33 (0)3 80 21 24 48

MONTAGNY

FRANÇOISE FEUILLAT-JUILLOT — 89/100

▼🖋 1er Cru 2013 : Attractive brilliant light gold. Muted nose showing mineral and stony accents. The palate displays beautiful substance, freshness and density. Aromatic expression is still shy but the wine is promising. Keep for a year or two.

Price approx.: 15,00 EUR
www.feuillat-juillot.com
Domaine Feuillat-Juillot
+33 (0)6 80 22 73 61

FRANÇOISE FEUILLAT-JUILLOT — 88/100

▼🖋 Camille 2013 : Limpid, light gold. Fairly elegant nose marrying white flowers with a mineral and buttery touch. Very fat, fresh palate showing beautiful balance. The nose aromatics carry through over substantial length. Wonderful typicality.

Price approx.: 12,00 EUR
www.feuillat-juillot.com
Domaine Feuillat-Juillot
+33 (0)6 80 22 73 61

MONTHÉLIE

GUY BOCARD   84/100

▼♪ Toisières 2011 : Young, light red. Endearing fruity nose suggestive of cherry flesh. On the palate, a polished attack with fairly upfront red fruit. The mid-palate introduces more tropical notes bordering on banana. A well-balanced yet atypical style.
Price approx.: 18,00 EUR
Domaine Guy Bocard
+33 (0)3 80 21 26 06

NUITS SAINT GEORGES

DOMAINE MICHEL GROS   88/100

▼♪ Vintage 2010 : Beautiful, young-looking red. Quite mature nose of red fruits, fairly reminiscent of stone fruits. A relatively mellow, harmonious wine with full-on fruit expression. Fairly lightweight structure making it suitable for drinking from now on.
Price approx.: 26,00 EUR
http://www.domaine-michel-gros.com
Domaine Michel Gros
+33 (0)3 80 61 04 69

PETIT CHABLIS

DOMAINE ALAIN GEOFFROY   87/100

▼♪ Vintage 2012 : Brilliant pale gold. Subdued, refined nose with mineral and smoke nuances and almond and hawthorn perfumes. Fat, mouth-coating attack leading into a more supple mid-palate where focused, persistent fruit shows through. A Petit Chablis in the major league.
Price approx.: 10,00 EUR
http://www.chablis-geoffroy.com
Domaine Alain Geoffroy
+33 (0)3 86 42 43 76

DOMAINE JOLLY ET FILS   86/100

▼♪ Vintage 2012 : Pale gold. Mineral and white fruit aromas on the nose with a whiff of smoke and linden. Soft palate boasting beautiful balance of freshness and acidity. Supple mouthfeel with noticeable fruit. A distinctive Petit Chablis, in full bloom.
Domaine Jolly et Fils
+33 (0)3 86 47 42 31

POUILLY-FUISSÉ

DOMAINE AUVIGUE   94/100

▼♪ Cuvée Hors Classe 2012 : Brilliant light yellow. Endearing nose intermixing ripe white fruits, tropical and floral notes and beautiful vanilla oak. On the palate, a velvety, concentrated and powerful wine with generous expression and a persistent, spicy finish. A top-flight Pouilly.
Price approx.: 17,00 EUR
http://www.auvigue.fr
Domaine Auvigue
+33 (0)3 85 34 17 36

CHÂTEAU POUILLY   92/100

▼♪ La Réserve 2010 : Brilliant yellow. Complex nose of white flowers, toast and vanilla notes backed by white fruits. The palate exudes superb mineral aromas entwined with spice. A fleshy, powerful and distinguished wine pairing best with shellfish.
Price approx.: 22,80 EUR
http://www.chateaupouilly.fr
Château de Pouilly
+33 (0)3 85 35 83 65

DOMAINE AUVIGUE   92/100

▼♪ Vieilles Vignes 2012 : Brilliant yellow with green tints. Expressive nose of spring flowers, white fruits and a tropical touch of mango. Full-bodied, rich palate boasting fat and liveliness. Aromas burst enthusiastically onto the palate and linger. A real pleasure.
Price approx.: 15,00 EUR
http://www.auvigue.fr
Domaine Auvigue
+33 (0)3 85 34 17 36

DOMAINE DENUZILLER   91/100

▼♪ Le Clos 2012 : Beautiful light gold with green tints. Generous nose intermixing fruit, mineral and milky scents. Round attack, concentrated, virile and fleshy palate framing beautiful freshness. Lingering spice-driven finish. Already enjoyable with lots of promise.
Price approx.: 14,00 EUR
Domaine Denuziller
+33 (0)3 85 35 80 77

DOMAINE ROGER LUQUET   90/100

▼♪ Au Bourg 2012 : Brilliant pale hue with some green tints. Elegant, mineral nose of flint and gunflint with white-fleshed fruits. The palate displays a fairly fat, concentrated and nervy mouthfeel. Still quite reticent yet full of promise for the future.
Price approx.: 19,50 EUR
http://www.domaine-luquet.com
Domaine Roger Luquet
+33 (0)3 85 35 60 91

MANOIR DU CAPUCIN   89/100

▼♪ Aux Morlays 2011 : Brilliant light yellow with green tints. Expressive creamy nose of ripe white fruits. Fleshy, generous palate showing refined vanilla and some spice supported by an invigorating freshness. The finish is still a

little angular. Keep for a while.
Price approx.: 15,00 EUR
Manoir du Capucin
+33 (0)3 85 35 87 74

DOMAINE DENUZILLER 89/100

▼♪ Prestige 2012 : Brilliant pale yellow with green tints. The nose is fairly muted yet promising, floral with a mineral dimension. Distinctive, racy palate showing more promise of beautiful aromatic exuberance. Tense and precise. A delicious Pouilly in 2-3 years time.
Price approx.: 12,50 EUR
Domaine Denuziller
+33 (0)3 85 35 80 77

CHÂTEAU POUILLY 88/100

▼♪ Cuvée 1551 2010 : Beautiful brilliant yellow. Expressive nose of ripe white fruits with honeyed, vanilla and floral touches. Round, concentrated and well-balanced palate driven by robust freshness. A few years cellaring will impart harmony and greater expression.
Price approx.: 17,80 EUR
http://www.chateaupouilly.fr
Château de Pouilly
+33 (0)3 85 35 83 65

DOMAINE DENUZILLER 88/100

▼♪ La Frérie 2012 : Brilliant pale gold with green tints. Racy nose of white flowers backed by nicely ripe white fruits. Beautiful harmonious, full and concentrated palate with refined, uplifting freshness. Very promising.
Price approx.: 12,50 EUR
Domaine Denuziller
+33 (0)3 85 35 80 77

DOMAINE ROGER LUQUET 86/100

▼♪ En Chatenet 2012 : Vibrant light yellow. On the nose, lovely mineral accents of gunflint backed by white fruits. Supple attack, charming, nervy and svelte palate showing medium concentration and a spice-infused finish. An enjoyable wine with freshness the key theme.
Price approx.: 15,80 EUR
http://www.domaine-luquet.com
Domaine Roger Luquet
+33 (0)3 85 35 60 91

POUILLY-VINZELLES

CHÂTEAU DE VINZELLES 88/100

▼♪ Les Pétaux 2011 : Light yellow with green tints. Toasted almond, white fruits and a mineral touch on the nose. A svelte wine on the palate that is full of vigour with generous aromatic expression and freshness ensuring exemplary balance. Pair with grilled fish.
Price approx.: 15,00 EUR
http://www.chateau-de-vinzelles.com
Château de Vinzelles
+33 (0)6 07 11 43 88

CHÂTEAU DE VINZELLES 87/100

▼♪ Cuvée Vauban 2011 : Brilliant pale yellow with green tints. On the nose, floral and fruity aromas work together pleasantly. The palate emphasises nervousness, it is svelte, tense and rich. Perfumed mid-palate showing mineral and spice touches. Perfect for Asian foods.
Price approx.: 13,00 EUR
http://www.chateau-de-vinzelles.com
Château de Vinzelles
+33 (0)6 07 11 43 88

PULIGNY-MONTRACHET

CHÂTEAU DE BEAUFORT 90/100

▼♪ 1er Cru Les Combettes 2010 : Bright, pale yellow. Refined nose showing delicate lemony, menthol and toast notes. Full, warm palate that is still fiery. Upfront exuberance imparts lovely length. The aromatic spectrum will become more complex over time.
www.david-de-beaufort.com
Château de Beaufort
+33 (0)6 28 27 10 38

RULLY

MANOIR DE MERCEY 87/100

▼♪ En Rosey 2012 : Attractive ruby with dark purple shades. Focused nose with crunchy aromas of red berry fruits. Delicate mousse notes in the background. Fairly lightweight on the palate with a fine texture and beautiful aromatic expression enhanced by a faint spice dimension.
www.berger-rive.fr
Domaine Gérard Berger-Rive & Fils
+33 (0)3 85 91 13 81

MANOIR DE MERCEY 87/100

▼♪ Cuvée Louise 2012 : Light yellow. Delightful, focused nose intermixing delicate lemony and vegetal notes with lightly toasted, refined oak. Fleshy attack with a silky texture. Supple and framed by a subtle sensation of freshness. Full and long.
www.berger-rive.fr
Domaine Gérard Berger-Rive & Fils
+33 (0)3 85 91 13 81

SAINT-VÉRAN

DOMAINE ROGER LUQUET   88/100

▼✏ Vieilles Vignes - élevé en fûts de chêne 2013 : Brilliant light yellow, green tints. Ripe nose of white fruits with tropical and vanilla notes and a refined mineral dimension. Concentrated, fleshy and lush palate with a welcome tension imparting liveliness. Harmoniously full. Pair with refined Asian foods.
Price approx.: 9,90 EUR
http://www.domaine-luquet.com
Domaine Roger Luquet
+33 (0)3 85 35 60 91

SANTENAY

DOMAINE CLAUDE NOUVEAU   90/100

▼✏ 1er Cru Grand Clos Rousseau 2011 : Ruby. Expressive nose showing red fruit overtones (cherry), toast and mineral-like notes after swirling. Beautiful presence, evident, refined and fleshy mouthfeel with wonderful fullness. An expressive, harmonious wine boasting great potential.
Price approx.: 16,50 EUR
http://www.claudenouveau.com
Domaine Claude Nouveau
+33 (0)3 85 91 13 34

DOMAINE MICHEL DELORME   89/100

▼✏ Vintage 2012 : Light yellow. Pure, focused nose intermixing floral notes, a lemony touch and subtle minerality. Soft, silky attack framed by delicious freshness that lingers. Precise fruit accompanied by a subtle touch of oak. Very charming.
Price approx.: 14,00 EUR
http://www.domainemicheldelorme.com
Domaine Michel Delorme
+33 (0)3 80 20 63 41

DOMAINE CLAUDE NOUVEAU   87/100

▼✏ Le Chainey 2012 : Limpid, light yellow. Racy nose of gunflint with a touch of toast and fruity and floral undertones. Balanced palate giving an impression of lightness and natural character with precise, albeit slightly subdued, aromas. Lively and enthusiastic. Good. Keep a little.
Price approx.: 14,50 EUR
http://www.claudenouveau.com
Domaine Claude Nouveau
+33 (0)3 85 91 13 34

DOMAINE MICHEL DELORME   87/100

▼✏ 1er Cru Grand Clos Rousseau 2010 : Limpid, lightly-coloured with evolved highlights. Mature nose with fruit aromas flowing into autumnal notes of undergrowth. Good staying power, fullness and a refined mouthfeel framed by fat. A sensation of suppleness yet also freshness.
Price approx.: 14,00 EUR
http://www.domainemicheldelorme.com
Domaine Michel Delorme
+33 (0)3 80 20 63 41

SAVIGNY LES BEAUNE

DOMAINE FOUGERAY DE BEAUCLAIR   88/100

▼✏ Les Golardes 2012 : Brilliant golden yellow. Racy nose intermixing flint, ripe white fruits, an exotic note and subtle ageing. Energetic palate with full-on expression, a round mouthfeel and medium concentration. Well-balanced. Needs a few more years bottle age.
Price approx.: 24,00 EUR
http://www.fougeraydebeauclair.fr
Domaine Fougeray de Beauclair
+33 (0)3 80 52 21 12

DOMAINE FOUGERAY DE BEAUCLAIR   88/100

▼✏ Les Golardes 2012 : Deep ruby, crimson tints. Delightful nose of morello cherry, redcurrant and fine spice. Fleshy attack, easy-drinking, rich and enjoyable palate with more perfume in reserve, some supporting tannins and subtle oak influence. All-set to become a great wine.
Price approx.: 21,00 EUR
http://www.fougeraydebeauclair.fr
Domaine Fougeray de Beauclair
+33 (0)3 80 52 21 12

VIRÉ-CLESSÉ

CAVE DE VIRÉ   88/100

▼✏ Viré d'Or 2012 : Bright pale gold with green tints. Quality vanilla oak on the nose with white fruits in the background. The palate stands out for its concentration, silkiness and fine spice. Fat mouthfeel that is lively and focused. Gets our approval.
Price approx.: 14,90 EUR
http://www.cavedevire.fr
Cave de Viré
+33 (0)3 85 32 25 50

CAVE DE VIRÉ   87/100

▼✏ Quintaine 2012 : Brilliant pale yellow with green tints. Refined nose blending spring flower notes and white fruits. Supple attack leading into a delicious, silky and

closely-integrated mouthfeel where a mineral streak imparts a hint of austerity.
Price approx.: 10,90 EUR
http://www.cavedevire.fr
Cave de Viré
+33 (0)3 85 32 25 50

CAVE DE VIRÉ 85/100

▼♪ Grande Réserve 2013 : Light gold with green tints. Expressive nose of white fruits with an elegant floral note. Supple attack. The palate's main calling card is its likeability. It is light, silky, harmonious and very welcoming. A wine that is suitable for any occasion.
Price approx.: 7,30 EUR
http://www.cavedevire.fr
Cave de Viré
+33 (0)3 85 32 25 50

VOLNAY

DOMAINE POULLEAU PÈRE & FILS 90/100

▼♪ Vintage 2012 : Beautiful limpid red. Racy nose showing refined spice, red fruits, morello cherry and subtle oak. Delicious, fleshy and fresh palate displaying vigorous fruit and spice. Vegetal finish with a trace of firmness. A convincing Volnay.
www.poulleau.com
Domaine Poulleau
+33 (0)3 80 21 26 52

VOSNE ROMANÉE

DOMAINE MICHEL GROS 96/100

▼♪ 1er Cru Clos des Réas - Monopole 2011 : Beautiful vibrant red. Outstanding quality fruit on the nose accompanied by a very delicate smoky tone. Volume, fruit and balance on the palate. The mid-palate and finish stay full with the archetypal smoke tone of the local terroir.
Price approx.: 50,00 EUR
http://www.domaine-michel-gros.com
Domaine Michel Gros
+33 (0)3 80 61 04 69

CHAMPAGNE

STILL SCALING THE HEIGHTS

Champagne can only be produced in the French region of the same name. Although its preparation may be linked to a specific set of skills and expertise, it is also associated with a terroir which is as influential as it is diverse. In other words, we should talk not of champagne, but instead of champagnes - each of which have their own individual characteristics and styles, making it possible for any champagne-lover to find a wine to astonish and delight, depending on individual taste and circumstances. To help you to know what to look for when choosing and tasting a champagne, we present a 'behind-the-scenes' look at this subtle brew.

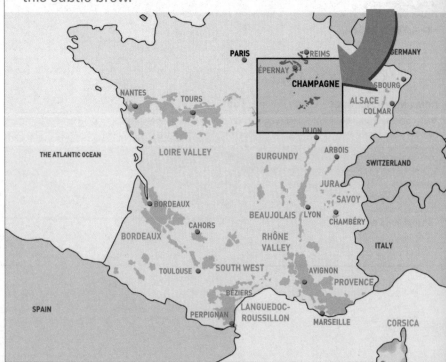

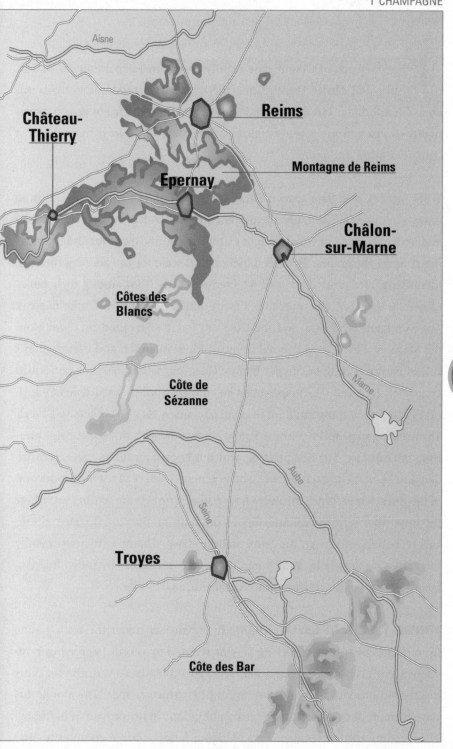

Aisne

Château-
Thierry

Reims

Montagne de Reims

Epernay

Châlon-
sur-Marne

Côtes des
Blancs

Côte de
Sézanne

Marne

163

Seine

Aube

Troyes

Côte des Bar

The vineyards of Champagne mainly cover three départements: Marne, Aube and Aisne. Three grape varieties are used predominantly in this area: Chardonnay, Pinot Noir and Pinot Meunier, which are grown across highly diverse terroirs. These fluctuations are due to various combinations of climate, subsoil and relief.

Three princes, one great terroir: There are a total of 313 crus produced in as many communes. The latter themselves are subdivided into parcels of land and lieux-dits, each of which impart extremely specific qualities and characteristics upon the grapes. There is a hierarchical scale for categorising the crus, identifying 17 Grands Crus and 41 Premiers Crus from among their ranks. Generally speaking, the three major grape varieties have their favourite areas. The Montagne de Reims and the Côte des Bar are favoured by Pinot Noir, the Marne Valley is the preferred home of Pinot Meunier, and Chardonnay's soil of choice is in the Côte des Blancs. Champagne harvesting is performed exclusively by hand. The grapes must be vinified whole, a requirement which necessitates their transportation in small containers such as baskets and crates. The pressing stage follows immediately afterwards, with three successive pressings taking place. The first pressing, which is known locally as cuvée, is considered to be of the highest quality, and is generally reserved for the production of the finest wines. Once the juices have passed through the settling vat, where the impurities separate off and sink to the bottom, they are transferred into vats or barrels and begin the fermentation phase. Champagne houses vinify the grapes separately by variety and - wherever possible - by individual cru, taking the particular structure into consideration.

WHERE TIME AND SKILL COMBINE: Having separated the resting wine from its lees by means of racking, a wine referred to as clair (signifying 'non-effervescent') is obtained. The cellarmaster then blends his various vins clairs together to produce one or more cuvées of a particular style. The aim at this stage is to produce the best possible combinations in the pursuit of harmony. There is universal agreement that blending lends a cuvée complexity. The artist's palette contains a wide variety of nuances: each vin clair exhibits the individual characteristics of its original grape, which will vary depending on cru, or - at a more basic level - on grape variety. Chardonnay's boast is that it lends refinement and ageing potential. Pinot Noir gives power and red fruit aromas. Pinot Meunier bestows fruitiness, and develops more quickly over time. The wine producer therefore makes a choice from among the grape varieties and crus from which the wines have been produced, but also - if the end product is not a vintage champagne - from among several different years. Of course, the blends depend on the various grapes at the producer's disposal, yet they must also conform to the "house style", not only as a means of differentiation from other champagnes, but also to satisfy the requirements of consumers whose loyalty depends on the year-to-year consistency of the wine. Creating a range of different types of wines also provides the producer with a wide range of styles and prices. Once blending has taken place, the wine is bottled along with a small quantity of sugar liqueur and a few yeasts, an addition which encourages the second fermentation. The law specifies a minimum of fifteen months' cellaring for non-vintage bruts and a full three years for vintage champagnes. During bottle fermentation, a deposit forms in the bottle. The process by which it is removed is known as remuage (riddling): the bottles are placed in a partially inverted position on slanted racks known as pupîtres and, over a period of several weeks, they are turned one quarter-turn per day while being gradually lifted further towards the vertical. The bottle ultimately ends up sur pointe (completely inverted) with the deposit settled in the neck. The old method of removing this deposit involved unstoppering the bottle and turning it over quickly; the pressure in the bottle would cause the deposit to be expelled. The preferred modern method is a simpler mechanical technique consisting of immersing the end of the bottle in a freezing 'bath' and then turning the bottle over, causing the plug of ice containing the deposit to be expelled by pressure. The bottle then receives its final cork, topped with a cap in the house colours; both of these are held in place by a muzzle. The package is completed by the addition of neck and body labels, and the champagne is ready to be sent out.

CHOOSING A CHAMPAGNE

Below is a presentation of the various types of champagne. Information on the following characteristics can be found on the bottle label, allowing you to make an informed choice.

• **GRAPE VARIETY** • Grape variety: the wine may have been blended from one or more varieties. Champagne produced solely from Chardonnay (a white grape with white juice) is known as blanc de blancs. Likewise, a champagne produced only from Pinot Noir and/or Pinot Meunier (black grapes with white juice) is known as a blanc de noirs. The liqueur d'expédition (the sweetening "dosage" - a mixture of sugar and wine added at the bottling stage in some cases) lends further nuances to the wine. Depending on the quantity of the dosage added, the wine will assume a more or less sweet character, classified as follows. 0-6g of sugar per litre: extra-brut; under 15 g: brut; 12-20g: extra-dry; 17-35g: sec; 33-50g: demi-sec; over 50g: doux.

• **NON-VINTAGE BRUT CHAMPAGNES** • These are the most common types of champagne, combining wines from a number of different years, and usually from a range of varieties and crus too. They include a proportion of reserve wine, preserving a degree of constant style.

• **VINTAGES** • These are produced from grapes from just one year (which determines the vintage); they may, however, come from a variety of crus. Vintages are not produced as a matter of course every year, but rather in years with particularly high-quality harvests.

• **PREMIERS AND GRANDS CRUS** • To be a Grand Cru, a wine must be produced exclusively from Grand Cru-classified terroirs; there are a total of 17 of these. Premiers Crus are produced using grapes taken from Premier Cru-classified communes, to which a proportion of Grand Cru may in some cases be added. Rosé champagnes: Champagne is the only French region where rosé wines may be produced from a combination of red and white wine. Rosé champagnes are therefore obtained in part by adding still red wine, but they can also be produced using the saignée (bleeding) technique; in other words, by macerating the juice of black grapes along with their skins to extract colour and aromas. Rosés may be vintage champagnes, or indeed be rated Grand Cru or Premier Cru.

RECENT VINTAGE

• **2009** • The beginning of the growing season was difficult, with frost followed by hailstorms, and a mildew problem in July. But there was a happy ending as the month of August was hot and dry, saving the harvest. With a good alcohol potential and level of acidity, this vintage should produce excellent blends.

• **2010** • unlike most other wine regions, Champagne did not fare well in this vintage. Yields were relatively low and ripeness only moderate. There will probably be some good dry wines for blending but generally speaking, the vintage will not make it into the history books.

• • •

2015
CHAMPAGNE WINES

CHAMPAGNE

CHAMPAGNE TAITTINGER   99/100

▼ ♪ Brut blanc de blancs Comtes de Champagne 2005 : Bright pale yellow with green tints. Delicate, subtle nose showing a mix of floral, fruity, mineral and creamy perfumes. Remarkably silky, fresh and ethereal palate. Full, fat and persistent. A consummate Champagne.
http://www.taittinger.fr
Champagne Taittinger
+33 (0)3 26 85 45 35

CHAMPAGNE DEUTZ   98/100

▼ ♪ Brut Amour de Deutz 2005 : Light yellow. Exotic aromas on the nose with mango and passion fruit. The palate combines fullness, elegance and aromatic precision with more of the lush yet restrained fruit aromatics. A remarkable Champagne showing outstanding length.
Price approx.: 129,00 EUR
http://www.champagne-deutz.com
Champagne Deutz
+33 (0)3 26 56 94 00

CHAMPAGNE HENRIOT   98/100

▼ ♪ Brut Cuvée des Enchanteleurs 1998 : Glistening light gold. Refined, expressive nose with accents of fresh fruit, warm bread, biscuit and a touch of rancio. The palate shows absolute textbook fullness, expression and harmony with the same delightful aromas and silky effervescence.
Price approx.: 120,00 EUR
http://www.champagne-henriot.com
Champagne Henriot
+33 (0)3 26 89 53 00

CHAMPAGNE CHARLES HEIDSIECK   97/100

▼ ♪ Brut blanc de blancs - Blanc des Millénaires 1995 : Very limpid pale gold. Racy, expressive nose with open aromas of toast and breadcrust. Still fresh and silky on the palate with remarkable complexity: notes of fresh fruit, dried fruit and mild spices. A very mature Champagne.
Price approx.: 140,00 EUR
http://www.piper-heidsieck.com
Cie Champenoise PH-CH. Piper Heidsieck
+33 (0)3 26 84 43 00

CHAMPAGNE DEUTZ   96/100

▼ ♪ Brut Cuvée William Deutz 2000 : Light yellow. Very refined nose expressing toast, ripe raspberry and patisserie aromatics. The palate shows extremely refined expression, silky effervescence and clear-cut perfumes. A very delicate Champagne across the palate.
Price approx.: 118,00 EUR
http://www.champagne-deutz.com
Champagne Deutz
+33 (0)3 26 56 94 00

CHAMPAGNE PHILIPPONNAT   95/100

▼ ♪ Brut Nature Royale Réserve : Pale yellow. Nose of grilled almonds with aromas of brioche bread and notes of white fruits (pear). Very refined, elegant palate showing more of the dried fruit and sublime acidity. Delicious finish intermixing fresh nuts and a mineral touch. Price approx.: 30,00 EUR
http://www.philipponnat.com
Champagne Philipponnat
+33 (0)3 26 56 93 00

CHAMPAGNE AMAZONE DE PALMER   95/100

▼ ♪ Brut : Old gold. Profound, mature nose showing aromas of dried fruits, orange peel and a patisserie note. On the palate, a full-bodied, vinous, lush and melted style with richness balanced by magnificent freshness. A consummate Champagne for meditation. Price approx.: 65,00 EUR
www.champagne-palmer.fr
Champagne Palmer & Co
+33 (0)3 26 07 35 07

CHAMPAGNE AYALA   95/100

▼ ♪ Brut Cuvée Perle d'Ayala 2005 : Light gold. Mature, profound and complex nose blending pastry, dried fruit and mocha perfumes. The palate shows seductive vinosity, fullness and fine bubbles yet also freshness. Creamy yet well-structured. A consummate Champagne.
Price approx.: 74,00 EUR
http://www.champagne-ayala.com
Champagne Ayala
+33 (0)3 26 55 15 44

GRAND SIÈCLE PAR LAURENT-PERRIER   95/100

▼ ♪ Brut Grande Cuvée : Beautiful gold. Profound, mature and complex nose intermixing dried fruits, citrus, toast and biscuity tones. The palate displays good balance of vinosity and freshness, lovely mellowness and above all, superb lingering freshness. Champagne for meditation
Price approx.: 125,00 EUR
http://www.laurent-perrier.fr
Champagne Laurent-Perrier
+33 (0)3 26 58 91 22

CHAMPAGNE GOSSET

97/100

▼ Extra Brut Celebris 2002

Beautiful deeply-coloured light gold. Refined, expressive nose blending tropical fruits and a creamy dimension. The palate shows seductive vinosity, fine-grained texture and exuberance highlighting mature fruit. A very compelling Champagne.

Price approx.: 126 EUR
Serving temperature: 9-11°
Ready to drink: From now on

Rossini-style crayfish tournedos

Ingredients: Two crayfish tails, 6 thick slices of raw foie gras, 5cl of Madeira, 1 tbsp flour, 2 tbsp oil, salt, pepper.
Method: Peel the crayfish tails and slice them into steaks.
Heat the oil, add the slices of crayfish.
Cook for 5 min. on each side with the lid on.
Keep warm.
Get the pan "white hot".
Dip the slices of foie gras in the flour and place them in the very hot pan.
Cook for 1 min on each side. Add pepper and remove.
Deglaze the pan with the Madeira, allow to reduce for 2 min. then scrape the bottom of the pan.
Put the crayfish tournedos on the plates with the foie gras on top. Pour over the Madeira juices. Serve.

Champagne Gosset
12, rue Godart Roger - 51200 Epernay
Tel: (+33) 3 26 56 99 56 - Fax: (+33) 3 26 51 55 88
E-mail: info@champagne-gosset.com
Website: http://www.champagne-gosset.com

CHAMPAGNE PHILIPPONNAT

97/100

▼ Brut Clos des Goisses 2004

Golden hue. Expressive nose blending dried apricot, citrus and gingerbread. Exuberance prevails over the classic vinous, lush style of this outstanding blend on the palate. Still young and fiery, this elegant 2004 needs more bottle time.

Price approx.: 140 EUR
Serving temperature: 9-11°
Ready to drink: From now on

The Philipponnat family has called Aÿ, the heart of the wine region, home since 1522, Pierre and Auguste Philipponnat moved to Mareuil sur Aÿ in 1910. They acquired magnificent cellars hewn thirty metres deep out of Champagne's chalk soils. In 1997, Champagne Philipponnat joined the Boizel Chanoine Champagne group and is managed by Charles Philipponnat, a descendant of the founders. Philipponnat offers an excellent range of Champagnes marked by clean fruit aromas and abundant freshness. Once again, a very special mention goes to the famous Clos des Goisses (5.5 hectares), one of Champagne's rare walled vineyards which has belonged to the house since 1935. The 2004 vintage has quite simply achieved perfection!

Champagne Philipponnat
13 rue du Pont - 51160 Mareuil sur Ay
Tel: (+33) 3 26 56 93 00 - Fax: (+33) 3 26 56 93 18
E-mail: charles.philipponnat@philipponnat.com
Website: http://www.philipponnat.com

CHAMPAGNE GOSSET

95/100

▼ Brut Grand Millésime 2004

Light gold. Subtle, racy nose with white-fleshed fruit aromas augmented by a slightly saline, mineral dimension. Lovely upright, exuberant palate with closely-integrated, fine bubbles.

Price approx.: 51 EUR
Serving temperature: 9-11°
Ready to drink: From now on

The oldest wine House in Champagne was founded in 1584 by Pierre Gosset, Mayor of Aÿ, who was producing a still wine 100 years before the méthode champenoise for producing sparkling wines was discovered. The House's grapes are today harvested among others in the districts of Aÿ, Bouzy, Mareuil and Rilly-la-Montagne. Gosset remains attached to its history and its traditions: for example, magnums and jeroboams are still riddled by hand. In addition, the elegant bottles of the Grandes Cuvées are the exact replicas of the 18th-century versions. The house produces a range of Champagnes of exceptionally high quality that are fruity, complex and endowed with remarkable personality; this year, in addition to the Celebris 2002, unbeatable since its launch, the House offers a premium Brut Grand Blanc de Blancs.

Champagne Gosset
12, rue Godart Roger - 51200 Epernay
Tel: (+33) 3 26 56 99 56 - Fax: (+33) 3 26 51 55 88
E-mail: info@champagne-gosset.com
Website: http://www.champagne-gosset.com

CHAMPAGNE PIPER HEIDSIECK

Brut Rare 2002

▼ Pale gold. Clean, expressive nose marrying white fruits and a biscuity tone. Assertive personality, intense crisp fruit aromas and creamy effervescence in the background. A mix of white fruits and a nicely restrained trace of sourness on the finish.

+33 3 26 84 43 00

95/100

CHAMPAGNE JEAN VESSELLE 95/100

▼ ♪ Brut grand cru Cuvée Le Petit Clos 2001 : Deep old gold. Mature, profound nose blending dried apricot, date and dried figs. Vinous, full and remarkably melted palate with freshness framing the whole. Superb persistency. A Champagne for meditation.
Price approx.: 58,00 EUR
www.champagnejeanvesselle.fr
Champagne Jean Vesselle
+33 (0)3 26 57 01 55

HAMPAGNE MICHEL GONET 94/100

▼ ♪ Extra brut grand cru Cuvée Authentique - fût de chêne 2005 : Deep gold bordering on amber. Profound, mature nose revealing pastry and dried fruit perfumes with an oak dimension. Well-structured, closely-integrated palate. Fresh and persistent with beautiful volume and substantial length. Drink with foie gras canape
Price approx.: 47,00 EUR
www.gonet.fr
Champagne Michel Gonet
+33 (0)3 26 57 50 56

CHAMPAGNE DEUTZ 94/100

▼ ♪ Brut rosé 2008 : Elegant light pink. Refined nose marrying red berry fruits and biscuit tones. Fleshy attack on the palate with abundant freshness and focused aromas. An extremely delicate rosé with vibrant fruit. Serve with food or as a pudding Champagne.
Price approx.: 57,00 EUR
http://www.champagne-deutz.com
Champagne Deutz
+33 (0)3 26 56 94 00

CHAMPAGNE COLLARD-PICARD 94/100

▼ ♪ Cuvée des Archives 2002 : Light gold. Profound, evolved nose blending honey notes, gingerbread, pastries and dried fruits. Beautiful freshness on the palate, fine-grained, well-integrated

texture and medium fullness counterbalanced by superb length. A top-notch Champagne.
Price approx.: 92,00 EUR
www.champagnecollardpicard.fr
Champagne Collard-Picard
+33 (0)3 26 52 36 93

CHAMPAGNE GUY CHARLEMAGNE 94/100

▼ ♪ Brut blanc de blancs grand cru Mesnillésime 2004 : Light gold. Racy, open nose intermixing a brioche character, dried fruits, a chalky dimension and a whiff of oak. Lush, full and melted palate showing persistency. A consummate Champagne from a great terroir and an expressive vintage.
Price approx.: 34,00 EUR
http://www.champagne-guy-charlemagne.fr
Champagne Guy Charlemagne
+33 (0)3 26 57 52 98

CHAMPAGNE TAITTINGER 94/100

▼ ♪ Brut 2006 : Beautiful bright pale yellow. Mature nose intermixing a floral and mineral dimension with lemon zest and a hint of almond. Full, silky and remarkably mellow attack leading into a mid-palate that is full yet fresh. Both lush and ethereal.
http://www.taittinger.fr
Champagne Taittinger
+33 (0)3 26 85 45 35

CHAMPAGNE MALARD 93/100

▼ ♪ Extra brut Lady Style : Beautiful light yellow-gold. Refined, mature nose blending creamy touches, dried and stewed fruits with fine brioche notes. Impeccable presence on the palate. Full, silky and driven by impertinent exuberance. A superlative Champagne that is full yet ether
Price approx.: 50,00 EUR
http://www.champagnemalard.com
Champagne Malard
+33 (0)3 26 32 40 11

CHAMPAGNE DRAPPIER

93/100

▼ Brut Grande Sendrée 2006

Light gold. Profound nose revealing a broad aromatic spectrum intermixing dried fruits, citrus, pastries and a patisserie note. Fullbodied, vinous and mellow palate framed by freshness. Lovely presence, volume and persistency. A consummate Champagne.

Price approx.: 70 EUR
Serving temperature: 9-11°
Ready to drink: From now on

The 53-hectare vineyard is located in the heart of the Côte des Bar along the hillside of Urville. Planted by the Gallo-Romans in the first years AD, it was one of the first to be farmed by the Cistercian monks from Clairvaux Abbey. More recently, the Drappier Champagne house prided itself on being a purveyor to Charles de Gaulle. The vineyard is planted to a predominant proportion of Pinot Noir, which covers 70 percent of the area under vine, alongside Chardonnay (15 percent) and Pinot Meunier (15 percent). It produces highly idiosyncratic Champagnes of extremely consistent quality which are housed in splendid vaulted cellars dating back to the 12th century.

Champagne Drappier
14 rue des Vignes - 10200 Urville
Tel: (+33) 3 25 27 40 15 - Fax: (+33) 3 25 27 41 19
E-mail: info@champagne-drappier.com
Website: http://www.champagne-drappier.com

CHAMPAGNE DEVAUX   93/100

▼ ♪ Brut D de Devaux rosé : Salmon-pink. Expressive nose revealing notes of blood orange and nicely ripe red fruit. Delightful fleshy and closely-integrated palate. Fine bubbles, upfront freshness and focused fruit that lingers. A stellar rosé Champagne.
Price approx.: 41,00 EUR
http://www.champagne-devaux.fr
Champagne Veuve A. Devaux
+33 (0)3 25 38 30 65

CHAMPAGNE DUVAL-LEROY   93/100

▼ ♪ Brut Rosé de saignée Femme de Champagne 2006 : Very elegant salmon-pink. Expressive nose with aromas of ripe citrus, orange peel and biscuit tones. The palate is vinous, invigorating yet also complex and persistent. More of the same delightful nose tones. A superlative rosé Champagne.
Price approx.: 103,40 EUR
http://www.duval-leroy.com
Champagne Duval-Leroy
+33 (0)3 26 52 10 75

CHAMPAGNE J. M. GOBILLARD & FILS   93/100

▼ ♪ Brut rosé Cuvée Prestige 2009 : Beautiful salmon-pink. Profound, focused nose revealing perfumes of ripe raspberry and cherry. The palate shows seductive fullness, vinosity and freshness. A full, harmonious and long rosé Champagne. Very compelling and suitable for any occasion.
Price approx.: 21,40 EUR
http://www.champagne-gobillard.com
Champagne J. M. Gobillard & fils
+33 (0)3 26 51 00 24

CHAMPAGNE PHILIPPONNAT   93/100

▼ DG Brut Réserve Rosée : Light coppery-orange. Refined, precise and mature nose marrying ripe raspberry, fresh strawberry and dried fruits. The palate is rich and full-bodied yet also shows superb freshness. Fine bubbles. Full yet ethereal across the palate. A successful Champagn
Price approx.: 36,00 EUR
http://www.philipponnat.com
Champagne Philipponnat
+33 (0)3 26 56 93 00

CHAMPAGNE FRANCK BONVILLE   93/100

▼ ♪ Brut blanc de blancs grand cru Les Belles Voyes : Light gold. Mature nose showing accents of dried fig, dried vegetal and faint toasted, patisserie touches. More of the same, slightly oxidative aromas on the palate showing abundant complexity. Superb length. Uncork for grilled shellfish.
Price approx.: 45,00 EUR
http://www.champagne-franck-bonville.com
Champagne Franck Bonville
+33 (0)3 26 57 52 30

CHAMPAGNE GEORGES VESSELLE   93/100

▼ ♪ Brut grand cru Cuvée Juline : Light gold. Profound, mature nose suggestive of dried fruits, fruit paste and a subtle patisserie touch. Delightful, lush palate showing crunchy fruit and seductive freshness and persistency. A very successful, party-style Champagne.
Price approx.: 32,90 EUR
http://www.champagne-vesselle.fr
Champagne Georges Vesselle
+33 (0)3 26 57 00 15

CHAMPAGNE HENRIOT   93/100

▼ ♪ Brut 2006 : Yellow-gold. The nose exudes notes of ripe raspberry and fresh bread. Fleshy attack showing evident freshness leading into a vinous mid-palate driven by persistent raspberry tones. An all-round, full and beautifully crafted Champagne.
Price approx.: 49,00 EUR
http://www.champagne-henriot.com
Champagne Henriot
+33 (0)3 26 89 53 00

CHAMPAGNE JACQUES COPINET   93/100

▼ ♪ Brut Cuvée Marie Etienne 2005 : Beautiful light gold. Mature nose revealing aromas of brioche, butter, candied lemon and wonderful minerality. Lovely full, fat and melted palate. Remarkable length showcasing very clearly-delineated aromas. A superlative Champagne.
Price approx.: 35,00 EUR
www.champagne-copinet.fr
Champagne Jacques Copinet
+33 (0)3 26 80 49 14

CHAMPAGNE LANSON   93/100

▼ ♪ Brut Extra Age : Light yellow. Delicate nose intermixing fruity, lemony notes and subtle brioche undertones with chalky notes. Lovely fullness, richness and beautiful balance of vinosity and freshness on the palate. The aromas evolve and linger on and on. Very compelling.
Price approx.: 50,00 EUR
http://www.lanson.com
Champagne Lanson
+33 (0)3 26 78 50 50

CHAMPAGNE MAURICE VESSELLE

92/100

▼ Extra Brut Grand Cru Les Hauts Chemins

Pinot noir 100% - Golden hue with amber nuances. Mature nose revealing perfumes of dried apricot and citrus, with a patisserie touch. The palate shows seductive vinosity, freshness and focused, mature fruity aromas.

Price approx.: n/a
Serving temperature: 9-11°
Ready to drink: From now on

Established in 1955, this vineyard is located in Bouzy, a great growth situated on the southern flank of the Montagne de Reims.
Didier and Thierry Vesselle have a profound respect for their terroir, ploughing deep into the soils to enhance its intrinsic qualities.
They are responsible for every stage of wine producing, from the vineyard to the cellar. Their Champagnes are blended from a majority proportion of Pinot Noir (85%) along with a balance of Chardonnay (15%). They do not undergo malolactic fermentation, thereby combining freshness and finesse with the specific characteristics of Pinot Noir. If you have a penchant for full-bodied, complex cuvées as well as older Champagnes (1976, 1985, 1988…), then this is one of the best addresses in Champagne!

Champagne Maurice Vesselle
2 rue Yvonnet - 51150 Bouzy
Tel: (+33) 3 26 57 00 81 - Fax: (+33) 3 26 57 83 08
E-mail: champagne.vesselle@wanadoo.fr
Website: http://www.champagnemauricevesselle.com

CHAMPAGNE NICOLAS FEUILLATTE — 93/100

▼ ♪ Brut Palmes d'Or 2002 : Light gold. The nose shows aromas of dried and stone fruits with fruit paste. On the palate, a full-bodied, vinous and powerful style with a very melted attack. A fresh, well-structured mid-palate imparts length and verticality. Serve with food.
Price approx.: 95,00 EUR
http://www.feuillatte.com
Champagne Nicolas Feuillatte
+33 (0)3 26 59 55 50

CHAMPAGNE PAUL DÉTHUNE — 93/100

▼ ♪ Brut grand cru Prestige : Bright golden hue. Profound, evolving nose opening up to almond and citrus then revealing dried fruit, patisserie and mineral perfumes. Subtle balance between vinosity and freshness on the palate which is very persistent throughout. A superlative Champagn
Price approx.: 35,00 EUR
www.champagne-dethune.com
Champagne Paul Déthune
+33 (0)3 26 57 01 88

CHAMPAGNE PHILIPPONNAT — 93/100

▼ ♪ Brut grand cru Cuvée 1522 2004 : Deep gold. Mature nose marrying candied citrus notes with a touch of rancio, patisserie and a mineral dimension. Remarkably well-balanced palate with vinosity and body nicely countered by lingering freshness. Beautiful presence on the palate.
Price approx.: 60,00 EUR
http://www.philipponnat.com
Champagne Philipponnat
+33 (0)3 26 56 93 00

CHAMPAGNE GEORGES VESSELLE — 92/100

▼ ♪ Extra brut grand cru blanc de noirs : Beautiful light gold. Profound nose revealing dried and stewed fruit perfumes. Impeccable presence on the palate, full, fleshy attack leading into a structured yet mellow mid-palate bordering on creamy. A very compelling Blanc de Noirs.
Price approx.: 29,50 EUR
http://www.champagne-vesselle.fr
Champagne Georges Vesselle
+33 (0)3 26 57 00 15

CHAMPAGNE CHARLES HEIDSIECK — 92/100

▼ ♪ Brut rosé 1999 : Light orange. Focused, expressive nose marrying notes of citrus fruits, blood orange and biscuit. The palate combines richness, exuberance, aromatic expression and length. A top-notch vintage, now fully mature.
Price approx.: 85,00 EUR
http://www.piper-heidsieck.com
Cie Champenoise PH-CH. Piper Heidsieck
+33 (0)3 26 84 43 00

CHAMPAGNE CHARLES MIGNON — 92/100

▼ ♪ Brut rosé grand cru Cuvée Comte de Marne : Orange-hued with coppery highlights. The nose opens up to notes of peaches in syrup, wild strawberries and a subtle patisserie note. The palate is full, fresh and mellow. Bold fruit aromas show elegant persistency. A highly successful rosé Champagne. Price approx.: 45,00 EUR
http://www.champagne-mignon.fr
Champagne Charles Mignon
+33 (0)3 26 58 33 33

CHAMPAGNE CHARPENTIER — 92/100

▼ ♪ Rosé Terre d'Emotion : Salmon-pink with orange. Profound, expressive nose intermixing ripe strawberry and blood orange notes. Lovely volume, full body and superb freshness on the palate showcasing fleshy, crunchy and precise fruit. A rosé Champagne boasting a robust personality
Price approx.: 36,00 EUR
www.champagne-charpentier.com
Champagne Charpentier
+33 (0)3 23 82 10 72

CHAMPAGNE JEAN VESSELLE — 92/100

▼ ♪ Brut Oeil de Perdrix : Light orange. Focused, refined nose reminiscent of orange flesh. Beautiful fleshy, crunchy attack. Lovely precise and persistent fruity aromas of citrus. A very compelling rosé Champagne that is generous yet light and fruity.
Price approx.: 18,00 EUR
www.champagnejeanvesselle.fr
Champagne Jean Vesselle
+33 (0)3 26 57 01 55

CHAMPAGNE PANNIER — 92/100

▼ ♪ Brt rosé de Saignée Egérie : Coppery orange hue. Mature, profound nose where dried fruit aromas (apricot, fig) blend with patisserie undertones. Fullness, vinosity and mellowness are key themes on the palate with freshness balancing the whole. A racy rosé Champagne for gourmet foods. Price approx.: 109,00 EUR
http://www.champagnepannier.com
Champagne Pannier
+33 (0)3 23 69 51 30

CHAMPAGNE PIERRE GIMONNET & FILS — 92/100

▼ ♪ Brut rosé de blancs : Orange hue. Wonderfully precise nose showing a mix of fresh red fruits and citrus notes. A rosé that is fresh yet fleshy and full with crunchy aromas. A stellar rosé Champagne, ideal as an aperitif or for a party.
Price approx.: 28,00 EUR
http://www.champagne-gimonnet.com
Champagne Pierre Gimonnet & fils
+33 (0)3 26 59 78 70

CHAMPAGNE GUY CHARBAUT

Brut blanc de blancs 1er cru Mémory 1998

▼ Old gold. Mature nose showing patisserie and brioche aromas with perfumes of dried fruits and almond paste. Fullness, fat and freshness underscore the same aromatic spectrum on the palate. Long, fresh finish leaving a long-lasting mineral sensation.

+33 3 26 52 60 59 **92/100**

CHAMPAGNE COLLARD-PICARD 92/100

▼ ♪ Brut Nature Essentiel 2006 : Beautiful deep gold. Mature nose combining stone fruits, patisserie and brioche notes and subtle toast. Beautiful presence on the palate, full body, vinosity and mellowness. Impeccable fruit expression with savoury freshness. A Champagne for meditation. Price approx.: 50,00 EUR
www.champagnecollardpicard.fr
Champagne Collard-Picard
+33 (0)3 26 52 36 93

CHAMPAGNE GEORGES VESSELLE 92/100

▼ ♪ Brut Nature grand cru Zéro 2008 : Golden hue. The nose blends dried fruits, apple flesh and a mineral dimension. Good framework on the palate that is tense yet closely-integrated and leaves a sensation of lingering freshness. A bone dry style that connoisseurs will enjoy.
Price approx.: 25,10 EUR
http://www.champagne-vesselle.fr
Champagne Georges Vesselle
+33 (0)3 26 57 00 15

CHAMPAGNE AYALA 92/100

▼ ♪ Brut blanc de blancs 2007 : Beautiful light yellow. Refined nose melding white flowers and delicate brioche notes. The palate shows seductive fullness, fine texture and balanced fat and freshness. A racy Blanc de Blancs, perfect for the aperitif. Very compelling.
Price approx.: 47,00 EUR
http://www.champagne-ayala.com
Champagne Ayala
+33 (0)3 26 55 15 44

CHAMPAGNE BEAUMONT DES CRAYÈRES 92/100

▼ ♪ Brut Nostalgie 2002 : Beautiful deep gold. Refined, mature nose opening up to dried fruits before delivering elegant patisserie and mineral touches. Lush palate framed by freshness, exuding powerful aromas of dried and candied fruits. Very

compelling. Price approx.: 56,00 EUR
http://www.champagne-beaumont.com
Champagne Beaumont des Crayères
+33 (0)3 26 55 29 40

CHAMPAGNE CHARLES HEIDSIECK 92/100

▼ ♪ Brut 2000 : Limpid pale gold. Expressive nose marrying notes of dried apricot and fig with a patisserie touch. On the palate, a beautiful taut, aromatic Champagne that lingers. The nose aromatics are augmented by a very enjoyable crisp dimension. Serve with food.
Price approx.: 75,00 EUR
http://www.piper-heidsieck.com
Cie Champenoise PH-CH. Piper Heidsieck
+33 (0)3 26 84 43 00

CHAMPAGNE DEVAUX 92/100

▼ ♪ Brut D - Magnum 2002 : Beautiful light gold. Extremely focused nose revealing aromas of citrus, dried fruits and pastry scents after swirling. Its mature character is more apparent on the palate which is full and mellow with notes of brioche and lots of freshness. Price approx.: 105,00 EUR
http://www.champagne-devaux.fr
Champagne Veuve A. Devaux
+33 (0)3 25 38 30 65

CHAMPAGNE HENRIOT 92/100

▼ ♪ Brut blanc de blancs : Pale gold. Refined nose suggestive of toasted almond and toast. Clean, closely-integrated attack on the palate leading into a rich, creamy mid-palate. The finish highlights very elegant Chardonnay perfumes. Racy mineral touch on the finish.
Price approx.: 35,00 EUR
http://www.champagne-henriot.com
Champagne Henriot
+33 (0)3 26 89 53 00

Detailed instructions are featured
at the start of the book.

CHAMPAGNE J. M. GOBILLARD & FILS 92/100

▼ ♪ Brut Privilège des Moines - élevé en fût de chêne : Light yellow. Delicate nose showing a floral and fruity character (pear) entwined with subtle vegetal notes. The predominant fruit prevails on the palate, nicely showcased by a fine texture and pleasant freshness with a touch of fresh oak on the finish. Price approx.: 22,30 EUR
http://www.champagne-gobillard.com
Champagne J. M. Gobillard & fils
+33 (0)3 26 51 00 24

CHAMPAGNE J. M. GOBILLARD & FILS 92/100

▼ ♪ Brut Cuvée Prestige 2009 : Light yellow, green tints. Fresh nose recalling white flowers, freshly-cut grass and fruit flesh with subtle tropical touches. The palate shows seductive fullness and ethereal character imparting stunning exuberance. A racy Champagne, still in its infancy
Price approx.: 20,70 EUR
http://www.champagne-gobillard.com
Champagne J. M. Gobillard & fils
+33 (0)3 26 51 00 24

CHAMPAGNE JACQUART 92/100

▼ ♪ Brut Cuvée Alpha 2006 : Beautiful deep gold. Profound, mature nose blending dried fruits, patisserie notes and gingerbread. Lush, mellow palate balanced by a touch of freshness that enhances the complex aromas. A generous Champagne for food. Price approx.: 80,00 EUR
http://www.champagne-jacquart.com
Champagne Jacquart
+33 (0)3 26 07 88 40

CHAMPAGNE JANISSON & FILS 92/100

▼ ♪ Brut blanc de blancs grand cru : Light yellow-gold. The nose opens up to refined brioche notes then reveals the full scale of its opulence with white-fleshed fruits and preserved lemon aromas. The palate is rich and mellow yet fresh. A racy, persistent Blanc de Blancs.
Price approx.: 25,00 EUR
www.janisson.com
Champagne Janisson & fils
+33 (0)3 26 49 40 19

CHAMPAGNE MICHEL GONET 92/100

▼ ♪ Brut blanc de blancs grand cru 2008 : Light yellow. Focused nose of white-fleshed fruits, mineral, chalky notes and fresh hazelnut. Excellent framework on the palate, well-structured yet refined and remarkably fresh. A beautiful Champagne that wine lovers will enjoy. Price approx.: 26,00 EUR
www.gonet.fr
Champagne Michel Gonet
+33 (0)3 26 57 50 56

CHAMPAGNE PANNIER 92/100

▼ ♪ Brut Cuvée Blanc Velours : Light yellow-gold. Refined nose revealing subtle notes of white flowers, fresh almond and chalk. Elegant, fresh and polished palate exuding more of the same delicate aromas. A top-flight, aptly-named Champagne. Drink from the aperitif onwards.
Price approx.: 79,00 EUR
http://www.champagnepannier.com
Champagne Pannier
+33 (0)3 23 69 51 30

CHAMPAGNE PERTOIS-MORISET 92/100

▼ ♪ Brut grand cru 2006 : Light gold. Mature nose developing notes of pastries, fresh bread and straw. Lush, mellow palate framed by a sensation of lingering freshness with fruit and mineral aromatics. A Champagne for gourmet foods.
Price approx.: 29,40 EUR
Champagne Pertois-Moriset
+33 (0)3 26 57 52 14

CHAMPAGNE PHILIPPONNAT 92/100

▼ ♪ Brut Grand Blanc 2006 : Intense light yellow-gold. After swirling, the nose reveals white flower notes, milk bread and lemony cream. Full, mouth-coating palate with a creamy texture supported by delicious freshness. A Champagne that is generous yet fresh. Price approx.: 47,00 EUR
http://www.philipponnat.com
Champagne Philipponnat
+33 (0)3 26 56 93 00

CHAMPAGNE VEUVE DOUSSOT 91/100

▼ ♪ Extra brut blanc de blancs Cuvée L by VD : Light yellow with green tints. Refined nose opening up to fairly heady floral notes then revealing perfumes of pear flesh with mineral undertones. Full, generous attack that is fleshy and nicely mellowed. Fresh mid-palate imparting a vertical dimension.
Price approx.: 60,00 EUR
http://www.champagneveuvedoussot.com
Champagne Veuve Doussot
+33 (0)3 25 29 60 61

CHAMPAGNE COLLARD-PICARD 91/100

CONV ▼ ♪ Brut rosé 1er cru Cuvée des Merveilles : Deep orange. Profound, focused nose blending ripe strawberry, cherry and other red fruits. Full-bodied, vinous palate yet also beautiful freshness enhancing an honest, persistent bouquet of fruit aromatics. A very compelling rosé Champagne for food.
Price approx.: 31,00 EUR
www.champagnecollardpicard.fr
Champagne Collard-Picard
+33 (0)3 26 52 36 93

CHAMPAGNE CHARLES ELLNER

91/100

▼ Brut Séduction 2005

Deep yellow-gold. The nose reveals milky, brioche-like perfumes and aromas of fresh hazelnut. Creamy texture, fullness and fat on the palate supported by a lively, fresh and clean structure. A beautiful elegant and mature Champagne.

Price approx.: 27 EUR
Serving temperature: 9-11°
Ready to drink: From now on

Charles-Emile Ellner, a riddler for a prominent Champagne house, created his own brand at the turn of the 20th century. His son Pierre inherited the brand and became a negociant in 1972. Jean-Pierre, one of Pierre's sons, manages the company, assisted by members of the fourth generation, Arnaud and Frédéric Ellner. The vineyards stretch over 50 hectares spread over 15 localities within the main Champagne regions. It is planted to 40% Chardonnay and 30% each of Pinot Noir and Pinot Meunier.
The Champagnes show consistent quality and a very attractive price tag.

Champagne Charles Ellner
6 rue Côte Legris - 51200 Epernay
Tel.: (+33) 3 26 55 60 25 - Fax: (+33) 3 26 51 54 00
E-mail: info@champagne-ellner.com
Website: http://www.champagne-ellner.com

CHAMPAGNE LAURENT-PERRIER   91/100

▼ ♪ Brut Cuvée Rosé : Orange-hued with coppery highlights. Mature nose reminiscent of stone fruits, candied citrus and dried fruits. The same aromatics are enhanced on the palate by a full, mellow and fresh structure. A very compelling, elegant Champagne for any occasion.
Price approx.: 71,00 EUR
http://www.laurent-perrier.fr
Champagne Laurent-Perrier
+33 (0)3 26 58 91 22

CHAMPAGNE PAUL DÉTHUNE   91/100

▼ ♪ Brut rosé grand cru : Deep orange. Highly expressive nose marrying red fruits and orange-flavoured fruits. Lovely aromatic precision on the palate with a delicious, fleshy and full character supported by mouth-filling freshness. Serve preferably with food. Price approx.: 24,00 EUR
www.champagne-dethune.com
Champagne Paul Déthune
+33 (0)3 26 57 01 88

CHAMPAGNE BESSERAT DE BELLEFON   91/100

▼ ♪ Brut Cuvée B de B : Pale yellow. Enticing nose opening up to fresh grape and white-fleshed fruits then revealing refined creamy notes. More of the same character at point of entry coupled with fine bubbles and lovely freshness. A dry Champagne with good staying power.
Price approx.: 60,00 EUR
http://www.besseratdebellefon.com
Champagne Besserat de Bellefon
+33 (0)3 26 78 52 16

CHAMPAGNE CHARPENTIER   91/100

▼ ♪ Brut blanc de noirs Terre d'Emotion : Light gold. Expressive nose suggestive of mirabelle and damson plum with black fruits. Full-bodied, vinous and closely-integrated on the palate with more of the signature fruit aromatics. A beautiful Blanc de Noirs pairing with poultry.
Price approx.: 32,00 EUR
www.champagne-charpentier.com
Champagne Charpentier
+33 (0)3 23 82 10 72

CHAMPAGNE DEVAUX   91/100

▼ ♪ Brut Ultra D de Devaux : Bright, pale yellow-gold. Expressive nose revealing aromas of exotic fruits with a touch of pastry. More of the same signature aromatics on the palate which is structured, taut and tinged with elegant firmness. More mineral finish. Price approx.: 36,00 EUR
http://www.champagne-devaux.fr
Champagne Veuve A. Devaux
+33 (0)3 25 38 30 65

CHAMPAGNE DRAPPIER   91/100

▼ ♪ Brut Millésime d'Exception 2008 : Beautiful pale gold. Refined nose revealing white-fleshed fruit, citrus and mineral perfumes after swirling. A well-structured Champagne on the palate showing lovely pervasive freshness and focused, persistent aromas.
Price approx.: 38,50 EUR
http://www.champagne-drappier.com
Champagne Drappier
+33 (0)3 25 27 40 15

CHAMPAGNE GIMONNET-GONET   91/100

▼ ♪ Brut blanc de blancs grand cru Carat du Mesnil : Beautiful yellow-gold. Profound nose recalling fresh hazelnut, fresh bread and almond on first pour then showing pastry scents. Wonderful presence on the palate, full, fat and silky with lovely freshness supporting the whole. A racy style.
Price approx.: 33,00 EUR
Champagne Gimonnet-Gonet
+33 (0)3 26 57 51 44

CHAMPAGNE GUY CHARLEMAGNE   91/100

▼ ♪ Brut blanc de blancs grand cru Cuvée Charlemagne 2008 : Light gold. Profound nose opening up to notes of dried fruits with beautiful mineral undercurrents. The palate shows seductive fullness and fat. A full, closely-integrated style with lovely freshness imparting length. A successful Champagne. Price approx.: 24,20 EUR
http://www.champagne-guy-charlemagne.fr
Champagne Guy Charlemagne
+33 (0)3 26 57 52 98

CHAMPAGNE JANISSON & FILS   91/100

▼ ♪ Brut blanc de noirs grand cru : Light yellow. Refined nose delivering delicate fruity notes yet also mineral accents. Lovely fullness, fine-grained, mellow texture, freshness and precise aromas on the palate. An idionsyncratic, elegant dry Champagne.
Price approx.: 30,00 EUR
www.janisson.com
Champagne Janisson & fils
+33 (0)3 26 49 40 19

CHAMPAGNE LECLERC BRIANT   91/100

Org▼ ♪ Brut 1er cru Les Chèvres Pierreuses : Brilliant light gold. Endearing nose blending citrus fruits, dried apricot and a chalky dimension in the background. Beautiful presence on the palate, a lively, upright structure and mineral presence. Quality length and focus. A pure style for connoisseur
Price approx.: 40,80 EUR
www.leclercbriant.com
Champagne Leclerc Briant
+33 (0)3 26 54 45 33

CHAMPAGNE MANDOIS 91/100

▼ ♪ Brut Victor Mandois - Vieilles Vignes 2005 : Limpid, light gold. Clean, elegant and expressive nose showing an almond note, white flowers and subtle mineral touch. More of the same on the palate which reveals great finesse, subtle effervescence and persistent aromas. A Champagne with class. Price approx.: 60,00 EUR
http://www.champagne-mandois.fr
Champagne Mandois
+33 (0)3 26 54 03 18

CHAMPAGNE PAUL MICHEL 91/100

▼ ♪ Brut blanc de blancs 1er cru Cuvée Prestige 2000 : Deep, bright yellow-gold. Mature nose with a mineral character asserting itself after swirling and almond notes. Full mouthfeel, superbly balanced fat and freshness, remarkably well-integrated and beautifully persistent brioche aromas. A superlative Champagne. Price approx.: 45,00 EUR
Champagne Paul Michel
+33 (0)3 26 59 79 77

CHAMPAGNE PHILIPPE GONET 91/100

▼ **DG** Brut blanc de blancs grand cru 2007 : Light gold. Expressive nose of white flowers, fresh lemon, a mineral note and a biscuit touch. On the palate, a delicate, fleshy and aromatic Champagne where the nose aromatics are augmented by a pleasant menthol and aniseed dimension. A delightful offeri Price approx.: 29,50 EUR
www.champagne-philippe-gonet.com
Champagne Philippe Gonet
+33 (0)3 26 57 53 47

CHAMPAGNE PHILIPPONNAT 91/100

▼ ♪ Brut Royale Réserve : Beautiful light yellow-gold. Refined nose where fruit aromas of apricot flesh and lemon are augmented by toasted almond notes. Wonderful presence with a very supple, vinous and mellow attack. Fresh, persistent mid-palate. A very compelling dry Champagne. Price approx.: 30,00 EUR
http://www.philipponnat.com
Champagne Philipponnat
+33 (0)3 26 56 93 00

CHAMPAGNE PIERRE GIMONNET & FILS 91/100

▼ ♪ Brut blanc de blancs 1er cru Spécial Club 2006 : Light yellow. The nose opens up to refined notes of milk bread, brioche, fresh butter and milk caramel. Lovely full, ethereal structure with fine bubbles on the palate. More of the predominant milky nose aromatics. Price approx.: 40,00 EUR
http://www.champagne-gimonnet.com
Champagne Pierre Gimonnet & fils
+33 (0)3 26 59 78 70

CHAMPAGNE PIERRE MONCUIT 91/100

▼ ♪ Brut blanc de blancs grand cru 2005 : Limpid pale yellow. Extremely distinctive nose marrying white fruits and chalky mineral notes. Fresh attack, character and a mineral and lemony mid-palate with deftly crafted aromatic persistence. A real classic.
Price approx.: 31,00 EUR
http://www.pierre-moncuit.fr
Champagne Pierre Moncuit
+33 (0)3 26 57 52 65

CHAMPAGNE VAZART-COQUART & FILS 91/100

▼ ♪ Brut blanc de blancs grand cru Grand Bouquet 2008 : Light yellow. Delightful focused nose unfurling floral perfumes, almond notes and beautiful minerality. The palate shows a seductively full attack, remarkably well-integrated, silky texture and very fresh, mineral mid-palate. Great persistency. Price approx.: 25,30 EUR
Champagne Vazart Coquart & fils
+33 (0)3 26 55 40 04

CHAMPAGNE GONET SULCOVA 90/100

▼ ♪ Extra brut grand cru : Light yellow. The nose displays a pronounced mineral character of chalk on first pour then opens up to white flowers and fresh hazelnut. Beautiful presence on the palate. Fleshy, creamy, vibrant and very well-integrated. Beautiful Chardonnay expression.
Price approx.: 20,00 EUR
http://www.champagne-gonet-sulcova.fr
Champagne Gonet Sulcova
+33 (0)3 26 54 37 63

CHAMPAGNE PHILIPPE GONET 90/100

▼ ♪ Extra brut blancs de blanc - 3210 : Light gold. Endearing, delicate nose delivering floral, mineral and white fruit notes. Fleshy palate on the attack leading into a fresh mid-palate revealing more of the same intense aromas. A delicious, honest and aromatic Champagne with substantial length. Price approx.: 29,50 EUR
www.champagne-philippe-gonet.com
Champagne Philippe Gonet
+33 (0)3 26 57 53 47

CHAMPAGNE JEAN VESSELLE 90/100

▼ ♪ demi-sec rosé Cuvée Friandise : Light ruby-red bordering on purple. Delightful nose suggestive of cherry flesh, raspberry and an array of garden fruits. Soft, fleshy and mild palate showing seductively crunchy fruit, freshness and precision. A superb treat for pudding. Price approx.: 19,00 EUR
www.champagnejeanvesselle.fr
Champagne Jean Vesselle
+33 (0)3 26 57 01 55

CHAMPAGNE PALMER & CO

Extra brut

▼ Light gold. Profound, expressive nose opening up to nicely ripe fruit and subtle toast notes. Beautiful presence on the palate, full, well-structured and melted with persistent freshness framing the whole. True character.

+33 3 26 07 35 07

90/100

CHAMPAGNE PIPER-HEIDSIECK   90/100

▼ ♪ Demi-sec Cuvée Sublime : Beautiful yellow-gold. Pleasant nose marrying candied fruits and toast. Excellent fullness on entry with freshness counterbalancing richness impeccably. Fresh, persistent finish. A sterling Champagne in this category.
Price approx.: 32,00 EUR
http://www.piper-heidsieck.com
Cie Champenoise PH-CH. Piper Heidsieck
+33 (0)3 26 84 43 00

CHAMPAGNE CHARLES HEIDSIECK   90/100

▼ ♪ Brut rosé Réserve : Light orange. Fairly subdued nose opening up to notes of citrus fruits and orange peel after swirling. Soft mouthfeel driven by more of the same delightful aromatics. A likeable rosé Champagne with a lingering crisp finish. Would work with duck à l'orange
Price approx.: 60,00 EUR
http://www.piper-heidsieck.com
Cie Champenoise PH-CH. Piper Heidsieck
+33 (0)3 26 84 43 00

CHAMPAGNE HENRIOT   90/100

▼ ♪ Brut rosé : Pale orange hue. Intense nose of red fruit with a citrus-like tone and a touch of toast after swirling. Highly aromatic at point of entry showing more of the same crisp aromatics. Lovely honest aromas, vinosity and power.
Price approx.: 40,00 EUR
http://www.champagne-henriot.com
Champagne Henriot
+33 (0)3 26 89 53 00

CHAMPAGNE JACQUES COPINET   90/100

▼ ♪ Brut rosé de saignée Cuvée Marie Etienne : Deep orange with bricking. Clean, profound nose suggestive of fruit butter. Full, generous and well-integrated palate revealing more of the focused fruit. Freshness is present throughout. A beautiful vinous rosé Champagne, ideal for food.

Price approx.: 60,00 EUR
www.champagne-copinet.fr
Champagne Jacques Copinet
+33 (0)3 26 80 49 14

CHAMPAGNE MAURICE VESSELLE   90/100

▼ ♪ Brut rosé grand cru : Orange hue with coppery highlights. Profound, expressive nose showing aromas of blood orange and red fruits. Beautiful presence on the palate. Full, vinous, mellow and balanced by freshness. Drink as a food Champagne with, say, duck breasts.
http://www.champagnemauricevesselle.com
Champagne Maurice Vesselle
+33 (0)3 26 57 00 81

CHAMPAGNE PAUL MICHEL   90/100

▼ DG Brut 1er Cru Cuvée Rosé Carte Blanche : Appealing salmon-pink. Delightful, focused nose blending red fruits and tangerine flesh. The palate shows seductive precision, crunchy fruit, freshness and immediate approachability. A beautiful and delicious rosé Champagne for pleasure.
Price approx.: 26,00 EUR
Champagne Paul Michel
+33 (0)3 26 59 79 77

CHAMPAGNE PERTOIS-MORISET   90/100

▼ ♪ Brut rosé grand cru : Orange-pink. Focused nose opening up to strawberry and white-fleshed fruit with chalky undertones. Beautiful staying power, full-bodied, rich, mellow and fresh palate underscoring precise fruit. A successful Champagne.
Price approx.: 25,50 EUR
Champagne Pertois-Moriset
+33 (0)3 26 57 52 14

CHAMPAGNE BLONDEL   90/100

▼ ♪ Brut 1er cru Prestige : Beautiful light gold. Profound, expressive nose blending a fruity dimension (white-fleshed fruits) and brioche notes.

CHAMPAGNE CHARLES HEIDSIECK

Brut Réserve

▼ Attractive pale hue. Expressive nose intermixing white fruits, toast and mild spice notes. Soft attack leading into a perfumed mid-palate and a lengthy, easy-drinking finish. A Champagne for top-end food.

+33 3 26 84 43 00

90/100

Wonderful presence on the palate, full-bodied yet fresh, closely-integrated and persistent. A stellar Champagne. Price approx.: 21,00 EUR
http://www.champagneblondel.com
Champagne Blondel
+33 (0)3 26 03 43 92

CHAMPAGNE BONNET GILMERT   90/100
▼ ♪ Brut blanc de blancs grand cru Précieuse d'Ambroise : Deeply-coloured light yellow. Expressive nose opening up to brioche and milky notes backed by ripe lemon and a chalky dimension. Beautiful presence on the palate. Full, mellow and creamy attack. Closely-integrated, persistent and framed by freshness.
Price approx.: 35,00 EUR
www.champagne-bonnet-gilmert.com
Champagne Bonnet Gilmert
+33 (0)3 26 59 49 47

CHAMPAGNE CHARPENTIER   90/100
▼ **DG** Brut blanc de blancs Terre d'Emotion : Light yellow with green tints. Precise nose revealing perfumes of white flowers, lemon and almond with mineral undertones. The palate shows seductive fullness, creamy texture and fine bubbles. Expressive and closely-integrated with beautiful freshness.
Price approx.: 32,00 EUR
www.champagne-charpentier.com
Champagne Charpentier
+33 (0)3 23 82 10 72

CHAMPAGNE CHARPENTIER   90/100
▼ ♪ Brut Vérité Terre d'Emotion : Light yellow with green tints. A mix of white-fleshed fruits (pear flesh), a subtle touch of almond and a creamy sensation on the nose. Full, closely-integrated palate blending vinosity and freshness which enhance precise aromas and a mineral finish. Price approx.: 29,00 EUR
www.champagne-charpentier.com
Champagne Charpentier
+33 (0)3 23 82 10 72

CHAMPAGNE CHASSENAY D'ARCE   90/100
▼ ♪ Extra brut Pinot Blanc 2005 : Bright, pale yellow. Distinctive, expressive nose intermixing white-fleshed fruits, fresh hazelnut and a mineral dimension. Full palate with a creamy texture and fine bubbles. Savoury freshness and persistent aromas. A well-made Extra Dry Champagne.
http://www.chassenay.com
Champagne Chassenay d'Arce
+33 (0)3 25 38 34 75

CHAMPAGNE CHASSENAY D'ARCE   90/100
▼ ♪ Brut Confidences : Light gold. Enticing fruity nose revealing notes of orange and red fruits after swirling. Lovely body and fullness on the palate yet also mellowness and freshness. Pleasant fruit-infused persistency. Harmonious.
http://www.chassenay.com
Champagne Chassenay d'Arce
+33 (0)3 25 38 34 75

CHAMPAGNE CLOS BOURMAULT   90/100
▼ ♪ Brut grand cru : Beautiful bright yellow-gold. Profound, racy nose blending dried fruits, a trace of citrus, pastry notes and a mineral dimension. Very compelling, full, closely-integrated and fresh palate that lingers, with subtle oak. A top-flight offering.
Price approx.: 68,00 EUR
Champagne Christian Bourmault
+33 (0)3 26 59 79 41

CHAMPAGNE DEUTZ   90/100
▼ ♪ Brut Classic : Light yellow. Delicate nose marrying white fruits with biscuit and wafer tones. Beautiful full, fresh attack on the palate leading into a velvety mid-palate then a soft, fruity finish that lingers. A refined style for the aperitif or a buffet.
Price approx.: 35,80 EUR
http://www.champagne-deutz.com
Champagne Deutz
+33 (0)3 26 56 94 00

CHAMPAGNE GUY CHARBAUT

Brut 1er cru 2005

▼ Light gold. Refined nose opening up after swirling to mature dried fruit notes. Beautiful presence on the palate, a full, remarkably melted yet fresh style. A focused, well-integrated dry Champagne displaying an elegant touch of austerity on the finish.

+33 3 26 52 60 59

90/100

CHAMPAGNE DEVAUX   90/100

▼ ♪ Brut D de Devaux : Light gold. Endearing nose centring on nicely ripe citrus and dried fruits with a patisserie touch. Delightful, harmonious palate showing crunchy fruit that is mellow yet fresh. A racy style for the aperitif or a party.
Price approx.: 32,00 EUR
http://www.champagne-devaux.fr
Champagne Veuve A. Devaux
+33 (0)3 25 38 30 65

CHAMPAGNE DIDIER DOUÉ   90/100

▼ ♪ Brut blanc de blancs 2005 : Brilliant yellow-gold. Distinctive, mature nose exuding fruit, dried vegetal, candied citrus and mineral aromas. Beautiful presence on the palate, a well-structured, expressive style with a remarkable freshness that lingers on and on and enhances personal
Price approx.: 19,00 EUR
www.champagne-didier-doue.fr
Champagne Didier Doué
+33 (0)3 25 79 44 33

CHAMPAGNE DRAPPIER   90/100

▼ ♪ Brut Carte d'Or - Magnum 1995 : Beautiful golden hue. Profound, mature nose opening up to dried fig and apricot with a patisserie note. Delicious, fleshy attack flowing into an extremely fresh yet also relatively firm mid-palate. Nearly 20 and still going strong.
Price approx.: 93,00 EUR
http://www.champagne-drappier.com
Champagne Drappier
+33 (0)3 25 27 40 15

CHAMPAGNE DUVAL-LEROY   90/100

▼ ♪ Brut Cuvée des Meilleurs Ouvriers de France Sommeliers : Light yellow. Endearing nose with creamy, brioche accents backed by white-fleshed fruits. Full, vinous and mellow palate supported by a persistent freshness showcasing the same aromas. Lovely fruity sensation. A racy dry Champagne for

a sophisticated aperitif. Price approx.: 37,25 EUR
http://www.duval-leroy.com
Champagne Duval-Leroy
+33 (0)3 26 52 10 75

CHAMPAGNE FRANCK BONVILLE   90/100

▼ ♪ Brut blanc de blancs grand cru : Beautiful pale gold. Intense, delicate nose marrying white flowers, stone fruits and abundant freshness. Very handsome texture on the palate, fine effervescence and more of the same, nicely highlighted aromas. An idiosyncratic Champagne.
Price approx.: 22,00 EUR
http://www.champagne-franck-bonville.com
Champagne Franck Bonville
+33 (0)3 26 57 52 30

CHAMPAGNE GIMONNET-GONET   90/100

▼ ♪ Brut blanc de blancs Cuvée Prestige 2008 : Light yellow with green tints. Refined nose opening up to fresh bread and almond cream notes. The palate shows seductive fullness, fine-grained, mellow and well-integrated texture, freshness and persistency. A Blanc de Blancs that is elegant and delicious Price approx.: 22,00 EUR
Champagne Gimonnet-Gonet
+33 (0)3 26 57 51 44

CHAMPAGNE H. GOUTORBE   90/100

▼ ♪ Brut grand cru Spécial Club 2005 : Light yellow. Refined, mature nose revealing delicate scents of dried fruits and fresh croissant. Elegant sensation of oak. Full, remarkably mellow attack showing beautiful vinosity and freshness throughout. A racy Champagne. Price approx.: 30,00 EUR
www.champagne-henri-goutorbe.com
Champagne Henri Goutorbe
+33 (0)3 26 55 21 70

CHAMPAGNE HENRIOT   90/100

▼ ♪ Brut Souverain : Limpid pale yellow. The nose offers up a compelling compromise between fruit

and toast notes. Extremely harmonious framework on the palate supported by a degree of exuberance. Lovely quality fruit and persistency. A beautifully crafted brut Champagne.
Price approx.: 30,00 EUR
http://www.champagne-henriot.com
Champagne Henriot
+33 (0)3 26 89 53 00

CHAMPAGNE J. M. GOBILLARD & FILS   90/100

▼ ♪ Brut blanc de noirs : Golden hue. Enticing nose bursting with grape, mirabelle plum and raspberry aromas. Full, lush and full-bodied palate beautifully balanced by a mouthfilling sensation of freshness. Focused, persistent fruit. A wonderful Champagne for food. Price approx.: 17,60 EUR
http://www.champagne-gobillard.com
Champagne J. M. Gobillard & fils
+33 (0)3 26 51 00 24

CHAMPAGNE JACQUART   90/100

▼ ♪ Brut blanc de blancs Vintage 2006 : Attractive pale gold. Delightful focused nose marrying white fruits, mineral and brioche notes. The palate is full-bodied, perfumed and reveals more of the nose aromatics with a more pronounced toast tone. A deftly crafted, successful and beautiful Champa
Price approx.: 31,75 EUR
http://www.champagne-jacquart.com
Champagne Jacquart
+33 (0)3 26 07 88 40

CHAMPAGNE JEAN VESSELLE   90/100

▼ ♪ Brut Réserve : Golden hue with subtle orange tints. Profound, fruit-driven nose of grape and red fruits. Lovely fleshy, full-bodied palate. Focused expression of the predominant Pinot grape. A delectable Champagne framed by freshness. Serve as an aperitif or with food.
Price approx.: 16,00 EUR
www.champagnejeanvesselle.fr
Champagne Jean Vesselle
+33 (0)3 26 57 01 55

CHAMPAGNE JEEPER   90/100

▼ ♪ Brut - Grand rosé : Attractive light salmon-pink. Delightful focused and fruity nose of raspberry, redcurrant and apple. The palate successfully combines vinosity and freshness. Mellow with a fine texture and bubbles enhancing focused, persistent fruit. A successful rosé. Price approx.: 22,00 EUR
http://www.champagne-jeeper.fr
Les Domaines Jeeper
+33 (0)3 26 05 08 98

CHAMPAGNE LANSON   90/100

▼ ♪ Brut Gold Label 2005 : Light gold. Focused nose blending white-fleshed fruits, delicate creamy

notes and a mineral dimension. Harmonious, full palate with refined texture and bubbles shot through with freshness. A racy, persistent style showcasing mineral aromatics.
Price approx.: 35,00 EUR
http://www.lanson.com
Champagne Lanson
+33 (0)3 26 78 50 50

CHAMPAGNE LOUIS DE SACY   90/100

▼ ♪ Brut blanc de blancs grand cru Cuvée Inédite : Light yellow, green tints. Refined nose intermixing white flowers with lemony notes and a chalky touch. The palate is full and exuberant with a fine texture and bubbles. Upfront aromas are primarily lemony and linger. A lively style for whetting the appet
Price approx.: 51,80 EUR
www.champagne-louis-de-sacy.fr
Champagne Louis de Sacy
+33 (0)3 26 97 91 13

CHAMPAGNE MICHEL TURGY   90/100

▼ ♪ Brut blanc de blancs grand cru 2006 : Light yellow. Initial nose of flowers and almonds flowing into lovely mineral notes with a whiff of toast. Beautiful full, mellow attack with full-on freshness. More of the mineral dimension augmented by a touch of butter and brioche.
www.champagne-turgy.com
Champagne Michel Turgy
+33 (0)3 26 57 53 43

CHAMPAGNE NICOLAS FEUILLATTE   90/100

▼ ♪ Brut 2006 : Beautiful light gold. Refined nose opening up to delicate biscuity and patisserie notes backed by subtle fruit. Good staying power on the palate. A well-structured, closely-integrated Champagne balanced by freshness. Excellent persistency. A successful 20
Price approx.: 32,50 EUR
http://www.feuillatte.com
Champagne Nicolas Feuillatte
+33 (0)3 26 59 55 50

CHAMPAGNE P. LANCELOT-ROYER   90/100

▼ ♪ Brut blanc de blancs grand cru Cuvée des Chevaliers : Beautiful light gold. Generous nose opening up to pastry, white-fleshed fruit and fresh hazelnut notes. Full, fat palate showing impeccable balance supported by persistent freshness. Elegant mineral touch.
Price approx.: 18,00 EUR
Champagne P. Lancelot-Royer
+33 (0)3 26 57 51 41

> Detailed instructions are featured
> at the start of the book.

CHAMPAGNE
PIERRE GIMONNET & FILS

90/100

▼ Brut Blanc de Blancs 1er Cru
Cuvée Fleuron 2006

Light yellow-gold. The nose opens up to notes of honey, white-fleshed fruits and subtle almond and pastry touches. Lovely clean attack, fine-grained texture and freshness on the palate. A generous, full and persistent wine.

Price approx.: 32 EUR
Serving temperature: 9-11°
Ready to drink: From now on

The Gimonnet family was already cultivating grapes in the district of Cuis before 1750, but it was only after the crisis of the 1930s that Pierre Gimonnet truly began to produce wine. Specialising in Blanc de Blancs (made from 100% Chardonnay), Olivier and Didier Gimonnet, Pierre's grandsons, tend a 28-hectare vineyard planted solely with Chardonnay in the terroirs of Cramant, Chouilly and Oger (Grands Crus), as well as in the districts of Cuis and Vertus (Premier Cru). The result is a very nice range of Blancs de Blancs with seductive freshness and balance, whose scores this year fall between 89 and 92/100. A House with Champagnes that merit a detour!

Champagne Pierre Gimonnet & fils
1 rue de la République - 51530 Cuis
Tel: (+33) 3 26 59 78 70 - Fax: (+33) 3 26 59 79 84
E-mail: info@champagne-gimonnet.com
Website: http://www.champagne-gimonnet.com

CHAMPAGNE PALMER & CO — 90/100

▼ ♪ Brut blanc de blancs 2007 : Light yellow. Refined, mature nose, floral and fruity on first pour then showing beautiful minerality with a hint of toast. Ample palate that is full yet ethereal. Lovely lively finish with full-on freshness prolonging the aromas. For a sophisticated aper
Price approx.: 38,00 EUR
www.champagne-palmer.fr
Champagne Palmer & Co
+33 (0)3 26 07 35 07

CHAMPAGNE PANNIER — 90/100

▼ ♪ Brut blanc de blancs 2005 : Light gold. Refined, mature nose showing delicate brioche aromatics followed by chalky notes after swirling. The palate reveals a seductive creamy character, fine texture and freshness. Closely-integrated with lovely, long-lasting, racy Chardonnay aromas.
Price approx.: 34,00 EUR
http://www.champagnepannier.com
Champagne Pannier
+33 (0)3 23 69 51 30

CHAMPAGNE PAUL DÉTHUNE — 90/100

▼ DG Brut grand cru : Light gold. Focused nose showing a delightful citrus and white-fleshed fruit character with pastry notes. Fleshy, round and closely-integrated palate with body counterbalanced by a sensation of freshness. A very pure, full style. Price approx.: 22,00 EUR
www.champagne-dethune.com
Champagne Paul Déthune
+33 (0)3 26 57 01 88

CHAMPAGNE PAUL MICHEL — 90/100

▼ ♪ Brut blanc de blancs 1er cru Carte Blanche 2008 : Light yellow, green tints. The nose is shy on first pour then opens up to fine chalky, lemony and buttery notes. Focused, precise palate showing lovely freshness and fine bubbles. More of the lemon and mineral character. Set aside for a sophisticated aper
Price approx.: 25,00 EUR
Champagne Paul Michel
+33 (0)3 26 59 79 77

CHAMPAGNE PIPER-HEIDSIECK — 90/100

▼ ♪ Brut 2006 : Beautiful light gold. Delicate, expressive nose marrying stone fruits with toast tones. Wonderfully defined fruit and freshness on the palate with the same, empyreumatic-like tone underscoring the whole. Extremely pleasurable.
Price approx.: 40,00 EUR
http://www.piper-heidsieck.com
Cie Champenoise PH-CH. Piper Heidsieck
+33 (0)3 26 84 43 00

CHAMPAGNE TAITTINGER — 90/100

▼ ♪ Brut Réserve : Light gold. The nose opens up to floral notes then reveals biscuit perfumes with subtle smoke undertones. Good staying power on the palate with beautiful balance of vinosity and freshness. Fine bubbles and lingering freshness. A nicely crafted dry Champag
http://www.taittinger.fr
Champagne Taittinger
+33 (0)3 26 85 45 35

CHAMPAGNE VEUVE DOUSSOT — 90/100

▼ ♪ Brut blanc de noirs Cuvée L by VD : Light gold. Profound, focused fruity nose with stewed accents flowing into dried fruits. On the palate, a full-bodied, rich and well-integrated style capped off with a pleasant touch of firmness. Works best with food such as white meats.
Price approx.: 50,00 EUR
http://www.champagneveuvedoussot.com
Champagne Veuve Doussot
+33 (0)3 25 29 60 61

CHAMPAGNE DIDIER DOUÉ — 89/100

▼ ♪ Extra brut Nature : Light gold. A mix of lemon and orange notes on the nose with a mineral dimension. Full, well-structured palate supported by freshness and a delicious firmness. The mineral character is displayed on the finish. A Champagne with good staying power.
Price approx.: 16,50 EUR
www.champagne-didier-doue.fr
Champagne Didier Doué
+33 (0)3 25 79 44 33

CHAMPAGNE PERRON-BEAUVINEAU — 89/100

▼ ♪ Extra dry Cuvée Elixir : Beautiful golden hue. Profound nose delivering refined stewed, biscuity and fruity notes. The palate shows seductive fullness, richness counterbalanced by freshness and overall harmony. A Champagne for gourmet foods.
Price approx.: 23,70 EUR
http://www.champagne-perron-beauvineau.com/
Champagne Perron-Beauvineau
+33 (0)3 25 27 40 56

CHAMPAGNE GONET SULCOVA — 89/100

▼ ♪ Brut rosé : Deep orange-pink. Honest, expressive nose suggestive of fresh strawberry. More of the same fruity flavours on the palate which is fleshy and full yet fresh. Beautiful presence. Serve either as an aperitif or with food.
Price approx.: 18,00 EUR
http://www.champagne-gonet-sulcova.fr
Champagne Gonet Sulcova
+33 (0)3 26 54 37 63

CHAMPAGNE H. GOUTORBE 89/100

▼ ♪ Brut rosé grand cru : Deep orange hue. Expressive nose blending red fruits and blood orange. On the palate, a full-bodied, well-structured style showing lovely fullness and freshness. Harmonious and pairing well with nibbles.
Price approx.: 19,45 EUR
www.champagne-henri-goutorbe.com
Champagne Henri Goutorbe
+33 (0)3 26 55 21 70

CHAMPAGNE J.M TISSIER 89/100

▼ ♪ Brut rosé de saignée - Cuvée Aphrodite : Deep orange with coppery nuances. Refined, expressive nose suggestive of ripe strawberry. Full, well-structured palate with vinosity counterbalanced by savoury freshness. A robust, perfumed and ambitious rosé Champagne. Perfect with food.
Price approx.: 18,90 EUR
www.champagne-jm-tissier.com
Champagne J.M Tissier
+33 (0)3 26 54 17 47

CHAMPAGNE JACQUART 89/100

▼ ♪ Brut Rosé : Salmon-pink. The nose delivers aromas of red and dried fruits after swirling. Well-balanced palate showing lovely mellowness, fullness and freshness. Fruit undertones are present, delicate and persistent. A rosé Champagne with good staying power.
Price approx.: 27,38 EUR
http://www.champagne-jacquart.com
Champagne Jacquart
+33 (0)3 26 07 88 40

CHAMPAGNE PIERRE MIGNON 89/100

▼ ♪ Brut Rosé de Saignée Prestige : Light coppery-orange. Focused, open nose revealing aromas of orange-flavoured biscuit. Lovely fleshy character, fruit and freshness on the palate. A full yet perfumed rosé Champagne drinking well from the aperitif through to dessert.
Price approx.: 18,40 EUR
http://www.pierre-mignon.com
Champagne Pierre Mignon
+33 (0)3 26 59 22 03

CHAMPAGNE TAITTINGER 89/100

▼ ♪ Brut rosé Prestige : Orange hue with coppery highlights. Expressive nose with cherries and plums taking centre stage. A full-bodied, vinous and full style on the palate showing more of the same lovely fruit aromas. A rosé Champagne that works best with food.
http://www.taittinger.fr
Champagne Taittinger
+33 (0)3 26 85 45 35

CHAMPAGNE BESSERAT DE BELLEFON 89/100

▼ **DG** Brut blanc de blancs Cuvée des Moines : Light gold. Rich, expressive nose with accents of white fruits, dried vegetal and mild spice aromas. Fine bubbles on the palate with very enjoyable freshness and delicate aromas. An invigorating, elegant wine that is long on the palate and pairs well with Price approx.: 41,00 EUR
http://www.besseratdebellefon.com
Champagne Besserat de Bellefon
+33 (0)3 26 78 52 16

CHAMPAGNE COLLARD-PICARD 89/100

▼ ♪ Brut blanc de blancs grand cru Cuvée Dom Picard : Attractive light yellow. Focused nose opening up to notes of white flowers, fresh hazelnut and lemon. The palate shows a seductive full attack, fine bubbles and beautiful crisp freshness revealing more of the lemon character and wonderful length.
Price approx.: 31,00 EUR
www.champagnecollardpicard.fr
Champagne Collard-Picard
+33 (0)3 26 52 36 93

CHAMPAGNE DE SAINT GALL 89/100

▼ ♪ Brut 1er cru 2007 : Light gold. Mature nose opening up to brioche and milk bread notes. The palate shows seductive fullness, creamy character and suppleness entwined with freshness. A well-made Blanc de Blancs for sophisticated pre-dinner drinks. Price approx.: 41,39 EUR
http://www.de-saint-gall.com
Champagne de Saint Gall
+33 (0)3 26 57 94 22

CHAMPAGNE DIDIER DOUÉ 89/100

▼ ♪ Brut Prestige : Brilliant light gold with green tints. Endearing, complex nose of toasted almond and ripe citrus with mineral presence. Silky attack, extremely seductive, svelte and concentrated palate that is tense and harmonious. A very stylish Pouilly Fumé. Price approx.: 18,00 EUR
www.champagne-didier-doue.fr
Champagne Didier Doué
+33 (0)3 25 79 44 33

CHAMPAGNE FRANCK BONVILLE 89/100

▼ ♪ Brut blanc de blancs grand cru Prestige : Light gold. Delicate nose showing white fruit expression with a faint tropical touch. The palate displays a degree of exuberance nicely framed by evident effervescence. A Champagne showing real drive with pleasant tangy perfumes.
Price approx.: 25,00 EUR
http://www.champagne-franck-bonville.com
Champagne Franck Bonville
+33 (0)3 26 57 52 30

CHAMPAGNE GEORGES VESSELLE 89/100

▼ ♪ Brut grand cru : Light gold. Honest fruity and expressive nose of red fruits and mirabelle plum. Fleshy, full-bodied attack. A well-structured Champagne balanced by freshness. Good fruit expression with a touch of fruit paste on the finish.
Price approx.: 20,50 EUR
http://www.champagne-vesselle.fr
Champagne Georges Vesselle
+33 (0)3 26 57 00 15

CHAMPAGNE GIMONNET-GONET 89/100

▼ ♪ Brut blanc de blancs grand cru Cuvée Or : Light yellow. Refined nose combining brioche tones, a touch of tropical fruits and almond cream in the background. Full, mellow palate showing savoury freshness, fine-grained texture and persistency. A very harmonious Champagne.
Price approx.: 17,00 EUR
Champagne Gimonnet-Gonet
+33 (0)3 26 57 51 44

CHAMPAGNE GUY CHARLEMAGNE 89/100

▼ ♪ Brut blanc de blancs grand cru Réserve : Light yellow with green tints. The nose opens up to mineral expression supported by notes of white fruits and straw. On the palate, a well-structured, clean style displaying elegant austerity. A characterful Champagne that connoisseurs will enjoy.
Price approx.: 19,90 EUR
http://www.champagne-guy-charlemagne.fr
Champagne Guy Charlemagne
+33 (0)3 26 57 52 98

CHAMPAGNE J. M. GOBILLARD & FILS 89/100

▼ ♪ Brut 1er cru Grande Réserve : Light yellow. The nose opens up to buttery and brioche notes then develops fruity perfumes of mirabelle plum and pear. Beautiful presence on the palate, fullness and mellowness and above all, stunning freshness. A harmonious Champagne, ideal for the aperi
Price approx.: 17,20 EUR
http://www.champagne-gobillard.com
Champagne J. M. Gobillard & fils
+33 (0)3 26 51 00 24

CHAMPAGNE LAURENT-PERRIER 89/100

▼ ♪ Brut : Beautiful light gold. Expressive nose with floral and fruity undertones augmented by a toast dimension. Fleshy, closely-integrated attack leading into a fresh mid-palate. Wonderful aromatic presence capped off with delicious pastry notes.
Price approx.: 36,00 EUR
http://www.laurent-perrier.fr
Champagne Laurent-Perrier
+33 (0)3 26 58 91 22

CHAMPAGNE LECLERC BRIANT 89/100

Org▼ ♪ Brut Cuvée Divine : Golden hue. Expressive nose revealing aromas of reserve wine, creamy, patisserie and dried fruit notes. The palate emphasises vinosity and fat. A powerful, lush style balanced by a touch of exuberance. Enjoy well-chilled with food.
Price approx.: 80,00 EUR
www.leclercbriant.com
Champagne Leclerc Briant
+33 (0)3 26 54 45 33

CHAMPAGNE MALARD 89/100

▼ ♪ Brut blanc de blancs grand cru Excellence : Beautiful, brightly-coloured light yellow. Inviting, focused nose marrying lemony, buttery and brioche notes. Wonderful presence on the palate. Full and mellow with lots of freshness. Beautiful crisp finish supporting aromatic length. A lovely Champagne.
Price approx.: 28,00 EUR
http://www.champagnemalard.com
Champagne Malard
+33 (0)3 26 32 40 11

CHAMPAGNE MAURICE VESSELLE 89/100

▼ ♪ Brut grand cru Cuvée Réservée : Light gold. Clean, profound nose displaying upfront fruit (red fruit and tangerine flesh). On the palate, a full-bodied yet fresh and lively style. A characterful Champagne that works well as an aperitif or for cocktail parties.
http://www.champagnemauricevesselle.com
Champagne Maurice Vesselle
+33 (0)3 26 57 00 81

CHAMPAGNE MONTAUDON 89/100

▼ ♪ Brut Classe M : Attractive yellow-gold. Delicate toast on the nose opening up to white fruit tones and notes of dried flowers. The palate is clearly fruit-forward on the attack with a pronounced grapefruit tone. A racy, complex and tropical style.
Price approx.: 30,87 EUR
www.champagnemontaudon.com
Champagne Montaudon
+33 (0)3 26 07 88 40

CHAMPAGNE NICOLAS FEUILLATTE 89/100

▼ ♪ Brut Cuvée Spéciale 2006 : Light gold. Subdued nose revealing aromas of fresh grape on first pour then almond notes. Full attack, refined, melted texture, fresh, pleasant aromatics with a more nervy finish. Vinous yet lively. Drink as an aperitif.
Price approx.: 38,00 EUR
http://www.feuillatte.com
Champagne Nicolas Feuillatte
+33 (0)3 26 59 55 50

CHAMPAGNE NOËL LEBLOND-LENOIR   89/100

▼ ♪ Brut Perle de Dizet : Light yellow. Clean, profound nose opening up to almond, fresh hazelnut, a buttery touch and white flower notes. The palate shows a seductive mellow and polished attack, balanced fat and freshness and focused aromas. A lovely Blanc de Blancs.
Price approx.: 16,80 EUR
Champagne Noël Leblond-Lenoir
+33 (0)3 25 38 53 33

CHAMPAGNE PIERRE GIMONNET & FILS   89/100

▼ ♪ Brut blanc de blancs 1er cru Cuvée Cuis : Light yellow. Refined, focused nose marrying white flowers, pear flesh and almonds. The palate is fresh, perfumed and closely-integrated with the full refinement of the Chardonnay. A Blanc de Blancs that is soft, elegant and delicious. The perfect appetis
Price approx.: 23,00 EUR
http://www.champagne-gimonnet.com
Champagne Pierre Gimonnet & fils
+33 (0)3 26 59 78 70

CHAMPAGNE PIERRE MONCUIT   89/100

▼ ♪ Brut blanc de blancs grand cru Cuvée Pierre Moncuit - Delos : Light yellow. Focused, expressive nose opening up to notes of white flowers, chalk, hazelnut and fresh almond. Lovely fleshy attack, fine bubbles, freshness and focused aromas. A delicious, racy Blanc de Blancs.
Price approx.: 19,50 EUR
http://www.pierre-moncuit.fr
Champagne Pierre Moncuit
+33 (0)3 26 57 52 65

CHAMPAGNE PIPER-HEIDSIECK   89/100

▼ ♪ Brut Essentiel : Beautiful limpid pale yellow. Expressive, ripe nose marrying notes of white fruits and toast. Fleshy, elegant attack on the palate with clearly-etched perfumes. Lovely long-lasting toast-infused finish. A potential partner for foie gras.
http://www.piper-heidsieck.com
Cie Champenoise PH-CH. Piper Heidsieck
+33 (0)3 26 84 43 00

CHAMPAGNE SADI MALOT   89/100

▼ ♪ Brut blanc de blancs 1er cru Vieille Réserve : Light yellow-gold. The nose reveals subtle white-fleshed fruit notes, white flowers and brioche. Good presence on the palate, a full, creamy and mellow style supported by freshness. Fine bubbles. A very convincing Champagne.
Price approx.: 17,00 EUR
http://www.champagne-sadi-malot.com
Champagne Sadi Malot
+33 (0)3 26 97 90 48

CHAMPAGNE TROUILLARD   89/100

▼ ♪ Brut Cuvée Elexium : Light yellow. Refined nose blending creamy notes, milk bread and pear flesh. Delightful palate showing a savoury, refined texture, freshness and fleshy character. Precise, persistent fruit aromas. A very compelling aperitif-style Champagne.
Price approx.: 19,70 EUR
http://www.champagne-trouillard.fr
Champagne Trouillard
+33 (0)3 26 55 37 55

CHAMPAGNE VAZART-COQUART & FILS   89/100

▼ ♪ Brut blanc de blancs grand cru Réserve : Light yellow. Refined, expressive nose with aromas of white flowers, hazelnut, fresh-cut grass with a chalky touch. Lovely fine-grained, well-integrated texture, freshness and aromatic focus on the palate. A beautiful, precise and persistent Blanc de Blan
Price approx.: 18,50 EUR
Champagne Vazart Coquart & fils
+33 (0)3 26 55 40 04

CHAMPAGNE FREDESTEL   88/100

▼ ♪ Extra brut blanc de blancs 1er cru Les Petits Pieds d'Emma 2008 : Attractive light yellow with green tints. Refined, racy nose opening up to mineral and fruit aromas. Beautiful lively, taut palate showing a lovely fine texture, upfront aroma and subtle note of sourness on the finish. A Champagne with real allure. Price approx.: 29,90 EUR
Champagne Fredestel
+33 (0)3 26 57 06 19

CHAMPAGNE JACQUART   88/100

▼ ♪ Extra brut : Beautiful light gold. Distinctive nose showing aromas of white-fleshed fruits augmented by notes of pastries and dried straw. Full-bodied, well-structured palate combining freshness and firmness. Bone dry, persistent and displaying a strong personality.
Price approx.: 26,29 EUR
http://www.champagne-jacquart.com
Champagne Jacquart
+33 (0)3 26 07 88 40

CHAMPAGNE PANNIER   88/100

▼ ♪ Extra brut Exact : Light gold. Expressive nose revealing notes of biscuit and pastry followed by white-fleshed fruits. Beautiful presence and fullness on the palate. Well-structured yet mellow and bordering on creamy. Good framework and boasting a strong personality.
Price approx.: 27,00 EUR
http://www.champagnepannier.com
Champagne Pannier
+33 (0)3 23 69 51 30

CHAMPAGNE PALMER & CO

Brut rosé

▼ Fairly deep orange-pink. Clean nose showing expressive fruit (cherry, strawberry...). On the palate, a full-bodied rosé marrying vinosity and freshness that showcase upfront fruit. A delectable, fresh Champagne that works well from the aperitif on.

contact@champagnepalmer.fr

88/100

CHAMPAGNE PERTOIS-MORISET   88/100

▼ ♪ Extra brut grand cru : Light yellow with green tints. Expressive nose showing pronounced minerality backed by beautiful apple flesh and a tropical touch. Well-structured, honest palate supported by beautiful exuberance. Full-bodied, long and fresh. Wonderful personality.
Price approx.: 24,90 EUR
Champagne Pertois-Moriset
+33 (0)3 26 57 52 14

CHAMPAGNE TROUILLARD   88/100

▼ ♪ Extra brut blanc de noirs : Light gold. Highly expressive nose with crunchy fruit perfumes of mirabelle plum and pear. The palate shows seductive fullness and balanced vinosity and freshness. More of the same crunchy fruit and exuberance. An honest Champagne.
Price approx.: 19,50 EUR
http://www.champagne-trouillard.fr
Champagne Trouillard
+33 (0)3 26 55 37 55

CHAMPAGNE DE CASTELLANE   88/100

▼ ♪ Brut rosé : Deeply-coloured light red. Assertive fruity nose showing clean cherry and raspberry aromas. More of the same delicious character on the palate, nicely supported by persistent freshness. A delightful rosé, equally delicious as an aperitif or with pudding. Price approx.: 25,00 EUR
www.castellane.com
Champagne de Castellane
+33 (0)3 26 51 19 19

CHAMPAGNE FABRICE BERTEMÈS   88/100

▼ ♪ Brut 1er cru rosé de saignée : Deep brick-red. Profound nose showing lovely, extremely precise aromas of cherry and raspberry. The palate is well-structured and vinous yet also remarkably well-balanced by freshness. A characterful Champagne pairing with red meats.

Price approx.: 21,90 EUR
http://www.champagne-bertemes.fr
Champagne Fabrice Bertemès
+33 (0)3 26 57 81 39

CHAMPAGNE MONTAUDON   88/100

▼ ♪ Brut Grande Rose : Orange with coppery nuances. Mature nose developing perfumes of citrus and dried fruits. Well-balanced palate showing lovely fullness, mellowness, freshness and above all, fruit expression. An enjoyable rosé that works well as an aperitif and with food.
Price approx.: 21,16 EUR
www.champagnemontaudon.com
Champagne Montaudon
+33 (0)3 26 07 88 40

CHAMPAGNE PANNIER   88/100

▼ ♪ Brut rosé : Orange-hued. Ripe fruity nose blending dried fruits, citrus notes (tangerine) and subtle toast touches. Delightful fleshy palate balanced by freshness. A party-style rosé Champagne that works equally well as an aperitif or with food. Price approx.: 29,00 EUR
http://www.champagnepannier.com
Champagne Pannier
+33 (0)3 23 69 51 30

CHAMAPGNE J.L GOULARD-GÉRARD   88/100

▼ ♪ Brut Sublime Elevé en fût de chêne : Light yellow. Endearing, refined nose opening up to fruity notes then revealing delicate fresh oak scents. Wonderful presence on the palate, full attack, fine, closely-integrated bubbles. Biscuit-like aromatics that linger pleasantly. Price approx.: 22,50 EUR
Champagne Jean Luc Goulard Gérard
+33 (0)3 26 03 18 78

Detailed instructions are featured
at the start of the book.

CHAMPAGNE BEAUMONT DES CRAYÈRES 88/100

▼ ♪ Brut Fleur de Prestige 2004 : Light yellow-gold. Expressive nose, still beautifully youthful with a blend of white-fleshed fruits and a subtle lemony note. Full and creamy on the palate yet also fresh. Closely-integrated and persistent across the palate. A top-notch Champagne.
Price approx.: 29,50 EUR
http://www.champagne-beaumont.com
Champagne Beaumont des Crayères
+33 (0)3 26 55 29 40

CHAMPAGNE CHARLES ELLNER 88/100

▼ ♪ Brut blanc de blancs : Limpid, light yellow. Distinctive nose intermixing white fruits, a subtle patisserie tone and a tropical touch of pineapple. Silky attack showing abundant freshness. More of the same delectable perfumes over quite substantial length. Price approx.: 19,60 EUR
http://www.champagne-ellner.com
Champagne Charles Ellner
+33 (0)3 26 55 60 25

CHAMPAGNE CHARLES MIGNON 88/100

▼ ♪ Brut grand cru Cuvée Comte de Marne : Light gold. Delightful nose blending tangerine flesh with notes of barley water. Full, generous palate combining vinosity with fine bubbles and pleasant freshness. Serve preferably as a food Champagne with poultry. Price approx.: 35,00 EUR
http://www.champagne-mignon.fr
Champagne Charles Mignon
+33 (0)3 26 58 33 33

CHAMPAGNE DE CASTELNAU 88/100

▼ ♪ Brut blanc de blancs 2002 : Pale gold. Delightfully expressive nose recalling ripe white fruits and biscuit. Beautiful attack on the palate increasing in power and fullness. More of the same focused aromas framed by creamy effervescence. Fresh, perfumed finish.
Price approx.: 39,00 EUR
http://www.champagne-de-castelnau.eu
Champagne de Castelnau
+33 (0)3 26 77 89 00

CHAMPAGNE FRANCIS COSSY 88/100

▼ ♪ Brut 2007 : Deep gold. Mature, expressive nose suggestive of stone fruits, dried fruits and a patisserie dimension. Generous palate bordering on lush, closely-integrated and fresh. A robust personality that would work marvellously as a food Champagne with white meats
Price approx.: 20,60 EUR
http://www.champagne-cossy.com
Champagne Francis Cossy
+33 (0)3 26 49 75 56

CHAMPAGNE GONET SULCOVA 88/100

▼ ♪ Brut blanc de blancs : Light yellow with green tints. Delicate nose revealing scents of white flowers and fresh almond and hazelnut. Fullness on the palate with a fine-grained texture, abundant freshness and the same spring-like aromas. A dashing Blanc de Blancs.
Price approx.: 17,00 EUR
http://www.champagne-gonet-sulcova.fr
Champagne Gonet Sulcova
+33 (0)3 26 54 37 63

CHAMPAGNE J. M. GOBILLARD & FILS 88/100

▼ DG Brut blanc de blancs : Pale yellow, green tints. Dashing, expressive nose suggestive of white flowers and almond. The palate combines freshness, creamy effervescence and distinctive aromatic expression with a menthol touch on the finish. An aperitif-style Champagne for sharing.
Price approx.: 17,60 EUR
http://www.champagne-gobillard.com
Champagne J. M. Gobillard & fils
+33 (0)3 26 51 00 24

CHAMPAGNE LE MESNIL 88/100

▼ ♪ Brut blanc de blancs grand cru : Light gold. Expressive and endearing nose intermixing white fruits, ripe lemon and chalky notes. On the palate, a well-structured Champagne showing impeccable balance, fullness and exuberance enhancing upfront, persistent aromas. Wonderful character.
Price approx.: 22,00 EUR
www.champagnelemesnil.com
Cave Coopérative U.P.R. Champagne Le Mesnil
+33 (0)3 26 57 53 23

CHAMPAGNE LECLERC BRIANT 88/100

Org▼ ♪ Brut 2006 : Deep gold. Mature nose revealing patisserie aromas and perfumes of dried fig and date. Powerful, lush and fat palate. A full style balanced by a touch of freshness on the finish. Enjoy with food.
Price approx.: 32,60 EUR
www.leclercbriant.com
Champagne Leclerc Briant
+33 (0)3 26 54 45 33

CHAMPAGNE P. LANCELOT-ROYER 88/100

▼ DG Brut blanc de blancs Cuvée de Réserve R.R. : Light gold. Delightful nose of ripe white fruits with delicate brioche notes in the background. The palate is soft and perfumed with the nose aromatics augmented by a pleasant mineral tone. A beautiful aperitif-style and also food-friendly Champagne.
Price approx.: 15,50 EUR
Champagne P. Lancelot-Royer
+33 (0)3 26 57 51 41

CHAMPAGNE CHARLES COLLIN

Extra brut

▼ Golden hue with subtle orange tints. Delightful, fruit-forward nose showing red fruits and plum flesh. Full-bodied, rich palate with a fruit-driven attack leading into a lively, closely-integrated mid-palate with mineral accents. A well-made Extra Dry.

+33 3 25 38 31 00

87/100

CHAMPAGNE PALMER & CO — 88/100

▼ ♪ Brut 2008 : Light gold. Very pure, delicate nose suggestive of pear flesh with a subtle biscuit note. Full, closely integrated attack leading into a fresh mid-palate and livelier, slightly sharp finish. Focused and persistent aromatic expression.
Price approx.: 38,00 EUR
www.champagne-palmer.fr
Champagne Palmer & Co
+33 (0)3 26 07 35 07

CHAMPAGNE PERTOIS-MORISET — 88/100

▼ ♪ Brut blanc de blancs grand cru : Limpid, light yellow. Focused nose blending white-fleshed fruits, breadcrust and delicate floral and mineral notes. Fleshy attack, creamy texture and lovely crisp freshness. A delightful, persistent Blanc de Blancs.
Price approx.: 23,50 EUR
Champagne Pertois-Moriset
+33 (0)3 26 57 52 14

CHAMPAGNE PICARD & BOYER — 88/100

▼ ♪ Brut Réserve de Famille : Light gold with amber shades. Mature nose opening up to dried fruits and patisserie notes. The palate shows seductive fullness, fine texture and above all, lingering freshness. Upfront biscuity fruit aromas showing beautiful precision.
Price approx.: 19,50 EUR
www.champagne-picard-boyer.fr
Champagne Picard & Boyer
+33 (0)3 26 85 11 69

CHAMPAGNE PIERRE MIGNON — 88/100

▼ ♪ Brut Année de Madame 2006 : Light yellow with green tints. Clean, youthful nose with upfront mirabelle plum and white-fleshed fruits. Good staying power, vinosity, freshness and lovely body on the whole. Price approx.: 21,40 EUR
http://www.pierre-mignon.com
Champagne Pierre Mignon
+33 (0)3 26 59 22 03

CHAMPAGNE ROYER PÈRE & FILS — 88/100

▼ ♪ Brut Vintage 2008 : Brightly-coloured light yellow. Refined nose revealing creamy, buttery perfumes backed by white-fleshed fruits. Beautiful full palate with fine texture and bubbles. Wonderful exuberance supports the whole, capped off with aromas of ripe lemon and citrus.
Price approx.: 17,75 EUR
www.champagne-royer.com
Champagne Royer père & fils
+33 (0)3 25 38 52 16

CHAMPAGNE RUFFIN ET FILS — 88/100

▼ ♪ Brut grand cru Cuvée Nobilis 2006 : Light gold. Expressive nose opening up to apple flesh then revealing notes of brioche and candied fruits after swirling. The palate focuses on body and vinosity. Mellow and lush yet also fresh. A Champagne with real food compatibility.
Price approx.: 30,00 EUR
www.champagnes-ruffin.com
Champagne Ruffin & fils
+33 (0)3 26 59 30 14

CHAMPAGNE SADI MALOT — 88/100

▼ ♪ Brut blanc de blancs 1er cru 2008 : Bright, light yellow. The nose marries lemony notes, a mineral, chalky dimension and a touch of brioche. Lively palate showing lovely fine bubbles and persistency. More of the same nose aromatics. A tense, perfumed Blanc de Blancs.
Price approx.: 22,00 EUR
http://www.champagne-sadi-malot.com
Champagne Sadi Malot
+33 (0)3 26 97 90 48

Prices mentioned in this book are guideline and can vary depending on point of sale.
The shops, wineries or publisher can in no way be held responsible for this.

CHAMPAGNE PLOYEZ-JACQUEMART — 87/100

▼ ♪ Extra-Brut blanc de blancs 2005 : Light yellow. Mature, expressive nose intermixing candied lemon and mirabelle plum with pleasant toast undertones. The palate is melted yet fresh with a crisp character. Focused, long and harmonious throughout. For a sophisticated aperitif. Price approx.: 38,00 EUR
http://www.ployez-jacquemart.fr
Champagne Ployez-Jacquemart
+33 (0)3 26 61 11 87

CHAMPAGNE DANY FÈVRE — 87/100

▼ ♪ Demi-sec rosé Gourmand : Orange-hued with pink tints. Beautiful fruit presence on the nose with red fruits and orange jam. The palate is lush and soft yet fresh. Precise fruit expression. Rich sweetness nicely framed by freshness. Delicious.
Price approx.: 14,70 EUR
Champagne Dany Fèvre
+33 (0)3 25 38 76 63

CHAMPAGNE CHASSENAY D'ARCE — 87/100

▼ ♪ Brut rosé : Deep orange-pink. Enticing, focused nose suggestive of red fruit jelly. The palate is soft, fleshy and fresh with the nose aromatics carrying through. A very charming rosé Champagne, appealing from the aperitif onwards.
http://www.chassenay.com
Champagne Chassenay d'Arce
+33 (0)3 25 38 34 75

CHAMPAGNE EUGÈNE RALLE — 87/100

▼ ♪ Brut rosé grand cru : Attractive light coppery-orange. Focused nose intermixing orange flesh, dried apricot and red fruits. Fleshy attack with crunchy fruit leading into a lively mid-palate boasting good persistency. Freshness and fruit make this rosé suitable as an aperitif.
Price approx.: 17,70 EUR
http://www.champagne-eugene-ralle.com
Champagne Eugène Ralle
+33 (0)3 26 49 40 12

CHAMPAGNE GUY CHARBAUT — 87/100

▼ ♪ Brut Rosé 1er cru : Orange hue. Mature nose of ripe red fruits and citrus. A full-bodied, vinous style on the palate with generosity nicely counterbalanced by a sensation of lingering freshness. Its richness makes it a marvellous food Champagne or partner for nibbles.
Price approx.: 22,70 EUR
http://www.champagne-guy-charbaut.com
Champagne Guy Charbaut
+33 (0)3 26 52 60 59

CHAMPAGNE MAURICE PHILIPPART — 87/100

▼ ♪ Brut rosé 1er cru : Orange-hued with coppery shades. Delightful nose of ripe red fruits coupled with blood orange notes. On the palate, a rosé brimming with freshness showcasing the same delectable aromas. Its structure and exuberance make it particularly suitable for food.
Price approx.: 17,30 EUR
http://www.champagne-mphilippart.com
Champagne Maurice Philippart
+33 (0)3 26 03 42 44

CHAMPAGNE PAUL LAURENT — 87/100

▼ ♪ Brut rosé Cuvée du Fondateur : Appealing orangy-pink. Focused nose recalling strawberry and raspberry. Full, fruity palate where vinosity is nicely balanced by freshness. A generous, honest and well-made rosé Champagne. Drink from the aperitif through to pudding. Price approx.: 19,00 EUR
http://www.champagnepaullaurent.com
Champagne Paul Laurent
+33 (0)3 26 81 91 11

CHAMPAGNE PIPER-HEIDSIECK — 87/100

▼ ♪ Brut rosé Sauvage : Clean pink. Intense nose of ripe red berry fruits primarily recalling strawberry. Marvellous combination of richness and nervousness, highlighting the same delightful perfumes. A lively, perfumed rosé pairing with food or drinking well as an aperitif.
Price approx.: 35,00 EUR
http://www.piper-heidsieck.com
Cie Champenoise PH-CH. Piper Heidsieck
+33 (0)3 26 84 43 00

CHAMPAGNE A. MARGAINE — 87/100

▼ ♪ Brut 1er cru Le Brut : Light yellow. Endearing nose opening up to fresh grape and white-fleshed fruit notes then revealing refined toasted notes. Delicious, full and generous palate. Fine bubbles and upfront freshness. A very charming dry Champagne. Price approx.: 15,50 EUR
http://www.champagne-a-margaine.com
Champagne A. Margaine
+33 (0)3 26 97 92 13

CHAMPAGNE ALAIN BAILLY — 87/100

▼ ♪ Brut Cuvée Prestige : Light yellow. Refined nose opening up to notes of white flowers, hazelnuts and fresh cut grass. Beautiful silky attack flowing into a lively mid-palate with a tangy character. Focused, persistent aromas. An appealing dry Champagne for the aperitif.
Price approx.: 16,40 EUR
http://www.champagne-bailly.com
Champagne Alain Bailly
+33 (0)3 26 97 41 58

CHAMPAGNE ANDRÉ ROBERT — 87/100

▼ ♪ Brut blanc de blancs grand cru Le Mesnil 2006 : Light gold. Mature nose of dried fruits,

patisserie notes and candied fruits. The palate is lively on the attack with intense aromas conveying a degree of freshness. The finish is perfumed and quite persistent. A Champagne with a real sense of place. Price approx.: 22,10 EUR
http://www.champagne-andre-robert.com
Champagne André Robert
+33 (0)3 26 57 59 41

CHAMPAGNE BEAUMONT DES CRAYÈRES   87/100

▼ ♪ Brut Grand Prestige : Golden hue. Mature nose blending fruity notes and a touch of nougat. The palate shows seductive fullness, a degree of opulence and a mellowness that envelops a pleasant sensation of freshness. A deftly crafted dry Champagne.
Price approx.: 23,50 EUR
http://www.champagne-beaumont.com
Champagne Beaumont des Crayères
+33 (0)3 26 55 29 40

CHAMPAGNE BERNARD RÉMY   87/100

▼ ♪ Brut grand cru : Beautiful light yellow. Enticing nose revealing pleasant fruity aromas, a touch of almond and a floral dimension. Wonderful presence on the palate, fine texture, exhilirating freshness and precise aromas. A single varietal Chardonnay, perfect for fish.
http://www.champagnebernardremy.com
Champagne Bernard Rémy
+33 (0)3 26 80 60 34

CHAMPAGNE BLONDEL   87/100

▼ ♪ Brut blanc de blancs 1er cru : Light yellow with green tints. Delightfully refined nose showing suggestions of fruit flesh (apple, kiwi, lemon). Lively, soft and perfumed palate displaying lots of exuberance and good length. An aperitif-style Blanc de Blancs. Price approx.: 18,00 EUR
http://www.champagneblondel.com
Champagne Blondel
+33 (0)3 26 03 43 92

CHAMPAGNE CUPERLY   87/100

▼ ♪ Brut blanc de noirs grand cru : Deep yellow-gold. Expressive, distinctive nose intermixing dried fruits and patisserie notes. Full-bodied, powerful attack displaying beautiful vinosity. Firmer, well-structured mid-palate tinged with a hint of sourness. Characterful and food-friendly.
Price approx.: 26,70 EUR
http://www.champagne-cuperly.com
Champagne Cuperly
+33 (0)3 26 05 44 60

CHAMPAGNE CUPERLY   87/100

▼ ♪ Brut grand cru : Appealing light yellow. Refined nose intermixing pear flesh and fresh

croissant. Lovely precise, lively palate. Refined bubbles and long-lasting perfumes. Perfect for whetting the appetite. Price approx.: 18,20 EUR
http://www.champagne-cuperly.com
Champagne Cuperly
+33 (0)3 26 05 44 60

CHAMPAGNE D. MASSIN   87/100

▼ ♪ Brut L'Envie T. 2010 : Light yellow-gold. Expressive nose opening up to delicious fruity notes of mirabelle plum and white-fleshed fruits. The palate shows seductive fullness, vinosity and body with refined texture and compelling exuberance nicely balancing the whole.
Price approx.: 28,00 EUR
http://www.champagne-dominique-massin.fr
Champagne D. Massin
+33 (0)3 25 38 74 97

CHAMPAGNE DANY FÈVRE   87/100

▼ ♪ Brut 2004 : Light gold. Mature nose opening up to patisserie notes, bitter almond and a buttery touch. Full, lush palate revealing a sensation of pronounced sweetness before ending with a trace of firmness. Serve preferably with food or as a pudding Champagne. Price approx.: 18,20 EUR
Champagne Dany Fèvre
+33 (0)3 25 38 76 63

CHAMPAGNE DE CASTELNAU   87/100

▼ ♪ Brut 2002 : Appealing yellow-gold. Highly endearing nose of toasted almond and dried fruits. Fleshy palate showing elegantly tense acidity and silky effervescence. The honest nose aromas carry through to the palate. A skilfully crafted Champagne. Price approx.: 36,96 EUR
http://www.champagne-de-castelnau.eu
Champagne de Castelnau
+33 (0)3 26 77 89 00

CHAMPAGNE DE SAINT GALL   87/100

▼ ♪ Brut blanc de blancs 1er cru : Light yellow. Fresh, focused nose blending white flowers, fresh hazelnut, brioche and chalky undertones. The palate is lively and tense with fine bubbles. Lovely persistency driven by mineral and lemony notes.
Price approx.: 35,80 EUR
http://www.de-saint-gall.com
Champagne de Saint Gall
+33 (0)3 26 57 94 22

CHAMPAGNE G. GRUET ET FILS

87/100

▼ Brut Blanc de Blancs

Light yellow. A mix of white-fleshed fruits and brioche notes on the nose. Full palate with a creamy texture. A generous style enveloped in freshness. A Blanc de Blancs pairing well with fish dishes.

Price approx.: 16 EUR
Serving temperature: 9-11°
Ready to drink: From now on

G. Gruet & Fils was founded in 1967 in Béthon by Gilbert Gruet whose aim was to establish a producers' group to target larger markets. The co-operative now has 100 members and still markets some of its wines under the G. Gruet & Fils label. The winery is open from Monday to Friday, from 9am to 12pm and from 1:30pm to 5:30pm, and on Saturdays from 9am to 12pm and from 2pm to 5:30pm. It is closed on Sundays and bank holidays as well as Saturday afternoons in July and August. Its Champagnes offer very good value for money. In addition to this Blanc de Blancs, the Grande Réserve and Rosé have also been selected this year.

Union Vinicole des Coteaux de Béthon
5 rue des Pressoirs - 51260 Béthon
Tel: (+33) 3 26 80 48 19 - Fax: (+33) 3 26 80 44 57
E-mail: champagne.g.gruetetfils@wanadoo.fr
Website: http://www.champagne-gruetetfils.fr

CHAMPAGNE FABRICE BERTEMÈS 87/100

▼ ♪ Brut blanc de blancs 1er cru Grande Sélection : Light gold. Focused, expressive nose opening to notes of lemon, candied fruits and a touch of pastry. Full attack with a refined texture and bubbles and savoury exuberance. Lovely freshness showcasing persistent fruity and buttery aromas. Robust personali

Price approx.: 16,50 EUR

http://www.champagne-bertemes.fr
Champagne Fabrice Bertemès
+33 (0)3 26 57 81 39

CHAMPAGNE FABRICE BERTEMÈS 87/100

▼ ♪ Brut blanc de blancs 1er cru 2006 : Very pure, attractive yellow-gold. The nose is open and fairly intense with white fruits, grapefruit, pineapple and a touch of toast in the background. A characterful Champagne with a full attack and honest aromas. Lovely persistent, ripe finish.

Price approx.: 23,00 EUR

http://www.champagne-bertemes.fr
Champagne Fabrice Bertemès
+33 (0)3 26 57 81 39

CCHAMPAGNE GEORGES CARTIER 87/100

▼ ♪ Brut Première Cuvée : Light gold. Mature nose intermixing patisserie notes, pastry and a touch of candied fruits. Lovely fullness, creamy texture and fresh finish on the palate. Good overall balance and finesse. Price approx.: 30,00 EUR

http://www.georgescartier.com
Champagne Georges Cartier
+33 (0)3 26 32 06 22

CHAMPAGNE GISÈLE DEVAVRY 87/100

▼ ♪ Brut Trésor de Cave 1998 : Amber-hued. Evolved nose revealing uninhibited scents of mature wine (dried fig, apricot and candied citrus...). These mature aromatics are enhanced on the palate by an almost youthful freshness with a trace of firmness on the finish. Drink with food.

Price approx.: 48,00 EUR

Champagne Bertrand Devavry
+33 (0)3 26 59 46 21

CHAMPAGNE GUY CHARBAUT 87/100

▼ ♪ Brut blanc de blancs 1er cru : Light yellow with green tints. Refined nose intermixing white flowers, fresh almond and a mineral dimension. Beautiful presence on the palate, fine texture, pronounced freshness and precise aromas. More of the tasteful chalky note on the finish.

Price approx.: 22,60 EUR

http://www.champagne-guy-charbaut.com
Champagne Guy Charbaut
+33 (0)3 26 52 60 59

CHAMPAGNE H. GOUTORBE 87/100

▼ ♪ Brut 1er Cru Cuvée Prestige : Beautiful light gold. Endearing nose intermixing dried fruits with a pastry note. Beautiful presence on the palate, full and fleshy yet fresh. Lovely length across the palate. Good performance throughout.

Price approx.: 17,05 EUR

www.champagne-henri-goutorbe.com
Champagne Henri Goutorbe
+33 (0)3 26 55 21 70

CHAMPAGNE HUGUENOT-TASSIN 87/100

▼ ♪ Brut Cuvée Prestige - les fioles : Bright, pale yellow. Refined nose unfurling lemony perfumes. Fleshy, full palate showing lovely fine bubbles and texture. Generous, lush almost and yet still very fresh and perfumed. An elegant Champagne.

Price approx.: 18,90 EUR

http://www.huguenot-tassin.com
Champagne Huguenot-Tassin
+33 (0)3 25 38 54 49

CHAMPAGNE JACQUART 87/100

▼ ♪ Brut Mosaïque : Light yellow. Endearing nose recalling white flowers, almond and white-fleshed fruits. Full, mellow and supple attack flowing into an enjoyable, livelier mid-palate. Well-balanced and persistent. An appealing Champagne for the aperitif.

Price approx.: 21,92 EUR

http://www.champagne-jacquart.com
Champagne Jacquart
+33 (0)3 26 07 88 40

CHAMPAGNE JACQUINOT & FILS 87/100

▼ ♪ Brut blanc de noirs : Golden hue with orange shades. Clean, focused nose with raspberry and stewed apple aromas taking centre stage. Fleshy, fairly full-bodied palate nicely balanced by freshness. Refined bubbles and precise perfumes. A charming Blanc de Noirs.

Price approx.: 22,00 EUR

http://www.champagne-jacquinot.com
Champagne Jacquinot & Fils
+33 (0)3 26 54 36 81

CHAMPAGNE JEAN VELUT 87/100

▼ ♪ Brut rosé : Light red. Expressive nose of red fruit with biscuit and brioche notes in the background. Lovely fleshy, full-bodied and perfumed palate balanced by savoury freshness. A characterful, expressive rosé Champagne for the aperitif or with food.

Price approx.: 17,40 EUR

http://www.champagne-velut.fr
Champagne Jean Velut
+33 (0)3 25 74 83 31

CHAMPAGNE JEAN-POL HAUTBOIS　　　87/100

▼ ✔ Brut blanc de blancs Cuvée Achille 2008 : Light yellow. Delicate nose of white flowers and refined fruit notes. Full, silky attack flowing into a more nervy, forthright mid-palate displaying a mineral tone. A vibrant, lively Blanc de Blancs that is still young and well-structured.

http://www.champagne-hautbois.com
Champagne Hautbois Jean-Pol
+33 (0)3 26 48 20 98

CHAMPAGNE JEEPER　　　87/100

▼ ✔ Brut - Grande Réserve : Light gold. Profound nose recalling stone fruits and dried fruits with a touch of apple after swirling. Full body and vinosity are key themes on the palate. A generous, lush style that works best with canapes or a sit-down meal.
Price approx.: 20,00 EUR
http://www.champagne-jeeper.fr
Les Domaines Jeeper
+33 (0)3 26 05 08 98

CHAMPAGNE JEEPER　　　87/100

▼ ✔ Brut - Grand assemblage : Light gold. Pleasant fruity nose suggestive of apple flesh and yellow plum. More of the same aromas on the palate which is generous and mellow supported by savoury freshness. An expressive, perfumed style. Drink as an aperitif.
Price approx.: 18,00 EUR
http://www.champagne-jeeper.fr
Les Domaines Jeeper
+33 (0)3 26 05 08 98

CHAMPAGNE L & S CHEURLIN　　　87/100

▼ ✔ Brut Coccinelle & Papillon 2008 : Pale gold. Alluring nose combining fruity notes with a floral, vegetal and mineral dimension. Fullness and savoury vinosity on the palate framed by freshness. A likeable, charming style that works well as an aperitif.
Price approx.: 21,00 EUR
Champagne L & S Cheurlin
+33 (0)3 25 38 55 04

CHAMPAGNE LINARD GONTIER　　　87/100

▼ ✔ Brut blanc de blancs : Light yellow, green tints. Notes of white flowers, fresh hazelnut and toast undertones on the nose. Fine-grained, closely-integrated texture on the palate. Soft attack leading into a fresh mid-palate. A focused Blanc de Blancs for whetting the appetite.
Price approx.: 17,00 EUR
http://www.champagne-gruetetfils.fr
Union Vinicole des Coteaux de Béthon
+33 (0)3 26 80 48 19

CHAMPAGNE LOUIS DE SACY　　　87/100

▼ ✔ Brut Originel : Light gold. Expressive nose revealing stewed and dried fruit aromas with a mineral dimension. Good staying power on the palate. Full attack leading into a lively, almost tangy mid-palate. Upright and persistent. Drinking well from the aperitif onwards.
Price approx.: 25,40 EUR
www.champagne-louis-de-sacy.fr
Champagne Louis de Sacy
+33 (0)3 26 97 91 13

CHAMPAGNE LOUIS DOUSSET　　　87/100

▼ ✔ Brut grand cru Assemblage : Deep golden hue. Distinctive nose developing perfumes of dried fruits, patisserie and brioche notes. Full-bodied, vinous palate. A well-structured, firm style balanced by a savoury sensation of freshness.
Price approx.: 26,00 EUR
http://www.louis-dousset.com/
Champagne Louis Dousset
+33 (0)3 26 83 99 08

CHAMPAGNE MICHEL TURGY　　　87/100

▼ ✔ Brut blanc de blancs grand cru Réserve Sélection : Light yellow. A mix of white flowers, white-fleshed fruits and chalk notes on the nose. Fleshy, fruity attack leading into a sensation of freshness revealing more of the mineral character. An appealing Blanc de Blancs for the aperitif.
www.champagne-turgy.com
Champagne Michel Turgy
+33 (0)3 26 57 53 43

CHAMPAGNE NICOLAS FEUILLATTE　　　87/100

▼ ✔ Brut Réserve : Pale yellow-gold. Focused, fruity nose opening up to apple and pear flesh with a subtle buttery, biscuity touch. Full-bodied, fleshy and full attack leading into a fresh middle palate. Harmonious and delightful. Serve as an aperitif.
Price approx.: 26,00 EUR
http://www.feuillatte.com
Champagne Nicolas Feuillatte
+33 (0)3 26 59 55 50

CHAMPAGNE NOMINÉ-RENARD　　　87/100

▼ ✔ Brut blanc de blancs : Glimmering light gold. Inviting nose of fresh fruits, particularly white fruits. Subtle touch of toast. Archetypal Chardonnay aromas on the palate which is ripe and rich with suggestions of toasted hazelnut and almond. A delicious partner for fish in a sa
Price approx.: 19,00 EUR
http://www.champagne-nomine-renard.com
Champagne Nominé-Renard
+33 (0)3 26 52 82 60

CHAMPAGNE
ROYER PÈRE & FILS

87/100

▼ Brut Prestige

Light yellow. The nose opens up to white-fleshed fruit notes with a subtle pastry touch. Lovely fullness, fat and above all, exuberance on the palate which imparts beautiful freshness. Fine bubbles. Set aside for the aperitif.

Price approx.: 16.75 EUR
Serving temperature: 9-11°
Ready to drink: From now on

Georges Royer planted his first vineyards in 1960 on the hillsides of Landreville, a village located in the heart of the Côte des Bar in Aube. The estate is currently run by his grandchildren who make well-balanced, elegant Champagnes from their 25- hectare vineyard. This year, four labels have been selected and scored between 85 and 88/100. The company's trump card is
its price range – from 13 to 16 euros. Visitors are welcomed from Monday to Friday during working hours and by appointment at weekends and on bank holidays.

Champagne Royer père & fils
120 Grande Rue - 10110 Landreville
Tel.: (+33) 3 25 38 52 16 - Fax: (+33) 3 25 38 37 17
E-mail: infos@champagne-royer.com
Website: www.champagne-royer.com

CHAMPAGNE PAUL MICHEL 87/100

▼ **DG** Brut 1er cru Carte Blanche : Attractive light gold. Very pure nose showing suggestions of white fruits with a delightful patisserie touch. Fresh palate revealing idiosyncratic crisp, invigorating perfumes of fruit that linger. An excellent Champagne for the aperitif.
Price approx.: 20,00 EUR
Champagne Paul Michel
+33 (0)3 26 59 79 77

CHAMPAGNE PHILIPPE GONET 87/100

▼ ♪ Brut blanc de blancs grand cru - Roy Soleil : Yellow-gold. The nose is expressive with biscuit tones, white fruits and breadcrust. Fairly lively yet highly perfumed attack revealing more of the same classic aromas. A dry, aperitif-style Champagne for sharing.
Price approx.: 33,75 EUR
www.champagne-philippe-gonet.com
Champagne Philippe Gonet
+33 (0)3 26 57 53 47

CHAMPAGNE PIPER-HEIDSIECK 87/100

▼ **DG** Brut : Light gold. Clean, expressive nose of ripe white fruits with a pleasant hint of almond. Polished, creamy attack on the palate showcasing the same fresh aromas. The finish stays crisp with drive and lingers. A Champagne for parties and sharing.
Price approx.: 30,00 EUR
http://www.piper-heidsieck.com
Cie Champenoise PH-CH. Piper Heidsieck
+33 (0)3 26 84 43 00

CHAMPAGNE RÉMY MASSIN & FILS 87/100

▼ ♪ Brut Spécial Club 2009 : Light gold. Clean nose driven by white fruit, hinting at beautiful freshness. The palate is dense and brings together full body, vinosity and harmony. A characterful, food-friendly Champagne that would pair with, say, white meats.
www.champagne-massin.com
Champagne Rémy Massin & fils
+33 (0)3 25 38 74 09

CHAMPAGNE SADI MALOT 87/100

▼ ♪ Brut blanc de blancs 1er cru Cuvée de Réserve : Light yellow. Pleasant nose opening up to white flowers with almond notes, fresh hazelnut and subtle lemony undertones. The palate shows seductive fine bubbles, exuberance and freshness. A nervy, focused and perfumed Blanc de Blancs.
Price approx.: 15,00 EUR
http://www.champagne-sadi-malot.com
Champagne Sadi Malot
+33 (0)3 26 97 90 48

CHAMPAGNE DANY FÈVRE 86/100

▼ ♪ Extra brut Sauvage : Light yellow-gold. Expressive nose with an assertive fruity character of mirabelle plum and a subtle patisserie touch. Full, fleshy and closely-integrated attack leading into very fresh, exuberant aromatics. The fruit aromas are augmented by a tropical no
Price approx.: 13,70 EUR
Champagne Dany Fèvre
+33 (0)3 25 38 76 63

CHAMPAGNE DENIS ROBERT 86/100

▼ ♪ Extra brut Cuvée Spontanée : Brilliant light yellow. Ripe nose suggestive of citrus, white-fleshed fruits and a faint patisserie touch. The palate is fairly lively on the attack yet also highly aromatic. The crisp nose aromatics carry through. An invigorating style. Price approx.: 14,90 EUR
www.roberdelph.fr
Champagne Roberdelph
+33 (0)3 23 82 11 74

CHAMPAGNE DUCHÊNE FLORENCE 86/100

▼ ♪ Extra brut Di Mangan : Light gold. Subdued nose revealing perfumes of dried fruits after swirling. Full-bodied, rich and well-structured palate. Well-balanced and robust with good staying power. Would work with food. Price approx.: 23,00 EUR
Champagne Duchêne
+33 (0)3 26 55 56 19

CHAMPAGNE FRANCIS COSSY 86/100

▼ ♪ Extra brut 1er cru 2007 : Brilliant golden hue. Honest, expressive nose blending dried fruits, dried vegetal aromas and a mineral dimension. The palate shows amazing fat, vinosity and mellowness. It exudes mature aromas of dried fruits and patisserie notes. Drink with food.
Price approx.: 16,50 EUR
http://www.champagne-cossy.com
Champagne Francis Cossy
+33 (0)3 26 49 75 56

CHAMPAGNE GIMONNET-GONET 86/100

▼ ♪ Extra brut grand cru blanc de blancs : Light yellow. Distinctive nose displaying a chalky character, fresh hazelnut notes then brioche. Full-bodied, vinous and well-structured palate showing a degree of firmness, a touch of austerity even. A no-frills Champagne boasting a sense of place.
Price approx.: 21,00 EUR
Champagne Gimonnet-Gonet
+33 (0)3 26 57 51 44

CHAMPAGNE BAUCHET PÈRE 86/100

▼ ♪ Brut rosé Séduction : Orange-pink. Focused fruity nose suggestive of fresh red fruits and

CHAMPAGNE CHARLES COLLIN

Brut blanc de noirs

▼ Light gold with faint orange tints. Enticing nose showing dried and fresh red fruits. Fleshy, full-bodied attack displaying a sensation of sweetness and richness. The finish is livelier and balances the whole, imparting depth. An appealing Blanc de Noirs.

+33 3 25 38 31 00

86/100

---

strawberry coulis. Well-balanced, supple palate showing more of the expressive, persistent fruit dimension. A soft style pairing with desserts. Price approx.: 20,00 EUR
http://www.champagne-bauchet.fr
Champagne Bauchet
+33 (0)3 26 58 92 12

CHAMPAGNE BEAUMONT DES CRAYÈRES   86/100
▼ ♪ Brut Grand rosé : Deep orange with copper highlights. Profound, honest nose intermixing red fruits and candied citrus. Generous, mellow and fruit-driven palate. Lovely focus and persistency. A food-friendly Champagne. Price approx.: 24,60 EUR
http://www.champagne-beaumont.com
Champagne Beaumont des Crayères
+33 (0)3 26 55 29 40

CHAMPAGNE CHARLES COLLIN   86/100
▼ ♪ Brut rosé : Deep orange-pink. Expressive fruity nose recalling ripe strawberry. Full-bodied, vinous yet also fresh palate. A well-structured, aromatic rosé Champagne showing a lovely crunchy finish. Serve preferably with pudding.
Price approx.: 19,00 EUR
http://www.champagne-charles-collin.fr
Champagne Charles Collin
+33 (0)3 25 38 31 00

CHAMPAGNE CHARLES ELLNER   86/100
▼ ♪ Brut rosé : Clean pink. Fruity nose revealing cherry perfumes. Full-bodied, vinous and perfumed on the palate showing lovely honesty. Freshness frames the whole. Will fully reveal itself with a sit-down meal or nibbles. Price approx.: 19,00 EUR
http://www.champagne-ellner.com
Champagne Charles Ellner
+33 (0)3 26 55 60 25

CHAMPAGNE DANY FÈVRE   86/100
▼ ♪ Brut rosé : Attractive orange-pink hue. Focused, profound nose suggestive of cherry and

strawberry. The palate combines full body, vinosity and freshness enhancing the same fruit aromas. Works best with food or as a pudding Champagne. Price approx.: 14,70 EUR
Champagne Dany Fèvre
+33 (0)3 25 38 76 63

CHAMPAGNE DENIS ROBERT   86/100
▼ ♪ Brut Cuvée Rosé : Bright, clean pink. Endearing nose of red fruits enhanced by floral notes. The palate is fresh and marries the same delightful aromas. A very refreshing, enjoyable aperitif-style rosé Champagne.
Price approx.: 15,50 EUR
www.roberdelph.fr
Champagne Roberdelph
+33 (0)3 23 82 11 74

CHAMPAGNE J.M TISSIER   86/100
▼ ♪ Brut rosé : Attractive orange hue. Focused nose reminiscent of orange biscuit with red fruit notes. Full, closely-integrated palate suported by savoury freshness enhancing the fruit. A pleasant rosé Champagne working well from the aperitif onwards. Price approx.: 16,20 EUR
www.champagne-jm-tissier.com
Champagne J.M Tissier
+33 (0)3 26 54 17 47

CHAMPAGNE LECLERC BRIANT   86/100
Org▼ ♪ Brut rosé : Light coppery orange. The nose opens up to notes of orange biscuit, gingerbread, rum baba and dried fruits. Full, lush palate showing more of the same aromatics. Lovely fresh, upright and firmer mineral finish. Price approx.: 30,60 EUR
www.leclercbriant.com
Champagne Leclerc Briant
+33 (0)3 26 54 45 33

> Detailed instructions are featured
> at the start of the book.

CHAMPAGNE NOËL LEBLOND-LENOIR — 86/100

▼ ♪ Brut Rosé Cuvé : Deeply-coloured light red. Honest nose showcasing cherry aromas. Full-bodied, well-structured palate displaying a lovely combination of vinosity and freshness. A robust rosé Champagne boasting a wonderful personality. A marvellous partner for red meats.
Price approx.: 14,80 EUR
Champagne Noël Leblond-Lenoir
+33 (0)3 25 38 53 33

CHAMPAGNE PIOT SÉVILLANO — 86/100

▼ ♪ Brut rosé : Deep orangy-pink. Enticing, focused nose blending white-fleshed fruits and ripe strawberry. A fleshy, full-bodied style framed by freshness with clearly-delineated fruit expression. Clean, perfumed and drinking well from the aperitif
Price approx.: 16,80 EUR
http://www.piot-sevillano.com
EARL Piot Sevillano
+33 (0)3 26 58 23 88

CHAMPAGNE ANDRÉ ROBERT — 86/100

▼ ♪ Brut Cuvée Séduction 2007 : Deep golden hue. Mature nose blending dried fruit notes, a vegetal touch and a patisserie dimension after swirling. On the palate, a lush, rich style nicely balanced by beautiful exuberance. A Champagne for food, pairing with white meats.
Price approx.: 23,60 EUR
http://www.champagne-andre-robert.com
Champagne André Robert
+33 (0)3 26 57 59 41

CHAMPAGNE BAUCHET PÈRE — 86/100

▼ ♪ Brut 1er cru Signature : Light yellow. The nose opens up to fruit notes, citrus, pineapple and a subtle touch of pastry. Full palate with a fine, closely-integrated texture and lovely persistent freshness. More of the same ripe, focused aromas that linger.
Price approx.: 18,90 EUR
http://www.champagne-bauchet.fr
Champagne Bauchet
+33 (0)3 26 58 92 12

CHAMPAGNE BERNARD ROBERT — 86/100

▼ ♪ Brut blanc de blancs Grande Réserve - Cuvée Le Treizot : Light gold. Extremely refined nose with tones of white flowers, hazelnut and a whiff of toast. Beautiful presence, abundant freshness, perfume and harmony on the palate. Creamy effervescence frames the finish.
Price approx.: 16,50 EUR
http://www.champagne-robert-voigny.com
Champagne Bernard Robert
+33 (0)3 25 27 11 53

CHAMPAGNE BOREL-LUCAS — 86/100

▼ ♪ Brut Art Divin : Light yellow. Delicate nose blending floral notes and fresh butter aromas. Good presence on the palate, a mouth-coating, fresh style showing lovely fine bubbles. The finish takes on a tangy character revealing lemony and biscuit notes.
Price approx.: 15,50 EUR
http://wwwchampagne-borel-lucas.com
Champagne Borel-Lucas
+33 (0)3 26 59 30 46

CHAMPAGNE CHARLES MIGNON — 86/100

▼ ♪ Brut 1er cru Premium Réserve : Light gold. The nose marries notes of white fruits with vegetal touches and menthol accents. The palate is very mellow at point of entry with a freshness that highlights invigorating fruity aromas. A refreshing Champagne for sharing. Price approx.: 25,00 EUR
http://www.champagne-mignon.fr
Champagne Charles Mignon
+33 (0)3 26 58 33 33

CHAMPAGNE CHASSENAY D'ARCE — 86/100

▼ ♪ Brut 2005 : Light gold. Focused fruity nose displaying a lovely youthfulness. Beautiful fleshy, focused and well-integrated attack. Fairly persistent, fresh mid-palate driven by fruit. A well-made dry Champagne showing lovely honesty.
http://www.chassenay.com
Champagne Chassenay d'Arce
+33 (0)3 25 38 34 75

CHAMPAGNE COLLARD-PICARD — 86/100

▼ ♪ Brut Cuvée Prestige : Light yellow-gold. Delightful, focused nose blending fruity and lemony notes. The same aromas carry through to the palate which is lively, tangy almost and shows a lovely fine-grained texture and persistency. A highly perfumed dry Champagne. Price approx.: 23,00 EUR
www.champagnecollardpicard.fr
Champagne Collard-Picard
+33 (0)3 26 52 36 93

CHAMPAGNE CUPERLY — 86/100

▼ ♪ Brut grand cru Grande Réserve : Attractive light yellow. Pleasant focused nose blending fruit character with almond and barley water. Good staying power, fleshy attack with refined, closely-integrated bubbles and lovely long-lasting freshness. A well-made dry Champagne for the aperitif.
Price approx.: 16,10 EUR
http://www.champagne-cuperly.com
Champagne Cuperly
+33 (0)3 26 05 44 60

CHAMPAGNE DANY FÈVRE — 86/100

▼ ♪ Brut Isabelle : Light yellow with green tints. Delightful, refined nose opening up to notes of

freshly-cut grass, white flowers and white-fleshed fruits. Beautiful presence, fullness and fat on the palate. A soft Champagne framed by freshness.
Price approx.: 15,60 EUR
Champagne Dany Fèvre
+33 (0)3 25 38 76 63

CHAMPAGNE DE CASTELLANE 86/100

▼ ♪ Brut : Light gold. Endearing nose blending white-fleshed fruit and citrus with biscuity aromas. Well-balanced palate that is fleshy yet fresh with the same aromas carrying through. A classic dry Champagne that makes a perfect appetiser.
Price approx.: 20,00 EUR
www.castellane.com
Champagne de Castellane
+33 (0)3 26 51 19 19

CHAMPAGNE DOM CAUDRON 86/100

▼ ♪ Brut Cuvée Cornalyne : Limpid pale gold. Ripe nose intermingling white fruits and patisserie tones. On the palate, a full, easy-drinking Champagne with upfront fruit expression. Lovely freshness and a degree of persistence on the finish.
Price approx.: 30,70 EUR
http://www.domcaudron.fr
Champagne Dom Caudron
+33 (0)3 26 52 45 17

CHAMPAGNE DUMÉNIL 86/100

▼ ♪ Brut 2005 : Light gold. Mature, refined nose with aromas of yellow-fleshed fruits and pastries. Good staying power, a full, fleshy and well-integrated style with freshness emphasising the fruit character. A 2005 still in its youth, drinking well as an aperitif. Price approx.: 25,50 EUR
www.champagne-dumenil.com
Champagne Duménil
+33 (0)3 26 03 44 48

CHAMPAGNE FOREST-MARIÉ 86/100

▼ ♪ Brut 1er Cru Cuvée St-Crespin : Light gold. Endearing fruity nose reminiscent of cherry flesh and raspberry. Full-bodied, mellow and delicious with more of the same focused fruit framed by freshness. A party-style Champagne, drinking well as an aperitif or late into the evening.
Price approx.: 16,00 EUR
Champagne Forest-Marié
+33 (0)3 26 03 13 23

CHAMPAGNE FRÉDÉRIC MALÉTREZ 86/100

▼ ♪ Brut 1er cru Sélection 2008 : Light gold. Mature nose with ripe fruity accents of stewed apple and subtle pastry notes in the background. Full palate with a generous, mellow and creamy attack

leading into a lively mid-palate imparting freshness.
Price approx.: 19,55 EUR
Champagne Maletrez Frédéric
+33 (0)3 26 97 63 92

CHAMPAGNE GUY CHARBAUT 86/100

▼ ♪ Brut 1er cru Cuvée de réserve : Light gold. Subdued nose opening up after swirling to pleasant notes of stone fruits. The palate shows seductively fine bubbles, exuberance and freshness. A classic, honest dry Champagne, drinking well as an aperitif. Price approx.: 22,00 EUR
http://www.champagne-guy-charbaut.com
Champagne Guy Charbaut
+33 (0)3 26 52 60 59

CHAMPAGNE J. M. GOBILLARD & FILS 86/100

▼ ♪ Brut Tradition : Light gold. Instantly accessible, focused nose showing upfront white-fleshed fruit. Clean, fleshy and fruity attack leading into a forthright mid-palate bursting with freshness. A nicely crafted dry Champagne that works well as an aperitif or for a party. Price approx.: 15,25 EUR
http://www.champagne-gobillard.com
Champagne J. M. Gobillard & fils
+33 (0)3 26 51 00 24

CHAMPAGNE J.M TISSIER 86/100

▼ ♪ Brut Réserve : Light yellow. The nose opens up to floral notes with a touch of white-fleshed fruits. Full, mellow palate with a fine-grained texture. Fat on the attack flows into a more nervy mid-palate with faint lemony accents. A compelling Champagne for the aperitif.
Price approx.: 16,00 EUR
www.champagne-jm-tissier.com
Champagne J.M Tissier
+33 (0)3 26 54 17 47

CHAMPAGNE J.M TISSIER 86/100

▼ ♪ Brut Apollon 2006 : Yellow-gold. Mature nose opening up to dried fruits then revealing lightly toasted perfumes. Rich, full-bodied and mouth-filling palate counterbalanced by savoury freshness. A generous yet lively Champagne.
Price approx.: 20,90 EUR
www.champagne-jm-tissier.com
Champagne J.M Tissier
+33 (0)3 26 54 17 47

Prices mentioned in this book are guideline and can vary depending on point of sale.
The shops, wineries or publisher
can in no way be held responsible for this.

CHAMPAGNE JACQUINOT & FILS — 86/100

▼ ♪ Brut Private Cuvée : Light yellow. Ripe fruit on the nose halfway between peach and pineapple. Clean at point of entry, a fleshy, fresh and closely-integrated style with lovely long-lasting aromas. A beautifully crafted dry Champagne for the aperitif.
Price approx.: 20,00 EUR
http://www.champagne-jacquinot.com
Champagne Jacquinot & Fils
+33 (0)3 26 54 36 81

CHAMPAGNE JEAN MICHEL PELLETIER — 86/100

▼ ♪ Brut Cuvée Origine : Light gold. Focused, endearing nose dominated by apricot flesh and white-fleshed fruits. Good staying power on the palate. Closely-integrated, fleshy attack leading into a fresh mid-palate with lengthy focused fruit expression. Trace of exuberance on the
Price approx.: 17,30 EUR
http://www.champagnejean-michelpelletier.fr
Champagne Jean-Michel Pelletier
+33 (0)3 26 52 65 86

CHAMPAGNE JEAN VALENTIN — 86/100

▼ ♪ Brut blanc de blancs 1er cru Saint Avertin : Light yellow. Refined, delicately mineral nose backed by white flowers and white-fleshed fruits. Good balance between vinosity and freshness. A full-bodied, well-structured Blanc de Blancs displaying wonderful personality.
Price approx.: 15,50 EUR
Champagne Jean Valentin & fils
+33 (0)3 26 49 21 91

CHAMPAGNE JEAN VELUT — 86/100

▼ ♪ Brut blanc de blancs : Light yellow. Subdued nose delivering mineral perfumes, white fruit and pastry aromas. Good presence, fullness and fat on the palate. A Blanc de Blancs that is well-structured yet mellow and shows persistent aromatics. Serve as an appetiser.
Price approx.: 17,80 EUR
http://www.champagne-velut.fr
Champagne Jean Velut
+33 (0)3 25 74 83 31

CHAMPAGNE JEAN-POL HAUTBOIS — 86/100

▼ ♪ Brut Grande Réserve : Bright pale yellow. Focused nose revealing refined lemony and brioche notes. Fine-grained texture and evident exuberance on the palate. Closely-integrated and full. Excellent fruit-driven persistency. An appealing, aperitif-style dry Champagne.
http://www.champagne-hautbois.com
Champagne Hautbois Jean-Pol
+33 (0)3 26 48 20 98

CHAMPAGNE LOUIS DOUSSET — 86/100

▼ ♪ Brut Original : Light gold. Endearing, focused nose with upfront white-fleshed fruits and a lemony touch. Clean, closely-integrated, fruit-driven attack. Texture and fine bubbles are perceptible mid-palate framed by freshness. A lovely dry Champagne for the aperitif.
Price approx.: 17,50 EUR
http://www.louis-dousset.com/
Champagne Louis Dousset
+33 (0)3 26 83 99 08

CHAMPAGNE MICHEL MAILLIARD — 86/100

▼ ♪ Brut Cuvée Prestige 2008 : Light yellow with green tints. Delightful nose blending white flowers and elegant vegetal notes of almond. The palate has good staying power and shows a lovely lively structure, fine texture and length. A fresh, clean style, perfect for whetting the appet
Price approx.: 24,00 EUR
http://www.champagne-michel-mailliard.com
Champagne Michel Mailliard
+33 (0)3 26 52 15 18

CHAMPAGNE MONTAUDON — 86/100

▼ ♪ Brut 2002 : Attractive yellow-gold. Mature nose suggestive of dried fruits with pastry and toast notes. Invigorating attack on the palate with noticeable perfume. Delicious mid-palate and finish showing mature aromatics.
Price approx.: 22,93 EUR
www.champagnemontaudon.com
Champagne Montaudon
+33 (0)3 26 07 88 40

CHAMPAGNE MONTAUDON — 86/100

▼ ♪ Brut Réserve Première : Light yellow. Focused, endearing nose of white fruits with subtle patisserie tones. Lively attack with fairly creamy effervescence emphasising the same perfumes with a pleasant toast tone on the finish. A beautiful, very invigorating Champagne.
Price approx.: 19,26 EUR
www.champagnemontaudon.com
Champagne Montaudon
+33 (0)3 26 07 88 40

CHAMPAGNE NOËL LEBLOND-LENOIR — 86/100

▼ ♪ Brut Cuvée Prestige : Light yellow with green tints. Endearing nose blending notes of almond and citrus then opening up to slightly creamy, toast notes. Full, closely-integrated attack with fine bubbles leading into a nervy mid-palate with lemony accents. A lively, perfumed st
Price approx.: 15,60 EUR
Champagne Noël Leblond-Lenoir
+33 (0)3 25 38 53 33

CHAMPAGNE NOMINÉ-RENARD 86/100

▼ ♪ Brut : Light yellow. Pleasant nose with floral and fruity perfumes backed by toast. Supple and fleshy at point of entry, a mellow, fresh style with persistent aromas. A good dry Champagne for the aperitif.
Price approx.: 16,00 EUR
http://www.champagne-nomine-renard.com
Champagne Nominé-Renard
+33 (0)3 26 52 82 60

CHAMPAGNE PALMER & CO 86/100

▼ ♪ Brut Réserve : Light yellow. Endearing, focused nose intermixing white-fleshed fruits, subtle lemony notes and a creamy touch. Well-balanced palate showing a lovely fleshy attack and freshness. Delicious fruit-driven entry with a faint vegetal trace on the finish.
Price approx.: 27,00 EUR
www.champagne-palmer.fr
Champagne Palmer & Co
+33 (0)3 26 07 35 07

CHAMPAGNE PANNIER 86/100

▼ ♪ Brut Sélection : Light gold. Focused nose opening up to fruity, creamy notes. More of the milky character with notes of milk bread on the palate which is round and mellow yet fresh. Drink as an aperitif.
Price approx.: 25,00 EUR
http://www.champagnepannier.com
Champagne Pannier
+33 (0)3 23 69 51 30

CHAMPAGNE PASCAL MAZET 86/100

▼ ♪ Brut 1er cru Tradition : Golden hue. Pleasant nose showing aromas of ripe raspberry and white-fleshed fruits. Delicious fleshy, fresh palate displaying lovely aromatic honesty and persistency. A nicely crafted dry Champagne for the aperitif or parties.
Price approx.: 16,50 EUR
http://www.champagne-mazet.com
Champagne Pascal Mazet
+33 (0)3 26 03 41 13

CHAMPAGNE PASCAL MAZET 86/100

▼ ♪ Brut 1er cru Grande Réserve : Deep golden hue. Mature nose dominated by dried fruits. Full-bodied, generous, rich and well-structured palate. A distinctive, expressive style that works well as a food wine with, say, poultry.
Price approx.: 23,00 EUR
http://www.champagne-mazet.com
Champagne Pascal Mazet
+33 (0)3 26 03 41 13

CHAMPAGNE PAUL LAURENT 86/100

▼ ♪ Brut Cuvée Prestige - L'Essentiel : Light yellow. The nose blends fruit character (white-fleshed fruits, touch of dried fruits) with vegetal nuances. Full, powerful and vinous style on the palate with a lovely mellow attack. Livelier mid-palate. A dry Champagne for the aperitif.
Price approx.: 19,00 EUR
http://www.champagnepaullaurent.com
Champagne Paul Laurent
+33 (0)3 26 81 91 11

CHAMPAGNE PIOT-SÉVILLANO 86/100

▼ ♪ Brut Cuvée Elégance : Beautiful light yellow hue. Focused nose showing delicate fruit (apple flesh) and refined lemony notes. The palate displays a lively, closely-integrated personality with refined bubbles and fruity aromas. Works well as an aperitif with fish-based nibbles.
Price approx.: 25,00 EUR
http://www.piot-sevillano.com
EARL Piot Sevillano
+33 (0)3 26 58 23 88

CHAMPAGNE ROYER PÈRE & FILS 86/100

▼ ♪ Brut blanc de blancs : Light yellow with green tints. The nose opens up to white flower and almond notes with fruit undercurrents. More of the same delightful aromatics on the palate which is lively and fresh with a lovely fine texture. Crisp finish bordering on lemony.
Price approx.: 15,50 EUR
www.champagne-royer.com
Champagne Royer père & fils
+33 (0)3 25 38 52 16

CHAMPAGNE STÉPHANE COQUILLETTE 86/100

▼ ♪ Brut blanc de noirs grand cru Les Clés : Light gold. Enticing fruity nose of cherry and plum flesh. Full-bodied palate displaying good balance of vinosity and freshness with lovely precise fruit aromas. A well-crafted Blanc de Noirs pairing with nibbles or a meal.
Price approx.: 20,80 EUR
Champagne Stéphane Coquillette
+33 (0)3 26 51 74 12

CHAMPAGNE TROUILLARD 86/100

▼ ♪ Brut Extra Sélection : Light gold. Endearing nose focusing on red and white-fleshed fruits. A degree of vinosity and body on the palate yet also wonderful exuberance imparting a forthright, persistent edge. A classic dry Champagne with good staying power. Price approx.: 17,10 EUR
http://www.champagne-trouillard.fr
Champagne Trouillard
+33 (0)3 26 55 37 55

CHAMPAGNE VEUVE DOUSSOT 86/100

▼ ♪ Brut Cuvée Ernestine 2009 : Light yellow-gold. Delicate focused fruit on the nose. The palate centres on exuberance and nervousness. A lively, upright style yet too green. Rejected.
Price approx.: 18,50 EUR
http://www.champagneveuvedoussot.com
Champagne Veuve Doussot
+33 (0)3 25 29 60 61

CHAMPAGNE CHRISTIAN BOURMAULT 85/100

▼ ♪ Extra brut Lettre à Terre : Beautiful light gold. Distinctive, mature nose intermixing overripe fruits and patisserie notes. Warmth and vinosity on the palate. A mellow, lush style capped off with a fresher note. A characterful Champagne that works best with food. Price approx.: 19,35 EUR
Champagne Christian Bourmault
+33 (0)3 26 59 79 41

CHAMPAGNE PASCAL MAZET 85/100

▼ ♪ Extra brut 1er cru : Golden hue. Expressive nose blending ripe red fruits, dried fruits and a mineral dimension. Good framework on the palate with a full, fresh attack leading into a structured mid-palate displaying a pleasant touch of firmness. A characterful Extra dry.
Price approx.: 18,00 EUR
http://www.champagne-mazet.com
Champagne Pascal Mazet
+33 (0)3 26 03 41 13

CHAMPAGNE PANNIER 85/100

▼ ♪ demi-sec Séduction : Light yellow-gold. Focused, expressive nose with accents of white-fleshed fruits and lemon. The nose aromatics carry through to the palate, enhanced by brioche notes. Evident mildness is framed by freshness. A deftly-crafted medium dry Champagne.
Price approx.: 25,00 EUR
http://www.champagnepannier.com
Champagne Pannier
+33 (0)3 23 69 51 30

CHAMPAGNE ANDREANI BESNIER 85/100

▼ ♪ Brut rosé : Orange-pink. Pleasant fruity nose suggestive of ripe raspberry and fresh strawberry. Fleshy attack with crunchy fruit. Fresh, perfumed mid-palate showing substantial persistency. A delicious, balanced rosé Champagne, enjoyable from the aperitif to dessert. Price approx.: 18,00 EUR
Andreani Besnier
+33 (0)447917992718

CHAMPAGNE BONNET GILMERT 85/100

▼ ♪ Brut rosé 1er cru Grand Assemblage : Lovely orange hue. Expressive nose revealing notes of apple flesh and ripe red fruits after swirling. Full, generous and closely-integrated palate. A fairly rich style, nicely balanced by focused fruit and a touch of freshness.
Price approx.: 18,00 EUR
www.champagne-bonnet-gilmert.com
Champagne Bonnet Gilmert
+33 (0)3 26 59 49 47

CHAMPAGNE CHARLES MIGNON 85/100

▼ ♪ Brut rosé 1er cru Premium Réserve : Orange-pink. Focused fruity nose showing accents of ripe strawberry. Clean attack on the palate with very precise fruity aromas. A simple, accessible and refreshing style. Set aside for the aperitif or dessert.
Price approx.: 30,00 EUR
http://www.champagne-mignon.fr
Champagne Charles Mignon
+33 (0)3 26 58 33 33

CHAMPAGNE J. M. GOBILLARD & FILS 85/100

▼ ♪ Brut rosé : Attractive light salmon-pink. Honest nose showing fruity accents of apple and red fruits. More of the same honesty on the palate which is well-balanced, fleshy and fresh. A rosé Champagne that is ideally suited to the aperitif.
Price approx.: 17,20 EUR
http://www.champagne-gobillard.com
Champagne J. M. Gobillard & fils
+33 (0)3 26 51 00 24

CHAMPAGNE JEAN MICHEL PELLETIER 85/100

▼ ♪ Brut rosé : Deep orange. Expressive fruity nose suggestive of orange biscuit. Full-bodied, generous, well-structured and nicely balanced palate with the same focused fruit aromas carrying through. Serve well-chilled as an appetiser or at a warmer temperature with foo
Price approx.: 15,10 EUR
http://www.champagnejean-michelpelletier.fr
Champagne Jean-Michel Pelletier
+33 (0)3 26 52 65 86

CHAMPAGNE BAUCHET PÈRE 85/100

▼ ♪ Brut blanc de blancs 1er cru Cuvée Saint-Nicaise 2007 : Light gold. Distinctive nose marrying chalk notes, white fruits and a pastry touch. The palate is invigorating and boasts creamy effervescence. The finish is harmonious, crisp and delicious. A wonderful aperitif-style Champagne.
Price approx.: 25,00 EUR
http://www.champagne-bauchet.fr
Champagne Bauchet
+33 (0)3 26 58 92 12

CHAMPAGNE BAUCHET PÈRE 85/100

▼ ♪ Brut Origine : Beautiful light yellow with golden highlights. Focused, endearing nose

blending lemony and biscuit notes. Good staying power on the palate with a savoury fleshy attack, exuberance and freshness. A compelling Champagne for the aperitif.
Price approx.: 16,95 EUR
http://www.champagne-bauchet.fr
Champagne Bauchet
+33 (0)3 26 58 92 12

CHAMPAGNE BEAUMONT DES CRAYÈRES 85/100

▼ ♪ Brut Grande Réserve : Golden hue. The nose opens up to white-fleshed fruit notes with a touch of dried straw. Fairly full-bodied, clean and mellow palate showing lovely fullness and a fresh finish. Well-balanced. A classic dry Champagne for the aperitif. Price approx.: 21,40 EUR
http://www.champagne-beaumont.com
Champagne Beaumont des Crayères
+33 (0)3 26 55 29 40

CHAMPAGNE BLONDEL 85/100

▼ ♪ Brut 1er cru Carte d'Or : Light gold. Focused, endearing nose centring on fruit with a subdued brioche touch in the background. Fleshy, perfumed attack leading into a very fresh mid-palate. A full-bodied yet nervy dry Champagne. Fruity, persistent and perfect for whetting the appe
Price approx.: 15,90 EUR
http://www.champagneblondel.com
Champagne Blondel
+33 (0)3 26 03 43 92

CHAMPAGNE CHARLES COLLIN 85/100

▼ ♪ Brut Sélection : Golden hue. Focused nose blending red fruits, dried fruits and subtle biscuity notes. Well-balanced palate that is fleshy and lush yet fresh. Good honesty and persistency. Drink as an aperitif or as a party Champagne.
Price approx.: 17,00 EUR
http://www.champagne-charles-collin.fr
Champagne Charles Collin
+33 (0)3 25 38 31 00

CHAMPAGNE CHARLES ELLNER 85/100

▼ ♪ Brut Grande Réserve : Light gold. A mix of ripe fruit notes and pastry touches on the nose. Well-balanced palate with vinosity countered by lovely exuberance. A taut, honest style that works well as an aperitif.
Price approx.: 18,35 EUR
http://www.champagne-ellner.com
Champagne Charles Ellner
+33 (0)3 26 55 60 25

CHAMPAGNE COLLARD-PICARD 85/100

▼ ♪ Brut Cuvée Sélection : Pale gold. Endearing nose of red berry fruits with stewed fruits. Fleshy, full-bodied and crunchy palate with rich fruit nicely balanced by a sensation of freshness. A charming Champagne for the aperitif.
Price approx.: 20,00 EUR
www.champagnecollardpicard.fr
Champagne Collard-Picard
+33 (0)3 26 52 36 93

CHAMPAGNE DANY FÈVRE 85/100

▼ ♪ Brut : Light yellow. Endearing nose with a fruity, lemony and subtly tropical perfume. Lovely texture and fine bubbles, closely-integrated exuberance, persistent fruity character and a touch of sweetness on the finish. A likeable party-style Champagne. Price approx.: 13,70 EUR
Champagne Dany Fèvre
+33 (0)3 25 38 76 63

CHAMPAGNE DE CASTELNAU 85/100

▼ ♪ Brut Réserve : Deep gold. Mature nose suggestive of dried and candied fruits with patisserie notes. Fullness and vinosity on the palate nicely balanced by lingering freshness. A deliciously generous dry Champagne for pairing with nibbles.
Price approx.: 25,56 EUR
http://www.champagne-de-castelnau.eu
Champagne de Castelnau
+33 (0)3 26 77 89 00

CHAMPAGNE DENIS ROBERT 85/100

▼ ♪ Brut Cuvée Tradition : Pale gold. Endearing nose of fresh fruits with a floral note. The palate is clean, crisp and highlights the same delightful fruity aromas. An excellent fresh and persistent aperitif-style Champagne. Price approx.: 14,00 EUR
www.roberdelph.fr
Champagne Roberdelph
+33 (0)3 23 82 11 74

CHAMPAGNE DIDIER DOUÉ 85/100

▼ ♪ Brut Sélection : Light gold. Subdued nose revealing floral and citrus fruit aromas after swirling. Deliciously well-balanced palate showing savoury fruit and freshness. Ideal as an appetiser or for a party. Price approx.: 15,00 EUR
www.champagne-didier-doue.fr
Champagne Didier Doué
+33 (0)3 25 79 44 33

CHAMPAGNE DOM CAUDRON 85/100

▼ ♪ Brut Vieilles Vignes : Light yellow. Nose of extremely fresh white fruits clearly recalling apple and pear. Slightly lively at point of entry yet a fruity mid-palate supported by effervescence. A very pleasurable style focusing on freshness and fruit.
Price approx.: 22,90 EUR
http://www.domcaudron.fr
Champagne Dom Caudron
+33 (0)3 26 52 45 17

CHAMPAGNE DROUILLY L.V. 85/100

▼ ♪ Brut Angéline : Light yellow. Medium focus on the nose with white-fleshed fruits (pear, mirabelle plum) in the background. A vibrant, fleshy style on the palate which reveals more of the same pleasant, persistent fruit. Enjoy as an aperitif.
Price approx.: 18,00 EUR
Champagne Drouilly LV
+33 (0)3 25 29 65 35

CHAMPAGNE EDWIGE FRANÇOIS 85/100

▼ ♪ Brut Tradition : Golden highlights. Pleasant fruity nose of white-fleshed fruits and apricot. Fresh, fleshy palate showing a lovely fruit bouquet. An honest style Champagne leaving a natural impression. Perfect for the aperitif.
Price approx.: 14,20 EUR
http://www.champagnefrancais.fr
Champagne Edwige François
+33 (0)3 23 82 11 26

CHAMPAGNE GERMAR BRETON 85/100

▼ ♪ Brut Blanc de Blancs : Beautiful light yellow. Refined nose blending a floral character with delicate lemony touches. Lovely freshness, refined texture and aromatic precision on the palate. A very fresh, focused Blanc de Blancs, perfect for whetting the appetite. Price approx.: 14,00 EUR
Champagne Germar Breton
+33 (0)3 25 27 73 03

CHAMPAGNE H. GOUTORBE 85/100

▼ ♪ Brut Cuvée Tradition : Light gold. Mature nose revealing perfumes of dried fruits and biscuit after swirling. Clean, fruit-driven attack leading into a lively mid-palate showing a degree of firmness and biscuit and smoke aromas. Drink as an appetiser.
Price approx.: 15,25 EUR
www.champagne-henri-goutorbe.com
Champagne Henri Goutorbe
+33 (0)3 26 55 21 70

CHAMPAGNE HUGUENOT-TASSIN 85/100

▼ ♪ Brut Cuvée Réserve : Light yellow-gold. The nose blends a fruity dimension with creamy notes. A harmonious, full and silky style on the palate which is fat yet fresh. A dry Champagne with good staying power that would sit nicely alongside fish-based nibbles. Price approx.: 15,20 EUR
http://www.huguenot-tassin.com
Champagne Huguenot-Tassin
+33 (0)3 25 38 54 49

CHAMPAGNE J.L GOULARD-GÉRARD 85/100

▼ ♪ Brut 2008 : Light yellow. Honest nose suggestive of white-fleshed fruits with subtle biscuit notes. Well-balanced, closely-integrated palate.

Fleshy attack with upfront fruit leading into a fresh mid-palate. Serve as an aperitif or for a party.
Price approx.: 18,00 EUR
Champagne Jean Luc Goulard Gérard
+33 (0)3 26 03 18 78

CHAMPAGNE JACQUES COPIN 85/100

▼ ♪ Brut Tradition : Brilliant light yellow. Focused fruity nose blending white-fleshed fruits and lemony notes. Freshness and exuberance take centre stage on the palate. The same lemon aromas carry through over good length. A lively Champagne for whetting the appetite. Price approx.: 15,00 EUR
www.champagne-jacques-copin.com
Champagne Jacques Copin
+33 (0)3 26 52 92 47

CHAMPAGNE JACQUINOT & FILS 85/100

▼ ♪ Brut blanc de blancs : Light yellow. Focused nose revealing perfumes of white flowers, brioche and a delicate lemony touch. The palate shows seductive freshness and refined bubbles.Fairly lively mid-palate and finish capped off with a hint of firmness. Price approx.: 22,00 EUR
http://www.champagne-jacquinot.com
Champagne Jacquinot & Fils
+33 (0)3 26 54 36 81

CHAMPAGNE JEAN VALENTIN 85/100

▼ ♪ Brut rosé 1er cru : Light red. Expressive nose recalling red fruit pulp (cherry). Fairly crunchy, fleshy attack showing more of the same focused aromas. Delightful and honest. Would work well as a pudding Champagne with a red fruit tart.
Price approx.: 14,75 EUR
Champagne Jean Valentin & fils
+33 (0)3 26 49 21 91

CHAMPAGNE JEAN VALENTIN 85/100

▼ ♪ Brut 2008 : Light yellow-gold. The nose reveals pleasurable floral and fruity notes (lemon) with fresh butter. Lovely texture, refined bubbles, freshness and persistency on the palate. The lemony aromas are augmented by a faint milky touch.
Price approx.: 15,60 EUR
Champagne Jean Valentin & fils
+33 (0)3 26 49 21 91

CHAMPAGNE JEAN VELUT 85/100

▼ ♪ Brut : Light yellow. Expressive nose showing suggestions of fresh almond and white flowers. Seductive, polished palate that is fresh yet fleshy. More of the same clean, persistent aromas. An appealing dry Champagne for the aperitif.
Price approx.: 15,00 EUR
http://www.champagne-velut.fr
Champagne Jean Velut
+33 (0)3 25 74 83 31

CHAMPAGNE JEAN-MARC VATEL 85/100

▼ ✦ Brut Cuvée Vieilles Vignes 2007 : Limpid, light gold. Ripe nose blending white fruits with a more candied dimension bordering on pastry. The same aromas carry through to the palate which shows fine effervescence and very ripe aromas. Beautiful freshness on the finish supports the whole.
Price approx.: 19,80 EUR
http://www.champagnevatel.fr
Champagne Jean Marc Vatel
+33 (0)3 26 52 94 67

CHAMPAGNE LIONEL CARREAU 85/100

▼ ✦ Brut Cuvée Préembulles : Light gold. Expressive nose focusing on honey notes and toast perfumes. Full, lush palate with mellowness the key theme. A sensation of freshness and faint bitterness lingering on the finish balances the whole. An unusual offering. Price approx.: 23,00 EUR
Champagne Lionel Carreau
+33 (0)3 25 38 57 27

CHAMPAGNE MALARD 85/100

▼ ✦ Brut blanc de noirs grand cru Excellence : Pale gold with golden highlights. The nose reveals fruity scents of grape and stone fruits. Full-bodied, generous and well-structured palate with vinosity balanced by a touch of freshness. A style that complements food and works with nibbles.
Price approx.: 28,00 EUR
http://www.champagnemalard.com
Champagne Malard
+33 (0)3 26 32 40 11

CHAMPAGNE MATHELIN 85/100

▼ ✦ Brut Prestige 2009 : Limpid, light gold. Appealing, focused nose with accents of dried flowers and fruits showing beautiful finesse. The palate is rich yet nervy with creamy effervescence framing the whole. More of the extremely aromatic Chardonnay character on the finish.
Price approx.: 20,10 EUR
http://www.champagne-mathelin.com
Champagne Mathelin
+33 (0)3 26 52 73 58

CHAMPAGNE MICHEL MAILLIARD 85/100

▼ ✦ Brut Mont Vergon 2005 : Light gold. Mature, ripe nose halfway between tropical fruits (pineapple) and a vegetal dimension (artichoke) backed by a touch of pastry. Well-structured palate. Full, generous and well-integrated attack. Nice fresh, firmer finish. Serve preferably with
Price approx.: 27,00 EUR
http://www.champagne-michel-mailliard.com
Champagne Michel Mailliard
+33 (0)3 26 52 15 18

CHAMPAGNE NICOLAS FEUILLATTE 85/100

▼ ✦ Brut Grande Réserve : Alluring pale gold. A mix of white-fleshed fruits, white flowers and vegetal notes on the nose. Generous, powerful and closely-integrated attack flowing into a livelier mid-palate. Hint of sourness on the finish revealing more of the vegetal nose aromatic
Price approx.: 24,90 EUR
http://www.feuillatte.com
Champagne Nicolas Feuillatte
+33 (0)3 26 59 55 50

CHAMPAGNE NICOLAS FEUILLATTE 85/100

▼ ✦ Brut : Brilliant, pale yellow-gold. Clean fruity nose suggestive of apple flesh and mirabelle plum. Fleshy attack with refined bubbles. Lively, forthright and well-balanced across the palate with the fruity nose aromatics recurring. A dry aperitif-style Champagne. Price approx.: 18,90 EUR
http://www.feuillatte.com
Champagne Nicolas Feuillatte
+33 (0)3 26 59 55 50

CHAMPAGNE PASCAL DEVILLIERS 85/100

▼ ✦ Brut 1er cru Tradition 2009 : Light gold. Expressive nose blending fruity notes, pastry touches and a slightly smoky sensation. Full, mellow and supple attack leading into an upright, lively mid-palate. A persistent, characterful Champagne that is perfect for the aperitif.
Price approx.: 13,50 EUR
www.champagne-devilliers.com
Champagne Pascal Devilliers
+33 (0)3 26 49 26 08

CHAMPAGNE PASCAL LEBLOND-LENOIR 85/100

▼ ✦ Brut 2009 : Light yellow. Endearing nose of mirabelle plums, red fruits and pleasant pastry notes. Full, closely-integrated, fresh and fruit-driven attack. More upright, firmer mid-palate with slightly smoky accents. Price approx.: 15,20 EUR
Champagne Leblond Lenoir Pascal
+33 (0)3 25 38 54 04

CHAMPAGNE PASCAL LEBLOND-LENOIR 85/100

▼ ✦ Brut Désir de Matthieu : Light yellow. Endearing fruity nose of white-fleshed fruits enhanced by subtle brioche touches. Full, fleshy, fresh and closely-integrated attack. A delicious, vibrant style that works best as an aperitif.
Price approx.: 14,70 EUR
Champagne Leblond Lenoir Pascal
+33 (0)3 25 38 54 04

> Detailed instructions are featured
> at the start of the book.

CHAMPAGNE PAUL LAURENT   85/100

▼ ♪ Brut Cuvée du Fondateur - Réserve : Light gold. Honest, endearing nose showing pronounced pear flesh and red fruit aromas. Rich, full palate with crunchy fruit. Mellow on the attack leading into a firmer mid-palate and finish. A characterful dry Champagne with seductive fruit perfumes.
Price approx.: 17,00 EUR
http://www.champagnepaullaurent.com
Champagne Paul Laurent
+33 (0)3 26 81 91 11

CHAMPAGNE PIERRE MIGNON   85/100

▼ ♪ Brut Prestige : Light gold. Endearing nose blending fruit character with brioche and patisserie notes. Full-bodied, ample palate with a full, generous attack. A livelier mid-palate reveals more of the fruity nose character (stewed apple). A characterful Champagne.
Price approx.: 17,50 EUR
http://www.pierre-mignon.com
Champagne Pierre Mignon
+33 (0)3 26 59 22 03

CHAMPAGNE PIOT-SÉVILLANO   85/100

▼ ♪ Brut Prestige : Deeply-coloured golden yellow. Distinctive, expressive nose focusing on patisserie and pastry notes with dried fruit. Lovely volume and richness on the palate nicely counterbalanced by a sensation of lingering freshness. Lush and perfumed in style. Price approx.: 18,90 EUR
http://www.piot-sevillano.com
EARL Piot Sevillano
+33 (0)3 26 58 23 88

CHAMPAGNE POINTILLART & FILS   85/100

▼ ♪ Brut 1er cru : Pale gold. Focused nose opening up to fruity notes of mirabelle and greengage plums. Full-bodied, vinous palate. Lush attack leading into a more structured mid-palate and finish with fruit driving the whole. A characterful Champagne.
Price approx.: 13,80 EUR
http://www.champagnepointillartetfils.com
Champagne Pointillart & fils
+33 (0)3 26 49 74 95

CHAMPAGNE ROYER PÈRE & FILS   85/100

▼ ♪ Brut Réserve : Light gold. Honest nose showing floral and fruity aromas. Full, mellow attack with fine bubbles flowing into a fleshy, fresh mid-palate. A deftly crafted dry Champagne that works well as an appetiser.
Price approx.: 14,75 EUR
www.champagne-royer.com
Champagne Royer père & fils
+33 (0)3 25 38 52 16

CHAMPAGNE RUFFIN ET FILS   85/100

▼ ♪ Brut L'Ame de Jean - vinifiée en fût de chêne : Light gold. Refined nose intermixing white-fleshed fruits, a subdued oak touch and subtle mild tobacco. The palate is fleshy and mellow yet also lively, nervy and highly perfumed with a crisp finish driven by lemony aromas. Will wake up your taste buds!
Price approx.: 40,00 EUR
www.champagnes-ruffin.com
Champagne Ruffin & fils
+33 (0)3 26 59 30 14

CHAMPAGNE POTEL-PRIEUX   84/100

▼ ♪ Extra brut Grand Nord : Light yellow-gold. Expressive nose delivering fruit and toast notes after swirling. Forthright, well-balanced palate supported by a sensation of freshness. A vegetal sensation and subtle touch of sourness cap off the whole.
Price approx.: 24,90 EUR
Champagne Potel-Prieux
+33 (0)3 26 58 48 59

CHAMPAGNE HÉNIN-DELOUVIN   84/100

▼ ♪ Brut rosé 1er cru : Attractive deep orange-pink. Delightful nose suggestive of cherries in syrup. The fruit character becomes more assertive on the palate which is fresh yet syrupy. A real treat that we recommend as a pudding Champagne with a red fruit tart.
Price approx.: 16,10 EUR
Champagne Hénin-Delouvin
+33 (0)3 26 54 01 81

CHAMPAGNE MALETREZ FRÉDÉRIC   84/100

▼ ♪ Brut rosé 1er cru : Orange-pink hue. After swirling, the nose delivers perfumes of nicely ripe raspberry and strawberry. More of the same aromas recalling coulis on the palate which is generous and fleshy yet lively. Serve preferably as a pudding Champagne.
Price approx.: 16,70 EUR
Champagne Maletrez Frédéric
+33 (0)3 26 97 63 92

CHAMPAGNE NICOLAS FEUILLATTE   84/100

▼ ♪ Brut rosé : Fairly deep, clean pink. Honest, expressive nose with aromas of cherry and wild strawberry. On the palate, a warm, full-bodied style that is powerful yet mellow with fruity aromas bordering on sweets. Serve preferably as a pudding Champagne.
Price approx.: 31,50 EUR
http://www.feuillatte.com
Champagne Nicolas Feuillatte
+33 (0)3 26 59 55 50

CHAMPAGNE RAINETEAU-GRIMET 84/100

▼ ♪ Brut rosé : Light red with bricking. Expressive nose displaying aromas of grape and black cherry. Vinosity, a sensation of richness and fruit are key themes on the palate. A lush rosé Champagne in a food-friendly style pairing with poultry, for example. Price approx.: 13,80 EUR
Champagne Raineteau-Grimet
+33 (0)3 26 83 90 32

CHAMPAGNE BERNARD ROBERT 84/100

▼ ♪ Brut blanc de blancs : Pale yellow. Distinctive nose marrying white flowers and nuts. Lively, crisp attack on the palate. Evident effervescence makes for a creamier mid-palate. A refreshing style that makes an ideal appetiser. Price approx.: 12,90 EUR
http://www.champagne-robert-voigny.com
Champagne Bernard Robert
+33 (0)3 25 27 11 53

CHAMPAGNE BERNARD ROBERT 84/100

▼ ♪ Brut Réserve : Limpid pale gold. The nose marries floral tones and ripe fruits. On the palate, wonderful full, clean attack leading into a vinous mid-palate and a powerful finish with accents of ripe fruits, bordering on jammy. A very honest Champagne for food. Price approx.: 12,30 EUR
http://www.champagne-robert-voigny.com
Champagne Bernard Robert
+33 (0)3 25 27 11 53

CHAMPAGNE BONNET GILMERT 84/100

▼ ♪ Brut blanc de blancs grand cru Cuvée de Réserve : Yellow-gold. Distinctive nose intermixing ripe fruits, tropical notes and a mineral dimension. Lush, well-structured palate with a creamy texture combining a sensation of richness and freshness. Serve preferably with food.
Price approx.: 17,00 EUR
www.champagne-bonnet-gilmert.com
Champagne Bonnet Gilmert
+33 (0)3 26 59 49 47

CHAMPAGNE BOREL-LUCAS 84/100

▼ ♪ Brut Cuvée de Réserve : Light yellow. Enticing nose blending white flowers, subtle fruit touches and a trace of lemon. Fleshy, closely-integrated and mellow attack leading into a livelier mid-palate. Fresh and focused. Perfect for whetting the appetite. Price approx.: 14,00 EUR
http://wwwchampagne-borel-lucas.com
Champagne Borel-Lucas
+33 (0)3 26 59 30 46

CHAMPAGNE BOUCHÉ PÈRE & FILS 84/100

▼ ♪ Brut Cuvée Saphir : Light yellow. A mix of ripe and candied lemon with a touch of toast on the nose. The palate combines power and exuberance. Fine texture and bubbles, freshness and lemony notes that take on a tangy character.
Price approx.: 28,00 EUR
www.champagne-bouche.fr
Champagne Bouché Père & fils
+33 (0)3 26 54 12 44

CHAMPAGNE CHARLES MIGNON 84/100

▼ ♪ Brut Premium Réserve : Attractive light gold. Medium intense nose of white fruits. Fairly lively attack on the palate with more of the fruit aromatics. The mid-palate and finish stay extremely invigorating. A Champagne for whetting the appetite. Price approx.: 20,00 EUR
http://www.champagne-mignon.fr
Champagne Charles Mignon
+33 (0)3 26 58 33 33

CHAMPAGNE CHASSENAY D'ARCE 84/100

▼ ♪ Brut Cuvée Première : Light yellow. Focused nose opening up to white-fleshed and red fruits. Clean, fruit-driven attack leading into a lively mid-palate. A fairly nervy, tense style, drinking well as an aperitif.
http://www.chassenay.com
Champagne Chassenay d'Arce
+33 (0)3 25 38 34 75

CHAMPAGNE DANIEL LECLERC & FILS 84/100

▼ ♪ Brut Cuvée Réserve : Golden hue with orange highlights. Profound nose recalling orange biscuits, dried fruits and a patisserie touch. Well-structured, powerful and full-bodied palate showing signature Pinot aromas. Equally suitable with a sit-down meal or a buffet. Price approx.: 14,50 EUR
www.champagne-daniel-leclerc.fr
Champagne Leclerc
+33 (0)3 25 38 51 12

CHAMPAGNE DROUILLY L.V. 84/100

▼ ♪ Brut : Deep gold with amber highlights. Expressive nose marked by dried apricot and orange zest. Full-bodied, vinous and well-structured palate, nicely enveloped in persistent, mouth-filling freshness. Drink with nibbles.
Price approx.: 14,00 EUR
Champagne Drouilly LV
+33 (0)3 25 29 65 35

CHAMPAGNE DUMÉNIL   84/100

▼ ♪ Brut 1er Cru Grande Réserve : Light yellow. Endearing fruity nose intermixing red fruits and white-fleshed fruits. More of the predominant fruit aromatics on the palate which is fleshy on the attack and lively mid-palate. A perfumed, fresh dry Champagne for the aperitif or parties.
Price approx.: 20,50 EUR
www.champagne-dumenil.com
Champagne Duménil
+33 (0)3 26 03 44 48

CHAMPAGNE EDWIGE FRANÇOIS   84/100

▼ ♪ Brut Ell'Ixir : Golden-hued with amber shades. The nose displays perfumes of dried and stewed fruits with pastries. Full-bodied, vinous palate. A rich, full style balanced by pronounced exuberance. An ambitious Champagne that will fully reveal itself with food.
Price approx.: 21,00 EUR
http://www.champagnefrancais.fr
Champagne Edwige François
+33 (0)3 23 82 11 26

CHAMPAGNE FENEUIL - POINTILLART   84/100

▼ ♪ Brut 1er cru Tradition : Light gold. Endearing fruity nose with a predominant red fruit streak. Fleshy attack leading into a livelier mid-palate counterbalanced by a sensation of rich fruit. Quite a drinkable, fruity style, that works well from the aperitif through to dessert.
Price approx.: 14,10 EUR
http://www.champagne-fp.com
Champagne Feneuil-Pointillart
+33 (0)3 26 97 62 35

CHAMPAGNE FRANCIS COSSY   84/100

▼ ♪ Brut 1er cru Eclat : Light gold. Endearing nose with scents of stone fruits, dried fruits and pastry notes. Full-bodied palate showing vinosity yet also freshness. More of the same very upfront, hallmark aromatics and personality.
Price approx.: 13,70 EUR
http://www.champagne-cossy.com
Champagne Francis Cossy
+33 (0)3 26 49 75 56

CHAMPAGNE FRÉDÉRIC MALÉTREZ   84/100

▼ ♪ Brut 1er cru Réserve : Light gold. Focused nose revealing fruity citrus aromas after swirling and faint patisserie notes. Fleshy, full-bodied attack with the same delicious fruit carrying through. Lively, forthright mid-palate. A balanced, robust dry Champagne pairing with nibb
Price approx.: 15,00 EUR
Champagne Maletrez Frédéric
+33 (0)3 26 97 63 92

CHAMPAGNE GEORGES CARTIER   84/100

▼ ♪ Brut Sélection : Light gold. Pleasant fruity nose of raspberry with subtle floral and vegetal notes. Fairly full-bodied, fleshy and closely-integrated palate. Upfront, expressive fruit aromas. A likeable, well-balanced dry Champagne for the aperitif or parties. Price approx.: 19,00 EUR
http://www.georgescartier.com
Champagne Georges Cartier
+33 (0)3 26 32 06 22

CHAMPAGNE HÉNIN-DELOUVIN   84/100

▼ ♪ Brut grand cru 2008 : Light yellow. After swirling, the nose opens up to fruit notes of apple and pear flesh with a subtle pastry touch. Ethereal attack, refined bubbles and texture and beautiful overall freshness. Lingering finish tinged with a hint of firmness. Price approx.: 17,20 EUR
Champagne Hénin-Delouvin
+33 (0)3 26 54 01 81

CHAMPAGNE J.M TISSIER   84/100

▼ ♪ Brut Tradition : Light gold. Endearing nose blending floral and fruit notes with subtle fresh almond touches. Lovely exuberance and fine bubbles on the palate yet also fat framing the whole. A lively dry Champagne for the aperitif.
Price approx.: 14,30 EUR
www.champagne-jm-tissier.com
Champagne J.M Tissier
+33 (0)3 26 54 17 47

CHAMPAGNE JEAN VALENTIN   84/100

▼ ♪ Brut Sélection : Beautiful light gold. A mix of red fruits and creamy, buttery notes on the nose. Fleshy, polished attack leading into a lively, clean mid-palate and fresh finish. The nose aromatics recur, coupled with a vegetal trace.
Price approx.: 14,30 EUR
Champagne Jean Valentin & fils
+33 (0)3 26 49 21 91

CHAMPAGNE LECLERC BRIANT   84/100

Org▼ ♪ Brut Réserve : Golden hue. Fruity nose opening up to perfumes of citrus and dried fruits with apple flesh in the background. Fleshy, fruit-forward palate framed by freshness. Naturalness comes across. Perfect for a party.
Price approx.: 29,50 EUR
www.leclercbriant.com
Champagne Leclerc Briant
+33 (0)3 26 54 45 33

CHAMPAGNE LIONEL CARREAU   84/100

▼ ♪ Brut Cuvée Réserve : Light yellow, green tints. Enticing fruity nose with mirabelle plum and raspberry notes. Delicious, well-balanced palate

showing lovely fleshy fruit, freshness and persistence. A party-style Champagne ideal for an aperitif or drinking well into the night. Price approx.: 16,00 EUR
Champagne Lionel Carreau
+33 (0)3 25 38 57 27

CHAMPAGNE MOUTARDIER   84/100
▼ ♪ Brut Carte d'Or : Beautiful light gold. Distinctive, focused nose marrying apple and a freshly-cut straw note. Delicious, fleshy and fruity attack balanced by lingering freshness. A pleasant, party-style Champagne for the aperitif or throughout the evening. Price approx.: 19,00 EUR
http://www.champagne-jean-moutardier.fr
Champagne Moutardier
+33 (0)3 26 59 21 09

CHAMPAGNE PASCAL LEBLOND-LENOIR   84/100
▼ ♪ Brut Esprit de Blancs 2008 : Beautiful brilliant light yellow. The nose marries white fruits with biscuit and patisserie notes. A lively style on the palate with floral and fruity accents that become very appetising on the finish. An ideal Champagne for the aperitif. Price approx.: 15,20 EUR
Champagne Leblond Lenoir Pascal
+33 (0)3 25 38 54 04

CHAMPAGNE PASCAL LEBLOND-LENOIR   84/100
▼ DG Brut Cuvée Prestige : Light yellow. Pleasant fruity nose suggestive of pear flesh. Lovely texture, fine bubbles and exuberance on the palate yet also a degree of body. A lively, focused dry Champagne for the aperitif. Price approx.: 14,90 EUR
Champagne Leblond Lenoir Pascal
+33 (0)3 25 38 54 04

CHAMPAGNE PICARD & BOYER   84/100
▼ ♪ Brut Esprit de Famille : Beautiful light gold. Distinctive nose blending white-fleshed fruits and freshly-cut straw. A fleshy, full-bodied and well-balanced style on the palate. Harmonious sensations of sweetness and freshness showcasing aroma. Drink as an aperitif or with puddin Price approx.: 16,00 EUR
www.champagne-picard-boyer.fr
Champagne Picard & Boyer
+33 (0)3 26 85 11 69

CHAMPAGNE PIERRE ARNOULD   84/100
▼ ♪ Brut grand cru Sélection : Light gold. Pronounced fruity character on the nose (red fruits and white-fleshed fruits). Generous, full-bodied palate with unrestrained fruit expression. A powerful, lush style for pairing with nibbles or a meal. Price approx.: 14,00 EUR

http://www.champagne-pierre-arnould.com
Champagne Pierre Arnould
+33 (0)3 26 49 40 12

CHAMPAGNE RAINETEAU-GRIMET   84/100
▼ ♪ Brut Cuvée Noir Tentation : Light gold. Endearing nose focusing on stone fruits and plum. Full-bodied palate showing lovely balance of vinosity and freshness. Focused fruit with a pleasant, cherry-driven finish. Serve with nibbles. Price approx.: 13,80 EUR
Champagne Raineteau-Grimet
+33 (0)3 26 83 90 32

CHAMPAGNE MARILYNE PERRON   83/100
▼ ♪ Extra brut blanc de noirs : Golden hue. Distinctive, expressive nose dominated by stewed apple, dried fruits, mineral and earthy undertones. Power and vinosity, a well-structured, lush Blanc de Noirs that stays bone dry with a note of sourness on the finish. Huge personality. Price approx.: 18,70 EUR
http://www.champagne-perron-beauvineau.com/
Champagne Perron-Beauvineau
+33 (0)3 25 27 40 56

CHAMPAGNE MATHELIN   83/100
▼ ♪ Extra brut : Deeply-coloured light gold. Focused nose opening up to ripe mirabelle plum and white-fleshed fruit notes with a hint of breadcrust. Good staying power on the palate, fresh, clean mid-palate. A well-balanced Champagne. Price approx.: 14,80 EUR
http://www.champagne-mathelin.com
Champagne Mathelin
+33 (0)3 26 52 73 58

CHAMPAGNE PIOT-SÉVILLANO   83/100
▼ ♪ Extra brut Tradition : Limpid, pale yellow. Pleasant nose marrying white fruits and biscuit notes. On the palate, a vibrant, taut and perfumed Champagne. Lovely creamy effervescence and lingering perfumes. A clean, honest style for immediate enjoyment. Price approx.: 15,40 EUR
http://www.piot-sevillano.com
EARL Piot Sevillano
+33 (0)3 26 58 23 88

CHAMPAGNE DANIEL LECLERC & FILS   83/100
▼ ♪ Brut rosé : Deep orange-pink. Expressive, mature nose suggestive of strawberry soup. Powerful, vinous palate. A well-structured style balanced by a touch of freshness with more of the same ultra ripe fruit. A rosé Champagne with real food compatibility. Price approx.: 13,50 EUR
www.champagne-daniel-leclerc.fr
Champagne Leclerc
+33 (0)3 25 38 51 12

CHAMPAGNE JEAN-MARC VATEL   83/100

▼ ♪ Brut rosé Cuvée La Vie en Rose : Orange-pink. Pleasant nose marrying notes of orange peel with a biscuit tone. On the palate, a fairly mature yet balanced style revealing more of the same aromas. An honest rosé Champagne that would work with, say, sweet and sour foods.
Price approx.: 16,80 EUR
http://www.champagnevatel.fr
Champagne Jean Marc Vatel
+33 (0)3 26 52 94 67

CHAMPAGNE LUTUN   83/100

▼ ♪ Brut rosé : Orangy-pink. The nose opens up to notes of red fruit syrup (strawberry, including wild strawberry). The same scents recur on the palate which is fresh and pleasantly approachable. A delightful rosé that works equally well as an apertif or with pudding. Price approx.: 16,90 EUR
http://www.champagne-lutun.com
SCEV Les Baronnies
+33 (0)3 26 59 41 33

CHAMPAGNE POTEL-PRIEUX   83/100

▼ ♪ Brut rosé : Salmon-pink. Fruity nose blending orange notes and red fruits. Fleshy, fruit-forward attack leading into a firmer mid-palate tinged with a hint of sourness. A rosé Champagne that works best as an aperitif or with dessert.
Price approx.: 15,43 EUR
Champagne Potel-Prieux
+33 (0)3 26 58 48 59

CHAMPAGNE ROYER PÈRE & FILS   83/100

▼ ♪ Brut Rosé : Light red. Profound, focused nose driven by strawberry and raspberry. The palate is also fruity and juxtaposes sensations of sweetness and liveliness. Vegetal touch on the finish. A rosé Champagne that works best with food or puddings.
Price approx.: 15,75 EUR
www.champagne-royer.com
Champagne Royer père & fils
+33 (0)3 25 38 52 16

CHAMPAGNE ANDREANI BESNIER   83/100

▼ ♪ Brut Réserve : Pale yellow with green tints. Endearing nose showing focused fruit with suggestions of apple flesh and a touch of raspberry. More of the same fruit aromas on the palate. Soft attack leading into a livelier mid-palate. A likeable, perfumed dry Champagne.
Price approx.: 16,00 EUR
Andreani Besnier
+33 (0)447917992718

> Detailed instructions are featured
> at the start of the book.

CHAMPAGNE BOUCHÉ PÈRE   83/100

▼ ♪ Brut Cuvée Réservée : Light gold. Expressive nose with aromas of dried fruits and a subtle patisserie touch. Fleshy, full-bodied palate where vinosity is nicely balanced by a touch of freshness. A mature style that works well with nibbles or a sit-down meal.
Price approx.: 18,00 EUR
www.champagne-bouche.fr
Champagne Bouché Père & fils
+33 (0)3 26 54 12 44

CHAMPAGNE DANIEL LECLERC & FILS   83/100

▼ ♪ Brut : Deep golden hue. Clean nose focusing on fruit (white-fleshed and dried fruits). Very honest and instantly accessible on the palate where the same fruity aromas follow through. A sensation of exuberance on the finish offsets the full-bodiedness.
Price approx.: 12,50 EUR
www.champagne-daniel-leclerc.fr
Champagne Leclerc
+33 (0)3 25 38 51 12

CHAMPAGNE DIDER LANGRY   83/100

▼ ♪ Brut Cuvée Prestige : Brightly-coloured light yellow. Endearing nose with ripe fruit aromas of grape and apple layered over subtle toast undertones. Full-bodied palate nicely balanced by savoury freshness. Clearly-delineated fruit aromas. Drink as an aperitif.
Price approx.: 15,50 EUR
http://www.champagne-didier-langry.com
Champagne Didier Langry
+33 (0)3 25 38 57 37

CHAMPAGNE GERMAR BRETON   83/100

▼ ♪ Brut Tradition : Beautiful light yellow. A blend of lemony, milky and brioche-like notes on the nose. The same aromatic spectrum, especially the crisp lemony edge, follows through to a lively, nervy and clean palate. A fiery, perfumed dry Champagne for the aperitif.
Price approx.: 12,00 EUR
Champagne Germar Breton
+33 (0)3 25 27 73 03

CHAMPAGNE GUY CHARBAUT   83/100

▼ DG Brut Sélection : Light gold. Nose of white fruits entwined with subtle floral and vegetal notes. The palate displays a slightly lively character but crisp fruity aromas impart a degree of harmony. Serve well-chilled as an appetiser.
Price approx.: 19,00 EUR
http://www.champagne-guy-charbaut.com
Champagne Guy Charbaut
+33 (0)3 26 52 60 59

CHAMPAGNE JEAN MICHEL PELLETIER 83/100

▼ ♪ Brut Sélection : Light gold. Distinctive nose intermixing white-fleshed fruits and straw notes. The palate is full-bodied and fairly vinous yet also fresh and mellow. A characterful dry Champagne that makes an enjoyable partner for nibbles.
Price approx.: 14,20 EUR
http://www.champagnejean-michelpelletier.fr
Champagne Jean-Michel Pelletier
+33 (0)3 26 52 65 86

CHAMPAGNE JEAN MICHEL PELLETIER 83/100

▼ ♪ Brut Cuvée Anaëlle 2006 : Light gold with faint amber. Distinctive, mature nose melding dried fruits and straw. Well-structured, full-bodied palate displaying a degree of firmness. More of the vegetal nose aromatics. A traditional style that works best with food.
Price approx.: 17,60 EUR
http://www.champagnejean-michelpelletier.fr
Champagne Jean-Michel Pelletier
+33 (0)3 26 52 65 86

CHAMPAGNE JEAN VALENTIN 83/100

▼ ♪ Brut 1er cru Tradition : Deep golden hue. Distinctive, profound nose with upfront fruit aromas of apple, cherry and dried fruits. Full-bodied, vinous palate. A rich, perfumed style balanced by good exuberance. Serve with petits fours.
Price approx.: 13,70 EUR
Champagne Jean Valentin & fils
+33 (0)3 26 49 21 91

CHAMPAGNE JEAN-BERNARD BOURGEOIS 83/100

▼ ♪ Brut 2006 : Limpid pale gold. Suggestions of red fruits with a faint jammy touch on the nose. Lush, aromatic and ripe on the palate revealing more of the same expressive perfumes. A Champagne for sharing, pairing well with white meats.
Price approx.: 18,80 EUR
Champagne Jean-Bernard Bourgeois
+33 (0)3 26 49 21 79

CHAMPAGNE JEAN-POL HAUTBOIS 83/100

▼ ♪ Brut Tradition : Light gold. Focused nose showing a lovely fruity character and delicate notes of pastries and patisserie. Fleshy, fruit-driven entry that is fresh and lively and reveals more of the fruit. A nice dry Champagne for the aperitif.
http://www.champagne-hautbois.com
Champagne Hautbois Jean-Pol
+33 (0)3 26 48 20 98

CHAMPAGNE L & S CHEURLIN 83/100

▼ ♪ Brut Lucie Cheurlin : Very pale yellow-green. The nose opens up to grape and mirabelle plum notes then reveals lightly toasted perfumes. More of

the unusual aromatic spectrum on the palate which is fleshy and mellow yet fresh. Try with spicy foods.
Price approx.: 16,00 EUR
Champagne L & S Cheurlin
+33 (0)3 25 38 55 04

CHAMPAGNE LECLERC BRIANT 83/100

Org▼ ♪ Brut : Deep gold. Distinctive nose opening up to citrus notes, dried fruits and a mineral dimension. Full-bodied, generous and lush palate displaying a sensation of suppleness. A mature style that works best with food. Price approx.: 25,50 EUR
www.leclercbriant.com
Champagne Leclerc Briant
+33 (0)3 26 54 45 33

CHAMPAGNE MAURICE PHILIPPART 83/100

▼ ♪ Brut 1er cru Carte d'Or : Pretty light gold. Very enticing nose of ripe raspberries with a heady floral tone. Delightful crunchy and fruit-driven palate with savoury patisserie tones. A dry Champagne with real drive for sharing over the aperitif.
Price approx.: 15,50 EUR
http://www.champagne-mphilippart.com
Champagne Maurice Philippart
+33 (0)3 26 03 42 44

CHAMPAGNE MICHEL MAILLIARD 83/100

▼ ♪ Brut Cuvée Grégory : Pale gold. Focused nose melding fruity notes, a touch of almond and a vegetal dimension. Pleasant fleshy, fruit-driven attack (mirabelle plum) leading into a fresh mid-palate. Well-balanced with a very faint touch of firmness on the finish. Price approx.: 16,70 EUR
http://www.champagne-michel-mailliard.com
Champagne Michel Mailliard
+33 (0)3 26 52 15 18

CHAMPAGNE NOËL LEBLOND-LENOIR 83/100

▼ ♪ Brut Grande réserve : Pale yellow. Honest, simple fruity nose. Good staying power on the palate. A fleshy yet fresh, upright style showing lovely aromatic focus. Drink as an appetiser.
Price approx.: 13,20 EUR
Champagne Noël Leblond-Lenoir
+33 (0)3 25 38 53 33

CHAMPAGNE RICHARD CHEURLIN 83/100

▼ ♪ Brut Cuvée Jeanne 2007 : Light yellow. Fruity nose opening up to pronounced toast notes. More of the same very upfront aromas on the palate which is full, well-integrated and fresh with a good framework. Its aromatic personality may come as a surprise. Drink with food.
Price approx.: 20,00 EUR
www.champagne-cheurlin.fr
Champagne Richard Cheurlin
+33 (0)3 25 38 55 04

CHAMPAGNE

CHAMPAGNE SOLEMME 83/100

▼ ♪ Brut 1er cru Terre de Solemme : Pale golden hue. Endearing fruity nose suggestive of orange biscuit with a touch of mirabelle plum. Full attack with vinosity nicely counterbalanced by a sensation of freshness. Perfumed and fruit-driven. A pleasant Champagne for the aperitif.
Price approx.: 17,50 EUR
Champagne Solemme
+33 (0)3 26 50 24 18

CHAMPAGNE STÉPHANE COQUILLETTE 83/100

▼ ♪ Brut blanc de blancs grand cru Cuvée Diane : Light yellow. Inviting nose suggestive of pear flesh with a touch of white flowers. On the palate, a creamy texture supported by a nervy structure. Perfumed and fairly persistent across the palate. Drink as an aperitif. Price approx.: 21,90 EUR
Champagne Stéphane Coquillette
+33 (0)3 26 51 74 12

CHAMPAGNE VIGNON PÈRE & FILS 83/100

▼ ♪ Brut grand cru Les Marquises 2007 : Light gold. Mature nose opening up to patisserie notes and dried fruits. The palate reveals vinosity yet also a lively structure displaying a measure of firmness. Slightly lean on the finish. Drink as an aromatic Champagne with nibbles. Price approx.: 24,50 EUR
Champagne Vignon Père & Fils
+33 (0)3 26 49 80 39

CHAMPAGNE BERNARD ROBERT 82/100

▼ ♪ Brut rosé : Brilliant, limpid salmon-pink. Powerful nose recalling red fruits in brandy. Beautiful freshness, fleshy stuffing and expressive, citrus-driven perfumes are predominant on the palate. A rosé Champagne with drive that would work with spicy or exotic foods. Price approx.: 14,00 EUR
http://www.champagne-robert-voigny.com
Champagne Bernard Robert
+33 (0)3 25 27 11 53

CHAMPAGNE CAMILLE PHILIPPE 82/100

▼ ♪ Brut rosé : Salmon-pink. Focused nose reminiscent of red fruits. Lively at point of entry with focused aromas of red fruits. A well-balanced Champagne that would work well with fruit-based desserts. Price approx.: 25,60 EUR
http://www.domcaudron.fr
Champagne Dom Caudron
+33 (0)3 26 52 45 17

CHAMPAGNE DE CASTELNAU 82/100

▼ ♪ Brut rosé : Deep orange hue. On the nose, aromas of blood orange combine with caramel notes. Vinosity, a measure of power, fat and a sensation of richness counterbalanced by quite

evident freshness that lingers on the palate. Serve preferably with food. Price approx.: 30,24 EUR
http://www.champagne-de-castelnau.eu
Champagne de Castelnau
+33 (0)3 26 77 89 00

CHAMPAGNE DE L'ARGENTAINE 82/100

▼ ♪ Brut Rosé : Deep orange-pink. The nose opens up to notes of orange biscuits, strawberry and vegetal undertones. Good staying power on the palate. A fleshy, full-bodied style balanced by freshness. An honest rosé Champagne, equally suitable as an aperitif or with food
Price approx.: 15,10 EUR
www.champagnedelargentaine.fr
Champagne de l'Argentaine
+33 (0)3 26 58 68 68

CHAMPAGNE EDWIGE FRANÇOIS 82/100

▼ ♪ Brut rosé Famous : Deep pink with orange tints. The nose opens up after swirling to red fruit notes with a vegetal touch. Rich palate with a soft, fruit-driven attack and a syrupy sensation counterbalancing a firmer finish. Set aside for red fruit-based desserts.
Price approx.: 16,00 EUR
http://www.champagnefrancais.fr
Champagne Edwige François
+33 (0)3 23 82 11 26

CHAMPAGNE NOËL LEBLOND-LENOIR 82/100

▼ ♪ Brut rosé : Orange-pink. Fruity nose marked by a sensation of sweetness. On the palate, a soft, fairly sweet and round style, bordering on medium-dry. Save for puddings. Price approx.: 13,50 EUR
Champagne Noël Leblond-Lenoir
+33 (0)3 25 38 53 33

CHAMPAGNE ALAIN BAILLY 82/100

▼ ♪ Brut Réserve : Light gold. Distinctive nose blending white-fleshed fruits and notes of straw. Full-bodied, vinous and mellow, counterbalanced by a sensation of exuberance. A dry Champagne pairing with nibbles. Price approx.: 14,30 EUR
http://www.champagne-bailly.com
Champagne Alain Bailly
+33 (0)3 26 97 41 58

CHAMPAGNE CHEURLIN-DANGIN 82/100

▼ ♪ Brut Cuvée Spéciale : Light gold. Honest fruity nose showing raspberry. Fairly full-bodied, rich and well-structured palate revealing more of the red fruit perfumes. A likeable, fruity and quite generous dry Champagne drinking best as an aperitif.
Price approx.: 15,80 EUR
www.cheurlin-daguin.fr
Champagne Cheurlin-Dangin
+33 (0)3 25 38 50 26

CHAMPAGNE CHRISTIAN BOURMAULT 82/100

▼ ♪ Brut Grand Eloge : Light gold. Fruity nose recalling apple flesh. Full, fairly rich and fruit-driven on the attack. Livelier, quite firm middle palate. A perfumed dry Champagne pairing with nibbles. Price approx.: 18,55 EUR
Champagne Christian Bourmault
+33 (0)3 26 59 79 41

CHAMPAGNE HUGUENOT-TASSIN 82/100

▼ ♪ Brut Cuvée Tradition : Light gold. Focused fruity nose bordering on grape with subtle raspberry notes and a vegetal touch. More of the same fruit aromatics on the palate which is round yet fresh. An instantly accessible dry Champagne that works well as an aperitif. Price approx.: 13,40 EUR
http://www.huguenot-tassin.com
Champagne Huguenot-Tassin
+33 (0)3 25 38 54 49

CHAMPAGNE JEAN-MARC VATEL 82/100

▼ ♪ Brut Cuvée Grande Réserve : Beautiful yellow-gold. Very mature nose of straw and dried vegetal aromas. A combination of exuberance and vinosity on the palate with more of the same honest, mature aromas. Drink very well-chilled as an appetiser. Price approx.: 16,40 EUR
http://www.champagnevatel.fr
Champagne Jean Marc Vatel
+33 (0)3 26 52 94 67

CHAMPAGNE NOËL LEBLOND-LENOIR 82/100

▼ ♪ Brut Tradition : Light yellow. Clean nose focusing on grape and white-fleshed fruits. The palate juxtaposes a sensation of fruity sweetness and a lively, nervy structure. Medium length and good accessibility. Drink as an aperitif. Price approx.: 12,50 EUR
Champagne Noël Leblond-Lenoir
+33 (0)3 25 38 53 33

CHAMPAGNE PASCAL LEBLOND-LENOIR 82/100

▼ ♪ Brut Tradition : Light yellow. Clean nose opening up to fruity notes then developing pastry aromatics. Full palate with vinosity nicely balanced by fine bubbles and a sensation of freshness. A fairly lively, classic dry Champagne. Price approx.: 12,50 EUR
Champagne Leblond Lenoir Pascal
+33 (0)3 25 38 54 04

CHAMPAGNE PASCAL LEBLOND-LENOIR 82/100

▼ ♪ Brut Grande Réserve : Light gold. Fruity nose reminiscent of mirabelle plum and dried apricot. Full-bodied, vinous palate. A fairly powerful, well-structured style that we would recommend as a food Champagne.

Price approx.: 13,20 EUR
Champagne Leblond Lenoir Pascal
+33 (0)3 25 38 54 04

CHAMPAGNE POTEL-PRIEUX 82/100

▼ ♪ Brut Grande Réserve : Light gold. Endearing fruity nose recalling stewed apple, subtle creamy touches and a vegetal touch. Full, warm and fleshy attack revealing more of the fruit expression. Enjoy well-chilled as an aperitif. Price approx.: 14,00 EUR
Champagne Potel-Prieux
+33 (0)3 26 58 48 59

CHAMPAGNE SOLEMME 82/100

▼ ♪ Brut 1er cru Exception de Solemme : Attractive pale yellow. The nose opens up to white-fleshed fruit notes (pear), freshly-cut grass and a subtle creamy touch. Pleasant attack supported by a fine-grained texture, fresh mid-palate and touch of leanness on the finish. Serve chilled as an aper Price approx.: 25,90 EUR
Champagne Solemme
+33 (0)3 26 50 24 18

CHAMPAGNE VEUVE DOUSSOT 82/100

▼ ♪ Brut Tradition : Light gold. Mature nose focusing on fruity aromas and reserve wine notes. Fleshy, fruit-driven attack enhanced by a sensation of sweetness bordering on honey. Livelier mid-palate. A soft dry Champagne for the aperitif. Price approx.: 14,20 EUR
http://www.champagneveuvedoussot.com
Champagne Veuve Doussot
+33 (0)3 25 29 60 61

CHAMPAGNE JEAN-BERNARD BOURGEOIS 81/100

▼ ♪ Brut rosé : Limpid orangy-pink. Heady nose of ultra ripe red fruits, citrus and a touch of fruits in brandy. The palate is extremely ripe with heady fruit perfumes. A fairly lush rosé Champagne for fruit-based desserts. Price approx.: 15,75 EUR
Champagne Jean-Bernard Bourgeois
+33 (0)3 26 49 21 79

CHAMPAGNE PERRON-BEAUVINEAU 81/100

▼ ♪ Extra dry rosé : Coppery light pink. Expressive nose with a fruity character (red fruits, orange flesh) and patisserie notes. More of the same aromatic personality on the palate which is warm yet mild. A food-friendly rosé that works well all the way through to dessert. Price approx.: 18,70 EUR
http://www.champagne-perron-beauvineau.com/
Champagne Perron-Beauvineau
+33 (0)3 25 27 40 56

CHAMPAGNE BOULACHIN-CHAPUT   81/100

▼ ♪ Brut nature Zéro dosage Sélection : Old gold with amber tints. Mature, distinctive nose blending dried fruits, dried vegetal aromas and patisserie notes. More of the same very pronounced aromatics on the palate which is full-bodied, fresh and lively. Pair with nibbles. Price approx.: 11,30 EUR
www.champagneboulachinchaput.com
Champagne Boulachin-Chaput
+33 (0)3 25 27 27 13

CHAMPAGNE BERNARD RÉMY   81/100

▼ ♪ Brut Carte Blanche : Brilliant light yellow. The nose opens up to notes of white-fleshed fruits, floral touches and a sensation of sweetness. Fairly lightweight, fresh palate showing more of the fruit. Faint vegetal dimension on the finish.
http://www.champagnebernardremy.com
Champagne Bernard Rémy
+33 (0)3 26 80 60 34

CHAMPAGNE LIONEL CARREAU   81/100

▼ ♪ Brut Tradition : Light gold. The nose blends a red fruit dimension and a vegetal touch. Powerful, generous and fruit-forward attack leading into a more linear mid-palate revealing its nervy character. An instantly accessible Champagne for the aperitif. Price approx.: 14,50 EUR
Champagne Lionel Carreau
+33 (0)3 25 38 57 27

CHAMPAGNE DE L'ARGENTAINE   80/100

▼ ♪ Brut Tradition : Light gold. Suggestions of white-fleshed fruits (apple flesh) on the nose with a floral and vegetal dimension. Clean attack leading into a lively mid-palate with focused fruit aromas. An instantly accessible, fresh dry Champagne. Drink as an aperitif. Price approx.: 13,80 EUR
www.champagnedelargentaine.fr
Champagne de l'Argentaine
+33 (0)3 26 58 68 68

CHAMPAGNE DIDIER LANGRY   80/100

▼ ♪ Brut : Light yellow. Fruity nose bordering on grape with subtle vegetal notes. More of these instantly perceptible fruit aromas on the palate which is fairly lively and nervy. An honest Champagne for the aperitif.
Price approx.: 13,20 EUR
http://www.champagne-didier-langry.com
Champagne Didier Langry
+33 (0)3 25 38 57 37

CHAMPAGNE GUSTAVE GOUSSARD   80/100

▼ ♪ Brut Respect N° 1 : Light gold with pale orange highlights. Endearing fruity nose blending pear flesh and a touch of red fruits. Fairly full-bodied, fleshy attack driven by fruit. Livelier, clean mid-palate. Well-balanced and fruity. Serve as an aperitif.Price approx.: 23,00 EUR
Champagne Gustave Goussard
+33 (0)3 25 29 30 03

CHAMPAGNE STÉPHANE FAUVET   80/100

▼ ♪ Brut Réserve : Golden hue. Distinctive nose reminiscent of apple flesh with a vegetal dimension. More of the same white-fleshed fruit aromas on the palate. Fairly vinous and closely-integrated, balanced by a trace of freshness. A rustic style pairing with nibbles. Price approx.: 13,80 EUR
Champagne Stéphane Fauvet
+33 (0)3 23 82 45 60

CHAMPAGNE GERMAR BRETON   79/100

▼ ♪ Brut Rosé : Deeply-coloured light red. Delectable nose of cherry and raspberry flesh with a subtle vegetal touch. The same character is framed on the palate by a sensation of sweetness and syrup. Drink preferably as a pudding-style rosé Champagne. Price approx.: 13,00 EUR
Champagne Germar Breton
+33 (0)3 25 27 73 03

CHAMPAGNE PASCAL LEBLOND-LENOIR   79/100

▼ ♪ Brut rosé : Light pink with orange tints. Subdued nose intermixing red fruits and vegetal touches. Supple attack displaying a degree of sweetness, leading into a firmer mid-palate tinged with faint sourness. A rosé whose sweetness makes it more of a pudding Champagne
Price approx.: 14,20 EUR
Champagne Leblond Lenoir Pascal
+33 (0)3 25 38 54 04

CHAMPAGNE LUTUN   79/100

▼ ♪ Brut : Pale yellow-gold. Subtle fruit on the nose bordering on grape. More of the same fruit presence on the palate which is fairly lively and well-balanced. An instantly accessible brut Champagne showing at its best served chilled as an aperitif. Price approx.: 14,20 EUR
http://www.champagne-lutun.com
SCEV Les Baronnies
+33 (0)3 26 59 41 33

CHAMPAGNE PIOT-SÉVILLANO   79/100

▼ ♪ Brut Tradition : Attractive golden hue. Distinctive nose intermixing fruity notes, white-fleshed and dried fruits with a touch of dried vegetal (straw). These aromas recur on a lively palate framed by a sensation of sweetness. A rustic style pairing with nibbles. Price approx.: 14,90 EUR
http://www.piot-sevillano.com
EARL Piot Sevillano
+33 (0)3 26 58 23 88

CHAMPAGNE RAINETEAU-GRIMET   79/100

▼ ♪ Brut Tradition : Golden highlights. Distinctive nose blending white-fleshed fruits (apple flesh) and dried vegetal aromas. These carry through to the palate which is lively with a degree of power. An instantly accessible brut that works well as an appetiser served well-ch
Price approx.: 12,80 EUR
Champagne Raineteau-Grimet
+33 (0)3 26 83 90 32

CHAMPAGNE SOLEMME   79/100

▼ ♪ Brut de Solemme : Deep gold with subtle orange highlights. Fruit-dominant nose (plum flesh, stewed fruits). Fleshy attack driven by the same fruit aromas, full-bodied mid-palate capped off with a trace of firmness on the finish. A distinctive, rustic style. Price approx.: 16,80 EUR
Champagne Solemme
+33 (0)3 26 50 24 18

CHAMPAGNE STÉPHANE COQUILLETTE   79/100

▼ ♪ Brut 1er cru Carte d'Or : Pale gold. Endearing fruity nose of fresh raspberry with floral notes. The palate displays evident bubbles and exuberance. The same fruit aromas recur coupled with a subtle vegetal dimension. Drink well-chilled as an appetiser. Price approx.: 17,80 EUR
Champagne Stéphane Coquillette
+33 (0)3 26 51 74 12

CHAMPAGNE CHEURLIN-DANGIN   78/100

▼ ♪ Brut Carte d'Or : Light yellow with green tints. Simple fruity, grape-like nose with white-fleshed fruit notes. The palate combines exuberance with a sensation of sweetness enhancing the same fruit aromatics. An instantly accessible dry Champagne for the aperitif or dessert. Price approx.: 14,50 EUR
www.cheurlin-daguin.fr
Champagne Cheurlin-Dangin
+33 (0)3 25 38 50 26

CHAMPAGNE MONSARRAT   75/100

▼ ♪ Brut Réserve : Brilliant pale gold. A mix of fruity notes, grape, mirabelle plum and vegetal notes on the nose. A sensation of sweetness prevails over a lively structure on the palate, revealing more of the vegetal dimension. A pudding-style Champagne. Price approx.: 12,00 EUR
http://www.meyblum-et-fils.com
MVP Wines
+33 (0)4 34 22 12 75

Detailed instructions are featured
at the start of the book.

COTEAUX CHAMPENOIS

MAURICE VESSELLE   86/100

▼ ♪ Bouzy Rouge 2006 : Medium intense orange-brown colour. Open nose where jammy aromas are entwined with undergrowth and gamey tones. Lightweight substance yet also fat on the palate. An ethereal, tense wine that works best served at room temperature with small game.
http://www.champagnemauricevesselle.com
Champagne Maurice Vesselle
+33 (0)3 26 57 00 81

RATAFIA

J.M TISSIER   89/100

▼ ♪ Beautiful amber hue with coppery highlights. Expressive, mature nose blending raisins, gingerbread and cigar box aromas. Full, closely-integrated palate with fairly restrained warmth. When served well chilled, it develops a delicious array of aromatics.
Price approx.: 13,90 EUR
www.champagne-jm-tissier.com
Champagne J.M Tissier
+33 (0)3 26 54 17 47

CORSICA

A VINEYARD WITH A DIFFERENCE

Although wine growing was introduced to Corsica, as it was to Provence, by the Greeks in Antiquity, making it one of France's oldest wine regions, centuries were to elapse before it prospered. After two world wars had left it on the wane, it enjoyed a new lease of life in the 1960s. Quality was initially poor, though gradually, promising wine regions emerged. Nowadays they form a ring around the island, like a crown studded with jewels, each one refined and expressive.

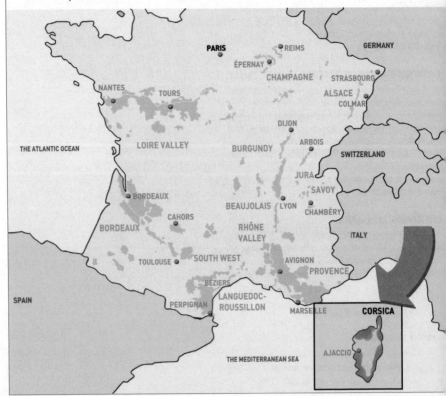

The north-south aligned mountain range stretching from one side of the island to the other harbours countless, highly idiosyncratic 'terroirs' embodied by myriad distinctive wines. Despite this diversity, soil formations can be divided into two major types - the upper western slopes are predominantly crystalline and granite, lacking in loam which makes them slightly prone to erosion. The eastern basin has a high proportion of shale and alpine type soils with large and sometimes recent deposits of sediment...

The island's idiosyncrasies also apply to its astonishing range of grape varieties,. Sciacarello and Niellucio are major varieties for

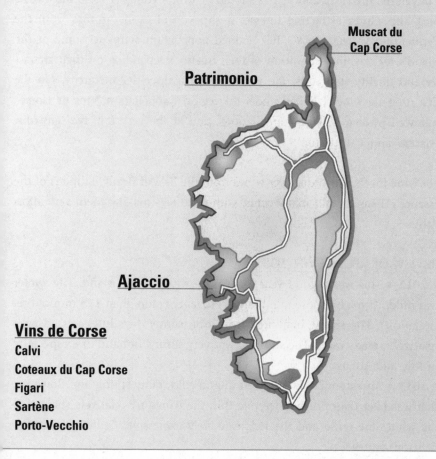

Muscat du Cap Corse

Patrimonio

Ajaccio

Vins de Corse
Calvi
Coteaux du Cap Corse
Figari
Sartène
Porto-Vecchio

the reds and rosés, along with Barbarossa, Grenache, Cinsault and Carignan. For the whites, Vermentino, otherwise known as Corsican Malvoisie, has become a household name and is the most prevalent white varietal. Other grape varieties play a minor role - such as Ugni Blanc - and some are even scarce, such as Rossola and Codivarta, both of which are only blended to make AC Vin de Corse-Coteaux du Cap Corse.

In terms of character, such a comprehensive range of grape varieties is reflected in a broad selection of wines. These can vary from light wines (like some Sciaccarello...) to more dense wines, like those made from Niellucio, which are described as well-balanced, round wines, suitable for lengthy cellaring. Conversely, the rosés and whites should be drunk young (two to three years old), the whites extracting finesse, freshness and exotic aromas from the Vermentino varietal. INAO has granted appellation status to some of the island's regions, in recognition of their quality. Depending on their character and quality standards, the wines follow a three-tier hierarchy. On the first rung are wines labelled under the regional appellation 'Vins de Corse', followed by five 'Villages' appellations, and at the very top, two growths, 'Ajaccio' and 'Patrimonio'...

For wine lovers yet to discover wines from the 'Isle of Beauty', time is of the essence. There are still many gems, with price tags making them very affordable.

REVIEW OF RECENT VINTAGE

• **2012** • This was a good year for winegrowing on the island. The winter was mild, with a bit more rain than in Provence (more than 125 mm of precipitation). The spring benefited from hot, sunny days interspersed with relatively steady rains. The summer was very sunny, hot and dry, especially in July and August.

• **2013** • An extremely late harvest after a cold, rainy spring and flowering that was later than normal. Despite this, the wines are relatively successful; the whites are tense and the reds extremely expressive. Quite a delightful, delicious vintage!

THE CORSICAN APPELLATIONS

A.C. AJACCIO

OVERVIEW: until 1984, this appellation was known as Coteaux d'Ajaccio. It stretches from the Gulf of Porto to the Sartène area, over 36 towns and villages. This highly-fragmented wine region is centred chiefly on the granite hillsides of the Gulf of Ajaccio and Sagone. Some vineyards are the highest in Corsica.

WINE STYLES: the majority of the wines are red, made from at least 40% Sciacarello. They are nervy, vigorous, fragrant wines (pepper, vanilla, dry leaf, roasted coffee, raspberry), with a solid framework. Firm when young, they have the potential to mature well. Try with red meat served with a sauce, game, or ewe milk cheese. The salmon-pink colour rosés display aromas of quince and grapefruit. They pair well with cured ham. The whites are drawn from at least 80% Vermentino and smell pleasantly of linden and freshly-cut hay. Try with shallow-fried red mullet or sauteed squid.

223

A.C. PATRIMONIO

OVERVIEW: situated in the southern part of Cap Corse between Bastia and the citadel of Saint-Florent, Patrimonio was the first area to be granted AC status in Corsica. Seven villages are entitled to the appellation. Patrimonio is made from 95% Niellucio for the red wines and Vermentino only for the whites. The wines are 50% red and 30% rosé. The vineyards are planted on hillside sites formed of limestone and clay scree. The soils are consistent, which is unusual for Corsica. The mountains form a buffer against the wind. Fog is prevalent both in the autumn and the winter.

WINE STYLES: the reds with their deep hue (ruby-red) exhibit balsamic fragrances (pine trees), dried fig, raspberry, violet and toasted aromas. They are powerful, dense, fleshy, warm and robust – more so than wines from Ajaccio - with a full mouthfeel. Try with game or goats cheese. The pleasant, fruity rosés are full-bodied with a slight acidulous note and pair with Corsican cooked cold pork meats. The pale yellow colour whites display floral and apple aromas. They are supple, fruity and well-structured. They are suitable for fish and shellfish.

A.C. VIN DE CORSE

OVERVIEW: these wines can be grown throughout the AC Corse production area (except for the Patrimonio region). Most Corsican wines (Vin de Corse) come from the hills overlooking the eastern plains and the middle Golo valley in the Corte area. A local appellation name (Sartène, Calvi, Cap-Corse, Figari, Porto-Vecchio) can be appended to AC Vin de Corse.

Native grapes are the most prevalent though Mediterranean varietals from the mainland are also grown. For red and rosé wines, the range comprises Nieluccio, Sciacarello and Grenache noir augmented with a maximum 50% of Cinsault, Mourvedre, Barbarossa, Syrah, Carignan and Vermentino (20% maximum for the latter two). For the whites, the range is simpler: Vermentino (75% minimum) and Ugni blanc (25% maximum).

WINE STYLES: the reds have a pleasant bouquet, are well-constituted, warm and supple. Aromas of fresh fruit and undergrowth are present, with gamey, spicy notes. Try with barbecues, roast meats (beef, goat), patés. The rosés have a deep colour, good vinosity and are clean. The whites are fat and supple with a slight bitterness. They pair with fish, sea urchins, goats or ewe milk cheese, and cooked cold pork meats.

VINS DE CORSE-CALVI: the appellation comes from Balagne, in the north-western part of the island. Vines grow mainly on the plains or Figarella and Regino valleys and along the coast. The reds are supple, concentrated and fragrant, the rosés are delicate, round and fruity. The whites are particularly complex and display great aromatic power. They should be drunk young.

VINS DE CORSE-CAP-CORSE: this is the island's most northerly wine area, set in the Regliano region. A broad selection of wines are made on a boutique scale. They range from particularly complex dry white wines with great aromatic power made from Malvoisie and Codivarta to red wines with good cellaring capacity and dessert wines known as 'rappus'... The region also boasts its own appellation - Muscat du Cap Corse - made from small-berry Muscat.

VINS DE CORSE-FIGARI: this is the Isle of Beauty's most southerly wine area. The gulf of Figari is dry and hot, making it highly conducive for growing red vines. The vines are planted on gently sloping hills, all facing south. The resultant wines are well-constituted and distinctive. They are considered to be amongst the island's best.

VINS DE CORSE-SARTÈNE: Sartène is situated in southern-western Corsica, near the Rizzanese river. It was the first wine growing region in Corsica to introduce modern techniques in the 19th century. 16 villages are entitled to the appellation. The reds, particularly those from the Montanaccio varietal, a local variation of Sciacarello, are round, distinctive and long on the palate. The rosés are robust with a pleasant bouquet. The whites are full and fragrant.

VINS DE CORSE-PORTO-VECCHIO: this appellation occupies the far south-eastern tip of Corsica, along the coast. Local farming focuses on wine, which is grown around Porto-Vecchio and Bonifacio. The reds are round, fruity, well-balanced and elegant. The rosés are delicate and aromatic. The whites are dry and fruity.

• • •

2015
CORSICA WINES

ILE DE BEAUTÉ

DOMAINE TERRA VECCHIA   **87/100**

▼ ♪ Vintage 2012 : Limpid red with youthful tints. Pleasurable nose of red fruits, chocolate, refined spice and herbs. Fairly virile, svelte palate showing real drive and offering up a beautiful array of aromatics mirroring the nose, supported by some fine tannins. Natural impression.
Price approx.: 4,10 EUR
Domaine Terra Vecchia
+33 (0)6 74 98 29 62

DOMAINE TERRA VECCHIA   **87/100**

▼ ♪ Vintage 2013 : Pale pink. Nose of crunchy red fruit sweets backed by spice and white pepper. A subtle, delicate rosé with generous substance and fat enhancing a range of spicy fruit aromatics. Fresh. Unrivalled with tapas.
Price approx.: 4,10 EUR
Domaine Terra Vecchia
+33 (0)6 74 98 29 62

VIN DE CORSE CALVI

A RONCA   **87/100**

Org▼ ♪ Vintage 2013 : Brilliant pale hue with yellow tints. Pleasurable nose intermixing citrus, red berry fruits and fine spices. Aromatic attack, virile palate showing great intensity and liveliness with spice and touches of maquis. Perfect for local gourmet cuisine. Price approx.: 8,50 EUR
www.domaine-figarella.com
Domaine A Ronca
+33 (0)4 95 61 06 69

A RONCA   **85/100**

CONV▼ ♪ Vintage 2012 : Deep garnet. Fairly subdued nose showing a strange iodine note entwined with blackberry and spice. Clean, expressive and robust palate with a touch of garrigue. Nervy and supported by a robust structure. An interesting wine. Price approx.: 8,00 EUR
www.domaine-figarella.com
Domaine A Ronca
+33 (0)4 95 61 06 69

A RONCA   **84/100**

CONV▼ ♪ Vintage 2013 : Brilliant pale gold with green tints. Alluring nose blending stone and white-

fleshed fruits. Lightness and freshness are key features on the palate. A touch of aniseed is entwined with the fruit. Lovely consistency and persistence.
Price approx.: 8,50 EUR
www.domaine-figarella.com
Domaine A Ronca
+33 (0)4 95 61 06 69

VIN DE CORSE PORTO-VECCHIO

DOMAINE DE TORRACCIA   **88/100**

Org▼ ♪ Vintage 2011 : Attractive limpid, slightly mature colour. The nose exudes splendid toast, spice, garrigue and ripe black berry aromas. Supple attack, lovely closely-integrated, rich and spicy presence framed by silky tannins. A convincing effort.
Price approx.: 9,24 EUR
Domaine de Torraccia
+33 (0)4 95 71 43 50

DOMAINE DE TORRACCIA   **87/100**

Org▼ ♪ Vintage 2013 : Brilliant salmon-pink. Refined, spicy nose with strawberry and citrus fruits. A rosé that is powerful yet soft. Beautifully arranged fruit laced with freshness. Pepper-infused finish. A beautiful rosé, excellent with tapas.
Price approx.: 9,24 EUR
Domaine de Torraccia
+33 (0)4 95 71 43 50

DOMAINE DE TORRACCIA   **84/100**

Org▼ ♪ Vintage 2013 : Light gold. Heady nose showing accents of white fruits, mild spices and meadow. Young, firm palate combining body, substance and fat. The flavours gradually unfurl. A generous Corsican wine that needs more time for full enjoyment.
Price approx.: 9,24 EUR
Domaine de Torraccia
+33 (0)4 95 71 43 50

VIN DE CORSE

CLOS POGGIALE   **89/100**

▼ ♪ Vintage 2012 : Deep crimson with dark purple tints. Pleasurable nose of cherry, strawberry, mild spices and herbs. The palate is powerful yet svelte, concentrated, tense and savoury with an elegant underlying structure. Lovely lightness. Bravo!
Price approx.: 7,60 EUR
Domaine Terra Vecchia
+33 (0)6 74 98 29 62

> Detailed instructions are featured
> at the start of the book.

DOMAINE DE TORRACCIA

90/100

▼ Oriu 2009 ORGANIC WINE

Limpid garnet, amber tints. Magnificent southern-style nose of spice, toast and animal aromas. Surprising lightness on the palate with velvety, full and spicy substance, an impression of harmony and a silky structure that is still present. Beautiful. Patience!

Price approx.: 19.20 EUR
Serving temperature: 15-17°
Ready to drink: From now on

Christian Imbert discovered Corsica on his return from Africa in the 1960s. He realised almost from the outset that this was prime wine growing land. However, instead of planting high-yielding, lucrative varieties he opted for the archetypal Corsican grapes Sciaccarellu, Niellucciu, Grenache and a little Syrah for the reds and rosés and Malvasia for the whites. Domaine Torracia was born on land clawed back from the maquis and granite soils and its wines are an admirable reflection of the generosity of the man who crafted them. The estate is extremely representative of the soul of Corsican wines and is a perfect illustration of the island's potential for wine growing.

Domaine de Torraccia
Torraccia - 20137 Porto Vecchio
Tel: (+33) 4 95 71 43 50 - Fax: (+33) 4 95 71 50 03
E-mail: torracciaoriu@wanadoo.fr

DOMAINE TERRA VECCHIA 88/100

▼ ♪ Vintage 2012 : Fairly deep, vibrant red. Shy nose of red fruits, cherry, refined spice and garrigue. Charming attack, with easy-drinking, fresh and svelte presence on the palate. A wine that proudly displays its Mediterranean personality, to our great delight. Price approx.: 5,95 EUR
Domaine Terra Vecchia
+33 (0)6 74 98 29 62

CLOS POGGIALE 88/100

▼ ♪ Vintage 2013 : Light pink. Complex mineral and menthol nose exuding perfumes of raspberry, violet and mild spices. Fleshy yet soft, powerful yet not overblown with perfume showcased throughout. A full mouthfeel makes pairing with food essential. Price approx.: 7,15 EUR
Domaine Terra Vecchia
+33 (0)6 74 98 29 62

DOMAINE TERRA VECCHIA 88/100

▼ ♪ Vintage 2013 : Pale pink. The nose reveals Mediterranean scents of pepper, ripe citrus, spice and wild flowers. Fleshy palate with mouthcoating substance and extremely generous aromatics. Persistent fruit and spice. Intense freshness. All the ingredients of a great rosé. Price approx.: 5,50 EUR
Domaine Terra Vecchia
+33 (0)6 74 98 29 62

DOMAINE DE LA PUNTA 88/100

▼ ♪ Vintage 2013 : Light yellow. Expressive nose with accents of white fruits, mild spices and wild flowers. Distinctive palate boasting a full mouthfeel, fat and lush texture. More of the rich nose aromatics with a refined note of sourness on the finish. Price approx.: 9,00 EUR
La Punta
+33 (0)4 95 30 60 68

WINE SCORES:

95-100/100: an outstanding wine, when a great 'terroir' meets exceptional winemaking expertise.

90-94/100: a superlative wine combining finesse, complexity and remarkable winemaking.

85-89/100: a wine of extremely high standard, which we enjoyed for its typicity and character.

80-84/100: a quality wine combining balance, structure and neatness for a pleasurable wine drinking experience.

75-79/100: a wine deemed acceptable.

70-74/100: a wine with defects, unacceptable.

65-69/100: a wine with major defects, inadmissible.

50-64/100: unacceptable wine, not worthy for sale.

Note: wines scoring less than 75/100 are not included in our publications.

LANGUEDOC-ROUSSILLON

STILL PUSHING THE BOUNDARIES OF QUALITY

Languedoc-Roussillon is France's leading wine region in terms of acreage. It is now an integral part of the country's wine scene, after ridding itself of its jug wines in the 1980s. It is a constant source of intrigue to wine lovers and has made such a quantum leap in quality that it is now a fully-fledged member of France's elite circle of premium wine regions. This has nurtured new talent, not only amongst the younger wine categories (including Vins de Pays d'Oc) but also the more traditional ones (Fitou, Corbières, Minervois, Saint-Chinian, Côtes du Roussillon-Villages…).

Malepère

Blanquette de Limoux

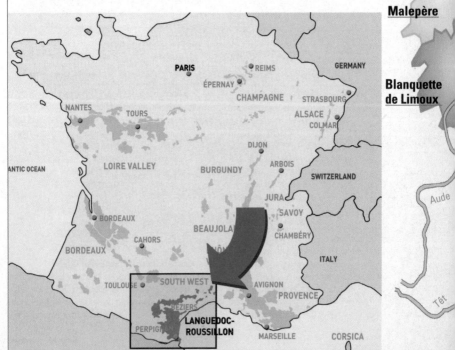

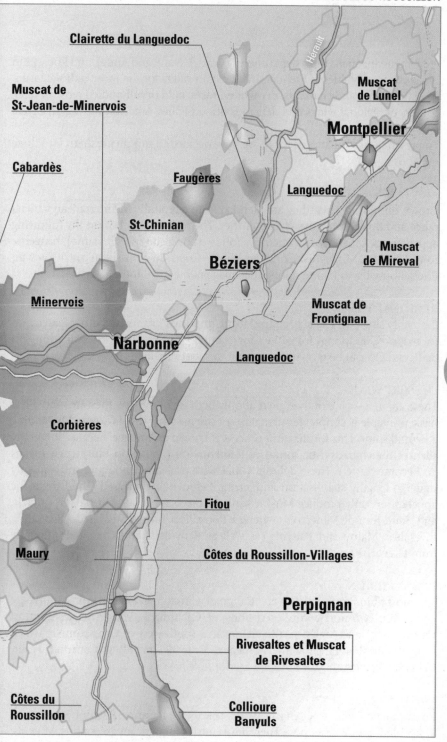

Clairette du Languedoc

Muscat de Lunel

Muscat de St-Jean-de-Minervois

Montpellier

Cabardès

Faugères

Languedoc

St-Chinian

Muscat de Mireval

Béziers

Minervois

Muscat de Frontignan

Narbonne

Languedoc

Corbières

Fitou

Maury

Côtes du Roussillon-Villages

Perpignan

Rivesaltes et Muscat de Rivesaltes

Côtes du Roussillon

Collioure Banyuls

Hérault

231

Languedoc spans three departments (Gard, Hérault and Aude), and Roussillon just one: Pyrénées-Orientales. The region caters for the most catholic tastes: sparkling wines and crémants, dry whites, rosés, light or full-bodied reds, all three colours of regional wines and delicious dessert wines, amongst the region's great hallmarks.

To present a clear picture of these, we have decided to sub-divide them into three categories:

APPELLATION WINES

Grown on hillside sites, they are blended from a typically Mediterranean varietal range and boast distinctive characteristics. The region plays host to the following appellations: Languedoc (sometimes followed by a site-specific name), Faugères, Saint-Chinian, Minervois, Corbières, Fitou, Côtes du Roussillon and Côtes du Roussillon-villages (some stating the village name), Collioure...

REGIONAL WINES

Generally single varietals, produced from 'imported' plants (Cabernet-Sauvignon for reds or Chardonnay for whites, for example). The regional denomination, Vin de Pays d'Oc, can be grown throughout this vast province.

DESSERT WINES

These are in a league of their own, if only because of the way they are made. The basic principle is simple: fermentation of the nascent wine is arrested by adding a neutral spirit. This fortification process is known as 'mutage' because it literally silences the characteristic sound of fermentation ('muter' in old French means 'to become mute'). These delicate wines with a pleasant bouquet subsequently undergo lengthy stabilisation and ageing before being released. The Languedoc appellations only produce Muscat wines in this way: Lunel, Mireval, Frontignan and Saint-Jean-de-Minervois, whereas Roussillon offers: Muscat de Rivesaltes, Rivesaltes, Maury and Banyuls (as well as Banyuls Grand Cru predominantly from Grenache noir).

RED VARIETALS

The most ubiquitous varietals are: Carignan, Cinsault, Grenache noir, Mourvedre and Syrah. Two noteworthy exceptions are Cabardès (a young AC set north of Carcassonne) and Malepère (an AC located south-west of Carcassonne) which supplement this range with 'Bordeaux' varietals including Cabernet Franc, Cabernet-Sauvignon, Cot noir and Merlot noir.

WHITE VARIETALS

Bourboulenc, Clairette, Grenache blanc, Macabeu, Marsanne, Picpoul, Roussanne, Terret blanc and Vermentino. There are a clutch of significant exceptions. Muscats:

in Languedoc, they are entirely drawn from the small berry Muscat; the Muscat de Rivesaltes appellation (Pyrénées-Orientales) also permits Muscat of Alexandria. Then there is Limoux where still white wines are made from Chardonnay, Chenin and Mauzac.

WINE STYLES

amongst the red wines, the elegance of Faugères, complexity of Corbières, tannic structure of Saint-Chinian, inimitable taste of 'terroir' in Fitou deserve a special mention. Of the whites, the most remarkable are without a doubt the fresh, aromatic Languedoc Picpoul de Pinet, Limoux and Vins de Pays d'Oc, though also the extremely distinctive character of the Muscats. Rounding off this selection are the Maury, Rivesaltes and Banyuls, the richest and most complex of our dessert wines.

REVIEW OF RECENT VINTAGES

• **2011** • At the risk of sounding repetitive, once again a dry, hot spring was followed by a very average summer saved by a delightful September. These southerly vineyards easily turned this to good account by producing plentiful volumes and aromatic, well-balanced wines. 2011 is definitely a year for wines from the South!

• **2012** • This region received a lot of sun and 20% less precipitation than usual in 2012. This resulted in healthy grapes apart from a bit of coulure (dropping of flowers) and powdery mildew. This vintage is still young, but is promising, with a good balance of sugar and acid.

• **2013** • A great year, occurring at an ideal time for the region which will be able to secure significant export markets due to the quality of the wines. The whites and rosés are fresh and vibrant and the wines in general are highly expressive, revealing a fullness that harks back to the balance displayed in the 1980s. The technical expertise built up over the last thirty years or so has yielded exceptional wines, that are extremely fashionable to boot.

THE LANGUEDOC-ROUSSILLON APPELLATIONS

BANYULS AND BANYULS GRAND CRU

OVERVIEW: Of all the Grand Roussillon dessert wine appellations, AC Banyuls is the best known. The area sits within the same boundaries as AC Collioure and embraces four towns and villages (Banyuls sur Mer, Collioure, Port Vendres, Cerbère). It climbs the abrupt hillsides on terraces propped up with dry stone walls. The skeletal soils lay on Cambrian shale. Banyuls is divided into a basic AC Banyuls and a Banyuls Grand Cru.

WINE-MAKING TECHNIQUES: Banyuls is a dessert wine made by the fortification process, whereby the wine grower adds 96% proof neutral spirit to grapes

233

during alcoholic fermentation in a ratio of 5 to 10% of must volume. By using this process, yeast activity is arrested before all the sugar has been turned into alcohol and aroma compounds can be fully extracted from young wines. The ageing phase begins two to four weeks after maceration. Banyuls Grand Cru must spend at least 30 months in oak whilst basic Banyuls is aged either in glass demi-johns or carefully sealed barrels kept in a cool, damp environment. They can also be stored outside to develop slightly oxidised aromas. Grenache noir, the appellation's primary varietal, must account for at least 50% of the blend for Banyuls and 75% for Banyuls Grand Cru. Some single vintage wines bottled prior to oxidation are labelled 'Rimage'.

WINE STYLES: AC Banyuls yields red, rosé and white dessert wines from the same varietal range. The red wines boast a ruby-red hue with mahogany tints in the early years, evolving into brick-red with copper tints over time. On the palate, they are supple, powerful, well-constituted, tannic wines with intense aromas of dried and crystallised fruits, morello cherries in brandy, vanilla, coffee…. Try as an appetiser or with desserts like chocolate cake. White Banyuls, with their elegant straw-yellow hue, are highly unusual. They can be made either as sweet, dry aged in new oak or medium sweet wines. Their character stems from the Grenache blanc varietal and they reveal delicate floral, citrus fruit and honeyed notes. Enjoy with foie gras, blue cheeses or desserts with honey.

AC BLANQUETTE DE LIMOUX

OVERVIEW: Blanquette de Limoux is one of Languedoc-Roussillon's oldest controlled appellations. The area is located 25 kilometres south of Carcassonne in the Aude department and covers 41 towns and villages. The vines grow on light, stony calcareous clay soils and the climate is unusual in that it alternates between Ocean and Mediterranean. The area specialises in sparkling wines made from the local varietal Mauzac, which can be blended with Chardonnay and Chenin blanc.

WINE-MAKING TECHNIQUES: there are two types of Blanquette: ancestral method Blanquette de Limoux is a single varietal made from Mauzac. It undergoes secondary (natural) fermentation in the bottle. Blanquette de Limoux itself is a blended wine: Mauzac (at least 90%), Chardonnay and Chenin. Like Crémant de Limoux it undergoes secondary fermentation in the bottle induced by adding a blend of yeast and sugar. This is when the bubbles form. The wines age for at least 9 months on the lees, following which they are disgorged (the sediment is removed by refrigeration) and the dosage is then added. This will determine whether a wine is dry or medium dry. Crémant de Limoux is made in the same way though it matures for longer than Blanquette, spending at least 15 months in the cellar.

WINE STYLES: Blanquette and Crémant de Limoux are sparkling wines with a pale hue highlighted with golden tints. Aromas of apricot, acacia, hawthorn, peach blossom or apple, citrus fruit and toast are present. They can be enjoyed as appetisers, with savoury or smoked canapés, red mullet, anchovies, squid, patés or white meat.

AC CABARDÈS

OVERVIEW: the Cabardès wine region is located a dozen kilometres north-west of Carcassonne. It extends outwards from the Minervois appellation and covers 18 towns and villages in the Aude department. Like its neighbour, it occupies the southern slopes of Mount Noire, with Carcassonne below in the plain. This is Languedoc-Roussillon's most westerly wine region and it plays host to a broad range of soil types: limestone stones on the valley floor followed by primary rocks (granite then shale and gneiss) at higher elevations. The most unusual feature of this region, however, is its climate: it is caught between Mediterranean and Ocean influences, augmented by the altitude factor. Cabardès is one of the few appellations combining varietals of Atlantic or Continental origin and Mediterranean grape varieties. Here, Cabernet-Sauvignon, Merlot, Cabernet Franc, Fer Servadou grow alongside Grenache, Syrah and Cinsault.

WINE STYLES: Cabardès appellation wines can be either red or rosé. The red wines are supple, full and complex, boasting a host of aromas (red and black fruit, prunes, crystallised fruit, spices, liquorice, undergrowth…). They pair well with cooked cold pork meats, poultry, mutton chops, cassoulet and goats cheese. The rosé wines are dry, lively, delicate and fruity. Try them with cooked cold pork meats, mutton kebabs, chicken with almonds or tagine.

AC CLAIRETTE DE BELLEGARDE

OVERVIEW: the Clairette de Bellegarde appellation area is set between Nîmes and Arles, in the Gard department. It covers a single town, Bellegarde, verging on the Costières de Nîmes appellation. Soil make-up is primarily formed of pebbles and sandstone and the Mediterranean-type climate is hot and dry, with plenty of sunshine and a favourable aspect. Wine styles: Clairette de Bellegarde is made from a single varietal, Clairette, and can be aged either in tanks or barrels. With its attractive pale gold hue, this dry white wine displays tell-tale aromas of walnuts, spices, fennel and a hint of grapefruit. It is soft and unctuous with relatively low acidity. The locals tend to pair it with grilled fish or shellfish.

AC COLLIOURE

OVERVIEW: the Collioure appellation area is set in the Pyrénées-Orientales department. The vines are planted on sheer hillsides sharing the same 'terroir' as Banyuls. Covering 727 hectares and four villages, the appellation stretches over poor, shale soils and basks in a hot, dry Mediterranean climate. The vines enjoy abundant sunshine, allowing the grapes - Grenache noir, Mourvedre, Carignan, Cinsault and Syrah - to achieve full ripeness (the proportion of Grenache noir, Mourvèdre and Syrah, either together or individually, must be at least 60% of the total blend with the highest single varietal accounting for anything up to 90%). Collioure wines are vinted traditionally at controlled temperatures, after des-temming and a prolonged two-week vatting period. The rosés are made from red varietals though also a maximum 30% of Grenache gris. The whites are blended from Grenache blanc, Grenache gris, Macabeu, Marsanne, Tourbat and Vermentino.

WINE STYLES: Collioure wines are either red or rosé. The red wines display a superb cherry-red hue. They are powerful, warm wines. In the early years, they exude fragrances of small black fruit (cherry, blackberry) and red fruit. As they age, they acquire their hallmark finesse and bouquet making them a perfect match for meat, stews and game. The rosé wines display a beautiful deep pink colour. They are harmonious, delicate, powerful and extremely aromatic (ripe red fruit). Try them with barbecued meat, fish, paella, mixed salads, cooked cold pork meats or Collioure anchovies. The white wines are rich, intense and driven by floral, exotic and mineral notes.

AC CORBIÈRES

OVERVIEW: the Corbières wine region spans from Narbonne to Perpignan and from Carcassonne to the Mediterranean. It embraces 105 towns and villages in the Aude department. The predominant soil type is calcareous clay interspersed with : shale, red sandstone, marl and stony terraces. Although the climate is strongly defined by the influence of the Mediterranean, the most westerly sites experience an Ocean climate.

The multifaceted nature of the region has led to the implementation of sub-zones. There are currently 11 such zones: Boutenac (recently promoted to 'growth' sta-tus), Durban, Fontfroide, Lagrasse, Lézignan, Montagne d'Alaric, Quéribus, Saint-Victor, Serviès, Sigean and Termenès. These converge into four major areas:
• The maritime Corbières form the western rim of the appellation and their defining characteristics are low elevation, predominantly limestone soils and a definite Mediterranean climate.
• The upper Corbières occupy the south-western portion of the area and its most mountainous section, home to the highest peaks in the Corbières. The climate therefore defines a threshold, restricting the development of vineyards. Vines do grow here however on predominantly shale-type soils conducive to producing top-flight wines.
• Alaric Corbières: located in the north-western part of the appellation, this area takes its name from Mount Alaric, a 600-metre-high summit overlooking the Aude valley. A multiplicity of soil types can be found here but the Mediterranean climate, strongly influenced by the Ocean, provides consistency throughout.
• The central Corbières: situated squarely in the middle of the Corbières, hence its name, this area boasts marl and sandstone soils as well as an extremely arid, hot climate.

WINE STYLES: AC Corbières wines come in all three colours. The reds (over 90% of total output) are blended from a classic selection of Mediterranean varieties: Carignan (less widespread in some areas), Grenache, Lladoner Pelut, Mouvedre, Syrah, Cinsault...The wines are fragrant, moderately tannic and warm though often need to mature for a few years. Aromatically, they cover a comprehensive range, evolving over time: red fruit fragrances (blackcurrant, blackberry), initially moving on to spices (pepper, liquorice, moorland, thyme, rosemary) then, a few years later, to worn leather, coffee, cocoa, undergrowth, game... This makes them suitable for a wide variety of food pairings: duck with orange, mutton stew, roast pigeon...

The rosés are blended from the same varietal range, augmented with Grenache gris, and are vinted using the 'bleeding' or direct to press method. Their hue embraces a broad spectrum, ranging from pale pink with salmon coloured tints to darker shades. They are aromatic wines (raspberry, violet, exotic fruits) and are fresh and round on the palate, often with a long finish. The white wines are drawn from Bourboulenc, Grenache blanc and Maccabeo (at least 50%), though also Clairette, Picpoul, Muscat, Terret, Marsanne, Roussanne and Vermentino. Direct press wines, they are robust and fat though remain fresh and well-balanced. Aromas of citrus fruit, pepper, cinnamon and floral notes are present. Some spend time in oak. They marry well with grilled fish, seafood, shellfish and chicken sauteed with mushrooms.

237

AC CORBIÈRES BOUTENAC

OVERVIEW: the Corbières Boutenac area is considered to be one of the appellation's finest terroirs and embraces 10 towns and villages between Lézignan and Thézan. The soils derive from the secondary (limestone and sandstone dolomitic outcrops) and tertiary eras (various types of molasse). Old vines plunge their roots deep into the ground in search of water, thereby ensuring the wines express optimum sense of place. The appellation was officially recognised in 2005 and only red wines are entitled to use it. Basic yields are lower than for Corbières (45 hl/ha instead of 50hl/ha) and wine making and ageing criteria are stricter.

AC CÔTES DU ROUSSILLON

OVERVIEW: AC Côtes du Roussillon covers an area stretching south of the Corbières down to the Albères on the Spanish border. 118 towns and villages in Pyrénées-Orientales qualify for the appellation which lines the Roussillon plain and climbs the surrounding hillsides. Several distinct sub-zones have been identified: the Agly, Têt and Tech valleys, the Aspres (a site-specific area embracing 37 towns and villages which can feature on labels. Only red wines are entitled to use it), the Albères and a coastal strip skirting the Mediterranean. The soils are generally littered with stones and run the gamut from red clay, granite, shale and gneiss to calcareous clay. The terrain is rugged, formed of rolling hills and poor, arid terraces (the Aspres, Fenouillèdes, Corbières and Albères hills). Summers are hot and rainfall occurs mainly in the autumn. The ripening process is enhanced by plentiful sunshine.

WINE STYLES: the ubiquitous red wines are required by law to come from a blend of at least three of the following varieties: Carignan (50% maximum), Grenache noir, Syrah, Mourvedre (these four varietals must account for at least 80% of the blend with the highest single varietal not exceeding 70%. The two latter varietals account for 25% of the blend, together or individually), Cinsault, Lladoner Pelut. The reds are full-bodied, fat, round, warm, well-constituted wines with good concentration and aromas (ripe red fruit, cherry, prune, wild berries, spices, liquorice). They boast great texture and depth. Try them with stews, grilled meats (lamb), beef stew with peppers, game and cheeses. Wines made by the whole grape fermentation process are sold shortly after the harvest and come primarily from the Carignan grape which is best suited to this process.

The rosés display an intense hue. They are slightly spicy, with aromas of red fruits (cherry), plum and liquorice. They are forward, fruity, full and powerful wines, relatively robust with well-balanced mellowness. The whites are blended from Grenache blanc, Macabeo, Tourbat (also known as Malvoisie in Roussillon), and can be supplemented with Marsanne, Grenache gris, Roussanne and Vermentino (50% maximum). They are delicate, fresh, vigorous, aromatic wines where the predominant aromas are floral. Enjoyable with fish (sardines), shellfish and snails.

AC CÔTES DU ROUSSILLON-VILLAGES

OVERVIEW: this region covers 32 towns and villages in Pyrénées-Orientales, dotted either side of the Agly valley. Soil types are varied but are frequently shale, gneiss and granite. Although Carignan is the mainstay of the varietal range, its share of the blend must not exceed 60%. Complementary varietals are Cinsault, Grenache, Lladoner Pelut, Syrah and Mourvedre (at least 30%). Four villages are entitled to add their name to the appellation and have now been promoted to 'growth' status: Latour-de-France, Lesquerde, Tautavel and Caramany, which must be blended from at least three varietals:

• Latour-de-France: 176 hectares in Latour-de-France and neighbouring villages. Soils are shale, calcareous clay and granite.

Lesquerde (granted in 1995): located in the far eastern part of the Agly valley, this village also covers plots in Lansac and Rasiguères.

• Tautavel: was created in 1997 on calcareous clay soils in the villages of Tautavel and Vingrau; growers use less Carignan here, tending to prefer Grenache and Lladoner Pelut. The wines must mature for at least a year.

• Caramany: gneiss soils along the Agly valley in Caramany, with a few outlying plots in Belesta and Cassagnes.

WINE STYLES: Côtes du Roussillon Villages are not only more robust than Côtes du Roussillon, they are also more harmonious, fleshy, powerful and complex. They are round, full, robust and long on the palate framed by firm tannins. A large proportion are oak-aged (three years). They display fragrances of small red fruits and stewed fruit (blackcurrant), spices (pepper), liquorice, bay and vanilla, gradually developing into scents of game, brandy and truffle. Try them with roasted red meats or meat in a sauce (rib steak), lamb, game and cheeses.

AC CRÉMANT DE LIMOUX

OVERVIEW: Crémant de Limoux was granted controlled appellation status in 1990. It bolsters the range of sparkling wines grown around Limoux: ancestral method Blanquette de Limoux and Blanquette de Limoux. It is grown within the same boundaries (41 towns and villages in Aude south of Carcassonne) though complies with different varietal and growing standards: an upper limit of 20% is applied to the traditional varietal Mauzac at the expense of Chardonnay and Chenin (20% minimum but less than 40%), the two main varieties (that can account for up to 90%). Secondary fermentation must occur in the bottle with 15 months bottle fermentation (versus 9 for Blanquette).

WINE STYLES: Crémant de Limoux is a sparkling wine with a pale hue highlighted with golden tints. It generally has a stronger structure than Blanquette though its fragrances can be more elusive: apricot, acacia, hawthorn, apple, toast… Excellent as an appetiser.

239

AC FAUGÈRES

OVERVIEW: Faugères is a small area covering 7 villages nestled amongst the lower slopes of Mount Noire which towers over the plain around Béziers. Soil types are reasonably consistent, with a predominant proportion of shale. Large chunks of scrubland have been cleared, particularly in the north, to make way for vineyards. The climate is Mediterranean, dry and hot, and the due south aspect of the vineyards promotes the ripening process. Great strides have been made in terms of varietal selection and the once ubiquitous Carignan grape has been joined by a host of other varieties over the last 25 years. Carignan and Cinsault (40% and 20% at most), Grenache and Lledoner Pelut (20% minimum) Syrah and Mourvedre (at least 5% for the latter one). The tiny proportion of white wines are labelled as Coteaux du Languedoc.

WINE STYLES: Faugères wines are red, rosé and white. The reds are heady, captivating, warm wines. Tannins are present but mellow and they frame a broad aromatic spectrum (cherry, raspberry, blackcurrant, crushed strawberries, liquorice, leather). All of this combines to produce silky wines with finesse. Try them with grilled beef tenderloin, partridge or wild boar fillet steak. The rosé wines are made using the 'bleeding' or direct to press method, and are round and harmonious. Aromas of red fruit, white flowers and smoky notes are present. A good match for cooked cold pork meats, starters and mixed salads. The whites are made from Roussane, Grenache blanc, Marsanne and Vermentino (Rolle) and draw impeccable minerality from the local schist soils.

AC FITOU

OVERVIEW: the Fitou appellation is located in southern Languedoc, between Perpignan and Narbonne. It embraces 9 villages divided into two wine growing regions in Aude: one following the coastline on calcareous clay soils, the other on higher elevations, where the soil is shallow shale. The climate is Mediterranean, humid on the coastline and more arid inland. Carignan forms the backbone of the varietal range (at least 30%), augmented with Grenache noir, Lladoner Pelut (these varietals must account for at least 70% of the blend), Syrah and Mourvedre, and a balance (10% at most) of Cinsault.

WINE STYLES: Fitou uses two different wine making techniques: traditional vinification methods (grapes crushed and destemmed) at controlled temperatures; and the whole grape fermentation process (grapes left uncrushed), primarily for Carignan. The resultant wines are often blended. They must age for at least 9 months. Blessed with a brilliant ruby-red hue, the wines are well-constituted, full, fat and generous with rich, complex aromas (wild flowers, moorland, red fruit (blackcurrant, cherry), spices, grilled almonds and leather layered onto venison and prune). Enjoy with game (wild boar, deer), roast beef with mushrooms or duck breast.

AC LANGUEDOC

OVERVIEW: the Languedoc appellation area (until recently Coteaux du Languedoc) follows the Mediterranean coastline from Nîmes to Narbonne. It covers 168 towns and villages spread over 3 departments (Aude, Hérault, Gard). To reflect the numerous 'terroirs' within this vast area (hard limestone in the scrublands, shale, gravel…) growers can add site-specific names to the appellation. There are 14 such sites for red and rosé wines and 2 for white wines. For reds and rosés, these are: La Clape, Quatourze, Cabrières, Montpeyroux, Saint-Saturnin, Pic-Saint-Loup, Saint-Georges-d'Orques, Les Coteaux de la Méjanelle, Saint-Drézéry, Saint-Christol and Les Coteaux de Vérargues, Grès de Montpellier, Terrasses du Larzac and Pézénas. For white wines: La Clape and Picpoul de Pinet. Five of these sites (growths) - La Clape, Grès de Montpellier, Terrasses du Larzac, Pézénas and Pic Saint Loup - are classed as geographical denominations within the appellation area. They have been officially recognised by AC law and comply with more restrictive production criteria. The same law allows the others to use their denomination as a village appellation.

The varietal range is Mediterranean: for reds and rosés: Carignan (40% maximum), Cinsault (40% maximum), Grenache, Lladoner Pelut, Syrah and Mourvedre. For whites: Grenache blanc, Clairette, Bourboulenc, Picpoul blanc (50% minimum), which can be augmented with Ugni blanc, Terret, Carignan, Maccabeo, Marsanne, Roussanne and Rolle.

WINE STYLES: AC Languedoc produces red, rosé and white wines. The reds are vinted either traditionally or using the whole grape fermentation process. They are generous, powerful, velvety, elegant wines with aromas of raspberry, blackcurrant and spices (pepper). Wines for cellaring have characteristic aromas of leather, bay and moorland fragrances (thyme, rosemary, juniper). Try them with grilled meats or meats served in a sauce. The rosés are made by the 'bleeding' process and are fruity and warm. They combine fullness, suppleness and finesse (redcurrant, raspberry, cherry, floral notes) and are well suited to hors d'œuvre, cooked cold pork meats, fish and shellfish. The white wines are increasingly fermented in oak. Full, round and displaying characteristic acidity, they conjure up aromas of apricot, peach, honey and floral and toasted notes. They are enjoyable with shellfish and grilled fish.

AC LANGUEDOC CABRIÈRES

OVERVIEW: this site-specific area fits within the broader Languedoc appellation and is located around the village of the same name, near Clermont-l'Hérault and Salagou lake. Primary shale is the predominant soil type playing host to vineyards here, imparting highly distinctive characteristics to the wines.

WINE STYLES: Cabrières produces both red and rosé wines. White wines grown in the same area are labelled Clairette du Languedoc. The red wines display a hallmark personality, and are generally very concentrated and well-balanced with aromas of red fruits (raspberry, strawberry, blackcurrant) and peony. Over time, these evolve and take on spicy, smoky undertones and toasted aromas of roasted coffee. They can be served with game, grilled meats or meats served with a sauce. The rosés, known as 'ruby-reds' are made chiefly from Cinsault and are pleasant, light wines with delicate aromas (floral, fruity notes). They are well suited to cooked cold pork meats and hors d'œuvre.

AC LANGUEDOC COTEAUX DE VÉRARGUES

OVERVIEW: the Vérargues wine area is set between Sommières (in the Gard department) and Lunel (in Hérault), in and around the towns and villages of Beaulieu, Boisseron, Lunel, Lunel-Viel, Restinclières, Saint Geniès Les Mourgues, Saint-Seriès, Saturargues and Vérargues. Vines grow on terrace sites and calcareous clay scree, pebbles and sand, where the climate is Mediterranean and dry.

WINE STYLES: the red wines of Vérargues are relatively supple and display great aromatic finesse (red and black fruit, vanilla). They marry well with duck with prunes, game and grilled meats. The rosés are delicate and elegant (red fruit, spices, aniseed) and pair with barbecued meats and cooked cold pork meats.

AC LANGUEDOC GRÈS DE MONTPELLIER

OVERVIEW: 46 towns and villages set on the outskirts of Montpellier in the Hérault department qualify for this appellation. The dry climate and damp warm air rising from the sea promote early ripening and good balance throughout the growing cycle. Grenache, Mourvedre and Syrah (at least 70% for all three varietals

241

combined and at least 20% Grenache) rub shoulders with a few old Carignan vines (30% maximum).

WINE STYLES: robust red wines to enjoy with red meat, meat in a sauce and game.

AC LANGUEDOC LA CLAPE

OVERVIEW: La Clape is a site-specific wine area (growth) within AC Languedoc. It is located east of Narbonne, in the Aude department, and embraces 5 villages: Armissan, Fleury, Salles-d'Aude, Vinassan and parts of Narbonne. La Clape boasts a variety of soil types: limestone plateaux clad in scrubland overlooking coombs which open up onto marl; Miocene molasse soils skirting the La Clape mountain range in the north, interspersed with limestone debris chiselled from the peaks as well as alluvial gravel. Frequent winds provide suitable ripening conditions for the grapes by curbing outbreaks of disease. The region is also blessed with low rainfall and plenty of sunshine.

WINE STYLES: La Clape produces primarily red wines but also yields some outstanding whites from Bourboulenc (also known locally as Malvoisie) and Grenache blanc, not to mention some extremely pleasant rosés. The red wines, drawn mainly from Grenache and Syrah, are fleshy, round and powerful. They display character and the tell-tale characteristics of their growing environment, exuding scents of the surrounding moorland and pine forests. Try with wild boar served with a sauce and red meats either grilled or served with a sauce. The rosé wines are light and well-balanced. Often described as a wine for immediate pleasure, they display floral (acacia, rose), peach, apricot and citrus notes. An ideal partner for barbecues, cooked cold pork meats or crudités. The white wines are powerful and complex, exhibiting a distinctive acidulous freshness. Fragrances of citrus fruit (grapefruit), exotic fruit, sweet almonds, peach and jasmine are present. Enjoy with fish soup or shellfish.

AC LANGUEDOC LA MÉJANELLE

OVERVIEW: La Méjanelle is a wine growing area located in four villages on the outskirts of Montpellier. The soil is scattered with pebbles of Alpine origin also known as 'grès'. The climate is Mediterranean with a maritime influence.

WINE STYLES: red wines from La Méjanelle are fleshy, fat and concentrated with aromas of ripe or crystallised red or black fruit, smoky notes, spices. Try with spit-roasted lamb or duck with olives. The rosés, drawn primarily from Grenache, are delicate and exhibit a host of aromas. The perfect match for barbecues and cooked cold pork meats.

AC LANGUEDOC MONTPEYROUX

OVERVIEW: Montpeyroux, which means 'Stony Mountain', is a wine growing area occupying the southern slopes of the Larzac, sandwiched between the plateau and the upper Hérault valley. The vines grow on sun-drenched soils littered with stones.

WINE STYLES: Montpeyroux red wines are on the whole warm and well-constituted. They are generous wines with mellow tannins and aromas bearing the tell-tale characteristics of their growing environment: the surrounding moorland (spices, stewed fruit, thyme, woody notes). Try with red meat or game.

AC LANGUEDOC PEZENAS

OVERVIEW: a newcomer to the Languedoc appellation system covering fifteen towns and villages around Pezenas in Hérault. Grenache, Mourvedre and Syrah must form at least 70% of the blend though the maximum percentage for a single varietal is 75%. Mourvedre and Syrah, either together or individually, must form at least 20% of the blend and if Carignan is included in the varietal range, at least 20% of Grenache must be used.

WINE STYLES: this particular area produces some sterling red wines due to a long-standing tradition of quality wine making by a handful of independent estates and co-operative wineries. Try with barbecues or meat served with a sauce.

AC LANGUEDOC PICPOUL DE PINET

OVERVIEW: the Picpoul de Pinet appellation area embraces six villages bordering Thau lake in the department of Hérault. With the exception of La Clape, it is the only area where white wines qualify for the Coteaux du Languedoc appellation. The soil make-up is characteristically formed of limestone gravel resulting from the decomposition of limestone marl dating from several different periods (from the Cretaceous to the Pliocene epoch). Picpoul de Pinet wines are vinted using the direct to press method and ferment at low temperatures. They often mature on the lees which imparts more fat and roundness.

WINE STYLES: Picpoul de Pinet is a dry white wine made from a single varietal, Piquepoul. Boasting a pale yellow hue with greenish tints, it is fresh and extremely aromatic (lemon, mango, white flesh fruits (banana), grapefruit, peach and vanilla)… On the palate, it displays a distinctive lemony flavour with undertones of dried fruit and freshly-cut hay. Try as an appetiser or with shellfish from the nearby Thau lake (Bouzigues oysters, clams) and grilled fish.

AC LANGUEDOC PIC SAINT LOUP

OVERVIEW: the Pic Saint Loup wine growing area takes its name from the local mountain which is located twenty kilometres or so north of Montpellier and reaches a peak of 658 metres. Of all the site-specific areas of Languedoc, this is the most northerly. Vines are grown in 13 villages amongst the lower foothills, on soils of limestone scree and Oligocene conglomerate where they thrive. At this elevation (vines are grown at an altitude of around 200 metres) springtime temperatures are cooler than in other parts and rainfall is higher.

243

WINE STYLES: the Pic Saint Loup appellation produces both red and rosé wines. The reds are powerful, concentrated and boast a distinctive silky texture. They exhibit aromas of ripe fruit, bay, spices, mint, cinnamon, liquorice and vanilla. They pair well with red meat, game and cheeses. The rosés are rich, full and fruity (raspberry, redcurrant, strawberry), providing the ideal match for barbecues, mixed salads and patés.

AC LANGUEDOC QUATOURZE

OVERVIEW: the Quatourze wine region occupies a stony plateau in the southern part of Narbonne in Aude. It enjoys a dry, hot climate, allowing the grapes to fully ripen.

WINE STYLES: the reds are warm, powerful wines which does not undermine their finesse (red fruits, spices, pepper). Of all the wines grown around Narbonne, they display the deepest colour and greatest structure and pair well with grilled meats, roast poultry and game (marcassin stew). The rosé wines are pleasant with a distinctive bouquet. Try them with cooked cold pork meats, barbecues or vegetable terrine.

AC LANGUEDOC SAINT-CHRISTOL

OVERVIEW: this area covers a single village, Saint-Christol in the department of Hérault. Villafranchian gravel and pebbles form the predominant soil type and the climate is dry and hot, allowing the grapes to fully ripen. Mourvedre, in particular, thrives here.

WINE STYLES: Saint-Christol produces wines with character, often displaying distinctive spice aromas. They are rich, velvety and extremely fragrant, providing the perfect match for a leg of lamb, game and grilled red meat. The appellation also produces rosé wines.

AC LANGUEDOC SAINT-DRÉZÉRY

OVERVIEW: the Saint-Drézéry wine region is located north of Montpellier, in and around the village of the same name. It is AC Languedoc's most diminutive geographical denomination. Villafranchian gravel forms the predominant soil type and the climate is dry and hot, allowing the grapes to fully ripen.

WINE STYLES: Saint-Drézéry wines are powerful, elegant and aromatic (red fruit) with spices. Pair with red meat, either grilled or served with a sauce.

AC LANGUEDOC SAINT-GEORGES D'ORQUES

OVERVIEW: the Saint-Georges d'Orques appellation area is located 8 kilometres west of Montpellier and covers five villages. Soil types are varied, alternating between calcareous clay and stones. Interspersed amongst these, is a good deal of flint mingled with decalcified clay, covering a significant portion of the area. The nearby sea has a moderating influence on the hot, dry Mediterranean climate.

WINE STYLES: Saint-Georges d'Orques boast a long-standing reputation for its wines. Prior to the advent of mass-produced wines, they were most certainly Languedoc-Roussillon's best known and loved red wines. They vary in style from rich, powerful wines with a great capacity for cellaring, to tender, flavoursome wines which reward early drinking. Either way, they are blessed with extremely delicate fruity characteristics (blackberry, cherry, morello cherry, vanilla, spices) and mild tannins. Try with red meat, game and cheeses.

AC LANGUEDOC SAINT-SATURNIN

OVERVIEW: the Saint-Saturnin wine region is nestled in the foothills of the Larzac. It covers the villages of Arboras, Jonquières, Saint-Guiraud and Saint Saturnin de Lucian. It occupies stony ground set on a subsoil of calcareous clay and enjoys a hot climate, sheltered from the wind. This particular site only produces classic red wines and 'overnight' wines which are vinted for just one night. The resultant wines are supple, easy-drinking and fruity.

WINE STYLES: the wines are supple, round and pleasant with a reasonably pale hue. They exhibit crunchy fruit flavours, freshness and good overall balance. Try with white meat, cooked cold pork meats, barbecues or jugged hare. The rosés, primarily drawn from Syrah, are fat, generous and fragrant wines (carnation, red fruit, pepper). They pair well with barbecues, cooked cold pork meats and hors d'œuvres.

245

AC LANGUEDOC TERRASSES DU LARZAC

OVERVIEW: The Terrases du Larzac area is one of the five specific AC Languedoc sites (growths). 32 towns and villages in the department of Hérault qualify for this appellation. The region covers an extensive, fragmented area. Grenache, Mourvedre and Syrah must form at least 60% of the blend, though the maximum percentage for a single varietal is 75%. Mourvedre and Syrah, either together or individually, must form at least 20% of the blend and if Carignan is included in the varietal range, at least 20% of Grenache must be used. The wines must be blended from grapes or wines drawn from at least two of the aforementioned grape varieties.

WINE STYLES: red wines only. Enjoy with barbecues or meat served with a sauce.

AC LIMOUX

OVERVIEW: although AC Limoux has a long history, it is still relatively unknown, mainly because for a long time it was in direct competition with local sparkling wines, Blanquette and Crémant de Limoux. It shares the same boundaries as its sparkling counterparts, covering 41 towns and villages in Aude, located south of Carcassonne. Its predominantly calcareous clay soils and especially its Ocean-cooled Mediterranean climate, are, however, particularly well-suited to growing top-flight still white wines. The reds (recognised in 2004) must be blended from at least three varietals: the primary varietals are Merlot (at least 50%), Cot, Syrah, Grenache and Carignan. The secondary varietals (at least 20%) are Cabernet Franc and Cabernet-Sauvignon.

WINE STYLES: The varietal range here comprises Mauzac (at least 15%), though also Chardonnay and Chenin which impart power, fat and aromatic complexity to the blend. Limoux is made on a boutique scale, with just over 1,000 hl made annually, though this is on an upward trend as demand for still white wines increases apace. The wines are fat and opulent and pair well with fish dishes and shellfish.

AC MALEPÈRE

OVERVIEW: AC Malpère is the most westerly of the Languedoc appellations. It sits squarely in the middle of a triangle formed by Carcassonne, Limoux and Castelnaudary, embracing 31 towns and villages in Aude. Vines grow on rolling hillsides of calcareous clay and gravely terraces, caught between Mediterranean and Ocean influences. The varietal range mirrors this unusual situation: Merlot, (40 % minimum), Cabernet Franc, Cot, Cabernet-Sauvignon, Grenache, Lledoner Pelut, Cinsaut for the reds, Cabernet Franc (40 % minimum), Cabernet-Sauvignon, Cinsaut, Cot, Grenache and Merlot for the rosés. The red wines are vinted traditionally at controlled temperatures. Some are aged in oak. The rosés are made using the 'bleeding' method and ferment at low temperatures.

WINE STYLES: Malepère produces both red and rosé wines. The red wines display a crimson hue with purple-blue tints. They are robust, well-structured, fruity and round on the palate. Initial aromas of very ripe red fruit take on spicy, gamey, undergrowth tones as they age. Try with cassoulet, Languedoc stew or beef bourguignon. The rosés are full and lively on the palate, frequently offering good balance and a long-lasting finish (blackcurrant, strawberry, raspberry). Enjoy with stuffed vine leaves, fricassee of monkfish, cooked cold pork meats.

AC MAURY

OVERVIEW: this region covers four villages in Pyrénées-Orientales. Although the climate is Mediterranean, the vines also enjoy occasional Atlantic influences. Soil type is predominantly black shale which retains heat during the day and releases it by night. The fruit is destemmed and whole berries are macerated to make Maury. Traditionally, neutral spirit is added with the pomace still in the tanks. Skin contact then lasts for two weeks or more, extracting greater aromas, colour and tannins. A quarter of the wines are aged traditionally in oak and the remaining three quarters in concrete tanks. They remain in the cellar until the first September of the second year after the harvest. The Maury appellation, which until now was restricted to dessert wines, can now be used for dry wines grown on the same site. The new appellation came into force for wines made from the 2011 vintage onwards.

WINE STYLES: Maury is a fruity, complex red dessert wine. It is drawn primarily from Grenache and Macabeu. On the palate, it shows concentrated aromas of red or black fruit, vanilla, spices, dried figs, beeswax, cocoa and mocha. It is a robust, fleshy wine with a mellow softness derived from its sweetness. It makes an ideal appetiser, or can be served with foie gras or a chocolate dessert.

AC MINERVOIS

OVERVIEW: the Minervois appellation area stretches across the departments of Aude and Hérault, east and south of Carcassonne, covering 61 towns and villages. The region is subdivided into four distinct zones, each with its own characteristic climate and soil types: the extremely arid central zone with terraces formed of pebbles, sandstone, shale or limestone; a zone with identical soil types but a damper climate due to Ocean influences; an area of higher elevations where the soils are shale or karst; and an area defined by a Mediterranean climate buffeted by strong winds and formed of stony terraces. Six different sites have also been defined: Canal du Midi, Les Causses, La Circulade et ses Mourels, Coteaux et Contreforts, Trois Vallées and Les Terrasses.

The varietal range comprises Grenache, Lladoner Pelut, Syrah and Mourvedre (at least 60% combined), with a secondary range of Carignan, Cinsault, Piquepoul, Terret and Riveirenc. The main white varietals are: Grenache blanc, Bourboulenc, Maccabeo, Marsanne, Roussanne and Vermentino; these can be supplemented with Clairette, Picpoul, Terret and small-berry Muscat, to within an upper limit of 20%.

WINE STYLES: Minervois wines come in all three colours though reds account for 95% of production. The red wines are expressive, robust, full and generous with aromas of blackcurrant, violet, cinnamon and vanilla, ageing into notes of leather, crystallised fruit and prune. Try with mountain hams and sausages, small wild game, cassoulet or lamb stew. The rosés are drawn primarily from Syrah and are made using the 'bleeding' method. Try them with pissaladière, stuffed veal rolls, chicken with tarragon or stuffed vine leaves. The white wines are made using the direct to press method and often ferment in oak. They are delicate and elegant (peach, pear, blossom…). Try with mussels or salmon steak either grilled or served with a sauce.

AC MINERVOIS LA LIVINIÈRE

OVERVIEW: 6 villages in the Minervois region (Azille, Azillanet, Cesseras, Siran, La Livinière and Felines-Minervois), covering around 200 hectares, qualify for the site-specific Minervois-la-Livinière appellation. Only red wines are grown here, with Grenache, Syrah and Mourvedre forming the compulsory backbone of the varietal range (at least 60%). Yields are lower and the wines are made and aged to stricter standards than basic Minervois.

WINE STYLES: Minervois-la-Livinière is a red wine only appellation: at least 60% of the blend is Grenache, Mourvedre and Syrah, and at least 40% Mourvedre and Syrah. Several prime movers provide the drive behind the appellation, going to great lengths (and sometimes concentration) to continually elevate the quality of the wines. Watch this space…

AC MUSCAT DE FONTIGNAN

OVERVIEW: Muscat de Frontignan is France's oldest Muscat appellation (recognised in 1936). The appellation sits north-east of Sète in the department of Hérault, embracing just two small towns: Frontignan and Vic-la-Gardiole. The local soil is red clay littered with limestone gravel and is home to a single grape variety: small berry Muscat, also known as Muscat de Frontignan. The wine of the same name is a dessert wine made by adding spirit - anywhere from 5 to 10% of total volume - to the fermenting must. This technique, known as 'mutage', arrests fermentation and retains some of the wine's natural sugars, called residual sugar (at least 110g per litre). The wines must be fortified in this way before December 31st and have a minimum alcohol content of 15%. Prior to their release, they must spend a minimum amount of time ageing. Fact: Muscat de Frontignan bottles have a unique cable type design.

WINE STYLES: these are archetypal Muscat wines at the far end of the sweetness scale, containing more residual sugar than other wines, with 125g per litre compared with 115g for Beaumes-de-Venise and 100g for Rivesaltes. This makes them extremely rich, very syrupy with good vinosity. They are powerful, generous, elegant, delicate and full, displaying a pale yellow hue with topaz tints and fragrances of honey, linden, fresh grapes, ripe fruit and citrus fruit. They can be enjoyed as an appetiser or served with melon, foie gras, Peking duck, Roquefort cheese or desserts. Fact: the appellation also produces a liqueur wine whereby spirit is added to the must prior to fermentation. The resultant nectar boasts 185g of residual sugar.

AC MUSCAT DE LUNEL

OVERVIEW: Muscat de Lunel is grown in Lunel, Lunel-Vieil, Vérargues and Saturargues, in the department of Hérault. The soils are red clay scattered with gravel and are home to small-berry Muscat. The wines are made by adding spirit to the fermenting must, a technique known as 'mutage'.

WINE STYLES: Muscat de Lunel are slightly different to Muscat de Frontignan. They are rich, delicate, elegant, unctuous, powerful wines, which are racy, well-balanced, harmonious and fresh. They boast a golden hue and their fragrances are floral (linden), though also grape, dried fruit (quince, fig, orange or tangerine peel, dried apricot), exotic fruit (lychee, mango) and citrus fruit. Try with chocolate gateau, fruit-based desserts, pear mousse, melon, foie gras, blue cheeses, asparagus and, of course, as an appetiser.

AC MUSCAT DE MIREVAL

OVERVIEW: the Muscat de Mireval area is adjacent to Frontignan, south-west of Montpellier. The small-berry Muscat grapes grow on stony ground with a subsoil of red clay, where the soils are arid and poor and Mount Gardiole acts as a natural barrier to the northerly winds. The wines are made by adding spirit to the fermenting must, a technique known as 'mutage'.

WINE STYLES: Muscat de Mireval bear many similarities with Muscat de Frontignan. They are extremely syrupy, powerful, fruity, elegant, delicate wines which are fresh, racy and harmonious with fragrances of honey, ripe grapes, rose and dried fruit. They can be enjoyed as appetisers or with a dessert (apricot charlotte and all fruit-based gateaux), but also throughout the meal: melon, foie gras or blue cheeses like Roquefort.

AC MUSCAT DE RIVESALTES

OVERVIEW: do not confuse AC Muscat de Rivesaltes, which is dedicated to white wines, with AC Rivesaltes. Covering 89 towns and villages in Pyrénées-Orientales and 9 in Aude, the Muscat de Rivesaltes region is the largest Muscat appellation in the world, with 5,342 hectares under vine. Soil types are therefore extremely varied, ranging from sandy or stony soil to loam, which soak up the dry, hot Mediterranean weather. Muscat de Rivesaltes are dessert wines made by arresting fermentation with spirit. Early bottling is a prerequisite to retain primary aromas and prevent oxidation.

WINE STYLES: Muscat de Rivesaltes are dessert wines that can only be made from small-berry Muscat and/or Muscat of Alexandria. They are powerful, fragrant white wines, though also suave and fresh with a long-lasting finish. They show pleasant notes of exotic fruits, pineapple, papaya and white peach, leading into vanilla, spicy, buttery, smoky overtones with grilled hazelnuts as they age. Enjoy as an appetiser, with foie gras or asparagus. The more mature wines pair well with cheeses (mature Cantal, Maroilles, Bleu d'Auvergne, goats cheese), marinated Collioure anchovies or desserts (chocolate mousse, lemon tart, sorbets).

AC MUSCAT DE SAINT-JEAN-DE-MINERVOIS

OVERVIEW: located in the heart of the Minervois wine region, forty or so kilo-metres north-west of Béziers in Hérault, this appellation area has the highest elevation of all of the Languedoc Muscats, reaching 300 metres in places. The vines grow on the limestone plateaux of the upper Minervois region, overlooking the river Cesse. The stony nature of the soil imparts the wines their hallmark characteristics. The wines are made from small-berry Muscat by adding spirit to the fermenting must, a technique known as 'mutage'.

WINE STYLES: Saint-Jean Muscats have a tell-tale touch of acidity which makes them different from the other Muscats. They are vigorous, generous, delicate wines with fragrances of flowers, honey, apricot, lemon and other citrus fruits. They can be enjoyed as appetisers or with a dessert (fruit-based gateaux, peach salad…).

AC RIVESALTES

OVERVIEW: AC Roussillon is located in the Roussillon basin and straddles two departments: Aude and Pyrénées-Orientales. Soil types are therefore extremely varied, ranging from limestone and calcareous clay to loam though also primary soils: Silurian shale, gneiss and granite. The climate is Mediterranean, hot and dry. High temperatures are in fact a prerequisite if the grapes are to achieve sufficient sugar concentration to be transformed into dessert wine. Like Banyuls, the red blends are fermented on the skins in an oxidised atmosphere, and the wines can age for no more than a year. There is no skin contact for the whites which are made using the direct to press method.

WINE STYLES: the Rivesaltes appellation is used for red, rosé and white dessert wines, drawn from Grenache noir, gris and blanc, Maccabeu, Muscat and Malvoisie, a varietal range which differentiates them from wines under the Muscat de Rivesaltes appellation. The "Grenats" are obtained by macerating the must for all or part of the red wine fermentation process (75% Grenache noir) and ageing them in a reducing atmosphere for at least months in the bottle. They display an attractive, extremely bright red hue which develops brick-red tints as they age. They are tannic, powerful, well-balanced wines with a long finish, boasting complex aromas (blackberry, raspberry, blackcurrant and cherry, leading into notes of cocoa, gingerbread, orange peel and crystallised fruit after spending time in oak). Try with strongly-flavoured food: game or duck. The red wines (50% Grenache noir) aged in an oxidative atmosphere until at least March 1st following the harvest are known as "tuilés" (or "bricked"). They are intense wines with notes of toast, cocoa, coffee, tobacco and candied fruits. The white wines are blessed with a pale yellow hue which turns amber after the same ageing duration in an oxidative atmosphere as the "tuilés". On the palate, they are round and supple, with hints of fennel and mint, leading into honeyed tones with dried fruit, vanilla, resin and cocoa. As they mature, they often develop slightly oxidised tones. Serve with fish marinated in ginger, lemon or mint. Mature Rivesaltes, both red and white, pair extremely well with desserts and a selection of cheeses.

AC SAINT-CHINIAN

OVERVIEW: the Saint-Chinian appellation area is located north of Béziers in the Hérault department. The area covers 20 towns and villages and its soil types are subdivided into two highly distinct zones: calcareous clay in the south, shale in the north. The climate is typically Mediterranean, hot and dry, and the varietal range, once dominated by Carignan, has changed considerably over the past 25 years : Carignan (40% maximum), Cinsault (30% maximum), Grenache, Lladoner Pelut, Syrah and Mourvedre. The latter four varietals must account for at least 60% of the blend including at least 10% for Syrah and Mourvèdre together and 20% for Grenache and Lladoner combined. Interestingly, the two village sites Roquebrun and Berlou, both on the appellation's shale soils, have recently been allowed to state their names on the label, alongside that of Saint-Chinian. However, only red wines are entitled to use these additional geographic denominations. The white wines (officially recognised in 2005) are primarily made from Grenache blanc, Marsanne, Roussanne, Vermentino, augmented with Bourboulenc, Clairette, Macabeu and Carignan blanc. They were previously label-led Coteaux du Languedoc.

WINE STYLES: the red wines display a 'cockerel blood' red hue. On the palate, they are rich, full and velvety, with aromas of red fruit (raspberry, blackcurrant), spices (pepper) and bay, leading into notes of cocoa, roasted coffee, fruit in brandy and jammy red fruit in time. The red wines grown on shale soils are more aromatic and supple, whilst those hailing from the calcareous clay soils are harder and more austere though with greater ageing capacity. Enjoy with game, duck salad or cassoulet. The rosés are fat, harmonious and boast distinctive freshness. Serve with marinated chicken kebabs, paella or a red fruit dessert.

• • •

2015
LANGUEDOC-
ROUSSILLON WINES

BANYULS

DOMAINE BERTA-MAILLOL   88/100

▼ ♪ Avis 2000 : Amber-hued, orange tints. Complex nose of stewed fruits, almond, liquorice, chocolate and coffee. The same broad-ranging, honest aromatics flow through to the palate over substantial length. Balance, freshness and generosity. A distinctive post-prandial Banyuls.
Price approx.: 35,00 EUR
www.bertamaillol.com
Domaine Berta-Maillol
+33 (0)4 68 88 00 54

DOMAINE BERTA-MAILLOL   86/100

▼ ♪ Rimage 2012 : Deep, young colour. Heady floral nose backed by cassis, cherry and blackberry with a hint of brandy. Well-balanced, fresh and full palate showcasing the liqueur-like fruit aromatics. A traditional Rimage that makes the perfect partner for chocolate desserts. Price approx.: 14,00 EUR
www.bertamaillol.com
Domaine Berta-Maillol
+33 (0)4 68 88 00 54

BLANQUETTE DE LIMOUX

DOMAINE ROSIER   87/100

▼ ♪ Brut : Light gold. Intense nose driven by white fruits, dried fruits, wild flowers... Refined and subtle with joyful bubbles. An unusual Blanquette for sharing with friends over a lengthy aperitif.
Price approx.: 4,60 EUR
Domaine Rosier
+33 (0)4 68 31 48 38

DOMAINE ROSIER   86/100

▼ ♪ Brut Cuvée 1531 : Light gold. Focused nose with accents of almond and lemon backed by flowers. A refined, supple and light Blanquette boasting a freshness which enhances fragrance. An enjoyable appetiser. Price approx.: 4,20 EUR
Domaine Rosier
+33 (0)4 68 31 48 38

GUINOT   85/100

▼ ♪ Brut Cuvée Réservée : Beautiful gold. Highly floral nose with peach, pear and fresh mushroom undercurrents. A soft Blanquette with fine effervescence. Freshness and crunchy flavours. A charming style for a mid-afternoon drink or delicately flavoured appetisers.
Price approx.: 7,20 EUR
www.blanquette.fr
Maison Guinot
+33 (0)4 68 31 01 33

DOMAINE ROSIER   85/100

▼ ♪ Brut Cuvée Spéciale : Light gold. The nose is driven by flowers, meadow and an intense lemony touch. Supple palate showing a delightful range of crisp aromatics and freshness. Classic and well-made.
Price approx.: 4,20 EUR
Domaine Rosier
+33 (0)4 68 31 48 38

DOMAINE DELMAS   82/100

Org ▼ ♪ Cuvée Tradition : Light gold. Suggestions of pear flesh on the nose coupled with a tropical touch. Simple, supple palate showing classic perfumes. A Limoux slightly lacking in personality. Drink as an aperitif.
Price approx.: 8,10 EUR
Domaine Delmas
+33 (0) 68 74 21 02

CABARDÈS

CHÂTEAU LA MIJEANNE   84/100

▼ ♪ Vintage 2012 : Beautiful deep, vibrant red. Nose of ripe black berry fruits with a mineral touch. Wonderful mouthfeel with fine, polished tannins and focused, fairly long-lasting fruit. A delightful wine drinking well now.
Price approx.: 3,00 EUR
Domaine de la Baquière
+33 (0)4 68 78 98 49

CÉVENNES

DOMAINE DE BERGUEROLLES   88/100

▼ ♪ Le Clos 2012 : Deep garnet. Very broad-ranging aromatics on the nose with vanilla oak, mild spices and fresh black fruits. A charming, elegant Cévennes with a soft mouthfeel showcasing perfume. Aromatic balance and no excessive power. A delicate wine from the South.
Price approx.: 10,50 EUR
Domaine de Berguerolles
+33 (0)4 66 24 01 84

TERRES D'HACHENE VIGNOBLE DES GARDIES 88/100

▼ ♪ Petraea 2011 : Deep colour, still in its youth. Endearing nose of ripe black fruits with a touch of

TERRES D'HACHENE

Petraea 2010

▼ Beautiful intense garnet. Rich nose driven by bigarreau cherry, garrigue, liquorice and mocha. A mature, ripe and balanced wine. Lovely freshness, supple mouthfeel, very sappy fruit and spicy finish. Perfect for leg of lamb.

PETRÆA
2010

VIN DE PAYS DES CÉVENNES

www.terresdhachene.com

88/100

---

garrigue, pepper and earth. Full, fleshy attack leading into a more supple mid-palate showing balanced, expressive fruit and spice perfumes that linger. Distinctive and refined. Price approx.: 18,00 EUR
http://www.terresdhachene.com
Terres d'Hachene Vignoble des Gardies
+33 (0)6 69 00 12 24

DOMAINE DE BERGUEROLLES 87/100

▼ ♪ Le Clos 2013 : Light gold. Very inviting nose halfway between pineapple, peach and white flowers and aniseed undertones. Round palate with a full mouthfeel and generous fruit displaying a degree of elegance and delicateness. Lingering white fruit finish. Well worth trying.
Price approx.: 11,00 EUR
Domaine de Berguerolles
+33 (0)4 66 24 01 84

TERRES D'HACHENE VIGNOBLE DES GARDIES 87/100

▼ ♪ Ilex 2011 : Young-looking colour. Refined floral and stone fruit nose with mild spice presence. An upright, focused style displaying balance and freshness. Aromatic presence with a welcome fruity suppleness. A southern wine that will easily find a captive audience. Price approx.: 22,00 EUR
http://www.terresdhachene.com
Terres d'Hachene Vignoble des Gardies
+33 (0)6 69 00 12 24

TERRES D'HACHENE VIGNOBLE DES GARDIES 87/100

▼ ♪ Ilex 2010 : Beautiful deep garnet. Lovely nose of spice and ripe stone fruits with a touch of mocha. Supple, well-balanced palate. Wonderful freshness enhancing distinctive aromas. Focused aromatic presence and an elegant mouthfeel. Stacks all the odds in its favour.
Price approx.: 22,00 EUR
http://www.terresdhachene.com
Terres d'Hachene Vignoble des Gardies
+33 (0)6 69 00 12 24

DOMAINE DE BERGUEROLLES 86/100

▼ ♪ Magnifica Preda 2013 : Light salmon-pink. Rich, mineral and floral nose backed by spice and ripe fruits. Full palate with focused aromas that linger. Savoury freshness throughout combined with generous perfumes. A complex, captivating rosé.
Price approx.: 10,50 EUR
Domaine de Berguerolles
+33 (0)4 66 24 01 84

TERRES D'HACHENE VIGNOBLE DES GARDIES 86/100

▼ ♪ Robur 2010 : Beautiful deep garnet. Endearing nose showing a lovely sense of place (spice, undergrowth, ripe stone fruit). More of the same on the palate, generous mouthfeel, freshness counterbalancing power and focused aromatic expression. A distinctive Cevennes, ready now.
Price approx.: 14,00 EUR
http://www.terresdhachene.com
Terres d'Hachene Vignoble des Gardies
+33 (0)6 69 00 12 24

TERRES D'HACHENE VIGNOBLE DES GARDIES 86/100

▼ ♪ Robur 2011 : Young, concentrated garnet. Intense nose showing peony on first pour then spicy fruit. Assertive palate that is full and chewy yet also reveals lovely aromatic presence. Consistent fruit with a spicy finish. A distinctive, successful southern wine. Price approx.: 14,00 EUR
http://www.terresdhachene.com
Terres d'Hachene Vignoble des Gardies
+33 (0)6 69 00 12 24

DOMAINE DE BERGUEROLLES 84/100

▼ ♪ Episode Cévenol blanc 2013 : Light gold. Appealing nose driven by peach and white flowers with floral undertones. Soft, refreshing palate with emphasis on delicious, user-friendly fresh fruit. An enjoyable wine for quaffing. Drink from the aperitif onwards. Price approx.: 6,80 EUR
Domaine de Berguerolles
+33 (0)4 66 24 01 84

DOMAINE DE BERGUEROLLES — 83/100

▼ ♪ Episode Cévenol rosé 2013 : Deep salmon-pink. Intense nose driven by citrus and ripe red fruits. An honest, full rosé revealing a generous array of aromatics. The finish is augmented by a touch of pepper. A focused, mature style.
Price approx.: 5,90 EUR
Domaine de Berguerolles
+33 (0)4 66 24 01 84

TERRES D'HACHENE VIGNOBLE DES GARDIES — 83/100

▼ ♪ Cerris 2012 : Light orange. Subtle floral and fruity nose. Supple palate already offering up ripe fruit with a generous mouthfeel and heat-driven finish. Drink from now on with barbecued foods.
Price approx.: 11,00 EUR
http://www.terresdhachene.com
Terres d'Hachene Vignoble des Gardies
+33 (0)6 69 00 12 24

CITÉ DE CARCASSONNE

L'ESPRIT DU DOMAINE DE SERRES — 85/100

▼ ♪ Vintage 2011 : Deeply-coloured with evolved highlights. Ripe nose halfway between jammy fruits and prune backed by earth and undergrowth. Well-balanced, chewy, terroir-driven palate. More of the honest, mature nose aromatics. Ready to drink now with game. Price approx.: 8,00 EUR
http://www.chateaudeserres.com
Château de Serres
+33 (0)4 68 25 29 82

SERRES — 81/100

▼ ♪ Vintage 2012 : Very young, deep colour. Nose of overripe fruits with heady floral undercurrents. Very light concentration on the palate which is supple and reveals fresh, yet low-key fruit. Designed in a crowd-pleasing style.
Price approx.: 6,00 EUR
http://www.chateaudeserres.com
Château de Serres
+33 (0)4 68 25 29 82

COLLIOURE

DOMAINE DU MAS BLANC — 89/100

▼ ♪ Les Junquets 2008 : Deeply-coloured with evolved highlights. Mature nose intermixing fruit character, a balsamic, menthol and oak dimension and cocoa note. Full, well-structured palate supported by good freshness lengthening aromatic exposure. Will keep.
Price approx.: 28,00 EUR
http://www.domainedumasblanc.com
Domaine du Mas Blanc
+33 (0)4 68 88 32 12

DOMAINE BERTA-MAILLOL — 87/100

▼ ♪ Arrels 2011 : Slightly evolved colour. The nose is subdued on first pour then opens up to notes of smoke, liquorice sweet, mocha, ripe fruits and spice. A distinctive, traditional Collioure with restrained power revolving around sun-filled perfumes. Nice rendition. Price approx.: 13,00 EUR
www.bertamaillol.com
Domaine Berta-Maillol
+33 (0)4 68 88 00 54

DOMAINE DU MAS BLANC — 86/100

▼ ♪ Terres de Schistes 2012 : Deep crimson. Fruit-driven nose of morello cherry, blackcurrant and cherry. Supple palate with a soft mouthfeel highlighting fruity freshness. A charming, accessible Collioure. Drink whilst still young.
Price approx.: 9,00 EUR
http://www.domainedumasblanc.com
Domaine du Mas Blanc
+33 (0)4 68 88 32 12

CORBIÈRES

CHÂTEAU DU GRAND CAUMONT — 90/100

▼ ♪ Impatience 2011 : Beautiful deep garnet. Rich, empyreumatic and spicy nose with morello cherry, cassis and raspberry. Powerful and warm, but above all balanced with mouth-coating, fruit-dominant substance. Racy, young and promising. A great wine with a bright future.
www.grandcaumont.com
Château du Grand Caumont
+33 (0)4 68 27 10 82

DOMAINE DE LONGUEROCHE — 90/100

▼ ♪ L'Ermitage 2010 : Deep colour, still in its youth. Hallmark Syrah nose of cassis and pepper backed by fine, toasted oak. Remarkable texture, restrained power and very persistent noble, racy perfumes with mellow oak. A consummate Corbières balancing typicity and modernity.
Price approx.: 29,90 EUR
http://www.longueroche.com
Domaine de Longueroche
+33 (0)4 68 41 48 26

CHÂTEAU DU GRAND CAUMONT — 88/100

▼ ♪ Cuvée Spéciale 2011 : Concentrated garnet. Superb nose infused with maquis, smoke, stone fruits, pepper, leather and olive paste. The broad-ranging aromatics carry through to the palate. Assertive power, tightly-wound tannins. A splendid generous and warm wine from the South.
www.grandcaumont.com
Château du Grand Caumont
+33 (0)4 68 27 10 82

DOMAINE DE FONTSAINTE 88/100

▼ ✶ Vintage 2011 : Deep, young colour. Enticing, distinctive nose driven by jammy black fruits with spice, pepper and olive paste. Silky mouthfeel enveloping the fruit and power framed by freshness. A racy, elegant Corbières. Recommended for herb-flavoured grilled meats.
Price approx.: 6,50 EUR
http://www.fontsainte.com
Domaine de Fontsainte
+33 (0)4 68 27 07 63

DOMAINE DE LONGUEROCHE 87/100

▼ ✶ Cuvée Raoul 2009 : Deeply-coloured garnet. Clean nose driven by stone fruits, spice and olive paste. The palate combines power with finesse, dense substance and distinctive, mouth-filling perfumes. An assertive, southern-style personality with a good measure of suppleness.
Price approx.: 15,90 EUR
http://www.longueroche.com
Domaine de Longueroche
+33 (0)4 68 41 48 26

CHÂTEAU DE L'ILLE 86/100

▼ ✶ Alexandre 2013 : Orange-pink hue. Joyful nose showing accents of red fruit sweets with a floral and spice touch. Supple palate, soft mouthfeel suffusing perfumes with a very delicate touch. A delectable rosé that makes the ideal companion for tapas. Price approx.: 6,50 EUR
www.chateaudelille.com
Château de l'Ille
+33 (0)4 68 41 05 96

DOMAINE DE FONTSAINTE 86/100

▼ ✶ La Demoiselle 2012 : Deep colour with young tints. Classic plummy nose with bigarreau cherry and jammy cassis. An honest, balanced Corbières with restrained power and focused, distinctive aromatic expression. Accessible, well-made and a perfect introduction to the appellation.
Price approx.: 8,00 EUR
http://www.fontsainte.com
Domaine de Fontsainte
+33 (0)4 68 27 07 63

CHÂTEAU BRUGAYROLE 85/100

▼ ✶ Cuvée Céleste 2013 : Deep purple-blue. Nose of wild black berries with mineral undercurrents. Robust palate with a powerful, sappy attack and tannins. The mid-palate and finish stay fresh with persistent, focused fruit. An enjoyable wine.
Price approx.: 12,00 EUR
http://www.dom-st-michel.com
Combe Long
+33 (0)4 68 43 36 62

CHÂTEAU MONT MILAN 85/100

▼ ✶ Vintage 2012 : Fairly deep garnet. Generous nose of ripe black fruits with a touch of spice. Powerful yet perfumed attack on the palate revealing more of the fruity nose character. Jam and spice notes are entwined on the finish. A very enjoyable, invigorating style.
http://www.rocbere.com
Les Caves Rocbère
+33 (0)4 68 48 28 05

DOMAINE DE LONGUEROCHE 85/100

▼ ✶ Cuvée Aurélien 2011 : Concentrated, young colour. Clean nose with accents of liquorice, black olive, garrigue and stone fruits. Warm palate displaying a typically Mediterranean range of lingering aromatics. A racy, well-balanced wine that calls for meats in a sauce.
Price approx.: 10,90 EUR
http://www.longueroche.com
Domaine de Longueroche
+33 (0)4 68 41 48 26

DOMAINE DE LONGUEROCHE 85/100

▼ ✶ Le Rosé 2013 : Light orange. Endearing nose of spicy fruit with floral undercurrents. Full-bodied attack leading into a more supple mid-palate with more mature aromatics. Focused fruit. A rosé with real food compatibility suitable for barbecues.
Price approx.: 6,40 EUR
http://www.longueroche.com
Domaine de Longueroche
+33 (0)4 68 41 48 26

CHÂTEAU DE L'ILLE 85/100

▼ ✶ Louis 2012 : Deeply-coloured garnet. Ripe nose with accents of undergrowth, stewed fruits and pepper. The mature nose aromatics follow through to the palate. Powerful and mouth-coating with ripe, focused perfumes. Warm with a real sense of place. Ready to drink now.
Price approx.: 15,00 EUR
www.chateaudelille.com
Château de l'Ille
+33 (0)4 68 41 05 96

CHÂTEAU DE L'ILLE 85/100

▼ ✶ Angélique 2011 : Concentrated garnet. Ripe nose showing accents of stone fruits, leather and garrigue. Fully mature palate revealing perfumes in full bloom. Nicely harnessed power yet also hallmark Languedoc aromas. Enjoyable from now on with pork and prunes.
Price approx.: 9,00 EUR
www.chateaudelille.com
Château de l'Ille
+33 (0)4 68 41 05 96

MONTMIJA 84/100

Org▼ ♪ Signature 2012 : Youthful highlights. Endearing nose driven by cassis, bigarreau cherry and plum. Supple palate with a soft mouthfeel and delicious fruit expression. A Corbières that works best chilled, drinking well now whilst still fruit-forward.
http://www.saint-auriol.com
Les Domaines Auriol
+33 (0)4 68 58 15 15

DOMAINE DE LONGUEROCHE 84/100

▼ ♪ Le Blanc 2013 : Light gold. Delectable nose driven by white fruits, peach, apricot and beautiful floral presence. A supple, soft wine showing savoury fresh perfume, a round mouthfeel and persistency. A white wine for opening up the palate.
Price approx.: 6,40 EUR
http://www.longueroche.com
Domaine de Longueroche
+33 (0)4 68 41 48 26

LES CAVES ROCBÈRE 83/100

▼ ♪ Grande Réserve 2012 : Garnet hue. Distinctive, expressive nose opening up to aromas of jammy red fruits, garrigue, spices and a touch of leather. Fullness, melted stuffing and power harnessed by a sensation of freshness. A nicely crafted wine. Price approx.: 3,00 EUR
http://www.rocbere.com
Les Caves Rocbère
+33 (0)4 68 48 28 05

CORBIÈRES BOUTENAC

DOMAINE DE FONTSAINTE 89/100

▼ ♪ Clos du Centurion 2011 : Deep garnet. Rich, empyreumatic nose driven by pepper, cinnamon and jammy stone fruits. Power and aromatic typicity at point of entry, expressive heat and a Southern-style finish driven by garrigue and thyme. An all-round, honest Boutenac. Price approx.: 12,00 EUR
http://www.fontsainte.com
Domaine de Fontsainte
+33 (0)4 68 27 07 63

CÔTE VERMEILLE

DOMAINE DU MAS BLANC 89/100

▼ ♪ Le Blanc des Junquets 2012 : Beautiful light gold. Rich, heady nose showing honeyed aromas backed by flowers (jasmine), yellow-fleshed and white fruits. Mouth-coating with a generous mouthfeel. Beautiful fruit presence and freshness. A very elegant, refined wine. Price approx.: 28,00 EUR
http://www.domainedumasblanc.com
Domaine du Mas Blanc
+33 (0)4 68 88 32 12

CÔTES CATALANES

TERRES DE LANSAC 88/100

▼ ♪ Vinifié et élevé en barriques 2012 : Pale gold. Appealing burnt vanilla on the nose backed by white and dried fruits. Power, substance and forthright oak that does not obscure the fruit. A proud Catalan wine with the capacity to mature still. Decant now with white meat in a cream sauce.
Price approx.: 8,90 EUR
Cave du Cellier de Trémoine
+33 (0)4 68 29 11 82

LES TERRES DE MALLYCE 87/100

Org▼ ♪ Pierres de Lune 2011 : Deep-hued with garnet tints. Refined nose of smoke and spice backed by stone fruits. Well-balanced palate showing seductive suppleness, mellowness and freshness whilst also developing intense, distinctive aromas. Spicy finish. Assertive southern character.
Price approx.: 13,00 EUR
Les Terres de Mallyce
+33 (0)4 68 73 86 37

CÔTES DE THONGUE

LES CHEMINS DE BASSAC 86/100

Org▼ ♪ Isa 2012 : Robe grenat. Nez mûr, entre fruits à noyau (bigarreau, prune) et notes épicées. Bouche charnue, à la puissance maîtrisée. Panoplie aromatique très méditerranéenne persistante. De la douceur en finale. Parfait pour accompagner de l'agneau rôti. Price approx.: 7,00 EUR
www.cheminsdebassac.com
Les Chemins de Bassac
+33 (0)4 67 36 09 67

DOMAINE MONTROSE 86/100

▼ ♪ Vintage 2013 : Pale orange-pink. Refined nose showing spice accents, red berry fruits and confectionary. Delicate palate combining suppleness and focused fruit expression framed by a generous mouthfeel. A rosé boasting lots of personality. Price approx.: 3,00 EUR
http://www.domaine-montrose.com
Domaine Montrose
+33 (0)4 67 98 63 33

LES CHEMINS DE BASSAC 83/100

Org▼ ♪ Isa 2013 : Light gold. Vegetal and floral aromatics (fern, moss, honeysuckle) adorn the nose with almond and peach in the background. A measure of sourness at point of entry coupled with ripe, focused fruit. Fairly full-bodied and pairing with fish in a sauce. Price approx.: 7,00 EUR
www.cheminsdebassac.com
Les Chemins de Bassac
+33 (0)4 67 36 09 67

CÔTES DU ROUSSILLON

DOMAINE DE SABBAT   90/100

CONV▼ ♪ Printemps 1900 2010 : Concentrated garnet. Rich nose driven by condiments, stone fruits and spice. Generous, distinctive palate retaining abundant freshness. Assertive Mediterranean aromatics set against a supple background. A successful wine. Uncork for stew.
Price approx.: 16,00 EUR
Domaine de Sabbat
+33 (0)6 75 48 19 74

DOMAINE DE SABBAT   89/100

CONV▼ **DG** Vintage 2011 : Gold. Rich nose of spicy oak backed by dried and white fruits with a touch of caramel. Full, warm and well-balanced palate. The generous range of nose aromatics follows through. A good rendition of white Roussillon. Enhances the flavour of pressed cheeses.
Price approx.: 14,00 EUR
Domaine de Sabbat
+33 (0)6 75 48 19 74

MAS ALART   88/100

▼ ♪ Les Trois Couronnes 2010 : Beautifully young colour. Delightful nose showing refined smoky vanilla oak backed by fresh black fruits. Very supple palate with freshness and fruit taking centre stage. The finish is infused with oak. A wine combining great drinkability with typicity.
Price approx.: 12,50 EUR
http://www.masalart.fr
Mas Alart
+33 (0)4 68 50 51 89

DOMAINE DE ROMBEAU   87/100

▼ ♪ Pierre de la Fabrègue - cuvée élevée en fûts de chêne 2010 : Deeply-coloured garnet. Smoky oak on the nose backed by stone fruits. Welcoming, mouth-coating palate with freshness and aromatic persistency nicely supported by oak. A Roussillon that has benefited from oak ageing and not lost its typicity. Price approx.: 11,50 EUR
Domaine de Rombeau
+33 (0)4 68 64 35 35

DOMAINE DE ROMBEAU   87/100

▼ ♪ Vintage 2012 : Light gold. Rich nose with honeyed accents, stewed white fruits, wild flowers and smoke. More of the same complexity on the palate. A generous, warm and full wine that will make the perfect partner for white meats after a little more bottle age.
Price approx.: 8,50 EUR
Domaine de Rombeau
+33 (0)4 68 64 35 35

MAS ALART   87/100

▼ ♪ dans la Vigne de Jules 2011 : The colour shows a youthful sparkle. Fresh blackcurrant, blackberry and raspberry drive the nose. Extremely supple palate centring on a zingy fruity freshness. A soft, accessible Roussillon, perfect for sharing over informal meals like barbecues.
Price approx.: 6,00 EUR
http://www.masalart.fr
Mas Alart
+33 (0)4 68 50 51 89

TRÉMOINE DE RASIGUÈRES   85/100

▼ ♪ Vintage 2012 : Garnet-red. Intense nose driven by ripe strawberry, raspberry and blackcurrant. Rich, lush palate exhibiting good balance of alcohol and freshness. Lovely long-lasting fruit. A good rosé with real food compatibility.
Price approx.: 6,30 EUR
Cave du Cellier de Trémoine
+33 (0)4 68 29 11 82

MAS ALART   85/100

▼ ♪ Les Trois Couronnes 2012 : Light gold. Slightly muted on the nose with perceptible oak, floral notes and white fruits in the background. A generous, full-bodied white with substance currently prevailing over aroma though oak is not invasive. Needs more time to fully reveal itself.
Price approx.: 9,00 EUR
http://www.masalart.fr
Mas Alart
+33 (0)4 68 50 51 89

INTENSE CLAUDE VIALADE   84/100

▼ ♪ Femme du Vin 2013 : Beautifully young colour. Very youthful, heady nose of peony, black cherry and cassis. A soft Roussillon with freshness and fruit to the fore. Mellow tannins. Very supple, drinking best whilst young and fruit-forward. Would work well with barbecued foods.
http://www.saint-auriol.com
Les Domaines Auriol
+33 (0)4 68 58 15 15

CHÂTEAU MONTANA   84/100

▼ ♪ Dialogue 2012 : Deep, young colour. The nose is midway between ripe stone fruits and vegetal notes. Generous palate boasting lovely fruity freshness. Fresh fruit and not heat is the overriding impression. A Roussillon showing seductive youthful character.
Price approx.: 4,90 EUR
www.chateaumontana.fr
Château Montana
+33 (0)4 68 37 54 84

CÔTES DU ROUSSILLON-VILLAGES

LES TERRES DE MALLYCE 90/100

CONV▼ .ℓ Del Amor 2009 : Mature highlights. Authentic nose of spice, stone fruits, undergrowth, leather and an empyreumatic touch. Fine-grained texture on the palate imparting suppleness. Freshness enhances lovely mature aromatics. Bravo.
Price approx.: 16,00 EUR
Les Terres de Mallyce
+33 (0)4 68 73 86 37

DOMAINE DE ROMBEAU 90/100

▼ .ℓ Elise - Vieilles Vignes 2011 : Concentrated dark purple. Rich nose of stone fruits and spices backed by toasted and mocha oak aromas. Velvety palate, silky mouthfeel with lifted perfumes enhanced by oak. Wonderful overall typicity. A very elegant, modern Roussillon with real allure.
Price approx.: 14,50 EUR
Domaine de Rombeau
+33 (0)4 68 64 35 35

DOMAINE DE ROMBEAU 88/100

Org▼ .ℓ Le Rouge 2012 : Youthful colour. Refined nose of stone fruits, black olive and oak undertones. Elegant palate with a silky mouthfeel and distinctive, focused perfumes. A noble, sound, all-round wine that is delicate yet still retains power. A prime candidate for mutton.
Price approx.: 9,50 EUR
Domaine de Rombeau
+33 (0)4 68 64 35 35

MAS DE LA DEVÈZE 88/100

▼ .ℓ Vintage 2012 : Deep, young hue. Vanilla oak is released on first pour then spice and stone fruits after swirling. Warm, chewy palate with assertive oak presence and fruit playing a supporting role. A Roussillon that will soon get up to speed. Ideal for marinated meats.
Price approx.: 13,00 EUR
http://www.masdeladeveze.fr
Mas de la Devèze
+33 (0)4 68 61 04 58

MOURA LYMPANY 88/100

▼ .ℓ Elevé en fûts de chêne 2011 : Deeply-coloured. Vanilla oak on the nose backed by ripe red and black fruits. Dense, well-balanced palate. Lovely marriage of fruit and quality oak, velvety mouthfeel. A supple Roussillon that has greatly benefited from ageing. Modern and distinctive.
Price approx.: 6,90 EUR
Cave du Cellier de Trémoine
+33 (0)4 68 29 11 82

CHÂTEAU PLANÈZES 88/100

▼ .ℓ Elevé en fûts de chêne 2010 : Deeply-coloured with garnet tints. Vanilla oak on the nose backed by ripe fruit. Supple palate. Melted attack, balanced perfumes with freshness driving the whole. A Village that has benefitted from quality ageing. Perfect for red meats.
Price approx.: 9,20 EUR
Cave du Cellier de Trémoine
+33 (0)4 68 29 11 82

DOMAINE RETY 87/100

CONV.ℓ L'Insolente 2012 : Young, deep colour. Refined nose driven by jammy fruit and spice. Suave palate boasting mellowness. Savoury aromatic presence framed by freshness. A soft, supple Roussillon in a fruity style. Grilled meat would fit the bill.
Price approx.: 9,90 EUR
http://www.domaine-rety.fr
Domaine Rety
+33 (0)8 11 69 67 35

DOMAINE RETY 87/100

.ℓ Vintage 2012 : Deep young colour. Endearing peppery nose with blackcurrant and black cherry. A supple Roussillon with delightful, distinctive aromas. Beautiful freshness supports the whole. Appealing youthfulness in a wine for pleasure. Pair with rib-eye steak in a wine sauce.
Price approx.: 14,95 EUR
http://www.domaine-rety.fr
Domaine Rety
+33 (0)8 11 69 67 35

CÔTES DU ROUSSILLON VILLAGES CARAMANY

EXCELLENCE DU CHÂTEAU CUCHOUS 89/100

▼ .ℓ Elevé en fûts de chêne 2011 : Deeply-coloured, young garnet. Refined smoky oak on the nose layered over stone fruit and spice. A full Caramany that is velvety, ample and powerful and displays good aromatic balance. Quality oak letting the fruit shine through. A successful wine.
Price approx.: 8,70 EUR
Cave du Cellier de Trémoine
+33 (0)4 68 29 11 82

Prices mentioned in this book are guideline and can vary depending on point of sale. The shops, wineries or publisher can in no way be held responsible for this.

CÔTES DU ROUSSILLON-VILLAGES TAUTAVEL

LES VINS DE LA DIFFÉRENCE   88/100

▼ ♪ La Racine carrée de la différence 2012 : Superb deep colour with youthful tints. Heady nose of toasted oak backed by peony and forest fruits. Supple palate centring on finesse and heat. More of the fruit nose aromatics over substantial length. Uncork for roast game. Price approx.: 9,95 EUR
Les Vins de la Différence
+33 (0)05 34 5628 18

CRÉMANT DE LIMOUX

DOMAINE DELMAS   89/100

Org▼ ♪ Cuvée des Sacres : Light gold. Complex nose driven by stewed pear, white flowers and a touch of mushroom. A superb Crémant that is rich and full-bodied with a broad-ranging spectrum of aromas. The complex nose aromatics are handsomely showcased by freshness. Superb.
Price approx.: 12,30 EUR
Domaine Delmas
+33 (0) 68 74 21 02

GUINOT   88/100

▼ ♪ Brut Créateur de Bull : Deep gold. Refined nose recalling breadcrust, breakfast pastries, almond and white flowers. Delicate texture on the palate with a silky effervescence and refined perfumes. A superlative sparkling wine. Uncork for fish en croute.Price approx.: 12,00 EUR
www.blanquette.fr
Maison Guinot
+33 (0)4 68 31 01 33

CHÂTEAU DE VILLELONGUE   88/100

▼ ♪ Brut : Light gold. Focused nose with lemony and sweet almond accents. Very refreshing, supple palate showing delicate balance. Sappy finish. A successful effort.
Price approx.: 5,60 EUR
Domaine Rosier
+33 (0)4 68 31 48 38

GUINOT   87/100

▼ ♪ Brut Tendre Impérial : Brilliant gold. Refined nose showing a hint of smoke, mineral aromas and breadcrust with lemony undertones. The complex nose aromatics are augmented by a lovely mellowness on the palate which enhances flavour. A delicate Crémant for finely-flavoured fish.
Price approx.: 10,05 EUR
www.blanquette.fr
Maison Guinot
+33 (0)4 68 31 01 33

FAUGÈRES

MAS NUY   91/100

▼ ♪ Le Fou du Rec 2011 : Deeply-coloured. Complex nose reminiscent of mocha, violet, liquorice, forest fruits and spice. The palate is of the same standard as the nose aromatics. Alluring youthfulness and restrained power showcasing the fruit. A superlative Faugères for game.
Price approx.: 28,00 EUR
Domaine du Mas Nuy
+33 (0)6 64 24 28 40

CHÂTEAU AUTIGNAC   88/100

▼ ♪ Réserve 2008 : Deeply-coloured, evolved garnet. Mature nose showing accents of leather, fresh undergrowth, stewed dark fruits and cinnamon. Well-balanced, mouth-coating palate boasting fleshiness and stature. The fruit is ripe and focused. A 2008 showing at its best.
Price approx.: 7,50 EUR
Domaine des Prés Lasses
+33 (0)6 86 55 89 20

CHÂTEAU DES ESTANILLES   88/100

Org▼ ♪ Inverso 2011 : Deep garnet. Distinctive nose driven by olive paste, liquorice sweets and stone fruits. The broad-ranging aromatics carry through to the palate with a finish augmented by spice. An assertive, clean, intense Languedoc fully revealing itself with stew. Stellar.
Price approx.: 15,00 EUR
Château des Estanilles
+33 (0)4 67 90 29 25

CHÂTEAU DES ESTANILLES   88/100

Org▼ ♪ Raison d'Etre 2011 : Deeply-coloured with beautiful glints. Refined nose of smoky oak backed by plum, jammy blackcurrant and wild berries. Full, silky mouthfeel showcasing balanced oak, fruit and spice aromatics. Refined power. A mouth-coating Faugères.
Price approx.: 35,00 EUR
Château des Estanilles
+33 (0)4 67 90 29 25

CHÂTEAU DES ESTANILLES   88/100

Org▼ ♪ Clos du Fou 2012 : Very concentrated colour, youthful tints. Heady nose halfway between wild flowers, plum, black cherry and a touch of graphite. Robust, powerful palate with very distinctive aromatics. Dense mouthfeel with warm length. A wonderfully unreasonable wine. Keep.
Price approx.: 20,00 EUR
Château des Estanilles
+33 (0)4 67 90 29 25

DOMAINE MAS NUY   88/100

▼ ♪ Le Rec 2011 : Cheekily young colour. Profound, heady nose driven by stone fruits, olive paste and spice. Supple palate with a soft, full mouthfeel and beautiful fruit presence. A feminine-style Faugères. Drink to your heart's content with roast partridge.Price approx.: 18,00 EUR
Domaine du Mas Nuy
+33 (0)6 64 24 28 40

CHÂTEAU AUTIGNAC   87/100

CONV▼ ♪ Réserve 2009 : Deep colour, still in its youth. Nose of fresh earth, ripe dark fruits and empyreumatic aromas. A racy, full and consistent Faugères, conveying archetypal Languedoc aromas and restrained power. Perfect for game in a sauce. Price approx.: 7,00 EUR
Domaine des Prés Lasses
+33 (0)6 86 55 89 20

DOMAINE MAS NUY   87/100

▼ ♪ La Catiéda 2012 : Light gold. Refined nose with accents of linden, wild flowers, verbena and white fruits. Young and well-structured, the palate shows more of the complex nose aromatics. Full, generous mouthfeel with abundant freshness. Serve with sophisticated dishes.
Price approx.: 18,00 EUR
Domaine du Mas Nuy
+33 (0)6 64 24 28 40

CHÂTEAU DES ESTANILLES   85/100

Org▼ ♪ L'impertinent 2012 : Very youthful dark purple. Refined nose with accents of black olive, spice and stone fruits. A supple, soft, well-balanced Faugères showing seductive aromatic freshness. Ready to drink and very accessible. A perfect partner for Sunday barbecues. Price approx.: 10,00 EUR
Château des Estanilles
+33 (0)4 67 90 29 25

CHÂTEAU DES ESTANILLES   84/100

Org ▼ ♪ Inverso 2013 : Light gold. Fairly subdued nose with a touch of white fruits and aniseed after swirling. Full-bodied with upfront substance slightly obscuring the fruit which is only revealed on the finish. Young with the structure to assert itself.
Price approx.: 15,00 EUR
Château des Estanilles
+33 (0)4 67 90 29 25

CHÂTEAU DES ESTANILLES   84/100

Org▼ ♪ L'impertinent 2013 : Light gold. Distinctive nose driven by almond, white fruits and wild flowers. Supple, forthright and lovely crisp palate. Focused, persistent aromas. An accurate rendition of a Rousanne-Marsanne style. Uncork for fennel-flavoured bass. Price approx.: 10,00 EUR
Château des Estanilles
+33 (0)4 67 90 29 25

CHÂTEAU DES ESTANILLES   75/100

Org▼ ♪ L'impertinent 2013 : Red with salmon-pink. Predominant vegetal aromas on the nose backed by fruit that is already ripe. Savoury acidity on the palate contrasting with ultra ripe aromatics. Vegetal-driven finish. Average personality.
Price approx.: 10,00 EUR
Château des Estanilles
+33 (0)4 67 90 29 25

LANGUEDOC

FRENCH CELLARS   88/100

▼ ♪ Vintage 2012 : Intense crimson with purple-blue. Concentrated, expressive nose intermixing black fruits, notes of bay, maquis and spice. A rich, opulent style on the palate that stays fresh. Excellent rendition of grapes from schist soils. Perfect for red meats.
Price approx.: 4,50 EUR
http://www.winesoverland.com
Wines Overland
+33 (0)1 45 08 87 87

MAS BRUNET   88/100

▼ ♪ Cuvée Tradition - élevée en fût de chêne 2012 : Beautiful gold. Rich nose with accents of smoke, toast and vanilla backed by stewed white fruits, honey and acacia. Generous, lush and warm palate revealing the complex range of nose aromatics with predominant oak. A great future lies ahead.
Price approx.: 11,70 EUR
http://masbrunet.unblog.fr/
Mas Brunet
+33 (0)4 67 73 10 57

CHÂTEAU DE FLAUGERGUES   88/100

▼ ♪ Noblesse 2013 : Pale gold with brilliant highlights. Very refined, floral nose backed by peach and white fruits. Young yet already very enjoyable with its balance, freshness, delicate substance and particularly well showcased range of nose aromatics. Delightful.
http://www.flaugergues.com
Château de Flaugergues
+33 (0)4 99 52 66 37

> Detailed instructions are featured
> at the start of the book.

LE ROSÉ DE LA BAUME

88/100

▼ Vintage 2013

Brilliant, limpid light pink. Suggestions of red fruit and spices on the nose. Delightful aromatics. The palate is supple yet also shows savoury freshness imparting lots of harmony. A rose for barbecues and tapas.

Price approx.: 9 EUR
Serving Temperature: 9-10°C
Ready to drink: From now on

La Baume's rose runs the gamut of Mediterranean flavours exuded by this magnificent terroir set in the heart of a totally unspoilt Natura 2000 protection area. It is made from a harmonious blend of Syrah and Grenache noir harvested on hillsides of limestone gravel from the Eocene period, lending the wines true personality. It is vinified using the bleeding process whereby tanks are filled with grapes and begin to macerate. The wine is then run-off once the desired colour and mouthfeel have been obtained. A highly aromatic, characterful rose that we found extremely compelling.

Château la Baume
34620 Puisserguier
Tel.: +33 4 67 38 16 22
E-mail: masdelabaume@gmail.fr

CHÂTEAU SAINT MARTIN DE LA GARRIGUE 88/100

▼ ♪ Bronzinelle 2011 : Black hue with garnet. Appealing Languedoc-style nose showing spice, pepper, stone fruits, black olives and liquorice. Robust with aromas gaining intensity across the palate. A racy Languedoc showing a real sense of place. Defintely gets our vote of approval.
Price approx.: 8,95 EUR
http://www.stmartingarrigue.com
Château Saint Martin de la Garrigue
+33 (0)4 67 24 00 40

CHÂTEAU CAPION 88/100

▼ ♪ Vintage 2011 : Attractive light yellow-gold. Expressive nose of ripe stone fruit with lovely smoky and honeyed touches in the background. On the palate, a fleshy, heady wine beautifully balanced by freshness. A generous style for fish in a sauce.
Price approx.: 25,00 EUR
www.chateaucapion.fr
Château Capion
+33 (0)4 67 57 71 37

DOMAINE GALTIER 87/100

▼ ♪ La Solana 2012 : Intense colour with crimson tints. Highly expressive, profound nose intermixing black fruits, liquorice, spice and minerality. Full, warm and well-structured palate with persistent Mediterranean aromas. Robust and powerful. Serve with wild boar stew.
Price approx.: 12,00 EUR
Domaine Galtier
+33 (0)4 67 37 85 14

CHÂTEAU DES HOSPITALIERS 87/100

▼ ♪ Réserve 2011 : Light gold. Menthol nose revealing a touch of pine, white fruits and acacia. Mouth-coating palate boasting fat and volume. Flavoursome balance of fruit, spice and flowers imparting a rich, intense range of aromatics. Set aside for sweet and sour foods.
Price approx.: 7,90 EUR
Château des Hospitaliers
+33 (0)4 67 86 03 50

DOMAINE D'ANGLAS 87/100

Org▼ ♪ Esprit de la Garrigue 2009 : Concentrated garnet. Jammy blackcurrant, plum and bigarreau cherry drive the nose backed by garrigue and pepper. Beautiful acidity on the attack revealing youthfulness. The mid palate is bursting with fruit. A supple, distinctive and authentic Languedoc.
Price approx.: 10,90 EUR
www.domaine-anglas.com
Domaine d'Anglas
+33 (0)4 67 73 70 18

CHÂTEAU SAINT MARTIN DE LA GARRIGUE 87/100

▼ ♪ Bronzinelle 2013 : Brilliant light gold. Appealing nose of white fruits, peach, almond and meadow. Mellow, soft, melt-in-the-mouth palate. Delicate fruit perfumes and volume on the finish. A refined white, perfect for cockle salads. A beautifully refreshing wine.
Price approx.: 8,95 EUR
http://www.stmartingarrigue.com
Château Saint Martin de la Garrigue
+33 (0)4 67 24 00 40

CHÂTEAU DE L'ILLE 87/100

▼ ♪ Emilie 2013 : Pale gold. Smoke-infused nose backed by white fruits and mild spices. Beautifully powerful, warm and fruit-driven at point of entry. More structured mid-palate dominated by smoke aromatics. A generous, complex wine that has yet to fully reveal itself.
Price approx.: 8,00 EUR
www.chateaudelille.com
Château de l'Ille
+33 (0)4 68 41 05 96

PLAN DE L'HOMME 87/100

CONV▼ ♪ Alpha 2011 : Beautiful light gold. Herbal infusion of linden and vanilla on the nose backed by almond and white fruits. Full-bodied, warm palate with subtle perfumes. Suggestions of fresh earth on the finish. Beautiful personality. Shows best with Provencal cuisine.
Price approx.: 21,00 EUR
Le Plan de L'homme
+33 (0)4 67 44 02 21

LE CHAI D'EMILIEN 86/100

▼ ♪ Edmond le Démon 2013 : Attractive orange-pink. Delightful nose of red fruit sweets, spice and eucalyptus. The palate combines elegance and substance. The range of aromatics is augmented by a crisp, mineral finish. Very enjoyable. Ideal for tapas. Price approx.: 8,00 EUR
http://lechaidemilien.com
Le Chai d'Emilien
+33 (0)6 99 50 45 38

CHÂTEAU DE FLAUGERGUES 86/100

▼ ♪ Les Comtes 2013 : Pale orange. Refined, floral and mineral nose flowing into red berry fruits, citrus and pepper. A very soft, very supple rosé showing crunchy freshness and fruit. Extremely charming crisp finish. A delicate wine for pleasure.
http://www.flaugergues.com
Château de Flaugergues
+33 (0)4 99 52 66 37

DOMAINE COSTEPLANE 86/100

Org▼ ✣ Pioch de l'Oule 2011 : Deeply-coloured with crimson shading. Concentrated nose showing aromas of black fruits, garrigue and pepper. Full palate with a closely-integrated mouthfeel. Lovely archetypal Mediterranean character of fruit and spice. Trace of firmness on the finish.
Price approx.: 9,00 EUR
http://www.costeplane.com
Domaine Costeplane
+33 (0)4 66 77 85 02

DOMAINE GALTIER 85/100

▼ ✣ Kermès 2011 : Intense colour, crimson tints. Concentrated nose opening up to dark fruit in brandy notes with a lovely spicy, liquoricy touch in the background. The palate is powerful and concentrated with a core of tannic extraction. A robust, perfumed style for game.
Price approx.: 8,00 EUR
Domaine Galtier
+33 (0)4 67 37 85 14

CHÂTEAU SAINT-JEAN D'AUMIÈRES 85/100

▼ ✣ Les Perles Roses 2013 : Orange-pink. Pleasant nose midway between mineral and fruit notes. On the palate, a dry, aromatic and no-frills rosé. Quite elegant and pairing equally well with salads and grilled meats. Price approx.: 6,50 EUR
Joseph Castan
+33 (0)4 67 40 00 64

CHÂTEAU SAINT-JEAN D'AUMIÈRES 85/100

▼ ✣ Les Perles Noires 2013 : Beautiful young, deep colour. Heady nose showing both flowers (peony) and fresh fruit (cherry, cassis, plum). Very supple, very soft palate with young, easy-drinking fruit. Freshness supports the whole. A Languedoc with youthful qualities. Price approx.: 7,50 EUR
Joseph Castan
+33 (0)4 67 40 00 64

LES VINS DE LA DIFFÉRENCE 85/100

▼ ✣ Le rosé de la racine carrée 2013 : Pale salmon-pink. Endearing nose driven by red berry fruits with mild spice notes and wild flowers. Soft, harmonious palate showing seductive fruity freshness and suppleness. Lovely spicy aniseed on the finish. A good rosé for tapas. Price approx.: 4,95 EUR
Les Vins de la Différence
+33 (0)05 34 5628 18

DOMAINE LE CLOS DU SERRES 85/100

CONV▼ ✣ Le Clos 2012 : Deeply-coloured with dark purple highlights. Intense nose driven by black fruit, liquorice sweet, spice and undergrowth.

Slightly austere, chewy palate. A wine that needs decanting to reveal the underlying fruit. Typicity needs to be confirmed over time.
Price approx.: 10,00 EUR
www.leclosduserres.fr
Le Clos du Serres
+33 (0)4 67 88 21 96

DOMAINE LES GRANDES COSTES 85/100

▼ ✣ Musardises 2012 : Deep, young colour. Crisp nose of fresh red and black berry fruits. Supple, soft palate placing fruity freshness centre stage whilst retaining a Mediterranean style. A perfect introduction to Languedoc wines. Price approx.: 9,25 EUR
http://www.grandes-costes.com
Les Grandes Costes
+33 (0)4 67 59 27 42

DOMAINE LES ANGES DE BACCHUS 85/100

▼ ✣ Angélique 2011 : Dark red. Distinctive nose dominated by jammy fruit notes bordering on blackcurrant and damp leather backed by a vegetal touch. Suppleness and a sensation of fruity sweetness are key themes on the palate. A likeable, soft style for foods in a sauce. Price approx.: 8,80 EUR
http://www.anges-bacchus.com
Domaine Les Anges de Bacchus
+33 (0)6 17 31 57 18

DOMAINE COSTEPLANE 84/100

Org▼ ✣ Arboussède 2011 : Appealing, medium intense colour. Endearing, delicate nose blending red fruits with vegetal and spice notes. Suppleness, refined texture and precise aromas are key themes on the palate. Light, yet also full and persistent.
Price approx.: 5,60 EUR
http://www.costeplane.com
Domaine Costeplane
+33 (0)4 66 77 85 02

DOMAINE COSTEPLANE 83/100

Org▼ ✣ Pioch de l'Oule 2012 : Brightly-coloured, pale yellow. Warm nose developing subtle floral and fruity notes after swirling. More of the power and fat on the palate augmented by a very faint trace of toast. Drink with fish in a sauce or white meats. Price approx.: 9,00 EUR
http://www.costeplane.com
Domaine Costeplane
+33 (0)4 66 77 85 02

DOMAINE GALTIER 81/100

▼ ✦ Tradition 2012 : Deeply-coloured with crimson highlights. Concentrated, focused nose opening up to dark fruits then revealing a liquorice and spice touch. Warm attack leading into a robust, firm mid-palate tinged with a hint of bitterness. Serve with grilled meats. Price approx.: 5,00 EUR
Domaine Galtier
+33 (0)4 67 37 85 14

CHÂTEAU SAINT MARTIN DE LA GARRIGUE 81/100

▼ ✦ Bronzinelle 2013 : Pale orange-pink. Nose of red berry fruits and spices. Light, crisp palate combining freshness and fruit. Displays a faint youthful beading. Drink preferably as an aperitif. Price approx.: 8,95 EUR
http://www.stmartingarrigue.com
Château Saint Martin de la Garrigue
+33 (0)4 67 24 00 40

LANGUEDOC GRÈS DE MONTPELLIER

N DE NOVI 95/100

▼ ✦ Vintage 2010 : Magnificent black hue. Complex, heady nose of chocolate and toasted oak backed by stone fruits, peony and graphite. Richly intense, balanced and silky palate. Fruit perfumes are on a par with ageing aromas. Remarkable volume. Sumptuous. Price approx.: 49,00 EUR
http://www.masdunovi.com
Domaine Saint-Jean du Noviciat
+33 (0)4 67 24 07 32

MAS DU NOVI 92/100

▼ ✦ Prestigi 2010 : Intense colour. Mellow oak on the nose with chocolate and jammy fruit presence showing plum and cherry. Balance, generous aromatics, restrained power and fine-grained tannins. A benchmark Southern wine enhanced by ageing. It would be a crime not to try it.
Price approx.: 10,90 EUR
http://www.masdunovi.com
Domaine Saint-Jean du Noviciat
+33 (0)4 67 24 07 32

NOVI 90/100

▼ ✦ Vintage 2007 : Intense hue with orange highlights. Mature nose revealing undergrowth aromas of humus and leather backed by jammy stone fruits. Very mature, well-balanced palate. Still under oak influence with assertive Languedoc aromas. In fine fettle.
Price approx.: 18,50 EUR
http://www.masdunovi.com
Domaine Saint-Jean du Noviciat
+33 (0)4 67 24 07 32

ABBAYE DE VALMAGNE 90/100

Org▼ ✦ Cardinal de Bonzi 2011 : Very dark, intense colour. Concentrated nose revealing a fruity (apple, black cherry) and mineral character with dark chocolate. Cherry and cocoa explode in the mouth. The palate is full and lush. A wine packed full of superlatives. Price approx.: 18,00 EUR
http://www.valmagne.com
Domaine de Valmagne
+33 (0)4 67 78 47 32

LE CHEMIN DE NOVI 88/100

CONV▼ ✦ Vintage 2012 : Young, deep colour. Delightful nose of fresh red and black fruits with spicy floral undercurrents. Very soft palate centring on freshness and suppleness and successfully focusing on crunchy fruit. A successful offering that will have you salivating. Very pure.
Price approx.: 9,00 EUR
http://www.masdunovi.com
Domaine Saint-Jean du Noviciat
+33 (0)4 67 24 07 32

CHÂTEAU SAINT MARTIN DE LA GARRIGUE 88/100

▼ ✦ Vintage 2011 : Intense hue tinged with garnet. Expressive nose showing accents of garrigue, maquis, spice and wild fruits. Clean, upright and distinctive palate. Spice perfumes are predominant with assertive Mediterranean aromatics. Heat is not a problem. A reliable choice.
Price approx.: 16,00 EUR
http://www.stmartingarrigue.com
Château Saint Martin de la Garrigue
+33 (0)4 67 24 00 40

LE CHAI D'EMILIEN 87/100

▼ ✦ Epopée 2013 : Deep, young colour. Refined nose of toasted oak backed by plum, bigarreau cherry and cassis. An elegant, supple wine, no excessive heat or oak. Fruit is present, upright and generous. Noticeable tannins on the finish. Decant and serve with leg of venison.
Price approx.: 13,00 EUR
http://lechaidemilien.com
Le Chai d'Emilien
+33 (0)6 99 50 45 38

CHÂTEAU-BAS D'AUMÉLAS 87/100

▼ ✦ Vintage 2012 : Light gold. Subtle nose with accents of flowers, herb tea, white fruits and a tropical touch. Young and pleasurable to drink, the palate shows seductive freshness, substantial perfume and length. Lovely note of bitterness on the finish. Generous in style. Price approx.: 8,00 EUR
http://www.chateaubasaumelas.fr
Château Bas d'Aumélas
+33 (0)4 30 40 60 29

CHÂTEAU-BAS D'AUMÉLAS 87/100

▼ ♪ L'Egérie 2011 : Deeply-coloured, young garnet. Intense nose showing a strong sense of place with animal notes, stone fruits and garrigue. Warm palate, refined oak (mocha) melding with sun-filled perfumes. Decanting is recommended to tone down the palate power. Price approx.: 19,00 EUR
http://www.chateaubasaumelas.fr
Château Bas d'Aumélas
+33 (0)4 30 40 60 29

CHÂTEAU DE FLAUGERGUES 86/100

▼ ♪ La Sommelière 2012 : Very young dark purple. Nose of black fruits with empyreumatic undertones and liquorice notes. Powerful, warm palate in a southern style. More of the fruit and spice. Honest and distinctive across the palate. Ideal for stews.
http://www.flaugergues.com
Château de Flaugergues
+33 (0)4 99 52 66 37

CHÂTEAU DE FLAUGERGUES 86/100

▼ ♪ Les Comtes 2012 : Young, dark purple. Endearing nose driven by blackcurrant, plum and black cherry backed by peppery spice. Soft, supple palate showing a successful fruit theme. Freshness, balance and roundness. An assertive Languedoc personality.
http://www.flaugergues.com
Château de Flaugergues
+33 (0)4 99 52 66 37

LANGUEDOC MONTPEYROUX

AUPILHAC 90/100

Org▼ ♪ Le Clos 2011 : Young, deep colour. Complex nose of toasted oak backed by morello cherry, plum and mild spices. Pleasure and elegance on the palate with mellow oak, intense, persistent fruit, a full mouthfeel, pervasive freshness. An all-round, racy wine all set for the future.
Price approx.: 38,80 EUR
www.aupilhac.com
Domaine d'Aupilhac
+33 (0)4 67 96 61 19

DOMAINE D'AUPILHAC 88/100

Org▼ ♪ Les Cocalières 2011 : Attractive deeply-coloured, dark purple. Distinctive, expressive nose with accents of jammy black fruits, bay, thyme and condiments. Very supple palate with an elegant mouthfeel, long-lasting perfume and prevailing freshness. An all-round Montpeyroux, ready now.
Price approx.: 16,40 EUR
www.aupilhac.com
Domaine d'Aupilhac
+33 (0)4 67 96 61 19

VILLA DONDONA 88/100

Org▼ ♪ Oppidum 2011 : Inky hue with dark purple tints. Fairly mild, endearing nose offering up ripe black fruits, mild spices and a chocolate note. A well-structured Montpeyroux offering power and generous aromatics. The palate is harnessed by freshness. A wonderful sun-filled wine.
Price approx.: 18,00 EUR
http://www.villadondona.com
Villa Dondona
+33 (0)4 67 96 68 34

COMTES DE ROCQUEFEUIL 88/100

▼ ♪ Grande Cuvée 2013 : Deep colour, dark purple tints. Refined nose showing beautifully dense fruit (plum, black cherry, cassis). Concentrated, full palate with a silky mouthfeel and beautiful fruit presence. Empyreumatic, peppery finish. Sourced from great sites. Perfect for duck breasts.
Price approx.: 13,10 EUR
http://www.montpeyroux.org
Montpeyroux Coopérative Artisanale
+33 (0)4 67 96 61 08

DOMAINE D'AUPILHAC 87/100

Org▼ ♪ La Boda 2011 : Deeply-coloured young garnet. Archetypal, ripe Mediterranean nose of spice, thyme and stone fruits. Supple, soft palate with spice and fruit overtones. Restrained power enhancing the fruit. Requires delicately flavoured foods like tournedos steak. Price approx.: 25,70 EUR
www.aupilhac.com
Domaine d'Aupilhac
+33 (0)4 67 96 61 19

DOMAINE D'AUPILHAC 87/100

Org▼ ♪ Vintage 2011 : Deep colour, still in its youth. Refined nose driven by plum and bigarreau cherry with a touch of spice and garrigue. No excessive power on the palate with crunchy fruit aromatics. A very supple, balanced and upright Montpeyroux. Undenialbe expertise.
Price approx.: 14,60 EUR
www.aupilhac.com
Domaine d'Aupilhac
+33 (0)4 67 96 61 19

DOMAINE SAINT ANDRIEU 87/100

CONV▼ ♪ Les Marnes Bleues 2010 : Mature garnet. Ripe nose showing a sense of place with accents of stewed plum and black cherry backed by woodland and undergrowth. Mature, supple and warm palate revealing more of the nose aromatics. Clear Languedoc personality. Serve with meats in a sauce. Price approx.: 16,80 EUR
www.saintandrieu-boisantin.com
Domaines de la Solane
+33 (0)4 67 96 61 37

DOMAINE SAINT ANDRIEU   86/100

CONV▼ .♪ La Séranne 2010 : Garnet. Lovely ripe nose with accents of jammy fruits, spice and sun-filled undergrowth. Body, personality and balance allowing aromas to fully reveal themselves. Fresh and ready to drink now.
Price approx.: 12,40 EUR
www.saintandrieu-boisantin.com
Domaines de la Solane
+33 (0)4 67 96 61 37

VILLA DONDONA   86/100

Org▼ .♪ Vintage 2012 : Deeply-coloured with dark purple tints. Powerful nose showing undergrowth aromas, leather notes, stone fruits and garrigue. Warm palate displaying archetypal Languedoc aromas of spice, jammy fruit, seasoning and sunshine. Set aside for game.
Price approx.: 11,00 EUR
http://www.villadondona.com
Villa Dondona
+33 (0)4 67 96 68 34

LE MAS DE BERTRAND   86/100

Org▼ .♪ Le 5 2011 : Intense colour with youthful highlights. Distinctive nose driven by stone fruit, condiments, liquorice sweet and wild spices. Upright, full and warm palate revealing generous aromatics. Beautiful length. A proud, representative Montpeyroux.
Price approx.: 3,60 EUR
http://www.domainemalavieille.com
Domaine de Malavieille
+33 (0)4 67 96 34 67

DOMAINE BOISANTIN   85/100

CONV▼ .♪ L'Embellie 2011 : Deeply-coloured with garnet tints. Ripe, mature nose of jammy stone fruits. Supple, soft palate centring on fruit. Generous mouthfeel with restrained power. A crowd-pleasing Montpeyroux pairing with grilled red meats.
Price approx.: 12,40 EUR
www.saintandrieu-boisantin.com
Domaines de la Solane
+33 (0)4 67 96 61 37

VILLA DONDONA   84/100

Org▼ .♪ Espérel 2012 : Brilliant hue with green tints. Delicate nose suggestive of meadow flowers with some white fruits. Suppleness, charm and accessibility are key themes on the palate. A succulent wine that would work well with fish or white meats.
Price approx.: 11,00 EUR
http://www.villadondona.com
Villa Dondona
+33 (0)4 67 96 68 34

COMTES DE ROCQUEFEUIL   84/100

▼ .♪ Montpeyroux 2013 : Crimson with purple-blue. The nose is driven by fresh red and black fruit with a touch of peony. Supple palate with a successful framework of fruity freshness and restrained power. Lovely perfume-infused length. An ideal Languedoc for a Sunday barbecue.
Price approx.: 5,50 EUR
http://www.montpeyroux.org
Montpyeroux Coopérative Artisanale
+33 (0)4 67 96 61 08

LANGUEDOC PIC SAINT-LOUP

DOMAINE LES GRANDES COSTES   87/100

▼ .♪ Vintage 2011 : Concentrated garnet. Nose of plum and bigarreau cherry backed by spicy oak. Melted, supple palate showing seductively well-defined perfume, fine-grained oak and a spice-infused finish. A crowd-pleasing Pic. Recommended for grilled meats. Price approx.: 18,50 EUR
http://www.grandes-costes.com
Les Grandes Costes
+33 (0)4 67 59 27 42

CLOS DES AUGUSTINS   87/100

CONV▼ .♪ Les Bambins 2011 : Beautiful concentrated hue, youthful sparkle. Heady spicy, floral and fruity nose (bigarreau cherry, blackcurrant and raspberry). Very supple palate, restrained power and mouth-coating freshness highlighting the fruit. Youthful qualities. Ready to drink.
Price approx.: 12,00 EUR
http://www.closdesaugustins.com
Clos des Augustins
+33 (0)4 67 54 73 45

DOMAINE DE LA VIEILLE   85/100

▼ .♪ Le Sang du Wisigoth 2010 : Deeply-coloured red. Profound, mature nose blending ripe red fruits, cocoa and spice. Warm, generous palate emphasising fullness and power. A lush, concentrated style framed by heat. Pair with game.
Price approx.: 10,00 EUR
http://www.domainedelavieille.fr
Domaine de la Vieille
+33 (0)4 67 55 35 17

LES AUGUSTINS   85/100

CONV▼ .♪ Les Bambins 2012 : Very youthful, deep colour. Fruit-driven nose of blackcurrant and bigarreau cherry with floral undertones. Supple palate with a soft mouthfeel promoting young fruit expression. An enjoyable wine ready to drink now. Perfect for grilled meats. Price approx.: 8,50 EUR
http://www.closdesaugustins.com
Clos des Augustins
+33 (0)4 67 54 73 45

LANGUEDOC PICPOUL DE PINET

CHÂTEAU SAINT MARTIN DE LA GARRIGUE   86/100

▼ .⸴ Vintage 2013 : Light gold. Distinctive nose driven by white fruits and wild flowers. Clean, soft palate with a strong fruit theme right through to the finish. A refined, elegant and superior Picpoul. Perfect for steamed foods.
Price approx.: 9,00 EUR
http://www.stmartingarrigue.com
Château Saint Martin de la Garrigue
+33 (0)4 67 24 00 40

LANGUEDOC SAINT-CHRISTOL

CHÂTEAU DES HOSPITALIERS   88/100

▼ .⸴ Sélection 2011 : Deeply-coloured garnet. Empyreumatic nose of smoke, spice and seasoning backed by plum and bigarreau cherry. Restrained heat on the palate with fine-grained tannins and Languedoc-style aromatics. Full and distinctive with the capacity to mature.
Price approx.: 10,70 EUR
Château des Hospitaliers
+33 (0)4 67 86 03 50

LANGUEDOC SAINT-SATURNIN

MAS D'ESTELLE   90/100

▼ .⸴ L'Afiamen 2011 : Deep ruby. Focused, profound nose focusing on jammy red fruit with subtle spice and oak in the background. Supple, rich attack on the palate. A heady style with fruit centre stage. The spice character takes a lead role on the middle palate. Price approx.: 25,00 EUR
Mas d'Estelle
+33 (0)4 67 96 11 63

MAS D'ESTELLE   87/100

▼ .⸴ Cor Rouge 2011 : Medium-deep garnet. Powerful nose showing undergrowth, smoke, garrigue and black fruit aromatics. Warm, well-balanced palate with an assertive Mediterranean aromatic personality. The powerfulness may come as a surprise. Decant or keep. Price approx.: 17,50 EUR
Mas d'Estelle
+33 (0)4 67 96 11 63

MAS D'ESTELLE   87/100

▼ .⸴ Lou Félibrige 2012 : Initial signs of evolution in the colour. Powerful nose of smoky pepper backed by stone fruits. Warm attack, extremely supple with predominant fruit on the finish. A wine that needs decanting to fully show itself off. Set aside for meats in a sauce.
Price approx.: 11,50 EUR
Mas d'Estelle
+33 (0)4 67 96 11 63

LE MAS DE BERTRAND   86/100

Org▼ .⸴ Saint Saturnin 2012 : Deep, dark purple. Refined nose driven by stone fruits, liquorice sweets and mild spices. A generous, supple wine boasting savoury aromatic freshness. Goes straight to the point with no heat issues or sharpness. Good with herb-flavoured red meats. Price approx.: 4,20 EUR
http://www.domainemalavieille.com
Domaine de Malavieille
+33 (0)4 67 96 34 67

LANGUEDOC TERRASSES DU LARZAC

CHÂTEAU CAPION   92/100

▼ .⸴ Vintage 2010 : Beautiful dense red with purple-blue. Appealing nose suggestive of ripe sloe with a mineral dimension after swirling. Great rectitude, power and freshness on the palate with perfume becoming more assertive on the finish. A very promising, racy wine. Price approx.: 29,00 EUR
www.chateaucapion.fr
Château Capion
+33 (0)4 67 57 71 37

DOMAINE D'ANGLAS   91/100

Org▼ .⸴ Le Chemin des Moutons 2009 : Concentrated hue. Chocolate-infused oak on the nose backed by black cherry with a smoky, spicy touch. Silky mouthfeel, fine-grained tannins and restrained power. Evident oak should soon take a back seat to the fruit. A moving experience.
Price approx.: 15,90 EUR
www.domaine-anglas.com
Domaine d'Anglas
+33 (0)4 67 73 70 18

PLAN DE L'HOMME   89/100

CONV▼ .⸴ Alpha 2011 : Concentrated, young colour. Mediterranean-style nose driven by liquorice, stone fruits, spices and condiments. More of the same aromatics on the palate supported by a generous, silky mouthfeel. Warmth framed by suppleness. A successful wine. Price approx.: 24,00 EUR
Le Plan de L'homme
+33 (0)4 67 44 02 21

LE CLOS DU SERRES   88/100

CONV▼ .⸴ Les Maros 2012 : Young and deeply-coloured. Powerful nose with accents of garrigue, rosemary, condiments and plum. Supple attack with fruit to the fore, fleshier mid-palate showing a Mediterranean character (fruit, spices, heat). A sterling wine. Price approx.: 15,00 EUR
www.leclosduserres.fr
Le Clos du Serres
+33 (0)4 67 88 21 96

PLAN DE L'HOMME 88/100

CONV▼ ✦ Sapiens 2011 : Concentrated, young hue. Intense nose of bigarreau cherry, plum and condiments backed by spice and graphite. The nose aromatics flow through to the palate where pepper and garrigue notes intensify. Characterful with a powerful backbone. Save for tagine.
Price approx.: 18,00 EUR
Le Plan de L'homme
+33 (0)4 67 44 02 21

MOLLARD & FILLON 87/100

CONV▼ ✦ Vintage 2012 : Concentrated hue, dark purple tints. Refined nose with accents of jammy plum, blackcurrant and cherry, and spicy, terroir-driven undertones. Fruit presence and freshness at point of entry, supple mouthfeel with restrained heat. Archetypal typicity.
Price approx.: 12,00 EUR
Mollard & Fillon
+33 (0)6 88 35 90 07

LE CLOS DU SERRES 87/100

CONV▼ ✦ La Blaca 2012 : Concentrated hue with very young highlights. Animal nose with accents of undergrowth, ripe stone fruits and a spicy peppery touch. Powerful, warm and displaying an assertive Languedoc personality making game in a sauce the obvious food choice.
Price approx.: 15,00 EUR
www.leclosduserres.fr
Le Clos du Serres
+33 (0)4 67 88 21 96

MAS BRUNET 87/100

▼ ✦ Cuvée Prestige - élevé en fût de chêne 2011 : Medium deep colour with mature highlights. Richly oaked nose (toast, smoke, empyreumatic aromas) backed by rosemary, pepper and stone fruits. Warm palate marked by ageing perfumes. Fruit comes to the fore on the finish. Racy and ripe.
Price approx.: 12,35 EUR
http://masbrunet.unblog.fr/
Mas Brunet
+33 (0)4 67 73 10 57

PLAN DE L'HOMME 87/100

CONV▼ ✦ Habilis 2011 : Young, deep colour. Distinctive nose showing accents of black olive, pine forest and stone fruits. Assertive power on the palate that does not obscure aromatic expression. Very Mediterranean in style, ideal for meat-based Provencal dishes.
Price approx.: 14,00 EUR
Le Plan de L'homme
+33 (0)4 67 44 02 21

LIMOUX

CHATEAU RIVES-BLANQUES 89/100

▼ ✦ La Trilogie 2012 : Deep yellow. Vanilla oak on the nose combining perfumes of dried fruits and white flowers. Ample, generous palate gradually opening up to fruit. Mellow, flavoursome mouthfeel. A multi-faceted flavour profile makes it a good partner for fish in a sauce. Price approx.: 20,00 EUR
http://www.rives-blanques.com
Château Rives-Blanques
+33 (0)4 68 31 43 20

MALEPÈRE

CHÂTEAU DE SERRES 85/100

▼ ✦ Vintage 2010 : Beautiful, intense garnet. Hallmark Cabernet nose of earth and undergrowth with ripe fruit undertones. Intense, terroir-driven palate developing ripe, mature aromas. Powerful. A Malepère with a real sense of place. Recommended for game. Price approx.: 10,00 EUR
http://www.chateaudeserres.com
Château de Serres
+33 (0)4 68 25 29 82

MAURY

MAS DE LA DEVÈZE 91/100

▼ ✦ Vintage 2012 : Inky hue. Vanilla oak and cocoa backed by condiments, stone fruits and spice on the nose. Dense, mouth-coating palate with assertive power that does not obscure the generous aromatics. Oak imparts abundant roundness. A must-try wine from the South.
Price approx.: 15,00 EUR
http://www.masdeladeveze.fr
Mas de la Devèze
+33 (0)4 68 61 04 58

MINERVOIS LA LIVINIÈRE

CHÂTEAU SAINTE-EULALIE 91/100

▼ ✦ Grand Vin 2012 : The colour shows a youthful sparkle. Rich nose of spice, toast and smoke with stone fruit undertones. Full mouthfeel, power coupled with freshness, suppleness and pervasive perfume. An elegant, distinctive La Livinière with substantial ageing potential.
Price approx.: 20,00 EUR
www.chateausainteeulalie.com
Château Sainte-Eulalie
+33 (0)4 68 91 42 72

DOMAINE ANCELY 90/100

▼ ✦ Les Vignes Oubliées 2009 : Deeply-coloured garnet-red. Profound, vibrant nose intermixing black fruits, cocoa, smoke and spice notes and a touch

of garrigue. Lush, full and melted palate with jammy accents. Very persistent. Finishes with a hint of bitterness. Price approx.: 14,50 EUR
Domaine Ancely
+33 (0)4 68 91 55 43

CHÂTEAU SAINTE-EULALIE   90/100

▼ ♪ La Cantilène 2011 : Deeply-coloured. Distinctive, inviting nose driven by black fruit, spice, condiments and graphite. Supple, velvety mouthfeel with focused aromatic presence. Peppery finish. Undeniable control of terroir expression. A perfect companion for roast poultry. Price approx.: 12,70 EUR
www.chateausainteeulalie.com
Château Sainte-Eulalie
+33 (0)4 68 91 42 72

DOMAINE AIMÉ   88/100

CONV▼ ♪ Au Gré du Vent 2011 : Deep colour. Intense nose of plum and cherry backed by spice and condiments. Lush, warm attack. The mouthfeel becomes fuller across the palate. Archetypal Southern-style perfumes. A La Livinière retaining its identity. Perfect for marinated game.
Price approx.: 10,00 EUR
www.domaineaimé.com
Domaine Aimé
+33 (0)4 68 91 14 10

LES FERRANDES   87/100

▼ ♪ Vintage 2011 : Deep colour, young tints. Distinctive, empyreumatic nose backed by olive paste, bigarreau cherry and plum. Supple palate with mellow oak and delicious fruit perfumes. A distinctive, refined Minervois that will fully reveal itself with grilled lamb cutlets.
http://www.saint-auriol.com
Les Domaines Auriol
+33 (0)4 68 58 15 15

MINERVOIS

CHÂTEAU SAINT-JACQUES D'ALBAS   91/100

▼ ♪ La Chapelle d'Albas 2010 : Deep colour, still in its youth. Complex nose of vanilla oak with menthol backed by peony, spice and stone fruits. The palate combines modernity and a sense of place. Balance, aromatic persistency and restrained power. Mocha-driven finish. Delicious.
Price approx.: 16,00 EUR
www.chateaustjacques.com
Saint-Jacques d'Albas
+33 (0)4 68 78 24 82

CHÂTEAU D'AGEL   91/100

▼ ♪ Vintage 2011 : Deep, young colour. Intense smoky vanilla oak on the nose backed by black

fruits. Oak recurs on the attack then fruit and spice are released. Silky mouthfeel, full body, restrained power. Young but with the qualities of a superlative wine.Price approx.: 44,00 EUR
http://www.chateaudagel.com
Château d'Agel
+33 (0)4 68 91 37 74

DOMAINE LA PRADE MARI   91/100

CONV▼ ♪ Trésor des Anges 2010 : Very concentrated colour. Refined nose of empyreumatic oak backed by condiments, rosemary and ripe stone fruits. Complex palate with power framed by freshness, lace-like substance and the full range of southern aromatics over substantial length. An all-rounder. Price approx.: 24,00 EUR
Domaine La Prade Mari
+33 (0)4 68 43 69 63

CHÂTEAU D'AGEL   90/100

▼ ♪ In extremis 2011 : Deep, young colour. Heady nose of vanilla oak backed by peony and forest fruits. Mouth-coating with silky substance, fine-grained tannins and nicely harnessed power enhancing perfume. Noble oak factors into the wine's success. A benchmark for quality.
Price approx.: 27,00 EUR
http://www.chateaudagel.com
Château d'Agel
+33 (0)4 68 91 37 74

DOMAINE PIERRE FIL   90/100

▼ ♪ Cuvée Orebus 2011 : Appealing dark red. Refined nose of red fruits enhanced by spice notes and eucalyptus. Full, melted and polished palate. Fruit takes a lead role on a stage that is generous yet fresh. A successful wine. Price approx.: 11,00 EUR
Domaine Pierre Fil
+33 (0)4 68 46 13 09

DOMAINE LA PRADE MARI   89/100

CONV▼ ♪ Gourmandise des Bois 2010 : Deeply-coloured with garnet highlights. Refined nose of toasted vanilla and mocha backed by plum, cassis and a menthol touch. Textbook balance, restrained power, freshness highlighting perfume and a combination of oak, fruit and spice. A very silky wine.
Price approx.: 17,00 EUR
Domaine La Prade Mari
+33 (0)4 68 43 69 63

Prices mentioned in this book are guideline and can vary depending on point of sale.
The shops, wineries or publisher can in no way be held responsible for this.

CHÂTEAU SAINT-JACQUES D'ALBAS 88/100

▼ ♪ Le Château d'Albas 2011 : Deep colour with garnet tints. Very jammy (currants and cherry), elegant nose showing a lovely oak framework. Very supple, extremely silky and delicate palate. Admirable blend of aromas (oak, fruit, spice) and mellow power. A seductive Minervois.
Price approx.: 9,25 EUR
www.chateaustjacques.com
Saint-Jacques d'Albas
+33 (0)4 68 78 24 82

CHÂTEAU D'AGEL 88/100

▼ ♪ Les Bonnes 2013 : Pale salmon-pink. Refined nose with confectionary accents, red berry fruits and floral undertones. A crunchy, fat rosé with a delicate crispness. Lots of fruit presence, flowers and intense freshness bordering on menthol. All the pleasure of drinking rosé. Price approx.: 7,00 EUR
http://www.chateaudagel.com
Château d'Agel
+33 (0)4 68 91 37 74

CHÂTEAU D'AGEL 88/100

▼ ♪ Les Bonnes 2013 : Pale gold. Rich, heady nose of almond, white fruits, wild flowers and linden. Full-bodied with generous, long-lasting perfume. A white wine showing delicate aromatic expression and therefore definite cellaring capacity. Very compelling.
Price approx.: 7,00 EUR
http://www.chateaudagel.com
Château d'Agel
+33 (0)4 68 91 37 74

DOMAINE LA PRADE MARI 88/100

CONV▼ ♪ Conte des Garrigues 2010 : Inky hue. Rich nose of toasted oak backed by plum, bigarreau cherry and rosemary. More of the same aromatic spectrum on the palate which is impeccably dense and balanced, framed by suave, silky substance with restrained power. A delicate Minervois.
Price approx.: 11,00 EUR
Domaine La Prade Mari
+33 (0)4 68 43 69 63

CHÂTEAU D'AGEL 87/100

▼ ♪ Caudios 2011 : Concentrated garnet. Intense nose of refined toasted vanilla oak backed by stone fruits and spice. Fleshy palate with a supple mouthfeel and restrained power. More of the fruit coupled with mellow oak. A clean, focused style that would sit well alongside game.
Price approx.: 14,00 EUR
http://www.chateaudagel.com
Château d'Agel
+33 (0)4 68 91 37 74

CHÂTEAU CANET 87/100

▼ ♪ Vintage 2011 : Deep garnet. Endearing nose marrying blackcurrant and cherry with a touch of liquorice and toast in the background. Supple palate showing medium concentration, good balance and freshness with mellow tannins. The finish is more spice-dominant.
Price approx.: 8,95 EUR
http://www.chateaucanet.com
Château Canet
+33 (0)4 68 79 28 25

CHÂTEAU CANET 87/100

▼ ♪ Vintage 2012 : Deep garnet. The nose centres on black fruits (cassis, blackberry) with cocoa undertones. Suppleness, fullness, freshness and black fruits are key themes on the palate. Well-structured tannins bode well for ageability. A Minervois pairing with cheese.
Price approx.: 8,95 EUR
http://www.chateaucanet.com
Château Canet
+33 (0)4 68 79 28 25

CHÂTEAU RIVIÈRE EN MINERVOIS 86/100

▼ ♪ Vintage 2013 : Beautiful, young-looking vibrant red. Very compelling nose of stone fruits with some spice notes. The same interesting aromatic personality carries through to the palate. Long, seductive finish in a fruit-forward style. A crunchy wine.
Price approx.: 2,95 EUR
Chantovent - Jean d'Alibert
+33 (0)1 30 98 59 79

CHÂTEAU SAINT-JACQUES D'ALBAS 86/100

▼ ♪ Le Domaine d'Albas 2012 : Deep colour with a youthful sparkle. Nose of ripe red and black fruits with spice undertones. More of the predominant fruit aromatics on the palate framed by a very supple mouthfeel. Heat is not an obstacle at all. A generous Minervois, ideal for grilled meats.
Price approx.: 6,10 EUR
www.chateaustjacques.com
Saint-Jacques d'Albas
+33 (0)4 68 78 24 82

DOMAINE AIMÉ 86/100

Org▼ ♪ Vintage 2012 : Concentrated colour with dark purple tints. Nose of stone fruits backed by spice and graphite. Chewy, powerful attack gaining fruit and suppleness on the finish. Assertive Mediterranean aromatics. A Minervois that works best with stew.
Price approx.: 6,00 EUR
www.domaineaimé.com
Domaine Aimé
+33 (0)4 68 91 14 10

CHÂTEAU TOUR BOISÉE 86/100

CONV▼ ✦ Marielle et Frédérique 2012 : Black-hued with dark purple tints. Nose of morello cherry, blackcurrant and raspberries in brandy. Powerful attack leading into a more supple mid-palate showing crisp, fresh fruit expression. A wine that will soon get up to speed.
Price approx.: 8,80 EUR
www.domainelatourboisee.com
Domaine La Tour Boisée
+33 (0)4 68 78 10 04

DOMAINE PIERRE FIL 86/100

▼ ✦ Cuvée Heledus 2012 : Attractive garnet with ruby highlights. Delightful, expressive nose with assertive aromas of wild red berry fruits, garrigue and spice. The same Mediterranean-style aromatics recur at point of entry which is supple, polished and generous yet fresh. Price approx.: 7,50 EUR
Domaine Pierre Fil
+33 (0)4 68 46 13 09

CHÂTEAU D'AGEL 85/100

▼ ✦ Grenu 2012 : Young colour. Fruit-driven nose of cassis, plum and black cherry. Intense, well-balanced palate with freshness countering power and focused fruit expression. A supple Minervois, drinking well from now on. A perfect introduction to the appellation. Price approx.: 12,00 EUR
http://www.chateaudagel.com
Château d'Agel
+33 (0)4 68 91 37 74

CHÂTEAU CANET 85/100

▽ ✦ Vintage 2013 : Pale gold. Pleasant plummy nose driven by citrus and tropical fruits (mango). Abundant freshness, suppleness and fullness on the palate with good concentration. Fruit is nicely showcased. Drink on its own or with fish.
Price approx.: 8,95 EUR
http://www.chateaucanet.com
Château Canet
+33 (0)4 68 79 28 25

JEAN D'ALIBERT 82/100

▼ ✦ Syrah - Grenache 2013 : Beautiful deep hue of a young red. Rather pleasant nose of black fruits with a touch of spice. Very supple framework on the palate with mellow tannins. Clear aromatic expression revealing delightful fruity and spicy aromas.
Price approx.: 2,90 EUR
Chantovent - Jean d'Alibert

Detailed instructions are featured
at the start of the book.

MUSCAT DE RIVESALTES

GOURMANDISE DE TRÉMOINE 87/100

▼ ✦ Light gold. Distinctive nose driven by orange marmalade and candied white fruit. A soft, supple and fresh Muscat with upfront fruit. A flavoursome wine that should be enjoyed whilst still young.
Price approx.: 9,60 EUR
Cave du Cellier de Trémoine
+33 (0)4 68 29 11 82

PAYS DE L'HÉRAULT - MONTS DE LA GRAGE

CHÂTEAU DE CASTIGNO 87/100

CONV▼ ✦ Terra Casta 2010 : Concentrated garnet. Appealing nose of stone fruits backed by spice, condiments and truffle. Supple palate with soft fruit. Chewier finish that stays fresh and perfumed. A distinctive southern-style wine pairing with waterfowl.
Price approx.: 8,50 EUR
http://www.chateaucastigno.com
Château de Castigno
+33 (0)4 67 38 05 50

PAYS D'HÉRAULT - COTEAUX DE MURVIEL

DOMAINE DE RAVANÈS 89/100

CONV▼ ✦ Les Gravières du Taurou - Grande Réserve 2009 : Concentrated, intense garnet. Smoky oak on the nose backed by jammy red and black fruits. Supple texture, silky mouthfeel and melted tannins on the palate. Impeccably balanced fruit and oak. Would work with grilled meats. A successful effort. Price approx.: 26,00 EUR
Domaine de Ravanès
+33 (0)4 67 36 00 02

DOMAINE DE RAVANÈS 89/100

CONV▼ ✦ Les Gravières du Taurou - Grande Réserve 2008 : Concentrated hue with subtle evolved highlights. Refined spicy oak on the nose backed by jammy fruits. Robust palate with fine-grained, upfront tannins. Fruit and ageing perfumes perform brilliantly. A chewy, sappy style with definite ageing potential. Price approx.: 25,00 EUR
Domaine de Ravanès
+33 (0)4 67 36 00 02

THE COLOUR OF THE WINES :

▼ Red wine	▼ Sparkling brut
▽ Dry white wine	▽ Sparkling brut rose
▼ Rose wine	▼ Brandy
▽ Sweet white wine	▼ Liqueur wine

DOMAINE DE RAVANÈS — 88/100

CONV▼ .* Le Renard Blanc 2011 : Beautiful light gold. Refined nose with accents of almond, white fruits and subtle spicy oak undertones. Full-bodied palate showing seductive strength and refined perfumes. Oak frames the whole. Calls for sophisticated foods. Price approx.: 15,00 EUR
Domaine de Ravanès
+33 (0)4 67 36 00 02

DOMAINE DE RAVANÈS — 87/100

CONV▼ .* Le Prime Verd - Grande Réserve 2009 : Inky hue. Oak on the nose with vegetal and ripe black fruit undertones. Warm, chewy palate with oak scents taking centre stage, enhanced with intense spice notes. Must be paired with marinated meats for full enjoyment.
Price approx.: 28,00 EUR
Domaine de Ravanès
+33 (0)4 67 36 00 02

DOMAINE DE RAVANÈS — 84/100

CONV▼ .* Merlot - Cabernet Sauvignon 2010 : Concentrated hue with mature highlights. Ripe nose halfway between earth and undergrowth notes and jammy fruits. A well-balanced, chewy wine with melted tannins. Focused aromatic presence. Well-suited to meats and drinking well from now on.
Price approx.: 6,00 EUR
Domaine de Ravanès
+33 (0)4 67 36 00 02

DOMAINE DE RAVANÈS — 82/100

CONV▼ .* L'Ibis Blanc 2012 : Light gold. Nose of ripe white fruits backed by spicy aniseed. Lots of sourness on the palate set against a warm backdrop. Fruit expression is still backward. An Ibis that has yet to get into its stride. Uncork for fennel-flavoured bass.
Price approx.: 5,00 EUR
Domaine de Ravanès
+33 (0)4 67 36 00 02

PAYS D'HÉRAULT

MOULIN DE GASSAC — 87/100

▼ .* Faune 2013 : Beautiful gold. Elegant nose with accents of peach, almond, linden and acacia. The pleasurable fruit aromatics are augmented on the palate by a tropical streak. Elegant mouthfeel, beautiful freshness. A seductive white that would be a good match for white meats.
Price approx.: 7,50 EUR
www.daumas-gassac.com
Mas de Daumas Gassac
+33 (0)4 67 57 71 28

FORTANT DE FRANCE — 86/100

▼ .* Réserve des Grands Monts - Carignan 2012 : Crimson with dark purple. Distinctive, profound nose recalling red and black berry fruits with a subtle wild smell. Fleshy attack leading into a well-structured yet mellow wine balanced by savoury freshness. Mineral dimension.
Price approx.: 8,90 EUR
http://www.skalli.com
Les Vins Skalli
+33 (0)4 90 83 58 35

DOMAINE DE SAINT DOMINIQUE — 86/100

▼ .* Vintage 2011 : Deeply-coloured with a youthful brilliance. Young nose dominated by vanilla oak with stone fruit perfumes after swirling. Supple, sappy palate with restrained power. Oak still prevails. More bottle age will reveal greater fruit presence.
Price approx.: 12,00 EUR
http://www.domainesaintdominique.com
Domaine de Saint Dominique
+33 (0)5 56 59 08 13

MOULIN DE GASSAC — 85/100

▼ .* Albaran Vielles Vignes 2012 : Young, black hue. Heady floral nose (peony, violet) with spice, black fruits and a vanilla touch. Supple palate with a soft, elegant mouthfeel. Power is counterbalanced by freshness. Southern-style aromatics pairing with game. More bottle age recommended.
Price approx.: 7,50 EUR
www.daumas-gassac.com
Mas de Daumas Gassac
+33 (0)4 67 57 71 28

CLOS GUILHEM — 85/100

Org▼ .* Vintage 2012 : Vibrant red. The nose unfurls gradually to red and black berry fruits. Lightweight style on the palate with emphasis on fruit. More of the same mouthwatering garden berry fruits. The finish shows a little more character. Set aside for white meats.
Price approx.: 12,00 EUR
Clos Guilhem
+33 (0)6 11 69 73 13

CLOS GUILHEM — 84/100

Org▼ .* Vintage 2013 : Beautiful deep gold. Highly floral, complex nose showing boxwood and notes of peach, mint and pine. Exuberant at point of entry rapidly flowing into predominant fruity perfumes supported by freshness. A fiery, elegant wine.
Price approx.: 8,00 EUR
Clos Guilhem
+33 (0)6 11 69 73 13

PAYS D'OC

MAS DU NOVI   88/100

▼ .♪ Lou Blanc 2012 : Light gold. Young, complex nose revealing perfumes of almond, stewed white fruits, wild flowers and mild spices. The nose aromatics carry through to the palate coupled with a youthful sourness. A white wine for top-end dining. Price approx.: 9,90 EUR
http://www.masdunovi.com
Domaine Saint-Jean du Noviciat
+33 (0)4 67 24 07 32

CHÂTEAU SAINT-JEAN D'AUMIÈRES   88/100

▼ .♪ Les Perles d'Or 2013 : Pale yellow with green tints. Suggestions of stone fruits, primarily white peach, on the nose. The palate is delicate, fresh and fruity. More of the same distinctive, enjoyable aromas. A characterful wine for fish or shellfish. Price approx.: 7,50 EUR
Joseph Castan
+33 (0)4 67 40 00 64

AUBAÏ MEMA   88/100

▼ .♪ Albion 2012 : Pale yellow. Delightful nose showing accents of peach, fruits in syrup and white fruits. Elegant, mouth-coating palate where heat does not obscure fruit expression. Attractive sourness on the finish. Two great varietals blended in an enjoyable wine. Price approx.: 10,00 EUR
Aubai Mema
+33 (0)4 66 73 52 76

L' ENCLOS DE LA CHANCE   87/100

▼ .♪ Les Jumeaux 2012 : Bright yellow-gold. Tropical nose reminiscent of mango with citrus notes. The same heady aromas are supported on the palate by a very fresh, balanced structure which balances the whole and lingers pleasantly. A successful wine. Price approx.: 11,00 EUR
http://www.chateauguiot.com
Château Guiot
+33 (0)4 66 73 30 86

DOMAINE SAINT-JEAN D'AUMIÈRES   87/100

▼ .♪ Les Marnes 2013 : Garnet with dark purple tints. Concentrated nose of red and black fruits. Supple, full, round and fleshy palate with free-rein aromatic expression. Smooth mouthfeel and balance. Delicious, generous style. Pair with ribsteak. Price approx.: 6,00 EUR
Joseph Castan
+33 (0)4 67 40 00 64

DOMAINE SAINT-JEAN D'AUMIÈRES   87/100

▼ .♪ Les Collines 2013 : Deep garnet with youthful highlights. The nose is driven by blackberry, cassis and blueberry. Velvety, supple and concentrated palate with clear-cut aromas. Polished tannins and harmonious across the palate. Powerful style. Drink with grilled meats. Price approx.: 6,00 EUR
Joseph Castan
+33 (0)4 67 40 00 64

AUBAÏ MEMA   87/100

▼ .♪ La Douzieme 2011 : Intense colour. Expressive nose driven by blackcurrant and pepper coupled with peach notes. A supple wine with a soft mouthfeel and beautiful fruity freshness. Lovely long finish. An enjoyable blend across the palate. A real find. Price approx.: 10,00 EUR
Aubai Mema
+33 (0)4 66 73 52 76

AUBAÏ MEMA   87/100

▼ .♪ L'Insoumise 2011 : Young, concentrated colour. Expressive nose showing accents of stone fruits and black olive. Generous, concentrated and fruit-driven palate. Its power underscores its provenance and the grape variety. Uncork for leg of venison. Accessible from now on.
Price approx.: 9,00 EUR
Aubai Mema
+33 (0)4 66 73 52 76

DOMAINE PAULET   87/100

▼ .♪ Texture 2013 : Crimson. Profound, focused nose intermixing red fruits and Mediterranean scents of garrigue and spice. Youthful, dense and lush palate. Lovely precise fruit. A full, promising wine that will improve with time. Price approx.: 12,00 EUR
Domaine Paulet
+33 (0)

L ENCLOS DE LA CHANCE   86/100

▼ .♪ les Aiguillettes 2013 : Young crimson. Heady nose suggestive of peony, blackberry, plum and blackcurrant. Very refined, lively palate with fresh perfumes. Freshness rapidly prevails over power and is entwined with distinctive fruit. An Oc drinking best in its youth. Price approx.: 6,00 EUR
http://www.chateauguiot.com
Château Guiot
+33 (0)4 66 73 30 86

ELEGANCE   86/100

▼ .♪ Chardonnay 2013 : Light gold. Compelling nose of white peach with a touch of apricot and honey. A Chardonnay for pleasure with fruit the key theme from the attack onwards. Full mouthfeel with upfront freshness. Delicious, fruity finish. A wine for sharing from the aperitif on. Price approx.: 5,00 EUR
Joseph Castan
+33 (0)4 67 40 00 64

ELEGANCE 86/100

▼ ♪ Merlot 2013 : Young garnet. Appealing nose of forest fruits and wild berries with garrigue and spice undertones. A soft, supple and fruity Merlot enveloped in a smooth mouthfeel. A real treat that works well with all grilled meats and should be shared with friends. Price approx.: 5,00 EUR
Joseph Castan
+33 (0)4 67 40 00 64

ELEGANCE 86/100

▼ ♪ Syrah 2013 : Young, dark purple. Delightful nose of black berry fruits, peony and mild spices. A crunchy, supple regional wine with very soft fruit. Beautiful overall freshness with a sappy mouthfeel. A wine for sharing, perfect for grilled foods.
Price approx.: 5,00 EUR
Joseph Castan
+33 (0)4 67 40 00 64

FORTANT DE FRANCE 86/100

▼ ♪ Terroir de Collines - Viognier 2013 : Light gold. Delightful nose blending floral notes with a touch of exotic fruits. More of the same pleasant aromatics on the palate which is fleshy, polished and framed by freshness. A successful Viognier, enjoyable from the aperitif onwards.
Price approx.: 6,00 EUR
http://www.skalli.com
Les Vins Skalli
+33 (0)4 90 83 58 35

FORTANT DE FRANCE 86/100

▼ ♪ Terroir de Collines - Pinot noir 2013 : Deeply-coloured crimson. Profound nose of black berry fruits with cherry. Beautiful presence on the palate, supple, mellow and fruity with a lovely ripeness. A full, expressive Pinot noir that works well with poultry. Price approx.: 6,00 EUR
http://www.skalli.com
Les Vins Skalli
+33 (0)4 90 83 58 35

VINITRIO 86/100

▼ ♪ Malbec 2013 : Deep colour, young tints. Intense, empyreumatic nose of plum, bigarreau cherry and floral undertones. Supple palate, polished mouthfeel, restrained power. The full volume of Malbec framed by elegance. A varietal with a strong personality. Serve with mutton chops.
Price approx.: 3,00 EUR
Domaine de la Baquière
+33 (0)4 68 78 98 49

DOMAINE DE LONGUEROCHE 86/100

▼ ♪ Viognier 2013 : Light yellow. Heady nose suffused with peach, pear and wild flowers. Freshness at point of entry, lovely suppleness and upfront fruit perfumes. A charming, crunchy Viognier for drinking at any time with seasonal salads.
Price approx.: 6,90 EUR
http://www.longueroche.com
Domaine de Longueroche
+33 (0)4 68 41 48 26

MAS D'ESTELLE 86/100

▼ ♪ Lou Blanc 2012 : Pale gold. Elegant nose driven by white peach, fresh almond, acacia and a tropical touch. Supple, soft and quite fleshy palate. Focused, refreshing expression of floral and fruity aromas. A regional wine drinking well from the aperitif to dessert. Price approx.: 14,50 EUR
Mas d'Estelle
+33 (0)4 67 96 11 63

L' ENCLOS DE LA CHANCE 85/100

▼ ♪ Les Aiguillettes 2013 : Orange-red. Fairly ripe nose driven by citrus and red fruits coupled with a floral and confectionary touch. Lovely freshness, roundness and delicious fruit at point of entry. The finish displays acidity and volume. A good food-friendly rosé.
Price approx.: 6,00 EUR
http://www.chateauguiot.com
Château Guiot
+33 (0)4 66 73 30 86

L' ENCLOS DE LA CHANCE 85/100

▼ ♪ Les Aiguillettes 2013 : Bright, pale yellow with green tints. Delightful, expressive nose blending floral notes, a touch of tropical fruits and a dash of lemon. Full, mellow attack showing lovely fat framed by a sensation of freshness. A very successful, perfumed Chardonnay.
Price approx.: 6,00 EUR
http://www.chateauguiot.com
Château Guiot
+33 (0)4 66 73 30 86

ELEGANCE 85/100

▼ ♪ Cabernet sauvignon 2013 : Crimson with dark purple. Dashing nose of violet, cassis and fresh raspberry. A soft, supple Cabernet with fruit in a lead role. Mellow with delicious, youthful expression. Drink with friends around the barbecue.
Price approx.: 5,00 EUR
Joseph Castan
+33 (0)4 67 40 00 64

FORTANT DE FRANCE 85/100

▼ ♪ Terroir de Collines - Chardonnay 2013 : Light yellow-gold. Focused, expressive nose with aromas of exotic fruits and a subtle vanilla touch. Racy Chardonnay expression on the palate which is supple

and fleshy yet fresh. Serve with a fish-based dish.
Price approx.: 6,00 EUR
http://www.skalli.com
Les Vins Skalli
+33 (0)4 90 83 58 35

FORTANT DE FRANCE — 85/100

▼ ♪ Réserve des Grands Monts - Chardonnay 2012 : Beautiful deep gold. Mature nose revealing buttery, brioche-like perfumes. Lovely fullness, volume, balanced fat and freshness and aromatic persistency on the palate. A Chardonnay for gourmet foods pairing with fish or white meats.
Price approx.: 8,90 EUR
http://www.skalli.com
Les Vins Skalli
+33 (0)4 90 83 58 35

FRENCH CELLARS — 85/100

▼ ♪ Grenache - Shiraz - Mourvèdre 2013 : Youthful sparkle. Distinctly southern-style, refined nose midway between stone fruits, spice and flowers. Very supple palate, delicious focus on freshness and fruit in a very easy-drinking style. A good wine for friends, perfect for gridled pork meats.
Price approx.: 2,58 EUR
http://www.winesoverland.com
Wines Overland
+33 (0)1 45 08 87 87

FRENCH CELLARS — 85/100

▼ ♪ Shiraz 2013 : Deeply-coloured with dark purple tints. Heady nose showing intense cassis backed by violet. The palate is defined by its fruity freshness. Very supple and light. A charming Shiraz that works well with barbecued food.
Price approx.: 2,52 EUR
http://www.winesoverland.com
Wines Overland
+33 (0)1 45 08 87 87

FRENCH CELLARS — 85/100

▼ ♪ Merlot 2013 : Deeply-coloured with dark purple tints. Fruit-driven nose of plum, raspberry and blueberry. Easy-drinking and fresh, very supple and showing delicious fruit immediately on entry. A simple Merlot for unrestrained enjoyment with others.
Price approx.: 2,48 EUR
http://www.winesoverland.com
Wines Overland
+33 (0)1 45 08 87 87

MONTMIJA — 85/100

Org▼ ♪ La Chapelle Winemaker's Reserve 2013 : Deeply-coloured dark purple. Heady nose driven by violet and red berry fruits. Delicious, supple palate with a soft mouthfeel in harmony with the fruity fresh-

ness. A Pays d'Oc for unrestrained enjoyment, pairing impeccably with cold cuts and cheeses.
http://www.saint-auriol.com
Les Domaines Auriol
+33 (0)4 68 58 15 15

MEYBLUM & FILS — 85/100

▼ ♪ Divin Nectar - Syrah boisée : Deeply-coloured dark purple. Heady nose driven by violet, cassis and vanilla. A very supple Syrah showing impeccable balance between fruit and oak perfumes. Very sappy and velvety. An enjoyable wine for all occasions.
Price approx.: 6,00 EUR
http://www.meyblum-et-fils.com
MVP Wines
+33 (0)4 34 22 12 75

DOMAINE SAINT MARTIN DES CHAMPS — 85/100

▼ ♪ Méli-Mélo 2013 : Light salmon-pink. Lovely fruity nose halfway between red berry fruits and citrus flesh. Extremely thirst-quenching palate blending freshness and fruit over good length. Beautiful overall acidity. A crunchy wine for sharing.
Price approx.: 6,20 EUR
www.saintmartindeschamps.com
Château Saint Martin des Champs
+33 (0)4 67 32 92 58

FORTANT DE FRANCE — 84/100

▼ ♪ Terroir de Collines - Merlot 2013 : Deeply-coloured with crimson tints. Endearing nose opening up to ripe blackberry with an oaked sensation. A rich wine on the palate, bordering on opulent, framing focused, long-lasting fruit. Well-integrated oak touch on the finish. A nicely crafted Merlot.
Price approx.: 6,00 EUR
http://www.skalli.com
Les Vins Skalli
+33 (0)4 90 83 58 35

FORTANT DE FRANCE — 84/100

▼ ♪ Terroir de Collines - Syrah 2013 : Deeply-coloured. After swirling, the nose reveals perfumes of red and black fruits framed by an oak sensation. A full, rich wine on the palate with a fine-grained, tightly-wound texture. A successful bottling fully revealing itself with grilled red meats.
Price approx.: 6,00 EUR
http://www.skalli.com
Les Vins Skalli
+33 (0)4 90 83 58 35

Detailed instructions are featured
at the start of the book.

FRENCH CELLARS 84/100

▼ ♪ Cabernet sauvignon 2013 : Deep, young colour. Nose of crunchy cassis and raspberry. The palate is supple yet displays tannin presence. The fruit recurs, coupled with a highly distinctive earthy Cabernet streak. Ideal for red meats.
Price approx.: 2,48 EUR
http://www.winesoverland.com
Wines Overland
+33 (0)1 45 08 87 87

MONTMIJA 84/100

Org▼ ♪ La Chapelle 2013 : Beautifully young colour. Endearing nose driven by cassis, blackberry, wild flowers and spice undertones. Supple palate showing lightweight concentration. Power takes a back seat to fruity freshness. A good wine for sharing with friends.
http://www.saint-auriol.com
Les Domaines Auriol
+33 (0)4 68 58 15 15

DOMAINE SAINT MARTIN DES CHAMPS 84/100

▼ ♪ Méli-Mélo 2013 : Light gold. Endearing nose midway between fresh peach, white fruits and floral notes. Supple, lightweight palate with gratifying perfume. Very soft with abundant freshness. Faint sourness on the finish. A wine for unrestrained, care-free enjoyment. Price approx.: 6,20 EUR
www.saintmartindeschamps.com
Château Saint Martin des Champs
+33 (0)4 67 32 92 58

CHANTAREL 83/100

▼ ♪ Merlot 2013 : Appealing, young-looking garnet. Focused fruit on the nose with accents of redcurrant and ripe cherry. More of the same aromatics on the palate showing lovely freshness and focus. An honest, well-balanced and delightful style.
Price approx.: 1,95 EUR
Chantovent - Jean d'Alibert

FORTANT DE FRANCE 83/100

▼ ♪ Terroir de Collines - Malbec 2013 : Deeply-coloured with dark purple tints. Profound nose reminiscent of cherry and ripe damsons enhanced by slightly spicy smoke notes. Full, rich and generous palate where fruit is entwined with oak flavours. A 'high-tech', oaked wine. Price approx.: 6,00 EUR
http://www.skalli.com
Les Vins Skalli
+33 (0)4 90 83 58 35

FORTANT DE FRANCE 83/100

▼ ♪ Terroir de Collines - Cabernet Sauvignon 2013 : Deeply-coloured with dark purple tints. The

nose opens up to aromas of red fruits then reveals subtle oak notes. Good framework on the palate with a polished texture. Fruit expression is supported by savoury freshness. A nicely crafted Cabernet.
Price approx.: 6,00 EUR
http://www.skalli.com
Les Vins Skalli
+33 (0)4 90 83 58 35

FRENCH CELLARS 83/100

▼ ♪ Chardonnay 2013 : Light yellow-gold. Endearing nose halfway between white-fleshed fruits and lemon. On the palate, a fleshy wine displaying good balance of fat and freshness with a slightly crisp dimension. A delicious, aromatic wine.
Price approx.: 5,50 EUR
http://www.winesoverland.com
Wines Overland
+33 (0)1 45 08 87 87

FORTANT DE FRANCE 82/100

▼ ♪ Réserve des Grands Monts - Pinot noir 2012 : Beautiful garnet hue. Open nose showing beautiful ripe Pinot expression with a touch of mild spices and an oak dimension. Full palate with a fine-grained, ample texture. Mellow attack leading into an upright mid-palate. Balance though average personality.
Price approx.: 8,90 EUR
http://www.skalli.com
Les Vins Skalli
+33 (0)4 90 83 58 35

COULEURS DU SUD 82/100

▼ ♪ Merlot 2013 : Fairly deep crimson. Suggestions of blackberry and black cherry on the nose. The palate is supple, mellow and clean. A likeable style with a pleasant fruitiness. Pair with barbecued foods. Price approx.: 3,30 EUR
http://www.skalli.com
Les Vins Skalli
+33 (0)4 90 83 58 35

FRENCH CELLARS 82/100

▼ ♪ Sauvignon blanc 2013 : Pale yellow with green tints. Distinctive nose with crunchy aromas of grapefruit and a vegetal touch. More of the archetypal varietal aromas on the palate which is lively, fresh and light. A very joyful, perfumed Sauvignon. Drink from the aperitif on. Price approx.: 2,75 EUR
http://www.winesoverland.com
Wines Overland
+33 (0)1 45 08 87 87

DOMAINE DE L'HERBE SAINTE 82/100

▼ ♪ Chardonnay 2013 : Light gold. Floral and white fruit aromas are predominant on the nose. The palate boasts fat and evident substance with fruit

consequently playing a supporting role. A wine that would work with fish terrine. Price approx.: 5,60 EUR
www.herbe-sainte.com
Domaine de l'Herbe Sainte
+33 (0)4 68 46 30 37

DOMAINE DE MALAVIEILLE — 82/100

Org▼ ♪ Charmille 2012 : Colour starting to evolve. Mature nose driven by jammy red and black fruits with a touch of undergrowth. Aromatic maturity fills the palate. A degree of firmness on the finish. Drink from now on with beef in a sauce. Price approx.: 2,80 EUR
http://www.domainemalavieille.com
Domaine de Malavieille
+33 (0)4 67 96 34 67

COULEURS DU SUD — 81/100

▼ ♪ Cabernet Sauvignon 2013 : Garnet with dark purple. Distinctive, focused nose blending red berry fruits and a subtle, pleasant vegetal dimension. On the palate, a round, likeable and fruity style. An instantly accessible wine, perfect for everyday enjoyment. Price approx.: 3,30 EUR
http://www.skalli.com
Les Vins Skalli
+33 (0)4 90 83 58 35

COULEURS DU SUD — 81/100

▼ ♪ Chardonnay 2013 : Light yellow-gold. Suggestions of pear flesh with a floral touch on the nose. A fat, mellow and fairly full style on the palate. A supple yet fresh Chardonnay displaying nice typicality. Price approx.: 3,30 EUR
http://www.skalli.com
Les Vins Skalli
+33 (0)4 90 83 58 35

COULEURS DU SUD — 81/100

▼ ♪ Grenache Rosé 2013 : Light pink. The nose opens up after swirling to subtle notes of red fruit sweets with a floral touch. Soft, polished palate revealing the same aromas. Instant accessibility. A rosé that is fat yet fresh and enjoyable from the aperitif onwards. Price approx.: 3,30 EUR
http://www.skalli.com
Les Vins Skalli
+33 (0)4 90 83 58 35

ELEGANCE — 80/100

▼ ♪ Syrah Grenache 2013 : Orange-red. Nose of ripe strawberry and tangerine. Powerful, warm palate displaying a range of open aromatics. A food-friendly rosé, drinking well from now on. Price approx.: 5,00 EUR
Joseph Castan
+33 (0)4 67 40 00 64

LES CONTEMPORAINS — 80/100

▼ ♪ Cabernet Sauvignon 2013 : Beautiful vibrant red. Pleasant nose of stone fruits, mainly recalling ripe cherry. On the palate, polished tannins and a refined mouthfeel. Aromas are nicely showcased with a delightful cherry flesh tone on the finish. Price approx.: 1,60 EUR
Chantovent - Jean d'Alibert

LES CONTEMPORAINS — 80/100

▼ ♪ Merlot 2013 : Fairly deep, vibrant red. Relatively subdued nose of black fruits. Extremely supple at point of entry, leading into a fleshy, expressive mid-palate where fruit and freshness impart beautiful harmony. Most certainly a wine for sharing. Price approx.: 1,60 EUR
Chantovent - Jean d'Alibert

LES CONTEMPORAINS — 80/100

▼ ♪ Sauvignon 2013 : Brilliant light yellow with green tints. Pleasant nose of citrus and white fruits. On the palate, a light wine showing more of the fruity nose aromatics in a very simple style, nicely enhanced by a fairly crunchy exuberance. An enjoyable wine. Price approx.: 1,60 EUR
Chantovent - Jean d'Alibert

RÉSERVE D'OC — 80/100

▼ ♪ Sauvignon - 1 litre 2013 : Brilliant light yellow with green tints. Pleasant nose intermixing white fruits and citrus. Honest palate revealing more of the nose aromatics. Lightweight, fairly crunchy and well-balanced across the palate. A simple, but well-made Sauvignon. Price approx.: 1,95 EUR
Chantovent - Jean d'Alibert

RÉSERVE D'OC — 80/100

▼ ♪ Syrah Grenache - 1 litre 2013 : Pale salmon-pink. Pleasant nose of strawberry with tangy floral notes. Fairly round, nervy palate showing good aromatic honesty and some spice coupled with crisp fruit. Relatively crunchy mid-palate with medium persistency. A simple, enjoyable rosé. Price approx.: 1,95 EUR
Chantovent - Jean d'Alibert

COULEURS DU SUD — 80/100

▼ ♪ Sauvignon blanc 2013 : Light yellow. Subtle nose opening up after swirling to notes of ripe lemon and white flowers. Supple, fleshy attack, fat and fruity on the palate. A Mediterranean style Sauvignon driven more by white fruits than citrus. Price approx.: 3,30 EUR
http://www.skalli.com
Les Vins Skalli
+33 (0)4 90 83 58 35

DOMAINE DES CARABINIERS 80/100

Org▼ .♪ Syrah 2012 : Light red. Subdued nose of red fruits. On the palate, a supple wine with light tannins showcasing the crunchy red fruit aromas. An easy, lightweight, accessible and crowd-pleasing style. Price approx.: 5,80 EUR
http://www.carabiniers-vin-biologique.fr
Domaine des Carabiniers
+33 (0)4 66 82 62 94

DOMAINE COSTEPLANE 78/100

Org▼ .♪ Plan de Savoulous 2011 : Garnet-hued. Expressive nose opening up to red fruits (ultra ripe strawberry) with a hint of spice in the backdrop. Full, generous palate showing super ripe aromas and developing a warm character. Touch of firmness on the finish. Price approx.: 8,70 EUR
http://www.costeplane.com
Domaine Costeplane
+33 (0)4 66 77 85 02

SAINT-CHINIAN

CHÂTEAU DE CASTIGNO 91/100

CONV▼ .♪ Vintage 2011 : Light gold. Complex nose of almond, linden, stewed fruits and wild plants. Powerful, refined palate. Generous, full and persistent perfume. Extremely rich, varied aromatic spectrum. A wine that still has lots left to give. Price approx.: 25,00 EUR
http://www.chateaucastigno.com
Château de Castigno
+33 (0)4 67 38 05 50

CHÂTEAU DE CASTIGNO 91/100

CONV▼ .♪ Vintage 2012 : Pale gold. Refined, mineral nose backed by wild flowers, peach and almond. A rich, delicate white wine. The complete range of complex nose aromatics gradually bursts forward. Mouth-coating with a warm, heady finish. Undeniable potential. Superb. Price approx.: 25,00 EUR
http://www.chateaucastigno.com
Château de Castigno
+33 (0)4 67 38 05 50

DOMAINE LA MAURINE 90/100

▼ .♪ Secrets de Paul 2011 : Concentrated colour with young tints. Refined nose of smoky vanilla oak backed by bigarreau cherry, blackcurrant, plum... A generous, full and powerful Saint-Chinian. Fine tannins and huge aromatic presence. Oak is in the melted phase. Rib steak it is! Price approx.: 11,50 EUR
http://www.chateaucastigno.com
Domaine La Maurine
+33 (0)6 82 96 28 00

CHÂTEAU VIRANEL 88/100

▼ .♪ Tradition 2013 : Light yellow. Refined nose with smoke and mineral aromas backed by white fruits. The palate shows surprisingly seductive mouth-coating substance, aromatic length, generosity and joyful character. Suitable from the aperitif on, showing at its best with cheese. Price approx.: 7,90 EUR
http://chateau-viranel.com
Château Viranel
+33 (0)4 67 89 60 59

CHÂTEAU FONSALADE 88/100

▼ .♪ Vintage 2011 : Deeply-coloured garnet. Empyreumatic nose of spice, seasoning, stone fruits and condiments. A racy Saint-Chinian convincingly exuding southern-style aromatics. Assertive power yet also freshness. Ideal for meats in a sauce. Price approx.: 12,50 EUR
http://www.fonsalade.com
Château Fonsalade
+33 (0)5 62 88 13 35

MAS DE CYNANQUE 88/100

CONV▼ .♪ Acutum 2010 : Deeply-coloured garnet. Distinctive nose driven by black olive, pepper, spice and stone fruits. Warm, concentrated palate displaying a typically Mediterranean bouquet. Long-lasting finish. Calls for foods in a sauce such as a casserole or a tagine. Price approx.: 12,00 EUR
http://www.masdecynanque.com
Mas de Cynanque
+33 (0)4 67 25 01 34

DOMAINE LA MAURINE 88/100

▼ .♪ Galopins 2011 : Medium deep colour. Distinctive nose driven by stone fruits, spice, smoke... Well-balanced palate showing seductive aromatic honesty. Nicely-harnessed yet still evident power. Long peppery and olive paste-infused finish. Already a superlative Galopins. Price approx.: 8,00 EUR
Domaine La Maurine
+33 (0)6 82 96 28 00

CHÂTEAU VIRANEL 87/100

▼ .♪ Tradition 2012 : Beautifully young, deep hue. Rich nose showing a touch of toast and smoke backed by ripe stone fruits. A well-structured Saint-Chinian with a personality based on aromatic honesty (fruit, spice), fleshy substance and clear power. A robust wine. Price approx.: 7,90 EUR
http://chateau-viranel.com
Château Viranel
+33 (0)4 67 89 60 59

CHÂTEAU LA BAUME

90/100

▼ Vintage 2013

Deeply-coloured orange-brown. Very open nose intermixing black cherry, prune, undergrowth and humus.
Sumptuous attack showing fat, fullness and presence flowing into a more mineral mid-palate (graphite) with wonderful persistency. Sterling effort.

Price approx.: 15 EUR
Serving Temperature: 15-17°C
Ready to drink: 2015-2017

Located in Puisserguier, around twenty kilometres from Béziers, and set amongst garrigue land in a Natura 2000 protected area, La Baume is a wine estate currently undergoing complete revitalisation. It already boasts 6 hectares under vine which will gradually increase to 18 hectares by 2015. The local soils, alternately limestone gravel and sandstone from the Eocene epoch, are outstanding. Syrah, Grenache and Mourvèdre vines averaging 20 years' old produce naturally healthy, concentrated grapes. During the wine making process, the overriding ambition is to bring out the maximum amount of fruit, freshness and minerality whilst avoiding excessive power and extraction. The result is convincing. An estate worth following.

Château la Baume
34620 Puisserguier
Tel.: +33 4 67 38 16 22
E-mail: masdelabaume@gmail.fr

CHÂTEAU MILHAU-LACUGUE

90/100

▼ Les Curées 2008

Intense colour. Profound, open nose showing delightful aromas of red fruits, stone fruits and garrigue with mineral undercurrents bordering on undergrowth. Full, lush, warm and melted palate. Lovely volume, power and persistency. A sterling wine.

Price approx.: 17 EUR
Serving temperature: 15-17°C
Ready to drink: From now on

A former Knights Hospitaller estate, Château Milhau-Lacugue farms vineyards facing South-South-East on clay-limestone soils from the Secondary and Tertiary periods formed by the whims of countless geological forces. Its 'Les Curées' blend mirrors all the qualities of a great growth with its idiosyncratic personality shaped by its boutique vineyard, a selection of Syrah and Grenache noir grapes and lengthy wine making process. As the air flows through the garrigue and along the valley floor, it imbues the grapes with myriad scents of wild plants that will later form part of the wine's unique personality. Power combines with elegance and the wine gradually matures after years of cellaring. Authentic, rich and distinguished, 'Les Curées' is a perfect match for the finest French cuisine.

Château Milhau-Lacugue
Route de Cazedarnes
34620 Puisserguier, France
Tel.: 04 67 93 64 79 - Fax: 04 67 93 64 79
E-mail: lacuguejean@yahoo.fr
Website: http://milhau-lacugue.com

CHÂTEAU MILHAU-LACUGUE

88/100

▼ Les Truffières 2010

Beautiful intense hue. Concentrated nose of red and black fruits, notes of liquorice and spice. Wonderful attack with a melted, fine-grained mouthfeel. Good length and freshness is displayed across the palate with the liquoricy, mineral character recurring on the finish.

Price approx.: 13 EUR
Serving temperature: 15-17°C
Ready to drink: From now on

'Les Truffières' by Château Milhau-Lacugue is a dense, elegant wine that takes its name from the truffle-bearing oak trees that grow wild here. The soils are clay-limestone with a South-South-East aspect exposed to a gentle daily breeze. In this unique location, Syrah and Grenache noir show outstanding expression, blending flowery and fruity elegance with dense, concentrated tannins. A wine displaying archetypal Mediterranean traits, it is rich and complex and will gradually reveal itself after a few years' cellaring. At a serving temperature of 17°C, 'Les Truffières' pairs well with all meat and game-based dishes, particularly slow-cooked meats.

Château Milhau-Lacugue
Route de Cazedarnes
34620 Puisserguier, France
Tel.: 04 67 93 64 79 - Fax: 04 67 93 64 79
E-mail: lacuguejean@yahoo.fr
Website: http://milhau-lacugue.com

DOMAINE SAINT MARTIN DES CHAMPS — 87/100

▼ ♪ Terrasses de Fonterilles 2008 : Concentrated colour that is beginning to evolve. Mature nose halfway between earth, undergrowth and jammy black fruit perfumes. Mature, full and generous palate with restrained power and high performance fruit. A distinctive Saint-Chinian, ready now with stew.
Price approx.: 13,40 EUR
www.saintmartindeschamps.com
Château Saint Martin des Champs
+33 (0)4 67 32 92 58

CHÂTEAU FONSALADE — 87/100

▼ ♪ Petit Bonheur 2013 : Salmon-pink. Very refined nose blending mild spices, white flowers, citrus and strawberry. The palate is worth discovering for its mildness, tangy freshness and soft, crunchy fruit. A delightful rosé augmented by beautiful substance.
Price approx.: 5,00 EUR
http://www.fonsalade.com
Château Fonsalade
+33 (0)5 62 88 13 35

CHÂTEAU FONSALADE — 87/100

▼ ♪ Felix Culpa 2011 : Deeply-coloured garnet. Heady nose showing accents of graphite, ripe dark fruits, wild spices and flowers. Supple palate with a smooth mouthfeel and effective, balanced perfumes. Lovely archetypal Languedoc aromatics. Definite cellaring capacity.
Price approx.: 20,00 EUR
http://www.fonsalade.com
Château Fonsalade
+33 (0)5 62 88 13 35

MAS DE CYNANQUE — 87/100

Org▼ ♪ Carissimo 2012 : Superb deep colour, youthful tints. Distinctive nose driven by olive paste and stone fruits. Beautiful aromatic attack, full mouthfeel and mellowness. Delicious, fruit-forward finish. A charming, already accessible Saint-Chinian. Uncork for braised duck.
Price approx.: 18,00 EUR
http://www.masdecynanque.com
Mas de Cynanque
+33 (0)4 67 25 01 34

MAS DE CYNANQUE — 87/100

Org▼ ♪ Althea 2012 : Brilliant light gold. Rich nose of sweet almond, jammy pears, flowers and spices. Well-balanced palate with a soft mouthfeel and focused, lingering perfumes. A refined white wine that works well with delicately-flavoured Mediterranean dishes. Price approx.: 11,50 EUR
http://www.masdecynanque.com
Mas de Cynanque
+33 (0)4 67 25 01 34

CHÂTEAU VIRANEL — 86/100

▼ ♪ Tradition 2013 : Brilliant red with orange. Nose of ripe red fruits coupled with spice and garrigue notes. A powerful, fleshy rosé with mouth-coating substance and focused, intense and distinctive fruit expression. Serve preferably with food such as grilled sardines.
Price approx.: 7,20 EUR
http://chateau-viranel.com
Château Viranel
+33 (0)4 67 89 60 59

DOMAINE SAINT MARTIN DES CHAMPS — 86/100

▼ ♪ Vieilles Vignes 2011 : Medium deep garnet. Refined nose of mellow toasted vanilla oak with ripe black fruit perfumes. Supple palate with a soft mouthfeel. Lovely aromatic balance. Oak takes a back seat to fruit expression. A mature Saint-Chinian, perfect for drinking now.
Price approx.: 8,30 EUR
www.saintmartindeschamps.com
Château Saint Martin des Champs
+33 (0)4 67 32 92 58

DOMAINE SAINT MARTIN DES CHAMPS — 86/100

▼ ♪ Sélection 2013 : Intense salmon-pink. Refined nose driven by ripe fruits, flowers and a touch of peppery spice. Full, round and generous palate driven by mature perfumes. Mouth-coating substance. A very good rosé for food, particularly barbecues.
Price approx.: 6,50 EUR
www.saintmartindeschamps.com
Château Saint Martin des Champs
+33 (0)4 67 32 92 58

DOMAINE GALTIER — 85/100

▼ ♪ L'Obstinée 2012 : Deeply-coloured with crimson highlights. Profound, mature nose recalling dark fruits and garrigue with mineral undertones. A warm, full and mellow style on the palate focusing on aromatic expression. An expressive, Mediterranean wine.
Price approx.: 7,00 EUR
Domaine Galtier
+33 (0)4 67 37 85 14

DOMAINE DES PRADELS QUARTIRONI — 85/100

▼ ♪ Vintage 2012 : Pale gold. Expressive nose with perfumes of ripe citrus, white fruits, almond and a touch of resin. Full-bodied palate. Very upfront substance obscuring the fruit. Still some bitterness on the finish. Serve preferably with fish in a sauce.
Price approx.: 7,20 EUR
www.vins-quartironi.com
Domaine des Pradels Quartironi
+33 (0)4 67 38 01 53

CHÂTEAU QUARTIRONI DE SARS   85/100

▼ ♪ La Cuvée Haut Priou 2009 : Deeply-coloured garnet. Intense, empyreumatic nose backed by olive paste and nicely ripe stone fruits. Ripe, warm palate, nevertheless boasting lovely mineral freshness. Archetypal Languedoc-style aromatics. A racy Saint-Chinian drinking well now.
Price approx.: 13,50 EUR
www.vins-quartironi.com
Domaine des Pradels Quartironi
+33 (0)4 67 38 01 53

MAS DE CYNANQUE   85/100

CONV▼ ♪ Plein Grès 2011 : Deep, young colour. Endearing nose driven by fresh black fruit, spice, pepper and a floral touch. Nicely restrained power on the palate. Aroma and freshness are emphasised yet the style remains true to Saint-Chinian. Ideal for kebabs. Price approx.: 8,50 EUR
http://www.masdecynanque.com
Mas de Cynanque
+33 (0)4 67 25 01 34

CHÂTEAU FONSALADE   83/100

▼ ♪ Petit Bonheur 2013 : Deep, young colour. Heady nose halfway between peony and red and black berry fruits. Sappy palate showing restrained power and upfront fruity freshness. A distinctive yet accessible wine. Recommended for a barbecue offering southern flavours. Price approx.: 5,00 EUR
http://www.fonsalade.com
Château Fonsalade
+33 (0)5 62 88 13 35

DOMAINE GALTIER   79/100

▼ ♪ L'Accompli 2011 : Intense colour. Mature, profound nose opening up to cassis, blackberry and spice. More of the same extrovert aromas on the palate. Supple, generous attack leading into a firmer, slightly lean mid-palate and finish. Meat in a sauce would be a good match.
Price approx.: 11,00 EUR
Domaine Galtier
+33 (0)4 67 37 85 14

SAINT-CHINIAN BERLOU

CHÂTEAU LES ALBIÈRES   86/100

▼ ♪ Vintage 2010 : Deep, young colour. Inviting, heady nose with black cherry, cassis, delicate smoky oak and cocoa undertones. A distinctive Saint-Chinian in terms of aromatics, nicely supported by ageing perfumes. Supple mouthfeel with restrained power. Accessible and well made.
http://www.saint-auriol.com
Les Domaines Auriol
+33 (0)4 68 58 15 15

ST GUILHEM LE DÉSERT

MAS DE DAUMAS GASSAC   90/100

▼ ♪ Vintage 2013 : Limpid hue. The nose reveals perfumes of plants, mild spices, white flowers, peach and white fruits. Pleasurable on point of entry with its lovely mellowness. Intense perfumes. Charming and rich. A successful wine.
Price approx.: 30,00 EUR
www.daumas-gassac.com
Mas de Daumas Gassac
+33 (0)4 67 57 71 28

MAS DE DAUMAS GASSAC   89/100

▼ ♪ Vintage 2012 : Young, concentrated colour. Refined nose with smoky oak accents. Focused fruit presence with currants and bigarreau cherry. Supple, the oak has already mellowed and leaves room for fruit expression. Harmonious and already accessible due to the fruit.
Price approx.: 30,00 EUR
www.daumas-gassac.com
Mas de Daumas Gassac
+33 (0)4 67 57 71 28

ST-GUILHEM-LE-DÉSERT - VAL DE MONTFERRAND

LES AUGUSTINS   87/100

▼ ♪ Les Bambins 2012 : Light yellow. Appealing spring-like and highly floral nose of honeysuckle and linden backed by almonds and white fruits. Soft, supple palate with an elegant mouthfeel, refined fruit and freshness. A delicate, lace-like regional wine.
Price approx.: 8,50 EUR
http://www.closdesaugustins.com
Clos des Augustins
+33 (0)4 67 54 73 45

LOIRE VALLEY

BRINGING FRESHNESS INTO THE EQUATION

Stretching 1,012 kilometres from start to finish, the Loire is France's longest river. It rises in the Massif Central and cuts through myriad landscapes before flowing into the Atlantic. Its catchment area covers an astounding 120,000 km2, giving some idea of the variety of wine styles the Loire can produce: dry, medium dry or sweet whites, sparkling wines, light rosés, smooth or robust reds suitable for ageing... providing an endless choice for discerning wine lovers.

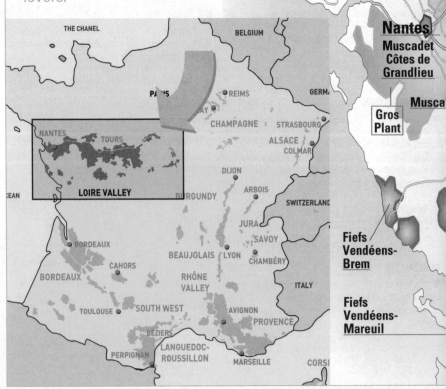

Nantes
Muscadet Côtes de Grandlieu

Musca

Gros Plant

Fiefs Vendéens-Brem

Fiefs Vendéens-Mareuil

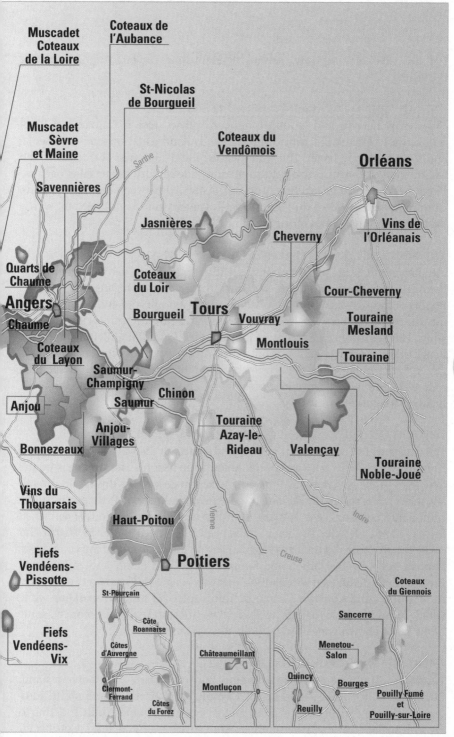

Muscadet
Coteaux
de la Loire

Coteaux de
l'Aubance

St-Nicolas
de Bourgueil

Muscadet
Sèvre
et Maine

Coteaux du
Vendômois

Orléans

Savennières

Jasnières

Cheverny

Vins de
l'Orléanais

Quarts de
Chaume

Coteaux
du Loir

Cour-Cheverny

Angers

Bourgueil

Tours

Vouvray

Touraine
Mesland

Chaume

Montlouis

Touraine

Coteaux
du Layon

Saumur-
Champigny

Anjou

Saumur

Chinon

Touraine
Azay-le-
Rideau

Valençay

Bonnezeaux

Anjou-
Villages

Touraine
Noble-Joué

Vins du
Thouarsais

Haut-Poitou

Fiefs
Vendéens-
Pissotte

Poitiers

Coteaux
du Giennois

St-Pourçain

Sancerre

Côte
Roannaise

Fiefs
Vendéens-
Vix

Côtes
d'Auvergne

Châteaumeillant

Menetou-
Salon

Quincy

Bourges

Clermont-
Ferrand

Montluçon

Reuilly

Pouilly Fumé
et
Pouilly-sur-Loire

Côtes
du Forez

Sarthe

Vienne

Indre

Creuse

285

For the sake of simplicity, several different zones can be identified, starting upstream:

THE AUVERGNE, BOURBONNAIS AND FOREZ REGIONS

Vines grow here in and around mountain valleys. This is Gamay and Pinot noir territory for the red wines. The climate is continental or semi-continental and the winters are harsh. The wines are light and fruity red and rosé, though Chardonnay, Sauvignon and a clutch of local varieties such as Tressalier or Saint-Pierre Doré are also grown here. The area is divided between four appellations: Côtes d'Auvergne, Côtes du Forez, Côte Roannaise and Saint-Pourçain, with a balance of regional wines including Vin de Pays d'Urfé.

THE BERRY, NIVERNAIS AND ORLÉANAIS REGIONS

Heading north from the Bourbonnais (Allier), you enter the Nivernais where the Allier river flows into the Loire. Between Nevers and Orléans (AC Sancerre, Pouilly-Fumé, Coteaux du Giennois) the winters are still cold and spring is fickle for wine growing. Berry is also home to vineyards starting with Menetou-Salon, which extends out from Sancerre in the east, then Quincy and Reuilly lining the banks of the Cher river and its tributary the Arnon, south of Vierzon. The area is famed for its white wines, made primarily from the Sauvignon grape, though the reds and rosés made from Pinot noir can be appealing and in some instances, highly distinguished wines.

THE TOURAINE REGION AND SURROUNDING AREAS

The vineyards of Touraine start in Blois and stretch all the way to the outskirts of Saumur (which is actually part of the Anjou wine region). The climate is milder here than in the Nivernais, as the warm ocean breezes sweep this far up the valley, though it is still partly defined by continental influences. Perhaps this subtle combination explains why Touraine (just like neighbouring Anjou) is renowned for its relaxed lifestyle. The kings of France certainly fell under its charm and chose the area to build their architectural jewels, the Châteaux of the Loire. Vines flourish here too. In Chinon and Bourgueil, Cabernet Franc, known locally as Breton, yields sterling red wines which in good vintages will keep for twenty years. In Montlouis and Vouvray, Chenin produces splendid still and sparkling white wines. Although these majestic wines rule the roost in terms of notoriety, some of the lesser-known wines also harbour some great surprises.

THERE ARE NINE TRUE TOURAINE APPELLATIONS

Touraine, Touraine-Amboise, Touraine-Azay-le-Rideau, Touraine-Mesland, Bourgueil, Saint-Nicolas de Bourgueil, Chinon, Vouvray and Montlouis. In addition to these are six peripheral appellations: Cheverny (which links Touraine to the Orléanais), Valençay (the south-eastern extension of Touraine), Coteaux du

Vendômois, Jasnières, Coteaux du Loir (in the north) and Haut-Poitou (heading south-west).

THE ANJOU AND SAUMUR REGIONS

Anjou is reached by crossing the border of Maine et Loire in the west. Initially, around Saumur, the landscape undergoes only minor changes. Its predominant feature is the chalky soil ('tuffeau') - hence the name 'white' Anjou - from which thousands of kilometres of caves have been carved out. The area is home to red wines, made primarily from Cabernet Franc, and renowned sparkling wines. Heading west, the dividing line between the Paris and Armorican basins marks the starting point of 'black' Anjou where the soil type is predominantly shale (slate). The resultant red wines are more robust and Chenin flourishes in some parts (the Layon valley) to produce superlative sweet wines. The rosés also deserve a mention. They can be dry though are more often medium sweet, making Anjou France's leading producer of this style, ahead of Provence.

All of this provides the context for a wide variety of appellations and wine styles.

THERE ARE MORE THAN TWENTY APPELLATIONS IN ALL

REDS: *Anjou, Anjou-Villages, Anjou-Gamay, Saumur, Saumur-Champigny.*
ROSÉS: *Rosé d'Anjou, Cabernet d'Anjou, Rosé de Loire,*
Cabernet de Saumur, Coteaux de Saumur.
SWEET WHITES: *Coteaux de l'Aubance, Anjou-Coteaux de la Loire, Coteaux du Layon, Chaume, Quarts de Chaume, Bonnezeaux.*
DRY WHITES: *Savennières (occasionally medium dry), Anjou*
SPARKLING: *Anjou Mousseux, Saumur Mousseux, Crémant de Loire.*

287

PAYS NANTAIS

The Pays Nantais region stretches west from Anjou, on the other side of Ingrandes. With around 20,000 hectares under vine, it is the most extensive area in the entire Loire valley. The Ocean type climate and cool soils (this is the Armorican mountain range) make production of dry white wines the natural choice. The summers are not hot enough to grow sweet wines and too changeable to make reds. Some red wine is grown on the border with Anjou (Coteaux d'Ancenis) and in Fiefs Vendéens around Les Sables d'Olonne, but only in diminutive quantities. The vast majority of the wines are white, made from Folle Blanche (known as Gros Plant) though chiefly Melon de Bourgogne (Muscadet). They yield dry, fragrant white wines (particularly the Muscadet) which form the perfect partners for the fruits of the sea, both shellfish and fish.

Pays Nantais boasts seven appellations: Coteaux d'Ancenis, Muscadet, Muscadet Sèvre et Maine, Muscadet des Coteaux de la Loire, Muscadet des Côtes de Grand-Lieu, Gros Plant du Pays Nantais and Fiefs Vendéens.

- **2011** • Like everywhere else, the vintage was challenging due to nature with a dry summer, almost too dry, then heavy rainfall, again slightly too heavy and too late in the season. However, the wines performed extremely well despite lower acidity than in 2010. Due to its acreage and wide array of grape varieties and sites, this favoured region always has something to offer.
- **2012** • The volume is low, but the wines are mature thanks to a sunny August and September. The Muscadets should be worthy of lying down, as well as the late-harvest whites, which have good acidity. The reds are clean and mature, with a nice fruity crunch. A vintage to enjoy!
- **2013** • A challenging yet fairly decent vintage. The weather wrought havoc across the entire region, particularly in Vouvray where several hailstorms in June destroyed over two thirds of the appellation's 2,200-hectare vineyard. Generally speaking, the wines are well made, with beautiful aromatic definition and a fruitiness that makes them suitable for early-drinking. The experience and hard work of the wine growers allowed the region to make the most of a tricky vintage.

THE LOIRE VALLEY APPELLATIONS

A.C. ANJOU

OVERVIEW: the appellation covers 188 towns and villages (southern half of the Maine-et-Loire department, some of Vienne and Deux-Sèvres). This vast area can be roughly divided into two different soil series: the first type, in the Armorican mountain range, is clayey shale or Silurian slate, and the second, in the Paris basin, is limestone and sandy clay. The various areas are referred to as 'black', 'blue' and 'white' Anjou.

WINE STYLES: the reds are made from Cabernet Franc, Cabernet Sauvignon and Pineau d'Aunis. They can vary from supple wines that are fresh, aromatic and easy-drinking to wines with a pronounced tannic framework imparted by prolonged maceration. Fragrances of raspberry, blackcurrant, green pepper and spices are present. Drink when young with cooked cold pork meats, white or red meat. The whites are blended from at least 80% Chenin (augmented with Chardonnay and Sauvignon) and are dry, elegant, distinctive and fragrant. The best examples hail from the shale soils. They proffer aromas of citrus fruit such as grapefruit as well as apple, peach stone and vegetal tones. Try with hors d'ouvre or fish. A small proportion of whites can be made as medium sweet or sweet. The rosés, which are constantly on the wane, are supple and soft.

A.C. ANJOU MOUSSEUX

Nine villages in the department of Vienne (subsumed into the Anjou appellation) are entitled to produce sparkling wines, including Pouancay, Berrie, Saint-Léger-de-Montbrillais, Ternay and Ranton. The minimum percentage of Chenin in the blend is 80%. Bottle fermentation takes place during a secondary fermentation in the bottle. These wines are recommended as appetisers or with desserts.

A.C. ANJOU COTEAUX DE LA LOIRE

OVERVIEW: this sweet wine appellation area covers 11 villages in Maine-et-Loire set on hillsides overlooking the Loire valley west of Angers. Production is centred primarily on the villages of Pommeraye and Montjean. All the grapes are hand-picked and sorted in batches. The soil is shale and limestone. The grape variety used is Chenin.

WINE STYLES: initially, they are drier than Coteaux du Layon though sub-sequently become round and silky as they mature. The wines display a brilliant hue with golden shades and greenish tints. They conjure up fragrances of ripe fruit such as vine peach though also honey, linden and freshly-cut hay. The shale soil promotes animal notes whilst the limestone imparts more mineral tones. Try as an appetiser or with trout, pear tart or cheeses (Bresse, Fourme).

A.C. ANJOU-GAMAY

OVERVIEW: only Gamay is permitted for this appellation, hence the name. The area covers the entire Anjou region, excluding the Saumur area.

WINE STYLES: these are round, supple, light and fruity wines. They are desig-ned to be drunk young and develop fragrances of red fruit such as red currant. Wines released soon after the harvest (primeur) display exotic fruit aromas as well. Recommended food pairings are poultry, grilled red meat, white meat and soft cheeses.

A.C. ANJOU-VILLAGES

OVERVIEW: 46 towns and villages within the Anjou appellation area are entitled to this red wine only appellation. Anjou-Villages differ from red Anjou both for their varietal range and wine making practices: there is no Pineau d'Aunis and vatting and ageing last longer. Another point of difference is that 'Villages' wines cannot be released until September 15th a year after the harvest. The best sites are located south of Angers, around Brissac, Thouarcé and Martigné-Briand...

WINE STYLES: made from Cabernet Franc and Cabernet Sauvignon, these wines are fruity and well-structured, and improve with age. Their hue ranges from crim-son to garnet-red and they display fragrances of red fruit (blackberry, strawberry, blackcurrant, cherry), undergrowth and spices, leading into leather and fruit stone over time. Try with game, fish in a red wine sauce, roast or grilled red meat or cheeses.

A.C. BONNEZEAUX

OVERVIEW: Bonnezeaux is one of two Coteaux du Layon great growths in Anjou. the vineyards are located south of the Loire, twenty or so kilometres from Angers in the village of Thouarcé. Three south-south-west facing hillsides over-looking the Layon - La Montagne, Beauregard and Fesles - are home to the vines. The overripe grapes are harvested by hand and painstakingly sorted as they ripen. Minimum alcohol content is 13.5%. The appellation is shared by around fifty different growers. The vines are planted on decomposed shale rich in sandstone, quartz and phtanite. The topsoil is shallow and littered with stones. Chenin is the only white varietal grown.

WINE STYLES: Bonnezeaux are fresh, well-balanced, delicate sweet wines that are complex and elegant. Bursting with fruit, they are opulent, fat and robust with a well-balanced mellowness. As they mature, they become full, unctuous and ample. Sporting a golden hue with greenish tints, they display fragrances of stewed apricot, orange, quince, pineapple, verbena, vanilla, honey, acacia, haw-thorn and linden. Try with foie gras and grapes, fish in a sauce such as turbot, blue cheeses…

A.C. BOURGUEIL

OVERVIEW: the Bourgueil area is spread over a 15 kilometre strip of land running perpendicular to the Loire, in Touraine. Eight villages are entitled to the appella-tion (Bourgueil, Saint-Nicolas de Bourgueil, Benais, Chouzé-sur-Loire, Ingrandes de Touraine, La Chapelle sur Loire, Restigné and Saint-Patrice). Historically, the wines were highly regarded by Louis XI, Rabelais and Ronsard.

The area can be divided into three zones: the banks of the Loire, where stony patches provide suitable plots for vines, then a terrace which provides the focal point for the area, and finally the chalk plateau ('tuffeau') through which a tribu-tary of the Loire - the Changeon - meanders.

WINE STYLES: Bourgueil produces mainly red wines from Cabernet Franc (Cabernet Sauvignon content is restricted to a maximum 10%). The different 'terroirs' are reflected in the wine styles. Gravely soils produce elegant, vigorous, delicate, supple, fruity wines. Conversely, chalk type soils yield well-structured, robust, tannic wines, which can be hard or firm when young. Bourgueil smells sweetly of violet, bell pepper, spices, raspberry and red currant and often exhibits gamey, earthy tones. Recommended food pairings include beef with morel mus-hrooms, stew, jugged hare, roast red meats…

A.C. CABERNET D'ANJOU

OVERVIEW: this rosé wine can be made in 188 towns and villages within the same boundaries as the Anjou appellation area. Soil types are varied, ranging from shale, to clay and limestone, very often covered in sand and gravel. The best sites are located along the hillsides of the upper and middle Layon valley. The area enjoys an ocean climate with mild winters, hot summers and low temperature variations between daytime and nightime.

WINE STYLES: most of the wines are medium sweet made from Cabernet Franc supported by a little Cabernet Sauvignon. They are fresh, light, soft and delicate with good length and are intended to be drunk young. Their orange or grenadine hue turns brick-red as they age. They display fragrances of raspberry, red currant, strawberry, fruit in brandy, vanilla and menthol notes though also exhibit floral nuances of iris, violet and rose. This charming wine can be served with mushroom pie, quiche, cooked cold pork meats, poultry, exotic dishes or fruit-based desserts (fruit mousse).

A.C. CABERNET DE SAUMUR

OVERVIEW: these rosé wines, made from Cabernet Franc and Cabernet Sauvignon, are grown in the same appellation area as Saumur, hence the name, on limestone soils.

Wine styles: these rosés are not only drier than Cabernet d'Anjou, they are also more elegant. They are soft, fresh and round. Try with cooked cold pork meats, poultry…

291

AC CHÂTEAUMEILLANT

OVERVIEW: the appellation is situated south-west of Saint-Amand-Montrond, 60 km from Bourges, in Berry. It is spread over two departments (Indre and Cher). The soils are silica with a predominant proportion of sand and sandy clay on a metamorphosed subsoil. Gamay thrives here on stony sandstone soils in a pre-mountain Limousin-type climate, though the area also grows Pinot noir and Pinot gris.

WINE STYLES: the reds are fruity, light quaffing wines which are lively and intended to be drunk young. Supple-menting them with a dash of Pinot noir and Pinot gris bolsters their framework though at the same time mellows them. Châteaumeillant exhibits a light hue and fragrances of wild strawberry and pepper. The rosés, known as 'vin gris', are fresh. Try with mixed salads or fresh goats cheese flavoured with herbs. Recom-mended pairings for the rosés are exotic cuisine from China, the Caribbean or Thailand.

A.C. CHEVERNY

OVERVIEW: this appellation is situated in north-eastern Touraine, between the Loire and the Sologne, near Blois. It embraces 24 towns and villages. The soils are sandy clay, sandy silica and calcareous clay. The area is home to stone quarries and the varietal range is comprised of Gamay, Cabernet, Pinot noir, Cot, Pineau d'Aunis, Pinot gris (reds), though also Chenin, Menu Pineau, Chardonnay, Romorantin and Sauvignon (whites).

WINE STYLES: the reds are lively, clean, fruity, light quaffing wines. Red and black fruit, blackcurrant and liquorice aromas are present. The whites, with their pale hue, are dry, lively and fresh with fragrances of hazelnut and honey. The rosés are supple and fresh. They display a salmon-pink colour and exude spicy, occasionally toasted notes. Cheverny wines are well suited to grilled veal, roast poultry, cheeses (reds), fish and shellfish (whites). The rosés are equally suitable as appetisers or with barbecues.

A.C. CHINON

OVERVIEW: the Chinon area sits at the point where Anjou, Saumur and Touraine meet. The appellation embraces 19 towns and villages (Beaumont-en-Véron, Avoine, Chinon, Cravant, Tavant, Avon les Roches…) set either side of the Vienne. There are three different soil types: gravel and sand along the banks of the Vienne, Senonian calcareous clay or silica clay hills and plateaux. Cabernet Franc and Cabernet Sauvignon (restricted to a maximum 10%) flourish on the south facing sites.

WINE STYLES: each 'terroir' produces a different style of wine. The reds grown on the gravely soils are light, fruity and extremely aromatic. They reward early drinking. Wines from the silica clay plateaux and hillside sites are well-constituted, robust, tannic and elegant. They display rich, dense aromas and are wines to keep which become full and deep down the years. With a ruby-red hue, Chinon exhibits aromas of blackcurrant, violet, mineral and vegetal notes. Humus and truffle, empyreumatic fragrances and animal notes occur as they mature.

Up until a few years ago, the character of Chinon wines was a result of blending wines from various sites. Nowadays, however, growers tend to separate site-specific wines and prefer old vines. Try with white and red meats (light Chinon), meats served in a sauce, game and cheeses (robust Chinon). Chinon also makes rosés with delicate, subtle aromas and limited edition whites from Chenin, which are dry and fruity.

AC CÔTES D'AUVERGNE

OVERVIEW: the Côtes d'Auvergne appellation is covering 54 towns and villages in Puy de Dôme (Auvergne). It boasts five growths which are entitled to add their name to the appellation: Corent, Boudes, Chanturgues, Châ-teaugay and Madargues, underscoring the diversity of the wines, despite the fact that the varietal range is restricted to Gamay for the reds and rosés and Chardonnay for the w hites (a tiny minority).

WINE STYLES: Corent, for instance, which surrounds the plateau of the same name, boasts calcareous clay soils and produces mainly rosés ('vin gris'). These are pleasant, fruity wines which develop fragrances of apricot, yellow fruit, candied fruit and peppery notes. Boudes, which also has a strong focus on rosé wines, covers soils where the limestone content is higher and fragments of basalt occur. The hillock at Châteaugay, north-west of Clermont-Ferrand, has soils with lower clay content and more sand with a higher proportion of volcanic debris. This particular 'terroir' yields firm, rustic wines with medium cellaring capacity that pair with barbecues.

In Chanturgues, the hillside is protected from erosion by Miocene basalt flows and calcareous clay soils show through on the slopes. This growth produces wines which are both well-structured and supple with smoky, spicy aromas, black cherry and violet. They show at their best after a few years' ageing.

A.C. CÔTE ROANNAISE

OVERVIEW: the Côte Roannaise appellation stretches over 14 villages along the left bank of the Loire. Gamay, known locally as Saint-Romain, is the only grape variety grown here. The soils are predominantly granite and basalt covered with sand and alluvium at the foot of the hills.

WINE STYLES: the red and rosé wines are made by the semi-carbonic maceration process, hence their fresh, clean, lively, fresh and harmonious style and capacity to be drunk young. With their ruby-red hue, they exhibit fragrances of red fruit such as blackcurrant, raspberry, strawberry, red currant and bilberry. They pair with chitterlings sausage, slicing sausage, tripe and white meat.

293

A.C. COTEAUX D'ANCENIS

OVERVIEW: the appellation is situated east of Nantes, either side of the Loire. It embraces 27 towns and villages straddling Maine-et-Loire and Loire-Atlantique. There are two different types of soil: micaschist and crimson schist north of the Loire and gneiss and green schist south of the Loire. The wines often mention the grape variety on the label: Chenin and Pinot gris for the whites and Cabernet Sauvignon, Cabernet Franc and Gamay for the reds.

WINE STYLES: the reds and rosés are fruity, light, lively quaffing wines. They display a brilliant colour and fragrances of red fruit. They are the perfect partner for hors d'ouvre, cooked cold pork meats, duck with cherries, barbecues and cheeses. The whites with their pale green hue and aromas of fruit and honey are soft, round and rich and will cellar well. They pair with fish and white meat in a sauce.

A.C. COTEAUX DE L'AUBANCE

OVERVIEW: this appellation is located west of the river Aubance, east of Brissac and north of the Loire in an area often described as 'black' Anjou because of the dark colour of the shale or sandstone soils of the Armorican mountain range. Ten villages are allowed to use the appellation. The region enjoys a particularly dry late autumn, allowing the Chenin grapes to become overripe. Vines growing on the hills overlooking the Aubance bask in plentiful sunshine.

WINE STYLES: although the Coteaux de l'Aubance appellation produces sweet wines, its major focus is on medium sweet wines. They are rich, soft, delicate, distinguished wines which are fruity, round, full and vigorous. They exhibit a limpid hue with green gold and straw-yellow gold tints and fragrances of quince paste, candied fruits, fig, lemon, honey, white flowers and mineral notes. They make marvellous appetisers served with refined canapes though also accompany fruit tarts, vol-au-vents…

A.C. COTEAUX DE SAUMUR

OVERVIEW: thirteen towns and villages in Maine-et-Loire and Vienne located north of the Saumur appellation are entitled to this appellation which covers sweet wines made from Chenin. The wines can only be made when the weather conditions are suitable. The grapes are handpicked and painstakingly sorted as they ripen. The soil type is 'tuffeau' chalk.

WINE STYLES: they are fruity, delicate, fat, lively and soft displaying a straw-yellow gold hue with greenish tints. They develop fragrances of roasted grapes, toasted almonds, honey, honeysuckle and hazelnut. They can be married with a whole array of foods: mushroom pie, foie gras, fish in a creamy sauce, cheeses (blue), sweetbreads in a cream sauce, oven-baked chitterlings sausage…

A.C. COTEAUX DU LAYON

OVERVIEW: this appellation is shared by 27 towns and villages on either side of the Layon river, a left bank tributary of the Loire. Seven of these are entitled to append their name to the Coteaux du Layon appellation (Beaulieu-sur-Layon, Faye d'Anjou, Rablay-sur-Layon, Rochefort-sur-Loire, Saint-Aubin-sur-Luigné, Saint-Lambert-du-Lattay and Chaume. The soils are stony with a predominant proportion of shale, clay shale and silica, interspersed with gravely sand and volcanic sediment. Chenin is the only grape variety grown here.

WINE STYLES: Coteaux du Layon are sweet white wines which are rich, intense, round, unctuous and fat rounded off with a superb fruity freshness. They display a green gold hue and develop fragrances of linden, acacia, honey, apricot and citrus fruit, evolving into aromas of wax, quince and candied fruit as they mature. They are delicious as appetisers or with foie gras, Roquefort, poultry in a cream sauce, gizzards, goats cheeses or blue cheeses, fish such as pike-perch and salmon, and of course desserts: apple pie and all nougatine-based gateaux.

A.C. CHAUME

OVERVIEW: this minute appellation area (70 hectares) within the Coteaux du Layon is situated in the village of Rochefort-sur-Loire, north of the hamlet of Chaume itself. The vast majority of the soils are carboniferous puddingstone though there are occasional shale formations (spilite and phanite). The vines enjoy a south-east aspect and are sheltered both from northerly winds and ocean influences. Chenin is the sole varietal.

WINE STYLES: they are fat, rich, delicate, well-structured and full wines that are fleshy, unctuous and elegant. They display a brilliant hue tinted with green and fragrances of candied fruits (apricots), white flowers, white peaches and a delicate bitterness. They are served with foie gras, fish in a hollandaise sauce, cheeses (blue), melon...

A.C. COTEAUX DU LOIR

OVERVIEW: this 80-hectare area, which is home to a varietal range comprised of Gamay, Pinot noir, Chenin and Pineau d'Aunis, is set on the left bank of the Loir (22 towns and villages in Sarthe and Indre-et-Loire). It is the most northerly of the Loire appellations. Most of the wines are grown in and around Lhomme, Ruillé-sur-Loir, Chahaines and Marçon. The soils are clay silica on a bedrock of chalk ('tuffeau') with occurrences of limestone marl. The region enjoys a mild climate defined by the Atlantic.

WINE STYLES: the reds are light, lively, fresh quaffing wines with a pleasant bouquet. They are highly reminiscent of Touraine wines. They display a pale hue and fragrances of morello cherry, cinnamon and spices (pepper). They can be served with cooked cold pork meats (potted meat, Vire andouille), white meats, grilled red meats, meat pie, black pudding with apples, poultry. The whites (Pineau de la Loire) are dry, vigorous wines for cellaring. They develop vegetal aromas. A good match for fish and seafood, cooked cold pork meats and white meat served in a sauce.

295

A.C. COTEAUX DU VENDÔMOIS

OVERVIEW: with its 150 hectares under vine, this area is situated in the Loir valley in Loir-et-Cher, between Vendôme and Montoire. The soils are formed of flint clay on a bedrock of limestone. The red varietals used are Pineau d'Aunis, the main grape which must account for at least 30% of the blend, Gamay (30% maximum), Pinot noir and Cabernet. For the white wines, Chenin and Chardonnay (no more than 20% of the blend).

WINE STYLES: the reds are intended to be drunk young and fresh, when they develop aromas of red fruit, banana and vanilla. The rosés are pale in shade with peppery notes. They are recommended with fried smelt.

A.C. COTEAUX DU GIENNOIS

OVERVIEW: this 150-hectare area occupies undulating land between Gien and Cosne-sur-Loire (16 villages in all). In the Nevers region, Aligny-Cosne, La Celle-sur-Loire, Cosne-sur-Loire, Cours-lès-Cosnes, Myennes, Pougny-Saint-Loup and Saint-Père are entitled to add the name Cosne-sur-Loire to the AC Côtes de Gien appellation. The soils are limestone, gravel and silica along ancient terraces of the Loire.

WINE STYLES: the Pinot noir reds exhibit a ruby-red hue and are lively, supple, fresh and fragrant. They pair with ham in puff pastry, grilled or roast meats, veal, ox tongue with gherkins and grilled black pudding. The whites with tell-tale Sauvignon scents, should be tried with freshwater fish (perch).

A.C. CÔTES DU FOREZ

OVERVIEW: this appellation verges on the Massif Central, north of Saint-Etienne. It embraces 21 towns and villages and roughly 200 hectares of vines. The soils contain less limestone than in Auvergne, though when they are derived from decomposed granite rocks they are 80% clay silica and 20% volcanic in origin. A large share of the wines are vinted and sold by the co-operative winery. The wines are made using the carbonic maceration or semi-carbonic maceration process.

WINE STYLES: the Gamay varietal reds are clean, aromatic, lively, supple and harmonious, and designed to be drunk young. The wines grown on basalt hillside sites are, however, more robust and richer in tannins and will keep for a few years. Try with cooked cold pork meats, grilled meats or poultry.

A.C. COUR CHEVERNY

OVERVIEW: Cour Cheverny wines are grown in Touraine, south-east of Blois (Loir-et-Cher department). The area covers a total 60 hectares spread over 11 villages in Sologne. Set north of the Cheverny area, this AC only produces white wines from a single grape variety -Romorantin - occasionally known as Donnery. Three rivers meander through the Cour Cheverny area: the Beuvron, the Cosson and the Bièvre. The vines are planted on clay silica, with occasional occurrences of calcareous clay.

WINE STYLES: with their straw-yellow hue, Cour Cheverny wines concentrate aromas of apple, pear, acacia flower, honey and mineral notes. Delicate on the palate, their attack conjures up empyreumatic fragrances. With a lively, long mouthfeel, some of the wines can even prove to be elegant and age for a few years. They can be served with cooked cold pork meats, freshwater fish, salmon, seafood or grilled young cockerel.

AC CRÉMANT DE LOIRE

OVERVIEW: Crémant is a sparkling wine made in the traditional way (secondary fermentation in the bottle). The appellation covers the Saumur, Anjou and Touraine areas though most Crémants are made in the departments of Maine-et-Loire and Indre-et-Loire. Crémant de Loire must be stored for at least a year in growers' cellars before it can be released.

WINE MAKING PROCESS: all of the Loire grape varieties can be used, except for Sauvignon. Chenin forms the backbone of the blend, which differentiates it from Crémants from other regions which are often drawn from Chardonnay and Pinots. The grapes are not only harvested by hand, they are also crushed in a chainless press. Bottle fermentation takes place during a secondary fermentation in the bottle after a blend of yeast and sugar has been added. The wines are aromatic, lively, intense and clean with delicate, long-lasting bubbles. Try as appetisers, or with shellfish, fish and goats cheese.

AC FIEFS VENDÉENS

OVERVIEW: the appellation stretches north of Les Sables d'Olonne between La Roche-sur-Yon and Luçon and around Fontenay-le-Comte. Back in 1955, growers began to replace hybrid varieties with noble grapes such as Pinot noir or Gamay. The current area under vine is around 500 hectares and most of the wines are red. Soil types are varied, ranging from clay silica, calcareous clay or gravel to sand. Four site-specific areas have been identified and are entitled to state the name of their main village on the label: Brem, Mareuil, Pissote and Vix.
WINE STYLES: they are light, pleasant and fruity. The reds display a deep garnet-red hue with fragrances of red fruits such as raspberry. Try pairing them with red or white meats or soft cheeses. They whites are a pale yellow colour with floral aromas and are the perfect partner for shellfish and fish.

AC GROS PLANT DU PAYS NANTAIS

OVERVIEW: in the 17th century, the Charentes varietal Folle blanche was introduced, courtesy of the Dutch. Local farmers dubbed it 'gros plant' because of the thickness of the vine's trunk. The area shares the same boundaries as Muscadet, though also spills over into the Retz area, bringing the total number of towns and villages up to around a hundred. Soil types are extremely varied, ranging from shale, micaschist and gneiss to Armorican mountain granite and a few pockets of Quaternary sand deposits.
The better quality wines come from Grand-Lieu lake where the soil is formed of sand and gravel. The climate is ocean, with mild winters and hot summers. A good deal of Gros Plant is vinted on the lees.
WINE STYLES: they are dry, light, vigorous, lively and fresh. They display a pale hue with greenish tints and develop fragrances of dried fruit, a slightly salty touch and mineral notes. Recommended food pairings include shellfish such as mussels, cockles, prawns, oysters or freshwater fish.

AC HAUT-POITOU

OVERVIEW: 47 towns and villages in Vienne and Deux-Sèvres are entitled to use this appellation. Virtually all the wines (95%) are made by the Neuville-de-Poitou co-operative winery and they grow on around 750 hectares of Jurassic calcareous clay and silica clay type soils.
WINE STYLES: the Gamay or Cabernet reds are aromatic, fresh, soft and lively. They

297

sport a ruby-red hue and exude fragrances of cherry, morello cherry and blackcurrant and are well-suited to dishes such as sauteed veal or duck. The whites (Sauvignon, Chardonnay) are fresh, harmonious and expressive. Try with fish (turbot).

A.C. JASNIÈRES

OVERVIEW: the Jasnières appellation, which sits within the boundaries of AC Coteaux du Loir, covers just two villages in Sarthe: Lhomme and Ruillé-sur-Loir, over a total 65 hectares. The villages provide an ideal setting for vines with a strip of land four kilometres long by just a few hundred metres wide with a due south aspect. 'Le Perche' hill acts as a buffer against the northerly winds. The soils are littered with stones and calcareous clay on a bedrock of 'tuffeau'. Frequent occurrences of flint are a feature of this area.

WINE STYLES: these white wines, made from Chenin, are extremely dry and vigorous when young but are capable of maturing. As they age, they become more full and silky, developing a pleasant bouquet. The wines display a deep straw-yellow hue and exude fragrances of linden, hawthorn, honey, acacia, broom, exotic fruits (pineapple) and peach. They boast a characteristic mineral aspect (gunflint). Try them with white meat or fish.

A.C. MENETOU-SALON

OVERVIEW: this appellation is set in the upper reaches of the Loire, south of Pouilly-sur-Loire and west of Sancerre, in Cher. It extends over 350 hectares divided between 10 villages - Aubinges, Humbligny, Menetou-Salon, Morogues, Parassy, Pigny, Quantilly, Saint Céols, Soulangis and Vignoux sous les Aix. The soils are extremely consistent covering a single geological formation of the Secondary era (Upper Cretaceous): light Saint-Doulchard marl (Kimmeridgian), highly conducive to growing Sauvignon blanc.

WINE STYLES: 65% of the wines are fresh, vigorous, lively whites which are light, full and aromatic with great length on the palate. They boast a yellow hue with greenish tints and exude floral and balsamic aromas, citrus (lemon, grapefruit), white peach, gunflint, pepper and mint. They are the perfect match for shellfish, fish served on its own or in puff pastry, goats cheese or snails. The Pinot noir-based reds and rosés are delicate, supple, pleasant, round, light and fruity. They are intended to be drunk soon after release. Their relatively pale hue exhibits ruby-red tints. On the nose, they reveal fragrances of cherry, raspberry and red currant. Recommended food pairings include grilled meat, cheeses (Beaufort) or rabbit terrine.

A.C. MONTLOUIS

OVERVIEW: situated between Tours and Amboise, AC Montlouis produces still and sparkling wines. Three villages feature within the appellation area

(Montlouis, Saint Martin le Beau and Lussault), between the Cher and the Loire, and total area under vine is around 400 hectares. When the weather conditions are right, Montlouis also produces some superlative sweet wines from Chenin grapes harvested in batches as they ripen. The soils are sandy clay or clayey sand on limestone plateaux and hillsides, on a bedrock of 'tuffeau'. A south-facing aspect provides maximum sunshine for hillside sites. The soils are lighter and sandier than in Vouvray.

WINE STYLES: Montlouis sparkling wines, which account for 40% of the entire AC, are light and pleasant. They undergo secondary fermentation in the bottle and are aged on laths for at least nine months. Dry Montlouis is quite similar in style to Vouvray. Less lively and perhaps more supple, it displays a more marked mineral character and is also more enjoyable in its early years. The calling card of sweet Montlouis is its aromatic complexity: verbena, bergamot, bitter almond, leading into dried honey, wax, quince jelly and candied angelica down the years. Try as an accompaniment to cooked cold pork meats, poultry, goats cheese, fish, shellfish or as an appetiser.

A.C. MUSCADET

OVERVIEW: the area stretches along the mouth of the Loire, from Anjou to the Retz region. Despite the local ocean climate, Muscadet is one of the first regions in France to start harvesting. A longer hang-time would jeopardise the wine's unique taste profile. Soils are extremely varied although two principal types can be identified: granite and eruptive rock, shale and micaschist. Within this vast area, three zones enjoy their own specific appellation: Muscadet de Sèvre-et-Maine (the largest), Muscadet des Coteaux de la Loire and Muscadet des Côtes de Grand-Lieu (see separate entries). The area covers a total 13,000 hectares under vine though only 2,000 are devoted to AC Muscadet.

WINE STYLES: made from the Melon de Bourgogne grape variety, Muscadet is a light, fresh white wine with well-balanced acidity, which requires early drinking. Often the wine is left on the lees for four to five months before bottling. This leaves a tiny remnant of carbonic gas, imparting a slight fizz which bolsters the wine's freshness (Muscadet sur Lie). Muscadet displays a pale yellow hue with greenish tints and develops floral (acacia, white flowers) and fruity fragrances (apple) and mineral notes. Try with oysters, shellfish (moules marinières), pike or crayfish fricassee.

A.C. MUSCADET COTEAUX DE LA LOIRE

OVERVIEW: this area extends over both banks of the Loire, in the localities of Ancenis, Carquefou, Champtoceaux, Ligné, Saint-Florent-le-Vieil and Varades. On the right bank of the Loire, the area overlaps Ancenis, whilst on the left bank it spills over into Anjou. Coteaux de Loire grow over some 300 hectares.

WINE STYLES: they are dry, fresh, elegant, supple, harmonious and fruity. They are more robust and well-constituted than Muscadet de Sèvre-et-Maine and can be cellared. Their hue is pale yellow with greenish tints and they develop mineral and gunflint notes due to the granite in the soil, though also fruity and floral aromas. Pair with oysters and seafood, grilled fish or fish served in a sauce (pike).

A.C. MUSCADET SÈVRE-ET-MAINE

OVERVIEW: two-thirds of Muscadet are grown in this area. The appellation is named after the Nantes branch of the Sèvre river and its tributary, the Petite Maine. 23 towns and villages with a combined area under vine of 10,000 hectares are entitled to the appellation. The soil, underpinned by an Armorican base, is varied: granite, shale, gabbro (dark brown soils) and gneiss, which promotes a certain diversity in wine styles within the appellation.

WINE STYLES: they are racy, elegant, fresh, supple, zippy and delicate, often with a slight sparkle. Muscadet sur Lie denotes a wine that has spent the winter in tanks on its lees allowing it to gain in complexity, finesse and bouquet. Muscadet de Sèvre-et-Maine displays a pale golden hue and reveals floral (acacia), fruity (unripe fruit, citronella, fresh grapes) and mineral fragrances. It is the perfect match for oysters, scallops, pike in a hot butter sauce, sole or crayfish fricassee.

A.C. MUSCADET CÔTES DE GRAND-LIEU

OVERVIEW: this appellation is located not far from Grand-Lieu lake, south-west of Nantes. It covers 250 hectares under vine, spread over 19 villages extending down to the tip of Vendée. Soil types are varied: micaschist, gneiss, sand with pebbles and even clayey sand south of the lake. The area enjoys a sunny, mild climate with plentiful rainfall which offsets the drying effect of the wind over the stony terrain.

WINE STYLES: they are delicate and relatively powerful. With their pale yellow hue, they exhibit a slightly salty taste, floral (acacia, white flowers), fruity (apple) and mineral fragrances. Recommended food pairings include oysters, seafood, grilled fish or fish served in a sauce.

A.C. POUILLY-FUMÉ

OVERVIEW: the appellation is named after the village of Pouilly-sur-Loire which sits on the right bank of the Loire. Although vines have grown here since at least the 7th century, in the 19th century the area chose to specialise in dessert grapes with a particular focus on the traditional varietal, Chasselas. Things have definitely moved on since then because nowadays Sauvignon (also know as Fumé) rules the roost here. Seven villages are entitled to the appellation including Pouilly, Saint-Andelain and Tracy. Soil types are varied: Kimmeridgian marl (white earth), hard limestone, flint interspersed with clay, and sandy or gravely terraces. The climate is temperate with a strong continental influence.

WINE STYLES: Pouilly-Fumé are fresh, lively fruity white wines which are powerful and elegant with a full mouthfeel. Their style does vary however depending on individual 'terroirs'. When they grow on limestone soils, blackcurrant bud and boxwood rise to the fore, whilst on flint, gunflint is the principal aroma. Marl soils coax floral fragrances out of the wines (tuberous, daffodils…). Try with shellfish, fish (pike, pike-perch, salmon) or white meat. An outstanding match for goats cheese.

A.C. POUILLY-SUR-LOIRE

OVERVIEW: the appellation area is the same as Pouilly-Fumé, on the right bank of the Loire in Nièvre, down-river from Nevers. Chasselas has been grown here since the 19th century and was shipped off to supply the Parisian market. The soils are clay silica and calcareous clay.

WINE STYLES: now in extremely short supply, these wines have low acidity, are dry, light supple, smooth, delicate and easy to drink. They are intended to be drunk young. The wines display a light golden hue and smoky, peppery fragrances with raisins and dried fruit, hazelnut, fresh almond, walnut and linden. They pair with trout mariniere, fried fish and goats cheeses.

301

A.C. QUARTS DE CHAUME

OVERVIEW: this area is located in Rochefort sur Loire and in Chaume, around the Layon river. The name of the appellation is a throwback to Mediaeval times when a lord would rent his land to an abbey in exchange for a quarter of the harvest. The noble-rotted grapes are picked in batches as they ripen. The vines are planted on shale soils covering 50 hectares on a south-facing hillside.

WINE STYLES: the wines are sweet, racy, firm, silky, delicate and rich. They have a full mouthfeel and are long on the palate, with a great propensity for ageing. Their well-defined structure and a certain austerity in their early years sets them apart from other Layons. They display a golden hue and reveal fragrances of wax, linden, candied fruits, honey, verbena and quince. Try with Roquefort in puff pastry, fish served with a sauce, poached poultry or turbot in a hollandaise sauce.

A.C. QUINCY

OVERVIEW: the appellation is situated in the villages of Quincy and Brinay (the left bank of the Cher). Sauvignon is the only permitted varietal. The vines occupy a plateau which is home to three different soil types: sandy gravel, sand, and sandy loam with sand and gravel. Silica and poor soils promote the ripening process. The area enjoys a hot, dry microclimate.

WINE STYLES: the wines are delicate, fruity, light, fresh and dry. These are elegant, distinguished wines that are also firm and vigorous. They can be drunk young though will also keep. They display a pale golden hue with the occasional greenish tint. On the nose, fragrances of almond, grapefruit, verbena, mushroom, fennel and thyme are present, and they can occasionally exude slightly smoky notes. Try them with fish, shellfish, cooked cold pork meats, goats cheeses, oysters, frogs legs...

A.C. REUILLY

OVERVIEW: the area occupies the banks of the Armon, in the villages of Reuilly, Dion, Cerbois, Chéry, Lazenay, Lury-sur-Armon and Preuilly. The soils are formed of limestone marl on the hillside sites, clayey sand and gravel on the upper terraces. In short, they form a bridge between soils in Sancerre and Quincy. Grape varieties used are Sauvignon (whites, the major variety) and Pinot noir (reds).
WINE STYLES: the reds are supple and light with fragrances of red fruit (cherry, raspberry) and flowers (violet). They are suitable partners for grilled meats, roast poultry or lentil soup. The soft, full rosés are delicate, flavoursome, easy-drinking wines which sport a magnificent coral pink hue and fruit tones. Perfect with paté roll, sauteed veal, mussel fritters. The whites are fresh, fruity and light with floral (acacia) and vegetal aromas (fern, mint). Serve with carp matelote or rabbit fricassee in wine.

A.C. ROSÉ D'ANJOU

OVERVIEW: these particular rosés are grown throughout Anjou, including the Saumur area. The Grolleau varietal forms the backbone of the blend but Cabernets, Gamay, Pineau d'Aunis and Cot can also be added, with no restriction on quantity.
WINE STYLES: they are fruity, light, thirst-quenching wines which are lively, round, soft, delicate, velvety and mild with a slightly sweet taste. Sugar content is offset by alcohol and acidity. They display a pale pink hue (onion peel) and predominantly fruity fragrances (raspberry, red currant, strawberry and pear drop). Recommended food pairings: cooked cold pork meats, white meat, grilled red meat and pork with grapefruit.

A.C. ROSÉ DE LOIRE

OVERVIEW: the catchment area for this appellation covers Anjou, Saumur and Touraine. Rosé de Loire must be made from at least 30% Cabernet Franc and/or Cabernet Sauvignon.
WINE STYLES: as a rule, they are clean, fresh, delicate, vigorous, fruity and light although diversity prevails in such a vast area. A statement that holds true for all of them though is that they are drier than Cabernet d'Anjou. Their hue covers a broad spectrum, from pale pink to grenadine red. Their fragrance is redolent of

red fruit (strawberry, raspberry, red currant, pear drop) and apple. The perfect partner for hors d'ouvre (mixed salads, cold cuts), barbecues and white meat.

A.C. SAINT-NICOLAS DE BOURGUEIL

OVERVIEW: only plots set in the village of Saint-Nicolas de Bourgueil (Touraine) can apply for this appellation (slightly over 1,000 hectares). The vines grow mainly on gravel terraces where the soils are clayey gravel, though, like in Bourgueil, there are occurrences of sloping vineyards on calcareous clay. The red varietals Cabernet Franc and Cabernet Franc coax the best out of these soils.

WINE STYLES: usually lighter than Bourgueil, they are supple, soft, well-balanced, mellow and approachable wines. Even when they evolve quickly, they should not be drunk too soon. The dividing line between wines grown on 'tuffeau' and on gravel is becoming increasingly sharper. 'Tuffeau' imparts greater body and structure, yielding wines with a crimson hue and fragrances of red fruits like raspberry, blackberry, red currant, violet, liquorice and spices. Conversely, gravel produces lighter wines that can be drunk chilled. Pair them with white meats (pork fillet, veal cutlet), cooked cold pork meats or cheeses.

AC SAINT-POURÇAIN

OVERVIEW: the appellation is located in the department of Allier, along the river of the same name and its tributary, the Sioule. It embraces twenty villages spread over a strip five to seven kilometres wide covering south-east facing hillsides. Nowadays, most of the wine is made by the local co-operative winery. The red wines are macerated for varying lengths of time, depending on the varietal: three to six days for Gamay, ten to fourteen days for Pinot noir. The white wines must be blended from at least 90% Chardonnay and Tressallier.

WINE STYLES: the reds and rosés are light, supple and fruity with a brilliant hue. Fragrances of red fruit (cherry), plum and liquorice are present. Try with roast chicken, poultry and fish such as pike, carp, eel or tench. The whites are supple, fresh, full, lively, vigorous and pleasing to the palate with a limpid, brilliant colour. They boast a pale golden hue and smell sweetly of apple, lemon, acacia and dried fruit (hazelnut, almond). Serve them with fried freshwater fish (bleak, roach), trout, frogs legs and of course, Auvergne cheeses.

A.C. SANCERRE

OVERVIEW: Sancerre's aptitude for vine growing has been known since Roman times. Until the early 20th century, Sancerre wines were made from Chasselas, until consumer demand led growers to switch over Sauvignon. The varietal thrives in ideal conditions here and enabled the area to forge a reputation for quality. The vines grow on a hillock overlooking the Loire in a setting combining rolling hills and the valley floor.

The appellation area embraces ten villages: Baunay, Bué, Crézancy, Menetou-Râtel, Ménétreol, Montigny, Thanvenay, Veaugne, Vigny and Vinon. Three different soil types can be identified: calcareous clay-based 'white earth' in the west ('terres blanches'), stony, flint-rich soils in the east ('silex') and a series of predominantly limestone hillocks and hills littered with stones known aptly as 'Caillotes'. The climate is continental though the river to the east and the forest to the west have a moderating influence. There are 3,000 hectares under vine altogether.

WINE STYLES: white Sancerre is fruity, generous, fresh and elegant with a clean attack and round mouthfeel, though its character varies according to the different vineyard sites. Sancerre from the 'terres blanches' site is full, robust and well-constituted. 'Caillotes' produces extremely elegant wines, whilst the 'silex' area yields firmer, more structured wines. Aromas of grapefruit, mint, fern, boxwood, broom, acacia, quince, apple, honey, blackcurrant bud and gunflint (on flint soils) are present. A handful of growers produce oak-aged wines. Try with shellfish, fish, Parma ham, goats cheese, crottin de Chavignol (produced locally) and cooked cold pork meats.

Sancerre also produces red and rosé wines from Pinot noir. They are light, fruity, pleasant wines with supple tannins and fragrances of morello cherry, strawberry or red currant jam, venison, violet.... Enjoy with poultry or grilled meats.

A.C. SAUMUR

OVERVIEW: 38 towns and villages stretching from the hills around Saumur (Montsoreau) as far as Vienne (Montreuil-Bellay) form this appellation area. 28 of them are located in Maine-et-Loire, nine in Vienne and one in Deux-Sèvres. Vines are established on hillsides and terraces overlooking the Loire and the Thouet. Soil types are varied although limestone prevails ('tuffeau') and the climate is characterised by low rainfall. A broad-ranging selection of grapes are grown here: Cabernet Franc, Cabernet Sauvignon and Pineau d'Aunis for the reds, Chenin, Chardonnay and Sauvignon (no more than 20%) for the whites.

WINE STYLES: Saumur reds are supple, clean, approachable wines with delicate tannins. Some of them gain in complexity and become more fleshy as they age. Fragrances of red fruits such as blackcurrant and raspberry are present and occasionally fresh mushroom notes can be detected, as a reminder of the local 'tuffeau' caves. Puy-Notre-Dame is one of the appellation's most dynamic and highly-regarded villages. The wines pair with an extensive array of food including barbecued meats, stuffed pork belly, roast meat and poultry (chicken) and veal kidneys.

The whites are elegant, fresh and light. They also display the tell-tale characteristics of the local 'tuffeau' which in Turquant and Brézé imparts aromas of gunflint. Fragrances of lime are present and there is even a slightly bitter touch. Try with eel matelote or pike in a hot butter sauce. The rosés, which are in short supply, make good partners for grilled chitterlings sausage and cooked cold pork meats.

A.C. SAUMUR-CHAMPIGNY

OVERVIEW: the appellation embraces nine villages, centred on the Loire, the Thouet and the Vienne. The soils are calcareous clay and the vines enjoy plentiful sunshine (in Latin, Champigny means 'fields of fire') on the characteristic white earth formed of 'tuffeau' limestone (Turonian chalk). The area is home to three red varietals: Cabernet Franc, Cabernet Sauvignon and Pineau d'Aunis.

WINE STYLES: Saumur-Champigny produces well-balanced, velvety wines which are relatively robust and full. With their elegant tannins though they can be drunk young. They have a deep ruby-red hue and exude fragrances of red and black fruit such as raspberry, red currant, blackberry and blackcurrant, soot and humus. As they mature, they take on spicy tones (pepper), tobacco and liquorice. The younger wines pair with red meat (beef fillet), grilled fish and soft cheeses, whilst the older examples match with poultry, rabbit, lamb and game.

305

A.C. SAUMUR MOUSSEUX

Within the boundaries of the Saumur appellation, 1,300 hectares are dedicated to producing sparkling wines from Chenin, using the traditional method. A clutch of large companies make most of the wines and have ensured their commercial success. Saumur Mousseux is equally delicious as an appetiser or with a meal.

AC SAUMUR PUY-NOTRE-DAME

The district of Puy-Notre-Dame is one of the most renowned and dynamic in the region, both in terms of tourism and winemaking. The vineyards grow on a Turonian limestone butte south of Saumur and were granted their own appellation in 2008.

WINE STYLES: The red wines are structured, made from Cabernet Franc grapes that attain depth and complexity in this terroir. These wines can be laid down and pair well with red meat and game.

A.C. SAVENNIÈRES

OVERVIEW: the appellation covers three villages north of the Loire and southwest of Angers, namely Savennières, Bouchemaine and Possonière, with a total area under vine of 150 hectares. It has been said that the vines here are real sun traps. Louis 11th used to compare Savennières to a drop of gold. Several hillside sites unquestionably boast ideal facings, including the highest site at Epiré, home to Coulée-de-Serrant (a 7-hectare walled vineyard) and La Roche-aux-Moines (25 ha). Such is the quality of these two site-specific vineyards that they enjoy their own appellations: Savennières Coulée de Serrant and Savennières Roche aux Moines. Just like Burgundy, Savennières has walled vineyards: Clos du Papillon, des Perrières, de la Bergerie, de Coulaine, Clos de la Goutte d'Or… The soils are formed of shale and purple sandstone of volcanic origin from the St George series with countless variations. Only Chenin is grown here.

WINE STYLES: Savennières is either a dry or medium dry white wine. It is full, delicate, elegant, rich and robust, which can be austere in the early years though is blessed with a fantastic potential for maturing. The wines display a golden straw-yellow hue and a complex bouquet with floral (acacia) and mineral fragrances, ripe white fruit, honey, flesh, sap, peach, and citrus fruit (apple). As they age, these lead into quince, candied fruit, peat, smoky and above all mineral shades. These sterling wines pair with fish in a sauce (pike, pike-perch, monkfish, salmon) and shellfish, roast white meats, goats cheeses and asparagus.

A.C. TOURAINE

OVERVIEW: the appellation covers an area stretching from Blois to Candes-Saint-Martin on the banks of the Loire and its tributaries (Cher, Indre and Vienne). A total 171 towns and villages are entitled to use the appellation, including 127 in Indre-et-Loire.

Soil types are extremely varied, ranging from calcareous clay ('aubuis'), clay and flint ('perruches'), to sand and light gravel, sand on shell sand and 'tuffeau'. The climate is temperate with an ocean influence to the west and continental influence to the east. Of all the red varietals grown here (Cabernet Franc, Cabernet Sauvignon, Gamay, Cot, Pinot Meunier, Pinot gris and Pineau d'Aunis), the dominant grape is Gamay. For whites, Chenin, Sauvignon, Menu Pineau and Chardonnay are grown. Sauvignon does particularly well in the Cher valley.

WINE STYLES: the reds and rosés are light, fruity, early-drinking wines when they are vinted as new or primeur wines. The reds blended from Gamay, Cabernet and Cot are well-structured and robust, with medium ageing potential. Recommended pairings are meat (kid goat) and cheeses. The whites are lively with floral fragrances leading into mineral notes as they age. Wines made from Sauvignon display shades of broom whilst Chenin wines are redolent of quince. Try them with fish, shellfish, seafood and potted meat. The rosés are fresh, fruity (red fruit) and refined. The perfect match for starters and cooked cold pork meats.

A.C. TOURAINE-AMBOISE

OVERVIEW: these wines grow either side of the Loire, upriver from Tours. The focal point of the appellation is the village of Cangey. The soils, which are stony or sandy on a limestone subsoil, are well-suited to the local grape varieties: Gamay, Cot, Cabernet Franc, Cabernet Sauvignon (reds) and Chenin (whites).

WINE STYLES: the reds are supple, easy-drinking wines when made from Gamay and stronger, fuller wines when blended. They are rich, delicate and fragrant. The duration of maceration makes Touraine-Amboise early-drinking wines or wines to be kept. They display a cherry-red hue and aromas of red fruit (cherry, blackcurrant) and slightly spicy notes. The rosés are delicate, fruity, approachable wines. The whites display a hue with pale yellow tints and fragrances of gunflint, acacia, apple, peach, apricot, dried fruit, liquorice and quince. Food pairings for the reds: grilled beef, leg of venison and cheese. For the whites: fish in a sauce. For the rosés: crudités, assortment of cold cuts, smoked salmon…

A.C. TOURAINE-AZAY-LE-RIDEAU

OVERVIEW: the appellation covers eight villages on both banks of the Indre. The soils are clay with flint ('perruches') and calcareous clay ('aubuis') with patches of eolian sand. Two-thirds of the wines are white. Most of the rosés are made using the direct-to-press method. No red wines are grown here.

WINE STYLES: the white wines, made from Chenin, are delicate, elegant, vigorous, well-balanced and aromatic, with good ageing potential. They have a straw colour and develop fragrances of quince, acacia, verbena and toasted almonds. They can be served with fish in a sauce or cheeses. The rosés, made from Grolleau, Gamay, Cot and Cabernet, can be fresher than Rosé d'Anjou. They are approachable, delicate wines with a pleasant bouquet, a pale, slightly purple-blue hue and floral, fruity notes. Perfect with crudités, cold cuts, poultry terrine and smoked fish.

A.C. TOURAINE-MESLAND

OVERVIEW: the appellation embraces six villages, including Mesland, along the right bank of the Loire in Loir-et-Cher. Production focuses mainly on red wines though there are some whites made from Chenin, augmented with Sauvignon or Chardonnay. The soil make-up comprises sand, clay and flint gravel.

WINE STYLES: the reds are easy-drinking, round, fruity, delicate wines with low tannin content. Wines blended from Cabernet, Cot and Gamay tend to be more robust with medium ageing capacity and fragrances of raspberry, red fruit and spices. Try with perch fillets in red wine, grilled beef or cheeses. The whites are warm, dry, vigorous wines with medium ageing capacity. They develop spring scents and aromas of linden. Try with fish and shellfish.

A.C. TOURAINE NOBLE JOUÉ

OVERVIEW: this tiny 25-hectare appellation is situated in the villages of Chambray-lès-Tours, Esvres, Joué-lès-Tours, Larçay and Saint Avertin in the Indre-et-Loire department. The wines are blended from three varietals: Pinot gris, Pinot Meunier and Pinot noir. They are vinted as 'vin gris', therefore undergoing a short maceration period before being pressed and fermented. Try with grilled fish or cooked cold pork meats.

A.C. VALENCAY

OVERVIEW: this appellation, which was promoted to AC status in 2003, is located on the banks of the Cher and its tributaries (the Fouzon and the Mondon), on the border of Touraine, Sologne and Berry. Red varietals account for 85% of the range and focus primarily on Cabernets, Gamay, Grolleau and Pinot noir. The vines occupy clay silica hillside sites and plateaux with a subsoil dating back to the Senonian and Eocene epochs. Gunflint is one of the soil's most essential components.

WINE STYLES: the reds are only lightly-coloured and display fragrances of cherry and blackberry. They are light, pleasant wines suitable for early drinking. They pair well with veal stew, veal breasts and rabbit with onions. The whites are vigorous, sharp and harmonious wines with character. They display a pale yellow hue and boast characteristic notes of gunflint and floral aromas. Perfect with goats cheeses.

AC ORLÉANAIS

OVERVIEW: from the Middle Ages to the 17th century, Orléans was the most extensive and famous wine region in the whole of the Loire. The appellation is situated on both banks of the Loire and covers 25 towns and villages (19 on the right bank and six on the left). The villages of Olivet, Saint-Hilaire, Saint-Mesman, Mareau-aux-Près, Mézières-les-Cléry and Cléry Saint-André produce 95% of the wines here and they are all on the left bank.

Pinot noir is referred to locally as Auvernat noir, Pinot Meunier as Gris Meunier and Chardonnay as Auvernat blanc. The soils are clay silica and gravel silica.

WINE STYLES: the reds and rosés are pleasant, light, round, well-balanced, lively and fruity and should be drunk young. The most noteworthy wine is made from Gris Meunier. The wines are pale in colour, displaying fragrances of cherry, red currant and wild strawberries with a smoky finish. Try the reds with roast partridge, cooked cold pork meats, mixed salads and fish in a sauce (tuna, pike). For the rosés: poultry terrine, cooked cold pork meats and barbecues.

AC THOUARSAIS

OVERVIEW: this tiny 40-hectare area is split between sixteen villages around Thouars, in the Deux-Sèvres department. Chenin and Chardonnay are grown here for the white wines, and Cabernet Sauvignon and Gamay for the red and rosé wines. The wines are made on a boutique scale, with no more than 20 hectares on-stream for the past few years. Try with fish (whites), cooked cold pork meats (rosés) and meats served in a sauce (reds).

A.C. VOUVRAY

OVERVIEW: vines have been grown here since Roman times though it was Saint-Martin, bishop of Tours, who expanded vine growing in the early Middle Ages. In the 14th century, the wines were popular with the Dutch though also Rabelais, who described them as "pure taffeta wine".

The AC is located upriver from Tours, on the outskirts of the city itself, along the northern banks of the Loire. Between Rochecorbon and Vouvray, the vineyards peer down over the 'tuffeau' cliff faces and subsequently drop down to follow the river Cisseau, as far as Vernou then on to Noizay. The soils are calcareous clay over a 'tuffeau' ('aubuis') or clay silica plateau with occurrences of flint ('perruches'). The site is carved out by the Loire and its tributaries and the soils follow several geological formations: Turonian, Senonian, Eocene. The vines are south-facing and the climate is ocean and continental. Chenin is the grape variety used here.

WINE STYLES: the dry whites are supple, fruity, quaffing wines which can be slightly pungent in their youth. They sport a straw-yellow hue and exhibit aromas of white flower, acacia, linden, apple, citrus fruit, crushed strawberries, peach, quince and lychee. The sweet wines are powerful, unctuous, concentrated and full with delicate, rich aromas: camomile, jasmine, freshly-cut hay, apricot, fig, quince jelly, honey, wax, brioche, dried fruit and occasionally notes of walnut and truffle. All of these wines boast excellent cellaring capacity. The appellation also produces sparkling wines displaying the tell-tale characteristics and slight bitterness of the Chenin grape. With a meal, the dry and medium dry wines sit nicely alongside eel matelote and especially Tours speciality cooked cold pork meats (potted meat, chitterlings sausage, pigs trotters). The sweet wines call for foie gras or mature, flavoursome cheeses.

• • •

2015
LOIRE VALLEY
WINES

ANJOU VILLAGES BRISSAC

Domaine de Terrebrune   89/100

▼ 🍷 Vintage 2011 : Young crimson hue. Very distinctive nose dominated by bell pepper, earth and forest fruits. Full, generous and juicy palate with very dashing perfumes and a full mouthfeel supporting the whole. A very faithful rendition of the Cabernet varietal.
Price approx.: 7,50 EUR
www.domainedeterrebrune.fr
Domaine de Terrebrune
+33 (0)2 41 54 01 99

DOMAINE DE MONTGILET   86/100

▼ 🍷 Vintage 2012 : Deep garnet with crimson tints. Expressive nose with beautiful floral touches backed by ripe black berries. The palate focuses on suppleness and lightness. Its elegant roundness is not lacking in charm. Some silky tannins frame the whole.
Price approx.: 8,20 EUR
www.montgilet.com
Domaine de Montgilet
+33 (0)2 41 91 90 48

ANJOU VILLAGES

DOMAINE DE SAINT-MAUR   87/100

▼ 🍷 Vintage 2011 : Beautiful deeply-coloured, young red. Profound nose blending red and black fruits with a mineral touch. Lovely construction on the palate, supple attack and polished tannins. Full, perfumed middle palate carrying over significant length.
Price approx.: 6,00 EUR
Domaine de Saint-Maur
+33 (0)2 41 57 30 24

ANJOU

DOMAINE DE SAINT-MAUR   89/100

▼ 🍷 Cuvée St Maur de Glanfeuille 2011 : Intense crimson. Profound, ripe nose with aromas of red and black fruits and liquorice. The palate shows seductive volume and mellowness. Full mouthfeel balanced by freshness.

Beautiful length revealing spice and liquorice aromas. A handsome Anjou.
Price approx.: 7,00 EUR
Domaine de Saint-Maur
+33 (0)2 41 57 30 24

ALLIANCE LOIRE   86/100

▼ 🍷 Prince Alexandre 2013 : Pale gold. The nose is driven by white fruit and bush peach. Harmonious palate showing crunchy fresh fruits with a mellow finish. A refreshing, thirst-quenching Anjou. Drinking well from the aperitif through to dessert. A highly perfumed wine.
Price approx.: 7,90 EUR
http://www.allianceloire.com
Alliance Loire
+33 (0)2 41 53 74 44

FAMILLE BOUGRIER   85/100

▼ 🍷 Chenin Blanc 2013 : Beautiful gold. Delightful nose of white fruits in syrup and apricot. The palate displays lovely restrained mellowness. Focused fruit presence with a tropical finish of pineapple. A charming, totally trustworthy Chenin.
Price approx.: 3,79 EUR
www.bougrier.fr
Bougrier SA
+33 (0)2 54 32 31 36

BARTON & GUESTIER PASSEPORT   85/100

▼ 🍷 Passeport 2013 : Brilliant deep pink. Nose of red berry fruits (strawberry), boiled sweets and mild spices in the background. Soft, supple and mouth-coating palate with clearly-defined aromas. Well-balanced and fresh. An enjoyable style to drink as an aperitif.
Price approx.: 6,00 EUR
http://www.barton-guestier.com
Barton & Guestier
+33 (0)5 56 95 48 00

DOMAINE DES IRIS   85/100

▼ 🍷 Vintage 2013 : Light yellow. Distinctive, mineral nose backed by fresh mushroom and white peach. A structured, full and powerful Anjou, still a little firm. Fruit expression should rapidly come to the fore. Tell-tale Chenin personality. Needs further confirmation.
Price approx.: 5,06 EUR
http://www.joseph-verdier.fr
Joseph Verdier-Logel
+33 (0)2 41 40 22 50

BAUMARD   85/100

CONV ▼ 🍷 Clos de la Folie 2009 : Slightly mature light red. Nose of jammy red fruits with a touch of undergrowth after swirling. On the palate, a melted wine showing mature fruit aromas. The finish introduces secondary or even tertiary aromas of undergrowth and humus.

Price approx.: 11,00 EUR
http://www.baumard.fr
Domaine des Baumard
+33 (0)2 41 78 70 03

DOMAINE DE TERREBRUNE — 85/100

▼ ♪ Sélection de Chenin 2013 : Light gold. Refined nose gradually opening up and developing aromas of fresh mushroom, bush peach and fresh oak. Slightly backward, youthful palate. The finish reveals distinctive, burgeoning Chenin aromas. Silky mouthfeel. Boasts potential.
Price approx.: 7,00 EUR
www.domainedeterrebrune.fr
Domaine de Terrebrune
+33 (0)2 41 54 01 99

DOMAINE DES IRIS — 84/100

▼ ♪ Elevé en fûts de chêne 2011 : Crimson with dark purple. Nose of refined vanilla oak backed by forest fruits. The palate is chewy with volume. Oak imparts firmness and although distinctive, the fruit stays in the background. A wine with a real sense of place. Pair with grilled meats.
Price approx.: 6,50 EUR
http://www.joseph-verdier.fr
Joseph Verdier-Logel
+33 (0)2 41 40 22 50

DOMAINE DES IRIS — 83/100

▼ ♪ Vintage 2013 : Young ruby. Nose of fresh red fruit. The palate retains its youthfulness due to beautiful overall freshness. A very supple, juicy style pairing with terrines.
Price approx.: 5,40 EUR
http://www.joseph-verdier.fr
Joseph Verdier-Logel
+33 (0)2 41 40 22 50

DOMAINE DES HAUTES OUCHES — 83/100

▼ ♪ Elevé en fûts de chêne 2011 : Deeply-coloured garnet. Intense nose of vegetal oak backed by ripe fruits with an earth note. The palate is more heavily influenced by oak which obscures the fruit. Power combines with a degree of firmness. A well-structured Anjou for game.
Price approx.: 6,60 EUR
http://www.joseph-verdier.fr
Joseph Verdier-Logel
+33 (0)2 41 40 22 50

DOMAINE DES HAUTES OUCHES — 83/100

▼ ♪ Vintage 2013 : Crimson with dark purple tints. Lovely youthful fruit on the nose with cherry, strawberry and raspberry. Supple, crunchy palate brimming with fruit. A simple wine for quaffing.
Price approx.: 5,20 EUR
http://www.joseph-verdier.fr
Joseph Verdier-Logel
+33 (0)2 41 40 22 50

ALLIANCE LOIRE — 80/100

▼ ♪ Le Paradis 2013 : Young cherry-red. Subtle floral and fruit aromas on the nose. Lightweight concentration on the palate, with present yet not very intense fruit, and freshness. An Anjou designed to suit all palates. Serve with barbecues and flank steaks for example.
Price approx.: 4,70 EUR
http://www.allianceloire.com
Alliance Loire
+33 (0)2 41 53 74 44

BOURGUEIL

DOMAINE DES OUCHES — 93/100

▼ ♪ Coteau des Ouches 2011 : Beautiful black hue tinged with dark purple. Endearing nose with fruit basket aromas of red and black fruits, a floral note and subtle oak. Superb velvety, concentrated and dense construction with a silky framework and lovely mellow impression. Bravo!
Price approx.: 9,60 EUR
www.domainedesouches.com
Domaine des Ouches
+33 (0)2 47 96 98 77

DOMAINE DES OUCHES — 88/100

▼ ♪ Igoranda 2013 : Beautiful crimson hue. Youthful qualities of fresh red and black fruits and a floral note on the nose. A lace-like Bourgueil with remarkable balance. Very supple with lengthy fruit expression. Elegant. Tannins on the finish. A seductive offering.
Price approx.: 7,20 EUR
www.domainedesouches.com
Domaine des Ouches
+33 (0)2 47 96 98 77

LE COUDRAY LA LANDE — 85/100

▼ ♪ Vieilles Vignes 2012 : Fairly deep ruby. The nose and the palate focus on delightful fresh wild berry fruits. Smooth tannins. A generous Bourgueil, very enjoyable whilst still young with its vibrant fruit. Serve with roast chicken.
Price approx.: 6,00 EUR
Domaine du Coudray La Lande
+33 (0)2 47 97 76 92

DOMAINE DU PETIT SOUPER   83/100

▼♪ Cuvée la Godinière 2013 : Youthful-looking dark purple. The nose is driven by fresh blackcurrant, cherry and strawberry. A delightful soft, fresh and light Bourgueil with seductive young aromatics, fruit to the fore. Drinking well from now on.

Price approx.: 5,50 EUR

http://www.joseph-verdier.fr

Joseph Verdier-Logel

+33 (0)2 41 40 22 50

CABERNET D'ANJOU

DOMAINE DE MONTGILET   87/100

▼♪ Millésime 2013 : Pale salmon-pink. Pleasant nose showing delicate suggestions of red fruits. Round attack, marvellous silky, mellow and lively mouthfeel with precise, clear-cut aromas. Accessible and welcoming. A beautiful soft rosé for fruit tarts.

Price approx.: 5,70 EUR

www.montgilet.com

Domaine de Montgilet

+33 (0)2 41 91 90 48

DOMAINE DES IRIS   85/100

▼♪ Vintage 2013 : Pale orange. Nose of orange flesh and fruit with earthy nuances. Soft palate showing a lovely mellow character that supports crunchy fruit perfumes. Pleasure in simplicity.

Price approx.: 5,30 EUR

http://www.joseph-verdier.fr

Joseph Verdier-Logel

+33 (0)2 41 40 22 50

DOMAINE DE LA SEIGNEURIE DES TOURELLES   85/100

▼♪ Vintage 2013 : Orange-pink. Nose of red fruits and sweets. Beautiful sweet attack nicely counterbalanced by freshness. Generous fruit presence tantalises the palate. A Cabernet providing guaranteed enjoyment.

Price approx.: 5,14 EUR

http://www.joseph-verdier.fr

Joseph Verdier-Logel

+33 (0)2 41 40 22 50

DOMAINE DE TERREBRUNE   85/100

▼♪ Vintage 2013 : Light red. Floral nose with red berry fruits. A soft, light Cabernet with a subtle sweetness that highlights the strawberry aromas. A very fresh, very thirst-quenching wine. Cabernet just the way we like it.

Price approx.: 4,50 EUR

www.domainedeterrebrune.fr

Domaine de Terrebrune

+33 (0)2 41 54 01 99

CAVES DE L'ANGEVINE   84/100

▼♪ Vintage 2013 : Salmon-pink. Delightful nose of fresh strawberries. A distinctive Cabernet with sweetness nicely offset by freshness. Fruit is focused and crunchy. Drink with friends over a selection of goats cheeses.

Price approx.: 3,79 EUR

www.bougrier.fr

Bougrier SA

+33 (0)2 54 32 31 36

DOMAINE DE FLINES   84/100

▼♪ Vintage 2013 : Brilliant salmon-pink. Pleasant nose of ripe red fruits with a patisserie touch. Round attack leading into an easy-drinking, full and fruity palate that is nervy and moderately clean (plastic) with a strange bitterness on the finish. Rejected.

Price approx.: 4,70 EUR

www.domainedeflines.com

Domaine de Flines

+33 (0)2 41 59 42 78

DOMAINE DES HAUTES OUCHES   84/100

▼♪ Vintage 2013 : Orange-red. Nose of ripe red fruits. Soft, well-balanced palate showing seductive freshness, fruit perfumes and sweetness. Distinctive. The ideal wine for a summer aperitif.

Price approx.: 4,60 EUR

http://www.joseph-verdier.fr

Joseph Verdier-Logel

+33 (0)2 41 40 22 50

CHÂTEAUMEILLANT

DOMAINE JACQUES ROUZÉ   82/100

▼♪ Grappes 2013 : Young dark purple. The nose is driven by red berry fruits. A very supple wine with a low level of concentration that showcases fresh fruity flavours. Works perfectly with everyday meals.

Price approx.: 7,00 EUR

http://www.jacques-rouze.com

Domaine Jacques Rouzé

+33 (0)2 48 51 35 61

CHEVERNY

DOMAINE MAISON PÈRE ET FILS   87/100

▼♪ Vintage 2012 : Limpid ruby. Seductive nose showing fruit bowl aromatics with floral notes. Clean, light and focused palate with lovely aromatic exuberance. Savoury succulence and roundness. Spicy finish with a hint of firmness. A well-made wine for pleasure.

Price approx.: 6,20 EUR

www.domainemaison.com

Domaine Maison père & fils

+33 (0)2 54 20 22 87

DOMAINE MAISON PÈRE ET FILS 87/100

✳🍷 Révélation 2013 : Pale yellow with green tints. Pleasant nose blending citrus, ripe white fruits and blackcurrant leaf. Fresh, energetic palate that is closely-integrated and fruity with persistent exuberant aromas. Mineral impression. A successful wine pairing with shellf
Price approx.: 7,70 EUR
www.domainemaison.com
Domaine Maison père & fils
+33 (0)2 54 20 22 87

DOMAINE SAUGER 84/100

🍷🍷 Tradition 2012 : Light yellow. Distinctive, expressive nose blending a vegetal dimension with crunchy grapefruit notes. Soft, fleshy attack displaying a sensation of mellowness. The fruit recurs and lingers pleasantly. An enjoyable Cheverny.
Price approx.: 5,80 EUR
http://www.domaine.sauger.com
Domaine Sauger
+33 (0)2 54 79 58 45

VIGNERONS DE MONT PRÈS CHAMBORD 83/100

🍷🍷 Vintage 2013 : Light orange. Pleasant nose halfway between red berry fruits and mineral notes. A light, crunchy and fruit-driven style on the palate bathed in a welcome freshness. A very enjoyable, light rosé for quaffing.
Price approx.: 4,45 EUR
http://www.vigneronsdemontpreschambord.com
Vignerons de Mont-Près-Chambord
+33 (0)2 54 70 71 15

DOMAINE SAUGER 79/100

🍷🍷 Millésime 2012 : Light hue with ruby · highlights. The nose opens up to notes of ripe red fruits with slightly peppery, vegetal undertones. Lightweight structure on the palate, a forthright style balanced by a touch of freshness. Hint of bitterness on the finish.
Price approx.: 5,80 EUR
http://www.domaine.sauger.com
Domaine Sauger
+33 (0)2 54 79 58 45

CHINON

CHÂTEAU DE LA BONNELIÈRE 92/100

🍷🍷 Chapelle 2011 : Intensely coloured with crimson highlights. Beautiful nose of black and red fruits, fine spice and violet. Delicious palate offering up a splendid full, rich, tense and fine-grain mouthfeel. Silky supporting tannins. Elegant and natural. Sterling work!
Price approx.: 11,60 EUR
http://www.plouzeau.com
Château de la Bonnelière
+33 (0)2 47 93 16 34

COULY-DUTHEIL 92/100

🍷🍷 Clos de l'Echo 2011 : Magnificent dark red. Profound nose with subtle notes of red and black fruits, flowers, spices and mineral tones. Fullness and stuffing on the palate. A melted, full, harmonious and persistent whole punctuated by elegant and subtle bitterness. Beautiful.
Price approx.: 19,45 EUR
www.coulydutheil-chinon.com
Maison Couly-Dutheil
+33 (0)2 47 97 20 20

CHÂTEAU DE LA BONNELIÈRE 91/100

🍷🍷 Chapelle 2012 : Deep, young-looking crimson. Refined nose that is still fairly backward. Quite rich, suave and delightful palate focusing on natural qualities and transparency. Svelte, succulent and fresh with a firm, spicy finish. 4-6 years' cellaring is recommended.
Price approx.: 11,60 EUR
http://www.plouzeau.com
Château de la Bonnelière
+33 (0)2 47 93 16 34

LE CLOS DE LA BONNELIÈRE 89/100

🍷🍷 Vintage 2011 : Deep crimson with dark purple tints. Inviting nose of peony and dark fruits. Seductive velvety, full and tense presence that fills the mouth. Freshness, some spice and an elegant, closely-integrated structure. Distinctive vegetal finish.
Price approx.: 9,50 EUR
http://www.plouzeau.com
Château de la Bonnelière
+33 (0)2 47 93 16 34

COULY-DUTHEIL 89/100

🍷🍷 Clos de l'Olive 2011 : Appealing garnet hue. Profound, expressive nose with fruit aromas augmented by mineral and spice notes. Full mouthfeel with a good framework showing a lovely mineral character and persistency. A generous wine with good ageability.
Price approx.: 18,95 EUR
www.coulydutheil-chinon.com
Maison Couly-Dutheil
+33 (0)2 47 97 20 20

COULY-DUTHEIL 88/100

🍷🍷 René Couly 2012 : Attractive, clean pink. Delightful nose blending strawberry and cherry with a pleasant vegetal and peppery dimension. Lovely freshness, fine-grained texture and a peppery and spicy character on the palate. A distinctive, expressive and well-crafted rosé.
Price approx.: 7,85 EUR
www.coulydutheil-chinon.com
Maison Couly-Dutheil
+33 (0)2 47 97 20 20

DOMAINE AUBERT-MONORY 88/100

▼🌶 Cuvée Prestige 2012 : Beautiful vibrant red. Distinctive nose marrying fruit and mineral notes. Wonderful clean attack. The middle palate offers up stuffing, freshness and fruit. A deftly crafted, silky wine that is already a pleasure to drink.

Price approx.: 5,70 EUR

http://www.aubert-monory-vindechinon.com

Domaine Aubert-Monory

+33 (0)2 47 93 33 73

DOMAINE DE LA DOZONNERIE 86/100

▼🌶 Vintage 2012 : Beautiful dark purple. Delightful floral and fruity nose of blackberry and raspberry with earthy undertones. Young palate marked by firmness. Fruit is more upfront on the finish. A distinctive, racy Chinon that needs to melt a little.

Price approx.: 5,50 EUR

Domaine de la Dozonnerie

+33 (0)2 47 93 16 72

COULY-DUTHEIL 86/100

❄🌶 Les Chanteaux 2012 : Brilliant light yellow with green tints. Pleasant, focused nose blending white flowers, peach flesh, white fruits... Full, generous palate balanced by a savoury sensation of freshness. Subtle sourness on the finish, enjoyable in this context.

Price approx.: 13,15 EUR

www.coulydutheil-chinon.com

Maison Couly-Dutheil

+33 (0)2 47 97 20 20

ALLIANCE LOIRE 85/100

❄🌶 Le Paradis 2013 : Young ruby. Nose of crunchy red and black berry fruits. A supple Chinon with a soft mouthfeel and delicious, focused fresh fruit presence. Ready to drink and accessible for all. Its festive character makes it ideal for a banquet, christening or a wedding.

Price approx.: 4,70 EUR

http://www.allianceloire.com

Alliance Loire

+33 (0)2 41 53 74 44

DOMAINE D'ETILLY 84/100

▼🌶 Vintage 2013 : Beautiful young ruby-red. Crunchy fresh strawberry, raspberry and redcurrant on the nose. A supple Chinon with a soft mouthfeel showcasing easy-drinking, crunchy young fruit. Drink now with barbecued foods.

Price approx.: 6,10 EUR

http://www.joseph-verdier.fr

Joseph Verdier-Logel

+33 (0)2 41 40 22 50

COULY-DUTHEIL 84/100

▼🌶 La Diligence 2012 : Attractive ruby with garnet

highlights. Endearing nose melding fresh cherry with pleasurable spicy and vegetal accents. On the palate, a fine-grained tannin framework and fairly pronounced vegetal dimension developing a tell-tale sensation of bitterness.

Price approx.: 9,45 EUR

www.coulydutheil-chinon.com

Maison Couly-Dutheil

+33 (0)2 47 97 20 20

COTEAUX DE L'AUBANCE

DOMAINE DE MONTGILET 95/100

▼🌶 Les Trois Schistes 2011 : Attractive, fairly deep, brilliant gold. Very delicate nose infused with ripe quince, candied yellow fruits and gingerbread. Mellow attack leading into a velvety, supple palate showing good sweetness and free-rein honeyed aromas. Harmonious.

Price approx.: 18,50 EUR

www.montgilet.com

Domaine de Montgilet

+33 (0)2 41 91 90 48

COTEAUX DE SAUMUR

CHÂTEAU DE TARGÉ 93/100

▼🌶 50 cl 2011 : Bright gold. Rich nose of honey, candied fruits, acacia and quince. A delicate sweet wine where sweetness is enveloped in freshness. The same elegant, rich aromatics recur on the palate. Melt-in-the-mouth finish. Art at its finest.

Price approx.: 21,00 EUR

www.chateaudetarge.fr

Château de Targé

+33 (0)2 41 38 11 50

COTEAUX DE TANNAY

DOMAINE MAISON CLAUDE DE LA PORTE 85/100

▼🌶 Cuvée élevée en fût de chêne - Pinot noir 2010 : Slightly mature light ruby. Pleasant nose showing elegant oak, cherry and some fine spice. Light, fresh palate exhibiting fruit and spice presence coupled with a vegetal dimension. Forward aromatics. Hint of dryness on the finish. Ready to drink.

Price approx.: 8,50 EUR

www.caves-tannay.com

Les Caves Tannaysiennes

+33 (0)3 86 29 31 59

DOMAINE MAISON CLAUDE DE LA PORTE
84/100

▼♪ Cuvée des Flotteurs - Melon 2011 : Brilliant light yellow. White fruits coupled with a floral tone on the nose. Clean, fairly round palate with fruit to the fore. A slight crunchiness supported by lovely freshness. An enjoyable wine pairing with white meats.
Price approx.: 9,90 EUR
www.caves-tannay.com
Les Caves Tannaysiennes
+33 (0)3 86 29 31 59

COTEAUX DU GIENNOIS

DOMAINE PHILIPPE RAIMBAULT   88/100

▼♪ Récolté sur les Coteaux de Saint Père 2013 : Brilliant pale gold with green tints. Intense nose driven by grapefruit with white fruits in the background. Fresh, full, supple and quite rich palate. Beautiful balance, elegant throughout. Powerful finish. A wine for special meals.
Price approx.: 6,70 EUR
www.philipperaimbault.fr
Philippe Raimbault
+33 (0)2 48 79 29 54

DOMAINE QUINTIN FRÈRES   86/100

▼♪ Rive Droite 2013 : Light yellow. Pleasant nose with delicate citrus scents. Round attack, lovely silky presence, striking lemony notes and an elegant underlying exuberance. Set aside for shellfish.
Price approx.: 6,00 EUR
Domaine Quintin Frères
+33 (0)3 86 28 31 77

DOMAINE PHILIPPE RAIMBAULT   85/100

▼♪ Récolté sur les Coteaux du Saint Père 2011 : Light red with bricking. Mature nose driven by ripe red fruits. Lightweight, evolved mouthfeel with accents of overripe red fruits. Powerful finish infused with mild spices. Drink from now on with red meats.
Price approx.: 6,50 EUR
www.philipperaimbault.fr
Philippe Raimbault
+33 (0)2 48 79 29 54

COTEAUX DU LAYON CHAUME

CHÂTEAU DE BELLEVUE   93/100

▼♪ 1er Cru 2011 : Limpid gold. Rich nose driven by apricot and passion fruit with smoky mineral undercurrents. Sumptuous and mouth-coating with freshness dovetailing impeccably with sweetness. Upfront perfume. A consummate Chaume that fully deserves first growth status.
Price approx.: 13,00 EUR
www.chateaudebellevue.fr
Château de Bellevue
+33 (0)2 41 78 33 11

COTEAUX DU VENDÔMOIS

ALLIANCE LOIRE   86/100

▼♪ Cuvée Prestige 2012 : Garnet. Nose of ripe red and black fruits backed by undergrowth and mild spices. More of the same aromatic trilogy on the palate highlighted by upfront, fine tannins and a generous mouthfeel. A Vendômois displaying a real sense of place.
Price approx.: 4,50 EUR
http://www.allianceloire.com
Alliance Loire
+33 (0)2 41 53 74 44

ALLIANCE LOIRE   84/100

▼♪ César de Vendôme 2012 : Lightly-coloured garnet. The nose is halfway between ripe red fruits, smoke and earth notes. A Vendômois with a supple attack and crunchy fruit. More secondary notes coupled with tannin presence mid-palate. A wine with a sense of place for red meats.
Price approx.: 4,50 EUR
http://www.allianceloire.com
Alliance Loire
+33 (0)2 41 53 74 44

CÔTES DE LA CHARITÉ

DOMAINE SERGE DAGUENEAU & FILLES
87/100

▼♪ Les Montées de Saint Lay 2012 : Vibrant, limpid red. Seductive nose of cherry, redcurrant and refined spices. Supple attack, a lovely suave, full and harmonious wine on the palate, deliciously drinkable. Persistent fruit and spice aromatics. A recommended choice.
Price approx.: 8,50 EUR
www.s-dagueneau-filles.fr
Domaine Serge Dagueneau & filles
+33 (0)3 86 39 11 18

CRÉMANT DE LOIRE

BOUVET   87/100

▼ ♪ Brut Excellence : Pale yellow, fine bubbles. Refined nose intermixing white flowers and white fruits. Beautiful aromatic intensity, suave, closely-integrated substance and a palate-caressing mousse. Yellow plum, crunchy sensation, great aromatic staying power.
Price approx.: 9,60 EUR
http://www.bouvet-ladubay.fr
Bouvet Ladubay
+33 (0)2 41 83 83 83

BOUVET   86/100

▼ ♪ Brut Rosé : Brilliant salmon-pink, fine bubbles. Pleasurable nose of ripe cherry with refined brioche and spice touches. Full-bodied, rich palate with an abundant, fine mousse imparting a sensation of harmony. A seductive wine that deserves to be served with food.
Price approx.: 9,60 EUR
http://www.bouvet-ladubay.fr
Bouvet Ladubay
+33 (0)2 41 83 83 83

ALLIANCE LOIRE   84/100

▼ ♪ Brut De Chanceny - Méthode traditionnelle : Light salmon-pink. The nose is driven by citrus and ripe red fruits. Intense palate showing savoury fruit presence, vinosity and freshness. An honest, balanced dry sparkling rosé that lovers of the style will enjoy. Uncork at the start of the meal.
Price approx.: 10,04 EUR
http://www.allianceloire.com
Alliance Loire
+33 (0)2 41 53 74 44

MENETOU SALON MOROGUES

JEAN-MAX ROGER   88/100

▼ ♪ Le Petit Clos 2012 : Light gold. Delightful nose with accents of tropical fruits, peach and wild flowers. Soft, supple palate bursting with freshness. Very enjoyable crunchy fruit that lingers. Uncork for fish served with peaches. Bravo!
Price approx.: 10,00 EUR
www.jean-max-roger.fr
Domaine Jean-Max Roger
+33 (0)2 48 54 32 20

MENETOU-SALON

DOMAINE DE L'ERMITAGE   88/100

▼ ♪ Vintage 2013 : Brilliant light hue with green tints. Expressive nose suggestive of boxwood and blackcurrant

leaf. On the palate, a sensation of roundness and fleshiness. A concentrated wine with striking, intense aromas supported by robust exuberance. Perfect for sushi.
Price approx.: 9,50 EUR
Domaine de l'Ermitage
+33 (0)6 64 74 02 58

ROGER CHAMPAULT   87/100

▼ ♪ Le Clos de la Cure 2013 : Brilliant pale hue with green tints. Intense nose of boxwood, lime, lemon and gunflint. Supple attack leading into a fine, full-bodied palate, uplifting, elegant exuberance and powerful, clear-cut and focused perfumes. A convincing wine.
Price approx.: 8,00 EUR
http://www.rogerchampaultetfils.fr
Roger Champault et Fils
+33 (0)2 48 79 00 03

DOMAINE DE L'ERMITAGE   87/100

▼ ♪ Vintage 2012 : Intense ruby. Exuberant nose suggestive of red fruits with a vegetal note. Supple palate showing lovely fullness. A concentrated wine conveying an impression of harmony. Hint of firmness on the finish. A beautiful bottling that will mature a little.
Price approx.: 9,80 EUR
Domaine de l'Ermitage
+33 (0)6 64 74 02 58

LE PRIEURÉ DE SAINT CÉOLS   87/100

▼ ♪ Vintage 2012 : Fairly deeply-coloured vibrant red. Powerful, spicy nose with cherry. Light, tense palate with real drive, lovely delicate, precise aromas and a thirst-quenching crunchiness. A successful wine, perfect for small game.
Price approx.: 7,40 EUR
http://www.menetou-salon-jacolin.com
Le Prieuré de Saint-Céols
+33 (0)2 48 64 40 75

LE PRIEURÉ DE SAINT CÉOLS   87/100

▼ ♪ Vintage 2013 : Brilliant pale hue with green tints. Refined nose of lemon and lime. Fresh, exuberant attack flowing into a very light palate revealing more of the citrus aromas and a natural sensation. A skilfully crafted Menetou for oysters.
Price approx.: 7,40 EUR
http://www.menetou-salon-jacolin.com
Le Prieuré de Saint-Céols
+33 (0)2 48 64 40 75

MUSCADET CÔTES DE GRANDLIEU

DOMAINE DES GILLIÈRES   85/100

▼ ♪ Vintage 2013 : Pale gold. Highly perfumed nose midway between lemon, grapefruit and wild flowers.

Lightweight palate with a lovely tangy edge. Pleasant, focused flavours. A classic, distinctive Muscadet, lovely for whetting the appetite and perfect for shellfish.

Price approx.: 4,20 EUR

Château des Gillières

+33 (0)2 40 54 80 05

MUSCADET SÈVRE ET MAINE CLISSON

CLISSON   93/100

▼ ♪ Vintage 2011 : Brilliant light gold, green tints. Inviting mineral and smoky nose with touches of tropical and white fruits. Supple attack, full, fleshy and generous palate with forthright expression. Beautiful combination of austerity and seduction. A great Muscadet.

Price approx.: 8,50 EUR

http://www.muscadet-grenaudiere.fr

Vignobles Ollivier Frères

+33 (0)2 28 01 07 07

MUSCADET SÈVRE ET MAINE SUR LIE

DOMAINE DE LA GRANGE   88/100

▼ ♪ Goulaine 2010 : Light gold. Complex nose of menthol and refined vanilla backed by ripe citrus and dried fruits. A full-bodied Muscadet with a full mouthfeel and delicate, refined flavours. Freshness blends nicely with sourness.

Price approx.: 12,20 EUR

www.domaine-r-delagrange.com

Domaine R de la Grange

+33 (0)2 40 06 45 65

DOMAINE SALMON   88/100

▼ ♪ Vieilles Vignes 2013 : Pale gold. Complex nose showing an array of yellow-fleshed fruit aromas, ripe citrus and minerality. A racy Muscadet with wonderful exuberance at point of entry making room for fruit mid-palate. Full with intense freshness. Ideal for crab or langoustine.

Price approx.: 3,90 EUR

Dominique Salmon

+33 (0)2 40 06 53 66

CHÂTEAU CHESNAIE-MORINIÈRE   88/100

▼ ♪ Vintage 2013 : Pale gold. Marine-style nose blending iodine and citrus fruits with a floral touch. A vibrant, tangy and extremely thirst-quenching Muscadet leaving the palate very fresh. Crunchy aromas. A successful effort.

Price approx.: 5,10 EUR

http://www.joseph-verdier.fr

Joseph Verdier-Logel

+33 (0)2 41 40 22 50

DOMAINE DE LA GRENAUDIÈRE   88/100

▼ ♪ Vintage 2013 : Brilliant light gold with green tints. Pleasant nose of white fruits with a mineral note. Supple attack, lovely round, savoury and expressive mouthfeel with a lemony note. Delicious across the palate and pairing well with trout and almonds.

Price approx.: 4,00 EUR

http://www.muscadet-grenaudiere.fr

Vignobles Ollivier Frères

+33 (0)2 28 01 07 07

DOMAINE DE LA GRENAUDIÈRE   88/100

▼ ♪ La Grenouille 2013 : Brilliant pale yellow. Fairly subdued nose of white fruits with some citrus against a floral backdrop. Supple attack, lovely silky, round and smooth mouthfeel supported by elegant freshness. The mid-palate flows into austerity on the finish that lingers.

Price approx.: 4,50 EUR

http://www.muscadet-grenaudiere.fr

Vignobles Ollivier Frères

+33 (0)2 28 01 07 07

DOMAINE LES TILLEULS   88/100

▼ ♪ Les Quatre Chanteaux - Vendangées à la main 2012 : Lightly-coloured with green tints. Pleasurable nose intermixing white fruits and a mineral dimension. On the palate, a fleshy, rich wine focusing on sense of place. Spice-infused mid-palate followed by some fruit (greengage, apple). A successful effort.

Price approx.: 5,20 EUR

www.domainedestilleuls.fr

Domaine des Tilleuls

+33 (0)2 40 33 60 04

VIGNOBLE DU CHÂTEAU BOIS BENOIST   87/100

▼ ♪ Vintage 2012 : Brilliant pale hue with green tints. Corked. Rejected.

Price approx.: 5,00 EUR

Château Bois Benoist

+33 (0)2 40 33 93 76

DOMAINE SALMON   87/100

▼ ♪ Réserve du Fief - vin n° 3 2013 : Pale gold. Distinctive nose blending citrus fruits with iodine and saline aromatics. A very soft wine gradually unfurling its aromatic personality. The finish retains freshness and fruitiness. A delicate style, perfect for oysters.

Price approx.: 3,50 EUR

Dominique Salmon

+33 (0)2 40 06 53 66

Detailed instructions are featured at

the start of the book.

MANOIR DE LA HERSANDIÈRE   87/100

▼🍷 Vintage 2013 : Brilliant light gold, young tints. Pleasant nose driven by white fruits, backed by patisserie notes of cream and butter. Supple attack, round, silky and mouthcoating palate. Smooth, balanced and harmonious mouthfeel. Wonderful fresh finish.

Domaine Source
+33 (0)2 51 71 70 34

DOMAINE DES AMOUREUX   87/100

▼🍷 Vintage 2013 : Brilliant pale gold. On the nose, a cornucopia of fruits with a tropical touch and floral dimension. The palate is airy and shows generous aromatics and freshness. A well-made wine showing at its best with seafood.

Price approx.: 3,90 EUR
http://www.muscadet-grenaudiere.fr
Vignobles Ollivier Frères
+33 (0)2 28 01 07 07

DOMAINE DE LA GRANGE   86/100

▼🍷 Vintage 2013 : Light gold. Intense nose driven by lime and grapefruit with a floral and mineral touch. The palate shows a seductive balance of acidity and fruit. Persistent, nervy and fresh. A Muscadet with an assertive personality.

Price approx.: 5,95 EUR
www.domaine-r-delagrange.com
Domaine R de la Grange
+33 (0)2 40 06 45 65

DOMAINE DE L'OLIVIER   86/100

▼🍷 Vintage 2013 : Brilliant pale hue. Pleasant nose of white flowers with a lemony touch. Supple attack, palate-caressing mouthfeel with an uplifting, delicate freshness. Expressive across the palate. A real treat as an appetiser with sardine rillettes.

Price approx.: 3,90 EUR
http://www.muscadet-grenaudiere.fr
Vignobles Ollivier Frères
+33 (0)2 28 01 07 07

CUVÉE CHARBONNIÈRE   86/100

▼🍷 Vintage 20123 : Brilliant pale yellow. On the nose, white fruits (pear) and a tangy dimension. Articulate mineral tones come to the fore on the palate. Lovely intensity. Apple recurs on the finish and lingers.

Price approx.: 3,50 EUR
http://www.muscadet-grenaudiere.fr
Vignobles Ollivier Frères
+33 (0)2 28 01 07 07

DOMAINE DE LA GRANGE   85/100

▼🍷 Vieilles Vignes 2013 : Pale gold. Endearing nose showing accents of lime with a floral and iodine touch. A distinctive, focused Muscadet offering up lovely ripe fruit and freshness. A loyal friend for a basket of oysters.

Price approx.: 6,80 EUR
www.domaine-r-delagrange.com
Domaine R de la Grange
+33 (0)2 40 06 45 65

DOMAINE DE LA BRONIÈRE   85/100

▼🍷 Vintage 2013 : Brilliant light yellow with green tints. Subdued nose driven by white fruits and white flowers. Lively attack leading into a supple, round and fairly rich palate. Faint, lingering minerality drives the finish. A balanced wine pairing with oily fish.

Domaine Source
+33 (0)2 51 71 70 34

CHÂTEAU LA NOË   85/100

▼🍷 Vintage 2013 : Bright, light gold. Suggestions of citrus fruits and white flowers on the nose. Supple, light, lively and fresh palate. Mineral finish. A polished wine pairing with a platter of seafoods.

Domaine Source
+33 (0)2 51 71 70 34

ALLIANCE LOIRE   85/100

▼🍷 Pierre 1er 2013 : Pale gold with green tints. Distinctive nose halfway between iodine and lime scents. A well-balanced Muscadet boasting savoury exuberance and menthol-infused freshness enhancing pleasant crisp fruit that lingers. Prompts the need to eat oysters.

Price approx.: 7,09 EUR
http://www.allianceloire.com
Alliance Loire
+33 (0)2 41 53 74 44

CHÂTEAU DE LA THÉBAUDIÈRE   85/100

▼🍷 Vintage 2013 : Pale gold. Distinctive iodine and lime nose. Lovely crisp, soft palate. Perfume makes a good impression and is coupled with a welcome freshness. Ideal for sea snails.

Price approx.: 5,10 EUR
http://www.joseph-verdier.fr
Joseph Verdier-Logel
+33 (0)2 41 40 22 50

CHÂTEAU DES GILLIÈRES   84/100

▼🍷 Vintage 2012 : Light gold. Refined nose with a lemony dimension backed by menthol and liquorice. The palate is firm and the fruit struggles to reveal itself such as the lushness of the mouthfeel. Sourness on the finish. A structured Muscadet for fish in a cream sauce.

Price approx.: 4,90 EUR
Château des Gillières
+33 (0)2 40 54 80 05

CHÂTEAU DE LA MOUCHETIÈRE   84/100

▼♪ Vintage 2013 : Brilliant pale gold with green tints. Pleasant nose driven by peach and white flowers. Beautiful freshness, suppleness and fruit overtones on the palate. Well-balanced with persistent liveliness. A wine drinking well from now on.

Domaine Source
+33 (0)2 51 71 70 34

DOMAINE DES TILLEULS   84/100

▼♪ Essentielle 2013 : Brilliant light colour with green tints. Lovely nose intermixing fruit scents of pear and lemon with crisp notes. Silky attack. Harmonious, light and closely-integrated presence with real drive. The finish is slightly austere.
Price approx.: 4,20 EUR
www.domainedestilleuls.fr
Domaine des Tilleuls
+33 (0)2 40 33 60 04

DOMAINE SALMON   82/100

▼♪ Réserve du Fief 2013 : Pale gold. Fairly subdued nose, opening up after swirling to lime notes. A light Muscadet. Fruity with beading on the attack leading into a more subtle mid-palate. Still quite shy. Uncork for shellfish.
Price approx.: 3,50 EUR
Dominique Salmon
+33 (0)2 40 06 53 66

MUSCADET
SÈVRE ET MAINE

VIGNOBLE POIRON - DABIN   84/100

▼♪ Vieilles Vignes 2013 : Brilliant pale yellow with green tints. The nose lacks focus on first pour then reveals citrus coupled with a mineral tone after swirling. Very energetic, crunchy palate revealing clear, delicate aromas. A likeable Muscadet that makes the perfect quaffer.
Price approx.: 5,00 EUR
http://www.muscadet-poiron.com
Domaine Poiron-Dabin
+33 (0)2 40 06 56 42

FAMILLE BOUGRIER   82/100

▼♪ Vintage 2013 : Pale gold. Very mineral and iodine-infused nose with flowers and lime. Tell-tale Muscadet characteristics at point of entry leading into lighter aromatics mid-palate. Freshness continues to call the shots. Serve as an aperitif or with shellfish.
Price approx.: 3,25 EUR
www.bougrier.fr
Bougrier SA
+33 (0)2 54 32 31 36

POUILLY-FUMÉ

DOMAINE PHILIPPE RAIMBAULT   92/100

▼♪ Les Lumeaux 2013 : Brilliant, limpid pale gold. Expressive nose suggestive of citrus fruits, white flowers and earthy undertones. Delicate, silky and delicious palate with clear-cut aromas. Impeccable balance, fresh finish. Extremely elegant - a real treat.
Price approx.: 9,60 EUR
www.philipperaimbault.fr
Philippe Raimbault
+33 (0)2 48 79 29 54

DOMAINE SERGE DAGUENEAU & FILLES   92/100

▼♪ La Léontine 2011 : Brilliant light gold with green tints. Endearing, complex nose of toasted almond and ripe citrus with mineral presence. Silky attack, extremely seductive, svelte and concentrated palate that is tense and harmonious. A very stylish Pouilly Fumé.
Price approx.: 2,00 EUR
www.s-dagueneau-filles.fr
Domaine Serge Dagueneau & filles
+33 (0)3 86 39 11 18

DOMAINE LANDRAT-GUYOLLOT   91/100

▼♪ Gemme de Feu 2012 : Crystalline hue. Rich nose intermixing mineral, tropical fruit, flower and spice aromas. A racy, full-bodied Pouilly boasting a full, fleshy mouthfeel, intense, distinctive fruit aromas, freshness and length. Superlative expression throughout.
www.landrat-guyollot.com
Domaine Landrat-Guyollot
+33 (0)3 86 39 11 83

JEAN PABIOT ET FILS   90/100

▼♪ Cuvée Séduction 2012 : Superb gold. Refined nose with a whiff of smoke and strong minerality opening up to notes of broom, almond, vanilla and jammy citrus. Full, elegant palate, revealing its charm tactfully and delicately, supported by its lees ageing. A superlative Pouilly.
Price approx.: 14,50 EUR
www.jean-pabiot.com
Jean Pabiot et Fils
+33 (0)3 86 39 10 25

DOMAINE CHAUVEAU   90/100

▼♪ Cuvée Sainte Clélie 2012 : Brilliant light hue tinged with green. Fairly subdued nose marrying citrus fruits and a mineral touch. Round attack, rich palate showing a lovely impression of harmony and mellowness. Elegant exuberance with finesse the key theme. Save for quality fish.
Price approx.: 10,00 EUR
www.domaine.chauveau.com
Domaine Chauveau
+33 (0)3 86 39 15 42

DOMAINE SERGE DAGUENEAU & FILLES
90/100

▼ ♪ Clos des Chaudoux 2012 : Brilliant light yellow with green tints. Racy nose offering up ripe citrus, chalk and a floral touch. Supple attack, rich, mellow palate with a beautifully curbed intensity. A deliciously compelling wine to set aside for Japanese fish-based dishes.
Price approx.: 18,00 EUR
www.s-dagueneau-filles.fr
Domaine Serge Dagueneau & filles
+33 (0)3 86 39 11 18

DOMAINE PHILIPPE RAIMBAULT
89/100

▼ ♪ Mosaïque 2013 : Light yellow with green tints. Extremely refined nose of citrus with mineral presence. The palate shows generous expression with incisive, exuberant and clearly-delineated fruit. A sterling quality Pouilly.
Price approx.: 9,40 EUR
www.philipperaimbault.fr
Philippe Raimbault
+33 (0)2 48 79 29 54

DOMAINE PATRICE MOREUX
88/100

▼ ♪ Vintage 2013 : Light yellow with green tints. Expressive nose of citrus, blackcurrant leaf and a touch of silica. The palate shows free-rein expression. It is generous and exuberant with lovely roundness, aromatic precision and just the right amount of freshness.
Price approx.: 8,30 EUR
http://www.pouilly.com
Domaine Patrice Moreux
+33 (0)3 86 39 13 55

DOMAINE LANDRAT-GUYOLLOT
88/100

▼ ♪ Gemme Océane 2012 : Pale gold with green tints. Refined nose revealing tropical nuances and white fruits with linden undertones. Full palate with a delicate crispness. Beautiful generous aromatics, length and personality. A Pouilly that proudly holds its own.
www.landrat-guyollot.com
Domaine Landrat-Guyollot
+33 (0)3 86 39 11 83

VILLEBOIS
87/100

▼ ♪ Vintage 2013 : Brilliant light hue tinged with green. Pleasurable nose of citrus and blackcurrant bud with a mineral dimension. A sensation of roundness and fullness on the palate. Vibrant acidity propels exuberant aromas. A Fumé that works best with salty seafoods.
Price approx.: 9,00 EUR
Villebois

GITTON PÈRE & FILS
87/100

▼ ♪ Clos Joanne d'Orion 2013 : Brilliant pale hue, green tints. Racy nose of silica, bush peach and ripe citrus. Round attack, fleshy, rich and lively palate that is still slightly inward-looking. Impression of precision and tenacity. Beautiful atypical wine.
Price approx.: 13,50 EUR
http://www.gitton.fr
Gitton Père & Fils
+33 (0)2 48 54 38 84

DOMAINE DES FINES CAILLOTES
86/100

▼ ♪ Vintage 2013 : Pale gold with brilliant highlights. Distinctive nose, still a little subdued, with perfumes of white fruits, citrus and meadow. Open, expressive palate showing seductive freshness, beautiful acidity and harmonious perfumes. A dashing, aromatic Pouilly.
Price approx.: 12,50 EUR
www.jean-pabiot.com
Jean Pabiot et Fils
+33 (0)3 86 39 10 25

DOMAINE CHAUVEAU
86/100

▼ ♪ La Charmette 2013 : Pale gold. Nose of fruits and white flowers. Young attack driven by intense, crisp aromas. Exuberance gradually fades, revealing archetypal Pouilly features. Still young and fiery. A little more bottle age would make for an even more enjoyable drink.
Price approx.: 8,00 EUR
www.domaine.chauveau.com
Domaine Chauveau
+33 (0)3 86 39 15 42

DOMAINE SERGE DAGUENEAU & FILLES
86/100

▼ ♪ Tradition 2013 : Light gold. Expressive nose of citrus fruits and lemon with a touch of crispness and subtle mineral note. Fresh palate, lovely supple mouthfeel showing generous expression and a very exuberant, spicy finish. Salmon baked in foil would be a good match.
Price approx.: 12,00 EUR
www.s-dagueneau-filles.fr
Domaine Serge Dagueneau & filles
+33 (0)3 86 39 11 18

DOMAINE CHAUVEAU
85/100

▼ ♪ Les Croqloups 2013 : Brilliant pale gold. Subdued nose driven by boxwood and nettle with citrus fruits. Upright, soft palate with a lovely tangy edge. Freshness dovetails well with perfume. A classic, well-made Pouilly, already drinking well. Serve with oysters and prawns.
Price approx.: 8,00 EUR
www.domaine.chauveau.com
Domaine Chauveau
+33 (0)3 86 39 15 42

QUARTS DE CHAUME

DOMAINE DES BAUMARD
92/100

CONV ▼ ♪ Vintage 2010 : Brightly-coloured gold.

Complex nose opening up to candied fruits with notes of honey and wax. Remarkable balance of richness and freshness showcasing clear-cut fruit aromas. The finish displays attractive youthful acidity. Undeniable potential.
Price approx.: 42,00 EUR
http://www.baumard.fr
Domaine des Baumard
+33 (0)2 41 78 70 03

QUINCY

DOMAINE ADÉLE ROUZÉ 88/100

▼✦ Vintage 2013 : Brilliant pale hue with green tints. Pleasurable, focused nose of lemon, citrus fruits and a touch of boxwood. Lightness and crunchiness are key themes on the palate with clearly-defined, focused aromas. Enjoyable as an aperitif and with goat's cheeses.
Price approx.: 7,10 EUR
Domaine Adèle Rouzé
+33 (0)2 48 58 93 08

DOMAINE JACQUES ROUZÉ 87/100

▼✦ Vintage 2013 : Light gold. Very welcoming nose showing floral perfumes of boxwood and acacia combined with crisp pineapple and pink grapefruit. Freshness immediately prevails on the palate, promoting very pure aromatic expression. Genuine pleasure.
Price approx.: 7,00 EUR
http://www.jacques-rouze.com
Domaine Jacques Rouzé
+33 (0)2 48 51 35 61

DOMAINE TROTEREAU 87/100

▼✦ Vintage 2013 : Light yellow with green tints. Subdued nose showing vegetal tones of ivy and boxwood with delicate spicy fruit undertones. Supple attack, round, generous and vigorous palate supported by elegant freshness. A successful if atypical Quincy.
Price approx.: 8,50 EUR
Domaine Trotereau
+33 (0)2 48 51 32 23

ROSÉ D'ANJOU

DOMAINE DES IRIS 86/100

▼✦ Vintage 2013 : Salmon-pink. Compelling nose of rose and red berry fruits. An easy-drinking, soft rosé boasting a lovely mellow character. Freshness and crunchy aromas. A true rosé for pleasure.
Price approx.: 4,90 EUR
http://www.joseph-verdier.fr
Joseph Verdier-Logel
+33 (0)2 41 40 22 50

CAVES DE L'ANGEVINE 85/100

▼✦ Vintage 2013 : Orange-red. Nose of red fruit sweets (strawberry). Very thirst-quenching palate showing a seductive fruity freshness, soft, mellow finish and young, bright and breezy fruit. An easy-drinking rosé offering instant pleasure.
Price approx.: 3,49 EUR
www.bougrier.fr
Bougrier SA
+33 (0)2 54 32 31 36

DOMAINE DES HAUTES OUCHES 84/100

▼✦ Vintage 2013 : Light salmon-pink. Subtle red fruit on the nose with earthy nuances. Flavoursome mellow palate showing pleasant crisp fruit aromatics and freshness. A classic, well-made Rosé d'Anjou. Recommended as an aperitif.
Price approx.: 4,76 EUR
http://www.joseph-verdier.fr
Joseph Verdier-Logel
+33 (0)2 41 40 22 50

DOMAINE DE FLINES 80/100

▼✦ Rosé d'Anjou 2013 : Light salmon-pink. Pleasurable nose of redcurrant, red fruits and a patisserie touch. Supple attack leading into a soft palate focusing on drinkability. Round, fairly perfumed and lively. A rosé for sharing.
Price approx.: 4,70 EUR
www.domainedeflines.com
Domaine de Flines
+33 (0)2 41 59 42 78

ROSÉ DE LOIRE

DOMAINE DE TERREBRUNE 85/100

▼✦ Chanteloup 2013 : Red with orange. Nose of crunchy red berry fruits (strawberry, raspberry). More of the delightful fresh fruit aromatics on the palate. Very supple, mellow and pleasurable. A delicious rosé for rillons and cold meats.
Price approx.: 4,50 EUR
www.domainedeterrebrune.fr
Domaine de Terrebrune
+33 (0)2 41 54 01 99

ANTOINE SIMONEAU 84/100

▼✦ Vintage 2013 : Pale salmon-pink. Refined nose driven by strawberry and raspberry with a touch of sweets. Lively attack flowing into a more supple mid-palate with fruit leading the way. A soft, fresh rosé that is very accessible from the aperitif onwards.
Price approx.: 3,35 EUR
http://www.antoinesimoneau.com
Domaine de la Rablais
+33 (0)2 54 71 36 14

DOMAINE DE LA COLLINE   81/100

▼♪ Vintage 2013 : Red with salmon-pink. Focused nose showing ripe red fruit and citrus accents. Fairly firm, powerful palate displaying lingering aromatic maturity. Serve preferably with food (barbecues).
Price approx.: 4,40 EUR
http://www.joseph-verdier.fr
Joseph Verdier-Logel
+33 (0)2 41 40 22 50

SAINT-NICOLAS-DE-BOURGUEIL

DOMAINE LORIEUX   86/100

▼♪ Cuvée les Barbeaux 2013 : Young dark purple. Crunchy strawberry and raspberry on the nose with a spicy earthy touch. An enjoyable, accessible Saint-Nicolas that gains in intensity and depth across the palate yet retains its lovely fruit. Uncork for poultry.
Price approx.: 7,50 EUR
http://www.joseph-verdier.fr
Joseph Verdier-Logel
+33 (0)2 41 40 22 50

VIGNOBLE DE LA JARNOTERIE   86/100

▼♪ Les Terres Noires 2012 : Deep, young-looking ruby. Fairly subdued nose with elegant floral and fruity tones. Round attack, ethereal yet full on the palate, a delicious wine revealing a beautiful, unexpected silky structure. Well-balanced, consistent and all-set for the future.
Price approx.: 11,00 EUR
http://www.mabileau-reze.com
Vignoble de la Jarnoterie
+33 (0)2 47 97 75 49

SANCERRE

DOMAINE PHILIPPE RAIMBAULT   93/100

▼♪ Les Chasseignes 2011 : Brilliant yellow. Racy nose of ripe white fruits, a patisserie touch and elegant toasted oak. On the palate, an ethereal, velvety and closely-integrated wine with delicious mellow aromas of smoke, spice and minerality. Aytpical and voluptuous.
Price approx.: 14,60 EUR
www.philipperaimbault.fr
Philippe Raimbault
+33 (0)2 48 79 29 54

JEAN-MAX ROGER   92/100

▼♪ Vieilles Vignes 2012 : Light gold. Mineral nose backed by freshly-cut grass, ripe citrus and a menthol touch. The palate is velvety, elegant and refined. Beautiful freshness enhancing perfumes of crunchy fruit. Lengthy finish. A consummate wine, already in great aromatic shape.
Price approx.: 20,00 EUR
www.jean-max-roger.fr
Domaine Jean-Max Roger
+33 (0)2 48 54 32 20

DOMAINE PATRICE MOREUX   92/100

▼♪ Cuvée Prestige - Les Bénédictins 2012 : Brilliant light hue with green tints. Racy nose of ripe citrus and gunflint with a patisserie touch. Tropical dimension on the palate. A svelte wine delivering an impression of opulence with superb fine, precise exuberance. A beautiful top-flight Sancerre
Price approx.: 17,50 EUR
http://www.pouilly.com
Domaine Patrice Moreux
+33 (0)3 86 39 13 55

DOMAINE HENRY NATTER   91/100

▼♪ François de La Grange de Montigny 2011 : Light gold. Profound nose revealing perfumes of candied lemon with mineral undertones. Lovely fat, fullness and silky texture on the palate yet also balance and persistency. A wine for gourmet foods, already nicely open.
www.henrynatter.fr
Domaine Henry Natter
+33 (0)2 48 69 58 85

JEAN-MAX ROGER   91/100

▼♪ Vieilles Vignes 2010 : Light garnet. Extremely pure cherry aromas on the nose. Suave, full and intense fruit-driven palate. The mouthfeel stays focused on elegance. Calls for roast game. A Sancerre that really does justice to Pinot noir. A superlative wine from central France.
Price approx.: 20,00 EUR
www.jean-max-roger.fr
Domaine Jean-Max Roger
+33 (0)2 48 54 32 20

PAUL PRIEUR & FILS   91/100

▼♪ Monts Damnés 2012 : Very pale, brilliant hue. Racy, refined nose intermixing delicate fruit with elegant minerality. Round attack, ripe, silky and easy-going palate showing gunflint and citrus. Aromatic expression is not lacking. Substantial persistency.
Price approx.: 14,00 EUR
Domaine Paul Prieur
+33 (0)2 48 79 35 86

MICHEL VATTAN   91/100

▼♪ Cuvée L-O 2012 : Light gold. Refined nose with tropical pineapple and peach accents and a mineral touch. Generous palate, suave mouthfeel with huge freshness showcasing very persistent, forthright crisp fruit aromas.

GITTON PÈRE & FILS

La Vigne du Larrey 2010

▼ Brilliant lemon-yellow, green tints. Racy mineral, vanilla nose with ripe citrus and bush peach. Lush, generous, lemony palate, still a tad angular with greengage and fine patisserie splashes. A superlative, atypical Sancerre all-set for a great future.

www.gitton.fr

92/100

Price approx.: 13,30 EUR
http://www.michel-vattan.com
Michel Vattan
+33 (0)2 48 79 40 98

MATTHIAS ET EMILE ROBLIN   91/100

▼ ♪ Ammonites 2012 : Pale yellow with green tints. Very expressive mineral nose with a faint petrol touch and delicate grapefruit notes. Clean, nervy and fiery palate framed by fat and mineral to boot. A highly expressive Sancerre.
Price approx.: 18,00 EUR
http://www.sancerre-roblin.com
Domaine Matthias et Emile Roblin
+33 (0)2 48 79 48 85

DOMAINE HENRY NATTER   90/100

▼ ♪ L'Enchantement 2010 : Beautiful cherry-red, beginning to mature. Refined, mature nose suggestive of cherries in brandy and prune flesh. The palate shows seductive fullness and fat yet also an ethereal, silky character. Beautiful length infused with freshness.
www.henrynatter.fr
Domaine Henry Natter
+33 (0)2 48 69 58 85

DOMAINE JEAN-PAUL PICARD   90/100

▼ ♪ Cuvée Prestige 2012 : Brilliant pale hue with green tints. On the nose, subtle tropical and vanilla notes with citrus in the background. Forward attack leading into a full, rich palate that is focused and dynamic. An unusual yet successful style pairing with grilled fish.
Price approx.: 11,00 EUR
Jean Paul Picard et Fils
+33 (0)2 48 54 16 13

JEAN-MARC & MATHIEU CROCHET   90/100

▼ ♪ MC 2011 : Beautiful gold. Rich nose of toasted oak backed by almond, white flowers and mineral aromas. Mouth-coating with majestic oak presence enveloping

impeccable fruit. Intense aromatic length. A top-flight wine showing a true sense of place.
Price approx.: 14,50 EUR
http://www.jean-marc-mathieu-crochet.com
Jean-Marc Crochet
+33 (0)2 48 54 11 30

MATTHIAS ET EMILE ROBLIN   90/100

▼ ♪ L'Enclos de Maimbray 2012 : Pale yellow. The nose opens up to mineral notes then reveals perfumes of lime and tropical fruits. The same fruit character carries through to the palate which is soft with a supple attack. A lovely crisp touch prolongs expression on the palate.
Price approx.: 13,00 EUR
http://www.sancerre-roblin.com
Domaine Matthias et Emile Roblin
+33 (0)2 48 79 48 85

MATTHIAS ET EMILE ROBLIN   90/100

▼ ♪ Origine 2012 : Pale yellow with green tints. Subdued nose asserting a mineral character after swirling with subtle grapefruit notes. Lovely focus, freshness and minerality on the palate. Fruit is forward, precise and persistent. A pretty Sancerre.
Price approx.: 12,00 EUR
http://www.sancerre-roblin.com
Domaine Matthias et Emile Roblin
+33 (0)2 48 79 48 85

VIGNERON ALBAN ROBLIN   89/100

▼ ♪ Héritage 2012 : Pale crystalline hue with green tints. Pleasant nose of white-fleshed fruits with a tropical touch and vanilla note. Delightful palate balanced by elegant freshness. Lime and lemon flavours with judicious use of oak. A very compelling wine.
Price approx.: 15,00 EUR
http://www.alban-roblin-sancerre.fr
Domaine Alban Roblin
+33 (0)2 48 79 31 15

VILLEBOIS 89/100

▼♪ Vintage 2013 : Brilliant pale hue with green tints. Refined nose of ripe citrus, flint and a chalky touch. Lace-like palate with beautiful elegant, precise aromas. An ethereal style with ample expression. Perfect with goat's cheeses.
Price approx.: 9,00 EUR
Villebois

DOMAINE PATRICE MOREUX 89/100

▼♪ Vintage 2013 : Brilliant light yellow with green tints. Refined, racy nose of citrus with a chalky impression. Very refined palate with precise, lace-like aromas that infuse a fleshy, rich mouthfeel. Every aspect of the wine is precision-made. Great craftmanship.
Price approx.: 8,50 EUR
http://www.pouilly.com
Domaine Patrice Moreux
+33 (0)3 86 39 13 55

MICHEL VATTAN 89/100

▼♪ Cuvée Argile 2013 : Pale yellow with green tints. Lovely finesse on the nose with floral, mineral and crisp notes. Dry character on the palate, very pure aromas with predominant floral and fruity notes. A characterful Sancerre pairing with prime quality fish.
Price approx.: 8,80 EUR
http://www.michel-vattan.com
Michel Vattan
+33 (0)2 48 79 40 98

MICHEL VATTAN 89/100

▼♪ Cuvée Calcaire 2013 : Pale yellow with green tints. Predominant mineral/gunflint tones on the nose with a varietal touch of white flowers. Rich attack, beautiful fullness on the palate. More of the mineral nose character giving the wine lots of personality.
Price approx.: 8,30 EUR
http://www.michel-vattan.com
Michel Vattan
+33 (0)2 48 79 40 98

DOMAINE JEAN-PAUL RICARD 89/100

▼♪ Vintage 2013 : Brilliant light hue with green tints. Subtle nose of silica and citrus fruits. The palate is more expressive, clearly projecting precise aromas. Fresh, focused, persistent and lemony throughout. A convincing Sancerre.
Price approx.: 8,70 EUR
Jean Paul Picard et Fils
+33 (0)2 48 54 16 13

DOMAINE PHILIPPE RAIMBAULT 89/100

▼♪ Les Godons 2013 : Light colour with green tints. Expressive nose of gunflint with citrus in the background. Lovely suave palate with a round, rich and dynamic mouthfeel and intense, persistent lemony aromas. A successful, textbook Sancerre.
Price approx.: 9,80 EUR
www.philipperaimbault.fr
Philippe Raimbault
+33 (0)2 48 79 29 54

DOMAINE SERGE LAPORTE 89/100

✳♪ Cuvée des M.a.g.e.s. 2012 : Brilliant pale gold, green tints. Appealing nose of super ripe citrus with a subtle vegetal touch. Suave attack, closely-integrated, concentrated substance driven by refined exuberance. Lovely fruit scents. Shows assertiveness. Gets our vote of approval.
Price approx.: 12,00 EUR
http://www.domainesergelaporte.com
Domaine Serge Laporte
+33 (0)2 48 54 30 10

DOMAINE HENRY NATTER 88/100

▼♪ Vintage 2010 : Medium intense colour with mature highlights. Mature nose showing aromas of ripe red fruits enhanced by a sensation of oak. The palate is amazingly fat and full with a mellow attack leading into a slightly firmer mid-palate and finish. Very compelling.
www.henrynatter.fr
Domaine Henry Natter
+33 (0)2 48 69 58 85

DOMAINE DE LA VILLAUDIÈRE 88/100

▼♪ Cuvée Héritage 2012 : Brilliant pale yellow, green tints. Fairly subdued nose intermixing vanilla and citrus fruit. Svelte, rich palate with a harmonious framework, lovely concentration and vigorous spicy lemony aromas with just the right amount of oak. A beautiful wine.
Price approx.: 13,00 EUR
http://www.lavillaudiere.com
Domaine de la Villaudière
+33 (0)2 48 79 30 84

JEAN PABIOT ET FILS 88/100

▼♪ La Merisière 2013 : Light gold. Reticent nose opening up to notes of grapefruit, chalk and wild flowers. Elegant palate with a beautiful crisp structure and distinctive, appealing fruit. A Sancerre that is both thirst-quenching yet complex.
Price approx.: 12,50 EUR
www.jean-pabiot.com
Jean Pabiot et Fils
+33 (0)3 86 39 10 25

DOMAINE DE LA CHÉZATTE 88/100

✳♪ Sancerre 2013 : Brilliant pale hue with green tints. Exuberant nose of boxwood, blackcurrant leaf, citrus. The palate is not backward in coming forward either with precise aromas, a touch of flint, crunchy freshness. A

distinctive wine pairing well with salty seafoods.
Price approx.: 7,00 EUR
Domaine De La Chezatte
+33 (0)2 48 78 03 21

VINCENT GRALL   88/100

▼♪ Le Manoir 2013 : Crystalline, light hue with green tints. Pleasant nose of vanilla with citrus in the background. Silky attack, a lace-like impression on the palate and great aromatic finesse supported by nicely present freshness. Pair with oysters and goat's cheeses.
Price approx.: 12,00 EUR
www.grall-vigneron-sancerre.com
Vincent Grall
+33 (0)2 48 78 00 42

GITTON PÈRE & FILS   88/100

▼♪ Les Herses 2012 : Brilliant yellow, green tints. Shy nose showing a touch of vanilla, ripe white fruits and peach. Silky attack, splendid lush, concentrated presence and fine patisserie touches. More adolescent citrus flavours drive the mid-palate. Will evolve gracefully.
Price approx.: 16,50 EUR
http://www.gitton.fr
Gitton Père & Fils
+33 (0)2 48 54 38 84

DOMAINE BIZET   88/100

▼♪ Dolium 2013 : Pale gold. Highly perfumed nose of white fruits flowing into tropical notes, wild flowers and confectionary. The palate is young and thirst-quenching with delicious fruit. A dashing, juicy Sancerre. Hugely successful with hot goat's cheese salad.
Price approx.: 9,50 EUR
http://www.sancerre-bizet.com
Domaine Bizet
+33 (0)2 48 79 34 43

DOMAINE JEAN-PAUL RIACRD   88/100

▼♪ Vintage 2013 : Light salmon-pink. Inviting nose of strawberry and red berry fruits with a crisp touch. Lovely natural impression with focused, precise expression mirroring the nose aromatics, rounded off with fine spice touches. Succulence and honesty. Serve with food.
Price approx.: 8,70 EUR
Jean Paul Picard et Fils
+33 (0)2 48 54 16 13

DOMAINE DANIEL REVERDY ET FILS   88/100

▼♪ Vintage 2013 : Brilliant pale hue with green tints. Racy nose blending citrus fruits, mango and a mineral touch. Round attack leading into a harmonious, rich and lively palate offering up lovely restrained exuberance and a hint of chalky firmness. We like it.
Price approx.: 7,30 EUR
Domaine Daniel Reverdy et fils
+33 (0)2 48 79 33 29

ROGER CHAMPAULT   88/100

▼♪ Les Pierris 2013 : Brilliant, pale salmon-pink. Pleasurable nose of redcurrant and strawberry with a tangy touch. The palate is light and lively with a refined crunchiness. Impeccably defined, precise fruit and spice aromas. A nicely crafted Sancerre.
Price approx.: 8,50 EUR
http://www.rogerchampaultetfils.fr
Roger Champault et Fils
+33 (0)2 48 79 00 03

PAUL PRIEUR & FILS   88/100

▼♪ Vendangé à la main 2013 : Brilliant pale hue with green tints. Refined nose showing suggestions of grapefruit and lemon. Supple attack leading into a very exuberant palate, beautiful ripe, focused and tense mouthfeel - lacks nothing. A convincing Sancerre pairing with shellfish.
Price approx.: 8,50 EUR
Domaine Paul Prieur
+33 (0)2 48 79 35 86

DOMAINE LA BARBOTAINE   88/100

▼♪ Vintage 2013 : Brilliant light gold. Refined, ripe nose showing delicate nuances of citrus fruits. Supple attack, beautiful round, polished and generous mouthfeel with a lovely, restrained aromatic exuberance. Harmonious throughout.
Price approx.: 8,00 EUR
http://www.sancerre-frederic-champault.fr
Domaine La Barbotaine
+33 (0)2 48 79 02 32

MICHEL VATTAN   88/100

▼♪ Vintage 2012 : Cherry red with young highlights. Appealing nose of jammy cherry, raspberry and strawberry. Full, generous palate driven by red fruit. Lovely crunchiness, freshness, suppleness and length. An excellent Pinot noir that is charming and soft.
Price approx.: 9,30 EUR
http://www.michel-vattan.com
Michel Vattan
+33 (0)2 48 79 40 98

JEAN-MARC & MATHIEU CROCHET   88/100

▼♪ Chêne Marchand 2012 : Light gold. Fresh, menthol-infused nose backed by white fruits, wild flowers and a mineral touch. The palate introduces honeyed aromatics on the attack. The mid-palate is more classic yet retains balance, freshness and perfume. Shows personality.
Price approx.: 11,50 EUR
http://www.jean-marc-mathieu-crochet.com
Jean-Marc Crochet
+33 (0)2 48 54 11 30

MATTHIAS ET EMILE ROBLIN   88/100

▼♪ Grande Côte de La Vallée 2012 : Beautiful deep colour. Focused nose with aromas of ripe cherry and plum. Velvety attack with concentrated fruit and a polished mouthfeel nicely balanced by a lively structure that imparts freshness. A fine Sancerre.
Price approx.: 18,00 EUR
http://www.sancerre-roblin.com
Domaine Matthias et Emile Roblin
+33 (0)2 48 79 48 85

VIGNERON ALBAN ROBLIN   87/100

▼♪ Vintage 2013 : Brilliant pale hue, green tints. Expressive nose of blackcurrant bud and citrus fruits. On the palate, supple, closely-integrated mouthfeel with lovely aromatic honesty, precise and intense lemony notes and beautiful persistency rounding off the whole.
Price approx.: 10,00 EUR
http://www.alban-roblin-sancerre.fr
Domaine Alban Roblin
+33 (0)2 48 79 31 15

DOMAINE DE LA GARENNE   87/100

▼♪ Les Bouffants 2013 : Brilliant pale gold. Distinctive nose showing floral aromas and crisp pink grapefruit. Young palate, already very pleasurable due to its finesse, suppleness and freshness, all of which emphasise the fruit. Calls for all types of goat's cheeses.
Price approx.: 9,20 EUR
http://www.sancerrelagarenne.com
Domaine de la Garenne
+33 (0)2 48 79 35 79

DOMAINE REVERDY DUCROUX   87/100

▼♪ Beau Regard 2012 : Cherry-red. Refined nose of fresh cassis, morello cherry and raspberry. More of the crunchy fruit aromatics on the palate. Very supple with elegant fruit. A delicious red Sancerre with staying power on the palate. Ideal for roast chicken.
Price approx.: 12,00 EUR
www.reverdy-ducroux.fr
Domaine Reverdy Ducroux
+33 (0)2 48 79 31 3

JEAN-MAX ROGER   87/100

▼♪ Cuvée La Grange Dîmière 2013 : Beautiful salmon-pink. Appealing nose of boiled sweets backed by red berry fruits. A charming rosé with seductively crunchy fruit, aromatic presence, freshness and a crisp finish. An easy-drinking wine for pleasure.
Price approx.: 11,00 EUR
www.jean-max-roger.fr
Domaine Jean-Max Roger
+33 (0)2 48 54 32 20

JEAN-MAX ROGER   87/100

▼♪ Cuvée G.C. 2012 : Beautiful light gold. Refined nose of blackcurrant bud backed by grapefruit, peach and a touch of smoke. A charming wine wavering between beautiful acidity and sweetness augmented by the tropical fruit aromas.
Price approx.: 12,00 EUR
www.jean-max-roger.fr
Domaine Jean-Max Roger
+33 (0)2 48 54 32 20

VINCENT GRALL   87/100

▼♪ Vintage 2013 : Pale crystalline hue with green tints. Refined nose with delicate fruity (citrus) and mineral touches. Lightweight palate with just the right amount of exuberance and intense, striking aromas of focused lemon. Lovely elegance and consistency.
Price approx.: 8,80 EUR
www.grall-vigneron-sancerre.com
Vincent Grall
+33 (0)2 48 78 00 42

MICHEL VATTAN   87/100

▼♪ Vintage 2013 : Beautiful pale orange. Fairly subdued nose of red berry fruits. A very lightweight rosé on the palate showing more of the red berry fruits coupled with a pleasant crisp dimension. Quite long-lasting, invigorating finish.
Price approx.: 8,30 EUR
http://www.michel-vattan.com
Michel Vattan
+33 (0)2 48 79 40 98

DOMAINE PHILIPPE RAIMBAULT   87/100

▼♪ Apud Sariacum 2013 : Light orangy pink. Crisp nose of red berry fruits. Delicate attack leading into a supple, round, full and velvety palate with upfront aroma. A delicious wine with a slightly spicy finish. Works well on its own as an aperitif or with sunny day meals.
Price approx.: 9,40 EUR
www.philipperaimbault.fr
Philippe Raimbault
+33 (0)2 48 79 29 54

DOMAINE PHILIPPE RAIMBAULT   87/100

▼♪ Apud Sariacum 2013 : Brilliant light yellow. Intense nose driven by blackcurrant bud with grapefruit in the background. Supple, rich palate with aroma supported by beautiful freshness. Persistent, fruit-forward finish.
Price approx.: 9,60 EUR
www.philipperaimbault.fr
Philippe Raimbault
+33 (0)2 48 79 29 54

DOMAINE SERGE LAPORTE   87/100

▼♪ Millésia 2013 : Brilliant light gold with green tints. Racy nose exuding nicely ripe fruit. Fairly round, focused palate with an elegant crunchiness perfumed with distinctive, focused aromas. A civilised style that would work with finely-flavoured fish.

Price approx.: 8,70 EUR

http://www.domainesergelaporte.com

Domaine Serge Laporte

+33 (0)2 48 54 30 10

DOMAINE HENRY NATTER   86/100

▼♪ Vintage 2013 : Light salmon-pink. Endearing, focused nose intermixing red berry fruits and tangerine notes. Fleshy attack, fine-grained texture and lovely persistent freshness. A vibrant wine showing well with fish.

www.henrynatter.fr

Domaine Henry Natter

+33 (0)2 48 69 58 85

DOMAINE HENRY NATTER   86/100

▼♪ Vintage 2013 : Limpid, light yellow with green tints. Expressive nose, floral on first pour then opening up to notes of grapefruit and tropical fruits. The palate is lively, nervy, upright and more subdued in terms of aroma with a pleasant mineral tone.

www.henrynatter.fr

Domaine Henry Natter

+33 (0)2 48 69 58 85

DOMAINE DE LA GARENNE   86/100

▼♪ Vintage 2013 : Pale gold. Highly aromatic nose wavering between pineapple, grapefruit and tropical fruits with subtle floral undertones. Supple, charming palate with crisp, crunchy fruit and freshness supporting the whole. A quaffer suitable for any occasion.

Price approx.: 8,50 EUR

http://www.sancerrelagarenne.com

Domaine de la Garenne

+33 (0)2 48 79 35 79

JEAN-MAX ROGER   86/100

▼♪ Cuvée G.C. 2013 : Light gold. Refined nose showing subtle boxwood and grapefruit aromas. Inviting palate boasting a faint youthful beading. The aromas are still a little fiery but should rapidly bond. Beautiful overall freshness. A Sancerre with good breeding.

Price approx.: 12,00 EUR

www.jean-max-roger.fr

Domaine Jean-Max Roger

+33 (0)2 48 54 32 20

DOMAINE JEAN-PAUL RICARD   86/100

▼♪ Vintage 2012 : Vibrant ruby. Expressive nose intermixing cherry, morello cherry, fine spice and a vegetal note. Vegetal and spice accents are predominant on the palate at the moment but fullness and some fine tannins ensure a harmonious future.

Price approx.: 8,70 EUR

Jean Paul Picard et Fils

+33 (0)2 48 54 16 13

ROGER CHAMPAULT   86/100

▼♪ Les Pierris 2013 : Attractive, brilliant cherry-red. Elegant nose recalling cherry and redcurrant. Lovely succulence, fullness and impression of harmony on the palate then closely-integrated, fine tannins and a spicy finish. Boasts undeniable qualities.

Price approx.: 9,20 EUR

http://www.rogerchampaultetfils.fr

Roger Champault et Fils

+33 (0)2 48 79 00 03

DOMAINE DES CHASSEIGNES   86/100

▼♪ Vintage 2013 : Brilliant pale yellow. Pleasurable nose of grapefruit and lemon with tangy notes. Fresh attack leading into a crunchy palate where a vegetal note combines with the fruit. Exuberant and well-balanced. A lovely Sancerre for the aperitif and seafood.

Price approx.: 6,80 EUR

Domaine des Chasseignes

+33 (0)2 48 79 36 84

DOMAINE SERGE LAPORTE   86/100

▼♪ Esprit 2012 : Slightly mature, limpid red. Fresh, floral nose of plum and cherry with oak undertones. Supple attack flowing into a full, fairly rich and delightful palate. Certainly doesn't lack charm. Spicy, vegetal, persistent finish.

Price approx.: 8,70 EUR

http://www.domainesergelaporte.com

Domaine Serge Laporte

+33 (0)2 48 54 30 10

JEAN-MARC & MATHIEU CROCHET   86/100

▼♪ Vintage 2013 : Pale gold. Floral-dominant nose backed by citrus, tropical fruits and a menthol touch. Heady palate showing appealing crunchy, tangy aromatics. Beautiful perfume-infused length. A distinctive Sancerre that you'll want to drink as soon as you smell it.

Price approx.: 8,70 EUR

http://www.jean-marc-mathieu-crochet.com

Jean-Marc Crochet

+33 (0)2 48 54 11 30

DOMAINE BIZET   85/100

▼♪ Célestin 2012 : Dark purple. Inviting nose driven by cherry and red berry fruits. Soft, light and fresh palate. A traditional, thirst-quenching Sancerre with enticing fruit. Ideal for mildly-flavoured terrines.

Price approx.: 9,50 EUR

http://www.sancerre-bizet.com

Domaine Bizet

+33 (0)2 48 79 34 43

DOMAINE PHILIPPE RAIMBAULT   85/100

▼♪ Les Godons 2011 : Fairly lightly-coloured red with crimson tints. Mature nose of ripe red berry fruits. Supple, full palate with predominant fruit. Ripe, mellow tannins. Intense, spice-driven finish. A wine for quaffing, drinking well from now on with grilled meats.
Price approx.: 9,40 EUR
www.philipperaimbault.fr
Philippe Raimbault
+33 (0)2 48 79 29 54

DOMAINE BIZET   85/100

▼♪ Vintage 2013 : Pale gold. Distinctive nose showing accents of grapefruit, pineapple and a floral setting. Very supple, very soft palate with a lovely crispness. Focused, persistent perfumes. A truly thirst-quenching Sancerre. Uncork from the aperitif onwards.
Price approx.: 7,20 EUR
http://www.sancerre-bizet.com
Domaine Bizet
+33 (0)2 48 79 34 43

DOMAINE DES CHASSEIGNES   85/100

▼♪ Vintage 2013 : Limpid salmon-pink. Delightful nose of red berry fruits such as strawberry with crisp tones. Supple attack flowing into a round, nervy palate showing refined spice. Fresh finish that is a tad angular. An enjoyable wine that works well with summery foods.
Price approx.: 6,80 EUR
Domaine des Chasseignes
+33 (0)2 48 79 36 84

MATHHIAS ET EMILE ROBLIN   84/100

▼♪ Origine 2012 : Garnet hue with crimson and dark purple shades. Ripe fruity nose recalling apple and cherry flesh. Cherry prevails on the palate which is supple, fleshy and jammy in style. A likeable wine showing at its best when young.
Price approx.: 13,00 EUR
http://www.sancerre-roblin.com
Domaine Matthias et Emile Roblin
+33 (0)2 48 79 48 85

DOMAINE BIZET   83/100

▼♪ Vintage 2013 : Dark purple. The nose is driven by cherry, cassis and raspberry. Very supple, light palate successfully focusing on fruity freshness. An easy-drinking style, enjoyable from now on over a meal with friends.
Price approx.: 7,20 EUR
http://www.sancerre-bizet.com
Domaine Bizet
+33 (0)2 48 79 34 43

SAUMUR CHAMPIGNY

CHÂTEAU DE TARGÉ   88/100

▼♪ Vintage 2012 : Young garnet. Distinctive nose driven by ripe forest fruits coupled with elegant earthy notes. Clean, full palate with intense, persistent perfumes. Hallmark Cabernet Franc aromas with an assertive sense of place. Perfect for roast poultry.
Price approx.: 9,00 EUR
www.chateaudetarge.fr
Château de Targé
+33 (0)2 41 38 11 50

CHÂTEAU DE CHAINTRES   88/100

CONV▼♪ Clos des Oratoriens 2008 : Beautiful concentrated garnet. Refined nose of melted oak with huge jammy red fruit presence and nicely ripe vegetal aromas. Generosity, fullness and huge fruit presence. A characterful Champigny that makes a perfect companion for roast game.
Price approx.: 15,00 EUR
http://www.chaintres.com
Château de Chaintres
+33 (0)2 41 52 90 54

CHÂTEAU DE CHAINTRES   86/100

CONV▼♪ Vintage 2010 : Deeply-coloured with young garnet tints. Distinctive, endearing nose with accents of blackberries and redcurrants backed by bell pepper. A delectable Champigny with silky, soft substance focusing on fruit and freshness. Drink whilst still fruit-forward.
Price approx.: 8,50 EUR
http://www.chaintres.com
Château de Chaintres
+33 (0)2 41 52 90 54

DOMAINE DES HAUTES TROGLODYTES 84/100

▼♪ Vintage 2013 : Young colour with dark purple tints. Nose of fresh red and black berry fruits coupled with a vegetal touch. Easy-drinking palate combining exuberance and fruity freshness. A style with real drive, showing at its best when young and still fruit-forward.
Price approx.: 6,22 EUR
http://www.joseph-verdier.fr
Joseph Verdier-Logel
+33 (0)2 41 40 22 50

SAUMUR

BOUVET   90/100

▼♪ Brut Trésor 2009 : Brilliant yellow, minute bubbles. Refined nose of ripe white-fleshed fruits, a creamy base and white pepper. Fleshy, rich palate with spicy, buttery touches, consistent, refined exuberance and an impression

of exotic wood.
Price approx.: 13,60 EUR
http://www.bouvet-ladubay.fr
Bouvet Ladubay
+33 (0)2 41 83 83 83

CHÂTEAU DE TARGÉ   88/100

▼♪ Brut 0 : Light gold. Refined nose with accents of peach and stewed white fruits backed by elegant mushroom aromas. Delicate palate with silky effervescence. Abundant freshness enveloping the fruit perfumes. A refined dry sparkling wine for canapes.
Price approx.: 9,50 EUR
www.chateaudetarge.fr
Château de Targé
+33 (0)2 41 38 11 50

DOMAINE DE MONTFORT   87/100

▼♪ Saveurs d'Antan 2011 : Deep garnet. Cassis, blackberry and redcurrant drive the nose with chalky and earthy undertones. Supple, full and robust palate showing generous fruit. The tannins are upfront and polished. Persistent spice and chalk-driven finish. A successful wine.
Price approx.: 15,00 EUR
http://www.domainedemontfort.com
Domaine de Montfort
+33 (0)6 19 65 22 00

DOMAINE DE LA SEIGNEURIE DES TOURELLES
87/100

▼♪ Vintage 2013 : Light gold. Enticing nose showing tropical nuances of peach and apricot with mineral undertones. Still a little firm at point of entry, fruit and freshness come to the fore on the finish. Generous mouthfeel. Substantial sense of place. Needs confirmation.
Price approx.: 5,72 EUR
http://www.joseph-verdier.fr
Joseph Verdier-Logel
+33 (0)2 41 40 22 50

DOMAINE DE MONTFORT   86/100

▼♪ La Chapelle 2012 : Deep garnet with crimson highlights. Pleasant nose intermixing red and black fruits, flowers and earthy undercurrents. Supple, round and chalky palate with fruit supported by wonderful freshness. A good Saumur.
Price approx.: 9,00 EUR
http://www.domainedemontfort.com
Domaine de Montfort
+33 (0)6 19 65 22 00

BOUVET   85/100

▼♪ Brut Vintage Saphir 2011 : Light yellow, good effervescence. Compelling nose of white-fleshed fruits and honeysuckle. Elegant palate with upright, focused aromas and a substantial freshness imparting a lovely crunchiness.

A successful offering with a richness making it suitable for
Price approx.: 9,60 EUR
http://www.bouvet-ladubay.fr
Bouvet Ladubay
+33 (0)2 41 83 83 83

DOMAINE DE MONTFORT   85/100

▼♪ Vintage 2012 : Deep garnet with crimson tints. Pleasurable nose of blackberry and cherry. Supple, full and powerful palate showing focused fruit expression. Concentrated structure with tightly-wound tannins. Hint of bitterness on the finish. A well-crafted Saumur.
Price approx.: 6,00 EUR
http://www.domainedemontfort.com
Domaine de Montfort
+33 (0)6 19 65 22 00

BOUVET   84/100

▼♪ Brut Saumur   : Light yellow with abundant effervescence. Pleasant nose suggestive of springtime flowers. Fairly vinous palate perfumed with intense aromas and supported by robust exuberance. Good persistency. A good Crémant for the aperitif, served with canapes.
Price approx.: 8,25 EUR
http://www.bouvet-ladubay.fr
Bouvet Ladubay
+33 (0)2 41 83 83 83

ALLIANCE LOIRE   84/100

▼♪ Duc de Berry 2013 : Young, morello-cherry red. Refined nose of wild berries with woodland and vegetal aromas. Fruit and freshness make it a supple, soft wine on the palate. Earthy nose and delicious palate - the prerequisite ingredients for a good barbecue wine.
Price approx.: 4,90 EUR
http://www.allianceloire.com
Alliance Loire
+33 (0)2 41 53 74 44

DOMAINE DE LA SEIGNEURIE DES TOURELLES
84/100

▼♪ Vintage 2013 : Young ruby. Distinctive Cabernet-style nose midway between bell pepper and ripe red fruits. Easy-drinking, supple palate with soft fruit and freshness. A pleasurable companion for an entire meal.
Price approx.: 5,50 EUR
http://www.joseph-verdier.fr
Joseph Verdier-Logel
+33 (0)2 41 40 22 50

SAVENNIÈRES

DOMAINE DES BAUMARD   93/100

CONV▼ ♪ Clos St Yves 2010 : Pale yellow. Pure nose marked by a mineral character, floral undertones and flower and honey notes. Remarkably full yet ethereal palate. Lingering freshness developing an assertive mineral character on the finish supports the whole.
Price approx.: 14,50 EUR
http://www.baumard.fr
Domaine des Baumard
+33 (0)2 41 78 70 03

DOMAINE DU CLOSEL   92/100

CONV▼ ♪ Clos du Papillon 2008 : Beautiful gold. The nose shows accents of candied fruits, mild spices and minerality. Full-bodied yet delicate, rich yet refined, mature and fully revealing its entire aromatic spectrum. A superlative wine for cellaring, pairing marvellously with lobster.
Price approx.: 25,00 EUR
www.savennieres-closel.com
Domaine du Closel
+33 (0)2 41 72 81 00

CHÂTEAU DE BELLEVUE   87/100

▼ ♪ La Croix Picot 2012 : Light gold. Fruit-driven nose halfway between white and tropical fruits. A full, supple Savennières where fruit takes a lead role. Lovely length and freshness. A pleasurable wine in its youth and a marvellous companion for flambeed king prawns.
Price approx.: 10,00 EUR
www.chateaudebellevue.fr
Château de Bellevue
+33 (0)2 41 78 33 11

TOURAINE AMBOISE

DOMAINE DUTERTRE   84/100

▼ ♪ Cuvée Prestige 2012 : Beautiful deep colour with dark purple tints. Unrefined oak prevails over the fruit on the nose. Ethereal palate where shy fruit notes (currants, blackberries) are still under oak influence. Firm, vegetal finish. Needs a little patience.
Price approx.: 6,30 EUR
http://www.domainedutertre.fr
Domaine Dutertre
+33 (0)2 47 30 10 69

TOURAINE CHENONCEAUX

DOMAINE DE LA ROCHETTE   89/100

▼ ♪ Sauvignon 2012 : Pale yellow. Refined, expressive nose driven by citrus notes of grapefruit augmented by a mineral dimension. Full, powerful attack leading into a lively, fresh mid-palate. Fine-grained texture. The fruit flows into a mineral character on the finish.
Price approx.: 8,00 EUR
http://www.vin-rochette-leclair.com
Domaine de la Rochette
+33 (0)2 54 71 44 02

DOMAINE DE LA RABLAIS   87/100

▼ ♪ Vintage 2012 : Beautiful young, deep colour. Refined, heady nose driven by peony, violet, wild blackberry and a touch of smoke. More of the same aromatics on the palate. Very honest, dense and expressive. Substantial floral edge. A Chenonceaux for grilled foods.
Price approx.: 8,00 EUR
http://www.antoinesimoneau.com
Domaine de la Rablais
+33 (0)2 54 71 36 14

TOURAINE

DOMAIN JOËL DELAUNAY   92/100

▼ ♪ La Voûte 2013 : Pale gold with green tints. Delicate nose intermixing white flowers and an assertive mineral dimension with citrus undertones. Wonderful fullness on the palate, silky texture and superb exuberance. More of the fruit and mineral nose character.
Price approx.: 7,20 EUR
http://www.joeldelaunay.com
Domaine Joël Delaunay
+33 (0)2 54 71 45 69

DOMAINE JOËL DELAUNAY   90/100

▼ ♪ Sauvignon 2013 : Pale yellow with green tints. Highly expressive nose revealing perfumes of grapefruit, blackcurrant bud and broom. The palate shows seductively balanced fat and exuberance. Fresh and persistent. A very compelling Touraine Sauvignon.
Price approx.: 5,90 EUR
http://www.joeldelaunay.com
Domaine Joël Delaunay
+33 (0)2 54 71 45 69

DOMAINE DE LA BROSSETTE   89/100

Org▼ ♪ Vintage 2012 : Appealing ruby, cherry-red tints. Precise, delicate nose opening up to red berry fruit aromas backed by pepper and spice with a delightful vegetal dimension. More of the same precision on the palate which is round and fresh with a fine, polished texture.
Price approx.: 8,50 EUR
http://www.joeldelaunay.com
Domaine Joël Delaunay
+33 (0)2 54 71 45 69

DOMAINE DE LA BROSSETTE 89/100

Org▼✔ Vintage 2013 : Attractive clean pink. The nose opens up to red fruits then delivers mineral and milky perfumes. Soft, closely-integrated attack leading into a fresh, upright mid-palate then a pleasant crisp finish. Lovely pure expression.
Price approx.: 8,50 EUR
http://www.joeldelaunay.com
Domaine Joël Delaunay
+33 (0)2 54 71 45 69

JEAN-FRANÇOIS MÉRIEAU 89/100

▼✔ Cent Visages 2010 : Beautiful deep red, crimson tints. Delightful, focused nose intermixing ripe strawberry, cherry, plum flesh and mineral undertones. Beautiful fleshy, crunchy, melted attack showing focused fruit expression framed by freshness, great persistence.
Price approx.: 10,00 EUR
http://www.merieau.com
Domaine Mérieau
+33 (0)2 54 32 14 23

DOMAINE GUENAULT 87/100

▼✔ Vintage 2013 : Light gold. Distinctive nose developing crunchy citrus and white fruit perfumes. Pronounced floral aromas of nettle and boxwood. A refreshing, impish and very supple Sauvignon. Long-lasting range of crisp aromatics. A wine for whetting the appetite.
Price approx.: 4,99 EUR
www.bougrier.fr
Bougrier SA
+33 (0)2 54 32 31 36

DOMAINE DE LA COLLINE 87/100

▼✔ Vintage 2013 : Pale gold. Appealing floral and fruity nose displaying citrus and exotic fruits. The palate shows real drive and boasts lovely exuberance. Pleasant, long-lasting crisp aromatics. A Sauvignon in a 'drink-me' style.
Price approx.: 5,02 EUR
http://www.joseph-verdier.fr
Joseph Verdier-Logel
+33 (0)2 41 40 22 50

DOMAINE DE LA ROCHETTE 87/100

▼✔ Sauvignon 2013 : Pale yellow-green. Expressive nose blending white-fleshed fruits, a mineral dimension and subtle citrus touches. Fleshy, crunchy attack with lovely fat framed by a tangy freshness. Pleasant saline sensation on the finish. Set aside for seafood.
Price approx.: 5,00 EUR
http://www.vin-rochette-leclair.com
Domaine de la Rochette
+33 (0)2 54 71 44 02

A. SIMONEAU 86/100

▼✔ Brut Rosé - Méthode traditionnelle : Brilliant salmon-pink. Nose of ripe red fruits and citrus. Delightful vinous, focused palate driven by ripe perfumes. Overall freshness. An honest, proud and intransigent rosé. Uncork for a tangerine tart.
Price approx.: 5,10 EUR
http://www.antoinesimoneau.com
Domaine de la Rablais
+33 (0)2 54 71 36 14

LES CAVES DE LA TOURANGELLE 86/100

▼✔ Sauvignon 2013 : Pale gold. Distinctive nose halfway between pink grapefruit, boxwood and blackcurrant bud. Light and easy-drinking with freshness supporting tangy aromas. A very thirst-quenching Sauvignon with delicious crunchy fruit. Perfect for soft goats cheese.
Price approx.: 4,39 EUR
www.bougrier.fr
Bougrier SA
+33 (0)2 54 32 31 36

VIGNOBLE DINOCHEAU 86/100

▼✔ Vintage 2011 : Very deep garnet. Mature nose blending spice, red fruits (cassis) and floral notes. Supple, full and fresh palate revealing all of the nose aromatics. Spice-driven finish with a mineral touch. A seductive Touraine, drinking well now.
Price approx.: 6,50 EUR
http://www.vignoble-dinocheau.fr/
Vignoble Dinocheau
+33 (0)2 54 71 73 08

DOMAINE DE LA CHARMOISE 86/100

▼✔ Sauvignon 2013 : Light golden yellow. Elegant nose intermixing floral touches with ripe apple. Aromatic attack, lively palate with an elegant crispness, faint beading and generous expression. A successful Sauvignon with character.
Price approx.: 6,50 EUR
http://www.henry-marionnet.com
Domaine de la Charmoise
+33 (0)2 54 98 70 73

DOMAINE DE LA CHARMOISE 86/100

▼✔ Henri Marionnet 2013 : Deep vibrant red with dark purple tints. Pleasant nose merging red fruits with a clutch of refined spices. Light, lively and delightful palate, showing a delicate crunchiness and more of the nose aromatics. Hint of firmness. A good Gamay.
Price approx.: 6,50 EUR
http://www.henry-marionnet.com
Domaine de la Charmoise
+33 (0)2 54 98 70 73

FAMILLE BOUGRIER 85/100

▼ ♪ Vintage 2013 : Pale gold with brilliant highlights. Refined nose with floral and white fruit accents and grapefruit aromas. An expressive Sauvignon boasting savoury exuberance on the attack, rapidly flowing into fruit. Tropical finish. Clear varietal character.
Price approx.: 4,39 EUR
www.bougrier.fr
Bougrier SA
+33 (0)2 54 32 31 36

ALLIANCE LOIRE 85/100

▼ ♪ Vallée Loire 2013 : Pale gold. Endearing nose showing refined floral aromas of blackcurrant bud backed by grapefruit and pineapple. A vibrant, crisp Sauvignon showcasing distinctive, focused perfumes. A very enjoyable wine for sharing and ideal for mussels.
Price approx.: 10,75 EUR
http://www.allianceloire.com
Alliance Loire
+33 (0)2 41 53 74 44

VILLEBOIS 84/100

▼ ♪ Vintage 2013 : Brilliant light hue with green tints. Refined nose of citrus tinged with fine minerality. The palate also focuses on finesse with precise, delicate aromas and nicely harnessed exuberance. Ethereal and pairing best with delicately-flavoured fish.
Price approx.: 6,00 EUR
Villebois

A. SIMONEAU 84/100

▼ ♪ Brut - Méthode Traditionnelle : Pale gold. Appealing mineral and bush peach aromas on the nose. Soft, supple palate with lovely vinosity. Focused fruit. Mellow finish. A good dry sparkling wine for the aperitif or petits fours.
Price approx.: 5,10 EUR
http://www.antoinesimoneau.com
Domaine de la Rablais
+33 (0)2 54 71 36 14

DOMAINE DE LA COLLINE 84/100

▼ ♪ Gamay 2013 : Ruby-hued. Nose of red berry fruits. Supple, light and soft palate showing seductive crunchy fruit. A traditional, easy-drinking Gamay that makes the perfect partner for grilled sausages.
Price approx.: 4,60 EUR
http://www.joseph-verdier.fr
Joseph Verdier-Logel
+33 (0)2 41 40 22 50

JEAN-FRANÇOIS MÉRIEAU 84/100

▼ ♪ Coeur de Roche 2010 : Limpid pale yellow. The nose combines a mineral dimension with notes of grapefruit. Warm attack on the palate leading into a lively, nervy mid-palate. More of the two aromatic nose components - minerality and grapefruit.
Price approx.: 12,00 EUR
http://www.merieau.com
Domaine Mérieau
+33 (0)2 54 32 14 23

DOMAINE DE LA ROCHETTE 83/100

▼ ♪ Fleur de Printemps 2013 : Light red. Fruit-driven nose showing accents of ripe cherry. The palate is supple, well-balanced and fruity. A real treat that would work well with a platter of cold meats.
Price approx.: 5,00 EUR
http://www.vin-rochette-leclair.com
Domaine de la Rochette
+33 (0)2 54 71 44 02

JEAN-FRANÇOIS MÉRIEAU 83/100

▼ ♪ L'alliance des générations 2005 : Appealing garnet hue. Focused, profound nose of ripe fruits, notes of undergrowth and a mineral dimension. Beautiful supple, silky and fresh attack. The middle palate is firmer, showing oak aromatics tinged with a faint bitterness. Ready to drink now.
Price approx.: 11,00 EUR
http://www.merieau.com
Domaine Mérieau
+33 (0)2 54 32 14 23

VILLEBOIS 82/100

▼ ♪ Prestige 2013 : Brilliant pale hue with green tints. Expressive nose of grapefruit, blackcurrant leaf and a mineral touch. Round, likeable and fresh palate showing character. The aromas could be a tad snappier. A focused wine that pairs best with fish curry.
Price approx.: 7,50 EUR
Villebois

VIGNOBLE DINOCHEAU 81/100

▼ ♪ Sauvignon Blanc 2013 : Brilliant pale yellow with green tints. Focused nose driven by grapefruit, gunflint and white flowers. Lively attack leading into a delicious, fresh, round palate revealing citrus fruits. Faint beading. A fiery wine drinking well in a year or two.
Price approx.: 6,00 EUR
http://www.vignoble-dinocheau.fr
Vignoble Dinocheau
+33 (0)2 54 71 73 08

VIGNOBLE DINOCHEAU 79/100

✳ ♪ Pineau d'Aunis 2013 : Light orange-pink. Subdued nose driven by red fruit notes. Focused freshness and lightweight mouthfeel with minerality prevailing over the fruit. Slightly sour finish. A rosé for food.
Price approx.: 6,00 EUR
http://www.vignoble-dinocheau.fr/
Vignoble Dinocheau
+33 (0)2 54 71 73 08

VAL DE LOIRE

DOMAINE DE LA RABLAIS 86/100

Cuvée St Georges 2013 : Pale gold with green tints. Charming nose showing accents of white fruits, peach and wild flowers. Distinctive palate with nicely harnessed exuberance. More of the same zippy nose aromatics. A beautiful opening wine that also pairs well with oysters.
Price approx.: 3,90 EUR
http://www.antoinesimoneau.com
Domaine de la Rablais
+33 (0)2 54 71 36 14

DOMAINE DES IRIS 85/100

Sauvignon 2013 : Pale-hued. Endearing nose showing accents of fruits in syrup, pineapple, pink grapefruit and meadow. A soft Sauvignon boasting roundness, freshness, fruit and balance. Enjoyable at any time of the day and on any occasion.
Price approx.: 4,60 EUR
http://www.joseph-verdier.fr
Joseph Verdier-Logel
+33 (0)2 41 40 22 50

MONTGILET 84/100

Sauvignon 2013 : Brilliant pale hue with green tints. Pleasant nose suggestive of citrus and blackcurrant bud. An easy-drinking, supple and likeable wine with distinctive, focused and clearly-delineated aromas. Very light and delicate. A good, versatile Sauvignon.
Price approx.: 5,30 EUR
www.montgilet.com
Domaine de Montgilet
+33 (0)2 41 91 90 48

VILLEBOIS 83/100

Petit Villebois 2013 : Pale hue with green tints. Distinctive nose of boxwood, blackcurrant leaf and citrus. Lightweight palate successfully aiming for drinkability with snappy aromas, crunchy exuberance and lovely aromatic intensity. A nice wine for the aperitif or seafood.
Price approx.: 4,90 EUR
Villebois

CAVES DE LA TOURANGELLE 83/100

Vintage 2013 : Orange-pink. Pleasant crisp nose showing perfumes of redcurrant and tangerine. A very supple, light rosé displaying seductive freshness and a delightful array of aromas. A simple wine for sharing. Pair with summer salads.
Price approx.: 3,99 EUR
www.bougrier.fr
Bougrier SA
+33 (0)2 54 32 31 36

DOMAINE DES IRIS 78/100

Chardonnay 2013 : Pale gold. Nose of white fruits and linden. Supple, light and perfumed palate showing freshness. A very accessible Chardonnay.
Price approx.: 4,60 EUR
http://www.joseph-verdier.fr
Joseph Verdier-Logel
+33 (0)2 41 40 22 50

VOUVRAY

DOMAINE DU CLOS DE L'EPINAY 88/100

CONV Cuvée Marcus 2011 : Light yellow. Distinctive nose with notes of bush peach backed by smoke and mineral aromas. Delicate palate brimming with freshness bordering on menthol which promotes focused Chenin expression. Intense fruit and mineral aromas.
Price approx.: 8,90 EUR
http://www.vinvouvray.com
Domaine du Clos de l'Epinay
+33 (0)2 47 52 61 90

BARTON & GUESTIER 86/100

Passeport 2012 : Light yellow. Fresh nose driven by bush peach with mineral and floral undertones. Soft, easy-drinking, crisp palate with some sweetness, highly aromatic, focused freshness. Lingering finish suffused with yellow fruits.
Price approx.: 7,00 EUR
http://www.barton-guestier.com
Barton & Guestier
+33 (0)5 56 95 48 00

ALLIANCE LOIRE 85/100

Brut Excellence - Tête de Cuvée - De Chanceny 2012 : Light gold. Vinous, mineral nose backed by fresh mushroom and ripe white fruits. The palate is augmented by a welcome floral touch. Clean freshness and savoury acidity. A distinctive Vouvray with presence, pairing with, say, goats cheese canapes.
Price approx.: 11,60 EUR
http://www.allianceloire.com
Alliance Loire
+33 (0)2 41 53 74 44

PROVENCE

MORE THAN JUST ROSÉ

The wine region of Provence begins south of Avignon, on the southern banks of the Durance, and ends up in the hills overlooking Nice. Flanked by the Mediterranean, the entire region basks in the balmy climate of the same name, whose defining characteristic is hot, dry summers. Its size and rugged terrain, however, (due to the nearby Alps) have shaped its diversity. Provence boasts no fewer than 9 appellations, the largest being AC Côtes de Provence spanning three departments: Bouches-du-Rhône, Var and Alpes-Maritimes.

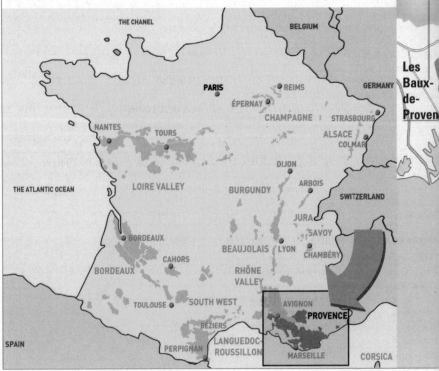

Les Baux-de-Proven

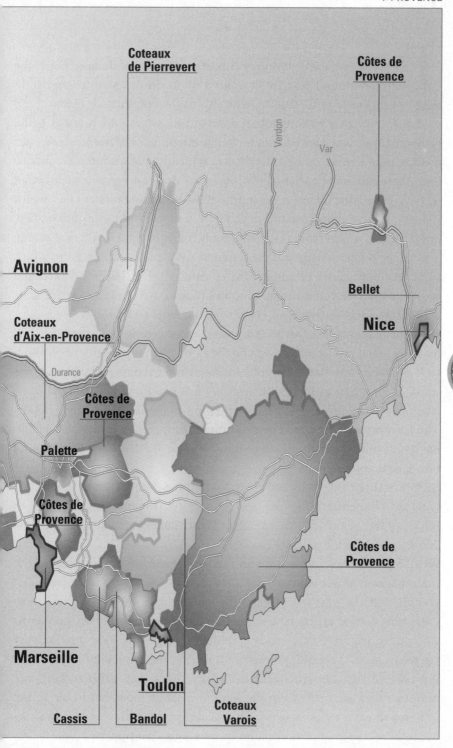

Coteaux
de Pierrevert

Côtes de
Provence

Verdon

Var

Avignon

Bellet

Coteaux
d'Aix-en-Provence

Nice

Durance

335

Côtes de
Provence

Palette

Côtes de
Provence

Côtes de
Provence

Marseille

Toulon

Cassis

Bandol

Coteaux
Varois

Travelling east, the environment undergoes a series of changes: limestone hillsides around Baux-de-Provence with its distinct Mediter-ranean climate - Montagne-Sainte-Victoire with its more continental climate and sandstone, clay soils yielding robust, idiosyncratic wines - the Beausset basin, between Cassis and Bandol, where the limestone terrain, swept over by sea breezes, produces warm, typically Provençal blends - the sea-influenced coastline where extremely ancient soils formed of shale and granite yield wines with character - the inland valley, north of the Maures mountain range which supplies a large chunk of the region's AC output, producing full-bodied, powerful reds drawn from clay-sand Cambrian soils - and finally, the rolling hills of the highland region, limestone remnants of the Alpine folds, which accounts for a quarter of output. The climate, which is harsh in winter and often extremely hot in summer, produces robust, well-structured yet delicate wines. They can take longer to mature and are more secret wines.

The climate and landscapes of Provence have for a long time attracted holidaymakers and investors from around the globe. The growing tide of pleasure-seeking consumers and a plentiful source of money obviousl y provide the stimulus for advances in quality by giving free rein to initiative. Sleepy wine farms have been given a new lease of life by enterprising, wealthy investors who leave no stone unturned in their quest to fully realise the 'terroir's' potential. Local initiatives also abound, however, and the resultant drive behind Provence is uplifting.

GRAPE VARIETALS: Reds and rosés: Grenache, Syrah, Cinsault, Mourvedre, Carignan, Cabernet, Tibouren and Cabernet-Sauvignon (Coteaux d'Aix); Whites: Rolle, Semillon, Clairette, Ugni Blanc, Sauvignon and Marsanne (the last three are specific to white Cassis).

WINE STYLES: Provence is the world's leading producer of rosé wines. Light, fresh, pleasant wines when young, their quality has improved in leaps and bounds over the past few years. Although some are still enjoyable 'thirst-quenching' wines, others have earned a place on well-set tables, partnering with grilled fish, shellfish, salads or white meat. Their success if reflected in the price tags of the top-flight wines, which can command up to 15 euros.

Provence though also produces red wines which are worth seeking out. Although they are made from the same varietal range, they run the gamut in terms of wine styles. A varietal like Carignan can yield superlative wines when the whole grape fermentation process is used. It imparts a host of aromas and freshness though requires early-drinking. Conversely, longer vatting periods for the reds extract more tannins, which are then often perfected by oak ageing; they have greater structure and need to spend a year or two in the bottle to mellow. The better vintages of these deep, complex wines can be laid down. Provence's greatest reds come from Bandol where the dominant varietal is Mourvedre (which is said only to realise its full potential when planted in sight of the sea). Bandol reds are powerful, though well-balanced. They are aged for a minimum of eighteen months (often in oak tuns) before being released, which imparts structure, depth and fullness. In the early years they display fruity, floral (violet) and spicy aromas (pepper, liquorice). As they age, their aromas span an even broader range and their mellow bouquet is occasionally reminiscent of leather, mushroom and undergrowth.

The white wines are produced on a more boutique scale (roughly 5%). They cover a broad aromatic spectrum, ranging from floral, fruity and acidulous to mineral. White wines from Provence flourish around Cassis, within the boundaries of the town which lent its name to the appellation (1936). Their unusual varietal combination imparts a genuine aromatic personality (thyme, sage, wild mint...), and they invariably display a delicious contrast between fat and vigour...

337

REVIEW OF RECENT VINTAGES

• **2010** • Volumes are generally up on 2009 probably due to rainfall in winter and spring and fairly low temperatures. The mistral wind dried out the vineyards and kept the crop disease-free. A good vintage!

• **2011** • A rainy winter, a hot, dry spring and intermittent storms over the summer: Provence experienced the same weather patterns as other parts of France. No serious damage occurred but the stormy weather led to the region's hallmark disparities from one area to another. Juice yields were often lower than in 2010, particularly in inland areas. Although output was still dominated by rosés, the vintage produced some superlative reds.

• **2012** • The 2012 vintage is quite good, although it varies considerably from one appellation to another, and even more so from one estate to another. Following a mild and very dry winter (just 53 mm of precipitation during the season), the spring was hot, especially from May onwards. During the summer, the drought was detrimental to the development and ripening of the grapes; only after several rains in September did ripening restart.

• **2013** • Despite a long, cold and wet winter and spring, and a two-week
delay in harvesting compared with 2012, the final outcome is actually quite
positive. Apart from shatter and shot berries in some western areas, reple-
nished water supplies enabled vineyards to avoid water stress and to deliver
yields promoting the production of quality wines. The rosés in particular
show fresh, intense and pure aromatics.

THE PROVENCE APPELLATIONS

A.C. BANDOL

OVERVIEW: AC Bandol embraces eight villages in the foothills of the Sainte
Baume mountain range overlooking the Mediterranean, where soil make-up
is formed of calcareous silica, sandstone and sandy marl. This particular site
enjoys 3,000 hours of sunshine annually, elevating both the fruitiness and
the quality of the wines. Mild winters, early springs and hot summers also
factor into this matrix. The reds are vinted traditionally and spend at least
18 months in oak tuns. Drawn from the same varietal range as the reds -
namely Mourvedre (at least 50%), Grenache, Cinsault and a tiny proportion
of Carignan and Syrah - the rosés are made using the direct to press method.
The less common whites come from Bourboulenc, Clairette and Ugni blanc,
with a balance of Sauvignon (no more than 40%).
WINE STYLES: Bandol is renowned above all for its reds and rosés. The red
wines (which account for 30% of output) exhibit a deep colour, are well-
structured, powerful and aromatic (morello cherry, raspberry, violet, blackcurrant, iris, dill); 4 to 5 years down the line, they exude aromas of truffle,
undergrowth, liquorice, cinnamon or musk. They boast an outstanding
lifespan. Enjoy with Sisteron lamb, goat meat with garlic or Provençal Banon
goat's cheese. The rosés (60% of output) with their extremely pale salmon-
pink hue, are well-balanced and conjure up aromas of ripe grapes and morello
cherries layered over spices. Enjoy with a courgette tart doused with olive oil,
fish or grilled white meat. The straw-yellow colour whites are dry, vigorous
and fragrant (citrus fruits, pear, linden and broom). Try them with shellfish,
fish and goat's cheeses.

A.C. BELLET

OVERVIEW: Bellet is a minute appellation set in the hills overlooking Nice.
Very few wines are actually produced here but their reputation is well-esta-

blished. Virtually all of them are sold in the hotels along the French Riviera, making them difficult to come by. Vineyard soils are formed of pebbles intermingled with very pale sand and the occasional seam of clay. The site also enjoys an outstanding micro-climate with 2,700 hours of sunshine annually and just the right amount of rainfall. The varietal range is quite unusual: Braquet, Folle noire, Cinsault and Grenache noir for the reds. Rolle, Roussanne, Spagnol as well as Clairette, Bourboulenc, Chardonnay, Pignerol and small-berry Muscat for the whites.

WINE STYLES: Bellet produces equal amounts of white, red and rosé wines. The whites, with their deep, bright hue, are full and suave. They develop aromas of hawthorn, honeysuckle and ripe pear and sit nicely alongside fish in a cream sauce, veal cutlets with mushrooms and Comté cheese. The rosés are soft, lively but not too sharp, with a delicate bouquet (wild rose, pepper). Served with lamb and sweet pepper kebabs, they form an unrivalled match. The reds are rich, elegant and vigorous. They exhibit pleasant aromas of peony, pepper and pine forests. Try them with a grilled leg of lamb with herbs or pork roast with prunes.

339

A.C. CASSIS

OVERVIEW: the Cassis appellation shares the same boundaries as the town of the same name in the Bouches-du-Rhône department, a few kilometres from Marseilles. Cretaceous limestone and limestone or marl scree are the constituent soil types of this site. The surrounding hillsides deflect the Mistral wind and gentle sea breezes comb through the vines which bask in 3,000 hours of sunshine and receive 670 mm of annual rainfall.

WINE STYLES: AC Cassis produces primarily white wines (70%) blended from a varietal range predominantly formed by Clairette, Marsanne, Sauvignon and Ugni blanc. The wines are dry and heady with a discrete nose (grapefruit, pear, quince, pine resin). They are fat and long on the palate. Pair with Bouillabaisse fish stew with garlic mayonnaise, bass with fennel, anchoïade or anchovy dip, sea urchins and fish served in a cream sauce. The rosés are blended from Barbaroux, Carignan, Cinsault, Grenache and Mourvedre; they are fruity, supple and delicate with a pleasant raspberry-pink colour. The red wines boast a cherry-red hue and display good balance, nice structure and powerful aromas (ripe fruit, havana, liquorice…). Enjoy with wild boar casserole or small game (thrush or lark).

A.C. COTEAUX D'AIX-EN-PROVENCE

OVERVIEW: the Coteaux d'Aix-en-Provence appellation area embraces 49 towns and villages in two departments: Var and Bouches-du-Rhône. The best known of these is, of course, Aix-en-Provence, though also Salon de Provence, Les Baux-de-Provence, (which has also been an appellation in its own right since 1995), Berre-L'Etang, Martigues, Ventabren, Fontvieille, Istres… A variety of soil types can be found here: stony calcareous clay, sand and gravel. The climate is Mediterranean with low rainfall and the vines bask for the most part in generous sunshine.

WINE STYLES: the vast majority of the wines are rosés, blended from Grenache, Cabernet-Sauvignon and Carignan, sometimes augmented with Cinsault, Syrah and Mourvedre. Made using the 'bleeding' technique, they display a pink hue with orangy tints. They are lively, fresh and fruity with good acidity. Try them with olive paste or Mediterranean fish and shellfish. The white wines, made from Ugni Blanc (no more than 40%), Sauvignon and Semillon (30%), Bourboulenc, Clairette, Grenache and Vermentino, are made by the direct to press method. They are light, fresh and delicate (white fruit, floral fragrances) and are a perfect match for grilled fish with herbs (fennel). The red wines, with their delicate tannins, are fruity and well-balanced. They exude aromas of leather, liquorice, black fruit (blackcurrant, prunes) and spicy notes. Enjoy with grilled meat.

A.C. COTEAUX VAROIS

OVERVIEW: entirely surrounded by the Côtes de Provence appellation, Coteaux Varois embraces 28 towns and villages located in the heart of the Var department. The appellation stretches from the Sainte-Baume mountain range to the Bessillons hills around the small town of Brignoles. The vast majority of the vines are planted on calcareous clay soils, for which the Argens river and its tributaries provide drainage. The prevailing climate is, of course, Mediterranean, though semi-continental influences exercise a moderating effect. These climatic conditions promote gradual ripening of the grapes depending on site elevation across the appellation area.

WINE STYLES: the lion's share of Coteaux Varois are rosés (70%) and reds (25%) with interesting potential. They are blended primarily from Grenache noir, Syrah, Mourvedre (at least 70%) though also Cabernet Sauvignon, Carignan and Cinsault. White wines are also made, on a boutique scale (from

Rolle, Semillon, Ugni blanc, Clairette and Grenache). The rosés are fresh and fruity and exhibit pleasant aromas of red fruit. The reds, with their vermilion hue, are rustic wines. They are well-structured though often display average concentration. They exude fragrances of violet, liquorice, leather, green pepper and black pepper, and they pair well with lamb kebabs, barbecued meat or an informal buffet lunch. The whites are dry and vigorous and conjure up aromas of citrus fruit (grapefruit). They are equally delicious as appetisers or with fish grilled on a bed of bay leaves.

A.C. COTEAUX-DE-PIERREVERT

OVERVIEW: Coteaux de Pierrevert, which is set in the upper reaches of Provence, gained AC status in 1998. The wines hail from villages nestled amongst the hills which run from Villeneuve and Manosque to Pierrevert and Corbières along the right bank of the Durance river and the southern slopes of the Valensole plateau. Coteaux de Pierrevert are the most northerly of the Provençal wines and are often subsumed into the Rhone Valley appellation system. The soils are predominantly limestone interspersed with patches of sand, loam, stones and sandstone. The area enjoys hot, sunny summers though the frequently high day/night temperature differentials can cause dramatic thunderstorms.

WINE STYLES: Rosés are the predominant wine style here. They are blended from Cinsault, Carignan, Grenache noir, Mourvedre and a balance of Oillade, Petite Syrah and Terret. Deep salmon-pink in colour, they are pleasant, floral, fruity wines (rose, lilac, pear drop). The red wines display a beautiful brilliant crimson hue. On the palate, they combine suppleness with vigour and exhibit aromas of ripe fruit (prune, bilberry), a touch of liquorice and a hint of vanilla. The white wines, blended from Grenache blanc, Marsanne, Picpoul, Ugni blanc and Vermentino exude fragrances of hawthorn, dried flowers and citrus fruit. The wines are made by two co-operative wineries and a dozen independent growers.

A.C. CÔTES DE PROVENCE

OVERVIEW: The winegrowing area of Côtes-de-Provence is extensive. It stretches from Marseille to the department of Alpes-Maritimes, covering 84 districts (68 in the Var, 15 in the Bouches-du-Rhône, and one, Villars-sur-Var, in Alpes-Maritimes). Over such a vast surface area, the terroirs are diverse. The

Massif des Maures and the coast form an area composed mainly of granite and schist. From Toulon to Saint-Raphaël, the soils are of sandy clay. The plateaux and hills of Provence consist of limestone. As a whole, the winegrowing region is fragmented, made up of isolated units. Most often, the vines grow up stepped terraces. The region has a Mediterranean climate with long, hot, dry summers, with rain in the spring and autumn. Recently, three new appellations were created: Côtes-de-Provence Sainte-Victoire, to the east of Aix-en-Provence; Côtes-de-Provence La Londe, near Hyères and Bormes-les-Mimosa; and Côtes-de-Provence Fréjus, on the other side of the region, between Saint-Raphaël and Trans-en-Provence. The Côtes de Provence La Londe appellation, near Hyères, was created in 2008.

WINE STYLES: Rosé wines are the predominant style (80%) though red wines (15%) are on the increase. The varietal range comprises Cinsault, Grenache, Mourvedre, Syrah and Tibouren, augmented with Cabernet-Sauvignon and Carignan. The rosés are made primarily using the 'bleeding' process. The initial stages of fermentation lift the pomace and when the right colour has been achieved after 12 to 24 hours of skin contact, part of the juice is run off and then continues to ferment off the pomace. The wines vary in hue from pale pink to very light red. Their defining characteristic is a clean, vigorous attack, a relatively steady body combined with mineral, exotic (mango, passion fruit, pomegranate) and floral fragrances. Pairings include grilled lamb chops. The reds are vinted traditionally and exhibit fine tannic structure. They are often matured in wooden tuns. On the palate, they display complex aromas of ripe fruit, bay, thyme, tobacco, cinnamon and venison. They are becoming increasingly popular. Try with local specialities or grilled ribsteak. The whites are vinted using the direct to press method. They are delicate, gracious, dry and vigorous and depending on the style can display floral, fruity or balsamic fragrances. The ideal partner for grilled red mullet or Bouillabaisse fish stew.

A.C. LES BAUX DE PROVENCE

OVERVIEW: initially subsumed into the Coteaux d'Aix en Provence AC area, the tiny region of Baux de Provence became an appellation in its own right in 1995. Its hot, dry climate, predominantly limestone soils and rugged terrain provide an ideal growing environment for the local grape varieties (Grenache, Syrah, Mourvedre, augmented with Counoise, Carignan and Cabernet-Sauvignon). Only red and rosé wines are made here.

A.C. PALETTE

OVERVIEW: the minute area of Palette is located in close proximity to Aix-en-Provence (Meyreuil, Le Tholonet and Aix-en-Provence) in Bouches-du-Rhône. It is currently one of France's smallest appellations, covering a diminutive thirty hectares or so. The lion's share of the wines are made by two independent growers, including the celebrated Château Simone, whilst the remaining grapes are delivered to the local co-operative. The soil is formed of Langesse lacustrine limestone and the climate is Mediterranean with low rainfall and plenty of sunshine.

WINE STYLES: Mourvedre, Grenache and Cinsault form the backbone of the red and rosé varietal range. The red wines are usually sourced from old vines then matured in oak (rarely new) for at least 18 months. They are dense wines with good cellaring capacity, boasting aromas of raspberry, blackcurrant, old leather and spices. The perfect match for a leg of mutton or game. The rosés are vinted using the 'bleeding' or direct to press method. They are fleshy and well-balanced, fruity and balsamic. The whites undergo classic vinification methods, and are subsequently matured on the lees in oak for at least 8 months. Delicate, elegant, suave wines, they are well-balanced and develop fragrances of spices, quince jelly, fig and hazelnut. Enjoy with foie gras terrine or lamb stew.

343

• • •

2015
PROVENCE WINES

ALPILLES

CHATEAU ROMANIN   89/100

Org ▼ ✔ Romanin 2013 : Brilliant pale gold. Refined nose of pear, apricot, mineral and floral touches. Ethereal, tense, clear-cut palate showing beautifully restrained exuberance and a natural impression. Very long-lasting, intense finish. A beautiful white for gourmet foods.
Price approx.: 15,00 EUR
http://www.romanin.fr
Château Romanin
+33 (0)4 90 92 45 87

BANDOL

DOMAINE LA SUFFRÈNE   93/100

▼ ✔ Les Lauves 2011 : Deeply-coloured garnet. Shy nose with faintly perceptible yet beautiful spice, animal, toast, roasted coffee and fruit notes. Generous, concentrated, velvety and very lively palate. Silky, closely-integrated tannins. A top-flight wine. Price approx.: 20,00 EUR
http://www.domaine-la-suffrene.com
Domaine La Suffrène
+33 (0)4 94 90 09 23

DOMAINE DE L'OLIVETTE   92/100

▼ ✔ Vintage 2009 : Deep colour, garnet tints. Ripe nose midway between jammy cassis and bigarreau cherry and undergrowth aromatics. The nose aromas carry through to the palate, showing restrained heat. Full, chewy mouthfeel and polished tannins. A Bandol with lots yet to reveal.
Price approx.: 16,50 EUR
www.domaine-olivette.com
Domaine de l'Olivette
+33 (0)04 94 985 885

CHÂTEAU ROMASSAN   92/100

▼ ✔ Coeur de Grain 2013 : Pale-coloured, light orange tinged with yellow. Expressive mineral nose with herbs, red fruits and bush peach. Welcoming palate at point of entry revealing a virile, rich and velvet-clad presence with fine spice. Harmonious. A convincing Bandol.
Price approx.: 22,92 EUR
www.domaines-ott.com
Domaines Ott
+33 (0)4 94 01 53 50

DOMAINE DE LA GARENNE   92/100

▼ ✔ Vintage 2013 : Light orange-pink. On the nose, strawberry, red berry fruits and subtle spice. On the palate, a fairly virile, generous and expressive wine. Layers of spice and minerality encourage you to indulge and linger. A sterling rosé for sophisticated foods.
Price approx.: 12,00 EUR
Domaine de la Garenne
+33 (0)4 94 90 03 01

DOMAINE LA SUFFRÈNE   91/100

▼ ✔ Vintage 2013 : Brilliant orange-pink. Expressive nose of red fruits, herbs and silica. Aromatic attack leading into a powerful, heady and rich palate showing lovely aromatic depth and heaps of personality. A splendid rosé for gourmet foods.
Price approx.: 12,00 EUR
http://www.domaine-la-suffrene.com
Domaine La Suffrène
+33 (0)4 94 90 09 23

DOMAINE LA SUFFRÈNE   91/100

▼ ✔ Vintage 2011 : Deep garnet, crimson tints. Very discrete nose of black fruits and vanilla. More expressive on the palate with morello cherry, plum, red berry fruits, lovely savoury toast and an elegant array of spice. Robust, underlying structure. Everything is in place.
Price approx.: 15,00 EUR
http://www.domaine-la-suffrene.com
Domaine La Suffrène
+33 (0)4 94 90 09 23

LE GALANTIN   90/100

▼ ✔ Vintage 2011 : Deep garnet with crimson tints. Beautiful spicy, warm and smoky nose with subtle oak. Suave attack, full, velvety mouthfeel that is quite seductive and supported by a robust, closely-integrated structure. Everything is in place, patience is needed now!
Price approx.: 13,00 EUR
www.le-galantin.com
Domaine Le Galantin
+33 (0)4 94 98 75 94

DOMAINE DE L'OLIVETTE   89/100

▼ ✔ Vintage 2013 : Light gold. Appealing nose of sweet almond, white fruits, menthol and anise. On the palate, the aromas blend together and complement one another with beautiful acidity guiding the whole. An elegant, delicate white wine pairing marvellously with scallops.
Price approx.: 15,50 EUR
www.domaine-olivette.com
Domaine de l'Olivette
+33 (0)04 94 985 885

DOMAINE DUPUY DE LÔME 89/100

Org ▼ .♪ Vintage 2011 : Deeply-coloured garnet. Endearing, savoury nose of toast, smoke, spice and liquorice. Supple entry, harmonious, concentrated and powerful palate where pepper and a vegetal element take centre stage. Closely-integrated structure. A good, traditional Bandol.
Price approx.: 16,00 EUR
http://www.dupuydelome.com
Domaine Dupuy de Lôme
+33 (0)4 94 05 22 99

DOMAINE DE L'OLIVETTE 88/100

▼ .♪ Vintage 2013 : Pale orange-pink. Highly mineral, complex nose backed by citrus and red fruit sweets. Rich, full-bodied palate marrying elegance and volume. Wonderful honest perfumes with a spicy finish. A rosé that plays in the big league. Price approx.: 14,20 EUR
www.domaine-olivette.com
Domaine de l'Olivette
+33 (0)04 94 985 885

CHÂTEAU ROMASSAN 88/100

▼ .♪ Vintage 2011 : Deeply-coloured garnet with some young highlights. Shy nose of mild spices, smoky and animal notes. Harmonious, velvety and rich framework on the palate with nicely harnessed power framed by silky tannins. A Bandol with elegance as its key feature.
Price approx.: 25,20 EUR
www.domaines-ott.com
Domaines Ott
+33 (0)4 94 01 53 50

LE GALANTIN 88/100

▼ .♪ Vintage 2013 : Light orange-pink with faint beading. Powerful nose combining fruity and mineral tones. Virile palate with intense fruity and spicy aromas and good exhilarating exuberance. Lacks neither personality nor assertiveness. A convincing Bandol.
Price approx.: 11,00 EUR
www.le-galantin.com
Domaine Le Galantin
+33 (0)4 94 98 75 94

DOMAINE LA SUFFRÈNE 88/100

▼ .♪ Vintage 2013 : Brilliant light yellow. Expressive nose blending white peach, orange and apricot. Generous presence and fullness on the palate which follows a spice route with exuberance fully doing its job. An all-round wine pairing with grilled fish.
Price approx.: 12,50 EUR
http://www.domaine-la-suffrene.com
Domaine La Suffrène
+33 (0)4 94 90 09 23

DOMAINE DUPUY DE LÔME 87/100

Org ▼ .♪ Vintage 2013 : Pale gold. Refined nose gradually coming together of almond, linden, white fruits, spices and meadow. Exuberance at point of entry, full body and perfume poised to gain in intensity. A Bandol that would benefit from cellaring. A little patience is needed.
Price approx.: 16,00 EUR
http://www.dupuydelome.com
Domaine Dupuy de Lôme
+33 (0)4 94 05 22 99

DOMAINE DUPUY DE LÔME 87/100

Org ▼ .♪ Vintage 2013 : Pale salmon-pink. Fine nose of spicy pepper backed by fresh red fruits and meadow. A delicate, refined rosé. Beautiful aromatic balance with fruit taking centre stage. Persistent freshness. Ideal as a prelude to an intimate dinner. Price approx.: 12,00 EUR
http://www.dupuydelome.com
Domaine Dupuy de Lôme
+33 (0)4 94 05 22 99

COTEAUX D'AIX EN PROVENCE

CHÂTEAU CALISSANNE 92/100

▼ .♪ Rocher Rouge 2009 : Deep garnet. Promising nose of mild spices, exotic wood and garrigue. Powerful palate displaying great elegance and splendid nascent complexity supported by silky tannins and wonderful invigorating exuberance. A deftly crafted, distinguished wine.
Price approx.: 30,00 EUR
www.calissanne.fr
La Jasso de Calissanne
+33 (0)4 90 42 63 03

CHÂTEAU CALISSANNE 91/100

▼ .♪ Clos Victoire 2009 : Dark garnet. Endearing nose of mild spices, red and black fruits, a trace of roasted coffee and subtle exotic wood. Virile, velvety, concentrated palate with a substantial structure and invigorating freshness. A far-reaching wine that needs to mature. Price approx.: 18,80 EUR
www.calissanne.fr
La Jasso de Calissanne
+33 (0)4 90 42 63 03

CHÂTEAU CALISSANNE 90/100

▼ .♪ Calisson de Calissanne 2013 : Brilliant salmon-pink with orange highlights. Expressive nose of red fruits with a trace of flowers and refined spices. Silky attack, round, robust and spicy palate with faint garrigue suggestions and lovely fullness. A beautiful harmonious rosé for food.
Price approx.: 14,95 EUR
www.calissanne.fr
La Jasso de Calissanne
+33 (0)4 90 42 63 03

CHÂTEAU CALISSANNE   88/100

▼ 🌶 Vintage 2013 : Light salmon-pink with orange tints. Expressive, crisp nose of strawberry and red fruits. The palate displays fairly virile body with lovely aromatic honesty. A spice dimension is revealed and effective exuberance brings balance to the whole.
Price approx.: 8,80 EUR
www.calissanne.fr
La Jasso de Calissanne
+33 (0)4 90 42 63 03

CHÂTEAU CALISSANNE   87/100

▼ 🌶 Vintage 2011 : Deep crimson. Pleasurable nose of cassis, redcurrant, fine spice and a touch of garrigue. The palate displays beautiful young, dynamic fruit, svelte proportions and the right measure of power. Firm, articulate finish. A successful wine.
Price approx.: 8,80 EUR
www.calissanne.fr
La Jasso de Calissanne
+33 (0)4 90 42 63 03

LES QUATRE TOURS   86/100

▼ 🌶 Signature 2013 : Light orange. Refined nose showing mineral freshness backed by red berry fruit presence with a touch of sweets. A very thirst-quenching rosé showcasing fruit and suppleness. Easy-drinking and pairing wonderfully with mozarella salad. Sheer pleasure.
Price approx.: 8,00 EUR
www.quatretours.com
Les Quatre Tours
+33 (0)4 42 54 71 11

LES QUATRE TOURS   85/100

▼ 🌶 Classique 2013 : Light orange. Appealing nose of red fruits, citrus and peach. A soft, supple rosé boasting freshness and highlighting delicious crisp fruit. Drinking well at any time of the day.
Price approx.: 7,00 EUR
www.quatretours.com
Les Quatre Tours
+33 (0)4 42 54 71 11

CÔTES DE PROVENCE

Clos Mireille   92/100

▼ DG2 Coeur de Grain 2013 : Pale orange with yellow highlights. Racy nose showing a mineral dimension with redcurrant and citrus. Suave entry with lovely velvety body, beautiful clear-cut, intense and persistent aromas with fine spice. Harmonious. Marvellous. Pair with top-end food.
Price approx.: 22,92 EUR
www.domaines-ott.com
Domaines Ott
+33 (0)4 94 01 53 50

LE CLOS PEYRASSOL   91/100

CONV ▼ 🌶 Vintage 2013 : Pale orange. Refined, racy nose gradually revealing floral and citrus tones. A fleshy, tightly-wound style on the palate opening up to citrus and mild spice flavours after swirling. A rosé that would probably benefit from a few more months' bottle age.
Price approx.: 26,00 EUR
http://www.peyrassol.com
Commanderie de Peyrassol
+33 (0)4 94 69 71 02

CHÂTEAU DE SELLE   91/100

▼ 🌶 Coeur de Grain 2013 : Very pale, brilliant hue with yellow tints. Enticing nose showing red fruit basket aromas with refined mineral and spice tones. A fairly crunchy, broad-shoulde red wine with a rich, precise and generously natured array of aromatics. Very beautiful.
Price approx.: 22,92 EUR
www.domaines-ott.com
Domaines Ott
+33 (0)4 94 01 53 50

DOMAINE DU DRAGON   91/100

▼ 🌶 Cuvée Saint-Michel - élevé en fûts de chêne 2009 : Evolving garnet hue. Endearing nose of toast, plum, morello cherry, fine spices and quality oak. Lightweight, silky and well-mannered palate showing complex, rich expression. Silky supporting tannins. A handsome wine.
Price approx.: 10,55 EUR
http://http://www.domainedudragon.com/
Domaine du Dragon
+33 (0)4 98 10 23 00

COMMANDERIE DE PEYRASSOL   90/100

CONV ▼ 🌶 Vintage 2011 : Beautiful deep garnet. Complex nose driven by smoke, incense, olive paste, stone fruits and mild spices. Suave palate with polished tannins, restrained power and focused, racy perfumes. A full wine that is only just beginning to evolve.
Price approx.: 11,70 EUR
http://www.peyrassol.com
Commanderie de Peyrassol
+33 (0)4 94 69 71 02

CHÂTEAU PEYRASSOL   90/100

CONV ▼ 🌶 Vintage 2013 : Pale orange. Delicate nose of citrus and white flowers. Dense, round and velvety attack on the palate leading into a mid-palate showing the same pronounced citrus perfumes. Delicate and persistent throughout.
Price approx.: 13,90 EUR
http://www.peyrassol.com
Commanderie de Peyrassol
+33 (0)4 94 69 71 02

CLOS MIREILLE 90/100

▼ ✔ Blanc de blancs 2013 : Brilliant light yellow, green tints. Refined nose blending white-fleshed fruits and fine floral and mineral notes. Round attack. Mellow, rich and velvety palate enveloping the mouth. Refined freshness. Fine, delicate, precise aromas. Very good tenacity.
Price approx.: 21,72 EUR
www.domaines-ott.com
Domaines Ott
+33 (0)4 94 01 53 50

CHÂTEAU ANGUEIROUN 90/100

▼ ✔ Prestige 2012 : Light yellow with green tints. Pleasurable nose of white-fleshed fruits and subtle vanilla oak. On the palate, roundness comes to the fore with a lovely fleshy, rich mouthfeel and vibrant spice. A beautiful wine pairing with creamy sauces.
Price approx.: 16,00 EUR
http://www.angueiroun.fr
Domaine de l'Angueiroun
+33 (0)4 94 71 11 39

CHÂTEAU DU GALOUPET 90/100

Cru Classé de Provence ▼ ✔ Vintage 2012 : Very alluring pale yellow. Highly inviting nose marrying citrus and mild spices with honey and flower notes. More of the same on a charming, expressive and elegant palate. Predominant fruit showing delectable tropical tones. Serve with grilled shellfish.
Price approx.: 12,85 EUR
www.galoupet.com
Château du Galoupet
+33 (0)4 94 66 40 07

CHÂTEAU DU GALOUPET 90/100

Cru Classé de Provence ▼ ✔ Vintage 2013 : Very pale colour with salmon-pink highlights. Delicate nose opening up after swirling to crisp, spicy tones and mineral undercurrents. Fine-textured palate showing delicate aromas and lingering freshness. A rosé for gourmet dining.
Price approx.: 11,40 EUR
www.galoupet.com
Château du Galoupet
+33 (0)4 94 66 40 07

CHÂTEAU DU GALOUPET 90/100

Cru Classé de Provence ▼ ✔ Empreinte 2010 : Dark hue, still in its youth. Profound, ripe nose marrying dark fruits with notes of garrigue and olive paste. Powerful attack with ripe tannins on the palate. Harmonious middle palate with assertive fruit presence. A wine with all-round balance.
Price approx.: 32,00 EUR
www.galoupet.com
Château du Galoupet
+33 (0)4 94 66 40 07

CHÂTEAU BARBEIRANNE 89/100

▼ ✔ Cuvée Camille 2013 : Light orange. Quality vanilla oak on the nose prevailing over red fruits. Upfront oak on the palate astutely augmenting a full, round and lively mouthfeel. Persistent, spice-infused finish. An ambitious rosé with real food compatibility.
Price approx.: 12,10 EUR
http://www.chateau-barbeiranne.com
Château Barbeiranne
+33 (0)4 94 48 84 46

COMMANDERIE DE PEYRASSOL 88/100

CONV ▼ ✔ Vintage 2013 : Pale orange. Pleasant, subdued nose intermixing floral notes, citrus, mild spices and orange peel. More of the same delightful array of aromatics on the palate with a delicate crisp persistency on the finish.
Price approx.: 9,95 EUR
http://www.peyrassol.com
Commanderie de Peyrassol
+33 (0)4 94 69 71 02

CHÂTEAU L'AFRIQUE 88/100

▼ ✔ Vintage 2013 : Pale pink. Refined nose showing mineral aromatics, perfumes of red berry fruits and rose. Mouthcoating palate revealing crunchy fruit. Beautiful freshness, wonderful substance and length. Has the makings of a superlative rosé. Perfect for tapas.
Price approx.: 11,00 EUR
www.sumeire.com
Châteaux Elie Sumeire
+33 (0)4 42 61 20 00

SAINT JEAN DE VILLECROZE 88/100

▼ ✔ Réserve 2013 : Brilliant pale orange. Compelling nose of focused red fruits with spice notes and a mineral impression. Supple attack leading into a rich, mellow and consistent mouthfeel. A powerful, enjoyable rosé that works best with grilled meat and fish.
Price approx.: 9,50 EUR
http://www.domaine-saint-jean.com
Domaine Saint-Jean de Villecroze
+33 (0)4 94 70 63 07

CHÂTEAU ESCARAVATIERS 88/100

▼ ✔ Vintage 2010 : Beautiful garnet with faint bricking. Racy nose intermixing red fruits and mild spices backed by refined oak. Svelte, generous palate with some tannins that still need to mellow. Lovely spicy, peppery and mineral intensity. Long-lasting finish. A successful wine.
Price approx.: 12,00 EUR
http://www.escaravatiers.com
Domaines BM Costamagna
+33 (0)4 94 19 88 22

CHÂTEAU ESCARAVATIERS 88/100

▼ ♪ Vintage 2013 : Brilliant light orange. On the nose, red fruits, a whiff of garrigue, some spice and ageing notes. Full on the palate with beautiful harmonious, rich, round and spicy presence that is fairly powerful. All the qualities of the quintessential Provencal wine.
Price approx.: 12,00 EUR
http://www.escaravatiers.com
Domaines BM Costamagna
+33 (0)4 94 19 88 22

CHÂTEAU PEYRASSOL 87/100

CONV ▼ ♪ Vintage 2011 : Limpid, pale yellow. Endearing, refined nose with notes of citrus fruits and mild spices. Delicious aromas on the palate showing more of the fruit, mild spices and flowers. A white for gourmet foods such as fish in a sauce.
Price approx.: 15,40 EUR
http://www.peyrassol.com
Commanderie de Peyrassol
+33 (0)4 94 69 71 02

CHÂTEAU RIOTOR 87/100

▼ ♪ Vintage 2013 : Salmon-pink. Inviting perfumed nose ranging from wild flowers, strawberry and mild spices to a mineral touch. Delightful, elegant palate developing crunchy fruit. Beautiful overall freshness. Drinking well from the aperitif onwards or throughout the meal.
Price approx.: 8,10 EUR
http://www.chateaumontredon.fr
Château Mont-Redon
+33 (0)4 90 83 72 75

CHÂTEAU DES VINGTINIÈRES 87/100

▼ ♪ Vintage 2012 : Deep, young crimson. Compelling nose of blackberry and redcurrant, with a floral element and refined pepper. The palate is primarily elegant, svelte and tense with lovely rich, spicy consistency and vegetal presence. Convincing. Keep for a while.
Price approx.: 6,50 EUR
http://www.pouilly.com
Domaine Patrice Moreux
+33 (0)3 86 39 13 55

CHÂTEAU DES VINGTINIÈRES 87/100

▼ ♪ Vintage 2013 : Pale orange hue with yellow highlights. Refined nose of red fruits with subtle crisp and peppery touches. A full wine on the palate revealing precise, lace-like, tenacious aromas with spice and impeccable balance. Deserves sophisticated cuisine.
Price approx.: 6,50 EUR
http://www.pouilly.com
Domaine Patrice Moreux
+33 (0)3 86 39 13 55

CHÂTEAU DU GALOUPET 87/100

Cru Classé de Provence ▼ ♪ Vintage 2011 : Beautiful deep garnet. Profound nose of ripe black fruits with an earthy mineral touch. Wonderful stuffing on the palate with powerful yet melted tannins and an upfront fruity freshness despite a hint of bitterness on the finish.
Price approx.: 13,25 EUR
www.galoupet.com
Château du Galoupet
+33 (0)4 94 66 40 07

SAINT JEAN DE VILLECROZE 86/100

▼ ♪ Réserve 2012 : Deep garnet. Pleasant nose of red and black fruits, spice and pepper notes and subtle herbs. Lovely generous aromatics on the palate with svelte, lively substance framed by a robust structure and vegetal presence on the finish.
Price approx.: 11,00 EUR
http://www.domaine-saint-jean.com
Domaine Saint-Jean de Villecroze
+33 (0)4 94 70 63 07

DOMAINE DES ESCARAVATIERS 86/100

▼ DG2 Vintage 2012 : Limpid ruby. Compelling nose of fern, red fruits and fine spices. Supple attack leading into a full, honest and easy-drinking palate showing some herbs. Accessible across the palate and supported by some fine-grained tannins. A successful offering.
Price approx.: 7,50 EUR
http://www.escaravatiers.com
Domaines BM Costamagna
+33 (0)4 94 19 88 22

CHÂTEAU ESCARAVATIERS 86/100

▼ ♪ Vintage 2013 : Pale crystalline hue tinged with green. Delightful nose intermixing white peach, pear and lovely vanilla oak. The palate is supported by refined freshness and is round, seductive, full and harmonious albeit dominated by oak at the moment. A good all-rounder.
Price approx.: 12,00 EUR
http://www.escaravatiers.com
Domaines BM Costamagna
+33 (0)4 94 19 88 22

DOMAINE ST MARC DES OMÈDES 85/100

▼ ♪ Cuvée L'Amiral 2008 : Colour starting to evolve. Mature nose blending jammy berry fruits, stone fruits and spice and balsamic notes. Sensation of fat and mellowness at point of entry leading into livelier, slightly firmer aromatics with well-integrated oak.
Price approx.: 8,33 EUR
www.stmarcdesomedes.com
Domaine Saint Marc des Omèdes
+33 (0)4 94 67 69 17

DOMAINE DES ESCARAVATIERS 85/100

▼ ♪ Vintage 2013 : Brilliant pale gold with green tints. Ripe nose suggestive of white peach and apricot. Round attack, lovely mellow, full and rich presence. Lively with an impression of harmony and more of the nose aromatics. Perfect for poultry in a korma sauce. Price approx.: 7,50 EUR
http://www.escaravatiers.com
Domaines BM Costamagna
+33 (0)4 94 19 88 22

DOMAINE DES ESCARAVATIERS 85/100

▼ ♪ Vintage 2013 : Brilliant pale hue with orangy tints. Pleasant nose suggestive of red berry fruits and fine spices with a tangy dimension. Lovely spicy and modern exuberance on the palate, an ethereal profile supported by beautiful liveliness.
Price approx.: 7,50 EUR
http://www.escaravatiers.com
Domaines BM Costamagna
+33 (0)4 94 19 88 22

DOMAINE DE LA GISCLE 85/100

▼ ♪ Moulin de l'Isle 2012 : Vibrant red. Ripe nose with accents of prune, black olive and a whiff of spice. Fairly robust framework on the palate with medium body. More of the same ripe, persistent aromas. Distinctly Provencal in style. Drink now.
Price approx.: 6,50 EUR
Domaine de la Giscle
+33 (0)4 94 43 21 26

CÔTES DE PROVENCE LA LONDE

CHÂTEAU ANGUEIROUN 91/100

▼ ♪ Prestige 2011 : Dark garnet with crimson tints. Black fruit basket aromas on the nose with fine spice and a touch of vanilla. Velvety, svelte and fresh palate framed by extremely refined tannins. Still fairly backward in coming forward but very promising.
Price approx.: 19,00 EUR
http://www.angueiroun.fr
Domaine de l'Angueiroun
+33 (0)4 94 71 11 39

CHÂTEAU ANGUEIROUN 90/100

▼ ♪ Prestige 2013 : Pale blush colour with salmon-pink. Extremely endearing nose with aromas of red fruits, citrus and flowers. Lovely fat, suppleness and silkiness on the palate yet also freshness that supports perfume over substantial length. A stellar rosé.
Price approx.: 14,00 EUR
http://www.angueiroun.fr
Domaine de l'Angueiroun
+33 (0)4 94 71 11 39

CÔTES DE PROVENCE SAINTE VICTOIRE

CHÂTEAU COUSSIN 91/100

▼ ♪ César à Sumeire 2013 : Pale pink. Complex smoky and mineral nose with substantial citrus and red fruit perfume. A full, powerful and sappy rosé. Fruit is present at point of entry and carries through across the palate. Not just a rosé, a consummate wine.
Price approx.: 26,00 EUR
www.sumeire.com
Châteaux Elie Sumeire
+33 (0)4 42 61 20 00

DOMAINE DE SAINT-SER 91/100

CONV ▼ ♪ Cuvée Prestige 2008 : Vibrant red, still in its youth. Pleasant nose showing accents of ripe red fruits bordering on jammy and a mineral touch. On the palate, beautiful, softish attack with velvety tannins. The finish is more powerful yet stays steeped in freshness. Lovely.
Price approx.: 12,00 EUR
http://www.saint-ser.com
Domaine de Saint Ser
+33 (0)4 42 66 30 81

CHÂTEAU COUSSIN 88/100

▼ ♪ Vintage 2013 : Pale orange. Complex mineral and smoky nose with focused floral and fruit presence. A full-bodied, proud rosé with an unctuous mouthfeel and focused, ripe fruit framed by freshness. A perfect food-friendly style pairing with, say, grilled fish. Real allure.
Price approx.: 12,50 EUR
www.sumeire.com
Châteaux Elie Sumeire
+33 (0)4 42 61 20 00

CHÂTEAU MAUPAGUE 88/100

▼ ♪ Vintage 2013 : Pale orange-pink. Rich nose showing ripe citrus and red fruit perfumes backed by flowers and spice. Abundant volume, fat and remarkable crisp freshness coupled with fruit on the palate. A rosé in a lovely crowd-pleasing style.
Price approx.: 8,50 EUR
www.sumeire.com
Châteaux Elie Sumeire
+33 (0)4 42 61 20 00

> Prices mentioned in this book are guideline and can vary depending on point of sale.
> The shops, wineries or publisher can in no way be held responsible for this.

LES BAUX DE PROVENCE

CHATEAU ROMANIN   92/100

Org ▼ ♪ Vintage 2008 : Beautiful deep garnet, starting to evolve. Mature nose of tobacco and mild spices with a trace of animal aromas. Svelte palate brimming with energy and exuding beautiful aromas. Elegant structure that needs to mellow. Powerful sense of place. Marvellous.
Price approx.: 20,00 EUR
http://www.romanin.fr
Château Romanin
+33 (0)4 90 92 45 87

CHATEAU ROMANIN   89/100

Org ▼ ♪ La Chapelle 2011 : Deeply-coloured garnet. Expressive nose of morello cherry, herbs and fine spice. Delicate attack, harmonious welcome leading into a silky, tense and very elegant palate with refined, closely-integrated tannins and a vegetal finish. A very promising wine.
Price approx.: 13,00 EUR
http://www.romanin.fr
Château Romanin
+33 (0)4 90 92 45 87

MAURES

DOMAINE DE L'ANGLADE   85/100

▼ ♪ Le Rosé d'Anna 2013 : Brilliant, pale salmon-pink. Elegant nose of strawberry and redcurrant with a tangy note. On the palate, a modern style intermixing fruit and spice showing exuberance and lovely aromatic honesty. Equally enjoyable as an aperitif or with summer salads.
Price approx.: 9,00 EUR
www.domainedelanglade.fr
Domaine de l'Anglade
+33 (0)4 94 71 10 89

DOMAINE DE L'ANGLADE   85/100

▼ ♪ Cuvée Tradition 2013 : Light salmon-pink. Pleasant nose of red berry fruits with a crisp note and creamy impression. Honest, rich palate with full-on expression, lovely intensity and aromatic precision. Some spice. Personality. An enjoyable wine. Price approx.: 9,00 EUR
www.domainedelanglade.fr
Domaine de l'Anglade
+33 (0)4 94 71 10 89

DOMAINE DE L'ANGLADE   84/100

▼ ♪ Vintage 2013 : Brilliant light hue with green tints. Pleasurable nose suggestive of white fruits with a floral touch. On the palate, a light, supple and lively wine revealing clean, honest aromas mirroring the nose. Fairly spicy, crunchy finish gaining intensity.
Price approx.: 9,00 EUR
www.domainedelanglade.fr
Domaine de l'Anglade
+33 (0)4 94 71 10 89

WINE SCORES:

95-100/100: an outstanding wine, when a great 'terroir' meets exceptional winemaking expertise.

90-94/100: a superlative wine combining finesse, complexity and remarkable winemaking.

85-89/100: a wine of extremely high standard, which we enjoyed for its typicity and character.

80-84/100: a quality wine combining balance, structure and neatness for a pleasurable wine drinking experience.

75-79/100: a wine deemed acceptable.

70-74/100: a wine with defects, unacceptable.

65-69/100: a wine with major defects, inadmissible.

50-64/100: unacceptable wine, not worthy for sale.

Note: wines scoring less than 75/100 are not included in our publications.

MÉDITERRANÉE

DOMAINE DE L'ATTILON **85/100**

Org ▼ Chardonnay 2013 : Brilliant light hue with green tints. Elegant nose of white flowers, pear and a crisp touch. Light palate showing lovely focused, clear-cut aromatics. The same aromas follow through. Lively across the palate and exuding a natural impression. Price approx.: 5,20 EUR
http://www.attilon.fr
Domaine de l'Attilon
+33 (0)4 90 98 70 04

DOMAINE DE L'ATTILON **84/100**

Org ▼ Marselan 2013 : Deeply-coloured dark purple. Welcoming youthful nose driven by peony, blackberry and redcurrant. Soft, supple and fresh palate. Savoury elegant fruit enhanced with a touch of spice and flowers on the finish. A welcoming red Marselan for pleasure. Price approx.: 5,70 EUR
http://www.attilon.fr
Domaine de l'Attilon
+33 (0)4 90 98 70 04

DOMAINE DE L'ATTILON **84/100**

Org ▼ Pinot Noir 2013 : Fairly intense ruby. Subdued nose of cherry, red fruits and a vegetal note. More expressive on the attack leading into a fresh, light palate with lovely, easy-drinking, young fruit to the fore, some spice and subtle oak. A little ageing would be beneficial.
Price approx.: 7,00 EUR
http://www.attilon.fr
Domaine de l'Attilon
+33 (0)4 90 98 70 04

DOMAINE DE L'ATTILON **83/100**

Org ▼ Merlot 2013 : Deeply-coloured with dark purple tints. Heady nose of peony and violet coupled with blackberry and redcurrant. Soft, light palate drinking well whilst young for its aromatic freshness and suppleness. A summery Merlot for barbecues. Price approx.: 4,60 EUR
http://www.attilon.fr
Domaine de l'Attilon
+33 (0)4 90 98 70 04

VAR

DOMAINE DES ESCARAVATIERS **85/100**

▼ Cinsault 2013 : Light salmon-pink. Pleasurable nose recalling red fruits. On the palate, a delightful fruity, crunchy and vibrant wine with a hint of spice. Accessible and enjoyable as a quaffer on a beautiful summer's day.
Price approx.: 8,50 EUR
http://www.escaravatiers.com
Domaines BM Costamagna
+33 (0)4 94 19 88 22

ESCARAVATIERS **85/100**

▼ Viognier 2013 : Brilliant pale gold. Expressive nose driven by peach, fruits in syrup and wild flowers. Supple and light with delightful perfume and overall freshness - this is the ultimate wine for instant pleasure. Perfect for a Sunday picnic.
Price approx.: 8,50 EUR
http://www.escaravatiers.com
Domaines BM Costamagna
+33 (0)4 94 19 88 22

SAINT JEAN DE VILLECROZE **84/100**

▼ La Petite Chapelle 2010 : Intense garnet. Expressive nose of ripe cassis, mild spices and a trace of smoke. Silky attack, ethereal, delicate, harmonious and well-balanced palate leading into a slightly blurred, weak finish. Interesting at first, ready to drink now.
Price approx.: 9,00 EUR
http://www.domaine-saint-jean.com
Domaine Saint-Jean de Villecroze
+33 (0)4 94 70 63 07

ESCARAVATIERS **84/100**

▼ Vintage 2013 : Brilliant pale hue with orange highlights. Pleasant nose of redcurrant, bush peach and a trace of citrus. On the palate, a crunchy, vibrant, focused and round wine with elegant spice touches and a fullness that allows it to be paired with white meats.
Price approx.: 5,20 EUR
http://www.escaravatiers.com
Domaines BM Costamagna
+33 (0)4 94 19 88 22

ESCARAVATIERS **84/100**

▼ Vintage 2013 : Brilliant pale hue with some green tints. Expressive nose with a faint crispness and pear, fresh grape and stone berry fruit aromatics. Ethereal palate driven by an effective crunchy exuberance. Well-balanced, honest and fairly fluid.
Price approx.: 5,20 EUR
http://www.escaravatiers.com
Domaines BM Costamagna
+33 (0)4 94 19 88 22

THE COLOUR OF THE WINES :

▼ Red wine	▼ Sparkling brut
▼ Dry white wine	▼ Sparkling brut rose
▼ Rose wine	▼ Brandy
▼ Sweet white wine	▼ Liqueur wine

RHONE VALLEY

CONTEMPORARY WINES

It has become customary to divide this extensive wine growing region into two completely different parts - the North, where vines grow on a thin strip of land alongside the Rhône, before widening out towards the South. This guide book is no exception. We will review the two parts separately, starting with the North.

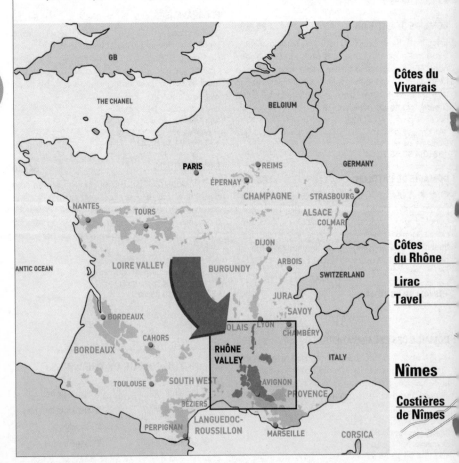

Côtes du Vivarais

Côtes du Rhône

Lirac

Tavel

Nîmes

Costières de Nîmes

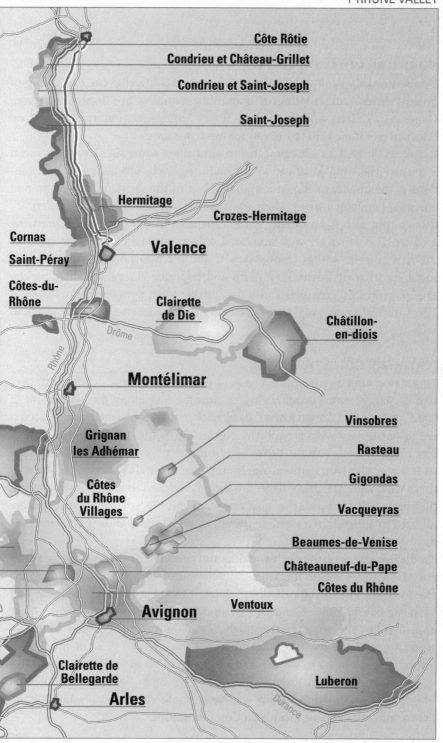

Côte Rôtie

Condrieu et Château-Grillet

Condrieu et Saint-Joseph

Saint-Joseph

Hermitage

Crozes-Hermitage

Cornas

Valence

Saint-Péray

Côtes-du-Rhône

Clairette de Die

Châtillon-en-diois

Drôme

Rhône

Montélimar

353

Vinsobres

Grignan les Adhémar

Rasteau

Gigondas

Côtes du Rhône Villages

Vacqueyras

Beaumes-de-Venise

Châteauneuf-du-Pape

Côtes du Rhône

Ventoux

Avignon

Clairette de Bellegarde

Luberon

Arles

Durance

NORTHERN CÔTES DU RHÔNE

Unquestionably a fully-fledged member of the world's elite circle of premium quality wines, with a string of household names (Côte Rôtie, Hermitage, Condrieu...). Here, vines cling to the Rhône Valley's steepest inclines, making it sometimes impossible to introduce mechanisation. In fact, as far back as winegrowers can remember, some sites have never seen a tractor. The only justification for enduring such adverse growing conditions is the quality of the wines (coaxed out of the outstanding 'terroir' and remarkable microclimate). Their reputation stems not only from the 'terroir', though, but also from quality grape varieties and the expertise of the wine growers. The wines are well-structured, robust, aromatic and complex. Both the reds and the whites (probably with the exception of the Viogniers) are suitable for laying down. Low yields and boutique vineyards, where harvesting can often be completed in a day, enable wine growers in the northern Côtes du Rhône to provide an extremely comprehensive range of wines in each appellation.

SOUTHERN CÔTES DU RHÔNE

This region stretches from the southern part of the Drôme department, over half of Vaucluse, the southern tip of Ardèche and along the right bank of Gard. The name 'Côte du Rhône' dates back to the 15th century when it referred to one of two areas around Uzès under the control of a magistrate which was branded onto barrels dispatched from the port of Roquemaure. Unlike its more northerly neighbour, single-crop farming is characteristic of the southern wine region. Many villages are entirely devoted to wine growing. 'Côtes du Rhône' wine is by far the most prevalent and the 'villages' (16 villages are allowed to append their name to the appellation) stand at the pinnacle of the local growths.

Producing vast quantities of wine does not preclude quality, neither at regional AC or Côtes du Rhône Villages level, and of course, even less so for the five local (or growth) appellations - Lirac, Tavel, Vacqueyras, Gigondas and Châteauneuf-du-Pape. Blending (see under varietals) is the norm for these appellations. The rosés (interestingly, Tavel only produces this colour of wine) are made by the 'bleeding' process or the direct-to-press method. Yield restrictions (35 hl/ha in Vaucluse and 42 to 48 hl/ha in Gard for the growths, 42 hl/ha for Côtes du Rhône Villages and 52 hl/ha for regional Côtes du Rhône) are one of the reasons why respectable cellars and restaurants, in France and abroad, stock southern Côtes du Rhône.

THE 'SATELLITE' WINE REGIONS
Five appellation areas are now joined to Côtes du Rhône, even though they are slightly further away from the river:
- DIE: Three appellations including two still wines (Clairette de Die, 88% of output) and Crémant de Die (12%), and one still wine appellation (Châtillon-en-Diois).
- GRIGNAN LES ADHÉMAR: Along the left bank of the Rhône in the Drôme department.
- CÔTES DU VENTOUX: Further south, stretching over 7,500 hectares amongst the foothills of Mont Ventoux, Provence's highest peak.
- CÔTES DU LUBERON: The second-largest area in Vaucluse, this proud 'terroir' growth is set within an area of outstanding natural beauty (the Luberon national park) north of the river Durance.
- COSTIÈRES DE NÎMES: This is the most southerly Rhône valley region, so much so that it borders on Languedoc (Gard department).

VARIETALS
Grenache, Mourvedre, Syrah and Cinsault take centre stage for the reds. The whites use primarily Clairette, Bourboulenc, Viognier, Roussanne and Marsanne. In Die, Clairette Pointue and Small Berry Muscat. Thirteen grape varieties are permitted in Châteauneuf-du-Pape: Clairette, Grenache, Mourvedre, Syrah, Picpoul, Cinsault, Counoise, Muscardin, Terret noir, Vaccarese, Picardan, Roussanne and Bourboulenc. In actual fact, though, few wines nowadays take full advantage of this huge potential.

WINE STYLES
the northern red growths are vigorous, and in some cases (see Châteauneuf-du-Pape) warm. They require several years' cellaring (at least three to five years and more for the likes of Côte Rôtie).
The Côtes du Rhône and Côtes du Rhône-villages are immediately more approachable, except when certain styles of winemaking or ageing are used.
The whites are also heady, fragrant, sunny-clime wines with a framework supported by their acidity. As they age (Châteauneuf-du-Pape again), some scale the heights for complexity and finesse.

REVIEW OF LATEST VINTAGES
- 2010 • Low quantities yet very high quality wines. The reds are dense, aromatic and complex. The white and rosés are pure and show wonderfully refined expression. The reds need to mature but should start to produce some

excellent efforts this year. Superlative wines in the north, definitely designed for cellaring.

• **2011** • an extraordinarily inconsistent year, particularly for red wines which account for the bulk of production. Harvesting began in late August, around 10 days early compared with 2010. For Syrah and Mourvèdre, the vintage is generally of an excellent standard with wonderful varietal expression and full, complex wines. Grenache shows clear differences depending on the area, where rainfall and harvest dates have a significant impact. The 2011s show abundant fruit and are similar in style to the 09s with aromas of cherry and prunes, a hint of over-ripeness and a warm edge.

• **2012** • This region experienced incessant rain combined with quite mild temperatures, causing the vines to grow exuberantly. This led to late ripening, which was compensated by uniform development. The reds are dense, with a tight tannic structure. The whites harvested early have retained a good level of acidity. A reasonable vintage.

• **2013** • As in many southern wine regions, the Rhone valley enjoyed an extremely successful vintage. Acidity levels are wonderful, the quality of the fruit is good and there is a welcome, yet not excessive, exuberance in the wines. The reds are deeply coloured, the whites are tense and the rosés display beautiful aromatic purity. Watch this space…

THE RHÔNE VALLEY APPELLATIONS

A.C. BEAUMES DE VENISE

OVERVIEW: previously subsumed into the Côtes du Rhône Villages appellation, Beaumes de Venise was recently promoted to growth status. The area stretches across the south-eastern face of the Dentelles de Montmiral range (at elevations ranging from 100 to 600m), in four villages in the Vaucluse department. The soil is derived from Oxfordian marl from the Upper Cretaceous series and the Triassic, unique to the Côtes du Rhône. The climate is particularly hot because the landform acts as a buffer against the Mistral wind.

WINE STYLES: Beaumes de Venise produces powerful, mellow red wines which are generous and aromatic. They make suitable partners for meat in a sauce and game.

A.C. CHÂTEAU GRILLET

OVERVIEW: Château Grillet is one of France's smallest appellations, covering just four hectares belonging to a single owner. The area forms an enclave within the Condrieu appellation along the right bank of the Rhône. Only white wines are made here from Viognier. The soils are formed of stony sand on a granite bedrock. The vines grow on sheer, south-facing terraces sheltered from the wind.

WINE STYLES: as the grapes are harvested earlier than for Condrieu, the wines tend to be more austere, less fragrant and heady. Blessed with an attractive pale golden hue and a fresh, delicate bouquet, they are subtle, well-structured wines with a long ageing capacity (10 to 20 years). Principal aromas are lychee and camomile. They can be paired with grilled fish, seafood, shellfish, goats cheese and mi-cuit foie gras.

A.C. CHÂTEAUNEUF-DU-PAPE

OVERVIEW: this area encompasses five towns and villages set in the southern part of the Rhône Valley - Châteauneuf-du-Pape, Bédarrides, Courthézon, Orange and Sorgues. The soil is extremely stony, covered with pebbles interspersed with red clay and sand. This type of soil retains heat during the day which it releases by night. Châteauneuf-du-Pape boasts the driest climate in the region with some 2,800 hours of sunshine annually. The wines are vinted traditionally at controlled temperatures. The reds are vatted for around three weeks to ensure maximum extraction. The permitted range of grape varieties is extensive, although many are not widely planted. For the reds: Grenache noir, Syrah, Mourvedre, Cinsault, Carignan, Terret noir, Counoise, Muscardin, Vaccarese, Camarese, Calitor and Picpoul noir. For the whites: Clairette, Bourboulenc, Roussanne, Grenache blanc, Picpoul blanc, Picardan, Marsanne, Viognier, Pascal blanc, Ugni blanc and Maccabeo.

WINE STYLES: the appellation produces both red and white wines. The red wines with their intense colour are redolent of red fruit, leather, aniseed, spices and the occasional balsamic note. They are round, unctuous, full and supple with good length on the palate. The white wines sport a translucid pale yellow colour. They are fresh and aromatic (floral notes reminiscent of vine flowers, honeysuckle and daffodils) with good staying power on the palate. The reds pair with game (leg of venison, jugged hare, roast woodpigeon) or cheese. The whites are equally delicious as appetisers or with grilled fish doused with olive oil, shellfish and rosemary-flavoured goats cheese.

A.C. CHÂTILLON-EN-DIOIS

OVERVIEW: a diminutive appellation area (60 hectares) located in the vicinity of Die, in the far eastern portion of the northern Rhône Valley. Although they are grown on the same soil types as Clairette de Die (stony hillsides, calcareous clay), wines from Châtillon-en-Diois come from the cooler zones of the Drôme Valley. **WINE STYLES:** the appellation produces light, fruity red wines from Gamay, Pinot noir and Syrah which reward early drinking or pleasant, vigorous still white wines from Chardonnay and Aligoté. The reds can be served with barbecued meats cooked on a wood fire and the whites with grilled fish.

A.C. CLAIRETTE DE DIE

OVERVIEW: this area covers 32 towns and villages dotted along the Drôme Valley. The soils are calcareous clay on stony hillsides. Once the grapes have been pressed, the juice is filtered and chilled and the partially fermented must is then bottled. Alcoholic fermentation continues in the bottle, resulting in a naturally sparkling wine. Sediment is removed at least six months after bottling.

WINE STYLES: Clairette de Die is a light, fruity sparkling wine with a brilliant golden hue. The wines develop aromas of green apple, white fruit and floral notes of rose. They can be served either as appetisers or with desserts, frozen sweets, chocolate or foie gras.

A.C. CONDRIEU

OVERVIEW: the Condrieu area, a producer of white wines, is situated 11 kilometres south of Vienne, on the right bank of the Rhône, just below the red wine appellation area Côte Rôtie. Seven villages feature within the area and the vines are planted on sheer granite slopes enriched with patches of loess. The steep inclines make mechanical harvesting impossible and the crop is therefore hand-picked. Low yields warrant the expensive price tag on these wines which are intended to be drunk in their youth (between two and four years old).

WINE STYLES: the appellation only produces white wines, made from the only permitted grape variety, Viognier. Pale gold in colour, they are heady, yet supple, rich and unctuous with a touch of acidity. Principal aromas are acacia honey, violet, musk, apricot and peach. They can be served with freshwater fish, mi-cuit foie gras, goats cheese, king prawns and duck breast with peaches.

A.C. CORNAS

OVERVIEW: this appellation area is set in the northern half of the Rhône Valley, opposite the town of Valence. The only permitted varietal is Syrah which forms the basis of the area's red wines. Similarly, only one village is entitled to the appellation, Cornas in Ardeche. The vines grow on terraces supported by dry stone walls and enjoy maximum sunshine which promotes good ripening. The neighbouring hills also shield the vines from the wind, resulting in significantly higher temperatures than in Hermitage, just 11 kilometres away. The soil is granite with patches of calcareous clay. At the base of the hills, they are sandy with decomposed granite whilst in the northern part of the appellation, there tends to be more limestone. The only varietal used is Syrah.

WINE STYLES: Cornas is a powerful, robust wine in its early years. Its tannins only begin to mellow several years down the line though even then, the wines remain robust with a dark hue. Strangely, it is unlike any of its northern Rhône Valley neighbours and is often described as rustic or wild. The younger wines display aromas of red fruit and pepper, leading into aromas of truffle, amber, hazelnut and liquorice after five to ten years' ageing. They pair with wild boar in a sauce, venison cutlets marinated in Cornas wine, roast venison or jugged hare.

A.C. COSTIÈRES DE NÎMES

OVERVIEW: an appellation situated between Arles and Nîmes, north of the Camargue. This is the most easterly of the Languedoc appellations although it is officially joined to the Rhône Valley. It covers 24 towns and villages in the Gard department, on ancient alluvial soils formed of pebbles, gravel and sand bordering one of the Rhône's former river beds.

The climate is Mediterranean and the varietal range is traditional. Carignan (40% maximum), Grenache (25% minimum), Syrah and Mourvedre (20% minimum) and Cinsault (40% maximum) for the reds. Clairette, Grenache, Bourboulenc, Ugni blanc (40% maximum), with a 50% maximum supporting range of Marsanne, Roussanne, Maccabeo and Rolle for the whites.

WINE STYLES: the red wines are expressive and well-balanced. They are powerful and robust when sourced in the southern part of the appellation (facing the sea). In the northern zone, they are more supple, fruity wines for quaffing. Their aromas belong to the red fruit, wild berry and small venison range. Try with grilled meat, Sète-style rabbit or small game. The rosés, which are made using the bleeding process, develop aromas of exotic fruit (mango) and citrus fruit. They are lively wines which pair remarkably well with shellfish fritters, squid in a sweet and sour sauce, cooked cold pork meats. Shellfish and fish are a perfect match for the white wines, which are mainly drawn from Grenache blanc and Clairette and are fresh and aromatic.

A.C. CÔTE RÔTIE

OVERVIEW: an appellation set in the far northern part of the Rhône Valley. The vines grow on terraces supported by dry stone walls facing south-east,

359

which provides them with maximum sunshine. Three villages are entitled to the appellation: Ampuis, Saint-Cyr-sur-le-Rhône and Tupin-et-Semons.

The Côte Rôtie area is divided into two parts: Côte Blonde and Côte Brune. Côte Blonde is home to steep granite terraces covered with a layer of siliceous limestone, whilst in Côte Brune the soil is iron oxide-rich clay. The wines are vinted traditionally with relatively long vatting periods (two to three weeks) and aged for 18 to 36 months in oak casks which are often new.

WINE STYLES: these red wines are single varietals made from Syrah, occasionally augmented with a tiny proportion of Viognier. Their deep red colour with purple tints takes on orangy-yellow tints when they reach 10 to 15 years of age. The wines are extremely well-structured, tannic and unctuous with a characteristic intense bouquet. Wines from Côte Blonde tend not to keep for as long as those from Côte Brune. They display aromas of violet, spices (pepper, vanilla), red fruit (raspberry), black fruit and undergrowth. They pair with water fowl, subtly-flavoured meats (roasted young wild boar), truffles and asparagus.

A.C. COTEAUX DE DIE

OVERVIEW: this is a young appellation set in the Die area, east of the northern Rhône Valley. The soils are primarily calcareous clay and shale marl. The grapes (Clairette) are sent straight to the press, vinted traditionally and then aged for six to eight months.

WINE STYLES: Coteaux de Die are still white wines sporting a golden hue with greenish tints. Usually dry and fresh, they develop fragrances of flowers and green apple. Recommended pairings include fish, shellfish and goats cheese.

A.C. CÔTES DU RHÔNE

OVERVIEW: this is the Rhône Valley's largest appellation (the second-largest in France, after Bordeaux). It covers 163 towns and villages spread over six departments, from Vienne to Avignon - Loire, Rhône, Ardèche, Gard, Drôme and Vaucluse, with most of the area under vine in the last three. The soils are granite in the north and alluvium on limestone in the south. Many areas are also home to gravel from the Alps mountain range.

The climate is Mediterranean with the characteristic Mistral wind. Seasonal rainfall, hot temperatures and outstanding sunshine are all distinctive features of the region. The wines are vinted traditionally at controlled temperatures. Most of the wines are aged in tanks though occasionally oak casks are used. The varietal range is extremely broad. Grenache noir, Syrah, Mourvedre, Cinsault, Carignan, Terret noir, Counoise, Muscardin, Vaccarese, Camarese, Calitor and

Picpoul noir for the reds. Clairette, Bourboulenc, Roussanne, Grenache blanc , Picpoul blanc, Picardan, Marsanne, Viognier, Pascal blanc, Ugni blanc and Maccabeo for the whites.

WINE STYLES: 95% of the wines grown in this appellation area are red and can be divided into two main styles. Some are rich, generous wines with mellow tannins that are intended for cellaring. Others are not unlike 'primeur' wines and are light, fruity and vigorous. Predominant aromas are small red and black fruit (red currant, blackcurrant, bilberry, blackberry), spicy and animal notes. Try with Provençal beef stew, leg of mutton with garlic, chicken sauteed with onions… The white and rosé wines, produced on a much smaller scale, are well-balanced and round. The rosés with their fruity bouquet of pear drop and quince paste, pair with barbecues and cooked cold pork meats. The whites exude floral fragrances (linden) or white peach and honey, depending on the varietal. Notes of kiwi and grapefruit may also be present. They are well suited to grilled fish and shellfish.

A.C. CÔTES DU RHÔNE VILLAGES

OVERVIEW: set within the Côtes du Rhône area, this appellation embraces 95 towns and villages spread over the departments of Drôme, Vaucluse, Gard and Ardèche. This takes it either side of the Rhône, from the south of Montélimar to the south of Avignon. Soil types vary from granite in the north, alluvium on a limestone bedrock in the south, both of which often come together in the shape of gravely terraces. The climate is Mediterranean, hot and dry, with the characteristic Mistral wind and maximum sunshine. The term Côtes du Rhône Villages can feature as such on the label or it can be extended with the name of one of 17 villages – Cairanne, Chusclan, Laudun, Puymeras, Roaix, Rochegude, Rousset, Sablet, Saint-Maurice, Saint-Gervais, Saint-Pantaléon, Séguret, Signargues, Valréas and Visan, as well as two site-specific areas: Plan de Dieu and Massif d'Uchaux.

WINE STYLES: AC Côtes du Rhône Villages produces sturdy, heady wines which do not go overboard on tannic astringency and have a silky finish. Principal aromas are fig, stone fruits and liquorice. They pair with cured mountain hams, wild boar stew, bull casserole and cheeses.

A.C. CÔTES DU RHÔNE VILLAGES CAIRANNE

OVERVIEW: Cairanne is situated in the Vaucluse department, in the southern Rhône Valley. Vines grow here on red soil, sandstone, clay terraces and sandy molasse. The appellation produces red, rosé and white wines.

WINE STYLES: the red wines are well-structured, unctuous and spicy with an elegant finish. They display aromas of small black fruit, leather and spices. This type of wine does in fact pair well with spices, Asian or exotic cuisine. The rosé wines are lively and well-balanced. The white wines are round and elegant with floral and vegetal tones (grilled fish).

A.C. CÔTES DU RHÔNE VILLAGES CHUSCLAN

OVERVIEW: an area spread over five villages in Gard. The vines occupy gravely hills and terraces and occasional sandy patches. The appellation produces red and rosé wines.

WINE STYLES: the reds are well-balanced, easy drinking wines with average strength. Try with stew or roast beef. The fleshy, unctuous rosés make good partners for subtly-flavoured cold cuts or barbecued meats.

A.C. CÔTES DU RHÔNE VILLAGES LAUDUN

OVERVIEW: the vines are planted on stony or gravely slopes, terraces formed of pebbles, covering three villages in Gard. Laudun produces red, rosé and white wines.

WINE STYLES: the red wines with their crimson hue are powerful and tannic. They exude aromas of stone fruit and spices. They can be served with meat, game or cheese. The delicate, supple rosé wines display enticing floral aromas. The fat, fruity white wines are buttressed by moorland notes. They pair with shellfish, grilled fish and poultry.

A.C. CÔTES DU RHÔNE VILLAGES MASSIF D'UCHAUX

OVERVIEW: AC Massif d'Uchaux is spread over five villages in Vaucluse. Soil type is mainly siliceous and limestone sandstone at elevations of between 100 and 280m.

WINE STYLES: tightly-woven red wines displaying attractive body and fat are grown here. The standard of quality is excellent and the wines are very consistent.

A.C. CÔTES DU RHÔNE VILLAGES PLAN DE DIEU

OVERVIEW: the area embraces four villages and occupies an extensive alluvial terrace topped with Quaternary limestone stones. Beneath the stones is either blue clay (Pliocene) or sandstone beds which draw up all-important water during the summer months. The name 'Plan de Dieu' is derived from the many local religious foundations which grew vines here over a long period of time.

WINE STYLES: Plan de Dieu produces powerful, well-balanced red wines suited to barbecues and meat served in a sauce.

A.C. CÔTES DU RHÔNE VILLAGES PUYMÉRAS

OVERVIEW: this area extends over five villages set in steep-sided valleys (elevations ranging from 220 to 600 metres) straddling Drôme and Vaucluse. It occupies stony terraces littered with pebbles.
WINE STYLES: Puyméras produces powerful, well-structured red wines.

A.C. CÔTES DU RHÔNE VILLAGES ROAIX

OVERVIEW: the Roaix area is set between Rasteau and Séguret. It stretches over land belonging to the village of the same name, in the Vaucluse department. The vines occupy stony or gravely terraces and decalcified clay slopes. Roaix produces red, rosé and white wines.
WINE STYLES: the reds are supple, delicate and extremely feminine wines with subtle tannins. They display aromas of red fruit and spices. The rosé wines are extremely fruity and refreshing. The white wines are fresh and well-balanced. The reds pair with game and red meat, the rosés barbecues and cooked cold pork meats and the whites, fish.

A.C. CÔTES DU RHÔNE VILLAGES ROCHEGUDE

OVERVIEW: the Rochegude area is spread over a single village of the same name in southern Drôme. It produces red, rosé and white wines.
WINE STYLES: the red wines are supple, round and warm with fragrances of black fruit and peach stone. The rosé wines are powerful and unctuous with a slightly acidulous flavour. They display aromas of red fruit (red currant, raspberry). The whites exhibit tell-tale vegetal flavours and floral tones (honeysuckle).

363

A.C. CÔTES DU RHÔNE VILLAGES ROUSSET-LES-VIGNES

OVERVIEW: the area covers just one village, Rousset-les-Vignes, in the Drôme department. Sheer hillside sites of sandstone and stone soils are home to the vines.
WINE STYLES: only red wines are grown here. They display a characteristic deep ruby-red hue, compact body, well-integrated tannins and woody flavour. They are suited to cellaring and reward a few years ageing by gaining finesse. They display fragrances of red fruit and are a perfect match for all types of meat.

A.C. CÔTES DU RHÔNE VILLAGES SABLET

OVERVIEW: the entire area is set in just one village, Sablet, which is adjacent to Gigondas in the Vaucluse department. The soils are sandy and clayey. Sablet produces red, rosé and white wines.

WINE STYLES: the red wines are full, round and well-structured, with elegant overtones. They display aromas of red fruit, violet and blackcurrant and pair well with game. The powerful, fat, warm rosés exhibit a fruity bouquet with predominant aromas of raspberry. They are a good match for barbecues. The white wines display well-integrated acidity and fragrances of green apple and freshly-cut hay, evolving over time into aromas of gingerbread. Try with fish and shellfish.

A.C. CÔTES DU RHÔNE VILLAGES SÉGURET

OVERVIEW: the area covers the village of Séguret in the Vaucluse department. Séguret produces red, rosé and white wines on hillside sites and calcareous clay terraces.

WINE STYLES: the red wines are supple and fruity with a fruity bouquet, almond and tobacco tones. They can be served with poultry. The rosés and the whites are delicate and elegant, developing a fruity bouquet brimming with freshness. Try with fish, seafood and cheese.

A.C. CÔTES DU RHÔNE VILLAGES SIGNARGUES

OVERVIEW: this is the most southerly of the Côtes du Rhône Villages appellations with a site specific name. Pebbled terraces, sand or Pliocene marl reddened by iron oxide at an average elevation of 150 metres above the Rhône, provide the context for the wines.

WINE STYLES: Signargues only produces red wines.

A.C. CÔTES DU RHÔNE VILLAGES SAINT-GERVAIS

OVERVIEW: the entire area covers the village of Saint-Gervais in the Gard department. The soils are sandstone on the hillside sites and more stony on the plateau. Saint-Gervais produces red, rosé and white wines.

WINE STYLES: the elegant, well-balanced, unctuous red wines are long on the palate and suitable for cellaring. They display aromas of red and stone fruit and are a good match for game, either roasted or served with a sauce. The rosé wines are elegant, fat and warm with fragrances of raspberry and strawberry. Try them with aubergine caviar, crudités, melon or Parma ham. The white wines are fresh and light with a fresh, floral bouquet. Marry them with grilled fish, prawn kebabs or shellfish.

A.C. CÔTES DU RHÔNE VILLAGES SAINT-MAURICE

OVERVIEW: the entire area covers the village of Saint-Maurice-sur-Eygues in the Drôme department. The soil is calcareous clay, with varying amounts of gravel, and some areas of lighter sandstone. Saint-Maurice produces red, rosé and white wines.

WINE STYLES: the red wines are elegant, not overly powerful, with a distinctively full attack and pleasant finish. They display a bouquet of red fruit leading into woody notes as they age. The rosés are characteristically fresh with a fresh, fruit-forward bouquet. The whites are extremely aromatic with fragrances of peach, apricot and violet.

A.C. CÔTES DU RHÔNE VILLAGES SAINT-PANTALÉON-LES-VIGNES

OVERVIEW: the area covers the village of Saint-Pantaléon, in the southern part of the Drôme department. The vines occupy calcareous clay hillsides with a few sandy patches and produce red and rosé wines.

WINE STYLES: the red wines are well-balanced with supple tannins and good length on the palate. The rosé wines are delicate, with a slight fruit flavour. Both the reds and the rosés display a fruity bouquet. The reds can be served with coq au vin or Provencal-style chicken. Cooked cold pork meats are the perfect match for the rosés.

A.C. CÔTES DU RHÔNE VILLAGES VALRÉAS

OVERVIEW: the are covers the village of Valréas, in the Vaucluse department. Hillside sites and terraces of red clay with varying amounts of stones are home to the vines. Valréas produces red, rosé and white wines.

WINE STYLES: the red wines are moderately powerful and are well-balanced and round. They display aromas of red fruit (raspberry, red currant and blackcurrant). The rosé wines are extremely fruity and acidulous. The white wines are dry, lively and aromatic, fruity with vanilla tones. The reds and the rosés can pair with barbecues and the whites with grilled fish and seafood.

A.C. CÔTES DU RHÔNE VILLAGES VISAN

OVERVIEW: the area covers the village of Visan in the Vaucluse department. The soil is calcareous clay and extremely stony. Visan produces red, rosé and white wines.

WINE STYLES: the red wines are full and supple with elegant tannins. They exhibit a complex bouquet of fruit, vanilla, blackcurrant and truffle. The rosés are elegant and fresh with a slight peppery touch. The whites are unctuous and fruity with fragrances of crushed grapes and lemon peel. All three are the perfect match for truffle-based dishes (scrambled eggs with truffles for example).

A.C. CÔTES DU VIVARAIS

OVERVIEW: situated in the north-western portion of the southern Côtes du Rhône, this area straddles the departments of Ardèche and Gard, with 577 hectares under vine. Of the 14 villages it embraces, only Orgnac, Saint-Remèze and Saint-Montan are entitled to add their name to the appellation. The soils are shallow calcareous clay. Varietals used are Syrah, Grenache, Mourvedre, Cinsault and Carignan.

WINE STYLES: the deeply-coloured red wines are well-balanced and well-structured with a long-lasting finish. Aromas of bell pepper, violet, blackcurrant and raspberry are present. Try them with meat served in a sauce or game. The rosés are harmonious, round and delicious (fragrances of red currant, blackcurrant, raspberry and floral notes) and pair with lamb loin chops. The whites are vigorous and well-balanced on the palate. They develop a floral bouquet (acacia, hawthorn), white fruit (quince, apple, peach) and a touch of hazelnut. Try with fish soup, trout or goats cheese.

A.C. CRÉMANT DE DIE

OVERVIEW: this appellation shares the same boundaries as Clairette de Die. The Clairette varietal forms the backbone of the blend, though a little Aligoté and small berry Muscat can be added. Crémant de Die is vinted traditionally. After pressing and initial must fermentation, secondary fermentation occurs in the bottle after a blend of sugar and yeasts has been added. The sediment (dead yeast deposits) is subsequently removed by disgorging.

WINE STYLES: Crémant de Die is a sparkling white wine with a brilliant, gold-tinted hue and small bubbles. As a rule, it is fresh, dry and soft with good length on the palate. Aromas of fresh flowers and a tell-tale buttery touch are present. Try as an appetiser or with fish.

A.C. CROZES-HERMITAGE

OVERVIEW: this area is set in the northern part of the Rhône Valley. It forms a boundary around Hermitage in the north and south and embraces 11 villages surrounding Tain-l'Hermitage. Soil types vary greatly with primarily granite hillside sites in the north and alluvium and terraces covered with pebbles of various origins in the south. The red wines are made from Syrah, the white wines from Marsanne and Roussanne.

WINE STYLES: the Crozes-Hermitage appellation produces red and white wines. The deeply-coloured red wines are supple and aromatic. They display aromas of blackcurrant, vanilla, cinnamon, liquorice and menthol notes. Try with a rack of lamb or roast chicken. The floral, elegant white wines are supple and fat, displaying fragrances of almond, passion fruit and white flowers. Serve them with eel in a parsley and garlic sauce, fish in a sauce or goats cheese.

A.C. GIGONDAS

OVERVIEW: this area is situated in the southern part of the Rhône valley, in the village of Gigondas (Vaucluse). The soils are formed of stony alluvium rich in red clay, spread over rolling hills or huge terraces. The climate is Mediterranean, characterised by a distinctive period of drought in the summer and the fierce Mistral wind. The vines bask in 2,800 hours of sunshine every year. The wines are vinted traditionally at controlled temperatures. They undergo prolonged vatting and are aged in oak tuns. The red varietal range is comprehensive: Grenache noir, Syrah, Mourvedre, Cinsault, Carignan, Terret noir, Counoise, Muscardin, Vaccarese, Camarese, Calitor and Picpoul noir.

WINE STYLES: the Gigondas appellation produces red and rosé wines. The red wines are robust, well-balanced and powerful though can occasionally be slightly severe in their youth. They are usually wines with a long cellaring capacity, developing finesse and elegance over time. The aromatic range, predominantly red and black fruit and kirsch over the first few years, leads into wilder aromas of undergrowth and animal notes with age. The deeply-coloured rosé wines are heady and generous, although they reward early drinking. They display fragrances of almond and stewed fruit. The reds pair with wild boar stew and the rosés with duck gizzards salad.

367

A.C. GRIGNAN LES ADHÉMAR

OVERVIEW: the area stretches over the left bank of the Rhône, from south of Montélimar to north of Bollène. It embraces 22 towns and villages in the Drôme department. The soil is formed of extremely stony ancient alluvium and sandy hillside sites. The red grape varieties used are typical of the Rhône: Grenache noir, Syrah, Mourvedre, Cinsault, Carignan, Terret noir, Counoise, Muscardin, Vaccarese, Camarese, Calitor and Picpoul noir.

WINE STYLES: AC Grignan les Adhémar produces red, rosé and white wines, although the latter two are grown more on a boutique scale. The red wines are robust and elegant with a pleasant bouquet, displaying aromas of raspberry, bell pepper and spices. Try with grilled lamb chops or grilled spatchcock. The rosés exhibit an elegant, bright salmon-pink hue. Round and warm, they develop fragrances of flowers (hawthorn) and fresh fruit. Try with pistou soup, tomato omelette or salad niçoise with anchovies. The whites display a bright, pale golden hue and scents of white flowers. They have a rich, full mouthfeel with a pronounced floral character. For shellfish or fish.

A.C. HERMITAGE

OVERVIEW: the appellation area is located in three villages set on the left bank of the Rhône, in the northern portion of the valley. Terraces chiselled into the sheer hillsides are home to the vines here. The soils are predominantly granite though for many years the area was divided into climate-specific sites, each with its own soil make-up. The climate sites situated along the far western end of the hill are formed of gravel and sand on a granite bedrock. On the lower climate sites, clay dominates, whilst calcareous clay occurs on the higher sites. The wines are vinted traditionally at controlled temperatures. Both the red and white wines can be aged either in tanks or oak casks.

WINE STYLES: the Hermitage appellation produces both red and white wines. As in the neighbouring appellations, the red wines are single varietal Syrah. As a rule of thumb, they display a deep red hue evolving into an orangy colour down the years, and an extremely fragrant nose. These wines are opulent, sumptuous, elegant and will keep for twenty to thirty years. Aromas of violet, peony, blackcurrant, raspberry, spices, truffle, leather and prune are present. Try with game served in a sauce, for example. The white wines are drawn from Marsanne, with a small proportion of Roussanne. They exhibit a pretty golden hue, are fat and full with an elegant framework. The best examples come from vineyards set on the highest elevations. They display fragrances of flowers, unroasted coffee, gunflint, vanilla and toasted almonds, leading into notes of honey and wax as they mature. They marry extremely well with lamb curry, pastilla or chicken tajine with lemon confit.

A.C. LIRAC

OVERVIEW: situated in the southern part of the Rhône Valley, this area stretches over four villages in Gard. The vines occupy pebbled terraces rich in loess and sand. The climate is typically Mediterranean with an average 2,700 hours of sunshine every year. The red wines undergo prolonged maceration. The rosés are made by the bleeding method. The varietal range is typically Mediterranean: Grenache noir, Syrah, Mourvedre, Cinsault and Carignan for the reds. Clairette, Grenache blanc, Bourboulenc, Ugni blanc, Marsanne and Roussanne for the whites.

WINE STYLES: the red wines boast an attractive, deep hue and are robust, generous and well-balanced. They reward ageing by becoming full and fleshy. Their aromatic range is dominated by red fruit and spices. Try with red meat or game. The rosé wines, also very popular, are elegant with a full mouthfeel. They marry very well with aioli, mixed salads, courgette or aubergine tart, or subtly-flavoured cold cuts. The white wines are lively and aromatic with good roundness on the palate. They exude floral notes. Enjoyable with grilled Mediterranean fish or seafood.

A.C. LUBERON

The second-largest winegrowing area in the Vaucluse, this proud terroir wine has its origin in a site of extraordinary natural beauty (Luberon Natural Park) north of the Durance River.

OVERVIEW: AC Côtes du Luberon extends over 3,500 hectares situated between Cavaillon and Apt, south-east of Avignon. The appellation area is adjacent to Côtes du Ventoux in the north and Coteaux de Pierrevert in the east. The appellation is divided between thirty-six towns and villages, all set within the Luberon national park. 80% of estates belong to the local co-operative wineries.

Soil types vary from stones on ancient terraces to sand on Miocene molasse and stones of glacial scree. The wines are vinted traditionally at controlled temperatures and most of them are tank aged, though some are aged in casks. Red varietals are Grenache noir, Syrah, Mourvedre, Cinsault and Carignan. White varietals are Grenache blanc, Clairette, Bourboulenc, Ugni blanc and Vermentino.

WINE STYLES: the appellation produces red, rosé and white wines. The red wines, with their crimson hue, are full and racy. They exhibit aromas of blackcurrant, blackberry, bilberry, notes of bell pepper, truffle, leather and undergrowth. Try with red meat and game (wild boar with sage, wild rabbit with savory). The rosés are well-structured and generous with great freshness and fragrances of raspberry and wild strawberry (fish, white meat, cooked cold pork meats). The white wines are harmonious, lively and well-balanced with good length on the palate. They display floral notes (linden, honeysuckle), vine peaches, apricot and unripe quince. They pair well with grilled fish or goats cheese.

369

A.C. MUSCAT DE BEAUMES DE VENISE

OVERVIEW: the village of Beaumes de Venise is situated in the Vaucluse department, at the foot of the famous Dentelles de Montmirail mountains which act as a natural buffer, deflecting the strong gusts of the Mistral wind. The soil is formed of soft limestone with patches of sandstone. As a whole, it is light with very few stones and the climate is Mediterranean, making it well-suited to the small berry Muscat grape variety.

WINE STYLES: AC Muscat de Beaumes de Venise produces a renowned dessert wine which displays a pretty, limpid, brilliant pale yellow hue with golden tints. On the palate, aromas are reminiscent of the nose, with characteristic scents of passion fruit, apricot and honey. There are also lashings of freshness underscored by notes of peppermint. These wines are generous, rich and should be served chilled when young. They are equally delicious as appetisers or with melon served with a slice of cured ham, fried foie gras or fruit sorbets.

A.C. RASTEAU

OVERVIEW: covering just one village of the same name in Vaucluse, Rasteau owes its reputation to its red and golden dessert wines drawn from the Grenache varietal. Only later was the village promoted to Rasteau appellation for its red wines. Rosés and whites are grown on a very small scale. The soils are limestone on a bedrock of marl or sandstone.

WINE STYLES: the red wines with their deep, brilliant hue are generous and well-balanced with good length on the palate enhanced by aromas of very ripe red fruit, vanilla and pepper. The rosés are heady and the whites fresh and fruity. The reds are a good match for rack of lamb or stew, the rosés for barbecues or mixed salads and the whites as appetisers or with grilled fish and seafood.

A.C. RASTEAU (SWEET WINES)

OVERVIEW: the Rasteau area is situated in the heart of the southern Rhône, north of Séguret and south of Vaison-la-Romaine. Rasteau is a dessert wine, which refers to sweet red and white wines made primarily from the Grenache grape variety. The wines are made by arresting fermentation with spirit ('mutage'). The juice is obtained either by the direct-to-press method or by bleeding. After settling for 24 hours, fermentation begins at a controlled temperature of 18° C. When natural grape sugar content has dropped to around 90g/l, 96% vol. brandy is added to arrest fermentation. Maceration continues for ten days or so after brandy has been added, followed by the ageing phase which lasts for about one year in old casks.

WINE STYLES: the whites display a superb bronze coloured hue with a taste that melts in the mouth and a lingering finish characterised by honey, toasted hazelnut and dried apricot. The reds display a deep red hue. On the palate, they are full and velvety, with overtones of ripe fruit leading into prune and cherries in brandy. The whites can be served with honey cake, fruit salad or orange-flavoured desserts. The reds are delicious either as appetisers or with chocolate-based desserts.

A.C. SAINT-JOSEPH

OVERVIEW: the Saint-Joseph area extends over fifty or so kilometres, along the right bank of the Rhône, between the Condrieu and Cornas appellations.

The appellation, which produces red and white wines, embraces 23 towns and villages in Ardèche and three in Loire. The soil is poor (shale and gneiss on a bedrock of granite).

WINE STYLES: Saint-Joseph red wines are fruity and pleasant. The best examples come from Mauves, Tournon, Saint-Jean-de-Mujols, Lemps, Vion and Glun, north of Cornas. They exhibit aromas of raspberry, blackcurrant, black cherry, violet and liquorice and pair well with braised ham or rabbit casserole. The white wines are fresh and relatively robust with good acidity and pleasant fruitiness, with fragrances of peach, apricot, pear, hawthorn, acacia and honey. They pair with rosemary-flavoured goats cheese or turbot in a mustard sauce.

A.C. SAINT-PÉRAY

OVERVIEW: situated on the right bank of the Rhône, south of AC Cornas, this area only produces still and sparkling white wines. Most of the soils are granite though there are also occurrences of limestone scree on the western slopes as well as Quaternary alluvium. The climate in this area is cooler than in other parts of the Valley. The still wines are vinted traditionally at controlled temperatures. The sparkling wines undergo secondary fermentation in the bottle using the traditional method. Marsanne and Roussanne are the two varietals blended to make the wines.

WINE STYLES: Saint-Péray produces primarily sparkling white wines (70%) though also a small amount of still white wines, reminiscent of Saint-Joseph. The sparkling wines are highly distinctive. Sporting a pale golden hue, they usually have better vinosity and lower acidity than other French sparklers. The still wines on the other hand are dry, vigorous and extremely floral. As they mature, they sometimes become more fat and round. They develop aromas of hawthorn, apricot, brioche notes, white fruit, almond and mineral notes. They can be served either as an appetiser or with young guinea-fowl cooked in honey.

A.C. TAVEL

OVERVIEW: situated in the southern part of the Rhône Valley, this area is restricted to a single village, Tavel. The soils are formed of fine sand covered with pebbles, interspersed with fine sandy clay and with limestone in the west. During the wine making process, after cold maceration, the grapes are pressed and the free-run juice is blended with the press juice prior to alcoholic fermentation. Grape varieties used are Grenache noir, Syrah, Cinsault, Clairette, Bourboulenc...

371

WINE STYLES: Tavel is a rosé wine only appellation boasting a long-standing reputation. Sporting an attractive onion skin colour with ruby-red tints evolving into livelier, more rosé style shades, Tavel is round on the palate with great aromatic power and a spicy finish. It is highly unusual in that it ages well. Tavel wines display fragrances of red fruit leading into notes of stone fruit and toasted almonds. They are suitable partners for fish, white or red meats though also exotic cuisine.

A.C. VACQUEYRAS
OVERVIEW: Vacqueyras covers two villages in Vaucluse, at the foot of the famous Dentelles de Montmirail mountains. The soil make-up is reasonably varied, ranging from stony terraces, to sandy soils on the hillside sites, sandstone, limestone and sandy marl. The climate here is Mediterranean, dry, hot and windy with long sunshine hours. The varietal range is extremely broad-ranging: Grenache noir, Syrah, Mourvedre, Cinsault, Carignan, Terret noir, Counoise, Muscardin, Vaccarese, Camarese, Calitor and Picpoul noir for the reds. Grenache blanc, Clairette, Bourboulenc, Marsanne, Roussanne and Viognier for the whites.
WINE STYLES: the appellation produces red, rosé and white wines. The red wines, with their deep tint, are robust and full, well-balanced and long. They exhibit aromas of fig, ripe stone fruit and black cherry with liquorice notes. As powerful wines, they pair well with game and meats served in a sauce. The full, generous rosés pair with barbecues and aioli. The whites are delicate and floral with their fragrances of honey, dried and acidulous fruit, flowers… Try with fish or shellfish.

A.C. VENTOUX
Farther south, these 7,500 hectares of vineyards stretch to the foothills of Mont Ventoux, the highest point in Provence.
OVERVIEW: 51 towns and villages, all in the Vaucluse department, share this appellation. The area is delineated in the north by Vaison-la-Romaine and by Apt, in the south. There are two distinct 'terroirs': a Rhône-style 'terroir' producing more robust wines and a more southerly-style 'terroir' where the wines are lighter, less concentrated. Eighty-five percent of the wines are made in co-operative wineries, with a balance of independent wineries. Soils vary from hard limestone to Tertiary sediment and scree littered with pebbles. The climate is Mediterranean although it enjoys the moderating influence of Mont Ventoux (harsher winters, wetter summers and cooler nights). Mont Ventoux, which reaches a peak at 1,912 metres, though also the Dentelles

de Montmirail and Monts du Vaucluse mountain ranges provide a buffer to the Mistral wind. The varietal range is typical of the Rhône. Grenache noir, Syrah, Mourvedre, Cinsault, Carignan, Counoise, Picpoul noir… for the reds. Clairette, Bourboulenc, Grenache blanc and Roussanne for the whites.

WINE STYLES: although they are well-constituted, red Côtes du Ventoux tend to be less powerful than neighbouring Côtes du Rhône. They boast characteristic fruit (blackcurrant, raspberry) and freshness, particularly in their youth. Fragrances of flowers and spices (pepper, liquorice) are also present. They are served with meat in a sauce, sophisticated dishes with truffles and game. The rosés display a hue ranging from pink with purple tints to salmon-pink. They boast fragrances of fresh fruit and white flowers. On the palate, they are elegant and fruity. The white wines, which are still made on a boutique scale, display an attractive pale yellow hue with greenish tints. They are lively, fresh and elegant with fragrances of flowers and citrus fruit. Try with shellfish or grilled fish.

A.C. VINSOBRES

OVERVIEW: centring on the village of Vinsobres, this area stretches over 7 kilometres of rolling hills in the Drôme department. Vines grow on stony and sandy marl hillsides, and similarly stony terraces. Vinsobres produces red, rosé and white wines.

WINE STYLES: the red wines are reasonably powerful with a certain amount of freshness, they are well-balanced and long on the palate. They can be served with strongly-flavoured meats. The generous rosés are quaffing wines with aromas of ripe fruit and citrus fruit. They are suitable for barbecues. The harmonious white wines are long on the palate and develop a complex bouquet of white flesh fruit (peach, apricot) and exotic notes. Perfect as appetisers or with shellfish.

• • •

373

2015
RHÔNE VALLEY WINES

ARDÈCHE

DOMAINE DE VIGIER   87/100

▼ ♪ Syrah 2011 : Deeply-coloured dark purple. Refined nose of fresh blackcurrant with empyreumatic undertones and a touch of toast. A supple, soft Syrah with crunchy flavours. Balanced oak and fruit aromas, elegant mouthfeel and clear-cut tannins. A successful wine.
Price approx.: 5,80 EUR
Domaine de Vigier
+33 (0)4 75 88 01 18

DOMAINE VIGIER   86/100

▼ ♪ Viognier Original 2013 : Beautiful gold. Very fresh nose driven by peach, tangerine and a menthol touch. The palate shows seductive sweetness at point of entry highlighting delicate tropical aromatics. A gourmet journey from the aperitif through to pudding. Price approx.: 7,50 EUR
Domaine de Vigier
+33 (0)4 75 88 01 18

DOMAINE VIGIER   86/100

▼ ♪ Viognier 2013 : Beautiful light gold. The nose is crisp and highly floral with wild flower aromas, backed by white peach and citrus. More of the same delicious aromas on the palate augmented by a mineral note. A traditional, joyful Viognier, drinking well at any time. Price approx.: 6,30 EUR
Domaine de Vigier
+33 (0)4 75 88 01 18

DOMAINE VIGIER   85/100

▼ ♪ Cuvée Mathilde 2012 : Deep gold. Liqueur-like nose driven by fruit paste, honey and acacia blossom. A well-balanced, fresh and generous sweet white infused with candied flavours. A successful, late harvest wine combining pleasure and complexity. Perfect for blue-veined cheeses.
Price approx.: 9,70 EUR
Domaine de Vigier
+33 (0)4 75 88 01 18

DOMAINE VIGIER   85/100

▼ ♪ Cuvée Inès 2012 : Light gold. The nose is dominated by intense toasted oak with subtler fruit and floral presence. Same sensation on the palate.

Oak is predominant but a lovely fruity sweetness can be sensed. Still needs to achieve greater balance. A very modern taste. Price approx.: 7,50 EUR
Domaine de Vigier
+33 (0)4 75 88 01 18

BEAUMES DE VENISE

DOMAINE SAINT AMANT   89/100

▼ ♪ Grangeneuve 2012 : Deep young colour. Appealing nose showing heady perfumes of peony, stone fruits and spice with smoky oak undertones. Soft, supple palate displaying a degree of sweetness. The aromas are nicely shown off and freshness is mouth-filling. A charming Beaumes.
Price approx.: 11,00 EUR
http://www.domainesaintamant.com
Domaine Saint Amant
+33 (0)4 90 62 99 25

DOMAINE SAINT AMANT   88/100

▼ ♪ Cuvée Nathalie 2012 : Very concentrated young colour. Distinctive, empyreumatic nose of burnt oak and vanilla toast backed by stone fruits and peony. Fleshy palate with restrained heat. Soft mouthfeel, impeccable aromatic balance with fruit standing on its own on the finish.
Price approx.: 25,00 EUR
http://www.domainesaintamant.com
Domaine Saint Amant
+33 (0)4 90 62 99 25

DOMAINE ROSEMERRY   88/100

CONV▼ ♪ Le Penchant 2012 : Robe concentrée, reflets violines. Nez fin, intense, aux accents de cassis confiturés, de poivre, de laurier, d'olive… Bouche ample, généreuse sur le plan aromatique. Belle fraîcheur d'ensemble, chaleur maîtrisée, tannins ciselés. Bel ouvrage. Price approx.: 12,00 EUR
Domaine Rosemerry
+33 (0)6 26 59 37 24

DOMAINE DES BERNARDINS   87/100

▼ ♪ Beaume de Venise 2012 : Intense red with crimson tints. Aromatic nose of blueberry, redcurrant, mocha and garrigue scents. Suave attack, splendid velvety, rich substance. A powerful wine in a typically southern style with fine pepper and a firm finish with vegetal notes. Patience!
Price approx.: 8,50 EUR
http://www.domaine-des-bernardins.com
Domaine des Bernardins
+33 (0)4 90 62 94 13

DOMAINE ROSEMERRY   86/100

CONV▼ ♪ Le Dos d'Ane 2012 : Youthful, concentrated colour. Intense nose driven by stone

fruits, spice and condiments. Full palate, warm attack flowing into a more supple middle palate with fruit to the fore. Good quality substance and honesty. True sense of place.
Price approx.: 10,00 EUR
Domaine Rosemerry
+33 (0)6 26 59 37 24

ARNOUX ET FILS   84/100

▼ *Les Ravards 2013 : Deep crimson. The nose delivers pleasant fruity perfumes of red fruits and plum with subtle spice undercurrents. Fleshy character, well-integrated substance and good balance of power and freshness enhance the fruit on the palate.
Price approx.: 9,20 EUR
http://htp://www.arnoux-vins.com
Arnoux et Fils
+33 (0)4 90 65 84 18

CHÂTEAUNEUF DU PAPE

MOURIESSE VINUM   95/100

▼ *Tour d'Ambre 2011 : Deeply-coloured with subtle orange highlights. Tertiary aromas of spice, undergrowth and stewed fruits on the nose. The palate shows abundant silkiness and elegance yet also assertive power and heat. Huge fruit and spice aromatic presence. Gold standard.
Price approx.: 38,00 EUR
http://www.mouriesse-vinum.com
Mouriesse Vinum
+33 (0)6 14 94 69 15

DOMAINE DE NALYS   94/100

▼ *Réserve 2011 : Garnet. The nose reveals true character with black fruit, liquorice and a mineral and animal dimension. Huge presence on the palate. A very full, dense wine with power nicely balancing wonderful freshness. More bottle time is a must for this beautiful offering.
Price approx.: 31,00 EUR
www.domainedenalys.com
Domaine de Nalys
+33 (0)4 90 83 72 52

MOURIESSE VINUM   93/100

▼ *Pierre d'Ambre 2011 : Deeply-coloured with mature highlights. Nose of jammy cassis and ripe cherry with forest aromatics. Remarkably supple, silky and fresh palate. Huge aromatic elegance and restrained power. A Châteauneuf that inspires respect.
Price approx.: 28,00 EUR
http://www.mouriesse-vinum.com
Mouriesse Vinum
+33 (0)6 14 94 69 15

DOMAINE DES RELAGNES   93/100

▼ *La Clef de St Thomas 2010 : Young, deep colour. The nose is already complex with mild spices, an animal note, garrigue and elegant oak. Powerful, distinguished, profound and pure palate with a freshness that offsets any heaviness. Very elegant. Velvet. Marvellous. Keep patiently.
Price approx.: 29,90 EUR
www.calissanne.fr
La Jasso de Calissanne
+33 (0)4 90 42 63 03

DOMAINE JULIETTE AVRIL   93/100

▼ *Cuvée Maxence 2012 : Beautiful young, deeply-coloured red. Expressive, complex nose with notes of cocoa, black fruits, liquorice and morello cherries in brandy. Delicate texture on the palate with very fine tannins. Still tightly-wound yet promising. Huge potential. Price approx.: 39,00 EUR
http://www.julietteavril.com
Domaine Juliette Avril
+33 (0)4 90 83 72 69

DOMAINE DES 3 CELLIER   92/100

▼ *Réserve 2011 : Beautiful deep gold. Burnt vanilla with mirabelle plum, peach and cinnamon perfumes on the nose. Huge volume, power and body. Intense empyreumatic presence that doesn't obscure the fruit. A very young, consummate white. Uncork for filet mignon or lobster.
Price approx.: 40,00 EUR
http://www.3cellier.fr
Les 3 Cellier
+33 (0)4 90 02 04 62

DOMAINE DES 3 CELLIER   92/100

CONV▼ *Eternelle 2012 : Deep, mature colour. Distinctive nose exuding empyreumatic aromas. A touch of venison, stone fruits, spices and tobacco. Textbook balance on the palate with restrained power enhancing a very broad range of aromas. The best is yet to come. Price approx.: 50,00 EUR
http://www.3cellier.fr
Les 3 Cellier
+33 (0)4 90 02 04 62

CHÂTEAU HUSSON   92/100

CONV▼ *Les Saumades 2011 : Mature highlights. Intense nose of jammy plum, bigarreau cherry and cassis backed by tobacco, mocha and spice. The palate is complex and robust yet delicious. The full range of nose aromatics recur, augmented by a liquoricy note. All-set for a great future. Price approx.: 19,95 EUR
www.royere-husson.com
Château Husson
+33 (0)4 90 76 87 76

DOMAINE DE LA RONCIÈRE — 92/100

CONV▼ ♪ Flor de Ronce 2011 : Garnet-hued. Powerful nose with accents of game, toasted vanilla, plum and cherries in brandy. Well-balanced palate with nicely harnessed heat. Complex range of aromatics enhanced with focused smoky oak. Calls for stews or meats in a sauce.
Price approx.: 33,00 EUR
Domaine de la Roncière
+33 (0)4 90 32 57 96

DOMAINE DE NALYS — 92/100

▼ ♪ Eicelenci 2012 : Pale yellow. The nose opens up to white flowers on first pour then delivers subtle toast notes after swirling. Fullness and fat come to the fore on the palate. Full, melted attack leading into a firmer mid-palate showing toasted oak influences. Price approx.: 32,00 EUR
www.domainedenalys.com
Domaine de Nalys
+33 (0)4 90 83 72 52

MOURIESSE VINUM — 91/100

▼ ♪ Terre d'Ambre 2013 : Pale gold, brilliant tints. Expressive nose driven by white fruits, dried flowers and a touch of anise. The palate shows more of the delightful nose aromatics framed by a generous, complex and elegant mouthfeel. Savoury youthful acidity. A superlative wine.
Price approx.: 23,00 EUR
http://www.mouriesse-vinum.com
Mouriesse Vinum
+33 (0)6 14 94 69 15

MAISON BOUACHON — 91/100

▼ ♪ La Tiare du Pape : Dark red. A mixture of black fruits, red fruits in brandy, liquorice and oak notes on the nose. Power and concentration are notable on the palate. A well-structured Châteauneuf, still in its youth with undeniable ageability.
Price approx.: 25,00 EUR
http://www.skalli.com
Les Vins Skalli
+33 (0)4 90 83 58 35

CHÂTEAU BEAUCHÊNE — 91/100

▼ ♪ Grande Réserve 2011 : Slightly evolved ruby. Intense nose driven by ripe black fruits, mild spices and cocoa undertones. Delicious, generous and powerful palate that is full and concentrated. Polished tannins. Fruit supported by freshness. Very spicy finish. A real treat!
Price approx.: 19,50 EUR
http://www.chateaubeauchene.com
Château Beauchêne
+33 (0)4 90 51 75 87

DOMAINE DE NALYS — 91/100

▼ ♪ Vintage 2011 : Garnet-hued. Seductive, focused nose revealing aromas of red fruits, cherries in brandy, spice and cocoa. Volume, refined, closely integrated mouthfeel and power harnessed by a touch of freshness on the palate. Very harmonious.
Price approx.: 18,00 EUR
www.domainedenalys.com
Domaine de Nalys
+33 (0)4 90 83 72 52

DOMAINE DE NALYS — 91/100

▼ ♪ Classique 2012 : Pale yellow. Refined, expressive nose of white flowers, honey, white peach notes and a subtle trace of aniseed. The palate combines power and exuberance. Lovely freshness and persistency. Full yet tense. A beautiful wine. Price approx.: 16,50 EUR
www.domainedenalys.com
Domaine de Nalys
+33 (0)4 90 83 72 52

DOMAINE L'OR DE LINE — 91/100

Org▼ ♪ Cuvée Paule Courtil 2012 : Deeply-coloured. Precise nose intermixing red fruits and delicate toast notes. Ample, full and melted attack driven by fruit. Firmer mid-palate and finish tinged with a faint bitterness adding to the overall harmony. Will keep.
Price approx.: 28,00 EUR
http://www.domaine-lor-de-line.com/
Domaine l'Or de Line
+33 (0)4 90 73 74 03

CHÂTEAU MONT - REDON — 90/100

▼ ♪ Vintage 2011 : Garnet nuances. Inviting nose showing spicy chocolate, a touch of stone fruits and tobacco. A well-balanced wine with supple tannins. Wide array of aromas supported by focused fruit. Tightly-wound finish holding the promise of a great future. Honest and sound.
Price approx.: 24,45 EUR
http://www.chateaumontredon.fr
Château Mont-Redon
+33 (0)4 90 83 72 75

CAVES SAINT-PIERRE — 90/100

▼ ♪ Vintage 2012 : Deeply-coloured garnet with crimson shades. Nose of ripe blackberry and forest fruits with a liquoricy touch. Full attack with a rich mouthfeel framed by a sensation of fat. A full, honest and perfumed style. An enjoyable Châteauneuf.
Price approx.: 17,99 EUR
http://www.skalli.com
Les Vins Skalli
+33 (0)4 90 83 58 35

CHÂTEAU FORTIA

90/100

▼ Cuvée du Baron 2012

Beautiful, fairly deep vibrant red. Muted nose delivering some mineral tones. Very beautiful attack on the palate showing lots of fullness and harmony. The range of aromatics is still very subdued but the wine seems promising. Keep.

Price approx.: 20 EUR
Serving temperature: 16-18°
Ready to drink: 2016-2018

Château Fortia is one of the oldest estates in Châteauneuf-du-Pape. According to local tradition, it was an outbuilding of the Papal castle and was used as stables by the cardinals. This is one estate visit not to be missed. The château was home to Baron Le Roy who spearheaded the transition to modern wine growing as well as the creation of the National Institute of Controlled Appellations and the appellation system itself. He moved to the estate in 1919 after marrying Edmée Bernard Le Saint and soon switched from being a legal expert to a wine grower. Wines grown here today remain true to his vision and are excellent ambassadors of this prestigious appellation. A key estate within the appellation.

Château Fortia
Route de Bédarrides - 84231 Châteauneuf du Pape
Tel.: (+33) 4 90 83 72 25 - Fax: (+33) 4 90 83 51 03
E-mail: fortia@terre-net.fr
Website: www.chateau-fortia.com

FRENCH CELLARS 90/100

▼ ♪ Vintage 2013 : Intense hue tinged with purple-blue. The nose delivers beautiful fruity aromas backed by subtle spice. Full, structured palate with delicious fruit, lovely freshness and persistency. A Chateauneuf still in its infancy, with some seriously positive assets.
Price approx.: 14,50 EUR
http://www.winesoverland.com
Wines Overland
+33 (0)1 45 08 87 87

CHÂTEAU BEAUCHÊNE 90/100

▼ ♪ Grande Réserve 2012 : Beautiful deep ruby. Expressive nose driven by lovely ripe fruit with floral notes in the background. Very supple attack, velvety palate with silky tannins. Wonderful well-balanced structure with fruit presence. Long-lasting spicy finish. Very elegant. Price approx.: 19,50 EUR
http://www.chateaubeauchene.com
Château Beauchêne
+33 (0)4 90 51 75 87

DOMAINE DE LA RONCIÈRE 90/100

CONV▼ ♪ Louis Geoffrey 2011 : Concentrated garnet. Distinctive, proud nose marrying stone fruits, garrigue, leather and undergrowth. A very chewy, supple style boasting volume. Mouth-coating, focused perfumes, substance and an empyreumatic finish. A beautiful rendition of Châteauneuf.
Price approx.: 26,00 EUR
Domaine de la Roncière
+33 (0)4 90 32 57 96

DOMAINE LA MEREUILLE 90/100

▼ ♪ Vintage 2009 : Deeply-coloured. Refined nose of toasted oak backed by liquorice, candied fruits and mild spices. Soft, velvety palate with marvellously restrained power and a broad-ranging aromatic spectrum supporting the whole. A racy, noble Châteauneuf.
Price approx.: 39,00 EUR
http://www.domainelamereuille.com
Domaine de la Mereuille
+33 (0)4 90 34 10 68

DOMAINE DES 3 CELLIER 89/100

CONV▼ ♪ Privilège 2012 : Concentrated colour with garnet tints. Evolving nose suggestive of smoke, mocha, liquorice, tobacco, plum and spice. Racy palate, power framed by freshness and focused, persistent aromas. Very supple on the finish. A successful wine with terrific momentum.
Price approx.: 38,00 EUR
http://www.3cellier.fr
Les 3 Cellier
+33 (0)4 90 02 04 62

CHÂTEAU HUSSON 89/100

CONV▼ ♪ Les Saintes Vierges 2012 : Pale yellow. Pleasurable nose opening up to floral tones, fresh almond and stone fruits after swirling. Delicate attack on the palate revealing more of the same delightful aromas. The mid-palate and finish stay fresh and perfumed.
Price approx.: 20,80 EUR
www.royere-husson.com
Château Husson
+33 (0)4 90 76 87 76

DOMAINE JULIETTE AVRIL 89/100

▼ ♪ Vintage 2012 : Clean red. Enticing, expressive nose of morello cherries in brandy. The palate is marked by a welcome freshness. Mellow tannins allow fruit expression to be revealed. An idiosyncratic finish introduces a welcome mineral touch.
Price approx.: 17,80 EUR
http://www.julietteavril.com
Domaine Juliette Avril
+33 (0)4 90 83 72 69

DOMAINE DES 3 CELLIER 88/100

▼ ♪ Alchimie 2012 : Colour starting to mature. Appealing nose of dark fruits and stone fruits with forest-like aromatics. A powerful, full-bodied Châteauneuf showing lovely mature aromas. Sappy and fresh. A real tribute to its local terroir.
Price approx.: 18,80 EUR
http://www.3cellier.fr
Les 3 Cellier
+33 (0)4 90 02 04 62

RÉSERVE DE BONPAS 88/100

▼ ♪ Vintage 2012 : Deeply-coloured garnet. Warm, expressive nose of jammy red fruits with subtle vegetal and spice touches. Lovely volume, density and mellowness on the palate. The same predominant fruit aromatics follow through, enhanced by a subtle touch of oak.
Price approx.: 19,90 EUR
Boisset La Famille des Grand Vins - Bonpas
+33 (0)4 90 83 58 35

DOMAINE DES 3 CELLIER 87/100

CONV▼ ♪ Insolente 2013 : Straw colour. Muted nose, delicately opening up to notes of smoke, plum and mild spices. Lush mouthfeel immediately leaving its mark. Backward fruit. A distinctive wine that needs more bottle age.
Price approx.: 21,20 EUR
http://www.3cellier.fr
Les 3 Cellier
+33 (0)4 90 02 04 62

DOMAINE DES 3 CELLIER   87/100

CONV▼ ♪ Marceau 2012 : Deeply-coloured garnet. Refined plummy nose driven by black cherry with a touch of mocha and liquorice. A well-balanced, upright Châteauneuf showing honest aromatics. Heat on the finish. An all-round, racy wine that needs a little more bottle time.
Price approx.: 21,00 EUR
http://www.3cellier.fr
Les 3 Cellier
+33 (0)4 90 02 04 62

CHÂTEAU FORTIA   87/100

▼ ♪ Tradition 2012 : Beautiful young red. The nose opens up gradually to mineral notes coupled with ripe fruits. Lovely framework on the palate with supple tannins allowing the fruit and spice notes to reveal themselves. Pleasant liquoricy tone on the finish. Price approx.: 18,50 EUR
www.chateau-fortia.com
Château Fortia
+33 (0)4 90 83 72 25

CHÂTEAU FORTIA   87/100

▼ ♪ Vintage 2012 : Pale gold. The nose is still shy and shows a mix of citrus, dried fruits and herbs. Warm attack framed by a sensation of fruity sweetness. The mid-palate is upright and still fiery revealing more of the vegetal character (fennel notes). Keep.
www.chateau-fortia.com
Château Fortia
+33 (0)4 90 83 72 25

CLAIRETTE DE DIE

MONGE GRANON   83/100

▼ ♪ Tradition : Light gold. The nose is driven by pear and apple flesh. Lovely sweetness on the palate coupled with freshness. A delicious Clairette showing archetypal features.
Price approx.: 6,50 EUR
www.clairette-mongegranon.com
Cave Monge Granon
+33 (0)4 75 21 74 93

CONDRIEU

DOMAINE RÉMI NIERO   94/100

▼ ♪ Chéry 2012 : Golden hue. Refined nose opening up to notes of pear flesh then developing a floral and tropical character. Full palate showing a lovely mellow freshness. Precise floral and fruity aromas displaying amazing persistency.
Price approx.: 35,00 EUR
Domaine Niero
+33 (0)4 74 56 86 99

DOMAINE RÉMI NIERO   91/100

▼ ♪ Les Ravines 2012 : Golden hued. Delicate nose showing floral and fruity notes (apricot, lychee) with a subtle, elegant oak dimension. The palate is full, generous and lush yet also reveals remarkable freshness enhancing its persistent floral dimension.
Price approx.: 28,50 EUR
Domaine Niero
+33 (0)4 74 56 86 99

DOMAINE DE CORPS DE LOUP   89/100

▼ ♪ Condrieu 2012 : Light gold with green tints. Pleasant nose of ripe white fruits, vanilla and a toasted, smoky note. Suave attack, fleshy yet ethereal palate, beautiful mellow mouthfeel and delicate freshness. A wine for pleasure.
Price approx.: 30,00 EUR
http://www.corpsdeloup.com
Domaine de Corps de Loup
+33 (0)4 74 56 84 64

COSTIÈRES DE NÎMES

MAS DES BRESSADES   90/100

▼ ♪ Quintessence 2012 : Dark garnet, crimson tints. Shy nose of red fruits, black berries, spice touches and quality oak in the background. Beautiful concentrated palate that is velvety and powerful in an archetypal southern style. Reveals a robust structure and substantial spice.
Price approx.: 15,00 EUR
www.masdesbressades.com
Mas des Bressades
+33 (0)4 66 01 66 00

CHÂTEAU MOURGUES DU GRES   89/100

CONV▼ ♪ Les Capitelles 2011 : Deep garnet with dark purple tints. Endearing nose of ripe black fruits, vanilla, refined spice and herbs. Suave attack, wonderful melted, concentrated, powerful and extremely vibrant mouthfeel. Good craftsmanship. Uncork with stew in a few years time.
Price approx.: 14,00 EUR
http://www.mourguesdugres.com
François Collard
+33 (0)4 66 59 46 10

CLOS DES AMÉRICAINS   88/100

▼ ♪ Prestige 2011 : Deeply-coloured garnet. Refined nose driven by cinnamon, vanilla, toast and ripe black fruits. Sappy mouthfeel with restrained empyreumatic perfumes, beautiful fruit presence and moderate heat. Modern and embodying trueness to terroir. ∩Price approx.: 12,00 EUR
http://www.clos-des-americains.com
Clos des Américains
+33 (0)4 66 88 85 61

MAS DES BRESSADES 88/100

▼ ♪ Cuvée Excellence 2012 : Dark garnet with young tints. Pleasant nose of mild spices, overripe black fruits and a vanilla note. Rich, heady and powerful palate with distinctive, focused aromas, a vegetal finish and a hint of firmness. A nicely crafted Nîmes. Keep for a while.
Price approx.: 10,00 EUR
www.masdesbressades.com
Mas des Bressades
+33 (0)4 66 01 66 00

CHÂTEAU LA TOUR DE BERAUD 88/100

CONV▼ ♪ Vieilles Vignes 2011 : Dark garnet. Warm, savoury showing refined spice, black fruits and a subtle vanilla touch. Suave attack, heady, generous palate supported by beautiful, closely-integrated freshness. Lovely clear, focused and persuasive Southern accent.
Price approx.: 8,50 EUR
http://www.mourguesdugres.com
François Collard
+33 (0)4 66 59 46 10

CLOS DES AMÉRICAINS 87/100

▼ ♪ Désirs de Bacchus 2012 : Beautifully young colour. Refined nose of jammy cherry and cassis backed by spicy pepper. Lots of volume and presence on the palate. Aromatic balance supported by nicely harnessed power. A successful wine that will shine with a wild boar casserole.
Price approx.: 8,00 EUR
http://www.clos-des-americains.com
Clos des Américains
+33 (0)4 66 88 85 61

MAS DES BRESSADES 87/100

▼ ♪ Cuvée Tradition 2013 : Deeply-coloured garnet with purple-blue tints. Lovely nose of red and black fruits with animal notes in the background. Powerful palate with tightly-wound tannins. Focused, precise aromas. Balanced with a persistent finish driven by some spice. Delicious!
Price approx.: 6,50 EUR
www.masdesbressades.com
Mas des Bressades
+33 (0)4 66 01 66 00

MEYBLUM & FILS 87/100

▼ ♪ Divin Nectar 2011 : Expressive nose of herbs, mild spices and a toast note. An easy-drinking, fresh wine on the palate with highly expressive, southern-style aromatics supported by some closely-integrated tannins. An exemplary, modern-style Nîmes pairing with meats in a sauce.
Price approx.: 9,50 EUR
http://www.meyblum-et-fils.com
MVP Wines
+33 (0)4 34 22 12 75

CHÂTEAU GUIOT 86/100

▼ ♪ Numa 2011 : Deeply-coloured garnet. Focused toasted oak on the nose backed by dark fruits and stone fruits. Supple, well-balanced palate boasting sappy oak which emphasises the fruit. Restrained heat. A modern yet distinctive Costières. Perfect for roast meats.
Price approx.: 11,00 EUR
http://www.chateauguiot.com
Château Guiot
+33 (0)4 66 73 30 86

CHÂTEAU VESSIÈRE 86/100

▼ ♪ Vintage 2013 : Light gold. Rich nose midway between acacia blossom, white fruits, white flowers and a touch of honey. Powerful, mouth-coating palate showing a seductive array of aromatics, steady freshness and a crisp finish. Pairs with seafood kebabs.
Price approx.: 6,00 EUR
http://www.chateau-vessiere.com
Château Vessière
+33 (0)4 66 73 30 66

CHÂTEAU GUIOT 85/100

▼ ♪ Vintage 2013 : Light red. Delectable nose of red fruit sweets with a floral and mineral touch. Very round palate with delightful crunchy fruit. The finish dons a spice tone. A rosé for pleasure, perfect for a hot goat's cheese salad.
Price approx.: 6,50 EUR
http://www.chateauguiot.com
Château Guiot
+33 (0)4 66 73 30 86

CHÂTEAU BEAUREGARD DU GRÈS 85/100

▼ ♪ Vintage 2013 : Deep, young colour. Appealing nose driven by blackcurrant, raspberry and cherry. Youthful palate showing delicious fresh fruit which carries right through to the finish. Powerful yet without undermining the fruit. An ideal Costières for a flank steak.
Price approx.: 5,00 EUR
Joseph Castan
+33 (0)4 67 40 00 64

Prices mentioned in this book are guideline and can vary depending on point of sale.
The shops, wineries or publisher can in no way be held responsible for this.

CÔTE RÔTIE

CHÂTEAU VESSIÈRE 85/100

▼ .● Vintage 2012 : Deep garnet. Expressive spicy nose with sun-filled red fruit aromas. Suave attack, impression of lightness and restraint on the palate. A wine that is virile yet invigorating with a hint of firmness and a vegetal note on the finish. A well made Nîmes. Price approx.: 6,00 EUR
http://www.chateau-vessiere.com
Château Vessière
+33 (0)4 66 73 30 66

CLOS DES AMÉRICAINS 84/100

▼ .● Année n° 6 2013 : Brilliant orange hue. Appealing nose of wild strawberries with a trace of flowers and liquorice. Soft, supple palate offering up freshness and fruit. A closely-integrated rosé that partners well with an entire summer meal. Price approx.: 5,00 EUR
http://www.clos-des-americains.com
Clos des Américains
+33 (0)4 66 88 85 61

CHÂTEAU GUIOT 84/100

▼ .● Vintage 2013 : Deeply-coloured dark purple. The nose is driven by plum and bigarreau cherry. Supple, soft palate offering up distinctive fruit and freshness. A generous Costières, enjoyable whilst fruit-forward. Ideal for getting to know the appellation. Price approx.: 6,50 EUR
http://www.chateauguiot.com
Château Guiot
+33 (0)4 66 73 30 86

CHÂTEAU SAINT-PÈRE 84/100

▼ .● Vintage 2013 : Crimson with dark purple. Nose of stone fruits with an empyreumatic spice touch. Welcoming palate with a supple attack, warmer mid-palate with distinctive, focused fruit and spice perfumes. A traditional, honest Costières pairing with all meats in a sauce. Price approx.: 5,00 EUR
Joseph Castan
+33 (0)4 67 40 00 64

CHÂTEAU GUIOT 82/100

▼ .● Nîmois Nitoi 2012 : Young, deep colour. Intense, warm nose with perfumes of black stone fruits, spice and leather. Distinctive palate with a fresh, fleshy attack. More supple mid-palate in a more classic style. An instantly accessible Costières for barbecues and cold cuts. Price approx.: 7,20 EUR
http://www.chateauguiot.com
Château Guiot
+33 (0)4 66 73 30 86

BENJAMIN ET DAVID DUCLAUX 95/100

▼ .● Maison Rouge 2012 : Intense hue with crimson highlights. Concentrated, reticent nose of red fruits, coffee and spice with a touch of toast. Amazingly full, melted and fresh palate with upfront power dovetailing with great elegance. Huge potential. Keep. Price approx.: 55,00 EUR
http://www.coterotie-duclaux.com
Domaine Benjamin et David Duclaux
+33 (0)4 74 59 56 30

DOMAINE RÉMI NIERO 95/100

▼ .● Eminence 2012 : Attractive garnet shades. Delightful, focused nose displaying raspberry and violet on first pour then a stunning spice bouquet. The palate shows seductive freshness, ethereal character and a refined mouthfeel. Restraint and superb persistency. Price approx.: 29,00 EUR
Domaine Niero
+33 (0)4 74 56 86 99

BENJAMIN ET DAVID DUCLAUX 94/100

▼ .● La Germine 2012 : Attractive garnet tints. Refined nose mingling violet, red fruits, spice and mineral character. The palate shows seductively precise aromatics, freshness, fine texture and substance. A delightful ethereal style. Noble yet instantly accessible. Very successful. Price approx.: 39,00 EUR
http://www.coterotie-duclaux.com
Domaine Benjamin et David Duclaux
+33 (0)4 74 59 56 30

DOMAINE GILLES BARGE 92/100

▼ .● Le Combard 2011 : Garnet. Suggestions of ultra ripe fruit on the nose with mineral and toast undercurrents. Medium-bodied yet harmonious palate. The fruit carries through with spice notes followed by a typical liquorice and tar finish. Needs aerating. Price approx.: 35,00 EUR
http://www.domainebarge.com
Domaine Gilles Barge
+33 (0)4 74 56 13 90

DOMAINE DE CORPS DE LOUP 88/100

▼ .● Corps de Loup 2010 : Beautiful vibrant, satin-like red. Distinctive nose with a floral, fruity and spice character. Supple, melted attack with fairly lightweight stuffing supported by a lively, still fiery structure. Young, would benefit from a few years' bottle age. Price approx.: 29,00 EUR
http://www.corpsdeloup.com
Domaine de Corps de Loup
+33 (0)4 74 56 84 64

DOMAINE DE CORPS DE LOUP — 87/100

▼ ♪ Corps de Loup 2011 : Garnet. Distinctive, endearing nose driven by peony, cassis and liquorice. A very supple wine showing medium concentration. Delicate mouthfeel with restrained aromatic presence and elegance. A wine that would benefit from a little bottle age. Serve with duck breasts.
Price approx.: 29,00 EUR
http://www.corpsdeloup.com
Domaine de Corps de Loup
+33 (0)4 74 56 84 64

CÔTES DU RHÔNE

DOMAINE SAINT AMANT — 89/100

▼ ♪ Cuvée Nathalie - Syrah 2010 : Deep garnet. Profound nose revealing beautiful ripe red fruit backed by garrigue and spice with subtle oak undertones. Full, well-structured and closely-integrated palate. Racy, perfumed Syrah expression. Huge potential.
Price approx.: 25,00 EUR
http://www.domainesaintamant.com
Domaine Saint Amant
+33 (0)4 90 62 99 25

DOMAINE NICOLAS CROZE — 88/100

▼ ♪ L'Epicurienne - Récolté en Vendange Manuelle 2011 : Deep garnet. Intense nose of lovely jammy fruits. Concentrated palate that is warm but not excessively so. Augmented by a peppery and stone fruit finish. Develops a flavoursome aromatic personality. Set aside for fine cuts of game.
Price approx.: 10,50 EUR
http://www.domaine-nicolas-croze.com
Domaine Nicolas Croze
+33 (0)4 75 04 67 11

DOMAINE NICOLAS CROZE — 88/100

▼ ♪ Vieilles Vignes - Récolté en Vendange Manuelle 2012 : Brilliant light yellow. Pleasant nose suggestive of ripe apricot and peach with a floral touch. Supple attack, delicious, crunchy and powerful palate showing fruit and refined spice. Hot, persistent finish. A successful white wine pairing with fish.
Price approx.: 10,50 EUR
http://www.domaine-nicolas-croze.com
Domaine Nicolas Croze
+33 (0)4 75 04 67 11

CHÂTEAU BEAUCHÊNE — 88/100

▼ ♪ Grande Réserve 2013 : Lightly-coloured ruby with dark purple tints. Subdued nose blending black fruits and a vegetal dimension. Freshness, tightly-wound tannins, lovely fruit and beautiful concentration. Very enjoyable, spice-driven finish. A promising wine for cellaring.
Price approx.: 6,00 EUR
http://www.chateaubeauchene.com
Château Beauchêne
+33 (0)4 90 51 75 87

DOMAINE DE L'ARNESQUE — 87/100

▼ ♪ Fleur de Guarrigues 2011 : Intense, young colour. Distinctive, rich nose with empyreumatic accents, undergrowth and stone fruits. Warm, mouth-coating palate. Huge fruit and spice presence. Assertive Mediterranean aromatics. Tradition is scrupulously abided by. A handsome wine. Price approx.: 5,80 EUR
http://www.arnesque.com
Domaine de l'Arnesque
+33 (0)4 90 40 32 84

DOMAINE NICOLAS CROZE — 87/100

▼ ♪ Coeur de Galets - Récolté en Vendange Manuelle 2011 : Deeply-coloured garnet. Refined vanilla oak on the nose backed by stone fruits and black olives. Very supple, soft palate. Oak melds with the fruit and spice. An impeccably balanced wine with an assertive Southern personality. A Rhone with real allure. Price approx.: 10,50 EUR
http://www.domaine-nicolas-croze.com
Domaine Nicolas Croze
+33 (0)4 75 04 67 11

CLOS DE CAVEAU — 87/100

Org▼ ♪ Les Bateliers 2013 : Deep crimson. Inviting nose showing a cornucopia of red and black fruits with herbs and fine spices. Round attack, full palate with generous, clearly-defined aroma, spontaneity and a natural impression. The mid-palate is lively and spicy. A successful wine.
Price approx.: 6,70 EUR
http://www.closdecaveau.com
Le Clos de Caveau
+33 (0)4 90 65 85 33

DOMAINE JULIEN DE L'EMBISQUE — 87/100

▼ ♪ Cuvée Plaisir 2011 : Vibrant, young red. Very inviting, profound nose marrying black fruit notes, olive paste and game. Very melted at point of entry with focused aromas. The finish stays perfumed and persistent in a very Southern style.
Price approx.: 6,70 EUR
http://www.st-julien-de-lembisque.fr
Domaine Julien de l'Embisque
+33 (0)4 90 30 56 34

DOMAINE DES ARCHES — 87/100

▼ ♪ Esprit des Arches 2012 : Deep, young-looking colour. Beautiful southern-style nose revealing a

basket of ripe fruits, fine spices and a touch of garrigue. Supple, accessible, generous and lively palate. A delicious generic displaying lovely harmony. Appealing spice and liquorice finish. Price approx.: 4,95 EUR
http://www.domaine-des-arches.com
Domaine des Arches
+33 (0)4 75 27 11 00

DOMAINE SAINT AMANT   86/100

▼ ♪ La Borry 2013 : Light gold. Appealing nose of white fruits in syrup, bush peach and fresh grape. The palate is young and fiery and delivers pleasant heady and fruity flavours. Fresh and delicious. Drink from the aperitif through to dessert. Price approx.: 9,00 EUR
http://www.domainesaintamant.com
Domaine Saint Amant
+33 (0)4 90 62 99 25

PAVILLON SAINT-PIERRE   86/100

▼ ♪ Réserve 2012 : Deep red, garnet tints. Endearing nose blending red fruits and mild spices. Fullness, a fine-grained, closely-integrated texture and savoury spice presence on the palate with a sensation of freshness supporting the whole. A well-made Côtes du Rhône. Price approx.: 8,50 EUR
http://www.skalli.com
Les Vins Skalli
+33 (0)4 90 83 58 35

FRENCH CELLARS   86/100

▼ ♪ Vintage 2012 : Attractive colour with dark purple tints. Precise nose with fruity aromas augmented by a subtle mineral and spice touch. Full, fat palate with fine, closely-integrated tannins. A delicious, fruit-driven style that works well with barbecued foods. Price approx.: 3,25 EUR
http://www.winesoverland.com
Wines Overland
+33 (0)1 45 08 87 87

CHÂTEAU HUSSON   86/100

CONV▼ ♪ Vintage 2012 : Deep, young colour. Intense nose driven by fresh stone fruits and spicy undercurrents. Supple palate with restrained heat. More of the same, quite delightful fruit. A Côtes du Rhône that will definitely attract a following. Price approx.: 6,80 EUR
www.royere-husson.com
Château Husson
+33 (0)4 90 76 87 76

DOMAINE DES FAVARDS   86/100

▼ ♪ Prestige 2012 : Intense crimson. Pleasurable nose marrying redcurrants, red berry fruits, black

pepper and violet. Lovely impression of lightness on the palate, beautiful freshness and precise, focused and exuberant aromas. Spicy finish. A nicely crafted generic. Price approx.: 5,50 EUR
www.favards.com
Domaine des Favards
+33 (0)4 90 70 94 64

DOMAINE DES FAVARDS   86/100

CONV▼ ♪ Les bons moments... 2013 : Brilliant salmon-pink. Generous nose of red fruits with a hint of crispness. On the palate, a fairly robust, generous, full and expressive rosé where spice dovetails with fruit. An all-round wine that would work with flavoursome foods. Price approx.: 4,90 EUR
www.favards.com
Domaine des Favards
+33 (0)4 90 70 94 64

DOMAINE DE L'AMANDINE   85/100

▼ ♪ Vintage 2012 : Deeply-coloured garnet. Nose of black fruits, stone fruits and a touch of spice. The palate is supple, fresh and sets the stage for fruit flavours. A distinctive, accessible Côtes du Rhône pairing with roast capon. Price approx.: 6,50 EUR
http://www.domaine-amandine.fr
Domaine de l'Amandine
+33 (0)4 90 46 12 39

ARNOUX ET FILS   85/100

▼ ♪ Vieux Clocher 2013 : Pale gold with brilliant highlights. Appealing nose showing perfumes of peach, pear and fresh grape. Freshness is forward from point of entry onwards and supports flavour over substantial length. An easy-drinking wine that would work with pear tart. Price approx.: 6,30 EUR
http://htp://www.arnoux-vins.com
Arnoux et Fils
+33 (0)4 90 65 84 18

DOMAINE BERNARD   85/100

▼ ♪ Vice versa 2011 : Fairly deep colour with garnet highlights. Nose of jammy fruits with aromas of cherry, redcurrant and raspberry in brandy. A well-balanced, chewy Côtes du Rhône offering up a mature, quality aromatic framework. Powerful and pairing with roasts. Price approx.: 5,00 EUR
Domaine Bernard
+33 (0)4 90 46 55 76

Detailed instructions are featured
at the start of the book.

DOMAINE SAINT AMANT 85/100

▼ ✦ Les Clapas 2012 : Appealing ruby. Focused nose with red fruit aromas augmented by a vegetal and spice note. Supple, fairly generous attack with a polished mouthfeel. More of the spice mid-palate and on the finish. A wine for instant pleasure. Enjoy whilst still fruit-driven.
Price approx.: 8,00 EUR
http://www.domainesaintamant.com
Domaine Saint Amant
+33 (0)4 90 62 99 25

DOMAINE DE L'AMANDINE 84/100

▼ ✦ Vintage 2013 : Pale gold. Refined nose driven by almond with white fruits and a touch of verbena. The palate shows sourness, heat and focused flavours. Balance, density and honesty characterises the whole. A wine for spice-flavoured fish.
Price approx.: 7,50 EUR
http://www.domaine-amandine.fr
Domaine de l'Amandine
+33 (0)4 90 46 12 39

DOMAINE SAINT AMANT 84/100

▼ ✦ Les Trois Roses 2013 : Light salmon-pink. Nose of crunchy red berry fruits and citrus with a spice touch. Very supple, very fresh palate showing delightful flavours recalling sweets. Works particularly well as an aperitif.
Price approx.: 10,00 EUR
http://www.domainesaintamant.com
Domaine Saint Amant
+33 (0)4 90 62 99 25

ARNOUX ET FILS 84/100

▼ ✦ Vieux Clocher 2013 : Young dark purple. Nose of fresh black fruits with garrigue, spice and pepper undertones. Warm, chewy and intense palate driven by spice perfumes. Fruit also features and shines through on the finish. A good Côtes du Rhône for grilled, herb-flavoured meats.
Price approx.: 5,70 EUR
http://htp://www.arnoux-vins.com
Arnoux et Fils
+33 (0)4 90 65 84 18

LAUDUN CHUSCLAN VIGNERONS 84/100

▼ ✦ Esprit du Rhône 2013 : Very young, deep colour. Nose of crunchy, fresh red and black berry fruits. Very supple, very soft palate showing seductive fruit presence, freshness and lightness. A Côtes du Rhône drinking best whilst still fruit-forward. Perfect for barbecued foods.
http://www.laudunchusclanvignerons.com
Laudun Chusclan Vignerons
+33 (0)4 66 90 53 46

LAUDUN CHUSCLAN VIGNERONS 84/100

▼ ✦ Prieurs de St-Julien 2013 : Very youthful, deep colour. Nose of crunchy, fresh red and black berry fruits. More of the delicious fruit aromas on the palate. Very supple mouthfeel allowing fruit to be released. Serve with grilled red meats.
http://www.laudunchusclanvignerons.com
Laudun Chusclan Vignerons
+33 (0)4 66 90 53 46

LAUDUN CHUSCLAN VIGNERONS 84/100

Org▼ ✦ Terra Vitae 2013 : Young ruby. Subtle fruit on the nose. Very supple palate with nicely harnessed power due to freshness. The fruit is focused and crunchy. A wine to be enjoyed for its youthful qualities, pairing with, say, flank steak.
Price approx.: 4,95 EUR
http://www.laudunchusclanvignerons.com
Laudun Chusclan Vignerons
+33 (0)4 66 90 53 46

FAMILLE VERGNIAUD-BERNARD 84/100

▼ ✦ Le Temps des Cerises 2013 : Lightly-coloured crimson with purple-blue tints. Focused nose driven by blackberry and cassis, liquorice and violet with spice undertones. Supple attack, round and full palate with full-on fruit expression. Youthful tannins. Firm, fruit-driven finish.
Price approx.: 5,00 EUR
http://www.chateaubeauchene.com
Château Beauchêne
+33 (0)4 90 51 75 87

DOMAINE JULIEN DE L'EMBISQUE 84/100

CONV▼ ✦ Cuvée Plaisir 2012 : Vibrant, young red. Pleasant nose of black fruits and spice. Supple attack on the palate leading into a slightly more structured mid-palate. Lovely aromatic personality and spice-infused finish. Serve with spice-flavoured red meats.
Price approx.: 6,70 EUR
http://www.st-julien-de-lembisque.fr
Domaine Julien de l'Embisque
+33 (0)4 90 30 56 34

DOMAINE JULIEN DE L'EMBISQUE 84/100

Org▼ ✦ Délice de Viognier 2013 : Limpid pale yellow. Expressive, heady nose intermixing notes of apricot, white flowers and honeyed touches. Good suppleness and fat on the palate framed by freshness. A well-balanced, perfumed and medium-bodied white wine.
Price approx.: 9,90 EUR
http://www.st-julien-de-lembisque.fr
Domaine Julien de l'Embisque
+33 (0)4 90 30 56 34

MAS DE LA LIONNE 84/100

▼ ♪ Ombre du Chateau Vieilles Vignes 2012 : Appealing garnet. The nose opens up to blackcurrant and raspberry with mineral notes. Honest attack with fairly tightwound tannins. Beautiful fullness on the palate in a warm setting. Classic in style.
Price approx.: 8,50 EUR
La Lionne
+33 (0)4 90 39 50 32

CAVE DES VIGNERONS DU CASTELAS 84/100

▼ ♪ Les Mésanges 2013 : Brilliant pale gold. Pleasurable nose suggestive of exotic fruits and white flowers. Full, supple and velvety palate with the range of nose aromatics carrying through. Good balance. Drink as an appetiser or with oily fish.
Price approx.: 4,90 EUR
http://www.vignerons-castelas.com
Cave des Vignerons du Castelas
+33 (0)4 90 26 62 66

CAVE DES VIGNERONS DU CASTELAS 84/100

▼ ♪ Vintage 2013 : Deep pink. Nose of red berry fruits with a lemony touch in the background. Beautiful exuberance on the attack. Supple, fruity palate showing lovely balance. Fresh finish. A pleasant rosé for the aperitif.
Price approx.: 3,90 EUR
http://www.vignerons-castelas.com
Cave des Vignerons du Castelas
+33 (0)4 90 26 62 66

ARNOUX ET FILS 83/100

▼ ♪ Seigneur de Lauris 2013 : Deep, young colour. The nose shows an earthy character halfway between vegetal, forest and stone fruit perfumes. Warm, powerful palate with noticeable tannins. Fruit in brandy flavours are heightened on the finish. Calls for meats in a sauce.
Price approx.: 6,80 EUR
http://htp://www.arnoux-vins.com
Arnoux et Fils
+33 (0)4 90 65 84 18

CAVE DES VIGNERONS DU CASTELAS 83/100

▼ ♪ Roca Fortis 2009 : Slightly evolved red. Mature nose opening up to animal notes and undergrowth backed by red fruits. Juxtaposition between a sensation of heat and exuberance on the palate. Still fiery. Pair with red meats or meat in a sauce.
Price approx.: 12,00 EUR
http://www.vignerons-castelas.com
Cave des Vignerons du Castelas
+33 (0)4 90 26 62 66

LAUDUN CHUSCLAN VIGNERONS 82/100

▼ ♪ Natura Vitis 2013 : Attractive ruby with dark purple highlights. Warm nose blending red fruits with vegetal and spice notes. Round, polished palate showing more of the same fruity perfumes. A pleasant, instantly-accessible and simple wine in a natural style.
http://www.laudunchusclanvignerons.com
Laudun Chusclan Vignerons
+33 (0)4 66 90 53 46

DOMAINE DU GRAND BELLY 82/100

▼ ♪ Vintage 2013 : Deep crimson with dark purple tints. Red fruits, a touch of garrigue and fine spice on a moderately clean nose (SO2). Full, concentrated and vigorous palate with spice playing a significant role. An accessible generic that would work with simple foods.
Price approx.: 4,10 EUR
http://www.vignerons-castelas.com
Cave des Vignerons du Castelas
+33 (0)4 90 26 62 66

CAVE DES VIGNERONS DU CASTELAS 82/100

▼ ♪ Cuvée d'Antan 2012 : Medium intense garnet. A mix of red fruit and vegetal notes on the palate. Supple, warm palate with a fairly light, closely-integrated mouthfeel. A harmonious, approachable style. Drink with barbecued foods.
Price approx.: 4,50 EUR
http://www.vignerons-castelas.com
Cave des Vignerons du Castelas
+33 (0)4 90 26 62 66

CAVES SAINT-PIERRE 81/100

▼ ♪ Sélection Vieilles Vignes 2012 : Deeply-coloured garnet. Plummy nose with cherry bordering on jammy and subtle spice notes. A warm, powerful and rich style with honest fruit expression. Set aside for barbecues or meats in a sauce.
Price approx.: 3,95 EUR
http://www.skalli.com
Les Vins Skalli
+33 (0)4 90 83 58 35

THE COLOUR OF THE WINES :

▼ Red wine	▼ Sparkling brut
▼ Dry white wine	▼ Sparkling brut rose
▼ Rose wine	▼ Brandy
▼ Sweet white wine	▼ Liqueur wine

BONPAS 81/100

▼ ♪ Grande Exception 2012 : Dark red. Nose of jammy ripe fruits and stone fruits. On the palate, a generous, lush and fruity Côtes du Rhône balanced by a touch of freshness. A robust wine for red meats. Price approx.: 4,90 EUR
Boisset La Famille des Grand Vins - Bonpas
+33 (0)4 90 83 58 35

CAVE DES VIGNERONS DU CASTELAS 78/100

▼ ♪ Vintage 2012 : Deeply-coloured, crimson tints. Focused, generous nose blending ripe black fruits and spice notes. Power and a sensation of heat are the focal points on the palate. Full, well-integrated stuffing capped off with a slightly disjointed note of exuberance.
Price approx.: 3,90 EUR
http://www.vignerons-castelas.com
Cave des Vignerons du Castelas
+33 (0)4 90 26 62 66

CÔTES DU RHÔNE-VILLAGES

DOMAINE SAINT AMANT 89/100

▼ ♪ La Tabardonne 2012 : Light gold. Rich, heady nose midway between smoky vanilla perfumes and notes of peach, pear and almond. Mouth-coating, very chewy and round on the palate. Extremely well-staged perfumes dominated by young, quality oak ageing. Great craftsmanship.
Price approx.: 15,00 EUR
http://www.domainesaintamant.com
Domaine Saint Amant
+33 (0)4 90 62 99 25

DOMAINE JULIEN DE L'EMBISQUE 88/100

▼ ♪ Cuvée Prestige 2011 : Deep, young-looking garnet. Profound nose of black fruits, spice, olive paste and garrigue notes. Beautiful mouthfeel with velvety tannins, a powerful mid-palate yet an aromatic, sun-filled finish. An idiosyncratic wine. Price approx.: 8,50 EUR
http://www.st-julien-de-lembisque.fr
Domaine Julien de l'Embisque
+33 (0)4 90 30 56 34

ARNOUX ET FILS 87/100

▼ ♪ Genus 2011 : Concentrated colour, still in its youth. Nose of jammy red and black fruits with floral and spice presence. Supple, soft mouthfeel with focused, crunchy and ripe fruit and freshness. Southern-style aromatics with no excessive power. Sterling work.
Price approx.: 7,00 EUR
http://htp://www.arnoux-vins.com
Arnoux et Fils
+33 (0)4 90 65 84 18

DOMAINE JULIEN DE L'EMBISQUE 84/100

▼ ♪ Cuvée Prestige 2012 : Young, vibrant red. Slightly muted on the nose with subtle mineral accents. A dense, tightly-wound wine that is fairly backward in terms of aromatics. Young, needs more bottle time. Price approx.: 7,70 EUR
http://www.st-julien-de-lembisque.fr
Domaine Julien de l'Embisque
+33 (0)4 90 30 56 34

DOMAINE DE CABASSE 83/100

▼ ♪ Primevères 2013 : Limpid pale yellow. Pleasant, focused nose marrying almond and white flower notes. Beautiful fruity attack leading into a well-balanced mid-palate with a tangy touch. A clean, enjoyable wine pairing with grilled fish.
Price approx.: 10,00 EUR
http://www.cabasse.fr
Domaine de Cabasse
+33 (0)4 90 46 91 12

CÔTES DU RHÔNE-VILLAGES CAIRANNE

DOMAINE ALARY 90/100

CONV▼ ♪ L'Estévenas 2011 : Dark-hued with dark purple tints. Racy nose showing smoke, herbs, fine spices, truffle and blackcurrant jelly. Virile palate displaying a delicious, lush mouthfeel with a harmonious structure framed by lovely velvety tannins. A superlative Cairanne.
Price approx.: 10,20 EUR
http://www.domaine-alary.fr
Domaine Alary
+33 (0)4 90 30 82 32

DOMAINE ALARY 89/100

CONV▼ ♪ La Jean de Verde 2011 : Deep garnet. Expressive, open nose with fruit and spice aromas augmented by a pleasant floral and vegetal dimension. Lush, rich and mellow palate revealing an explosion of jammy and Mediterranean flavours. An opulent wine. Price approx.: 13,00 EUR
http://www.domaine-alary.fr
Domaine Alary
+33 (0)4 90 30 82 32

CHÂTEAU LE PLAISIR 89/100

▼ ♪ Vintage 2011 : Intense colour with crimson tints. Refined, expressive nose revealing beautiful floral, fruity and spicy aromas. The palate shows a seductive full, polished and melted attack with precise aromas and a touch of freshness framing the whole. A successful wine.
Price approx.: 11,40 EUR
Château Le Plaisir
+33 (0)4 90 46 84 05

DOMAINE ALARY   88/100

CONV▼ ♪ La Brunote 2011 : Dark garnet. Powerful nose of toast, fine spices and garrigue. Velvety, heady and luxurious palate showing splendid nascent, complex southern-style aromas supported by a silky structure. Will need time to fully reveal itself. Price approx.: 8,80 EUR
http://www.domaine-alary.fr
Domaine Alary
+33 (0)4 90 30 82 32

CHÂTEAU LE PLAISIR   88/100

▼ ♪ Vintage 2012 : Intense colour with crimson tints. The nose is wild and still fiery, revealing black fruit, liquorice and spice aromas after swirling. Beautiful presence on the palate, warm, full, lush, melted and perfumed. Would work with meats in a sauce. Price approx.: 11,95 EUR
Château Le Plaisir
+33 (0)4 90 46 84 05

L'AMEILLAUD   87/100

▼ ♪ Vintage 2012 : Dark garnet, young tints. Reticent nose with a floral note and ripe black fruits. More expressive on the palate. A virile wine revealing redcurrant, black berries, pepper, herbs and a trace of jam. Lively with a vegetal presence. A recommendable Cairanne. Price approx.: 9,30 EUR
http://www.ameillaud.com
Domaine de l'Ameillaud
+33 (0)4 90 30 82 02

ARNOUX ET FILS   86/100

▼ ♪ Vieux Clocher - Secret de Terroir 2013 : Beautiful deep colour with garnet nuances. Seductive nose with a spice character matching the delicious fruit. Fleshy, polished attack leading into a full mid-palate. Well-balanced with distinctive aromas that linger. Ideal for grilled beef. Price approx.: 8,15 EUR
http://htp://www.arnoux-vins.com
Arnoux et Fils
+33 (0)4 90 65 84 18

CÔTES DU RHÔNE-VILLAGES CHUSCLAN

LAUDUN CHUSCLAN VIGNERONS   87/100

▼ ♪ Agapa 2013 : Deep colour with very young tints. Distinctive, fruit-driven nose of bigarreau cherry, plum and raspberry. A full, supple Chusclan with power nicely counterbalanced by freshness, all of which showcases aroma. Spicy finish. A successful wine ready now.
http://www.laudunchusclanvignerons.com
Laudun Chusclan Vignerons
+33 (0)4 66 90 53 46

LAUDUN CHUSCLAN VIGNERONS   86/100

▼ ♪ Excellence 2013 : Magnificent crimson with dark purple. Refined nose driven by plum, cassis, black cherry and mild spices. Soft palate with a silky mouthfeel. A sensation of suppleness is revealed on the attack, lovely fruit presence. A very harmonious, accessible Chusclan.
Price approx.: 11,80 EUR
http://www.laudunchusclanvignerons.com
Laudun Chusclan Vignerons
+33 (0)4 66 90 53 46

LAUDUN CHUSCLAN VIGNERONS   86/100

▼ ♪ Les Genets 2013 : Black with youthful tints. Compelling nose of dark fruits and stone fruits with peony and violet undertones. Supple palate with a soft mouthfeel. Beautiful fruity freshness (plum, cherry). A delicate Chusclan, ideal as an introduction to the appellation.
Price approx.: 8,20 EUR
http://www.laudunchusclanvignerons.com
Laudun Chusclan Vignerons
+33 (0)4 66 90 53 46

DOMAINE DE LA BARANIÈRE   85/100

▼ ♪ Vintage 2013 : Beautifully youthful, concentrated hue. Distinctive nose with upfront spice and stone fruits. Full, focused and fruit-driven palate showing an assertive Mediterranean style. Powerful. Finish of prunes and spice. Recommended for game in a sauce.
http://www.laudunchusclanvignerons.com
Laudun Chusclan Vignerons
+33 (0)4 66 90 53 46

DOMAINE DE L'OLIVETTE   84/100

▼ ♪ Vintage 2013 : Deeply-coloured crimson with purple-blue. Lovely nose of fresh stone fruits. The palate is augmented by a delicious black olive nuance. The mouthfeel stays supple and soft. A Chusclan drinking best whilst still young and crunchy.
http://www.laudunchusclanvignerons.com
Laudun Chusclan Vignerons
+33 (0)4 66 90 53 46

LAUDUN CHUSCLAN VIGNERONS   82/100

▼ ♪ Les Monticauts 2013 : Intense hue with crimson and dark purple. Young nose with fresh red and black fruit. Delightful, supple palate. Pleasurable fruit encounter. A Chusclan suitable for any occasion, particularly with grilled red meats.
Price approx.: 8,20 EUR
http://www.laudunchusclanvignerons.com
Laudun Chusclan Vignerons
+33 (0)4 66 90 53 46

CÔTES DU RHÔNE-VILLAGES LAUDUN

DOMAINE ROUVRE SAINT LÉGER 91/100

▼ ✦ Vintage 2012 : Magnificent young dark purple. Charming nose showing crunchy fresh, wild berries, plum and morello cherry backed by refined spice. Remarkably balanced palate with a dense, full mouthfeel, assertive power, silky aromatic texture. A superlative, noble, racy Laudun.
Price approx.: 15,00 EUR
http://www.rouvresaintleger.com
Domaine Rouvre Saint Léger
+33 (0)6 17 33 80 26

DOMAINE ROUVRE SAINT LÉGER 91/100

▼ ✦ Vintage 2013 : Light gold. Delicate nose infused with apricot, dried and yellow fruits with a floral touch in the background. Suave, velvety and silky palate that is extremely delicate. Good concentration with clear-cut aromas. A very elegant wine. Price approx.: 15,00 EUR
http://www.rouvresaintleger.com
Domaine Rouvre Saint Léger
+33 (0)6 17 33 80 26

CLOS DE TAMAN 87/100

▼ ✦ Vintage 2013 : Intense hue tinged with purple-blue. Expressive, distinctive nose intermixing red fruits, liquorice, spice and a floral dimension. On the palate, a full, generous and rich wine balanced by a pleasant sensation of freshness. Harmonious and crunchy. Price approx.: 8,20 EUR
http://www.laudunchusclanvignerons.com
Laudun Chusclan Vignerons
+33 (0)4 66 90 53 46

LAUDUN CHUSCLAN VIGNERONS 87/100

▼ ✦ Agapa 2013 : Brilliant light yellow. Compelling nose with a floral dimension and lovely tropical and stone berry fruit tones. Round attack, seductive silky and rich yet lively palate with apricot and vanilla. A successful wine that works best with exotic dishes.
http://www.laudunchusclanvignerons.com
Laudun Chusclan Vignerons
+33 (0)4 66 90 53 46

LAUDUN CHUSCLAN VIGNERONS 87/100

▼ ✦ Les Dolia 2013 : Crimson with purple-blue. Profound, distinctive nose where ripe red and black fruit perfumes are coupled with liquorice and spice. Rich, full palate showing lovely aromatic precision. A generous, mellow and persistent Laudun.
Price approx.: 8,20 EUR
http://www.laudunchusclanvignerons.com
Laudun Chusclan Vignerons
+33 (0)4 66 90 53 46

LAUDUN CHUSCLAN VIGNERONS 87/100

Org▼ ✦ Terra Vitae 2013 : Light yellow. Refined nose with almond, white peach and white flower nuances. Round palate boasting savoury acidity. Focused, persistent aromatic presence. An absolute must-try in white. Perfect for freshwater fish.
Price approx.: 7,00 EUR
http://www.laudunchusclanvignerons.com
Laudun Chusclan Vignerons
+33 (0)4 66 90 53 46

LAUDUN CHUSCLAN VIGNERONS 86/100

Org▼ ✦ Natura Vitis 2013 : Light yellow. Nose of dried fruits, white fruits and floral undertones. Fat, suppleness and freshness enhancing focused perfumes. The finish is augmented by a touch of verbena. A pretty Laudun that would make a marvellous partner for trout with almonds.
http://www.laudunchusclanvignerons.com
Laudun Chusclan Vignerons
+33 (0)4 66 90 53 46

LAUDUN CHUSCLAN VIGNERONS 85/100

▼ ✦ Excellence 2013 : Light yellow. A mix of white fruits and apricot backed by vanilla oak on the nose. Supple attack, lovely round, full and mellow presence on the palate with fine, closely-integrated exuberance. Fairly reticent fruit aromas, oak still prevails. Promising. Price approx.: 9,10 EUR
http://www.laudunchusclanvignerons.com
Laudun Chusclan Vignerons
+33 (0)4 66 90 53 46

LAUDUN CHUSCLAN VIGNERONS 80/100

Org▼ ✦ Natura Vitis 2013 : Young crimson with purple-blue. Fairly subdued nose halfway between fresh fruit and vegetal notes. The palate shows faint beading and boasts lovely fresh fruit. A very approachable Laudun, already drinking well now.
http://www.laudunchusclanvignerons.com
Laudun Chusclan Vignerons
+33 (0)4 66 90 53 46

LAUDUN CHUSCLAN VIGNERONS 80/100

Org▼ ✦ Terra Vitae 2013 : Young colour. Subdued nose with vegetal-type aromas. Fruit is more forthcoming on the palate (cherry, raspberry) which is supple and light. Drinking well from now on. Recommended for a platter of cold cuts.
Price approx.: 7,00 EUR
http://www.laudunchusclanvignerons.com
Laudun Chusclan Vignerons
+33 (0)4 66 90 53 46

Detailed instructions are featured
at the start of the book.

CÔTES DU RHÔNE-VILLAGES PLAN DE DIEU

DOMAINE DES PASQUIERS   90/100

▼ .✿ L' Envy 2011 : Beautiful deeply-coloured garnet. Very compelling, intense nose suggestive of black fruits, spices and liquorice backed by cocoa. Generous, velvety, full and fruity palate with polished tannins. Lingering spicy finish. A superlative, powerful wine. Price approx.: 20,00 EUR
http://www.domainedespasquiers.fr
Les Vignobles des Pasquiers
+33 (0)4 90 46 83 97

DOMAINE DES FAVARDS   88/100

▼ .✿ Vintage 2010 : Deeply-coloured garnet. Endearing nose of mild spices, cocoa, red fruits and subtle oak. Virile palate showing delicate aromas of mild tobacco, cigar box and some fine tannins with a vegetal mid-palate. Gets our approval. A little more bottle time is recommended.
Price approx.: 8,60 EUR
www.favards.com
Domaine des Favards
+33 (0)4 90 70 94 64

DOMAINE DE L'ARNESQUE   87/100

▼ .✿ Plan de Dieu 2011 : Deep, young colour. Nose of fresh red and black fruits with spice undertones. Supple palate, power counterbalanced by heat and nicely showcased fruit and spice perfumes that linger. A distinctive, youthful Plan de Dieu which is gradually settling down.
Price approx.: 8,20 EUR
http://www.arnesque.com
Domaine de l'Arnesque
+33 (0)4 90 40 32 84

DOMAINE DES PASQUIERS   87/100

▼ .✿ Vintage 2012 : Deeply-coloured garnet with young tints. Pleasant nose marrying spice, black fruits and dried grass backed by cocoa. Supple, full, delicious palate showing beautiful concentration and tight-knit tannins. Fresh, fruit-forward finish. Drink with red meats. Price approx.: 8,50 EUR
http://www.domainedespasquiers.fr
Les Vignobles des Pasquiers
+33 (0)4 90 46 83 97

FRENCH CELLARS   86/100

▼ .✿ Vintage 2012 : Crimson with purple-blue. Expressive nose marrying ripe red fruits, spices and mineral and liquorice undertones. Powerful, warm palate enveloping full, mellow substance. Slightly firmer finish imparting a degree of length.
Price approx.: 3,60 EUR
http://www.winesoverland.com

Wines Overland
+33 (0)1 45 08 87 87

JOSEPH CASTAN   85/100

▼ .✿ Sélection Plan de Dieu 2012 : Beautiful, fairly deep vibrant red. Nose of black fruits, spices and ripe olive. On the palate, lovely round, fruity attack leading into a compelling fleshy, fresh mid-palate. Pleasant liquorice and garrigue-driven finish.
Price approx.: 6,00 EUR
Joseph Castan
+33 (0)4 67 40 00 64

BONPAS   85/100

▼ .✿ Grande Exception 2013 : Deeply-coloured crimson. Concentrated nose blending dark fruits, black olives and a touch of spice. Lush palate showing lovely quality aromatics and mellowness. Beautiful spice-driven length. Serve with rib-steak.
Price approx.: 6,75 EUR
Boisset La Famille des Grand Vins - Bonpas
+33 (0)4 90 83 58 35

CÔTES DU RHÔNE-VILLAGES PUYMÉRAS

DOMAINE BERNARD   87/100

▼ .✿ Cuvée Augustin 2010 : Deep garnet. Expressive nose of black fruits, mild spices, herbs and subtle oak. A virile, concentrated wine in an archetypal southern style with beautiful uplifting exuberance. Everything is in place. A well-made Villages deserving a little more bottle time.
Price approx.: 9,50 EUR
Domaine Bernard
+33 (0)4 90 46 55 76

DOMAINE BERNARD   86/100

▼ .✿ Puyméras 2010 : Deep garnet, mature tints. Compelling nose showing overripe fruit basket aromas, hay, jammy notes, toast and spice. Silky attack leading into a full-bodied yet lively palate with the same lovely nose exuberance carrying through. Impression of heat, some tannins.
Price approx.: 7,50 EUR
Domaine Bernard
+33 (0)4 90 46 55 76

CÔTES DU RHÔNE-VILLAGES SABLET

DOMAINE DES PASQUIERS — 88/100

▼ ✦ Vintage 2012 : Deeply-coloured garnet with dark purple tints. Profound nose of ripe black fruits, spice and vegetal notes. Supple attack. Heat, power and fruit on the palate with velvety tannins and persistent spice. Well-balanced, harmonious and silky. A successful wine.
Price approx.: 8,50 EUR
http://www.domainedespasquiers.fr
Les Vignobles des Pasquiers
+33 (0)4 90 46 83 97

CÔTES DU RHÔNE-VILLAGES SÉGURET

DOMAINE DE L'AMAUVE — 88/100

▼ ✦ Réserve 2010 : Dark crimson tinged with dark purple. Endearing nose of blackberry, blackcurrant, liquorice and mild spice with subtle oak. Powerful, robust and virile palate supported by a substantial, lively structure with no heaviness. Firm finish. A successful wine.
Price approx.: 14,00 EUR
http://www.domainedelamauve.fr
Domaine de l'Amauve
+33 (0)4 90 46 82 81

DOMAINE DE L'AMAUVE — 87/100

▼ ✦ La Daurèle 2012 : Brilliant pale hue. Compelling nose recalling plum, fennel and linden. On the palate, a round, full wine revealing generous, honest aromatics. Fresh with a spicy mid-palate. Serve with grilled fish.
Price approx.: 9,50 EUR
http://www.domainedelamauve.fr
Domaine de l'Amauve
+33 (0)4 90 46 82 81

DOMAINE DE L'AMAUVE — 87/100

▼ ✦ Les Merrelies 2012 : Limpid crimson with youthful highlights. Promising nose of red and black fruits with mild spices and subtle oak in the background. Silky attack, a powerful yet delightful wine with fully open fruit and spice aromas. Firm, vegetal finish.
Price approx.: 11,50 EUR
http://www.domainedelamauve.fr
Domaine de l'Amauve
+33 (0)4 90 46 82 81

DOMAINE DE L'AMAUVE — 86/100

▼ ✦ Laurances 2011 : Dark garnet with dark purple tints. Pleasurable nose of blackberry and raspberry with refined spice. A welcoming, spontaneous and robust wine on the palate showing lovely exuberance and freshness. Firm, spicy finish. A successful effort. Price approx.: 9,50 EUR
http://www.domainedelamauve.fr
Domaine de l'Amauve
+33 (0)4 90 46 82 81

DOMAINE DE L'AMAUVE — 86/100

▼ ✦ Laurances 2012 : Crimson, dark purple tints. Pleasurable nose with abundant red and black fruits, an elegant vegetal dimension and mild spices. The palate displays drive, supported by a silky structure with a vegetal mid-palate. A successful Séguret. Keep for 2-3 years. Price approx.: 9,50 EUR
http://www.domainedelamauve.fr
Domaine de l'Amauve
+33 (0)4 90 46 82 81

DOMAINE DE CABASSE — 85/100

▼ ✦ Casa Bassa 2010 : Subtle mature highlights. Mature, fruit-driven nose showing stewed red and black fruits coupled with smoke and dried spice notes. Fleshy, warm and very mature palate. The oak is mellow and contributes to overall balance. A Séguret ready to drink now.
Price approx.: 16,00 EUR
http://www.cabasse.fr
Domaine de Cabasse
+33 (0)4 90 46 91 12

DOMAINE DE CABASSE — 85/100

▼ ✦ Cuvée Garnacho 2010 : Bold garnet. Ripe nose of stewed fruits backed by undergrowth, liquorice and liquorice sweets. Upright palate showing restrained power. Lovely full-on mature aromatics. A balanced Séguret pairing perfectly with roast pheasant. Price approx.: 11,00 EUR
http://www.cabasse.fr
Domaine de Cabasse
+33 (0)4 90 46 91 12

DOMAINE DE CABASSE — 83/100

▼ ✦ Le Rosé 2013 : Appealing, clean, honest pink. Nose of red fruits and sweets. Fresh, crunchy attack on the palate delivering more of the delightful nose aromas. An aromatic rosé for sharing over summer barbecues. Price approx.: 8,50 EUR
http://www.cabasse.fr
Domaine de Cabasse
+33 (0)4 90 46 91 12

CÔTES DU RHÔNE-VILLAGES SIGNARGUES

DOMAINE DU FOURNIER — 87/100

▼ ✦ Vintage 2013 : Deep garnet, dark purple tints. Subdued nose driven by dark fruits and violet.

Fairly lively attack leading into a generous, full and very drinkable, balanced palate. Fruit is supported by freshness on the finish. A powerful, promising wine. Keep for 2-3 years.
Price approx.: 5,90 EUR
http://www.vignerons-castelas.com
Cave des Vignerons du Castelas
+33 (0)4 90 26 62 66

CAVE DES VIGNERONS DU CASTELAS 84/100

▼ ♪ Cuvée Saint-Sébastien 2012 : Vibrant red with crimson tints. Distinctive nose opening up to chocolatey, fruity and spicy notes. Warm, ample palate framing a fairly full mouthfeel. A well-balanced, instantly accessible wine pairing well with barbecued foods.
Price approx.: 5,10 EUR
http://www.vignerons-castelas.com
Cave des Vignerons du Castelas
+33 (0)4 90 26 62 66

CAVE DES VIGNERONS DU CASTELAS 82/100

▼ ♪ Vieilles Vignes 2012 : Vibrant red tinged with crimson. Focused, distinctive nose merging red fruits, spices and cocoa notes. Full, melted attack flowing into a firm mid-palate with slightly dry, vegetal tannins. Pair with red meats.
Price approx.: 6,40 EUR
http://www.vignerons-castelas.com
Cave des Vignerons du Castelas
+33 (0)4 90 26 62 66

CÔTES DU RHÔNE-VILLAGES VISAN

DOMAINE DE LUCÉNA 91/100

▼ ♪ Frison 2009 : Intense hue with garnet tints. Concentrated nose where the oak character dovetails impeccably with the wine's aromatic personality (dark fruits, liquorice, spice). Full, well-structured palate displaying beautiful harmony. Complex, precise and persistent aromas.
Price approx.: 13,00 EUR
www.domainelucena.free.fr
Domaine de Lucéna
+33 (0)4 90 28 71 22

DOMAINE DE LUCÉNA 89/100

▼ ♪ Passo Fino 2011 : Deep garnet. Generous, expressive nose blending dark fruits, liquorice and spice. On the palate, a warm, full style showing great balance and developing a spicy, liquorice character over substantial length. A successful wine.
Price approx.: 7,20 EUR
www.domainelucena.free.fr
Domaine de Lucéna
+33 (0)4 90 28 71 22

VIGNOBLE ART MAS 85/100

CONV▼ ♪ Classic 2011 : Deep, young colour. Nose of cherry and cassis in brandy. Powerful palate augmented by intense spicy and floral notes. Evident substance and warmth. An assertive Mediterranean style. Recommended for meats in a sauce. Price approx.: 13,00 EUR
http://www.artmas.fr/
Vignoble Art Mas
+33 (0)4 90 28 75 60

VIGNOBLE ART MAS 84/100

Org▼ ♪ Il était une fois 2012 : Garnet. Expressive nose blending a fruity character, smoky notes and touches of spice. Powerful, warm and closely-integrated attack. Firmer mid-palate and finish revealing pronounced tannins tinged with a hint of bitterness. Drink with game.
Price approx.: 7,00 EUR
http://www.artmas.fr/
Vignoble Art Mas
+33 (0)4 90 28 75 60

CÔTES DU VIVARAIS

DOMAINE VIGIER 88/100

▼ ♪ L'Intemporel 2011 : Deeply-coloured garnet. Balsamic nose showing smoke, black fruits and stone fruits. The palate is racy and powerful with rich, mouth-coating substance and focused fruit and oak presence - the prerequisites for ageing well. Ideal for roast poultry. Price approx.: 8,00 EUR
Domaine de Vigier
+33 (0)4 75 88 01 18

DOMAINE VIGIER 84/100

▼ ♪ Vintage 2013 : Orange hue. Nose of ripe citrus and raspberry with spice and pepper undercurrents. Fleshy, powerful attack leading into a more supple, fresher mid-palate revealing savoury fruit. A good rosé for cold cuts.
Price approx.: 3,85 EUR
Domaine de Vigier
+33 (0)4 75 88 01 18

CROZES-HERMITAGE

DOMAINE MICHELAS SAINT JEMMS 91/100

▼ ♪ La Chasselière 2012 : Deep, young crimson. Inviting nose of blackberry, raspberry, violet and elegant vanilla oak. Silky attack, dense, virile, lush and highly seductive palate supported by fine-grain tannins. Wonderful aromatic consistency. Lively with no heaviness. Bravo! Price approx.: 20,00 EUR
http://www.michelas-st-jemms.fr
Domaine Michelas Saint Jemms
+33 (0)4 75 07 86 70

DOMAINE MELODY   91/100

▼ ✦ Etoile Noire 2012 : Beautiful dark hue with dark purple tints. Endearing nose blending red fruits, pepper, fine spice and a touch of garrigue. Full attack, a broad-shouldered, richly constituted wine with an exhilarating freshness. Firm finish. All set for a wonderful future. Price approx.: 18,00 EUR
Domaine Melody
+33 (0)4 75 08 16 51

ARNOUX ET FILS   89/100

▼ ✦ Petites Collines 2011 : Concentrated young garnet. Empyreumatic nose driven by plum, jammy blackcurrant, smoke, liquorice and mild spices. Fleshy palate with a full mouthfeel showing full-on rich perfumes covering a broad spectrum. An elegant, rich and consummate wine.
Price approx.: 10,10 EUR
http://htp://www.arnoux-vins.com
Arnoux et Fils
+33 (0)4 90 65 84 18

DOMAINE MICHELAS SAINT JEMMS   89/100

▼ ✦ Signature 2012 : Dark, young-looking crimson. Pleasurable nose of blackberry, raspberry, refined spice and a floral note. Suave attack, delicious palate leaving an impression of purity and natural quality. Faint firmness on the finish. Exuberant and precise. Sheer pleasure.
Price approx.: 15,00 EUR
http://www.michelas-st-jemms.fr
Domaine Michelas Saint Jemms
+33 (0)4 75 07 86 70

DOMAINE DES REMIZIÈRES   89/100

▼ ✦ Cuvée Christophe 2012 : Young, deep colour. Refined nose of toasted oak backed by jammy cassis. Elegant palate with silky tannins. Very round, very focused fruit and oak perfumes that are impeccably entwined. Velvety mouthfeel. A successful wine with lots left to reveal.
Price approx.: 15,00 EUR
http://www.domaineremizieres.com
Domaine des Remizières
+33 (0)4 75 07 44 28

DOMAINE DU PAVILLON   88/100

▼ ✦ Vintage 2012 : Deep, young colour. Heady nose of peony backed by fresh black fruits. The palate is supple, elegant and consistent. Fruit influence carries through with the same youthfulness. A charming, distinctive Crozes that needs more bottle time.
Price approx.: 13,00 EUR
www.pavillon-mercurol.fr
Domaine du Pavillon
+33 (0)4 75 07 99 12

DOMAINE PHILIPPE ET VINCENT JABOULET   88/100

▼ ✦ Vintage 2010 : Dark garnet with crimson highlights. Expressive nose transporting us to the countryside, halfway between orchards and garrigue. Velvety, full and powerful palate with a measure of drive. Peppery and vegetal. Refined, nicely matured. Good craftmanship.
Price approx.: 12,00 EUR
www.jaboulet-philippe-vincent.fr
Jaboulet Philippe et Vincent
+33 (0)4 75 07 44 32

DOMAINE MELODY   87/100

▼ ✦ Premier Regard 2012 : Deep crimson with dark purple tints. Shy nose of blackberry, raspberry and violet with a spice dimension. Clean, nervy and well-balanced palate with a faint crunchiness and more of the spice and pepper. Light, natural impression. Some fine tannins.
Price approx.: 13,50 EUR
Domaine Melody
+33 (0)4 75 08 16 51

DOMAINE DES REMIZIÈRES   87/100

▼ ✦ Cuvée Particulière 2012 : Delicate nose intermixing stone fruits and tones of rose petal. Soft attack on the palate with focused aromas dominated by white fruit with a pleasant almond touch on the finish. A distinctive, refreshing style drinking well from now on.
Price approx.: 9,50 EUR
http://www.domaineremizieres.com
Domaine des Remizières
+33 (0)4 75 07 44 28

DOMAINE MICHELAS SAINT JEMMS   86/100

▼ ✦ Fleur de Syrahne 2013 : Deep crimson with dark purple. Powerful yet muddled nose. After swirling, aromas of redcurrant, cassis, pepper, hint of violet. Fresh, silky and virile palate showing a lovely impression of purity and more nose aromatics. Small, well-integrated framework.
Price approx.: 12,00 EUR
http://www.michelas-st-jemms.fr
Domaine Michelas Saint Jemms
+33 (0)4 75 07 86 70

DOMAINE JEAN-CLAUDE MARSANNE   86/100

▼ ✦ Vintage 2011 : Dark purple. Distinctive nose driven by fresh blackcurrant and blueberry. An elegant, supple and already melted Crozes. Lovely focused, lengthy fruit exposure. Classic and well-made. Ideal for grilled meats.
Price approx.: 15,00 EUR
http://www.domainemarsanne.com
Domaine Jean-Claude Marsanne
+33 (0)4 75 08 86 26

GIGONDAS

ARNOUX ET FILS   89/100

▼ ♪ Seigneur de Lauris 2011 : Deeply-coloured, faintly mature hue. Mature nose focusing on spice, balsamic and cocoa aromas with red fruits in brandy in the background. The palate is warm, full and mellow with predominant balsamic aromas. Still young. A good match for game.
Price approx.: 19,85 EUR
http://htp://www.arnoux-vins.com
Arnoux et Fils
+33 (0)4 90 65 84 18

ARNOUX ET FILS   88/100

▼ ♪ Vieux Clocher - Nobles Terrasses 2013 : Brilliant deep crimson. Expressive, refined nose with fruit and spice aromas augmented by a mineral tone. Fleshy attack with a fine-grained texture and crunchy fruit expression. Mineral and spice-driven mid-palate. A lovely upright, precise wine. .
Price approx.: 14,80 EUR
http://htp://www.arnoux-vins.com
Arnoux et Fils
+33 (0)4 90 65 84 18

CAVES SAINT-PIERRE   88/100

▼ ♪ Vintage 2012 : Dark red with garnet shades. Profound nose with red and black fruit aromas bolstered by a subtle touch of spice and olive paste. Beautiful presence on the palate. Full, well-structured, closely-integrated and persistent. A fine bottling.
Price approx.: 9,99 EUR
http://www.skalli.com
Les Vins Skalli
+33 (0)4 90 83 58 35

BONPAS   85/100

▼ ♪ Grande Exception 2012 : Deeply-coloured garnet. Expressive nose suggestive of plum and cherry flesh with subtle spice notes. Full, warm attack enveloping a fruity mouthfeel. An instantly accessible, honest Gigondas. Drink with red meats.
Price approx.: 14,25 EUR
Boisset La Famille des Grand Vins - Bonpas
+33 (0)4 90 83 58 35

GRIGNAN LES ADHÉMAR

DOMAINE DE MONTINE   88/100

▼ ♪ Emotion 2012 : Vibrant red, still in its youth. Expressive nose blending vanilla oak, black fruits, mild spices and liquorice. Velvety, powerful, profound and lively palate with wonderful restraint capped off with a lingering cocoa and pepper finish. A convincing wine.

Price approx.: 9,00 EUR
http://www.domaine-de-montine.com
Domaine de Montine
+33 (0)4 75 46 56 18

DOMAINE DE MONTINE   87/100

▼ ♪ Viognier 2013 : Brightly-coloured pale yellow. The nose opens up to apricot, white flowers and a patisserie touch. Delicious round and concentrated palate with spice accents. Focused fruit supported by savoury freshness. A quality Viognier drinking well as an aperitif. Price approx.: 9,00 EUR
http://www.domaine-de-montine.com
Domaine de Montine
+33 (0)4 75 46 56 18

HERMITAGE

DOMAINE PHILIPPE ET VINCENT JABOULET   93/100

▼ ♪ Vintage 2010 : Brilliant golden yellow. Racy nose of ripe white fruits, fresh almond, a floral note and subtle oak. Sensual, concentrated and powerful palate exuding wonderful, still primary aromas. Spice and mineral notes. Fresh with no heaviness. Very successful. Price approx.: 35,00 EUR
www.jaboulet-philippe-vincent.fr
Jaboulet Philippe et Vincent
+33 (0)4 75 07 44 32

LIRAC

CHÂTEAU LA GENESTIÈRE   90/100

▼ ♪ Cuvée Raphaël 2012 : Limpid pale yellow. Expressive, elegant nose marrying white flowers, almond notes and stone fruits. Abundant freshness, stuffing and lively, persistent aromas on the palate. A full, aromatic and distinctive wine.
Price approx.: 9,20 EUR
http://domaine-genestiere.com
Domaine la Genestière
+33 (0)4 66 50 07 03

DOMAINE DES CARABINIERS   89/100

Org▼ ♪ Vintage 2012 : Vibrant red. Distinctive, focused and zippy nose intermixing ripe morello cherry and a touch of violet and spice. Beautiful full, melted attack flowing into an aromatic mid-palate and persistent finish. Many positive traits for this very well-crafted wine. Price approx.: 10,80 EUR
http://www.carabiniers-vin-biologique.fr
Domaine des Carabiniers
+33 (0)4 66 82 62 94

Detailed instructions are featured
at the start of the book.

CHATEAU LE DEVOY MARTINE 88/100

▼ ♪ Via Secreta 2012 : Fairly deeply-coloured garnet. Expressive nose driven by violet, blackberry, pepper and liquorice. Crunchy, warm, concentrated and velvety palate exuding fruit and spice. Well-balanced with an intense, spice-infused finish. A handsome wine.
Price approx.: 8,50 EUR
http://www.chateauledevoymartine.fr
Château Le Devoy Martine
+33 (0)4 66 50 01 23

CHÂTEAU LA GENESTIÈRE 88/100

▼ ♪ Cuvée Raphaël 2011 : Beautiful garnet red. Ripe nose with accents of morello cherry and prune jam. Fairly powerful attack on the palate leading into a full mid-palate and a fresh, perfumed finish. A lush, heady and aromatic style. Set aside for game.
Price approx.: 9,00 EUR
http://domaine-genestiere.com
Domaine la Genestière
+33 (0)4 66 50 07 03

DOMAINE SAINT-NICOLAS 87/100

▼ ♪ Vintage 2013 : Deeply-coloured with crimson tints. Nose of red fruits and spices revealing a floral and vegetal character. Fleshy, closely-integrated and soft attack with a sensation of freshness mid-palate. A charming, delicious Lirac, enjoyable from now on.
Price approx.: 8,50 EUR
http://www.laudunchusclanvignerons.com
Laudun Chusclan Vignerons
+33 (0)4 66 90 53 46

CHÂTEAU LE DEVOY MARTINE 86/100

▼ ♪ Via Secreta 2013 : Lightly-coloured with green tints. Pleasurable nose of pear, mirabelle plum and floral tones. An impression of lightness on the palate conceals power. Some spice is entwined with the fruit and a faint crunchiness drives the whole.
Price approx.: 8,50 EUR
http://www.chateauledevoymartine.fr
Château Le Devoy Martine
+33 (0)4 66 50 01 23

DOMAINE DE GEORAND 84/100

▼ ♪ Vintage 2013 : Beautiful dark purple. Intense nose with lots of spice, backed by stone fruits. The palate dispalys suppleness and aromatic freshness. Crunchy, focused fruit. Restrained heat. A Lirac showing well from now on. Works best with grilled meats.
http://www.laudunchusclanvignerons.com
Laudun Chusclan Vignerons
+33 (0)4 66 90 53 46

DOMAINE DES CARABINIERS 83/100

Org▼ ♪ Vintage 2012 : Light yellow. The nose is halfway between smoke, dried fruits and white fruits. Powerful, warm palate with a youthful sourness showing through. Backward perfume. A Lirac that needs decanting or more bottle age for full enjoyment. Price approx.: 10,80 EUR
http://www.carabiniers-vin-biologique.fr
Domaine des Carabiniers
+33 (0)4 66 82 62 94

LUBERON

CHÂTEAU LA VERRERIE 90/100

CONV▼ ♪ Grand Deffand 2012 : Deeply-coloured, limpid dark purple. The nose exudes fruit aromas of cassis, cherry and blackberry with peony, violet and eucalyptus. Racy palate with inward-looking power, freshness supporting the fruit, spice and flowers. A very elegant, superlative wine.
Price approx.: 29,00 EUR
http://www.chateau-la-verrerie.fr
Château La Verrerie
+33 (0)4 90 08 32 98

CHÂTEAU LA VERRERIE 88/100

CONV▼ ♪ Vintage 2011 : Deep colour still in its youth. Compelling, empyreumatic nose driven by mild spice, blackberry, plum and bigarreau cherry. Charming, fleshy palate where aroma and identity rapidly fall into place. Restrained power. A sound, genuine Luberon. Price approx.: 14,00 EUR
http://www.chateau-la-verrerie.fr
Château La Verrerie
+33 (0)4 90 08 32 98

CHÂTEAU LA VERRERIE 87/100

Org▼ ♪ Vintage 2013 : Light gold. Young, complex nose delivering a sensation of smoke backed by citrus and ripe white fruits. Lovely acidity at point of entry which fades and leads into fruit, freshness, full body and sourness. Set aside for spicy foods. Price approx.: 12,00 EUR
http://www.chateau-la-verrerie.fr
Château La Verrerie
+33 (0)4 90 08 32 98

CHÂTEAU LA VERRERIE 87/100

CONV▼ ♪ Esprit Bastide 2012 : Deep, young colour. Reticent nose opening up to notes of garrigue and stone fruits. Supple, fruity attack, elegant mouthfeel and freshness. A soft Luberon showcasing aromas. Drinking best whilst still young with barbecues. Price approx.: 9,50 EUR
http://www.chateau-la-verrerie.fr
Château La Verrerie
+33 (0)4 90 08 32 98

CHÂTEAU VAL JOANIS   87/100

▼ ♪ Réserve Les Griottes 2011 : Deep-hued, young tints. Smoky vanilla oak on the nose backed by cassis and morello cherry. Youthful palate dominated by oak that doesn't obscure the quality fruit all-set for the future. Evident tannins, assertive power. A great rendition of southern Syrah. Price approx.: 12,50 EUR
http://www.val-joanis.com
Château Val Joanis
+33 (0)4 90 79 20 77

DOMAINE DE MARIE   87/100

▼ ♪ N° 1 2006 : Evolved highlights. Refined nose of undergrowth and stewed red and black fruits. A mature, supple Luberon showing a generous range of aromatics and retaining balance and substance. A beautifully mature wine. Serve with leg of lamb. Price approx.: 13,00 EUR
http://www.domainedemarie.com
Domaine de Marie
+33 (0)4 90 72 54 23

CHÂTEAU VAL JOANIS   86/100

▼ ♪ Tradition 2013 : Beautiful, fairly deep salmon-pink. Expressive nose of crisp red berry fruits. Supple, fresh and concentrated palate showing crisp, clean and delicious fruit. A well-balanced, structured rosé that works well as an appetiser. Price approx.: 7,20 EUR
http://www.val-joanis.com
Château Val Joanis
+33 (0)4 90 79 20 77

DOMAINE DE LA ROYÈRE   84/100

▼ ♪ L'Oppidum 2012 : Crimson tinged with ruby. Pleasant nose intermixing raspberry, violet and dried fig with mild spice undertones. Fairly lively, fruit-driven attack with a supple, lightweight mouthfeel and spicy finish. A Luberon for pleasure, pairing with barbecued foods. Price approx.: 7,40 EUR
www.royere-husson.com
Château Husson
+33 (0)4 90 76 87 76

MUSCAT DE BEAUMES DE VENISE

DOMAINE DES BERNARDINS   95/100

▼ ♪ Hommage - 50 cl : Magnificent amber-orange hue. Complex nose suggestive of cherries in brandy, liquorice, white chocolate, creme brulee and fig. The palate shows sumptuous balance and length. Freshness constantly lifts the aromas. The crème de la crème. Price approx.: 15,90 EUR
http://www.domaine-des-bernardins.com
Domaine des Bernardins
+33 (0)4 90 62 94 13

DOMAINE DE LA PIGEADE   90/100

▼ ♪ Vintage 2012 : Light gold. Endearing nose with accents of apricot, orange and tangerine marmalade. Lush, elegant palate that has opted for freshness over power. Focused, soft and distinctive perfumes. A top-flight Muscat with definite ageability. Price approx.: 13,00 EUR
http://www.lapigeade.fr
Domaine de la Pigeade
+33 (0)4 90 62 90 00

DOMAINE DES BERNARDINS   85/100

▼ ♪ Muscat Beaume de Venise 2013 : Golden hue with orange tints. Distinctive Muscat-style nose driven by candied orange. Rich, fleshy palate showing jammy fruit aromas. Intense finish infused with mild spices. A well made, balanced and elegant wine. Price approx.: 12,60 EUR
http://www.domaine-des-bernardins.com
Domaine des Bernardins
+33 (0)4 90 62 94 13

RASTEAU

DOMAINE DES CARABINIERS   87/100

Org▼ ♪ Vintage 2012 : Dark hue. Focused, warm nose opening up to red fruits with mineral and spice undertones. On the palate, a warm, full style with a refined mouthfeel framed by power. More of the same flavoursome aromas of spice and a mineral-infused finish. Price approx.: 7,80 EUR
http://www.carabiniers-vin-biologique.fr
Domaine des Carabiniers
+33 (0)4 66 82 62 94

CAVES SAINT-PIERRE   85/100

▼ ♪ Vintage 2012 : Deeply-coloured garnet. Warm nose revealing aromas of nicely ripe red fruits with a delicate hint of spice. Beautiful presence on the palate. A rich, full, generous and mellow style with the nose aromatics carrying through. Drink with game. Price approx.: 6,45 EUR
http://www.skalli.com
Les Vins Skalli
+33 (0)4 90 83 58 35

Prices mentioned in this book are guideline
and can vary depending on point of sale.
The shops, wineries or publisher
can in no way be held responsible for this.

SAINT-JOSEPH

DOMAINE ROCHEVINE 95/100

▼ ♪ Coeur de Rochevine 2011 : Appealing crimson. Extremely precise, profound nose of red berry fruits, spice and a mineral dimension. Remarkable balance on the palate. Full, polished, fresh and showing crunchy fruit and delicious mineral aromas. Hugely successful.
Price approx.: 30,00 EUR
http://www.cave-saint-desirat.com
Cave Saint-Désirat
+33 (0)4 75 34 22 05

DOMAINE MICHELAS SAINT JEMMS 93/100

▼ ♪ Sainte Epine 2012 : Intense crimson, dark purple tints. Expressive nose of redcurrant, blackberry, violet and a mineral impression. A svelte, powerful and velvety wine brimming with vigour. Refined, well-integrated tannins, subtle oak, persistent peppery finish. Magnificent.
Price approx.: 20,00 EUR
http://www.michelas-st-jemms.fr
Domaine Michelas Saint Jemms
+33 (0)4 75 07 86 70

GUY FARGE 91/100

▼ ♪ Terre de granit 2011 : Alluring colour with garnet tints and crimson nuances. Refined, elegant nose with a mineral dimension framed by fruity, floral and spicy aromas. The palate focuses on finesse, freshness and persistence. An elegant, racy and unassuming Saint Joseph. Price approx.: 14,00 EUR
http://www.vigneron-guy-farge-rhone.com/
Domaine Guy Farge
+33 (0)4 75 06 58 49

ARNOUX ET FILS 88/100

▼ ♪ Les Echamps 2012 : Deeply-coloured ruby, crimson tints. Violet vies with red fruits on a beautifully focused nose. Fine-grained, closely-integrated texture on the palate. Structured and generous yet also fresh and persistent. Still young.
Price approx.: 12,80 EUR
http://htp://www.arnoux-vins.com
Arnoux et Fils
+33 (0)4 90 65 84 18

DOMAINE DE LA CÔTE SAINTE-EPINE 88/100

▼ ♪ Vieilles Vignes 2012 : Young-looking limpid garnet. Expressive nose intermixing spice, black fruits and subtle oak. Powerful palate showing lovely vigorous spice, fruit and mineral aromatics. A Saint-Joseph made with a successful respect for tradition.
Price approx.: 15,00 EUR
Domaine de la Côte Sainte Epine
+33 (0)4 75 08 85 35

CAVE SAINT-DÉSIRAT 88/100

▼ ♪ Septentrio 2011 : Intensely-coloured. Profound nose showing red and black fruit and spice aromas coupled with evident oak revealing graphite accents. Dense mouthfeel framed by freshness and upfront tannins underscoring oak influence.
Price approx.: 14,50 EUR
http://www.cave-saint-desirat.com
Cave Saint-Désirat
+33 (0)4 75 34 22 05

DOMAINE JEAN-CLAUDE MARSANNE 88/100

▼ ♪ Vintage 2011 : Dark purple. Refined nose with accents of blackberry, blackcurrant and blueberry and delicate oak. Young and promising, a supple wine with silky oak nicely supporting the fruit. Beautiful acidity on the finish. A Saint-Joseph with the best yet to come. Price approx.: 18,50 EUR
http://www.domainemarsanne.com
Domaine Jean-Claude Marsanne
+33 (0)4 75 08 86 26

TAVEL

DOMAINE DES CARABINIERS 85/100

Org▼ ♪ Vintage 2012 : Mature light red. Nose of ripe fruits coupled with spice notes. Soft, suave palate. Lovely marriage of archetypal Mediterranean-style spice-infused fruit. A generous Tavel. Price approx.: 10,50 EUR
http://www.carabiniers-vin-biologique.fr
Domaine des Carabiniers
+33 (0)4 66 82 62 94

VACQUEYRAS

CLOS DE CAVEAU 92/100

Org▼ ♪ Iao muse 2011 : Dark garnet. Ripe red fruits, mild spices and herbs on the nose with vanilla oak in the background. Profound, concentrated palate adorned with a delicious, silky mouthfeel. Lovely natural impression. Hides its virility well. Marvellous. Price approx.: 25,00 EUR
http://www.closdecaveau.com
Le Clos de Caveau
+33 (0)4 90 65 85 33

CLOS DE CAVEAU 89/100

Org▼ ♪ Carmin Brillant 2011 : Bright, deeply-coloured garnet. Shy nose of pepper, liquorice, red fruits and subtle ageing aromas. A delightful, broad-shouldered wine on the palate displaying amazing lightness. Expressive and lively with blackcurrant and mild spices. Price approx.: 14,75 EUR
http://www.closdecaveau.com
Le Clos de Caveau
+33 (0)4 90 65 85 33

ARNOUX ET FILS

Château Lestours Clocher 2012

▼ Beautiful, fairly deep garnet. Profound, refined nose with fruit enhanced by an elegant oak touch infused with fine spice. Full, generous and rich palate framed by a full mouthfeel. Focused, evolving and persistent aromas. A very compelling Vacqueyras.

+33 4 90 65 84 18

90/100

ARNOUX ET FILS

Cuvée 1717 Vintage 2012

▼ Intense hue, crimson tints. Focused, racy nose combining berry fruits with elegant oak, spice and balsamic undertones. More of the same aromatics on a superbly built, polished and closely-integrated palate. Still extrovert, will increase in depth.

+33 4 90 65 84 18

90/100

CLOS DE CAVEAU   89/100

Org▼ ♪ Fruit Sauvage 2012 : Deep crimson. Seductive nose of peony, smoke, red fruits and mild spices. Velvety attack, delightful, powerful and rich palate with fine, precise aromas. Dynamic, taut and supported by very elegant tannins. A convincing, modern style. Price approx.: 11,55 EUR
http://www.closdecaveau.com
Le Clos de Caveau
+33 (0)4 90 65 85 33

CHÂTEAU LESTOURS CLOCHER   88/100

▼ ♪ Les Pénitents 2012 : Fairly deep colour with garnet nuances. Suggestions of red fruits in brandy on the nose backed by subtle oak and spice. The palate is seductively supple and velvety yet also shows a warm character and persistency. Good presence on the palate.
Price approx.: 14,45 EUR
http://htp://www.arnoux-vins.com
Arnoux et Fils
+33 (0)4 90 65 84 18

ARNOUX ET FILS   87/100

▼ ♪ Jean Marie Arnoux 2013 : Deeply-coloured crimson. Young nose displaying beautiful red fruit entwined with spice and subtle toast undertones. Fleshy palate showing lovely velvety tannins, mellowness and persistency. A full, perfumed Vacqueyras pairing well with prime cuts of beef. Price approx.: 12,40 EUR
http://htp://www.arnoux-vins.com
Arnoux et Fils
+33 (0)4 90 65 84 18

ARNOUX ET FILS   86/100

▼ ♪ Vieux Clocher 2013 : Pale gold with brilliant highlights. A mix of mineral, wild flower, white fruit and boiled sweet perfumes on the nose. The palate reveals a mellower, more heady streak emphasising the delicious fruit. Refined spice on the finish. Price approx.: 12,40 EUR
http://htp://www.arnoux-vins.com
Arnoux et Fils
+33 (0)4 90 65 84 18

ARNOUX ET FILS — 86/100

▼ ♪ Seigneur de Lauris - Vieilles Vignes 2011 : Medium intense, slightly mature colour. Focused nose of red berry fruits in brandy with a touch of cocoa. Full, warm palate framing upfront, mellow substance. A traditional, generous style that will fully reveal itself with meats in a sauce.
Price approx.: 15,00 EUR
http://htp://www.arnoux-vins.com
Arnoux et Fils
+33 (0)4 90 65 84 18

ARNOUX ET FILS — 86/100

▼ ♪ Vieux Clocher - Classic 2013 : Attractive crimson. Endearing nose showing a lovely fruit and spice character. Good fullness and suppleness on the palate with a refined, well-integrated mouthfeel. Upfront freshness coupled with tasteful generosity. Serve with ribsteak.
Price approx.: 10,95 EUR
http://htp://www.arnoux-vins.com
Arnoux et Fils
+33 (0)4 90 65 84 18

ARNOUX ET FILS — 85/100

▼ ♪ Jean Marie Arnoux 2012 : Beautiful, brilliant garnet. Expressive nose intermixing red fruits, spice notes and garrigue. Lovely supple, full attack leading into a warm mid-palate. Distinctive and balanced across the palate. Ideal for grilled meats.
Price approx.: 12,40 EUR
http://htp://www.arnoux-vins.com
Arnoux et Fils
+33 (0)4 90 65 84 18

ARNOUX ET FILS — 85/100

▼ ♪ Vieux Clocher - Classic 2012 : Medium intense hue tinged with ruby. Suggestions of jammy red fruits on the nose with subtle spice undertones. Fairly lightweight mouthfeel with medium body and fat. A supple, balanced and instantly accessible Vacqueyras showing delightful aromas.
Price approx.: 10,95 EUR
http://htp://www.arnoux-vins.com
Arnoux et Fils
+33 (0)4 90 65 84 18

CLOS DE CAVEAU — 83/100

Org▼ ♪ La Rose du Clos 2013 : Light candy pink. Shy nose of red fruits. Suave attack. The palate is also fairly reticent yet shows lovely full, rich presence. Shy spices gradually reveal themselves. Freshness marks the finish.
Price approx.: 7,90 EUR
http://www.closdecaveau.com
Le Clos de Caveau
+33 (0)4 90 65 85 33

VAUCLUSE - PRINCIPAUTÉ D'ORANGE

DOMAINE DES CAMBADES — 88/100

CONV▼ ♪ Ivoire 2012 : Brilliant pale hue with green tints. Pleasant nose intermixing apricot, vanilla and floral notes. Suave attack leading into a style combining richness and freshness with seductive, focused perfumes. Personality. A successful offering.
Price approx.: 8,50 EUR
Domaine des Cambades
+33 (0)6 89 07 13 03

VAUCLUSE

CHÂTEAU LA VERRERIE — 86/100

Org▼ ♪ Viognier 2013 : Pale gold. Charming nose showing accents of peach, white fruits in syrup and boiled sweets. Light, soft palate displaying an array of very thirst-quenching aromatics. Abundant freshness. Ideal as a seductive aperitif.
Price approx.: 11,00 EUR
http://www.chateau-la-verrerie.fr
Château La Verrerie
+33 (0)4 90 08 32 98

ARNOUX ET FILS — 85/100

▼ ♪ P'tit Clocher 2013 : Pale gold. Intense nose driven by fresh grape and pear. Soft, light palate with crunchy flavours. Beautiful balance of acidity and freshness. An ideal after-work wine that pairs well with tapas and foods grilled on a hot plate.
Price approx.: 4,35 EUR
http://htp://www.arnoux-vins.com
Arnoux et Fils
+33 (0)4 90 65 84 18

DOMAINE DE TARA — 85/100

▼ ♪ Terre d'Ocres 2013 : Light orange hue. Elegant nose suggestive of red fruits. Full attack leading into an honest, lively palate revealing more of the fruit. Focused and well-balanced. A delicious rosé that makes an enjoyable aperitif or partner for pizzas. Price approx.: 6,80 EUR
www.domainedetara.com
Domaine de Tara
+33 (0)4 90 05 74 87

DOMAINE DE LA PIGEADE — 85/100

▼ ♪ Petits Grains de Folie 2012 : Light gold. Refined nose suggestive of orange marmalade, pear, almond and wild flowers. Very flavoursome sweetness on the palate tinged with sourness. More of the same elegant nose aromatics. Ideal with, say, melon or asparagus. Price approx.: 8,50 EUR
http://www.lapigeade.fr
Domaine de la Pigeade
+33 (0)4 90 62 90 00

DOMAINE DE L'AMAUVE 85/100

▼ 🍷 Vintage 2012 : Crimson with dark purple highlights. Pleasurable nose of raspberry and red fruits with a floral dimension. Clean, vigorous palate showing drive and fruit and drinking well served chilled. Spicy, vegetal finish. Perfect for a platter of cold meats.
Price approx.: 4,50 EUR
http://www.domainedelamauve.fr
Domaine de l'Amauve
+33 (0)4 90 46 82 81

DOMAINE DES ANGES 85/100

▼ 🍷 Chérubin 2012 : Pale yellow with green tints. Pleasant nose of white fruits and apricot with a creamy touch. Round attack, full, ripe and delicious palate balanced by well-integrated freshness. Hint of firmness on the finish. Set aside for fish gratin.
Price approx.: 9,00 EUR
www.domainedesanges.com
Domaine des Anges
+33 (0) 90 61 88 78

ARNOUX ET FILS 84/100

▼ 🍷 P'tit Clocher 2013 : Light salmon-pink. Delightful nose showing accents of confectionary with citrus and red fruit sweet aromas. Fairly round, soft palate revealing seductively compelling fruit perfumes. An easy-drinking rosé for instant, effortless pleasure. Ideal for tapas.
Price approx.: 3,75 EUR
http://htp://www.arnoux-vins.com
Arnoux et Fils
+33 (0)4 90 65 84 18

ARNOUX ET FILS 84/100

▼ 🍷 P'tit Clocher 2013 : Young-looking colour. Nose of black berry fruits and peony. Fresh, soft palate with simple, crunchy fruit flavours. Lovely mellowness throughout. A hassle-free wine, ideal for barbecues.
Price approx.: 3,75 EUR
http://htp://www.arnoux-vins.com
Arnoux et Fils
+33 (0)4 90 65 84 18

DOMAINE JULIETTE AVRIL 83/100

▼ 🍷 le Merlot 2012 : Beautiful deeply-coloured, young red. Appealing nose of ripe cherries. The palate is supple with silky tannins and emphasises the same, quite delightful aromas. An easy-drinking wine that works perfectly with barbecues.
Price approx.: 6,20 EUR
http://www.julietteavril.com
Domaine Juliette Avril
+33 (0)4 90 83 72 69

VENTOUX

CHÂTEAU JUVENAL 88/100

Org▼ 🍷 La Terre du Petit Homme 2012 : Dark hue, crimson tints. Pleasurable nose of toast, spice and vanilla, backed by red fruits. Velvety, powerful and profound palate, lively with a backbone of closely-integrated, silky tannins. Lingering aromatic finish. A beautiful Ventoux. Price approx.: 12,00 EUR
http://www.chateau-juvenal-provence.com
Le Graveyron
+33 (0)4 90 62 31 78

DOMAINE DE TARA 87/100

▼ 🍷 Hautes Pierres 2011 : Deep garnet. Delightful nose with accents of ripe red and black fruits. Delicate palate with the nose aromatics carrying through. Polished tannins. Lingering, liquorice-infused finish. A warm, generous wine.
Price approx.: 12,00 EUR
www.domainedetara.com
Domaine de Tara
+33 (0)4 90 05 74 87

DOMAINE DES CAMBADES 87/100

CONV▼ 🍷 Crépuscule 2011 : Deeply-coloured garnet. Predominant, focused vanilla oak on the nose with stone fruit scents after swirling. A modern Ventoux, still under the influence of oak ageing. Powerful and distinctive, though a little more bottle age is recommended. Price approx.: 14,00 EUR
Domaine des Cambades
+33 (0)6 89 07 13 03

DOMAINE DE LA PIGEADE 86/100

▼ 🍷 Les Sables 2012 : Young-looking colour. Endearing plummy nose with bigarreau cherry, spice and smoke. A supple Ventoux with a soft mouthfeel. Lovely generous aromatics nicely supported by freshness. No sign of excessive heat at all. A wine designed for sharing.
Price approx.: 6,00 EUR
http://www.lapigeade.fr
Domaine de la Pigeade
+33 (0)4 90 62 90 00

CHÂTEAU JUVENAL 86/100

Org▼ 🍷 Les Ribes du Vallat 2012 : Deep crimson. Distinctive nose blending herbs, fine spice and red fruits. Suave attack, delightful palate driven by raspberry and spice and running the gamut through freshness, power and warmth. Vegetal note. Robust structure on the finish.
Price approx.: 8,20 EUR
http://www.chateau-juvenal-provence.com
Le Graveyron
+33 (0)4 90 62 31 78

DOMAINE DU BON REMÈDE   86/100

▼ ♪ La Grange Delay 2012 : Deep, young colour. Distinctive nose of black cherry and plum backed by peppery garrigue aromas. Powerful, dense and well-balanced palate. Beautiful aromatic presence allowing perfume to carry through. Power is part of its personality. Calls for game.
Price approx.: 8,00 EUR
http://www.domainedubonremede.com
Domaine du Bon Remède
+33 (0)4 90 69 69 76

DOMAINE DE TARA   85/100

▼ ♪ Hautes Pierres 2012 : Brilliant light gold. Lovely nose blending citrus fruits and floral notes. Delicious mouth-coating and robust palate with spice presence. Freshness, intensity and an array of aromatics. A successful wine pairing with white meats.
Price approx.: 12,00 EUR
www.domainedetara.com
Domaine de Tara
+33 (0)4 90 05 74 87

DOMAINE DES ANGES   85/100

▼ ♪ Archange 2012 : Brilliant light hue with green tints. Endearing nose blending herbs, white fruits and subtle vanilla undertones. Round attack, rich, generous and powerful palate mirroring the nose aromatics. Slightly more upfront oak influence. A successful effort.
Price approx.: 15,00 EUR
www.domainedesanges.com
Domaine des Anges
+33 (0) 90 61 88 78

ARNOUX ET FILS   84/100

▼ ♪ Vieux Clocher 2013 : Light orange. Lovely inviting nose of ripe red fruits and citrus. A supple rosé with a soft mouthfeel and abundant freshness enhancing focused fruit and very upright expression. Works well with cold cuts.
Price approx.: 5,30 EUR
http://htp://www.arnoux-vins.com
Arnoux et Fils
+33 (0)4 90 65 84 18

DOMAINE DE TARA   84/100

▼ ♪ Terre d'Ocres 2013 : Brilliant pale yellow. Floral and fruity nose showing peach, apricot and some citrus with a creamy touch. Fairly lively attack leading into a supple, round, fruity and fresh palate. Well-balanced. Drinking well with summer starters.
Price approx.: 7,50 EUR
www.domainedetara.com
Domaine de Tara
+33 (0)4 90 05 74 87

DOMAINE DES ANGES   84/100

▼ ♪ Vintage 2011 : Slightly mature colour. Nose of ripe red fruits developing spice and mineral aromas of graphite. Warm, generous palate with a melted attack. More of the same well-established aromatic personality. Subtle bitterness on the finish.
Price approx.: 7,00 EUR
www.domainedesanges.com
Domaine des Anges
+33 (0) 90 61 88 78

DOMAINE DU BON REMÈDE   84/100

▼ ♪ Vieilles Vignes 2012 : Young red. The nose is dominated by mineral tones and leather with very backward fruit. Beautiful attack balanced by a sappy quality. The nose aromatics carry through to a finish showing more fruit.
Price approx.: 7,00 EUR
http://www.domainedubonremede.com
Domaine du Bon Remède
+33 (0)4 90 69 69 76

DOMAINE DU BON REMÈDE   84/100

▼ ♪ Pensée Sauvage 2013 : Light salmon-pink. Fairly subdued nose driven by red fruit notes with mineral undertones. Supple, rich palate with focused fruit supported by beautiful freshness. Quite forthright on the finish. A simple wine for sharing.
Price approx.: 6,00 EUR
http://www.domainedubonremede.com
Domaine du Bon Remède
+33 (0)4 90 69 69 76

ARNOUX ET FILS   83/100

▼ ♪ Vieux Clocher 2013 : Ruby with crimson nuances. The nose displays a Mediterranean-style character intermixing red fruits and garrigue notes. Good framework on the palate with a lightweight mouthfeel framed by restrained power and savoury freshness. Enjoyable.
Price approx.: 5,10 EUR
http://htp://www.arnoux-vins.com
Arnoux et Fils
+33 (0)4 90 65 84 18

DOMAINE DE TARA   82/100

▼ ♪ Terre d'Ocres 2013 : Deeply-coloured garnet with young highlights. A mix of black and red fruits with a floral touch on the nose. Supple attack flowing into a round palate with upfront tannins. Powerful and fruity. Slightly bitter finish. Drink with red meats.
Price approx.: 7,50 EUR
www.domainedetara.com
Domaine de Tara
+33 (0)4 90 05 74 87

SAVOY

A BRAND NEW IMAGE

A land of contrasts is the calling card of this alpine province. Production is centred primarily in Savoie, with 80,000 hectolitres, with a balance of 8,000 hl produced in Haute-Savoie, divided between 30% reds and rosés (truly) and 70% whites. The vines follow the contours of Lake Geneva, stretch southwards alongside the Rhone, circle Lake Bourget and hug the flanks of Savoy Coomb, after occupying the scree slopes of Mount Granier. The diversity of landforms illustrates the determination of Savoy wine producers in the face of such a borderline climate for growing grapes.

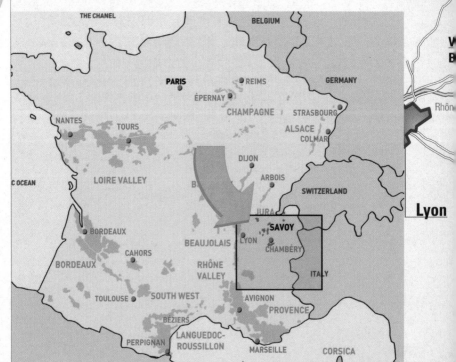

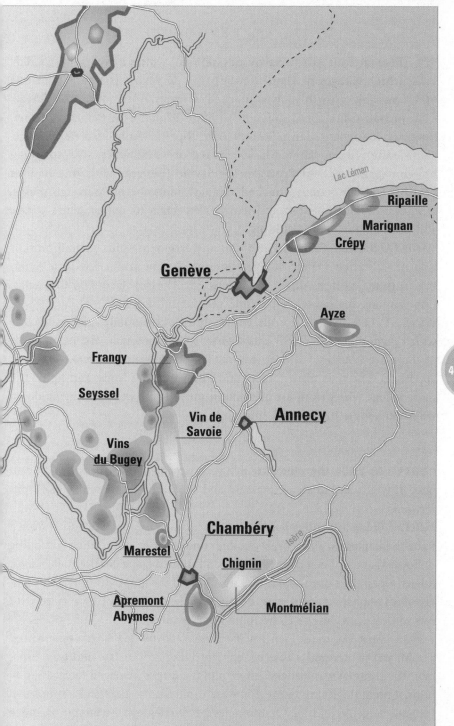

403

There are four ACs in Savoy: Seyssel (still whites or sparkling); Crépy (three villages in Haute-Savoie); Vin de Savoie (perhaps with one of 17 possible growth names attached: Abymes, Apremont, Arbin, Ayze, Char-pignat, Chautagne, Chignin, Chignin-Bergeron or Bergeron, Cruet, Jongieux, Marignan, Marin, Montmélian, Ripaille, Saint-Jean de la Porte, Saint-Jeoire Prieuré, Sainte-Marie), for red or white wines, still, sparkling or semi-sparkling; and Roussette de Savoie (perhaps with one of four possible growth names attached: Frangy, Marestel or Marestel-Altesse, Monterminod and Monthoux) which also refers to red or white wines, still, sparkling or semi-sparkling.

VARIETALS: Reds: Gamay, Pinot noir and Mondeuse plus a small proportion of Cabernets (Franc and Sauvignon), Persan and a few local varieties in Isère. Whites: Aligoté, Roussette (or Altesse), Jacquère, Chasselas, Chardonnay, augmented with some 'secondary' varieties.

WINE STYLES: lively, vigorous, fruity whites, occasionally aged on the lees which gives them their delicious slightly sparkling touch. The best known of these are Roussette and Apremont. The sparkling wines make excellent appetisers. The reds from Gamay and Pinot noir are fruity and light. The more robust wines from Mondeuse can prove to be excellent laying down wines on a more full-bodied, spicy note.

REVIEW OF RECENT VINTAGES

- **2011** - As a rule, the whites are rich yet crisp and show structure and freshness. The reds and rosés are pleasant and should be drunk whilst still fruit-forward.

- **2012** - This was a difficult year that was mainly rainy and cool apart from a quite mild autumn. These unfavourable conditions caused coulure (dropping of flowers) and millerandage (irregular and stunted grape development), until August when the return of hot weather allowed the grapes to ripen. This vintage does not herald a bad wine, but the volume is very low (the average yield was sometimes as low as 20 hectolitres per hectare!).

- **2013** - Just like other French wine regions, Savoy and Bugey experienced a cold, wet winter and a dire spring. Flowering arrived late and was disparate. The summer was hot and sunny and the grapes managed to catch up to normal physiological ripeness. There are some highly successful examples in Chignin Bergeron and the Chardonnays, Roussettes and the famous Jacquère are showing promise. A low-yielding yet good quality vintage in Savoy.

THE SAVOY APPELLATIONS

AC BUGEY

OVERVIEW: this 450-hectare area is set on the right bank of the Rhone, between Chanay and Lagnieu, mostly in the Ain department, embracing a total 65 towns and villages. Fifteen or so of these are entitled to a specific growth name: Virieu-le-Grand, Manicle, Machuraz, Montagnieu and Cerdon. Neighbouring Lake Bourget creates a microclimate suitable for vine growing. White wines from Chardonnay, Altesse (or Roussette), Aligoté, Jacquère, Pinot gris and Molette are made here, as well as sparkling wines, including Cerdon. The red grape varietals used are Gamay, Pinot noir, Poulsard and Mondeuse.

WINE STYLES: the whites are clean, vigorous, lively, fresh and round, with a pleasant bouquet. They are delicate with good length on the palate, developing fragrances of white flowers, citrus fruit and a mineral touch. Try with freshwater fish, fish paté or quenelles. The reds made from Gamay are lively, supple, fruity and light, whilst the Pinots are more delicate and rich. Try with red meat or good Reblochon cheese.

A.C. CRÉPY

OVERVIEW: the Crépy appellation area, covering around 70 ha, is set on the southern-eastern shores of Lake Geneva between Thonon-les-Bains and Geneva. Three villages in Ain and Isère are entitled to the appellation: Douvaine, Ballaison and Loisin. The soils are formed of limestone scree, mostly moranic in origin, and are littered with stones. Mountain peaks act as a buffer against the cold winds and the reflection off Lake Geneva increases sunlight. Chas-selas, the only varietal grown locally, is also known in Valais as Fendant.

WINE STYLES: these wines are dry white, light, fresh, delicate and lively with a slight sparkle. They are similar to Swiss wines such as Vaud Dorin and Valais Fendant. They reward early drinking although they can be kept for a few years. Their acidity increases their lifespan though as they age they do lose some of their freshness. They display a pale green hue and fragrances of hazelnut, unripe almond, gunflint, violet and hawthorn. They are suitable as appetisers, or with poached crayfish, whitebait, shellfish, trout, calf's brains or Tomme de Savoie cheese.

A.C. ROUSSETTE DE SAVOIE

OVERVIEW: the appellation is situated west of Lake Bourget. The name Roussette is derived from the russset shades the wine acquires as it matures.

In Savoy, this grape variety is also called Altesse. Four zones are entitled to growth status: Frangy, north-west of Annecy, Marestel and Monthoux, along the left bank of the Rhone and Monterminod near Chambéry.

WINE STYLES: these white wines are fruity, delicate, racy, full and unctuous with acidulous notes. They can be laid down for a few years. Roussette produces a range of aromas known as 'peacock's fan' because they stretch across the whole palate. The wines display a golden green hue and fragrances of dried fruit, predominantly apricot, almond, honey and hazelnut, enhanced by floral notes. They can be served with lightly poached trout, whitebait, crayfish, white meats…

AC ROUSSETTE DU BUGEY

OVERVIEW: Roussette is the name of a grape variety, also called Altesse. It is usually blended with a small proportion of Chardonnay. Situated in the south-eastern tip of Ain, near the border between Savoie and Haute-Savoie, this area stretches from Bourg-en-Bresse to Belley. The limestone soil marks a boundary between the southern part of Revermont in Jura and the foothills of the Alps.

WINE STYLES: these are distinctive, robust, aromatic white wines, which are delicate, elegant and occasionally soft. Bugey's best Roussette wines hail from six growths: Lagnieu, Montagnieu, Virieu-le-Grand, Arbignieu, Anglefort and Chanay. Suitable for laying down. They display fragrances of peach and apricot, evolving over time into honey and beeswax scents. They can pair with quenelles, grilled freshwater fish or fish in a sauce, fondues, raclette and soft cheeses.

A.C. SEYSSEL

OVERVIEW: Seyssel wines are grown in the twin villages of Seyssel in Haute-Savoie and Seyssel-Corbonod, over 80 or so hectares in Ain. The steep slopes of the upper Rhone valley, where the soil is stony moranic or sandy molasse, provide a foothold for the vines. The best hillside sites are 'Les Michalettes', 'La Tour', 'Les Chênes', 'Les Vérones' and 'La Péclette'. The still and sparkling white wines are made primarily from Altesse and Molette.

WINE STYLES: white Seyssels display a pale hue and a floral bouquet with dominant aromas of violet, bergamot pear and passion fruit. A touch of flint is also present. On the palate, they are light, delicate, soft, dry, racy wines with well-balanced mellowness. They are velvety, supple, refreshing and long on the palate with good acidity. The best examples will keep for a few years. Try with cheeses such as Reblochon, Beaufort and Emmenthal, though also quenelles, poached crayfish, fish (trout, lavaret), raclette or cheese fondue. The sparkling wines have a distinct 'terroir' taste and are suitable as an appetiser or with a dessert.

A.C. VIN DE SAVOIE

OVERVIEW: the production area stretches over 75 km from Thonon-les-Bains to Chambéry. Vineyard sites cover 59 towns and villages: 29 in Savoie, 26 in Haute-Savoie, 2 in Ain and 2 in Isère, totalling just under 2,000 hectares. Most of the vineyards are not contiguous but scattered over the valley floor and along the shores of the lakes. White wines hold a majority share of production. Wines drawn from a single varietal are often labelled as such. The most noteworthy wines are the 17 growths entitled to append their name to that of the appellation.

Soil types are varied, ranging from limestone, to limestone marl, glacial morain, shale and rocky scree. The lakes moderate the effect of the continental climate whilst the mountains form a buffer against the rain fronts. Winters are long and harsh, springs are mild and damp, summers hot and stormy and there are long sunshine hours. Red varietals used: Gamay, Mondeuse, Pinot noir, Persan and Cabernet. For the whites: Jacquère, Altesse, Aligoté, Chardonnay, Malvoisie, Mondeuse blanche, Gringet, Roussette d'Ayze and Chasselas.

WINE STYLES: the whites have an unusual character. They are dry, vigorous and pleasant to drink, developing fragrances of white flowers (hawthorn, honeysuckle). The reds are fresh, pleasant, upfront wines which should be drunk young when they are made from Gamay. Wines made from Mondeuse are more rustic and fruity and improve with age. They display aromas of strawberry, violet and spices. The whites are suitable partners for cheese fondue, raclette, Beaufort soufflé, quenelles and cooked cold pork meats. The reds can pair with potatoes Savoyard, round fillet of veal or game.

SAVOY GROWTHS: 17 of them can add their name to AC Vin de Savoie. Site-specific growing conditions and higher production standards create a point of difference with other local wines. The growths are: Abymes, Apremont, Arbin, Ayze, Charpignat (uncommon), Chautagne, Chignin, Chignin-Bergeron, Cruet, Jongieux, Ma-rignan, Marin, Montmélian, Ripaille, Sainte-Marie-d'Alloix, Saint-Jeoire-Pri-euré and Saint-Jean-de-la-Porte.

VIN DE SAVOIE ABYMES: the production area is located in the villages of Mylans and Chapareillan and part of Marches and Apremont. It yields white wines with a crystalline hue tinted with greenish shades. They are dry, light and often slightly sparkling. They display floral fragrances, primarily violet. Made from the Jacquère varietal they should be drunk chilled and young.

VIN DE SAVOIE APREMONT: dry white wines are made here on soils with patches of limestone. The area is 20 km from Chambéry and occupies the slopes of Mount Granier. The wines are light, supple and fruity, conjuring up a touch of gunflint and honeysuckle. They pair with seafood, shellfish and fish.

VIN DE SAVOIE ARBIN: red and white wines are grown here on calcareous clay soils. The wines are grown in the villages of Arbin and Saint-Jean-de-la-Porte. The reds display aromas of blackberry, raspberry and bilberry, with a touch of spice. They are supple wines with good length on the palate. They are served with red meat or cheese. The red wines are made from the Mondeuse varietal.

VIN DE SAVOIE AYZE: this growth is situated in the villages of Ayze, Bonneville and Marignier. It produces sparkling wines from the Gringet, Altesse, Mondeuse blanche and Roussette d'Ayze grape varieties on the south-eastern and south-western flanks of Mount Môle. They can be labelled either as Mousseux de Savoie or Pétillant de Savoie. The soils are formed of glacial alluvium, scree or molasse. The wines are fresh, lively, distinctive, aromatic and supple. They pair best with fish, cheese fondue or desserts.

VIN DE SAVOIE CHAUTAGNE: this growth is situated in north-western Savoy in the villages of Motz, Serrières-en-Chau-tagne, Ruffieux and Chindrieux. Red and white wines are grown on a 10 km strip of land below Mount Gros Foug on the northern tip of Lake Bourget. The soils are formed of glacial scree and alluvium. The well-known red wines with their ruby-red hue are fleshy, solid, well-constituted, complex and tannic with floral and fruity fragrances. They can be savoured with wild boar, venison, cured mountain ham or cheese.

VIN DE SAVOIE CHIGNIN: the vineyards stretch over the villages of Chignin, Francin and Montmélian. The white wines, made from Jacquère, are generous, with a pleasant bouquet and slight sparkle. The reds, made from Gamay or Mondeuse, are flavoursome wines.

VIN DE SAVOIE CHIGNIN-BERGERON: although this wine comes from the same area as Chignin, it is made from the Bergeron varietal, otherwise known as Roussane de l'Hermitage. It is delicate, elegant, aromatic (hazelnut and almond), and capable of withstanding the test of time. It is one of Savoy's finest examples of white wine.

VIN DE SAVOIE CRUET: this area is set on the flanks of Bauges mountain, on calcareous clay soils and stony Jurassic scree. The whites are dry, lively and vigorous with fragrances of exotic fruits. The reds, made from Mondeuse, are delicate.

VIN DE SAVOIE JONGIEUX: this growth occupies the upper reaches of the Monthoux and Marestel appellation areas on calcareous clay soils. Red Jongieux sports a cherry-red hue. It is a supple, light wine with a bouquet of raspberry, strawberry, cherry and blackcurrant. The majority of the wines are red. The rosés are light and pleasant to drink.

VIN DE SAVOIE MARIGNAN: this growth is situated in the villages of Marignan and Sciez. The wines are slightly sparkling, dry and fragrant with predominant aromas of gunflint and hazelnut. The area owes its existence to the single-minded determination of Filly abbey. The wines are made from Chasselas.

VIN DE SAVOIE MARIN: these are dry white wines grown in the most northerly portion of Haute-Savoie, on the edge of Dranse valley. The vineyards enjoy a microclimate and are planted on south-south-west facing slopes. The wines made from Chasselas and are fruity, delicate quaffing wines with aromas of almond.
Vin de Savoie Montmélian: set in the villages of Montmélian and Francin, the vines grow here on limestone scree. The area is well suited to Jacquère and Mondeuse positively thrives here, yielding amazingly full-bodied wines.

VIN DE SAVOIE RIPAILLE: an area located along the shores of Lake Geneva, in the villages of Ripaille and Thonons-les-Bains. The soil is gravely and permeable. It produces fresh, fruity, dry white wines from Chasselas, reminiscent of Crépy.

VIN DE SAVOIE SAINT-JEAN-DE-LA-PORTE: scree and alluvial fans on the north-western flanks of Savoy Coomb provide a foothold for vines here. The reds display a crimson hue. They are rich, aromatic and mature extremely well. Mondeuse is the only permitted grape varietal.

409

J U R A

GREAT DISCOVERIES

This region borders the western edge of the Jura mountain range, adjoining Revermont, a vast, west-facing region of rolling hills overlooking the plains of the Saone. The Franche-Comté wine region boasts some real gems (including «vin de paille» and «vin jaune»). There are six appellations: Côtes du Jura, Arbois, Château Chalon, l'Etoile (only white and «yellow»), Crémant du Jura (sparkling) and Macvin (a liqueur wine). The growths forge their inimitable personalities from their individual terroirs and grape varieties and invariably create a long-lasting impression. «Vin jaune» for instance, (which is a term and not an appellation) is a unique growth which spends six years and three months in casks without being topped up before release. Any other wine would succumb to such shock treatment, not «vin jaune». As it ages, it acquires its famous «yellow taste» prized by wine lovers. Don't tarry, try it !

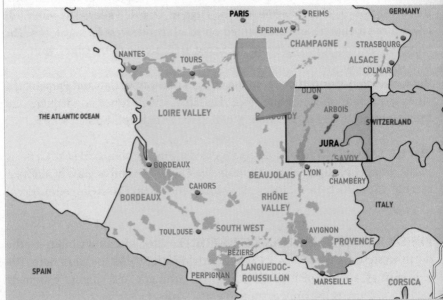

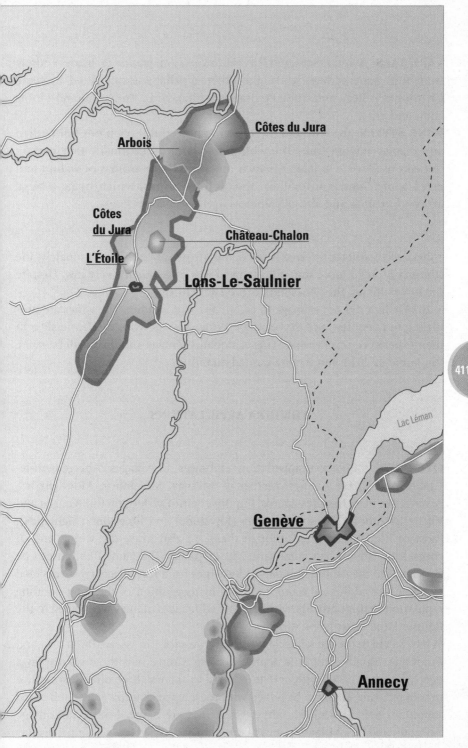

VARIETALS: Whites: Savagnin (or Na-turé). «Vin jaune» is made entirely from this grape variety, whilst the other appellations can blend in some Chardonnay. Reds and rosés: Poulsard (or Ploussard), Trousseau and Pinots (noir and gris).

WINE STYLES: the reds and the rosés are powerful though not full-bodied and display intense fruit. The whites are warm. Occasionally they mature in casks used for «vin jaune», which imparts tell-tale aromas of walnut and green apple. Similar aromas for the 'yellow' wines, which boast a huge array of aromas and virtually endless ageing capacity.

REVIEW OF RECENT VINTAGE

- **2012** • His vintage received more rain than any since 1977! Fortunately, the summer brought more sun, but the yield was consequently very low. Despite the low volumes, the wines have a good structure.
- **2013** • Jura did not manage to escape the bad weather. The wines are promising but very few and far between. Wine growers worked relentlessly and their experience was decisive. This is a quality vintage and there will be some Vin Jaune in 2013, but in very limited quantities.

THE JURA APPELLATIONS

A.C. ARBOIS

OVERVIEW: the Arbois appellation embraces 12 villages: Abergement-le-Grand, Arbois, Les Arsures, Mathenay, Mesnay, Molamboz, Montigny-les-Arsures, Les Planches-près-Arbois, Pupillin, Saint-Cyr-Montmalin, Vadans and Vilette-lès-Arbois. The soils are clay (lowlands) and limestone (highlands). Most of the wines are red, though there are also rosés, dry whites and of course, the famous 'vin jaune' and 'vin de paille'. The name Pupillin can be appended to the Arbois appellation for wines from the village. INAO decided to allow the additional name in 1970, in recognition of the long-standing reputation of this particular vineyard site which is extremely well-suited to the Poulsard and other grape varieties.

WINE STYLES: the red wines, made from Poulsard, Trousseau, Pinot noir and Pinot gris, usually have little depth of colour. Conversely, the rosés display a deep hue, often tinted with orange, referred to as coral. Both offer delicate aromas of red fruit. They can be served with roast leg of chamois (reds) and cured mountain ham (rosés). The dry white wines are drawn from Chardonnay, Savagnin and Pinot blanc. Wines matured in casks used for 'vin jaune' display aromas of mocha, dried fruit and green apple. Try these lively, intense, fat, sweet wines with morel mushrooms in a creamy sauce, button mushroom fricassee and of course Comté cheese.

'VINS JAUNES': 'vins jaunes' from Arbois display characteristic aromas of unripe walnuts, green apples and spices. Try with Roquefort cheese in puff pastry, chicken cooked with morel mushrooms and 'vin jaune', and walnut cake.

'VINS DE PAILLE': 'vins de Paille' are made from dessicated grapes which have been laid on a bed of straw to dry or hung up in a dry, well-aired room for around three months. The berries, which by now have extremely high sugar concentrations, are pressed at Christmas (100kg of grapes can yield less than 20 litres of must). Fermentation in small casks is a long drawn out process, lasting up to four years. Once the ageing process is over, most 'vins jaunes' have an alcohol content of 15% vol. and are suitable for lengthy bottle ageing. Try with Bresse fatted chicken in a cream sauce or Morbier cheese.

A.C. CHÂTEAU CHALON

OVERVIEW: this prestigious Jura appellation is both the name of a cliff top village and an appellation embracing 4 villages producing 'vin jaune', viz Château Chalon, Ménétru, Domblans and Nevy-sur-Seille. The sloping vineyards grow primarily on limestone scree intermingled with Lias marl on the steepest gradients. More consistent black marl type soils are also present. The climate is continental, with extremely cold winters and frequent autumn frosts.

413

WINE MAKING METHODS: Château Chalon is one of France's greatest white wines, even if the descriptor 'white' is not entirely accurate because Château Chalon is in fact 'yellow'. A ripe crop is a prerequisite for making this type of wine (204g/l of natural sugar at least). Made using conventional wine making techniques, the wines are aged for six years and three months in partly-filled 228-litre oak casks. They are neither racked nor topped up, allowing a kind of yeast veil similar to the flor fungus in Sherry to form on the surface. This yeast veil, which grows during the summer (due to variations in temperature), entices out the characteristic aromas found in the wines. The actual wine making process is in fact extremely tricky as the risk of volatile acidity is very high. As the wines mature, a large proportion of them evaporates, hence the unusual size of the traditional Jura wine bottle. The 62 cl 'clavelin' contains the amount left per litre of matured wine. To maintain high quality standards, growers do not apply for AC approval in years when they consider their wines to be anything less than top notch.

WINE STYLES: Château Chalon only produces 'vin jaune' from Savagnin, a temperamental, low-yielding grape variety which some consider to be on a par with Tokay wines or Sherry. With its inimitable taste of unripe walnuts, green apple and spices (nutmeg, cinnamon), and its deep colour which sometimes turns amber down the years, this wine is extremely well-constituted and rich in alcohol (minimum 12% vol.). It boasts an extensive lifespan (up to 100 years with no deterioration) and shows at its best when it has matured for at least ten to fifteen years. Enjoy with Comté cheese, poultry served in a cream sauce... Drink at room temperature (12-15°C).

A.C. CÔTES DU JURA

OVERVIEW: the Côtes du Jura appellation area covers over 600 hectares divided between 12 villages, with a focal point around Lons-le-Saunier, Poligny and Salins-les-Bains. A full range of soil types is present. At the highest elevations, limestone is interspersed with organic sediment whilst lower down, marl covers stones and on the lowlands, the soil is almost entirely clay. Red varietals used are Pinot noir, Poulsard and Trousseau and white varietals, Chardonnay and Savagnin.

WINE STYLES: red wines made from Trousseau are reasonably tannic. Conversely, Poulsard yields more supple wines with aromas of morello cherry, wild cherry and raspberry. They pair with mountain pork meats and small cuts of venison. The dry whites boast distinctive mocha, dried fruit and green apple aromas, often imparted by the casks they are stored in, previously used for 'vin jaune'.

The 'vins jaunes' themselves develop fragrances of unripe walnut, fir tree honey and bitter almond. The 'vins de paille' display scents of toast, acacia honey, almond, nutmeg and gingerbread.

A.C. CRÉMANT DU JURA

OVERVIEW: Crémant du Jura shares the same appellation area as Côtes du Jura. This fruity wine is made from Savagnin and Chardonnay for the whites and Poulsard, Pinot noir, Pinot gris and Trousseau for the reds. The local climate promotes good acidity in the grapes, making Jura suitable for producing sparkling Crémant wines. This particular type of sparkler undergoes secondary fermentation in the bottle.

WINE STYLES: the wines are sparkling with a pale yellow hue highlighted with greenish tints. They display tiny bubbles and long-lasting aromas of toast, honey, green apple and citrus fruit. Both fruity and floral, they are refreshing on the palate with a hint of pear and hawthorn. They are equally delicious as appetisers or with a dessert.

A.C. L'ETOILE

OVERVIEW: this small appellation area in Jura embraces the villages of l'Etoile, Plainoiseau, Quintigny and Saint-Didier where the soil is black or blue marl from the Lower Jurassic period. The climate is continental, with extremely cold winters and frequent autumn frosts. The white wines are blended from three permitted grape varieties (Chardonnay, Poulsard and Savagnin) and are frequently aged on the lees.

WINE STYLES: the entire regional white range is made here, from white itself to 'yellow', sparkling and 'vin de paille'. The white wines are lively and intense yet also fat and mellow. They pair well with fish and cooked shellfish. 'Vins de paille' are extremely concentrated and syrupy, exhibiting a beautiful amber hue and a rich, smooth taste. The extremely powerful 'vins jaunes' display a clean attack, fine structure and smooth, silky finish. They develop aromas of unripe walnut, fir tree honey and bitter almond.

415

A.C. MACVIN DU JURA

OVERVIEW: Macvin, previously known as 'Galant des Abbesses', is a liqueur wine made by adding spirit to the grape must to arrest fermentation. Villers-Farlay, Salins, Arbois, Poligny, Sellières, Voiteur, Bletterans, Conliège, Lons-le-Saunier, Beaufort, Saint-Amour and Saint-Julien, are all involved in producing it. The varietal range comprises Poulsard, Trousseau, Pinot noir, Pinot gris, Chardonnay and Savagnin. Macvin is made from the sweetest grapes sourced in prime vineyard sites. It is produced using the 'mutage' technique whereby fermentation is arrested by adding pomace brandy or Franche-Comté brandy made by the grower himself. The ratio is one litre of 50% proof spirit to three litres of must. 'Fine' brandy is not permitted. Macvin is aged in small casks for a year or more and must have an ABV ranging from 16 to 22%.

WINE STYLES: several components factor into the popularity of this liqueur wine: its hue, which can vary from yellow to dark brown depending on its age, its sweet flavour, generous bouquet and length on the palate. Adding brandy to the must preserves full fruit aromas. Several years in casks are required before the grape aromas integrate with the alcohol to produce greater finesse. Macvin can be served either as an appetiser or with a dessert.

• • •

2015
SAVOY-JURA WINES

SAVOY

ROUSSETTE DE SAVOIE MONTHOUX

Jean Perrier & Fils **87/100**

▼ ♪ Fleur d'Altesse 2013 : Beautiful light gold. Very mineral, heady nose backed by peach, apricot and orange. Fleshy, full-bodied palate boasting fat. More of the rich nose aromatics. A racy, well-structured Savoie pairing with rockfish.
Price approx.: 14,50 EUR
http://www.vins-perrier.com
Jean Perrier & fils
+33 (0)4 79 28 11 45

ROUSSETTE DE SAVOIE

Château Mont Termineau **88/100**

▼ ♪ Vintage 2012 : Light gold. Intense nose of marmalade, white-fleshed fruits and a touch of honey. A focused, intense and full-bodied Roussette. Freshness counters power and enhances fruit perfumes. A successful wine, perfect for tartiflette.
http://www.vins-perrier.com
Jean Perrier & fils
+33 (0)4 79 28 11 45

Domaine de Rouzan **87/100**

▼ ♪ Altesse 2013 : Light gold. Pleasurable nose of pear, peach and white flowers. Supple, round, full and generous palate where aromas are supported by beautiful freshness. Almond and hazelnut drive the finish. Elegant across the palate. Pair with oily fish.
Price approx.: 5,80 EUR
http://www.vinssavoie.fr
Domaine de Rouzan
+33 (0)4 79 28 25 58

THE COLOUR OF THE WINES :

▼ Red wine
▽ Dry white wine
▽ Rose wine
▽ Sweet white wine
▽ Sparkling brut
▽ Sparkling brut rose
▼ Brandy
▼ Liqueur wine

VIN DE SAVOIE APREMONT

Domaine de Rouzan **86/100**

▼ ♪ Cuvée Prestige 2013 : Brilliant pale yellow. Pleasant nose driven by white fruits and white flowers. Lively palate showing intense, focused aromas. Fresh and well-balanced. Faint minerality on the finish. A successful wine pairing with fish dishes.
Price approx.: 5,40 EUR
http://www.vinssavoie.fr
Domaine de Rouzan
+33 (0)4 79 28 25 58

VIN DE SAVOIE CHIGNIN-BERGERON

Jean Perrier & Fils **87/100**

▼ ♪ Cuvée Gastronomie 2013 : Light gold. Refined nose driven by almond, wild flowers and jammy white fruits. Lush, robust palate. Perfume is already mature and framed by substance. A wine for gourmet foods. Price approx.: 16,50 EUR
http://www.vins-perrier.com
Jean Perrier & fils
+33 (0)4 79 28 11 45

VIN DE SAVOIE MONDEUSE

Domaine Dupasquier **87/100**

▼ ♪ Mondeuse 2011 : Garnet-hued. Inviting nose of jammy cherry, raspberry and blueberry. Extremely supple palate showcasing freshness and fruit. Pleasant crispness. A delightful Mondeuse that pairs well with food cooked on a hot stone.
Price approx.: 10,00 EUR
Domaine Dupasquier
+33 (0)4 79 44 02 23

Jean Perrier & Fils **86/100**

▼ ♪ Cuvée Gastronomie 2012 : Alluring dark purple. Delightful nose of cherry, blackcurrant and wild strawberry. A charming, supple and soft Mondeuse focusing on freshness and fruit with all the prerequisite qualities of a Mondeuse. Perfect for smoked ham. Price approx.: 11,90 EUR
http://www.vins-perrier.com
Jean Perrier & fils
+33 (0)4 79 28 11 45

VIN DE SAVOIE RIPAILLE

Château de Ripaille **86/100**

▼ ♪ Vintage 2013 : Brilliant light yellow. Pleasant nose reminiscent of white-fleshed fruits. Ethereal palate showing seductive honesty, crunchiness, exuberance and more of the same nose aromatics. A very suitable partner for fish in a sauce.
Price approx.: 6,60 EUR
http://www.ripaille.com
Domaine de Ripaille
+33 (0)4 50 71 75 12

JEAN PERRIER & FILS

Cuvée Gastronomie 2013

▼ Pale gold. Inviting nose with accents of meadow, grapefruit and tangerine. Light, supple palate with a lovely crispness. Beautiful fruity freshness. A very thirst-quenching wine that would pair with a platter of oysters.

+33 4 79 28 11 45

86/100

VIN DE SAVOIE

Domaine Dupasquier   **88/100**

▼ ♪ Roussette Altesse 2011 : Light gold. Rich nose reminiscent of plum flesh and stewed pear with floral and smoky undertones. Delectable full and generous palate driven by perfume and freshness. Complex yet thirst-quenching. A successful wine.
Price approx.: 11,00 EUR
Domaine Dupasquier
+33 (0)4 79 44 02 23

Domaine Dupasquier   **86/100**

▼ ♪ Jacquère 2012 : Light gold. Intense nose with accents of citrus zest, white flowers and almonds. A supple, soft Jacquère with a delightful fruitiness. Beautiful crisp presence on the finish. A wine for pleasure.
Price approx.: 8,00 EUR
Domaine Dupasquier
+33 (0)4 79 44 02 23

Jean Perrier & Fils   **85/100**

▼ ♪ Pure Rosé 2013 : Orange-pink. Delightful nose driven by red fruits sweets. Soft, round and fat palate. Lovely red fruit presence. A crunchy rosé laden with fruit, ideal for drinking with a platter of cold cuts.
Price approx.: 14,00 EUR
http://www.vins-perrier.com
Jean Perrier & fils
+33 (0)4 79 28 11 45

JURA

ARBOIS

Domaine Jacques Tissot   **86/100**

▼ ♪ Chardonnay 2010 : Brilliant pale yellow. Refined nose intermixing white fruits and a floral note. On the palate, a supple wine showing fullness, precision and freshness. An enjoyable, idiosyncratic Chardonnay that would work with, say, Asian foods.
Price approx.: 8,30 EUR
www.domaine-jacques-tissot.fr
Domaine Jacques Tissot
+33 (0)3 84 66 14 27

CHÂTEAU-CHALON

Domaine Berthet-Bondet   **87/100**

▼ ♪ Vin Jaune 2007 : Beautiful bright golden yellow. Expressive nose showing iodine, dried fruits and mild spices. Fresh palate centring on elegance. Precise, honest and generous aromas with restrained austerity. A well-crafted wine.
Price approx.: 33,70 EUR
http://www.berthet-bondet.net
Domaine Berthet-Bondet
+33 (0)3 84 44 60 48

Prices mentioned in this book are guideline and can vary depending on point of sale.
The shops, wineries or publisher can in no way be held responsible for this.

Detailed instructions are featured at the start of the book.

SOUTH-WEST

AN IMPRESSIVE LINE-UP OF TALENT

South-West is the name given to a raft of wine areas located in South-Western France, between Bordeaux to the west and Languedoc-Roussillon in the east. Interestingly, although Bordeaux is also located in South-Western France, it is never referred to as such. The South-West is too attached to its own specific qualities to share its name. It thereby protects its internationally-renowned identity.

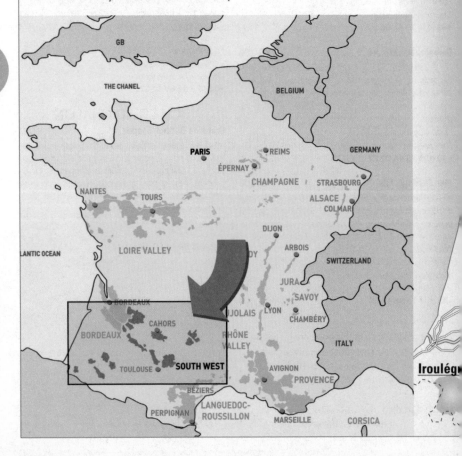

Bois Ordinaires

Borderies

Grande Champagne

Charente

Fins Bois

COGNAC

Angoulême

Bons Bois

Petite Champagne

Bois Ordinaires

Pécharmant-Rosette

Bergerac

Vins d'Entraygues et du Fel

Bordeaux

Montravel

Saussignac

Monbazillac

Côtes de Duras

Côtes Bergerac

Cahors

Côtes du Marmandais

Marcillac

Buzet

Garonne

Côtes du Brulhois

Vins de Lavilledieu

Vins d'Estaing

Bas-Armagnac

Ténarèze

Gaillac

Armagnac

Côtes du Frontonnais

Tursan

Toulouse

Béarn

Pau

Gers

St-Mont

Jurançon

Madiran et Pacherenc du Vic Bilh

Dordogne

419

South-West is the name given to a raft of wine areas located in South-Western France, between Bordeaux to the west and Languedoc-Roussillon in the east. Interestingly, although Bordeaux is also located in South-Western France, it is never referred to as such. The South-West is too attached to its own specific qualities to share its name. It thereby protects its internationally-renowned identity.

It is difficult to sum up the myriad wine styles and diversity of the South-West in just a few lines. In this land of Cockaigne, the choice of gourmet delights is endless: dry or sweet wines, supple or robust reds, rosés for quaffing, sparkling wines, brandies, liqueur wines… This diversity stems from a vast array of 'terroirs' though also from highly individual varietal ranges. Although the Bordeaux varietals (Cabernet-Sauvignon, Merlot, Sauvi-gnon…) are ubiquitous in some areas, elsewhere originality prevails (see the various appellations).

To simplify, the thirty or so appellations can be roughly divided into five different geographical areas:

THE BERGERAC REGION

This important wine region is the eastward extension of Bordeaux, travelling upstream and stretching over the Dordogne department. Although the varietal range and climate differ only slightly from its prestigious neighbour, the soil types change quite significantly: north of the Dordogne river, the soils are Perigordian sand whilst to the south, they are a combination of molasse, marl and limestone. This region is home to red wines (Bergerac, Côtes de Bergerac, Pécharmant), dry whites (Bergerac sec, Montravel) and sweet whites (Monbazillac, Rosette, Côtes de Montravel…).

THE WINE REGIONS OF THE GARONNE AND ITS TRIBUTARIES

These highly diverse regions stretch over the departments of Lot-et-Garonne, Tarn et Garonne, Tarn, Lot and Haute-Garonne. This is red wine territory, and the wines are predominantly dense and robust: Buzet, Côtes de Duras, Marmandais, Gaillac, Fronton, Cahors… some of which are drawn from a highly unusual range of varietals.

THE WINE REGIONS OF AVEYRON

Set in the heart of the Massif Central, these regions cover only a small area and the wines (mostly reds) are drunk locally. Marcillac is the best known.

THE PYRENEAN WINE REGION

This covers Béarn, Gascony and the Basque country, three regions with a strong personality. In the appellation areas of Irouleguy, Tursan, Madiran, Côtes de Saint-Mont and Béarn, growers are proud to produce robust, concentrated wines which can take the first-time drinker aback but are ideal partners for local specialities which abound in preserved meats or meats served with a sauce. At the other end of the spectrum, Jurançon and Pacherenc du Vic Bilh produce the most wonderful sweet wines. Armagnac rounds off the selection with its famous brandies.

THE COGNAC REGION

Although technically it is north of Bordeaux, Cognac belongs to the South-West and is famous the world over for its brandies. An increasing amount of wines labelled as Vin de Pays Charentais are grown there too. Refer to the chapter on 'brandies'.

REVIEW OF RECENT VINTAGES

• **2010** • Defying the effects of climate change, harvesting in the region was generally several days later than usual, sometimes more. The wines are off to a promising start, both in terms of fruit and acidity and should produce some great efforts, particularly reds. Watch this space…

• **2011** • After several small crops, the region returned to more normal levels with good quality due to favourable weather patterns. Like other parts of France, weather in the spring was outstanding but July was wet and punctuated by stormy episodes. August and September were absolutely wonderful, providing ideal conditions for harvesting from late August onwards, eight days earlier than usual. Excellent potential, both for the whites (freshness, fruit) and the reds (colour, structure, fruit).

• **2012** • Following a tricky spring, the region experienced a hot, dry summer that impeded the ripening of the berries. The whites suffered, but the reds reached a good level of maturity. Generally a decent vintage, more than likely one that will be ready to drink soon.

• **2013** • The weather was challenging almost everywhere across the region with traces of shatter, mildew and botrytis. Despite this, the wines are relatively good quality, though yields are low. Cahors was affected by hail in June and witnessed a severe decline in production, as did Duras. In the Bergerac area, early-ripening Merlot suffered but the Cabernets fared well. The dry and sweet whites (Monbazillac) are extremely well made. 2013 also produced some very good quality wines in Jurançon, too, with some wonderful late harvests.

THE SOUTH-WEST APPELLATIONS

A.C. BERGERAC

OVERVIEW: the Bergerac appellation area is located in the Dordogne department, on both banks of the river of the same name. 90 towns and villages

are entitled to use the appellation. With almost 10,000 hectares under vine, the area has an extremely varied soil make-up, ranging from calcareous clay soils, to Perigordian sand and gravel, molasse… The climate is defined predominantly by the ocean, moderated by the coolness of the Dordogne. Red varietals here are Cabernet-Sauvignon, Cabernet Franc, Merlot, Malbec, Fer Servadou and Merille. White varietals: Semillon, Sauvignon, Muscadelle, augmented with a secondary range of Ondenc, Chenin blanc and Ugni blanc.
WINE STYLES: AC Bergerac produces red, rosés and dry white wines. The red wines are delicate and fruity, supple and elegant. They develop aromas of red fruit (strawberry, blackcurrant) and vanilla notes. They should be drunk within two or three years of being harvested and make a pleasant partner for preserved meats, cooked cold pork meats, poultry and small game birds (quail, thrush…). The rosés, made from Cabernet-Sauvignon, display an attractive salmon-pink hue. They are delicate, supple and extremely fruit-forward with great freshness. They display a fruity (raspberry, banana, blackcurrant) and floral bouquet (violet). Excellent with cooked cold pork meats, grilled meat or fish. The white wines are dry, fresh, with a pleasant bouquet. They boast a distinctively lively attack and good length on the palate. Their aromas range from toasted, spicy and dried flowers to citrus fruit and vanilla. Try as an appetiser, with fish or shellfish.

A.C. BUZET

OVERVIEW: the Buzet appellation area embraces 27 towns and villages in the Lot-et-Garonne department, along the left bank of the Garonne between Agen and Marmande. Soil types are reasonably varied, ranging from gravel and calcareous clay on hillside sites, to 'boulbènes' (slaked loamy soils) along the plateau and the ridge. Red varietals are: Merlot, Cabernet-Sauvignon, Cabernet Franc and Malbec. For whites: Semillon, Sauvignon and Muscadelle.
WINE STYLES: the appellation produces red, rosé and white wines. With their attractive cherry colour, the reds are powerful, deep, fleshy, tannic wines, reminiscent of wines from Graves. Both wines in fact share virtually identical varietal ranges. Predominant aromas for the reds are ripe red fruit, animal notes and spices. The rosés are fresh and fruity, they are pleasantly nervous without becoming acidic. They exhibit fragrances of small red fruit and pear drops. The white wines are delicate, with a pleasant bouquet, nervous yet well-balanced, they retain freshness. They display floral notes, toasted almonds, ripe fruit (peach). The red wines pair with duck breast, preserved meats, rabbit with prunes. The rosés match with cooked cold pork meats, grilled white or red meats and the whites with foie gras, fish, freshwater whitebait or goats' cheese.

A.C. CAHORS

OVERVIEW: the Cahors region is located in the Lot department. The soils lay on a bed of ancient alluvium shaped into terraces or gently rolling hills. They are meagre, laden with quartz pebbles and siliceous gravel, interspersed with red clay and iron-rich sand. Along the plateau, the soil is more limestone. The valley enjoys an extremely unusual microclimate. The area is prone to some treacherous frost in the winter, though it is not particularly wet and autumn is usually sunny which promotes ripening.

WINE STYLES: Cahors only produces red wines from the Auxerrois grape variety (also known as Cot or Malbec). Occasionally, Merlot is added to the blend to soften the wines. Often dubbed 'black wine' because of its extremely dark hue and highly-present tannins, it is fruity and fleshy when young. Over the first two to three years, it remains closed before subsequently acquiring fullness and roundness. Predominant aromas are mushroom, spices, strawberry, prune, mineral notes and slightly toasted fragrances. In the early years, Cahors pairs extremely well with foie gras, duck confit or a leg of mutton. A few years down the line and it can be enjoyed with truffle croustade, ribsteak with ceps or game.

423

AC COTEAUX DU QUERCY

OVERVIEW: this 1999-established AOVDQS embraces 15 villages in the Lot department and 18 in Lot-et-Garonne, primarily located between Cahors and Montauban. Cabernet Franc (40% minimum, 60% maximum), though also Cot, Gamay, Merlot and Tannat (which individually must not exceed 20% of the varietal range) are grown here.

WINE STYLES: the red wines, which are relatively robust though less tannic than neighbouring Cahors, sit well alongside local specialities such as preserved meats and cassoulet. The rosés pair with cooked cold pork meats, fish or white meat.

A.C. CÔTES DE BERGERAC

OVERVIEW: the Côtes de Bergerac appellation, which can be applied to different colour wines, shares the same boundaries as AC Bergerac, in the Dordogne department, east of Bordeaux. Soil types are calcareous clay, sand, Perigordian gravel and molasse from several periods, with the climate strongly defined by the ocean.

WINE STYLES: AC Côtes de Bergerac produces red and white wines. The whites range from medium-dry to sweet depending on residual sugar content. The red wines, with their intense, deep colour, exhibit aromas of crystallised fruit (prune), blackcurrant, spices and vanilla. They are rich, well-structured and fruity with an excellent propensity for ageing. Enjoy with duck or goose confit, duck breasts or cassoulet. The sweet white wines display an attractive golden hue. They combine aromatic freshness (crystallised fruit, honey, citrus fruit, exotic fruit) with roundness on the palate. As they mature they develop a remarkably full mouthfeel. They pair well with foie gras, poultry, white meat, fish served with mousseline sauce, or desserts.

A.C. CÔTES DE DURAS

OVERVIEW: the Côtes de Duras appellation area is situated in Aquitaine. Every style of wine is grown here: reds, rosés, dry and sweet whites, on soils of molasse and compact clay mixed with various types of limestone.

WINE STYLES: the red wines, drawn from Cabernet Sauvignon, Cabernet Franc, Merlot and Malbec boast an attractive colour. They are powerful, fleshy, round wines displaying aromas of red fruit in brandy and spices. They can be served with garbure soup, black pudding, boiled chicken…

The rosés are made using the 'bleeding' process, and display a floral nose with red fruit (blackcurrant). They are lively, ethereal wines, well-balanced, combining freshness, roundness and fruitiness with a long aromatic finish. They are perfect partners for cooked cold pork meats. The dry white wines (Semillon, Sauvignon, Muscadelle, Chenin blanc, Ugni blanc) are racy and lively (tangerine, lemon, floral notes, hazelnut). Enjoy them with shad in a sorrel sauce or eel in a parsley and garlic sauce.

The sweet white wines, made from overripe grapes, exhibit a brilliant straw-yellow hue. They are unctuous, fat and well-balanced with great aromatic length. Aromas of crystallised fruit, acacia, honey, caramel, prune, crystallised orange… are all present. Perfect with foie gras or desserts.

AC CÔTES DE MILLAU

OVERVIEW: Côtes de Millau is the last region in Aveyron to be granted appellation status (AOVDQS since 1994). The vineyards wend their way along the Tarn river, embracing 17 towns and villages in Aveyron. The soil is calcareous clay on a bed of scree in the east and sandstone to the west. Mediterranean and mountain influences define the climate. Red varietals are: Gamay, Syrah, Cabernet-Sauvignon, Fer Servadou, Duras. White grapes are Chenin and Mauzac.

WINE STYLES: Côtes de Millau can be made as reds, rosés or whites. The red wines are round, well-balanced and harmonious with aromas of wild fruit (blackberry, wild raspberry). In their early years they can be served with cooked cold pork meats or poultry. A little patience allows the tannins to mellow. The rosé wines are fresh and fruity, and the whites well-balanced and supple on the palate.

A.C. CÔTES DE MONTRAVEL AND HAUT MONTRAVEL

OVERVIEW: the Côtes de Montravel and Haut Montravel appellation areas share the same location as Montravel. It is widely held that there is little difference between the two; the only reason there are two names is apparently because of a local feud. The vines are planted on a plateau and calcareous clay hillside sites. The climate is defined predominantly by the ocean, with the moderating influence of the Dordogne. Only white grape varieties are grown here: Semillon, Sauvignon and Muscadelle.

WINE STYLES: both appellations produce sweet or noble-rotted wines which display an unctuous attack, are harmonious, rich, complex and have good cellaring capacity. Some of the them can also be labelled as Bergerac moelleux. Predominant aromas are crystallised fruit, orange peel and lemon. They are suitable as appetisers, with fish served in a sauce and parsley-flavoured cheeses.

AC SAINT-MONT

OVERVIEW: the Saint-Mont region is situated exactly half way between the Atlantic Ocean and the Pyrenees, in the Adour valley. It covers the departments of Gers and Landes, centring on the towns of Saint-Mont, Plaisance, Aignan and Riscle. The soils are gravely (primeur wines), clayey (more distinctive wines) and calcareous clay (the realm of the white wines). The vineyards enjoy the dual climatic influence of the Pyrenees and the ocean. Long sunny days in the summer and autumn promote good ripening. Red varietals are Tannat, Cabernet Sauvignon, Cabernet Franc and Fer Servadou. White varieties are Arrufiac, Clairette, Courbu, Gros Manseng and Petit Manseng.

WINE STYLES: the appellation produces red, rosé and white wines. The red wines are rich, fleshy, fruity and heady, though at the same time elegant (aromas of black fruit, prune, cherry, blackberry, mild spices). The rosés are fresh, fruity and well-constituted with a full mouthfeel. The white wines are full, round and aromatic. The reds can be paired with red meat, poultry, game served with a sauce and cheeses. The rosés are well suited to barbecues (particularly lamb), paella, starters and mixed salads. The whites complement white meat (stuffed veal rolls, chicken Basquaise), shellfish and fish.

AC CÔTES DU BRULHOIS

OVERVIEW: Côtes du Brulhois wines are grown south of the Garonne valley, in an area straddling the departments of Lot-et-Garonne, Tarn-et-Garonne and Gers over 42 towns and villages. The soil is shaped into terraces or spread over stony, gravely and calcareous clay hillsides. The climate is defined both by ocean and Mediterranean influences. The area is home to Cabernet Sauvignon, Cabernet Franc, Merlot, Malbec, Fer Servadou and Tannat.

WINE STYLES: Côtes du Brulhois can be either red or rosé. The red wines, which are described locally as 'black wines', are powerful, full and velvety. They are rustic wines displaying aromas of blackcurrant, cherry, redcurrant, leather, toast and spices. Try with preserved meats, ceps, cassoulet or red meat. The rosé wines are made on a boutique scale and are also powerful and fruity. They should be served at a sit-down meal, with cooked cold pork meats or barbecued meats.

A.C. FRONTON

OVERVIEW: the Fronton wine region (Côtes du Frontonnais prior to 2007) is near Toulouse in the Tarn-et-Garonne and Haute-Garonne departments. The vines are grown on alluvium gravel terraces on a bedrock of molasse. Ocean and Mediterranean-type climates meet here and although the varietal range is varied – Gamay, Merille, Cinsault, Mauzac – the dominant grape is Negrette. **WINE STYLES:** Fronton can be either red or rosé. The red wines are powerful with a ruby-red hue. They are well-structured and elegant with aromas of blackcurrant, raspberry, prune, floral notes (peony, violet) and spices (pepper). The rosés are both distinguished and easy-drinking wines. On the palate, they are aromatic with slightly acidulous notes (raspberry, blackcurrant, peach, pear, acacia blossom). The reds pair well with cassoulet, grilled red meats or game. The rosés can be served with fatty fish, barbecues or mixed salads.

A.C. CÔTES DU MARMANDAIS

OVERVIEW: set on the border with Gironde, in Lot-et-Garonne, Côtes du Marmandais is the natural extension of Graves and Entre-deux-Mers. It covers 27 towns and villages, 18 of which are located along the right bank of the Garonne and 9 on the left bank. The soils are gravely and calcareous clay on a bedrock of limestone molasse. The climate is defined primarily by the ocean although it is also influenced by the Pyrenees. The vines enjoy a favourable aspect, with plentiful sunshine, which promotes optimum ripeness. The varietal range embraces Cabernet Sauvignon, Cabernet Franc, Merlot, Abouriou, Cot, Fer, Gamay and Syrah. For the whites: Sauvignon, Semillon, Ugni blanc and Muscadelle. **WINE STYLES:** the appellation produces red wines, rosés made predominantly using the 'bleeding' method, and white wines. The red wines are supple and aromatic: stewed fruit (prune, blackcurrant, raspberry) and spices (pepper, vanilla). Try with poultry, leg of lamb, grilled meat, game or cheese. The rosés are fresh, pleasant wines (red fruit, exotic fruit). They combine power with finesse, which makes them the ideal partner for barbecued meats, delicately-flavoured cooked cold pork meats, white meat, or fruit salad. The white wines are dry, aromatic and extremely fruity. They sit nicely alongside shellfish or fish.

A.C. FLOC DE GASCOGNE

OVERVIEW: AC Floc de Gascogne is a liqueur wine blended from grape juice and Armagnac, grown in the Gers, Landes and Lot-et-Garonne departments. The appellation covers an area under vine of 750 hectares and the wines can only be made within the confines of the Armagnac appellation area. Every year, 10% of Armagnac is actually used to make Floc de Gascogne, which is blended from two-thirds fresh grape juice drawn from Gascony grape varieties, and one third young Armagnac. Once the two are blended, the resultant wine then spends the next ten months in the cellar.

WINE STYLES: Floc de Gascogne can be either white or rosé and should be drunk within its first year. The whites are made from the white varietals Colombard, Ugni blanc and Gros Manseng. They are rich, generous and full, with a freshness that provides balance. The rosés are drawn from Cabernet Franc, Cabernet Sauvignon and Merlot. They are soft and extremely aromatic with predominant flavours of kirsch. The whites make perfect appetisers or can be paired with foie gras, melon and desserts (fresh fruit salad for instance). The rosés pair with apple tart, foie gras or melon.

427

A.C. GAILLAC

OVERVIEW: the Gaillac wine region is situated 50 kilometres from Toulouse in the Tarn department. It stretches northwards along both banks of the river Tarn to the mediaeval walled town of Cordes. Gaillac can be divided into four clear-cut 'terroirs': the terraces along the left banks of the Tarn with their poor gravel soils, the valley floor and its sand and deep gravel, the clay and calcareous clay along the hillocks and the predominantly limestone plateau. Wet springs and long, dry late autumns are the defining climatic characteristics. The sparkling wines are made either by the handcrafted method using natural grape sugars or by the traditional method. Either way, secondary fermentation takes place in the bottle. Harnessing the gas produced during alcoholic or malolactic fermentation gives dry whites a slight sparkle.

WINE STYLES: Gaillac wines cover a broad range of styles, from reds to dry whites, sweet whites or sparkling. Red wines are the region's mainstay, with an 80% share, and they are well-balanced, fragrant quaffing wines when they hail from the plateau. The hillside sites produce more robust wines with mellowed tannins and a harmonious finish. Wines grown along the gravel soils of the left bank are powerful with dense body and well-integrated tannins. Aromas of blackcurrant, green pepper and spices (pepper) are present. Try with beef and vegetable stew, duck casserole or rabbit stew.

The dry whites are slightly sparkling, fruity, floral wines with abundant freshness and suppleness. They are perfect with freshwater fish. The Mauzac varietal sweet white wines are rich and mild (musk, apple pips). They pair well with foie gras, roquefort cheese or gateaux. The sparkling wines display characteristic notes of apple, citrus fruit, ripe fruit and honey. Drink as an appetiser.

A.C. IROULEGUY

OVERVIEW: the Irouleguy wine region is located in the Pyrenees-Atlantiques department, in Basque country. The vines grow on siliceous clay and calcareous clay hillside sites with high iron oxide content where they enjoy a favourable aspect and are sheltered from the wind. This allows them to soak up maximum sunshine, particularly in the autumn. The co-operative winery is the region's foremost producer though there are also some independent wineries.

WINE STYLES: the red wines (Cabernet Franc, Cabernet Sauvignon, Tannat) display a bright, deep hue and boast a solid framework. They are often compared to Madiran though possibly have less body, are more rustic and exhibit great fragrance. They display an intense bouquet of wild red and black fruit (bilberries, blackberries) and pepper (Espelette). Try with cooked cold pork meats, roast meats (lamb) or ewe milk cheeses. The rosés, which are lively and quite light, pair well with tomato and pepper omelette, fish or seafood. The white wines (Courbu, Manseng) are fat and well-balanced. Their floral, exotic fruit (mango) and grapefruit tones give their freshness a boost. Perfect with fish and shellfish.

A.C. JURANÇON

OVERVIEW: the Jurançon wine region covers 700 hectares located south and west of Pau, in the foothills of the Pyrenees. Soil types are calcareous clay and siliceous clay and the ground is scattered with pebbles which retain heat during the day and release it by night. The vines grow here in a unique environment. The climate combines ocean influences (well-distributed rainfall) with mountain-type characteristics (risk of spring frosts). The south south-east facing plots enjoy plentiful sunshine and are sheltered from northerly winds. The vines grow at heights of 1.7 m. The Camaralet (15% maximum), Courbu, Gros Manseng, Lauzet (15% maximum) and Petit Manseng thrive in these conditions. A combination of hot daytime temperatures followed by cool nights is highly conducive to the production of sweet wines as it boosts the natural sugar content in the grapes. Fruit for the noble-rotted wines is harvested late in the season (November, or occasionally December).

WINE STYLES: the appellation only produces dry and sweet white wines. The dry white wines are fruity and aromatic (aromas of broom, acacia and passion fruit leading into toasted almond, dried fruit and truffle tones as they age). They can be served with shellfish and fish. The noble-rotted wines are fleshy, silky and harmonious. By and large they boast excellent cellaring capacity. The fruit on the nose is repeated on the palate: honey, white flowers (acacia, wild rose, hawthorn), candied fruit (apricot, orange, quince), fresh, warm bread and spices. Serve with foie gras or Pyrenean cheeses.

AC LAVILLEDIEU

OVERVIEW: the Lavilledieu wine region is situated west of Montauban in the Tarn-et-Garonne department. It covers 13 villages. Soil types are fine loam and silica on a bedrock of large stones or iron-rich hardpan. The climate is defined by both ocean and Mediterranean influences. The wines are aged either in tanks or barrels.

WINE STYLES: Lavilledieu wines can be either red or rosé and are blended from Negrette, Mauzac, Bordelais, Morterille, Chalosse, Gamay, Syrah and Fer Servadou. The red wines are well-constituted with well-integrated tannins. They are delicate and harmonious with aromas of red and black fruit (raspberry, blackcurrant, bilberry, strawberry) and liquorice and vanilla notes. A good match for duck or goose confit. The rosés are light, soft, highly-fragrant quaffing wines (floral and fruity notes, fragrances reminiscent of grenadine and pear drops). They pair well with barbecued meats, cooked cold pork meats and starters.

429

A.C. MADIRAN

OVERVIEW: Madiran stretches across three departments: Gers, Hautes-Pyrenees and Pyrenees-Atlantiques, embracing 36 towns and villages (27 in Pyrenees-Atlantiques, 6 in Hautes-Pyrenees and 3 in Gers). It shares the same area as the Pacherenc du Vic Bilh appellation where the soils are siliceous clay and calcareous clay. The nearby Atlantic has a moderating influence on the climate, making it slightly milder and wetter.

WINE STYLES: AC Madiran is a red wine only appellation where the primary varietal is Tannat. With their dense, extremely deep garnet-red colour, Madiran wines are rich in tannins, powerful, robust and well-constituted. They have an outstanding capacity to age though as young wines they can be harsh, particularly when Tannat is the mainstay of the blend. Principal aromas are black fruit, roasted coffee and spices. Food pairings include duck confit or breast, meat served with a sauce, lamb and ewe milk cheeses.

A.C. MARCILLAC

OVERVIEW: the Aveyron department is home to this appellation, which stretches over a dozen villages west of Rodez. The soils are made up of clay with high iron oxide content as well as limestone and marl, along the rim of the limestone plateau. The area is blessed with a microclimate conducive to growing vines which enjoy a favourable aspect due to their situation, on extremely steep hillside sites or terraces supported by dry stone walls. The wines are vinted traditionally at controlled temperatures and are aged either in tanks or barrels.

WINE STYLES: Marcillac produces both red wines from the Fer Servadou grape variety and rosés. The red wines are tannic, clean and warm with aromas of red fruit, spices, fern and green pepper. They pair well with sophisticated meat dishes, aligot (a local speciality made from mashed potatoes, fresh cheese and garlic), tripe or Bleu des Causses cheese. The rosés, which in some respects are a reflection of the 'terroir', are a great match for cooked cold pork meats.

A.C. MONBAZILLAC

OVERVIEW: the Monbazillac wine region is located south of Bergerac, along the left bank of the Dordogne. It is France's largest producer of noble-rotted sweet wines (with an average annual production of 50,000 hl). The vines (Semillon, Sauvignon and Muscadelle) are planted on hillside sites and calcareous clay plateaux. A mantle of fog frequently covers the vines on Autumn mornings, lifting during the day to make way for radiant sunshine. This provides ideal conditions for the formation of botrytis cinerea, a prerequisite for producing great sweet wines. As with Sauternes, the grapes are harvested by painstakingly combing through the vineyards time after time as each berry 'roasts'. Once they have been pressed, the resultant juice may have a natural content of up to 20% by volume. The wines are made in the ordinary way and then undergo ageing, usually in barrels, for at least a year.

WINE STYLES: Monbazillac can only produce noble-rotted white wines. They display a golden hue and boast unrivalled fat and unctuousness, bolstered by a touch of nervousness on the finish. They have an excellent propensity for ageing. Principal aromas are honey, acacia, peach, candied fruit. Suitable food pairings include foie gras, fatted chicken in a cream sauce, blue cheese from Auvergne or Roquefort cheese.

A.C. MONTRAVEL

OVERVIEW: the Montravel appellation area sits between Bordeaux and Bergerac. It forms an enclave, surrounded by Côtes-de-Castillon, from which it extends outwards, Entre-deux-Mers and the Sainte-Foy-Bordeaux area. Fifteen villages stretching along the right bank of the Dordogne are entitled to the appellation. The vines grow either on a calcareous clay plateau or on gravely terraces over an Asteries limestone bedrock.

The climate is strongly defined by the ocean and is hot though with the moderating coolness of the Dordogne. Some wines are vinted and aged on the lees which imparts greater structure and roundness.

WINE STYLES: Montravel is a dry white wine drawn from Semillon, Sauvignon and Muscadelle. Boasting a pale yellow hue, they are lively on the palate though not acidic. Growers who choose to do so can label their wines as Bergerac sec. However, red and rosé wines grown within this area are only entitled to the Bergerac or Côtes de Bergerac appellations. The aromas are floral, mineral (gunflint) and blackcurrant bud. They can be served with poached trout or pike with melted butter.

A.C. PACHERENC DU VIC BILH

OVERVIEW: the Pacherenc du Vic Bilh appellation shares the same area as Madiran, embracing 36 towns and villages split between three departments: Gers, Hautes-Pyrenees and Pyrenees-Atlantiques. The soils are siliceous clay and calcareous clay. The climate is defined by the ocean and is thus mild and damp.

WINE STYLES: the appellation produces white wine which can range from dry to sweet depending on the weather. It is made from Arrufiac, Courbu, Petit Manseng, Gros Manseng, Sauvignon and Semillon. The dry white wines usually display a lively attack leading into a round mouthfeel. They develop aromas of white flowers and exotic fruits with an extremely pleasant acidulous finish. Try with shellfish or fish in a sauce. The sweet wines are powerful, warm and extremely fragrant (pineapple, orange peel, honey). On the palate, their freshness is unexpected. They are enjoyable as appetisers or with foie gras or ewe milk cheese.

A.C. PINEAU DES CHARENTES

OVERVIEW: Pineau des Charentes is produced in both Charente departments, in the same area as Cognac. It is actually a blend of fresh grape juice and Cognac (mistelle). Once the fruit is pressed, the juice is left for 24 hours in tanks before oak-aged Cognac is added to arrest fermentation. Pineau then matures in oak barrels for at least 1 year before being bottled. These liqueur wines are made from Ugni blanc, Colombard, Folle blanche, Cabernet, Malbec and Merlot. To warrant the appellation, Pineau must comply with stringent regulations. The Cognac must come from the same farm as the fresh grapes and must have an ABV of at least 60%. The resultant Pineau has an ABV of between 16 and 22%.

WINE STYLES: Pineau des Charentes can be either white or rosé. The whites display an amber-yellow colour with golden tints. They are fat, round and aromatic with great length on the palate: dried fruit (walnuts, almonds), honey, quince paste and often slightly oxidised notes, of varying intensity. The rosés display a crimson hue with brick-red tints. They are delicate and extremely fruity, both on the nose and on the palate: red and black fruit (blackberry, blackcurrant, morello cherry). The whites and the rosés can be savoured as appetisers, or partnered with foie gras, fruit-based desserts (melon, tarts, fruit salad) or chocolate.

A.C. ROSETTE

OVERVIEW: Rosette is set in rolling hills near Bergerac in the Dordogne department. Urban sprawl has reduced its area under vine to less than 100 hectares. The vines are planted on gravely clay soils and the climate is defined by the ocean though with a southerly influence. The noble-rotted grapes are picked in stages then pressed, vinted and subsequently aged, primarily in oak. **WINE STYLES:** the appellation only produces sweet white wines on a boutique scale, blended from Semillon, Sauvignon and Muscadelle. They are straw-yellow in colour, supple, fat and elegant; their freshness imparts balance. As for aromas, their bouquet is floral and fruity. Rosette can be served as an appetiser, with seafood, mushroom or truffle-based starters or foie gras.

A.C. SAUSSIGNAC

OVERVIEW: Saussignac is grown west of Bergerac, along the left bank of the Dordogne. The area embraces four villages. The soils are calcareous clay or fine grain sandy clay ('boulbènes') which can easily become impermeable. The noble-rotted grapes are picked in stages then pressed in the normal way, vinted and subsequently aged, primarily in oak. **WINE STYLES:** the Saussignac appellation produces only sweet white or noble-rotted wines. The sweet whites are supple and well-balanced. The noble-rotted wines are full, rich and fat and will only fully reveal their opulence after a few years' ageing. Predominant aromas for the sweet whites are honey, flower (linden) and citrus fruit (grapefruit), whilst the noble-rotted wines display primarily floral (acacia) and fruit aromas (peach, nectarine). Serve with foie gras, cream soups and desserts.

AC TURSAN

OVERVIEW: the Tursan wine region is situated south-east of Mont-de-Marsan, in the Landes and Gers departments where it embraces 41 towns and villages. The vines occupy rolling hills where the soil make-up is clayey silica, limestone and stones. The region enjoys a mild, temperate ocean climate. A broad range of grape varietals is grown here: Tannat, Bouchy, Cabernet

Sauvignon, Cabernet Franc, Fer Servadou and Pinenc for the reds. Baroque, Sauvignon, Petit Manseng, Gros Manseng, Claverie, Cruchinet, Raffiat, Gers Claret and Clairette for the whites.

WINE STYLES: the red wines are powerful, well-constituted and full of finessse (wild fruit and fern notes). They enhance duck or goose breast, wood pigeon casserole, jugged hare, roast beef or foie gras with grapes. The rosés are fresh, fruity quaffing wines which reward early drinking and pair with cooked cold pork meats and mixed salads. The white wines are dry, lively, fruity and pleasing to the palate. They are a particularly good match for oysters, fish (salmon, trout), hors d'ouvre or foie gras.

AC VINS D'ENTRAYGUES ET DU FEL

OVERVIEW: Entraygues et du Fel wines are grown in the departments of Aveyron and Cantal. The area covers around 20 hectares under vine on shale hillsides in Fel and 'barene' type and granite soils in Entraygues. A broad range of grape varietals is grown here: Cabernet Sauvignon, Cabernet Franc, Fer Servadou, Abouriou, Gamay, Jurançon noir, Merlot, Mouyssages, Negrette, Pinot noir, Duras and Castel for the reds. Chenin blanc, Roussellou and Mauzac for the whites.

433

WINE STYLES: the wines of Entraygues et du Fel can be either red, rosé or white. The red wines are sturdy and bear the hallmark characteristics of their 'terroir'. Occasionally they are described as rough though they can also be approachable quaffing wines intended for early drinking. Try with tripe, Auvergne-style stew or lamb. The rosés are aromatic (red fruit and almond notes), racy and velvety. They pair well with cooked cold pork meats and barbecued meat. The white wines are dry, vigorous and extremely fragrant (broom, acacia, linden, gunflint, citrus fruit). On the palate, they reveal aromas of apple and almond. Try with shellfish.

AC VINS D'ESTAING

OVERVIEW: AOVDQS Estaing wines are grown in the departments of Cantal and Aveyron. The shale or calcareous clay soils provide a foothold for the vines along the abrupt hillsides overlooking the Lot valley.

WINE STYLES: Estaing wines can be either red or white. The red wines are delicate and fruity (red fruit, green pepper) and reward early drinking with roast meat and game (jugged hare, leg of venison…). The white wines are dry and fruity with an after-taste of gunflint. They are good partners for fish and seafood.

• • •

2015
SOUTH WEST WINES

BERGERAC SEC

LE CLOS DU BREIL — 88/100

▼ Expression 2013 : Light gold. Rich nose of toast and smoke backed by peach and candied orange. Mouth-coating and powerful. Intense oak with complex, yet still backward fruit. The finish offers up savoury exuberance. A superlative Bergerac, still in its youth and very promising.
Price approx.: 10,10 EUR
Le Clos du Breil
+33 (0)5 53 58 75 55

CHÂTEAU BELINGARD — 87/100

▼ Blanche de Bosredon 2012 : Light gold. Complex nose of citrus marmalade and dried flowers with spicy vanilla oak undertones. Powerful, full-bodied palate. Undeniable youthful qualities dominated by ageing perfumes. Sappy with substance. Shows promise for the future.
Price approx.: 8,00 EUR
http://www.belingard.com
Château Bélingard
+33 (0)5 53 58 28 03

CHÂTEAU DE FAYOLLE — 86/100

▼ Vintage 2012 : Pale gold. Inviting floral and citrus-driven nose. Supple, light, soft palate supported by a delightful fruity freshness. A Sauvignon for pleasure that would go down well as an aperitif.
Price approx.: 6,80 EUR
www.chateaufayolle.com
Château de Fayolle
+33 (0)5 53 74 32 02

BERGERAC

CHÂTEAU ROQUE-PEYRE — 85/100

▼ Fraîcheur 2013 : Light salmon-pink. Focused nose with accents of ripe red berry fruits and spice and earth undercurrents. Lovely sweetness on the palate nicely countered by freshness. Savoury, consistent fruit perfumes. A charming rosé for drinking at any time of the day.
Price approx.: 4,95 EUR
Vignobles Vallette
+33 (0)5 53 24 77 98

CHÂTEAU RIFFAUD — 85/100

▼ Fraîcheur 2013 : Light salmon-pink. Fairly subdued nose of ripe fruits and spice. A soft rosé showing a lovely smoothness that coats the palate without obscuring the fruit. An easy-drinking wine, perfect for between meals.
Price approx.: 4,95 EUR
Vignobles Vallette
+33 (0)5 53 24 77 98

CHÂTEAU DE FAYOLLE — 85/100

▼ Vintage 2012 : Concentrated hue with purple-blue tints. Intense nose of red and black berry fruits with spice undertones. A generous Bergerac with fine tannins and a melted mouthfeel. The fruit is nicely showcased. Calls for red meats.
Price approx.: 6,80 EUR
www.chateaufayolle.com
Château de Fayolle
+33 (0)5 53 74 32 02

CHÂTEAU ROQUE-PEYRE — 83/100

▼ Elégance 2012 : Deep, young colour. Fruit-driven nose of blackcurrant, blackberry and raspberry with earthy undertones. Supple, mellow palate with restrained power. The nose aromatics recur. A distinctive, classic Bergerac drinking well from now on.
Price approx.: 5,10 EUR
Vignobles Vallette
+33 (0)5 53 24 77 98

CHÂTEAU RIFFAUD — 82/100

▼ Vintage 2012 : Deep, young colour. Fruit-driven nose of cassis, raspberry and redcurrant. A supple Bergerac showing low concentration. Mellow tannins with fruit presence. Ready to drink now.
Price approx.: 5,10 EUR
Vignobles Vallette
+33 (0)5 53 24 77 98

BRULHOIS

LES VIGNERONS DU BRULHOIS — 87/100

▼ Terressence 2011 : Dark garnet with crimson tints. Fairly subdued nose of red and black fruits, violet and exotic wood. Silky, full, invigorating and concentrated palate. A virile wine supported by a robust structure. Successful and ambitious, needs 3-5 years more bottle age.
Price approx.: 18,00 EUR
http://www.vigneronsdubrulhois.com
Les Vignerons du Brulhois
+33 (0)5 63 39 91 92

CHÂTEAU GRAND CHÊNE — 86/100

▼ Vintage 2010 : Deep garnet. Pleasurable nose showing a basket of red and black fruits, cherry, fine

spices and subtle oak. Fairly dense, honest and svelte palate framed by a robust structure. Balanced across the palate. Needs a few more years bottle age to fully blossom.
Price approx.: 7,40 EUR
http://www.vigneronsdubrulhois.com
Les Vignerons du Brulhois
+33 (0)5 63 39 91 92

BUZET

COURÈGE-LONGUE   88/100

CONV▼.♪ Vieilles Vignes 2012 : Deep garnet. Delectable nose driven by blackberry, cassis, redcurrant and raspberry backed by oak. Delightful palate with a range of aromatics supported by freshness. Smooth tannins. Persistent, fruit-forward finish. A robust, successful Buzet..
Price approx.: 13,10 EUR
http://www.couregelongue.fr
Domaine Courège-Longue
+33 (0)5 49 95 45 14

COURÈGE-LONGUE   87/100

CONV▼.♪ Family Réserve 2012 : Appealing deeply-coloured garnet with dark purple tints. Endearing nose driven by fruity notes of currants and raspberry. The palate shows seductive supple and refined tannins. Fruit is supported by freshness. A delightful Buzet. Will keep.
Price approx.: 8,10 EUR
http://www.couregelongue.fr
Domaine Courège-Longue
+33 (0)5 49 95 45 14

CAHORS

CHÂTEAU LAMARTINE   92/100

▼.♪ Expression 2011 : Beautiful deep colour tinged with crimson. Expressive nose of cassis, blackberry, vanilla oak and violet. Delicate, silky and concentrated palate with nicely crafted tannins. Free-rein fruit expression. Persistent finish driven by fruit and spice. Top-notch.
Price approx.: 23,00 EUR
http://www.cahorslamartine.com
Château Lamartine
+33 (0)5 65 36 54 14

CHÂTEAU PINERAIE   92/100

▼.♪ L'Authentique 2011 : Magnificent inky hue. Refined nose of toasted, smoky oak backed by flowers and wild berries. Full palate with silky tannins and oak impeccably integrated into the fruit. A majestic Cahors in a refined setting. Substantial cellaring capacity.
Price approx.: 20,00 EUR
http://www.chateaupineraie.com
Château Pineraie
+33 (0)5 65 30 82 07

CHÂTEAU NOZIÈRES   89/100

▼.♪ L'Elégance 2011 : Deep garnet with purple-blue tints. Elegant nose of black fruits, violet and spice backed by liquorice. Velvety, concentrated and well-structured palate with evident tannins and focused fruit. Persistent, liquorice-infused finish. A characterful Cahors.
Price approx.: 14,00 EUR
www.chateaunozieres.com
Château Nozières
+33 (0)5 65 36 52 73

LA TOUR SAINT-SERNIN   88/100

▼.♪ Vintage 2010 : Concentrated, young colour. Heady oaked nose halfway between toasted, vanilla perfumes and peony backed by ripe black fruits. Well-balanced palate with a silky mouthfeel. Expressive fruit and oak presence. An elegant Cahors needing a little more patience.
Price approx.: 18,00 EUR
http://www.chateau-st-sernin.com
Cavalié
+33 (0)5 65 20 13 26

CHÂTEAU LAMARTINE   88/100

▼.♪ Cuvée Particulière 2011 : Deeply-coloured with crimson highlights. Lovely profound nose of ripe black fruits, violet and vanilla oak. Supple, soft, velvety and balanced palate with fine-grained tannins. Upfront fruit. Beautiful harmony. A seductive Cahors pairing with red meats.
Price approx.: 11,00 EUR
http://www.cahorslamartine.com
Château Lamartine
+33 (0)5 65 36 54 14

CHÂTEAU NOZIÈRES   88/100

▼.♪ Ambroise de l'Her 2012 : Deeply-coloured with dark purple tints. Expressive nose mingling black fruits, oak notes and flowers with mineral undertones. Round, full and velvety palate with polished tannins. Full-on fruit expression. Spicy, liquoricy finish. A charming, quality Cahors.
Price approx.: 6,50 EUR
www.chateaunozieres.com
Château Nozières
+33 (0)5 65 36 52 73

CHÂTEAU PINERAIE   88/100

▼.♪ Vintage 2011 : Black hue. Very floral, heady nose backed by currants and mellow oak. A supple Cahors with a soft mouthfeel and bold fruit. Well-integrated oak. Delightful, fresh aromatics. Uncork from now on with grilled meats.
Price approx.: 8,00 EUR
http://www.chateaupineraie.com
Château Pineraie
+33 (0)5 65 30 82 07

CHÂTEAU NOZIÈRES 88/100

▼♪ L'Elégance 2010 : Superb young black hue. Heady nose midway between flowers and jammy fruits with refined oak. A distinctive, lace-like Cahors with a generous, rich mouthfeel and persistent, well-balanced aromatic presence. A very good Cahors that would enhance game in a sauce.
Price approx.: 14,00 EUR
www.chateaunozieres.com
Château Nozières
+33 (0)5 65 36 52 73

CHÂTEAU DE GAUDOU 87/100

▼♪ Renaissance - Cuvée boisée 2012 : Young, deep black hue. Predominant oak on the nose with flowers and fruit in the background. Mouth-coating, robust palate with upfront tannins and oak. Will develop fruit, suppleness and freshness once it gets into its stride. A Cahors for cellaring.
Price approx.: 16,00 EUR
www.chateaudegaudou.com
Durou et Fils
+33 (0)5 65 36 52 93

CHÂTEAU NOZIÈRES 87/100

▼♪ Signature Malbec 2011 : Deeply-coloured with crimson tints. Refined nose combining dark fruits, oak, vanilla and liquorice undertones. Powerful, velvety and well-balanced palate with freshness supporting a range of aromatics. Slightly firm finish. A successful Cahors.
Price approx.: 9,50 EUR
www.chateaunozieres.com
Château Nozières
+33 (0)5 65 36 52 73

CHÂTEAU NOZIÈRES 87/100

▼♪ Ambroise de l'Her - élevé en fûts de chêne 2011 : Inky hue with purple-blue tints. Endearing nose of toasted vanilla oak backed by violet and young fruits. Very supple, well-balanced palate showing good quality oak influence. Fruit-driven finish. Undeniable craftsmanship.
Price approx.: 6,30 EUR
www.chateaunozieres.com
Château Nozières
+33 (0)5 65 36 52 73

CHÂTEAU DE HAUTERIVE 86/100

▼♪ Cuvée Prestige - élevé en fûts de chêne 2011 : Intense black tinged with garnet. Complex nose of roasted coffee and oak backed by ripe fruits, flowers and a touch of mocha. Very supple, soft palate boasting nicely mellowed oak which enhances the fruit and floral flavours. A harmonious wine.
Price approx.: 8,80 EUR
http://www.chateaudehauterive.fr
Château de Hauterive
+33 (0)5 65 36 52 84

CHÂTEAU DE GAUDOU 85/100

▼♪ Tradition 2013 : Beautiful dark hue with dark purple tints. On the nose, jammy cassis and blackberry with a floral note and subtle oak. Honest attack leading into a svelte palate with generous aromatic expression, a robust framework, spice dimension, chalky touch and vegetal finish.
Price approx.: 6,00 EUR
www.chateaudegaudou.com
Durou et Fils
+33 (0)5 65 36 52 93

CHÂTEAU FANTOU 85/100

▼♪ Grande Terrasse 2012 : Beautifully youthful colour. Predominant peony and violet on the nose with beautiful blackcurrant and cherry presence. Soft, supple palate with upfront fruity freshness. A wine made in a crowd-pleasing style. Ideal for becoming familiar with the appellation.
Price approx.: 10,00 EUR
Château Fantou
+33 (0)5 65 30 61 85

CHÂTEAU DE HAUTERIVE 84/100

▼♪ Chemin de Compostelle 2011 : Very deep colour with garnet tints. Fresh, heady nose revealing notes of peony, blackberry and redcurrant. Well-structured palate with noticeable tannins providing the perfect setting for the nose aromatics which expand. Drinking well whilst fruit-forward.
Price approx.: 7,20 EUR
http://www.chateaudehauterive.fr
Château de Hauterive
+33 (0)5 65 36 52 84

CHÂTEAU DE GAUDOU 84/100

▼♪ Grande Lignée 2012 : Dark crimson. Generous nose of black fruits, fine spices and upfront oak. On the palate, a substantial structure, a compact, svelte and rich wine leading into predominant oak notes mid-palate. Fairly severe on the finish. A good traditional wine. Keep.
Price approx.: 8,00 EUR
www.chateaudegaudou.com
Durou et Fils
+33 (0)5 65 36 52 93

CHÂTEAU NOZIÈRES 84/100

▼♪ Vintage 2012 : Youthful sparkle to the colour. Delightful, heady nose with aromas of violet, raspberry and blackcurrant. A supple Cahors with a soft mouthfeel and fruit presence. Drinking nicely in its youth.
Price approx.: 4,50 EUR
www.chateaunozieres.com
Château Nozières
+33 (0)5 65 36 52 73

CHÂTEAU EUGÉNIE 91/100

▼♪ Cuvée Réservée de l'Aïeul 2011 : Deep purple-blue hue. Profound nose showing black fruit, spice and a degree of minerality. The palate combines power and delicateness. Aromas are present and persistent even though oak also has its say. Lovely, extremely sappy wine.

Price approx.: 10,50 EUR

couture@chateaueugenie.com

Château Eugénie

+33 (0)5 65 30 73 51

CHÂTEAU EUGÉNIE   87/100

▼♪ Cuvée Pierre le Grand 2011 : Young, vibrant red. Ripe nose with accents of prune and jammy cherry. A clean, full-bodied wine on the palate with nicely balanced fruit, freshness and tannins. A distinctive, crowd-pleasing style.

Price approx.: 7,50 EUR

couture@chateaueugenie.com

Château Eugénie

+33 (0)5 65 30 73 51

CHÂTEAU EUGÉNIE   94/100

▼♪ Haute Collection 2011 : Deep purple-blue. Profound, delicate nose gradually unfurling mineral, oak and graphite notes with black fruits. Lovely sappy palate with extremely refined aromatics recalling the nose aromas. Persistent, full and captivating finish.

Price approx.: 20,00 EUR

couture@chateaueugenie.com

Château Eugénie

+33 (0)5 65 30 73 51

COMTÉ TOLOSAN

L'INSTANT PAPILLON   83/100

▼♪ Vintage 2013 : Pale gold. Nose of orange and apricot marmalade. A light, sweet white wine showing a pleasant combination of freshness and fruit. Simple, well-made and working best with desserts.

Price approx.: 5,50 EUR

Domaine de Revel

+33 (0)5 63 30 92 97

COTEAUX DU QUERCY

GRAINS DE REVEL   85/100

▼♪ Vintage 2013 : Light orange hue. Alluring nose of ripe strawberry and citrus fruits. Savoury, supple and crisp palate. Lovely overall freshness for a rosé focusing on fruit. Perfect as an appetiser followed by a barbecue.

Price approx.: 5,00 EUR

Domaine de Revel

+33 (0)5 63 30 92 97

CÔTES DE BERGERAC

CHÂTEAU BÉLINGARD   89/100

▼♪ Cuvée Blanche de Bosredon 2012 : Appealing deep red with youthful highlights. Elegant nose blending blackberry and raspberry with oak and liquoricy notes. Harmonious, concentrated palate with fine-grained tannins and upfront fruit. An ambitious, successful Côtes de Bergerac.

Price approx.: 8,75 EUR

http://www.belingard.com

Château Bélingard

+33 (0)5 53 58 28 03

LE CLOS DU BREIL   87/100

▼♪ Expression 2012 : Very concentrated, superb colour, youthful tints. Focused nose of ripe forest fruits with floral undertones. Chewy, well-structured palate with upfront, polished tannins. More of the delicious fruit aromas. A Bergerac displaying typicity, pairing with game.

Price approx.: 10,10 EUR

Le Clos du Breil

+33 (0)5 53 58 75 55

CHÂTEAU DE PANISSEAU   85/100

▼♪ Cuvée Alcéa 2013 : Light yellow with green tints. Compelling nose of citrus fruits, blackcurrant leaf and boxwood. Ethereal, lively palate with nicely harnessed exuberance and lovely focused, dynamic aromas. A delightful wine for the aperitif and seafoods.

Price approx.: 6,25 EUR

Château de Panisseau

+33 (0)5 53 58 40 03

CHÂTEAU DE PANISSEAU   84/100

▼♪ Vintage 2013 : Limpid cherry-red. Fairly shy nose showing a floral note with strawberry and red fruits in the background. No hesitation on the palate which reveals bold fruit expression augmented by a spice note. A delicious, honest wine pairing with cold meats.

Price approx.: 6,25 EUR

Château de Panisseau

+33 (0)5 53 58 40 03

CÔTES DE DURAS

DOMAINE DE FERRANT   85/100

▼♪ Tradition 2012 : Light gold. Ripe nose of toasted oak backed by citrus fruits and white peach. On the palate, oak is focused yet not pervasive. Fruit is still a little backward. Generous, full mouthfeel. A match for white meats in a cream sauce.

Price approx.: 6,00 EUR

Domaine de Ferrant

+33 (0)5 53 84 45 02

DOMAINE DE FERRANT   83/100

▼♪ C de Ferrant 2010 : Garnet. Ripe nose driven by blackcurrant, plum and cherry with vegetal oak undertones. Beautiful aromatic attack on the palate leading into a lighter mid-palate and finish showing oak influence. A mature Duras, drinking well from now on.

Price approx.: 10,00 EUR
Domaine de Ferrant
+33 (0)5 53 84 45 02

CÔTES DE GASCOGNE

DOMAINE CHIROULET   90/100

▼♪ Vent d'Hiver 2011 : Beautiful deep gold. Very honeyed, rich nose of acacia blossom backed by candied apricot. Beautiful liqueur-like palate. Balanced sweetness and freshness with archetypal perfumes that linger. Impeccable use of the drying (passerillage) process.

Price approx.: 17,40 EUR
http://www.chiroulet.com
Domaine Chiroulet
+33 (0)5 62 28 02 21

DOMAINE CHIROULET   89/100

▼♪ La Côte d'Heux 2012 : Light yellow. Elegant nose showing smoky vanilla aromas backed by white fruits and acacia. Refined, silky palate. Lovely fullness and aromatic balance. The oak melts into the fruit. Enjoyable mellow finish. Try now.

Price approx.: 8,40 EUR
http://www.chiroulet.com
Domaine Chiroulet
+33 (0)5 62 28 02 21

DOMAINE DE LAGUILLE   88/100

▼♪ Petit Manseng 2011 : Brilliant yellow with golden tints. Expressive nose of tropical and white fruits, toasted almond, candied, patisserie dimensions and a vanilla touch. Silky attack leading into a mellow, rich palate with a lovely impression of harmony. Very compelling.

Price approx.: 7,90 EUR
Domaine de Laguille
+33 (0)5 62 09 77 05

DOMAINE CHIROULET   88/100

▼♪ Grande Réserve 2009 : Colour still in its youth. Refined toasted oak on the nose backed by forest fruits. Supple palate with polished tannins and aromatic balance dominated by fruit. A racy, full Gascogne that still has plenty left to offer. Perfect for mutton chops.

Price approx.: 13,35 EUR
http://www.chiroulet.com
Domaine Chiroulet
+33 (0)5 62 28 02 21

LE DOMAINE DE HERREBOUC   87/100

Org▼♪ La Sélection Merlot 2011 : Deeply-coloured dark purple. Intense nose of ripe red and black fruits backed by spice and maquis. Well-structured, mouth-coating palate showcasing abundant fruit and spice aromas with an assertive sense of place. Recommended for game.

Price approx.: 10,00 EUR
Domaine de Herrebouc
+33 (0)5 62 64 68 34

LE DOMAINE DE HERREBOUC   87/100

CONV▼♪ Merlot 2009 : Concentrated garnet. Intense nose with accents of plum and cherry backed by spice and undergrowth. Warm palate displaying ultra ripe, intense perfumes. Alcohol presence bolsters the character of the wine. Set aside for meats in a sauce.

Price approx.: 9,00 EUR
Domaine de Herrebouc
+33 (0)5 62 64 68 34

LA TOUR DE HERREBOUC   87/100

▼♪ Sélection Cabernet Sauvignon 2006 : Concentrated garnet. Intense nose of wilderness, undergrowth and leather backed by nicely ripe red and black fruits. Chewy, warm palate confirming the nose aromatics. Mellow oak and polished tannins. A wine for game and foods in a sauce.

Price approx.: 12,00 EUR
Domaine de Herrebouc
+33 (0)5 62 64 68 34

DOMAINE DE LAGUILLE   86/100

▼♪ Gros Manseng 2013 : Brilliant pale hue with green tints. Inviting nose of blackcurrant leaf, citrus and white fruits. Suave attack leading into a delightful, medium-dry palate revealing a proud range of spice, fruit and refined tropical aromas supporting crunchy exuberance.

Price approx.: 6,60 EUR
Domaine de Laguille
+33 (0)5 62 09 77 05

PETIT M   86/100

▼♪ Tahi 2011 : Deep garnet. Complex nose intermixing mild spices, truffle, red fruits and morello cherry. On the palate, a harmonious wine focusing on elegance with beautiful tension driving its powerful aromas. The structure will soon mellow. A characterful Gascon wine.

Price approx.: 10,00 EUR
Domaine de la Higuère
+33 (0)5 62 65 18 05

DOMAINE DE JOŸ   86/100

▼♪ Attitude 2011 : Attractive yellow-gold. Rich, expressive nose with accents of tropical fruits and mild spices. On the palate, a rich yet nevertheless fresh wine. A lush style that works well with poultry in a cream sauce.

Price approx.: 12,00 EUR
http://www.domaine-joy.com
Domaine de Joÿ
+33 (0)5 62 09 03 20

DOMAINE CHIROULET 86/100

▼ ♪ Terres Blanches 2013 : Pale yellow. Harmonious nose halfway between mellow flowers and crisp fruit. More of the same delightful aromatics on the palate with a delicious tropical finish. A thirst-quenching style for sharing. Instant enjoyment.
Price approx.: 6,85 EUR
http://www.chiroulet.com
Domaine Chiroulet
+33 (0)5 62 28 02 21

DOMAINE CHIROULET 85/100

▼ ♪ Le Temps des Fleurs 2013 : Cherry-pink. Delectable nose of red fruit sweets with spice undercurrents. Full, generous palate showing more of the delightful fruit aromatics. A powerful rosé showing at its best with barbecued foods.
Price approx.: 6,60 EUR
http://www.chiroulet.com
Domaine Chiroulet
+33 (0)5 62 28 02 21

DOMAINE DE JOŸ 83/100

▼ ♪ Odes à la Joie 2012 : Limpid light yellow. Nose of stone fruits suggestive of ripe apricot. Rich at point of entry leading into a crisper mid-palate. A dense yet nervy style that works equally well with fish or foie gras.
Price approx.: 6,50 EUR
http://www.domaine-joy.com
Domaine de Joÿ
+33 (0)5 62 09 03 20

DOMAINE DE LAGUILLE 82/100

▼ ♪ Ugni Blanc -Colombard 2013 : Brilliant pale hue with green tints. Powerful nose of blackcurrant bud and grapefruit. On the palate, a supple, round wine with crunchy exuberance, medium intense, focused aromas and a slightly weak finish. A pleasant partner for whitebait.
Price approx.: 4,70 EUR
Domaine de Laguille
+33 (0)5 62 09 77 05

DOMAINE DE JOŸ 80/100

▼ ♪ Nuances 2012 : Pale yellow with green tints. Pleasant nose marrying floral notes and white fruits with a touch of crispness. On the palate, delightful fruity aromatics blending freshness and snap. A party-style wine for sharing.
Price approx.: 4,95 EUR
http://www.domaine-joy.com
Domaine de Joÿ
+33 (0)5 62 09 03 20

CÔTES DE MONTRAVEL

CHÂTEAU ROQUE-PEYRE 83/100

▼ ♪ Douceur 2013 : Pale gold. Nose of white fruits in syrup with floral undercurrents. A supple, soft wine with restrained sweetness and upfront freshness. Would work well as a pudding wine.
Price approx.: 5,10 EUR
Vignobles Vallette
+33 (0)5 53 24 77 98

CHÂTEAU RIFFAUD 81/100

▼ ♪ Douceur 2013 : Pale gold. Nose of white fruits in syrup with a floral touch of rose. A very light sweet white wine that is supple, fresh and shows pleasant fruit aromatics. Simple yet enjoyable. Perfect as a pudding wine.
Price approx.: 5,10 EUR
Vignobles Vallette
+33 (0)5 53 24 77 98

CÔTES DU LOT

CHÂTEAU NOZIÈRES 84/100

▼ ♪ Le Gravis 2013 : Light red. Intense nose suggestive of red fruit sweets with a floral and mineral touch. Fat, roundness, freshness and upfront substance leading into a powerful finish. A food-friendly rosé pairing preferably with grilled meats.
Price approx.: 4,30 EUR
www.chateaunozieres.com
Château Nozières
+33 (0)5 65 36 52 73

CÔTES DU TARN

COMTE DE THUN 91/100

▼ ♪ La Tarabelle 2009 : Dark garnet. Beautiful complex nose of fine spices, ripe plum, garrigue, mocha, toast and a touch of truffle. Silky, rich and svelte mouthfeel. Invigorating with vibrant aromas and silky tannins bordering on mellow. Heading towards its peak. Superb.
Price approx.: 35,00 EUR
http://www.comtedethun.com
Domaine du Comte de Thun
+33 (0)5 63 56 14 02

Detailed instructions are featured at
the start of the book.

COMTE DE THUN 89/100

▼♪ Le Parrazal 2009 : Deeply-coloured garnet. Generous nose of mild spices, exotic wood, garrigue and graphite. Velvety, rich and nervy presence on the palate exuding splendid racy aromas and a robust structure still marking the finish. A fine wine that needs more bottle time.
Price approx.: 15,00 EUR
http://www.comtedethun.com
Domaine du Comte de Thun
+33 (0)5 63 56 14 02

DAVID 87/100

▼♪ Sauvignon & Mauzac 2013 : Pale gold. Crisp nose showing tell-tale Sauvignon aromas on first pour (grapefruit, boxwood) then flowing into more mellow notes of sweets. More of the same pronounced aromas on the palate. A juicy, light, supple and soft wine. Would work with Asian foods.
Price approx.: 3,80 EUR
http://www.clement-termes.com
Château Clément Termes
+33 (0)5 63 40 47 80

DAVID 85/100

▼♪ Syrah & Braucol 2013 : Orange-red hue. Nose of ripe fruits and citrus with spice undertones. Full, generous palate driven by fruit perfumes. Beautiful ripeness. A food-friendly rosé, perfect for grilled meats or Mediterranean salads.
Price approx.: 3,80 EUR
http://www.clement-termes.com
Château Clément Termes
+33 (0)5 63 40 47 80

DAVID 81/100

▼♪ Merlot & Duras 2013 : Young colour. Fruit-driven nose of raspberry, blackberry and blackcurrant with subtle spice undertones. The palate successfully focuses on fresh fruit and suppleness. Drinking well from now on with barbecued foods.
Price approx.: 3,80 EUR
http://www.clement-termes.com
Château Clément Termes
+33 (0)5 63 40 47 80

FRONTON

THIBAUT DE PLAISANCE 87/100

Org▼♪ Vintage 2011 : Deeply-coloured garnet. A mix of ripe black fruits and spices (liquorice) on the nose with forest undertones. Chewy palate with present, polished tannins, power and gushing fruit. Honest sense of place. Calls for roast game.
Price approx.: 10,00 EUR

www.chateau-plaisance.fr
Château Plaisance
+33 (0)5 61 84 97 41

CHÂTEAU PLAISANCE 87/100

Org▼♪ Vintage 2012 : Deep, young colour. Appealing nose of fresh cassis, blackberry and plum with floral undertones. The palate shows seductive freshness at point of entry, highlighting fruit flavours nicely framed by fine, present tannins. Spicy finish. An honest, sound Fronton.
Price approx.: 11,00 EUR
www.chateau-plaisance.fr
Château Plaisance
+33 (0)5 61 84 97 41

CASSIN 86/100

▼♪ Sunshine 2012 : Dark purple highlights. Floral and fruity nose showing blackcurrant, blackberry, violet... Supple, soft mouthfeel successfully focusing on fresh perfumes. An easy-drinking Fronton, ideal for a platter of cold cuts and cheeses.
Price approx.: 8,00 EUR
http://www.chateau-cassin.fr
Le Fronton Nez
+33 (0)5 61 82 93 29

GAILLAC MOUSSEUX

CHÂTEAU LECUSSE 87/100

▼♪ Extra Brut Méthode Traditionnelle 2008 : Brilliant light gold. Intense nose driven by brioche, creamy and buttery notes, white flowers and white fruits. Well-balanced, fresh and crisp palate with a persistent, fruit-forward finish. A successful sparkling Gaillac.
Price approx.: 5,86 EUR
Château Lecusse
+33 (0)5 63 33 90 09

CHÂTEAU LECUSSE 86/100

▼♪ Extra Brut Méthode Traditionnelle 2010 : Bright gold. The nose is driven by milky and patisserie notes coupled with dried fruits. Lively, well-balanced and fresh palate with upfront fruit. Pleasant and harmonious across the palate. Drink as an aperitif.
Price approx.: 5,86 EUR
Château Lecusse
+33 (0)5 63 33 90 09

GAILLAC

CLOS ROCAILLEUX 88/100

▼♪ Duras rosé 2012 : Light salmon-pink. Appealing nose of red fruits with a pepper note. A rich, full-bodied

rosé revealing a generous range of aromatics. The complexity of aroma (fruit, spice) captivates the palate. A successful wine that belongs up with the top-tier rosés.
Price approx.: 9,50 EUR
http://closrocailleux.com
Clos Rocailleux
+33 (0)9 67 20 89 75

CHÂTEAU LECUSSE   87/100

▼♪ Grande Cuvée Prestige - Syrah 2012 : Young-looking deep crimson. Expressive nose of red fruits, violet and spice touches. Ethereal palate with generous, exuberant aromas. Tense, full of life, without artifice. Some silky supporting tannins. An enjoyable wine for grilled meats.
Price approx.: 6,64 EUR
Château Lecusse
+33 (0)5 63 33 90 09

CHÂTEAU LECUSSE   87/100

▼♪ Grande Cuvée Prestige - Duras 2012 : Deep crimson, dark purple tints. Pleasant nose of blackberry and redcurrant with a peppery note and subtle oak. Likeable, light and natural palate showing fruit sweets. Full-on expression provides an enjoyable drink. Fresh, focused, easy-drinking. Real pleasure.
Price approx.: 6,64 EUR
Château Lecusse
+33 (0)5 63 33 90 09

CHÂTEAU LECUSSE   87/100

▼♪ Grande Cuvée Prestige - Fer Servadou 2012 : Deep, young crimson. Pleasant nose of black fruits and peony with a trace of spice. Supple attack leading into a likeable round, aromatic and juicy palate supported by effective freshness. Hint of firmness and vegetal presence on the finish. Lovely natural sensation.
Price approx.: 6,64 EUR
Château Lecusse
+33 (0)5 63 33 90 09

CHÂTEAU LECUSSE   86/100

▼♪ Cuvée Spéciale 2012 : Deep crimson. Powerful nose of cassis, redcurrant, pepper and fine spices. Exuberant fruit driven by crunchy freshness on the palate. A broad, chewy and dense wine with a firm finish, still under oak influence. Lovely natural impression. Good.
Price approx.: 4,30 EUR
Château Lecusse
+33 (0)5 63 33 90 09

CHÂTEAU CLÉMENT TERMES   86/100

▼♪ Vintage 2013 : Orange-red. Nose of ripe red fruits and citrus with earthy undertones. Fat, fullness and flavoursome mature aromatics not lacking in freshness. A lush, generous rosé, perfect for terrines.
Price approx.: 4,80 EUR

http://www.clement-termes.com
Château Clément Termes
+33 (0)5 63 40 47 80

CHÂTEAU CLÉMENT TERMES   86/100

▼♪ Vintage 2013 : Pale gold. Refined nose displaying sweet white fruit, tropical fruit and wild flower aromatics. Soft palate with a lovely crispness. Very fresh and supple. Crunchy tropical finish. A real pleasure to drink.
Price approx.: 4,80 EUR
http://www.clement-termes.com
Château Clément Termes
+33 (0)5 63 40 47 80

CHÂTEAU DE MAYRAGUES   85/100

Org▼♪ Les Mages 2012 : Deep, young colour. Heady nose driven by peony and fresh fruit. Generous, supple and intense palate infused with fruity freshness. Exuberance and acidity balance out on the finish. A Gaillac with a true sense of place. Keep for a while for full enjoyment.
Price approx.: 11,50 EUR
http://www.chateau-de-mayragues.com
Château de Mayragues
+33 (0)5 63 33 94 08

MAS DES COMBES   84/100

▼♪ Coteaux d'Oustry 2011 : Robe grenat, légèrement évoluée. Nez épanoui mêlant fruits rouges, notes florales sur fond minéral et de sous-bois. La bouche est ronde, souple, fruitée. Les tanins sont polis. Bon équilibre. Finale épicée persistante. A apprécier sur viande rouge.
Price approx.: 7,00 EUR
Mas des Combes
+33 (0)5 63 57 06 13

MAS DES COMBES   84/100

▼♪ Vintage 2013 : Pale gold. Enticing nose driven by spice, wild flowers and grapefruit. Supple, light palate boasting savoury exuberance. Focused, refreshing perfumes. A good wine for stimulating the appetite.
Price approx.: 4,80 EUR
Mas des Combes
+33 (0)5 63 57 06 13

CHÂTEAU CLÉMENT TERMES   84/100

▼♪ Vintage 2012 : Young, dark purple. Nose of crunchy blackcurrant, blackberry and redcurrant backed by spice. Well-balanced, supple palate with a lovely fruit theme. Mellow tannins and freshness. Youthful qualities that should be fully enjoyed.
Price approx.: 5,50 EUR
http://www.clement-termes.com
Château Clément Termes
+33 (0)5 63 40 47 80

CLOS ROCAILLEUX   84/100

▼✦ Mauzac 2012 : Pale gold. Nose of white fruits backed by meadow aromas. A soft, supple and well-balanced Mauzac with substance nicely supporting aromatic expression. A potential partner for Sushi.
Price approx.: 11,00 EUR
http://closrocailleux.com
Clos Rocailleux
+33 (0)9 67 20 89 75

MAS DES COMBES   83/100

▼✦ Millésime 2013 : Robe rouge orangé. Nez de fruits rouges mûrs, touche fumée. Un rosé chaleureux, gras, sur une maturité aromatique affirmée. Conviendra mieux à des grillades qu'à l'apéritif.
Price approx.: 4,80 EUR
Mas des Combes
+33 (0)5 63 57 06 13

JURANÇON SEC

DOMAINE BRU-BACHÉ   90/100

Org▼✦ Les Casterasses 2011 : Appealing deep amber. Mature nose revealing perfumes of dried apricot, fig and fresh mushroom. Beautiful full, generous attack with lovely fat. Opulence combined with a very persistent, bone dry style. A very compelling wine.
Price approx.: 12,00 EUR
Domaine Bru-Baché
+33 (0)5 59 21 36 34

DOMAINE CAUHAPÉ   88/100

▼✦ Geyser 2013 : Light gold. Attractive nose of white fruits and fruits in syrup with a hint of confectionary. Crunchy, elegant palate boasting beautiful exuberance supporting perfume. Sorbet-driven finish. A very dynamic wine for shaping up the palate from the aperitif on.

Price approx.: 11,70 EUR
www.cauhape.com
Domaine Cauhapé
+33 (0)5 59 21 33 02

DOMAINE CAUHAPÉ   88/100

▼✦ Chant des Vignes 2013 : Robe or clair. Nez intense, aux accents exotiques et d'agrumes, arrière-plan épicé poivré. La bouche possède de l'étoffe, du gras associés à une palette aromatique croquante et désaltérante. Toutes les qualités du vin de plaisir immédiat.
Price approx.: 11,70 EUR
www.cauhape.com
Domaine Cauhapé
+33 (0)5 59 21 33 02

DOMAINE NIGRI   88/100

CONV▼✦ Pierre de Lune 2012 : Beautiful limpid pale yellow. The nose marries citrus, tropical fruits and peppermint. Freshness, aromatic expression and balance are clear themes on the palate. Evident tropical drive on the finish with perfumes of pomelo and mango.
Price approx.: 9,00 EUR
Domaine Nigri
+33 (0)5 59 21 42 01

JURANÇON

DOMAINE BRU-BACHÉ   95/100

Org▼✦ L'Eminence 2011 : Old gold with amber. Complex nose combining dried fruits, fresh mushroom, and a mineral dimension with a slightly oxidised character. The palate shows amazing volume and fullness. Superb freshness ensures balance. A monumental wine.
Price approx.: 51,00 EUR
Domaine Bru-Baché
+33 (0)5 59 21 36 34

DOMAINE BRU-BACHÉ   93/100

Org▼✦ La Quintessence 2011 : Beautiful light gold with amber. Profound nose blending dried apricot, orange zest, roasted notes and a touch of honey. The palate is lush yet fresh and remarkablly soft. Fruit is present and precise and the palate stays clean. A consummate wine.
Price approx.: 21,00 EUR
Domaine Bru-Baché
+33 (0)5 59 21 36 34

DOMAINE BRU-BACHÉ   90/100

Org▼✦ Les Casterasses 2011 : Yellow-gold with faint amber. The nose opens up to floral, honeyed notes backed by gingerbread and dried fruits. Silky palate showing savoury freshness, impeccably balanced with a sensation of sweetness. Very charming and light.
Price approx.: 14,00 EUR
Domaine Bru-Baché
+33 (0)5 59 21 36 34

DOMAINE NIGRI   90/100

CONV▼✦ Toute une Histoire 2012 : Golden hue. Expressive, alluring nose with accents of candied apricot and honey. On the palate, concentration is transcended by freshness. Lovely clearly-etched aromas that linger with more of the nose aromatics. A real treat.
Price approx.: 15,00 EUR
Domaine Nigri
+33 (0)5 59 21 42 01

CLOS LAPLUME 88/100

▼✦ Esprit de l'ambroisie 2011 : Light gold. Smoky oak on the nose backed by apricot, orange, peach... Lovely youthful exuberance, mellowness and freshness on the palate. Honeyed finish. A distinctive Jurançon that will reach its peak in 2 to 3 years' time.
Price approx.: 11,00 EUR
http://www.clos-laplume.fr
Clos Laplume
+33 (0)5 59 21 27 60

LANDES

ARGILÉUS 89/100

▼✦ Vintage 2009 : Concentrated colour with youthful tints. Intense nose of morello cherries, blackcurrant and refined vanilla oak. Full, rich palate. Impeccably balanced fruit and ageing aromas. Silky tannins. Assertive character with undeniable presence. A successful wine.
Price approx.: 14,50 EUR
www.tursan-dulucq.com
Château de Perchade
+33 (0)5 58 44 50 68

MONTRAVEL

CHÂTEAU MOULIN CARESSE 89/100

▼✦ Cuvée CENT pour 100 2009 : Beautiful deep red. Ripe nose marrying notes of red fruits and slightly spicy oak tones. Wonderful attack on the palate with ripe tannins and highly expressive, mature fruit. A deftly crafted wine at its peak now.
Price approx.: 15,20 EUR
Château Moulin Caresse
+33 (0)5 53 27 55 58

CHÂTEAU RIFFAUD 86/100

▼✦ Subtilité 2013 : Pale yellow. Appealing tropical and citrus nose backed by wild flowers. Beautiful acidity at point of entry heralds in pervasive fruit perfumes. Wonderful overall freshness. A Montravel for sharing over salads or goat's cheeses.
Price approx.: 4,95 EUR
Vignobles Vallette
+33 (0)5 53 24 77 98

CHÂTEAU ROQUE-PEYRE 85/100

▼✦ Subtilité 2013 : Pale gold. Subtle floral and fruity nose (white fruits). The palate is dominated by savoury exuberance, focused crisp perfumes and freshness. A wine providing instant pleasure as soon as the warm weather arrives.

Price approx.: 4,95 EUR
Vignobles Vallette
+33 (0)5 53 24 77 98

PINEAU DES CHARENTES

DOMAINE ANDRÉ PETIT 87/100

▼✦ Sélection - blanc 2010 : Golden amber. Distinctive nose halfway between vanilla, cinnamon, almond and cherries in brandy. Characteristic, generous palate showing power nicely counterbalanced by freshness. Focused, uplifting perfumes. Classic Pineau.
Price approx.: 11,00 EUR
Domaine André Petit & fils
+33 (0)5 45 78 55 44

DOMAINE ANDRÉ PETIT 85/100

▼✦ Sélection - rouge : Garnet. Nose of jammy red fruits and red fruits in brandy. Freshness provides lovely support for the aromas from point of entry on. A well-balanced, honest and straightforward red Pineau. Best served chilled as an aperitif.
Price approx.: 11,00 EUR
Domaine André Petit & fils
+33 (0)5 45 78 55 44

TURSAN

CHÂTEAU DE PERCHADE 87/100

▼✦ Vintage 2011 : Concentrated hue. Focused nose of ripe black fruits with a hint of spice. Generous palate with fine, melted tannins. Powerful with focused, ripe fruit. An idiosyncratic Tursan that calls for red meats.
Price approx.: 6,00 EUR
www.tursan-dulucq.com
Château de Perchade
+33 (0)5 58 44 50 68

2015
ENTRY LEVEL TABLE WINES

VIN DE FRANCE

VINITRIO   87/100
▼ ♪ Carignan 2013 : Concentrated hue, young tints. The nose is driven by stone fruits, condiments, spices and mocha. A generous, full and structured Carignan. Power does not overshadow the array of aromatics. An impeccable rendition of a beautiful varietal. Calls for meat in a sauce.
Price approx.: 3,00 EUR
Domaine de la Baquière
+33 (0)4 68 78 98 49

COSTE LONGUIÈRE   87/100
CONV ▼ ♪ Camaieu 2012 : Deep, young colour. Inviting nose halfway between forest fruits, violet and mild spice. Full, fleshy palate with youthful qualities and freshness supporting heady perfumes that linger. A revelation. Uncork for chocolate cake.
Price approx.: 12,00 EUR
Coste Longuiere Repellin
+33 (0)4 66 83 00 56

ELEGANCE   86/100
▼ ♪ Sauvignon 2013 : Light yellow. Very tropical, charming nose showing pineapple, mango and passion fruit aromas. Delicious palate with the same aromatics carrying through coupled with a pleasant, persistent crispness. Floral finish. A Sauvignon to titillate your taste buds.
Price approx.: 5,00 EUR
Joseph Castan
+33 (0)4 67 40 00 64

AUBAÏ MEMA   86/100
▼ ♪ Lunatico 2011 : Concentrated hue with mature highlights. Refined nose showing accents of olive paste, spice and stone fruits. Warm, concentrated palate that is mouth-coating and chewy. Very focused, already mature aromas. Meats in a sauce would be a good match.
Price approx.: 18,00 EUR
Aubai Mema
+33 (0)4 66 73 52 76

MAISON CLAUDE DE LA PORTE   86/100
▼ DG2 Ratafia rouge : Limpid red. Generous nose of candied red fruits, kirsch, a balsamic touch and smooth oak in the background. Mild, suave and round palate showing an effective, uplifting freshness. A Ratafia with a good measure of personality.
Price approx.: 15,00 EUR
www.caves-tannay.com
Les Caves Tannaysiennes
+33 (0)3 86 29 31 59

PETIT LOUPART   85/100
▼ ♪ Chenin Blanc 2013 : Brilliant pale hue, green tints. Expressive nose of ripe white-fleshed fruits bolstered by a trace of flowers. Generous at point of entry. Round, full palate that is fleshy yet invigorating. Aromatic intensity doesn't play hard to get. Sheer pleasure. Price approx.: 5,00 EUR
www.villebois.eu
Villebois

COSTE LONGUIÈRE   85/100
CONV ▼ ♪ Coquelicot 2011 : Concentrated colour with youthful highlights. Heady nose showing accents of violet, peony and wild berries. Joyful, supple palate showcasing perfume. A wine for quaffing.
Price approx.: 8,00 EUR
Coste Longuiere Repellin
+33 (0)4 66 83 00 56

LES VIGNERONS DU BRULHOIS   81/100
▼ ♪ Grain d'amour - doux : Light salmon-pink. Compelling nose suggestive of fresh grape and red berry fruits. On the palate, a medium-dry wine with honest, crunchy fruits. Well-balanced across the palate and enjoyable at any time of day when served well-chilled.
Price approx.: 5,70 EUR
http://www.vigneronsdubrulhois.com
Les Vignerons du Brulhois
+33 (0)5 63 39 91 92

VENT & TERROIR   81/100
▼ ♪ Le Cers - 1 litre 2013 : Light salmon-pink with orange tints. Shy nose of strawberry and redcurrant. More expressive on the palate. An upright, easy-drinking and fresh wine with a fruity simplicity that makes it the perfect partner for pizzas and salads.
Price approx.: 1,95 EUR
Chantovent - Jean d'Alibert
+33 (0)1 30 98 59 79

LA HAIE   80/100
Org ▼ ♪ Cabernet Sauvignon 2011 : Very dark hue with purple-blue tints. The nose shows no fruit but reveals venison tones and earthy notes. A mature, melted style on the palate displaying a real sense of place. Fruitier finish recalling cassis.
Château La Haie
+33 (0)6 72 94 53 37

VIN DE TABLE DE FRANCE

COSTE LONGUIÈRE 84/100

▼ ♪ La Cour à Mouton 2008 : Concentrated colour with subtle mature highlights. Powerful nose of mocha, liquorice, cinnamon, smoke, stone fruits and spice. Chewy, warm palate with a robust mouthfeel and predominant empyreumatic perfumes. An assertive Mediterranean rendition.
Price approx.: 13,00 EUR
Coste Longuiere Repellin
+33 (0)4 66 83 00 56

VIN MOUSSEUX (BRUT)

KYSTIN 88/100

▼ ♪ Cuvée Pûr - Poiré : Beautiful yellow-gold. Intense nose of white fruits with a whiff of caramel and toast. On the palate, wonderful clean attack with a fairly creamy mousse. Perfumed finish tinged with a hint of sourness and brimming with freshness. Beautiful finesse.
Price approx.: 12,00 EUR
Kystin
+33 (0)6 20 25 68 88

CHÂTEAU DE CASTIGNO 85/100

CONV ▼ ♪ Brut nature 2011 : Pale salmon-pink. Nose of strawberry, orange and tangerine flesh. Supple, well-balanced palate. Generous mouthfeel gradually revealing fruit aromas. Mellow finish. An elegant dry sparkling wine.
Price approx.: 16,50 EUR
http://www.chateaucastigno.com
Château de Castigno
+33 (0)4 67 38 05 50

KYSTIN 85/100

▼ ♪ Cuvée XVII - cidre châtaigne : Old gold. Suggestions of confectionery and almond paste on the nose. Fairly fruit-forward on the attack then flowing into more patisserie-like notes on the finish. An unusual, easy-drinking style that works well with puddings for instance.
Price approx.: 12,00 EUR
Kystin
+33 (0)6 20 25 68 88

FINES PERLES DES TILLEULS 83/100

▼ ♪ Brut - Méthode traditionnelle 2011 : Brilliant pale hue with medium effervescence. Subdued nose suggestive of white-fleshed fruits. An ethereal style on the palate. An honest, focused and well-balanced wine, still fruit forward with savoury, crunchy freshness. The finish is a tad austere.
Price approx.: 6,10 EUR
www.domainedestilleuls.fr
Domaine des Tilleuls
+33 (0)2 40 33 60 04

L'EXCEPTION DE GALOUPET 80/100

▼ ♪ Vintage 2011 : Attractive amber highlights. Endearing nose of ripe grape. Lively palate with accents of lime and crisp white fruits. A style with lots of drive that would work well as an aperitif. An unusual wine well worth discovering.
Price approx.: 19,50 EUR
www.galoupet.com
Château du Galoupet
+33 (0)4 94 66 40 07

MARQUISE DE LEROY-BEAUVAL 79/100

▼ ♪ Brut rosé : Light orange-pink. Nose of red berries and strawberry candy. Fairly lively at point of entry flowing into a more closely-integrated mid-palate. Fruit is nicely underscored with a trace of sweetness on the finish. Drink very well-chilled as an aperitif.
Price approx.: 10,00 EUR
Château Leroy-Beauval
+33 (0)5 35 38 61 65

WINE SCORES:

95-100/100: an outstanding wine, when a great 'terroir' meets exceptional winemaking expertise.

90-94/100: a superlative wine combining finesse, complexity and remarkable winemaking.

85-89/100: a wine of extremely high standard, which we enjoyed for its typicity and character.

80-84/100: a quality wine combining balance, structure and neatness for a pleasurable wine drinking experience.

75-79/100: a wine deemed acceptable.

70-74/100: a wine with defects, unacceptable.

65-69/100: a wine with major defects, inadmissible.

50-64/100: unacceptable wine, not worthy for sale.

Note: wines scoring less than 75/100 are not included in our publications.

2015 BRANDIES

CALVADOS

COMTE LOUIS DE LAURISTON 86/100

▼ ♪ Fine Calvados : Beautiful brilliant light yellow. Very focused, pleasant nose suggestive of ripe apple with a crisp tone. Clean attack on the palate, wonderful balance driven by the same fruit aromatics with a hint of spice on the finish. Would work in cocktails.
Price approx.: 23,60 EUR
www.calvados-lauriston.com
Les Chais du Verger Normand
+33 (0)2 33 38 53 96

CALVADOS DOMFRONTAIS

COMTE LOUIS DE LAURISTON 91/100

▼ ♪ Vintage 1975 : Beautiful amber hue with ginger tints. Very compelling nose with accents of cooked apples and tarte tatin. On the palate, fruit is impeccably showcased and enhanced by pleasant spice notes. The finish flows smoothly across the palate.
Price approx.: 165,00 EUR
www.calvados-lauriston.com
Les Chais du Verger Normand
+33 (0)2 33 38 53 96

COMTE LOUIS DE LAURISTON 89/100

▼ ♪ Vintage 1964 : Coppery-orange. Complex nose showing tropical tones with stewed apple flowing into subtle spice perfumes. On the palate, a characterful offering revealing more of the same aromatic features. The finish is still powerful.
Price approx.: 244,00 EUR
www.calvados-lauriston.com
Les Chais du Verger Normand
+33 (0)2 33 38 53 96

COMTE LOUIS DE LAURISTON 88/100

▼ ♪ Hors d'Age : Attractive coppery-orange. Predominantly tangy and spicy perfumes on the nose. The palate shows seductive harmony, freshness and persistent perfumes. Fruit gradually makes way for spice tones. A beautiful and very consistent offering.
www.calvados-lauriston.com
Les Chais du Verger Normand
+33 (0)2 33 38 53 96

CALVADOS PAYS D'AUGE

CALVADOS CHRISTIAN DROUIN 94/100

▼ ♪ Vintage 1974 : Coppery-orange hue. Mature nose marrying stewed apple and spice notes of cinnamon, nutmeg and clove. Soft, velvety and savoury attack on the palate leading into a fresh, harmonious mid-palate interspersed with delightful fruity and spice perfumes.
Price approx.: 235,00 EUR
http://www.calvados-drouin.com
Calvados Christian Drouin
+33 (0)2 31 64 30 05

CALVADOS CHRISTIAN DROUIN 94/100

▼ ♪ Vintage 1964 : Orange hue. Extremely mature nose of sugar cane, spice and brown sugar. Fleshy attack on the palate bordering on crunchy despite its age. Pronounced spicy aromatic expression. Stays fresh, persistent and in its prime.
Price approx.: 360,00 EUR
http://www.calvados-drouin.com
Calvados Christian Drouin
+33 (0)2 31 64 30 05

CALVADOS CHRISTIAN DROUIN 92/100

▼ ♪ Vintage 1984 : Beautiful coppery-orange hue. Delightful nose marrying jammy fruits with a mild spice tone and cinnamon. On the palate, a full, velvety and delectable offering showing more of the same harmonious aromatic blend. A fairly complex, charming style. Price approx.: 165,00 EUR
http://www.calvados-drouin.com
Calvados Christian Drouin
+33 (0)2 31 64 30 05

CALVADOS CHRISTIAN DROUIN 90/100

▼ ♪ Vintage 1994 : Coppery-orange hue. Powerful nose showing predominant cooked fruit and stewed apple perfumes. Clean, aromatic attack with the apple carrying through. A classic style capped off with a spicy finish. Quite convincing. Price approx.: 89,00 EUR
http://www.calvados-drouin.com
Calvados Christian Drouin
+33 (0)2 31 64 30 05

CALVADOS CHRISTIAN DROUIN 90/100

▼ ♪ 25 ans : Beautiful orange hue tinged with bronze. Nice, fruit-driven nose recalling ripe apple and tarte tatin. Very charming palate with intense aromas ranging from fruit to patisserie notes with a salted butter caramel touch on the finish.
Price approx.: 72,00 EUR
http://www.calvados-drouin.com
Calvados Christian Drouin
+33 (0)2 31 64 30 05

CALVADOS CHRISTIAN DROUIN — 87/100

▼ ♪ VSOP : Brilliant orange hue. Fairly endearing nose of candied fruits with mild spices. Beautiful aromatic presence, fullness and spice notes on the palate. An honest, accessible style that works best as a long drink.
Price approx.: 45,50 EUR
http://www.calvados-drouin.com
Calvados Christian Drouin
+33 (0)2 31 64 30 05

BAS ARMAGNAC

CASTARÈDE — 95/100

▼ ♪ Vintage 1974 : Beautiful deep hue with bronze highlights. Delicate, spicy nose gradually revealing delicious candied fruit tones. The palate shows seductive elegance, harmony and very progressive aromatic intensity. Reaches an aromatic climax on the finish.
Price approx.: 135,00 EUR
http://www.armagnac-castarede.fr
Castarède
+33 (0)5 53 65 50 06

DOMAINE D'OGNOAS — 87/100

▼ ♪ Vintage 2002 : Beautiful orange hue with bronze highlights. Pleasant heady nose showing floral notes and mild spices with a tropical streak. Powerful attack on the palate with predominant citrus and spice aromas. A massive, powerful style, still very young.
Price approx.: 21,64 EUR
http://www.domaine-ognoas.com
Domaine d'Ognoas
+33 (0)5 58 45 22 11

COGNAC BORDERIES

CAMUS COGNAC — 90/100

▼ ♪ Borderies XO : Orange hue with mahogany highlights. The nose opens up to tones of dried flowers, prune and violet. Suave attack leading into a degree of power mid-palate. A lovely impression of fullness is exuded across the palate.
Price approx.: 130,00 EUR
http://www.camus.fr
Camus Cognacs
+33 (0)5 45 32 28 28

COGNAC FINE CHAMPAGNE

COGNAC GODET — 92/100

▼ ♪ XO Extra Old : Coppery orange hue. Delicate nose offering fruit on first pour (prune, stewed apple) with delicate spice touches in the background. On the palate, a very melted style displaying a degree of roundness. More

idiosyncratic finish with lingering spice aromas.
www.cognacgodet.com
Cognac Godet
+33 (0)5 46 41 10 66

COGNAC FINS BOIS

BERNARD BOUTINET — 91/100

▼ ♪ VSOP : Brilliant coppery orange. Very delicate, appealing nose of dried fruits and spices. Full palate revealing more of the same racy aromas augmented by fairly substantial length. A VSOP of a remarkable standard.
Price approx.: 33,00 EUR
http://www.cognacboutiet.com
Bernard Boutinet
+33 (0)5 45 80 86 63

COGNAC GRANDE CHAMPAGNE

PIERRE FERRAND — 93/100

▼ ♪ 1er cru Ancestrale : Deep coppery colour with mahogany highlights. Subtle nose intermixing oak and spice notes with tobacco. The nose of a very old Cognac. Full, mellow and delicate palate showing remarkable freshness and aromatic expression. Lingering spice-driven finish.
Price approx.: 475,00 EUR
http://www.pierreferrandcognac.com
Pierre Ferrand
+33 (0)5 45 36 62 50

PIERRE FERRAND — 92/100

▼ ♪ 1er cru Sélection des Anges : Amber hue. Extremely mellow nose marrying dried flower tones with dried fruit. Very mellow on the attack coupled with freshness. Highly aromatic mid-palate and finish with the same delicious aromas carrying through.
Price approx.: 125,00 EUR
http://www.pierreferrandcognac.com
Pierre Ferrand
+33 (0)5 45 36 62 50

COGNAC GRANDE FINE CHAMPAGNE

DROUET ET FILS — 94/100

▼ ♪ Paradis de Famille : Beautiful coppery orange. Expressive nose marrying dried fruits, orange peel notes and mild spices. Velvety attack on the palate, racy, expressive aromas augmented by significant length. A very full Cognac.
Price approx.: 112,00 EUR
www.cognac-drouet.fr
Domaine Drouet & fils
+33 (0)5 45 83 63 13

COGNAC

COGNAC GODET 93/100

▼ ♪ XO : Fairly deep orange hue with copper highlights. Extremely archetypal nose revealing prune, violet and spice. Rich and harmonious at point of entry leading into a perfumed mid-palate and a finish displaying predominant spice. A great classic.
www.cognacgodet.com
Cognac Godet
+33 (0)5 46 41 10 66

CAMUS 92/100

▼ ♪ XO Elégance : Coppery orange hue. Profound nose of candied prune and spice showing true elegance. The palate reveals a seductively velvety texture, mellowness and aromatic precision. The finish introduces subtle honeyed and spicy persistency. A highly successful Cognac
Price approx.: 119,00 EUR
http://www.camus.fr
Camus Cognacs
+33 (0)5 45 32 28 28

COGNAC GODET 90/100

▼ ♪ Epicure - Folle Blanche : Appealing colour with amber and copper tints. Delicate nose marrying dried flowers, mild spices and oriental tones. Extraordinary roundness on the palate. Full attack flowing into a mid-palate revealing a degree of power and a highly aromatic, long finish
www.cognacgodet.com
Cognac Godet
+33 (0)5 46 41 10 66

CAMUS 89/100

▼ ♪ VSOP Elégance : Beautiful coppery-orange hue. Pleasant nose of dried flowers and dried fruits. Velvety at point of entry with more of the same delightful, upfront aromatics. A highly aromatic, round, polished Cognac in quite a seductive style.
Price approx.: 36,00 EUR
http://www.camus.fr
Camus Cognacs
+33 (0)5 45 32 28 28

PASCAL DUMONT 89/100

▼ ♪ Fine : Coppery hue with bronze tints. Pleasantly focused nose of dried fruits and dried flowers. Velvety and harmonious at point of entry with the nose aromas flowing into a persistent spice dimension. A full, generous style drinking well at the end of a meal.
Price approx.: 45,00 EUR
Pascal Dumont
+33 (0)5 45 81 69 16

CAMUS COGNAC 87/100

▼ ♪ Ile de Ré - Fine Island Cognac - Double Matured : Amber hue with orange highlights. Quite enticing nose of prune and candied fruits. Lovely roundness on the palate with a more upfront spice tone. A delightful aromatic Cognac for sharing.
Price approx.: 50,00 EUR
http://www.camus.fr
Camus Cognacs
+33 (0)5 45 32 28 28

OTHER SPIRITS

ANTONIO MASCARO, S.L. 92/100

▼ ♪ Brandi : Very vibrant orange. The nose intimates hints of date, cinnamon and clove. The palate reveals refined toast notes and expresses the authenticity of the grape. Elegant warmth is displayed over substantial length. Excellent.
Price approx.: 11,50 EUR
http://www.mascaro.es/
Antonio Mascaro, S.L.
+33 (0)34938901628

CHRISTIAN DROUIN 90/100

▼ ♪ Eau-de-vie de cidre Vintage 1948 : Coppery-orange with bronze tints. Powerful nose showing a floral tone of heather with delightful patisserie notes. A surprising predominant mineral streak on the palate, faintly reminiscent of chalk. Apple aromas are more present on the finish. Unusual.
Price approx.: 210,00 EUR
http://www.calvados-drouin.com
Calvados Christian Drouin
+33 (0)2 31 64 30 05

ANTONIO MASCARO, S.L. 83/100

▼ ♪ Brandi : Golden hue with vibrant orange highlights. Relatively mature nose intermixing raisin, walnut, hazelnut and almond aromas. The palate delivers a sensation of suave sweetness then flows into a warm finish.
Price approx.: 5,80 EUR
http://www.mascaro.es/
Antonio Mascaro, S.L.
+33 (0)34938901628

2015
WINES OF THE WORLD

• • • • • • • • • • • • • • • •

ARGENTINA

Mendoza
MENDOZA

Condor Andino   **87/100**

▼♪ Réserve Malbec 2013 : Beautiful vibrant red with young highlights. Profound nose of black fruits, cassis, sloe and a mineral touch. Lovely sappy palate with polished tannins and delightful focused aromatic expression with fruit playing a lead role.
Price approx.: 3,23 EUR
http://www.winesoverland.com
Wines Overland
+01 45 08 87 87

CONDOR ANDINO   **86/100**

▼♪ Cabernet Sauvignon 2013 : Clean red. Ripe nose suggestive of red berry garden fruits. Robust attack on the palate, substantial tannin density yet pleasant balance. More of the nose aromatics with a touch of liquorice on the finish.
Price approx.: 2,16 EUR
http://www.winesoverland.com
Wines Overland
+33 (0)1 45 08 87 87

CONDOR ANDINO   **85/100**

▼♪ Chardonnay 2013 : Pale yellow with green tints. Pleasurable nose intermixing citrus fruits, vanilla, floral notes and a mineral touch. Lively, fresh and very fruity palate. Fairly warm, persistent finish. A seductive Chardonnay that connoisseurs will enjoy. Drink as an aperitif.
Price approx.: 2,16 EUR
http://www.winesoverland.com
Wines Overland
+33 (0)1 45 08 87 87

CONDOR ANDINO   **84/100**

▼♪ Malbec 2013 : Young-looking garnet. The nose is ripe and fruity and delivers perfumes of dark fruits and sloe. The palate displays a fairly tannic, dense attack. The mid-

palate stays firm yet well-balanced and shows more of the same honest aromas.
Price approx.: 2,16 EUR
http://www.winesoverland.com
Wines Overland
+33 (0)1 45 08 87 87

• • • • • • • • • • • • • • • •

CHINA

(ALL REGIONS)

CHÂTEAU NINE PEAKS   **90/100**

▼♪ Reserva 2012 : Faint mature tints. The nose opens up to beautiful aromas of jammy and dried fruits backed by touches of undergrowth and spice. Full, well-integrated attack with refined tannins. Beautiful presence and good persistency. Needs to be decanted. A sterling wine.
Price approx.: 13,00 EUR
http://www.greatriverhill.com
Qingdao Great River Hill Winery Co.,Ltd.
+86 53290000000

CHATEAU NINE PEAKS   **87/100**

▼♪ Chardonnay 2013 : Limpid, light yellow. Very fruity, focused nose with aromas of white-fleshed fruits, banana and a touch of vanilla. Full, fat and powerful palate also revealing a sensation of freshness. A lush, generous and exotic Chardonnay.
Price approx.: 10,00 EUR
http://www.greatriverhill.com
Qingdao Great River Hill Winery Co.,Ltd.
+86 53290000000

CHÂTEAU NINE PEAKS   **87/100**

▼♪ Vintage 2012 : Fairly light colour with bricking. Highly expressive, mature nose combining ultra ripe red berry fruit notes, bigarreau cherry and lightly spiced refined oak. Full, warm attack with quite a light, mellow mouthfeel. Lovely presence and persistency.
Price approx.: 8,00 EUR
http://www.greatriverhill.com
Qingdao Great River Hill Winery Co.,Ltd.
+86 53290000000

• • • • • • • • • • • • • • • • • •

ITALY

AOSTA VALLEY

VALLE D'AOSTA D.O.C.

LA SOURCE DI CELI STEFANO & C   90/100

▼♪ Torrette 2012 : Ruby-red. Intense nose of violet and berry jam with lovely notes of wet asphalt and sweet liquorice. Persistent palate with elegant tannins and aromas of red fruits with a subtle touch of bitterness. Serve with meat.
http://www.lasource.it
La Source di Celi Stefano & C
+390166000000

LA SOURCE DI CELI STEFANO & C   90/100

▼♪ Gamay 2012 : Ruby-red. Pleasant, young nose intermixing red fruits with refined balsamic and eucalyptus notes. On the palate, a fresh, fruity style with balanced tannins and an elegant finish showing good quality oak influence. Excellent with meat.
http://www.lasource.it
La Source di Celi Stefano & C
+390166000000

LA SOURCE DI CELI STEFANO & C   90/100

▼♪ Petit Arvine 2012 : Straw-yellow. Intense, mineral nose opening up to apple, blackcurrant and pear. On the palate, lovely level of acidity, persistence, fresh fruit aromas and a balsamic finish. An enjoyable wine, drinking well on its own or with cheese.
http://www.lasource.it
La Source di Celi Stefano & C
+390166000000

LA SOURCE DI CELI STEFANO & C   88/100

▼♪ Torrette Superiore 2011 : Ruby-red. Intense, complex nose of wild cherry and earth combined with balsamic and liquorice notes. On the palate, an intense, persistent wine with refined, balanced tannins marked by predominant spice. Serve with elaborate meals.
http://www.lasource.it
La Source di Celi Stefano & C
+390166000000

LA SOURCE DI CELI STEFANO & C   88/100

▼♪ Cornalin 2012 : Ruby-red. Elegant nose of red fruits, wild berries, refined spice notes, vanilla and liquorice.

Good presence on the palate marrying red fruit and fine-grained oak with light, elegant tannins. A compelling wine pairing with meat.
http://www.lasource.it
La Source di Celi Stefano & C
+390166000000

ABRUZZO

MONTEPULCIANO D'ABRUZZO D.O.C.

PASETTI   86/100

▼♪ Harimann 2007 : Intense red. Warm nose of red fruits in brandy, spice, a touch of oak and a liquorice note. Highly aromatic, persistent palate framed by a subtle sensation of freshness. Ideal for red meats or meats in a sauce.
Price approx.: 35,00 EUR
http://www.pasettivini.it
Pasetti
+0 8 56 18 75

PASETTI   84/100

▼♪ Testarossa 2009 : Deep ruby-red. Nose of forest fruits revealing scents of blackberry and raspberry with faint spicy oak notes and a touch of toasted almond. The palate shows seductively supple tannins and aromatic complexity nicely infused with spice.
Price approx.: 17,00 EUR
http://www.pasettivini.it
Pasetti
+0 8 56 18 75

APULIA

**AZIENDA AGRICOLA MASSERIA NEL SOLE
SOC. AGR.   87/100**

▼♪ Metodo Classico Pas Dosè 2011 : Straw-yellow with a fine, persistent mousse. Nose of white flowers, magnolia, tropical fruits, pineapple, mango and papaya with a subtle touch of yeast. On the palate, a focused, fresh and subtly perfumed wine. Ideal for the aperitif.
Price approx.: 11,59 EUR
http://www.masserianelsole.it
Azienda Agricola Masseria Nel Sole Soc. Agr.
+390882000000

DAUNIA I.G.T.

AZIENDA AGRICOLA MASSERIA NEL SOLE
SOC. AGR.   87/100

Org ▼♪ Dedicato 2012 : Straw-yellow with pale green tints. Highly expressive nose intermixing white flowers and tropical fruits such as pineapple and papaya. Intense and persistent on the palate, displaying beautiful acidity. Ideal for fish-based dishes.

Price approx.: 5,49 EUR
http://www.masserianelsole.it
Azienda Agricola Masseria Nel Sole Soc. Agr.
+390882000000

AZIENDA AGRICOLA MASSERIA NEL SOLE
SOC. AGR.   84/100

Org ▼♪ Madame 2012 : Brilliant cherry-pink. Delicate bouquet of flowers and red fruits. On the palate, a fresh wine supported by good acidity, revealing fruit perfumes and interesting minerality. Ideal for the aperitif or with raw fish.

Price approx.: 5,49 EUR
http://www.masserianelsole.it
Azienda Agricola Masseria Nel Sole Soc. Agr.
+390882000000

PRIMITIVO DI MANDURIA
D.O.C.

JORCHE ANTICA MASSERIA   85/100

▼♪ Primitivo di Manduria Riserva 2010 : Deep ruby-red. Complex and refined nose of blackberry, cocoa, coffee and liquorice. Robust, supple and persistent on the palate, revealing elegant tannins. Would pair with rich, flavoursome foods like meats in a sauce.

Price approx.: 15,00 EUR
http://www.jorche.it
Jorche Antica Masseria
+391000000000

CAMPANIA

GRECO DI TUFO D.O.C.G

ESTERINA CENTRELLA VITICOLTORE   89/100

▼♪ Ester 2010 : Intense yellow-gold. Expressive nose blending ripe apricot, Williams pear, aniseed and liquorice. On the palate, tightly-wound tannins are noticeable but also lovely fruity roundness and beautiful acidity. Excellent for fish dishes served with a sauce.

http://www.esterinacentrella.com
Esterina Centrella Viticoltore
+390825998272

ESTERINA CENTRELLA VITICOLTORE   88/100

▼♪ Ester 2009 : Deeply-coloured golden yellow. Intense nose of tropical fruits, cedar wood and almond with a chalky touch. On the palate, a fresh, persistent style revealing balsamic accents of liquorice and eucalyptus. Perfect on its own or with shellfish.

http://www.esterinacentrella.com
Esterina Centrella Viticoltore
+390825998272

IRPINIA CAMPI TAURASINI
D.O.C.

IRPINIA CAMPI TAURASINI DOC
BORGODANGELO   89/100

▼♪ Irpinia Campi Taurasini 2010 : Very intense ruby-red. Complex nose driven by spice notes of tobacco and damp oak, as well as mint and plums in brandy. Very enjoyable full and fruity palate boasting round, seamless tannins. Makes an ideal partner for meat.

Price approx.: 11,00 EUR
http://www.borgodangelo.it
Borgodangelo
+39082773027

IRPINIA D.O.C

IRPINIA CAMPI TAURASINI DOC
BORGODANGELO   86/100

▼♪ Irpinia Campi Taurasini 2009 : Ruby. Instantly accessible fruity nose marked by ripe red fruits. On the palate, a warm, melted, bone dry wine showing seductive elegant tannins and a lengthy, spice-infused finish. Perfect for traditional cuisine, starters and meat courses.

Price approx.: 11,00 EUR
http://www.borgodangelo.it
Borgodangelo
+39082773027

IRPINIA ROSATO D.O.C.

IRPINIA ROSATO DOC BORGODANGELO 88/100

▼♪ Irpinia Rosato 2013 : Deeply-coloured pink with cherry tints. Intense nose of flowers and fresh strawberry and raspberry that lingers. On the palate, wonderful level of acidity and fine-grain tannins. Ideal as an appetiser or for summer meals.

Price approx.: 13,00 EUR
http://www.borgodangelo.it
Borgodangelo
+39082773027

LACRYMA CHRISTI DEL VESUVIO D.O.C.

AZIENDA AGRICOLA SORRENTINO   86/100

▼♪ Versacrum Lacryma Christi 2013 : Light pink. Warm nose with mineral hints and compelling cocoa notes. A round, persistent wine on the palate boasting good acidity and revealing more of the mineral character. Perfect for fish or soft cheeses.

Price approx.: 5,00 EUR
Lambrusco di Modena Doc Rosato «Opera Rosè»»
Az Ag Sorrentino di Angela Cascone
08 18 58 49 63

AZIENDA AGRICOLA SORRENTINO   85/100

▼♪ Versacrum Lacryma Christi 2013 : Ruby with purple tints. The nose recalls a bouquet of violets and forest fruits. The palate is fruity and fresh, showing a lovely long, focused finish supported by dense, enveloping tannins. Ideal for meat.

Price approx.: 5,00 EUR
Lambrusco di Modena Doc Rosato «Opera Rosè»»
Az Ag Sorrentino di Angela Cascone
08 18 58 49 63

POMPEIANO I.G.T.

AZIENDA AGRICOLA SORRENTINO   85/100

▼♪ Versacrum Falanghina 2013 : Pale straw-yellow. Intense, well-balanced nose with warm, aromatic, mineral notes. The mineral scents filter through to the palate. A wine displaying beautiful acidity and a long finish. Ideal for fish or as an aperitif.

Price approx.: 5,00 EUR
Lambrusco di Modena Doc Rosato «Opera Rosè»»
Az Ag Sorrentino di Angela Cascone
08 18 58 49 63

AZIENDA AGRICOLA SORRENTINO   84/100

▼♪ Don Paolo 2010 : Impenetrable ruby. Intense nose of cherry and dark chocolate. Peppery palate with persistent spicy oak accents. Firm yet not intrusive tannins. Clean finish. A wine pairing well with full-flavoured meats.

Price approx.: 10,00 EUR
Lambrusco di Modena Doc Rosato «Opera Rosè»»
Az Ag Sorrentino di Angela Cascone
08 18 58 49 63

AZIENDA AGRICOLA SORRENTINO   84/100

▼♪ Frupa 2011 : Intense ruby-r ed. Expressive nose combining aromas of potpourri, forest fruits in brandy and a faint spice note. Persistent palate with firm tannins and lovely focus. Ideal for meat.

Price approx.: 14,00 EUR

Lambrusco di Modena Doc Rosato «Opera Rosè»»
Az Ag Sorrentino di Angela Cascone
08 18 58 49 63

TAURASI D.O.C.G

OPERA MIA   90/100

▼♪ Taurasi 2008 : Garnet-red. Intense, elegant nose of ripe red fruits, molasses, mild spices and liquorice. Fresh palate with tightly-wound tannins that stays extremely focused and ends with a tobacco and oak-driven finish. A meditation wine.

Price approx.: 16,00 EUR
http://www.tenutapepe.it
Tenuta Cavalier Pepe
+39082773766

TAURASI DOCG BORGODANGELO   88/100

▼♪ Taurasi 2009 : Intense ruby. Expressive nose opening up to plums and blackberries in brandy then revealing a spicy oak character and tobacco notes. On the palate, a full yet fresh wine with persistent aromas. Refined and racy.

Price approx.: 21,00 EUR
http://www.borgodangelo.it
Borgodangelo
+39082773027

EMILIA-ROMAGNA

FORLI I.G.T.

CONDE' AZ. VITIVIN.   92/100

Eco▼♪ Rosso Massera 2011 : Intense colour with purple-blue tints. Expressive, harmonious nose showing a broad range of balsamic and mineral notes, crunchy cassis perfumes and a whiff of toast. The palate is focused, well-balanced and delicious with compact, silky tannins.

Price approx.: 120,00 EUR
http://www.conde.it
Conde' Az. Vitivin.
+390543940860

Prices mentioned in this book are guideline and can vary depending on point of sale. The shops, wineries or publisher can in no way be held responsible for this.

LAMBRUSCO DI MODENA D.O.C.

CLETO CHIARLI   **85/100**

▼♪ Pruno Nero Spumante Dry 2013 : Brilliant ruby. Crimson mousse. Expressive nose of morello cherry jam and sweet cherry with vegetal notes that are a tad resinous and herbal. Fresh, zippy and refeshing palate. Faint tannic trace counterbalanced by beautifully balanced sweetness.
Price approx.: 4,60 EUR
http://www.chiarli.it
Cleto Chiarli
390593163311

LAMBRUSCO DI SORBARA D.O.C

CLETO CHIARLI   **89/100**

▼♪ Vecchia Modena Premium 2013 : Light ruby. Expressive nose showing notes of wild strawberry, redcurrant and pomegranate entwined with floral aromas of violet and rose. Extremely fresh and very savoury palate. Long, clean and fruity finish.
Price approx.: 4,80 EUR
http://www.chiarli.it
Cleto Chiarli
390593163311

LAMBRUSCO GRASPAROSSA DI CASTELVETRO D.O.C

CLETO CHIARLI   **87/100**

▼♪ Vigneto Cialdini 2013 : Ruby with a crimson mousse. Fruit-based array of aromatics on the nose: raspberry, blackberry and redcurrant yet also floral and vegetal notes of hyacinth, eucalyptus and undergrowth. Refined creamy, savoury palate with abundant freshness. Long, clean finish.
Price approx.: 4,80 EUR
http://www.chiarli.it
Cleto Chiarli
390593163311

RUBICONE I.G.T.

AZIENDA VINICOLA ENIO OTTAVIANI & C. S.N.C.   **85/100**

▼♪ Merlot 2011 : Ruby-red with garnet highlights. Intense nose of spice, liquorice and gum arabic. Warm palate with firm tannins boasting lovely persistency and a focused finish. Pairs with game or meats in a sauce.
Price approx.: 19,00 EUR
http://www.enioottaviani.it
AZIENDA VINICOLA ENIO OTTAVIANI & C. S.n.c.
05 41 95 26 08

SANGIOVESE DI ROMAGNA D.O.C.

CONDE' AZ. VITIVIN.   **90/100**

Eco▼♪ Superiore Riserva 2010 : Brilliant ruby. The nose exudes a complex and elegant range of perfumes: violet, cherry, notes of roasted cocoa and coffee, incense, spice and graphite. Supple attack, pronounced freshness and rich yet velvety tannins.
Price approx.: 32,00 EUR
http://www.conde.it
Conde' Az. Vitivin.
390543940860

VINO SPUMANTE

CLETO CHIARLI   **84/100**

▼♪ Rosé Brut de Noir»» 2013 : Beautiful mousse and brilliant coral hue. Simple yet honest and perfumed nose centring on raspberry, reducurrant, undergrowth and tobacco leaf aromas. Very fresh, slender, savoury and lively palate with the nose aromatics flowing through.
Price approx.: 4,60 EUR
http://www.chiarli.it
Cleto Chiarli
390593163311

FRIULI - VENEZIA GIULIA

COLLIO D.O.C.

VILLA RUSSIZ   **91/100**

▼♪ Sauvignon De La Tour 2013 : Straw-yellow. Intense with persistent, tell-tale varietal aromas of tropical fruit (pineapple and papaya) enveloping the nose, enhanced by mineral notes. A fresh, balsamic and persistent style on the palate for lengthy enjoyment. Ideal for an entire meal.
Price approx.: 22,00 EUR
http://www.villarussiz.it
Villa Russiz
39048180047

BROY   **90/100**

▼♪ Collio Bianco 2012 : Intense straw-yellow with golden highlights. Highly expressive nose developing floral and tropical fruit scents of papaya and pineapple. Fresh, perfumed palate with almond, capped off with a faint note of sourness, attractive in this context.
http://www.collavini.it
Collavini - Eugenio Collavini Viticultori
390432753222

VENICA&VENICA   90/100

▼♪ Ronco delle Cime - Friulano 2013 : Deeply-coloured straw-yellow. Intense, complex, mineral (flint) and vegetal nose (herbs). The same expressive aromas carry through to the palate augmented by balsamic notes and supported by beautiful acidity. Would work well with cheese.
Price approx.: 18,00 EUR
http://www.venica.it
Venica & Venica - Dolegna del Collio
39048161264

VILLA RUSSIZ   90/100

▼♪ Pinot Bianco 2013 : Straw-yellow. Intense, complex nose blending white flowers, mineral notes and a sensation of sweetness (vanilla). On the palate, a polished, fresh wine displaying balsamic and mineral aromatics. Ideal for fish dishes.
Price approx.: 13,00 EUR
http://www.villarussiz.it
Villa Russiz
39048180047

VENICA&VENICA   89/100

▼♪ Tre Vignis - Collio Bianco 2011 : Straw-yellow with golden highlights. Complex nose intermixing mineral notes, herbs and exotic fruits. Lovely freshness on the palate showcasing the balsamic and mineral character. Ideal for fish-based meals.
Price approx.: 22,00 EUR
http://www.venica.it
Venica & Venica - Dolegna del Collio
39048161264

VENICA&VENICA   89/100

▼♪ Ronco delle Mele - Sauvignon 2013 : Light straw-yellow. Intense nose of tropical fruits (pineapple, mango and papaya) augmented by a faint balsamic note. Round, persistent, fruity and balsamic on the palate with a mineral dimension. Ideal for cheeses, meat and fish.
Price approx.: 27,00 EUR
http://www.venica.it
Venica & Venica - Dolegna del Collio
39048161264

VENICA&VENICA   88/100

▼♪ Tàlis - Pinot Bianco 2013 : Brilliant straw-yellow. Harmonious nose revealing mineral accents backed by white flowers and golden delicious apple. Good acidity makes for a fresh palate. Persistent finish with a faint balsamic streak. Perfect for fish.
Price approx.: 16,00 EUR
http://www.venica.it
Venica & Venica - Dolegna del Collio
39048161264

RONCO DEI PINI PINOT BIANCO   85/100

▼♪ Pinot bianco 2012 : Straw-yellow. Clean nose blending white flowers and fresh fruits (green apple). Fresh palate ending on a bitter almond note. A user-friendly wine drinking well as an appetiser, with fish-based antipasti or soft cheeses.
Price approx.: 11,50 EUR
http://www.roncodeipini.it
Ronco dei pini di Novello
390432713239

RONCO DEI PINI SAUVIGNON   85/100

▼♪ Sauvignon 2012 : Pale yellow. Slightly herbaceous nose opening up to freshly-cut hay and white-fleshed fruit scents of pear. Fruity, perfumed palate augmented by a subtle bitter almond touch. A summer wine for drinking on its own or with shellfish.
Price approx.: 12,50 EUR
http://www.roncodeipini.it
Ronco dei pini di Novello
390432713239

RONCO DEI PINI CHARDONNAY   85/100

▼♪ Chardonnay 2012 : Pale yellow with straw-yellow highlights. Immediately accessible nose of fresh white flowers. The palate combines mellowness with a subtle sensation of freshness. An easy drinking wine that works well as a summer aperitif or with fish.
Price approx.: 13,50 EUR
http://www.roncodeipini.it
Ronco dei pini di Novello
390432713239

FRIULI COLLI ORIENTALI
D.O.C

ROBERTO SCUBLA AZ.AGR.   92/100

▼♪ Cratis Vertduzzo Friulano 2009 : Intense yellow with amber tints. Expressive nose recalling apricot jam and tropical fruits (papaya). Nicely balanced exuberance, mellowness and power and a lovely almond-driven finish. Drink with cheese or puddings.
Price approx.: 23,60 EUR
http://www.scubla.com
Roberto Scubla Az.Agr.
393356919043

GRILLO FRIULANO   88/100

▼♪ Friulano 2012 : Straw-yellow. Complex nose opening up to dried fruits, almond and coffee bean then revealing chalky notes after swirling. Perfumed, persistent palate enhanced by a balsamic and liquoricy dimension. Drink on its own or with food.
Price approx.: 9,00 EUR
http://www.vinigrillo.it
Azienda Agricola Grillo
393284696888

TURIAN   88/100

▼♪ Turian Schioppettino 2006 : Ruby-red. Complex, expressive nose of ripe red fruits backed by spicy oak and a touch of leather. Beautiful palate supported by pronounced freshness and fairly supple tannins. A characterful wine drinking well with flavoursome foods.
http://www.collavini.it
Collavini - Eugenio Collavini Viticultori
390432753222

GRILLO SAUVIGNON   87/100

▼♪ Grillo Sauvignon 2012 : Fairly pale straw-yellow. Highly perfumed intense nose marked by vegetal notes including sage. The palate shows seductive persistency, a subtle almond touch and delicate trace of sourness on the finish. An interesting, harmonious wine.
Price approx.: 9,00 EUR
http://www.vinigrillo.it
Azienda Agricola Grillo
393284696888

IL RONCAL AZIENDA AGRICOLA   87/100

▼♪ Civon 2009 : Intense ruby-red. Mature nose blending forest fruits in brandy with notes of spicy oak and tobacco. Warm, persistent palate with melted, closely-integrated tannins. Refined across the palate, showing perfume and flavour.
Price approx.: 13,80 EUR
http://www.ilroncal.it
Il Roncal Azienda Agricola
390432730138

GRILLO SAUVIGNON BLANC   86/100

▼♪ IL 2011 : Pale yellow with straw tints. Highly aromatic, expressive nose showing forthright exotic fruits, papaya, mango and pineapple. Fresh on the palate with almond accents capped off with a hint of sourness. Serve with soft cheeses.
Price approx.: 11,00 EUR
http://www.vinigrillo.it
Azienda Agricola Grillo
393284696888

FORRÉSCO   86/100

▼♪ Forresco Rosso 2006 : Ruby with garnet highlights. Intense nose of wild fruits in brandy enhanced by a spicy oak and balsamic dimension of eucalyptus. Warm palate with firm tannins and a finish tinged with subtle bitterness.
http://www.collavini.it
Collavini - Eugenio Collavini Viticultori
390432753222

IL RONCAL AZIENDA AGRICOLA   85/100

▼♪ Merlot 2011 : Intense ruby. Expressive nose revealing perfumes of undergrowth, cherry and a subtle spice touch. The palate is fresh and persistent, displaying subtle

astringency. An instantly accessible style pairing with meats or flavoursome foods.
Price approx.: 9,70 EUR
http://www.ilroncal.it
Il Roncal Azienda Agricola
390432730138

LE VIGNE DEL NORD EST   85/100

▼♪ Friulano 2013 : Brilliant straw-yellow. Expressive nose blending mineral and vegetal notes. Fresh with balsamic accents leaving the palate clean. Very enjoyable across the palate. Ideal on its own or with a seafood platter.
Price approx.: 5,00 EUR
http://www.lvne.it
Le vigne del Nord Est
39 0432 753-554

ROBERTO SCUBLA AZ.AGR.   85/100

▼♪ Merlot 2011 : Intense ruby-red. Nose of red fruits coupled with spice notes, oak and wet leather. Intense, persistent palate with mellow tannins and aromas of green pepper. Ideal for rare-cooked beef.
Price approx.: 11,30 EUR
http://www.scubla.com
Roberto Scubla Az.Agr.
393356919043

ROBERTO SCUBLA AZ.AGR.   84/100

▼♪ Pinot Bianco 2012 : Pale yellow. Mineral nose opening up to white flowers, white fruits, pear. Fairly persistent, warm palate enhanced by a trace of bitter almond. Ideal as an aperitif or with fish.
Price approx.: 10,80 EUR
http://www.scubla.com
Roberto Scubla Az.Agr.
393356919043

ROBERTO SCUBLA AZ.AGR.   83/100

▼♪ Sauvignon 2012 : Fairly pale straw-yellow. Nose of white flowers (magnolia) and tropical fruits rounding off the archetypal varietal signature aromatics. Warm and lush on the palate, revealing more of the same aromas. Would work with fish in a sauce.
Price approx.: 10,80 EUR
http://www.scubla.com
Roberto Scubla Az.Agr.
393356919043

ROBERTO SCUBLA AZ.AGR.   83/100

▼♪ Bianco Pomedes 2011 : Straw-yellow with pale highlights. Nose of macerated yellow fruits enhanced by a mineral note. The palate reveals a mellow yet warm style displaying lovely aromatic persistency. Well-balanced and pairing with mature cheeses.
Price approx.: 17,00 EUR
http://www.scubla.com
Roberto Scubla Az.Agr.
393356919043

AZIENDA AGRICOLA RUBINI PIETRO E FIGLI DI L. DOTT. 82/100

Org▼♪ Merlosco 2011 : Deep ruby-red with crimson tints. Fairly complex nose intermixing red fruits in brandy with damp wood. On the palate, a spice dimension and pronounced tannins capped off with a faint bitterness. Ideal for meats and cheeses.
Price approx.: 9,95 EUR
http://www.villarubini.net
Azienda Agricola Rubini
04 32 71 61 41

GRAVE DEL FRIULI D.O.C

FOSSA MALA 90/100

▼♪ Chardonnay 2013 : Intense straw-yellow. Persistent nose of lily-of-the-valley, apple and peach with butter and vanilla notes. Mouth-coating, fruity and aromatic palate. Ideal for fish and cheese.
Price approx.: 4,60 EUR
http://www.fossamala.it
Fossa Mala
390434957997

LE DUE TORRI AZIENDA AGRICOLA 88/100

CV Eco ▼♪ Pinot Grigio 2013 : Straw-yellow. Intense nose of ripe white fruits, wildflowers, ginger, thyme and mineral scents. Savoury palate showing abundant freshness and heat. Persistent finish consistent with the nose.
Price approx.: 5,00 EUR
http://www.le2torri.com
Le Due Torri
390432759150

ANTONUTTI CASA VINICOLA 87/100

▼♪ Merlot Linea Antonutti 2012 : Intense ruby-red. Harmonious nose driven by ripe fruit aromas of cherry and blackberry then round spicy notes, a touch of liquorice and a pepper-driven finish. Supple palate with a subtle, compact tannin framework. Fruity finish.
Price approx.: 5,50 EUR
http://www.antonuttivini.it
Antonutti Casa Vinicola
390432662001

FOSSA MALA 87/100

▼♪ Sauvignon 2013 : Straw-yellow. Expressive, aromatic nose of ripe tropical fruits, particularly pineapple and mango, with mild vanilla notes. Lush, mouth-coating palate showing good acidity and savoury fruit notes. Ideal for the summer, with fish.
Price approx.: 4,60 EUR
http://www.fossamala.it
Fossa Mala
390434957997

LE DUE TORRI AZIENDA AGRICOLA 87/100

CV Eco ▼♪ Friulano 2013 : Straw-yellow with green tints. Instantly accessible, pleasurable nose showing notes of lemon, sage and dried fruits. Deliciously refined palate showing abundant freshness. More of the nose aromatics. Long, focused finish.
Price approx.: 5,00 EUR
http://www.le2torri.com
Le Due Torri
390432759150

LE DUE TORRI AZIENDA AGRICOLA 87/100

CV Eco ▼♪ Sauvignon 2013 : Straw-yellow with green tints. Fresh, vibrant, simple and elegant bouquet driven by notes of kiwi, mint and grapefruit. Well-structured palate boasting excellent balance between acidity and heat.
Price approx.: 5,00 EUR
http://www.le2torri.com
Le Due Torri
390432759150

FOSSA MALA 86/100

▼♪ Merlot 2012 : Intense ruby-red. Spicy nose of leather and oak with strong red fruit in brandy accents, primarily morello cherry. A warm wine with upfront tannins that leaves the palate clean. Ideal for cold cuts and mature cheeses.
Price approx.: 4,90 EUR
http://www.fossamala.it
Fossa Mala
390434957997

ANTONUTTI CASA VINICOLA 84/100

▼♪ Pinot Grigio Linea Antonutti 2013 : Brilliant straw-yellow. Simple, immediately accessible nose of white-fleshed fruits, hazelnut and wild flowers. Mellow palate showing medium concentration yet nevertheless elegant, easy-drinking, fresh, savoury and consistent with the nose.
Price approx.: 5,50 EUR
http://www.antonuttivini.it
Antonutti Casa Vinicola
390432662001

ISONZO DEL FRIULI D.O.C

LIS NERIS CHARDONNAY 90/100

▼♪ Jurosa 2011 : Pale straw-yellow. Highly expressive, complex nose of fresh white flowers, ripe yellow fruits (Abate Fetel pear, golden delicious apple) with a delightful mineral touch in the background. Enveloping palate with mineral and fruit notes. Ideal for cheese.
Price approx.: 16,00 EUR
http://www.lisneris.it
Lis Neris Agricola
39048180105

LIS NERIS FRIULANO 89/100

▼♪ La Vila 2012 : Straw-yellow. Fruity nose revealing apple, pear and pineapple accompanied by mineral notes in the background. Beautiful acidity and a savoury fruity note on the palate. Ideal as an aperitif or with white fish.
Price approx.: 16,00 EUR
http://www.lisneris.it
Lis Neris Agricola
39048180105

LIS NERIS SAUVIGNON BLANC 89/100

▼♪ Picol 2012 : Pale straw-yellow. Highly expressive and aromatic nose with distinctive varietal character offering up pleasant mineral and herbal notes. Intense, balsamic palate with beautiful acidity. Long finish. Excellent with shellfish.
Price approx.: 16,00 EUR
http://www.lisneris.it
Lis Neris Agricola
39048180105

DRIUS MAURO AZIENDA AGRICOLA 88/100

▼♪ Pinot Bianco 2008 : Intense straw-yellow with golden highlights. Mineral nose intermixing chalk, pumice stone and mild spices. An intense, persistent wine on the palate with balsamic and spice aromas. Complex flavour profile, ideal for cold cuts and white meats.
Price approx.: 10,00 EUR
http://www.driusmauro.it
Drius Mauro Azienda Agricola
39048160998

LIS NERIS PINOT GRIGIO 88/100

▼♪ Gris 2011 : Straw-yellow. Mature nose driven by mineral, floral and faint fruity notes with recognisable aromas of golden delicious apple. Mineral palate showing light aromatics and beautiful acidity. Ideal as an aperitif or with whitefish.
Price approx.: 16,00 EUR
http://www.lisneris.it
Lis Neris Agricola
39048180105

DRIUS MAURO AZIENDA AGRICOLA 86/100

▼♪ Vignis di Siris 2011 : Intense straw-yellow. Complex nose of mild spices and mineral aromas with well-structured balsamic notes. Well-balanced palate showing more of the balsamic and mineral aromas. Ideal for cold cuts and mature cheeses.
Price approx.: 12,00 EUR
http://www.driusmauro.it
Drius Mauro Azienda Agricola
39048160998

VENEZIA GIULIA I.G.T

LIS NERIS 93/100

▼♪ Lis 2009 : Intense straw-yellow. Intense, complex bouquet driven by mineral and fruit notes of ripe yellow-fleshed fruits with mild spices and pleasurable eucalyptus accents. More of the intensity and the mineral and spice aromas on the palate. Ideal for spicy dishes.
Price approx.: 23,00 EUR
http://www.lisneris.it
Lis Neris Agricola
39048180105

LIS NERIS 93/100

▼♪ Confini 2010 : Straw-yellow bordering on gold. Complex mineral and herbal nose showing Mediterranean aromas with compelling aromatic notes in the background. These recur on the palate with balsamic aromas and notes of bitter almond. An enjoyable partner for fish and meat.
Price approx.: 23,00 EUR
http://www.lisneris.it
Lis Neris Agricola
39048180105

LIS NERIS 90/100

▼♪ Tal Lùc 2010 : Brilliant amber-yellow. Inviting, intense bouquet of yellow flowers, orange blossom and apricot and orange jam. Aromatic, persistent and fruity palate boasting beautifully balanced acidity. Perfect for cheese and biscuits.
Price approx.: 50,00 EUR
http://www.lisneris.it
Lis Neris Agricola
39048180105

LE VIGNE DEL NORD EST 88/100

▼♪ Cru Priòra 2011 : Intense straw-yellow. Complex nose combining coffee, chalk and mild spice aromas of cinnamon. The spice character recurs on the palate with a volcanic mineral dimension and a persistent balsamic finish. Serve on its own or with fish.
Price approx.: 11,90 EUR
http://www.lvne.it
Le vigne del Nord Est
39 0432 753-554

LE DUE TORRI AZIENDA AGRICOLA 86/100

CV Eco▼♪ Cabernet Sauvignon 2011 : Ruby with purple-blue. The nose is still young and driven by herbal notes of bell pepper, tomato leaf, bark, undergrowth, redcurrant and raspberry. Fresh, savoury and well-balanced palate with a lively, sharp tannin framework. Long, focused finish.
Price approx.: 5,00 EUR
http://www.le2torri.com
Le Due Torri
390432759150

LE VIGNE DEL NORD EST 86/100

▼♪ Cru Altera 2011 : Intense hue with ruby tints. Highly expressive nose intermixing spice, dried flowers, forest fruits in brandy and an oak dimension. The palate offers up good acidity, fine-grained tannins and a fairly persistent finish. Ideal for meat, hot or cold.
Price approx.: 11,90 EUR
http://www.lvne.it
Le vigne del Nord Est
39 0432 753-554

LE VIGNE DEL NORD EST 85/100

▼♪ Pinot Grigio 2013 : Intense straw-yellow with pink highlights. Mineral nose revealing perfumes of white flowers and green apple. More subdued aromas on the palate lead into a persistent mineral finish. Ideal for shellfish.
Price approx.: 5,00 EUR
http://www.lvne.it
Le vigne del Nord Est
39 0432 753-554

LE VIGNE DEL NORD EST 84/100

▼♪ Tramonti Pinot Grigio 2013 : Light straw colour. Persistent, mineral nose opening up to fruity notes of green apple. On the palate, the bouquet is augmented by faint balsamic touches with the mineral nose character flowing through. Ideal on its own or with fish-based starters.
Price approx.: 3,20 EUR
http://www.lvne.it
Le vigne del Nord Est
39 0432 753-554

LE VIGNE DEL NORD EST 83/100

▼♪ Tramonti Merlot 2013 : Ruby-red. Warm, intense nose of blackberry and raspberry in brandy and spicy oak notes. Powerful, generous palate with mouth-coating tannins capped off with a more subdued finish. Ideal for meat.
Price approx.: 3,20 EUR
http://www.lvne.it
Le vigne del Nord Est
39 0432 753-554

LE VIGNE DEL NORD EST 83/100

▼♪ Tramonti Chardonnay 2013 : Pale yellow with green tints. Silky nose intermixing white flowers and subtle green apple notes. A more nervy, firm style on the palate showing more of the apple aromas layered over pleasant mineral undertones. Set aside for the aperitif.
Price approx.: 3,20 EUR
http://www.lvne.it
Le vigne del Nord Est
39 0432 753-554

VENEZIE I.G.T

LE DUE TORRI AZIENDA AGRICOLA 89/100

CV Eco ▼♪ Malvasia 2013 : The bouquet reveals beautifully balanced notes of cedar, bergamot orange, yellow-fleshed fruits and herbs. Fresh, succulent palate showing fruity and floral suggestions along the same lines as the nose. Beautiful length.
Price approx.: 6,00 EUR
http://www.le2torri.com
Le Due Torri
+390432759150

VINO DA TAVOLA ROSSO

RONCO DEI PINI VINO LIMES 87/100

▼♪ Limes 2007 : Intense ruby. Expressive nose suggestive of blackberry jam backed by spicy oak and leather notes. Fresh, savoury palate with a subtle trace of austerity due to the Cabernet Franc. A wine pairing with meat.
Price approx.: 28,00 EUR
http://www.roncodeipini.it
Ronco dei pini di Novello
+390432713239

VINO SPUMANTE

RIBOLLA GIALLA SPUMANTE BRUT 87/100

▼♪ Ribolla Gialla 2009 : Straw-yellow with fairly persistent, fine effervescence. The nose exudes fragrances of bread crust and white flowers. Refined texture, good length and a faint salinity on the palate. Perfect as an appetiser or with fish dishes.
http://www.collavini.it
Collavini - Eugenio Collavini Viticultori
+390432753222

PIERA MARTELLOZZO S.P.A. 86/100

▼♪ 075 Carati Ribolla Gialla Brut 2013 : Straw-yellow with fine bubbles. Delicate nose of lily-of-the-valley and magnolia flowers. The palate is elegant and fruity with good acidity, capped off with a touch of toasted almonds. Ideal as an aperitif.
Price approx.: 5,40 EUR
http://www.pieramartellozzo.com
Piera Martellozzo S.p.A.
+390434963100

Detailed instructions are featured at the start of the book.

LE DUE TORRI AZIENDA AGRICOLA — 85/100

CV Eco▼✔ Ribolla Gialla Spumante Extra Dry 2013 : Brilliant straw-yellow with green tints. Refined, persistent bubbles. Delicate nose with aromas of nectarine, white fig, green apple and mineral notes. Fresh, supple and well-structured palate flowing into lemony aromatics. Persistent finish.
Price approx.: 7,00 EUR
http://www.le2torri.com
Le Due Torri
+390432759150

LAZIO

FRASCATI D.O.C.G. SUPERIORE

PRINCIPE PALLAVICINI — 88/100

Eco▼✔ Poggio Verde 2013 : Brilliant straw-yellow. Compelling, expressive nose showing aromatic freshness with grapefruit, lime, white-fleshed fruits, wild flowers and herbs. Robust, persistent palate displaying a lemony freshness.
Price approx.: 6,00 EUR
http://www.principepallavicini.com
Terre dei Pallavicini
+69438816

FRASCATI D.O.C

TERRE DEI PALLAVICINI — 85/100

Eco▼✔ Frascati 2013 : Straw-yellow with green tints. Very fresh, instantly accessible nose showing delicate scents recalling lemon, fruit and flowers. The palate is lively, balanced and slender yet not linear. A wine with real drinkability and good persistency.
Price approx.: 3,50 EUR
http://www.principepallavicini.com
Terre dei Pallavicini
+69438816

LAZIO I.G.T.

PRINCIPE PALLAVICINI — 92/100

Eco▼✔ Casa Romana 2011 : Deep ruby. Harmonious and complex nose of blackberry, resin, garrigue, undergrowth, anise, sandalwood and cocoa. The palate is very fresh and offers up more of the same nose aromatics. Tightly-wound, noble tannin framework. Long, saline finish.
Price approx.: 19,00 EUR
http://www.principepallavicini.com
Terre dei Pallavicini
+69438816

PRINCIPE PALLAVICINI — 90/100

Eco▼✔ Stillato 2012 : Old gold. Full, harmonious nose intermixing candied lemon zest, wildflower honey, vanilla, dates and saffron. Deliciously rich, concentrated palate, generously sweet with refreshing acidity. Substantial length.
Price approx.: 12,50 EUR
http://www.principepallavicini.com
Terre dei Pallavicini
+69438816

PRINCIPE PALLAVICINI — 89/100

Eco▼✔ Amarasco 2012 : Ruby with purple-blue. Expressive, refined nose showing fresh and jammy black fruits, juniper, balsamic notes and faint charred accents of coffee and tobacco. Very fresh palate, bordering on saline, with evident yet mellow tannins.
Price approx.: 10,00 EUR
http://www.principepallavicini.com
Terre dei Pallavicini
+69438816

TERRE DEI PALLAVICINI — 87/100

Eco▼✔ Syrah 2013 : Ruby with purple-blue. Intense nose of cassis and morello cherry with spice (white pepper), mineral and balsamic garrigue notes. Very fresh, crunchy, succulent palate boasting a vibrant tannin framework and persistency.
Price approx.: 7,00 EUR
http://www.principepallavicini.com
Terre dei Pallavicini
+69438816

PRINCIPE PALLAVICINI — 85/100

Eco▼✔ Rubillo 2013 : Intense ruby. Simple, endearing and instantly accessible nose revealing young, vinous and pleasantly rustic aromas of wild berry fruits, raspberry, sweetbriar and violet. Fresh, savoury palate with a clean finish showing evident tannins.
Price approx.: 4,20 EUR
http://www.principepallavicini.com
Terre dei Pallavicini
+69438816

ROMA D.O.C.

TERRE DEI PALLAVICINI — 87/100

Eco▼✔ Malvasia Puntinata 2013 : Straw-yellow with green tints. Expressive, refined nose showing a broad array of floral (lily-of-the-valley, hawthorn) fruity and lemony aromas entwined with iodine and gunflint notes. Robust, supple palate with beautiful acidity. Enjoyable length.
Price approx.: 5,50 EUR
http://www.principepallavicini.com
Terre dei Pallavicini
+69438816

LOMBARDY

CURTEFRANCA D.O.C

RICCI CURBASTRO AZIENDA AGRICOLA 90/100

Eco▼⫶ Vigna Bosco Alto 2010 : The colour shows yellow-gold highlights. Harmonious nose of pastry cream, toasted hazelnut, gunflint, flowers, sweet almond and oak. On the palate, body, fat and a touch of honey. Just the right amount of oak. Long, savoury and mineral-driven finish.
Price approx.: 8,00 EUR
http://www.riccicurbastro.it
Ricci Curbastro Azienda Agricola
+39030736094

LA FIOCA 89/100

Eco▼⫶ Rosso del Diavolo Allegro 2009 : Brilliant ruby-garnet. Elegant, harmonious nose of flowers, morello cherry, raspberry, graphite, menthol, tobacco. Balanced tannin framework, not very massive yet mellow and refined. Savoury and mineral mid-palate. Suggestions of incense on the finish.
Price approx.: 6,00 EUR
http://www.lafioca.com
Societa' Agricola La Fioca
+390309826313

CA' DEL BOSCO S.R.L - SOCIETA' AGRICOLA 85/100

▼⫶ Rosso 2010 : Ruby with crimson tints. Honest nose showing medium power yet immediate aroma of crystallised violet, tobacco leaf and ink. Savoury palate, bordering on overripeness with a subtle tannin framework. Initially supple then flowing into a faint sensation of bitterness.
Price approx.: 14,40 EUR
http://www.cadelbosco.com
Ca' del Bosco S.r.l. - Societa' Agricola
+390307766111

CA' DEL BOSCO S.R.L - SOCIETA' AGRICOLA 85/100

▼⫶ Bianco 2013 : Brilliant straw-yellow. Classic, intense and endearing nose of banana, golden delicious apple, pineapple, hawthorn and sugared almonds. Fairly well-structured, very supple palate that is fruity, savoury and fresh with good lemon-driven length.
Price approx.: 15,00 EUR
http://www.cadelbosco.com
Ca' del Bosco S.r.l. - Societa' Agricola
+390307766111

FRANCIACORTA D.O.C.G

CASTELLO DI GUSSAGO LA SANTISSIMA 91/100

CV Eco▼⫶ Rosé Brut 0 : Intense, brilliant coppery hue. Rich, seductive nose of citrus zest, cigar, bark, humus, morello cherry, breadcrust and berry fruit tart. Robust, vinous, savoury palate that is rich and mellow with beautiful persistency.
Price approx.: 22,00 EUR
http://www.castellodigussago.it
Castello di Gussago La Santissima
+302069967

QUADRA 91/100

▼⫶ Extra Brut Millesimato QZero 2009 : Fine mousse. Intense, elegant and harmonious nose of resin, balm, linden, lily-of-the-valley, white fruits and anise. Vibrant palate. Beautiful trace of acidity. Savoury mineral aromas mid-palate. Long, dry yet not bitter finish. Fresh rather than muscular. Young.
Price approx.: 18,90 EUR
http://www.quadrafranciacorta.it
Quadra S.r.l.
+390307157314

RICCI CURBASTRO AZIENDA AGRICOLA 91/100

Eco▼⫶ Satèn Brut 2010 : Brilliant straw-yellow with green tints. Mineral, saline notes on the nose with scents of musk, undergrowth then gooseberry and pear. Very creamy palate flowing into harmonious, juicy aromas then a vibrant, savoury finish.
Price approx.: 14,84 EUR
http://www.riccicurbastro.it
Ricci Curbastro Azienda Agricola
+39030736094

LA FIOCA 91/100

Eco▼⫶ Riserva Satèn Brut 2005 : Brilliant straw-yellow. Austere, refined and slightly oxidative on the nose with breadcrust, chestnut honey, rubber and mineral notes. More dynamic, creamy and refined palate showing beautiful freshness. Very savoury, vibrant minerality. Good length.
Price approx.: 18,00 EUR
http://www.lafioca.com
Societa' Agricola La Fioca
+390309826313

ANTICA CANTINA FRATTA 90/100

▼⫶ Brut Essence 2008 : Appealing mousse. Harmonious and refined nose showing great complexity and driven by notes of sweet almond, hawthorn, chalk and mineral scents. The palate is very creamy, fresh, savoury and mineral and shows balance. Long clean finish suffused with lemon.
Price approx.: 14,80 EUR
http://www.anticafratta.com
Antica Cantina Fratta
+30652068

Detailed instructions are featured at
the start of the book.

LE MARCHESINE S.S. 90/100

▼♪ Riserva Dosage Zero Secolo Novo 2007 : Straw-yellow with green tints. The nose opens up gradually to white flower and talc scents with saline and mineral notes. Silky, robust palate flowing into fresh, savoury and mineral-driven aromatics. A trace of sourness on the finish. Still youthful.

http://www.lemarchesine.it
Az Ag Le Marchesine S.S.
+39030657005

FRATELLI BERLUCCHI 90/100

Eco▼♪ Freccianera Brut 2007 : Persistent mousse. Complex, harmonious nose of yellow flowers, melon, yellow peach, tobacco leaf and butter notes. Creamy, endearing and mellow palate flowing into savoury aromatics with mineral notes. Long, focused finish.

Price approx.: 22,00 EUR
http://www.fratelliberlucchi.it
Azienda Agricola Fratelli Berlucchi S.r.l.
+39030984451

BERSI SERLINI SOCIETA' AGRICOLA S.R.L. 90/100

▼♪ Brut Anteprima 0 : Intense straw-yellow. Unusual nose showing interesting aromas of fresh butter, dried flowers, almond and mild spices. Creamy, characterful palate flowing into savoury aromatics with mineral notes. Long, Havana cigar-driven finish.

Price approx.: 17,00 EUR
http://www.bersiserlini.it
Bersi Serlini
+390309823338

GUIDO BERLUCCHI & C. S.P.A. 90/100

CV Eco▼♪ Palazzo Lana Satèn Riserva 2006 : Intense straw-yellow. Full, refined and endearing bouquet of yellow flowers, nougat, vanilla and mineral aromas. Velvety, succulent palate. Long savoury and fresh finish. Promise for the future.

Price approx.: 22,00 EUR
http://www.berlucchi.it
Guido Berlucchi & C. s.p.a.
+39030984381

LANTIERI DE PARATICO AZIENDA AGRICOLA 90/100

CONV▼♪ Satèn 0 : Intense straw-yellow. Ripe bouquet with a rich personality showing notes of gunflint, rubber, cigar, tropical fruits and fresh croissant. Fairly supple, very velvety, fresh and clean palate. Long finish, a tad sour.

Price approx.: 13,50 EUR
http://www.lantierideparatico.it
Lantieri de Paratico Azienda Agricola
+39030736151

LE MARCHESINE S.S. 89/100

▼♪ Rosé Brut Millesimato 2009 : Brilliant, intense coppery hue. Characterful nose that is supple, harmonious and elegant with a mix of mineral and gypsum notes, talc and cherry. More of the same on the palate which is structured, savoury and fresh. Long finish driven by sugared almonds.

http://www.lemarchesine.it
Az Ag Le Marchesine S.S.
+39030657005

CORTEBIANCA 89/100

Org▼♪ Satèn Millesimato 2009 : Brilliant straw-yellow. Full, refined nose of dried fruits, hay, cigar and hot spices. Very creamy, intense palate showing fresher, lemony aromatics mid-palate and on the finish which is long and savoury.

Price approx.: 19,00 EUR
http://www.corte-bianca.it
CorteBianca
+30983293

LA BOSCAIOLA AZIENDA AGRICOLA 89/100

▼♪ Satèn Brut 0 : Brilliant straw-yellow. Intense, endearing nose of yellow flowers (broom), tea and chamomile. Lush, elegant, creamy and savoury palate that is extremely mellow and persistent.

http://www.laboscaiola.com
La Boscaiola Azienda Agricola
+390307156386

1701 88/100

CONV▼♪ Vintage Brut 2009 : An appealing mousse and brilliant straw-yellow hue form the prelude to a slightly muted nose on first pour, opening up to notes of chestnut honey, yellow flowers and cigar. Creamy, robust palate that is fresh, harmonious and savoury.

Price approx.: 24,00 EUR
http://www.1701franciacorta.it
1701
+307750875

CA' DEL BOSCO S.R.L. - SOCIETA' AGRICOLA 88/100

▼♪ Vintage Collection Satèn 2009 : Brilliant, intense straw-yellow. The bouquet boasts personality with notes of cigar, rubber, a mineral touch and tar. Very fresh, creamy and savoury palate showing lots of volume. Hint of astringency. Highly unusual, medium-length finish.

Price approx.: 43,00 EUR
http://www.cadelbosco.com
Ca' del Bosco S.r.l. - Societa' Agricola
+390307766111

GUIDO BERLUCCHI & C. S.P.A. 88/100

CV Eco▼♪ 61 Rosé Brut 0 : Coppery hue. Characterful nose driven by mineral and iron notes with aromas of wheat flour and fresh almond flowing into notes of root, bark and morello cherry. Supple, velvety palate leading into a savoury, fresh mid-palate and a long, mineral finish.

Price approx.: 15,00 EUR

http://www.berlucchi.it
Guido Berlucchi & C. s.p.a.
+39030984381

GUIDO BERLUCCHI & C. S.P.A. 88/100

CV Eco▼.✦ Cellarius Pas Dosé 2008 : Straw-yellow with green tints. Classic, refined and mineral nose showing notes of gypsum, toasted breadcrust, white fruits and gooseberry. Very creamy, fresh and savoury palate. Long focused finish.
Price approx.: 16,80 EUR
http://www.berlucchi.it
Guido Berlucchi & C. s.p.a.
+39030984381

MONTE ROSSA S.R.L. 88/100

▼.✦ Salvadèk Extra Brut 2009 : Fine bubbles, brilliant, warm straw-yellow hue. Delightful, round and rich palate with patisserie, vanilla and mild tobacco notes. The palate shows volume and freshness, flowing into fairly strict aromatics. Tobacco-driven finish focusing nicely on sourness.
Price approx.: 17,00 EUR
http://www.monterossa.com
Monte Rossa S.r.l.
+39030725066

QUADRA 88/100

▼.✦ Brut QBlack 0 : Brilliant straw-yellow. Intense, fresh nose of wheat flour, almond, anise, grapefruit and lemongrass. Precise, mineral palate with a velvety mousse. A vibrant, warm wine showing a long, harmonious finish of mild tobacco.
Price approx.: 14,00 EUR
http://www.quadrafranciacorta.it
Quadra S.r.l.
+390307157314

TENUTA AMBROSINI 88/100

▼.✦ Brut Il Millesimo 2009 : Warm, brilliant straw-yellow. Refined, endearing and supple bouquet of hawthorn, ripe white peach and sugared almonds. Very flavoursome, round, fresh and mellow palate with resin and balsamic accents and mineral notes. Good persistency.
Price approx.: 20,10 EUR
http://www.tenutambrosini.it/
Tenuta Ambrosini
+307254850

VIGNA DORATA 88/100

▼.✦ Franciacorta Satèn Millesimato 2008 : Deep straw-yellow with fine, persistent bubbles. Expressive nose intermixing white flowers, ripe fruits, pear and pineapple. The palate is round and fruity and displays pleasant acidity with slightly salty notes. Perfect with fish.
Price approx.: 19,00 EUR

http://www.vignadorata.it
VIGNA DORATA
+390307254275

1701 87/100

CONV▼.✦ Brut 0 : Straw-yellow. Expressive nose intermixing hay, tobacco leaves, dried yellow flowers and yellow peach. Savoury, creamy and fresh palate. A likeable, refreshing style with abundant mousse. The finish is tinged with a hint of sourness.
Price approx.: 14,00 EUR
http://www.1701franciacorta.it
1701
+307750875

AZIENDA AGRICOLA UGO VEZZOLI 87/100

▼.✦ Rosé Brut 0 : Coppery hue. The nose is slightly muted on first pour then opens up to pleasurable yet simple notes of raspberry, pomegranate and seductive boiled sweet nuances. Very supple, creamy palate enhanced by a beautiful trace of exuberance. Long, clean finish.
Price approx.: 13,40 EUR
http://www.vezzolifranciacorta.it
Az Agr Vezzoli Ugo
+30738018

FRATELLI BERLUCCHI 87/100

Eco▼.✦ Brut 25 0 : Straw-yellow. Appealing nose showing notes of ginger, dried flowers and yellow-fleshed fruits. Very refined and balanced. Silky, fairly robust palate with perceptible freshness, flavour and persistency.
Price approx.: 18,00 EUR
http://www.fratelliberlucchi.it
Azienda Agricola Fratelli Berlucchi S.r.l.
+39030984451

BERSI SERLINI SOCIETA' AGRICOLA S.R.L. 87/100

▼.✦ Brut Anniversario 0 : Straw-yellow with green tints. Polished, shy and elegant nose of white flowers, fresh butter and apple. Refined, mellow and savoury palate that is fresh with a persistent finish. A convincing dry sparkling wine.
Price approx.: 17,00 EUR
http://www.bersiserlini.it
Bersi Serlini
+39030982338

BERSI SERLINI SOCIETA' AGRICOLA S.R.L. 87/100

▼.✦ Extra Brut Millesimato 2010 : Straw-yellow with green tints. Refined, full nose with aromas of white flowers, almond and white peach. Creamy, supple and savoury palate. Lemony mid-palate showing lime and lemongrass. A bone dry style displaying pleasant austerity.
Price approx.: 20,00 EUR
http://www.bersiserlini.it
Bersi Serlini
+39030982338

BIONDELLI 87/100

CONV▼♪ Satèn Brut 0 : Appealing straw-yellow. Very fresh, inviting nose showing aromas of resin, pine needle, undergrowth, roots and star anise. The palate is fairly robust and centres primarily on freshness and accessibility. Beautiful austere yet slightly short finish.
Price approx.: 12,40 EUR
http://www.biondelli.com
Biondelli
+390307759896

CA' DEL BOSCO S.R.L. - SOCIETA' AGRICOLA 87/100

▼♪ Cuvée Annamaria Clementi Rosé 2006 : Brilliant coppery hue. Austere, elegant and harmonious nose of chalk, bark, root, undergrowth and cigar. Creamy, robust and savoury palate showing good persistency. The finish is tinged with a trace of sourness.
Price approx.: 140,00 EUR
http://www.cadelbosco.com
Ca' del Bosco S.r.l. - Societa' Agricola
+390307766111

CA' DEL BOSCO S.R.L. - SOCIETA' AGRICOLA 87/100

▼♪ Cuvée Prestige Rosé Brut 0 : Brilliant coral hue. The nose is subtle yet boasts personality with notes of gunpowder, talc, cherry, cassis and almond. Savoury, fresh palate with a tannin framework of moderate concentration. Long finish with a sourness that is attractive in this context.
Price approx.: 35,00 EUR
http://www.cadelbosco.com
Ca' del Bosco S.r.l. - Societa' Agricola
+390307766111

CASTELLO DI GUSSAGO LA SANTISSIMA 87/100

CV Eco▼♪ Brut Millesimato 2008 : Brilliant hue. Abundant mousse. Mature, endearing nose intermixing cigar tones, gunflint and rubber. The palate is structured yet creamy and focuses on a pleasant oxidative character of aroma rather than instantly noticeable freshness.
Price approx.: 30,00 EUR
http://www.castellodigussago.it
Castello di Gussago La Santissima
+302069967

GUIDO BERLUCCHI & C. S.P.A. 87/100

CV Eco▼♪ Cuvée Imperiale Vintage Brut 2008 : Straw-yellow with abundant mousse. Full, fresh, delicate and harmonious nose showing notes of resin, menthol, talc, freshly-ground wheat flour and fresh almond. Lightweight structure on the palate yet also balance, refinement, freshness and flavour.
Price approx.: 15,95 EUR
http://www.berlucchi.it
Guido Berlucchi & C. s.p.a.
+39030984381

MONTE ROSSA S.R.L. 87/100

▼♪ P.R. Rosé Brut 0 : The colour displays onion skin highlights. Expressive nose intermixing smoke, nougat, citrus zest, toast and cigar notes. Creamy palate. Supple attack leading into a savoury mid-palate and a long finish suggestive of quinine root.
Price approx.: 14,50 EUR
http://www.monterossa.com
Monte Rossa S.r.l.
+39030725066

RICCI CURBASTRO AZIENDA AGRICOLA 87/100

Eco▼♪ Extra Brut 2010 : Brilliant straw-yellow, green tints. Expressive nose with a fruity attack of apple, pear and peach leading into sweet almond notes. Supple, robust attack on the palate with lovely fat flowing into very focused lemony aromatics on the mid-palate and finish.
Price approx.: 14,84 EUR
http://www.riccicurbastro.it
Ricci Curbastro Azienda Agricola
+39030736094

MONTENISA DI ALBIERA ALLEGRA E ALESSIA ANTINORI 87/100

▼♪ Satèn Brut 0 : Warm straw-yellow. Refined, elegant nose of gooseberry, acacia flowers, lime and white peach. Creamy, fresh and savoury palate with personality. Perhaps a little austere for a Satèn but still a very pleasant wine.
Price approx.: 13,50 EUR
http://www.montenisa.it
Tenuta Montenisa
+390307750838

VIGNA DORATA 87/100

▼♪ Franciacorta Satèn : Deep straw-yellow with a fine, persistent mousse. The nose opens up to lovely notes of breadcrust, acacia flowers and ripe pear flesh. On the palate, lovely fruit and pleasant acidity. Ideal as an aperitif.
Price approx.: 19,00 EUR
http://www.vignadorata.it
VIGNA DORATA
+390307254275

VILLA FRANCIACORTA 87/100

Eco▼♪ Satèn Brut Millesimato 2010 : Straw-yellow with golden tints. Harmonious, seductive nose showing personality with supple notes of butter, pastry, creme brulee and apricot croissant. Rich palate boasting a beautiful mouthfeel and abundant mousse. Fresh, savoury finish.
Price approx.: 13,50 EUR
http://www.villafranciacorta.it
Villa Franciacorta
+30652329

ANTICA CANTINA FRATTA 86/100

▼♪ Riserva Extra Brut Quintessence 2007 : Abundant mousse with brilliant straw-yellow shades. Delicate nose of

apricot, white flowers and redcurrants. Very supple, robust and silky palate. Faint touch of sourness on the finish.
Price approx.: 25,00 EUR
http://www.anticafratta.com
Antica Cantina Fratta
+30652068

LE MARCHESINE S.S.   86/100

▼. Brut Blanc de Noirs Millesimato 2010 : Straw-yellow with green tints. Refined nose intermixing mineral notes of chalk, freshly-ground wheat flour and fresh almond. Robust palate boasting pronounced exuberance with faint lemon suggestions and a slightly astringent finish.
http://www.lemarchesine.it
Az Ag Le Marchesine S.S.
+39030657005

BERSI SERLINI SOCIETA' AGRICOLA S.R.L. 86/100

▼. Satèn Brut 2010 : Brilliant straw-yellow tinged with green. Classic, refined and compelling nose of wheat flour, yeast, toated breadcrust and chalk. Velvety, elegant, mellow and savoury palate, slightly backward in terms of aromatics.
Price approx.: 17,00 EUR
http://www.bersiserlini.it
Bersi Serlini
+390309823338

CASTELLO DI GUSSAGO LA SANTISSIMA 86/100

CV Eco▼. Pas Dosé Millesimato 2009 : Brilliant straw-yellow with green tints. The nose is very fresh with notes of resin, freshly-ground wheat flour and rubber. Very creamy, vibrant palate that is mineral, savoury and punctuated by a firmer finish.
Price approx.: 30,00 EUR
http://www.castellodigussago.it
Castello di Gussago La Santissima
+302069967

CORTEBIANCA   86/100

Org▼. Rosé Extra Brut Millesimato 2009 : Brilliant coral. Inviting, harmonious and refined nose intermixing mineral notes of chalk, berry fruits, tobacco and raspberry tart. More of the nose aromatics on the palate which is fairly robust and savoury mid-palate. Very fresh, lemony almost, finish.
Price approx.: 17,00 EUR
http://www.corte-bianca.it
CorteBianca
+30983293

GUIDO BERLUCCHI & C. S.P.A.   86/100

CV Eco▼. Cuvée Imperiale Max Rosé Extra Dry 0 : Intense coppery, brilliant hue. The nose is slightly muted on first pour then opens up to sappy notes of bark and crunchy raspberry. Creamy, round, savoury and fresh palate. Good finish suffused with wild strawberry. A consummate wine.
Price approx.: 13,50 EUR

http://www.berlucchi.it
Guido Berlucchi & C. s.p.a.
+39030984381

VILLA FRANCIACORTA   86/100

Eco▼. Selezione Brut Millesimato 2005 : Deep straw-yellow. Expressive, ripe nose intermixing notes of honey, cigar and bark with smoky, mineral and rubber aromas. Fairly abundant mousse on the palate, a fresh mid-palate and liquorice-like finish.
Price approx.: 12,00 EUR
http://www.villafranciacorta.it
Villa Franciacorta
+30652329

AZIENDA AGRICOLA UGO VEZZOLI   85/100

▼. Brut Millesimato 2009 : Straw-yellow. Simple, refined and mellow nose intermixing notes of wildflower honey, dried yellow flowers and cigar aromas. Very supple palate flowing into honey aromatics. A touch of acidity would not have gone amiss. Fairly pronounced maturity.
Price approx.: 17,00 EUR
http://www.vezzolifranciacorta.it
Az Agr Vezzoli Ugo
+30738018

AZIENDA AGRICOLA UGO VEZZOLI   85/100

▼. Satèn Brut 0 : Brilliant straw-yellow. Highly expressive, supple nose showing notes of apple, yellow peach and fruit salad. Creamy, somewhat linear palate. Fresh, savoury mid-palate and finish with a trace of lemon.
Price approx.: 15,30 EUR
http://www.vezzolifranciacorta.it
Az Agr Vezzoli Ugo
+30738018

BERSI SERLINI SOCIETA' AGRICOLA S.R.L.   85/100

▼. Brut Cuvée Rosé 0 : Intense coppery hue. Harmonious resinous and mineral nose showing scents of pine needles, bark and chalk, capped off with red berry fruit notes. The palate reveals wild strawberry flavours leading into a degree of exuberance.
Price approx.: 17,00 EUR
http://www.bersiserlini.it
Bersi Serlini
+390309823338

BERSI SERLINI SOCIETA' AGRICOLA S.R.L.   85/100

▼. Brut Cuvée n.4 Millesimato 2010 : Brilliant straw-yellow, green tints. Shy, instantly accessible nose that is simple and delicate with white flower and fresh almond aromas. Fairly robust, supple and delightfully fresh palate yet slightly incisive. An above average wine true to the appellation.
Price approx.: 20,00 EUR
http://www.bersiserlini.it
Bersi Serlini
+390309823338

CA' DEL BOSCO S.R.L. - SOCIETA' AGRICOLA   85/100

▼✔ Vintage Collection Brut 2009 : Brilliant straw-yellow with very abundant mousse. Simple, yet elegant nose driven by mineral notes of stone and chalk with resin aromas. The palate is along the same lines. It is simple, refined, harmonious and almost a textbook wine.

Price approx.: 43,00 EUR

http://www.cadelbosco.com

Ca' del Bosco S.r.l. - Societa' Agricola

390307766111

CASTELLO DI GUSSAGO LA SANTISSIMA 85/100

CV Eco▼✔ 0 : Intense, brilliant straw-yellow. Fresh nose with plentiful musk-like, sappy and mineral notes. Creamy attack on the palate, leading into a savoury mid-palate showing more of the same aromas. Medium length.

Price approx.: 22,00 EUR

http://www.castellodigussago.it

Castello di Gussago La Santissima

+302069967

CASTELLO DI GUSSAGO LA SANTISSIMA 85/100

CV Eco▼✔ Brut 0 : Beautiful warm tones. Elegant nose of yellow flowers, peach and a mineral touch. The palate is fairly mellow and offers up volume and a beautiful lemony streak mid-palate. Medium length, savoury and mineral-driven finish.

Price approx.: 20,00 EUR

http://www.castellodigussago.it

Castello di Gussago La Santissima

+302069967

GUIDO BERLUCCHI & C. S.P.A   85/100

CV Eco▼✔ Cuvée Imperiale Demi-Sec 0 : Warm straw-yellow. Polished, refined and well-balanced nose showing notes of fresh butter, vanilla and tropical fruits. Very creamy palate enhanced by decent freshness and fairly good harmony centring on the right sweetness and sourness ratio. Persistent.

Price approx.: 13,20 EUR

http://www.berlucchi.it

Guido Berlucchi & C. s.p.a.

+39030984381

GUIDO BERLUCCHI & C. S.P.A.   85/100

CV Eco▼✔ 61 Brut 0 : Straw-yellow with green tints. Pleasurable, shy, simple and instantly accessible nose of acacia and hawthorn, fresh almond and hay. Aside from the mousse, a tad too exuberant, the palate is robust, dry and mineral. Medium persistency.

Price approx.: 13,40 EUR

http://www.berlucchi.it

Guido Berlucchi & C. s.p.a.

+39030984381

GUIDO BERLUCCHI & C. S.P.A.   85/100

CV Eco▼✔ 61 Satèn Brut 0 : Exuberant, young nose driven by extremely mineral notes of gypsum with yeast, wheat flour and fresh almond. The palate is very accessible and flows into saline aromatics. There is perhaps slightly too much mousse for a Satèn.

Price approx.: 15,00 EUR

http://www.berlucchi.it

Guido Berlucchi & C. s.p.a.

+39030984381

LA BOSCAIOLA AZIENDA AGRICOLA   85/100

▼✔ Brut 0 : Brilliant straw-yellow. Fairly penetrating, refined and harmonious aromas of white flowers, anise and mineral notes on the nose. Abundant volume on the palate, flowing into savoury, fresh lemony aromatics. Medium length.

http://www.laboscaiola.com

La Boscaiola Azienda Agricola

+390307156386

LANTIERI DE PARATICO AZIENDA AGRICOLA   85/100

CONV▼✔ Arcadia Lantieri Brut Millesimato 2010 : Persistent bubbles. Nose of dried yellow flowers with a touch of lime honey. Polished and harmonious with aroma hitting you instantly. Very mellow, creamy and savoury palate boasting pronounced acidity.

Price approx.: 16,00 EUR

http://www.lantierideparatico.it

Lantieri de Paratico Azienda Agricola

+39030736151

MONTE ROSSA S.R.L.   85/100

▼✔ Cabochon Brut 2009 : Brilliant straw-yellow. Harmonious, expressive nose of white-fleshed fruits, tobacco leaf, undergrowth, dried mushroom and bark. Creamy palate centring on suppleness rather than exuberance. Cigar note on the finish.

Price approx.: 28,00 EUR

http://www.monterossa.com

Monte Rossa S.r.l.

39030725066

RICCI CURBASTRO AZIENDA AGRICOLA 85/100

Eco▼✔ Museum Release Satèn Brut 2006 : Brilliant straw-yellow. Endearing, refined and classic nose with perfumes of butter, croissant, toast and apricot. Very creamy, supple, well-balanced and long palate. A trace of acidity wouldn't have gone amiss!

Price approx.: 20,41 EUR

http://www.riccicurbastro.it

Ricci Curbastro Azienda Agricola

+39030736094

LA FIOCA   85/100

Eco▼✔ Rosé Brut 0 : Coppery hue. Expressive nose intermixing wild strawberry, bark, root, undergrowth and mineral notes. Silky, flavoursome palate showing lovely warmth. Vinous, savoury mid-palate. Supple finish. A touch

more acidity would not have gone amiss!
Price approx.: 13,33 EUR
http://www.lafioca.com
Societa' Agricola La Fioca
+390309826313

TENUTA AMBROSINI 85/100

▼⬩ Dosaggio Zero Nihil 0 : Straw-yellow. Beautifully full, unusual nose showing lemony notes, anise, cigar and chestnut flour. Precise attack on the palate with a faintly sour mid-palate and abundant freshness. Fairly good persistency.
Price approx.: 14,90 EUR
http://www.tenutambrosini.it/
Tenuta Ambrosini
+307254850

VIGNA DORATA 85/100

▼⬩ Franciacorta Extra Brut : Deep straw-yellow with fine bubbles. Enticing floral and fruity nose blending lily-of-the-valley and pear nectar. Focused, persistent palate capped off with a faint touch of sourness, enjoyable in this context. Ideal as an aperitif or with cold meats.
Price approx.: 24,00 EUR
http://www.vignadorata.it
VIGNA DORATA
+390307254275

1701 84/100

CONV▼⬩ Satèn Brut 0 : Abundant mousse. Brilliant straw-yellow. Unusual nose displaying wild aromas, spice and a vegetal touch suggestive of ginger. Succulent palate. Supple attack flowing into more vibrant aromatics with lemony accents.
Price approx.: 14,00 EUR
http://www.1701franciacorta.it
1701
+307750875

LANTIERI DE PARATICO AZIENDA AGRICOLA 84/100

CONV▼⬩ Origines Lantieri Riserva Dosaggio Zero 2008 : Brilliant straw-yellow. Nose of spice, mild tobacco and patisserie flowing into tropical aromatics. Fairly fresh, savoury and creamy palate. Resin-driven finish. Good quality bubbles. Perhaps a little too supple for a zero dosage sparkling wine.
Price approx.: 28,00 EUR
http://www.lantierideparatico.it
Lantieri de Paratico Azienda Agricola
39030736151

MONTE ROSSA S.R.L. 84/100

▼⬩ Coupé Non Dosato 0 : A pretty ring of bubbles forms a prelude to an unusual, spicy nose recalling gingerbread, mild tobacco and smoke scents. The palate displays volume and structure, with broad expression rather than vertical acidity. Fairly long.

Price approx.: 14,00 EUR
http://www.monterossa.com
Monte Rossa S.r.l.
+39030725066

RICCI CURBASTRO AZIENDA AGRICOLA 84/100

Eco▼⬩ Rosé Brut 0 : Brilliant coppery hue. Fairly subdued nose opening up to dried flower perfumes, hay and wild notes. Fairly elegant. Clean, saline palate with the nose aromatics following through. Balanced and fresh. Boasts personality.
Price approx.: 15,66 EUR
http://www.riccicurbastro.it
Ricci Curbastro Azienda Agricola
+39030736094

LA FIOCA 84/100

Eco▼⬩ Satèn Brut 0 : Brilliant straw-yellow. Expressive nose of nougat, gingerbread, anise, graphite, white flowers, yeast and mineral notes. More subdued palate displaying little mousse and abundant freshness. Fairly lightweight.
Price approx.: 12,50 EUR
http://www.lafioca.com
Societa' Agricola La Fioca
+390309826313

MONTENISA DI ALBIERA ALLEGRA E ALESSIA ANTINORI 84/100

▼⬩ Rosé Brut 0 : Brilliant copper hue with onion skin highlights. The nose is relatively lush and supple with notes of marzipan, pomegranate, cherry and raspberry. A moderately robust, subtle yet savoury wine boasting a finish that is a tad firm and crisp.
Price approx.: 17,70 EUR
http://www.montenisa.it
Tenuta Montenisa
+390307750838

VILLA FRANCIACORTA 84/100

Eco▼⬩ Bokè Rosé Brut Millesimato 2010 : Coppery hue with faint yellow highlights. Unusual nose of ginger, dried yellow flowers and citrus. Quite robust, velvety palate showing subtle freshness. Medium length.
Price approx.: 13,50 EUR
http://www.villafranciacorta.it
Villa Franciacorta
+30652329

1701 83/100

CONV▼⬩ Rosé Brut 0 : Fairly intense, brilliant coppery hue. The nose opens up to vegetal aromas of hay, then nougat and coffee, and ends with a touch of raspberry. Slighty free-flowing palate, bitter rather than fresh. Harmony has not yet been totally achieved.
Price approx.: 14,00 EUR
http://www.1701franciacorta.it
1701
+307750875

ANTICA CANTINA FRATTA   83/100

▼✦ Satèn Brut Essence 2010 : Brilliant straw-yellow tinged with green. Simple, immediately accessible nose showing notes of gooseberry, white flowers, wheat flour and mineral touches. On the palate, the mousse is slightly too abundant for a Satèn.
Price approx.: 15,40 EUR
http://www.anticafratta.com
Antica Cantina Fratta
+30652068

LE MARCHESINE S.S.   83/100

▼✦ Brut Secolo Novo Millesimato 2008 : Straw-yellow with green tints. Beautiful mousse. Balsamic nose exuding refined notes of resin, talc and menthol. Very supple, creamy attack on the palate flowing into wild strawberry scents. Not very robust or persistent.
http://www.lemarchesine.it
Az Ag Le Marchesine S.S.
+39030657005

FRATELLI BERLUCCHI   83/100

Eco▼✦ Brut Millesimato 2010 : Beautiful mousse introducing a bouquet of chestnut honey, undergrowth and hazelnut. Fairly creamy, well-balanced palate combining suppleness and a touch of sourness. A little extra acidity would have been welcome.
Price approx.: 22,00 EUR
http://www.fratelliberlucchi.it
Azienda Agricola Fratelli Berlucchi S.r.l.
+39030984451

BIONDELLI   83/100

CONV▼✦ Brut 0 : Brilliant straw-yellow with green tints. Pleasantly simple, delicate nose showing notes of yeast, anise and gooseberry. Fairly well-structured palate marked by a mousse that is slightly too fizzy. The finish tails off a little too quickly.
Price approx.: 10,90 EUR
http://www.biondelli.com
Biondelli
+390307759896

CA' DEL BOSCO S.R.L. - SOCIETA' AGRICOLA 83/100

▼✦ Vintage Collection Dosage Zéro 2009 : Brilliant straw-yellow, green tints. The nose is slightly muted on first pour then opens up to simple yet enjoyable notes of white flowers, wheat flour and fresh almond. Medium balance on the palate, sour rather than fresh. Suggestions of cigar on the finish.
Price approx.: 43,00 EUR
http://www.cadelbosco.com
Ca' del Bosco S.r.l. - Societa' Agricola
+390307766111

GUIDO BERLUCCHI & C. S.P.A.   83/100

CV Eco▼✦ Cuvée Imperiale Brut 0 : Straw-yellow with green tints. Refined, interesting bouquet driven by resin and

balsamic notes, spice aromas of anise, flowers and fruit (white peach). The palate is very supple and enjoyable with an abundant mousse. Slight lack of balance.
Price approx.: 12,50 EUR
http://www.berlucchi.it
Guido Berlucchi & C. s.p.a.
+39030984381

RICCI CURBASTRO AZIENDA AGRICOLA 83/100

Eco▼✦ Museum Release Extra Brut 2006 : Straw-yellow. The nose shows toasted and tertiary accents, patisserie, creme brulee and vanilla flowing into more austere notes of cigar and chestnut honey. Supple, robust and creamy palate with a touch of oak. Structured rather than refined.
Price approx.: 20,41 EUR
http://www.riccicurbastro.it
Ricci Curbastro Azienda Agricola
+39030736094

EMOZIONE BRUT MILLESIMATO   83/100

Eco▼✦ 2010 : Deep straw-yellow. Rich, delightful yet mature nose of gooseberry, candied fruits and ripe tropical fruits. Creamy, supple, vinous, robust and concentrated palate where slightly more pronounced, invigorating acidity would have been nice. Serve with food.
Price approx.: 12,00 EUR
http://www.villafranciacorta.it
Villa Franciacorta
30652329

BERSI SERLINI SOCIETA' AGRICOLA S.R.L. 82/100

▼✦ Demi-Sec 0 : Brilliant straw-yellow. Fairly full, harmonious nose exuding notes of peach, apple, yellow flowers, tobacco and ginger. The palate is slightly more backward than the nose. Creamy attack leading into a round mid-palate that is fairly short and reticent.
Price approx.: 14,00 EUR
http://www.bersiserlini.it
Bersi Serlini
+390309823338

CORTEBIANCA   82/100

Org▼✦ Extra Brut 0 : Brilliant straw-yellow. Unusual nose showing faint milky accents, casein and then aromas of chestnut flour and white flowers. Upright, precise palate bordering on lemony and displaying a slight firmness.
Price approx.: 15,00 EUR
http://www.corte-bianca.it
CorteBianca
+30983293

LA FIOCA   82/100

Eco▼✦ Brut 0 : Brilliant straw-yellow with green tints. Shy, delicate nose exuding flower notes of acacia and hawthorn, and almond aromas. Very creamy, slightly linear

palate displaying a touch of sourness on the finish.
Price approx.: 0,11 EUR
http://www.lafioca.com
Societa' Agricola La Fioca
+390309826313

LA FIOCA 82/100

Eco▼♪ Dosaggio Zero 2008 : Brilliant straw-yellow.
Simple, instantly accessible nose of gooseberry, ginger and
nougat. Moderately robust palate. Beautifully supple attack
leading into a fairly crisp mid-palate. A touch of sourness
on the finish.
Price approx.: 15,00 EUR
http://www.lafioca.com
Societa' Agricola La Fioca
+390309826313

TENUTA AMBROSINI 82/100

▼♪ Satèn Brut 0 : Intense, brilliant straw-yellow. Spicy,
mineral and metallic nose opening up to a faint touch of
redcurrant. The palate is creamy and more reticent, with
fairly rich dosage, a hint of firmness and medium length.
Price approx.: 14,50 EUR
http://www.tenutambrosini.it
Tenuta Ambrosini
+307254850

MONTENISA DI ALBIERA ALLEGRA E ALESSIA
ANTINORI 82/100

▼♪ Satèn Brut 2009 : Brilliant straw-yellow with green
tints. The nose is slightly muted on first pour then opens up to
notes of anise, grapefruit and fresh almond. On the palate,
freshness and flavour flow into a faint sourness on the finish.
Medium length.
Price approx.: 19,40 EUR
http://www.montenisa.it
Tenuta Montenisa
+390307750838

ANTICA CANTINA FRATTA 81/100

▼♪ Brut 0 : Straw-yellow. Shy, simple nose driven by
garrigue, berry, undergrowth and fresh almond notes. The
palate is slightly linear with a degree of opposition between
sweetness and sourness. Fairly good freshness.
Price approx.: 11,65 EUR
http://www.anticafratta.com
Antica Cantina Fratta
+30652068

AZIENDA AGRICOLA UGO VEZZOLI 81/100

▼♪ Brut 0 : Straw-yellow with green tints. Simple bouquet
revealing notes of white flowers (acacia), damp hay, humus
and undergrowth. The palate is consistent with the nose and
reveals subtle harmony.

Price approx.: 13,30 EUR
http://www.vezzolifranciacorta.it
Az Agr Vezzoli Ugo
+30738018

CA' DEL BOSCO S.R.L. - SOCIETA' AGRICOLA 80/100

▼♪ Cuvée Prestige Brut 0 : Brilliant straw-yellow with
green tints. Supple nose of sweet almond, nougat and
tropical fruits. Immediately forthcoming yet harmonious
and pleasurable bouquet. Surprising palate revealing an
atypical array of aromas. The finish displays a degree of
bitterness.
Price approx.: 26,00 EUR
http://www.cadelbosco.com
Ca' del Bosco S.r.l. - Societa' Agricola
+390307766111

MONTENISA DI ALBIERA ALLEGRA E ALESSIA
ANTINORI 80/100

▼♪ Cuvée Speciale Brut 0 : Brilliant, warm straw-
yellow. Slightly veiled aromas on the nose intermixing
anise, gingerbread, vegetal and cigar notes. Moderately
harmonious palate with abundant mousse. The finish is
slightly wild and reveals more of the vegetal character.
Price approx.: 15,20 EUR
http://www.montenisa.it
Tenuta Montenisa
+390307750838

LUGANA D.O.C

ANCILLA LUGANA-AZIENDA AGRICOLA LA
GHIDINA DI BENEDETTI LUISELLA 85/100

▼♪ Ancilla Lugana 2011 : Pale yellow. Intense, perfumed
and highly aromatic nose. Fairly refined, mellow and
persistent palate displaying a savoury character on the
finish. Would work as an aperitif or paired with fish.
Price approx.: 18,00 EUR
http://www.ancillalugana.it
Ancilla Lugana-Azienda Agricola La Ghidina di Benedetti
Luisella
+39 045 51 35 67

SEBINO I.G.T

CA' DEL BOSCO S.R.L - SOCIETA' AGRICOLA 90/100

▼♪ Rosso Maurizio Zanella 2008 : Dark ruby with purple-
blue. Intense, full and austere bouquet of undergrowth, bark
and Indian ink with a charred chocolate touch. Silky yet
very vibrant tannin framework. Fresh, elegant, harmonious,
mature and vibrant with saline notes and a cocoa finish.
Price approx.: 47,00 EUR
http://www.cadelbosco.com
Ca' del Bosco S.r.l. - Societa' Agricola
+390307766111

LA FIOCA — 87/100

Eco▼♪ 2012 : Straw-yellow with green tints. Elegant nose of white-fleshed melon, white peach and dried fruit (hazelnut, almond) with a lovely personality. Well-structured, fairly fresh and persistent palate. Citrus notes of lemon and grapefruit on the finish.
Price approx.: 5,00 EUR
http://www.lafioca.com
Societa' Agricola La Fioca
+390309826313

SFORZATO DI VALTELLINA D.O.C.G

NINO NEGRI — 93/100

▼♪ Sfursat 5 Stelle 2010 : Brilliant ruby. Intense, rich and elegant nose of forest fruit jam, morello cherries in brandy, mushroom, graphite, a charred touch of cocoa and coffee. Lush, coherent palate. Massive yet mellow and silky tannin framework. Long, mineral-driven finish.
Price approx.: 50,00 EUR
http://www.ninonegri.it
Nino Negri
+390342485211

MARCHE

MARCHE I.G.T.

LA CANOSA — 86/100

▼♪ Musè 2011 : Intense ruby. Fruity nose of blackberry and plum in brandy with a liquoricy and balsamic touch coupled with slightly spicy oak. The palate is fresh and persistent and displays beautiful tannins and more balsamic flavours. Set aside for red meat.
Price approx.: 12,00 EUR
http://www.lacanosaagricola.it
La Canosa
+390736000000

LA CANOSA — 83/100

▼♪ Nullius 2011 : Ruby-red. Fruity nose of wild blackberries and strawberries in brandy enhanced by faint notes of spice, tobacco and a subtle balsamic note. Good presence on the palate supported by fine-grain tannins. Fairly persistent and working well with meat.
Price approx.: 12,00 EUR
http://www.lacanosaagricola.it
La Canosa
+390736000000

OFFIDA D.O.C.G. PECORINO

LA CANOSA — 84/100

▼♪ Peko' 2012 : Straw-yellow. Slightly salty, mineral nose with notes of Mediterranean maquis. The saline sensation carries through to the palate, coupled with a hint of toasted almond. Fresh and persistent, ideal as an appetiser or with fish or cheese.
Price approx.: 6,50 EUR
http://www.lacanosaagricola.it
La Canosa
+390736000000

ROSSO PICENO DOC SUPERIORE

LA CANOSA — 86/100

▼♪ Nummaria 2011 : Impenetrable ruby-red. Complex nose of red fruits in brandy, blackberry and raspberry with notes of liquorice and spice. The palate is concentrated yet mellow with upfront tannins. Serve with meat.
Price approx.: 7,50 EUR
http://www.lacanosaagricola.it
La Canosa
+390736000000

PIEDMONT

BARBARESCO D.O.C.G.

BATTAGLIO AZIENDA — 90/100

▼♪ Barbaresco Docg 2010 : Intense garnet-red. Elegant nose of blackberry, cherry and raspberry in brandy with mild spice notes of cloves. The palate is round and persistent and driven by spice and balsamic notes. An elegant wine drinking well even on its own.
Price approx.: 18,00 EUR
http://www.battaglio.com
Battaglio Azienda
+39017365423

BAROLO D.O.C.G.

BATTAGLIO AZIENDA — 90/100

▼♪ Barolo Docg 2010 : Garnet-red. Mature, elegant nose intermixing mild spice and balsamic notes of eucalyptus and liquorice with ultra ripe red fruits. Elegant palate displaying beautiful acidity with aromas of pepper. Persistent. A wine for cellaring or serving with cheese.
Price approx.: 20,00 EUR
http://www.battaglio.com
Battaglio Azienda
+39017365423

DOGLIANI D.O.C.G.

CLAVESANA SIAMO DOLCETTO   86/100

▼✎ Clavesana 2012 : Intense ruby. Open nose suggestive of dried flowers, blackberry and cherries in brandy, enhanced by a touch of mint and liquorice. The palate is fresh, mellow and warm and suffused with spice on the finish. Perfect for red meats or cheeses.
Price approx.: 4,80 EUR
http://www.inclavesana.it
Cantina Clavesana Sca
+390173790451

DOLCETTO DI DOGLIANI SUPERIORE D.O.C.G

CLAVESANA SIAMO DOLCETTO   88/100

▼✎ Il Clou 2011 : Intense ruby. Elegant nose intermixing jammy wild fruits, dried red flowers and a subtle balsamic note. The palate is fresh yet intense with a crunchy finish. A full-bodied wine drinking well with mature cheeses.
Price approx.: 6,50 EUR
http://www.inclavesana.it
Cantina Clavesana Sca
+390173790451

ERBALUCE DI CALUSO D.O.C.G.

LA MASERA   90/100

Eco▼✎ Macaria 2012 : Intense straw-yellow. Complex nose revealing successive aromas of sage, thyme, acacia blossom, eucalyptus and star anise. Very fresh, mellow and refined palate. The end flavour and suppleness coat the palate.
Price approx.: 7,50 EUR
http://www.lamasera.it
La Masera
+113164161

LA MASERA   88/100

Eco▼✎ Anima 2013 : Brilliant straw-yellow. Fairly complex, refined nose driven by floral notes of linden and acacia, with apple and white peach and citrus notes of grapefruit. The palate shows the perfect combination of mellowness, freshness, power and mineral flavours.
Price approx.: 6,00 EUR
http://www.lamasera.it
La Masera
+113164161

GAVI D.O.C.G. DEL COMUNE DI GAVI

MAGDA PEDRINI   92/100

▼✎ Riserva Vigna Domino 2012 : Intense straw-yellow. Very mineral nose with scents of iodine and gunflint. Elegant bouquet enhanced by floral notes of hawthorn and fruit aromas of white peach. Robust, powerful, savoury and fresh palate. Very long persistency.
Price approx.: 11,90 EUR
http://www.magdapedrini.it
Magda Pedrini
+143667923

MAGDA PEDRINI   89/100

▼✎ Domino 2012 : Intense straw-yellow. The nose delivers buttery, vanilla, crystallised cedar, ripe pineapple and mineral notes on first pour. Very well-structured, balanced and harmoniously fresh. Long savoury finish of almond and vanilla.
Price approx.: 8,90 EUR
http://www.magdapedrini.it
Magda Pedrini
+143667923

MAGDA PEDRINI   87/100

▼✎ La Piacentina 2013 : Brilliant straw-yellow. Elegant, supple and mineral nose of flint and chalk with ripe citrus and pineapple, acacia and hawthorn. Endearing, fresh, robust and warm palate with a savoury trace of acidity. Long-lasting persistency.
Price approx.: 7,25 EUR
http://www.magdapedrini.it
Magda Pedrini
+143667923

MONFERRATO D.O.C

MAGDA PEDRINI   90/100

▼✎ Il Pettirosso 2012 : Intense ruby. Vibrant, perfumed nose driven by red fruit aromas of morello cherry, raspberry and plum with black pepper, cocoa, undergrowth and rhubarb. Structured, crunchy palate offering up beautifully balanced exuberance and warmth. Long clean finish.
Price approx.: 7,80 EUR
http://www.magdapedrini.it
Magda Pedrini
143667923

MOSCATO D'ASTI D.O.C.G

BATTAGLIO AZIENDA　　　　　　**88/100**

▼✔ Moscato D'Asti 2013 : Straw-yellow with fine bubbles. The nose opens up to pleasant, aromatic scents of peach blossom, magnolia and white-fleshed fruits. Sweet and fruity palate recalling apricot jam. Ideal for cream-based desserts.
Price approx.: 7,00 EUR
http://www.battaglio.com
Battaglio Azienda
39017365423

NEBBIOLO D'ALBA D.O.C.

BATTAGLIO AZIENDA　　　　　　**90/100**

▼✔ Nebbiolo D'Alba Superiore Valmaggiore 2011 : Garnet-red. Expressive, complex nose of spice, leather, red fruits in brandy and toasted tobacco. More of the spice on the palate which is persistent with balsamic aromas of liquorice. Beautiful exuberance. A wine for cellaring.
Price approx.: 14,00 EUR
http://www.battaglio.com
Battaglio Azienda
+39017365423

CA RICHETA AZ. AGR.　　　　　　**88/100**

▼✔ Crussi 2011 : Garnet. Intense nose of spices, toast and red fruits in brandy (redcurrant, cassis). A warm, mellow style on the palate with aromas of liquorice and pepper. Ideal for raw-cooked meats or herb-flavoured cheeses.
Price approx.: 12,00 EUR
http://www.caricheta.com
Ca Richeta Az. Agr.
+393336894199

ROERO D.O.C.

BATTAGLIO AZIENDA　　　　　　**86/100**

▼✔ Piasì 2013 : Straw-yellow. Delicate, fresh and herbal nose backed by mineral notes, extremely typical of the varietal. Easy-drinking, consistent palate offering up the same well-balanced exuberance and herbal aromas. Excellent as an aperitif, with fish or cheese.
Price approx.: 7,00 EUR
http://www.battaglio.com
Battaglio Azienda
+39017365423

SICILIA

SICILIA D.O.C.

FONDO ANTICO　　　　　　**88/100**

▼✔ Grillo Parlante 2013 : Straw-yellow with green tints. Intense, complex nose of yellow fruits with herbal and mineral scents of pumice stone. More of the same minerality and intensity on the palate flowing into a slightly balsamic finish. Excellent with fish.
http://www.fondoantico.it
Fondo Antico
+390923864339

CORBERA　　　　　　**87/100**

▼✔ Grillo 2013 : Straw-yellow. Expressive nose opening up to flowers and white-fleshed fruits then revealing a mineral character. A good level of acidity on the palate, persistent aromas and a finish suffused with vanilla accents. Drink as an aperitif or with fish.
Price approx.: 3,00 EUR
http://www.cantinacorbera.com
Cantina Sociale Corbera Soc.Coop.
+39092531377

CORBERA　　　　　　**85/100**

▼✔ Nero d'Avola 2012 : Ruby-red with crimson highlights. Intense nose suggestive of jammy forest fruits with a creamy, vanilla and liquoricy touch. Full mouthfeel with polished tannins revealing more of the balsamic character. Serve with meat.
Price approx.: 3,00 EUR
http://www.cantinacorbera.com
Cantina Sociale Corbera Soc.Coop.
+39092531377

SICILIA I.G.T

TENUTA RAPITALÀ　　　　　　**90/100**

▼✔ Chardonnay Grand Cru 2012 : Golden straw-yellow. Rich, harmonious, complex nose of pineapple, peach, pear, pastry cream and mild tobacco. Well-balanced, fat and concentrated palate that is fresh, warm and buttery with the nose aromas flowing through. Long, savoury and mineral finish.
Price approx.: 20,00 EUR
http://www.rapitala.it
Tenuta Rapitalà
+39092437233

TENUTA DI CASTELLARO　　　　　　**87/100**

Org▼✔ Bianco Pomice 2011 : Intense straw-yellow. Expressive nose of fresh white flowers (lily-of-the-valley). Fruit prevails on the palate augmented by a pleasant hint of bitter almond on the finish. Good acidity. Ideal as an appetiser or with white fish.
Price approx.: 12,80 EUR
http://www.tenutadicastellaro.it
Tenuta di Castellaro
+39035233337

TENUTA DI CASTELLARO　　　　　　**87/100**

Org▼✔ Nero Ossidiana 2011 : Ruby with crimson highlights. Nose of fresh flowers and forest fruits enhanced by faint balsamic notes in the background. The palate shows delicate tannins driven by pleasant spice notes. Ideal for a tartare or cheese.

Price approx.: 13,90 EUR

http://www.tenutadicastellaro.it

Tenuta di Castellaro

+39035233337

TRENTINO

TRENTO D.O.C.

FERRARI F.LLI LUNELLI   96/100

▼✦ Giulio Ferrari Riserva del Fondatore 2004 : Brilliant yellow-gold. Opulent nose of mild tobacco, cocoa butter, Mediterranean garrigue, quince and pineapple also revealing toast and mineral notes. Supple, silky and savoury palate. Lemony, iodine-driven finish over excellent length.

Price approx.: 54,00 EUR

http://www.cantineferrari.it

Ferrari F.lli Lunelli

+39 046 19 72 311

FERRARI F.LLI LUNELLI   94/100

▼✦ Ferrari Perlé Nero 2008 : Golden hue. Complex nose showing fruity notes of raspberry, wild strawberry, morello cherry, redcurrant and cedar then burnt wood, herbs and gunflint. Fleshy, mellow and mineral-driven palate. Good length and an almond-infused finish.

Price approx.: 36,50 EUR

http://www.cantineferrari.it

Ferrari F.lli Lunelli

+39 046 19 72 311

FERRARI F.LLI LUNELLI   92/100

▼✦ Ferrari Perlé 2008 : Intense, brilliant straw-yellow. Expressive vegetal bouquet of lemongrass with fruit (lime and melon), flowing into yellow flowers and pastry cream. Very savoury attack leading into a fresh, lemony yet also supple mid-palate. Iodine drives the finish.

Price approx.: 19,25 EUR

http://www.cantineferrari.it

Ferrari F.lli Lunelli

+39 046 19 72 311

CANTINA ALDENO   91/100

▼✦ Riserva Altinum 2009 : Golden straw-yellow. Full, rich nose of ripe tropical fruits, white flowers (acacia, hawthorn), toast, croissant, pastries and gunflint. Full, creamy and fresh palate with a strong mineral streak. Savoury and persistent.

Price approx.: 22,00 EUR

http://www.cantinaaldeno.com

Cantina Aldeno

+390461842511

FERRARI F.LLI LUNELLI   89/100

▼✦ Ferrari Maximum Brut 0 : Brilliant straw-yellow. Lightly toasted nose of bread and hazelnut opening up to fruity notes of pineapple, orange, cedar and peach with pastries and mineral scents. Fresh, creamy, mellow palate matching the flow of aromatics.

Price approx.: 15,25 EUR

http://www.cantineferrari.it

Ferrari F.lli Lunelli

+39 046 19 72 311

CANTINA ALDENO   87/100

▼✦ Altinum 2010 : Endearing, fresh and instantly accessible nose intermixing lime, pineapple, apple, peach, hazelnut and more subtle balsamic and musk-like aromas. Fairly robust, easy-drinking palate showing supple, balanced freshness. Focused, lemony finish.

Price approx.: 11,10 EUR

http://www.cantinaaldeno.com

Cantina Aldeno

+390461842511

TUSCANY

ANSONICA COSTA DELL'ARGENTARIO D.O.C

IL PONTE   86/100

▼✦ T-Lex 2013 : Straw-yellow with green tints. Elegant nose showing perfumes of herbs, loquat, apricot, iodine and damp rock notes. Harmonious palate that is refined, fresh, balanced and capped off with a long, clean, saline and mineral finish.

Price approx.: 5,00 EUR

http://www.agricolailponte.com

Il Ponte

+3334843966

BOLGHERI D.O.C. SUPERIORE

TAM   87/100

▼✦ Bolgheri Superiore 2009 : Deep ruby. The nose reveals intense perfumes of red fruits in brandy and blackberry framed by subtle spice aromatics. The same focused fruit carries through to the palate enhanced by a balsamic touch and fine tannins. A well-balanced, characterful wine.

Price approx.: 30,00 EUR

http://www.batzella.com

Batzella S.S.A.

+393393975888

BOLGHERI D.O.C.

PEÀN   88/100

▼♪ Bolgheri rosso 2010 : Intense ruby. Expressive nose opening up to wild berries and raspberry. Warm, melted palate deliciously capped off with a typical terroir note. Subtle, well-integrated oak. An ideal wine for pairing with red meats.

Price approx.: 18,00 EUR
http://www.batzella.com
Batzella S.S.A.
+393393975888

BRUNELLO DI MONTALCINO D.O.C.G.

TENUTA GREPPO - FRANCO BIONDI SANTI 96/100

▼♪ Riserva Tenuta Greppo 2008 : Intense garnet. Very complex nose of redcurrant, morello cherry, blackberry then undergrowth, fern, medicinal herbs, iodine, tobacco, leather and graphite. Warm, endearing palate - an iron fist in a velvet glove. Very long, mineral and balsamic finish.

http://biondisanti.it
Tenuta Greppo - Franco Biondi Santi
+390577848087

MARCHESI DE' FRESCOBALDI   93/100

▼♪ Castelgiocondo Brunello di Montalcino 2009 : Impenetrable ruby-red. Complex, intense bouquet of pot pourri, red fruit jam and mild liquorice. Supple, intense and mouth-coating palate. An elegant wine encouraging meditation.

http://www.frescobaldi.it
Marchesi de' Frescobaldi
+3905527141

TENUTA GREPPO - FRANCO BIONDI SANTI
93/100

▼♪ Tenuta Greppo 2009 : Garnet with ruby highlights. Full, harmonious nose of rose, violet and undergrowth with fruit notes of morello cherry, redcurrant and citrus then mint, tobacco and sandalwood. Delicious palate showing elegantly austere, noble tannins. Very fresh and long.

Price approx.: 55,00 EUR
http://biondisanti.it
Tenuta Greppo - Franco Biondi Santi
+390577848087

BOTTEGA   90/100

▼♪ Il Vino dei Poeti 2009 : Crimson red. The nose reveals smoke notes on first pour then shows undergrowth, berry fruits, morello cherries in brandy, liquorice and graphite. Powerful palate with an evident tannin framework, freshness and a long spicy finish.

http://www.bottegaspa.com
Bottega SpA
+4384067

CAPALBIO D.O.C.

IL PONTE   87/100

▼♪ T-lex 2012 : Ruby-garnet. Rich nose of morello cherry, cherry, rose, violet, burnt oak and undergrowth. The palate is well-structured and displays a trace of exuberance consistent with the vibrant tannin framework and power. Delicious, clean finish.

Price approx.: 5,00 EUR
http://www.agricolailponte.com
Il Ponte
+3334843966

CHIANTI CLASSICO D.O.C.G. GRAN SELEZIONE

FATTORIA LORNANO   92/100

▼♪ Gran Selezione 2010 : Deep ruby. Complex nose recalling tar, undergrowth, musk, graphite and then more delicate scents of prune and mild spices. Succulent palate. The tannins are still young yet refined and nicely mellowed, combining freshness and full flavour.

Price approx.: 45,00 EUR
http://www.fattorialornano.it
Fattoria Lornano
+390577309059

SOC. AGR. LOSI QUERCIAVALLE   92/100

▼♪ Gran Selezione LOSI Millennium 2009 : Beautifully intense ruby. Full, refined nose of ripe cherry, plum and delicate tertiary notes of leather and tobacco with a faint toasted touch of chocolate. Delicious, incisive palate with a massive, generous tannin framework that is focused and fresh.

Price approx.: 15,00 EUR
http://www.aziendagricolalosi.it
Soc. Agr. Losi Querciavalle
+390577356842

IL MOLINO DI GRACE   91/100

CONV▼♪ Gran Selezione Il Margone 2010 : Ruby-garnet. Refined nose intermixing raspberry, black cherry, violet, humus, dried mushroom yet also rhubarb, tobacco and leather. The palate is extremely flavoursome and combines a fine tannin framework with beautiful freshness. Long mineral finish.

Price approx.: 16,00 EUR
http://www.ilmolinodigrace.it
Il Molino di Grace
+390558561010

RUFFINO   90/100

▼♪ Riserva Ducale Oro 2010 : Intense ruby. Expressive nose of cherry, blackberry, bark and undergrowth capped off with mellower aromas of cinnamon. Harmonious on the palate, offering elegant, silky tannins and a long, fresh finish.

Price approx.: 14,50 EUR

http://www.ruffino.it

Ruffino

+3905583605

CHIANTI CLASSICO D.O.C.G. RISERVA

CASTELLO DI MELETO   90/100

▼● Riserva Vigna Casi Castello di Meleto 2011 : Intense ruby. Full, refined nose of blackberry jam, aromatic wood (sandalwood), anise, incense, toasted touches of coffee, cocoa and liquorice. Harmonious, elegant and characterful palate that is extremely fresh and savoury.

Price approx.: 8,90 EUR

market@castellomeleto.it

Castello di Meleto

+390577749217

LE MICCINE   90/100

CONV▼● Riserva 2011 : Vibrant ruby. Refined, focused nose showing crunchy raspberry and citrus notes, pencil lead, mushroom, prune and clove. The tannins have mellowed nicely yet remain intense. The palate is dynamic, juicy, fresh and savoury.

Price approx.: 21,00 EUR

http://www.lemiccine.com

Le Miccine

+390577749526

SOC. AGR. LOSI QUERCIAVALLE   90/100

▼● Riserva Querciavalle 2010 : Brilliant ruby hue displaying a full, harmonious bouquet of ripe black berry fruits, balsamic, resinous notes of root and bark with round spices. Supple palate with a massive tannin framework that is mellow yet lively. Long, fresh finish.

Price approx.: 12,00 EUR

http://www.aziendagricolalosi.it

Soc. Agr. Losi Querciavalle

+390577356842

SOCIETA AGRICOLA TERZONA SRL   90/100

CV Eco▼● Gàudio 2011 : Deep ruby. Intense, full bouquet perfumed with berry fruits, liquorice, fern, pepper, resin, cocoa, mint and mild spices. The palate displays mouth-coating suppleness from the glycerol followed by the bite of the tannins. Lengthy finish.

Price approx.: 16,00 EUR

http://www.carusvini.it

Societa Agricola Terzona SRL

TERRA DI SETA - AZIENDA AGRICOLA LE MACIE DI M. PELLEGRINI   90/100

Eco▼● Riserva 2010 : Brilliant ruby. Intense nose of black cherry, blackberry juice, candied violet, graphite, liquorice

and herbs opening up elegantly to balsamic aromas. Powerful, fresh and mineral-driven palate with a robust yet delicious tannin framework.

Price approx.: 18,00 EUR

http://www.terradiseta.it

Terra di Seta - Azienda Agricola Le Macie di M. Pellegrini

+05 77 32 24 28

LA CASA DI BRICCIANO   89/100

Org▼ Riserva Biologico 2010 : Ruby-hued. A mix of mild spice, wild berry fruits, cassis, violet and milk chocolate notes on the nose. The palate shows substance and tightly-wound, compelling tannins coupled with a trace of freshness and acidity.

Price approx.: 21,35 EUR

http://www.lacasadibricciano.it

La Casa di Bricciano

+390577749297

VILLA MANGIACANE S.R.L.   89/100

▼● Riserva Villa Mangiacane 2011 : Intense ruby. Nose of morello cherry, wild blackberry, Indian ink, wilted rose, leather, cigar, mocha, pencil lead and garrigue. The palate shows thickness and a tightly-wound tannin framework. Supple and mouth-coating. A wine boasting good persistency.

Price approx.: 11,60 EUR

http://www.mangiacane.com

Villa Mangiacane S.r.l.

+390558000000

VILLA CERNA CHIANTI CLASSICO RISERVA 88/100

▼● Villa Cerna 2010 : Deep ruby. Intense nose with balsamic and spice accents and a touch of liquorice. More of the refined spice aromatics on the palate framed by melted, velvety tannins. A meditation wine drinking well with traditional regional cuisine.

Price approx.: 10,00 EUR

http://www.cecchi.net

Cecchi

+39057754311

CHIANTI CLASSICO D.O.C.G.

FELSINA   94/100

CONV▼● Rancia Berardenga Riserva 2011 : Brilliant ruby. A full, complex range of aromatics on the nose: Indian ink, liquorice, rhubarb on top of pleasurable notes of morello cherry, mint and rose petals. Acidity is toned down by the suppleness of the palate and the right balance of tannins.

Price approx.: 20,00 EUR

http://www.felsina.it

Fèlsina

+390577355117

FELSINA 90/100

CONV▼⬧ Berardenga 2012 : Intense ruby. Concentrated nose with notes of cherry and blackberry juice, wilted violet, pencil lead, roots and thyme. Powerful, vigorous palate boasting fresh acidity and massive, savoury tannins. Long, smoke-infused finish.
Price approx.: 9,50 EUR
http://www.felsina.it
Fèlsina
+390577355117

PODERE CASTELLINUZZA 90/100

Eco▼⬧ Podere Castellinuzza 2011 : Vibrant ruby. Full, harmonious nose exuding notes of coffee, cardamom, humus, ripe fruits and balsamic aromas of eucalyptus. Very savoury, mineral and fresh palate. Beautiful tannin presence. Long, clean finish.
Price approx.: 12,00 EUR
http://www.castellinuzza.it
Podere Castellinuzza
+558549052

POGGIO A CAMPOLI 90/100

Eco▼⬧ Campolaia 2010 : Compact ruby. Expressive nose of blackberry jam and cocoa flowing into more austere notes of liquorice, black pepper, humus and bark. Velvety palate showing vibrant acidity, harmonious tannins and a clean, spice-driven finish.
Price approx.: 6,00 EUR
http://www.mastrocecco.com
Poggio a Campoli
+39 340 26 29 728

TENUTA DI BIBBIANO 90/100

Org▼⬧ Vigna del Capannino 2010 : Impenetrable ruby-red. Intense nose of macerated wild blueberries and raspberries with balsamic notes of eucalyptus and liquorice with a hint of vanilla. Warm, mouth-coating palate. Serve with meat.
Price approx.: 21,00 EUR
http://www.tenutadibibbiano.it
Tenuta di Bibbiano
+39 057 77 43 065

CASTELLO DI SELVOLE 89/100

▼⬧ Gran Selezione 2011 : Garnet starting to mature. Reserved nose opening up to black fruit notes, tobacco and a floral touch. Clean attack on the palate with a velvety texture. Fine tannins and fullness as well as aromatic persistency.
Price approx.: 20,00 EUR
http://www.selvole.com
Castello di Selvole Eri
+390577322662

POGGIO TORSELLI 89/100

▼⬧ Riserva 2010 : Bright ruby. Intense nose of black berry fruits, dried flowers, orange peel, graphite, undergrowth and Oriental spices. The palate displays incisive, tightly-wound tannins in harmony with the acidity, warmth and minerality.
Price approx.: 8,00 EUR
http://www.poggiotorselli.it
Poggio Torselli
+558290241

FATTORIA LORNANO 88/100

▼⬧ Lornano 2011 : Intense ruby. The nose is immediate yet full, intermixing fruity notes of morello cherry, floral aromas of violet and touches of cardamom and tobacco. More of the same on the palate which is very enjoyable, mellow, savoury, saline and infused with iodine.
Price approx.: 12,00 EUR
http://www.fattorialornano.it
Fattoria Lornano
+390577309059

IL MOLINO DI GRACE 88/100

CONV▼⬧ 2012 : Ruby-hued. Exuberant nose that is mineral yet fruity, showing red fruits accompanied by humus, cardamom, liquorice and herbs. Intense flavour on the palate coupled with explosive freshness and superlative quality tannins. A beautiful wine.
Price approx.: 6,35 EUR
http://www.ilmolinodigrace.it
Il Molino di Grace
+390558561010

SOC. AGR. LOSI QUERCIAVALLE 88/100

Eco▼⬧ Querciavalle 2011 : Brilliant ruby. Classic nose of red berry fruits, morello cherries in brandy and vegetal notes of liquorice, undergrowth and dried mushrooms. Dynamic, supple yet also fresh and savoury palate. Vibrant tannin framework.
Price approx.: 8,00 EUR
http://www.aziendagricolalosi.it
Soc. Agr. Losi Querciavalle
+390577356842

TERRA DI SETA - AZIENDA AGRICOLA LE MACIE DI M. PELLEGRINI 88/100

Eco▼⬧ 2010 : Brilliant ruby. Elegant, harmonious nose driven by floral notes of rose and violet with cherry and pepper. Fairly fresh palate with a vibrant tannin framework and a savoury finish driven by fruit notes.
Price approx.: 12,00 EUR
http://www.terradiseta.it
Terra di Seta - Azienda Agricola Le Macie di M. Pellegrini
+05 77 32 24 28

TENUTA SAN VINCENTI 87/100

▼✎ Tenuta San Vincenti 2011 : Brilliant ruby. Full, harmonious nose of morello cherries in brandy, iron, Indian ink, rhubarb, eucalyptus, liquorice and herbs. Fresh, dynamic palate with a beautiful, vibrant tannin framework. Very savoury.
Price approx.: 6,50 EUR
http://www.sanvincenti.it
Azienda Agricola San Vincenti
+39577734047

CASTELLO DI MELETO 87/100

▼✎ Castello di Meleto 2011 : Limpid, brilliant ruby. Refined nose of wild flowers and forest fruits then spice, orange peel, medicinal herbs and garrigue. The palate is very fresh, focused and harmonious with a tightly-wound, mellow, noble tannin framework. Lengthy finish.
Price approx.: 5,90 EUR
market@castellomeleto.it
Castello di Meleto
+390577749217

CASTELLO DI SELVOLE 87/100

▼✎ Riserva 2011 : Attractive garnet. The nose is generous and shows suggestions of ripe stone fruits. Robust, powerful attack on the palate with upfront yet restrained tannins. Perfumed finish exuding more of the pleasant stone fruit notes.
Price approx.: 15,00 EUR
http://www.selvole.com
Castello di Selvole Eri
+390577322662

LE MICCINE 87/100

CONV▼✎ 2011 : Brilliant ruby. The nose opens up to scents of raspberry, morello cherry and redcurrant then flows into notes of bark, liquorice root and a toasted touch of cocoa. Refined, elegant and very powerful palate that is crunchy, fresh and savoury.
Price approx.: 13,00 EUR
http://www.lemiccine.com
Le Miccine
+390577749526

TENUTA DI BIBBIANO 87/100

Org▼✎ Bibbiano 2012 : Ruby with garnet highlights. Soft, intense nose revealing lovely spicy oak notes in the background. On the palate, a fairly dense, round wine with mellow tannins. Ideal for meats or mature cheeses.
Price approx.: 13,00 EUR
http://www.tenutadibibbiano.it
Tenuta di Bibbiano
+39 057 77 43 065

VILLA MANGIACANE S.R.L. 86/100

▼✎ Villa Mangiacane 2011 : Limpid ruby. Fruity bouquet of citrus, plum and morello cherry with floral aromas of rose

and geranium, vegetal notes of rhubarb, and a touch of leather and spice. Dynamic, fresh and savoury palate with a vibrant tannin framework and a persistent finish.
http://www.mangiacane.com
Villa Mangiacane S.r.l.
+390558000000

CHIANTI D.O.C.G.

FATTORIA DIANELLA 89/100

▼✎ Riserva Dianella 2011 : Attractive, brilliant ruby. Classic, refined and well-balanced nose of cherry, raspberry and redcurrant with touches of undergrowth, bark and liquorice root. Very upfront yet mild, elegant tannins on the palate. A savoury, fresh and long wine.
Price approx.: 15,00 EUR
http://villadianella.it
Fattoria Dianella
+390571508166

NATIO CHIANTI 86/100

Org▼✎ Natio 2012 : Ruby-red. Intense nose of wild fruits in brandy (blackberry). The palate displays a certain amount of tannins yet also a fresh, lingering finish leaving the palate clean. A young wine pairing with mature cheeses and red meats.
Price approx.: 4,00 EUR
http://www.cecchi.net
Cecchi
+39057754311

FATTORIA DIANELLA 86/100

▼✎ Dianella 2013 : Ruby with purple-blue tints. The nose exudes aromas that are still very youthful, fruity and vinous with notes of garrigue and balsamic touches. Slender yet very pleasant, well-balanced and fresh palate with vibrant tannins. A delicious, crunchy wine.
Price approx.: 6,00 EUR
http://villadianella.it
Fattoria Dianella
+390571508166

MAREMMA TOSCANA D.O.C.

PIÙ TANTO 86/100

▼✎ Pugnitello 2010 : Impenetrable ruby-red. Expressive nose of forest fruits and cherry. Fresh, vertical and fruity palate showing lovely fine, elegant tannins. A harmonious wine drinking well with traditional cuisine.
Price approx.: 18,00 EUR
http://www.sassalsole.com
Az Ag Podere Il Poggio» di Spinelli Silvia»
+393286372145

MONTECUCCO D.O.C

SASS'ALSOLE 88/100

▼♪ Montecucco 2009 : Garnet-red. Intense nose suggestive of instant coffee and plum and fig jam. The same fruit aromatics flow through to the palate and are enhanced by round, elegant tannins. A potential partner for herb-flavoured cheeses or chocolate fondant.

Price approx.: 9,50 EUR

http://www.sassalsole.com

Az Ag Podere Il Poggio» di Spinelli Silvia»

+393286372145

MONTEREGIO D.O.C.

BICOCCHI FRANCESCA AZ. AGR. 88/100

Org▼♪ Armonia di Moreta Monteregio di Massa Marittima 2011 : Ruby-hued. Open nose driven by wild fruits with a faint spice dimension. Fresh, polished palate augmented by good acidity and displaying a savoury character on the finish. Focused across the palate. Would work best with hearty foods.

Price approx.: 8,30 EUR

http://www.bicocchiwine.it

Bicocchi Francesca Az. agr.

+390566919162

BICOCCHI FRANCESCA AZ. AGR. 88/100

▼♪ Sor'Emilio Monteregio di Massa Marittima 2009 : Ruby-hued with garnet tints. Complex nose recalling a bouquet of dried flowers combined with balsamic, liquorice and oak notes. Warm, closely-integrated palate with velvety tannins and a savoury finish. An interesting wine.

Price approx.: 10,50 EUR

http://www.bicocchiwine.it

Bicocchi Francesca Az. agr.

+390566919162

MORELLINO DI SCANSANO D.O.C.G

JACOPO BIONDI SANTI CASTELLO DI MONTEPO 89/100

▼♪ 2010 : Deep ruby. Refined, interesting bouquet of fresh and jammy red fruits accompanied by floral notes of rose and geranium, and spicy white pepper aromas. Very fresh, supple, warm and savoury palate. Polished tannins. Good persistency.

Price approx.: 11,50 EUR

http://www.biondisantimontepo.com

Biondi Santi - Castello di Montepo

+390577848238

FATTORIA DI MAGLIANO 88/100

▼♪ Heba 2012 : Ruby-red. Intense bouquet of violet and jammy strawberry and raspberry with faint balsamic and

spice notes of clove. On the palate, an intense, persistent wine with delicate tannins. Ideal for cold meats.

Price approx.: 5,90 EUR

http://www.fattoriadimagliano.it

Fattoria Di Magliano

+3905645933040

CECCHI 87/100

▼♪ Val Delle Rose 2010 : Ruby-hued. Nicely open, intense nose intermixing red fruit jam with faint mint and eucalyptus notes. Robust, persistent palate with melted tannins and a slightly vegetal spice note. A full-bodied wine with an assertive personality.

Price approx.: 85,00 EUR

http://www.cecchi.net

Cecchi

+39057754311

ROSSO DI MONTALCINO D.O.C.

TENUTA GREPPO - FRANCO BIONDI SANTI 88/100

▼♪ Tenuta Greppo 2010 : Ruby with garnet. Elegant nose of fern, plum and carob with balsamic notes of resin and eucalyptus. The palate is savoury and still tense with abundant freshness and incisive tannins. Long finish with the nose aromatics carrying through.

Price approx.: 17,50 EUR

http://biondisanti.it

Tenuta Greppo - Franco Biondi Santi

+390577848087

ROSSO DI MONTEPULCIANO D.O.C.

VILLA S. ANNA 88/100

Eco▼♪ 2011 : Brilliant ruby. Vibrant nose delivering crunchy notes of cherries in brandy, wild strawberry jam, raspberry and rose petal. Full, well-structured and very fresh palate accompanying robust, feisty tannins.

http://www.villasantanna.it

Villa S. Anna

+578708017

AZ AG LE BERTILLE 87/100

▼♪ 2012 : Ruby with crimson nuances. The nose delivers notes of cherry, liquorice and musk plus a classic touch of wilted violet. Lovely sappy, fresh palate with dense, mellow tannins. A firm, focused and perfumed style.

Price approx.: 5,00 EUR

http://www.lebertille.com

Az Ag Le Bertille

+390578758330

FATTORIA DI PALAZZO VECCHIO 87/100

Eco▼🍷 Dogana 2013 : Ruby, purple-blue tints. Fruity nose of morello cherry and plum flowing into vegetal notes of liquorice, Indian ink and undergrowth, balsamic aromas of juniper and charred milk chocolate notes. Very fresh palate, upfront structure. Tannins still very young.
Price approx.: 6,40 EUR
http://www.vinonobile.it
Fattoria di Palazzo Vecchio
+390578724170

TOSCANA I.G.T.

FELSINA 96/100

CONV▼🍷 Fontalloro Sangiovese 2011 : Full, complex and refined bouquet with intense notes of cherry and raspberry coupled with scents of undergrowth, pencil lead, leather and Mediterranean garrigue. Lovely saline and mineral flavours, tannin framework and balance on the palate. Personality.
Price approx.: 23,00 EUR
http://www.felsina.it
Fèlsina
+390577355117

TENUTA LUCE DELLA VITE 96/100

CONV▼🍷 Luce 2010 : Intense garnet with crimson tints. Very compelling, pure nose of red fruits enhanced with delicate liquorice, menthol and spice-infused oak. Amazingly full, mellow and fresh palate. Dense yet polished, full and fresh. Remarkable!
Price approx.: 90,00 EUR
http://www.lucedellavite.com
Tenuta Luce della Vite

JACOPO BIONDI SANTI CASTELLO DI MONTEPO 93/100

▼🍷 Schidione 2004 : Intense ruby. Profound nose driven by blackberry and cassis notes, charred aromas of milk chocolate and cinnamon and a balsamic touch of sandalwood. Austere yet supple palate. Noble, tightly-wound tannin framework. Long, fruity and mineral finish.
Price approx.: 90,00 EUR
http://www.biondisantimontepo.com
Biondi Santi - Castello di Montepo
+390577848238

CASTELLO DEL TERRICCIO 92/100

▼🍷 Tassinaia 2008 : Ruby with garnet tints. Nose of jammy berry fruits and Mediterranean berries (juniper, myrtle) with balsamic, spice and mineral notes of graphite. Intense palate with tightly-wound, velvety tannins. Fresh, mineral mid-palate. Long almond-driven finish.
Price approx.: 13,00 EUR
http://www.terriccio.it
Castello del Terriccio
+39050699709

IL MOLINO DI GRACE 91/100

CONV▼🍷 Gratius 2009 : Ruby with garnet tints. The nose reveals powerful notes of cherry, including morello, forest fruits and red flowers, followed by liquorice, graphite and rhubarb. The palate is fresh, delicious and supported by tightly-wound tannins and lovely exuberance.
Price approx.: 15,50 EUR
http://www.ilmolinodigrace.it
Il Molino di Grace
+390558561010

TENUTA LUCE DELLA VITE 91/100

CONV▼🍷 Lucente 2011 : Intense hue with crimson highlights. Profound nose intermixing red and black fruits, stone fruits and mild spice notes with subtle oak. Warm, full palate with mellow, polished tannins. A successful wine.
Price approx.: 30,00 EUR
http://www.lucedellavite.com
Tenuta Luce della Vite

CECCHI 90/100

▼🍷 Coevo 2010 : Intense ruby. Refined, persistent nose showing mild spices entwined with balsamic and liquorice notes. Concentrated palate revealing elegant oak notes and melted tannins. Beautiful acidity imparting ageability.
Price approx.: 25,00 EUR
http://www.cecchi.net
Cecchi
+39057754311

DEI DI MARIA CATERINA DEI 90/100

▼🍷 Sancta Catharina 2010 : Ruby with crimson nuances. Complex, mellow bouquet exhuding scents of cassis, liquorice, dark chocolate, wilted violet and graphite. Fleshy, supple palate with incisive yet velvety tannins and a fruit and spice-driven finish.
Price approx.: 15,00 EUR
http://www.cantinedei.com
Dei di Maria Caterina Dei
+390578716878

FATTORIA DIANELLA 90/100

▼🍷 Il Matto delle Giuncaie 2012 : Brilliant ruby. Refined fruit on the nose with a touch of liquorice. Fresh, savoury and harmonious palate. A simple yet not at all run of the mill wine, drinking extremely well.
Price approx.: 18,00 EUR
http://villadianella.it
Fattoria Dianella
+390571508166

Detailed instructions are featured at

the start of the book.

FATTORIA LORNANO — 90/100

▼⚑ Commendator Enrico 2009 : Concentrated ruby. Elegant, characterful nose driven by menthol tones, fruit (morello cherry), herb and spice touches. The palate delivers ideal balance between the heat of the alcohol, freshness and the silkiness of the tannins.
Price approx.: 21,00 EUR
http://www.fattorialornano.it
Fattoria Lornano
+390577309059

FERRARI F.LLI LUNELLI — 90/100

Org▼⚑ Aliotto - Tenuta Podernovo 2012 : Vibrant ruby. Expressive nose of morello cherry, cherry, violet and sandalwood leading into balsamic and herb scents. Very savoury palate with an elegant, velvety tannin framework. Supple, fruity and spice-driven finish.
Price approx.: 6,50 EUR
http://www.cantineferrari.it
Ferrari F.lli Lunelli
+39 046 19 72 311

LA CASA DI BRICCIANO — 90/100

Org▼⚑ Rosso Il Ritrovo Biologico 2010 : Deep ruby. Full, mellow nose intermixing blackberry, blueberry, plum, cassis, violet and herbs with racy notes of humus. Elegant, well-structured palate displaying mellow tannins and a supple, spice-driven finish over good length.
Price approx.: 42,70 EUR
http://www.lacasadibricciano.it
La Casa di Bricciano
+390577749297

VILLA MANGIACANE S.R.L. — 90/100

▼⚑ Aleah 2009 : Intense ruby. The nose exudes perfumes of wild blackcurrant, dark chocolate, pepper, rhubarb and chervil notes. Full, warm palate with a tightly-wound, soft tannin framework. Long, fresh finish.
http://www.mangiacane.com
Villa Mangiacane S.r.l.
+390558000000

JACOPO BIONDI SANTI CASTELLO DI MONTEPO — 89/100

▼⚑ Sassoalloro 2010 : Deep garnet. Rich, elegant nose of morello cherry, plum, blueberry, mint, clove then floral notes of herbs with graphite. Noble tannin framework. Fresh, savoury mid-palate. Lemony and mineral finish.
Price approx.: 12,50 EUR
http://www.biondisantimontepo.com
Biondi Santi - Castello di Montepo
+390577848238

IL PONTE — 89/100

▼⚑ Balto 2010 : Dark ruby. Full, elegant and intense nose of rose, cherry, blackberry, eucalyptus, resin and pepper.

Well-structured palate with a tightly-wound, incisive tannin framework, mineral and vegetal notes of the garrigue. Lengthy finish.
Price approx.: 7,50 EUR
http://www.agricolailponte.com
Il Ponte
+3334843966

MEZZODÌ — 88/100

▼⚑ Toscana IGT Bianco 2012 : Straw-yellow. Focused nose of yellow-fleshed fruits like pear and pineapple augmented by an alluring mineral note of gypsum. The palate is fresh yet generous, mellow and balanced by a pleasant fruity sensation. Stands well on its own.
Price approx.: 14,00 EUR
http://www.batzella.com
Batzella S.S.A.
+393393975888

JACOPO BIONDI SANTI CASTELLO DI MONTEPO — 88/100

▼⚑ Braccale Rosso 2011 : Ruby with garnet tints. Expressive nose of quinine root, ink, graphite then violet, plum, morello cherry and menthol-infused tobacco. Harmonious palate with the nose aromas carrying through. Very fresh, persistent and saline. Velvety tannin framework.
Price approx.: 7,00 EUR
http://www.biondisantimontepo.com
Biondi Santi - Castello di Montepo
+390577848238

IL MOLINO DI GRACE — 88/100

CONV▼⚑ Il Volano 2011 : Brilliant ruby. Extremely broad-ranging spectrum of aromas on the nose with notes of cherry, rose petal, leather, mild spices and graphite. The palate is very fresh and consistent with the nose, enhanced by velvety tannins. Long, almond-driven finish.
Price approx.: 3,35 EUR
http://www.ilmolinodigrace.it
Il Molino di Grace
+390558561010

LA CASA DI BRICCIANO — 88/100

Org▼⚑ Sangiovese Biologico 2010 : Vibrant ruby. Rich, balsamic nose opening up to blackberry, redcurrant, cherry jam, rose petal, milk chocolate and liquorice. Heat and softness are impeccably balanced on the palate. Fine-grained tannin framework and a long finish.
Price approx.: 32,03 EUR
http://www.lacasadibricciano.it
La Casa di Bricciano
+390577749297

RUFFINO — 88/100

▼⚑ Modus 2011 : Brilliant ruby. Terroir-driven nose revealing notes of graphite, violet, morello cherry, black forest fruits, touches of tobacco and pepper. Succulent, savoury palate with tightly-wound yet round tannins. A hint of roasted coffee on the finish.

Price approx.: 15,00 EUR

http://www.ruffino.it

Ruffino

+3905583605

SOCIETA AGRICOLA TERZONA SRL   88/100

CV Eco▼. Tespero 2011 : Deep ruby. Complex nose intermixing ripe cassis and blueberry with a balsamic touch of resin and eucalyptus and more austere notes of quinine and rhubarb, plus a dash of black pepper. Fleshy, persistent and fresh palate with elegant tannins.

Price approx.: 14,00 EUR

http://www.carusvini.it

Societa Agricola Terzona SRL

TUSCANY LUXURY   87/100

▼. Dè Ré 2011 : Garnet. Intense nose of red fruits in brandy with pleasant spice and tobacco notes. The palate displays a degree of austerity revealing oak influence. Its intensity and persistence make it suitable for meats in a sauce.

Price approx.: 20,00 EUR

http://www.tuscanyluxury.it

Tuscany Luxury

+39335464848

VAL DELLE ROSE VERMENTINO   86/100

▼. Litorale 2012 : Straw-yellow with green tints. Young nose dominated by white flower perfumes. The palate shows a seductive mineral character and good level of acidity. An instantly approachable wine showing at its best in the summer.

Price approx.: 5,00 EUR

http://www.cecchi.net

Cecchi

+39057754311

BICOCCHI FRANCESCA AZ. AGR.   85/100

Org▼. Cardaelis Alicante Alicante 2012 : Ruby-red. Complex nose intermixing floral notes of musk rose with blackcurrant, raspberry and coffee. Fresh and expressive on the palate boasting good persistency. Drink as a summer wine with simple cheese or meat-based dishes.

Price approx.: 8,30 EUR

http://www.bicocchiwine.it

Bicocchi Francesca Az. agr.

+390566919162

I BALZINI   84/100

▼. White Label 2009 : Ruby-red with an intense nose of forest fruits, fig and mild spices. A round, fairly fresh and intense wine on the palate with elegant tannins. Tobacco notes and a mineral touch are accompanied by good

acidity. Ideal for red meats and cheeses.

Price approx.: 30,00 EUR

http://www.ibalzini.it

I Balzini

+558075503

VILLA MANGIACANE S.R.L.   84/100

▼. Shamiso 2013 : Brilliant cherry-pink. The nose is fresh and shows crunchy fruit notes of wild strawberry and ripe cherry flowing into balsamic and mineral scents. Dynamic, juicy palate coupled with very fresh, vibrant acidity. Savoury finish.

http://www.mangiacane.com

Villa Mangiacane S.r.l.

+390558000000

I BALZINI   82/100

▼. Red Label 2011 : Impenetrable ruby-red. Delightful nose with aromas of ripe forest fruits, raspberry and blueberry with a faint spice note. More austerity and a degree of persistency on the palate with subtle saline notes. Serve with meats cooked rare.

Price approx.: 18,00 EUR

http://www.ibalzini.it

I Balzini

+558075503

VERNACCIA DI SAN GIMIGNANO D.O.C.G

CASTELLO MONTAUTO VERNACCIA DI SAN GIMIGNANO   86/100

▼. Castello Montauto 2012 : Limpid straw-yellow. Instantly accessible nose blending white flowers and fresh fruits (predominant apple notes) layered over pleasant mineral undertones. Fresh, round palate that stays fairly backward in terms of aromatics.

Price approx.: 5,20 EUR

http://www.cecchi.net

Cecchi

+39057754311

VINO NOBILE DE MONTEPULCIANO D.O.C.G

DEI DI MARIA CATERINA DEI   94/100

▼. Vino Nobile di Montepulciano Riserva Bossona 2009 : Brilliant ruby. Full, harmonious nose displaying red berry fruit jam, a medley of flowers and fern, quinine root, leather and nutmeg. Fresh, savoury and warm palate revealing massive tannins that are refined yet still impetuous.

Price approx.: 18,00 EUR

http://www.cantinedei.com

Dei di Maria Caterina Dei

+390578716878

FATTORIA DI PALAZZO VECCHIO 93/100

Eco▼♪ Terrarossa 2009 : Brilliant ruby. The nose combines aromas of violet, morello cherry, pepper and graphite with balsamic notes of garrigue, undergrowth, humus and bark. Full, lush palate with a velvety tannin framework and savoury exuberance. Long almond-driven finish.
Price approx.: 16,00 EUR
http://www.vinonobile.it
Fattoria di Palazzo Vecchio
+390578724170

AZ AG LE BERTILLE 92/100

▼♪ Riserva 2008 : Ruby. Complex nose suggestive of blackberry, Mediterranean maquis, a touch of liquorice, herbs and balsamic vinegar. The palate combines elegance and power. A full, round and well-balanced style that is very fresh and long-lasting.
Price approx.: 10,00 EUR
http://www.lebertille.com
Az Ag Le Bertille
+390578758330

DEI DI MARIA CATERINA DEI 92/100

▼♪ Vino Nobile di Montepulciano 2011 : Ruby. Endearing, elegant nose of chocolate, cherries in brandy, Indian ink, incense, violet and menthol-infused tobacco. Crunchy, full, delicious and fresh palate with evident tannins. Long, almond-driven finish.
Price approx.: 10,00 EUR
http://www.cantinedei.com
Dei di Maria Caterina Dei
+390578716878

FATTORIA DI PALAZZO VECCHIO 91/100

Eco▼♪ Maestro 2011 : Intense ruby. Remarkable, highly expressive, harmonious nose of cherry, black pepper, liquorice, humus, bark and quinine root. Well-structured palate, high in tannins, mellowed by sustained warmth. Long, spice infused finish.
Price approx.: 9,40 EUR
http://www.vinonobile.it
Fattoria di Palazzo Vecchio
+390578724170

AZ AG LE BERTILLE 90/100

▼♪ 2010 : Expressive, harmonious nose intermixing notes of cherry, plum jam, forest fruits, graphite, liquorice, tobacco, leather and violet. Warm, well-structured palate boasting good acidity and tannins that are still slightly severe. Lovely length.
Price approx.: 8,00 EUR
http://www.lebertille.com
Az Ag Le Bertille
+390578758330

VILLA S. ANNA 90/100

Eco▼♪ 2010 : Ruby with garnet highlights. Nose of morello cherry, violet and Indian ink with distinguished notes of menthol-infused tobacco, graphite and faint tar accents. Rich, tense palate, still evolving and boasting a firm tannin framework.
http://www.villasantanna.it
Villa S. Anna
+578708017

VILLA S. ANNA 90/100

Eco▼♪ Poldo 2007 : Powerful nose of blackberry, juniper, talc, wilted violet and notes of chocolate and medicinal herbs. Characterful, powerful and invigorating palate enhanced by a robust yet elegant tannin framework. Pleasant contrast between flavour and alcohol.
http://www.villasantanna.it
Villa S. Anna
+578708017

UMBRIA

COLLI MARTANI D.O.C

TERRE DE LA CUSTODIA 90/100

Eco▼♪ Gladius Spumante Metodo Classico 2009 : Straw-yellow showing good intensity with fine, persistent and active bubbles. Harmonious nose intermixing floral notes of linden and acacia with sweet almond aromas and a mineral touch. The palate is very fresh, lush, well-balanced and persistent.
http://www.terredelacustodia.it
Terre De La Custodia
+742929529

ARNALDO CAPRAI 88/100

Eco▼♪ Grechetto Grecante 2013 : Straw-yellow, green tints. Delicate, fine and harmonious nose showing honest expression driven by fruity notes of green apple, blackberry, citrus, grapefruit and a touch of sage. The palate is fresh, focused and enjoyable. Mild attack, saline finish.
Price approx.: 10,00 EUR
http://arnaldocaprai.it
Arnaldo Caprai
+390742378802

TERRE DE LA CUSTODIA 87/100

Eco▼♪ Grechetto 2013 : Brilliant straw-yellow with green tints. Distinctive, pleasant nose alternately revealing perfumes of medlar, sage and tomato leaf. On the palate, a fresh, fruity style, moderately powerful and capped off with a touch of almond.
http://www.terredelacustodia.it
Terre De La Custodia
+742929529

TERRE DE LA CUSTODIA   85/100

Eco▼𝄞 Alissa (Senza solfiti aggiunti) 2013 : Brilliant straw-yellow. Refined, young and pleasurable nose of grapefruit and lemon, pineapple, sage and verbena. Very fresh, polished palate combining beautiful acidity with a sourness that is attractive in this context. Persistent saline note on the finish.

http://www.terredelacustodia.it
Terre De La Custodia
+742929529

MONTEFALCO D.O.C.

AZIENDA AGRARIA SCACCIADIAVOLI   92/100

Eco▼𝄞 Rosso 2011 : Ruby-hued. Harmonious nose revealing fruity aromas of plum and cherry with peony, a spicy touch of pink peppercorn and tobacco. Abundant freshness on the palate combined with upfront yet mellow, velvety tannins. Good persistency.

Price approx.: 6,50 EUR
http://www.scacciadiavoli.it
Azienda Agraria Scacciadiavoli
+390742371210

FERRARI F.LLI LUNELLI   92/100

CONV▼𝄞 Rosso Riserva Lampante - Tenuta Castelbuono 2009 : Brilliant ruby. Lush bouquet that is vegetal with herbs such as thyme and marjoram, floral and fruity with cherries, including morello cherry, and plums, with damson. Fresh, juicy palate with elegant tannins and a lengthy almond-driven finish.

Price approx.: 12,00 EUR
http://www.cantineferrari.it/
Ferrari F.lli Lunelli
+39 046 19 72 311

ARNALDO CAPRAI   91/100

Eco▼𝄞 Rosso 2012 : Ruby-hued. Refined, harmonious nose revealing fragrances of blackberry, juniper berries, liquorice and spice. The palate is seductively crunchy and fresh with a tightly-wound, fine and silky tannin framework. Power and mellowness balance the whole.

Price approx.: 11,00 EUR
http://arnaldocaprai.it
Arnaldo Caprai
+390742378802

TERRE DE LA CUSTODIA   91/100

Eco▼𝄞 Rosso 2011 : Ruby with garnet nuances. Expressive nose recalling ripe plum and sun-dried tomato enhanced by a touch of wild fennel and myrtle imparting freshness. The palate is fresh and delicious with dense yet fine-grained tannins. Long, cocoa-driven finish.

http://www.terredelacustodia.it
Terre De La Custodia
+742929529

AZIENDA AGRARIA SCACCIADIAVOLI   90/100

Eco▼𝄞 Bianco 2012 : Straw-yellow. Expressive nose with balsamic and vegetal accents typical of the Grechetto varietal, bolstered by more complex toast notes from the oak-fermented Chardonnay and the lees-fermented Trebbiano. Structured, mouth-coating and persistent palate.

Price approx.: 7,00 EUR
http://www.scacciadiavoli.it
Azienda Agraria Scacciadiavoli
+390742371210

CANTINE BRIZIARELLI   90/100

▼𝄞 Rosso Mattone 2010 : Ruby-hued. Highly expressive nose recalling blackberry, liquorice and undergrowth with cinnamon and black pepper in the background. Rich, fleshy palate with mild, tightly-wound tannins. Good balance between heat and acidity showcases the whole.

Price approx.: 7,90 EUR
http://www.cantinebriziarelli.it
Cantine Briziarelli
+75602784

PERTICAIA   89/100

Eco▼𝄞 Rosso 2011 : Brilliant, deep ruby. The nose shows cherry perfumes with a spicy touch of nutmeg and black pepper. Refined, harmonious bouquet. Good freshness on the palate, mouth-caressing tannins and sustained alcoholic warmth. Good persistency.

Price approx.: 6,50 EUR
http://www.perticaia.it
Az Ag Perticaia
390742379014

CANTINA COLLE CIOCCO - AGRICOLA
SPACCHETTI SS   87/100

Eco▼𝄞 Rosso 2010 : Deep ruby. Pronounced aromas of undergrowth, mild spices (cinnamon, clove) and ripe fruits (blueberry jam) on the nose. The palate is tannic and lively yet mild with good aromatic persistency, mirroring the nose.

Price approx.: 9,00 EUR
http://www.colleciocco.it
Cantina Colle Ciocco - Agricola Spacchetti SS
390742379859

CANTINE BRIZIARELLI   85/100

▼𝄞 Rosso 2010 : Glimmering ruby. Floral and fruity tones on the nose enhanced by mild aromas of spice. The palate is well-balanced and offers up a pleasurable sensation with refined, velvety tannins and savoury balance of fat and exuberance.

Price approx.: 4,60 EUR
http://www.cantinebriziarelli.it
Cantine Briziarelli
+75602784

MONTEFALCO SAGRANTINO D.O.C.G

ARNALDO CAPRAI 95/100

Eco▼ 🖋 25 Anni 2010 : Deeply-coloured ruby. Powerful, complex nose intermixing spice, cloves, white pepper, mint-flavoured chocolate and cinnamon, backed by cherry jam. Mellow, mouth-coating, fresh palate with velvety tannins. Long finish revealing tobacco accents.

Price approx.: 55,00 EUR

http://arnaldocaprai.it

Arnaldo Caprai

+390742378802

TERRE DE LA CUSTODIA · 95/100

Eco▼ 🖋 Exubera 2004 : Ruby with garnet highlights. Beautiful perfumes of cherry jam, prune, leather notes and dried mushrooms. Elegant, silky and harmonious palate that lingers. A wine at its peak that will still keep.

http://www.terredelacustodia.it

Terre De La Custodia

+742929529

AZIENDA AGRARIA SCACCIADIAVOLI 94/100

Eco▼ 🖋 2009 : Intense ruby. Ripe red fruits, refined spice, toast, vanilla and chocoate notes, pipe tobacco and mineral, graphite undertones envelop the nose. The palate shows dense, upfront tannins, a warm style and good acidity. Long, spicy finish.

Price approx.: 12,90 EUR

http://www.scacciadiavoli.it

Azienda Agraria Scacciadiavoli

+390742371210

TERRE DE LA CUSTODIA 94/100

Eco▼ 🖋 2009 : Ruby-garnet. The nose opens up to intense morello cherry jam, tobacco, anise and chocolate aromas. The palate is elegant and harmonious with tightly-wound, elegant tannins. True nectar, successfully reconciling the demands of tradition with modern-day styles.

http://www.terredelacustodia.it

Terre De La Custodia

+742929529

ARNALDO CAPRAI 93/100

Eco▼ 🖋 Collepiano 2008 : Brilliant ruby with garnet highlights. Endearing nose intermixing cassis and blackberry with cherry, augmented by a trace of cinnamon and a touch of mint. Well-structured, full and warm palate with supple tannins.

Price approx.: 27,00 EUR

http://arnaldocaprai.it

Arnaldo Caprai

+390742378802

PERTICAIA 93/100

Eco▼ 🖋 2010 : Deep ruby. Full, refined nose showing floral notes of rose, fruity aromas of strawberry jam, balsamic tones of sandalwood and juniper berries. Very fresh palate with vibrant tannins still in their youth and savoury, warm accents.

Price approx.: 13,90 EUR

http://www.perticaia.it

Az Ag Perticaia

+390742379014

FERRARI F.LLI LUNELLI 93/100

CONV▼ 🖋 Carapace - Tenuta Castelbuono 2009 : Deep ruby. Full, fruity nose of cherries in brandy and blackberry with spice (cloves, cinnamon, nutmeg) and vegetal notes (carob), eucalyptus and rose. Dense, powerful yet succulent and mild tannins. Fruity and chocolatey finish.

Price approx.: 15,70 EUR

http://www.cantineferrari.it/

Ferrari F.lli Lunelli

+39 046 19 72 311

ARNALDO CAPRAI 92/100

Eco▼ 🖋 Collepiano 2010 : Intense ruby. Elegant, expressive nose blending strong red fruit notes with a touch of spice and balsamic vinegar. On the palate, a generous yet fresh and well-balanced style with dense tannins. Good persistency on the finish.

Price approx.: 27,00 EUR

http://arnaldocaprai.it

Arnaldo Caprai

+390742378802

TERRE DE LA CUSTODIA 92/100

Eco✳ 🖋 Passito Melanto 2009 : Intense ruby. Full, well-balanced nose melding black cherry jam with cassis, vegetal notes of liquorice, rhubarb and roasted cocoa. Harmonious on the palate, with impeccably balanced acidity, sweetness, power and velvety tannins.

http://www.terredelacustodia.it

Terre De La Custodia

+742929529

CANTINA COLLE CIOCCO - AGRICOLA SPACCHETTI SS 90/100

Eco▼ 🖋 2008 : Ruby-garnet. A fairly broad-ranging spectrum of harmonioius nose aromatics with notes of violet, liquorice, mocha and cigar box. Abundant freshness with tightly-wound yet soft tannins caressing the palate. Long plummy finish.

Price approx.: 20,00 EUR

http://www.colleciocco.it

Cantina Colle Ciocco - Agricola Spacchetti SS

+390742379859

TENUTA ALZATURA MONTEFALCO SAGRANTINO 89/100

▼⌁ Uno di dodici 2009 : Garnet hue. Intense, complex nose mingling red fruits in brandy with elegant oak notes and a balsamic touch. Fresh, racy, fruity palate with upfront tannins. More bottle age would be a definite bonus.
Price approx.: 12,80 EUR
http://www.cecchi.net
Cecchi
+39057754311

FERRARI F.LLI LUNELLI 88/100

CONV✳ ⌁ Passito - Tenuta Castelbuono 2010 : Dark ruby. Endearing nose of cassis, prune and chocolate flowing into more vegetal tones of heather, root, liquorice and rhubarb. The tannins are incisive yet restrained. A wine offering balanced sweetness and acidity. Very fresh.
Price approx.: 15,70 EUR
http://www.cantineferrari.it/
Ferrari F.lli Lunelli
+39 046 19 72 311

CANTINE BRIZIARELLI 87/100

▼⌁ Vitruvio 2008 : Bright ruby. Rich, expressive nose suggestive of ripe cherry, incense, cinnamon, milk chocolate and balsamic notes. Invigorating freshness and elegant, vibrant tannins form a lovely structure supported by warmer undertones.
Price approx.: 19,00 EUR
http://www.cantinebriziarelli.it
Cantine Briziarelli
+75602784

CANTINA COLLE CIOCCO - AGRICOLA SPACCHETTI SS 86/100

Eco▼⌁ Passito 2009 : Produced from grapes dried on straw mats for 3 months then fermented in steel tanks and aged in oak casks, the wine exudes exuberant perfumes of black cherries in syrup, raspberry jam and tobacco. Good balance of sweetness and acidity. Very fresh.
Price approx.: 25,00 EUR
http://www.colleciocco.it
Cantina Colle Ciocco - Agricola Spacchetti SS
+390742379859

UMBRIA I.G.T.

CANTINA COLLE CIOCCO - AGRICOLA SPACCHETTI SS 88/100

Eco▼⌁ Bianco Tempestivo 2012 : Fairly intense straw-yellow. Expressive nose releasing harmonious aromas of peach, mango and plum nicely entwined with characteristic varietal herb aromas. The palate shows a blend of freshness,

a mineral and saline sensation and a savoury fruity finish.
Price approx.: 8,00 EUR
http://www.colleciocco.it
Cantina Colle Ciocco - Agricola Spacchetti SS
+390742379859

PERTICAIA 87/100

Eco▼⌁ Trebbiano Spoletino 2013 : Intense straw-yellow, golden tints. Fresh, fruity nose of apple, lychee and grapefruit with floral aromas of hawthorn and typical varietal notes of sage. Judicious trace of acidity on the palate. Very flavourful, framed by good, supple fleshiness. Clean finish.
Price approx.: 5,50 EUR
http://www.perticaia.it
Az Ag Perticaia
+390742379014

AZIENDA AGRARIA SCACCIADIAVOLI 87/100

Eco▼⌁ Bianco Grechetto dell'Umbria 2013 : Bright straw-yellow with green tints. Refined, harmonious and fruity nose recalling pear and loquat, enhanced with elegant mineral notes. The palate is taut, lively and saline, supported by beautiful acidity and leading into a lovely citrus-driven finish.
Price approx.: 4,20 EUR
http://www.scacciadiavoli.it
Azienda Agraria Scacciadiavoli
+390742371210

CANTINA COLLE CIOCCO - AGRICOLA SPACCHETTI SS 85/100

Eco▼⌁ Bianco Clarignano 2013 : Straw-yellow. The nose reveals floral and fruity sensations of pineapple and papaya with herbs including marjoram. The palate is focused and offers up a lovely blend of warmth and a crisp mineral dimension.
Price approx.: 8,00 EUR
http://www.colleciocco.it
Cantina Colle Ciocco - Agricola Spacchetti SS
+390742379859

VENETIAN

BISOL DESIDERIO & FIGLI 92/100

▼⌁ VSQ Talento Metodo Classico Pas Dosé Millesimato 2002 : Brilliant gold. Refined nose with a whiff of smoke and notes of acacia honey, dried fruits and crema catalana. Velvety, silky, mellow palate that is fresh and savoury. Long finish revealing more of the nose aromatics.
Price approx.: 18,30 EUR
http://www.bisol.it
Bisol Desiderio & Figli
+390423900138

LE VIGNE DI ALICE 90/100

▼🍷 Angelo Metodo Classico Pas Dosé 2009 : Intense straw-yellow with golden tints. Intense, elegant nose with strong mineral aromas of gunflint, chalk and burnt oak. The palate is slightly austere yet savoury and fresh with dried fruit and mineral aromas. Long finish driven by Havana cigar flavours.

Price approx.: 9,90 EUR

http://www.levignedialice.it

Le Vigne di Alice

+390438920818

AZIENDA AGRICOLA CONTE COLLALTO 87/100

▼🍷 Rosso Vinciguerra 2008 : Deep ruby. Expressive nose with aromas of kirsch and dark chocolate - a lovely duo of fruit and roasted coffee aromas. Very fine, tightly-wound tannins make for a savoury wine with accents of ink and violet. Long finish recalling quinine root.

Price approx.: 10,50 EUR

http://www.cantine-collalto.it

Azienda Agricola Conte Collalto

+390438738241

BISOL DESIDERIO & FIGLI 86/100

▼🍷 VSQ Relio Metodo Classico Extra Brut 2009 : Brilliant straw-yellow. Very expressive nose of bread, toasted almond, hazelnut, yellow flowers and nougat. Pleasant, classic bouquet true to the appellation. Abundant mousse, clean, fresh and savoury palate. Good persistency.

Price approx.: 19,95 EUR

http://www.bisol.it

Bisol Desiderio & Figli

+390423900138

TENUTE TOMASELLA 86/100

▼🍷 Rigole Brut 2012 : Straw-yellow with a fine, persistent mousse. Intense bouquet of flowers and white fruits with predominant apple and pear aromas and pleasant vanilla and butter notes. Lovely persistency on the palate. Ideal as an aperitif.

http://www.tenute-tomasella.it

Tenute Tomasella

+39 042 28 50 043

SOCIETÀ AGRICOLA CA' DI RAJO 85/100

▼🍷 Epsilon Pink 2013 : Pink with cherry tints and fine bubbles. Floral nose recalling rose. The palate is fairly persistent and places emphasis on vinosity and red fruits, ending on a sweet note. Drink as an appetiser.

Price approx.: 8,80 EUR

http://www.cadirajo.it

Società Agricola Ca' di Rajo

+390422855885

SOCIETÀ AGRICOLA CA' DI RAJO 85/100

▼🍷 Epsilon Gold 2012 : Intense straw-yellow with persistent bubbles. Fruity nose showing precise notes of fresh tropical fruits. Bone dry and fairly persistent, leaving the palate clean. Ideal as an appetiser.

Price approx.: 8,60 EUR

http://www.cadirajo.it

Società Agricola Ca' di Rajo

+390422855885

SOCIETÀ AGRICOLA VIGNALTA 85/100

▼🍷 Brut Nature : Brilliant straw-yellow with fine, persistent bubbles. Refined nose recalling yeast and crusty bread. Focused, fresh palate with well-integrated acidity and a whiff of bitter almond. Ideal as an aperitif or with cold meats.

Price approx.: 23,00 EUR

http://www.vignalta.it

Società Agricola Vignalta

+390429777305

AZIENDA AGRICOLA CONTE COLLALTO 83/100

▼🍷 VSQ Manzoni Moscato Rosé Extra Dry 0 : Coppery colour with onion skin highlights. The nose shows bulb flowers (hyacinth), gunflint, wild strawberries and cherry. Honest, supple and endearing. The palate is very creamy, quite savoury and fresh. Medium-length finish tinged with a little bitterness.

Price approx.: 5,50 EUR

http://www.cantine-collalto.it

Azienda Agricola Conte Collalto

+390438738241

AZIENDA AGRICOLA DRUSIAN FRANCESCO 82/100

▼🍷 VS Rosé Mari Extra Dry 0 : Coral hue with brilliant coppery highlights. Persistent mousse. Mineral, harmonious and quite refined nose showing medium fullness and aromas of chalk, wheat flour, pomegranate and raspberry. Creamy, savoury and fresh palate. Slightly bitter finish.

Price approx.: 7,50 EUR

http://www.drusian.it

Azienda Agricola Drusian Francesco

+390423982151

LA TORDERA AZIENDA AGRICOLA 80/100

Eco▼🍷 VS Gabry Rosé Extra Dry 2013 : Brilliant coral hue with onion skin highlights. Expressive, mellow nose with aromas of wild strawberries, raspberry, redcurrant and fruit tart. Fairly savoury, round, creamy attack on the palate. Medium length and freshness.

Price approx.: 5,20 EUR

http://www.latordera.it/

La Tordera Azienda Agricola

+39 042 39 85 362

AZIENDA AGRICOLA ALTHEA DI DRUSIAN
MARIKA 77/100

▼♪ VS Rosato Extra Dry 0 : Intense, brilliant coppery hue with coral highlights. Unusual nose of wild strawberry, bark, sap, undergrowth, chalk and redcurrant. The palate disappoints after the nose: it is linear, free-flowing and short. Bitter finish.
Price approx.: 6,20 EUR
http:// www.agriturismoalthea.it
Azienda Agricola Althea di Drusian Marika
+390438560511

AMARONE DELLA VALPOLICELLA D.O.C.G

CA' BOTTA 84/100

▼♪ Tenuta Cajò 2010 : Opaque ruby. Intense nose of liquorice, immediately delivering a warm character with toasted oak aromas. Generous, powerful palate with strong scents of oak and black pepper. A characterful wine pairing with red meats.
Price approx.: 50,00 EUR
http://www.cabotta.it
Ca' Botta
+39045982875

AMARONE VALPOLICELLA CLASSICO D.O.C.

RISERVA LE ORIGINI 91/100

▼♪ Riserva Le Origini 2008 : Refined, expressive nose showing fruity notes of morello cherry, plum, spicy nutmeg and mineral aromas of graphite and even a touch of liquorice and cocoa. Mineral, warm, round, fat and silky palate. Long finish driven by balsamic nuances.
Price approx.: 44,00 EUR
http://www.bolla.it
Bolla S.p.A
+39 045 683 65 55

COLLI EUGANEI D.O.C

SOCIETÀ AGRICOLA VIGNALTA 84/100

▼♪ Gemola 2009 : Intense, almost impenetrable ruby. Balsamic and spicy nose rounded off with notes of red fruits in brandy and an oak dimension. Fairly persistent palate showing a peppery, spicy character and refined tannins. Ideal for meat.
Price approx.: 27,00 EUR
http://www.vignalta.it
Società Agricola Vignalta
390429777305

SOCIETÀ AGRICOLA VIGNALTA 82/100

▼♪ Sirio Moscato Secco 2013 : Pale straw-yellow. Mineral and vegetal nose opening up to a broader array of aromatics after swirling. Expressive, persistent palate driven by upfront acidity. Ideal with shellfish, oily fish or, alternatively, as an aperitif.
Price approx.: 9,50 EUR
http://www.vignalta.it
Società Agricola Vignalta
390429777305

COLLI EUGANEI FIOR D'ARANCIO D.O.C.G.

SOCIETÀ AGRICOLA VIGNALTA 87/100

▼♪ Alpianae Passito 2011 : Golden yellow. Expressive nose of orange blossom, peach, apricots in syrup and honey. Warm, persistent palate boasting beautiful acidity followed by compelling scents of apricot and honey. Perfect at the end of a meal with shortcrust pastries or on its own.
Price approx.: 18,90 EUR
http://www.vignalta.it
Società Agricola Vignalta
390429777305

SOCIETÀ AGRICOLA VIGNALTA 85/100

▼♪ Spumante Fior d'Arancio 2013 : Pale straw-yellow. Fine bubbles. Aromas of orange blossom, apricots in syrup and honey pervade the nose. The palate shows sweetness and beautiful acidity with more of the apricot jam, honey and toasted almond. Serve as a pudding wine.
Price approx.: 10,00 EUR
http://www.vignalta.it
Società Agricola Vignalta
390429777305

CONEGLIANO VALDOBBIADENE D.O.C.G. PROSECCO SUPERIORE

BELLENDA 90/100

▼♪ Extra Dry Miraval Millesimato 2013 : A truly memorable Prosecco! Extremely classic, refined and harmonious nose showing notes of fresh wheat flour, white peach, sage and green apple. The palate is fresh, lemony, savoury and full. Enjoyable long, clean finish driven by almond aromas.
Price approx.: 6,80 EUR
http://www.bellenda.it
Bellenda
390438920025

RUGGERI 90/100

▼✔ Vecchie Viti Brut 2013 : Brilliant straw-yellow, green tints. Very refined, polished nose showing notes of fresh wheat flour, almond, hazelnut and white flowers. Very robust, mineral and dry palate that is substantial, mellow and persistent. Floral and fruity finish driven by peach.
Price approx.: 12,00 EUR
http://www.ruggeri.it
Ruggeri & C. S.p.A.
3904239092

AZIENDA AGRICOLA DRUSIAN FRANCESCO
89/100

▼✔ Extra Dry 0 : Brilliant straw-yellow with green tints. Full, endearing nose driven by aromas of white peach, hawthorn, gooseberry and sugared almonds. The palate is creamy, fresh, very savoury and harmonious, offering up volume. Focused, persistent finish.
Price approx.: 6,60 EUR
http://www.drusian.it
Azienda Agricola Drusian Francesco
390423982151

BISOL DESIDERIO & FIGLI 89/100

▼✔ Extra Dry Vigneti del Fol 2013 : Beautiful mousse. The nose shows a full bouquet with idiosyncratic aromas of boiled sweets, wild strawberries and yellow flowers. The palate is mineral and mellow, displaying volume and beautiful freshness. Very persistent, focused finish.
Price approx.: 11,90 EUR
http://www.bisol.it
Bisol Desiderio & Figli
390423900138

TENUTA COL SANDAGO 89/100

▼✔ 11» Undici Dry» 2013 : Attractive, brilliant straw-yellow with green tints. Intense, refined, harmonious and full nose exuding aromas of peach, yellow flowers and mineral notes. Creamy, robust, very fresh and savoury palate. Long, supple finish of citrus and almond.
Price approx.: 7,00 EUR
http://www.casebianche.it
Case Bianche Srl
39043864468

LA TORDERA AZIENDA AGRICOLA 89/100

Eco▼✔ Brunei Brut 2013 : Fine bubbles and a brilliant straw-yellow hue with green tints intimate at a charming nose with scents of chalk, fresh almond and wheat flour. Tense, savoury and fresh palate that is mineral-driven, austere, long and focused.
Price approx.: 6,20 EUR
http://www.latordera.it/
La Tordera Azienda Agricola
+39 042 39 85 362

VAL D'OCA S.R.L. 89/100

▼✔ Rive di Colbertaldo Extra Dry 2013 : Straw-yellow with green tints. Lovely classic nose blending mineral notes of gypsum with white flowers, fresh almond and yellow apple. Very creamy, robust and fairly supple palate that is fresh, savoury and persistent.
http://www.valdoca.com/
Val d'Oca s.r.l.
390423982070

AZIENDA AGRICOLA ANDREOLA 88/100

▼✔ 6° Senso Dry 2013 : Brilliant straw-yellow, green tints. Simple, yet harmonious, unusual and endearing nose showing notes of chalk, yellow butter, white flowers and peach. Consistent, supple and well-balanced palate that is savoury and mineral-driven. Persistent apple notes.
Price approx.: 7,30 EUR
http://www.andreola.eu
Azienda Agricola Andreola
39438989379

AZIENDA AGRICOLA BORTOLIN ANGELO 88/100

▼✔ Extra Dry 2013 : Straw-yellow with green tints. Elegant, refined and very harmonious nose where white flowers and gysum notes flow into wheat flower and white peach. Very creamy, well-balanced palate. Refined, focused and savoury lemony aromatics mark the finish.
Price approx.: 6,70 EUR
http://www.bortolinangelo.com/
Azienda Agricola Bortolin Angelo
390423900125

AZIENDA AGRICOLA BORTOLIN ANGELO 88/100

▼✔ Brut 2013 : Superbe straw-yellow. Very mineral-driven (gypsum, gunflint) complex nose showing acacia blossom and broom with a touch of fruit salad. Tense, focused and mineral palate that is austere, lemony, savoury and sharp. Still in its youth.
Price approx.: 6,70 EUR
http://www.bortolinangelo.com/
Azienda Agricola Bortolin Angelo
390423900125

AZIENDA AGRICOLA CONTE COLLALTO 88/100

▼✔ Extra Dry 2013 : Fine, persistent mousse. The nose is harmonious and classic, opening up to mineral notes of chalk, then revealing floral aromas of broom and linden with apple and peach. Creamy, rich and fresh palate that is lemony, savoury and focused.
Price approx.: 6,10 EUR
http://www.cantine-collalto.it
Azienda Agricola Conte Collalto
390438738241

BELLENDA 88/100

▼✔ Extra Dry Prima Cuvée 2013 : Brilliant straw-yellow. Persistent mousse. The nose boasts personality with

endearing notes of resin, bark and toasted hazelnut. The palate is slightly austere yet creamy and velvety, flowing into savoury lemon aromatics. Long finish.
Price approx.: 7,90 EUR
http://www.bellenda.it
Bellenda
390438920025

CASE BIANCHE SRL 88/100

▼♪ Vigna del Cuc Brut 2013 : Brilliant hue. The nose is fairly mineral in style, intermixing chalk notes, white flowers and yellow apples. Velvety, fleshy palate showing a classic, varietal character. Savoury, lemon-infused mid-palate. Long finish.
Price approx.: 6,00 EUR
http://www.casebianche.it
Case Bianche Srl
39043864468

LE VIGNE DI ALICE 88/100

▼♪ Alice.G Metodo Classico 2011 : Intense straw-yellow. Refined, elegant nose of acacia honey, chalk, gunflint and white flowers. Creamy, velvety and savoury palate with a clear mineral streak. Very fresh, well-balanced and persistent.
Price approx.: 9,90 EUR
http://www.levignedialice.it
Le Vigne di Alice
390438920818

LE RIVE DI OGLIANO 88/100

Eco▼♪ Rive di Ogliano Extra Dry 2013 : Straw-yellow, green tints. Full, harmonious nose intermixing notes of pineapple, citrus and white flowers with a pleasant touch of anise in the background. Mellow, creamy and fresh palate recalling wheat flour. Persistent finish infused with sweet almond.
Price approx.: 26,00 EUR
http://www.masottina.it
Masottina
390438400775

RUGGERI 88/100

▼♪ Giustino B. Extra Dry 2013 : Straw-yellow tinged with green. Full, supple and fruity bouquet of yellow apple, dried flowers, yellow peach and tropical notes. Mellow, creamy and fresh palate with impeccable dosage. Long lemony finish.
Price approx.: 11,00 EUR
http://www.ruggeri.it
Ruggeri & C. S.p.A.
3904239092

SOCIETÀ AGRICOLA CA' DI RAJO 88/100

▼♪ Cuvee del Fondatore Brut 2013 : Pale yellow. Mineral nose of chalk revealing notes of white flowers and fruits (green apple, pear). On the palate, fruit presence is confirmed and shows intensity with freshness and focus. Ideal as an appetiser.
Price approx.: 7,80 EUR
http://www.cadirajo.it
Società Agricola Ca' di Rajo
390422855885

AZIENDA AGRICOLA MALIBRAN DI FAVREL MAURIZIO 87/100

Eco▼♪ Brut 5 Grammi 2013 : Straw-yellow with green tints. Highly elegant nose exuding aromas of acacia and hawthorn, with lemongrass and sage. The palate is robust, fresh and mineral, bordering on saline, and displays a long, focused finish suffused with lemon.
Price approx.: 7,80 EUR
http://www.malibranvini.it
Az Ag Malibran
438781410

AZIENDA AGRICOLA ANDREOLA 87/100

▼♪ Dry 2013 : Expressive, harmonious and elegant nose driven by notes of chalk, fresh wheat flour, sweet almond, peach and yellow flowers, capped off with a tropical touch. Creamy, clean, fresh and savoury palate. Very supple, persistent finish.
Price approx.: 6,95 EUR
http://www.andreola.eu
Azienda Agricola Andreola
39438989379

AZIENDA AGRICOLA ANDREOLA 87/100

▼♪ Rive di Soligo Mas de Fer Extra Dry 2013 : Persistent mousse. Tense, mineral nose of chalk with fresh wheat flour notes, acacia and hawthorn. The palate is similarly compelling, creamy, well-balanced and fresh. Focused, persistent finish.
Price approx.: 6,15 EUR
http://www.andreola.eu
Azienda Agricola Andreola
39438989379

AZIENDA AGRICOLA CONTE COLLALTO 87/100

▼♪ Brut 2013 : Beautiful brilliant hue. Refined, elegant nose with accents of citrus and broom. The best is revealed on the palate though which is fleshy, savoury and mineral, flowing into an austere mid-palate and a long, focused finish.
Price approx.: 6,10 EUR
http://www.cantine-collalto.it
Azienda Agricola Conte Collalto
390438738241

Detailed instructions are featured at
the start of the book.

CASE BIANCHE SRL   87/100

▼✦ Extra Dry 2013 : Sparkling wine with a brilliant hue. Supple, endearing nose of chalk, bordering on menthol, then opening up to tropical fruits and a touch of banana. The palate is more low-key - creamy, very fresh, savoury and mineral-driven. Very persistent, focused finish.
Price approx.: 6,00 EUR
http://www.casebianche.it
Case Bianche Srl
39043864468

SOCIETÀ AGRICOLA CA' DI RAJO   87/100

▼✦ Prosecco Superiore millesimato extra Dry 2013 : Straw-yellow with a fine, persistent mousse. Fresh, perfumed and fruity nose suggestive of golden delicious apples and peach. The palate stays focused and shows pleasant fruity notes. Ideal for kicking off a meal or with cream-based desserts.
Price approx.: 7,50 EUR
http://www.cadirajo.it
Società Agricola Ca' di Rajo
390422855885

SPAGNOL   87/100

▼✦ Col del Sas Brut 2013 : Brilliant straw-yellow with green tints and persistent bubbles. Rich, ripe, varietal nose showing notes of sage, apple, dried yellow flowers and lime honey. Robust, creamy and savoury palate that is fresh and lemony with an average finish.
Price approx.: 6,80 EUR
http://www.coldelsas.it
Spagnol Col del Sas
423987177

BISOL DESIDERIO & FIGLI   86/100

▼✦ Brut Crede 2013 : Brilliant pale yellow with green tints. The bouquet is fairly subdued, refined and vegetal with saline notes and a touch of fresh almond. Velvety, savoury and fresh palate driven by classic notes of apple and citrus. Fairly good persistency.
Price approx.: 9,85 EUR
http://www.bisol.it
Bisol Desiderio & Figli
390423900138

CARPENE MALVOLTI SPA   86/100

▼✦ 1868 Extra Dry 2013 : Straw-yellow with green tints. Expressive, mineral and saline nose that is supple and blends varietal notes of apple, yellow peach and sage. The same aromatics follow through. The palate is classic, creamy and round. Lemony notes mid-palate and a focused finish.
http://www.carpene-malvolti.com
Carpene Malvolti SpA
390438364611

LE BERTOLE   86/100

▼✦ Brut 2013 : Straw-yellow with a fine mousse. Pleasant nose blending white flowers and white-fleshed fruits (apple, pear). Focused palate showing beautiful acidity and persistent fruity aromas. Ideal as an appetiser.
Price approx.: 6,30 EUR
http://www.lebertole.it
Le Bertole
390423975332

LE VIGNE DI ALICE   86/100

▼✦ Alice Extra Dry 2013 : Bright straw-yellow. Mineral nose with aromas of chalk and a faint toast note followed by vegetal touches of sap, bark and resin. A velvety style, slightly dry for an extra dry. Fairly good freshness and a hint of sourness on the finish.
Price approx.: 6,80 EUR
http://www.levignedialice.it
Le Vigne di Alice
390438920818

CONTRADA GRANDA   86/100

Eco▼✦ Rive di Ogliano Brut 2013 : Pale yellow with green tints. Inviting varietal nose recalling green apple, sage and a mineral dimension. The palate is lush, mellow and harmonious showing a very fresh mid-palate and a savoury tangy, sour note on the finish.
Price approx.: 26,00 EUR
http://www.masottina.it
Masottina
390438400775

SAN GIUSEPPE   86/100

▼✦ Extra Dry Millesimato 2013 : Intense, classic and refined nose driven by yellow flower, white peach and apple aromas capped off with a touch of wildflower honey. Slighty mature, robust palate showing a delightful savoury and focused freshness.
Price approx.: 6,50 EUR
http://www.aziendaagricolasangiuseppe.it
San Giuseppe Azienda Agricola
390438450526

AZIENDA AGRICOLA ANDREOLA   85/100

▼✦ Vigneto Dirupo Brut 2013 : Brilliant straw-yellow tinged with green. Harmonious nose of yellow apple, white flowers, sugared almonds and mineral notes. Creamy, savoury palate with a fresh, lemony mid-palate and a clean finish.
Price approx.: 5,95 EUR
http://www.andreola.eu
Azienda Agricola Andreola
39438989379

AZIENDA AGRICOLA BORTOLIN ANGELO 85/100

▼✦ Desiderio Dry 2013 : Brilliant straw-yellow topped with a beautiful mousse. Very mineral-driven, refined, harmonious and supple nose with white flower, sage and

white peach notes. Creamy palate with a subtle freshness that is sweet yet bitter. Long finish.
Price approx.: 7,50 EUR
http://www.bortolinangelo.com/
Azienda Agricola Bortolin Angelo
390423900125

AZIENDA AGRICOLA DRUSIAN FRANCESCO 85/100

▼♪ Brut 0 : Brilliant straw-yellow, green tints. Fairly subdued yet pleasant, harmonious nose showing varietal scents of sage, apple, yellow flowers, sugared almonds. The palate is less structured yet consistent with the nose. Beautiful savoury and lemony mid-palate.
Price approx.: 6,60 EUR
http://www.drusian.it
Azienda Agricola Drusian Francesco
390423982151

CASE BIANCHE SRL 85/100

▼♪ Antico - Bottle Rifermentation 2013 : Fittingly hazy straw-yellow. Lemony nose of chinotto, grapefruit then root, bark and dried flowers. Unusual. Velvety yet slightly linear mouthfeel with a savoury mid-palate and a finish tinged with a little bitterness.
Price approx.: 5,60 EUR
http://www.casebianche.it
Case Bianche Srl
39043864468

LE BERTOLE 85/100

▼♪ Extra Dry 2013 : Pale straw-yellow with a fine mousse. Pleasant nose intermixing lily-of-the-valley and fruity notes of green apple flesh. The palate shows seductive freshness, persistency and fruit aromas, with more green apple. Ideal as an appetiser.
Price approx.: 6,30 EUR
http://www.lebertole.it
Le Bertole
390423975332

MONGARDA 85/100

▼♪ Brut 0 : Brilliant light straw-yellow. Mineral-driven nose showing fresh almond, white flowers and chamomile notes. Creamy, supple palate revealing a subtle sweet/sour balance. A tense, savoury, mineral and focused wine.
Price approx.: 7,00 EUR
http://www.mongarda.it
Mongarda
438989168

SPAGNOL 85/100

▼♪ Rive di Solighetto Brut 2012 : An appealing ring of bubbles and straw-yellow nuances with green tints introduce a subtle yet harmonious bouquet of white flowers, honey and a mineral touch. Creamy, austere and focused palate with fresh, mineral-driven acidity. Medium length.

Price approx.: 8,40 EUR
http://www.coldelsas.it
Spagnol Col del Sas
423987177

VAL D'OCA S.R.L. 85/100

▼♪ Rive di San Pietro di Barbozza Brut 2013 : Bright straw-yellow. Bouquet of light honey scents rounded out with notes of dried yellow flowers (mimosa and broom). Focused, precise palate with creamy accents flowing into persistent lemony aromatics that carry through to the finish.
http://www.valdoca.com/
Val d'Oca s.r.l.
390423982070

VAL D'OCA S.R.L. 85/100

▼♪ Uvaggio Storico Dry 2013 : Brilliant green. Simple yet refined nose showing notes of citrus, butter and lemongrass leaf. Robust, upright palate, as pleasurable as the nose. Fresh, savoury and showing good persistency.
http://www.valdoca.com/
Val d'Oca s.r.l.
390423982070

ZARDETTO 85/100

▼♪ Extra Dry Molin 2013 : Abundant mousse. The nose shows a harmonious, refined and mineral-driven bouquet (gypsum) with notes of white flowers, fresh almond and freshly-milled flour. The palate is fairly expressive and displays volume and persistency.
Price approx.: 7,20 EUR
http://www.zardettoprosecco.com
Zardetto Spumanti
390438394969

AZIENDA AGRICOLA MALIBRAN DI FAVREL MAURIZIO 84/100

Eco▼♪ Brut Ruio 2013 : Refined, persistent bubbles form the prelude to a shy, mineral and saline nose that is simple yet refined and harmonious with white flower aromas. Creamy palate, a tad too austere and bitter, yet nonetheless showing a long, focused finish.
Price approx.: 5,80 EUR
http://www.malibranvini.it
Az Ag Malibran
438781410

BELLENDA 84/100

▼♪ Brut San Fermo Millesimato 2013 : Abundant mousse and a brilliant straw-yellow hue. Refined, shy nose of dried yellow flowers, chamomile, mineral and saline notes. The palate is supple on entry then tinged with a hint of sourness. An enjoyable, simple and sleek Prosecco.
Price approx.: 6,80 EUR
http://www.bellenda.it
Bellenda
390438920025

LA FARRA AZIENDA AGRICOLA S.S 84/100

Eco▼🌱 Rive di Farra di Soligo Extra Dry Millesimato 2013 : Straw-yellow with brilliant green nuances and a persistent mousse. Refined nose showing aromas of yellow flowers (broom), mineral notes and chalk with lime honey. Very creamy palate where the sweet component stands out more than acidity. A pleasant wine.

Price approx.: 6,20 EUR
http://www.lafarra.it
La Farra Azienda Agricola s.s
+39 043 88 01 242

LE COLTURE AZIENDA AGRICOLA 84/100

▼🌱 Fagher Brut 2013 : Very abundant mousse. The nose is relatively complex with notes of chalk, yellow flowers and apple. The palate falls just below expectations. It is supple, fairly balanced, slightly lean and of average length.

Price approx.: 7,50 EUR
http://www.lecolture.it
Le Colture Azienda Agricola
390423900192

LE VIGNE DI ALICE 84/100

▼🌱 Doro Brut 2013 : Warm straw-yellow. Subdued, refined nose of dried yellow flowers, chalk, chamomile and tea. Supple attack on the palate leading into a slender, slightly linear mid-palate and a finish tinged with a trace of sourness. Simple and easy-drinking.

Price approx.: 6,80 EUR
http://www.levignedialice.it
Le Vigne di Alice
390438920818

MONGARDA 84/100

▼🌱 Extra Dry 0 : Beautiful brilliant straw-yellow with green tints. Unusual nose of hazelnut, almond and lily-of-the-valley. Subtle, elegant bouquet. Very supple, creamy palate. The finish is tinged with a hint of sourness.

Price approx.: 7,00 EUR
http://www.mongarda.it
Mongarda
438989168

AZIENDA AGRICOLA ALTHEA DI DRUSIAN MARIKA 83/100

▼🌱 Brut 2013 : Straw-yellow with green tints. Persistent mousse. Elegant nose of white flowers, fresh almond and wheat flour with mineral notes. The palate is slightly lean, fairly fresh and well-balanced and less mineral-driven than the nose.

Price approx.: 5,00 EUR
http:// www.agriturismoalthea.it
Azienda Agricola Althea di Drusian Marika
390438560511

LA FARRA AZIENDA AGRICOLA S.S 83/100

Eco▼🌱 Rive di Farra di Soligo Brut Millesimato 2013 : Brilliant straw-yellow with green tints. Persistent mousse. Delicate, harmonious nose intermixing multi-floral honey, dried yellow flower pot pourri and chamomile. Fresh, precise palate boasting a beautiful mineral verve and slight astringency.

Price approx.: 6,20 EUR
http://www.lafarra.it
La Farra Azienda Agricola s.s
+39 043 88 01 242

LA GIOIOSA 83/100

Eco▼🌱 Extra Dry 0 : Persistent mousse. Very fruity nose showing suggestions of melon flesh. The palate displays a degree of volume, fat and good balance. The finish is slightly firmer and tinged with a subtle pungency. Drink chilled as an appetiser.

http://www.lagioiosa.it
La Gioiosa
+39 042 38 607

LA GIOIOSA 83/100

Eco▼🌱 Brut Millesimato 2013 : Bright, limpid straw-yellow. Fairly intense nose blending sweet almond, dried yellow flowers and honey. Round style on the palate recalling a regular dry sparkling wine. Subtle freshness and satisfactory balance.

http://www.lagioiosa.it
La Gioiosa
+39 042 38 607

PERLAGE 83/100

Org▼🌱 Col di Manza» - Rive di Ogliano - Millesimato Bio Extra Dry» 2013 : Brilliant straw-yellow. The nose shows a mineral streak of gypsum followed by floral notes of linden and a touch of acacia honey. Creamy palate but the sweet component lacks balance and flows into sour almond flavours.

Price approx.: 13,00 EUR
http://www.perlagewines.com
Perlage SRL
390438900203

ZARDETTO 83/100

▼🌱 Fondego Dry 2013 : Brilliant green. Fine, persistent mousse. Round, harmonious, classic nose that opens up immediately to vanilla sugar, mimosa and yellow peach. Fairly intense, creamy attack leading into quite a short finish.

Price approx.: 7,20 EUR
http://www.zardettoprosecco.com
Zardetto Spumanti
390438394969

LE COLTURE AZIENDA AGRICOLA 82/100

▼🌱 Rive di Santo Stefano Gerardo Brut 2013 : Straw-yellow with green tints. Shy, mineral nose with notes of white flowers. Simple yet refined. Precise, austere palate. A wine

that is still a little young with an average finish.
Price approx.: 8,80 EUR
http://www.lecolture.it
Le Colture Azienda Agricola
390423900192

RUGGERI   82/100

▼.✶ Quartese Brut 0 : Very abundant mousse. Brilliant straw-yellow hue with green tints. The nose is backward, a little shy, simple and slightly muted, showing notes of apple and dried yellow flowers. Quite an unusual palate with wild notes. Has yet to fully mellow.
Price approx.: 9,00 EUR
http://www.ruggeri.it
Ruggeri & C. S.p.A.
3904239092

VAL D'OCA S.R.L.   82/100

▼.✶ Extra Dry Millesimato 2013 : Light yellow. The nose is shy on first pour then opens up after swirling to perfumes of dried yellow flowers and hay. The palate displays beautiful volume, subtle freshness and a hint of salinity. Medium persistency across the palate.
http://www.valdoca.com/
Val d'Oca s.r.l.
390423982070

ZARDETTO   82/100

▼.✶ Rive di Ogliano Tre Venti Brut 2013 : Brilliant straw-yellow shades with green tints. Fine, persistent mousse. Honey-driven nose with scents of dried yellow flower pot pourri. Mineral-infused palate displaying volume and abundant mousse. A simple, yet refined wine. Slightly short.
Price approx.: 8,00 EUR
http://www.zardettoprosecco.com
Zardetto Spumanti
390438394969

AZIENDA AGRICOLA BORTOLIN ANGELO 81/100

▼.✶ Rive di Guia Brut 2013 : Straw-yellow with green tints. Unusual nose showing perfumes of toasted hazelnut, almond and white flowers. The nose aromatics carry through to the palate. The mid-palate is slightly lean and the finish bitter.
Price approx.: 7,50 EUR
http://www.bortolinangelo.com/
Azienda Agricola Bortolin Angelo
390423900125

BISOL DESIDERIO & FIGLI   80/100

▼.✶ Jeio no SO2 - senza solforosa aggiunta Brut Millesimato 2012 : Warm straw-yellow. Not very elegant, mature nose of rubber, toasted hazelnut and smoke notes. Austere palate, totally consistent with the nose. The flavour profile is slightly out of the ordinary and oxidative in style.

Price approx.: 11,30 EUR
http://www.bisol.it
Bisol Desiderio & Figli
390423900138

GARDA DOC.

CA' BOTTA RIESLING   87/100

▼.✶ Tenuta Rossino 2013 : Brilliant straw-yellow. Intense nose reminiscent of white flowers with tropical fruits (pineapple, mango, papaya). On the palate, a fresh wine boasting good acidity and savoury fruit. Subtle salty touch in the background. Ideal for fish.
Price approx.: 10,00 EUR
http://www.cabotta.it
Ca' Botta
39045982875

LESSINI DURELLO D.O.C.

CORTE MOSCHINA   90/100

▼.✶ Riserva Spumante Metodo Classico Extra Brut 2008 : Very vibrant colour. Unusual nose with extremely pronounced tertiary notes that stay very fresh: sweet flowers, wild strawberries, undergrowth, bark, mushrooms and toast. Substantial yet easy-drinking palate. Creamy, full, elegant, savoury and mineral.
http://www.cortemoschina.it
Corte Moschina
457460788

FATTORI   90/100

▼.✶ Spumante Metodo Classico Brut Millesimato 2010 : Brilliant straw-yellow. Persistent mousse. Elegant, no-frills nose showing mineral aromas of damp rock, plus breadcrust, undergrowth, humus, smoke notes and dried fruits. Creamy, refined, mellow, saline and fresh palate. Long, clean finish.
Price approx.: 12,00 EUR
http://www.fattoriwines.com
Fattori
390457460041

MARCA TREVIGIANA

SOCIETÀ AGRICOLA CA' DI RAJO   89/100

▼.✶ Marinò 2010 : Impenetrable ruby-red. Intense nose of blackberry and raspberry with notes of mild liquorice and cloves. Good presence on the palate with fine-grain tannins, balsamic flavours and lovely persistency. Drink with meat.
Price approx.: 12,80 EUR
http://www.cadirajo.it
Società Agricola Ca' di Rajo
390422855885

PIAVE D.O.C.

SOCIETÀ AGRICOLA CA' DI RAJO — 89/100

▼♪ Notti di luna Piena 2007 : Intense ruby. Expressive nose of blackberry and raspberry liqueur enhanced by notes of spice and tobacco. Warm, welcoming palate with mellow tannins recalling the spicy oak nose aromatics. Ideal for red meats.

Price approx.: 19,80 EUR
http://www.cadirajo.it
Società Agricola Ca' di Rajo
390422855885

SOCIETÀ AGRICOLA CA' DI RAJO — 87/100

▼♪ Sangue del Diavolo Raboso 2009 : Ruby-red. Fairly intense bouquet of red fruits and spicy oak. Warm, mellow and aromatic palate revealing peppery and liquoricy flavours. Oak presence is quite pronounced. Ideal for red meats.

Price approx.: 10,80 EUR
http://www.cadirajo.it
Società Agricola Ca' di Rajo
390422855885

PROSECCO D.O.C. TREVISO

TENUTE TOMASELLA — 85/100

▼♪ Pro' 2013 : Pale straw-yellow with fine, persistent bubbles. A mix of floral (acacia) and fruit notes (ripe pear) on the nose. Seductive, persistent palate revealing more of the pleasant pear flavours. Drink as an appetiser.

http://www.tenute-tomasella.it
Tenute Tomasella
+39 042 28 50 043

PROSECCO D.O.C.

BELLENDA — 85/100

▼♪ Brut Col di Luna Etichetta Nera Millesimato 2013 : Fine bubbles and a brilliant straw-yellow hue. Inviting, classic nose showing signature varietal aromas of green apple, sage and recurring mineral notes. Creamy, robust palate flowing into bone dry flavours. Slightly lean finish.

Price approx.: 5,50 EUR
http://www.bellenda.it
Bellenda
390438920025

BELLENDA — 84/100

▼♪ Extra Dry Prima Cuvée 2013 : Warm, brilliant straw-yellow. Shy, refined nose recalling dried yellow flower and wildflower honey scents. Creamy, velvety, supple and robust palate.

Price approx.: 6,00 EUR
http://www.bellenda.it
Bellenda
390438920025

BISOL DESIDERIO & FIGLI — 83/100

▼♪ Bel Star Cult Extra Dry 0 : Attractive straw-yellow with green tints. Very refined, shy and simple nose driven by hawthorn and acacia notes with almond and wheat flour. Fairly robust, savoury palate with a fresh mid-palate leading into a beautiful lemon-infused finish.

Price approx.: 6,18 EUR
http://www.bisol.it
Bisol Desiderio & Figli
390423900138

BELLENDA — 82/100

▼♪ Extra Dry Col di Luna Millesimato 2013 : Persistent bubbles. Simple, instantly accessible nose of white flowers and fresh almond flowing into mineral notes. Supple palate showing sufficient creaminess yet relatively backward in terms of aroma. The finish is tinged with sourness.

Price approx.: 5,50 EUR
http://www.bellenda.it
Bellenda
390438920025

COSTA FARNEL — 82/100

▼♪ Extra Dry : Straw-yellow with fine, persistent bubbles. Floral nose recalling fresh white flowers and lily-of-the-valley. On the palate, a fruity, focused and fairly persistent wine. Works equally well as an aperitif or with starters.

Price approx.: 8,00 EUR
http://www.lacanosaagricola.it
La Canosa
390736000000

RECIOTO DI SOAVE D.O.C.G

FATTORI — 88/100

▼♪ Motto Piane 2012 : Intense yellow-gold. Round, slightly oxidative nose of dried apricots and figs, candied fruits, vanilla, fudge and dried fruits. Very fresh, fleshy and mellow palate. The finish is tinged with a hint of sourness.

Price approx.: 19,00 EUR
http://www.fattoriwines.com
Fattori
390457460041

SOAVE D.O.C

MARCO MOSCONI — 90/100

▼♪ Corte Paradiso 2013 : Brilliant straw-yellow. Refined nose of talc, damp rock, pear and geranium. The bouquet is unusual yet typical. Very mineral, saline and supple palate boasting fat. A complex yet easy-drinking wine. Long, clean finish.

http://www.marcomosconi.it
Marco Mosconi
456529109

CORTE ADAMI 88/100

▼♪ Vigna della Corte 2012 : Straw-yellow. Full, harmonious nose showing mineral aromatics with notes of damp rock, chalk then almond, fresh wheat flour, white flowers and peach. Supple, fleshy mouthfeel with a flavoursome mid-palate. Long saline and iodine-infused finish.
Price approx.: 9,50 EUR
http://www.corteadami.it
Corte Adami
457680423

CORTE ADAMI 88/100

▼♪ Soave 2013 : Brilliant straw-yellow with green tints. Aromatic nose of herbs, fern and elderberry flowing into white peach and almond. Very supple mouthfeel with a mineral, saline mid-palate making it a subtle wine, in keeping with the style of the appellation.
Price approx.: 6,50 EUR
http://www.corteadami.it
Corte Adami
457680423

CORTE MOSCHINA 88/100

▼♪ Evaos 2013 : Brilliant straw-yellow tinged with green. Floral nose of lime and acacia with fruit aromas of yellow peach followed by classic mineral notes. Delicate, refined bouquet. Very savoury, fleshy palate bordering on saline and showing warmth. Fairly long finish.
http://www.cortemoschina.it
Corte Moschina
457460788

MARCO MOSCONI 88/100

▼♪ Rosetta 2013 : Straw-yellow with green highlights. Full, harmonious nose revealing notes of musk, bark, yellow peach, anise and damp rock. Very fresh, mineral and fleshy palate. Long, savoury almond-driven finish.
http://www.marcomosconi.it
Marco Mosconi
456529109

PORTINARI 88/100

▼♪ Le Albare 2013 : Brilliant straw-yellow. Needs a little aerating to reveal beautiful notes of white flowers, almond, wheat flour, gunflint and talc. Warm palate boasting fat. Mineral and saline with savoury acidity and a hint of sourness.
Portinari Umberto
456175087

BERTANI 87/100

▼♪ 2012 : Brilliant straw-yellow. Mineral and smoky nose enhanced by notes of broom and a touch of candied citrus and dried apricot. Ripe yet elegant bouquet. Flavoursome, mellow palate that is robust, mineral and fresh with a clean finish.
http://www.bertani.net
Bertani
390458658444

SANDRO DE BRUNO 87/100

▼♪ Colli Scaligeri 2012 : Brilliant straw-yellow. Very mineral nose driven by notes of dried yellow flowers, hay and wild aromas. Full, savoury and fresh palate. Focused, persistent finish.
Price approx.: 10,00 EUR
http://www.sandrodebruno.it
Sandro De Bruno
456540465

VICENTINI 87/100

▼♪ Terrelunghe 2013 : Appealing, brilliant straw-yellow. Harmonious, unusual nose of powder, talc, red berry fruits and sugared almonds. Very drinkable, supple palate. Beautiful savoury and mineral mid-palate, simpler and more immediate than the complex nose aromatics.
http://www.vinivicentini.com
Vicentini
457650539

BERTANI 83/100

▼♪ Serèole 2013 : Unusual nose revealing notes of talc, white-fleshed fruits, white flowers, fresh almond, wheat flour and a touch of raspberry. The palate is simple and immediately accessible. Fairly fresh and robust with a slightly predominant sour touch of bitter almond.
http://www.bertani.net
Bertani
390458658444

SOAVE DOC CLASSICO

MONTETONDO 93/100

▼♪ Casette Foscarin 2011 : Intense straw-yellow. Very mineral nose with notes of stone, chalk then scents of wheat flour, fresh almond and graphite. A wine true to the appellation with a consistent, precise and savoury palate that is elegant and mellow. Long, clean, saline finish.
Price approx.: 11,00 EUR
http://www.montetondo.it
Montetondo
390457680347

COFFELE 92/100

▼♪ Soave Classico 2013 : Full, young, elegant and mineral nose of rock with a vegetal and menthol touch, floral and fruity scents of white peach, pear and fresh almond. The palate is supple, savoury, fresh and mineral and boasts fat. Long, clean finish. Still in its youth.
Price approx.: 9,00 EUR
http://www.coffele.it
Coffele
390457680007

GINI 92/100

▼ La Froscà 2012 : Brilliant straw-yellow. Mineral, full and complex nose of damp rock then musk, undergrowth, white peach, pear and dried fruits. Rich, supple palate boasting fat. Fresh, savoury mid-palate showing tropical notes. Focused and persistent.
Price approx.: 16,00 EUR
http://www.ginivini.com
Gini
390457611908

CANTINA DI MONTEFORTE 91/100

▼ il Vicario 2013 : Straw-yellow, green tints. Refined nose showing elegant austerity with damp stone, mineral, root, dried yellow flowers and white peach aromas. The palate is consistent with the nose, boasting body and fat yet also elegance, focus and harmony. Mineral finish.
http://www.cantinadimonteforte.it
Cantina di Monteforte
390457610110

CA' RUGATE 90/100

▼ San Michele 2013 : Brilliant straw-yellow with green tints. Intriguing, complex nose of damp rock, fresh almond, citrus (citron, grapefruit) and pastries. Fleshy palate showing elegant austerity. Savoury, very mineral and warm. Long clean finish.
Price approx.: 8,00 EUR
http://www.carugate.it
Ca' Rugate
390456176328

LE MANDOLARE 90/100

▼ Corte Menini 2013 : Very brilliant hue. Rich, delightful nose of tropical fruits, flowers, a touch of honey, candied fruits and a subtle touch of mushroom. The palate is more austere, fresh and mineral flowing into lemony aromatics mid-palate. Long, dry, almond-driven finish.
Price approx.: 6,00 EUR
http://www.cantinalemandolare.com
Le Mandolare
456175083

CORTE MAINENTE 89/100

▼ Nettroir 2012 : Straw-yellow. Harmonious, mineral bouquet of gunflint followed by scents of apricot and yellow peach. Fruit aromas and terroir notes fuse beautifully. Fleshy, fresh and savoury palate with an almond flavour. Welcome trace of sourness on the finish.
http://www.cortemainente.com
Corte Mainente
457680303

GUERRIERI RIZZARDI 89/100

▼ Soave Classico 2013 : Brilliant straw-yellow. Full, intriguing nose of graphite, mineral notes, dried flowers, yellow peach, lemony aromas of citron and grapefruit. Consistent, precise, rocky palate showing vitality. Saline finish. Good length.
http://www.guerrieri-rizzardi.it
Guerrieri Rizzardi
390457210028

LE BATTISTELLE 89/100

▼ Le Battistelle 2012 : Brilliant straw-yellow with green tints. The nose is still young and intense with aromas of grapefruit and citron, flowers and yellow peaches, and mineral notes of gunflint. Savoury, mineral palate, fresh on the mid-palate. Long, clean, almond-driven finish.
Price approx.: 11,00 EUR
http://www.lebattistelle.it
Le Battistelle
+456175621

MONTETONDO 88/100

▼ Monte Tondo 2013 : Intense, complex nose revealing pinapple, dried and jammy apricot, vegetal scents of musk and undergrowth and rock notes. Well-structured, savoury and fresh palate boasting fat. The fruit notes dovetail with the vegetal aromas.
Price approx.: 7,50 EUR
http://www.montetondo.it
Montetondo
+390457680347

LE BATTISTELLE 87/100

▼ Roccolo del Durlo 2012 : Straw-yellow. Elegant, harmonious nose revealing scents of yellow peach, dried flowers then musk notes and mineral aromas of damp rock. The palate shows elegant austerity and is savoury, very fresh and focused. Lengthy finish tinged with a welcome sourness.
Price approx.: 15,00 EUR
http://www.lebattistelle.it
Le Battistelle
+456175621

LE MANDOLARE 87/100

▼ Il Roccolo 2013 : Intense straw-yellow. Full, harmonious nose showing scents of pastries, mild tobacco, flowers, tropical notes and almond. An exotic yet elegant array of aromas. Very fresh, savoury, focused and fleshy palate. Red fruit drives the finish.
Price approx.: 8,00 EUR
http://www.cantinalemandolare.com
Le Mandolare
+456175083

MARCATO 87/100

▼ Monte Tenda 2013 : Straw-yellow with green tints. Intense nose of cedar, rapidly opening up to elegant aromas of menthol, chlorophyll and mineral notes. The palate is perfectly in keeping with the nose. It is fresh and savoury rather than concentrated. Refined, long and lemony.

http://www.marcatovini.it

Marcato

+457460070

CANTINA DI MONTEFORTE   86/100

▼♪ Clivus 2013 : Brilliant straw-yellow. Interesting, unusual bouquet driven by notes of butter, smoke, dried yellow flowers and mild spices. Fairly easy-drinking, compelling palate with the nose aromatics flowing through. Savoury lemony finish.

http://www.cantinadimonteforte.it

Cantina di Monteforte

+390457610110

COFFELE   85/100

▼♪ Ca' Visco 2013 : Very mineral, shy nose with cave accents followed by almond, fresh wheat flour, white flowers (acacia and hawthorn) and peach. Fairly fresh, robust mouthfeel with a mid-palate tinged with bitterness. Medium finish.

Price approx.: 12,50 EUR

http://www.coffele.it

Coffele

+390457680007

GUERRIERI RIZZARDI   85/100

▼♪ Costeggiola 2013 : Straw-yellow. Shy nose of wheat flour, fresh almond, talc, acacia, hawthorn and white melon. The palate shows beautiful austerity. It is mineral, savoury and slightly sour with root aromas. Fairly persistent, long finish.

Price approx.: 9,00 EUR

http://www.guerrieri-rizzardi.it

Guerrieri Rizzardi

+390457210028

MARCATO   85/100

▼♪ Pigno 2012 : Intense straw-yellow. Expressive, unusual nose of cedar, tropical fruits, sugared almond, mild tobacco and menthol. Fairly good structure and freshness on the palate expressing slightly vegetal and wild aromas. Medium finish.

http://www.marcatovini.it

Marcato

+457460070

PORTINARI   85/100

▼♪ Ronchetto 2013 : Brilliant straw-yellow, green tints. Unusual, ripe nose driven by boiled sweets, dried yellow flowers and peaches in syrup. The nose aromas follow through to the palate which is savoury and persistent with a beautiful trace of acidity. Slightly dry finish.

Portinari Umberto

456175087

SOAVE
SUPERIORE D.O.C.G

LE MANDOLARE   92/100

▼♪ Monte Sella 2011 : An excellent Soave with an archetypal, harmonious and elegant bouquet of mineral and musk notes, cave, undergrowth, peach, melon and broom. Fleshy, supple, well-balanced and fresh palate that is savoury, long and focused with a final touch of candied fruits.

Price approx.: 13,00 EUR

http://www.cantinalemandolare.com

Le Mandolare

456175083

CANTINA DI MONTEFORTE   90/100

▼♪ Classico Vigneti di Castellaro 2012 : Intense straw-yellow. Full nose still in its youth showing smoke, mineral notes of damp rock, pear, peach, humus and undergrowth. Saline and iodine-driven palate that is fresh with a long, clean, supple and fruity finish.

Price approx.: 9,00 EUR

http://www.cantinadimonteforte.it

Cantina di Monteforte

390457610110

CANTINA DI SOAVE   89/100

▼♪ Classico Castelcerino 2012 : Brilliant straw-yellow. Full, elegant nose of tropical fruits, balm, menthol, dried apricot and pastries with mineral notes and wild aromas. The palate is robust, mellow, very savoury, mineral and fresh. Very persistent, clean finish.

Price approx.: 13,00 EUR

http://www.cantinasoave.it

Cantina di Soave

390456139811

SANDRO DE BRUNO   89/100

▼♪ Monte San Piero 2011 : Straw-yellow with golden highlights. Intense nose with pronounced aromas of candied citrus peel, ginger, smoke and mineral notes then whiffs of chestnut honey. Rich, savoury, fresh and warm palate that lingers with tropical flavours.

http://www.sandrodebruno.it

Sandro De Bruno

456540465

Prices mentioned in this book are guideline and can vary depending on point of sale. The shops, wineries or publisher can in no way be held responsible for this.

VALDOBBIADENE SUPERIORE DI CARTIZZE D.O.C.G.

BISOL DESIDERIO & FIGLI   90/100

▼ 🍷 Cartizze Dry 2013 : Attractive, brilliant straw-yellow. Shy yet elegant nose that is sappy with resin, sage and white peach aromas. Highly perfumed bouquet. Very creamy, full, savoury and mellow palate, with saline and iodine-like aromas. Pleasant long, focused finish.
Price approx.: 15,85 EUR
http://www.bisol.it
Bisol Desiderio & Figli
+390423900138

BISOL DESIDERIO & FIGLI   88/100

▼ 🍷 Cartizze Private Rifermentato in bottiglia Non Dosato 2011 : Intense straw-yellow. Expressive, rich and austere nose of toasted breadcrust, dried fruits, peanut butter and dried flowers. The palate shows volume in a slightly oxidative style. A savoury, mineral, fresh and dry wine. Focused finish.
Price approx.: 28,00 EUR
http://www.bisol.it
Bisol Desiderio & Figli
+390423900138

ZARDETTO   87/100

▼ 🍷 Cartizze Dry 2013 : Straw-yellow with green tints. Fine, persistent mousse. Refined, full and harmonious nose of vanilla sugar, flour, fresh almond, white peach, gooseberry and sage. Creamy, focused and well-balanced palate. Long lemony finish.
Price approx.: 13,00 EUR
http://www.zardettoprosecco.com
Zardetto Spumanti
+390438394969

CARPENE MALVOLTI SPA   82/100

▼ 🍷 1868 Cartizze Dry 2013 : Brilliant straw-yellow with green tints. The bouquet is endearing and refined, showing yellow apple, multi-floral honey, peach and yellow flowers. Fresh, savoury palate albeit slightly linear and free-flowing for a Cartizze. Slightly short finish.
http://www.carpene-malvolti.com
Carpene Malvolti SpA
+390438364611

VALPOLICELLA D.O.C.

CORTE ADAMI   90/100

▼ 🍷 Valpolicella Superiore 2011 : Ruby-red. Intense nose of leather and damp wood enhanced by notes of ground coffee. The palate is rich and persistent and reveals aromas of pepper and spice. Ideal with a platter of cold cuts or full-flavoured meats.
Price approx.: 9,50 EUR
http://www.corteadami.it
Corte Adami
+457680423

VALPOLICELLA RIPASSO D.O.C. SUPERIORE

CA' BOTTA   85/100

▼ 🍷 Tenuta Costa Rossa 2010 : Intense ruby. Expressive nose suggestive of cherry liqueur, liquorice and balsamic perfumes with a faint tobacco note. Warm, persistent palate showing predominant fruity and peppery flavours. Serve with rare-cooked meats.
Price approx.: 25,00 EUR
http://www.cabotta.it
Ca' Botta
+39045982875

VALPOLICELLA RIPASSO D.O.C

CORTE ADAMI   90/100

▼ 🍷 Valpolicella Ripasso Superiore 2011 : Intense ruby. Floral nose reminiscent of dried flowers and cherry notes with a pleasant sensation of liquorice. Clearly-defined tannins on the palate with upfront balsamic and peppery aromas. A characterful wine pairing well with meat.
Price approx.: 12,00 EUR
http://www.corteadami.it
Corte Adami
+457680423

• • • • • • • • • • • • • • • •

LEBANON

BÉKAA

BÉKAA-OUEST

CHÂTEAU QANAFAR   93/100

▼ 🍷 Vintage 2011 : Dark colour with dark purple tints. Refined nose of ripe black fruit basket aromas, a floral note and fine spice. Silky, full and tense substance with precise aromas that cannot fail to impress. Menthol touch. Well-integrated velvety tannins. Superb.
Price approx.: 30,00 EUR
http://www.chateauqanafar.com
Chateau Qanafar
+961 1 398 782

CHÂTEAU KSARA 92/100

▼✦ Le Souverain 2010 : Young, deeply-coloured garnet. Endearing nose of mild spices, ripe cassis and blackberry, roasted coffee and fine oak. Svelte, virile palate that is profound, nervy and precise. Oak influence on the finish. A distinguished wine rewarding patience. Bravo!
Price approx.: 30,00 EUR
http://www.chateauksara.com
Château Ksara
+961 1 200 715

DOMAINE WARDY 92/100

▼✦ Private Selection 2007 : Dark hue with bricking. Delectable, expressive nose with accents of jammy fruits, truffle, liquorice and a touch of herbs. The palate displays a very interesting sensation of harmony and freshness. Aromas explode on the finish.
Price approx.: 20,00 EUR
Domaine Wardy
+9618930141

CHÂTEAU KSARA 88/100

▼✦ Cuvée du Troisième Millénaire 2011 : Deep ruby with dark purple tints. Shy nose of ripe black fruits with fine spices and subtle ageing scents. Full, silky and fresh palate with rich fruit aromatics, a menthol note and fine proportions framed by velvety tannins. Wonderful craftmanship.
Price approx.: 20,00 EUR
http://www.chateauksara.com
Château Ksara
+961 1 200 715

CHÂTEAU KSARA 86/100

▼✦ Réserve du Couvent 2012 : Limpid, deeply-coloured garnet. Expressive nose of mild spices, currants and vanilla oak in the background. Virile, robust and lively palate that is well-balanced with more of the nose aromatics. Firm finish. Will open up with a little more bottle time.
Price approx.: 5,00 EUR
http://www.chateauksara.com
Château Ksara
+961 1 200 715

CHÂTEAU KSARA 85/100

▼✦ Le Prieuré 2012 : Deep garnet with crimson tints. Pleasant nose of peony, cassis, black pepper and fine spice. Supple attack leading into a svelte, easy-drinking and fresh palate with good aromatic intensity, depth and a robust framework. Patience!
Price approx.: 3,00 EUR
http://www.chateauksara.com
Château Ksara
+961 1 200 715

LEBANON (ALL REGIONS)

VIN DU LIBAN

CHÂTEAU FAKRA 89/100

CONV▼✦ Collection Privée 2010 : Very young, deep purple-blue. Racy nose marrying black fruits, spice, notes of olive and olive paste. A fairly subtle range of aromatics on the palate with complex, evolving and persistent aromas. Notes of truffle, liquorice and liquorice sweet on the finish.
Price approx.: 13,35 EUR
Château Fakra
+961 9 635 111

CHÂTEAU FAKRA 87/100

CONV▼✦ Pinacle 2011 : Beautiful young red. Pleasant, profound nose marrying floral, fruity and spice notes. Beautiful elegance. Fruit-forward attack on the palate rapidly flowing into a mid-palate with a fairly dense mouthfeel. The finish stays harmonious and perfumed.
Price approx.: 4,75 EUR
Château Fakra
+961 9 635 111

CHÂTEAU FAKRA 86/100

CONV▼✦ Merlon 2011 : Young, light red. Nose of ripe red and black fruits with notes of liquorice and spice. The palate shows seductive suppleness, fruit and balance. It displays more of the delightful nose aromatics with a long-lasting finish of liquorice sweet.
Price approx.: 3,45 EUR
Château Fakra
+961 9 635 111

CHÂTEAU FAKRA 86/100

CONV▼✦ La Fleur 2013 : Light orange-pink. On the nose, a mixture of ripe red fruits and mineral, gunflint notes. A crunchy, fruity and spicy rosé on the palate. Fleshy, aromatic and idiosyncratic in style. Set aside for barbecues and summery foods.
Price approx.: 5,50 EUR
Château Fakra
+961 9 635 111

CHÂTEAU FAKRA 84/100

CONV▼✦ Cuvée du Temple 2013 : Young, light red. Fruity nose tinged with vegetal notes. Lovely mellowness, suppleness and aroma on the palate with fruit flowing into spice on the finish. A very enjoyable, crunchy and accessible style.
Price approx.: 3,00 EUR
Château Fakra
+961 9 635 111

CHÂTEAU FAKRA   84/100

CONV ▼ ♪ Blanc de blancs 2013 : Pale yellow. Endearing nose suggestive of white and stone fruits with a floral touch. The same, quite intense, heady aromas follow through to the palate. A fairly lush style that should be served well-chilled with grilled fish or seafood.
Price approx.: 5,50 EUR
Château Fakra
+961 9 635 111

MONT LIBAN

CHOUF

CHÂTEAU FLORENTINE   91/100

▼ ♪ Vintage 2011 : Deep garnet. Expressive, creamy nose of mild spices, blackberry, cassis and quality oak. Robust, profound palate driven by beautiful tension, a menthol note and a very compelling array of aromatics framed by silky tannins. Absolutely wonderful.
Price approx.: 25,00 EUR
http://www.chateauflorentine.com
Château Florentine
+961 1 204898

NORTH

BATROUN

ATIBAIA   91/100

▼ ♪ Vintage 2010 : Deep, young red. Expressive nose marrying black berries with a mineral and spice dimension. Polished, racy attack on the palate with mellow tannins and a focused, harmonious mid-palate showcasing the same, highly elegant perfumes.
Price approx.: 30,00 EUR
http://www.atibaiawine.com
Atibaia
+961 3 363 941

• • • • • • • • • • • • • • • • •

PORTUGAL

LISBOA

BUCELAS A.O.P.

QUINTA DA MURTA   84/100

▼ ♪ The Wine of Shakepeare 2012 : Brilliant light yellow. Pronounced mineral nose revealing lemony perfumes after swirling. Full, warm and rich attack leading into a nervy mid-palate imparting freshness. Robust personality. Perfect as an appetiser.
Price approx.: 9,00 EUR
http://www.quintadamurta.pt
Quinta da Murta
+351210155190

LISBOA V.R.

MURTA   88/100

▼ ♪ Vintage 2011 : Deep garnet with crimson. Expressive nose delivering slightly oaky, spice perfumes backed by fresh red fruits. Full palate showing a lovely fine texture, freshness and persistency. A nice wine.
Price approx.: 9,00 EUR
http://www.quintadamurta.pt
Quinta da Murta
+351210155190

• • • • • • • • • • • • • • • • •

SOUTH AFRICA

COASTAL REGION

PAARL W.O.

PLAISIR DE MERLE   87/100

▼ ♪ Cabernet Sauvignon 2010 : Dark garnet, with attractive herbal hints of mint & tobacco leaf on the nose, this wine is packed with blackberries, cassis & other dark forest fruit. It has soft tannins & a rich mouthfeel, finishing dry.
Price approx.: 15,00 EUR
http://www.capelegends.co.za
Cape Legends
+218097000

PLAISIR DE MERLE   84/100

▼ ♪ Merlot 2012 : Dark, youthful ruby red. Attractive nose of ripe blackberries with a gentle whiff of vanilla. On the palate, soft & well rounded with ripe red plums, a drizzle of dark chocolate & a hint of liquorice on the finish.
Price approx.: 15,00 EUR
http://www.capelegends.co.za
Cape Legends
+218097000

STELLENBOSCH W.O.

THE FMC   95/100

▼ ♪ Chenin Blanc 2012 : Liquid gold, made from fully ripe & wild-fermented grapes, this is a rich, honeyed wine

with a hint of vanilla. Dried apricots dominate on the nose & palate, the latter full-bodied but remarkably fresh with freshly baked bread & savoury spice notes.
Price approx.: 43,00 EUR
Ken Forrester Wines
+270219000000

FLEUR DU CAP   94/100

▼♪ Lazlo 2008 : Deep garnet, this perfectly integrated Bordeaux-style blend is developing secondary hints of leather & tobacco in addition to mulberries, black cherries & plums, joined on the palate by a rich nuttiness, almost like marzipan, as well as dark chocolate.
Price approx.: 21,00 EUR
http://www.capelegends.co.za/
Cape Legends
+218097000

FAMILY RESERVE OLD BUSH VINE CHENIN BLANC   93/100

▼♪ Chenin Blanc 2012 : Spun gold colour with ripe peaches & apricots on the nose, so concentrated that they taste almost sun-dried on the palate, with zesty orange adding freshness while hints of grapefruit pith & pine nut add savoury complexity.
Price approx.: 14,00 EUR
http://www.kleinezalze.co.za
Kleine Zalze
+27218800717

FLEUR DU CAP   91/100

▼♪ Cabernet Sauvignon Unfiltered 2011 : Dark inky colour with floral aromas as well as a hint of lead pencil adding to cassis appeal. Complex flavours include blackberry, mocha & liquorice with an intriguing metallic edge. Tannins are firm but ripe.
Price approx.: 14,00 EUR
http://www.capelegends.co.za/
Cape Legends
+218097000

FAMILY RESERVE CABERNET SAUVIGNON   91/100

▼♪ Cabernet Sauvignon 2009 : Dark inky core with a narrow garnet rim. Blackcurrant-flavoured Ribena concentrate on the nose, with ultra-ripe black plum & dark chocolate sweetness balanced by quite mouthwatering acidity & a dry, lingering finish.
Price approx.: 28,00 EUR
http://www.kleinezalze.co.za
Kleine Zalze
+27218800717

FLEUR DU CAP   88/100

▼♪ Cabernet Sauvignon 2012 : Still youthfully dark purple, this medium-bodied wine has ripe dark berries as

well as hints of vanilla & toasted hazelnuts on the nose. Red cherries & raspberries play on the palate, soft & ripe yet with refreshing acidity.
Price approx.: 7,50 EUR
http://www.capelegends.co.za/
Cape Legends
+218097000

FLEUR DU CAP   88/100

▼♪ Sauvignon Blanc 2014 : Brilliantly clear tinged with green, also some green apples & leafy herbaceous notes on the nose, but mostly intense tropical passionfruit & guava flavours from free-run juice, with tangy lime from mouthwatering acidity, finishing very crisp & dry.
Price approx.: 9,00 EUR
http://www.capelegends.co.za/
Cape Legends
+218097000

FAMILY RESERVE SHIRAZ   88/100

▼♪ Shiraz 2009 : Still densely purple, with ripe plums (almost prunes) on the nose, hints of vanilla & all-spice adding to the overall impression of sweetness, with black pepper & smoked meat adding savoury appeal. An unashamedly big wine but with good balance.
Price approx.: 26,00 EUR
http://www.kleinezalze.co.za
Kleine Zalze
+27218800717

ZONNEBLOEM   80/100

▼♪ Cabernet Sauvignon 2012 : Deep ruby core, garnet at the edges. Red & black berries on the nose but also leafy & herbal hints, which carry through to palate. Medium-bodied with soft tannins, rich plum notes enlived by a green stalkiness, & a hint of bitter coffee on the finish.
Price approx.: 9,00 EUR
http://www.capelegends.co.za/
Cape Legends
+218097000

SWARTLAND W.O.

BRYAN MACROBERT WINES CC   91/100

Org▼♪ Tobias Shiraz, Cinsault, Mourvedre 2013 : Youthful purple rim, almost inky black core. Mulberries on nose as well as savoury notes of smoked meat & fynbos scrub. On palate, red cherries dipped in dark chocolate, a medium-bodied, silky wine with lovely fresh acidity & long finish.
Price approx.: 11,00 EUR
Bryan MacRobert Wines CC
+27 (0)71-223-3129

BRYAN MACROBERT WINES CC — 90/100

Org ▼ ♪ Tobias Steen 2013 : Made from 100% old-vine chenin blanc, pale gold with enticing peach & passionfruit perfume. Waxy mouthfeel with apricot & a hint of honey but overall impression is fresh & savoury with citrus peel, wet stone minerality & rye notes adding to complexity.
Price approx.: 11,00 EUR
Bryan MacRobert Wines CC
+27 (0)71-223-3129

SOUTH AFRICA (ALL REGIONS)

WESTERN CAPE

THE GYPSY — 93/100

▼ ♪ Rhone-style blend 2010 : Dark crimson with concentrated red fruit (cherries & wild strawberries) as well as hints of nutmeg & cinnamon. On the palate, sinewy rather than bulky, with layers of intense, wild fruit plus savoury notes of black olive & pepper. Powerful but elegant.
Price approx.: 43,00 EUR
Ken Forrester Wines
+270219000000

FLEUR DU CAP — 89/100

▼ ♪ Chardonnay 2013 : Bright & clear with green-gold hue, orange blossom & pear drop aromas. Although dry, citrus sweetness & vanilla oak spice come through. Smooth, rich texture elegantly balanced with lively acidity.
Price approx.: 9,00 EUR
http://www.capelegends.co.za
Cape Legends
+218097000

FAMILY RESERVE SAUVIGNON BLANC SUR LIE — 89/100

▼ ♪ Sauvignon Blanc 2012 : Pale straw with green fig, melon & pea aromas. On the palate, medium-bodied with a leesy, slightly bitter pithiness as well as melon, gooseberry & a pinch of crushed herbs. Lime acidity & a slight petillance add crisp zing.
Price approx.: 14,00 EUR
http://www.kleinezalze.co.za
Kleine Zalze
+27218800717

PONGRACZ — 86/100

▼ ♪ Brut 0 : Pale gold with a fine, persistent bead, this Méthode Cap Classique (traditional method) sparkling wine has aromas of crisp green apple as well as a hint of blackberry. On the palate, a dry, fruity, foamy mouthful with toasty, nutty notes & a long finish.
Price approx.: 13,00 EUR
http://www.capelegends.co.za
Cape Legends
+218097000

PONGRACZ — 84/100

▼ ♪ Rose 0 : An enchanting pale salmon pink, this Méthode Cap Classique (traditional method) sparkling wine has a strawberry shortcake nose with flavours of cranberry & ruby grapefruit, very dry with biscuit notes from two years on the lees before dégorgement.
Price approx.: 13,00 EUR
http://www.capelegends.co.za
Cape Legends
+218097000

ZONNEBLOEM — 83/100

▼ ♪ Chardonnay 2013 : Pale straw with flashes of lime, fragrant & fruity with crisp green apples & pears on the nose, zesty tangerine & lime on the palate. From light oak caress, creamy mouthfeel is nicely balanced by refreshing acidity.
Price approx.: 6,00 EUR
http://www.capelegends.co.za
Cape Legends
+218097000

● ● ● ● ● ● ● ● ● ● ● ● ● ●

SPAIN

BASQUE COUNTRY

CHACOLI DE BIZCAIA - BIZKAIKOTXAKOLINA D.O.

BERROJA — 90/100

Org ▼ ♪ B 2012 : Light yellow with green tints. Pleasant nose of white flowers, meadow, stone fruits and a touch of gunflint. The same complex aromatics carry through to the palate which combines fat, freshness and expression. A delightful wine for fish in a sauce.
Price approx.: 6,75 EUR
Berroja
+34 944 10 62 54

BODEGA BERROJA — 84/100

▼ ♪ Aguirrebeko 2012 : Pale yellow with green tints. Subtle fruit on the nose recalling mainly white fruits and stone fruits. On the palate, a clean, fruit-driven wine with quite simple yet well-focused aromas. Uncork for seafood and grilled fish.
Price approx.: 4,50 EUR
Berroja
+34 944 10 62 54

CASTILE - LA MANCHA

LA MANCHA D.O.

CASA GUALDA　　　　　　　　**90/100**

▼✦ Tempranillo 2013 : Archetypal varietal and terroir-driven nose intermixing blackberry and sloe with a subtle white pepper note. A well-structu▼with upfront tannins on the palate, displaying fine overall balance and medium length. A delicious, joyful wine.

http://www.casagualda.com
Casa Gualda
+969387173

PALACIO GALIANA S.L., BODEGAS　　**84/100**

▼✦ Luna Negra Reserva 2009 : Ruby-red. Precise nose of ripe red fruits augmented by a delicate touch of truffle and smoke. On the palate, a well-balanced wine where fruit and toasted oak are impeccably entwined and delicious acidity supports the whole. A good wine.

Price approx.: 2,70 EUR
Palacio Galiana S.L., Bodegas
+034 926 6471

PALACIO GALIANA S.L., BODEGAS　　**79/100**

▼✦ Luna Negra Crianza 2011 : Garnet with dark purple nuances. Nose of ripe red fruits and jammy cherry with fresh mint undertones. The palate reveals subtle fruit, a mellow structure and light oak. Ideal as an accompaniment to tapas.

Price approx.: 2,00 EUR
Palacio Galiana S.L., Bodegas
+034 926 6471

PALACIO GALIANA S.L., BODEGAS　　**77/100**

▼✦ Luna Negra 2013 : Very appealing red with purple-blue. The nose marries mild notes of ripe and candied fruit with spice perfumes. An easy-drinking, light wine on the palate where fruit and freshness prevail. A good everyday companion to food.

Price approx.: 1,50 EUR
Palacio Galiana S.L., Bodegas
+034 926 6471

MÉNTRIDA D.O.

EXPORT IBERIA, ABANICO　　　**88/100**

▼✦ Tierra Fuerte Graciano 2011 : Intense crimson bordering on black. The nose delivers perfumes of breadcrust, black fruits and toasted oak. Firm, robust attack marked by pepper and caramel flowing into a more restrained mid-palate with fruit expression and freshness.

http://www.exportiberia.com
Export Iberia, Abanico
+34 93 812 56 76

RIBERA DEL JUCAR D.O.

CASA GUALDA　　　　　　　　**88/100**

▼✦ Syrah 2013 : The nose reveals perfumes of black forest fruits and black pepper. Lightweight palate showing lovely balance between freshness, alcoholic power and supple tannins. A pleasant, easy-drinking wine for any occasion.

http://www.casagualda.com
Casa Gualda
+969387173

VALDEPENAS D.O.

BODEGAS NAVARRO LÓPEZ　　**93/100**

▼✦ Laguna de la Nava Gran Reserva 2008 : Intense red. Captivating elegance and aromatic complexity on the nose with spice, pepper and ripe red fruit aromas. The same fruit aromatics coupled with butter caramel flavours carry through to the palate. An excellent wine.

Price approx.: 3,50 EUR
http://www.bodegasnavarrolopez.com
Bodegas Navarro López
+34902193431

BODEGAS NAVARRO LÓPEZ　　**85/100**

▼✦ Laguna de la Nava Reserva 2009 : Intense garnet. A mix of ripe fruits and snuff and leather notes from the oak barrels on the nose. A wine boasting personality on the palate with crunchy fruit flowing into warmer aromatics. Toast-infused finish.

Price approx.: 2,70 EUR
http://www.bodegasnavarrolopez.com
Bodegas Navarro López
+34902193431

BODEGAS NAVARRO LÓPEZ　　**84/100**

▼✦ Pergolas Old Vines Crianza 2011 : Intense garnet. Unusual nose exuding spice notes of oregano and dill with wild berry aromas. The palate is fresh with fine-grained tannins and a mellow structure. An excellent conversational wine.

Price approx.: 2,00 EUR
http://www.bodegasnavarrolopez.com/
Bodegas Navarro López
+34902193431

BODEGAS NAVARRO LÓPEZ　　**79/100**

▼✦ Laguna de la Nava Rosado 2013 : Brilliant pale pink. The nose exudes perfumes of fresh strawberry and citrus as well as a mineral dimension. The palate is fresh with fruit overtones. Quite a pleasurable, thought-provoking wine.

Price approx.: 1,50 EUR
http://www.bodegasnavarrolopez.com/
Bodegas Navarro López
+34902193431

BODEGAS NAVARRO LÓPEZ 78/100

▼✔ Laguna de la Nava Verdejo 2013 : Pale yellow-gold with green tints. The nose marries tropical notes of fresh pineapple, white peach perfumes and mineral undertones which impart freshness. Well-balanced acidity and persistent fruit on the palate.
Price approx.: 1,50 EUR
http://www.bodegasnavarrolopez.com
Bodegas Navarro López
+34902193431

VT CASTILLA

AURUM RED 98/100

▼✔ Aurum Red White 2013 : Elegant nose with mineral accents of silica enhanced by notes of citrus, hawthorn and freshly-cut hay. Very subtle palate with impeccably integrated freshness and a mouth-coating mid-palate. An extremely stylish, pure, honest wine.
http://www.aurumwine.com
Aurum Red
+34967160464

VERUM S.L., BODEGAS Y VIÑEDOS 92/100

▼✔ Verum Roble 2011 : Ruby with bricking. A mix of cloves, ginger, ripe fruits and black pepper on the nose. On the palate, magnificent fruit presence and beautiful acidity fusing with supple tannins and mellow oak.
Price approx.: 7,97 EUR
http://www.bodegasverum.com
Verum S.L., Bodegas y Viñedos
+34926511404

VERUM S.L., BODEGAS Y VIÑEDOS 90/100

▼✔ Verum Blanco Sauvignon Blanc Gewürztraminer 2013 : Pale gold with onion skin tints. Highly perfumed nose intermixing tropical fruits (lychee), apple and floral notes of rose. The palate is savoury, balanced and fruity and supported by beautiful acidity bringing harmony to the whole. Refined and persistent.
Price approx.: 7,62 EUR
http://www.bodegasverum.com
Verum S.L., Bodegas y Viñedos
+34926511404

VIÑEDOS BALMORAL S.L 89/100

▼✔ Maravides 12 Meses 2010 : Intense garnet bordering on black. The nose marries spice notes and fruity sweetness with a perceptible delicate toast and smoke note. The palate reveals a very balanced wine showing seductively refined tannins and a velvety texture.
http://www.vinedosbalmoral.com
Viñedos Balmoral, Finca El Moralejo
+34967675723

CALAR DEL RÍO MUNDO 86/100

▼✔ Tempranillo 2011 : Intense hue with garnet-ruby tints. The nose blends jammy red fruits and woody notes of vanilla and fresh oak. Fullness and power come to the fore on the palate. A warm, closely-integrated style capped off with a hint of firmness.
Price approx.: 11,50 EUR
http://www.bodegascalar.com
Bodegas Calar
+34915751130

ÁBREGO 84/100

▼✔ Tempranillo 2011 : Deep ruby with garnet tints. Powerful nose showing assertive ripe red fruit. The palate is robust, generous and concentrated with the same impression carrying through. Firmer finish marked by oak. Drink with meats in a sauce.
Price approx.: 5,50 EUR
http://www.bodegascalar.com
Bodegas Calar
+34915751130

ORGANIC SIGNATURE WINES 82/100

Org▼✔ Cambrius 2013 : Medium intense garnet. The nose shows a pronounced floral character of violet enhanced by fresh raspberry and damp earth notes. Lovely complexity. On the palate, a delicate style showing abundant freshness. A wine to get people talking.
http://www.franchete.com
Organic Signature Wines
+34967472503

VIÑEDOS BALMORAL S.L 82/100

▼✔ Maravides Mediterraneo 2012 : Intense purple. A mix of red fruit notes with a touch of spice and liquorice on the nose. Clean, delicious attack driven by sweets, gradually gaining a little in complexity towards the mid-palate. Lovely acidity and refined structure.
http://www.vinedosbalmoral.com
Viñedos Balmoral, Finca El Moralejo
+34967675723

BODEGAS NAVARRO LÓPEZ 80/100

▼✔ Laguna de la Nava Rojo 2013 : Intense colour with purple-blue. Nose of jammy blackberry bolstered by herb and spice notes. An easy-drinking, mellow, mild wine showing very good balance on the palate. A good companion for everyday foods.
Price approx.: 1,50 EUR
http://www.bodegasnavarrolopez.com
Bodegas Navarro López
+34902193431

VERUM S.L., BODEGAS Y VIÑEDOS 80/100

▼✔ Terra de Verum Airén de Pie Franco 2013 : Pale gold with green tints. The nose opens up to floral and vegetal notes suggestive of freshly-cut grass backed by tropical fruits. Mineral-driven palate combining fresh acidity and a

sensation of bitterness typical of the varietal.
Price approx.: 7,56 EUR
http://www.bodegasverum.com
Verum S.L., Bodegas y Viñedos
+34926511404

VIÑEDOS BALMORAL S.L   79/100

▼♪ Edone Rose Gran Cuvee 2010 : Attractive pink with an elegant mousse forming persistent rings. The nose reveals perfumes of grape and fresh strawberry. The palate displays balanced acidity, good effervescence and crunchy red fruit aromas.
http://www.vinedosbalmoral.com
Viñedos Balmoral, Finca El Moralejo
+34967675723

VERUM S.L., BODEGAS Y VIÑEDOS   77/100

▼♪ Verum Rosado 2013 : Intense pink. Explosive fruity nose reminiscent of strawberry jam then revealing floral perfumes. Warm, fruit-dominant palate flowing into aromatics recalling caramel. Drink well-chilled.
Price approx.: 6,35 EUR
http://www.bodegasverum.com
Verum S.L., Bodegas y Viñedos
+34926511404

VIÑEDOS BALMORAL S.L   75/100

▼♪ Edone Cuvee de María 2011 : Pale gold with active bubbles forming regular rings. The nose opens up to notes of fresh bread, tropical fruits, citrus and subtle mineral undertones. The palate is fresh and lively with suggestions of ripe pineapple. Set aside for the aperitif.
http://www.vinedosbalmoral.com
Viñedos Balmoral, Finca El Moralejo
+34967675723

VIÑEDOS BALMORAL S.L   75/100

▼♪ Edone Gran Cuvee 2009 : Intense yellow-gold. Persistent mousse with an unbroken ring of bubbles. A mix of citrus notes and a milky touch on the nose. Acidity is nicely balanced on the palate and enhances aromas of cooked fruit and green apple.
http://www.vinedosbalmoral.com
Viñedos Balmoral, Finca El Moralejo
+34967675723

CASTILE AND LEON

BIERZO D.O.

EXPORT IBERIA, ABANICO   89/100

▼♪ Manium 2010 : Ruby with purple-blue tints. A mix of black fruit jam aromas, tobacco and pepper notes on the nose. Expressive, savoury palate marked by fruit and presence suffused with toast flavours. The tannins are refined and delicate.

http://www.exportiberia.com
Export Iberia, Abanico
+34 93 812 56 76

RIBERA DEL DUERO D.O.

EXPORT IBERIA, ABANICO   94/100

▼♪ Cathar Reserva 2006 : Deep ruby with purple-blue tints. Elegant nose combining caramel sweet notes and fruit expression. Seductive fruit character and freshness at point of entry flowing into pleasant mocha aromas. Excellent.
http://www.exportiberia.com
Export Iberia, Abanico
+34 93 812 56 76

DEHESA VALDELAGUNA S.L   92/100

▼♪ Montelaguna Selección 2010 : Intense garnet. Refined, expressive nose of jammy black fruits augmented by spice notes recalling black pepper with delicate menthol undertones. A good wine displaying perfect balance between acidity and structure. Excellent.
Price approx.: 21,50 EUR
http://www.montelaguna.es
Dehesa Valdelaguna, S.L
+921142325

BODEGAS TRUS S.L, GRUPO PALACIOS
VINOTECA S.L   92/100

▼♪ Trus Crianza 2011 : Deep red. The nose is dominated by spice with roasted coffe enhanced by a milky, buttery touch. Delicious palate offering up a robust, fruity sensation, beautiful body and substantial length. An excellent wine.
Price approx.: 8,00 EUR
http://www.palaciosvinoteca.com
Palacios Vinoteca
+941444418

DEHESA VALDELAGUNA S.L   87/100

▼♪ Montelaguna Crianza 2010 : Intense garnet. Nose of ripe red fruits enhanced by a delicate milk and sweet note. A characterful, mouth-filling wine leaving a fruity sensation on the palate. Lovely persistent oak notes of roasted coffee.
Price approx.: 14,00 EUR
http://www.montelaguna.es
Dehesa Valdelaguna, S.L
+921142325

DEHESA VALDELAGUNA S.L   82/100

▼✔ Montelaguna 2012 : Intense colour with purple-blue tints. Black berry fruits dominate the nose, flowing into notes of humus and truffle. The palate offers up very good balance between acidity, fruit expression and structure. Ripe, savoury tannins.

Price approx.: 8,20 EUR

http://www.montelaguna.es/

Dehesa Valdelaguna, S.L

+921142325

BODEGAS TRUS S.L, GRUPO PALACIOS VINOTECA S.L   80/100

▼✔ Trus Roble 2012 : Medium intense red. The nose reveals perfumes of ripe black fruits backed by spice. On the palate, a flavoursome wine with lingering fruit enhanced by toast notes. Its freshness makes it a suitable partner for spicy foods.

Price approx.: 4,50 EUR

http://www.palaciosvinoteca.com

Palacios Vinoteca

+941444418

RUEDA D.O.

BODEGAS NAVARRO LÓPEZ   88/100

▼✔ Lirum 2013 : Pale yellow-gold. Aromas of orange blossom are entwined with a refined tropical touch of lychee and mineral undertones on the nose. The palate displays savoury freshness due to the successful fusion of acidity and citrus aromas. A very compelling wine.

Price approx.: 2,40 EUR

http://www.bodegasnavarrolopez.com

Bodegas Navarro López

+34902193431

EMW GRANDES VINOS DE ESPAÑA   86/100

▼✔ El Gordo del Circo 2013 : Yellow-gold with green tints. The nose delivers intense perfumes of fresh pineapple against a very tropical backdrop. A highly aromatic wine on the palate supported by a very enjoyable sensation of exuberance. Very good.

http://www.emw.es

EMW Grandes Vinos de España

+34968151520

EXPORT IBERIA, ABANICO   86/100

▼✔ Piedra Blanca Verdejo 2013 : Very pale yellow tinged with green. The nose is mineral on first pour then opens up after swirling to notes of citrus and tropical aromas. Delicious palate showing forceful fruit expression that stays nicely fresh right through to the finish.

http://www.exportiberia.com

Export Iberia, Abanico

+34 93 812 56 76

BODEGA PAGO TRASLAGARES S.L   84/100

Org ▼✔ Oro Pálido, Verdejo Ecológico 2013 : Intense gold with green tints. Very fresh fragrances of green apple and elegant floral notes can be sensed on the nose. Firm at point of entry then flowing into a dominant mineral dimension which does not obscure savoury fruit undercurrents.

http://www.traslagares.com/

Bodega Pago Traslagares S.L

+34983667023

BODEGA PAGO TRASLAGARES S.L   79/100

▼✔ Traslagares Verdejo 2013 : Pale yellow with brilliant green tints. Pleasantly refined nose opening up to floral notes of lilac then flowing into perfumes of peach. The palate is rich yet nicely fresh due to pronounced acidity. Set aside for the aperitif.

http://www.traslagares.com

Bodega Pago Traslagares S.L

+34983667023

TORO D.O.

EXPORT IBERIA, ABANICO   93/100

▼✔ Los Colmillos 2009 : Deeply-coloured crimson. The nose shows a lovely combination of fruit perfumes, butter, spice and toasted oak. Assertive fruit character on the palate enhanced by a delicate structure and delicious toast aromatics. Excellent.

http://www.exportiberia.com

Export Iberia, Abanico

+34 93 812 56 76

CATALONIA

CAVA D.O.

CAVA AGUSTÍ TORELLÓ MATA   93/100

▼✔ Kripta 2007 : Brilliant pale yellow-green with a ring of very fine, persistent bubbles. Lovely harmony between the citrus and toast notes on the nose. A very fresh, highly aromatic style on the palate. An extremely elegant Cava.

Price approx.: 45,00 EUR

http://www.agustitorellomata.com

Cava Agustí Torelló Mata

+34938911173

CAVA AGUSTÍ TORELLÓ MATA   88/100

▼✔ Brut Nature Barrica Gran Reserva 2009 : Pale gold with green tints, a persistent mousse and fine bubbles forming a perfect ring. A mix of tropical fruit, citrus notes and an elegant yeast touch on the nose. On the palate, a fresh wine with a very elegant character.

Price approx.: 20,00 EUR

http://www.agustitorellomata.com

Cava Agustí Torelló Mata

+34938911173

ANTONIO MASCARO, S.L. 83/100

▼♪ Antonio Mascaró Gran Reserva Brut Nature 2010 : Pale gold with green tints and very persistent bubbles. Mineral nose enhanced by citrus perfumes and floral notes. Fresh palate with noteworthy acidity and persistent fruit undertones. A good Cava.
Price approx.: 10,70 EUR
http://www.mascaro.es
Antonio Mascaro, S.L.
+34938901628

PENEDES D.O.

CELLER CREDO 94/100

Org ▼♪ Can Credo 2010 : Refined vanilla oak on the nose unfurling perfumes of honey, butter, flowers and fennel yet also a strong mineral personality of chalk and petrol. The palate is fresh and well-balanced, long and complex. Ideal for grilled sole.
Price approx.: 18,00 EUR
http://www.celercredo.cat
Celler Credo
938910214

ANTONIO MASCARO, S.L. 92/100

▼♪ Brandi : Very vibrant orange. The nose intimates hints of date, cinnamon and clove. The palate reveals refined toast notes and expresses the authenticity of the grape. Elegant warmth is displayed over substantial length. Excellent.
Price approx.: 11,50 EUR
http://www.mascaro.es
Antonio Mascaro, S.L.
+34938901628

CELLER CREDO 92/100

Org ▼♪ Aloers 2012 : Remarkably mineral nose opening up to perfumes of spice, garrigue (rosemary, fresh bay) and lime zest. Fresh and well-balanced on the palate, subtle, long and complex. A handsome wine for the aperitif or with lemon-flavoured chicken.
Price approx.: 12,00 EUR
http://www.celercredo.cat
Celler Credo
+938910214

ALBET I NOYA 89/100

▼♪ Belat 2009 : The nose reveals perfumes of blueberry, floral notes of violet, black pepper, dark fruits and liquorice. Fat on the palate, mellow, lush and very fruity at point of entry. Subtle cigar box notes. Light, mellow and extremely charming.
http://www.albetinoya.cat
Albet I Noya
+34938994812

CELLER MAS CANDI (RAMON JANE GARRIGA) 89/100

▼♪ Quatre Xarel.los 2011 : Harmonious nose combining citrus notes, refined oak and a vegetal dimension. Full palate enhanced by beautiful acidity recalling lemon zest and fruity apple aromas. Well-integrated oak imparts good balance to the whole.
Price approx.: 10,00 EUR
http://www.mascandi.com
Celler Mas Candi (Ramon Jane Garriga)
+34680765275

VILADELLOPS VINICOLA, S.L 89/100

▼♪ Xarel.lo 2012 : Deep yellow. Pleasant nose blending vegetal and fruit notes of apple and citrus with a touch of vanilla and some very subtle oak. Full on the palate with good overall balance and pronounced freshness. Lovely lingering finish.
Viladellops Vinicola, S.L
+93 8188371

PARATO VINICOLA, S.L. 88/100

▼♪ Parató Negre classic 2004 : Evolved nose revealing notes of coffee, black cherry, cigar box, new leather, black pepper and paprika. Warm, full palate with slightly dry tannins. Medium intense finish marked by ripe vegetal accents.
Price approx.: 9,75 EUR
Parato Vinicola, S.L.
+34 93 898 81 82

VILADELLOPS VINICOLA, S.L 88/100

▼♪ Tinto 2010 : Pleasant nose of nicely ripe cherry, orange peel, black pepper, leather and mineral undertones. Good overall balance, well-integrated tannins and medium persistency on the finish. Grenache and Syrah go hand in hand and each imparts its own personality.
Viladellops Vinicola, S.L
+93 8188371

ALBET I NOYA 87/100

▼♪ La Milana 2009 : Open nose of black pepper, ripe black fruits and balsamic accents. On the palate, a concentrated, expressive and warm wine that is well-structured and tannic. Robust personality. Designed to last. Pair with red meats.
http://www.albetinoya.cat
Albet I Noya
+34938994812

Prices mentioned in this book are guideline and can vary depending on point of sale. The shops, wineries or publisher can in no way be held responsible for this.

ALBET I NOYA 87/100

🍷🌿 El Fanio 2012 : Medium intense yellow. Pronounced toasted notes on the nose with vegetal and white pepper aromas. On the palate, a fairly warm style displaying vegetal aromatics. A balanced wine with medium length that is instantly accessible.
http://www.albetinoya.cat
Albet I Noya
34938994812

LLOPART CAVA, S.A. 87/100

Org🍷🌿 Clos dels Fòssils 2012 : The nose opens up to citrus fruits, white flowers and nectarine with a whiff of white pepper in the background. Mouth-coating, well-structured palate with faint vegetal aromas. Medium length. The various components need time to meld.
Price approx.: 10,50 EUR
http://www.llopart.es
Llopart Cava
+34938993125

ALBET I NOYA 86/100

🍷🌿 Reserva Martí 2008 : Expressive nose intermixing black pepper and dark fruits. The palate shows seductively beautiful acidity, drinkability and elegant tannins. Oak is fairly upfront and persistent on the finish. Would sit well alongside grilled foods.
http://www.albetinoya.cat
Albet I Noya
+34938994812

BODEGA J. MIQUEL JANÉ 86/100

🍷🌿 Cabernet Sauvignon 2012 : Strawberry-red. Nose of boiled sweets, chocolate, white pepper, red fruits and paprika. Fresh and fairly long on the palate with a pronounced bitter finish. A very accessible wine with an assertive vegetal character. Ideal for grilled white meats.
Price approx.: 7,00 EUR
http://www.jmiqueljane.com
Bodega J. Miquel Jané
+34 93 891 02 14

CELLER MAS CANDI (RAMON JANE GARRIGA) 86/100

🍷🌿 Les Forques 2009 : Expressive nose marked by a strong mineral dimension of graphite, notes of ripe cherry, black pepper and meat. The palate displays strong acidity dominating the whole. Tannins are present with ripe vegetal aromatics.
Price approx.: 9,00 EUR
http://www.mascandi.com
Celler Mas Candi (Ramon Jane Garriga)
+34680765275

LLOPART CAVA, S.A. 86/100

Org🍷🌿 Castell de Subirats 2009 : Expressive nose intermixing green pepper, smoke, toast (coffee), black pepper, earth notes and a touch of dried orange peel. Light attack, well-integrated tannins and a good overall structure dominated by a sensation of heat. Serve slightly chilled.
Price approx.: 12,50 EUR
http://www.llopart.es
Llopart Cava
+34938993125

LLOPART CAVA, S.A. 86/100

Org🍷🌿 Llopart Vitis 2012 : Appealing pale yellow. Mild, Muscat varietal aromas on the nose enhanced by citrus and fresh grape notes. The predominant citrus aromas recur on the palate. A light, perfumed and easy-drinking wine, suitable for any occasion.
Price approx.: 9,00 EUR
http://www.llopart.es
Llopart Cava
+34938993125

BODEGA J. MIQUEL JANÉ 85/100

🍷🌿 Blanc Baltana 2012 : Brilliant pale yellow. Expressive nose intermixing lemon, bay, hay, white pepper and white flowers. Fresh, fairly full-bodied palate displaying a hint of sourness. A pleasant, approachable wine, dry on the finish and pairing with grilled fish.
Price approx.: 6,50 EUR
http://www.jmiqueljane.com
Bodega J. Miquel Jané
+34 93 891 02 14

BODEGA J. MIQUEL JANÉ 84/100

🍷🌿 Miquel Jané Baltana Selecció 2010 : Garnet-red. Ripe nose of dark fruits, black pepper and Indian ink with a touch of old oak, vanilla and smoke. Well-integrated yet slightly dry tannins on the palate backed by caramel and a vegetal note. Serve with grilled red meats.
Price approx.: 9,50 EUR
http://www.jmiqueljane.com
Bodega J. Miquel Jané
+34 93 891 02 14

PLA DE BAGES D.O.

BODEGAS ABADAL, S.L. (MASIA ROQUETA) 91/100

🍷🌿 Abadal 3.9 2009 : Deep ruby. The nose reveals perfumes of dried fruits, hazelnut, blackberry jam and rosemary. A very elegant wine on the palate where roasted coffee and caramel flavours do not obscure fruit expression or freshness.
http://www.abadal.net
Bodegas Abadal, S.L. (Masia Roqueta)
+93 874 35 11

BODEGAS ABADAL, S.L. (MASIA ROQUETA)
88/100

▼🍷 Abadal Crianza 2010 : Intense ruby. A lovely blend of ripe wild fruits, pepper and herbs on the nose with a tobacco note in the background. The wine seems nicely balanced on the palate with aromas of fruit and sweets and persistent acidity.
http://www.abadal.net
Bodegas Abadal, S.L. (Masia Roqueta)
+93 874 35 11

BODEGAS ABADAL, S.L. (MASIA ROQUETA)
85/100

▼🍷 Abadall Picapoll 2013 : Bright, pale yellow with green tints. A mix of tropical fruits like fresh pineapple with white peach, citrus then floral notes in the background. The palate opens up to fruit and freshness then delivers the archetypal warmth stemming from the varietal.
http://www.abadal.net
Bodegas Abadal, S.L. (Masia Roqueta)
+93 874 35 11

PRIORATO D.O.

TERRA DE VEREMA
92/100

▼🍷 Corelium 2005 : Intense hue, ruby tints. Warm nose of ripe fruits augmented by a fresh oak note. The palate reveals a substantial structure yet retains a persistent mellow character. Beautiful acidity and quality fruit are noteworthy features of this 2005. Top-notch.
Price approx.: 35,00 EUR
http://www.teradeverema.com
Terra de Verema
+34667726330

EMW GRANDES VINOS DE ESPAÑA
90/100

▼🍷 Casa Rojo Maquinon 2013 : Intense red with dark purple. The nose shows pronounced candied black fruits, blackberry and blackcurrant jam, revealing a delicate truffle aroma. A characterful wine on the palate with an intense fruity attack flowing into refined notes of toasted caramel.
http://www.emw.es/
EMW Grandes Vinos de España
+34968151520

TERRA DE VEREMA
87/100

▼🍷 Triumvirat 2009 : Intense garnet. Expressive, intense and complex nose intermixing ripe fruits and elegant spice notes. The palate reveals aromas of sweets, chocolate and dark fruit jam. A very elegant wine combining character and freshness.
Price approx.: 18,00 EUR
http://www.teradeverema.com
Terra de Verema
34667726330

TERRA ALTA D.O.

EXPORT IBERIA, ABANICO
94/100

▼🍷 Herencia Altés L'Estel 2013 : Brilliant crimson-red. Dominant fruit and floral notes on the nose blending harmoniously with aromas of tobacco and leather that are exuded after swirling. A powerful attack flows into elegant fruit supported by good acidity.
http://www.exportiberia.com
Export Iberia, Abanico
+34 93 812 56 76

EXPORT IBERIA, ABANICO
92/100

▼🍷 Herencia Altés Garnatxia Blanca 2013 : Light yellow with onion skin highlights. Highly unusual nose blending freshly-cut grass perfumes with a fresh pineapple note. On the palate, this savoury wine boasts personality and well-balanced acidity. Persistent toast-infused finish.
http://www.exportiberia.com
Export Iberia, Abanico
+34 93 812 56 76

EXPORT IBERIA, ABANICO
88/100

▼🍷 Herencia Altés Cupatge 2013 : Intense crimson bordering on black. The nose is dominated by fresh black fruit notes coupled with spice and a subtle leather touch. Structure is initially displayed on the palate then flows into fruit expression and freshness.
http://www.exportiberia.com
Export Iberia, Abanico
+34 93 812 56 76

EXPORT IBERIA, ABANICO
87/100

▼🍷 Herencia Altés La Serra 2012 : Deep red, purple-blue tints. Aromas of candied fruits and fig take centre stage on the nose entwined with pepper and chocolate. The palate reveals a very fruity wine with lots of personality and beautiful acidity. Roasted coffee accents mark the finish.
http://www.exportiberia.com
Export Iberia, Abanico
+34 93 812 56 76

EXPORT IBERIA, ABANICO
87/100

▼🍷 Herencia Altés Benufet 2013 : Yellow-gold with green tints. A mineral dimension, citrus notes and a delicate toast sensation intermingle on the nose. A strong personality is displayed on the palate with surprising acidity and freshness. Savoury fruit persistency.
http://www.exportiberia.com
Export Iberia, Abanico
+34 93 812 56 76

EXPORT IBERIA, ABANICO 79/100

▼♪ Herencia Altés Garnatxia Negra 2013 : Ruby with purple-blue tints. The nose is dominated by aromas of vanilla and toast entwined with ripe red fruit. Delicious fruity palate with a supple structure and fine-grained tannins. Persistent finish showing accents of vanilla and caramel.

http://www.exportiberia.com

Export Iberia, Abanico

+34 93 812 56 76

EXTREMADURA

RIBERA DEL GUADIANA D.O.

BODEGAS TORIBIO 91/100

▼♪ Viña Puebla BFB 2012 : Pale yellow with green tints. The nose reveals a broad array of aromas with nicely combined mineral notes, fruit and breadcrust. Lovely balanced mineral character on the palate with fruit and acidity. Very elegant.

Price approx.: 4,60 EUR

http://www.bodegastoribio.com

Bodegas Toribio

+924551449

COOPERATIVA SAN ISIDRO DE VILLAFRANCA 91/100

▼♪ Valdequemao Blanco en barrica 2013 : Bright yellow-gold. The nose opens up to fruity notes then reveals toast accents from the oak. The palate combines fat and beautiful acidity. Delicate sourness and an elegant touch of toast on the finish add to the complexity.

http://www.cooperativasanisidro.com

Cooperativa San Isidro de Villafranca

+33924324136

COOPERATIVA SAN ISIDRO DE VILLAFRANCA 87/100

▼♪ Valdequemao Blanco 2013 : Light yellow with green tints. The nose is a nice halfway house between tropical, citrus notes and a mineral dimension. Citrus-dominant attack leading into a palate supported by acidity and minerality imparting freshness. An honest, characterful wine.

Price approx.: 1,80 EUR

http://www.cooperativasanisidro.com

Cooperativa San Isidro de Villafranca

+33924324136

SOC. COOP. MONTEVIRGEN 87/100

▼♪ Marques Montevirgen de Villalba : Light yellow-gold. The nose displays mineral tones enhanced by tropical fruit and grapefruit perfumes. A strict, full wine on the palate with a mineral character blending with a touch of sourness and elegant acidity.

Soc. Coop. Montevirgen

+924 68 50 25

BODEGAS CARABAL 85/100

▼♪ Carabal Cávea 2009 : Crimson displaying faint signs of maturing. Expressive nose of ripe black fruits, spice and subtle, mellow oak. More of the same blend of fruit and oak on the palate enhanced by a subtle vegetal tone. A round wine that has nicely matured.

Price approx.: 12,00 EUR

http://www.carabal.es

Bodegas Carabal

+34917346152

SOC. COOP. SANTA MARTA VIRGEN 85/100

▼♪ Puerta de la Coracha 2012 : Ruby-red with purple-blue tints. The nose offers up aromas of blackberry and ripe cherry. Lovely, delicate notes of oak, spice and black pepper. Fine-grained tannins on the palate. Mellow finish driven by a bitterness that imparts complexity.

Price approx.: 3,00 EUR

Soc. Coop. Santa Marta Virgen

+924 69 02 18

BODEGAS CARABAL 84/100

▼♪ Carabal Rasgo 2010 : Intense red with purple-blue. Expressive nose intermixing black plum, spice and mineral notes (graphite). On the palate, a harmonious wine exuding blackberry and damp earth aromas, nicely combined with upfront acidity. A savoury wine boasting personality.

Price approx.: 7,50 EUR

http://www.carabal.es

Bodegas Carabal

+34917346152

BODEGAS ROMALE, S.L. 84/100

▼♪ Privilegio de Romale 2010 : Attractive ruby. Pleasant nose intermixing aromas of forest fruits, fresh plum and notes of violet and spice. Fleshy, full-bodied palate showing seductively precise fruit dominated by black cherry. Harmonious across the palate.

Price approx.: 3,00 EUR

http://www.romale.com

Bodegas Romale, S.L.

+34924667255

BODEGAS VIA DE LA PLATA, S.L. 84/100

▼♪ Via de la Plata Brut Nature Chardonnay 2012 : Light gold with green tints, fine bubbles. The nose opens up to apple, yeast and milk notes then reveals fresh perfumes of citrus and mineral notes. A fresh attack on the palate contrasts with a warm mid-palate and suave fruit.

Price approx.: 5,50 EUR

http://www.bodegasviadelaplata.es

Bodegas Via de la Plata, S.L.

+34924661155

PAGO LOS BALANCINES, S.L.   84/100

▼♪ Vasos de la Luz 2009 : Intense crimson. Highly aromatic nose revealing notes of ripe fruits and damp earth. Aromas of ripe fruits on the palate coupled with notes of burnt oak and an interesting, light vegetal touch.
Price approx.: 49,00 EUR
Pago Los Balancines, S.L.
+620 27 33 11

SOC. COOP. SAN MARCOS DE ALMENDRALEJO
    84/100

▼♪ Campobarro Pardina 2013 : Pale yellow with green tints. The nose reveals aromas of lemon and flowers. A warm attack on the palate and abundant freshness combine to make a very well-balanced and persistent wine.
Soc. Coop. San Marcos de Almendralejo
+924 67 04 10

SOC. COOP. SANTA MARTA VIRGEN   84/100

▼♪ Blason del Turra 2013 : Pale yellow-gold tinged with green. Highly perfumed nose exuding vegetal notes of asparagus and tropical fruit aromas of mango and pineapple. Extremely pronounced tropical notes on the palate with beautiful freshness. An unusual style wine.
Price approx.: 2,50 EUR
Soc. Coop. Santa Marta Virgen
+924 69 02 18

SOC. COOP. VIÑAOLIVA   84/100

▼♪ Zaleo Pardina 2013 : Pale yellow with green tints. Highly floral nose showing great aromatic elegance with fresh notes of lemon. Excellent acidity on the palate with persistent freshness and a faint trace of sourness imparting complexity.
Price approx.: 1,50 EUR
Soc. Coop. Vĩaoliva
+924 67 73 21

BODEGAS MARTINEZ PAIVA, S.A.T.   82/100

▼♪ Payva Reserva 2007 : Ruby-red with bricking. The nose reveals aromas of ripe red fruits, cherry and burnt oak backed by herbal aromas. Generous attack on the palate, a traditionally styled wine showing fruit and oak capped off with a soft, vegetal finish.
Price approx.: 6,50 EUR
http://www.payva.es
Bodegas Martinez Paiva, S.A.T.
+34 924 67 11 30

BODEGAS ROMALE, S.L.   82/100

Org▼♪ Privilegio de Romale Cava 2012 : Light yellow with very active, persistent bubbles. The nose shows a blend of citrus fruits and mineral notes with fresh pineapple and a touch of yeast. The palate shows seductively focused fruit, citrus aromas and a subtle touch of sourness on the finish.
Price approx.: 2,80 EUR

http://www.romale.com
Bodegas Romale, S.L.
34924667255

COOPERATIVA NUESTRA SEÑORA DE LA SOLEDAD   82/100

▼♪ Orgullo de Barros Tempranillo 2013 : Ruby with crimson shades. Nose of red and black berry fruits such as cassis with elegant milk undertones. The palate is round, supple and well-balanced and boasts good acidity. An easy-drinking wine for everyday meals.
Price approx.: 1,80 EUR
http://www.bodegaslasoledad.com
Cooperativa Nuestra Señora de la Soledad
34924680228

SOC. COOP. VIÑAOLIVA   82/100

▼♪ Zaleo Blanco Semidulce 2013 : Yellow and light gold. Expressive nose blending honey, vegetal notes (asparagus) and a touch of lemon zest. A sweet wine on the palate balanced by a sensation of freshness imparted by the citrus and lemon flavours. An unusual wine.
Price approx.: 1,80 EUR
Soc. Coop. Vĩaoliva
924 67 73 21

BODEGAS CARABAL   80/100

▼♪ Carabal Gulae 2010 : Intense crimson. Expressive nose revealing perfumes of plum, blackberry and dark fruits combined with mineral notes, spices and vanilla. Full palate introducing flavours of coffee, liquorice, oak and black pepper.
Price approx.: 20,50 EUR
http://www.carabal.es
Bodegas Carabal
34917346152

BODEGAS MARTINEZ PAIVA, S.A.T.   80/100

▼♪ Payva Cosecha 2013 : Attractive, intense violet with shades near to black. Expressive nose intermixing forest fruits with notes of caramel and spice. Well-structured, mellow palate marked by fruit presence. The finish is slightly bitter yet delicate.
Price approx.: 2,60 EUR
http://www.payva.es
Bodegas Martinez Paiva, S.A.T.
+34 924 67 11 30

BODEGAS ORAN S.L.L.   80/100

▼♪ Senturio de Oran Blanco 2013 : Bright, pale yellow. The nose shows pronounced vegetal notes, lime and a mineral dimension in the background. Warm attack with subtle acidity and freshness imparted by citrus aromas. Serve chilled as an aperitif or with cold meals.
Bodegas Oran S.L.L.
662 95 28 01

BODEGAS VIA DE LA PLATA, S.L.   80/100

▼✦ Vía de la Plata Brut Rosé 2012 : Strawberry-pink with faint orange. Floral nose enhanced by notes of strawberry and blackberry. The palate is round, generous and fruity. An honest, well-balanced, easy-drinking wine that works well chilled with desserts.

Price approx.: 3,60 EUR
http://www.bodegasviadelaplata.es
Bodegas Via de la Plata, S.L.
34924661155

VIÑAS DE ALANGE, S.A.   80/100

CONV▼✦ Palacio Quemado La Zarcita 2013 : Attractive crimson with very deep purple shades. Harmonious nose of concentrated cherry, oak and mild spices. More of the cherry, oak and mild spices on the palate with delicate fruit. Persistent charred finish. An easy-drinking wine.

Price approx.: 9,00 EUR
http://www.palacioquemado.com
Viñas de Alange, S.A.
34924120296

BODEGAS MARCELINO DIAZ, S.A.   79/100

▼✦ Cava Brut Puerta Palma   : Golden yellow with medium, persistent bubbles. A Cava boasting aromas of white flowers, lemon zest and soft perfumes of tropical fruits backed by apple. Notes of apple recur on the palate with abundant freshness.

Price approx.: 3,50 EUR
Bodegas Marcelino Diaz, S.A.
924 67 75 48

COOPERATIVA SANTA MARÍA EGIPCIADA
    79/100

▼✦ Conde de la Corte Tempranillo 2013 : Deep ruby with purple-blue highlights. Fruit perfumes prevail on the nose interspersed with toast notes. Beautiful harmonious attack that is mellow yet fresh, contrasting with a firmer, vegetal mid-palate and finish.

Price approx.: 1,66 EUR
http://www.bodegaslacorte.com
Cooperativa Santa María Egipciada
33924693014

PAGO LOS BALANCINES, S.L.   79/100

▼✦ Los Balancines Huno 2011 : Deep ruby-red with very intense purple glints. The nose reveals perfumes of liquorice, spice and red fruits with delicate oak notes in the background. Substantial fruit concentration on the palate with beautiful acidity.

Price approx.: 12,00 EUR
Pago Los Balancines, S.L.
620 27 33 11

SOC. COOP. VIÑAOLIVA   79/100

▼✦ Zaleo Premium 2012 : Very deep crimson and purple. Extremely intense nose with accents of cherry, a touch of anise and pepper. On the palate, a wine boasting a beautiful fruity attack, marrying impeccably with delicate vegetal notes.

Price approx.: 3,50 EUR
Soc. Coop. Vlñaoliva
924 67 73 21

SOC. COOP. VIÑAOLIVA   79/100

▼✦ Zaleo Tempranillo 2013 : Intense purple. A mix of fresh fruits and spice undertones on the nose. The palate opens up to a mellow attack then displays greater firmness and a faint sensation of sourness. A wine that works best in its youth.

Price approx.: 1,50 EUR
Soc. Coop. Vlñaoliva
924 67 73 21

VIÑAS DE ALANGE, S.A.   79/100

CONV▼✦ Palacio Quemado Los Acilates 2011 : Deep ruby-red. Aromas of black fruits, oak and leather on the nose. The palate shows perceptible fruit presence coupled with savoury acidity and beautiful burnt oak presence leaving a sensation of caramel.

Price approx.: 15,50 EUR
http://www.palacioquemado.com
Viñas de Alange, S.A.
34924120296

BODEGAS ORAN S.L.L.   78/100

▼✦ Señorío de Oran Flor 2012 : Ruby-red with purple nuances. The nose exudes roasted coffee, paprika and cured meat notes. A lightweight wine on the palate showing delicate fruit presence and persistent roasted coffee notes.

Bodegas Oran S.L.L.
662 95 28 01

BODEGAS ORAN S.L.L.   78/100

▼✦ Entremares Rosado 2013 : Strawberry-pink with orange glints. More of the ripe strawberry on the nose coupled with a vegetal touch in the background. A fresh wine on the palate with fruit overtones yet very subdued acidity.

Bodegas Oran S.L.L.
662 95 28 01

BODEGAS VIA DE LA PLATA, S.L.   78/100

▼✦ Vía de la Plata Brut   : Pale gold with persistent bubbles. Expressive nose suggestive of apple flesh and citrus fruits. Fleshy attack, bone-dry style dominated by citrus fruits with a subtle vegetal touch. A refreshing wine that shows at its best when served well-chilled.

Price approx.: 3,60 EUR
http://www.bodegasviadelaplata.es
Bodegas Via de la Plata, S.L.
34924661155

BODEGAS VIA DE LA PLATA, S.L. 78/100

▼✎ Vía de la Plata Brut Nature Coupage 2012 : Bright pale yellow with fine, persistent bubbles. Lovely expressive perfumes of green apple and ripe pear on the palate. A warm attack flows into fruit and vegetal aromatics before finishing with a subtle touch of sourness.
Price approx.: 3,65 EUR
http://www.bodegasviadelaplata.es
Bodegas Via de la Plata, S.L.
34924661155

BODEGAS TORIBIO 77/100

▼✎ Viña Puebla Verdejo 2013 : Light yellow with green tints. A mix of tropical fruits and milky notes on the nose. Good balance, subtle aromas and upfront freshness on the palate, rounded off with the refined sourness of the grapefruit aromas. Serve as an aperitif.
Price approx.: 3,80 EUR
http://www.bodegastoribio.com
Bodegas Toribio
924551449

SOC. COOP. VIÑAOLIVA 77/100

▼✎ Zaleo Rosado 2013 : Cherry-pink with orange highlights. Nose of fresh morello cherry developing an unusual perfume of freshly-mowed meadow. Warm at point of entry flowing into distinctive exuberance with fruit and vegetal notes.
Price approx.: 1,50 EUR
Soc. Coop. Vlñaoliva
924 67 73 21

COOPERATIVA SANTA MARÍA EGIPCIADA 76/100

▼✎ Conde de la Corte 2013 : Bright pale yellow-gold. The nose opens up to vegetal notes then reveals a tropical character of fresh pineapple and a subtle milky touch. Warm palate balanced by a trace of acidity on the finish. Drink chilled as an appetiser.
Price approx.: 1,33 EUR
http://www.bodegaslacorte.com
Cooperativa Santa María Egipciada
33924693014

BODEGAS VITICOLTORES DE BARROS 75/100

▼✎ Vizana 2010 : Deep crimson with purple shades. The nose offers up notes of red fruits, blackberry, a spice character and a vegetal touch. The palate is warm, structured and vegetal and boasts round tannins and abundant freshness. Very fruity finish.
Price approx.: 5,00 EUR
Bodegas Viticoltores de Barros
+34 924 66 48 52

PAGO LOS BALANCINES, S.L. 75/100

▼✎ Blanco sobre Lias 2013 : Pale yellow-gold. The nose reveals vegetal notes melded with watermelon and melon aromas on first pour. Warm at point of entry flowing into refreshing exuberance. Delicate finish driven by apple skin aromas.
Price approx.: 5,50 EUR
Pago Los Balancines, S.L.
620 27 33 11

VT EXTREMARDURA

BODEGAS HABLA 94/100

▼✎ Habla N° 11 2010 : Ruby with purple-blue tints. Endearing nose intermixing liquorice, fresh red fruits and a whiff of smoke. On the palate, an elegant style wine with upfront fruit, impeccable acidity, refined tannins and delicate oak. Excellent.
Price approx.: 15,30 EUR
http://www.bodegashabla.com
Bodegas Habla
34927659180

BODEGAS HABLA 92/100

▼✎ Habla N° 12 2011 : Intense purple-blue bordering on black. Expressive, elegant nose marrying spice, red fruits and a delicate anise note in the background. Plenty of fruit on the palate enhanced by notes of leather, mellow tannins and well-integrated oak. Very compelling.
Price approx.: 15,30 EUR
http://www.bodegashabla.com
Bodegas Habla
34927659180

VIÑA SANTA MARINA 88/100

▼✎ Miraculus 2007 : Intense crimson. Classic nose of wild black berry fruits enhanced by subtle notes of smoky oak and spice. Well-balanced palate with a warm attack nicely counterbalanced by good acidity, ripe tannins and persistent fruit.
Price approx.: 19,00 EUR
http://www.vsantamarina.com
Viña Santa Marina
902506364

BODEGAS HABLA 87/100

▼✎ Habla del Silencio 2011 : Red with dark purple highights. The nose opens up to notes of mint and black pepper then reveals perfumes of fresh black fruits and violet. Delicious, savoury and fruity palate balanced by good acidity and a hint of oak.
Price approx.: 6,85 EUR
http://www.bodegashabla.com
Bodegas Habla
34927659180

BODEGA DE MIRABEL 85/100

Org ▼ ♪ Pagos de Mirabel Blanco 2013 : Pale gold with green tints. Mature nose dominated by perfumes of hazelnut. The palate is balanced, warm and marked by flavours of toasted nuts and toast. A very unusual wine.

Price approx.: 27,00 EUR
Bodega de mirabel
34927323154

BODEGAS DE OCCIDENTE 84/100

▼ ♪ Buche 2012 : Ruby-red. Lovely refined oak aromas on the nose melding beautifully with the red fruit and spice. An easy-drinking style on the palate where fruit, freshness and oak unite well. Nicely crafted.

http://www.bodegasoccidente.com
Bodegas de Occidente
34662952801

BODEGAS CARLOS PLAZA 80/100

▼ ♪ Carlos Plaza Joven 2013 : Intense colour with crimson tints. The nose marries fresh red fruit perfumes with vegetal notes and spice undertones. Lightweight, fruity structure on the palate displaying a good level of acidity. An easy-drinking style.

Price approx.: 4,00 EUR
http://www.bodegascarlosplaza.com
Bodegas Carlos Plaza
34924687932

BODEGAS HABLA 79/100

▼ ♪ Habla de la Tierra 2013 : Intense purple-blue. Suggestions of fresh blackberry and plum flesh with vegetal and milky undertones. More of the wild fruits on the palate coupled with a sensation of toast supported by a warm structure.

Price approx.: 3,75 EUR
http://www.bodegashabla.com
Bodegas Habla
34927659180

BODEGAS MCR 79/100

▼ ♪ Ines del Alma Mia 2013 : Yellow-gold. Fresh nose with accents of pineapple and banana. On the palate, an unusual wine with an honest, fruit-driven attack flowing into a crisp range of aromatics. Drink as an appetiser.

Price approx.: 3,50 EUR
http://www.bodegasmcr.com
Bodegas MCR
34924677337

VIÑA SANTA MARINA 79/100

▼ ♪ Gladiator 2008 : Intense ruby. Expressive nose combining ripe fruits, toasted oak notes and a touch of caramel. Warm attack leading into a mid-palate marked by vanilla aromas. A traditional style wine.

Price approx.: 21,00 EUR
http://www.vsantamarina.com
Viña Santa Marina
902506364

BODEGAS DE OCCIDENTE 78/100

▼ ♪ Gran Buche 2010 : Deep ruby. Nose of red fruits augmented by a faint vegetal touch. Warm at point of entry with a fine-grained texture. Mellow mid-palate and finish tinged with a hint of bitterness. A wine with real approachability.

http://www.bodegasoccidente.com
Bodegas de Occidente
34662952801

BODEGAS CARLOS PLAZA 77/100

▼ ♪ Carlos Plaza Selección 2011 : Ruby with bricking. The nose displays aromas of ripe fruits coupled with spicy and toasted oak. Nicely balanced acidity and alcoholic warmth on the palate with fruit and oak also complementing each other.

Price approx.: 7,00 EUR
http://www.bodegascarlosplaza.com
Bodegas Carlos Plaza
34924687932

VIÑA SANTA MARINA 77/100

▼ ♪ Viña Santa Martina Cabernet Sauvignon y Syrah 2010 : Intense crimson. Nose of ripe black fruits and spice with vegetal undertones. Upfront acidity on the palate and a vegetal sensation that leads into ripe fruit aromas on the finish. A wine with real accessibility.

Price approx.: 7,98 EUR
http://www.vsantamarina.com
Viña Santa Marina
902506364

GALICIA

RIAS BAIXAS D.O.

BODEGAS SANTIAGO ROMA, S.L. 91/100

▼ ♪ Albariño Selección 2013 : Bright yellow-gold. A mix of mineral and citrus notes on the nose with a fine touch of gunpowder imparting beautiful aromatic freshness. Fresh and bubbly on the palate, well-balanced and leaving a delicious fruity aftertaste. Very good.

Price approx.: 6,45 EUR
http://wwwsantiagoroma.com
Bodegas Santiago Roma, S.L.
34986718477

VIÑA CARTÍN, S.L. 88/100

▼ ♪ Terras de Lantaño 2013 : Medium intense yellow with green tints. Subdued nose of hay and citrus enhanced by a subtle touch of spice and white flowers. Balanced and fresh on the palate showing medium persistency. Makes an ideal aperitif.

VIÑA CARTÍN, S.L.
34986154239

ADEGAS LUZ 87/100

▼ ♪ Abadía de Tortóreos - Albariño 2012 : Pale yellow. Expressive nose blending vegetal notes of hay with stewed lemon zest, russet apple and white truffle. Good presence on the palate, a warm style revealing banana notes. Fairly persistent finish.

http://adegasluz.es
Adegasluz
986648559

VIÑA CARTÍN, S.L. 87/100

▼ ♪ Viña Cartín 2013 : Light yellow-green. Expressive nose of hay, lemon zest, a whiff of white pepper and pineapple. Fresh, light and seductive palate. An honest, pleasurable style showing a lovely long finish with faint bitterness. Perfect for seafood.

VIÑA CARTÍN, S.L.
34986154239

BODEGAS COTO REDONDO, S.L (PERNOD RICARD) 86/100

▼ ♪ Manuel D'Amaro Pedral 2011 : Red with purple-blue, bordering on black. The nose shows notes of menthol entwined with perfumes of blackberry and pepper. Lovely fine-grained texture, balance, mouth-filling fruit, freshness and a finish recalling sweets.

http://www.bodegas-cotoredondo.com
Bodegas Coto Redondo, S.L
+34 986 66 72 12

EXPORT IBERIA, ABANICO 85/100

▼ ♪ Diluvio 2013 : Pale yellow with pronounced green tints. Tropical notes of lychee and white peach backed by mineral aromas are displayed on the nose. The palate is fresh and even more mineral-driven, revealing a marked contrast with the nose aromatics.

http://www.exportiberia.com
Export Iberia, Abanico
+34 93 812 56 76

BODEGAS SANTIAGO ROMA, S.L. 84/100

▼ ♪ Colleita de Martís 2013 : Intense yellow-gold. Assertive tropical notes on the nose enhanced by a refined touch of butter. Lovely freshness, savoury character and persistent fruit notes on the palate. An elegant wine.

http://wwwsantiagoroma.com
Bodegas Santiago Roma, S.L.
34986718477

BODEGAS VINUS ORIGINALES, GRUPO PALACIOS VINOTECA 84/100

▼ ♪ Sete Bois 2013 : Yellow-gold. Expressive, complex nose marked by tropical fruits, floral notes and a mineral dimension. On the palate, a robust, idiosyncratic wine showing a good level of acidity. Good Albarino varietal expression.

Price approx.: 4,50 EUR
http://www.palaciosvinoteca.com
Palacios Vinoteca
941444418

EMW GRANDES VINOS DE ESPAÑA 82/100

▼ ♪ La Marimorena 2013 : Pale yellow-gold. A mix of delicate tropical fruit aromas, floral notes and lemon zest on the nose. Very fresh, fruity palate supported by good acidity making it a delicious wine. Ideal for hot afternoons.

http://www.emw.es
EMW Grandes Vinos de España
34968151520

BODEGAS COTO REDONDO, S.L (PERNOD RICARD) 80/100

▼ ♪ Señorio de Rubios Sousón 2013 : Intense colour with crimson tints. On the nose, perfumes of wild berry jam, milky notes and snuff can be sensed. Suave on the palate, supported by upfront acidity which imparts freshness. A wine conducive to conversation.

http://www.bodegas-cotoredondo.com
Bodegas Coto Redondo, S.L
+34 986 66 72 12

BODEGAS COTO REDONDO, S.L (PERNOD RICARD) 79/100

▼ ♪ Señorio de Rubios Albariño 2013 : Yellow-gold with green tints. The nose opens up to floral notes then reveals subtle aromas of banana and lemon zest. The palate is not lacking in personality with minerality and acidity combining to create a fresh wine.

http://www.bodegas-cotoredondo.com/
Bodegas Coto Redondo, S.L
+34 986 66 72 12

BODEGAS COTO REDONDO, S.L (PERNOD RICARD) 79/100

▼ ♪ Señorio de Rubios (Pernod Ricard) : Bright yellow-gold with persistent bubbles and a fine mousse. A mix of floral notes, honey and tropical fruits on the nose. On the palate, a fresh, fruity and persistent wine boasting good acidity.

http://www.bodegas-cotoredondo.com/
Bodegas Coto Redondo, S.L
+34 986 66 72 12

BODEGAS SANTIAGO ROMA, S.L. 79/100

▼ ♪ Albariño 2013 : Bright yellow-gold. Tropical accents on the nose delivering delicate aromas of ripe banana and pineapple with delicate mineral undertones. Amazing freshness and minerality on the palate. A perfect wine for light summer meals.

http://wwwsantiagoroma.com
Bodegas Santiago Roma, S.L.
34986718477

BODEGAS COTO REDONDO, S.L (PERNOD RICARD) 78/100

▼✔ Señorío de Rubios Condado Do Tea Blanco 2013 : Yellow-gold with green tints. The nose reveals perfumes of tropical fruits such as pineapple and lychee, coupled with a mineral dimension. On the palate, acidity and freshness are on a par with the fruit and citrus flavours.
http://www.bodegas-cotoredondo.com/
Bodegas Coto Redondo, S.L
+34 986 66 72 12

RIBEIRO D.O.

TERRA MINEI 89/100

▼✔ Treixadura 2012 : The palate shows vegetal accents with aromas of yellow flowers, walnuts plus a hint of white pepper. Subtle saline touch backed by citrus fruits. Well-balanced, closely-integrated palate revealing more of the citrus fruit. Good length.
Price approx.: 9,00 EUR
Terra Minei - Adegas Fernández
988489077

VALDERROAS D.O.

MARIA TERESA NUÑEZ 86/100

▼✔ Bioca. Godello Selección. 2013 : Light yellow with green tints. Floral nose of white flowers with hay and ripe citrus aromas. Fat and warm on the attack flowing into drier aromas mid-palate. Medium persistency. Leaves a sensation of lightness.
Price approx.: 5,00 EUR
Maria Teresa Nuñez
34609250665

LA RIOJA

RIOJA D.O.CA.

BODEGAS DE LA MARQUESA, S.L 94/100

▼✔ Valserrano Mazuelo 2009 : Deep purple-blue bordering on black. The nose displays intense perfumes of violet, blackberry jam and chocolate. Unbridled fruit expression on the palate supported by a mellow structure and good acidity. Elegant and excellent.
Price approx.: 19,00 EUR
Bodegas de la Marquesa, S.L
+34 945 60 90 85

CASTILLO DE CUZCURRITA, S.L. 94/100

▼✔ Señorío de Cuzcurrita 2008 : Elegant, complex nose showing accents of coffee, white pepper, blueberries and subtle basil. Very mineral, refined oak. The palate is seductive, pleasurable and balanced with the refinement of a great wine. Lengthy finish.

http://www.castillodecuzcurrita.com
Castillo de Cuzcurrita, S.L.
34941328022

CASTILLO DE CUZCURRITA, S.L. 93/100

CONV▼✔ Cerrado del Castillo 2008 : Highly elegant nose with pronounced blueberry, white pepper, refined oak, faint roasted coffee aromas and mineral undertones. A fresh wine with fine-grained, well-integrated tannins boasting substantial potential for development. One the firm's top offerings.
http://www.castillodecuzcurrita.com
Castillo de Cuzcurrita, S.L.
34941328022

BODEGAS CAMPO VIEJO 92/100

▼✔ Azpilicueta Reserva 2008 : Intense garnet. The nose offers up a delicious blend of ripe red fruits and refined oak with milky and snuff accents. The palate is well-balanced and elegant, boasting magnificent complexity and persistency. Excellent.
http://www.campoviejo.com
Bodegas Campo Viejo
+34 941 27 99 00

BODEGAS DE LA MARQUESA, S.L 92/100

▼✔ Valserrano Blanco Premium Gran Reserva 2008 : Pale yellow-gold with green tints. The nose combines tropical fruits and expressive oak recalling caramel, vanilla and toast. The palate reveals an elegant wine with balanced acidity and a great combination of fruit and oak. Excellent.
Price approx.: 25,00 EUR
Bodegas de la Marquesa, S.L
+34 945 60 90 85

BODEGAS LACUS 92/100

▼✔ Inedito Blanco 2012 : Bright yellow with green tints. Expressive nose blending pineapple and lychee with herbs. The palate is delicious, fresh and full and boasts true, mouth-watering character. Definitely deserves a try.
Price approx.: 7,00 EUR
Bodegas Lacus
34649331799

MARQUÉS DEL ATRIO, S.L., HACIENDA Y VIÑEDOS 92/100

▼✔ Marques del Atrio Single Vineyard 2007 : Deep garnet. The nose displays spice aromas backed by fruit. The oak is remarkably mellow. Beautifully refined, full palate nicely combining tannins and acidity. An excellent wine.
Price approx.: 17,00 EUR
Marqués del Atrio, S.L., Hacienda y Viñedos
948 37 99 94

OLIVIER RIVIÈRE 92/100

▼ 🔖 Jequitibá 2013 : Pale golden yellow with green tints. A mix of floral notes (orange blossom), citrus, a delicate tropical touch and a mineral dimension. The palate shows seductive personality, balanced acidity and a very fresh fruit character. An excellent wine.
Price approx.: 17,00 EUR
http://www.olivier-riviere.com
Olivier Rivière
34690733541

VIÑA VALORIA, S.A. 92/100

▼ 🔖 Reserva 2008 : Intense garnet. Pleasant nose marrying fresh red fruit, floral undertones and notes of spice and rosemary. Well-balanced palate showing lovely refined oak, delicate tannins and exceptional aromatic expression. An excellent wine.
Price approx.: 5,62 EUR
http://www.bvaloria.com
Viña Valoria, S.A.
+34 941 20 40 59

BODEGAS CAMPO VIEJO 90/100

▼ 🔖 Félix Azpilicueta Colección Privada 2012 : Intense, bright yellow-gold. The nose exudes delicate perfumes of tropical fruits, fresh pineapple and a subtle candy note. Assertive personality on the palate, the culmination of a successful blend of fruit, oak and acidity.
http://www.campoviejo.com
Bodegas Campo Viejo
+34 941 27 99 00

OLIVIER RIVIÈRE 90/100

▼ 🔖 Rayos UVA 2013 : Deep purple. Refined nose with ripe red fruit perfumes harmoniously entwined with liquorice and herbs. The palate is elegant with strong fruit presence, refined oak and delicious acidity.
Price approx.: 8,00 EUR
http://www.olivier-riviere.com
Olivier Rivière
34690733541

BODEGAS DE LA MARQUESA, S.L 89/100

▼ 🔖 Valserrano Gran Reserva 2005 : Ruby with intense purple-blue tints. A nicely combined mix of ripe black fruit aromas, milky notes, caramel and a touch of toast on the nose. A characterful wine on the palate where fruit fuses with the vanilla aromas from the oak.
Price approx.: 20,00 EUR
Bodegas de la Marquesa, S.L
+34 945 60 90 85

LEZA GARCÍA, C.B., BODEGAS 89/100

▼ 🔖 Nube de Leza Semi-dulce 2013 : Brilliant hue with salmon-pink tints. Pleasant nose of red fruit sweets. The palate shows a seductive level of acidity, precise, delicious fruit and a very well-integrated touch of sweetness. Would pair well with Asian foods.
Price approx.: 5,50 EUR
http://www.bodegasleza.com
Leza García, C.B., Bodegas
+34 941 37 11 42

BODEGAS CAMPO VIEJO 88/100

▼ 🔖 Félix Azpilicueta Crianza 2009 : Deep ruby. The nose exudes pleasant aromas of damp earth entwined with toast notes and a delicate scent of cassis in the background. A refined, fruity wine on the palate boasting a supple structure and good persistency.
http://www.campoviejo.com
Bodegas Campo Viejo
+34 941 27 99 00

BODEGAS CAMPO VIEJO 88/100

▼ 🔖 Azpilicueta Rosado 2013 : Bright pink. Very refined nose dominated by floral notes and fresh cherry then revealing a mineral dimension. Delicious palate supported by exuberance which enhances the fruit. An outstanding rosé.
http://www.campoviejo.com
Bodegas Campo Viejo
+34 941 27 99 00

BODEGAS DE LA MARQUESA, S.L 88/100

▼ 🔖 Valserrano Reserva 2009 : Intense red with purple. The nose reveals perfumes of jammy forest fruits entwined with spice notes of black pepper and snuff. Assertive personality, good structure, fine-grained tannins and upfront fruit in the palate.
Price approx.: 13,00 EUR
Bodegas de la Marquesa, S.L
+34 945 60 90 85

EXPORT IBERIA, ABANICO 88/100

▼ 🔖 Hazaña Tradición 2011 : Ruby-red with purple highlights. Expressive nose combining ripe black fruits, spice notes and rosemary and vanilla undertones. An elegant wine on the palate showing lovely balance between fruit, acidity and oak. A successful bottling.
http://www.exportiberia.com
Export Iberia, Abanico
+34 93 812 56 76

MARQUÉS DEL ATRIO, S.L., HACIENDA Y VIÑEDOS 88/100

▼ 🔖 Faustino Rivero Uclecia Silver Label, Reserva 2008 : Deep garnet. Lovely aromas of candied fruits on the nose with a touch of snuff adding to the complexity. Beautiful palate offering up everything one would expect: structure, fruit and toast notes.
Price approx.: 7,25 EUR
Marqués del Atrio, S.L., Hacienda y Viñedos
948 37 99 94

MARQUÉS DEL ATRIO, S.L., HACIENDA Y VIÑEDOS   88/100

▼🍷 Marques del Atrio Reserva 2008 : Garnet-red bordering on black. A mix of ripe red fruit presence, very refined spice notes, almond and milky touches on the nose. A delicious wine with a hallmark fruity finish that lingers on and on. Very elegant.
Price approx.: 9,25 EUR
Marqués del Atrio, S.L., Hacienda y Viñedos
948 37 99 94

BODEGAS CAMPO VIEJO   87/100

▼🍷 Campo Viejo Reserva 2009 : Very dark, intense ruby. The nose recalls hazelnut and a walk through the undergrowth with tobacco and fruit undertones. A polished, well-balanced wine with a mellow structure and pronounced acidity. More of the fruit along with roasted coffee.
http://www.campoviejo.com
Bodegas Campo Viejo
+34 941 27 99 00

BODEGAS CAMPO VIEJO   87/100

▼🍷 Campo Viejo Garnacha 2013 : Lovely red with purple-blue. The nose unfurls pronounced perfumes of jammy fruits with a subtle touch of leather. The palate shows more of the same fruit aromatics augmented by toast flavours. A highly unusual bottling.
http://www.campoviejo.com
Bodegas Campo Viejo
+34 941 27 99 00

LEZA GARCÍA, C.B., BODEGAS   87/100

▼🍷 LG de Leza Garcia 2010 : Deeply-coloured. Endearing nose blending toasted oak, blueberry and black pepper. The palate displays well-integrated tannins, a sensation of freshness and a touch of caramel. Firmer finish revealing more vegetal aromatics. Ideal for Iberian hams.
Price approx.: 18,00 EUR
http://www.bodegasleza.com
Leza García, C.B., Bodegas
+34 941 37 11 42

LEZA GARCÍA, C.B., BODEGAS   87/100

▼🍷 Leza Garcia Reserva 2008 : Classic nose with well-integrated oak revealing perfumes of varnish, ash, black pepper and black fruits. Fairly persistent, fresh palate combining a degree of acidity and evident tannins. Serve with braised meats.
Price approx.: 11,00 EUR
http://www.bodegasleza.com
Leza García, C.B., Bodegas
+34 941 37 11 42

BODEGAS CAMPO VIEJO   86/100

▼🍷 Azpilicueta Crianza 2010 : Intense garnet-red. A blend of spice notes (oregano, pepper) and black fruits on the nose with a touch of snuff. The palate reveals a delicate

fruity style with supple tannins. Tastes like a delicious sweet!
http://www.campoviejo.com
Bodegas Campo Viejo
+34 941 27 99 00

BODEGAS DE LA MARQUESA, S.L   86/100

▼🍷 Valserrano Blanco 2013 : Brilliant pale yellow with green tints. The nose shows tropical aromatics of fresh pineapple and jasmine with mineral undercurrents. Very fruity style on the palate, nicely enhanced by savoury freshness. Long aromatic persistency.
Price approx.: 9,00 EUR
Bodegas de la Marquesa, S.L
+34 945 60 90 85

BODEGAS DE LA MARQUESA, S.L   86/100

▼🍷 Valserrano Crianza 2010 : Ruby with dark purple nuances. Perfumes of jammy black fruits, prune and hazelnut with a touch of vanilla on the nose. A savoury wine on the palate with abundant fruit and toast notes. The structure is mellow and persistent.
Price approx.: 9,00 EUR
Bodegas de la Marquesa, S.L
+34 945 60 90 85

LEZA GARCÍA, C.B., BODEGAS   86/100

▼🍷 Valdepalacios crianza 2011 : Expressive, oaked nose intermixing black pepper, notes of caramel and roasted coffee. On the palate, lightweight substance displaying a vegetal character. Immediately accessible and pairing well with red meats.
Price approx.: 6,00 EUR
http://www.bodegasleza.com
Leza García, C.B., Bodegas
+34 941 37 11 42

LEZA GARCÍA, C.B., BODEGAS   86/100

▼🍷 Leza Garcia tinto Familia 2011 : Expressive nose intermixing perfumes of oak, black pepper, menthol and coffee rounded off with notes of ripe dark fruits and smoky accents. Powerful, warm palate with mellow tannins. The finish is firmer and marked by oak. Serve with game.
Price approx.: 9,00 EUR
http://www.bodegasleza.com
Leza García, C.B., Bodegas
+34 941 37 11 42

VIÑA VALORIA, S.A.   86/100

▼🍷 Gran Reserva 2001 : Deeply-coloured red. The nose shows a delightful blend of ripe fruit notes and spicy, toast accents delivered by the oak. Delicate palate opening up to fruit then flowing elegantly into warmer aromatics. A fine wine.
Price approx.: 9,22 EUR
http://www.bvaloria.com
Viña Valoria, S.A.
+34 941 20 40 59

ZUAZO GASTÓN, S.C., BODEGAS Y VIÑEDOS
86/100

▼✦ Reserva 2009 : Intense garnet. Expressive nose revealing perfumes of ripe and candied red fruits with liquorice and cinnamon notes. Robust, characterful attack flowing into perfectly balanced freshness and fruit. A very well-made wine.
Price approx.: 6,00 EUR
http://www.zuazongaston.com
Zuazo Gastón, S.C., Bodegas y Viñedos
+34945 60 15 26

BODEGAS CAMPO VIEJO
85/100

▼✦ Campo Viejo Tempranillo 2012 : Red with purple-blue tints. Expressive nose showing a harmonious blend of fruit and spice then revealing perfumes of caramel and vanilla. A robust personality on the palate with assertive fruit presence enhanced by a toast dimension.
http://www.campoviejo.com
Bodegas Campo Viejo
+34 941 27 99 00

VIÑA VALORIA, S.A.
85/100

▼✦ Crianza 2011 : Intense garnet. Predominant ripe fruit and cassis on the nose with notes of leather and snuff in the background. The palate is delicate and suave, opening up to fruit then revealing the spice and vanilla character of the oak.
Price approx.: 3,82 EUR
http://www.bvaloria.com
Viña Valoria, S.A.
+34 941 20 40 59

BODEGAS CAMPO VIEJO
84/100

▼✦ Campo Viejo Gran Reserva 2009 : Ruby. The nose reveals very fresh, pleasant aromas of flowers and plum on first pour then opens up to liquorice, pepper and fresh bread. A characterful wine on the palate with a warm attack leading into a livelier, fruity mid-palate.
http://www.campoviejo.com
Bodegas Campo Viejo
+34 941 27 99 00

BODEGAS DE LA MARQUESA, S.L
84/100

▼✦ Valserrano Garnacha 2009 : Deep red with purple-blue. Notes of cassis and ripe strawberry entwined with toast and vanilla perfumes from the oak on the nose. The palate is warm and oaky at point of entry then reveals freshness and persistent fruit.
Price approx.: 19,00 EUR
Bodegas de la Marquesa, S.L
+34 945 60 90 85

BODEGAS LACUS
84/100

▼✦ Inédito H12 2009 : Deep, intense red. The nose opens up to aromas of prune and tobacco, revealing complex yet unusual aromatic expression. Acidity imparts freshness on the palate and fruit marries with elegant oak. A surprising wine.

Price approx.: 9,00 EUR
Bodegas Lacus
34649331799

MARQUÉS DEL ATRIO, S.L., HACIENDA Y VIÑEDOS
84/100

▼✦ Faustino Rivero Uclecia Silver Label, Crianza 2011 : Garnet. Expressive nose intermixing ripe red fruits with notes of pepper and candy in the background. Well-balanced, supple palate driven by good acidity with full-on freshness and lingering fruit accompanied by toast notes.
Price approx.: 4,25 EUR
Marqués del Atrio, S.L., Hacienda y Viñedos
948 37 99 94

OLIVIER RIVIÈRE
84/100

▼✦ Ganko 2012 : Beautiful crimson hue. The nose displays ripe black fruit and cassis notes with leather and snuff undertones increasing complexity. A well-balanced wine on the palate with abundant fruit, refined tannins and a rich finish of roasted coffee.
Price approx.: 20,00 EUR
http://www.olivier-riviere.com
Olivier Rivière
34690733541

BODEGAS CAMPO VIEJO
83/100

▼✦ Azpilicueta Blanco 2013 : Pale gold with green tints. The nose intermixes perfumes of citrus fruits and wild flowers before being bolstered by mineral undertones after swirling. An expressive wine on the palate, displaying good acidity which imparts freshness and savoury persistency.
http://www.campoviejo.com
Bodegas Campo Viejo
+34 941 27 99 00

BODEGAS DE LA MARQUESA, S.L
82/100

▼✦ Valserrano Finca Monteviejo 2008 : Intense ruby with purple. The nose reveals notes of pepper, toast, a touch of cassis and a trace of milk in the background. Huge personality on the palate, chocolate on the attack followed by very rich fruit underscored by a welcome acidity.
Price approx.: 20,00 EUR
Bodegas de la Marquesa, S.L
+34 945 60 90 85

ZUAZO GASTÓN, S.C., BODEGAS Y VIÑEDOS
82/100

▼✦ Crianza 2011 : Brilliant colour with purple highlights. Nose of dried fruits augmented by notes of vanilla and snuff. A mouth-filling, delicate wine. Lovely freshness and subtle tannins. Drink with spicy foods.
Price approx.: 4,00 EUR
http://www.zuazongaston.com
Zuazo Gastón, S.C., Bodegas y Viñedos
+34945 60 15 26

EMW GRANDES VINOS DE ESPAÑA   80/100

▼✔ The invisible Man 2011 : Intense red with purple-blue. The nose reveals aromas of ripe and candied red fruits, cassis and mild menthol-like perfumes. The oak comes centre-stage at first on the palate then melds with the fruit. Savoury, well-balanced acidity.
http://www.emw.es
EMW Grandes Vinos de España
34968151520

BODEGAS NIVARIUS, GRUPO PALACIOS VINOTECA   80/100

▼✔ Nivei 2013 : Brilliant pale gold. Nose of tropical fruits (lychee) combined with mineral accents and vegetal notes. The wine displays personality on the palate. Although the attack is firm, aroma is upfront and persistent. A well-made wine.
Price approx.: 3,50 EUR
http://www.palaciosvinoteca.com
Palacios Vinoteca
941444418

BODEGAS CAMPO VIEJO   79/100

▼✔ Gran Cava Brut Reserva : Pale gold with green tints, explosive bubbles forming rings and a persistent mousse. A mix of yeast notes, citrus perfumes and a floral dimension on the nose. Very fresh, fruity palate boasting beautiful acidity. Drink as an appetiser.
http://www.campoviejo.com
Bodegas Campo Viejo
+34 941 27 99 00

BODEGAS DE LA MARQUESA, S.L   79/100

▼✔ Valserrano Graciano 2009 : Dark purple. The nose opens up to spice and herb notes (thyme) on first pour then releases ripe black fruit undertones. Mellow structure, freshness and fruit on the palate. A conversational wine.
Price approx.: 19,00 EUR
Bodegas de la Marquesa, S.L
+34 945 60 90 85

VIÑA VALORIA, S.A.   79/100

▼✔ Vendimia Seleccionada 2013 : Garnet-red. Red fruit notes coupled with spice and smoke aromatics on the nose. A delicate wine on the palate with good acidity fusing with the fruit. An everyday wine.
Price approx.: 2,43 EUR
http://www.bvaloria.com
Viña Valoria, S.A.
+34 941 20 40 59

BODEGAS CAMPO VIEJO   78/100

▼✔ Gran Cava Brut Rose : Very attractive pink with a fine mousse and ring of persistent bubbles. The nose displays perfumes of fresh strawberry with mineral undercurrents. The palate shows very mild fruit scents balanced by a good

level of acidity. Unusual.
http://www.campoviejo.com
Bodegas Campo Viejo
+34 941 27 99 00

BODEGAS LACUS   78/100

▼✔ Inedito 2011 : Intense, vibrant red. Expressive nose blending notes of hazelnut and plum jam, quite dissimilar to the varietal norm. A mellow wine on the palate with aromas of ripe fruits displaying good acidity. Unusual.
Price approx.: 5,50 EUR
Bodegas Lacus
34649331799

ZUAZO GASTÓN, S.C., BODEGAS Y VIÑEDOS   78/100

▼✔ Vendimia Seleccionada 2012 : Intense purple hue. Harmonious nose of fresh red fruits marked by beautiful spice presence of black pepper. An easy-drinking wine for everyday enjoyment. Well-balanced and persistent on the palate.
Price approx.: 3,00 EUR
http://www.zuazongaston.com
Zuazo Gastón, S.C., Bodegas y Viñedos
+34945 60 15 26

MADRID

MADRID D.O.

FINCA VALQUEJIGOSO   98/100

▼✔ V1 2008 : Complex nose intermixing a mineral dimension, chili pepper, undergrowth and tobacco backed by ripe black fruit and red meat. Delicate undertones. The palate shows seductive freshness, delicious character, a finely-etched framework, fullness and persistency.
Price approx.: 420,00 EUR
http://www.valquejigoso.com
Valquejigoso S.L.
91 813 68 41

FINCA VALQUEJIGOSO   97/100

▼✔ V2 2005 : Open nose with accents of spice, black fruits, Indian ink, undergrowth and an animal and leather touch flowing into Mediterranean herbs. Elegant, fresh palate with a delicious attack, powerful yet melted tannins and a persistent finish.
Price approx.: 55,00 EUR
http://www.valquejigoso.com
Valquejigoso S.L.
91 813 68 41

FINCA VALQUEJIGOSO   95/100

▼✔ V2 2007 : Complex mineral nose intermixing tobacco, black pepper, Indian ink, black olive, leather, blackcurrant and smoke notes flowing into vanilla after swirling. Elegant tannins, fresh across the palate and a seductive finish. Substantial maturing potential.

Price approx.: 55,00 EUR

http://www.valquejigoso.com

Valquejigoso S.L.

91 813 68 41

FINCA VALQUEJIGOSO 94/100

▼✦ V2 2009 : Mineral nose (graphite, granite) intermixing blueberry, tobacco, black pepper, notes of meat and leather. Tightly-wound palate with elegant tannins. Fresh, well-balanced and showing a lovely ripe, long and faintly vegetal finish. Huge potential.

Price approx.: 62,97 EUR

http://www.valquejigoso.com

Valquejigoso S.L.

91 813 68 41

FINCA VALQUEJIGOSO 94/100

▼✦ V2 2008 : Expressive mineral and melted nose showing subtle scents of tobacco, spice, dark chocolate, ripe black fruits and a trace of roasted coffee. A very fresh, profound wine on the palate with dense tannins capped off with a note of undergrowth.

Price approx.: 58,85 EUR

http://www.valquejigoso.com

Valquejigoso S.L.

91 813 68 41

MURCIE

JUMILLA D.O.

VIÑEDOS Y BODEGAS J.M. MARTÍNEZ VERDÚ, S.L. 94/100

▼✦ Xenysel 12 Meses 2012 : Ruby with purple-blue tints. The nose reveals spice notes, black pepper, rosemary and violet. Menthol undertones and graphite notes are also perceptible. Very well-balanced and elegant on the palate with impeccably integrated oak backed by fruit.

Price approx.: 9,00 EUR

Viñedos y Bodegas J.M. Martínez Verdú, S.L.

34968756240

BODEGAS Y VINEDOS CASA DE LA ERMITA, S.L. 91/100

▼✦ Casa de la Ermita crianza 2010 : Highly floral, fresh nose opening up to notes of blueberry, spice (cardamom), black plum, liquorice and graphite with a subtle touch of bell pepper. Beautiful, fairly powerful and fresh palate showing good balance. A seductive, complex and joyful style.

Price approx.: 3,95 EUR

http://www.casadelaermita.com

Bodegas y Vinedos Casa de la Ermita, S.L.

34968783035

EGO BODEGAS 91/100

Org▼✦ Goru El Blanco 2013 : Seductive nose showing perfumes of white flowers (orange blossom), fruits (melon and nectarine) and white pepper, rounded off with a hint of citrus (tangerine zest). Mellow, fresh and lively on the palate, displaying lovely length.

Price approx.: 2,50 EUR

http://www.egobodegas.com

Ego Bodegas

34968964326

EGO BODEGAS 90/100

Org▼✦ Infinito 2011 : Expressive nose opening up to perfumes of black pepper, stewed black fruits, a subtle touch of caramel and refined, liquoricy oak undertones. Full, mouth-coating palate that is fresh, persistent and combines power and well-integrated tannins.

Price approx.: 11,00 EUR

http://www.egobodegas.com

Ego Bodegas

34968964326

EGO BODEGAS 90/100

Org▼✦ Talento ecológico 2013 : Aromatic and fresh, intermixing subtle notes of black pepper, wild berries (blackberries and blueberries), plum and liquorice – typical varietal aromas. Delicious, well-balanced and persistent palate. A very enjoyable wine boasting great seductive powers.

Price approx.: 3,00 EUR

http://www.egobodegas.com

Ego Bodegas

34968964326

EGO BODEGAS 90/100

Org▼✦ Goru organic 2013 : Intense ruby. Very fresh nose suggestive of freshly-picked forest fruits (blackberry), plum, liquorice and a whiff of black pepper. Vibrant, well-balanced and joyful, this is a seductive wine with supple, well-integrated tannins. Persistent and very enjoyable.

Price approx.: 3,00 EUR

http://www.egobodegas.com

Ego Bodegas

34968964326

EGO BODEGAS 90/100

▼✦ Talento by Ego 2012 : Elegant nose showing refined oak and suggestions of plum, black pepper, caramel, coffee and toast. A lovely earthy note imparts depth to the whole. Very well-balanced, fresh and polished on the palate with a wonderfully seductive persistency.

Price approx.: 3,00 EUR

http://www.egobodegas.com

Ego Bodegas

34968964326

EGO BODEGAS   90/100

Org▼✦ Clos Lagoru 2013 : Endearing nose intermixing plum, black pepper, blueberry, blackberry and liquorice with refined, subtle oak in the background. Fairly concentrated, mouth-coating palate with all the components nicely integrated. Polished tannins on a delicious, seductive palate.
Price approx.: 3,00 EUR
http://www.egobodegas.com
Ego Bodegas
34968964326

EGO BODEGAS   89/100

▼✦ Goru Monastrell 2010 : Nose of ripe berry fruits, spices, black plum and liquorice with a hint of chocolate and roasted coffee. Easy-flowing on the palate, fresh with evident tannins backed by ripe fruit and well-integrated vegetal aromas. Persistent and slightly firm on the finish.
Price approx.: 10,00 EUR
http://www.egobodegas.com
Ego Bodegas
34968964326

EMW GRANDES VINOS DE ESPAÑA   89/100

▼✦ Macho Man Monastrell Casa Rojo 2012 : Generous nose intermixing liquorice, leather, plum, red and black fruits (ripe blackcurrant) and white pepper. Round tannins, good structure. A well-balanced, fresh wine capped off with a well-integrated touch of bitterness that imparts depth to the whole.
Price approx.: 4,50 EUR
http://www.emw.es/
EMW Grandes Vinos de España
34968151520

BODEGAS CARCHELO   88/100

▼✦ Sierva 2011 : Garnet-hued. Refined, elegant nose suggestive of sweets and forest fruits with oak notes of vanilla, cinnamon and cocoa. Fresh on the palate and supported by oak tannins, combining a fruit dimension with subtle smoke notes.
http://www.carchelo.com
Bodegas Carchelo
34968435137

BODEGAS CARCHELO   88/100

▼✦ C 2012 : Purple-blue hue. Expressive nose of crunchy fresh forest fruits and rose in bloom. On the palate, oak is fairly upfront with spice and smoke aromatics. Slightly vegetal aromas round off the whole.
http://www.carchelo.com
Bodegas Carchelo
34968435137

BODEGAS Y VINEDOS CASA DE LA ERMITA, S.L.   88/100

▼✦ Casa de la Ermita Roble 2012 : Endearing nose of fresh blueberries, vanilla, patchouli, caramel and black pepper. On the palate, black fruits (plum) and liquorice prevail, before flowing into persistent toasted oak aromas. New World in style.
Price approx.: 2,50 EUR
http://www.casadelaermita.com
Bodegas y Vinedos Casa de la Ermita, S.L.
34968783035

EGO BODEGAS   88/100

Org▼✦ Goru Monastrell 2011 : Open nose intermixing prune, ripe blueberry, liquorice and a subtle touch of black pepper, rounded off with well-integrated oak and notes of coffee in the background. Well-balanced on the palate and supported by polished tannins. An enjoyable, persistent wine.
Price approx.: 6,00 EUR
http://www.egobodegas.com
Ego Bodegas
34968964326

EGO BODEGAS   88/100

▼✦ Goru 2013 : Mature nose intermixing prune, ripe blueberry, liquorice and black pepper rounded off with refined, well-integrated oak in the background. Well-balanced on the palate, boasting savoury, polished tannins. Also shows a seductively persistent finish.
Price approx.: 3,00 EUR
http://www.egobodegas.com
Ego Bodegas
34968964326

EGO BODEGAS   88/100

▼✦ Fuerza 2011 : The nose reveals perfumes of black pepper, graphite, cassis and plum with subtle liquorice and caramel undercurrents. Enjoyable and fresh on the palate with a well-balanced structure and a lingering finish.
Price approx.: 6,00 EUR
http://www.egobodegas.com
Ego Bodegas
34968964326

EGO BODEGAS   88/100

▼✦ Clos Lagoru 2012 : Medium intense crimson. The nose boasts a degree of elegance with aromas of black plum, liquorice, undergrowth and spice. Mellow and well-balanced on the palate, it displays aniseedy undertones and a pleasant vegetal finish.
Price approx.: 7,00 EUR
http://www.egobodegas.com
Ego Bodegas
34968964326

EGO BODEGAS 87/100

▼✦ Marionette 2013 : Intense garnet. The nose opens up after swirling to aromas of caramel, coffee, ripe black fruits and black pepper with a subtle touch of black berry fruits in the background. Light, well-balanced and joyful palate in an easy-drinking style. Simple and enjoyable.
Price approx.: 3,00 EUR
http://www.egobodegas.com
Ego Bodegas
34968964326

VIÑEDOS Y BODEGAS J.M. MARTÍNEZ VERDÚ, S.L. 87/100

▼✦ Xenysel Pie Franco 2013 : Intense colour with purple-blue. Nose of ripe black fruits enhanced by notes of cinnamon, coffee and caramel. Delicious palate nicely balanced by elegant acidity and showing more of the fruit coupled with refined oak that lingers.
Price approx.: 5,00 EUR
Viñedos y Bodegas J.M. Martínez Verdú, S.L.
34968756240

EGO BODEGAS 86/100

Org▼✦ Goru organic 2012 : Medium intense garnet with fawn highlights. Evolved nose of spice, damp earth, subtle notes of black plum and liquorice with oak scents. Warm palate with slightly dry tannins displaying a faintly vegetal character.
Price approx.: 5,50 EUR
http://www.egobodegas.com
Ego Bodegas
34968964326

VIÑEDOS Y BODEGAS J.M. MARTÍNEZ VERDÚ, S.L. 80/100

Org▼✦ Xenysel Orgánico 2103 : Beautiful intense red with purple-blue. Suggestions of forest fruit jam backed by delicate vegetal and spice aromas on the nose. The palate is fat and well-structured and blends fruit character with caramel notes. Good persistency.
Price approx.: 5,00 EUR
Viñedos y Bodegas J.M. Martínez Verdú, S.L.
34968756240

NAVARRA

NAVARRA D.O.

BODEGAS JULIÁN CHIVITE, S.L. 92/100

▼✦ Chivite Colección 125 Blanco fermentado en barrica 2010 : Refined nose suggestive of lemon zest, butter and subtle smoke notes (cigar box) flowing into white pepper, white flowers and pear. Fat and ripe on the palate, displaying persistent freshness and a long finish. Good balance.
Price approx.: 59,00 EUR
http://www.chivite.com
J. Chivite Family Estate, SL
34948555285

BODEGAS JULIÁN CHIVITE, S.L. 88/100

▼✦ Chivite Colección 125 Reserva 2009 : Brilliant garnet. The nose exudes perfumes of blueberry and blackcurrant with violet, as well as black pepper, bay and smoke notes. The fruit is more subdued on the palate due to upfront oak. Good persistency.
Price approx.: 25,00 EUR
http://www.chivite.com
J. Chivite Family Estate, SL
34948555285

BODEGAS JULIÁN CHIVITE, S.L. 88/100

▼✦ Finca Villatuerta Chardonnay sobre lías 2012 : Pale gold. Pleasant nose with buttery, smoky and lemony accents and well-integrated oak. Instantly approachable, fresh palate reflecting true varietal character. A subtle touch of sourness on the finish gives depth to the whole.
Price approx.: 15,00 EUR
http://www.chivite.com
J. Chivite Family Estate, SL
34948555285

BODEGAS JULIÁN CHIVITE, S.L. 86/100

▼✦ Chivite Colección 125 Rosado Fermentado en barrica 2011 : Raspberry colour. Subdued nose showing perfumes of white pepper, cigar box and smoke notes. The palate is lively and more expressive, revealing aromas of citrus and vanilla. The finish displays pronounced toasted oak.
Price approx.: 28,00 EUR
http://www.chivite.com
J. Chivite Family Estate, SL
34948555285

BODEGAS JULIÁN CHIVITE, S.L. 86/100

▼✦ Finca Villatuerta Syrah 2011 : Deep crimson. Warm nose of ripe cassis and blueberry augmented by notes of toasted oak and black pepper. Mouth-coating palate with ripe, well-integrated tannins. Subtle touch of firmness on the finish.
Price approx.: 16,00 EUR
http://www.chivite.com
J. Chivite Family Estate, SL
34948555285

Detailed instructions are featured at the start of the book.

BODEGAS JULIÁN CHIVITE, S.L.   86/100

▼♪ Finca Villatuerta Selección Especial 2009 : Garnet-hued. Expressive nose intermixing blueberry, black pepper, coffee and oak notes. On the palate, polished tannins, good acidity and relatively predominant oak. The finish displays subtle bitterness. Serve with red meats.
Price approx.: 13,00 EUR
http://www.chivite.com
J. Chivite Family Estate, SL
34948555285

VALENCE

ALICANTE D.O.

BODEGAS BOCOPA   86/100

▼♪ Marques de Alicante 2013 : Intense crimson with purple-blue. The nose is dominated by spice aromas revealing a mix of clove and liquorice. Personality and character are displayed on the palate, with balanced acidity and upfront fruit.
http://www.bocopa.com
Bodegas Bocopa
34966950489

BODEGAS BOCOPA   79/100

▼♪ Conde de Alicante Selección 2013 : Intense purple. Expressive nose blending floral notes, red fruits, toasted oak and chocolate. A suave wine on the palate with fruit and toast flavours enhanced by good acidity. A conversational wine.
http://www.bocopa.com
Bodegas Bocopa
34966950489

UTIEL-REQUENA D.O.

BODEGAS MURVIEDRO S.A   79/100

▼♪ DNA Murviedro Classic Bobal 2013 : Garnet with crimson tints. The nose reveals perfumes of black fruits, fresh blackberry, spice and white pepper. An enjoyable, easy-drinking wine displaying archetypal varietal characteristics. A good companion to everyday food.
Price approx.: 2,00 EUR
http://www.murviedro.es
Murviedro bodegas
34962329003

VALENCIA D.O.

BODEGAS MURVIEDRO S.A   86/100

▼♪ Murviedro Colección Crianza 2011 : Garnet-red.

The nose reveals lovely complex fresh red and black fruit aromas combined with delicate buttery and smoky undertones. Fresh, characterful attack on the palate, fruit expression and a touch of heat on the finish.
Price approx.: 2,80 EUR
http://www.murviedro.es
Murviedro bodegas
34962329003

BODEGAS MURVIEDRO S.A   85/100

▼♪ Murviedro Colección Reserva 2010 : Deeply-coloured red. A mix of ripe fruits and cassis on the nose with delicate spice undercurrents. The palate reveals a refined style with a suave attack showing lovely expressive fruit and fine oak accents. A very well-made wine.
Price approx.: 3,60 EUR
http://www.murviedro.es
Murviedro bodegas
34962329003

VT CASTELLO

BODEGAS Y VINEDOS BARON D'ALBA SL CLOS DESGARRACORDES   89/100

▼♪ Clos d'Esgarracordes 2012 : The nose blends citrus fruits, a vegetal dimension and a pleasant touch of white pepper. On the palate, good acidity levels and well-integrated power. Persistent finish tinged with a hint of bitterness which gives depth to the whole.
http://www.barondalba.com
Bodegas y Vinedos Baron d'Alba SL Clos Desgarracordes
34608032884

BODEGAS Y VINEDOS BARON D'ALBA SL CLOS DESGARRACORDES   88/100

▼♪ Clos d'Esgarracordes vino tinto barrica 2011 : Fresh, fruity nose suggestive of blueberry, red fruits, a hint of vanilla, caramel and refined oak. Well-balanced on the palate with polished tannins and savoury predominant fruit. Good length. Ideal for simple meals.

http://www.barondalba.com
Bodegas y Vinedos Baron d'Alba SL Clos Desgarracordes
34608032884

Prices mentioned in this book are guideline and can vary depending on point of sale. The shops, wineries or publisher can in no way be held responsible for this.

TURKEY
(ALL REGIONS)

CHAMLIJA 85/100

▼♪ Cabernet Sauvignon 2012 : Intense, dark colour. Concentrated nose revealing aromas of ripe red and black fruits with a subtle liquorice touch. Full, concentrated, warm and balanced palate. Closely-integrated tannins. Displays an interesting personality.
Price approx.: 15,00 EUR
Chamlija
905338000000

CHAMLIJA 85/100

▼♪ Pinot Noir 2013 : Attractive deeply-coloured crimson. On the nose, red fruit aromas are augmented by a pleasant touch of toast and a graphite note. More of the same aromas on the palate which is dense and concentrated. The slightly firm oak sensation lingers on the finish.
Price approx.: 15,00 EUR
Chamlija
905338000000

CHAMLIJA 83/100

▼♪ Istranca 2012 : Intense colour. Warm nose intermixing black cherry with a vegetal and spice dimension. Supple attack leading into a firmer mid-palate revealing slightly vegetal tannins. The sensation of fruity sweetness flows into a faint bitterness on the finish.
Price approx.: 12,00 EUR
Chamlija
905338000000

OUR LAST TASTING FROM ITALY

FRIULI VENEZIA GIULIA
FRIULI COLLI ORIENTALI D.O.C

ARZENTON MAURIZIO AZIENDA AGRICOLA
90/100

▼♪ Pinot Grigio – 2013: Pale straw-yellow. Highly expressive, mineral-driven nose of pumice stone with delightful scents of lemon leaf and cedar wood. The palate is persistent, round, very mineral and displays a savoury finish. Ideal for fish and cheeses.
Price approx.: 5,50 EUR
+39 0432 716139

ARZENTON MAURIZIO AZIENDA AGRICOLA
90/100

▼♪ Sauvignon – 2013: Intense straw-yellow. Harmonious nose intermixing ripe tropical fruit aromas of pineapple and papaya with herbal perfumes of garrigue. Intense, fruity and persistent palate. Shows well on its own or paired with full-flavoured fish dishes.
Price approx.: 6,00 EUR
+39 0432 716139

ARZENTON MAURIZIO AZIENDA AGRICOLA
88/100

▼♪ Friulano – 2013: Straw-yellow. Round, mineral nose with faint balsamic and fruit notes of citrus. On the palate, a persistent wine with more of the balsamic aromas and a savoury after-taste. The perfect partner for mature cheeses and white meats.
Price approx.: 5,50 EUR
+39 0432 716139

B

INDEX OF WINES AND PRODUCERS

C

INDEX OF WINES AND PRODUCERS

INDEX OF WINES AND PRODUCERS

D

E

F

G

H

INDEX OF WINES AND PRODUCERS

I

J

INDEX OF WINES AND PRODUCERS

K

L

INDEX OF WINES AND PRODUCERS

M

N

O

P

Q

INDEX OF WINES AND PRODUCERS

S

T

U

V

W

Z

D

E

F

G

H

I

J

L

M

N.

O

P

Q

R

S

INDEX OF APPELLATIONS

W

GILBERT & GAILLARD

INTERNATIONAL

WINE GUIDE

Publisher: Vinipresse - 7 Parc des Fontenelles 78870 Bailly - FRANCE

Publishing managers: François Gilbert & Philippe Gaillard - **Editor:** Sylvain Patard

With the collaboration of:
FRANCE: Frédéric Comet, Annick Delauneux, Olivier Delorme, Isabel Ferran, Gwendoline Jobelot, Michèle Huyard, Emma Rakotomalala, Nicolas Sanseigne and James Turnbull.
USA: Jamal Rayyis
ITALY: Isabel Ferran
PORTUGAL, SPAIN AND SOUTH-AMERICA: Evelyn Israel

Translation: Elise Bradbury, Sharon Nagel.

Distributed in the United States by

BookMasters Distribution Services, Inc.

30 Amberwood Parkway - Ashland, OH 44805

Distributed in Canada by

BookMasters Distribution Services, Inc.

c/o Jacqueline Gross Associates - 165 Dufferin Street

Toronto, Ontario, Canada M6K 3H6

Distributed in UK, Ireland, East Europa and Asia by:

Vinehouse Distribution Ltd

The Old Mill House, Mill Lane, Uckfield, East Sussex - TN22 5AA

Phone: 01825 767396

email: sales@vinehouseuk.co.uk

Printed by La Tipografica Varese (Varese - Italy)

Copyright: December 2014